Crimes of the Internet

Edited by

Frank Schmalleger
Distinguished Professor Emeritus, University of North Carolina at Pembroke

Michael Pittaro
Executive Director, Council on Alcohol and Drug Abuse, Allentown, Pennsylvania

Adjunct Criminal Justice Professor, Cedar Crest College, Allentown, Pennsylvania

PEARSON
Prentice
Hall

Upper Saddle River, New Jersey 07458

Library of Congress Cataloging-in-Publication Data

Crimes of the Internet / edited by Frank Schmalleger, Michael Pittaro.
   p. cm.
Includes bibliographical references and index.
ISBN-13: 978-0-13-231886-0 (pbk. : alk. paper)
ISBN-10: 0-13-231886-5 (pbk. : alk. paper)
  1. Computer crimes. I. Schmalleger, Frank. II. Pittaro, Michael.
HV6773.C765 2008
364.16'8—dc22

2007052871

Editor in Chief: Vernon R. Anthony
Senior Acquisitions Editor: Tim Peyton
Editorial Assistant: Alicia Kelly
Director of Marketing: David Gesell
Marketing Manager: Adam Kloza
Marketing Coordinator: Alicia Dysert
Production Manager: Kathy Sleys
Creative Director: Jayne Conte
Cover Design: Bruce Kenselaar
Cover Illustration/Photo: Comstock Images/Jupiter Images, Inc.
Full-Service Project Management/Composition: Babitha Balan/GGS Book Services
Printer/Binder: R. R. Donnelley & Sons, Inc.

Pearson Education LTD.
Pearson Education Singapore, Pte. Ltd
Pearson Education, Canada, Ltd
Pearson Education–Japan

Pearson Education Australia PTY, Limited
Pearson Education North Asia Ltd
Pearson Educación de Mexico, S.A. de C.V.
Pearson Education Malaysia, Pte. Ltd

10 9 8 7 6 5 4 3 2 1
ISBN-13: 978-0-13-231886-0
ISBN-10:   0-13-231886-5

Dedication

For Jason Star, the most brilliant scientist I know.
Frank Schmalleger

To my beautiful and incredibly compassionate wife, Christine and my sons, Dakota and Darrian.
Michael Pittaro

Contents

v

Contents

Foreword

By
Susan W. Brenner*

As some of us know, cyber crime takes many guises, and for that and other reasons constitutes a new and highly problematic threat to governments around the world. The chapters Professor Pittaro and Dr. Schmalleger have assembled in this volume examine the varied facets of this still-new phenomenon.

As I explain below, they address topics ranging from substantive law (the statutory offenses we can use to prosecute cyber criminals) to procedural law (Fourth Amendment and other laws that constrain what law enforcement can do in investigating these crimes) to what is probably the most difficult issue of all: the transnational nature of cyber crime. The chapters provide a comprehensive, current treatment of these issues and, in so doing, will give the reader an understanding, and an appreciation, of why we should all be concerned about this very different category of criminal activity.

As to substantive law, the book includes a series of impressive chapters that deal with particular types of cyber crime. Some deal with what experts and civilians alike agree as a particularly heinous category of cyber crime: crimes against children. These chapters examine the dangers that arise when pedophiles use the Internet to stalk and lure child victims and the related problem of online child pornography.

As those familiar with cyber crime know, the creation and dissemination of child pornography has exploded into cyberspace, for several reasons; pedophiles who would never have been willing to risk exposure by seeking out child pornography in the real-world can now acquire it anonymously online, with little risk of exposure. And we see a very similar phenomenon with regard to child stalking and luring; cyberspace makes it possible for pedophiles to interact directly with potential victims, engaging them in online chats that can, and do, result in a pedophile's luring children to a rendezvous, where the pedophile intends to attack the child. Cyberspace, in effect, lets pedophiles breach the security of our homes in their search for potential victims. In the same way and for the same reasons, it also facilitates other types of stalking and a very new phenomenon: cyber bullying. The book includes an entire chapter devoted to cyber bullying, a topic that has so far been rather neglected. This chapter does an excellent job of describing the nature and parameters of cyber bullying; its contribution is also distinctive because the author provides us with a transnational perspective on the problem.

There are additional chapters dealing with the substantive law of cyber crime, all of which do an excellent job of surveying the more important varieties of cyber crime. There is, for example, a very thoughtful chapter dealing with identity theft, which has become a problem

---

*NCR Distinguished Professor of Law and Technology, University of Dayton School of Law, Dayton, OH.

of almost epidemic proportions in the United States and many other countries. Other, equally thoughtful chapters deal with the difficult legal and policy issues raised by online gambling and by the online sale of pharmaceuticals; another insightful chapter examines the related issues of fraud and spam and a companion piece deals with a crime that remains obscure to many: phishing. Other substantive law chapters deal with the very lucrative, and very elusive, phenomenon of online copyright infringement, a serious global phenomenon.

There are also chapters dealing with a type of cyber crime that is emerging as a very real concern for governments around the world: cyber terrorism. As these chapters explain, cyber terrorism is a concern because so many activities in the modern world—e.g., transportation, communications, commerce, utilities, and even governance—depend on computer systems. This creates an area of vulnerability terrorists can, and certainly will, exploit. In 2006, the U.S. Department of Homeland Security and the Secret Service ran a mock cyber terrorism exercise that encompassed all of these sectors and lasted for several days; the exercise, which included some international participation, revealed that civilian and governmental systems are woefully vulnerable to the kind of tactics these chapters examine.

In what I would deem the category of procedural law, there are chapters dealing with how the Fourth Amendment impacts on law enforcement's efforts to investigate these and other online crimes and with the particularly intricate problem of adapting our traditional rules of evidence to the unique characteristics of digital evidence. A related chapter examines the process of investigating cyber crime; it analyzes the similarities and differences between traditional criminal investigations and cyber crime investigations and offers guidance for improving how law enforcement officers pursue the latter. Like this chapter, other chapters provide a more theoretical perspective on aspects of cyber crime; these chapters examine issues such as trends in online crime, the politics of cyber crime and criminological perspectives on cyber crime.

The transnational aspect of cyber crime is an issue the treatment of which is woven throughout most, if not all, of the chapters in the book. It makes the application of both substantive and procedural law problematic. If, for example, a citizen living in a country where gambling is illegal accesses an online casino located in another country where gambling is legal, has a crime been committed? Here, we have conduct that would be a crime if it had been committed entirely within the territory of the country where gambling is illegal, but it has not; cyberspace breaks the conduct into pieces, so that part of it occurs in the country where gambling is illegal and another part occurs in a country where gambling is legal. This creates a conundrum: How are we to apply substantive law, the law that defines what is and is not a crime, to conduct, which is at once legal and illegal? Moreover, if we can get past that hurdle, how do we decide which country's law will govern the investigation of the crime?

Our laws, both substantive and procedural, were created for a physical world in which travel from one jurisdiction was possible, but time-consuming and difficult. Travel in the real world has become much easier and faster over the last, say, 50 years, but cyberspace takes the concept to an entirely new level. As I sit in my office in the United States, I can more easily access an extraterritorial online casino or Warez site or (if I were so inclined) child pornography site than I can the shop down the street. As you will learn from this book, cyberspace lets criminals attack us with relative impunity from halfway around the globe, and that is yet another issue we must address.

I am confident you will find this book to be more than worth your time: it is at once interesting, instructive, and thought provoking. I think we all owe a vote of thanks to Professor Pittaro and Dr. Schmalleger for assembling such a valuable contribution to scholarship in this area.

Preface

Crimes of the Internet was expressly created for undergraduate and graduate criminal justice students, but it will undoubtedly appeal to a much wider audience interested in learning more about the growing number of Internet crimes; hereafter referred to as cyber crimes. This edited collection of original, previously unpublished articles has attempted to illuminate and explore some of the most technologically sophisticated crimes to surface since the dawn of the Internet. This book examines the changing nature of cyber crime that has specifically occurred with the evolution of the Internet. Our world, as we know it, has come to rely on the size, capability, and velocity of the Internet to locate and identify enormous quantities of personal and professional information. We have come to rely on the Internet as a tool for exploration and data gathering, and the Internet has enabled us to swiftly communicate with virtually anyone, anywhere, and at anytime across the globe.

The anonymity, accessibility, and ubiquitous availability of the Internet, coupled with its relatively low costs, have made it attractive and incredibly valuable to many people, including those who have turned to the Internet for unlawful, deviant purposes. Consequently, the Internet presents new challenges for law enforcement officials that, for the most part, transcend all geographical boundaries and borders, and evade many investigative and prosecutorial procedures that have traditionally been used to detect, prosecute, and punish criminal activity. As this book will show, the Internet has become a fertile breeding ground for an entirely new and unique type of criminal offender—the cyber criminal—who continues to elude law enforcement and avoid prosecution by engaging in crimes that are particularly difficult to prosecute under laws.

ORGANIZATION OF THE BOOK

Crimes of the Internet is an edited volume of original scholarly articles authored by many of the world's top experts on cyber crimes. As of this writing, the research into cyber crime activities has been limited to a few "not so well known" studies, which although often insightful, have unfortunately been confined mainly to academic journals that cater predominantly to college students, faculty, and researchers. Unfortunately, these findings seldom reach the desks of law enforcement officials, prosecutors, and policymakers. Outside of academia, cyber crime coverage is largely restricted to identity theft and child pornography—a shortcoming that this book seeks to address.

Crimes of the Internet is divided into five major sections. Part I is titled "Online Predatory Child Victimization and Exploitation," because it addresses the challenges and tribulations of combating child pornography and online predatory behaviors by pedophiles and other sexual sadists who have turned to the Internet for sexual gratification. Also included are the problems associated with cyber bullying. Childhood offenses that were once confined to the school playground have now entered cyberspace with far-reaching consequences to victims, while presenting unique challenges to law enforcement agencies, school officials, and parents. Chapter 1 addresses Internet sexual addiction, which is considered by some to be an emerging clinical disorder. The search for online pornography and chat rooms that cater to sexual conversations has become a compulsive addiction for a number of individuals. These people spend countless hours searching for, downloading, viewing, and exchanging explicit pornographic images or engaging in sexually enticing text communication while displaying some of the same behaviors and actions as other documented clinical disorders.

Part II is titled "Emerging Global Crimes of the Internet" and this section introduces readers to developing Internet crimes about which there is limited information. Some of the topics provide a glimpse into the growing trend of online pharmaceutical sales, fraudulent online pharmacies, and illicit cyber drug-dealing within the United States and abroad. In this section, readers also learn about consumer credit card fraud taking place in Ghana, a country located on the western coast of Africa, from a researcher who spent a semester in Ghana exploring how a third-world community uses Internet technology to commit consumer credit card fraud. Chapter 8 compares and contrasts traditional offline stalking with that of online cyberstalking, and identifies the challenges associated with regulating such behaviors in cyberspace. Chapter 9 gives readers a glimpse into the world of Internet gambling and, in particular, the efforts of the federal government in the United States to sanction such activity. Chapter 10 discusses the role of Internet phishing, a technique used by scammers to gather personal information from their victims, typically by sending e-mails that purport to be from reputable companies or simulating legitimate Web sites. Chapter 11 introduces readers to an email scam that is neither costly nor sophisticated; yet, the scam remains the most ubiquitous and well known of all cyber crimes. Chapter 12 highlights how the Internet as the so-called "information superhighway" has made it faster and easier to steal personal information in comparison to the traditional "dumpster diving" method of stealing personal information than ever before.

Part III is titled "Criminological Perspectives on Cyber Crime." Chapter 14, which is the first one presented to readers in this section describes the "Space Transition Theory" of cyber crime behavior. Chapter 15 applies Marcus Felson's Routine Activity Theory (RAT) to Internet crime. RAT has been applied to most traditional crimes; however, the ability to "surf" the Web. Chapter 16 examines hacking activities from the perspective of the hackers themselves and the neutralization techniques that they use to justify their actions. Chapter 17 that follows presents an insider's look into the social organization of hackers' culture. Chapter 18 explains how the explosion of digital media, coupled with the rapid development of high-speed computer networks, has resulted in a spike in piracy, allowing digital files to be distributed illegally yet efficiently to millions of file sharers. Chapter 19 is unique in that it introduces readers to the highly organized, domestic, and transnational groups that compete to illegally amass huge quantities of digital media in the secretive online world known as, the Warez scene. These groups are considered responsible for the vast majority of illegal digital media available on the Internet. Chapter 20 discusses the impact of the Internet on traditional forms of crimes that do not entail the use of new technologies, an area that the author says has never been addressed in the social science literature. Chapter 21 approaches online gambling from that of its companion Chapter 9. Many see the virtual casino as liberating, and think that its lure of readily accessible 24-hours-a-day entertainment is not only highly desirable but also inevitable. Others see the virtual casino as embodying a multitude of dangers that will magnify the problems associated with conventional casino gambling while introducing new and perhaps, yet unimagined dangers to vulnerable populations.

Part IV highlights the challenges associated with "Investigating and Prosecuting Cyber Crimes." Chapter 22 emphasizes how computer crimes are requiring law enforcement departments and criminal investigators to tailor an increasing amount of their efforts toward successfully identifying, apprehending, and assisting in the successful prosecution of cyber crime perpetrators. The authors of Chapter 23 note that crime in cyberspace, like most traditional crime, is about making money. They note that highly organized groups of cyber criminals have successfully perpetrated large-scale raids on financial institutions across the globe, and that much of that activity originates in countries like China, India, Russia, Romania, and Latin America, which puts perpetrators out of reach of U.S. law enforcement agencies. Chapter 24 focuses on the understanding of, and issues surrounding the prevention, detection, and investigation of electronic crime. Chapter 25 identifies inadequacies associated with investigating and prosecuting online predators using traditional law enforcement techniques, yet it shows how the media has been effective in locating and apprehending sexual predators on the Internet using highly successful sting operations. The Internet has been a great vehicle for individuals involved in both financial fraud and child pornography. In prosecuting both types of cases, one of the most frequent evidence issues involves the right to search and seize a suspect's computer. Chapter 26 answers this and other questions regarding prosecutorial limitations and proposed solutions to prosecuting Internet crimes. In recent years, the proliferation of crimes committed on the Internet or with the help of the Internet has forced politicians and policymakers to react with laws and policies that have attempted to reduce the incidence of such crimes. These topics are addressed in Chapter 27. Lastly, Chapter 29 emphasizes the importance of the exclusionary rule and the Fourth Amendment in electronic investigations. The courts' assessment of electronic evidence (E-Discovery) and the guidelines for E-Discovery are presented. The chapter also provides some explanation of the process of investigation of electronic evidence, types of electronic evidence, the analysis of electronic evidence, and the misconceptions of digital evidence.

Part V is titled "Cyber Terrorism: The 'New' Face of Terrorism." The Internet has brought about revolutionary change, and one of the greatest changes has been the growing connectivity between all "corners" of the world. In many ways, this has provided new economic and social opportunities. There is also, however, a dark side to such enhanced connectivity. The Internet is an extraordinary medium for the advancement of terrorist ideology because it is relatively inexpensive and attracts a large audience. The Internet also provides an outstanding tool for communicating with current and potential group members. Finally, the Internet provides access to vital information that can be used to injure terrorist targets (like governments) or to collect reconnaissance information to plan attacks. With every passing day, the world becomes more dependent on the myriad of activities carried out via the Internet; yet terrorists have capitalized on that increased dependence in many ways. Consequently, cyber-terrorist activities hold the potential to be highly destructive. As this section shows, cyber terrorism is essentially the convergence of terrorism and cyberspace. Chapter 30 examines cyber terrorism, the potential impact of cyber terrorism as well as cyber terrorism prevention, and control. Finally, the author of Chapter 31 asks whether countries should create new laws to combat cyber terrorism or use existing laws since many statutes that have been created to combat terrorism include language that can be applied to cyber terrorism.

ACKNOWLEDGMENTS

We would like to acknowledge the following individuals for their steadfast support, guidance, and patience throughout the production stages of this peer-reviewed, edited volume of original cyber crime articles. First, we would be remiss if we did not thank all of the contributing authors. Without them, we could have never produced a book of this caliber. We genuinely appreciate their commitment and dedication in seeing this project through from the beginning to the very end. Our sincerest gratitude goes out to each of them.

We would also like to thank those contributing authors who voluntarily participated in the peer review process: Ryan Baker, Indiana University; Wendy Cukier, Ryerson University, Canada; Laura Finley, Florida Atlantic University; Kelli Frakes, Eastern Kentucky University; Gilbert Geis, University of California–Irvine; Thomas Holt, University of North Carolina; Wilson Huang, Valdosta State University; K. Jaishankar, Manonmaniam Sundaranar University, India; Madhava Soma Sundaram, Manonmaniam Sundaranar University, India; Marc Ouimet, University of Montreal, Canada; Wayne Pitts, University of Memphis; Cliff Roberson, Washburn University; Marc Rogers, Purdue University; Cristina San Martin, Purdue University; Kay Scarborough, Eastern Kentucky University; Daniel Shoemaker, University of Detroit–Michigan; Orly Turgeman-Goldschmidt, Bar-Ilan University, Israel.

Finally, we would also like to extend our sincerest appreciation and gratitude to all of the wonderful and incredibly helpful and talented people at Prentice Hall, namely Tim Peyton, senior acquisitions editor, and Alicia Kelly, editorial assistant.

About the Editors

Frank Schmalleger

Frank Schmalleger, Ph.D., is Distinguished Professor Emeritus at the University of North Carolina at Pembroke. He holds degrees from the University of Notre Dame and Ohio State University, having earned both a master's (1970) and a doctorate in sociology (1974) from Ohio State University, with a special emphasis in criminology. From 1976 to 1994, he taught criminology and criminal justice courses at the University of North Carolina at Pembroke. For the last 16 of those years, he chaired the university's Department of Sociology, Social Work, and Criminal Justice. The university named him Distinguished Professor in 1991.

Schmalleger has taught in the online graduate program of the New School for Social Research, helping to build the world's first electronic classrooms in support of distance leaning through computer telecommunications. As an adjunct professor with Webster University in St. Louis, Missouri, Schmalleger helped develop the university's graduate program in security administration and loss prevention. He taught courses in that curriculum for more than a decade.

Frank Schmalleger is the author of numerous articles and more than 30 books, including the widely used *Criminal Justice: A Brief Introduction* (Prentice Hall, 2008), *Criminology Today* (Prentice Hall, 2009), and *Criminal Law Today* (Prentice Hall, 2006).

Schmalleger is also founding editor of the journal *Criminal Justice Studies*. He has served as editor for the Prentice Hall series *Criminal Justice in the Twenty-First first Century* and as imprint adviser for Greenwood Publishing Group's criminal justice reference series.

Schmalleger's philosophy of both teaching and writing can be summed up in these words: "In order to communicate knowledge we must first catch, then hold, a person's interest—be it student, colleague, or policymaker. Our writing, our speaking, and our teaching must be relevant to the problems facing people today, and they must in some way help solve those problems." Visit the author's Web site at http://www.schmalleger.com.

Michael Pittaro

Michael Pittaro, MPA, is the Executive Director of the Council on Alcohol and Drug Abuse in Allentown, Pennsylvania. He is also an adjunct criminal justice professor with Cedar Crest College in Allentown, Pennsylvania. Prior to assuming his current position, Pittaro was the Chair of the Legal Studies Department at Lehigh Valley College, Pennsylvania. In addition to teaching, he serves as a criminal justice curriculum specialist for the Pennsylvania Department of Education's Degree Granting Team and as a criminal justice subject matter expert for the Accrediting Council for Independent Colleges and Schools (ACICS), Washington, D.C. Most recently, Professor Pittaro's criminal justice associate degree program, which he chaired, was ranked 16th in the nation in a June 2007 report titled "*Top 100 Associate Degree Producers,*" in the publication Community College Week, 19 (21).

Professor Pittaro is the recipient of numerous awards for his philosophy, style, and approach to teaching. He has twice been nominated for Who's Who Among America's

Teachers (2006 and 2005), Madison's Who's Who Among Business Professionals (2007), a finalist in Career Education Corporation's "Educator of the Year" (2006), the recipient of Lehigh Valley College's VIP Award, and the Alpha Beta Kappa National Honor Society award for exemplary performance. In addition to serving on a number of local advisory boards, Pittaro also serves on the academic advisory boards for Career Education Corporation's National Criminal Justice Advisory Board as well as Wadsworth Publishing's *National Career Education Criminal Justice Advisory Board*.

Professor Pittaro holds a master's degree in public administration (summa cum laude, 2000) and a bachelor's degree in criminal justice (Who's Who Among Students in Colleges and Universities, 1989) from Kutztown University, Pennsylvania. He is presently a 4.0 doctoral student and student ambassador enrolled in Capella University's School of Public Safety where he is pursuing his Ph.D. in criminal justice.

Prior to teaching, he worked for the Northampton County Department of Corrections in Easton, Pennsylvania, where he served in a number of administrative roles, including time spent as the lead internal affairs investigator, inmate treatment division coordinator, criminal records administrator, and field investigations officer. He has nearly 20 years of professional field experience working with both juvenile and adult criminal offenders and victims. He has also served as a youth advocate and mentor, a group facilitator for sexual offenders, a drug and alcohol counselor, and most recently as a child custody supervisor Northampton County Pennsylvania's Orphans Court.

Professor Pittaro has authored several journal articles and has contributed to several book publications. Most recently, he authored the nation's first and only criminal justice "quick study" academic reference guide. In addition to coediting this particular volume, he also assisted the copyeditor in the final production stages of John Dempsey's *Introduction to Private Security* text (Wadsworth, 2007); and is on the editorial board for the *International Journal of Criminal Justice Sciences*. Professor Pittaro is a member of the Academy of Criminal Justice Sciences, the American Society of Criminology, and the Pennsylvania Association of Criminal Justice Educators.

Visit the author's Web site at http://www.MichaelPittaro.com.

PART I

Online Predatory Child Victimization and Exploitation

Chapter 1

Sexual Addiction to the Internet: From Curiosity to Compulsive Behavior

Michael Pittaro
Council on Alcohol and Drug Abuse, Pennsylvania

Michael Pittaro, MPA, is the Executive Director of the Council on Alcohol and Drug Abuse in Allentown, Pennsylvania, and an adjunct professor with Cedar Crest College's (Allentown, Pennsylvania) Criminal Justice Department. Prior to assuming his current position, Pittaro was the Chair of the Legal Studies Department at Lehigh Valley College, Pennsylvania. He is the author of several publications, including the nation's first and only criminal justice quick study reference guide, and has been the honored recipient of several awards for his teaching style and practice. Pittaro is the coauthor and editor of *Crimes of the Internet* and a member of the Editorial Board for the *International Journal of Criminal Justice Sciences*. Professor Pittaro has nearly 20 years of professional criminal justice field experience. The holder of a master's degree in public administration and a bachelor's degree in criminal justice from Kutztown University, he is currently pursuing a Ph.D. in criminal justice from Capella University.

Abstract

The Internet is undoubtedly the most valuable technological resource available to millions of people across the globe. With a simple click of the mouse, one can retrieve information on virtually every topic imaginable in that the Internet gives users access to millions of personal and professional Web sites. By and large, Internet users enter cyberspace to conduct business, research information, and communicate with others in virtually every corner of the globe, but the Internet has a dark side. The search for pornographic text, videos, and images has become a compulsive addiction for many men and women who spend countless hours searching for explicit pornographic images or sexually engaging text communication. As a result, a new psychological disorder has emerged. Sexual addiction to the Internet has slowly emerged as a clinical disorder like any other addictive disorder that requires intervention and treatment. This paper will provide an in-depth analysis into an emerging addictive disorder that is difficult to detect and challenging to control.

INTRODUCTION

As of February 2002, 54 percent of all Americans used the Internet on a regular basis, and more than half of all households in the United States had an Internet provider at home (Schneider 2003). The overwhelming majority of those who use the Internet use it for both legitimate, law-abiding personal and professional purposes. Most users could safely be identified and classified as recreational users, whereas a smaller population has recently emerged with questionable addictive behaviors and tendencies. Internet usage, in general, and the duration of time spent in Internet activities, in particular, is staggering (Cooper et al. 1999).

Without question, the Internet has become the most valuable technological resource since its conception. With a simple click of the mouse, one can retrieve information on virtually every topic imaginable. Over the past several decades, society has struggled to create an accurate definition that would help identify and describe pornography. In 1973, the United States Supreme Court in *Miller v. California* called for a definition of pornography based on the average person applying contemporary community standards (Dilevko and Gottlieb 2004). The subjectivity and impermanence of this definition is perhaps best illustrated by Justice Potter Stewart's famous comment in reference to pornography, "I know it when I see it" (Dilevko and Gottlieb 2004).

As described by Cooper et al. (1999), the amount of information available on the Internet is virtually limitless, and a sizeable portion of it is related to the topic of sex. Prior to the Internet, most individuals refrained from fully embracing pornography out of fear of public exposure and likely humiliation if one were to get caught in an adult bookstore renting X-rated tapes or any other adult sexual paraphernalia, or while going into an X-rated theater, especially alone (Philaretou 2005). According to Bissette (2004), 25 percent of total search engine requests are porn-related. Consequently, Internet pornography can be enjoyed in the comforts and anonymity of one's home (Philaretou 2005). It is for this reason that the search for Internet pornography has become a compulsive addiction to millions, mostly men, who spend countless hours viewing, downloading, and exchanging explicit sexual images and movies, including child pornography. Stein et al. (2001) characterize this particular behavior as psychiatric in general, sexual pathology in particular.

Far worse than child pornography is the fact that the Internet has also become a fertile breeding ground for sexual offenders, specifically pedophiles, who use the Internet to prey upon the weak, vulnerable, and innocent. **Sexual addiction** to pornography crosses all demographic boundaries regardless of one's religious, racial, ethnic, or cultural background and experiences. Even though women do not represent a large segment of those labeled as compulsive, there is a growing interest in the number of women accessing the Internet, especially chat rooms, for sexual gratification. Unlike print, video, and film pornography, Internet sex can also be interactive through real-time exchanges of words and video pictures that are more enticing to the viewer (Schneider 2003). Some of the many advantages of the Internet are that it is widely accessible, inexpensive, legal, available in the privacy of one's home, anonymous, and does not put the user at risk of contracting a sexually transmitted disease or an unplanned pregnancy (Schneider 2003).

THE PORNOGRAPHY EMPIRE

One cannot address the issue of sexual addiction to Internet pornography without first having discussed the enormous wealth and profitability of the pornography empire. The adult entertainment industry generates an estimated $57 billion in worldwide revenue (Bissette 2004). Twelve billion dollars of which originates in the United States alone, more than all combined revenues of ABC, CBS, and NBC news affiliates (Bissette 2004). In fact, it is one of the fastest growing economies in the world with the porn industry making an estimated 6,000 movies a year and growing (Rice-Hughes 2005). The Internet pornography business, in particular, is alleged to have grown significantly since 1985 when its profits are believed to have exceeded $75 million to an estimated $665 million in 1996. In fact, there are an estimated 1.3 million pornography Web sites, and this number is continuing to grow at unprecedented rates each year, particularly amongst amateurs who post their sexual adventures on the Internet for the simple thrill and excitement of doing so (Rice-Hughes 2005). The search engine, Google, now examines over three billion Web pages with sex continuously being the most searched topic on the Internet (Cooper 2004). As one could imagine, the pornography industry, as a whole, consists of a vast empire that will continue to expand as more and more users access the Internet in search of pornography.

According to a massive study conducted by Comscore Media Metrix, 71.9 million people visited adult Web sites and viewed an incredible 15 billion pages of adult content in August 2005, reaching 42.7 percent of the Internet (Rice-Hughes 2005). The two largest individual buyers of bandwidth are firms in the United States' adult online industry (Rice-Hughes 2005). By 1997, there were roughly 900 pornography sites on the Web. One year later, this number had grown to approximately 30,000, and is estimated to climb at an unprecedented rate to meet the needs and demands of Internet surfers (Stack, Wasserman, and Kern 2004).

THE ETIOLOGY OF SEXUAL ADDICTION

Before embarking on this research-oriented journey, one must be familiar with the etiology of sexual addiction and the behaviors associated with this disorder. Sexual addiction is a subcategory of Internet Addiction Disorder, a term that was first proposed by Dr. Ivan Goldberg to explain pathological, compulsive Internet usage (King 1996). It has been suggested that an Internet addiction disorder has similar features to that of a gambling addiction, and therefore, one must approach this problem in much the same manner as one would approach an addiction to gambling (Young 1996). One must be cognizant of the fact that it is not the technology that is addictive, but rather the behaviors being expressed when one uses the Internet for sexual purposes (Grohl 2005). According to Young (n.d.), Internet addiction, like many drug addictions, provide the euphoria that some individuals desperately seek to feel normal. Consequently, this behavior is often displayed in individuals who are depressed, anxious, or experiencing problematic relational issues.

Sexual addiction to the Internet, for the most part, has been under-researched, but it has recently gained the attention of criminologists and criminal justice practitioners (Seegers 2003). The question remains unresolved as to whether sexual addiction is a bona fide addiction like other addictive disorders such as substance abuse (Griffiths 2001). Some still approach the subject of sexual addiction to the Internet with a strong degree of skepticism and rightfully so. Therefore, it is important to look deeply into the etiology of addictive disorders to fully appreciate and understand the potential problematic behaviors that this disorder, like the others, has on individuals, the individuals' families, community, and workplace (Seegers 2003).

As with any addiction, there are many plausible causes and explanations that may help to explain how someone becomes an addict. Addiction has been linked to biological, neurological, and physiological factors, yet one's peers, family, and community can also influence one's decisions (Seegers 2003). Early literature in the sexual addiction field placed a heavy emphasis on the role of childhood maltreatment, mainly physical and sexual abuse, as the primary cause of most sexually addictive behaviors (Blanchard and Tabachnick 2002). Sexual addiction to the Internet has since become widely recognized by clinicians in the fields of psychology, sexology, and psychiatry as a behavioral disorder warranting further review and investigation (Blanchard and Tabachnick 2002). Today, there are many causal explanations for this type of behavior with the evidence suggesting a correlation between sexual addiction and many well-known disorders. For example, studies have shown that sexual addicts also suffer from **obsessive-compulsive disorders** (OCD), attention deficit hyperactivity disorders, bipolar disorders, anxiety disorders, brain injuries, hormonal abnormalities, chemical imbalances, endocrine abnormalities, diabetic hyperglycemia, hypoglycemia, or any combination of the aforementioned (Blanchard and Tabachnick 2002).

Cooper et al. (2004) credit Young (1996) for being one of the first to write about Internet addiction as an emerging clinical disorder warranting further research. Over the past decade, there have been dozens of studies conducted with a few researchers becoming self-proclaimed Internet addiction experts. Cooper et al. (1999) were the first to conduct a large-scale study of online sexual activity. The results of this particular study are scattered throughout this chapter. The Cooper et al. study (1999) is considered by many to be one of the most detailed and widely cited articles written on the subject.

Sexual addiction to the Internet usually implies a psychological dependence on the Internet, typically for 11 or more hours per week, that is frequently characterized by an increasing investment of time, resources, and attention (Cooper et al. 1999). Like most addicts who are initially confronted by family and friends, most will deny that a problem behavior exists. Denial is a common characteristic that most sexual addicts display once exposed. One must be cautious in assigning this label to individuals who may be using the Internet for lengthy periods of time to complete legitimate personal or professional business. For example, an online student will typically spend more than 11 hours per week online to perform research and complete weekly assignments in a timely manner. However, if one begins to neglect family, friends, school, and work in favor of spending time online in search of pornography or sexually enticing communication, one may be labeled as a sexual addict, especially when the Internet usage causes significant problems in one's life.

The attention that this disorder has received over the past few years has resulted in scholars and practitioners acknowledging that **Internet sexuality** can be pathological (Cooper et al. 1999). The other issue to emerge is the growing acceptance that the Internet invites sexual exploration through sexual fantasies that would otherwise be extinguished if it were not for reinforcement of the immediate feedback (Cooper et al. 1999). The Internet is appealing and attractive in so many ways, yet it is feasible for some to rely on it as the drug of choice to fulfill certain needs and expectations.

Cooper et al. (2004) are credited with first introducing the concept of the *Triple A Engine*. The Triple A Engine highlights three characteristics of the Internet that undoubtedly explain its tempting influence over its users: accessibility, anonymity, and affordability. The Triple A Engine is said to turbocharge, that is accelerate and intensify online sexual activity, and is believed to be the precursor to the new sexual revolution (Byers, Menzies, and O'Grady 2004). The anonymity coupled with easy access and affordability leads to a sense of freedom and disinhibition, which can enhance self-disclosure and a willingness to talk frankly about sexual matters in general, and sexual fantasies in particular (Byers, Menzies, and O'Grady 2004). Some people adopt a completely different persona since physical and emotional characteristics like attractiveness and shyness can easily be concealed in secrecy from other online users. For instance, some homosexual men reveal their sexual orientation first in cyberspace to test the reactions of others to the announcement before doing so in the real world (Byers, Menzies, and O'Grady 2004).

Expanding on the Triple A Engine approach, Griffiths (2000) suggested additional facets such as convenience, escape, and social acceptability must also be examined and considered as powerful lures to Internet sexuality. In particular, it is the social aspect of computer-assisted communication and the interpersonal exchange with others, which is so stimulating, rewarding, and reinforcing that some find it difficult to stop this type of behavior from continuing (King 1996). In addition to the chat room experience, the Internet users have access to an enormous amount of information to anonymously solicit and trade massive amounts of pornography (Cluff 2005). Like some other addictions, sexual addiction to the Internet is often held in secrecy from family and friends. In fact, nearly 70 percent of those who download pornography keep it a secret from family, friends, and intimate partners (Rice-Hughes 2005).

THE EMERGENCE OF THE NEW SEXUAL REVOLUTION

As alluded to earlier, more and more people are using the Internet as an alternative to venturing out into the traditional bars, single clubs, and dating services to meet other people (Cooper and Griffin-Shelley 2002). People are uninhibited by the Internet and, thereby, not afraid to reveal fantasy-laden thoughts over the Internet as would be the case in a direct, face-to-face interaction. In other words, the Internet brings out behaviors that otherwise would not be openly discussed in most sexual relationships for fear of rejection or embarrassment. Unfortunately, the reference to the so-called sexual revolution has not yet been fully explained and lacks empirical evidence to substantiate its claims (Byers, Menzies, and O'Grady 2004). Revolutionary radical changes for women are not expected since women do not use the Internet in the same large numbers and for the same purposes as men have shown to do in almost all studies conducted to date (Byers, Menzies, and O'Grady 2004). However, more than 80 percent of women who have this particular addiction will take this behavior offline and are more likely than men to act out these behaviors in real life, including having multiple partners, casual sex, or an extra-marital affair (Rice-Hughes 2005).

Definition of Internet Sexuality

Internet sexuality has been defined as the use of the Internet for any activity, including audio, text, graphics, or any other Internet medium that involves sexuality (Cooper et al. 2004). This definition also includes recreational use, entertainment, exploration, support around sexual concerns, education, purchasing sexual materials, trying to find sexual partners, and so forth (Cooper et al. 2004). Given that the Internet allows rapid access to sexual materials and even sexual partners, sexual behavior in this context is especially interesting to researchers who continue to focus on the uninhibited nature of Internet sexuality (Stein et al. 2001).

Cybersex is a subcategory often associated with any conversation pertaining to Internet sexual activity. The term has been repeatedly described as using the Internet to engage in sexually gratifying behaviors (Cooper et al. 2004). This would entail looking at pictures and movies, and engaging in other sexually gratifying behaviors, including sexual chat communication, exchanging sexually explicit e-mails and files, and *cybering* (Cooper et al. 2004). *Cybering* is a term coined by Cooper et al. (2004) to describe the sharing of fantasies over the Internet, which entails being sexual together while one or more of those participants masturbate to the shared fantasy.

It is considered an addiction if the individual is obsessed with spending a great deal of time fantasizing, planning, or thinking about sexual behavior in pursuit of the perfect image, story, or erotic material that fulfills a favorite fantasy (Cooper et al. 2004). Fantasy, when coupled with online pornography, can produce a potentially dangerous situation, one in which intimacy can be superficially gained and wrongly substituted for actual intimate contact (Bloem 2005). With fantasy, one can imagine anything one likes, however unrealistic, without experiencing embarrassment or rejection or social or legal restrictions or consequences (Bloem 2005). Sexual compulsivity is often used interchangeably with sexual addiction. Sexual compulsivity, however, is defined as an irresistible urge to perform an irrational sexual act that may be difficult to discontinue without intervention (Cooper et al. 2004). Those who suffer from sexual addiction depict this type of behavior as being unmanageable, chaotic, relentless, and unstoppable (Birchard 2004).

TYPOLOGY OF CYBERSEX USERS

Cooper et al. (2004) divide cybersex users into three distinct types. The first type of cybersex users are the recreational users who search for sexual material or engage in sexual chat rooms on a casual, recreational basis. The second type is the sexually compulsive users who typically have a prior history of past difficulties or challenges with sex or sexuality. And finally, the third type is identified as being truly at-risk, the most critical category of cybersex users. These are the individuals with no history of sexual problems and would be unlikely to develop a problem if not for the Triple A Engine of accessibility, anonymity, and affordability (Cooper et al. 2004).

Those who suffer from low self-esteem, a severely distorted body image, untreated sexual dysfunction, or a prior sexual addiction are more at risk of developing cybersexual addictions (Griffiths 2001). This is not meant to declare that people who suffer from these problems will become sexually addicted to the Internet. Even for those individuals who are confident and lack any known sexual behavior problems cybersex can be the first expression of an addictive disorder that is similar to the increased crack cocaine abuse by the previously occasional cocaine user (Griffiths 2001).

The at-risk groups are divided further into three subtypes: the stress-reactive, depressive, and fantasy types (Cooper et al. 2004). The stress-reactive type is one with a tendency to engage in online sexual behavior during times of high stress to escape or cope with sexually stressful situations. The depressive subtype refers to individuals who are generally depressed, dysthymic, or anxious individuals who use Internet sexual behavior to bring about relief from the dysphoria. The final subtype is one that surfaced unexpectedly during the Cooper et al. study (2004). Individuals in this subtype use the Internet to engage in sexual activities that normally would not be encountered in real life. These individuals are more likely to experiment sexually online because users feel encouraged to engage in secret fantasies and validated by the acceptance received by the cyberspace culture (Cooper et al. 2004).

Paraphilia on the Internet

According to Healey (2005), paraphilia is defined as sexual arousal through deviant means. Paraphilias run the gamut from the seemingly harmless fetishisms such as being sexually aroused by a woman's feet to those that have been deemed criminal by society such as child pornography (Healey 2005). According to Healey (2005), the *Diagnostic and Statistical Manual of Mental Disorders*, fourth edition, hereafter known as DSM-IV, depicts paraphilia as behavior characterized by recurrent intense sexual urges and sexually arousing fantasies. To be properly diagnosed, these urges and fantasies must last at least 6 months and involve nonhuman objects, the suffering or humiliation of oneself or one's partner or children or other nonconsenting people (Healey 2005). There are so many paraphilias out there on the Internet that one could easily spend countless hours identifying and describing each one from amomaxia, sex in a parked car, to Ylophilia, an arousal to forests. For the purposes of this project, it would be best to confine this discussion to only the most heinous paraphilias such as those that involve sexual arousal and violence.

There has been an enormous emergence of violent pornography over the past decade. Increased anonymity has surely led to an increased demand, making various forms of violent pornography more appealing and available than in past years (Cluff 2005). What is disturbing is that some viewers become desensitized to the violence and aggression being portrayed in the images; most of which are staged (Cluff 2005). As an illustrative example of classical conditioning, violence and sexual excitement become paired and reinforced (Cluff 2005). For some viewers, this may become the desired fantasy scenario required to achieve a sense of sexual gratification (Cluff 2005).

In addition to rape, torture, degradation, and mutilation, there is an increasing demand for snuff films that depict the victim being killed at the end of the sexual encounter (Cluff 2005). Whether snuff films are actually real or simply urban legend is not nearly as important as the increased interest people have shown in acquiring such films or images for sexual gratification (Cluff 2005). The Internet pornography industry continues to cater to the needs of its consumers by providing even the most abhorrent images and films that most could not even fathom, especially since there is an incredibly large demand for such graphic images.

CHILD PORNOGRAPHY

According to Bissette (2004), 12 percent of total Web sites are pornographic. An astounding 100,000 of those Web sites offer illegal child pornography that has been estimated to generate nearly $3 billion annually even though child pornography is banned worldwide (Bissette 2004). A staggering 20,000 images of child pornography are posted on the Internet every week, and this figure is growing at an alarming pace (Rice-Hughes 2005). What is even more frightening is the demand for pornographic images of babies and toddlers on the Internet, a paraphilia that is soaring, and it should be noted that the images are more tortuous and sadistic than previously known (Rice-Hughes 2005). The average age of children being portrayed in these images is between 6 and 12 years; however, the profile is getting much younger as the demand for child pornography continues to mount (Rice-Hughes 2005). Moreover, more than half of the illegal sites are hosted in the United States.

The average age of first Internet exposure to pornography is 11 years and the largest consumer of Internet pornography is the 12–17 age group (Bissette 2004). One study concluded that 66 percent of adult content sites visited displayed a warning that the site contained adult content, consequently 25 percent prevented users, whether accidental or not, from exiting the site, a strategy known as *mouse trapping* (Rice-Hughes 2005). According to information posted by Rice-Hughes (2005), one out of 33 youths was sexually solicited online and asked to either meet, call, or send pictures to a predator soliciting the minor, and only 25 percent of youth who were sexually solicited online told their parents. Children must be continuously warned of the dangers and risks of pornography and online chat discussions, even if the discussion initially appears to be an innocent one. Sexual predators have been known to access chat rooms specifically in search of young children and adolescents for the sole purpose of soliciting these minors for sex.

Common sense should prevail in knowing that not every child exposed to Internet pornography will become a sexual deviant or sexual addict. This same argument is often applied to any child who is raised in a poor, inner-city neighborhood surrounded by crime. A child raised in this type of environment will not necessarily be drawn to a life of crime. There are definitely higher probabilities that one will succumb to the temptations of one's social environment, but it should not be perceived as one's fate. The best advice for parents would simply be to monitor and supervise their children's online activities. It would be advisable to err on the side of caution by an occasional visit to the child's or adolescent's computer. Privacy is important for an individual, even if that individual is a child; however, that privacy has limits in that certain conditions exist, and therefore, should only be permissible to a certain degree. The child's safety and security are paramount, and therefore, the child's safety takes precedence over the child's privacy.

Children and adolescents are not exempt from online sexual addiction. During childhood, a child's brain is being programmed for sexual orientation. Exposure to pornography and unhealthy sexual behaviors may affect the child's views of sexuality and sexual orientation (Rice-Hughes 1998). Pornography is believed to distort the normal personality development of a child by supplying misinformation about the child's sexuality, sense of self and body, that subsequently leaves the child confused, changed, and emotionally damaged (Rice-Hughes 1998). If a child's early stimulus for sexual release was pornography, that child can conceivably be conditioned to become sexually aroused mostly by pornography, especially if the experience is positively reinforced a number of times (Rice-Hughes 1998).

It cannot be emphasized enough that consistent exposure to pornography, especially for children and adolescents, can lead to distorted perceptions of sex and one's own sexuality. In one study, adult male subjects were exposed to as little as 6 weeks worth of standard hardcore Internet pornography, which resulted in obvious distorted changes in sexuality perception (Rice-Hughes 1998). Rice-Hughes (1998) claimed that the male subjects developed an increased sexual callousness toward women; began to trivialize rape; developed an appetite for more deviant, bizarre, or violent pornography; and viewed nonmonogamous relationships as normal and natural behavior. Imagine the negative impact this same study would have if children and adolescents served as the study's participants. Ethically, this could never be made possible, but the thought is frightening.

Even with the introduction of such stringent legislative acts as *Megan's Law* and the *Jacob Wetterling Sexually Violent Crimes Against Children Act*, sexual predators continue to roam cyberspace relatively undetected in an effort to lure in unsuspecting, vulnerable victims, including women and children. Law enforcement agencies throughout the nation have created cyber crime units in pursuit of sexual offenders who have chosen to use the Internet as the weapon of choice. These units are not as effective and successful in apprehending offenders as one would hope. There is no denying that the number of offenders being caught in police sting operations across the nation has risen significantly, yet there are literally thousands who have gone and will continue to go undetected unless law enforcement efforts are intensified further.

In fact, many sexual predators have gone underground to form criminal subcultures that disseminate and exchange images, movies, and other pertinent, personal information on children and adolescent victims. There is no doubt that sexual predators have formed deviant subcultures that exist and operate outside the realm of the dominant culture. Deviant subcultures affect individual behavior through shared values, norms, and beliefs (Stack, Wasserman, and Kern 2004). This problem is not confined solely to the United States but abroad as well. In fact, many foreign countries cater to these individuals and are more than willing to sell or rent children for sexual purposes at a modest, nominal fee.

Visual Stimuli, Pornography, and Men

There is clear evidence that gender constitutes a definitive variable that distinguishes users of sexually explicit Internet sites (Cooper et al. 1999). As most would suspect, males account for an estimated two-thirds of Internet users (Cooper et al. 1999). Men frequent Internet sites daily and feel more competent and comfortable using the Internet when compared to women (Cooper et al. 1999). According to a 2001 Nielsen Netrating study, 158 million users had access to the Internet in 12 different countries. According to Cooper et al. (1999), men prefer accessing Web sites featuring visual erotica; therefore, downloading pornographic images to stimulate arousal is significantly higher for men than women. In reference to pornography, most men would prefer to surf the Internet for pornography from the comfort and perceived security of one's home. For many men, access to Internet pornography aids in eliminating the fear of being seen at an adult bookstore, contracting a sexually transmitted disease from a stranger or a prostitute, or being rejected by one's spouse or one's partner (Griffiths 2001). This perceived fear of rejection may stem from an underlying problem with premature ejaculation, impotence, or any other embarrassing sexual dysfunction that some men may encounter (Griffiths 2001).

In addition to accessing pornography from one's home, men will also surprisingly frequent pornographic sites during the course of a normal workday. In one study, 20 percent of men admitted to accessing pornography at work whereas an unforeseen 13 percent of women admitted to doing the same (Bissette 2004). It is readily apparent that society has become more tolerant of pornography and sex in general. Partial nudity, sexuality, and references to sex are consistently being displayed on television, even during prime-time hours in television sitcoms that often cater to adolescents. At times, it is difficult to determine what constitutes normal and abusive behavior in terms of pornographic consumption (Bloem 2005). In other words, how much is too much? It is truly difficult to answer this question because there are so many variables to consider.

From a feminist perspective, one would agree that one aspect of pornography is the obvious objectification of women. The literature has overwhelmingly supported the notion that exposure to Internet pornography objectifies women in a negative light. Women are perceived as being weak, vulnerable, and submissive. Rape is illustrated as being sexually arousing and inviting to women. Men are perceived as being virile, powerful, and dominating. According to Seegers (2003), men will often behave in ways that objectify the partners and minimize emotional involvement, whereas the women will often use sex as a way to gain power, control, and attention.

The Intimacy and Infidelity Issues Associated with Sexual Chat Rooms

Women prefer to enter chat rooms where the ongoing discussions provide social interaction and can assist in the development of intimate relationships. Women are less interested in visual pornographic stimuli in comparison to men and prefer discussions and fantasies displayed through written communication (Cooper et al. 1999). Chat rooms are ideal for the computer savvy woman because chat room activities can be concealed from one's spouse or partner (Schneider 2003). This is worrisome to many mental health professionals. This combined with the improbability of any local, real life repercussions for online social activity produces a new and poorly understood psychological phenomena whereby people, mostly women, feel free to express themselves in an unrestrained manner (King 1996). Very rarely does the chat room conversation leave an obvious trail of evidence of the sexual encounter; making it fairly difficult to retrace the online user's infidelity (Schneider 2003). However, if one is exposed, the discovery of an online affair can be emotionally devastating to the spouse or partner. In fact, adults who have been surveyed perceive this type of infidelity as being similar to that of a real-life physical affair (Schneider 2003). In essence, the Internet allows users to play out hidden or repressed sexual fantasies with little fear of being caught. For the curious, cybersex offers a private, safe, and anonymous way to explore those sexual fantasies without the fear of rejection or embarrassment (Griffiths 2001).

There are many possible explanations for why women enter chat rooms. Loneliness and low self-esteem have been found to be correlated with sexual compulsivity in women, even for those actively involved in a relationship (Cooper et al. 1999). Internet addicts suffer from relationship problems in 75 percent of the cases studied and use chat rooms as a safe way of establishing new relationships and improving one's self-esteem and confidence (Young n.d.). Women who engage in cybersex use the elusive chat room as a form of sexual expressionism (Cooper et al. 1999). This sexual expression can range from simple curiosity to obsession. According to McCormick and Leonard (1996), chat rooms are appealing to women because physical attractiveness, age, and disability can be hidden; sexual feelings and fantasies can be expressed without fear or rejection; and, computer romances have no physical boundaries. Women prefer cybersex because it removes the social stigma that women should not enjoy sex and it creates a safe environment for women to explore sexuality in new, uninhibited ways (Griffiths 2001).

What may take months or years to establish in an offline relationship may only take a few hours, days, or weeks online (Griffiths 2001). Cybersex enables women to take sexual risks that would unlikely be voiced or attempted in real life. However, when a female chooses to take the behavior offline, there is a tendency to engage in dangerous sexual activities with complete strangers, thereby increasing the risk of contracting a sexually transmitted disease, being exploited, or being abused (Seegers 2003). Another critical factor is that chat room's disinhibiting effect is inherent in online activity (King 1996). Disinhibition is clearly one of the Internet's key appeals as there is little doubt that the anonymity associated with the Internet makes people less inhibited (Griffiths 2001).

There can also be a voyeuristic aspect to cyberspace participation whereby individuals, men and women alike, can simply sit back and read the ongoing discussions in sexually oriented chat rooms (King 1996). The ability to witness others interacting in an uninhibited fashion is sexually stimulating and arousing to some men and women (King 1996). Voyeurism is a characteristic more likely to be expressed by males; however, some women may be attracted to the sexual excitement it provides. Voyeuristic peeping may be perceived as a way to observe what others are saying and doing in cyberspace before deciding on whether one should participate in the same discussion or create a new discussion to guide the conversation in another direction.

Physiological Explanations

Many mistakenly believe that one's sexual desires and urges stem from one's genitalia but the fantasy originates in one's mind, specifically the brain since there is a biological, neurological, and physiological reaction to sex (Seegers 2003). There are chemical reactions that increase in the brain during sexual stimulation that often start with the simplest sexual fantasy. With continued exposure to pornography for sexual stimulation, the brain chemistry becomes altered, which then requires the individual to engage in compulsive sexual activity to reach the same euphoric high (Seegers 2003). It is very similar to the biological process of drug and alcohol addiction and the concept of tolerance. Tolerance occurs when a subject's reaction to a drug or, in this case, pornographic visual stimuli decreases so that a larger quantity is required to achieve the same desired effect. One could say that a tolerance develops when heightened sexual behavior is needed to reach the climax that one wants to achieve through the desired activity.

From a biological perspective, testosterone levels are predictive of hypersexual behavior in men; therefore, it should come as no surprise that men are more than six times more likely than women to use cyber pornography (Stack, Wasserman, and Kern 2004). Nevertheless, atypical sexuality, including hypersexuality, has repeatedly been linked to closed head trauma as well as injury and disease that cause damage to the frontal and temporal lobes of the brain (Blanchard and Tabachnick 2002). Blanchard and Tabachnick (2002) claim that temporal lobe epilepsy has been repeatedly thought to be a causal factor in the development of certain paraphiliac sexual addictions. Brain damage or neuropsychological deficit is significantly associated with criminal sexual activity (Blanchard and Tabachnick 2002). For example, sexual serial killer, John Wayne Gacy, suffered from severe seizures as a child that were thought to have originated from a childhood accident in which Gacy sustained a head injury. In an older, but relevant study, abnormal readings of quantitative electroencephalograms were found in 100 percent of sexual abusers (Corley et al. 1994). One would approach this study's findings with a strong degree of skepticism since absolute findings are rare.

Personality and Other Psychiatric Disorders

Research trends indicate that Internet addicts suffer from emotional problems, particularly depression and anxiety-related disorders. These individuals often use the fantasy world of the Internet to psychologically escape and, in a sense, cope with unpleasant feelings or stressful situations (Young n.d.). Psychological studies of pornography use have speculated that factors such as personality disorders like mood, anxiety, and depression may be related to compulsive Internet pornography use (Stack, Wasserman, and Kern 2004). This type of neurotic behavior can result in increased levels of anxiety or stress as one lives in constant fear of the behavior being discovered (Reece and Dodge 2004). The feeling of shame and guilt may intensify as the addiction affects the individual's values, beliefs, and spirituality (Reece and Dodge 2004). Depression is likely to follow which creates further despair since stress and depression have been found to play a significant role in the development of pathological Internet use. The studies pertaining to depression and anxiety-related disorders suggest that this compulsive behavior may be related to psychological difficulties stemming from social isolation and loneliness (Cooper et al. 1999). Consequently, engaging in Internet sexual activity may be used as an escape, distraction, or means of coping with uncomfortable feelings that arise from such stressful situations (Cooper et al. 2004).

CRIMINOLOGICAL EXPLANATIONS

Behavior theory can be applied to the study of Internet addiction. It has often been referred to as the stimulus response approach to human behavior (Schmalleger 2005). When an individual's behavior results in rewards or positive feedback, or when the behavior is regarded as pleasurable and desirable, it is likely that behavior will be repeated via the concept of positive reinforcement (Schmalleger 2005). Viewing and downloading pornography becomes a pleasurable activity that invokes strong, positive feelings regarding one's sexual feelings, desires, and urges. The same argument could be applied to Internet chat rooms since such avenues provide a positive outlet for many women who find the experience pleasing and rewarding. As applied to sexual addiction, this behavior is likely to continue because it has been positively reinforced through past pleasurable experiences. Reinforcement is a powerful psychological concept, and its application to the study of Internet sexuality is quite relevant.

If one were to apply the philosophy of the early classical school works of criminology theorists such as Beccaria and Bentham, one would speculate that human behavior could be viewed from a rational choice perspective. One of the major principles of the classical school is that human beings are fundamentally rational and most human behavior is the result of free will coupled with rational choice (Schmalleger 2005). Pain and pleasure are the two central determinants of human behavior. If the pleasure is greater than the pain, the behavior is likely to continue.

According to Bentham, who coined the term, *hedonistic calculus*, the value of any pleasure could be calculated by its intensity, duration, certainty, and immediacy (Schmalleger 2005). Humans are inherently pleasure-seeking organisms and are likely to engage in activities that maximize pleasure and minimize pain. The sexual pleasure that one receives from Internet pornography or chat room communication is immense, yet the risks associated with this particular addiction are minimal. It is likely that most sexual addicts will continue to engage in this type of behavior because of the pleasure and positive reinforcement that it produces to its users.

As applied to modern day theory, Cooper et al. (1999) cited three psychological reinforcements underlying Internet addiction. In short, the Internet can be used to meet and socialize with new people; establishing relationships or viewing pornography can be a sexually fulfilling experience; and, the anonymity of the Internet allows one to create an imaginary persona (Cooper et al. 1999). In other words, the Internet allows people to live out unfulfilled sexual fantasies or sexual acts that typically would not be attempted in a real-world setting. It is a fantasy world where one can be virtually anyone else but him or herself and interact with anyone whether real or imaginary (Cooper et al. 1999).

Attachment Theory

Giugliano (2004) applied Bowlby's attachment theory that was first introduced in the 1950s to the study of sexual addiction. Attachment theory has become increasingly popular among researchers and scholars (Giugliano 2004). Bowlby viewed attachment as a strong affectional bond between the primary caregiver and the child. If the bond did not exist or did not properly form, the maladjusted child would have unresolved emotional attachment issues as an adult (Schmalleger 2005). Alley (2005) contends that there is a connection between childhood trauma and sexual acting out where the adult may be trying to recapture, albeit destructive, feelings of belonging and love from the presexualization encounter. As with most addictions, there can be co-occurring disorders (Blankenship and Laaser 2004). Blankenship and Laaser (2004) claim that 97 percent of sexual addicts have experienced some type of emotional, physical, or sexual trauma in childhood or adolescence.

ADHD and Sexual Addiction

In 2002 and again in 2004, Blankenship and Laaser determined that there is a strong link between attention deficit hyperactive disorder (ADHD) and sexual addiction. For some of these individuals, sex becomes a form of self-medication, a term researchers refer to as hyperfocused hypersexuality (Blanchard and Tabachnick 2002). The impulsive nature of individuals suffering from ADHD may explain the acting out behavior and the compulsive nature of the addictive tendencies. The link between ADHD and other addictive, delinquent, and criminal behaviors has been the subject of many studies for several decades.

Depression

As has been repeatedly mentioned, the link between major depression and sexual addiction is incredibly strong. Major depression, according to Weiss (2004), is listed in DSM-IV-TR. The symptoms include a depressed mood, diminished interest or pleasure in activities, significant weight loss or gain, insomnia or hyperinsomnia, fatigue, feelings of worthlessness and guilt, diminished ability to think or concentrate, and recurrent thoughts about death (Weiss 2004). Depression can be successfully treated with proper medication, and if needed, psychological counseling.

Bipolar disorder or manic-depressive illness is characterized by dramatic swings in mood from depressive to manic. Studies have consistently revealed elevated rates of addictive behaviors among bipolar patients, especially those with drug or alcohol addictions (Blanchard and Tabachnick 2002). For men, bipolar disorder typically emerges, on average, around the age of 18 when testosterone levels are elevated (Blanchard and Tabachnick 2002). In some cases, individuals with any one of the aforementioned disorders have an inherent risk that this behavior may manifest itself to the point where one needs to act out the sexual fantasy in real life. Heasman (2005) found that sex offenders, like Internet sexual addicts, suffer from comorbid psychiatric disorders, specifically major depression along with a history of one or more anxiety disorders.

OCD

OCD is also linked to sexual disturbances and sexual disorders. For example, compulsive masturbation, exhibitionism, and other sexually addictive behaviors have long been associated with an OCD diagnosis (Blanchard and Tabachnick 2002). As with any diagnosis mentioned throughout this chapter, one should proceed with caution in assuming that individuals suffering from any of these disorders will engage in sexual deviancy or criminality. In fact, there have only been a small number of cases in which OCD, if left untreated, has caused an individual to drift into exploitive or criminal behavior (Blanchard and Tabachnick 2002).

SOCIAL BOND THEORY

Hirschi's social bond theory can also be applied to the study of sexual addiction to the Internet as to how some people may be more at risk of developing such behaviors. In short, Hirschi argued that through successful socialization, a bond forms between individuals and the social group (Schmalleger 2005). When the bond is broken or weakened, deviance and crime may result (Schmalleger 2005). For the purpose of this chapter, the discussion will pertain to the deviance aspect of Hirschi's theory. Hirschi described four components of the social bond, namely attachment, commitment, involvement, and belief.

> Taken individually, attachment refers to a person's shared interest with others; commitment is the amount of energy and effort put into activities with others; involvement is the amount of time spent with others in shared activities; and finally, belief is a shared value and moral system. (Schmalleger 2005)

Those with the strongest bonds to conventional society will be less likely than others to become socially isolated and resort to compulsive Internet pornography and other sexually addictive activities for sexual gratification.

Hirschi's social bond theory could easily be applied to contemporary studies of Internet addiction. Stack, Wasserman, and Kern (2004) found that the strongest predictors of use of Internet pornography were weak ties to religion and an unhappy marriage or relationship. Those individuals with stronger marital bonds were likely to refrain from such activity when compared to those individuals in an unhealthy relationship in which one or both partners are unhappy (Stack, Wasserman, and Kern 2004).

Sexually compulsive users, on average, are comprised of those people who have had past or present difficulties with sexual issues, yet find the Internet to be an effective venue by which to pursue uninhibited sexual interests (Cooper et al. 2004). The Sexual Behavior Sequence is a social psychological model of the antecedents and consequences of sexual behavior that can be applied to conceptualizing experience with Internet sexuality (Fisher and Barak 2001). Further, it directly addresses the question of how the effects of experiences with Internet sexuality may influence an individual's future sexual behavior (Fisher and Barak 2001). According to Fisher and Barak (2001), a positive outcome will strengthen the future likelihood of further contact with sexual stimuli on the Internet. This behavior may trigger overt experimentation with a partner in a real-life setting.

For example, if one continues to search for a particular sexual image that is especially arousing, that individual may want to experiment with a partner in the same manner. Fisher and Barak's study (2001) cited an example of an individual who was sexually aroused by images of men ejaculating on the breasts of women. According to Fisher and Barak (2001), that individual may be inclined to ask a partner to act out that particular fantasy. The man will only approach the sexual partner if a positive response is to be expected. If the sexual suggestion is anticipated to invoke a negative reaction, the individual might choose to confine this covert fantasy to masturbating to pornographic images. The problem lies in the fact that some individuals, especially teenagers, may expect this type of sexual activity to take place outside of the cyberworld based on the duration of time spent viewing pornographic images and movies on the Internet. For those with limited sexual experience, pornography generates distorted perceptions between fantasy and reality, which could potentially lead to problematic behaviors, including those that violate the law.

INTERVENTION

There are several obstacles to intervening and treating this disorder. Finding a qualified mental health professional who acknowledges this condition and specializes in this type of treatment may be a cumbersome task to accomplish (King 1996). As mentioned, sexual addiction does not occur in a vacuum. Frequently, there are coexisting disorders or problems that also need to be addressed in therapy. Counselors who treat this condition should adopt a holistic approach to treating the entire person and the environmental variables that may play a significant role in the addiction itself. Those individuals who engage in online sexual activity may be suffering from a number of problems including, but not limited to, negative financial, legal, occupational, relational, and personal issues that can easily escalate involvement in sexually deviant Internet behaviors (Cooper 2004).

Unfortunately, the *Diagnostic and Statistical Manual of Mental Disorders* does not acknowledge pornography as an addiction with a primary diagnosis, yet it meets the criteria noted in the DSM-IV for other addictive disorders (Bloem 2005). Treatment for online sexual addiction is best when conducted with a multimodal approach that is similar to other non-chemical process disorders (Cooper 2004). To facilitate long-term changes in behavior requires ongoing treatment, such as individual or couples therapy (Cooper 2004). To effectively confront this disorder, Cooper (2004) recommends focusing on what is commonly referred to as the three R's—relationship, resistance, and reality.

In short, individuals must work on identifying, tolerating, and processing intense emotions, including interpersonal issues such as trust, vulnerability, and intimacy (Cooper 2004). Couples are encouraged to strive for a deeper level of intimacy and strengthen the relationship through improved communication, increased honesty, and commitment to the ongoing problem (Schneider 2002). Group therapy is also an integral part of treatment because groups offer support for changing behaviors 24 hours a day, and it provides an opportunity for the client to practice new healthy behaviors (Cooper and Griffin-Shelley 2002).

At present, treatment for sexual addiction usually includes inpatient, outpatient, and aftercare support, and self-help groups (Griffiths 2001). Outpatient is the preferred treatment intervention, whereas inpatient treatment is reserved primarily for those with chronic, possibly criminal, sexual tendencies. Treatment may also consist of family counseling programs, support groups, and educational workshops for addicts and families (Griffiths 2001). Treatment for online sexual addiction needs to be centered on breaking the denial and isolation frequently associated with the sexually addictive personality disorder (Cooper et al. 1999). This is illustrated in a study whereby 92 percent of those surveyed felt that the compulsive online sexual behavior was not problematic (Cooper et al. 1999).

Women, for the most part, are often more difficult to treat because the addiction rarely has anything to do with sex itself, but is a desperate search for intimacy, love, touch, affirmation, and acceptance (Seegers 2003). Treatment is based more on emotional need or the lack of the aforementioned in one's life. In the search for love, women often have sex with multiple partners; therefore, the shame of sexual addiction is greater for women than it is for men (Seegers 2003). Women are more likely than men to be labeled as promiscuous for engaging in such immoral acts that are shunned by society.

The efficacy of treatment must consider other co-occurring problems. Issues such as ADHD, generalized anxiety disorder, OCD, posttraumatic stress, dysthymia, major depression, and bipolar disorder may have a significant impact upon the speed and quality of the addict's recovery (Blankenship and Laaser 2004). It may be difficult to determine with true exactness which came first, the sexual addiction or one or more of the psychological disorders listed above.

The Application of the Behavioral Economics Model to Internet Addiction

If one were to view sexual addiction to the Internet from the Behavioral Economics Model, one could apply the economic law of supply and demand (Vuchinich 1999). There are very little constraints on access to Internet pornography with the exception of child pornography. Even though the availability of alternative activities exists, most sexual addicts choose to engage in online sexual activities at the expense of normal, healthy relationships. The Behavioral Economics Model claims that consumption is based on economic costs. Gaining access to the Internet is fairly inexpensive, making it extremely appealing to even those individuals with limited incomes. The Internet is easily accessible and available wherever one travels, whether it be at home, work, school, or a public library for that matter. Therefore, it is relatively easy to access, and costs associated with Internet access are minimal at best.

Demand is the primary dependent variable in microeconomics and refers to the amount of a commodity that is purchased (Vuchinich 1999). Further, the basic demand curve plots consumption as a function of its price, and the general economic Law of Demand suggests an inverse relationship between consumption and price (Vuchinich 1999). The demand for Internet pornography is incredibly high therefore; distributors of pornography will provide a steady supply of licit and illicit pornography based on consumer demands. As mentioned, researchers have seen an increasing demand for child pornography and violent pornography that is particularly disturbing to most people. The pornography industry has repeatedly shown that it will provide virtually any image, movie, or discussion if there is a demand for such material. For the consumer, Internet pornography is relatively inexpensive. The pornography business continues to thrive, and will obligingly vary the content of Internet sex Web sites to meet individual consumer demands and needs (Philaretou 2005). The opportunity and easy access to the Internet makes it very appealing to its users. Research into other socially acceptable but potentially problematic behaviors such as drinking alcohol and gambling has demonstrated that increased accessibility leads to increased regular use (Griffiths 2003). The increased usage may lead to an increase in problematic behaviors (Griffiths 2003). The Behavioral Economics Model can easily be applied to the study of sexual addiction to the Internet as it has shown that economics and behavior are key indicators of compulsive Internet usage.

The Use of Harm Reduction

Although not widely pursued in the United States, a more balanced approach to supply and demand reduction strategies has emerged in other nations employing harm reduction programs (Tucker 1999). Harm reduction, as applied to sexual addiction to the Internet, could be used as a public health approach aimed at reducing the harmful consequences of this addictive disorder for both the user and the community (Tucker 1999). Any change in behavior that reduces harm or the risk of harm is encouraged and accepted; even if it falls short of abstinence (Tucker 1999). Total abstinence is not the goal of any intervention used to control the compulsiveness of this particular behavior unless, of course, the behavior is criminal such as the downloading of child pornography.

It is essential that the treatment intervention employed resembles that of an individual who is dieting by reducing caloric intake. Like dieting, the goal is to reduce the compulsive behavior of its user. The traditional approach to substance abuse is quite different, whereas groups such as Alcoholics Anonymous (AA) or Narcotics Anonymous (NA) require its members to abstain from drinking alcohol or using drugs. Contrarily, sexual addicts are led back into a normal, healthy sex life much in the same way that those suffering from eating disorders must relearn healthy eating patterns (Griffiths 2001). It would be illogical for one to consider abstaining from sex since sexual desires and urges are inherent human qualities that cannot be discounted. Avoiding the Internet is also not a realistic option. Total computer abstinence would be difficult, if not impossible, to adhere to considering that the Internet is used both personally and professionally in today's technological age.

Eliminating Internet usage altogether is simply not plausible or realistic in today's contemporary society since there is a heavy reliance on Internet usage both at work and at home. According to King (1996), mental health professionals may want to recommend that the client create a calendar schedule to record one's time online, which can be used to establish a baseline for the behavior and tracking recovery progress. In addition, King (1996) suggested that users could create a program that flashes a warning message at regular intervals, reminding the user to stop momentarily and evaluate whether continuing Internet activity is warranted or not.

Dr. Young suggests implementing a treatment program based on cognitive-behavioral techniques to achieve moderation and controlled use along with a comprehensive psychosocial approach to address the underlying problems. This could be illustrated using an analogy similar to that of controlled or moderate drinking as a viable alternative to abstinence. The debate over controlled drinking has stirred up quite a bit of controversy since it was first introduced in early 1960s when the prominent British physician D. L. Davies (1962) published a paper documenting his observation that a percentage of patients in an abstinence-based program had come to drink innocuously (Westermeyer n.d.). According to Westermeyer (n.d.), it was not until Mark and Linda Sobell's study of chronic male alcoholics gained international attention in the late 1970s that this idea was revisited as a treatment alternative to the large majority of problem drinkers that are not dependent on alcohol. The same argument could be applied here as well. The objective behind harm reduction is to reduce the harmful consequences for the user and the community, and any change that reduces harm or risk of harm is encouraged and accepted, even if it falls short of abstinence (Tucker 1999). The goal is to reduce the compulsive behavior of sexual addicts who use the Internet for sexual gratification.

THE PUBLIC HEALTH APPROACH TO AWARENESS AND EDUCATION

The public health perspective often utilizes policies and programs already in place and approaches the issue of prevention through a multidisciplinary scientific approach (Blanchard and Tabachnick 2002). To begin, there must be a mature national public dialogue on issues of sexuality, sexual health, and responsible sexual behavior (Blanchard and Tabachnick 2002). Society has often viewed sexuality as a taboo subject to avoid discussing at all costs. To combat the problems of sexuality, and sexual addiction in particular, society must call on all individuals, communities, the media, private businesses, and the government from local to national to assist in prevention and education efforts (Blanchard and Tabachnick 2002). Blanchard and Tabachnick (2002) suggested that education must begin by increasing public awareness of sexual health and responsible sexual behavior. Responsibility must include providing the intervention necessary to promote sexual health and responsible sexual behavior (Blanchard and Tabachnick 2002). Blanchard and Tabachnick (2002) also suggest investing in scientific research related to sexual health and disseminating those findings both in and out of the world of academia.

Blanchard and Tabachnick (2002) recommend that early detection, diagnosis, and viable treatment options are essential to the public health perspective. Society must recognize the early warning signs and intervene before any harm is done. Reducing harm through the harm reduction philosophy of the public health perspective is a key ingredient to awareness and education. Those in the sex abuse and sex addiction treatment fields must unite and orchestrate a grassroots educational approach in which these issues could be addressed in the schools, with parent groups, with health care professionals, and with civic organizations (Blanchard and Tabachnick 2002).

There is an undeniable need to create an environment that would encourage and invite families and individuals who have been affected by this disorder to come out, speak publicly, and provide awareness regarding this disorder. Those who work in the sexual addiction field must initiate collaboration with the various educational organizations to broaden the existing knowledge of the medical, psychological, and environmental factors that give rise to inappropriate sexual behaviors (Blanchard and Tabachnick 2002).

The public need to be educated as to the dangers of the Internet, especially for those individuals who are at risk for developing online sexually compulsive behavior (Cooper et al. 1999). Programs are needed to help individuals develop healthy sexual self-esteem and behaviors, especially the disenfranchised populations such as those who are physically unattractive or emotionally insecure, who may struggle with sexuality issues (Cooper et al. 1999). As mentioned, there are coexisting problems or co-occurring psychiatric problems that must be addressed to reduce the harm being done to the individual as well as to the community.

It would also be helpful if the Internet service providers and major providers of online adult entertainment posted warnings about the potential negative effects of online sexual pursuits (Cooper et al. 1999). Surprisingly, the adult entertainment industry has been very responsive to public opinion and pressure and has been supportive of Web site monitors like CyberNanny and the requiring of credit card numbers to access certain Web sites (Cooper et al. 1999). One would think that the adult entertainment industry would be resistant to such suggestions but the industry has been very receptive to the implementation of warnings and other attempts to block children and adolescents from accessing adult content sites, specifically those pornographic Web sites that may be emotionally traumatizing to this segment of the population.

It is imperative that mental health professionals and others identify those who may be at risk. By adopting a public health approach to sexual addiction, researchers can understand how to address societal factors and social norms that discourage most from discussing sexual behavior, especially unhealthy sexual behaviors that can possibly be treated and managed (Blanchard and Tabachnick 2002). There must be a willingness to start providing awareness and education to the public about the possible dangers of the Internet, specifically the dangers of pornography and the lure of chat rooms.

SOCIAL REPERCUSSIONS

Sexual addiction to the Internet can have a profound effect on family and friends. In particular, partners may feel lonely, ignored, unimportant, neglected, and obviously, angry because the user spends an inordinate amount of time online (Schneider 2003). The couple's sexual relationship may also suffer because the user views and downloads images and movies of sexual behaviors that are often hidden from one's spouse or significant partner. These images and movies take the place of healthy relational sex. Schneider (2003) cited a study in which divorce and separation were two of the unfortunate consequences of a sexual addiction to pornography, including the use of sexually intimate chat rooms.

Many users feel a sense of distrust and betrayal when the partner discovers an online romance. Even though actual physical encounters rarely occur between the two users, there is an elevated level of intimacy that is revealed and the sexual fantasies can escalate to the point of mutual masturbation amongst the cybersex users. The intensity of the sexual addiction may adversely affect the sexual relationships between couples. In a recent study, 68 percent of the study's respondents, either one or both partners, reported having infrequent sexual relations or lost interest in sexual relations altogether (Schneider 2003). Some of those cited in the Schneider study (2003) were labeled as sexual anorexics because Internet sex was substituted for relational sex. This is clearly an indication that a problem behavior exists and must be confronted to save the relationship.

Whitty's study (2003) supported the hypothesis that women were more likely than men to perceive online sexual behavior as violations of fidelity. An unhappy marriage does not necessarily mean that sexual deviance is likely to emerge. However, there is strong evidence of a correlation between marital happiness and sexual addiction. Those who were unhappy or unsatisfied in an existing relationship are more at-risk of engaging in sexually explicit chat room conversations and more inclined to take that relationship to an offline sexual encounter. Those who suffer from sexual addiction to the Internet may jeopardize family and marriage relationships and job performance (Seegers 2003).

INTERNET PORNOGRAPHY AND THE WORKPLACE

According to the research, 30–40 percent of employee Internet activity is nonbusiness-related, costing millions of dollars in productivity loss (Bissette 2004). Nearly 70 percent of all Internet pornography traffic occurs during the typical nine-to-five workday (Bissette 2004). These individuals recognize the consequences of the behavior but most are unable to control this compulsive behavior without receiving appropriate treatment intervention (Seegers 2003). It takes a very daring person to view and download pornography at work. The risk of detection is high and the penalties may be severe, including termination.

According to Cooper (2004), the increasing use of the Internet in the workplace provides a brand new avenue for the availability, spread, and distribution of sexually related material and its consumption by employees with jobs that require online access. In a 2002 study, almost 20 percent of the 40,000 adults surveyed reported engaging in online sexual activity while at work (Cooper et al. 2002). This study corroborates data from other sources that adult content sites are astonishingly the fourth most visited category at work (Delmonico, Griffin, and Carnes 2002).

Cybersexual Internet abuse is a term coined by Griffiths (2003) which involves the abuse of adult Web sites for cybersex and cyber porn during work hours. It includes conventional soft-core Web sites like Playboy and unconventional Web sites that consist primarily of hard-core pornography (Griffiths 2003). In addition to the above, there are also pornographic picture libraries, videos, video clips, live strip shows, live sex shows, and voyeuristic Web cam sites that can easily be accessed while at work (Griffiths 2003).

LEGAL RAMIFICATIONS

In an attempt to curb the number of adults, mainly men, who are viewing, downloading, and trading child pornography, law enforcement is continuously fighting back. Law enforcement has responded by establishing controversial sting programs offering child pornography and a chance to meet children to gullible Americans, many of whom have never been in any prior legal trouble (Cooper 2004). The Communications Decency Act, enacted as part of the Telecommunication Act of 1996, criminalized the knowing transmission of obscene or indecent messages or images through telecommunications to recipients under age 18 (McCarthy 2005). This is just one of the many legislative acts passed in recent years to combat the problem of child pornography and solicitation over the Internet.

There are several other legislative acts worth mentioning briefly that have had a significant role in protecting children and adolescents of the dangers of Internet activity. The Children's Internet Protection Act of 2000 focuses on the recipients rather than the senders of transmission. It requires public libraries and school districts receiving federal technology funds to implement Internet safety procedures, specifically filters that protect against harmful images (McCarthy 2005). The Child Online Protection Act has generated the most litigation because it prohibits content harmful to minors under age 17 from being distributed for commercial purposes through the Internet (McCarthy 2005).

The Supreme Court decision in *Ashcroft v. ACLU* was a major disappointment to antipornography groups and a win for the adult pornography empire since the power and protection of the First Amendment remains somewhat elusive (McCarthy 2005). The United States Supreme Court ruled that the government's attempt to restrict access to online pornography is too restrictive. One has to question whether America's forefathers intended to protect sexual deviants and predators under the First Amendment's protection of the right to freedom of religion and freedom of expression from government interference. The Supreme Court has struggled with the intent of the First Amendment's right to freedom of speech, a clause that allows individuals to express themselves without interference or constraint by the government.

It is difficult, if not impossible, to adequately monitor or regulate the Internet effectively; therefore, one cannot accurately understand the negative impact that society will experience (Cluff 2005). To complicate matters further, those with the potential for developing deviant interests and sexual addiction have access to more sexually explicit, violent, and even illegal materials without ever having to leave the comfort of one's home (Cluff 2005). The anonymity of the Internet allows one to accumulate and trade mass amounts of pornography. Unlike a substance abuse addiction, there is a steady, constant supply of pornography that one could obtain relatively cheap and with minimal risk. The global nature of the Internet has created considerable challenges for the various law enforcement agencies throughout the world who desperately need to unite in a cooperative effort to effectively monitor Internet activity (Philaretou 2005).

Even after the behavior is exposed, the person being questioned will typically deny that the behavior is problematic. If the material being downloaded or shared with others is illegal, there could be numerous legal implications that follow. There may be a loss of professional status or licensure (Reece and Dodge 2004); however, the ultimate fear and the most likely to occur if one is downloading child pornography would be imprisonment. The downloading of illegal material, specifically child pornography, is likely to result in a sentence of imprisonment. Those who are sent to prison for child pornography are perceived by the inmate population to be child molesters even though that individual may not have had direct contact with a child. Child molesters are even loathed in prison and must be segregated from the general inmate population for fear of being victimized.

Unfortunately, treatment in prison is often confined to confrontational therapy, which, according to Williams (2004), may be ineffective or counterproductive to treating sex offenders. Despite its popularity, the confrontational approach has a damaging effect on individuals and it does not encourage change (Williams 2004). The scare tactic of confrontation therapy is to get the offender to admit to the crimes and accept responsibility for those actions. Coercion and other forceful acts may be effective in getting a confession or admission but this approach is not effective in producing positive change in this type of offender.

INCARCERATION

Incarceration is only a temporary solution to a societal problem that is growing at an alarming rate. The literature strongly suggests that sexual offenders have compulsively used pornography to stimulate deviant sexual fantasies. For some, the fantasy may not be enough to satisfy the insatiable sexual appetite or other compulsive behaviors. These individuals may act out the fantasies if the conditions are right and the intended victim meets the role of the fantasized victim. If one were to use an analogy, incarceration is like putting a band-aid on a serious wound. It may be effective in the short term but unlikely to do the job in the long term. American society has concentrated all of its efforts on managing sexual offenders who have already been caught and subsequently convicted and sentenced to prison. However, to truly move forward, society must change the way it thinks about sexual abuse and addiction, and expand efforts to address this epidemic (Blanchard and Tabachnick 2002).

DISCUSSION

To respond compassionately and effectively and to assist the sexual addict in recovery, professionals must set aside personal biases and judgments and treat this problem as a clinical disorder. The stigma, specifically shame and guilt, that accompanies behaviors of this kind make it difficult for people to come forward on their own accord. By providing a respectful, caring, and safe therapeutic environment where one might feel comfortable in revealing and examining those hidden secrets, further exploitation can be prevented. The first step starts with society accepting that discussions about sex and sexual behavior are vital to addressing the issue headfirst. Prevention and intervention arc critical ingredients to the successful treatment of sexual addiction to the Internet. The updated *Diagnostic and Statistical Manual of Mental Disorders* is due to be released in 2011. Until that time, sexual addiction to the Internet will continue to be viewed as a problem issue, not necessarily a recognizable addiction. The society should take a proactive rather than a reactive approach to the problem before the problem escalates to one of epidemic proportions.

Law enforcement, policymakers, and political legislators are struggling to respond to fears of new forms of sexual violence via the Internet. These emerging scenarios include online harassment, cyberstalking, cyber peeping, rape Web sites, child seduction, cybersex with minors, child pornography, male violence, and online pedophilia (Cooper 2004). These challenges are not new but the Internet has made it easier to access such material and significantly lowered the risk of detection, apprehension, and prosecution. The Internet has become the new playground for the child molester. All one needs is access to the Internet and everything imaginable is virtually at one's fingertips.

In summary, anything that can safely, quickly, and completely satisfy such basic human desires is bound to be addictive to some (King 1996). Further empirical evidence is warranted that would hopefully yield more promising results into intervention strategy suggestions and alternative viable treatment options that are inexpensive, yet effective. The Internet is one of the most resourceful pieces of technology to have ever been created by humankind but it also has a malevolent side that cannot be discounted. The problems associated with sexual addiction to the Internet might grow exponentially as technology becomes more sophisticated than humankind has ever imagined.

Internet sexuality   Obsessive compulsive disorder (OCD)
Sexual addiction

REFERENCES

Alley, D. 2005. "Attachment disturbances and sexual offending." In *Sex Crimes and Paraphilia*, edited by E. Hickey, 15–23. New Jersey: Pearson/Prentice Hall.

Birchard, T. 2004. The snake and the seraph—Sexual addiction and religious behaviour. *Counseling Psychology Quarterly* 17 (1): 81–8.

Bissette, D. C. 2004. Internet pornography statistics: 2003. Retrieved November 14, 2005, from http://healthymind.com/s-port-stats.html

Blanchard, G., and J. Tabachnick. 2002. The prevention of sexual abuse: Psychological and public health perspectives. *Sexual Addiction & Compulsivity* 9 (1): 1–13.

Blankenship, R., and M. Laaser. 2004. Sexual addiction and ADHD: Is there a connection? *Sexual Addiction & Compulsivity* 11 (1/2): 7–20.

Bloem, F. 2005. "Pornography and obscene material." In *Sex Crimes and Paraphilia*, edited by E. Hickey, 45–9. New Jersey: Pearson/Prentice Hall.

Byers, L. J., K. S. Menzies, and W. L. O'Grady. 2004. The impact of computer variables on the viewing and sending of sexually explicit material on the Internet: Testing Cooper's "triple a engine." *The Canadian Journal of Human Sexuality* 13 (3): 3–4.

Cluff, L. 2005. "Snuff films, pornography, and violent behavior." In *Sex Crimes and Paraphilia*, edited by E. Hickey, 25–31. New Jersey: Pearson/Prentice Hall.

Cooper, A. 2004. Online sexual activity in the new millennium. *Contemporary Sexuality* 38 (3): i–vii.

Cooper, A., D. Delomico, E. Griffin-Shelley, and R. Mathy. 2004. Online sexual activity: An examination of potentially problematic behaviors. *Sexual Addiction & Compulsivity* 11 (3): 129–43.

Cooper, A., and E. Griffin-Shelley. 2002. "Introduction: The Internet: The next sexual revolution." In *Sex and the Internet: A Guidebook for Clinicians*, edited by A. Cooper, 1–15. New York: Brunner & Routledge.

Cooper, A., J. Morahan-Martin, R. M. Mathy, and M. Maheu. 2002. Toward an increased understanding of user demographics in online sexual activities. *Journal of Sex and Marital Therapy* 28: 105–29.

Cooper, A., C. R. Scherer, S. C. Boies, and B. L. Gordon. 1999. Sexuality on the Internet: From sexual exploitation to pathological expression. *Professional Psychology: Research and Practice* 30 (2): 154–64.

Corley, A., M. Corley, J. Walker, and S. Walker. 1994. The possibility of organic left posterior hemisphere dysfunction as a contributing factor in sex-offending behavior. *Sexual Addiction & Compulsivity* 1 (4): 337–46.

Delmonico, D. L., E. Griffin, and P. J. Carnes. 2002. "Treating online compulsive sexual behavior: When cybersex is the drug of choice." In *Sex and the Internet: A Guidebook for Clinicians*, edited by A. Cooper. New York: Brunner & Routledge.

Dilevko, J., and L. Gottlieb. 2004. Selection and cataloging of adult pornography web sites for academic libraries. *The Journal of Academic Librarianship* 30 (1): 36–50.

Fisher, W. A., and A. Barak. 2001. Internet pornography: A social psychological perspective on Internet sexuality. *The Journal of Sex Research* 38 (4): 312–23.

Giugliano, J. 2004. A sociohistorical perspective of sexual health: The clinician's role. *Sexual Addiction & Compulsivity* 11 (1/2): 43–55.

Griffiths, M. 2000. Excessive Internet use: Implications for sexual behavior. *Cyberpsychology & Behavior* 3 (4): 537–52.

Griffiths, M. 2001. Sex on the Internet: Observations and implications for Internet sex addiction. *Journal of Sex Research* 38 (4): 333–43.

Griffiths, M. 2003. Internet abuse in the workplace: Issues and concerns for employers and employment counselors. *Journal of Employment Counseling* 40 (2): 87–96.

Grohl, J. M. 2005. Internet addiction guide. Retrieved November 11, 2005, from Dr. John Grohl's Psych Central Web site http://psychcentral.com/netaddiction/

Healey, J. 2005. "The etiology of paraphilia: A dichotomous model." In *Sex Crimes and Paraphilia*, edited by E. Hickey, 57–68. New Jersey: Pearson/Prentice Hall.

Heasman, A. 2005. "Personality and psychiatric disorder comorbidity in sex offenders." In *Sex Crimes and Paraphilia*, edited by E. Hickey, 25–31. New Jersey: Pearson/Prentice Hall.

King, S. A. 1996. Is the Internet addictive or are addicts using the Internet? Retrieved November 23, 2005, from http://webpages.charter.net/stormking/iad.html

McCarthy, M. 2005. The continuing saga of Internet censorship: The Child Online Protection Act. *Brigham Young University Education & Law Journal* 1 (2): 83–101.

McCormick, N., and J. Leonard. 1996. Gender and sexuality in the cyberspace frontier. *Women & Therapy* 19 (4): 109–19.

Philaretou, A. G. 2005. Sexuality and the Internet. *Journal of Sex Research* 42 (2): 180–81.

Reece, M., and B. Dodge. 2004. Exploring indicators of sexual compulsivity among men who cruise for sex on campus. *Sexual Addiction & Compulsivity* 11 (3): 87–113.

Rice-Hughes, D. 1998. How pornography harms children. Retrieved November 16, 2005, from http://www.protectkids.com/effects/harms.htm

Rice-Hughes, D. 2005. Recent statistics on Internet dangers. Retrieved November 16, 2005, from http://www.protectkids.com/dangers/stats.htm

Schmalleger, F. 2005. *Criminology Today: An Integrative Introduction*, 4th ed. Upper Saddle River, NJ: Pearson/Prentice Hall.

Schneider, J. P. 2002. "The new 'elephant in the living room': Effects of compulsive cybersex behaviors on the spouse." In *Sex on the Internet: A Guidebook for Clinicians*, edited by A. Cooper. New York: Brunner & Routledge.

Schneider, J. P. 2003. The impact of compulsive cybersex behaviours on the family. *Sexual and Relationship Therapy* 18 (3): 1468–79.

Seegers, J. 2003. The prevalence of sexual addiction symptoms on the college campus. *Sexual Addiction & Compulsivity* 10 (4): 247–58.

Stack, S., I. Wasserman, and R. Kern. 2004. Adult social bonds and use of Internet pornography. *Social Science Quarterly* 85 (1): 75–88.

Stein, D. J., D. W. Black, N. A. Shapira, and R. L. Spitzer. 2001. Hypersexual disorder and preoccupation with Internet pornography. *The American Journal of Psychiatry* 158 (10): 1590–95.

Tucker, J. A. 1999. "Changing addictive behavior: Historical and contemporary perspectives." In *Changing Addictive Behavior: Bridging Clinical and Public Health Strategies*, edited by J. A. Tucker, D. M. Donovan, and G. A. Marlatt, 3–44. New York: The Guilford Press.

Vuchinich, R. E. 1999. "Behavioral economics as a framework for organizing the expanded range of substance abuse interventions." In *Changing Addictive Behavior: Bridging Clinical and Public Health Strategies*, edited by J. A. Tucker, D. M. Donovan, and G. A. Marlatt, 191–218. New York: The Guilford Press.

Weiss, D. 2004. The prevalence of depression in male sex addicts residing in the United States. *Sexual Addiction & Compulsivity* 11 (1/2): 57–69.

Westermeyer, R. W. n.d. Harm reduction and moderation as an alternative to heavy drinking. Retrieved December 5, 2005, from http://www.habitsmart.com/cntrldnk.html

Whitty, M. T. 2003. Pushing the wrong buttons: Men's and women's attitudes toward online and offline infidelity. *CyberPsychology and Behavior* 6 (6): 569–79.

Williams, D. 2004. Sexual offenders' perceptions of correctional therapy: What can we learn? *Sexual Addiction & Compulsivity* 11 (3): 145–62.

Young, K. S. August 1996. Internet addiction: The emergence of a new clinical disorder. Paper presented at the 104th Annual Convention of the American Psychological Association, Toronto, Ontario, Canada.

Young, K. S. n.d. Frequently asked questions about Internet addiction. Retrieved November 11, 2005, from http://www.netaddiction.com/faqsindex.htm

Chapter 2

Pedophilia, Pornography, and Stalking: Analyzing Child Victimization on the Internet

K. Jaishankar
Manonmaniam Sundaranar University, India

Debarati Halder
Manonmaniam Sundaranar University, India

and

S. Ramdoss
University of Madras, India

Dr. K. Jaishankar is a lecturer in the Department of Criminology and Criminal Justice, Manonmaniam Sundaranar University, Tirunelveli, India. He is the founding editor in chief of the *International Journal of Cyber Criminology*, the founding editor of "Crime and Justice Perspective"—the official organ of the Criminal Justice Forum (CJF), India, and the founding managing editor of the *International Journal of Criminal Justice Sciences*. He serves in the international editorial boards of *Journal of Social Change* (U.S.), *Electronic Journal of Sociology* (Canada), *Crime, Punishment and Law: An International Journal* (U.S.), *Journal of Physical Security* (U.S.), and *Graduate Journal of Social Science* (UK). He is the national focal point for India for the International Police Executive Symposium's working paper series and Expert of World Police Database at www.coginta.com. He is a coinvestigator of the International Project on Cyber Bullying funded by SSHRC, Canada, involving eight countries, along with the principal investigator Dr. Shaheen Shariff, McGill University. He is a pioneer in developing the new field Cyber Criminology and is the proponent of *Space Transition Theory*, which gives an explanation for the criminal behavior in cyberspace. He is a recognized expert in the field of cyber criminology and invited by various universities in the United States to deliver lectures on his Space Transition Theory of Cyber Crimes. His areas of academic competence are cyber criminology, crime mapping, GIS, communal violence, victimology, policing, and crime prevention.

Ms. Debarati Halder is a lawyer. She is presently a research assistant in the International Project on Cyber Bullying in the Department of Criminology and Criminal Justice, Manonmaniam Sundaranar University, Tirunelveli, India. She received her LLB degree from the University of Calcutta and master's degree in International and Constitutional Law from the University of Madras. Her research interests include constitutional law, cyber laws, international law, and international criminal justice.

Dr. S. Ramdoss is a lecturer in the Department of Criminology, University of Madras, Chennai, India. Ramdoss's areas of interest are Victimology and Correctional Administration, and he specifically focuses on the bonded labor victims in India. He holds a master's and a Ph.D. degree in criminology from the University of Madras. He was awarded the prestigious UGC Junior Research Fellowship for his doctoral research. His doctoral dissertation is in the field of victimology with special reference to victimization of bonded laborers in tobacco industries. He is a Life Member of Indian Society of Criminology and Indian Society of Victimology.

Abstract

Children have always been vulnerable to victimization. Their trusting nature and naiveté make them perfect targets for perpetrators—both people they know and whom they don't. Today, an estimated 10 million children are using the Internet. With so many children online, today's predators can easily find and exploit them. For predators, the Internet is a new, effective, and more anonymous way to seek out and groom children for sexual activity. Before the Internet came along, pedophiles were lonely and hunted individuals. Today, networks of child abusers are proliferating worldwide. Child victimization on the information superhighway or Internet is escalating at an alarming rate. Many children are being sexually exploited/solicited by individuals who are using the online services as their new playgrounds. There are many reasons for this increase, and some of these are discussed in this chapter. Also analyzed in this chapter are the three types of crimes being committed against children using the online services (i.e., pedophilia, child pornography, and stalking), and the ways through which children can lower the risk of becoming victimized while online.

INTRODUCTION

The development of the **Internet** has been called the most profound change in the way we communicate since the invention of the printing press. Users can access an almost limitless array of rewarding content at the click of a mouse. Familiarity with this technology is vital to our children's future. For today's children to lead tomorrow's world, they must acquire the skills to access the enormous benefits of the Internet, safely. It is especially important that they develop key job skills and an awareness of the increasingly global community. The Internet can empower children, giving them the ability to communicate and share ideas and information on a worldwide basis (Aftab and Polly 1997).

As wonderful as the future of the Internet may be, the extensive media coverage of various "potholes" on the information highway is not an exercise in fiction—there are problems, which cannot be swept under the rug. These problems must be addressed squarely in order to protect our children and maximize the potential of the Internet (Aftab and Polly 1997). While the World Wide Web has made the world shrink, it has also made it more dangerous for children. While we should encourage our children to take advantage of the benefits of the Internet, we must also ensure that they are aware of the dangers and that we take the necessary steps to protect them.

Millions of children are online, either in their own homes, in public libraries, in schools, or at a friend's house. When children who return from school find that there's nobody in their house, they may turn to the Internet as much as they used to turn on the television. They may not feel any threat by talking to someone online, and after a few weeks or months of communication, they are not strangers any more. The Internet is not governed by anyone, and it does not respect any global boundaries. This makes it difficult to police. Experienced users can operate with virtual anonymity, although law enforcement in some parts of the world is struggling to find out the original identity of the users. Those countries have recognized this new form of child sexual exploitation and have begun to dedicate the necessary resources and attention to this growing problem (Canadian Resource Center for Victims of Crime 2000). Although there have been some highly publicized cases of abuse involving the Internet and online services, reported cases are relatively infrequent. Of course, like most crimes against children, many cases go unreported, especially if the child is engaged in an activity that he or she does not want to discuss with a parent (Armagh 1998).

The potential dangers facing children on the Internet (Canadian Resource Center for Victims of Crime 2000) are:

1. Children may be exposed to inappropriate material that is sexual, hateful, or violent in nature, or encouraged to take up activities that are dangerous or illegal (e.g., there are sites that instruct people how to build pipe bombs);

2. Pedophiles may "meet" a child online through e-mail, bulletin board systems (which are the most popular source of child pornography), and chat rooms. They gain a child's confidence and then arrange a face-to-face meeting. They target kids who are lonely or having trouble at home (just as they do in the real world; Canadian Resource Center for Victims of Crime 2000);

3. Children may not feel threatened talking to someone online, and after a few weeks or months of communication, they are no longer strangers. The young person may feel comfortable and provide personal information. If they send a photo, the predator may alter or "morph" it to put the child into explicit positions and use it as blackmail (Canadian Resource Center for Victims of Crime 2000);

4. Internet provides an underground market for child pornography;

5. Adults who normally would not actively seek child pornography may become interested through the easy access of the Internet;

6. Pedophiles will share methods and means to reduce a child's inhibitions and facilitate exploitation;

7. The Internet can be used to facilitate the sex trade/tourism. Web sites offer information about locations of places/countries to go where laws protecting children from sexual abuse may be lax or not be enforced;

8. Children may be "stalked" or harassed on the Internet through unsolicited e-mails, mail bombs, spreading of rumors, negative Web pages, impersonation of victim, providing personal information online, etc. In one reported U.S. case, a man posted the name and number of a 9-year-old girl on the Internet saying she wanted to have sex. In another case, a man impersonated a woman and posted her name and address saying she wanted to be raped—six men showed up at her door in the middle of the night (Canadian Resource Center for Victims of Crime 2000).

Child Victimization on the Internet

Child victimization on the Internet is escalating at an alarming rate. Many children are being sexually exploited/solicited by individuals who are using the online services as their new playgrounds (Zwicke 2000). In this chapter, child victimization on the Internet is analyzed under three types:

1. *Pedophiles:* Individuals who sexually exploit/solicit children.

2. *Child Pornography:* Mostly involves adults getting kids involved in child pornography or distributing pornography to minors.

3. *Stalkers*: Individuals who become obsessed with another individual and they follow their victim from board to board, seeking and compiling various information that their victim may have posted on the boards, with the intent to locate personal information on their victim such as address, telephone number, date of birth, or the city/state in which they live. They then use this information to harass, threaten, and intimidate their victim both online and offline (Zwicke 2000).

PEDOPHILIA

Computer technology and the Internet enable pedophiles to locate and interact with other pedophiles more readily than ever before. Although pedophiles luring kids on the Internet is a horrifying problem, the long-term organizational aspects are more terrifying. The common meeting place and the resultant support child predators provide to each other is probably their most significant advantage—and the most troublesome for a concerned public. The computer, a common household fixture, is now a place where pedophiles can go to hear others say, "You're okay and what you're doing is okay; don't listen to the rest of the world, just listen to us." The ability to receive and offer comfort within the support of their like-minded group reinforces pedophiles with the belief that their attraction to children and adult–child sex are an acceptable way of life (Mahoney and Faulkner 1997; Carr 2003; Krone 2005).

With the advent of the Internet, pedophilic activity has exploded. Pedophiles could use their own computers to make instant copies of pictures grabbed from an Internet club on a Web site located in, say, Moscow and send them to like-minded friends around the world (ECPAT 2004). The Internet has been transformed in recent years into a big store where pedophiles and voyeurs can look or shop around for "articles." They can go to Web sites for the provision of photos and films; to newsgroups for the sharing of mailing lists and URLs (the link to a particular Internet site); to Internet Relay Chats (IRCs) in order to identify, groom, and approach children; and to systems of instant messages. These are enhanced through encrypted plug-ins (software that adds extra features to these programs; ECPAT 2004).

Men who had fantasies that they were once ashamed to admit or afraid to act upon now found a "community" online clubs and chat rooms devoted to preteen sex. Via the Internet, they could enter a home, introduce themselves to children, and carry on a long process of seduction (Nordland and Bartholet 2001a, b; ECPAT 2004). Pedophiles may use the Internet for a variety of reasons, including validation (communication with like-minded people), to find potential victims, and to trade child pornography. Pedophiles who use the Internet to search new victims may be the predatory type, who have above-average intelligence and have the economic means to operate the Internet (Office of Juvenile Justice and Delinquency Prevention 1999). Many pedophiles never act on their urges, while others commit acts of cruelty that are, simply, unthinkable (Nordland and Bartholet 2001a, b).

The Internet allows pedophiles the following (Mahoney and Faulkner 1997; ECPAT 2004):

- Instant access to other predators worldwide;
- Open discussion of their sexual desires;
- Shared ideas about ways to lure victims;

- Mutual support of their adult–child sex philosophies;
- Instant access to potential child victims worldwide;
- Disguised identities for approaching children, even to the point of presenting as a member of teen groups;
- Ready access to "teen chat rooms" to find out how and who to target as potential victims;
- Means to identify and track down home contact information; and
- Ability to build a long-term "Internet" relationship with a potential victim, prior to attempting to engage the child in physical contact (Mahoney and Faulkner 1997).

How Do They Operate?

a) Many of the offenders sign on the services giving false personal information.

b) Seek child/teen victim in the kid's areas on the services, such as the Teens BB, Games BB, or chat areas where the kids gather.

c) Make contact through e-mail.

d) Befriend child/teen.

e) Extract personal information from child/teen.

f) Write sexually explicit e-mails to the child/teen.

g) Set up a "meet"—molest child/teen (Zwicke 2000; Taylor and Quayle 2003).

Many pedophiles will also make telephone contact with the victim, usually by having the child call so that his telephone number don't show up on the parents' bill (Taylor and Quayle 2003; Smith, Grabosky, and Urbas 2004). Two main reasons why they want telephone contact are

a) To engage the child in "phone sex," and

b) To make sure that they are communicating with a child and not with a law enforcement agent.

Child predators are forming an online community and bond that is unparalleled in history. They are openly uniting against legal authorities and discussing ways to influence public thinking and legislation on child exploitation. While pedophile Web sites are being tracked down and removed from the Internet servers in countries all over the world, they are still easily finding ways to post Web sites, Webrings, forums, and chat rooms. Recent online topics have even focused on fund-raising efforts and plan to purchase a dedicated server for their Web sites. It is easy to find and read messages between pedophiles supporting adult–child sex. It is also increasingly common to observe pedophiles in chat rooms promoting one another to move forward with advances on new victims and their families, in what they define as "loving relationships." The advancement of Internet technology allows pedophiles to exchange information about children in an organized forum. They are able to meet in "online chat rooms" and educate each other. These online discussions include sharing schemes about how to meet, attract, and exploit children, and how to lure the parents of their victims into a false sense of security about their presence within the sanctity of the family structure. It has become an online "How To" seminar in **pedophilia** activities (Mahoney and Faulkner 1997).

Scale of the Problem

Some Internet pedophiles raided during United Kingdom law enforcement operations in recent years have been found to be in possession of magazines, videos, and CDs (as well as computer images), and to be downloading images from the Internet onto CDs for distribution by post (National Criminal Intelligence Service 1999). Operation Starburst was the first operation in the United Kingdom to target pedophiles who were using the Internet for communications. Information provided by the U.S. Customs led to the identification of a researcher at Birmingham University who was using the university computer to store 11,850 images, of which 1,875 were pedophilic pictures. Investigations by the West Midlands Police Commercial Vice Unit enabled other individuals, who had copied some of these images, to be identified and located. Police forces in Australia, Germany, South Africa, Singapore, the United Kingdom, and the United States then cooperated and coordinated arrests to prevent the targets from using the Internet to tip each other off. Evidence seized in the original operation led to follow-up investigations, and to date, there have been over 20 prosecutions in the United Kingdom and over 100 worldwide (National Criminal Intelligence Service 1999).

Operation Cathedral, a law enforcement operation across 15 different countries against the "Wonderland" pedophile ring, resulted in autumn 1998 in the largest ever worldwide seizure of pedophile material. In the 12 European countries alone, over a quarter of a million pedophilic images were uncovered from computers, plus hundreds of CDs and thousands of videos and floppy disks containing such material. In the United Kingdom, eight suspects were charged with the conspiracy of distributing obscene images of children, one suspect with the possession of such images, and another (in Scotland) with the possession and distribution of obscene material. Another suspect was not proceeded against, but was already serving a 12-year sentence following conviction of child abuse offences. In other countries, law enforcement agencies sought to identify over 110 targets and, where identified, either charged suspects or continued their investigations (National Criminal Intelligence Service 1999).

The Internet has become an essential medium for facilitation of pedophiles in Korea; as of 2006, the Koreans had spent more time on the Internet than citizens of any other country. Almost all Korean Internet portal sites have chat rooms frequented by teenagers. One search of a portal's chat service revealed 869 individual chat sites, with some obscurely titled "friends of the other gender," where men can meet girls and arrange to provide them with money in exchange for sexual relations. After locating girls online, men usually meet them at subway stations and then proceed to inns or hotels (McCoy 2005). A survey released by Chulalongkorn University of Thailand in early 2003 found that many students provide sexual services through IRC, a form of real-time text communication via the Internet. It allows students and prospective "clients" to communicate in Thai and set up chat rooms with names such as "High School Girls for Sale," "Hi-So[ciety] Girls for Sale," and "Hi-School Gay Room." Adults looking for sex with students often ask for their telephone numbers and a digital photo (McCoy 2005). In India, the pedophilic activity is considered as a crime of Western origin even though there are some cases of pedophiles actively involving in the abuse of children (Bindra 2001).

CHILD PORNOGRAPHY

Child pornography is different from other pornography, and consequently receives more stringent legal treatment. It is distinguished as an issue of child abuse—in its production and/or in the way it is used by pedophiles to desensitize their victims. The growth of the Internet has provided child pornographers with a distribution vehicle, which is perceived to be relatively anonymous (Akdeniz 1997; Taylor and Quayle 2003; Krone 2004, 2005). In its project "Innocent Images," the FBI specified (*Weekly Standard,* April 14, 1997) that the bureau has a database of at least 4,000 cases of child pornography being distributed online. Child pornography makes most people turn away with profound revulsion. Other people will dismiss the problem as one of lone perverts trading dirty pictures. However, that very instinct—to turn away—serves well the child pornographers. The fact is, thousands of children around the world have been brutally abused to create these images, and the demand for the pictures is burgeoning, fuelled by the Internet (Akdeniz 1997; Taylor and Quayle 2003). This in turn encourages more abuse. Child pornography comes in many forms, ranging from photos of kids in baths to the terrible images of child sexual involvement. Some are old images that have been scanned into computers; others are new. It is sad to know that the thousands of children in the photos, tapes, and videos pinging around the Internet were likely forced to partake in the above (Nordland and Bartholet 2001a, b; Taylor and Quayle 2003).

Many times persons involved in child pornography deceive their victims into sending pictures of themselves to the people. Some of the ways they do this is by stating they are photographers and that they can help the child get into modeling, and many times offer them several hundred dollars to pose. Another way is, after they build a "close" relationship with their victim, they tell them they want "sexy" pictures for their viewing only. The pictures are scanned and put on disk. Even if the victim sends his/her photo that is not sexually explicit, there are graphic programs that allow one to alter these photos, such as morphing the face of the victim with the nude body of another person. These pictures are then distributed via modem to others. The pictures are many times posted on the Internet without the victim's knowledge and are used to trade with others involved in child pornography (Akdeniz 1997; Zwicke 2000; Taylor and Quayle 2003).

The distribution of child pornography, through utilizing the online services, is rapidly increasing at an alarming rate. The most common way of distribution is by sending the graphic images to another person's e-mail. Pedophiles will use this method in attempts to "excite" the child and to lead them into other sexual conversation/acts (Krone 2004, 2005). They will also send child porn, as well as adult porn, to the child in attempts to desensitize them to a degree that the child feels everyone is doing these things, and there is nothing wrong with taking these kinds of sexually graphic pictures. When an individual sends these files through e-mail, he will many times coach the kids as to how to get rid of any evidence of having received the files. Some of the things they will be coached to do are as follows:

a) Download the files to floppy disk rather than the hard drive;

b) Label the disk with the name of a game or other child-appropriate program so that the parents will not suspect;

c) Change the file extension after downloading. For example, when the file originally named "teenxxx.jpg" is renamed as "checkers.exe," parents would think the file was a checkers game; besides, even if they attempt to execute the file, they would receive an execution error message and would not be able to open the file. When the child wants to view the graphic, all she/he has to do is rename the file with the correct extension to it. Individuals will also assign a password to the child allowing them to enter their account to download graphic files from their e-mail. Example: Prodigy allows the "A" member (the account holder) to add five other members to their accounts using sub ids B–F. The "A" member will set up a sub id# with a false name and date of birth, then give the password to the child so that he/she can sign on to his/her account using a sub id#. The individual will then send the porn from his "A" membership e-mail to the sub id e-mail. If he is writing sexually explicit letters to the child, he will also send them to the sub id#. The child downloads the files, reads the letters, replies to the individual, sending it back to the "A" id, deletes the e-mail/files in the sub id e-mail box, and then signs off of the service. This is done to keep the parents who do monitor their children's e-mail from becoming aware that someone is distributing porn or writing sexually explicit letters to their children. Since all of the communication between the child and the individual is taking place in the individual's account, parents are unaware of these exchanges (Zwicke 2000; Taylor and Quayle 2003; Krone 2004, 2005).

Scale of the Problem

In the United Kingdom, since December 1996, the Internet Watch Foundation (IWF) has operated a telephone and e-mail hotline for members of the public to report material encountered on the Internet, which they consider illegal. While it would be presumptuous to interpret the figures as indicating an increase in pedophile activity on the Internet, they do at least represent a growing awareness of the presence of obscene material on this medium. It is also important to note that the vast majority of these complaints (about 95%) relate to material originating outside of the United Kingdom (mostly from the United States and Japan). Supplementing the hotline, the IWF also routinely monitors certain newsgroups, which have a record of accomplishment of carrying potentially illegal material; in January 1998, about 40 such newsgroups were watched (National Criminal Intelligence Service 1999).

The National Center for Missing and Exploited Children of United States (NCMEC) Cyber Tip Line receives over 200 leads a week from parents and concerned citizens about child pornography, child solicitation of enticement, child prostitution, child sex tourism, etc. (Magid 1998). In March 1998, the Tip Line received over 10,000 tips about online child pornography alone (remarks by U.S. Deputy Attorney General Eric Holder at the International Conference on Combating Child pornography on the Internet, Vienna, Australia, September 29, 1999). Because Canada has no such tip line, some Canadians have reportedly called the NCMEC line.

In a 2-week period in January 1998, research by the COPINE project of University College Cork in United Kingdom identified 6,033 erotic and pornographic pictures of children posted in 23 child-sex-related newsgroups. In a repeated exercise in April 1998, 7,303 such pictures were found, although the number of newsgroups had fallen to 16. Two-thirds of the images were deemed to be arguably erotic rather than pornographic, with the latter comprising largely either old European photos or more recent ones featuring Asian children (National Criminal Intelligence Service 1999). In the United States, in 1996, child protection services reported at least 23 cases of "cyber solicitation." The U.S. law enforcement, though, has had some success with a proactive approach to this threat. Teams will pose as children upon chat channels and gather evidence through online conversations. Thus, the anonymity of the Internet—the inability to determine gender or age or trustworthiness—can work both for and against the offender (National Criminal Intelligence Service 1999).

The 2000 Annual Report of the Criminal Intelligence Service Canada warns that the "distribution of child pornography is expanding proportionately with the Internet use in Canada. Chat rooms available throughout the Internet global community further facilitate and compound this problem." The report presents the following statistics: Interpol Ottawa (which coordinates international investigation of child pornography) received 164 requests for assistance in 1999 (101 from international law enforcement). In the first 6 months of 2000, 89 cases were received and forwarded to Canadian jurisdictions (78 from international law enforcement). In the same period, one pornography unit investigated 100 incidents and laid 92 charges (in 1999 for the same time period, they did 52 investigations and laid 55 charges).

In 1999, one police service handled 116 files related to child pornography on the Internet. The report concludes that the "sexual exploitation of children and child pornography . . . remains an area of criminal activity that is largely undetected or not reported." The report warns that as "technology provides more opportunities for anonymity and the easy transfer of images and information on the Internet, the distribution of child pornography by pedophiles may increase." The report recommends, "partnerships among police forces, governments and other agencies will be increasingly required to facilitate provincial, national, and international investigations." Prior to the Internet, it was more difficult for pedophiles to find child pornography and to link with others who had similar interests. By the late 1980s, police had cut the flow of child pornography to a trickle (Canadian Police College 1998, 16).

Given the secretive nature of this type of activity, the size of the Internet, and the anonymity it provides, accurate estimates are virtually impossible, although some say there are over one million sexually explicit images of children on the Internet (Canadian Police College 1998, 16). The policing of child pornography should be considered as proactive police work. According to a report from the Attorney General of New Jersey (2000), about 70 percent of convicted child molesters also collect child pornography . The former director of the U.S. Customs Cyber Smuggling Center says that 75 percent of registered sex offenders routinely surf the Internet (Attorney General of New Jersey 2000). About half of the 700 pedophiles arrested in Los Angeles had child pornography in their possession, and a study in England showed nearly all child molesters arrested had child pornography in their possession (Canadian Police College 1998, 8).

When the U.S. Customs set up a child porn Web page for investigative purposes, it had over 70,000 visitors in the first two months (Canadian Police College 1998, 16). In 1997, the FBI probed 301 child pornography cases, 698 in 1998, and 1,500 in 1999 (*Ottawa Sun,* April 11, 2000). In 1999, the FBI opened 1,497 new cases and obtained over 185 search warrants, made almost 200 arrests, and had over 100 convictions (Federal Bureau of Investigation 2000). In 1998, there were 700 documented cases of sexual predators working on the Internet in the United States (*Vancouver Province* 2000). There were almost 800 traveler (someone who meets a potential victim on the Internet and is willing to travel to meet them) cases identified in 1999 alone, with over 300 being investigated by the FBI (Crimes Against Children Research Centre 2000).

The U.S. federal prosecutions have increased 10 percent every year since 1995, with over 400 cases per year now being prosecuted in federal courts alone (Holder 1999). Child pornography offences have increased over 129 percent in 1996 (Attorney General of New Jersey 2000). The U.S. Postal Inspection Service and the FBI made over 450 arrests involving the exchange of child pornography on the Internet (Attorney General of New Jersey 2000). Ninety-five percent of the child pornography that comes into the United States is via the Internet (Attorney General of New Jersey 2000). By May 1999, there were over 21,000 documented Web sites on the Internet devoted to child pornography and pedophilia, which was up from only four months earlier (Attorney General of New Jersey 2000).

The problem seems to be growing in Canada as well. For example, the workload of the Ontario Provincial Police's Child Pornography Unit doubled in 2000. The unit has grown to 14 full-time officers. Vancouver's Organized Crime Agency of BC has seen an increasing consumer demand from Canada for child pornography and access to children. They point to an increase in the use of computers in child pornography offences and to help facilitate other offences. They had at least 10 "luring" cases in 1999 including one case involving a 12-year-old boy and a 55-year-old man from the United States. Ottawa Carleton Regional Police Staff Sergeant Randy Brennan told the *Ottawa Sun* (March 6, 2000) that if all his five-person team deals with Internet child pornography and pedophiles online, they "could take someone down everyday." Canadian Customs intercepts over 200 shipments of child pornography and obscenity with children every year. Follow-up investigations reveal many importers to be working or volunteering with children (teachers, volunteers, etc.) and most are unknown to police.

An unanswered question is the proportion of users of child pornography who are also child abusers. West Midlands Police estimated that 35 percent of those targeted by Operation Starburst in 1995 had physically abused children. The FBI's research of child pornographers in 1998 suggested that less than 50 percent of collectors of material had, as far as investigations could tell, committed physical offences. Whether there is a tendency for collectors, in time, to move on to actual child abuse, however, is also a pertinent question (National Criminal Intelligence Service 1999; Wolak, Mitchell, and Finkelhor 2003).

Reason for Concern Research conducted at Carnegie Mellon University in Pittsburgh, PA, shows the reason for such concerns. Drawing on computer records of online activity, researchers measured the material being downloaded in comparison with the stated reasons for Internet use. The results were enlightening. In an 18-month study, the research team reviewed 917,410 images that were downloaded; 83.5 percent were pornographic. Trading sexually explicit images is currently one of the largest recreational applications of users of computer networks. At one university, 13 of the 40 most frequently visited newsgroups featured sexually explicit posts. The study demonstrated that these materials go beyond the soft-core pornography on magazine racks. The online market features images of pedophilia (nude photographs of children in various poses), hebephilia (youth/teens), and paraphilia (images of bondage, sadomasochism, urination, defecation, and sex acts with animals; Rimm 1995; Wolak, Mitchell, and Finkelhor 2003).

Internet child pornography is an international problem; all countries that are tied to the **cyberspace** face this problem. In 2000, three men from Indonesia and Russia, and a couple from Texas, were charged with selling pictures and videos of children having sex with adults through Web sites named "child rape" and "Lolita hardcore." Some of these children were as young as four. The Texas couple charged $29.95 per month for access to the sites from which they made $1.1 million a year. Two-thirds of that money was paid to the Web masters in Indonesia and Russia. Their customers extended to several continents (Make-IT-safe 2005). A 2002 National Police Agency report of Japan indicated that teenage prostitution and pornography was the most common Internet crime, with 408 cases encountered in that year alone. The prostitution of teenagers via Internet dating accounted for 268 of these cases, a 230 percent increase from 2001 (McCoy 2005).

The latest situation of child pornography is mind-boggling. The IWF has reported a fourfold rise in online images depicting the most severe form of child sexual abuse. The IWF 2006 Annual Report warns of a growing demand for more severe images, and claims that nearly 60 percent of commercial child-abuse Web sites sell images of child rape. Some 80 percent of the children in abusive images are female, according to the report, and 91 percent appear to be under 12 years. The United States and Russia seem to be the main havens for hosting such sites, with 82.5 percent of all the Web sites linked these countries up from 67.9 percent in 2005. The IWF has claimed a 34 percent increase in reports processed by its "Hotline," leading to the confirmation of 10,656 URLs on 3,077 Web sites containing potentially illegal content. Less than one percent of all child abuse content has been hosted in the United Kingdom since 2003, and in 2006 the IWF provided 11 evidential statements supporting UK police enquiries and gave evidence at five UK trials (Williams 2007).

STALKING

There are over a hundred million Internet users across the world. The overwhelming majority is people who use Internet for work, research, or to communicate with family and friends. However, even if cyberstalkers and predators represent only a small percentage of users, we are still talking about a significant number of offenders and potential victims. In 1999, a U.S. report "Cyberstalking: A new challenge for law enforcement and industry" specified that **cyberstalking** was a serious and growing problem (U.S. Attorney General 1999). Both the Los Angeles and the Manhattan DA's offices said that 20 percent of their stalking cases involved cyberstalking. Twenty-five percent of female college students have been cyberstalked. The majority of victims do not report it to the police. When they do, many police officers do not know how to investigate and do not take it seriously.

How Do They Operate? (Zwicke 2000)

a) Stalkers follow their victims from board to board. They "hangout" on the same BBs as their victims do, many times posting notes to the victim, making sure the victim is aware that he/she is being followed. Many times they "flame" their victim (becoming argumentative or insulting) to get their attention.

b) They accumulate personal information of their victims. Many times members post personal information such as address, date of birth, or telephone number, on the various bulletin boards. The stalker will accumulate any information that he can of his victim.

c) Stalkers almost always make contact with their victims through e-mail. The letters may be loving, threatening, or sexually explicit. Many times he uses multiple names when contacting the victim.

d) They contact victims via telephone. If the stalker is able to access the victim's telephone number, he will call the victim many times to threaten, harass, or intimidate.

e) They track the victims to their home.

Scale of the Problem

A 1999 study done in the United States (Crimes against Children Research Centre 2000) sampled 1,500 youth that regularly use the Internet, and the findings are as follows: 1/5 received a sexual solicitation or approach over the Internet; 1/33 received an aggressive sexual solicitation—asked to meet, called them on the phone, sent them e-mails or gifts; 1/4 had unwanted exposure to pictures of naked people or people having sex; 1/17 was threatened or harassed; less than 10 percent of sexual solicitation and only 3 percent of unwanted exposure episodes were reported to authorities such as a law enforcement agency, an Internet service provider, or a hotline.

A Novell survey in 1998 (of 810 people using e-mail at work) found that half the sample had received unwanted e-mails from a persistent sender. Thirty-five percent of the offensive messages comprised unsolicited pornography. To date, however, there have been no known criminal cases in the United Kingdom concerning cyberstalking. However, as Internet usage grows, NCIS assesses that occurrences of harassment will escalate (National Criminal Intelligence Service 1999). Online stalking of children is on the rise in the United States. In 2003, the Cyber Tip Line received 2,600 complaints about online sexual predators, up 23 percent from the previous year. A United Kingdom national survey in 2004 of online experience of more than 1,500 young people aged 9–19 found a third had received unwanted sexual or nasty comments online. Also, 46 percent said they had given out personal information online. A national U.S. survey in 2001 found that almost one in five of the young people aged 10–17 had received an unwanted sexual solicitation in the past year, two-thirds of those were in chat rooms. An online ECPAT survey in Thailand in 2000 found 92 percent of the young respondents had been persuaded to chat about sex online, and only a quarter told their parents about it. In 2002, Japanese police listed teen prostitution and pornography as the most common **cyber crime**, with half their cases related to prostitution by teenagers via Internet dating (Make-IT-safe 2005).

Cyberstalking has attracted much concern in the United States, and 17 states have reportedly passed laws against online stalking or harassment. A court in Texas issued the first temporary restraining order on an online stalker in October 1996; the individual had been harassing the employees of a Dallas-based ISP. In addition, the first prison sentence for an e-mail hate crime was handed out in May 1998. A student in California was convicted of violating the civil rights of 59 students by sending racially targeted threats to them in 1996; he was sentenced to one year imprisonment (National Criminal Intelligence Service 1999).

Vicious online statements and rumors may be used against the victim. Two especially nasty cases have reportedly occurred in the United States. In 1997, someone allegedly posted a child's name, age, and telephone number on 14 pedophile chat rooms, giving false sexual messages which led pedophiles to call on the girl's home. In January 1999, a Californian man was arrested after allegedly impersonating a girl (who had spurned his advances) on the Internet. He, posing as she, is believed to have placed an ad on a bulletin board, seeking male partners to live out a gang rape fantasy and giving (the girl's) name, address, and telephone number, and even instructions on how to bypass her house's burglar alarm. Several men responded to the ad with telephone calls and visits to the girl's home (National Criminal Intelligence Service 1999).

E-mail harassment shares similarities with the posting of hate e-mails and the making of obscene telephone calls. Notably, the stalker does not have to terrorize the victim face-to-face. However, compared with those traditional forms of pestering, the Internet offers advantages to the stalker. No forensic evidence is left on the message (which may occur with letters); there is no need to confront the victim in real time (as on the phone); there is no danger of voice or handwriting recognition; and there are various ways in which it is possible to attain relative anonymity (so there is less risk of the connection being traced, as with telephone calls; National Criminal Intelligence Service 1999).

In the period 1996–98, the NCIS Kidnap and Extortion Desk of the United States was notified of two cases of blackmail by e-mail. This figure is small in comparison with the total number of notified blackmails in this time (96 cases). As with cyberstalking, the Internet offers a number of advantages to the electronic extortionist. There is no danger of fingerprints, and steps can be taken to hide identity. However, the blackmailer will need a physical interface in order to access their ill-gotten gains (National Criminal Intelligence Service 1999).

CONCLUSION

Our society is beginning to learn the dark side of the Internet only now. The cases referred at the beginning of this chapter make it clear that this is an emerging problem, and the sexual exploitation of children is only one of many other types of crimes being committed online. Sabotage, fraud, hacking all present major problems for companies, individuals, and governments, and all deserve a law enforcement response. However, there is no more precious commodity than our children, and no more important priority than their well-being. Most children do not understand online risks, and few parents are sufficiently familiar with them and/or Internet technology to effectively guard against them. These problems must be addressed. This requires unprecedented collaboration and cooperation among government entities (including law enforcement agencies), the Internet industry, schools, corporations, families, and others. Broad access to quality content on the Internet must be a community priority, where all involved identify and implement appropriate solutions (Internet Crimes Against Children Task Force 2000; Williams 2007).

KEY TERMS

Child victimization   Cyberstalking
Cyber crime   Internet
Cyberspace   Pedophilia

REFERENCES

Aftab, P., and J. A. Polly. 1997. Child safety online. Paper presented at the Internet online summit: Focus on children, Washington, DC, December 1–3, 1997. Retrieved May 19, 2006, from http://www.prevent-abuse-now.com/home.htm

Akdeniz, Y. 1997. The regulation of pornography and child pornography on the internet. *Journal of Information Law and Technology*. Retrieved May 19, 2006, from http://www2.warwick.ac.UnitedKingdom/fac/soc/law/elj/jilt/1997_1/akdeniz1/

Armagh, D. 1998. A safety net for the Internet: Protecting our children. *Juvenile Justice Journal* V (1). Retrieved May 19, 2006, from http://ojjdp.ncjrs.org/jjjournal/jjjournal598/contents.html

Attorney General of New Jersey. June 2000. Computer crime.

Bindra, P. S. 2001. Log on to the reality. *The Week* (August 12).

Canadian Police College. May 1998. Innocence exploited: Child pornography in the electronic age. Canadian Police College, 16.

Canadian Resource Center for Victims of Crime. 2000. Child sexual exploitation and the Internet. Report prepared by the Canadian Resource Center for Victims of Crime. Retrieved July 12, 2005, from http://www.crcvc.ca/Resources/childsexualexploitation.pdf

Carr, J. 2003. *Child Abuse, Child Pornography and the Internet*. London: National Children's Home.

Crimes against Children Research Centre. 2000. Online victimization—A report on the nation's youth.

ECPAT. July 2004. A challenge for the real world. *ECPAT Newsletter*, No. 48.

Federal Bureau of Investigation. 2000. Congressional statement (February 16).

Holder, E. 1999. Remarks at the international conference on combating child pornography on the Internet, Vienna, Australia, September 29, 1999.

Internet Crimes against Children Task Force. 2000. Retrieved May 19, 2006, from http://www.troopers.state.ny.us/CrimInv/Icac/IcacIntro.html

Krone, T. 2004. A typology of online child pornography offending. *Trends & Issues in Crime and Criminal Justice*, No. 279. Australian Institute of Criminology.

Krone, T. 2005. International police operations against online child pornography. *Trends & Issues in Crime and Criminal Justice*. No. 296. Australian Institute of Criminology.

Magid, L. J. 1998. *Child Safety on the Information Highway*. National Center for Missing and Exploited Children. Retrieved May 19, 2006, from http://www.safekids.com/child_safety.htm

Mahoney, D., and N. Faulkner. 1997. Brief overview of pedophiles on the Web. Submitted by request to the Child Advocacy Task Force on The Internet Online Summit: Focus on Children, Washington, DC, December 1, 1997. Retrieved May 19, 2006, from http://www.prevent-abuse-now.com/summit.htm

Make-IT-safe. April 2005. Fact sheet #1: Children, young people and IT 1. Retrieved May 19, 2006, from www.makeitsafe.com

McCoy, A. 2005. Blaming children for their own exploitation: The situation in East Asia. ECPAT 7th report on the implementation of the agenda for action 1 against the commercial sexual exploitation of children.

National Criminal Intelligence Service. 1999. Project Trawler: Crime on the information highways. Retrieved May 29, 2006, from http://www.cyber-rights.org

Nordland, R., and J. Bartholet. 2001a. Blue babies of the web. *The Week* (August 12).

Nordland, R., and J. Bartholet. 2001b. The Web's dark secret. Special Report, *Newsweek* (March 19).

Office of Juvenile Justice and Delinquency Prevention. 1999. Use of computers in the sexual exploitation of children.

Rimm, M. 1995. Marketing pornography on the information highway. *Georgetown Law Journal* 83: 1849.

Smith, R., P. Grabosky, and G. Urbas. 2004. *Cyber Criminals on Trial*. Cambridge: Cambridge University Press.

Taylor, M., and E. Quayle. 2003. *Child Pornography: An Internet Crime*. Hove: Brunner & Routledge.

U.S. Attorney General. 1999. Cyberstalking: A new challenge for law enforcement and industry. Report prepared by the U.S. Attorney General.

Williams, I. 2007. Internet child porn on the rise: More prolific and more severe content than ever before. Retrieved May 29, 2007, from http://www.vnunet.com/vnunet/news/2187930/internet-child-porn-rise

Wolak, J., K. Mitchell, and D. Finkelhor. 2003. *Internet Sex Crimes Against Minors: The Response of Law Enforcement*. New Hampshire: National Center for Missing and Exploited Children.

Zwicke, L. 2000. Crime on the superhighway: A guide to online safety. Retrieved May 19, 2006, from http://www.geocities.com/CapitolHill/6647/rings.html

Chapter 3

Internet Child Sexual Exploitation: Offenses, Offenders, and Victims

Wilson Huang, Mathew Earl Leopard, and Andrea Brockman
Valdosta State University, Georgia

Wilson Huang is an associate professor in the Department of Sociology, Anthropology, and Criminal Justice at Valdosta State University. He received his Ph.D. in criminal justice and criminology from the University of Maryland, College Park. His teaching and research interests include police–community relations, comparative criminal justice, research methodology, and cyber crime.

Mathew Earl Leopard is a former criminal justice student at Valdosta State University. He holds an Associate of Science degree in criminal justice from Middle Georgia College and is currently pursuing his bachelor's degree from Valdosta State University on a part-time basis and also hopes to pursue a master's degree. While at Valdosta State, Mathew became a member of the Criminal Justice Honor Society, Alpha Phi Sigma, and was the President of the Society from January 2006 to January 2007. Mathew currently resides in Perry, GA, with his beautiful wife Tiffany and works for the Perry Police Department as a patrol officer.

Andrea Brockman is a criminal justice graduate from Valdosta State University. She works for the Department of Corrections as a full-time correctional counselor at Valdosta State Prison. She holds a bachelor's degree in both psychology and criminal justice. Andrea actively participates in the Big Brothers Big Sisters program of South Georgia. She also plans to attend a doctorate program with a focus in forensic psychology.

Abstract

Factors contributing to the explosive growth of child sexual exploitation in cyberspace can be linked to online accessibility and anonymity, increasing commercialization of exploitation features, and greater digitization in the production and dissemination of images. As Internet applications advance, legislative initiations and modifications are continuously evolving in defining offenses of child sexual exploitation. But the nature and distribution of child exploitation cases by characteristics of both offenders and victims are found to remain similar over time and across studies. Efforts of criminal justice responses can be concentrated on emerging challenges so that online child exploitation can be prevented and contained ahead.

INTRODUCTION

Sexual exploitation of children is a heartless crime detestable to any individual conscious of civil responsibility. It deprives the dignity of an innocent child, and in the worst of cases it even takes the life of the young victim. The despicable nature of the crime can be illustrated in two appalling cases. In the first, 6-year-old Thea Pumbroek, who had appeared in a number of child pornography videos, died of a cocaine overdose while being filmed in Amsterdam (Taylor and Quayle 2003). Information about the overdose and circumstances surrounding her death were misplaced or unknown. No social campaigns were created under her name to tackle the problem. The second case, which occurred more recently in Pennsylvania, involved a 2-year-old girl (Ove 2005). The girl's own mother took her to a man's residence for sexual acts and pornographic images, which were sent online to others. Subsequently five men were convicted. One of the convicts was also charged with using a Web camera to send pornographic images of his own 4-year-old daughter over the Net. He pled guilty and was sentenced to 71 months in prison.

Thea's story and that of the Pennsylvanian 2-year-old are more than isolated tragedies in a civilized world. They are reflective how helpless, exploited children suffer and how the pleasures of wrongdoers can be built upon the suffering of children—shockingly, in some cases, their own children. Shocking also is that the possession of child pornography is still not a crime in 138 countries, according to a study by the International Centre for Missing and Exploited Children (ICMEC) (2006), and that stories like Thea's and the 2-year-old's are just the tip of a rapidly growing iceberg.

In fact, a 2005 survey of online **victimization** of youths by the National Center of Missing and Exploited Children (NCMEC) found that about 13 percent of the young respondents received at least one sexual solicitation over the Internet in the previous year (Wolak, Mitchell, and Finkelhor 2006). Of these victims being solicited, only a few of them (5%) reported their victimization to law enforcement agents; the majority did not disclose the solicitation to anyone. An emerging problem discovered by the NCMEC survey was the solicitation of sexual photographs of youths: 56 percent of victims mentioned that their solicitors had asked them for photographs of themselves. In 27 percent of these incidents, solicitors asked specifically for sexual photographs. As the level of Internet use among youths continues to climb, the prevalence of the child pornography problem in the cyberspace is unavoidably and unfortunately expanding.

THE GROWTH OF CHILD EXPLOITATION IMAGES IN CYBERSPACE

Child pornography (CP) and the Internet have become inseparable in this information era. Before the advent of the Internet, photographs, films, and videocassettes portraying erotic or sexual images of minors were distributed through conventional means such as the postal service, pornographic stores, or commercial dealers (Burgess, Clark, and Books 1984; Durkin 1997; Hughes 2002). Mainstream adult magazines, *Playboy, Penthouse*, and *Hustler*, also occasionally carried pornographic depictions of youthful adult models. One study by the Justice Department revealed that 20 percent of images of teen models shown in these magazines involve nudity or sexual activity and about 16 percent include sexual contact with an adult (Taylor et al. 2006). Though these traditional distributions remain operational, their role has been replaced gradually and largely by electronic transmissions via the Internet. In 1995, an inspector of Greater Manchester in the United Kingdom seized only 12 child pornographic images displayed in the form of photographs or videos. In 1999, when the Internet began to boom, the CP images seized increased to 41,000, and almost all of those originated from the Internet (Carr 2001). In the United States, the percentages of CP cases related to the Internet increased from 32 percent in 1998 to 77 percent in 2000, according to a U.S. Postal Inspection Service investigator (Hughes 2002). This represented an average 15 percent annual increase. These observations from law enforcement officials have indicated a persistent upward trend since the late 1990s in the distribution of CP materials by the Internet.

Accompanying this Internet trend is the skyrocketing number of CP sites. The Internet Watch Foundation (IWF), a watchdog group headquartered in the United Kingdom, has tracked CP Web sites around the world through citizen reports since 1996. In the first reporting year, the foundation processed 615 reports of CP Web sites. By 2006, that number had grown to 27,750 (Internet Watch Foundation 2006). IWF stated that the organization has processed more than 100,000 reports since its inception and that the average has reached about 1,000 reports a month. Among these reports to IWF, more than 31,000 Web sites had been found to contain potentially illegal child abuse content. Statistics from NCMEC, which has monitored online sexual exploitation in the United States since 1990s, are even more astonishing. Scherer (2005) estimated that the number of CP sites has grown by almost 400 percent in the last 4 years. Further NCMEC statistics showed that complaints of child exploitation to its telephone hotline increased from 20,000 in 2000 to more than 390,000 in 2006. About 90 percent of these hotline complaints involved CP (Barton and Johnson 2006). In addition to the creation of numerous Web sites, the number of CP images has increased dramatically as well. According to the hotline data maintained by the British IWF, there were around 1 million images of child exploitation in circulation on the Internet and this number is growing at the rate of about 200 per day (Chetty 2003). In New Hampshire, McLaughlin (2000) and his team in the Keene Police Department seized more than 2 million CP images over a 3-year investigation. Most recently, the Internet Crimes Against Children Task Force program sponsored by the federal government claimed the number at 6.5 million (Koch 2006).

Factors contributing to this rapid growth can best be summarized by the so-called Triple-A Engine of access, affordability, and anonymity (Cooper 2002). Accessibility and speed are clear advantages of the Internet over traditional delivery methods. The Internet allows child pornographers to receive images instantly through downloads, electronic attachments, Webcams, etc., 24 hours a day, 365 days a year in the privacy of their homes (Chetty 2003). They no longer need to visit adult bookstores or make face-to-face contact to purchase pornographic materials. The pornographer's name, address, or other identifying information is no longer necessary to view pornographic images. Moreover, the expense of exploring sexual images on the Internet is minimal, often costing no more than a $30 monthly connection fee. Once on the Net, search engines that have not filtered their links are obviously offering free services to CP seekers and collectors. Maintaining anonymity is always of greatest concern to child pornographers, in particular, pedophiles (Armstrong and Forde 2003). The Internet to them is the best choice of communication, because it can be used as a shield to disguise their identity in full. For instance, when child pornographers search for targets on the Web, they can use falsified information to misrepresent their identity. When they need to communicate within their own network, they activate private channels or one-to-one communication to prevent their exchanges from being exposed to others. The Internet has provided all necessary nutrition for CP to grow on this platform. Unless the criminal justice system is able to contain CP effectively, it is inevitable that the problem will increase directly with the use of the Internet.

The commercialization of CP is another force that has accelerated its growth. The U.S. Customs Service estimates that revenues for the domestic market range from about $200 million to more than $1 billion per year (Hughes 2001). Some experts estimate that overall revenues from the entire CP industry may exceed $50 billion annually (Barton and Johnson 2006). In one recent case, two citizens of Belarus were convicted in a U.S. federal court and sentenced to 25 years in prison for operating a global Internet pornography business that had thousands of paid memberships to erotic sites featuring children (Sampson 2006). Between June 2002 and July 2003, the two men processed between $2.5 million and $7 million in credit card transactions for dozens of Web sites that offered images of prepubescent children engaged in sex acts. The authorities identified 270,000 subscribers from the seized billing records and subsequent investigations have resulted in more than 1,200 arrests in 12 countries.

To attract potential customers, commercial CP Web sites usually exhibit the words "hard-core child pornography" on their home pages (Save the Children European Group 2003). These sites typically display "child erotica" for anyone who visit their site, but suggest that "stronger" materials are available to subscribers who pay, typically by credit card. Viewing fees commonly range from a few U.S. dollars per image viewed (Hughes 2001; Save the Children Sweden n.d.) to $20–50 for unlimited monthly access. Records from Save the Children hotlines show that the number of such paid sites has grown fast in recent years. The organization has discovered that many of these Web sites operate in Russia, Romania, the Czech Republic, and Baltic countries (Save the Children Sweden n.d.) and that the financial transactions also take place in these East European countries. For example, in the Belarusian case, two U.S. companies in California and Florida processed the credit card verification and the payment was funneled to bank accounts in the Baltic country Latvia. This electronic billing process is instantaneous and highly commercialized to meet the needs of the CP market. But it is definitely a serious threat to the welfare of children.

Digitization and its associated technology also facilitate the production and dissemination of images in the network of child pornographers. Congressional reports accompanying recent legislative changes in federal statutes (18 U.S.C. §2251) have found that the vast majority of CP prosecutions today involve images stored on computer hard drives, computer disks, or related new media. Prior to the invention of the Internet, many CP images were duplicated into hardcopies and recycled in the pedophilia subculture. Now, any printed pictures or video programs can be easily digitized through a scanner, camera, cellular phone, or other image-capture device into an electronic file saved in a regular computer, laptop, or handheld PC. A simple click can then send hundreds of images to a member in the subculture network in less than a minute. Hughes (2002) found that pedophiles have regularly transformed single video clips to 200–300 still images and then sent them to pedophile newsgroups or uploaded them to a Web site. In some cases, pedophiles have employed encryption technology to conceal their identities when sending files to other members in the "cottage industry" (Scherer 1998; Taylor et al. 2006). Hughes (2002) also noted that many currently circulating images were originally made in the 1970s. These images have been digitized and exchanged among pedophiles (Save the Children European Group 2003). Hughes (2001) estimated that about 50 percent of current images were digitized from old images, although others indicate that as many as 70–80 percent were (Save the Children Sweden n.d.). Digitized files can be maintained in a more organized manner than hardcopy files. They can be sorted, saved, and duplicated in different ways by the preference of the CP possessor. Furthermore, the current user-friendly equipment and features enable a CP collector to easily assume the role of distributor. If the upward trend in digitization continues, the functions of CP distribution can be more commercialized in lieu of the profit and growth of adult pornography.

LEGAL DEFINITION AND SCOPE OF CHILD SEXUAL EXPLOITATION

Laws against production, distribution, and possession of **child sexual exploitation** materials are in existence under federal statutes in all 50 states. Though the legal definition and scope of CP may vary from state to state, U.S. federal laws have set a strong foundation for the prohibition of and prosecution for child sexual exploitation. Many states have adopted federal statutes to enact their legislation against child sexual exploitation. States have also followed the federal lead to combat CP and exploitation (Wortley and Smallbone 2006). At the federal level, legislative activities banning child sexual exploitation have been very active in the past 20 years. More than 10 congressional acts have been enacted to better protect children from being sexually exploited. These acts are manifestations of the dynamic interrelations of the ever-changing technology and the diverse aspects of child exploitation in the society. The following discussions examine these legislative initiations and modifications that have taken part in shaping the legal definition of CP in recent decades.

The series of legislative campaigns against child sexual exploitation began in 1977 when Congress passed the Protection of Children Against Sexual Exploitation Act (Public Law 95-225). This 1977 Act prohibited sexual exploitation of children under age 16. The statutes prohibited any person from employing, enticing, or coercing any minor to engage in any sexually explicit conduct for the purpose of producing any visual or print medium of such conduct. The Act also prohibited transporting or mailing these sexual materials of minors for sale or distribution. Under the act, persons convicted for the offenses shall be fined up to $10,000 or imprisoned for a maximum of 10 years, or both. These statutes formally recognize the prohibition and penalty against the production and commercial distribution of sexually explicit activities involving children. The provisions were codified as amended to sections 2251–2253 under Title 18 of U.S. Code. A few years later, the Supreme Court affirmed the prohibition in *New York v. Ferber* (1982). The Court held that a New York criminal statute prohibiting the promotion of sexual performances by children under 16 is constitutional. The court reasoned that visual depictions of sexual conduct by children without serious literary, artistic, or scientific value are harmful to the physiological, emotional, and mental health of the victimized child and that government entities have a compelling interest in protecting children from these harms. As such, CP, like obscenity, is not entitled to the First Amendment protection.

After the 1982 landmark case, several congressional acts were passed to tighten provisions banning the exploitive use of minors in the production, distribution, and possession of sexual depictions. First, the Child Protection Act of 1984 (Public Law 98-292) raised the age of a minor from 16 to 18 to ease the proof for prosecution. The Act also prohibited any person from knowingly reproducing any visual depiction of child sexual exploitation for distribution. In addition, this 1984 Act removed the commercial clause that required distribution for sale; this removal enabled the law to ban not-for-profit distribution of child sexual depiction. Previously, only commercial distribution of these images was prohibited. Two years later, the Child Sex Abuse and Pornography Act of 1986 (Public Law 99-628) began prohibiting the production and use of advertisements for seeking or offering CP. In 1988, the Child Protection and Obscenity Enforcement Act (Public Law 100-690) further banned the use of computers to transport, distribute, or receive CP. Then in 1990, the Child Protection Restoration and Penalties Enhancement Act (Public Law 101-647) penalized any person who knowingly possesses three or more books, magazines, periodicals, films, video tapes, or other matter which contain any visual depiction of child sexual activities. The above four acts were codified as amended at 18 U.S.C. §2251–2256.

All prohibitions at this stage meant sexual exploitation of real children in the depiction. In the mid-1990s, rapidly advancing computer technology in conjunction with Internet growth necessitated new legislation to include images producible by computer. Congress has found that contemporary computer imaging technologies such as morphing software can generate visual depictions that are virtually indistinguishable from actual children engaging in sexual activities. Films, videos, and photos can also be altered in a way that makes it virtually impossible for viewers to identify children or determine if the offending material was produced using real children (Public Law 104-208, 110 Stat. 3009). This ability along with the concerns for the potential harm to children gave birth to the Child Pornography Prevention Act (CPPA) of 1996. Major amendments were introduced by Congress to ban mailing, receiving, distributing, and possessing CP as amended at 18 U.S.C. §2251(A), and virtual CP as amended at 18 U.S.C. §2256. In the CPPA, the statutes define CP as any visual depiction, including computer-generated images, of sexually explicit conduct, where

(A) the production of such visual depiction involves the use of a minor engaging in sexually explicit conduct;

(B) such visual depiction is, or appears to be, of a minor engaging in sexually explicit conduct;

(C) such visual depiction has been created, adapted, or modified to appear that an identifiable minor is engaging in sexually explicit conduct; or

(D) such visual depiction is advertised, promoted, presented, described, or distributed in such a manner that conveys the impression that the material is or contains a visual depiction of a minor engaging in sexually explicit conduct.

As defined by the 1996 statutes, sexually explicit conduct means actual or simulated: "(A) sexual intercourse, including genital–genital, oral–genital, anal–genital, or oral–anal, whether between persons of the same or opposite sex; (B) bestiality; (C) masturbation; (D) sadistic or masochistic abuse; or (E) lascivious exhibition of the genitals or pubic area of any person" (18 U.S.C. §2256). Simulated conduct here refers mainly to simulated sexual acts performed by an adult who appears to be underage and pretends acts of a minor. A simulation can also be an acting performance instead of a real act. The intention of the statutes is to prohibit to the fullest extent the production of any CP.

The CPPA definitions codified and amended at 18 U.S.C. §2256(8)(A)(B)(C)(D) encountered immediate allegations for violating the First Amendment protection, and were challenged legally by the Free Speech Coalition, a trade association founded in 1991 by businesses in the production of pornographic materials (Mota 2002). The Coalition alleges that certain provisions of CPPA are unconstitutionally overbroad and vague, and constitute impermissible content-specific regulations on free speech. At the lower court, the judge held that CPPA was neither overbroad nor vague. The CPPA was not overbroad because it prohibited only those works necessary to prevent the malicious effects of CP from reaching minors. The CPPA was not void for vagueness, as it gave sufficient guidance to a person of reasonable intelligence as to what it prohibited. But in 1999, the Court of Appeals for the Ninth Circuit reversed the district court's ruling in *Free Speech Coalition v. Reno* (198 F.3d 1083; 9th Cir.). Judges of the appellate court found that the CPPA's two phrases "appear to be a minor" and "conveys the impression" were highly subjective. The CPPA did not specify an explicit standard as to what the provisions containing the questionable phrases mean. The appellate court found that the provisions provided no measure to guide an ordinarily intelligent person about prohibited conduct, and any such person could not be reasonably assured about whose perspectives define the appearance of a minor.

In *Ashcroft v. Free Speech Coalition* (122 S. Ct. 1389, 2002), the Supreme Court affirmed the Ninth Circuit's decision. It was decided that the 2256(8)(B) and 2256(8)(D) phrases were overbroad and violative of the First Amendment. The majority of the Court held that the overbreadth of 2256(8)(B) had implicitly banned a range of sexually explicit images, including "virtual child pornography" and some works which possibly have significant literary, artistic, political, or scientific merit. Cited examples included the Academy Award-nominated films *Traffic* and *American Beauty*, in which underage sexual relations were portrayed. The ban on virtual CP also could not be justified because, unlike real CP, it was not intrinsically related to the sexual abuse of real children. The link between virtual images and actual instances of child abuse was contingent and indirect. As to 2256(8)(D), the Court also found it unconstitutionally vague. Mainly, the "conveys the impression" provision required little judgment about the image's content. The provision seemed to indicate that even if a film contains no sexually explicit scenes involving minors, it can be treated as CP if the title and trailers convey the impression that such scenes are to be found in the movie. The Court advised that the 1996 statutes require a more precise restriction on the meaning of CP.

The constitutional controversy has resulted in noticeable consequences on governmental prosecutions after *Ashcroft v. Free Speech Coalition*. The case establishes that the government carries the burden to determine and identify a real child who was actually used in a depiction. Because it places the burden on the prosecutor's side, defendants have become less likely to plead guilty. If defendants plead not guilty, cases are less likely to result in guilty verdict (Farhangian 2003). In the Ninth Circuit, prosecutions have been brought in the most clear-cut cases where the child in the depiction or the origin of the image can be identified specifically as a real minor. The adverse effect of the decision on the federal government's ability to prosecute CP offenders was evident (Public Law No. 108-21, Section 501). In response to the ruling and finding, Congress enacted the "Prosecutorial Remedies and Other Tools to End the Exploitation of Children Today Act of 2003" or the PROTECT Act to modify the two controversial phrases (Public Law No. 108-21, Section 502). The Act amended the four 2256 subsections by revising 2256(8)(B) provision and striking down 2256(8)(D) in entirety.

CP is today defined at 18 U.S.C. §2256(8) as any visual depiction, including any photograph, film, video, picture, or computer-generated image or picture, whether made or produced by electronic, mechanical, or other means, of sexually explicit conduct, where

(A)   the production of such visual depiction involves the use of a minor engaging in sexually explicit conduct;

(B)   such visual depiction is a digital image, computer image, or computer-generated image that is, or is indistinguishable from, that of a minor engaging in sexually explicit conduct; or

(C)   such visual depiction has been created, adapted, or modified to appear that an identifiable minor is engaging in sexually explicit conduct.

In (B), the term indistinguishable means that the depiction must be so realistic that a viewer would conclude that such depiction is of an actual minor engaged in sexually explicit conduct.

A main purpose of 18 U.S.C. §2256(8) as amended in the PROTECT Act is clearly to ban virtual CP. The terms "digital image," "computer image," and "computer-generated image" in the Act are used purposely to prohibit virtual or composite child sexual images. Such prohibition, however, remains constitutionally deficient, claimed Farhangian (2003). She argued that the words "indistinguishable from" are subject to the same problem as "appears to be" from a constitutional standpoint. That term and other language are similarly overbroad in that they may criminalize innocent speech and innovative work which may have literary or artistic value. The statutory overbreadth would make artists or filmmakers vulnerable to prosecution where their artistic products were created without the use of a real child.

In addition to the ban of virtual CP, the 2003 PROTECT Act also prohibits Web site owners from using domain names that will draw Internet users into viewing materials constituting obscenity. An owner who intentionally deceives a minor into viewing material that is harmful to minors will be punished more harshly. In 2006, the Adam Walsh Child Protection and Safety Act (Public Law 109-248) expands the prohibitions to any words or digital images embedded into the source code of a Web site. This definition covers both viewable and non-viewable images available at the Web site (Baron-Evans and Noonan 2006). Under the Adam Walsh Act, any person who knowingly embeds such words or digital images will receive an even harsher punishment than the one involving misleading domain names. This ban is codified and amended at 18 U.S.C. §2252(C). Below is a summarized list of the key statutes and penalty associated with child sexual exploitation in the current U.S. Code:

18 U.S.C. §2251: Sexual exploitation of children in the production of child pornography, 30 years maximum for 1st offense;

18 U.S.C. §2251A: Selling or buying children for sexual exploitation, life sentence maximum;

18 U.S.C. §2252: Transportation, distribution, and possession of visual depiction involving child sexual exploitation, 20 years maximum for 1st offense;

18 U.S.C. §2252A: Mailing, transportation, distribution, and possession of child pornography, 20 years maximum for 1st offense;

18 U.S.C. §2252B: Misleading domain names on the Internet, 10 years maximum; and

18 U.S.C. §2252C: Misleading words or digital images on the Internet, 20 years maximum.

NATURE OF CHILD ABUSE IMAGES

In dealing with child sexual exploitation, there is a tendency for investigators worldwide to use the term "child abuse image" (CAI) instead of "child pornography." Trifiletti (2005) noted from his law enforcement experience that the former term can more accurately describe the dramatic and long-lasting effects of the images on victimized children. Lanning (2001), a former FBI expert in child sexual exploitation, has classified CAIs as commercial or homemade depending on whether they were created for sale or not. In his investigative guide, Lanning reported that commercial CAIs are usually produced in foreign countries and smuggled into the United States. U.S. customers appear to be the main buyer of these materials. Homemade images are not produced for profit; however, they may be used for exchange within the pedophile network. For instance, "Operation Hamlet" executed in the United States and six European countries uncovered a pedophile ring of more than 15 members who exploited their own children to produce homemade images. These depictions were not produced for commercial profit, but rather were made for and disseminated primarily to other members of the network (Cable News Network 2002). Once homemade CAIs were released to the network; these images were reproduced and circulated over and over again in the pedophile community. Child advocates have found that a substantial part of the images currently circulating are homemade (Save the Children European Group 2003). Jenkins (2001) uncovered that these homemade CAIs are very graphic, frequently depicting the perpetrators' ongoing acts of sexual assault against young family members or neighbors. Digital technology has enabled home producers to enhance the quality of their images, thereby decreasing the difference between the quality of commercial and homemade CAIs. Fortunately, according to Lanning (2001), forensic examiners and technicians are able to distinguish the difference between the two.

Another categorization of CAIs mentioned by Lanning (2001) is the dichotomy of CP and child erotica. In Lanning's practical view, CP is a permanent record of the sexual exploitation of an actual child in the form of photographs, negatives, slides, magazines, movies, videotapes, or computer disks. CP, therefore, is illegal and it has harmed the victim through sexual exploitation. Child erotica, on the other hand, is usually not illegal. It is frequently used to serve "a sexual purpose for a given individual" (Lanning 2001, 65). These materials, which may be considered pedophile paraphernalia, include erotic novels, letters, drawings, or other written fantasies in e-mails or diaries. Though child erotica can be in a wide array of visual or written formats, many investigators have used the term child erotica to refer only to images of naked children in nonsexual settings. These images are referred by Jenkins (2001) as "soft-core." In Jenkins' investigation, lots of soft-core photographs were taken in nudist camps or on nude beaches showing children playing games or sports. These images were captured without causing direct harm to the children. Some other sources of soft-core photos may come from nonpornographic works of art photographers, underwear or swimsuit advertisements, photos of teen gymnasts, or glamour shots. These images become child erotica when they are used for sexual gratification of culprits (Jenkins 2001). In contrast to the soft-core images, hard-core images involve explicit sexual conduct or obscene poses by a minor. Jenkins disclosed that most of these hard-core images are associated with oral sex or mutual masturbation. Penetration is rare due to the young age of the subject; however, some depictions did involve genital and anal penetration. Jenkins (2001) noted that hard-core images exist in abundance. Some of them were from the magazines of the 1970s; many were produced in recent years.

EXTENT OF CAI'S

Several empirical studies on the extent of CAIs have been conducted by academicians and child advocates in the United States (Wolak, Finkelhor, and Mitchell 2005) and Great Britain (Gallagher et al. 2006; Taylor, Holland, and Quayle 2001; Taylor and Quayle 2003). The National Juvenile Online Victimization (N-JOV) Study was a large-scale survey conducted by researchers of NCMEC (Wolak, Finkelhor, and Mitchell 2004, 2005) in an effort to understand Internet-related sex offenses committed against children. The study sent out questionnaires to more than 2,500 local, county, state, and federal agencies asking if they had made arrests related to Internet child sexual exploitation during the period between July 1, 2000, and June 30, 2001. From cases reported by the responding agencies, the study was able to track down 612 arrestees via phone interviews. Among the 612 offenders, 429 were arrested for offenses related directly to child sexual exploitation or pornography involving the Internet. Descriptive data of these 429 arrestees showed that 96 percent of them had CAIs stored on a hard drive or removable media and 39 percent had moving pictures in digital or other video formats. About half of the arrestees possessed more than 100 still images; 14 percent possessed more than 1,000 images. Of the 429 offenders, the study also discovered that

- 92 percent had graphic images showing genitals or explicit sexual activity,
- 80 percent had images showing the sexual penetration of a child, including oral sex,
- 79 percent had images showing nude or seminude children and that some of these images displayed minors being sexually victimized, and
- 71 percent had images showing sexual contact between adults and minors, such as an adult touching the genitals or breasts of a minor or vise versa.

The N-JOV findings strongly suggest that a large majority of child pornographers own hard-core images involving sexual violence against a minor. This type of highly graphic, strong image is a possessor's favorite and target collection. However, in terms of numbers, violent hard-core images remain a minority collection. Wolak, Finkelhor, and Mitchell (2005) reported that about 21 percent had depictions showing bondage, rape, or torture. Possession of these cruel, hard-core images should be considered a very serious crime.

In Great Britain, Gallagher et al. (2006) gathered data from Her Majesty's Revenue and Customs (HMRC) on cases prosecuted for importation of CP images. Eighty-two cases prosecuted between 2001 and 2004 were examined. HMRC classified these cases into three categories: (1) indicative (i.e., borderline images which suggests a sexual interest in children), (2) indecent (i.e., images of naked children), and (3) obscene (i.e., images of children being sexually abused). The study found that the majority of the exploitive images imported into the United Kingdom were either indicative or indecent. Obscene images account for only a tiny proportion of all seizures of CP. The study also reviewed investigative reports on cases involving Internet-based CAIs in three police jurisdictions. Their reviews of police reports revealed that content of CAIs varied greatly, ranging from photos of children taken on a beach to depictions of rape, torture, and other sexual violence. Their findings indicated that the relation between seriousness of depictions and the number of such depictions is inverse. The most serious depiction is the least likely to be found on the Internet.

The Combating Paedophile Information Networks in Europe (COPINE) project administered at the University College Cork, Ireland, is well known for its comprehensive effort in research of CAIs. The COPINE project has collected more than 150,000 still images and more than 400 video clips since its archival initiation in the mid-1990s (Taylor and Quayle 2003). COPINE researchers have created a 10-point continuum system to grade still and serial images of child abuse pictures. The grading system is constructed to reflect the level of child sexual victimization and adult sexual interest in children. The higher the level, the greater the degree of severity of victimization dramatization. In this rating system, the 10 categories are as follows: (1) indicative (e.g., children in their underwear or bathing suits), (2) nudist (e.g., naked children in an appropriate setting), (3) erotic (e.g., children showing varying degrees of nakedness in safe play areas), (4) posing (e.g., partially clothed or naked children in deliberate poses), (5) erotic posing (e.g., partially clothed or naked children in sexualized poses), (6) explicit erotic posing (e.g., emphasizing genital areas of partially or fully naked children), (7) explicit sexual activity (e.g., masturbation, oral sex, or intercourse by child not involving an adult), (8) assault (e.g., children being sexually assaulted by adults), (9) gross assault (e.g., obscene depiction of penetrative sex or oral sex involving adults), and (10) sadistic/bestiality (e.g., pain is implied in pictures showing a child is tied, beaten, or whipped).

Taylor and Quayle (2003) applied the grading system to their analysis of a sample of over 3,000 still images derived from about 100 individual picture series featuring girls aged 1.5 to 7. They found that most of the pictures in the series fell within level 6 or below, suggesting that the majority of these pictures did not show explicit sexual activities. A very distressing discovery from the analysis was that those pictures of level 7 and above were portrayed mainly by few repeatedly exploited girls, one of whom was photographed over time from a very young age of 3 to about 7. Sadly, none of these exploited girls nor the producers were identified at the time of their analysis. This inability to identify a child victim of an image has been a continuing problem in the investigation of child sexual exploitation cases.

REASONS FOR COLLECTIONS OF CAI'S

A number of explanations have been discussed by researchers and investigators as to why child pornographers possess and catalog exploitive images of children (Carr 2001; Jenkins 2001; Lanning 2001; Taylor and Quayle 2003). Sexual gratification may be the most direct incentive for possession of CAI by child pornographers. CP enthusiasts may use the images to satisfy their sexual fantasies or to stimulate their sexual arousal for immediate gratification. But sex may not be a sole reason why child pornographers eagerly seek and collect CAI. Obviously, such gratification can be achieved legally and more conveniently through adult pornography. Sometimes, CAI possession and collection may start purely incidentally (Carr 2001). One may encounter an exploitative image in cyberspace accidentally the first time. This may pique an interest in searching for more, which gradually evolves into a compulsive habit. Jenkins (2001) suggests that a "collector fetish" may be a main motivation for possession of CAI. Collecting CAI can function as a hobby, much like collecting stamps, coins, sports cards, badges, or other memorabilia. Possessors of CAIs may collect the images as souvenirs or trophies for their intended purposes (Lanning 2001). Like other seasoned collectors, CP enthusiasts can be obsessed with a particular type of CAI. They may strive for a sense of completion and perfection by collecting CAI of a particular series or subject. A perfect completion signifies a great sense of dominance and control over the CAI collection. If a child pornographer is able to fill missing images in a CAI serial, the person can gain a strong sense of pride (Lanning 2001). This filling contribution can also gain status for person who posts the image in the network of CAI collectors.

Another main reason for the collection of CAIs is to use those images as a medium of exchange for validation. Through newsgroups, chat rooms, bulletin boards, and other Internet channels, child pornographers communicate frequently to exchange information and sexual images in their own network. They actively look for new, hard-core images to enlarge and strengthen their collections. Lanning (2001) has found that the younger the victim and the more bizarre the sexual act is, the higher the value of the image is for exchange in the network. The psychological utility of the exchange is for validation (Lanning 2001; Taylor and Quayle 2003). The networking with similar others reduces their sense of guilt and helps legitimize their collection activities. Collection and distribution reinforce their values on acceptance of CAI. By distributing and exchanging CAI in their own network, collectors gain a sense of commonality and legitimacy. This false sense of common acceptance can validate what they have done and believe. As explained by Lanning (2001), continuous collection and updates help child pornographers fulfill their mental needs for validation.

For pedophiles and child molesters, CAI may be used to groom their young prey (Moore 2005). By showing sexual images of a child of the same age to the target child, pedophiles are able to reduce the minor's resistance to real sexual acts. During the grooming process, pedophiles frequently show the images to propel the minor's interest and curiosity in sex. Lowering the minor's sexual inhibition enables the pedophile to entice a minor to pose for sexual photos or engage in sexual acts. This technique is commonly employed by pedophiles on the Internet to groom a minor into sex activity. Once the child is sexually abused, the images may be saved in a computer as a souvenir of the relationship established with the minor. The images may also be used by the predator as blackmail to coerce the victim in keeping the secret (Lanning 2001). Because victimized children are typically afraid of letting their parents know about the abuse incident, the molester's threat to reveal the images to the victim's parents allows the molester to continuously exploit the child in secrecy.

The ongoing collection of CAIs may eventually turn the CP possessor into a CP producer. At a certain point, the possessor may find new images are difficult to acquire unless he can contribute new images to the collection group. Unfortunately, this demand and pressure for new images may lead to a predator to produce images from children of his immediate social networks such as family, school, and neighborhood. The following scripts taken from a pedophile during an interview by Taylor and Quayle (2003) illustrate this distressing progression:

> The progression for me came when I started offending against my daughter . . . I was in the chat room . . . and obviously chatting to a lot of other people who were trading images . . . people would send lists of material that they had . . . and they were reluctant to give me access to any of that material unless I could come up with my new material . . . I was sort of let out of this sort of arena that was going on, this trading of private pictures . . . my motivation was to come up with some images that I could trade for this new material . . . it was then that I thought about steps of . . . of involving my daughter in . . . in creating video to actually trade to get the material that I wanted. (p. 161)

Though the above case depicts a link between CAI collection and production, no empirical study has been conducted to establish this linkage by causal analysis. There is some evidence suggesting that CAI possession is quite common among child molesters. For example, Carr (2001) examined police records from the Chicago police, U.S. Postal Service, and U.S. Customs Service, and found that child molesters arrested for sexual abuse always possess and collect CAI. Taylor et al. (2006) reviewed prior research on the link and also reported that CP is a potential facilitator in the commission of child molestation. These reviews suggest a correlation but do not demonstrate a causality. Systematic, scientific research is needed to verify such link that possession causes production and molestation.

EXAMINING CHARACTERISTICS OF CP OFFENDERS

Several empirical studies adopting sampling methodology have been carried out to understand the types of CP and personal characteristics of those who produce and collect it. In their analysis on official data gathered by the National Incident-Based Reporting System (or NIBRS in abbreviation), Finkelhor and Ormrod (2004) studied 677 CP incidents known to the police between 1997 and 2000. They classified cases into two categories: CP involving victims (this includes the production of CP and the use of pornography in the seduction of a child) and CP involving possession and distribution only. Their classification showed that the large majority (84%) of CP offenses were limited to possession and distribution of exploitive materials. Only 111 cases (16%) involved incidents where an identifiable child victim was found. Huang, Leopard, and Brockman (2006) have used a similar classification of offenders in their content analysis of Internet CP cases. They sought cases reported by major U.S. newspapers during the year 2005 and utilized the LexisNexis newspapers database as their primary source of data. Their search procedures using "child pornography" and "Internet" resulted in a total of 354 offenders. Their findings reported that 83 percent of cases were possession and distribution charges, the other 17 percent involved not only possession/distribution but also contacts with minors.

The large scale N-JOV Study directed by Wolak, Finkelhor, and Mitchell (2005) created a slightly different classification. They categorized their 429 arrest cases into three groups: CP possession, child sexual victimization, and CP solicitation to undercover investigator. They found that about 52 percent of offenders were charged for CP possession, 31 percent involved actual child victims, and the remaining offenders (17 percent) were arrested for CP solicitations over the Internet. These solicitation arrestees were neither CP possessors nor victimizers. If we recount only the first two categories, the percentages change to 63 percent for possession and 37 percent for child sexual victimizations. Another recent study conducted by Alexy, Burgess, and Baker (2005) also designed a typology of three categories. They reviewed newspaper articles published between 1996 and 2002 and generated a convenience sample of 225 cases. In these cases, 59 percent were categorized as traders, 22 percent as travelers, and the rest (19%) involved a combination of both roles. In the study, traders were defined as collectors of online CP, while travelers were vigorous offenders who approached children for sexual purposes either online or face-to-face. A comparison of these percentages with those of the N-JOV Study shows similarities. Table 3-1 highlights findings of these offender types described above.

TABLE 3-1 Offender Types of Internet Child Pornography

Authors	Offender Types	Percentages of Total
Finkelhor and Ormrod (2004)	CP possession and distribution	84%
	CP involving victims	16%
Huang, Leopard, and Brockman (2006)	CP without contact	83%
	CP involving personal contact	17%
Wolak, Finkelhor, and Mitchell (2004, 2005)	CP possession	53%
	CP with victimization	31%
	CP solicitation to undercover Investigator	16%
Alexy, Burgess, and Baker (2005)	CP traders	59%
	CP travelers	22%
	Combination of both	19%

In addition to types of CP offenders, researchers have also investigated offenders' few personal characteristics, such as gender, age, and vocational types. Table 3-2 displays gender and age distributions found in recent studies. It can be observed that results regarding gender have been fairly consistent in that offenders have been predominantly male. When females are involved, they are usually acting in concert with their male counterparts (Gallagher et al. 2006). It appears that the role of CP female offenders tends to be that of facilitator rather than perpetrator, but females can be active CP providers, taking a role in the production of CAIs through exploitation of their own children (Ove 2005). Unlike gender distribution, ages of CP offenders vary widely, ranging from 17 to 70 years (Huang, Leopard, and Brockman 2006). The majority range between 35 and 55 years. CP predators tend to be slightly younger than possessors. Even though the majority of CP offenders were middle aged, Wolak, Finkelhor, and Mitchell (2005) found that more than half (62%) of possessors were not married. These men were never married, separated, divorced, or widowed at the time of their crime.

Similar to the diversity in age, vocational background of CP offenders differs greatly by types. Alexy, Burgess, and Baker (2005) found that in 64 percent of their CP cases, the offenders were considered professional, 11.2 percent were laborers, 8.8 percent were unemployed, 7.2 percent were students, and 5.6 percent were in the military. Clergy accounted for 3.2 percent. Huang, Leopard, and Brockman (2006) have created similar categories and have found that 42 percent work in governmental agencies, another 42 percent work in private business or nonprofit organizations, 3 percent are students, and 2 percent are in the military. Clergy accounted for 7 percent, and 5 percent were unemployed or retired. Wolak, Finkelhor, and Mitchell (2005) found that among offenders who were employed at the time of their arrest, most were working full time. Findings from the above studies suggest that CP offenders are typically full-time workers who may come from almost any occupation or socioeconomic status. For example, previous arrestees have included lawyers, medical doctors, college administrators,

TABLE 3-2 Gender and Age of Child Pornography Offenders

Finkelhor and Ormrod (2004)

	CP Involving Victims	CP Possessors and Distributors
Males	85%	86%
Females	8%	8%
Mixed gender	7%	6%
Adults	83%	90%
Juveniles <18	14%	8%
Mix age	3%	2%

Wolak, Finkelhor, and Mitchell (2004, 2005)

	CP Involving Victims	CP Possessors
Males	99%	100%
Females	1%	<1%
Younger than 18	1%	3%
18–25	23%	11%
26–39	41%	41%
40 or more	35%	45%

Alexy, Burgess, and Baker (2005)

	CP Travelers	CP Traders
Males	95.9%	94.7%
Females	4.1%	5.3%
Younger than 20	–	3.0%
20–29	22.4%	21.8%
30–39	36.7%	34.6%
40 or more	30.6%	30.1%
Unknown	10.2%	10.5%

Huang, Leopard, and Brockman (2006)

	CP Involving Contact	CP Without Contact
Males	98.3%	100%
Females	1.7%	<1%
Younger than 18	–	.3%
18–25	8.3%	9.9%
26–39	40%	30.3%
40 or more	48.3%	52%
Unknown	3.4%	7.5%

teachers, youth counselors, janitors, police officers, and a spokesman for the federal homeland security department (Kalfrin 2006).

The N-JOV Study has investigated additional characteristics related to the social and economic backgrounds of arrested CP possessors. With regard to race, Wolak, Finkelhor, and Mitchell (2005) found that whites accounted for a total of 91 percent of cases. The majority of offenders did not have biological children (53%), nor did they live with a minor (65%). Educational backgrounds of possessors were quite diversified: 5 percent did not finish high school, 38 percent had a high school diploma, 21 percent had some college education, 20 percent had college degree or higher. For 17 percent, information concerning education was not available. Similar diversity was found at income levels: 18 percent had an annual salary of less than $20,000, 41 percent earned between $20,000 and $50,000, 17 percent earned between $50,001 and $80,000, and 10 percent earned more than $80,000 annually. An examination of criminal histories for CP possessors showed that the majority had no record of sexual offenses, violence incidents, drugs, or mental illness. These findings suggest that the typical CP possessor is a white, single, middle-aged, middle-income man, with a high school diploma and possibly some college education, and no criminal record.

Characteristics of computer use by CP offenders were also examined by the 2005 N-JOV Study. Findings of Wolak, Finkelhor, and Mitchell indicate that 91 percent of CP possessors employed home computers as their primary access to CP materials; the other 9 percent relied on computers at work, libraries, or rental venues as their primary means. Using sophisticated technology to hide CP images was uncommon among offenders. The study found that only 20 percent of CP possessors used some sort of hiding methods such as password protection, encryption, or evidence-elimination software. However, the actual percentage of CP possessors using these methods may be higher, because CP possessors who are knowledgeable of computer technology may be more capable of hindering detection (Wolak, Finkelhor, and Mitchell 2005, 10). This suggests that CP criminal investigators should be well equipped with timely and proficient knowledge of computer technology so that they can stay informed of hiding techniques employed by CP possessors.

UNDERSTANDING THE VICTIM CHARACTERISTICS

Few studies have examined victim characteristics by gender, age, race, and other factors. A common issue addressed by previous researchers was whether a girl or boy is more likely to be victimized. In their study of CAIs, Wolak, Finkelhor, and Mitchell (2005) reported that girls are more likely than boys to be depicted in pictures. They found that 62 percent of CP possessors hold mostly pictures of girls, 17 percent own mostly pictures of boys, and 15 percent possess pictures of about equal numbers of girls and boys. Regarding ages of children depicted on the images, Wolak, Finkelhor, and Mitchell (2005) found that 83 percent of arrested possessors had images of children 6–12 years old, 75 percent had pictures of children aged 13–17, 39 percent had images of 3–5 year olds, and 19 percent had CP pictures showing children younger than 3. Like ages of offenders, victims' ages vary greatly—from newborn to age 18.

Table 3-3 reports gender and age distributions for children victimized or contacted by sexual perpetrators. Finkelhor and Ormrod (2004) found that the percentages were about 62 for girls and 38 for boys. Wolak, Finkelhor, and Mitchell (2004) reported the ratio is about

TABLE 3-3 Gender and Age of Victims

Finkelhor and Ormrod (2004)

Males	38%
Females	62%
Younger than 6	13%
6–11	28%
12–17	59%

Wolak, Finkelhor, and Mitchell (2004)

Males	25%
Females	75%
12	1%
13	26%
14	22%
15	28%
16	14%
17	7%

Huang, Leopard, and Brockman (2006)

Males	34.1%
Females	65.9%
Younger than 6	18.9%
6–11	40.6%
12–17	40.5%

3:1, i.e., 75 percent girls and 25 percent boys. Consistent with the two prior studies, Huang, Leopard, and Brockman (2006) found that the majority of victims were girls, which accounted for 66 percent of contact cases. As to ages, results reveal that the 12- to 17-year-old group seems to be at the greatest risk of sexual attacks. These teenagers are frequent users of chat rooms, instant messaging, blogs, or some other social networking systems, which may expose them to sexual predators on the Internet. Table 3-3 also indicates that children under age 6 accounted for a little over 10 percent of victims. Though this percentage is smaller than those of the other two older groups, these very young children are most defenseless and should be protected with greater attention. Medical professionals, daycare teachers, and pre-kindergarten activity providers play an important role in detecting and reporting the possible victimizations of these young children.

Family and economic backgrounds of victims were rarely examined in prior research due to confidentiality and safety reasons. However, Wolak, Finkelhor, and Mitchell (2004) overcame difficulties and were able to provide valuable information on these personal characteristics. The study, conducted in the United States, found that most victims (81%) were non-Hispanic whites. Other ethnic groups had a much smaller percentages:

African-American, 7 percent; Asian, 5 percent; Hispanic white, 3 percent; others, 1 percent. Sixty-one percent of victims lived with both biological parents at the time of the incident. Though information about parents' highest level of education was missing for 40 percent of the cases, valid percentages suggest that victims are equally likely to come from families whose parents had either college degrees or a high school education or less. Incomes of victims' households were not available for 23 percent of cases; percentages of victims by other income brackets were: 4 percent, less than $20,000; 42 percent, $20,000–$50,000; and 30 percent, more than $50,000. Results appear that victims are most likely to come from low- to moderate-income families. This finding to some degree overlaps with Gallagher's observation (Gallagher et al. 2006) that victims are most likely to come from a disadvantaged background. Vieth and Ragland (2005) also noted that children living in small rural communities supply a significant proportion of commercially exploited children in the United States.

The harmful consequences of sexual exploitation on victimized children could be devastating and long lasting, but hopefully curable. To evaluate the short- and long-term effects, Silbert (1989) studied 100 victims of child sexual abuse over various periods of the victims' involvement. During the period of the exploitation, Silbert reported that victims suffered a great deal of soreness and irritation around genital areas, and some somatic symptoms such as vomiting, headaches, sleeplessness, and loss of appetite. Later, many victims developed emotional withdrawal, moodiness, a sense of helplessness, feelings of anxiety and shame, etc. These negative responses might develop into extremely low self-concept, strong sense of guilt, and deep despair. Silbert (1989) also noted that some psychological malfunctions would continue even after the abuse had been disclosed. The victim might experience an initial relief from the disclosure, but negative symptoms such as nightmares and paranoia might subsequently arise. Without proper treatment and counseling, victims might develop learned helplessness and fall into long-term depression. Layden and Smith (2005) have conducted clinical observations of several adult survivors of child sexual exploitation concerning negative consequences in adulthood. Outcomes showed that these adult survivors continuously suffered a variety of psychological disorders such as depression, posttraumatic stress disorder, substance abuse disorder, and social problems like divorce and unemployment. They (Layden and Smith 2005) advised that victims need to learn some coping strategies and problem-solving skills to improve their healing process. Those who suffer physical and psychological damages during childhood must work to rise from being victims to being winning survivors.

EMERGING ISSUES IN FIGHTING ONLINE CHILD EXPLOITATION

As Internet usage and technology continues to grow, the ability to effectively protect a child's innocence becomes more threatened. Many enforcement and prevention programs have been created within and outside the United States to crack down on this new phase of child sexual exploitation (Wortley and Smallbone 2006). Criminal Justice professionals have successfully prosecuted numerous child pornographers and members of molestation rings. But the potential applications of the Internet are so immense and fast-changing that it is difficult for governmental responses to meet and control the spread of the problem. Congress has recently passed the 2006 Adam Walsh Act, creating more resources and programs to prevent child sexual exploitation while promoting Internet safety. A new bill, Deleting Online Predators Act (DOPA), was passed overwhelmingly 410-15 by the House in July 2006, but was unable to be approved by the Senate before the closing of the last session. DOPA, which intends to limit public access to social networking sites such as MySpace, Xanga, LiveJournal, and Facebook, may be reviewed again by both the House and the Senate in their 2007 session. But passing DOPA remains opposed by the American Library Association and some educators. Their concerns are that access limitations placed on schools and libraries will take away an educational environment where teachers and librarians can show how Internet applications are used for collaboration, business, and learning (American Library Association 2006). Further, the bill would deprive socially disadvantaged youths of access to online social networking, while others are able to have 24-hour access to all features of the Internet (Borger 2006; Jenkins 2006).

The increasing popularity of online social networking is a real threat to the protection of innocent children. A keyword search on cases related to CP and MySpace in the LexisNexis newspaper database showed only one case in 2005. Quite amazingly, the same keyword search using the 2006 database resulted in more than 20 unique cases. It seems that social net-working sites have been utilized by some child predators as a platform for preying on victims of their choice. Teens' online profiles, which they post on the sites, provide entry points for sexual predators to become acquainted with their chosen targets. The sites' interactive, multimedia features like blogs, photos, videos, and chat rooms help create relationship, intimacy, and excitement, all of which facilitate the predators' grooming process. Without legal regulations and strong safeguards installed, the social networking sites can be a dangerous virtual ground for these aggressive perpetrators to harm unguarded children.

Another alarming phenomenon is the mutual blending of the CP producer and victim. A front-page story reported by Eichenwald (2005a) in the *New York Times* illustrates how an underage teenager, Justin Berry, built up his own business by exposing himself live in front of a Webcam. Over a period of 5 years, Justin performed a wide array of sexually explicit activities following real-time instructions provided by viewers. He claimed more than 1,500 online subscribers had paid fees to watch him undressing or performing sexual acts. Though the Webcam sites that featured Justin's images and videos have since been shut down, other portals featuring girls still operate actively (Eichenwald 2005b). A congressional testimony (Mattar 2006) revealed that 80 percent of female prostitutes enter the market before the age of 18. Even if only a tiny proportion of this potential pool of female minors is involved in Webcam pornography, the impact of its large number on Internet CP activities will be substantial. In his investigation of Webcam CP, Eichenwald (2005a) reported that more than 500 sites were created by teenagers to advertise pornographic showing. In a one-week period, Eichenwald discovered Webcam images of 98 minors. The profit, fame, and gifts received by the operating minor, along with the ease of site creation and social network, will potentially drive more teens to attempt opening their own online CP business. To viewers, the interactive nature of Webcam broadcasting makes sexual materials more exciting and participative. The instant display also allows viewers to evaluate and determine whether the subject is a minor or not. This identification facet has made the Webcam delivery of images more appealing to child pornographers, while more challenging to undercover police investigations.

The lack of universal criminalization of CP is another obstacle to the crackdown of child sexual exploitation. A recent survey of 186 Interpol member nations by ICMEC showed that 95 countries have no legislation specifically addressing the CP issue. Of those countries that do have CP legislation, 41 do not criminalize possession of CP (International Centre for Missing and Exploited Children n.d.). The ICMEC has recommended a model

CP law to help establish standards on the definition of CP. Mattar (2006) has also recommended an international convention or declaration against Internet sexual exploitation to solidify global efforts in combating CP. If universal prohibition and enforcement are not established, Web portals and other individual sites can still operate in countries that have loose laws about CP. As long as these sites are up and running on the Net, they can deliver sexual depictions to meet the desires of child pornographers around the world. Engagements in international and interagency collaborations are hence crucial in winning the war against child sexual exploitation.

The invention and power of the Internet have without question changed the nature and extent of child sexual exploitation. New challenges have come subsequently with the outgrowth of the Internet. These challenges can best be addressed by holistic efforts involving governments, private sectors, parents, and concerned citizens. Law enforcement agencies have to cooperate professionally with stakeholders in the investigation and conviction of child exploitation cases. Internet service providers, chat and Webcam sites, social networking portals, and other Web hosting services are obligated to maintain a safe environment for usage by children. Banks and credit card billing companies should block financial transactions between CP buyers and sellers, and develop tracking procedures for law enforcement purposes. Schools can offer Internet safety awareness programs to teach students and their parents about the hazards of online communication. Meanwhile, parents are to be highly cognizant of the Internet use by their children, and monitor closely their children's online activities. Also, citizens should be vigilant in reporting CP and exploitation to hotlines and authorities. With these efforts combined and solidified, the society will be able to move toward a stronger position in protecting the well-being of children of this Internet generation.

KEY TERMS

Child sexual exploitation
Digitization
Victimization

REFERENCES

Alexy, E., A. Burgess, and T. Baker. 2005. Internet offenders: Traders, travelers, and combination trader-travelers. *Journal of International Violence* 20 (7): 804–12.

American Library Association. 2006. Why does it matter to libraries? Retrieved February 5, 2007, from http://www.ala.org/ala/washoff/WOissues/techinttele/dopa/dopa.htm

Armstrong, H., and P. Forde. 2003. Internet anonymity practices in computer crime. *Information Management and Computer Security* 11 (5): 209–15.

Baron-Evans, A., and N. Noonan. October 19, 2006. Memorandum regarding Adam Walsh Act, Part I. Office of Defender Services/Training Branch of the Administrative Office of the U.S. Courts. Retrieved January 2, 2007 from http://www.fd.org/pdf_lib/Adam%20Walsh%20MemoPt%201.pdf

Barton, G., and A. Johnson. 2006. Web fuels child porn resurgence. *Journal Sentinel Online*. Retrieved December 12, 2006, from http://www.jsonline.com/story/index.aspx?id=431464

Borger, J. 2006. Chatrooms may be banned in US schools to combat sexual predators. *The Guardian* (London). Retrieved February 5, 2007, from LexisNexis data base.

Burgess, A., M. Clark, and L. Books. 1984. *Child Pornography and Sex Rings*. Lexington, MA: Lexington Books.

Cable News Network. August 9, 2002. Customs service announces child pornography bust. CNN.COM Transcripts. Retrieved January 8, 2007, from http://transcripts.cnn.com/TRANSCRIPTS/0208/09/se.01.html

Carr, J. 2001. Theme paper on child pornography for the 2nd World Congress on commercial sexual exploitation of children. Retrieved January 27, 2007, from http://www.ecpat.net/eng/Ecpat_inter/projects/monitoring/wc2/yokohama_theme_child_pornography.pdf

Chetty, I. 2003. Child abuse images and the Internet. Retrieved November 22, 2006, from http://www.ispa.org.za/iweek/2003/presentations/ichetty.doc

Cooper, A. 2002. *Sex and the Internet: A Guidebook for Clinicians*. New York: Brunner & Routledge.

Durkin, K. 1997. Misuse of the internet by pedophiles: Implications for law enforcement and probation practice. *Federal Probation* 6 (192): 14–18.

Eichenwald, K. December 19, 2005a. Through his Webcam, a boy joins a sordid online world. *New York Times*. Retrieved January 5, 2007, from LexisNexis data base.

Eichenwald, K. December 30, 2005b. Child pornography sites face new obstacles. *New York Times*. Retrieved January 5, 2007, from LexisNexis data base.

Farhangian, J. 2003. A problem of "virtual" proportions: The difficulty inherent in tailoring virtual child pornography laws to meet constitutional standards. *Journal of Law and Policy* 12 (1): 241–86.

Finkelhor, D., and R. Ormrod. 2004. Child pornography: Patterns from NIBRS. *Juvenile Justice Bulletin*. Office of Justice Program, U.S. Department of Justice.

Gallagher, B., C. Fraser, K. Christmann, and B. Hodgson. 2006. International and Internet child sexual abuse and exploitation. Research Report, Center for Applied Childhood Studies, University of Huddersfield, England.

Huang, W., M. Leopard, and A. Brockman. 2006. A content analysis of child pornography cases involving the Internet. Paper presented at the 2006 annual meeting of the Criminal Justice Association of Georgia, November 16–18, 2006, Savannah, Georgia.

Hughes, D. R. 2001. Recent statistics on Internet dangers. Retrieved December 16, 2006, from http://www.protectkids.com/dangers/stats.htm

Hughes, D. M. 2002. The use of new communications and information technologies for sexual exploitation of women and children. *Hastings Women's Law Journal* 13 (1): 129–48.

International Centre for Missing and Exploited Children. April 6, 2006. New study reveals child pornography not a crime in most countries. Press Release. Retrieved December 20, 2006, from http://www.missingkids.com/missingkids/servlet/NewsEventServlet?LanguageCountry=en_US&PageId=2336

International Centre for Missing and Exploited Children. n.d.. Global campaign against child pornography. Retrieved December 12, 2006, from http://www.icmec.org/missingkids/servlet/PageServlet?LanguageCountry=en_X1&PageId=1736

Internet Watch Foundation. October 24, 2006. IWF reveals 10 year statistics on child abuse images online. IWF News. Retrieved December 13, 2006, from http://www.iwf.org.uk/media/news.179.htm

Jenkins, P. 2001. *Beyond Tolerance: Child Pornography on the Internet*. New York: New York University Press.

Jenkins, H. 2006. Congress wigs out over MySpace. *The Boston Globe*. Retrieved February 5, 2007, from LexisNexis data base.

Kalfrin, V. April 6, 2006. Spokesman arrested in child-porn sting. *The Tampa Tribune*. The Tribune Co. Retrieved February 1, 2007, from LexisNexis Academic database.

Koch, W. October 17, 2006. In shadows of Net, War on child porn rages. *USA Today*. Gannett Company, Inc. Retrieved December 11, 2006, from LexisNexis Academic database.

Lanning, K. 2001. *Child Molesters: A Behavioral Analysis*. 4th ed. Washington, DC: National Center for Missing and Exploited Children.

Layden, M., and L. Smith. 2005. "Adult survivors of the child sexual exploitation industry: Psychological profiles." In *Medical, Legal, Social Science Aspects of Child Sexual Exploitation: Comprehensive Review of Pornography, Prostitution, and Internet Crimes,* edited by Cooper et al., 155–77. St. Louis, Missouri: G.W. Medical Publishing, Inc.

Mattar, M. 2006. Protecting children: The battle against child pornography and other forms of sexual exploitation. Congressional hearing before the Commission on Security and Cooperation in Europe, September 27, 2006. Retrieved December 23, 2006, from http://sharedhope.org/images/ct_drmohamed.doc

McLaughlin, J. 2000. Cyber child offender typology. Keene Police Department, New Hampshire. Retrieved December 14, 2006, from http://www.ci.keene.nh.us/police/typology.html

Moore, R. 2005. *Cybercrime: Investigating High-Technology Computer Crime.* Cincinnati, TN: Anderson Publishing.

Mota, S. A. 2002. The U.S. Supreme Court addresses the Child Pornography Prevention Act and Child Online Protection Act in *Ashcroft v. Free Speech Coalition* and *Ashcroft v. American Civil Liberties. Federal Communication Laws Journal* 55 (1): 85–98.

Ove, T. September 14, 2005. Man admits to sex with girl, 2, and mom. *The Pittsburgh Post-Gazette.* P.G. Publishing Co. Retrieved December 16, 2006, from LexisNexis Academic database.

Sampson, P. August 9, 2006. Child porn duo to serve 25 years. *The Record.* North Jersey Media Group Inc. Retrieved December 16, 2006, from LexisNexis Academic database.

Save the Children European Group. 2003. Child pornography and Internet-related sexual exploitation of children. Retrieved December 16, 2006, from http://www.ecpat.no/dokumenter/alliance%20child%20pornography%20on%20the%20internet.doc

Save the Children Sweden. n.d. Helping children in need. Retrieved December 16, 2006, from www.rb.se/NR/rdonlyres/98BD1213-4948-4209-AC0B-0AC81E383315/0/Centre.pdf

Scherer, R. December 17, 1998. New vice squads troll the Web for child porn. *Christian Science Monitor.* Retrieved December 20, 2006, from http://www.csmonitor.com/1998/1217/121798.us.us.3.html

Scherer, R. August 18, 2005. Child porn rising on Web. *The Christian Science Monitor.* Retrieved November 26, 2006, from http://www.csmonitor.com/2005/0818/p01s01-stct.html

Silbert, M. 1989. "The effects on juveniles of being used for pornography and prostitution." In *Pornography: Research Advances and Policy Considerations,* edited by D. Zillmann and J. Bryant, 215–34. Hillsdale, NJ: Lawrence Erlbaum Associates, Inc.

Taylor, M., G. Holland, and E. Quayle. 2001. Typology of paedophile picture collections. *Police Journal* 74 (2): 97–107.

Taylor, M., and E. Quayle. 2003. *Child Pornography: An Internet Crime.* New York, NY: Brunner & Routledge.

Taylor, R., T. Caeti, D. Loper, E. Fritsch, and J. Liederbach. 2006. *Digital Crime and Digital Terrorism.* Upper Saddle River, NJ: Pearson Education, Inc.

Trifiletti, C. 2005. "Investigating Internet child exploitation cases." In *Medical, Legal, Social Science Aspects of Child Sexual Exploitation: Comprehensive Review of Pornography, Prostitution, and Internet Crimes,* edited by Cooper et al., 609–34. St. Louis, MO: G.W. Medical Publishing, Inc.

Vieth, V., and E. Ragland. 2005. "Shadow children: Addressing the commercial exploitation of children in rural America." In *Medical, Legal, Social Science Aspects of Child Sexual Exploitation: Comprehensive Review of Pornography, Prostitution, and Internet Crimes,* edited by Cooper et al., 1027–39. St. Louis, MO: G.W. Medical Publishing, Inc.

Wolak, J., D. Finkelhor, and K. Mitchell. 2004. Internet-initiated sex crimes against minors: Implications for prevention based on findings from a national study. *Journal of Adolescent Health* 35 (5): 424.e11–424.e20.

Wolak, J., D. Finkelhor, and K. Mitchell. 2005. Child pornography possessors arrested in Internet-related crime. Findings from the National Juvenile Online Victimization Study, National Center of Missing and Exploited Children.

Wolak, J., K. Mitchell, and D. Finkelhor. 2006. Online victimization of youth: Five years later. National Center of Missing and Exploited Children.

Wortley, R., and S. Smallbone. 2006. Child pornography on the Internet. U.S. Department of Justice, Office of Community Oriented Policing Services. Retrieved January 29, 2007, from http://www.cops.usdoj.gov/mime/open.pdf?Item=1729

Chapter 4

Cyber Bullying: A Transnational Perspective

K. Jaishankar
Manonmaniam Sundaranar University, India

Shaheen Shariff
McGill University, Canada

Dr. K. Jaishankar is a lecturer in the Department of Criminology and Criminal Justice, Manonmaniam Sundaranar University, Tirunelveli, India. He is the founding editor in chief of the *International Journal of Cyber Criminology*, the founding editor of "Crime and Justice Perspective"—the official organ of the Criminal Justice Forum (CJF), India, and the founding managing editor of the *International Journal of Criminal Justice Sciences*. He serves in the international editorial boards of *Journal of Social Change* (U.S.), *Electronic Journal of Sociology* (Canada), *Crime, Punishment and Law: An International Journal* (U.S.), *Journal of Physical Security* (U.S.), and *Graduate Journal of Social Science* (UK). He is the national focal point for India for the International Police Executive Symposium's working paper series and Expert of World Police Database at www.coginta.com. He is a coinvestigator of the International Project on Cyber Bullying funded by SSHRC, Canada involving eight countries, along with the principal investigator Dr. Shaheen Shariff, McGill University. He is a pioneer in developing the new field, Cyber Criminology and is the proponent of "Space Transition Theory" which gives an explanation for the criminal behavior in cyberspace. He is a recognized expert in the field of cyber criminology and invited by various universities in the United States to deliver lectures on his Space Transition Theory of Cyber Crimes. His areas of academic competence are cyber criminology, crime mapping, GIS, communal violence, victimology, policing, and crime prevention.

Dr. Shaheen Shariff is an assistant professor in the Faculty of Education, McGill University, Montreal, Quebec, Canada. Her appointment is in leadership, policy studies and education law, informed by human rights, legal pluralism, and tort law and constitutional law. She is principal investigator on two grants funded by Social Science and Humanities Research Council of Canada to develop a profile of cyber bullying, inform the current policy vacuum, and develop guidelines to help schools address cyber bullying. She has published numerous journal articles and book chapters on cyber bullying, and she is also writing two books on this topic: *Cyber-bullying: Issues and Solutions for the School, the Classroom, and the Home* (Routledge, UK); and *Cyber-bullying: What Schools Need to Know to Control Misconduct and Avoid Legal Consequences* (Cambridge University Press). Dr. Shariff has presented many papers nationally and internationally on cyber bullying and has also contributed to a round-table consultation on violence against children organized by the United Nations Secretary General in June 2005. Her work on cyber bullying has drawn significant public and media interest, placing her among Canada's top 20 most frequently interviewed and quoted experts according to a recent media relations survey.

Abstract

Cyber bullying is a psychologically devastating form of social cruelty among adolescents and others. This chapter reviews the international scenario of cyber bullying and emphasizes the current policy vacuum across the world on this malicious act. It opens with a description and definition of cyber bullying, followed by a brief discussion of the international responses to cyber bullying. A detailed comparative analysis of cyber bullying in the United States, United Kingdom, Canada, Australia, China, Japan, India, South Korea, and Thailand will be presented.

INTRODUCTION

Parents can often be heard complaining that once their children reach adolescence, they crave for independence and prefer that their parents' care and affection are not obvious to public. Their primary focus turns on clothes, physical appearance, music, and friends. Adolescence is a period of abrupt biological and social change. Specifically, the rapid body changes associated with the onset of adolescence, in particular, puberty, and changes from elementary to high school initiate dramatic changes in the youngster's peer group composition and status. Changes in peer group availability, an individual's status within the said groups, and peer pressure confront youngsters as they are entering new, larger, and typically impersonal secondary high schools. One way in which peer status is often achieved in these sorts of environments, especially for boys, is through the selective use of aggression and other agonistic strategies.

This is typically a time when a young person's reputation amongst his or her peers is of crucial importance, and when the slightest insult, derogatory statement, or threat can result in extreme feelings of shame and humiliation (Rigby 2005; Shariff and Johnny 2007). This sense of shame is exacerbated as the offensive peer group increases in size (Salmivalli et al. 1996; Pellegrini and Bartini 2000). Bullying is a problem behavior that concerns students, educators, and parents because of its potential detriment to the students' well-being (Nansel et al. 2001, 2003; Haynie et al. 2001). Most school violence, particularly during adolescence, involves students bullying their peers (Boulton and Underwood 1992; Boulton 1993).

In the 1990s, the United States saw an epidemic of school shootings (of which the most notorious was the Columbine High School massacre). Many of the children behind these shootings claimed that they were victims of bullying and that they resorted to violence only after the school administrators repeatedly failed to intervene. In many of these cases, the victims of the shooters sued the shooters' families and the school district. In fact, many victims have filed suit against the bullies directly for intentional infliction of emotional distress. Because of these school violence trends, schools in many countries strongly discouraged bullying, with programs designed to teach students on how to cooperate and respect each other's differences, as well as to train peer moderators in intervention and dispute resolution techniques. According to Hoover and Olsen (2001), "up to 15% of students in American schools are frequently or severely harassed by their peers. . . . Only a slim majority of 4th through 12th graders . . . (55.2%) reported neither having been picked on nor picking on others." Further, bully–victim cycles are found where individuals are both bullies and victims (Ma 2001; Pellegrini and Bartini 2000; Schwartz, Dodge, and Coie 1993; Schwartz et al. 1997).

More importantly, it is reported that in many school-shooting cases, bullying played a major role (Dedman 2001).

Bullying among school children is certainly a very old phenomenon, though it was not until the early 1970s, that it was made the object of systematic research. In schools, bullying usually occurs in areas where there is minimal or no adult supervision. It can occur in nearly any part in or around the school building, though it more often occurs in gym, exploratory classes, hallways, bathrooms, classes that require group work, and/or after school activities. Bullying in some school instances consists of a group of students taking advantage over a student (a boy or girl), or isolating one student in particular, and outnumbering him/her. The typical targets of bullying in school are often pupils who are considered strange or different by their peers to begin with, making the situation harder for them to deal with. Teachers who fail to intervene on behalf of the victim may actually be partly responsible for perpetrating the bullying incidents further.

From a historical perspective, bullying was not perceived to be a problem that necessarily needed attention but rather has been accepted as a fundamental and normal part of childhood similar to a rite of passage (Limber and Small 2003; Campbell 2005). In the last two decades, however, this view has changed and schoolyard bullying is now perceived to be a serious problem that warrants further attention. Bullying is an age-old societal problem, beginning in the schoolyard and often progressing to the boardroom later in life (McCarthy et al. 2001; Campbell 2005). "Bullying" is often defined as being an aggressive, intentional act or behavior that is carried out by a group or an individual repeatedly against a victim who cannot easily defend himself or herself (Whitney and Smith 1993; Olweus 1991; Campbell 2005). It is a form of abuse that is based on an imbalance of power; in that way, it can be defined as a systematic abuse of power (Smith and Sharp 1994; Rigby 2002). Bullying may involve physical assault, including behaviors such as hitting, punching, and spitting, or it may involve language that is similar to browbeating using verbal assaults, teasing, ridicule, sarcasm, and scapegoating (DiGiulio 2001; Slee and Rigby 1993; Campbell 2005). It involves a minimum of two people, typically the perpetrator and the victim. However, a large number of people, bystanders who are witnesses to the bullying incidents, may be perceived as an audience. These bystanders may be other students who witness the bullying event, yet remain uninvolved. They are frequently afraid of becoming the next victim if they do choose to interfere. They often feel powerless and show a loss of self-respect and self-confidence (Harris and Petrie 2002; Campbell 2005).

In the recent years, a new form of bullying has emerged that makes use of the diverse range of technology that is now available. **Cyber bullying**, as coined by Canadian Bill Belsey (2007), or bullying using technology, is a phenomenon that children and **adolescents** seem to be increasingly using to harm others (National Children's Home 2002; Campbell 2005). Cyber bullying using e-mail, text, chat rooms, mobile phones, mobile phone cameras, and Web sites is surfacing as a new medium used by today's bullies. Methods include "texting" derogatory messages on mobile phones, with students showing the message to others before sending it to the target; sending threatening e-mails; and forwarding a confidential e-mail to all address book contacts, thus publicly humiliating the first sender. Others gang up on one student and bombard him/her with "flame" (sending derogatory messages to a person(s) e mails) (Snider 2004; Campbell 2005).

Another way to cyber bully is to set up a derogatory Web site dedicated to a targeted student, and then e-mail others about the targeted victim's address or Web site to invite their comments.

In addition, Web sites can be set up for others to vote on the biggest geek, or sluttiest girl in the school (Snider 2004; Campbell 2005). In one widely reported incident, a self-made film of a 15-year-old Quebec boy emulating a Star Wars fight was posted on the Internet by his classmates. Millions of people downloaded the film, with the media dubbing him the Star Wars Kid (Snider 2004; Campbell 2005). In another incident, an overweight boy in the school's changing room was photographed by another student with a mobile phone camera, and the picture was subsequently posted on the Internet (Mitchell 2004; Campbell 2005). Cyber bullying can also be carried out in chat rooms with the participants ragging a targeted student or continually excluding someone (Williams, Cheung, and Choi 2000; Campbell 2005).

CYBER BULLYING: DEFINITIONS AND CONCEPTUALIZATION

There is no dearth of definitions regarding cyber bullying. Cyber bullying is defined by various scholars (Willard 2003; Belsey 2005; Smith et al. 2004; Shariff 2005; Patchin and Hinduja 2006). Bill Belsey defined cyber bullying as *"the use of information and communication technologies such as e-mail, cell phone and pager* **text messages***, instant messaging, defamatory personal Web sites, and defamatory online personal polling Web sites, to support deliberate, repeated, and hostile behavior by an individual or group, that is intended to harm others."* According to Nancy Willard, Director for the Center for Safe and Responsible Internet Use, cyber bullying is speech that is *"defamatory, constitutes bullying, harassment, or discrimination, discloses personal information, or contains offensive, vulgar, or derogatory comments"* (Willard 2003). The numerous tactics students can employ include flaming (sending derogatory messages to a person(s)), harassing and denigrating (put-downs), masquerading, outing, and excluding (Willard n.d.). Shariff (2005) defines cyber bullying as follows: "Cyber bullying consists of covert, psychological bullying, conveyed through the electronic mediums such as cell-phones, web-logs and web-sites, on-line chat rooms, 'MUD' rooms (multi-user domains where individuals take on different characters) and Xangas (on-line personal profiles where some adolescents create lists of people they do not like)."

Patchin and Hinduja (2006) define cyber bullying as "willful and repeated harm inflicted through the medium of electronic text." Smith et al. (2004) defines cyber bullying as "an aggressive, intentional act carried out by a group or individual, using electronic forms of contact, repeatedly and over time against a victim who cannot easily defend him or herself." Cyber bullying is a form of bullying which has, in recent years, become more apparent, as the use of electronic devices such as computers and mobile phones by young people has increased. Cyber bullying can take many forms, and for the sake of this chapter, the concept of "cyber bullying" is subdivided (Smith et al. 2004) into seven subcategories:

- Text message bullying
- Picture/video clip bullying (via mobile phone cameras)
- Phone call bullying (via mobile phone)
- E-mail bullying
- Chat room bullying
- Bullying through instant messaging
- Bullying via Web sites.

These subcategories were chosen because "cyber bullying" is a very broad term, and the subcategories would help get a better understanding of the range of cyber bullying and of forms that were most prevalent. Three aspects of cyber bullying make it a challenge for schools to supervise and monitor. First, cyber bullying is anonymous. For example, in Li's (2005) study, 41 percent of the students surveyed did not know the identity of their perpetrators. Second, it allows participation by an infinite audience. A third concern is that sexual harassment is a prevalent aspect of cyber bullying.

Anonymity

Most cyber bullying is anonymous because perpetrators are shielded by screen names that protect their identity. Anonymity in cyberspace adds to the challenges for schools (Harmon 2004). Furthermore, although cyber bullying begins anonymously in the *virtual* environment, it influences learning in the *physical* school environment. The consequences can be psychologically devastating for victims, and socially detrimental for all students (Gáti et al. 2002). Fear of unknown cyber perpetrators among classmates and bullying that continues at school distracts *all* students (victims, bystanders, and perpetrators alike) from schoolwork. It creates a hostile physical school environment where students feel unwelcome and unsafe. In such an atmosphere, equal opportunities to learn are greatly reduced (Devlin 1997; Shariff and Strong-Wilson 2005).

An Infinite Audience

Research on general bullying finds that 30 percent of onlookers and bystanders support the perpetrators instead of victims (Salmivalli et al. 1996; Boulton 1993). The longer it persists, the more bystanders join in on the abuse (Henderson et al. 2002), creating a power imbalance between victims and perpetrators. Isolation renders victims vulnerable to continued abuse, and the cycle repeats itself. What might begin in the physical school environment as friendly banter can quickly turn into verbal bullying that continues in cyberspace as covert psychological bullying. The difference in cyberspace is that hundreds of perpetrators can get involved in the abuse, and classmates who may not engage in the bullying at school can hide themselves using technology to inflict the most serious abuse (see examples in Shariff 2004; Shariff and Strong-Wilson 2005).

Prevalence of Sexual Harassment

Preliminary research suggests that although both genders engage in cyber bullying, there are considerable gender differences (Chu 2005; Li 2005). It has been argued that children who engage in any form of bullying are victims. However, studies have shown that teenage girls have more often been at the receiving end of cyber bullying (Dibbell 1993; Evard 1996).

A review of the scholarly literature (Shariff and Gouin 2005) finds that according to Herring (2002), 25 percent of Internet users aged 10–17 were exposed to unwanted pornographic images in the past year; 8 percent of the images involved violence, in addition to sex and nudity. Mitchell et al. (2001, cited in Barak 2005), who conducted a survey of American teenagers found that 19 percent of these youths (mostly older girls) had experienced at least one sexual solicitation online in the preceding year. According to Adams (2001), one in three female children reported online harassment in 2001. Moreover, adolescent hormones rage and influence social relationships as children negotiate social and romantic relationships and become more physically self-conscious, independent, and insecure (Boyd 2000). Research on dating and harassment practices at the middle-school level shows that peer pressure causes males to engage in increased homophobic bullying of male peers and increased sexual harassment of female peers to establish their manhood (Tolman et al. 2001). During this confusing stage of adolescent life, the conditions are ripe for bullying to take place. The Internet media provides a perfect platform for adolescent anxieties to play themselves out.

These three aspects of cyber bullying present a number of unprecedented legal and educational concerns for schools. The first involves a determination of the boundaries of supervision. Schools find it difficult to monitor students' online discourses. This is because cyber bullying typically occurs outside supervision boundaries, and this raises important legal questions about the extent to which schools can be expected to intervene when their students cyber bully off campus, outside school hours, and from home computers. Currently, the legal boundaries regarding freedom of expression, student privacy, and protection in cyberspace remain unresolved (Wallace 1999; Shariff and Johnny 2007). Meanwhile, frustrated parents are beginning to sue schools for failing to protect their children from online harassment and abuse.

CYBER BULLYING: THE INTERNATIONAL SCENARIO

Numerous surveys of students have found that face-to-face bullying by peers in school is a frequent experience for many children (Genta et al. 1996; Kumpulainen et al. 1998; Whitney and Smith 1993). It has been found that one in six children reported having being bullied at least once a week (Rigby 1997; Zubrick et al. 1997) although that figure was as high as 50 percent if the duration of the bullying is taken as lasting only one week (Smith and Shu 2000). In another study, 40 percent of adolescents reported having been bullied at some time during their schooling (Mynard, Joseph, and Alexander 2000). However, the percentage of students who have reported long-term bullying of 6 months or more decreases between 15 and 17 percent (Slee 1995; Slee and Rigby 1993).

A cursory review of cyber bullying internationally discloses the following statistical realities. Twelve percent of Australian children under age 10 use text messaging daily, increasing to 49 percent of 10- to 14-year-olds and 80 percent of 15- to 17-year-olds. Sixty-one percent of Australian homes have computers and 46 percent of those have Internet access. Finally, 46 percent of 14-year-old Australian youth, 55 percent of 15-year-olds, and 73 percent of 16-year-olds have their own cell phones (Lee 2005). In Japan, children are exposed to digital gadgets at a very early age but only 20 percent are regular users (Dickie et al. 2004). In Great Britain, over 80 percent of children and teens access home computers, and 75 percent of 11-year-olds own a cell phone (Dickie et al. 2004). Of these, 16 percent reported receiving threatening text messages or Internet threats (NCH 2002). In the United States, approximately 70 percent of children, aged 4–6 have used computers, and 68 percent under the age 2 have used screen media. A United States survey of 3,700 middle-school students found that 18 percent of students were cyber bullied (Chu 2005). Finally, Canadian statistics confirm that 99 percent of Canadian teens use the Internet. An Alberta middle-school study, disclosed that 23 percent of the 177 respondents were bullied by e-mail, 35 percent in chat rooms, 41 percent by cell phone text messaging, 32 percent by known schoolmates, 11 percent by people outside school, and 16 percent by multiple sources including schoolmates (Li 2005).

United States

In the year 2000, a University of New Hampshire study found that one out of every 17, or 6 percent of kids in the United States, had been threatened or harassed online. However, in March 2006, statistics showed that 75–80 percent of 12- to 14-year-olds had been cyber bullied. Furthermore, 20 percent of kids under 18 have received a sexual solicitation. Therefore, cyber bullying is clearly on the rise, and it affects both genders. An American Educational Research Association study shows that female bullies preferred the use of text messaging harassment versus face-to-face bullying by two to one (Toppo 2006).

Ybarra and Mitchell (2004) in the United States reported that 15 percent of their sample identified themselves as Internet bullies while 7 percent said they had been targeted online. It also seems that cyber bullying is a growing problem. The growth of cyberspace harassment has been recognized as far back as 1999 with a report from the U.S. Attorney General (Janet Reno) to the former Vice President, Al Gore, suggesting that incidents were an increasing problem for law enforcement officials (Beckerman and Nocero 2002). An American Web site I-Safe reports research on cyber bullying, from a survey of 1,500 students from grades 4 to 8 (aged 9 to 13 years). The main findings (cited from www.mmu.k12.vt.us) determined that 42 percent of children claimed to have been bullied while online, that 35 percent had been threatened online, and that 21 percent had received threatening e-mails or other messages. Fifty-three percent of students surveyed admitted being mean or hurtful online, and 58 percent had said nothing to their parents if they had been threatened online. Again, how respondents were recruited is not specified.

Another organization in the United States that monitors young peoples' use of the Internet is Wirekids.org, which asserts that 1,500 youth report either being bullied, are guilty of cyber bullying, or know someone who was bullied. In fact, the *Portsmouth Herald* (2005) reports that cyber bullies or perpetrators, averaging 9 to 14 years of age, use anonymity to cyber bully. In Westchester County, New York, school officials invited 600 students, parents, educators, and law-enforcement officials to a one-half day conference on cyber bullying. When officials asked approximately 200 students if they had personally been a cyber victim or perpetrator, or knew a friend who was either, 194 students raised their hands (Swartz 2005).

Hinduja and Patchin's (2005) study of 1,500 Internet-using adolescents found that over one-third of youth reported being victimized online and over 16 percent of respondents admitted to cyber bullying others. While most of the instances of cyber bullying involved relatively minor behavior (40 percent were disrespected and 18 percent were called names), over 12 percent were physically threatened and about 5 percent were scared for their safety. Notably, less than 15 percent of victims told an adult about the incident. Additional research by Hinduja and Patchin (2007) found that online bullying victimization is related to offline problem behaviors. That is, youth who report being victims of cyber bullying also experience stress or strain that is related to offline problem behaviors (an index of 11 deviant behaviors includes running away from home, cheating on a school test, skipping school, using alcohol or marijuana, among others). However, both of these studies provide only preliminary information about the nature and consequences of online bullying, owing to the methodological challenges associated with an online survey.

A recent poll commissioned by Fight Crime: Invest in Kids (2007) found that more than 13 million children in the United States, aged 6–17, are victims of cyber bullying. One-third of all teens and one-sixth of all pre-teens have had mean, threatening, or embarrassing things written about them online.

Canada

Canadian research on cyber bullying is currently emerging in a major way (Shariff 2005, 2006a, b; Shariff and Gouin 2005; Shariff and Johnny 2007; Shariff and Strong-Wilson 2005). Although there have been studies on students' Internet use over the last few years, few have focused on cyber bullying (Li 2005, 2006, 2007; Shariff 2003, 2005; Shariff and Hoff, 2007). A Canadian study researched the legal obligations of Canadian schools to address cyber bullying in Quebec and British Columbia (Shariff 2005).

Li's (2006) study in Canada investigates the nature and the extent of adolescents' experience of cyber bullying. A survey study of 264 students from three junior high schools was conducted. The results shows that close to half of the students were bully victims and about one in four had been cyber bullied. Over half of the students reported that they knew someone being cyber bullied. Almost half of the cyber bullies used electronic means to harass others more than three times. The majority of the cyber bully victims and bystanders did not report the incidents to adults. When gender was considered, significant differences were identified in terms of bullying and cyber bullying. Males were more likely to be bullies and cyber bullies when compared with their female counterparts. In addition, female cyber bully victims were more likely to inform adults than their male counterparts. Another study by Li (2005) was a comparative analysis of the nature and extent of Canadian and Chinese Adolescent school students' cyber bullying experiences. This study found some similar patterns as well as different trends between Canadian and Chinese adolescents' experiences in cyber bullying.

United Kingdom

The National Children's Home (2002) study in Great Britain found that one in four children reported being bullied by mobile phone or on the Internet. According to a survey by the National Children's Home charity and Tesco Mobile (NCH 2005) of 770 youth between the ages of 11 and 19, 20 percent of respondents revealed that they had been bullied via electronic means. Almost three-quarters (73 percent) stated that they knew the bully, while 26 percent stated that the offender was a stranger. Another interesting finding was that 10 percent indicated that another person had taken a picture of them via a cellular phone camera, consequently making them feel uncomfortable, embarrassed, or threatened. Many youths were reluctant to tell an authority figure about their cyber bullying victimization; while 24 percent and 14 percent told a parent or teacher, respectively, 28 percent did not tell anyone while 41 percent told a friend. A survey by the Crimes against Children Research Center at the University of New Hampshire in 2000 found that 6 percent of the young people in the survey had experienced some form of harassment including threats and negative rumors and 2 percent had suffered distressing harassment (Finkelhor, Mitchell, and Wolak 2000).

A survey of over 500 British 12- to 15-year-olds has found that 1 in 10 has experienced cyber bullying, most commonly through threatening e-mails, exclusion from online conversations, or through the spread of rumors about them on the Internet. The MSN cyber bullying report, *Blogging, instant messaging and email bullying amongst today's teens*, was published by MSN using data from a British market research company, YouGov that conducted a study on 518 young people and their parents in January 2006. The major findings from the report are as follows:

- More than twice as many girls (18 percent) as boys (7 percent) reported that they had been "cyber bullied," while twice as many girls (34 percent) as boys (17 percent) knew someone who had experienced cyber bullying.

- One in 20 respondents admitted their involvement in bullying someone online. One in eight reported sending threats to others, while one in 12 admitted to posting fabricated information about someone on a blog (online diary).

- Thirteen percent of respondents judged cyber bullying to be "worse than physical bullying."

- Seventy-four percent of respondents did not approach anyone for help after experiencing cyber bullying.

- Forty-eight percent of parents were "unaware of the phenomenon of cyber bullying."

- Over half of the young people surveyed had Instant Messenger (IM) conversations at least once daily, while 33 percent chatted on IM several times a day.

- One in 10 respondents reported visiting online blogs (diaries) daily, and 48 percent of those surveyed said that they checked their e-mail at least once daily. (MSN UK 2006)

Australia

An article in www.theinquirer.net, an Australian news Web site, provides brief statistics on cyber bullying, taken from a study by the Queensland University of Technology. The statistics given are that 13 percent of students have already experienced cyber bullying by age 8, and that 25 percent of students knew somebody who had experienced cyber bullying. This article also reports that more than half the students of the study thought that the phenomenon was on the rise. There is an unspecified time frame or sample size for this study, and the method of collecting data is not known from the article provided.

Campbell (2005) conducted a study of 120 Australian students in Grade 8. Her results indicate that over one-quarter reveal they know someone who had been bullied using technology. Further, 11 percent of the students admit that they have cyber bullied, and 14 percent reveal that they were targets. Campbell's (2005) study also reveals that most of the targets are bullied through text messaging, followed closely by chat rooms and then by e-mail.

A recent case (2007) of cyber bullying led an Australian state to ban the popular Internet film-sharing Web site "YouTube" from school computers (Bartlett 2007; Smith 2007). A group of school boys had filmed themselves sexually abusing and degrading a female classmate and then uploaded the video onto YouTube. The film showed a group of 12 youths surrounding the 17-year-old girl, who has a mild mental disability, bullying her to perform sex acts, urinating on her, and setting her hair alight. The education minister in Southern Victoria State, where the attack took place, said the state's 1,600 public schools would block access to YouTube. "The government has never tolerated bullying in schools and this zero tolerance approach extends to the online world," said the minister. The director of the Australian police's High Tech Crime Centre, Kevin Zuccato, said at the time of the attack on the girl late last year that it was a disturbing example of cyber bullying. "Cyber bullying between children online is on the rise," he said. "Social networking sites are also putting children at risk. The dark side is too dark" (Bartlett 2007).

India

Bullying is predominantly considered as a serious issue in Western countries. In India, bullying is part of certain cultures. Even though school bullying or college bullying is prevalent in the name of *ragging*, the connotation of bullying is not present in the Indian context. Even though there are new laws regarding ragging in schools and colleges, bullying per se has not been condoned. The use of modern technologies such as Internet and mobile phones has increased the prevalence of bullying by school and college students. Today, Internet and mobile phones have become part of everybody's lives, including school students.

If u think they r hot . . . Well, let me tell u they're not. They're ugly, they're fat, they look like ratz!!!! Even alienz look better dan dat!!!!! This was an e-mail sent out by the 10th standard class students of a respected Mumbai school, about the students of a rival school. While this may seem to be more of a playful prank than a serious offense, it is only the beginning of a trend that can escalate into a serious problem in the near future. In this case, the teachers intervened and the problem was eventually resolved. In India, where younger and younger kids are discovering the power of the Internet, cyber bullying has already started trapping Indian teenagers in its insidious Web (Kapoor 2003).

Apart from the cyber bullying by school students, a cursory look in to www.orkut.com (a social networking site) will show how much cyber bullying is occurring in India. Orkut came to India only in February 2006 with a mission statement claiming to help people to create a closer, more intimate network of friends and hoping to put them on the path to social bliss. It is apparent from the mission statement that it was established to enable people to interact with each other across the globe by bridging geographical distances. However, it has since been used for superfluous activities leading to moral degradation and upheaval (Rahul 2007). A 19-year-old student has been accused of making a fake account of a girl. The police arrested a management student from Mumbai following a girl's complaint about tarnishing her image in Orkut. The boy was trying to entice the girl for some time. He threatened her with dire consequences when she resisted his advances. Later, he posted an obscene profile of her in Orkut portal along with her mobile number. The profile has been sketched in such a way that it draws lewd comments from many who visit her profile. Later, the boy was arrested under section 67 of Information Technology Act, 2000 (India has no separate law for cyber bullying). A brief search in the Orkut profile will reveal many such profiles with pictures of beautiful girls (Sengupta 2006).

In another case of Orkut cyber bullying, a malicious profile of a Delhi school girl was uploaded on the site. The mischief mongers have actually posted obscene photographs and contact details such as her home address and telephone numbers on the profile, using suggestive names like "sex teacher" for her. Authorities knew about the matter after the girl's family started receiving vulgar calls; thereafter, her father contacted the Cyber Cell of Delhi Police's Economic Offences Wing. According to the Delhi police sources, the girl is a student in a

South Delhi school. Her father told the police that somebody had misused the social networking Web site to falsify her profile and circulate obscene pictures and information on her profile. The family received the first call almost a month back when the caller wanted to speak to her, following a series of similar calls, referring to Orkut. Two strangers knocked at the girl's door, thinking that the girl had invited them for sex through Internet. This is the second incident demonstrating Orkut's misuse in New Delhi. Earlier, an airhostess alleged that someone has opened an account in her name on the Web site, in which she was described as a "sex struck woman."

In another interesting case of school cyber bullying in Orkut, a few students from Bombay Scottish School, angered over a few things, started a discussion, "All those who hate DPN" (DPN here are the initials of the principal DPN Prasad). Many students seem to have a grouse against the authorities, and the post flourished with quite uncharitable comments. The school authorities noticed it, and the students were made to apologize and delete their offensive posts. Quite on the heels of this incident, another similarly unpleasant incident was reported in the papers in Mumbai. A few Students at MMK College in Mumbai started a forum, "Give your opinion about the principal" on Orkut. In the forum, reportedly, five students posted comments that were not only uncharitable but also derogatory and slanderous in nature. Once again, college officials made the students apologize and edit their posts. These are only tip of the iceberg of Orkut cyber bullying in India. There are hundreds of communities involving hate against students, teachers, actors, politicians, etc.

Though there are many Western studies related to cyber bullying, there are no empirical researches in India to unearth this modern phenomenon. One study by Anil Kumar and Jaishankar (2007) found that mobile bullying is common among the school students. This study investigated the nature and the extent of school students' experience of cyber bullying using mobile phones. The results showed that 65 percent of the students were victims of cyber bullying using mobile phones. Interestingly, 60 percent of the respondents have also involved in bullying others using mobile phones. This study is a pioneering one in this area, even though a sweeping generalization was not determined. This survey is the only of its kind so far conducted in India at Tirunelveli city.

In the United States, United Kingdom, and Canada, antibullying sites and support groups have mushroomed to redress this problem. For example, Bullying.ca, Be Safe Online, and Bully Online are just some of the hundreds of sites that offer advice, support, and resources to counter cyber bullying; however, there are no such organizations in India, as the concept of cyber bullying is still not widespread in India (Kapoor 2003).

Japan

In Japan, a country considered to be digitally ahead of the rest of the world by at least two generations (Mitchell 2004), children are exposed to digital gadgets at a very early age. Approximately half of Japanese children aged 11 use the Internet; however, only about 20 percent of them are regular users (Dickie et al. 2004). As Internet use by children is on the rise, cases of cyber bullying have also increased.

In a brief study, Julie d'Eon and Senoo (2007) tried to analyze the prevalence of cyber bullying in Japan and provided insights on some cases. In what is believed to be the first case of cyber bullying in Japan, a few 9th grade girls bullied a 7th grade girl using a cell phone camera. Several girls took the girl to a restroom in one shopping mall, took off her clothing, and proceeded to take naked pictures of her with two-group member's cell phones. These two bullies showed the pictures to some friends and threatened the victim that they would spread her picture around the school if she reported the incident to teachers. One of them sent the picture to friends by cell phone. In this case, the school interfered, deleted the picture, and stopped the picture from being circulated further (Hasegawa 2007; Senoo 2007).

In another case in Japan, one young girl resorted to murdering her classmate over a contentious Web site (*New York Times* 2004). According to a University of Adelaide academic, "In Japan, 80% of bullying or cyber bullying is carried out by a group, rather than an individual. It happens in close friendships where the victim is not excluded from the group, but harassed for a period before it is someone else's turn. 'Good students' are involved in bullying, instead of 'problem kids' " (Gibson 2006).

There is also a new trend in Japan involving mobile bullying, which is steadily increasing. Accessed mainly via mobile phones, these so-called "gakko ura saito" (clandestine school sites), have created a new form of group bullying that is spurring a whole generation of anonymous slanderers who make old-fashioned bullies seem almost preferable by comparison. After all, in old-style "ijime" (bullying in Japanese), at least you know who the tormentor is. The electronic version is just as vicious, if not more so, because electronic communications afford complete anonymity. And of course, it is far more difficult for school authorities to intervene, let alone identify the instigators, or implement disciplinary measures. In November 2006, a first-year high-school student in Sapporo was discovered to have posted moving images of himself undergoing physical bullying by several classmates. Two of the offenders, one boy and one girl, were subsequently suspended from the school. In December 2006, eight members of a high-school baseball team in Nagano Prefecture were found to have slandered a teammate on a bulletin board. Six offenders were ordered restricted to their homes, and the team was banned from competition for 3 months. In February 2007, six middle-school girls in Kobe used their cell phones' digital cameras to photograph one another nude. They posted the photos on a bulletin board, with an invitation for visitors to rank their favorites. The Kobe Prefectural Police filed charges for engaging in obscene acts (Aera 2007).

China

Li's comparative study (2005) on the nature and extent of Canadian and Chinese adolescents' cyber bullying experiences gives some insights into Chinese cyber bullying. However, more studies are needed on China to understand the true extent of cyber bullying. There are some cases of cyber bullying in China worth noting. A noteworthy case of cyber bullying developed in April 2006, when a man posted information about another man who allegedly had an affair with his wife. He identified his wife's suspected lover by his Web name, which led to a series of postings that revealed the man's name, phone number, and address. Thousands of Web postings denounced the lover, while Internet users telephoned or showed up at his home to verbally abuse him and his family. Lawyers are now calling on the government to protect people from having their personal information made public on the Internet (Bartlett 2007).

In one case involving a young student in China, someone posted a very common and normal picture of the student on the Internet. Nobody could have anticipated that his picture would attract so many hackers who would eventually alter the picture for fun. Many considered the pictures as being funny, and everybody liked the protagonist and they call him "Little Fat Boy" (Yan 2005). In a recent case of cyber bullying in China, a video was posted on

YouTube involving students bullying a teacher. The students were cursing at the teacher and taking other hurtful actions that were intended to belittle their teacher. Many protested this incident (Belew 2007).

South Korea

In South Korea, a law aimed at cracking down on Internet misuse is intended to stop cyber bullies who were previously able to hide behind false identities. When the new law takes effect in July 2007, the "Internet real-name system" will mean that cyber bullies can be traced because major portals and news media Web sites will be compelled to record the real IDs of users when they post entries. Portal operators will be obliged to disclose personal information such as names and addresses of cyber attackers when their victims want to sue them for libel or infringement upon privacy. "South Korea is an Internet powerhouse and it is probably the most wired country in the world. But sadly, the dark side is too dark," ministry director Lee Ta-Hee told AFP. "Victims have so far been unable to trace cyber attackers when the attackers use false IDs," he said (Bartlett 2007).

Online mobs first demonize those they disagree with, and then the victims' home address, credit card details, and even their boss's phone numbers are circulated around. All of Korea's police stations now have a cyber terror unit to help deal with the problem. The number of cases referred to Korea's Internet Commission tripled last year. "Often using other people's login to a website, these people spread bad rumors aimed at affecting the victim's social status," said Chun Seong Lee, Liaison Officer at the Cyber Terror Response Centre. "It's happening a lot. In these situations, people could lose their job, or it could affect their social life, even causing mental distress. That's all happening because of the development of the Internet, of course." Next year a new law will come into effect which will force the Koreans to reveal their name and ID number before they share their opinions online (Simmons 2006).

Thailand

Sending cruel and sometimes threatening messages, racial, or ethnic slurs online are frequent. Because computer proficiency is second nature to many of today's youngsters, it is not surprising that many create Web sites that have audio-based stories, cartoons, and pictures that ridicule others. Dave Knight, a Canadian, was told to check out a certain Web site. To his horror, the Web site was titled, "Welcome to the page that makes fun of Dave Knight." At least one similar Web site has ridiculed a Bangkok student, but, understandably, she did not want to share the site address with Learning Post readers. Pictures of classmates are often posted online along with questions asking students to rate the pictured classmate. For example, "Who is the biggest .... (choose your own derogatory term)?" Hacking into an e-mail account and sending vicious or embarrassing material to others are also becoming common practices in Bangkok. Somsak (not his real name), a local 14-year-old student, walked into class to find everyone glaring at him. A boy he barely knew approached him and shouted, "Why did you call me a [disparaging term]?" Somsak was as shocked as the boy making the complaint. Eventually, the problem was resolved, but Somsak still has no idea who accessed his account to send the offensive e-mail. Another technique is to engage someone in instant messaging by tricking that person into revealing sensitive personal information, and, in turn, forwarding that information to others. The practice of taking a picture of a person in the locker room or toilet using a camera phone and sending that picture to others is another method that is gaining momentum (Payne 2007).

CONCLUSION

Bullying among schoolchildren is certainly a very old phenomenon. However, in recent years, a new form of bullying has emerged that makes use of the diverse range of technology now available. Cyber bullying is a phenomenon that children and adolescents seem to be increasingly using to harm others. Cyber bullying using e-mail, text, chat rooms, mobile phones, mobile phone cameras, and Web sites is surfacing as a new medium used by bullies. Many countries are struggling to stop this form of Internet harassment by establishing new laws and policies. There is an urgent need for researchers to address the policy vacuum on cyber bullying from an interdisciplinary and international perspective. Recently, a project is funded by SSHRC Canada to develop a set of guidelines that inform sustainable and legally defensible international policies on cyber bullying that respect children's rights, for which the authors Jaishankar and Shaheen Shareef are co-investigator and principal investigator, respectively. This project (2007–2009) will develop an international profile of cyber bullying through a review of multidisciplinary research on its forms, prevalence, and impact in Australia, New Zealand, Great Britain, the United States, Japan, China, and India. This project (http://www.cyberbullying.co.nr) is expected to address the policy vacuum on cyber bullying internationally.

KEY TERMS

Adolescents
Cyber bullying
Text message

REFERENCES

Adams, A. 2001. "Cyberstalking: Gender and computer ethics." In *Virtual Gender: Technology, Consumption and Identity*, edited by E. Green and A. Adam, 209–24. New York: Routledge.

Aera. 2007. In the hands of mean teens, cell phones becoming WMDs. *Mainichi Daily News*, March 21, 2007. Retrieved May 15, 2007, from http://mdn.mainichi-msn.co.jp/waiwai/news/20070321 p2g00m0dm002000c.html

Anil Kumar R., and K. Jaishankar. 2007. Cyber bullying using Mobile Phones: A study on victimization and perpetration among school students. Paper presented at the Second International Conference on Victimology and Sixth Biennial Conference of the Indian Society of Victimology, Chennai, India 9–11, February 2007.

Barak, A. 2005. Sexual harassment on the Internet. *Social Science Computer Review* 23 (1): 77–92.

Bartlett, L. 2007. Cyber bully concern grows. Retrieved May 15, 2007, from http://cooltech. iafrica.com/features/729468.htm

Beckerman, L., and J. Nocero. 2002. You've got hate mail. *Principal Leadership (High School Ed.)* 3 (4): 38–41.

Belsey, B. 2005. Internet usage: Facts and news. Retrieved February 15, 2007, from http://www.cyberbullying.ca/fact.html

Bill, B. 2007. The biz of knowledge. Retrieved June 1, 2007, from http://www.thebizofknowledge.com/2007/05/cyberbullying_in_china_student.html

Boulton, M. J. 1993. A comparison of adults' and children's abilities to distinguish between aggressive and playful fighting in middle school pupils. Implications for playground supervision and behaviour management. *Educational Studies* 19: 193–203.

Boulton, M. J., and K. Underwood. 1992. Bully/victim problems among middle school children. *British Journal of Educational Psychology* 62: 73–87.

Boyd, F. B. 2000. The cross-aged literacy program: Developing mediational activity to assist ninth-grade African-American students who struggle with literacy learning and schooling. *Reading and Writing Quarterly* 16 (4).

Campbell, M. 2005. Cyber bullying: An older problem in a new guise? *Australian Journal of Guidance and Counselling* 15 (1): 68–76.

Chu, J. August 8, 2005. You wanna take this online? Cyberspace is the 21st century bully's playground where girls play rougher than boys. *Time* (Toronto): 42–3.

Dedman, B. 2001. Schools may miss mark on preventing violence. Retrieved January 26, 2007, from http://www-suntimes.com/shoot/shoot16.html

Devlin, A. 1997. "Offenders at school: Links between school failure and aggressive behaviour." In *Bullying: Home, School and Community*, edited by D. Tattum and H. Graham, 149–58. London: David Fulton.

Dibbell, J. December 21, 1993. A rape in cyberspace. *Village Voice* 38.

Dickie, M., K. Merchant, M. Nakamoto, C. Nuttall, E. Terazono, and H. Yeager. April 13, 2004. Digital media. *Financial Times* 8.

DiGiulio, R. C. 2001. *Educate, Medicate, or Litigate? What Teachers, Parents, and Administrators Must Do ABOUT Student Behavior*. Thousand Oaks, CA: Corwin Press.

Evard, M. 1996. "'So please stop, thank you': Girls online." In *Wired Women: Gender and New Realities in Cyberspace*, edited by L. Cherny and E. R. Weise, 188–204. Toronto: Seal Press.

Fight Crime: Invest in Kids. 2007. 1 of 3 Teens and 1 of 6 preteens are victims of cyber bullying. Retrieved January 21, 2007, from http://www.fightcrime.org/releases.php?id=231

Finkelhor, D., K. Mitchell, and J. Wolak. 2000. *Online Victimization: A Report on the Nation's Youth*. Alexandria, VA: National Centre for Missing & Exploited Children. Retrieved January 9, 2006, from http://www.unh.edu/ccrc/Youth_Internet_info_page.html

Gáti, Á., T. Tényi, F. Túry, and M. Wildmann. 2002. Anorexia nervosa following sexual harassment on the Internet: A case report. *International Journal of Eating Disorders* 31 (4): 474–77.

Genta, M. L., E. Menesini, A. Fonzi, A. Costabile, and P. K. Smith. 1996. Bullies and victims in schools in central and southern Italy. *European Journal of Psychology of Education* 11: 97–110.

Gibson, C. August 2006. Standing up to cyber bullies. *Adelaidean*. Retrieved November 28, 2006, from http://www.adelaide.edu.au/adelaidean/issues/13601/news13683.html

Harmon, A. August 26, 2004. Internet gives teenage bullies weapons . . . from afar. *New York Times*. Accessed August 26, 2004, from http://www.nytimes.com./2004/08/26/education

Harris, S., and G. Petrie. 2002. A study of bullying in the middle school. *National Association of Secondary School Principals (NASSP) Bulletin* 86 (633): 42–53.

Hasegawa, M. 2007. Discussion with Yasuko Senoo in Japanese on cyber bullying. Study material provided in the First International Summit of the collaborators of the cyber bullying project, Montreal, Canada, February 9–11, 2007.

Haynie, D. L., T. R. Nansel, P. Eitel, A. D. Crump, K. Saylor, K. Yu, and B. Simons-Morton. 2001. Bullies, victims, and bully/victims: Distinct groups of at-risk youth. *Journal of Early Adolescence* 21: 29–49.

Henderson, M., D. Wight, G. M. Raab, C. Abraham, K. Buston, G. Hart, and S. Scott. 2002 Heterosexual risk behaviour among young teenagers in Scotland. *Journal of Adolescence* 25: 483–94.

Herring, S. C. 2002. Cyber violence: Recognizing and resisting abuse in online environments. *Asian Women* 14: 187–212.

Hinduja, S., and J. Patchin. 2005. Cyberbullying victimization among an adolescent population—Executive summary. Retrieved January 4, 2006, from http://www.cyberbullying.us/cyberbullying_victimization.pdf

Hinduja, S. and J. Patchin. 2007. Cyber bullying: An exploratory analysis of factors related to offending and victimization. *Deviant Behavior*.

Hoover, J., and G. Olsen. 2001. *Teasing and Harassment: The Frames and Scripts Approach for Teachers and Parents*. Bloomington, IN: National Educational Service.

Julie d'Eon and Senoo. 2007. Cyber bullies in Japan: A cultural perspective. Study material provided in the First International Summit of the collaborators of the cyber bullying project, Montreal, Canada, February 9–11, 2007.

Kapoor, G. 2003. School spats: Fights, squabbles and school rivalries take a nasty turn online. Accessed May 26, 2003, from http://www.rediff.com/netguide/features.htm

Kumpulainen, K., E. Raesaenen, I. Henttonen, F. Almqvist, K. Kresanov, S.L. Linna, I. Moilanen, J. Piha, K. Puura, and T. Tamminen. 1998. Bullying and psychiatric symptoms among elementary school-age children. *Child Abuse and Neglect* 22: 705–17.

Li, Q. 2005. "Cyber-bullying in schools: A comparison of Canadian and Chinese adolescents' experience." In *Proceedings of World Conference on E-Learning in Corporate, Government, Healthcare, and Higher Education 2005*, edited by G. Richards, 878–84. Chesapeake, VA: AACE.

Li, Q. 2006. Computer-mediated communication: A meta-analysis of male and female altitudes and behaviors. *International Journal on E-Learning* 5 (4): 525–70.

Li, Q. 2007. New bottle but old wine: A research on cyberbullying in schools. *Computers and Human Behavior* 23 (4): 1777–91.

Limber, S. P., and M. A. Small. 2003. State laws and policies to address bullying in schools. *School Psychology Review* 32.

McCarthy, P., J. Rylance, R. Bennet, and H. Zimmermann. 2001. *Bullying from the Backyard to Boardroom*. 2nd ed. Leichhardt, New South Wales: The Federation Press.

Mitchell, A. January 24, 2004. Bullied by the click of a mouse. Retrieved September 24, 2005, from http://www.cyberbullying.ca/globe-mail_January_24_2004.html

MSN UK. 2006. MSN cyber bullying report: Blogging, instant messaging and email bullying amongst today's teens. Microsoft retrieved December 27, 2006, from http://www.msn.co.uk/customercare/protect/cyberbullying/Default.asp?MSPSA=1

Mynard, H., S. Joseph, and J. Alexander. 2000. Peer victimisation and post traumatic stress in adolescents. *Personality and Individual Differences* 29: 815–21.

Nansel, T., M. Overpeck, D. Haynie, J. Ruan, and P. Scheidt. 2003. Relationships between bullying and violence among US youth. *Archives of Pediatric and Adolescent Medicine* 157: 348–53.

Nansel, T., M. Overpeck, R. Pilla, J. Ruan, B. Simons-Morton, and P. Scheidt. 2001. Bullying behaviors among U.S. youth: Prevalence and association with psychosocial adjustment. *Journal of the American Medical Association* 285: 2094–100.

NCH (National Children's Home). 2002. Text bullying survey. Retrieved December 17, 2005, from http://www.nch.org.uk/information/index.php?i=237

NCH (National Children's Home). 2005. Putting U in the picture. Mobile Bullying Survey 2005. Retrieved December 27, 2005, from http://www.nch.org.uk/uploads/documents/Mobile_bullying_%20report.pdf

New York Times. 2004. Japanese girl fatally stabs a classmate. *New York Times* 153 (52868): A12.

Olweus, D. 1991. "Bully/victim problems among schoolchildren: Basic facts and effects of a school based intervention program." In *The Development and Treatment of Childhood Aggression*, edited by D. Pepler and K. Rubin. Hillsdale, NJ: Erlbaum.

Patchin, J. W., and S. Hinduja. 2006. Bullies move beyond the schoolyard: A preliminary look at cyber bullying *Youth Violence and Juvenile Justice* 4 (2): 148–69.

Payne, S. 2007. Cyber-bullying: It's not "cool," it's cruel. Retrieved May 15, 2007, from http://www.bangkokpost.net/education/index.htm

Pellegrini, A., and M. Bartini. 2000. A longitudinal study of bullying, victimization, and peer affiliation during the transition from primary school to middle school. *American Educational Research Journal* 37 (3): 699–725.

Portsmouth Herald. 2005. Internet age brings new form of harassment: Cyber bullying. Retrieved September 2005, from http://www.seacoastonline.com/news/03302005/editorial/72651.htm

Rahul. 2007. Orkut: The sex hub! Retrieved April 22, 2007, from http://www.merinews.com/catFull.jsp?articleID=124543

Rigby, K. 1997. Reflections on Tom Brown's schooldays and the problem of bullying today. *Australian Journal of Social Science* 4 (1): 85–96.

Rigby, K. 2002. How successful are anti-bullying programs for schools? Invited paper. Australian Institute of Criminology in conjunction with the Department of Education, Employment and Training, Victoria and Crime Prevention, Victoria, Melbourne.

Rigby, K. 2005. Why do some children bully at school? The contributions of negative attitudes towards victims and the perceived expectations of friends, parents and teachers. *School Psychology International* 26:147–61.

Salmivalli, C., K. Lagerspetz, K. Bjorqvist, K. Osterman, and A. Kaukianen. 1996. Bullying as a group process: Participant roles and their relations to social status within the group. *Aggressive Behavior* 25: 81–9.

Schwartz, D., K. Dodge, and J. Coie. 1993. The emergence of chronic peer victimization. *Child Development* 64: 1755–72.

Schwartz, D., G. Pettit, K. Dodge, and J. Bates. 1997. The early socialization and adjustment of aggressive victims of bullying. *Child Development* 68: 665–75.

Sengupta, S. 2006. Orkut: The new danger. Retrieved December 20, 2006, from http://www.merinews.com/index.jsp;jsessionid=7225B40ACCB0D3FEFD9353D185401576

Scnoo, Y. 2007. Translation of Japanese discussion with Hasegawa on cyber bullying. Study material provided in the First International Summit of the collaborators of the cyber bullying project, Montreal, Canada, February 9–11, 2007.

Shariff, S. 2003. A system on trial: Identifying legal standards for educational, ethical and legally defensible approaches to bullying in schools. Doctoral diss., Simon Fraser University, Burnaby, B.C.

Shariff, S. 2004. Keeping schools out of court: Legally defensible models of leadership to reduce cyber-bullying. Educational Forum, *Delta Kappa Pi* 68 (3): 222–33.

Shariff, S. 2005. Cyber-dilemmas in the new millennium. *McGill Journal of Education* 40 (3): 467–87.

Shariff, S. 2006a. Cyber-dilemmas: Balancing free expression and learning in a virtual school environment. *International Journal of Learning* 12 (4): 269–78.

Shariff, S. 2006b. "Cyber-hierarchies: A new arsenal of weapons for gendered violence in schools." In *Combating Gender Violence in and around Schools*, edited by C. Mitchell and F. Leech. London: Trentham Books.

Shariff, S., and R. Gouin. 2005. Cyber-dilemmas: Gendered hierarchies, free expression and cyber-safety in schools. Paper presented at Oxford Internet Institute, Oxford University, U.K. International Conference on Cyber-Safety. Retrieved February 15, 2007, from www.oii.ox.ac.uk/cybersafety

Shariff, S., and D. Hoff. 2007. Cyber bullying: Clarifying legal boundaries for school supervision in cyberspace. *International Journal of Cyber Criminology* 1 (1): 76–118. Retrieved February 15, 2007, from http://www40.brinkster.com/ccjournal/Shaheen&Hoffijcc.htm

Shariff, S., and L. Johnny. 2007. "The role of the charter in balancing freedom of expression, safety and equality in a virtual school environment." In *Courts, Charter and the Schools: The Impact of Judicial Decisions on Educational Policy and Practice*, edited by M. Manley-Casimir. Toronto: University of Toronto Press (20 pages, page numbers not allocated).

Shariff, S. and T. Strong-Wilson. (2005). "Bullying and new technologies." In *Classroom Teaching: An Introduction*, edited by J. Kincheloe, 219–40 (Ch. 14). New York: David Lang.

Simmons, D. 2006. Cyber bullying rises in S Korea. BBC Click Online, November 3, 2006. Retrieved March 30, 2007, from http://news.bbc.co.uk/2/hi/programmes/click_online/6112754.stm

Slee, P. T. 1995. Peer victimization and its relationship to depression among Australian primary school students. *Personality and Individual Differences* 18: 57–62.

Slee, P. T., and K. Rigby. 1993 Australian school children's self-appraisal of interpersonal relations: The bullying experience. *Child Psychiatry and Human Development* 23: 272–83.

Smith, B. 2007. Schools ban YouTube sites in cyber-bully fight. Retrieved June 13, 2007, from http://www.theage.com.au/news/national/schools-ban-youtube-sites-in-cyberbully-fight/2007/03/01/1172338796092.html

Smith, P., J. Mahdavi, M. Carvalho and N. Tippett. 2004. An investigation into cyberbullying, its forms, awareness and impact, and the relationship between age and gender in cyberbullying. A report to the Anti Bullying alliance. Unit for School and Family Studies, Goldsmiths College, University of London. Retrieved February 15, 2007, from http://www.anti-bullyingalliance.org.uk/downloads/pdf/cyberbullyingreportfinal230106_000.pdf

Smith, P. K., and S. Sharp, eds. 1994. *School Bullying: Insights and Perspectives*. New York: Routledge.

Smith, P. K., and S. Shu. 2000. What good schools can do about bullying: Findings from a survey in English schools after a decade of research and action. *Childhood* 7:193–212.

Snider, M. May 24, 2004. Stalked by a Cyberbully. *Maclean's* 117 (21/22): 76.

Swartz, J. March 7, 2005. Schoolyard bullies get nastier online. *USA Today*. Retrieved September 2005, from http://www.usatoday.com/tech/news/2005-03-06-cover-cyberbullies_x.htm

Tolman, D. L., R. Spencer, M. Rosen-Reynoso, and M. Porches. April 13, 2001. "He's the man!" Gender ideologies and early adolescents' experiences with sexual harassment. Paper presented at the American Educational Researchers Association (AERA), Seattle, Washington.

Toppo, G. April 2006. High-tech bullying may be on the rise. *USA Today*, 8. Retrieved August 7, 2006, from Ebsco.

Wallace, P. 1999. *The Psychology of the Internet*. Cambridge, UK: Cambridge University Press.

Whitney, I., and P. K. Smith. 1993. A survey of the nature and extent of bullying in junior/middle and secondary schools. *Educational Research* 35: 3–25.

Willard, N. 2003. Off-campus, harmful online student speech. *Journal of School Violence* 1 (2): 65–93.

Willard, N. n.d. Retrieved September 2005, from http://www.cyberbully.org

Williams, K. D., C. K. T. Cheung, and W. Choi. 2000. Cyberostracism: Effects of being ignored over the Internet. *Journal of Personality and Social Psychology* 79: 748–62.

Yan. 2005. Cyber bullying in China. In Sandy Peter's blog used to engage students in a project which was an integral part of an ESL writing class taught by Sandy Peters at Michigan State University. Comment posted by Yan on April 30, 2005 at 08:03 AM. Retrieved on February 15, 2007, from http://sandeelee.blogs.com/bullying/2005/02/bullying_moves_.html

Ybarra, M. L., and J. K. Mitchell. 2004. Online aggressor/targets, aggressors and targets: A comparison of associated youth characteristics. *Journal of Child Psychology and Psychiatry* 45: 1308–16.

Zubrick, S. R., S. R. Silburn, H. J. Teoh, J. Carlton, C. Shepherd, and D. Lawrence. 1997. *Western Australian Child Health Survey: Education, Health and Competency Catalogue 4305.5*. Perth, WA: Australian Bureau of Statistics.

Chapter 5

Internet Crimes: Youth and Children

R. K. Raghavan
Chairman, Committee on Ragging in Educational Institutions, India

Sheetal Ranjan
William Paterson University, New Jersey

and

Vidya Reddy
Executive Director, Tulir—Centre for the Prevention and Healing of Child Sexual Abuse (CPHCSA), India

Dr. R. K. Raghavan is the former Director of the Central Bureau of Investigation (CBI) in India. He obtained his Ph.D. in 1985 from Karnatak University, Dharwar, and holds a master's degree in criminal justice from Temple University. In 1994, he was a Visiting Fellow at the School of Criminal Justice, Rutgers University, and in 2001, he was a Visiting Fellow in the Human Rights Program at Harvard Law School. He was recently appointed as Chairman of the Committee on Ragging in Educational Institutions by the Supreme Court of India.

Dr. Raghavan has many publications to his credit, among which are the two books *Indian Police: Planning, Personnel and Perspectives* (1989, Manohar Publications, New Delhi) and *Policing a Democracy: A Comparative Study of India and the U.S.* (1999, Manohar Publications, New Delhi). He has contributed a chapter on the Indian Police in Francine Frankel et al.'s (eds) *Transforming India: Social and Political Dynamics of Democracy* (Oxford University Press, 2000). He is a frequent contributor to *The Hindu*, one of India's leading national newspapers. He now writes a column on Law and Order for *Frontline*, a leading publication of *The Hindu* group of newspapers, and a fortnightly column on cyber security for the *Business Line*, the business daily newspaper of *The Hindu* group.

Dr. Raghavan's current interests include human rights, police reforms, cyber security, cyber crime, bank security, counterterrorism and anticorruption in the field of public administration. He is presently an Adviser for Tata Consultancy Services (TCS), India's largest software company, where he is responsible for corporate security issues spanning the globe. He is also the President of the Indian Society of Victimology and a member of the Board of Governors for the Bharathidasan Institute of Management, Tiruchy, Tamil Nadu.

Sheetal Ranjan holds a master's degree in criminology from John Jay College of Criminal Justice, New York, and is presently a faculty in the Department of Sociology at William Paterson University, New Jersey. She is also a doctoral student in criminal justice at the Graduate Center—City University of New York. Sheetal's research interests are diverse, the chief areas being stalking, domestic violence, and other forms of victimization of women and children. She has presented numerous research papers in the field of victimization of women and children in national and international conferences. She is also interested in comparative international and cross-cultural research and was involved in the "International Crime Data Project" at the John Jay College of Criminal Justice where she evaluated face validity of international crime statistics for the United Nations and Interpol. Sheetal uses crime mapping technologies to study crime patterns in various cities. She has taught numerous courses at John Jay College of Criminal Justice including statistics, research methods, computer applications in criminal justice, corrections in juvenile justice administration, and crime in Asia. She enjoys using various computer applications and software both in her research and in her teaching. She is a member of several professional organizations including the American Society of Criminology.

Vidya Reddy is executive director of the Tulir—Centre for the Prevention and Healing of Child Sexual Abuse (CPHCSA), Chennai. Tulir—CPHCSA is a nongovernmental, nonprofit organization committed to working against child sexual abuse in India. Its programs range from training and consultancy, advocacy and networking, resource development, research and documentation, healing and socio legal assistance to the dissemination of personal safety education.

Considering the growth and spread of ICTs in India and with the realization of the impact they have in reshaping the contours of sexual crime against children, Tulir has initiated and is continuing dialogue with industry, policy makers, law enforcement, educators, and the larger community as well, to ensure that all efforts are made within each of their professional and community responsibilities to ensure that children's experience with the new technologies is enjoyable.

Abstract

The Internet has both a positive and a negative impact on society. It is known to facilitate crimes of a wide spectrum against children. Bodily harm of children, including sexual assault, using the Internet is an unfortunate modern phenomenon which is widely prevalent. Governments have brought in new law to checkmate this. But legislation has been found to be ineffective in neutralizing pedophile gangs that use the cyberspace to gratify their lust and greed. Law enforcement agencies have also done their bid, but their success has been modest. All these efforts will not succeed unless the community rises in support and relentlessly stands against the wrongdoers.

INTRODUCTION

There is an inconclusive debate across the globe whether the Internet is a blessing or a curse. It would be facile to take a categorical stand in favor of either view. This is because it is hardly possible to exaggerate the positive role played by this powerful medium, which disseminates knowledge and promotes an enduring relationship between nations and communities that are otherwise divided by conflicting political philosophies, economic disparities, and cultural differences. Perhaps, half the advances made in modern science and medicine would not have been possible without a healthy exchange of views over cyberspace. Having said that, it is a sad fact that the Internet has been grievously misused for promoting hatred and violence, as is evidenced by confirmed reports of terrorists employing this medium to circulate appeals for violence against lawfully established governments and peace-loving individuals and groups. Besides this, there is an additional phenomenon in which dubious persons explore the Internet for downright greed and lust. It has been more than well established that the Internet now facilitates crimes against the youth and children. This misuse is not confined to one particular ethnic group or any geographic region. Surprisingly, it is also not poverty that has driven this evil. Many affluent countries in the West have reported a surge in this form of questionable activity. Groups and individuals in the developing countries such as India have also fallen prey to this. The problem is slowly getting out of hand. Governments in these countries are conscious of this trend and have been reasonably sensitive. But what they have done till now has had only a marginal impact. It is disturbing to see the signs of a losing battle and hence we would like to place a few facts before readers in the hope these would help to build world opinion and generate a massive international exercise against perpetrators of online crime against youth and children.

Children access the Internet on a regular basis to learn, to play games, and to network with their friends. The Internet is an integral part of childhood learning and growing up. This is good as far as it goes. We need to promote such healthy use of the cyberspace. Along with the benefits of the Internet are the risks associated with it. In this chapter, we explore the benefits and risks of Internet use for children and youth, examine available usage statistics, discuss in brief the legislation in various countries and its consequences for the community, examine the research initiatives undertaken by various governmental and nongovernmental organizations, examine the policing initiatives to combat the problem, and survey the work of NGOs and other agencies. We conclude with a brief discussion about the difficulties involved in the legislation and policing of the Internet and about how educating the parents, teachers, and children can be first steps to combating the problem.

THE INTERNET PENETRATION

As of June 10, 2007, 1.133 billion people use the Internet; North America has the highest penetration rate (ratio of Internet usage to population) at about 69 percent. Close to 9 in 10 teens are Internet users (Lenhart 2005). A survey by the Pew Internet & American Life Project in November 2004 finds that 87 percent of teenagers between the ages of 12 and 17 use the Internet—about 21 million youth (Lenhart and Madden 2005). Various other studies have reflected that 75 percent of 9- to 19-year-olds have Internet access at home (ahead of adults), 92 percent have access at school (and few have no access at all), and 84 percent use the Internet at least weekly (Livingstone and Bober 2005). Younger children, 37 percent of 5- to 6-year-olds and 64 percent of 7- to 8-year-olds are also the users of the Internet (Childwise 2006). About half (48 percent) of all children of age 6 and below have used a computer; by the time they are in the 4- to 6-year-old range, 7 out of 10 (70 percent) have used a computer. Those who use a computer spend an average of just over an hour at the keyboard (Rideout, Vandewater, and Wartella 2003). Nearly half (48%) of children aged between 8 and 11 use the Internet at home, and two-thirds (65 percent) of children aged between 12 and 15 do so (OFCOM n.d.). Almost 70 percent of adults (69.6 percent) say that the children in their households spend the right amount of time online (Center for the Digital Future 2007). Solitary usage is also common among kids.

HOW CHILDREN USE THE INTERNET

Education, entertainment, and communication are amongst the most common uses for children. Education can involve access to educational Web sites, libraries, globally relevant information, news Web sites, technological Web sites, and the like. Children may access these Web sites as part of their school education and projects or out of their own curiosity and interest. Internet is a major part of entertainment in the lifestyle of children across the world. Children access the Internet to play (or download) games, download (or listen to) music or movies, view pictures and videos (e.g., YouTube), shop online, visit hobby Web sites, or join fan forums. Internet is one of the primary means of communication for children. E-mail, online chatting, networking sites (e.g., Myspace and Facebook), blogs, message boards, and Internet phones (e.g., Skype) are frequently used not only to communicate with their friends and family but also to make new friends or network with other people. Some youth and children also host their own Web sites on the Internet. Apart from education, entertainment, and communication, children may use the Internet to seek information or advice about emotional, health, or sexual issues; whereas others may be interested in civic and political participation and find the Internet to be a good medium to connect with other community members.

The OFCOM study found that the top two uses of the Internet for children in each age group are school work and playing games. Children aged between 12 and 15 make a broader use of the Internet than those aged 8–11 (OFCOM n.d.). Children and adults continue to express conflicting views about the importance of the Internet for schoolwork. Of Internet users aged 18 and below, 80.5 percent say that going online is very important or extremely important. However, almost three-quarters of adults say that since their household acquired the Internet, the grades of children in their households had stayed the same (Center for the Digital Future 2007).

Half of the teenagers in a study in Ireland said they had chatted on the Internet, whereas only a quarter of the preteens have ever chatted. A large majority of teens (71 percent) have established online profiles (including those on social networking sites such as MySpace, Friendster, and Xanga), up from 61 percent in 2006; about 47 percent have an Internet profile that is public and viewable by everyone (Cox Communications, NCMEC, and Walsh 2007). It is no surprise that a medium as pervasive as the Internet brings with it certain risks.

INTERNET RISKS

Internet risks for children and youth can broadly be grouped into two categories, offending risks and victimization risks. It is important to understand the specific offending risks that Internet-use can create for young users. Yet, the greater interest and concern worldwide is about the victimization risks for young users. Here, we attempt to understand the different offending and victimization risks. We also examine current statistics and some cases.

Offending Risks

Offending risks are specifically those actions that either completely go against the law or border on the illegal. Children may unwittingly commit such offenses or may knowledgeably involve themselves as a manifestation of the thrill-seeking behavior common among children and youth. Very often, children and youth commit such offenses as a reaction to emotional distress or because of psychological problems.

Internet offenses that children commonly get involved in are

- Pirating music and software
- Viewing pornography
- Libel or defamation
- Writing computer codes to create viruses that damage other computers
- Hacking into other people's computers and networks
- Credit card and other financial abuse
- Online con games
- Gambling
- Cyber bullying

Other very serious forms of offending can include terrorism, self-harm (suicide, anorexia), illegal purchase and distribution of narcotics and weapons, etc. Children might also be perpetrators of sexual exploitation or harassment against other children or adults. More recently, children are becoming perpetrators of cyber bullying (willful and repeated harm inflicted through the medium of electronic text) (Patchin and Hinduja 2006).

In 2003, the Recording Industry Association of America filed 261 copyright infringement lawsuits on behalf of major record labels. Many parents were unaware of the risks involved in sharing music, but they were held responsible for their kids' actions. In one such case, the mother of a 12 year-old settled the case with a payment of $2,000 (Harmon 2003).

Various research studies have tried to measure the extent of the problem; they have differing methodologies, age groups, and samples; some have questioned parents and others children, some others have questioned both. Here is a brief of what these studies suggest: 12 percent of 12- to 19-year-olds seek porn online on purpose (UCLA 2003); 57 percent Internet users have seen porn online via pop-ups (38 percent), junk mail (25 percent), e-mail from contact (9 percent); 10 percent had visited porn sites on purpose and over half reported "not bothered" by porn, whereas one-fifth were "disgusted" (Livingstone and Bober 2005). A study in Australia reports that 38 percent of boys and 2 percent of girls have searched for sex on Web sites (Flood and Hamilton 2003); 19 percent of children aged 10–17 years were involved in online aggression (Ybarra and Mitchell 2004). A study in Ireland reports that 26 percent of children (mostly boys) had visited hateful sites and about 35 percent had visited pornographic sites (Agebäck 2004).

In a recent online survey of approximately 1,500 Internet-using adolescents, about 16.7 percent of the youth are known to have bullied others online. A nontrivial number have also threatened (4.1 percent) others and made others scared for their own safety (2.7 percent) (Hinduja and Patchin 2007). These findings are reiterated in the MSN bullying survey, where about 5 percent of the children reported bullying other children (MSN 2006). While these statistics provide a basic understanding about violent, sexual, or offensive behavior, there is no study to date that measures the types of pornography that has been viewed. Much information about other Internet offences is not easily available because these are usually prosecuted under general local or central laws.

Victimization Risks

Just as a child on the street is exposed to risk of accident or kidnapping, a child on the information superhighway is exposed to certain victimization risks. Victimization risks for children using the Internet range from mild to severe forms or could be the precursor to other more serious forms of victimization. Victimization risks on the Internet can broadly be divided into content risks and contact risks.

Content Risks

Content risks involve exposure to harmful content on Web sites or in e-mail. Common forms of content risks include exposure to nudity and age-inappropriate sexually explicit material; harmful, violent, or offensive content; and promotional material about tobacco, alcohol, or drugs. Other types of content risks include information about satanic, cult, or terrorist groups; recipes for making bombs or other explosives; Web sites that defraud children or commercially exploit them; and hacking of personal information, etc.

Eighteen percent of European parents and caregivers of children less than 18 years of age believe that their children had encountered harmful or illegal content on the Internet, the rate being higher for teens than for younger children (Eurobarometer 2005–2006). Sixteen percent of 8- to 15-year-olds have come across "nasty, worrying or frightening" material online (OFCOM n.d.). The Online Victimization of Youth Survey in 2006 reported an increased exposure to sexual material (34 percent vs. 25 percent) compared to its previous survey (Wolak et al. 2006).

Contact Risks

Contact risks involve communicating with strangers, pedophiles, hate groups, kidnappers, online bullies, stalkers, harassers, etc. Sometimes, the strangers may misrepresent themselves as children and "groom the children" to gain trust and later lure them into real physical meetings resulting in serious harm to them. The first Youth Internet Safety Survey (YISS-1) using a sample of 10- to17-year-olds indicated that 20 percent of children received sexual solicitation online in the past year, of which 3 percent reported aggressive sexual solicitation. One in 17 children was threatened or harassed online. Depressed teenagers are more likely to receive unwanted sexual solicitations and are emotionally distressed by such incidents. Only a few children reported the incident to their parents or any elder (Finkelhor, Mitchell, and Wolak 2000).

The second survey (YISS-2) was conducted between March and June of 2005. It interviewed 1,500 youth Internet users, aged 10–17, and reported an increased incidence of online harassment (9 percent vs. 6 percent) and less unwanted sexual solicitations (13 percent vs. 19 percent) in recent years. Four percent of them had been asked for nude or sexually explicit photos of themselves, and the number of children distressed by it increased (9 percent vs. 6 percent). Most of the unwanted solicitations were reported from acquaintances but not from strangers, indicating that the risks were not necessarily associated with exposure to strangers (Wolak et al. 2006).

A study in Ireland of 9- to 16-year-olds reported that 27 percent of the children who met someone new online were asked for their photos, phone number, street address, or the name of the school he or she attended. Most children gave false information or ignored the request. Younger children were much more likely to give all the information they were asked. Ten percent of the children gave all the demanded information. The study also found that 23 percent of the children had received unwanted sexual comments on the Internet, with boys receiving twice as much as girls. Nineteen percent of those who use the chat room said that they had been harassed, upset, bothered, threatened, or embarrassed by someone during the process. Seven percent have met someone dangerous in real life that they had first met on the Internet, and a worrying 24 percent of those who met face to face said that someone who introduced himself or herself as a child on the Internet turned out to be an adult (WebWise n.d.).

More recently, social networking has become one of the major uses of Internet for children. In a large-scale study of teenagers in Holland, about 40 percent reported that they had a social networking profile. Eighty-two percent of boys and 73 percent girls flirted online in the past 6 months, and about 25 percent of boys and 20 percent of girls had cybersexual experiences. The Internet has increasingly become the prime media for sexual exposure for 9- to 16-year-olds, about 72 percent boys and 83 percent of girls reported received sexual questions online; 40 percent boys and 57 percent girls were asked to undress on Webcam, and about 33 percent of boys and 10 percent of girls were actually doing it. About 47 percent girls received an unwanted request for a sexual act on the Webcam, with about 2 percent complying. Many girls (62 percent) and fewer boys (13 percent) expressed a dislike for receiving sexual questions online. Thirty-five percent of girls and 12 percent boys claimed a negative experience in receiving sexual questions. Many kids (9 percent girls and 3 percent boys) in this study had posted sexual photos online and later regretted it. It is interesting to note that most of these children were aware of "pedophiles," but they were unclear about boundaries among teens (Remco Pijpers Foundation 2006). Such contact risks are especially of greater concern to parents, as reports about dubious ownership of these sites emerge. Stickam is one such social networking Web site which has about 600,000 registered users. Recently, a former employee reported that Stickam shares officespace, employees, and computer systems with pornographic Web sites. The owner of Stickam is apparently a Japanese businessman who owns at least 49 pornography sites and a pornography film production company (Stone 2007).

Cyber bullying is also emerging as a major form of victimization risk for children. A recent online survey of cyber bullying indicates that over one-third (33.4 percent) of the youth had been victimized through cyber bullying. Among that group, the most frequent types of cyber bullying victimization include being ignored (43.2 percent) and disrespected (39.8 percent). The primary cyber locations in which victimization occurs are chat rooms (55.6 percent), instant message (48.9 percent), and email (28.0 percent). More than one-third of the victims felt frustrated, 30.6 percent felt angry, and 21.8 percent felt sad (Patchin and Hinduja 2006). The National Bullying Survey (2006) conducted in the UK reported that 69 percent pupils were bullied in the past year (half of those were physically hurt) of which 7 percent said that they received unpleasant or bullying e-mails/IM/text messages. Per the MSN (2006) cyber bullying report, 11 percent of 12- to 15-year-olds were cyber-bullied (18 percent girls and 7 percent boys), 74 percent told no one, and 62 percent knew someone who has been bullied online.

RELEVANT LEGISLATION

The overwhelming growth of the Internet, high usage among youngsters, and accompanying risks have brought with them a need for regulation and legislation. It is very difficult for regulations and legislations to keep pace with emerging technologies. Yet, almost all major governments have tried to regulate it in some form or the other. Legislation and regulations have a variety of objectives:

- protect children
- assist law enforcement
- raise public awareness
- promote basic civil rights
- find solutions within the Internet industry.

Legislation and regulation in most countries involve a two-pronged approach: governmental legislation (or rulings) and industry **self-regulation** attempts. This provides a combined effort on the part of both the government and the industries to make the information superhighway a safe place for children of all ages. In the ensuing paragraphs, we will examine the legislation in a few regions of the world, compare them, and discuss their successes and shortcomings.

United States Legislations and Regulations

Many crimes of the Internet are prosecuted under the Criminal Code. Apart from this, specific Congressional Legislations and Federal Agency Rulemakings to combat Internet risks for children in the United States are the following.

Child Online Protection Act (COPA) was designed specifically to provide both criminal and civil penalties for transmitting sexually explicit materials and communications over the World Wide Web that are available to minors and harmful to them (47 U.S.C. § 231). Recently, on March 22, 2007, the Child Online Protection Act was struck down again. U.S. District Judge Reed found that the law on the face of it violates the First and Fifth Amendments of the U. S. Constitution. He issued an order permanently prohibiting the government from enforcing COPA.

There is also the *Child Abuse Act of 1990*, which, after an amendment, included the reporting of child pornography by electronic communication. Section 226 regarding this was added to the act by the 27th January 1998 Amendment.

Government-Mandated Filtering in schools and libraries require schools, libraries, and other places where the computers are bought with public funds, to install blocking and filtering technologies. Overall, the American Library Association, educators, and civil liberties groups object to government-mandated filtering. They feel that schools should decide what their students are allowed to view online and the same applies to librarians as well.

The Children's Online Privacy Protection Act, effective April 21, 2000, pertains to the online collection of personal information from children under the age of 13. The new rules spell out what a Web site operator must include in a privacy policy, when and how to seek verifiable consent from a parent, and what responsibilities an operator has in order to protect children's privacy and safety online. The primary objective of the Act is protection of the identity and privacy of children on the Internet. It works on a sliding scale system, in which, if the information is used for internal purposes, e-mail can be used to get parental consent. When a child's personal information is made publicly available through a chat room or message board, a more reliable method of consent is required. Some of these methods of consent include: verifying a credit card number; getting a signed form from the parent via postal mail or facsimile; accepting calls from parents through a toll-free telephone number staffed by trained personnel; receiving e-mail accompanied by digital signature; and receiving e-mail accompanied by a PIN or password obtained through one of the verification methods mentioned above.

Deleting Online Predators Act 2007 is a bill brought before the U.S. House of Representatives and is pending legislation. The bill, if enacted, would amend the Communications Act of 1934, requiring schools and libraries that receive E-rate funding to protect minors from online predators in the absence of parental supervision when using "Commercial Social Networking Websites" and "Chat Rooms." The Deleting Online Predators Act of 2007 would require schools and libraries that receive federal funding to block children's access to social networking Web sites or chat rooms unless supervised. The proposed Act also mandates the creation of an online clearinghouse Web site to educate parents, teachers, and students about the potential dangers of social networking sites and chat rooms. It would also require the Federal Trade Commission to issue consumer alerts regarding dangerous sites and suspicious activity, for parents and teachers.

Industry self-regulation efforts provide safety and protection to children on the information super highway, some of which are briefly explained below.

The Children's Advertising Review Unit (CARU) is a voluntary organization founded in 1974 to promote advertisements for making children more responsible. It is an alliance of major advertising trade associations working through the National Advertising Review Council. CARU is directed at self-regulation of child-directed advertising in all media and online privacy practices where they affect children. It has created self-regulatory guidelines for children's advertising. It works through the voluntary cooperation of advertisers.

Trade associations such as the Better Business Bureaus' online effort known as BBBOnLine and the Direct Marketing Association (DMA) have also taken measures to create programs to make members of their associations comply with privacy standards. The Association of National Advertisers, Inc. and the American Association of Advertising Agencies have also been participating in discussions involving data collection and electronic commerce. Some of these efforts are directed specifically at children, but most of them involve regulations and standards applicable to both adults and children.

Online Privacy Alliance is a group comprising 80 corporations and industry trade associations in an effort to promote privacy practices among its business members. The Alliance has a specific set of principles around children's privacy.

The United Kingdom Legislations and Regulations

Like the United States, in the United Kingdom also, the legislation related to Internet and crimes against children is a combination of criminal codes, other acts, and some case laws. Some of the acts that are specifically used to prosecute child abuse images are:

- Protection of Children Act 1978 (England and Wales)
- Civic Government Act, 1982 (Scotland)
- Sexual Offences Act 2003: Key Changes (England and Wales)
- Memorandum of Understanding: Section 46 Sexual Offences Act 2003
- Obscene Publications Act 1959 and 1964.

Racial hatred content perpetrated over the Internet is prosecuted using the *Public Order Act 1986* where Incitement to Racial Hatred was adopted into the Public Order Act in 1986. Directive applicable to the liability of Internet Service Providers is found under the *Liability Of Intermediary Service Provider's Directive 2002.*

Some judicial rulings have helped clarify the position of the judiciary on matters relating to victimization of children on the Internet. For instance, *R v Oliver, Hartrey & Baldwin* clarifies the definitions proposed by the Sentencing Panel in relation to Images of Child Abuse. *R v Bowden* held that the downloading of an indecent image of a child was an act of "making" under the Protection of Children Act 1978. In *R v Fellows & Arnold*, the court held that the wording of the Protection of Children Act 1978 covered the use of the Internet to distribute indecent images. *R v Jayson* concluded that the act of deliberately downloading an image from the Internet was "making an image." *R v Perrin* brought residents of the United Kingdom who use offshore servers for distribution, into the jurisdiction of the U.K. Law for obscene content. *R v Smith* (Wallace Duncan) concluded that a person can be guilty of an offence if a "substantial part of the crime" was committed in the United Kingdom. This was relevant to fraud cases but could be considered for Cases of Incitement to Racial Hatred, as part of the Public Order Act 1986.

INTERNATIONAL CONVENTIONS AND TREATIES

The United Nations Convention on the Rights of the Child, entered into force in September 1990, specifically safeguards the interest of children. Article 34 states that the participants of the convention will undertake actions to protect the children from all forms of sexual exploitation and sexual abuse. And they shall also take appropriate national, bilateral, and multilateral measures to prevent the inducement or coercion of a child to engage in any unlawful sexual activity; the exploitative use of children in prostitution or other unlawful sexual practices, and the exploitative use of children in pornographic performances and materials.

The United Nations Optional Protocol to the Convention on the Rights of the Child on the Sale of Children, Child Prostitution and Child Pornography, entered into force in January 2002, addresses all issues about the rights of children. Several articles of the convention are specifically relevant to the use of Internet. These pertain to issues such as the right to freedom of expression, obligation to protect their privacy and attacks on their honor or reputation, responsibility of the mass media to partake in protecting these rights and to disseminate information, and commitment of the member states to protect children from all kinds of exploitation, including pornography. The Protocol specifically supports the worldwide criminalization of the "production, distribution, exportation, transmission, importation, intentional possession and advertising of child pornography." It also stresses the need for cooperation among nations and between the Internet industry and the governments.

The United Nations Convention on Cybercrime came into force in July 2004. The Convention is the first international treaty on crimes committed via the Internet and other computer networks. It deals with a variety of Internet crimes, child pornography being one among them. It also contains a series of powers and procedures such as the search of computer networks and interception. Its main objective, set out in the preamble, is to pursue a common criminal policy aimed at the protection of society against cyber crime, especially by adopting appropriate legislation and fostering international cooperation.

PREVENTION AND ENFORCEMENT INITIATIVES

Internet crimes need specialized law enforcement initiatives. Crimes against children on the Internet need constant monitoring of chat rooms, access to pornographic content, etc. Prevention initiatives are directed to educate the children, parents, and educators about safety on the Internet. In the following section, we will examine the law enforcement initiatives to combat victimization of children in the United States and United Kingdom. We will also discuss initiatives in other parts of the world and the role of governmental and nongovernmental agencies in prevention.

United States Law Enforcement and Prevention Measures

Law enforcement agencies in the West are visibly exercised over the abuse of children through the Internet. A major Federal Bureau of Investigation exercise to fight child pornography is the *Innocent Images National Initiative* (IINI), which focuses its attention on organizations and individuals engaged in exploiting children to produce and distribute obscene child images for a price. It also keeps a tab on individuals who travel from place to place for the purpose of gratifying themselves through children. Mere possessors of child pornography also receive the IINI's attention. Identifying child victims and rendering them assistance falls within its scope. As part of the FBI's cyber division, this strategic unit has managed to muster substantial international cooperation. An idea of the volume of work turned out is available from the statistics put out by the FBI. More than one-third of all investigations by the Bureau's cyber division emanates from the IINI. Since 1996, when the Initiative was first set up, the number of cases unearthed has gone up beyond expectations. During the decade that ended in 2006, the increase was more than 1,700 percent. About 18,000 cases were registered during this period, leading to the arrest of 7,700 persons and successful prosecution of 5,840 individuals.

The Office of Juvenile Justice and Delinquency Prevention (OJJDP) is a component of the Office of Justice Programs, U.S. Department of Justice. Its primary mission is to develop and implement effective programs for juveniles. The Office strives to strengthen the efforts of juvenile justice system to protect public, hold offenders accountable, and provide services that address the needs of youth and their families. Programs sponsored by OJJDP to meet its objectives with regards to crimes of the Internet include:

> *The Crimes Against Children Research Center* combats crimes against children by providing high-quality research and statistics to the public, policymakers, law enforcement personnel, and other child welfare practitioners.
>
> *i-SAFE America* provides Internet safety information to students, parents, and other community members.
>
> *Internet Crimes Against Children Task Force Program* helps state and local law enforcement agencies develop an effective response to cyber enticement and child pornography cases.
>
> *National Center for Missing and Exploited Children* collects and distributes data regarding missing and exploited children and operates a national toll-free hotline.

The work of nongovernmental and not-for-profit agencies cannot be discounted either. Some of these agencies maintain comprehensive informational Web sites to educate parents and other caregivers about safe use of the Internet. Some agencies in the United States that are doing an excellent work in this area are the Netsmartz and Safeteens.

United Kingdom Law Enforcement and Prevention Measures

The *Child Exploitation and Online Protection* (CEOP) *Centre* is a law enforcement agency that works in both online and offline environments. The Centre works across the United Kingdom and uses international links to deal with child sex abuse wherever and whenever it happens. The Center achieves this by providing Internet safety advice for parents and by also offering a virtual police station for reporting abuse on the Internet.

The *Internet Watch Foundation* (IWF) is a key component in the UK's industry/police/government partnership for tackling illegal content online. The IWF is the only recognized nonstatutory organization in the United Kingdom operating an Internet "Hotline" for the reporting of exposure to potentially illegal content online. The IWF strives to minimize the availability of potentially illegal Internet content, such as **child sexual abuse** images hosted anywhere in the world, criminally obscene content hosted in the United Kingdom, and incitement to racial hatred content hosted in the United Kingdom. The IWF has been very successful in the United Kingdom in reducing the percentage of Web sites hosting illegal content; apparently down to 1 percent in 2006 from 18 percent in 1997 according to information on its Web site. The IWF works in collaboration with all police agencies. It achieves its objectives by maintaining collaboration with agencies such as the Child Exploitation and Online Protection Centre (CEOP), Virtual Global Taskforce, Serious Organized Crime Agency (SOCA), The Metropolitan Police Paedophile Unit, West Midlands Police Hi Tech Crime team, Greater Manchester Police Abusive Images Unit, and The National Hi-Tech Crime Unit Scotland (NHTCUS).

Other nongovernmental and not-for-profit agencies also do a commendable job in creating awareness to keep children safe online. Among these are SafeKids, NCH—the children's charity, and the like.

International Law Enforcement and Prevention Measures

The Lyon-based *International Criminal Police Organization* (ICPO) generally referred to as the *Interpol* got involved in the investigation of offenses against children in 1989 following the adoption of the UN Convention on Rights of the Child. Interpol works globally with several partners raising awareness. It focuses on the need for international partnerships while emphasizing a local perspective on the issue. It has a specialist group to tackle crimes against children. This group focuses on four different arenas; commercial exploitation and trafficking in children, sex offenders, serious violent crimes against children, and child pornography. The Interpol presents itself as a worldwide forum of specialists dealing with these issues. It has activities in different regions of the world to ensure that law enforcement officers understand the need to act upon requests involving children at risk. Interpol creates a global understanding to address victim identification and help rescue children being sexually abused and pornographically exploited.

Child sexual exploitation on the Internet includes posed photos and video recordings of sex crimes against children. To help police in different countries fight this type of crime, the

Interpol Child Abuse Image Database (ICAID) was created in 2001. This database consists of thousands of images of child sexual abuse submitted by member countries. This sharing of images by the Interpol with member countries helps in identifying old versus new crimes and is a great aid in tracking down the criminals. The Interpol, as part of its commitment to eradicate sexual abuse of children, has passed several resolutions making crimes against children as one of its top international policing priorities.

Operationally, Interpol supports member-states in carrying out large investigative operations involving the commercial exploitation of children by pedophile networks. It also provides support in ongoing cases. The Interpol is authorized to issue Green Notices on offenders who travel to commit their crime.

Virtual Global Task Force (VGT) is another initiative to fight child pornography. This task force forms the basis of forging close relations between law-enforcement agencies in the United States, the United Kingdom, Canada, and Australia. The VGT brings together officers from the four countries for exchange of information and for collaboration in investigation. VGT was established in 2003, and since then it has set up a 24/7 watch-system where agencies of VGT member-countries operate by turn as an "On-call Internet Police Officer." This arrangement enables instantaneous response to imminent threats to children. For instance, in a recent case, a man in England was identified to be planning molestation of his children. A joint team of U.S. and U.K. authorities moved in swiftly to arrest him and foil the attempt. Such an initiative need not necessarily come from agencies alone. Suspicious online activity can be reported to the VGT by individual Internet users as well.

In an international meeting held in Washington in February 2007, the VGT launched a 60-second commercial that is being distributed all over the world to a projected audience of 450 million. This conference has proposed a European task force and an educational and awareness program for all Internet users, especially for those in the United Kingdom. A manual of good practice for investigators across the globe is also a distinct possibility. The VGT Web site will become more informative in due course so as to facilitate a quicker law enforcement response to any report on child abuse.

CONCLUSION

Even though a model legislation for pornography was proposed by the *International Center for Missing and Exploited Children* (ICEMC), and with a research study indicating there are now fewer dismissals and acquittals for Internet sex crimes against minors than for conventional child sexual abuse prosecutions, it cannot be said with confidence that our children are completely protected. This is especially true in light of a recent report according to which state prosecutors have discovered that nearly 141 convicted New Jersey sex offenders were using MySpace (Maddux 2007). Discovering these sex offenders was not very hard for the prosecutors, but bringing them to justice was. The problems in arresting and convicting online predators usually center on issues of masked identities, jurisdiction, problems in gathering evidence and following the electronic trail. Chief of the FBI's cyber division, Raul O. Roldan (2006) testified to Congress that, "Even after . . . a thorough analysis of all information is conducted, there is rarely enough probable cause established to request a search warrant on the customer's residence."

The Internet is under assault from many quarters, especially from people who have distinct evil intentions. Some of them are downright perverts. What we should be more concerned about are the activities of international gangs who want to earn a living out of child pornography. Such pornography has many dimensions. The most serious ones are physical assaults on children after their pictures had been carried by the Internet and are lured into face-to-face contact with those who peddle images. Governmental authorities can only do a little. The role of parents is much more crucial and effective. They need to monitor surfing by children so that their access to total strangers is denied. Once such access becomes difficult, it will be possible to eliminate from cyberspace those strangers who are out to exploit the children. Not many parents are clued up on this, and there is a need to educate them.

KEY TERMS

Child sexual abuse
Internet risks
Self-regulation

REFERENCES

Agebäck, A. K. 2004. What do children do online? Facts from the SAFT project. Accessed June 2007, from http://www.multirio.rj.gov.br/riomidia/imgs/PP_Rio.pdf

Center for the Digital Future. 2007. 2007 USC-Annenberg digital future project. Retrieved June 2007, from http://www.digitalcenter.org/pages/current_report.asp

Childwise. 2006. Childwise monitor report 2005–2006. Retrieved June 2007, from http://www.bbc.co.uk/commissioning/marketresearch/flash/html/chart751.shtml

Cox Communications, NCMEC, and J. Walsh. 2007. Teen internet safety survey wave II. Retrieved June 2007, from http://www.cox.com/takeCharge/survey_results.asp

Deleting Online Predators Act of 2007. H. R. 5319 (RFS), 109th Cong., 2nd Sess. (2007).

Eurobarometer. 2005–2006. Eurobarometer report 2005–2006. Retrieved June 2007, from http://ec.europa.eu/public_opinion/index_en.htm

Finkelhor, D., K. J. Mitchell, and J. Wolak. 2000. Online victimization: A report on the nation's youth. Retrieved June 2007, from http://www.unh.edu/ccrc/pdf/Victimization_Online_Survey.pdf

Flood, M., and C. Hamilton. 2003. *Youth and Pornography in Australia: Evidence on the Extent of Exposure and Likely Effects.* Canberra, Australia: Australia Institute.

Harmon, A. 2003. New parent-to-child chat: Do you download music? *New York Times* (September 10).

Hinduja, S., and J. W. Patchin. 2007. What kids do on MySpace. *Technology & Learning* 27 (7): 7.

Lenhart, A. 2005. Protecting teens online. Pew Internet & American Life Project, Washington, DC. Retrieved June 19, 2007, from http://www.pewinternet.org/pdfs/PIP_Filters_Report.pdf

Lenhart, A., and M. Madden. 2005. Teens and technology: Youth are leading the transition to a wired and mobile nation. Retrieved June 19, 2007, from http://www.pewinternet.org/pdfs/PIP_Teens_Tech_July2005web.pdf

Livingstone, S., and M. Bober. 2005. UK children go online: Final report of key project findings. Retrieved June 2007, from http://www.york.ac.uk/res/e-society/projects/1/UKCGOExecSummary.pdf

Maddux, M. 2007. Online predators beyond laws arm. *Record* (North Jersey; July 8).

MSN. 2006. MSN cyberbullying report: Blogging, instant messaging and email bullying amongst today's teens. Retrieved June 2007, from http://www.msn.co.uk/img/specials/portal/cyberbullying/cyberbullying_tall_revised3.pdf

OFCOM. n.d.. Report on media literacy amongst children. Retrieved 2007, from http://www.ofcom.org.
    uk/advice/media_literacy/medlitpub/medlitpubrss/children/children.pdf

Patchin, J. W., and S. Hinduja. 2006. Bullies move beyond the schoolyard: A preliminary look at
    cyberbullying. *Youth Violence and Juvenile Justice* 4 (2): 148–69.

Remco Pijpers Foundation. 2006. My child online. Retrieved June 2007, from www.mijnkindonline.nl

Rideout, V. J., E. A. Vandewater, and E. A. Wartella. 2003. Zero to six: Electronic media in the lives of
    infants, toddlers and preschoolers. Retrieved July 12, 2007, from http://www.kff.org/entmedia/loader.
    cfm?url=/commonspot/security/getfile.cfm&PageID=22754

Roldan, R. O. Section Chief, Cyber Division, FBI. 2006. Aggressively combating child sexual
    exploitation via the Internet: Hearings before the House Committee on Energy and Commerce, May 3,
    2006 (testimony).

Stone, B. 2007. Accuser says Web site has X-rated link. *New York Times* (NY; June 11).

The National Bullying Survey. (2006). Retrieved June 2007, from http://www.bullying.co.uk/
    thenationalbullyingsurvey_results.pdf

UCLA. 2003. *The UCLA Internet Report: Surveying the Digital Future—Year Three.* UCLA Center for
    Communication Policy.

WebWise. (n.d.). BBC's guide to using the Internet. Retrieved June 2007, from http://www.bbc.
    co.uk/webwise/

Wolak, J., K. Mitchell, D. Finkelhor, National Center for Missing & Exploited Children (US),
    University of New Hampshire Crimes Against Children Research Center, and United States Office of
    Juvenile Justice and Delinquency Prevention. 2006. *Online Victimization of Youth: Five Years Later.*
    National Center for Missing & Exploited Children.

Ybarra, M. L., and K. J. Mitchell. 2004. Youth engaging in online harassment: Associations with
    caregiver–child relationships, internet use, and personal characteristics. *Journal of Adolescence* 27 (3):
    319–36.

Ybarra, M. L., K. J. Mitchell, J. Wolak, and D. Finkelhor. 2006. Examining characteristics and
    associated distress related to Internet harassment: findings from the Second Youth Internet Safety
    Survey. *Pediatrics* 118 (4): e1169–77.

PART II

Emerging Global Crimes of the Internet

Chapter 6

Online Pharmaceutical Sales and the Challenge for Law Enforcement

Laura L. Finley
Florida Atlantic University, Boca Raton

Laura Finley, Ph.D., is Director of Social Change at Women In Distress of Broward County, Inc., a domestic violence agency in South Florida. She has also been visiting professor of sociology at Florida Atlantic University, and has taught at several colleges and universities in Florida, Colorado, and Michigan since earning her Ph.D. in 2002. She is co-author of two books, has edited an encyclopedia, and has two individually authored books forthcoming in fall, 2007. Her work has been published in numerous journals as well.

Abstract

In recent years, the number of people using, misusing, and abusing prescription drugs has risen dramatically in the United States and in the rest of the world. Paralleling that rise has been an increase in people using the Internet to make a variety of personal purchases—of legal as well as illegal products. This chapter chronicles the scope and extent of prescription drug sales on the Web. It provides a brief overview of applicable laws, a description of prescription drugs available on the Web, and how Web-based sales may be altering the stereotypical profile of drug users and dealers. The chapter concludes with an examination of the challenges of Web-based sales for law enforcement.

INTRODUCTION

From worries about availability and cost to concerns about over-prescription, misuse, and abuse, prescription drugs have been a hot topic in the United States since the early 1990s. During the same time period, the Web has become a marketplace for all kinds of products, and drugs are no exception. Because it is so convenient and can reach so many, it is no surprise that needy users and enterprising dealers have turned to the Web to buy and sell their wares. An increasing number of Web sites are devoted to drug sales of all sorts. Buyers and sellers also use chat rooms, e-mail, and private Web rings to exchange information and products. Indeed, prescription drugs and the Internet are both changing how we conceive of drug users, drug dealers, and the war on drugs.

This chapter explores the topic of online pharmaceutical sales and the challenges they bring for law enforcement. It begins with an examination of the rise in prescription drug use and abuse. This is followed by a description of the widespread use of the Internet. The chapter then presents a profile of Internet prescription drug dealers and buyers, illustrating how this is considerably different than the stereotypical image of drug users and dealers. Since one of the major challenges for drug warriors is finding and applying applicable law, the chapter provides a brief historical overview of legal issues regarding prescription drugs. It then presents a description of prescription drug sales online, discussing ease of access, lack of prescriptions required, and concerns about purity and safety. Integrated in this section are analyses of sites purveying specific pharmaceuticals. The chapter ends with a discussion of the challenges for policing prescription drug sales on the Web, as well as successes to date.

PRESCRIPTION DRUG USE

Prescription drug sales have grown tremendously in the last two decades. Prescription drug sales are up almost 400 percent since 1990 (Birnhanemaskel 2005). From 2000 to 2004, the lawful distribution of pharmaceuticals increased over 100 percent, making these products widely available in the United States and even internationally (National Drug Intelligence Center (NDIC) 2006). Simply put, Americans use a lot of drugs. In 1993, the average American received seven prescriptions per year. In 2000, that was up to eleven, and by 2004, twelve. In 2004, close to half of all Americans took at least one prescription daily, with one in six taking three or more each day (Critser 2005). Citizens of the United States currently spend more than $200 billion per year on medications. Spending on prescription drugs is the fastest growing part of American health care costs, rising 13–19 percent each year. The average amount spent per capita on medications in the United States is 65 percent higher than anywhere else in the developed world (Avorn 2004). A good part of the increase in prescription drug use can be traced to the rise in direct to consumer advertisements, or DTC. While in 1980 the amount spent on DTC was $2 million, in 2004 it was $4.35 billion and continues to rise (Critser 2005).

Drug prescriptions in recent years in the United States are increasingly for "me too" substances—those drugs that contain no new active ingredients and are virtually the same as drugs already on the market. Because they are cheap and easy for pharmaceutical companies, they are the most highly marketed drugs. They are also more costly than the other substances already available—for instance, Nexium is the same thing as Prilosec, but in 2004, over-the-counter Prilosec cost $24 and Nexium cost $171 (Riedberg 2006). Costs for all prescription drugs have risen to the point that many simply cannot afford to buy the drugs prescribed for them. The cost of prescription drugs rose in the double digits each year between 1995 and 2003 (Critser 2005). The inability to pay for needed and/or desired drugs has led some to look for these substances outside the legitimate marketplace.

Prescription drugs are not just for old people anymore. Between 2000 and 2003, spending on medicines intended to treat the behavioral concerns of children and adolescents rose 77 percent, and 65 percent of young people who take a drug for their behavior take an anti-depressant (Critser 2005). Prescriptions for young people for antidepressants such as Prozac and ADD drug Ritalin more than doubled between 1991 and 1995 (Lichtenstein 2005). Current estimates suggest 15–20 percent of boys in the United States are taking methylphenidate, or Ritalin (Mercogliano 2003). A 2003 study found Ritalin prescriptions for 2- to 4-year-olds increased 300 percent between 1991 and 1995 (Mercogliano 2003). The FDA found that, since 1994, more than 3000 prescriptions for Ritalin have been written for children under 1-year-old (Mercogliano 2003).

This is not just a U.S. issue, however. In 2005, there were 359,600 prescriptions for Ritalin in the UK, a 180 percent increase since 1991 (PR.com 2006). Between 1994 and 2001, Ritalin prescriptions in Canada rose 142 percent (PR.com 2006). NIMH (2007) reported that the number of children prescribed Ritalin in Singapore doubled between 1999 and 2004.

PRESCRIPTION DRUG ABUSE

According to the Drug Enforcement Agency data, as early as the 1990s the majority of abused **controlled substances** in the United States were prescription drugs. Common opioids such as Vicodin and sedatives such as Xanax and Valium were on the list of top 20 most abused controlled substances (Colvin 1995). In some states, **prescription drug abuse** is considered one of the worst problems. In the second half of 2000, Florida state officials announced that there had been more deaths from overdose of OxyContin and Vicodin than from heroin and cocaine (Meier 2003). Jim McDonough, Drug Czar in Florida, announced prescription drug abuse to be the state's biggest drug problem in 2005, stating that six people die each day in Florida due to prescription drug abuse (Join Together Online, October 31, 2005). Between 2004 and 2005, emergency room visits for nonmedical use of prescription and over-the-counter drugs rose 21 percent, according to the Substance Abuse and Mental Health Services Administration (SAMHSA 2005).

SAMHSA released a new analysis of the 2004 National Survey on Drug Use and Health (NSDUH) in 2005 in which they found that more Americans used narcotic pain medicines recreationally than all other drugs except alcohol. While there were 2.1 million new marijuana users in the year, there were 2.4 million new recreational narcotics. The most commonly abused pain medications were Vicodin, Lortab, or Lorcet, followed by Darvocet, Darvon, or Tylenol with Codeine (Join Together Online, June 22, 2006). The NSDUH found six million people in the United States admitted to using psychotherapeutic drugs for nonmedical purposes, and 31.8 million admitted using painkillers nonmedically (Kweder 2006).

Prescription drug misuse and abuse is a global social problem. The International Narcotics Control Board (INCB) announced in 2006 that prescription drug abuse is a major problem in all of North America, including Mexico, Canada, and the United States (Join Together Online, March 3, 2006a). Despite combined efforts involving the DEA, the RxNet Task Force, and Border Patrol, prescription drugs regularly make it across the Mexican border and into the United States, with college students representing a large part of the demand (Join Together Online, October 28, 2004).

Some teens are experimenting with many prescription drugs in order to get buzzed. The Federal Substance Abuse and Mental Health Services Administration says prescription drugs are second only to marijuana on the list of most abused substances by people age 12–24 (Birnhanemaskel 2005), while The National Survey of American Attitudes on Substance Abuse found that between April 2004 and June 2005, 86 percent of students surveyed knew a friend of classmate who had abused prescription drugs (Eberstadt 2005). According to Girl Life, 14 percent of high school seniors have used prescription drugs for nonmedicinal purposes, 20 percent of U.S. teens have abused the pain reliever Vicodin, and 10 percent have abused Ritalin and/or Adderall (Monarch Avalon 2005). It is not just the ADD/ADHD drugs, however. Klonopine, called "K-pins" by young people, are antianxiety pills that are sold for $2 to $5 to get high (Join Together Online, February 8, 2006). In 2002, 28 teens in

Philadelphia took Xanax at lunch. Twelve needed to be hospitalized. Shortly thereafter, four Houston teens were also hospitalized. "Xanies" or "Blues," as they are often called, can be purchased for $1 to $3 per pill (MSNBC 2002).

This, too, is not just an American problem. In 2003, 24-year-old Liam Brackell of England killed himself after becoming addicted to numerous prescription drugs he purchased online. When he died, he had tried 23 different drugs. After his death, it was found that many of the drugs he purchased were counterfeits (Firth 2006). In 2003, the BBC reported that Ritalin is being sold on playgrounds for £0.50 to £1 per pill (Midgely 2003). Scottish authorities report increased usage by teens of Temazepam, a tranquilizer, when heroin is unavailable (Global Youth Network 2006). In 2002, the Australian *Sun-Herald* reported young people "swopping, sharing, and selling" prescription drugs at school, and death of 14 students in the Hunter region in March 2006 prompted numerous federal inquiries (Piriani 2006).

Young people are mixing prescription drugs in very dangerous ways. Nicklin (2000) maintains that "People tend to be less picky these days and more willing to try new combinations," the most common being the mix of Ritalin or Valium with other substances. Critser (2005) tells of the "California cocktail," a mix of Neurontin (a medication used to treat epilepsy and bipolar disorder), Wellbutrin (an antidepressant), and Ritalin. Some teens are holding what they call "pharm parties," where everyone brings whatever pharmaceutical products they can find to share. Typically, teens find these drugs by rummaging through the family medicine cabinet, called "pharming," or even ordering them online. There are even names for the various combinations. For instance, bowls and bags of random assortments are called "trail mix" (Ratcliffe and Kohler 2006).

Not all of the prescription drugs are being misused to obtain a high. Teens and college-aged students are increasingly turning to prescription drugs for academic or quasi-academic purposes. One survey of University of Delaware Business majors found 90 percent had used Adderall, Ritalin, or Provigil as a study aid for exams and finals. Only one quarter had a legitimate prescription to do so (Join Together Online, June 28, 2006a). In another study, one student explained that Adderall helped him balance school, sports, and a social life, and argued it even helped him think more deeply about a subject (Join Together Online, May 9, 2005).

Although there is clearly a great concern about prescription drug use by young people, another group that is prone to dangerous misuse and abuse but that receives little attention is the elderly. In the mid-1990s, people over 65 constituted 13 percent of the U.S. population, but consumed 30 percent of all prescription drugs. Many take six medications in one day, increasing the chance of misuse. Each year, 25 percent of nursing home admissions are a result of concern that a senior is unable to use medications safely (Colvin 1995). Elderly people are increasingly being arrested for selling their prescription drugs. Between April 2004 and December 2005, more than 40 people over the age of 60 were arrested for illegally selling prescription drugs in the state of Kentucky alone. One Kentucky physician regularly hears from addicted persons that they got their drugs from their elderly neighbors, so now she requires her patients submit to a drug test to ensure they are taking, not selling, their prescriptions (Join Together Online, December 13, 2005).

Prescription drug abusers are quite different than the typical image of a "druggie." Dr. Clifford Bernstein, a pain and addiction specialist at the Waismann Institute, explained "What we are seeing now are bright, aggressive people—some at the crest of their careers—who may start out on the drug for, say, a weekend sprained ankle, then find out how great it feels to be on it" (Critser 2005, 160). Sara Simpson, supervisor of the Rx Task Force of the Pharmaceutical Narcotic Enforcement Team asserts, "The people who are addicted to these drugs are people that work just like you and me. We arrest police officers, nurses, airline pilots, school teachers" (Join Together Online, October 28, 2004). Most of the new recreational users surveyed by the NSDUH admitted to previous use of illicit drugs. More than half the new users were female (Join Together Online, June 22, 2006). Women and the elderly are two to three times more likely to become addicted to prescription drugs (Medindia, n.d.). While historically males have constituted the greatest portion of drug users, girls are more likely to abuse prescription drugs (Join Together Online, February 9, 2006). Lawrence Diller (1998) explains why prescription drugs appeal to teens. Teens "think that since their younger brother takes it under a doctor's prescription, it must be safe" (p. 42). An executive friend of Greg Critser's (2005) described to him about "Vicodin Fridays." Each Friday, someone would make the rounds of the office, dispensing the prescription-only painkiller. The drugs helped the executives, "numb out" for a long weekend of script reading. Critser (2005) comments: "There was no fun in Vicodin Fridays, no rebellion or even any major highly cool posing. The pills had simply become part of work" (p. 159). He goes on to explain, however, that these stories did not just happen with elite executives; rather, pill-popping to confront life's daily challenges was widespread among middle- to upper-class suburbanites.

The problem is not the drugs, per se. As Sullum (2003) explains, no drug is purely "good" or "bad." Rather, it is how each substance is used, the amount used, the purity of the substance, the drug interactions, and a host of other things that determine a drug's effects.

> Taking drugs can hurt you; not taking drugs can hurt you. Tens of millions of people are alive today who would be dead without their medicines, and tens of millions more have far less life-crushing disability because of prescriptions their doctors have written. Some others—though mercifully a much smaller number—become disabled or die when a drug's risk-benefit balance goes horribly wrong. Each year sees the introduction of new discoveries that hold enormous clinical promise if used well, and each year the nation's pharmaceutical bill is considerably larger. The price of our drug appetite now takes an ever larger bite out of already strained health care budgets. It has grown at an unsustainable annual rate of 15 to 19 percent over the last few years, making prescription drugs the fastest-rising component of all health-care expenditures. (Avorn 2004, 17)

In sum, more and more people take prescription drugs for assorted pains, woes, and pleasures. At the same time, the cost of many prescription drugs has increased astronomically. Many who legitimately need certain drugs find it difficult to get them lawfully. In search of affordable access to what they need and want, many have turned to the Internet to shop. Online sales of pharmaceuticals from Canadian pharmacies grew from a total of $50 million in 2000 to $800 million in 2003 (Crowley 2004). One pharmaceutical expert has called the Internet "the Mall of America for prescription drugs" (Crowley 2004). Similarly, many who seek a reprieve from their mundane existence in the form of a chemical high have looked to the Internet as a less dangerous and more convenient means of finding the desired product. Critser (2005) discusses how the ". . . suburban drug sprawl marked the same kind of pharmaceutical populism that was going on in college dorms. If you knew what 'worked,' why engage a doctor's advice? Who cared about the intent of the drug? Just get the pills. It is an attitude that has exploded with the onslaught of Internet prescription drug sites . . ."

(pp. 160–61). The NDIC (2006) says that prescription drug abuse in the United States is largely due to doctor shopping, forged prescriptions, theft, and the Internet.

INTERNET USE EXPLODES

Since it was conceived in the 1960s, Internet has exploded as a method of worldwide broadcasting, information dissemination, and as a medium for collaboration without regard for geography. Worldwide, over 957,000,000 people are connected, representing 14.9 percent of the world's population (Internetworldstats.com 2005). In the United States, 68.5 percent of people are said to regularly use the Internet (Internetworldstats.com 2005). Adolescents and young adults constitute the largest group of users, with more than 40 million people under the age of 18 online (Office of National Drug Control Policy 2002). Since 2001, Internet usage by teens has grown 24 percent (Lenhart, Madden, and Hilton 2005). On an average, teens spend 16.7 hours per week online—more than they do watching television (Office of National Drug Control Policy 2002). A 2005 Pew Internet & American Life Project found 51 percent of teenagers are online each day, a 9 percent increase since 2000 (Kershaw 2005). The next age group, college-aged students, is even more likely to be online—one study found 93 percent of college students have Internet access (Davis 2003).

There's no doubt that the Internet is changing the way we all live and work. As with any technology, whether that change is largely good or bad depends on circumstances and perspective. On the "good" side, surely the Web has allowed people to learn more about an array of topics that previously would have required hours of frustrating labor in the library. The Supreme Court has lauded the Internet for providing diverse thought and instant access, while Judge Stuart Dalzell of the U.S. District Court for the Eastern District of Pennsylvania has called it "the most participatory form of mass speech yet developed" (cited in Corn-Revere 2002, 2).

On the "bad" side, some doctors have even diagnosed patients as being onlineaholics, calling their problem Internet Addiction Disorder. These mental health specialists maintain that approximately 6 to 10 percent of the 189 million Internet users in the United States are Internet-dependent, and that this dependency can be as destructive to their lives as alcoholism or drug addiction is (Kershaw 2005). Further, experts maintain the majority of obsessive users are using the Internet to further other addictions, such as gambling or viewing pornography. To addicts, the Internet offers a cheap escape from reality, is easily accessible, and at least the appearance of anonymity (Kershaw 2005). Blackberry, a wireless e-mail device, is considered so addictive it has been called "crackberry" (Kershaw 2005).

PRESCRIPTION DRUGS AND THE INTERNET

Sale of prescription drugs is the easiest form of online drug sale (Reaves 2002). Illegal online pharmaceutical sales take a number of forms. Some people sell unapproved drugs via the Internet, some dispense FDA approved drugs without prescriptions, others make fraudulent claims about prescription medications, and other sites provide illegal or doctored up versions of approved medicines (Hubbard 2004a). The U.S. Food and Drug Administration estimated there were over 1,000 Internet pharmacies in 2004 (Veronin and Youan 2004). International

Narcotics Control Board (INCB) member Herbert Okun said, "It started as a trickle and—wham!—now it's a mushroom cloud," in reference to the growth of Internet drug sales (Pisik 2001, 27). In 2005, the online prescription drug industry was estimated to be worth $23 million to $1 billion per year (BuySafeDrugs.info 2005).

Easy Access

In 2006, the INCB recognized the Internet as a major conduit for questionable sales of the more than 10 million illegal shipments entering the United States each year (Join Together Online, March 3, 2006a). It is obvious that prescription drugs are easy to obtain online. One study found 495 Web sites selling prescription drugs in just one week of analysis, and verification of an actual prescription was only required on 6 percent of those sites (Sullivan 2004). Many of these sites offered highly addictive drugs, like Oxycontin, Percocet, and Darvon (Sullivan 2004). In an interview with *Nightline* reporter Chris Cuomo (2006), federal Drug Enforcement Agency (DEA) agent Tim Stover demonstrated how easy it is to find prescription drugs on the Web. A search for no-prescription hydrocodone gave 141,000 listings. In 2004, the General Accounting Office (GAO), the investigating arm of Congress, found it easy to purchase prescription drugs on the Internet, and cautioned that many are mishandled, sold without proper prescriptions, or are missing important warning information. Researchers purchased 11 different drugs from 68 Internet pharmacies located in 12 different countries.

Goldberg (2006) explains that, in real life, if a person has no regular supplier of their drugs, they may need to spend weeks in search of a dealer. With the Internet, however, the next dealer is merely a click away. In addition, in contrast to the covert nature of traditional illegal drug sales, online dealers can advertise their product—not only to a local market, but to a global one. Certainly anyone who has an e-mail account has received prescription drug spam. In 2004, the top spam terms were related to pharmaceutical items, especially Vioxx and Viagra (Join Together Online, December 29, 2004). Sixty-three percent of Internet users said they received unsolicited e-mail advertising sexual health medications, 55 percent received unsolicited e-mail about prescription drugs, and 40 percent said they received unsolicited e-mail about an over-the-counter drug on the Pew Internet American Life survey (Fox 2004). According to Internet security experts, almost one-quarter of all spam, approximately 15 billion messages per day, is spam advertising drugs (Grow, Elgin, and Weintraub 2006). Although the author had received drug-related spam prior to writing this paper, it has increased exponentially since she began. Each day, 6 to 10 advertisements for prescription medications appear in her hotmail inbox, with approximately the same number landing promptly in junk mail. Med Zone, AwesomeRx, Meds Delivered, Pharmacy Warehouse, Fantastic Meds, and Pharmacy Here all want her to buy from them, and Pharmacy Here tells her in their tag line she needs no prescription to do so.

Prescriptions Needed?

The 2004 research by the GAO found pharmacies based in Canada proved to be the most legitimate. They found that all of the 18 Canadian pharmacies required a valid prescription, but only 5 of the 29 U.S.-based pharmacies did. The remaining U.S. sites, as well as the other 21 sites from foreign countries, relied on medical questionnaires or required nothing prior to arranging a sale. The National Center on Addiction and Substance Abuse (CASA) released their analysis of Web-based prescription drug sales in July 2006. Their analysis involved 185 Web sites. No prescription was needed on 89 percent of the sites. Thirty percent of the sites actually boasted that no prescription is needed, another 60 percent offered online consultations, and 10 percent simply made no mention about prescriptions (Join Together Online, July 14, 2006). Even those where a prescription is required allow users to fax the prescription in, which is hardly an exact measure (Join Together Online, July 14, 2006). Only two of the 185 sites were licensed by the National Association of Boards of Pharmacy. Even those where a prescription is required allow users to fax the prescription in, which is hardly an exact measure (Join Together Online, July 14, 2006). According to Colvin (1995), prescription forgery is popular because it can be financially lucrative, offenders perceive it as a victimless offense, chances of being apprehended are small, and penalties are slight. Additionally, some 85 percent of forged prescriptions are filled. The United Nations' International Narcotics Board (INCB) says approximately 90 percent of pharmaceutical sales made online are done without a prescription (Join Together Online, March 2, 2005).

Even if a prescription is required, many sites boast of online consultations so as to provide the appearance of meeting the requirement (Sullivan 2004). DEA deputy assistant administrator Joseph Rannazzisi testified before a House subcommittee on Oversight and Investigations, saying, "Perhaps most disturbing is that many of these Internet pharmaceutical sites . . . are hiding behind a façade of legitimacy by pretending to ask customers health question" (Lyons 2007, 2). Federal law prohibits purchasing controlled substances online. This includes pain relievers like OxyContin and Vicotin, sedatives like Xanax and Ambien, stimulants like phentermine, Adderall, and Ritalin, and anabolic steroids without a valid doctor's prescription. The U.S. Department of Justice does not consider cyber doctors who use online questionnaires to be legitimate (Consumer alert, n.d.).

Safety Concerns

Clearly, there is tremendous risk when patients take potentially dangerous substances without the knowledge and advice of their physicians.

> However well or poorly we physicians handle information about drugs, a separate flood of communication washes over our patients once they leave the office. Each year consumers have access to more medicine-related information, a growing stream with its own torrents and whirlpools, crystal-clear eddies, and toxic outflows. In olden times, before the Internet and consumer advertising, the doctor's consulting room and the drugstore were the main places where such information was transferred to the patients. (Avorn 2004, 285–6)

In the GAO research, only the Canadian sites included instructions for use, and only one-third of the non-Canadian sites provided warning information. Most of the drugs did contain the proper active ingredients, although two were counterfeits and two had different chemical compositions (*USA Today* 2004). The FDA has reported that almost 90 percent of prescription drugs coming into the United States and purchased via mail or ordered online are dangerous (Tinnin 2005).

An investigation conducted by the National Association of Boards of Pharmacy (NABP), prompted by drug company Eli Lilly, found that a vast majority of the pills available online contain dangerous levels of impurities (Herper 2005). While some online pharmaceutical products are not effective because they barely contain the required active components, the reverse is also true. Ambient knock-offs purchased online were as much as twice as strong (Herper 2005). In 2005, a team of investigative journalists attempted to make online purchases of a number of prescription drugs. They found this to be quite easy. Once the drugs arrived, they made arrangements with Pfizer to have them tested. According to Joe Theriault, Vice President of Global Secuirty, "They [online pharmaceutical companies] are selling an array of junk that frankly I would be afraid to put in my system." The Norvasc, a blood pressure medicine, the team ordered was fake, and the Viagra they received had only a small amount of the active ingredient (BuySafeDrugs.info 2005). Phony Viagra from Thailand has been found containing vodka (Grow, Elgin, and Weintraub 2006). According to the *U.S. News & World Report* (2004), the top 10 most frequently counterfeited drugs in 2004, all sold regularly on the Internet, were Viagra, Lipitor, OxyContin, Procrit, Zoloft, Cipro, Celebrex, Serostim, Albuterol, and Crixivan.

The General Accounting Office cautions that the worst countries in regards to drug impurities and fakes are Argentina, Costa Rica, Fiji, India, Mexico, Pakistan, the Philippines, Spain, Thailand, and Turkey. *Business Week* reported in December 2006 about a counterfeit pill mill operating out of Belize. There, workers compiled knock-off Viagra, Lipitor, and Ambien from raw ingredients shipped from China (Grow, Elgin, and Weintraub 2006).

Stoppler (2005) warned that drugs purchased from illegal **online pharmacies** might be outdated or expired, manufactured in substandard facilities, contain dangerous ingredients or have been improperly stored, be too strong or too weak, may be the wrong drugs, or may be outright fakes. The NABP has claimed that almost half of all online pharmacies offering prescribing services are located outside the United States (Stoppler 2005). In addition to varying levels of ingredients and contaminants, Hickman (2006) cautions that only one-quarter of drugs purchased online actually arrive. William Hubbard reported to the United States Senate that in 2003, the FDA and Customs opened 1,153 shipments of pharmaceuticals coming into the United States. Of these, 88 percent were unapproved drugs. They also found controlled substances and drugs that are no longer allowed in the United States (Hubbard 2004a).

In 2007, the FDA found people ordering Ambien, Xanax, Lexapro, and Ativan online were being shipped a schizophrenia medication, haloperidol, which caused three people to seek emergency room attention (Lopes 2007).

Access by Young People

Since prescription drugs are the second most abused substance by young people (next to marijuana), it is important that research identify the extent and scope of Internet sales, as well as the ways the Web might contribute to drug abuse in general. In July 2006, drug czar John Walters hosted a roundtable discussion with teenagers to discuss the ways they used technology to further substance abuse. One 17-year-old told Walters "I was always searching [the Internet] for new ways to get high." He said he learned how to grow marijuana and how to crush pills, and would regularly instant message his friends so they could access his favorite drug sites. And, when his parents decided to give him a drug test, he found out how to detox online (Lexis Nexis 2006).

Sanders (2006) who work with polydrug using street youth found that while many were given penethylamines in clubs, by either acquaintances or strangers, others admitted to having searched them out on the Web; 178 peneythylamines are available online (Sanders 2006). The UK has a blanket ban on penethylamines (Sanders 2006), but in other locations the drug is not illegal.

In 2004, a mother authorized her 14-year-old son to order Xanax online as part of their family's investigation of online drug sales. With a few clicks of his mouse, he lied on a medical questionnaire and purchased $170 worth of Xanax from a Central America-based pharmaceutical seller. The drugs arrived in less than one month (KZAT 2004).

INTERNET BUYERS AND SELLERS

The Buyers

The Pew Internet & American Life Project surveyed 2,200 randomly selected adults aged 18 and older on their use of the Web to learn about and purchase prescription drugs. They found 45 percent of American adults, approximately 91 million people, take some type of prescription drug regularly. Just over one-quarter of Americans have researched prescription drugs online. This population tended to be older, more educated, have high-speed connections at home and work, and have been online for 6 or more years. Much of the population—62 percent—is concerned about online purchases, believing them to be less safe than making the same purchase at the local pharmacy. Still, 28 percent feels online purchases are every bit as safe. Only 4 percent admitted to ever making an online purchase of prescription drugs. These people cited convenience as the number one reason for doing so. Three-quarters of the purchases were for chronic medical conditions, like arthritis or high blood pressure, while the remaining quarter were for some other purpose like weight loss or sexual performance. It is likely that these numbers will grow, as 90 percent of the sample said they planned to fill a prescription online in the future (Fox 2004). In fact, the *New York Times* reported an increase in the use of televised and Internet-based mental health counseling in June 2006, an appealing form of help for those living in rural communities (Join Together Online, June 28, 2006b).

According to Boehm et al. (2003), Medicare recipients in search of deals and diabetics looking for easy refills make many of the online prescription drug purchases. In October 2005, health watchdogs issued a lookout for an increase in online sales connected to the bird flu scare. Because of all the attention to a potential shortage of Tamiflu, experts were concerned that worried consumers would turn to the Web to make their purchases (Ingham 2005). In 2006, *The Observer* (England) reported that cancer patients who cannot get the drugs they want from the National Health System are ordering directly from the Internet without their doctor's knowledge. Patients are also self-prescribing treatments and ordering them on the Web (Revill 2006).

The INCB, however, has said it actually costs more and that most insurance companies and medical aid systems do not reimburse for the price of drugs purchased online. Hence, the INCB argues the vast majority of Internet prescription drug purchases are made by people who do not have lawful prescriptions (Join Together Online, February 3, 2005). According to Hinkel (2000), one survey found a person could save as much as 29 percent by purchasing their prescription drugs online, while another in the same year (1999) found Viagra and Propecia cost 10 percent more than they did at a local pharmacy.

The anonymity of the Web is appealing to many users, but especially to those wishing to purchase drugs illegally. In particular, teenagers may be comforted by the fact that they can purchase drugs without having to deal with a traditional "drug dealer" (Cuomo 2006). According to Joseph Califano of CASA, a large part of the appeal is "You don't have to deal with a dirty drug dealers like they might have to with cocaine or marijuana or heroin," yet users can get a slow-down of the central nervous system much like an alcohol-induced high (MSNBC 2002). In New Zealand, for instance, social service providers are expressing concern that teens are using the Internet to learn about drugs they wish to try. This most frequently involves some type of prescription drug, such as Ritalin (Tiffen 2005). Carol Falkowski, director of research communications for the Hazeldon foundation explains that prescription drugs are popular with young people because, in many social circles, they are viewed as more acceptable. Catherine Harnett, chief of demand reduction for the DEA, explains that teens often see prescription drug use as safe because it is "medicine," which seems sanitary and safe. Also, many teens begin using as a way of self-medicating for depression and anxiety (Leinwand 2006). One 18-year-old explained that he used OxyContin, or "OCs" because they were easier to obtain than pot (Leinwand 2006). U.S. Representative Ed Whitfield, R-Ky, testified before a House subcommittee on Oversight and Investigations in December 2005. "For young people in particular, online pharmacies seem especially seductive. For this generation, the Internet is a familiar medium and it feels safe. The seduction and convenience of the Internet coupled with the wide availability of controlled substances raises a disturbing prospect of many young people hooked on drugs with the ease of logging on to a computer" (Lyons 2007, 3).

Addicts say it is easy to get a prescription for pain medication. Joe Leonetti told the Des Moines Register he would get Vicodin and Oxycontin when he told emergency room or clinical doctors he had back pain or other difficult-to-diagnose ailments. Fellow addicts also shared tips (Join Together Online, March 3, 2006b). The Waismann Method, an opiate dependency treatment, found that one-quarter of patients who had sought treatment for prescription painkiller addiction used the Web to find or obtain drugs (*Drug Week* 2005).

The Sellers

The NDIC (2006) says there is little involvement by drug trafficking organizations (DTOs) in pharmaceutical trafficking. Most online sales to date are for small amounts. The NDIC does caution that DTOs could step up trafficking if access was limited. In particular, they argue limitations on access in the United States would increase the trafficking by Mexican DTOs (NDIC 2006).

Unlike typical illicit drug sellers, online sellers may be actual doctors. Or, the seller may work with an actual doctor to provide online consultation or "prescriptions." The NDIC says doctors are paid up to $1,500 per day for writing fake prescriptions online (National Drug Information Center, 2004).

One of the biggest challenges regarding prescription drug abuse in general, which is exacerbated by the ease of access on the Web, is the lack of oversight and appropriate law. The following section offers a brief historical summary of laws regarding pharmaceuticals.

PRESCRIPTION DRUGS AND THE LAW: A BRIEF HISTORY

Prior to the 20th century, there was really no attention paid to what we today call prescription drug abuse, nor were there laws in place to address abuses and misuses. According to Spillane (2004a), the American pharmaceutical industry, in the 19th century, was a small operation that generally supplied botanical items to physicians on demand. In the early 1800s, chemists discovered that the painkilling power of opium, commonly used to treat diarrhea as well as to "calm" upset babies, really came from its constituent substance, Morphine. Consequently, use of Morphine became widespread. Other chemicals were soon isolated from opium, including thebaine, the starter material for oxycodone. Despite the positive uses, it was clear by mid-19th century that Morphine was highly addictive. At the start of the 19th century, there were already some 300,000 addicts, many of whom became addicted when the painkiller was used to treat war-related injuries or illnesses (Meier 2003). In addition to soldiers who had become addicted, others became addicted after a physician prescribed them the painkiller, called iatrogenic addiction (Meier 2003).

Two distinct groups of drug manufacturers began to emerge after the Civil War; ethical drug firms, who provided products for medical use only, and unethical firms, who cashed in on sales of all kinds. Ethical companies included Bayer, E.R. Squibb, and Parke Davis (Crellin 2004). By the turn of the century, new pill-making machines made the work of pharmaceutical companies far easier, hence greater numbers of drugs in circulation. Further, in the 1880s and 1890s, these companies realized that not only could they provide the products demanded by physicians, but that they could also develop their own drug products. During this decade, drug companies began to conduct their own studies and publish favorable results in an effort to market their drugs. Foreshadowing concerns of the 21st century, the health professions began to worry that physicians and pharmacists would become "mere slaves to the pharmaceutical trade" and that the "corporate desire for profit would overwhelm care for public health and safety" (Spillane 2004a, 3). Alongside the ethical pharmaceutical industry, firms selling "patent" medicines developed. At the turn of the century, some 5,398 of these companies were listed (Spillane 2004a). These companies also marketed medicinal products. The primary difference between them and their ethical counterparts was their market; these companies marketed directly to consumers, rather than to physicians. In fact, many of them denounced physicians, claiming that consumers could do just as well on their own (Spillane 2004a).

In the 1860s and 1870s, states established pharmacy laws, setting standards for the handling of pharmaceutical drugs. Early laws focused on the inclusion of opium and cocaine in medicinal products (Spillane 2004a). Most of these laws, however, were designed to regulate, not prohibit, and there is little documented evidence of enforcement efforts (Spillane 2004a), partly because most people did not desire federal intervention at this time (Spillane 2004a). In 1867, the East River Medical Association of New York requested pharmacists refrain from renewing prescriptions without permission from physicians. This move was intended to curtail problems with excessive use of prescription substances (Swann 2004). The American Pharmaceutical Association (APhA) admitted there was a problem, but did not support the New York group's resolution (Swann 2004). In 1922, however, APha revised their code of ethics to include the concern about refilling prescriptions, recommending that pharmacists consult with physicians whenever they were to refill a prescription.

The 1904 Pure Food and Drug Act was a dramatic victory for those who did favor a national standard, including the American Medical Association's Council on Pharmacy and

Chemistry. It required a national labeling system detailing the presence of certain drugs in the product. Those drugs included morphine, opium, cocaine, heroin, alpha or beta eucaine, chloroform, cannabis indica, chloral hydrate, acetanilide, or any derivative of these substances (Spillane 2004a). Generally, early enforcement of the Act dealt with mislabeling, rather than with false or misleading claims. Further, food violations were the primary focus (Swann 2004a). Only 135 of the first 1,000 cases brought under the 1906 law involved drugs (Temin 1980). One year later, the Sherley Amendment prohibited manufacturers from making fraudulent or false claims about the curative or therapeutic of foods or drugs on their labels (Temin 1980).

At the start of the 20th century, patients did not have to obtain medicines from their doctors—medicines were readily available and were widely advertised to the public and to doctors. People were free to select the substance of their choosing (Temin 1980). In essence, purity was the main concern. No coordinated efforts were in place to address whether medications were actually useful, or whether their risks outweighed their benefits. It wasn't until three decades later that legislation required medications to be nonlethal (Avorn 2004).

The Harrison Narcotics Act required dealers of narcotics to register with the Internal Revenue Service and to pay an annual tax. Pharmacists were only allowed to dispense narcotics with a written prescription from a doctor or dentist. Orally issued narcotic prescriptions were prohibited, as were prescription refills (Swann 2004). It also required a record of drug orders, although physicians were exempted from this requirement. Even at this time, the pharmaceutical industry had become powerful lobbyists and had achieved an exemption for products containing small amounts of cocaine, heroin, and morphine. Another loophole allowed manufacturers to market drugs that did not conform to strength, quality and purity standards, as long as this was clearly stated on the product label (Swann 2004).

Perhaps the most controversial portion of the Act was section 8, which made possession of any of the regulated substances presumptive evidence of a violation of the Act. Individuals then had to prove that their purchases were legitimate. Penalties for violations included prison terms of no more than 5 years or a fine of $2,000 (Spillane 2004b). In 1916, the Supreme Court dealt with the constitutionality of Section 8. In *United States v. Fuey Moy* 214 U.S. 394 (1916), the court determined section 8 to be unlawful (Spillane 2004b). A 1919 Supreme Court decision interpreted the Harrison Act as banning the prescription of narcotics to addicts, and by the late 1930s, more than 25,000 doctors had been charged with violating the law (Meier 2003).

The Prohibition era was a difficult time for regulation of pharmaceutical drugs. Banning alcohol served to move manufacture and sales underground. One vehicle for black market sales was through illegal prescriptions of medicinal alcohol (Swann 2004). In the 1920s, less than one-third of medicines were purchased based on a doctor's prescription (Temin 1980). Surveys in the 1920s showed that between 9 and 24 percent of addicts first started using Morphine when it was prescribed for them (Meier 2003).

Rising concern about abuse of barbiturates prompted over half the states to enact laws regulating their sale in the 1920s and 1930s (Crellin 2004). After the 1937 Massengill Massacre, in which more than one hundred patients—including many children—died from a sulfinalamide product that had been manufactured with a toxic solvent, the Congress strengthened the Pure Food and Drug Act with the Food, Drug, and Cosmetic Act. The revised Act allowed the federal government to require that drug products not be poisonous. "But there was still no requirement that the drugs needed to work" (Avorn 2004, 43). The Food, Drug, and Cosmetic Act attempted to control misbranded drugs. Misbranded drugs included those that lacked adequate directions for use and failed to carry adequate safety warnings for patients. The FDA was given the authority to exempt any drug from the use requirements provision. Another provision required a warning that certain narcotic and hypnotic substances could be habit forming, but any substance filled from a written, nonrefillable prescription written by a physician, dentist, or veterinarian was exempted. A drug that was dangerous when used as the directions stated was considered misbranded. Finally, the Act prohibited the marketing of any new drugs without FDA approval (Swann 2004).

By 1941, the FDA had identified 20 drugs that were too dangerous to sell without a physician's prescription, yet they still did not consider this a hard and fast list but rather a list of examples (Swann 2004). In order to control the growing problem of barbiturate abuse, the FDA focused on abuses by pharmacists in the 1940s (Swann 2004). In 1946, the FDA reported a pharmacy repeatedly refilling a prescription for Nembutal to a customer for 18 months, and in 1945, a pharmacy in Waco, Texas, dispensed over 45,000 doses of barbiturates over 18 months without any prescription (Swann 2004). At that time, investigations typically involved an investigator posing as a customer and making a number of purchases at a targeted pharmacy. These efforts then prompted a records search of the pharmacy, a check to see if all the required written records were present. The Supreme Court affirmed the FDA's efforts in 1944 (Swann 2004). Early on, some expressed concern that FDA inspectors were not simply investigating pharmacies under suspicion of wrongdoing, but conducting wide sweeps in areas in order to intimidate pharmacists (Swann 2004). Another challenge was that pharmacies were not the only source of illegal barbiturates. Bootleg sources, including truck stops, cafes, bars, and individual dealers were also popular, and likely reached a wider audience (Swann 2004). To police these bootleg sources, the FDA had to get creative. In the 1950s, inspectors enrolled in truck driving school and attended specialized conferences to help conduct stings (Swann 2004).

In the 1950s, the majority of medicines were prescribed by doctors, and by 1969, more than four-fifths of medicines in use had been physician-prescribed (Temin 1980). The Durham-Humphrey Amendment of 1951 clarified what was considered a prescription drug. The definition covered any habit-forming drug, any drug so harmful or toxic it required supervision, and any new drug approved under the 1938 Act requiring supervision. Substances meeting at least one of those criteria were to contain the label, "Caution: Federal law prohibits dispensing without prescription." Over-the-counter drugs were not required to carry the label. Manufacturers still made the decision whether a drug was over-the-counter or prescription, but the FDA could now issue advisory lists (Musto 2002a).

The FDA continued to go after both pharmacies and nontraditional sellers through the 1950s and into the 1960s, but by the mid-1960s, they were taking more action against nontraditional sellers (Swann 2004). The Thalidomide tragedy of the early 1960s prompted a new wave of legislation across the world. In 1962, following tragic reports of babies being born with horrific abnormalities of their arms and legs because their mothers had taken thalidomide during the first trimester of pregnancy, the Kefauver Act passed through Congress unanimously (Musto 2002a). The Kefauver-Harris Amendments to the 1938 Food, Drug, and Cosmetic Act banned the sale of harmful drugs without medical advice and prescription (Crellin 2004). It was the first time the Food and Drug Administration required prescriptions be proven effective before they were sold in the United States (Avorn 2004). Musto (2002b) maintained, however, that the prohibitionist strategy of drug control was, and arguably still is, ineffective at addressing substance abuse and misuse.

In the later 1980s, several "pain management" advocates popularized the term, "pseudoaddiction." Their argument was that doctors might mistake patients who are in tremendous pain as drug addicts because they exhibit similar characteristics, including seeking out multiple doctors for prescriptions for narcotics. Rather than drug addicted, these people maintain that the patient is actually under or inadequately medicated (Meier 2004). Much of this was based on anecdote and what appeared to be common sense, rather than scientific studies, yet likely served to increase the number of prescriptions being written (Meier 2004). In 1988, Congress enacted the Prescription Drug Marketing Act (PDMA) to prevent substandard, counterfeit, and ineffective drugs. The PDMA was in response to concern about the more than two million unapproved birth control pills that had been imported from Panama (Hubbard 2004b).

In the 1990s, many states established prescription monitoring systems, intended to track physician's that were prescribing controlled substances in great volumes, known as "pill mills." Both the American Medical Association and drug companies opposed these measures, arguing they would prevent doctors from prescribing needed medications (Meier 2004). In 1994, Congress passed the Dietary Supplement and Health Education Act, nicknamed the Snake-oil Protection Act, which continued the practice that, if a substance was named a "supplement," it was not subject to efficacy or safety tests and remained beyond the reach of most governmental regulation (Avorn 2004). As Avorn (2004) comments, "The Dietary Supplement and Health Education Act of 1994 may have dealt a blow to science, but it did wonders for the supplements industry, which now sucks $18 billion a year from the pockets of a nation that can't seem to find enough money to pay for the real drugs its citizens need. During the 1990s, use of herbal remedies increased some 400 percent, and by 2002, two Americans in five were taking some kind of supplement or related nostrum" (p. 66). In the 1990s, manufacturers of a number of products came to realize that calling something an herbal remedy or nutritional supplement allowed them to evade the standards set for conventional prescription products (Avorn 2004), hence a new category of sketchy products emerged.

From the origin of the war on illicit drugs in the 1960s, there were critics. As prescription drugs entered the scene of abused substances, the drug war extended to them, and critics extended their concerns. Szasz (1996) explains,

> The laws that deny healthy people 'recreational' drugs also deny sick people 'therapeutic' drugs. This is partly because some of the same drugs—including our favorite scapegoats drugs, cocaine, heroin, and marijuana—have both recreational and therapeutic uses, and partly because certain drugs believed to be therapeutic for serious diseases (and sometimes available abroad) have not (yet) been approved by the FDA as both effective and safe, the basic criteria drugs must meet under present U.S. law. (p. 67)

Further, "The fact that our drug laws require people to secure a prescription for many of the drugs they want (but cannot get on the free market) fosters a mutually degrading dishonesty between physicians and patients . . ." (Szasz 1996, 134).

By 2000, counterfeiting medicine had become a significant problem. Between 2000 and 2004, the FDA saw an almost 10-fold increase of cases involving counterfeits, with one case alone involving a counterfeited medicine that may have reached some 600,000 patients (Eban 2005). The Internet was one vehicle to create and disseminate counterfeits. One could easily purchase a second-hand pill-making machine on eBay. Because prescription drug abuse and misuse had become such considerable problems, in Florida in 2003 Governor Jeb Bush signed the Prescription Drug Protection Act, which imposed restrictions on wholesalers, required background checks for those wanting license to dispense prescription drugs, and authorized serious penalties for people trafficking adultered drugs (Eban 2005).

PHARMACY SITE ANALYSES

It is absolutely unbelievable how many drugs are available on the Web and how easy they are to find. Avorn (2004) describes trying to find out what a "typical net-surfing American patient or doctor might find" on the perplexing issue of whether women should continue hormone replacement therapy. A Google search for "estrogen" revealed a wealth of information, including prominently featured shopping sites (shopping.com and yesnutritionworks.com), as well as teamestrogen.com (marketing women's bicycling apparel), estrogenmusic.com (an abandoned musician's site), a link to the *Journal of the American Medical Association*, eeletter.com (a newsletter about chemicals that interfere with hormone function), dmeb.net (home of the Darth maul Estrogen Brigade, female *Star Wars* fans), and a site for online casino and video games. Even a "medical search" using WebMD, the most widely used medical site on the net, showed advertisements before anything else (Avorn 2004).

In order to research what is available and how it is marketed, the author and her research assistants conducted Google searches of a number of the most abused prescription drugs. Of the first 10 links available in a Google search for "buy Darvon," seven clearly required no prescription and it was unclear whether two others required them. These links were to the same source, drugstore.com, which says a prescription will be required at the end of the purchase. Several of the others blatantly advertised that no prescription was needed, or provided a set of links to other online pharmacies where no prescriptions were needed. Buydarvon.net offered the following information: "Shipping and delivery is by default discreet in order to protect personal privacy and security." Losepain.com cautions users, "Before purchasing Darvon, make sure you have consulted your physician," and reminds users it is their responsibility, not that of anyone affiliated with the site, to ensure use is safe and appropriate. All the sites featured information about the drug, directions and cautions for use, side effects, and drug interactions. Pharmacyseek.com features a list of popular drugs on the left so users can link to find information and make purchases of those substances as well. It also features links to "join and save on meds," links to pharmaceutical sites requiring no prescription, and links to doctors who do phone consultations.

Another Google search, this time for "buy hydrocodone," revealed more of the same—information about the drug, links to places to buy it, and in general, no prescription required. One interesting feature of this search was the number of sites that were dead ends—that is, once you clicked to link, you were unable to go back to the previous page by clicking the back button on the computer. No prescriptions were required in the first 10 links in a search for "buy Vicodin" either. Links were either dead, offered to sell the medication without prescription, or provided links to other sites doing so. Some sites even offer a free 30-day trial period for purchasing assorted medications, such as USrxLeader.com and SafeUSMeds.com. Searches for "buy Percocet," "buy Ativan," and "buy Tamaepam" revealed more of the same—most sites provide links to other sites offering no prescription needed sales. Some provide an automatic redirect, most frequently to topmeds10.com, which offers more links to no doctor visit, no prescription sales.

Viagra, the prescription drug used to assist those with erectile dysfunction, is equally easy to obtain. The very first link that appears, the blue highlighted "sponsored link," advertises next day delivery in discreet packaging and requires no prescription. Again, only one of these top 10 links did require a prescription. Several others advertised online consultations.

Prescription drugs more commonly used by children and teens are also easy to obtain. A simple Google search for "buy Ritalin" conducted by the author revealed numerous sites where someone could purchase the substance. Perhaps the most obvious was noprescriptionneeded .com, featuring the offer, "Buy Ritalin Online through No Prescription Needed Pharmacies." Only one of the links listed on Google's first page of "hits" instructed users that Ritalin is a Schedule II substance and cannot be purchased without a valid prescription. Several of the sites specifically advertised that no prescription was needed. One site was clearly marketed to parents, as it began with this introduction: "Does your child have ADHD? Let's face it, having to go to your doctor's office each and every month for a new prescription for your child's Ritalin, Concerta, or Metadate is very inconvenient." Some sites serve as clearinghouses and link users to numerous sites where Ritalin can be obtained in a variety of dosages and amounts. Findrxonlin.com/Ritalin.htm links users to a site where the drug can be purchased. This site makes the claim, "We will provide you with info on: U.S. Doctors who will set you up with consultations over the phone and provide you with legit prescriptions for meds like Vicodin, Lortab, Lorcet, Xanax, and Valium." Most feature "Buy Now" links like those used on amazon.com to purchase books and CDs. One link, RxList.com, connected to a message board where a user had posted, "Where can I buy Ritalin without a prescription?" At the time of the search, in July 2006, the post had been viewed 1,230 times, although many of the responses did caution "Anthony" about the dangers of buying Ritalin online. As evidence of the federal government's concern about the ease in which people can purchase this drug and the potential for misuse, the first link to appear is deadiversion.usdoj.gov/consumer_ alert.htm. This is a U.S. Department of Justice Drug Enforcement Agency site cautioning users against purchasing drugs online, lists several medications that are prohibited by federal law to be purchased online, features links to stories about DEA efforts to crack down on online drug sales, and offers tips on identifying rogue pharmacies and detecting pharmaceutical drug abuse.

Similarly, a search for "buy Adderall" revealed many purveyors, and having a valid prescription does not seem to be a barrier to purchasing the amphetamine. At Drugstorescripts.com, a user is asked to complete an online questionnaire and to name a Primary Care Physician, but it is not clear that there is any follow-up with the named doctor for prescription information. One site, Drugstore.com, did emphasize that Adderall is a controlled substance that should be kept out of reach of children and never shared with others for whom it was not prescribed. Buymedsquick.com serves as a clearinghouse to connect users to online pharmacies. The site explicitly states they are not selling any drugs; rather, they connect users ONLY to legally licensed pharmacies.

Tryptamines are easy to find online. Although the DEA issued an emergency classification of some tryptamines as controlled substance, others were not classified as such, leaving some gaps that sellers and buyers can exploit. A Google search for "buy trypatamines" revealed a plethora of sites set up like e-Bay, the online auction site. Many of the sites specifically advertised "research chemicals" in their tag lines. These sites at first appear to be purely academic, describing the chemical make-up of the various tryptamines and their effects. The "offer to buy" and "offer to sell" links are more discreet than with other sites offering drugs. The Green Party Drug Group from the UK was the ninth link to appear on the day of the search, August 14, 2006. That site features information about drug-related books, information about a variety of substances, and a "Health on Drugs" section that details the effects of each substance, how to be safe using them, and how to use supplements to make them work better. Another link was to a blog where a user described his first experience with the tryptamine DIPT. The user described how he took DIPT in his dorm room in 2000, along with propranolol, a drug for heart conditions. He describes the impact on his senses, as well as the fact that he had a slightly more intense orgasm.

In addition to finding substances to purchase, someone trolling the Internet can easily find advice on doctoring pharmaceuticals and illicit drugs. A study published in June 2006 in *Drug and Alcohol Dependence* described the surge in people using the Internet to find information and exchange advice about how to tamper prescription drugs to get high. The study cited examples of Web sites where users share advice to crush and then snort time-released drugs like Ritalin or recommending that users chew pain-killing skin patches to slowly release fentanyl. Users also explain on the Web how to mix amphetamines with other chemicals in order to alter their pH, as well as which drugs should be mixed with tranquilizers (Muir 2006). The author of the study, Edward Cone, a toxicologist at ConeChem Research in Maryland, explained that people obtain prescription drugs in a variety of ways, including buying them from rogue Internet pharmacies, using other people's prescriptions, and conning doctors into writing prescriptions for bogus ailments. Cone argues that Web sites detailing with how to use prescription drugs recreationally, including recipes for how to get a better high, are the latest trend, and that these sites cause tremendous traffic. One site featuring personal accounts of drug experiences, both illicit and prescription, receives an average of 420,000 hits per day.

Toxicologists warn that tampering with prescription drugs, which surged after users realized they could get an immediate high from the time-released painkiller OxyContin by chewing them or crushing and snorting them, can be deadly. There are no official statistics on how frequently drug tampering is fatal, but it is estimated there are approximately 200 deaths in the state of Florida alone. Estimates are that in 2004, there were almost 40,000 emergency room admissions due to misuse of OxyContin, nicknamed "hillbilly heroin." One expert said he had previously been reluctant to discuss the issue publicly, for fear of giving users ideas. But now, claims toxicologist Bruce Goldberger, the information is so widespread anyone can access it through a simple Google search. Some companies are taking efforts to reduce tampering by making tablets that are harder to crush, and Novartis, makers of Ritalin, have released a one-a-day tablet that parents can give their children before school, which lessens the risk the drugs get into the wrong hands (Muir 2006). Cone, however, maintains this will do little, claiming "I just touched the tip of the iceberg in my review" (Join Together Online, July 27, 2006). "This [the Internet] clearly is a way for illegal organizations to communicate. They use it to give directions to people working for them or to sell the product itself," said Jack Riley, assistant special agent in charge of the St. Louis office of the DEA (Ratcliffe and Kohler 2006).

A simple search for "drug recipes" on Google reveals numerous sites where one can learn not only to make their own drugs, but how to combine them in unique ways. Totse.com features a page called "Speedy Drugs" where one can find recipes for making methamphetamines, as well as cocaine pudding, "half-ass crank," and "how to make crack like a drug dealer." Online recipes for making methamphetamines are one of the main reasons for the spread of meth from the west to east coasts (Sexton 2006). Neonjointcom/drugreceipes.index.html offers users recipes for LSD, methamphetamines, crack, Liquid E (Ecstasy). In addition, users of the site can learn how to get high from cough medicines and motion sickness pills, poppy seeds and nutmeg, as well as psychoactive toads. Also featured is advice on obtaining pharmaceuticals. According to McHugh (2006), recipes for crystal meth, known as "Ice" or "Tina," can be found easily online.

POLICING ONLINE PHARMACEUTICAL SALES

The sale of illegal drugs online is so big it has overwhelmed law enforcement. Government agencies claim that, while they are aware of the problem, they can do little to control these sales without significantly more resources and funding. "The system we have in place has been overrun by the volume of illegal Internet drug sales," according to Richard Stana, director of the homeland security and justice team in the General Accounting Office, which is the investigative arm of Congress (Sullivan 2004).

In the U.S., several agencies are charged, at least in part, with dealing with online drug sales. The Office of National Drug Control Policy (ONDCP), The Department of Justice (DOJ), the Federal Bureau of Investigations (FBI), the Immigration and Naturalization Service (INS), the Coast Guard, the State Department, the Central Intelligence Agency (CIA), the U.S. Agency for International Development (AID), the Food and Drug Administration (FDA), and the Federal Trade Commission (FTC) are all involved, although to what degree is unclear (Levine 1998; Posner 2000). Prevention efforts come largely from the Department of Health and Human Services and the Department of Education (Levine 1998). Many of these organizations are not well-prepared to police the Internet (Posner 2000). Utilizing skills gained from investigations of online child predators, investigators are starting to troll the Internet for drug dealers. Officers in Albany, New York, set up a sting operation when they ordered steroids, Ritalin, and methadone for a 4-foot-tall, heroin addicted airline pilot. They were able to track down and arrest the seller, Dr. David Stephenson, after the drugs arrived. DEA agents acknowledge, however, they will never be able to catch up with all the dealers this way (Skoloff 2007).

A particular difficulty is that many sites offering prescription meds originate outside the U.S., where large drug firms may make copycat pills that would be illegal here but are not there due to dramatically different safety and production standards (Herper 2005). For instance, in Brazil the law provides for three classes of drugs: the brand-names sold by big-time firms; the generics; and the similares, medicines which supposedly have the same amount of active ingredients but have not been tested on humans (Herper 2005).

Even in the U.S., online prescription drug sales is a, "very fuzzy area of the law," according to Dr. Frank Palumbo, director of the University of Maryland's Center on Drugs and Public Policy (Reaves 2002). Some designer drugs can lawfully be purchased for "research purpose," something somewhat difficult to discern (TheSite.org 2004). The Food, Drug, and Cosmetic Act (FDCA) prohibits the manufacture and distribution of misbranded and adulterated drugs. A prescription drug may be considered misbranded if it is dispensed without a proper physician's prescription (Posner 2000). Racketeer Influences and Corrupt

Organizations (RICO) laws might apply to large-scale online sellers (Levine 1998). Yet many of the sites, as noted above, offer online diagnoses and prescriptions. As each state regulates their own pharmacies, varying rules apply to Internet sites and to the issue of whether online diagnoses and prescriptions violate the FDCA (Posner 2000). To date, only one state has a full-time investigator looking into doctors writing prescriptions for online sales (Gaul and Flaherty 2003), although Kansas, Maryland, and Washington have taken legal action against doctors, pharmacies, and Web sites that provide prescription drugs with only online questionnaires (Posner 2000). The FDA has asked physicians and pharmacists for help, encouraging them to take action against those who prescribe online (Marwick 1999), and the State Federation of Medical Boards has declared that the prescription of medications based on an electronic questionnaire alone is not an acceptable standards of care (Posner 2000). Yet state laws vary regarding the issue of online questionnaires. New York and Florida prohibit physicians and pharmacists from dispensing medications without a face-to-face meeting, but in Utah doctors can prescribe Viagra and some other substances without an exam (Skoloff 2007).

It is possible to apply the Controlled Substances Act to online sales. The Controlled Substances Act prohibits the dispensing of a controlled substance without a valid prescription, so applying it also depends on whether a prescription made via an online questionnaire is valid (Posner 2000).

Since most sites purveying drugs operate by making certain claims to potential consumers, they might be regulated under the Federal Trade Commission Act (FTCA), which authorizes the Justice Department to investigate the claims made by Web sites and to bring civil proceedings if they are unfair or deceptive (Posner 2000). If an online pharmacy defrauds consumers, it is also possible to enforce federal mail and wire fraud statutes, which might be civil or criminal (Posner 2000). Generally speaking, the "learned intermediary doctrine" is the guiding principle regarding who holds the responsibility for warning clients about the possible effects of prescription medications. This doctrine has generally been interpreted to absolve manufacturers from responsibility and making doctors the responsible party. Yet this clearly becomes far more complicated when the drug is purchased online. Austin, Texas attorney J.D. Horne questions, "Never mind 'learned.' Is there an intermediary here at all?" (Tinnin 2005).

Even if they can crack down on Internet-based sales, another difficulty arises in intercepting the actual shipments. A 2003 investigation found an overwhelming number of prescription drug shipments at U.S. mail facilities. The House Energy and Commerce Subcommittee on Oversight and Investigations heard testimony describing this surge in prescription drug shipments, many of which are counterfeit, illegal, or unapproved. They also heard testimony about the rise in online sales, as well as criminal involvement in prescription drug sales. Members of Congress then discussed the role of high U.S. drug prices and inadequate Medicare coverage of prescriptions, both of which might turn people to the Internet in search of affordable drugs. Witnesses cautioned that international mail facilities are simply overwhelmed with the number of prescription drug shipments they are required to process, and thus cannot do a thorough job of investigating the shipments. For instance, the Miami international mail facility alone receives an estimated seven million drug shipments annually. In addition, because of the way the Food and Drug Administration interprets federal law, shipments identified as improper cannot quickly be destroyed, detained, or returned to sender (*USA Today* 2003).

As noted, one of the most significant challenges is the global nature of the sales. According to John Taylor, the FDA's associate commissioner for regulatory affairs, his agency is doing all that it can but is daunted by the task. "Each day thousands of individual packages containing prescription drugs are imported illegally into the U.S. simply because the sheer volume has grown to exceed the capability of FDA field personnel to properly process it" (Sullivan 2004). Jason Surks, a 19-year-old sophomore at Rutgers University, died from an overdose of prescription drugs. A look at his computer revealed that he had an account with several different online pharmacies based in Mexico (Cuomo 2006). DEA Agent Misha Pastro says it is easy to get prescription drugs in Mexico, and Mexican authorities have not been terribly cooperative in addressing the problem. Tijuana, Mexico, walking distance from the U.S. border, is home to some 1,400 pharmacies (Join Together Online, October 28, 2004).

While the FDA, DEA, Customs, and other federal agencies have apprehended some online sellers through coordinated efforts, these are merely the tip of the iceberg. They must still rely heavily on foreign law enforcement agents to collaborate. While some countries have been cooperative, others are not. In 2005, authorities announced a crackdown on sales of narcotics and psychotropic drugs being exported from India to the United States via Internet pharmacies. Indian doctors were prescribing the drugs, while U.S. citizens operated the servers, Web sites, and e-mail communications. Vicodin, Oxycontin, Ritalin, Steroids, and Viagra were all being sold through this collaboration (Siddharth 2005).

Adding to the challenge for law enforcement, the Web allows people to easily change identity and location (Reaves 2002). Further, lawmakers are, probably rightfully, concerned with censoring the Web. In 2000, the FDA, GAO, and several members of the House of Representatives called for a requirement that all online pharmacies be required to disclose their owners, their location, the doctors involved, their affiliated pharmacies, and their telephone numbers, but the legislation went nowhere. According to William Hubbard of the FDA, "getting a bill regulating the Internet is about as hard as it gets" (Gaul and Flaherty 2003). Further, Web-based material is protected as free speech, in general.

Law enforcement officers have admitted that the illegal prescription drug market in general poses a challenge, and that Web-based sales make it even more difficult. Officials at the DEA admit they are understaffed for this type of problem, and thus tend to only go after the major organizations diverting pharmaceuticals to the street market (Colvin 1995). Unlike street drug rings, which tend to cluster in major cities, illegal prescription drug sales are geographically spread out (Colvin 1995). Many states lack adequate laws to protect against "doctor shopping," thus the small-time prescription drug offender is difficult to prosecute (Colvin 1995).

SUCCESSFUL EFFORTS

There have been some successes, however. Some of the earliest successes occurred in 1998–99. The Department of Justice opened 30 cases involving drug sales on the Internet, 20 of which involved online pharmacies, with a total of over 60 different sites involved. The U.S. Attorney's office in Maryland prosecuted Dr. Pietr Herzog in 1999, who ran an Internet business in which he sold phentermine and fenfluramine, both controlled substances, based only on e-mail requests. Other prosecutions involved the unapproved online sale of gamma butyrolactone (GBL), a precursor chemical for GHB, and an indictment in Hawaii for fraudulent sales of Viagra. Two individuals were convicted in Florida for selling drugs on the Internet without a prescription with the intent to defraud and mislead (Posner 2000). In July of 1999, the Federal Trade Commission (FTC) inaugurated "Operation Cure-All," an effort to stop bogus Internet claims for products and treatments touted as cure-alls. In two years, they had identified over 800 sites and numerous usenet newsgroups offering questionable promotions (Hinkel 2000).

In March of 2004, the Bush administration announced a $138 million program to address illegal diversion of prescription drugs, including greater labeling requirements for pain medications, methods to identify individuals filling prescriptions from multiple physicians, developing training for physicians to identify patients seeking prescription drugs for illegal purposes, and cracking down on Internet sales. The program is a joint effort between the Drug Enforcement Agency, the Food and Drug Administration, the Department of Health and Human Services, and the White House Office of National Drug Control Policy. Prompting the program was evidence of rising prescription drug abuse, such as the fact that emergency room visits due to abuse of narcotic pain relievers increased 163 percent between 1995 and 2004 (Health 2004). In July 2004, the DEA arrested 10 people across the country as part of their Operation Web Try, an effort to crack down on Web-based distribution of designer drugs classified falsely by sellers as research chemicals. As part of the investigations, DEA officers intercepted an e-mail one defendant wrote to another saying he joined a Yahoo! chat room as a means of drumming up business. The response was that this was a great idea, and that the Web was how that individual initially learned about new chemicals (U.S. Drug Enforcement Agency 2005).

In 2005, Mark Kolovitch, owner of World Express Rx, pled guilty to a number of charges involving his unlawful online sale of prescription drugs. The site required only a health questionnaire and a $35 "doctors" fee in order to make a purchase. There never was a doctor, however. World Express Rx distributed Viagra, Cialis, Propecia, Celebrex, and many other prescription drugs. Owners of another online company, MyRxforless of Florida, were also charged because they purchased and then sold the drugs from Kolovitch's site (Tryon 2005). In October 2005, Sarasota, Florida attorney Ted Eastmoore filed a lawsuit targeting 17 Internet-based doctors and 19 Internet pharmacies for their role in the overdose death of 44-year-old Robin Bartlett in 2003. Bartlett purchased over 4,000 doses of prescription drugs, including hydrocodone, Alprazolam, Adipex, Carisoprodol, and Methocarbamol, online in the last 3½ months of her life alone (Tryon 2005).

In September 2005, the DEA announced they had completed Operation CYBERRx, a collaborative drug task force investigation targeting pharmaceutical drug traffickers. They arrested 18 people they called the "ringleaders" of 4,600 pharmacy Web sites for selling illegal pharmaceutical drugs (States News Service 2005). Another operation, Cyber Chase, netted the arrest of doctor Akhil Bansal, who was working with his father in Philadelphia to supply millions of pharmaceutical products made in India without prescriptions. The federal government seized $4 million from his bank account, in addition to the more than five million pills and 238 pounds of ketamine, known as a club drug (Smith 2005). A lawyer who helped an online pharmacy acquire narcotics and assisted the founder in hiding company assets was indicted in early 2006. He was charged with conspiracy to distribute and dispense controlled substances, wire fraud, and unlawful distribution and dispensing of controlled substance and misbranded drugs. Daniel Adkins allegedly helped Xpress Pharmacy Direct fill 72,000 illegal prescriptions for narcotic painkillers. He faces up to 20 years in prison and a $250,000 fine (Associated Press 2006). In another effort to end prescription drug abuse, the

DEA launched a toll-free number in 2005 (1-877-RxAbuse) for reporting abuse (United States Drug Enforcement Agency 2005). In June, 2006, the ONDCP announced the first Synthetic Drug Control Strategy, aimed at controlling methamphetamine production and prescription drug abuse (Join Together Online, July 20, 2006). In addition, many states are using the Web to "out" people convicted of making or selling methamphetamines. Montana, Tennessee, Minnesota, and Illinois have these online lists, and Georgia, Maine, Oklahoma, Oregon, Washington, and West Virginia are considering them. Interestingly, Graham Boyd, director of the ACLU's Drug Policy Litigation Project, has argued that these online lists might be a good resource for people to learn where to buy meth (Join Together Online, August 25, 2006).

Pharmaceutical companies are obviously interested in shutting down rogue pharmacy sites. In February 2006, Richard Cowley was convicted of counterfeit labeling and providing false trademarks on pharmaceutical drugs. Investigators at Eli Lilly and Company first discovered Cowley was using the Web site bestonlineviagra.com to advertise and sell prescription drugs such as Cialis (manufactured by Eli Lilly) at prices they thought suggested the drugs were stolen or counterfeit. Lilly investigators purchased the substances and arranged a meeting via email. When they obtained the drugs, they found them to be indeed counterfeit. The investigators notified the FBI in April 2005. The FBI eventually arrested Cowley as well as his supply source in China. Chinese officials seized 440,000 counterfeit Viagra and Cialis pills as well as pill bottles and labeling materials (States News Service 2006). In 2006, a 71-year-old Shreveport, Louisiana doctor was one of seven convicted of approving thousands of online prescriptions for patients. Edward Schwab never saw any of the people for whom he authorized 19,000 prescriptions. Schwab received $8 for every prescription he wrote (Join Together Online, April 11, 2006). The National Association of Boards of Pharmacies (NABP) has developed a list of licensed online pharmacies, available at www.nabp.info. To help consumers identify which online pharmacies are in compliance with state and federal guidelines, the NABP has created the Verified Internet Pharmacy Practice Sites Seal as well (Stoppler 2005). Many of the major pharmaceutical companies are paying third parties to observe blogs about their products (Pharma Marketletter 2006).

Other countries have dealt with the problem differently. Russia has perhaps taken the most extreme response, banning all sites offering drugs (ITAR-TASS News Agency 2006). In 2005, Canada's Health Minister Ujjal Dosanjh announced the country would be restricting Internet pharmacies from selling drugs to U.S. consumers.

One suggestion to reduce the number of online purchases of prescription drugs is to work with domain registrars to eliminate access to certain domain names. According to Joshua Halpern, Vice President of IntegirChain, explained to a House subcommittee on Energy and Commerce that, "Consumers become accustomed to accessing a Web site via its domain name. So, if we can force Web sites to change their domain names with increased frequency . . . that would make it more difficult for consumers to get to the Web sites" (Thompson 2006, 108).

In August 2006, Republican Senator Jeff Sessions and Democrat Dianne Feinstein introduced a bill to regulate online pharmaceutical sales and sales of controlled substances. The Online Pharmacy Consumer Protection Act of 2006 would prohibit sale of controlled substances and prescription drugs without a prescription and make unlawful distribution of those drugs online a criminal act. In introducing the legislation, Feinstein acknowledged the case of Ryan Haight, a San Diego teen who had become addicted to painkillers he purchased online with a debit card his parents gave him to buy baseball cards. Haight eventually overdosed (Sessions 2006).

In conclusion, it is clear that the Internet has helped facilitate increasing prescription drug abuse rates, and that popular stereotypes of the typical user and dealer are in flux as this book goes to press. What is less clear is how, or even if, law enforcement should respond to the challenges listed above. Should the drug war be extended to better address prescription drug abuse? Should drug warriors prepare themselves to police the Web? These are questions that will be grappled with in the coming years.

KEY TERMS

Controlled substance
Online pharmacy
Prescription drug abuse

REFERENCES

Associated Press. January 25, 2006. Lawyer indicted for alleged role in illegal Internet pharmacy case. Retrieved February 6, 2006 from Lexis Nexis Academic database.

Avorn, J. 2004. *Powerful Medicines*. NY: Alfred A. Knopf.

Birnhanemaskel, M. March 23, 2005. Addiction. *Rocky Mountain News*, B1.

Boehm, E., B. Holmes, L. Bishop, and S. McAuley. January 13, 2003. Who buys prescription drugs online? Retrieved August 17, 2006, from www.forrester.com

BuySafeDrugs.info. November 14, 2005. I-team 10 investigation: The hidden dangers of online drugs. Retrieved August 17, 2006, from www.buysafedrugs.info/reorts/nbsreport.html

Colvin, R. 1995. *Prescription Drug Abuse: The Hidden Epidemic*. Omaha, NE: Addicus Books.

Consumer alert. n.d. DEADiversion. Retrieved June 26, 2006, from www.deadiversion.usdoj.gov/consumer_alert.html

Corn-Revere, R. July 24, 2002. Caught in the seamless Web: Does the Internet's Global reach justify less freedom of speech? *CATO Institute Briefing Papers*, 71.

Crellin, J. 2004. *A Social History of Medicines in the Twentieth Century*. Binghampton, NY: Pharmaceutical Products Press.

Critser, G. 2005. *Generation Rx*. Boston, MA: Houghton-Mifflin.

Crowley, B. 2004. Lower prescription drug costs don't tell the whole story. Retrieved August 29, 2006, from, www.aims.ca/library/prI1.pdf

Cuomo, C. March 9, 2006. Pharm country: Internet prescriptions. Nightline—ABC News transcripts. Retrieved March 22, 2006, from Lexis Nexis database.

Davis, H. November 13, 2003. One-click shopping for illegal drugs. Penn Current Online. Retrieved November 1, 2005, from www.upenn.edu/pennnews/current/2003/111303/research.html

Diller, L. 1998. *Running on Ritalin*. New York: Bantam.

Drug Week. April 29, 2005. Survey indicates drug dependencies often supported via the Internet. p. 324.

Eban. K. 2005. *Dangerous Doses*. Orlando, FL: Harcourt.

Eberstadt, M. September 25, 2005. A prescribed threat: Among the harshest critics of the child wonderdrug regimen? Think rock icons. *Los Angeles Times*: 5.

Firth, M. April 18, 2006. Mypills.co.uk. *The Independent [London]*: 36.

Fox, S. 2004, October 10. Prescription drugs online. Pew Internet & American Life Project. Retrieved June 26, 2006, from www.pewinternet.org

Gaul, G., and M. Flaherty. October 20, 2003. Internet trafficking in narcotics has surged. *Washington Post* [Online version].

Global Youth Network. 2006. Illicit use of Tamazepam. Retrieved August 29, 2006, from www.unodc.org/youthnet_action_good_practice_temaepam.html

Goldberg, C. January 26, 2006. Studies link psychosis, teenage marijuana use. *The Boston Globe*: A1.

Grow, B., B. Elgin, and A. Weintraub. December 18, 2006. Bitter pills: More and more people are buying prescription drugs from shady online marketers. That could be hazardous to their health. *BusinessWeek* [Online edition]: 110.

Health, E. March 1, 2004. Internet pharmacies targeted in crackdown of drug abuse. *CongressDaily*: 7–9.

Herper, M. May 23, 2005. Bad medicine. *Forbes*: 202.

Hickman, M. June 22, 2006. "Russian roulette" of buying prescription drugs on the Internet. *The Independent* [online version]. Retrieved June 26, 2006, from http://news.independent.co.uk/uk/health_medical/article1094701.ece

Hinkel, J. January–February 2000. Buying drugs online: Convenient and private, but beware of 'rogue sites.' U.S. Food and Drug Administration. Available at www.fda.gov/fdac/features/200/100_online.html

Hubbard, W. March 18, 2004a. Statement before United States Food and Drug Administration. Retrieved October 28, 2005, from www.fda.gov/ola/2004/internetdrugs0318.html

Hubbard, W. July, 14, 2004b. Statement before the Committee on the Judiciary, U.S. Senate. Retrieved August 29, 2006, from www.usfda.gov/ola/2004/importeddrugs0714.html

Ingham, R. October 18, 2005. Internet and Tamiflu: Bird flu scare exposes glaring loophole. Agence France Presse. Retrieved February 6, 2006, from Lexis Nexis Academic database.

Internetworldstats.com. September 30, 2005. World Internet users and population statistics. Retrieved November 1, 2005, from www.internetworldstats.com/stats.html

ITAR-TASS News Agency. January 27, 2006. Russia bans Internet sites offering drugs. Retrieved January 27, 2006, from Lexis Nexis Academic database.

Join Together Online. October 28, 2004. U.S. unable to stop flow of prescription drugs from Mexico. Retrieved March 4, 2006, from www.jointogetheronline.org

Join Together Online. December 29, 2004. Drugs, phishing top 2004 list of spam terms. Retrieved January 27, 2006, from www.jointogetheronline.org

Join Together Online. February 3, 2005. Drug sales soaring online. Retrieved October 20, 2005, from www.jointogtheronline.com

Join Together Online. March 2, 2005. Most online drug sales illegal, UN says. Received March 4, 2005, from www.jointogether.org/sa/news/summaries

Join Together Online. May 9, 2005. Adderall used to boost school performance. Retrieved May 11, 2005, from www.jointogether.org

Join Together Online. October 31, 2005. Prescription meds Florida's top drug problem. Retrieved November 2, 2005, from www.jointogetheronline.com

Join Together Online. December 13, 2005. Elderly caught selling prescription drugs. Retrieved December 15, 2005, from www.jointogetheronline.org

Join Together Online. February 8, 2006. Suicide brings attention to teen prescription drug use. Retrieved February 8, 2006, from www.jointogetheronline.org

Join Together Online. February 9, 2006. Prescription drug abuse, smoking higher among teen girls. Retrieved February 11, 2006, from www.jointogtheronline.org

Join Together Online. March 3, 2006a. Abuse of prescription drugs seen as global problem. Retrieved March 4, 2006, from www.jointogetheronline.org

Join Together Online. March 3, 2006b. Addict says it's easy to con docs for prescription meds. Retrieved March 4, 2006, from www.jointogetheronline.org

Join Together Online. April 11, 2006. Local Iowa pharmacy an Internet drug hub. Retrieved April 12, 2006, from www.jointogetheronline.org

Join Together Online. June 22, 2006. Narcotic pain meds become drug of choice. Available at www.jointogetheronline.com

Join Together Online. June 28, 2006. Students turn to 'smart pills' to boost performance. Retrieved June 30, 2006, from www.jointogether.org

Join Together Online. June 28, 2006. Telemedicine taking off, especially in rural communities. Retrieved June 30, 2006, from www.jointogetheronline.org

Join Together Online. July 14, 2006. More web sites offer unfettered prescription drug sales, CASA says. Retrieved July 17, 2006, from www.jointogetheronline.org

Join Together Online. July 20, 2006. ONDCP releases prescription tracking strategy. Available at www.jointogetheronline.com

Join Together Online. July 27, 2006. Internet offers how-to's for drug use. Retrieved July 28, 2006, from www.jointogetheronline.com

Join Together Online. August 25, 2006. Some states 'out' methamphetamine dealers online. Retrieved August 28, 2006, from www.jointogetheronline.org

Kershaw, S. December 1, 2005. Hooked on the web: Help is on the way. *The New York Times—Late edition*: G1.

Kweder, S. July 26, 2006. Statement before subcommittee on Criminal Justice, Drug Policy, and Human Rights, U.S. House of Representatives. Retrieved August 29, 2006, from www.fda.gov/ola/2006/rxdrugabuse0726.html

KZAT. March 4, 2004. 14-year-old buys prescription drugs online. Retrieved August 17, 2006, from www.kzat.com/news/2897160.html

Leinwand. D. June 13, 2006. Prescription drugs find place in teen culture. *USA Today*: 1A.

Lenhart, A., M. Madden, and P. Hilton. July 27, 2005. Teens and technology: Youth are leading the transition to a fully wired and mobile nation. Pew Internet Surveys. Retrieved November 1, 2005, from www.pew.internet.org/PPF/r/162/report_display.asp

Levine, H. 1998. *The Drug Problem*. Austin, TX: Raintree Steck-Vaughn.

Lexis Nexis. July 18, 2006. Teens, technology, and drugs: An inside look. PR Newswire. Retrieved August 15, 2006, from Lexis Nexis Academic database.

Lichtenstein, R. June 2005. Preschoolers in the Prozac nursery. Health A-Z. Retrieved September 15, 2005, from www.healthatoz/com/healthatoz/Atoz/hc/chi/kids/alert03252000.jsp

Lopes, G. February 17, 2007. Patients get wrong drugs online: Anti-psychotic substituted for depression, insomnia medicine. *The Washington Times*: C11.

Lyons, B. March 4, 2007. Internet brings drug dealing into the home. *The Times-Union*.

Marwick, C. 1999. FDA has asked physicians and pharmacists for help. *Journal of the American Medical Association* 281 (100): 975–6.

McHugh, H. May 7, 2006. Recipes for danger sex drug found on Internet. *The People*: 31.

Medindia. n.d. Prescription drug abuse. Retrieved August 29, 2006 from www.medindia.net/patients/patientinfo/drugtoxicity-abuse.html

Meergaard, L. July 21, 2006. Drug errors plentiful, costly. *The Miami Herald*: 5A.

Meier, B. 2003. *Painkiller: A "Wonder" Drug's Trail of Addiction and Death*. NY: Rodale.

Mercogliano, C. 2003. *Teaching the Restless*. Boston, MA: Beacon

Midgely, C. February 21, 2003. Kiddie coke: A new peril in the playground. TimesOnline. Retrieved December 1, 2007, from www.timesonline.co.uk/tol/life_and_style/article884809.ece

Monarch Avalon. October 2005. Prescription for trouble. *Girl's Life* 12 (2): 68.

MSNBC. January 29, 2002. Xanax often abused. Retrieved August 17, 2006, from www.benzo.org/uk/msnbc1.html

Muir, H. June 3, 2006. An epidemic of home-made hits. *New Scientist* 190.

Musto, D. (Ed.). 2002a. *Drugs in America: A Documentary History*. NY: New York University Press.

Musto, D. 2002b. *The Quick Fix Drug Control: Politics and Policies in a Period of Increasing Substance Abuse, 1963–1981*. NY: New York University Press.

National Drug Intelligence Center. November 2004. Pharmaceutical drug threat assessment. Retrieved August 16, 2006, from www.doj.gov/ndic

NIMH. March 6, 2007. Reference for reference page should read National Institute of Mental Health. Global use of ADHD medications rises dramatically. NIMH Sciencce Update. Retrieved December 1, 2007, from www.nimh.nih.gov/science-news/2007/global_use_of_adhd_medications_rises_dramatically.shtml

Nicklin, J. June 9, 2000. The latest trend: Mixing prescription drugs with other substances. *Chronicle of Higher Education* [Online version].

Office of National Drug Control Policy. October 2002. Drugs, Youth, and the Internet. Department of Justice Information Bulletin.

Pharma Marketletter. July 26, 2006. Drug firm keeps out of on-line conversation. Marketletter Publications Ltd. Retrieved August 15, 2006, from Lexis Nexis Academic database.

Piriani, C. March 27, 2006. Child drugs linked to heart attack. The Australian News. Retrieved December 1, 2007, from www.theaustraliannews.com/au/story/0,20867,18614238-2702,00.html

Pisik, B. April 16, 2001. Online traffickers feed 'pill-popping culture.' *Insight on The News*: 27.

Posner, E. May 25, 2000. Statement of Ethan M. Posner. Retrieved October 28, 2005, from www.cybercrime.gov/posner.html

PR.com. July 24, 2006. Canada's ADHD drug warning lifts lid on questionable diagnosis. Retrieved August 17, 2006, from www.pr.com/press-release/13298

Ratcliffe, H., and J. Kohler, J. May 19, 2006. Using Internet for drug deals is not unusual, authorities say. *St. Louis Post-Dispatch*: C4.

Reaves, J. February 27, 2002. Clicking for fix: Drugs online. *Time* [Online version].

Revill, J. November 5, 2006. Cancer patients turn to Internet for cheap drugs. *The Observer* England [online edition]: p. 1.

Riedberg, R. (Producer) 2006. *Big Business, Big Pharma* [Motion picture]. Media Education Foundation.

Sanders, W. August 11, 2006. Penethylemene use amongst young people. Paper presented at the Society for the Study of Social Problems annual conference, Montreal, Canada.

Sessions, J. August 4, 2006. Sessions and Feinstein introduce online pharmacy bill. *Congressional Quarterly*. Retrieved August 15, 2006, from Lexis Nexis Academic database.

Sexton, R. August 11, 2006. Impact of peudoephedrine legislation on illicit methamphetamines production "cooking" in rural Kentucky and Arkansas. Paper presented at the Society for the Study of Social Problems annual conference, Montreal, Canada.

Siddharth, S. April 27, 2005. Illegal drug trade outsourced to India, too. *Asia Times* [Online version]. Retrieved October 28, 2005, from www.asiatimes.com

Skoloff, B. March 17, 2007. *Illicit Internet Pharmacies called '21st Century Drug Traffickers.'* The Associated Press.

Smith, J. September 19, 2005. For young doc, Internet drug case 'is a nightmare.' *Philadelphia Daily News*. Retrieved February 6, 2006, from Lexis Nexis Academic database.

Spillane, J. 2004a. "The road to the Harrison Narcotics Act: Drugs and their control, 1875–1918." In *Federal Drug Control: The Evolution of Policy and Practice*, edited by J. Erlen and J. Spillanne, 1–24. Binghamton, NY: Pharmaceutical Products Press.

Spillane, J. 2004b. "Building a drug control regime, 1919–1930." In *Federal Drug Control: The Evolution of Policy and Practice*, edited by J. Erlen and J. Spillanne, 25–59. Binghamton, NY: Pharmaceutical Products Press.

States News Service. September 21, 2005. DEA disables major pharmaceutical Internet scheme. Retrieved March 22, 2006, from Lexis Nexis Academic database.

States News Service. February 6, 2006. Internet distributor of counterfeit Pharmaceutical drugs convicted. Retrieved March 22, 2006, from Lexis Nexis Academic database.

Stoppler, M. May 17, 2005. Buying prescription drugs online—are the risks worth it? Retrieved June 26, 2006, from www.medicinenet.com

Substance Abuse and Mental Health Services Administration. 2005. Drug Abuse Warning Network Report, 2005. Available at www.samhsa.gov

Sullivan, M. August 4, 2004. Online drug sales targeted. *PC World* [Online Version].

Sullum, J. 2003. *Saying Yes*. NY: Jeremy P. Tarcher/Putnam.

Swann, J. 2004. "The FDA and the practice of pharmacy: Prescription drug regulation before 1968." In *Federal Drug Control: The Evolution of Policy and Practice*, edited by J. Erlen and J. Spillane, 145–74. Binghamton, NY: Pharmaceutical Products Press.

Szasz, T. 1996. *Our Right to Drugs*. Syracuse, NY: Syracuse University Press.

Temin, P. 1980. *Taking Your Medicine*. Cambridge, MA: Harvard University Press.

TheSite.org. 2004. Buying Drugs Online. Retrieved October 28, 2005, from www.thesite.org/drinkanddrugs/drugsafety/thelaw/buyingdrugsonline.html

Thompson, C. January 15, 2006. Internet experts testify about illegal drug sales. *American Journal of Health System-Pharmacy*: 108, 110.

Tiffen, R. October 15, 2005. Teenagers research drugs on Internet. *The New Zealand Herald*. Retrieved October 15, 2005, from www.nzherald.co.nz

Tinnin, A. October 19, 2005. Online pharmacies are new vehicle for raising some old legal issues. *Kansas City Missouri Daily Record* [online version].

Tryon, T. October 2005. Wife's death leads husband to sue Internet prescription purveyors. *Sarasota herald-Tribune*: F1.

United States Drug Enforcement Agency. April 30, 2006. International Internet drug ring shattered. Retrieved August 29, 2006, from www.dea.gov/pubs/pressrel/pr042005.html

USA Today. June 25, 2003. Problems grow with drugs bought on Net. p. 5B.

USA Today. June 18, 2004. Some Internet drug sales put buyers at risk. p. 3B.

U.S. Department of Justice. 2005. Internet pharmaceutical operator receives 51 month prison sentence. Retrieved August 16, 2006, from www.doj.gov/opg/pr/2005/January/05

U.S. Drug Enforcement Agency. 2005. U.S. arrests Internet merchants of designer drugs. Retrieved August 17, 2006, from www.dea.gov/pubs/stats/newrel/nyco72304.html

U.S. News & World Report. September 20, 2004. Shams and scams, 137 (9): 50.

Veronin, M., and B. Youan, B. July 23, 2004. Magic bullet gone astray: Medications and the Internet. *Science*: 481.

Chapter 7

Charges Without Borders: Consumer Credit Card Fraud in Ghana

Elizabeth L. Davison
Appalachian State University, North Carolina

Elizabeth L. Davison is an associate professor in the Department of Sociology and Social Work at Appalachian State University. She primarily teaches research methods and statistics. During the summer months, she enjoys traveling with her students to Ghana to share with them a resilient culture and introduce them to some of the friendliest people on the planet. Her primary research interests are in the areas of neighborhood crime and Internet studies. She has recently produced documentaries about her travels to Ghana and Appalachian history.

Abstract

This chapter reports on consumer credit card fraud originating from Ghana. Ghana is a developing West African country where less than 5 percent of the population has ever used a computer. As access to the super highway of global information spreads throughout Ghana, so are the misuses of the emerging Internet technologies to access first-world resources. This chapter reports on the processes of how some Ghanaians are using their computer skills and public Internet cafes to process stolen credit card numbers and for online panhandling. The chapter discusses (1) how the stolen credit card numbers are obtained; (2) how the credit card numbers are used to purchase merchandise from the United States and have it shipped to Ghana; and (3) reveals the elaborate international networking that is required to sustain the illegal Internet activities.

The following story is based on fictional characters, places, and organizations from composite information I collected while researching Internet usage in Ghana.

Denise Sederick checked into the Bacana Hotel in Accra, the capital city of Ghana, the night before her flight back to the United States. Her employer, Global Hands, funds clean water supplies and provides childhood immunizations for remote villages around the world. She had spent an intense month traveling throughout Ghana monitoring the operations of Global Hands Organization–sponsored sites. Her nonprofit work is very meaningful and fulfilling, but the travel takes its toll. She is looking forward to returning home to her dogs, hot showers, and processed sugary foods.

The Bacana Hotel is a four-star resort hotel and costs around $150 a night, which is comparable to U.S. lodging costs. As is customary in many parts of the world, Denise uses her credit card to pay for her room since she has spent all her Cedis (Ghanaian currency) prior to her departure. Despite the modern hotel with all the expected amenities of a four-star establishment, her credit card is imprinted on a carbon copy machine instead of swiped into a computer system that connects immediately to a credit card authorization data bank, as you would expect in the United States. Little does Denise know she is leaving behind more than the imprint of her credit card for the room charge.

When registering at the hotel, Denise is asked for her passport information and home address to assist in processing her credit card information. To Denise, the registration protocol seems fairly customary for international hotels. Working behind the registration desk on the day Denise checks in is Isaac Kufuor, Reservations General Manager. Isaac speaks great American English and is quite personable. He has interacted with numerous tourists and knows the questions to ask to put them at ease, such as "Have you enjoyed your visit to Ghana?," "Have you seen other parts of Africa?," "Did you try fufu?" . . . He has worked at the Bacana Hotel for six years and now earns around $50 a month. His friends envy his cushy job in the posh hotel and the money he earns, but they are especially jealous of his connections to Obrunies (the Ghanaian term for foreigners).

Not long after Denise was back home in the States enjoying a cappuccino and cheese cake with her friends, Isaac had started an elaborate processing of her credit card that would ultimately lead to more charges than just a night's stay at the Bacana Hotel. Isaac took Denise's credit card information to the streets of Accra to sell to the highest bidder. Since he had complete credit card information (i.e., a credit card number, expiration date, and home address), he is able to sell the credit information for a fetching price of $50.

Isaac sells the information to Kwesi, a college student at Central Cape University. Kwesi is a business major hoping to start his own restaurant soon after he graduates in a year. Kwesi buys stolen credit card numbers from time to time. Compared to the majority of Ghanaians who live on $2 a day, Kwesi's family is well off and he has the necessary discretionary funds to buy stolen credit cards.

Kwesi resides in a crowded dorm room with four other college students. They attend classes and have limited access (long lines) to the few aging computer labs on campus. However, Kwesi manages to be online more than most college students do. He is a regular at the Central City's Internet Café that has satellite Internet connection and modern computer stations for the tourists traveling through the area. He maintains friendship with most of the Internet Café staff and has learned how to surf the Net, IM, and word process.

Using the computers at the Internet Café is a bit pricey, around 80 cents an hour. Kwesi always pays for one hour of browsing but when the hour elapses, he reboots the system in a "certain way" that his staff friends have shown him to bypass the login system. No one seems to notice or care that Kwesi is at the Internet Café for hours, despite only paying for one hour.

Kwesi has planned to order a laptop for awhile but was waiting for the right time, and more importantly, the right credit card. Finally, Kwesi will be able to purchase a laptop with the newly acquired credit card! But first he has a bit of ground work to do. He will order the laptop from the American Electronics "R" Us Company, but he knows that this company, as with most American businesses, will not ship to Ghana. Kwesi, who has never traveled outside of Ghana, has to have someone residing in the United States to ship him the computer. He logs on to his romancematchmaker.com account, which he joined using a previously purchased stolen credit card number, and checks his messages. Melissa has left him a note! Because of the 6-hour time difference, Kwesi rarely gets to exchange messages with Melissa in real time, but for three months they have consistently written to each other about their lives, interests, and love for each other.

Melissa is one of several online romances that Kwesi maintains. He has created an online persona for all his cyber pals. Online he is a 32-year-old single male who runs a National Government Organization (NGOs are nonprofit organization) for homeless kids, a cause he knows will tug at the hearts of many European and American women. In his e-mails, Kwesi writes and weaves a story about the kids he is helping and often invites Melissa (and others) to come to Ghana. Until now, Kwesi has never asked Melissa for anything and has always responded to her messages. He frequently tells her she is a beautiful, wonderful person and hopes that God will continue to bless her.

Now Kwesi composes a response to Melissa's latest e-mail. He is glad to hear things are better for her at work, and he talks a bit about the success and excitement of Ghana's national soccer team. Kwesi then adds he has ordered a laptop for his NGO and explains the computer company will not ship to Ghana and asks if she will ship the box to him.

Upon reading Kwesi's e-mail the next day, Melissa considers his request and decides to forward the package. She figures she will have to pay for the shipment from the United States to Ghana, but she trusts her Ghanaian friend and likes the idea of being able to help the less fortunate children that Kwesi's organization assists. The shipping request sounds reasonable, and she doesn't think a thing about whether Kwesi is able to afford the laptop or how he paid for it. Like most Americans, Melissa has no idea of how low the wages are in Ghana and assumes that most world citizens have credit cards and are able to shop online. Melissa agrees to ship the computer to Kwesi and in doing so, is unknowingly becoming an accessory to a crime.

Since Kwesi is uncertain how "fresh" the credit card information is, he goes to a known online credit card verification Web site to make certain the credit card account is still active. Verifying that the credit card information is still good, Kwesi proceeds to order the laptop giving Melissa's address for the shipping information. Over the next few days he tracks the shipping information, like most online consumers, waiting for Melissa to receive the package. He continues to write to Melissa to maintain the friendship and ensure that she will ship him the package.

As instructed, Melissa mails the package overseas to Kwesi's post office box in Ghana. He has provided her with the address and a fabricated last name. Kwesi knows the package will take two to three weeks to arrive in Ghana where his post office "friend" is on the lookout for the package. Kwesi has to pay dearly for his post office pal to deliver the box, usually around $20 a box depending on what is shipped, and sometimes offers him some of the merchandise. Kwesi is hoping the post office friend will not open the box and discover the laptop because if this happens, he will probably have to pay a higher bribe.

All goes as planned! Approximately two months after Denise's stay at the Bacana Hotel, Kwesi has his laptop and Denise has an unexpected $1,200 charge on her credit card statement.

COMPUTER TECHNOLOGIES IN GHANA

Ghana, with a population of 22 million, is a country located on the western coast of Africa. It is a developing country where the GDP per capita is $2,600 compared to $43,500 in the United States (Central Intelligence Agency 2006). Ghana is considered one of the more economically advanced, progressive, and stable sub-Sahara African countries, but despite its relative good standing among other African nations, Ghana lags behind many Asian countries, the United States, and Western Europe in **computer technology**.

Meager incomes do not provide enough money for buying computers and all the necessary software and accessories. Most Ghanaian public schools cannot provide textbooks for their pupils, and can afford only less computer access. Few businesses, government organizations, and medical facilities are able to take advantage of existing computer technologies. Whereas Pew Internet & American Life Project (2006) report that 73 percent of the U.S. adults (over 18) are online, the best estimate for Ghana is that only about 1 percent of Ghanaians have used a computer, as of 2002 (Central Intelligence Agency 2006).

Zachary (2004) provides a great discussion of the technological challenges Ghana faces in keeping step with the rest of the wired world. Ghana lacks the government policy and fiscal support to bring computers to the Republic on a massive scale. Furthermore, there is a national lack of a knowledge base on how to build, use, and maintain the technology. Few technologically skilled people stay in Ghana (i.e., brain drain), and few places in Ghana offer adequate affordable training. There is also the issue of assimilation; the technological standards that are implemented in the Western world cannot seamlessly be adopted in a culture with different values and circumstances. Frequent power outages and a complicated land ownership system prohibit many businesses from establishing roots in Ghana.

Despite the many obstacles, Ghanaian Internet users are growing by leaps and bounds. I believe the rate of computer technology diffusion is happening at a faster pace than can be documented. Thanks to satellite technology, **Internet cafés** can bypass the concerns over infrastructure, such as lack of phone lines, to connect to the Internet. As a result, Internet cafés have sprung up all over Ghana. As typical in most places, the access is more widely available in urban areas, but increasingly the Ghanaian population is logging onto the Internet.

THE RESEARCH SETTING

During the spring of 2004, I spent a semester in Ghana exploring how a third-world community uses Internet technology. Given that Ghanaians have different values and circumstances than the U.S. citizens, I was curious if Ghanaian use of the emerging computer technologies would differ from that found in the United States. I wondered if the standard technologies (such as Microsoft operating systems, e-mail, and word processing) and human nature (such as it is) would determine universal computer usage, or would cultural differences supersede all else leading to different practices of Internet technologies? Although I found a lot of typical applications of computer technology in Ghana, I also discovered some highly innovative misuse of the Internet and computer technology that is largely determined by third-world circumstances.

While visiting Ghana I stayed in an urban area along the coast where a satellite linked Internet café had opened up four months prior to my arrival. The cost of using the Internet café per hour was around 78 cents. Put in perspective this is expensive, even from an American standpoint. Given that most Americans get unlimited Internet connection at home for around $20 a month, less than a dollar a day, the 78 cents an hour is expensive. Even the staff at the Internet café, where I collected my data, made only 17 cents an hour or around $28 a month and could not afford to browse the Net beyond the two free hours they were allotted a month.

Although there were several Internet cafés in the area where I was staying, the satellite linked café did the bulk of the business. It was not the cheapest Internet café in town, but it offered the highest number of modern computer stations, lots of staff assistants, and foremost, it had the fastest Internet connection. The cost to use the more modern Internet café was only about 10 cents an hour more than the other smaller outfits in town, and most people felt the faster connection justified the higher price. I estimated that around 80 percent of all the computer use in the area transpired at this one Internet café. Very few businesses in the area used computers; the university, bank, and hospital are the main exceptions. I met Ghanaian business leaders and college professors who used the Internet café as their primary source for computer resources since a fast Internet connection was not standard in universities and businesses.

RESEARCH METHODS

I conducted interviews and made observations over a 10-week period while hanging out at the Internet café. I generally would be at the café for a couple of hours a day and tried to vary the times of day I visited. In addition to the 32 computer stations, the café offered scanning, printing, typing, telephone, and faxing services. There were usually three to four workers on hand that were easily identified by their uniforms: a white golf shirt with the Café's logo and blue pants. The Internet café was owned by an American and employed around 20 Ghanaian workers, most of which were male.

Since my initial research focus was to study how Ghanaians used Internet and computer technologies, I made observations, conducted interviews, and administered an online survey. The survey turned out to be a disaster because Ghanaians are not as familiar with taking surveys as Americans. As a result, what I thought would take 10 minutes to complete took my subjects 45 minutes to read and then type in their responses. Many of the respondents became frustrated and left their surveys incomplete.

Around the third week, I became suspicious of a few guys who always congregated in the back corner of the Café and appeared to hide their work. They would minimize their windows if I came by or huddle around a workstation to block the monitor's views from outsiders. At first I thought they were trying to hide porn but after inquiring, I found out about the stolen credit card numbers. Once I realized what was going on, I started asking more questions. As with any qualitative analysis into deviant or criminal behavior, I had to assure everyone involved they could trust me if they disclosed information about their illegal activities. Eventually, I conducted several interviews with the café workers who were familiar with the process (informants), and they introduced me to a couple of guys who used the stolen credit cards on a regular basis. Other than the staff members, I purposely never learned the names of the stolen credit card users.

HOW IT WORKS: SPINNING STOLEN CREDIT CARD NUMBERS

When I try to describe the typical business in Ghana, I tell folks to imagine walking through a flea market where people are selling odd sundries or a limited product line. That is the type of business you will see while walking the streets of Ghana. People are selling a few wares or food items in their stands or on their makeshift tables. Larger urban areas in Ghana will have indoor marts that are more in-line with how Westerners are used to shopping (lots of inventory). There are no McDonalds or other familiar chains, but you can find a few typical gas station convenience stores scattered throughout Ghana.

The reality is that most businesses in Ghana do not have computers, hardly any capital, and they certainly are not set up to accept credit cards as legal tender! The exception to the use of credit cards in Ghana is the resort hotels that cater to tourists and accept credit cards as payment. The hotels are the primary place where credit card numbers are compromised by the employees behind the desk.

In addition to limited credit card usages in Ghana, few Ghanaians are able to obtain credit cards. It is hard to imagine a world where credit card applications do not flood your mailbox or where they are not offered to you at the checkout line, but that is the reality in Ghana.

The stolen credit card information is usually sold in the streets of Accra, the capital city. The more complete the information (card number, expiration date, name, and address) is, the higher is the selling price. Price ranges for the credit cards with complete information are from $40–50, but everything is negotiable as with any purchase in Ghana. Credit card numbers with less complete information are sold in bulk; typically, a person buys five numbers to start out. The buyer is not guaranteed that the numbers will work but if none of the numbers work, there may be some negotiation about receiving credit for future card numbers.

Once credit card numbers are purchased, the challenge is to be able to successfully use the card. There are many Web sites like elfquin.com where a credit card's account status can be verified. The likelihood that hotel credit card numbers are still active is usually good since the victims are not aware their credit card number is hijacked until they see a felonious charge on their statement. By only stealing the card information and not the card itself, there is a greater possibility that the card information can be used. By contrast, having a wallet stolen or actually misplacing a credit card usually prompts someone to immediately close a credit card account.

Processing a credit card online takes computer skills and money (a point that will be analyzed later in this chapter). College students and Internet café employees are typical people who have both the skills and the time to be online to use the stolen card numbers. They are also likely to have discretionary funds to buy the cards. One other note, I have never heard of any women involved in the stolen credit card networks. Sexism is alive and well in Ghana, and I suspect in the Ghanaian black market, men are unwilling to sell illegal information to women.

Although the majority of ill-gotten credit card numbers are funneled into the streets from hotels, one person I interviewed showed me an e-mail he received from an individual in the United States. Attached to the e-mail was a scanned page of credit card numbers (some with the extra three-digit security codes), expiration dates, time and amount of purchases, laid out like a spreadsheet. At the top of the page was a store identification number for a Walgreens in Tennessee and the cashier's name. Another person mentioned there are Web sites that generate credit card numbers and expiration dates that could be tried or checked online for validity.

The downside to all the credit card numbers in the Walgreen e-mail attachment or numbers generated from Web sites is that they are harder to use without a name or address for each number. One interviewee explained how he spends a lot of time online looking for consumer sites that let you place orders with minimal credit card information.

Finding Internet sites that will process the stolen credit card information requires a network of folks who are constantly browsing the Web (Google Yellow Pages is a great help) looking for places to make purchases with the available credit card information. Similar to sharing trade secrets, there was a subculture around the Internet café that exchanged useful information about which Web locations are the best to use with what credit card information.

If the complete credit card information is available, a popular site to spend the credit is at QVC. I think the attraction to the QVC Web site is the variety of merchandise they offer. I was told that Best Buy and plaza101 are favorite sites for purchasing electronics. The favorite items to purchase with the credit cards are electronics that are hard to find in Ghana. These include computers and computer equipment, Sony walkmans (I guess iPods are all the rage now), DVDs and DVD players, digital cameras, cell phones, and sporty sunglasses. Usually items are purchased in bulk. Sports clothing with popular logos are also popular, and just like in America, Ghanaians are all about the latest sports footwear. Although the credit card users occasionally purchase items for their personal use, most often the merchandise is liquidated through sales on the street.

However, there is a huge catch to these spending sprees with stolen credit cards. Many U.S. online merchants do not ship to post office boxes outside the United States. The credit card thieves have to find someone in the United States to ship them their orders. American women are the primary target for shipping the ill-gotten gains to Ghana. White, divorced, American women, aged 30 and older, are the best candidates for shipping. They are the most likely to feel sympathetic to the Ghanaians and the stories they concoct such as purchasing necessities for their NGOs, school supplies, or their dying relatives. The only men that forward shipments to Ghana are established Ghanaian friends of the scammers that are staying in the United States.

The credit card crooks meet potential shippers, innocent accessories to these crimes, through dating sites like afroconnections.com or imatchup.com and often use stolen credit cards to pay for their memberships to these sites. They spend a lot of time online nurturing friendships. For each relationship, they make up an identity. They tell the women how beautiful they are and express desires to date them or be their boyfriends. They also fabricate stories about their lives in Africa, usually portraying themselves as do-gooders that are trying to make a difference in difficult circumstances. The more long-term cyber relationships they can maintain, the more potential shippers they have for their credit card merchandise.

The credit card purchases arrive, from their shippers, in Ghana via air carrier to the capital city airport or to the post office. Both require payoffs to employees to keep them from stealing the shipments. The airport is the favored portal into Ghana despite having to pay the custom officials to avoid duty and stealing. Airport employees are less likely to tamper with the boxes and easier to pay off, and packages are readily tracked so that credit card crooks know exactly when to expect delivery. On several occasions, I saw guys huddled around a computer tracking a FedEx shipment online. They were able to find out the exact flight their shipment was arriving on. If they expected a big package of purchases to be sold for a profit, they would spread the word to meet at a certain airport gate on the night the shipment arrived in Ghana. All goods were sold immediately upon delivery of the shipment.

One day I had a conversation with an expat who had stayed at a Ghanaian hotel and had her credit card number compromised. She called her overseas bank to report the exact hotel where her credit card number was stolen. The hotel was the only place she had used her credit card in months, thus the most logical place where her credit information was stolen. To her knowledge, nothing ever became of the reported criminal incident despite providing the bank with incriminating details of the crime.

Ghanaians know there is little chance of getting caught for these crimes. American and European credit card companies stand little to gain from the expense of tracking down someone using a public Internet café in Ghana. Also the shippers, if ever contacted, are truly innocent of their actions and can only provide vague information of the persons they ship to. Any information they share about their Ghanaian cyber friends would turn up to be fabricated identities. Another problem is that many Ghanaians share very common names. Often Ghanaians are named after the day of the week they were born on. This leads to 14 very common names; seven names for days of the week for men (e.g., Kofi and Kwesi) and seven names for days of the week for women (e.g., Akosua and Aba). Also, Americans who forward the shipments do not realize, as I did not until traveling there myself, that Ghanaians do not have credit cards.

An Internet café staff informed me that the café workers were once instructed to crack down on the college students who were processing the stolen credit cards. As a result, the student credit card hustlers rebelled by convincing their friends to boycott the café. The decrease in the number of college students patronizing the café seemed to hurt business enough that the café has since "turned a blind eye" to their activities. Also, because a few staff members were processing credit card numbers, their policing efforts were perceived as hypocritical. Now the college students come mainly at night to run their credit card numbers knowing that nothing will be said about their activities.

Since I conducted my research in 2004, a Ghanaian friend has written to me that the Internet cafés throughout Ghana are starting to crack down on these illegal practices. The government has put forth an effort to train police officers to monitor the cafés. Pretty much a Ghanaian purchasing anything online would be a flag since the only way to purchase online is through credit, which most Ghanaians do not have. I do not know what effect, if any, these efforts are having on the stolen credit card culture. As recently as Spring 2006, after giving a lecture in class about this topic, a female student spoke with me after class and shared that she had a Ghanaian Internet pal that had recently asked her to ship something for him! I cautioned her that there is no way he could have legally made the purchase. Shippers beware!!!

ONLINE PANHANDLING AND OTHER INNOVATIVE INTERNET USAGE

My research revealed that some of the Ghanaian Internet users establish cyber friendships for more than just the novelty of having international contacts or pen pals (as is probably the case for many Americans). International contacts, especially from the United States and Western Europe, represent a hope for possible financial gains. I learned that many users meet someone online through a chat room, establish a friendship, and eventually ask for financial assistance. They offer justifications for the financial assistance along the lines of needing money for school, business purposes, or illnesses. Often the requests are based on fictitious scenarios of desperation (like fabricating they cannot afford their school fees) that are meant to gain sympathy in the form of monetary support.

One thing that stood out to me as odd behavior at the Internet café was watching a guy chatting online while aiming a Webcam at a woman using the computer beside him. This also happened to an American friend of mine; while using the Internet café one day she looked up to find the guy sitting next to her had pointed his Webcam on her! When inquiring about this unusual behavior, I discovered the guys were posing as women online to flirt with the men they hope would send them money. Whereas women are most likely to forward shipments to Ghana, men are more likely to wire money to their Ghanaian "girlfriends." The Webcams are used during initial contacts to convince their targets of their female identity. The next time the scammers chat with their cyber "boyfriends," they write that the Webcam is broken so that they do not have to keep up their false appearance. Another way these con artists faked their identity was to display a scanned picture of a woman, usually the pictures were of their real girlfriends.

The male scammers write to the Western men saying they are in love with them, how good looking they are, or offer to show them around Ghana. Eventually, the scammers ask the men for money to fund their education or maybe for health reasons. The men often send the money (perhaps a couple hundred dollars) to their "Ghana girlfriend" (i.e., the hustlers). For a few guys at the Internet café, running these scams was a full-time job.

One day I approached two young boys (around 6–8 years of age) while they were waiting to use the Internet at the café (often there was a wait during peak hours). Upon asking them if they had any international Internet friends, they produced a small handwritten note. On the back of the note were six e-mail addresses they obtained, probably from tourists they had met in the area (I was often asked for my e-mail address by strangers I met in the street). On the front of the note was a message they were planning to type and e-mail to the six contacts. It appeared that the note was written by someone else and given to the boys to use at the Internet café. The boys wanted me to read the note and asked me to make corrections (spelling and grammar). The boys could barely type much less spell. As you can see below, the note had many English errors that are typical in most Ghanaian e-mail messages.

> Dear friend,
>
> I am very happy to write you this letter. Please how are you, I hope you are fine by the grace of God. Please can you send me some money. Please I want to tell you all my secret so that you can help me. Please my mother have travel my father too have travel. They give me only 10,000 and it has finish and my parent haven't came so I want you to help me a little goodbye.
>
> Yours Sincerely,

The boys told me they have received wired money sent by an Internet contact. The most common way to receive financial contributions in Ghana is through Western Union wiring services. It is well known, and I have since discovered for myself, that the postal service cannot be trusted to deliver mail containing money or goods since most government employees try to supplement their inadequate incomes in any way possible.

Some of the Ghanaians know or have met face-to-face their international Internet contacts, such as friends or family members living in other countries or tourists they have met in the streets of Ghana (or at the Internet cafés). I have received several requests for money since my return to the United States.

Admittedly, my first reaction to using computer technology to hustle and beg for money was disapproving and disappointing. I feel there are more constructive ways to use computers, such as providing information and awareness, increasing education, and learning marketable skills. However, I now have a better understanding of the fact that these computer contacts for many Ghanaians are the only hope for financial advancement given the extremely low wages and lack of jobs in Ghana. For example, staff members of the Internet café reported working hard rarely led to a promotion or to raises. In fact, staff members often worked more than their designated hours but were not compensated. Besides, asking someone to send money for school is not a stretch. Ghana has a 28 percent illiteracy rate (Central Intelligence Agency 2006). With many Ghanaians unable to afford the school fees, the educational needs are great in Ghana.

THEORETICAL CONSIDERATIONS

Theories such as Routine Activities Approach that emphasize the importance of the geographical proximity between the criminal and the crime victim, in understanding why crime events occur, may need to rethink the theoretical applications to Internet crimes. The importance of a geographical convergence is not necessary for many Internet crimes.

An insightful perspective for understanding these credit card crimes is Cloward and Ohlin's (1960) Differential Opportunity theory. Differential Opportunity theory recognizes that the distribution of legitimate and illegitimate opportunities varies for each person and place. The impoverished conditions of Ghana make **credit card fraud** very attractive and very plausible with the arrival of the Internet and the subsequent blossoming of an online cashless commerce. For the criminally inclined in developing countries, the Internet provides them conduits to people who have money and places to spend money.

An important characteristic of these cyber credit card criminals is that they were mostly employed (hotel clerks) or in college (college students). These positions allow them to take advantage of opportunities to obtain and process credit cards through the Internet. Hotel clerks are the few Ghanaians that have access to foreigners' credit cards and college students have the necessary computer skills to process the stolen credit card numbers. These circumstances are important considerations when trying to understand how these crimes are most likely rational acts of opportunity.

Further, I believe a perceived low risk of getting caught inform these criminal actions. Throughout my interviews, I only heard of one alleged account of a person caught using stolen credit cards in an Internet café and sent to jail for a short time. I could never get any specific information about this arrest. I also have never heard of American credit card companies pursuing these criminals, pressing charges, or prosecuting cases. The 6,000 miles between the United States and Ghana is a great buffer for these crimes.

I also sense that the criminals neutralize their crimes by believing that no one, other than the "greedy capitalist credit card companies," is directly hurt by their crimes. Americans and American companies are seen as gluttons in terms of world resources. One person I interviewed justified his actions by expressing how Africa was a forgotten continent in terms of real economic help and investments, and he felt the credit card heists are somewhat of a payback for American neglect. Since they perceive Americans as fat cats, they believe no real losses are felt when fraudulent charges occur. What is a gold mine to a Ghanaian is barely a pinch to Americans.

Another interesting note, I learned that some of the guys were using their credit card assets as a gateway into establishing legitimate businesses. The credit card proceeds allowed them to obtain the necessary capital to start their businesses that would not otherwise be attainable. One interview shared a story of Ghanaians that bought 20 laptops over 3 years and subsequently opened up their own Internet café. I heard another story of a Ghanaian purchasing plane tickets to sell through the tourist business he was starting.

CONCLUSION

Since there are few prosperous outlets for computer savvy Ghanaians, I am not surprised to find a few Ghanaians using their Internet skills to take advantage of first-world resources by either stealing credit card numbers or asking for money directly. They have purchased laptops, clothing, and DVD players. They have strangers or acquaintances wire them money and send them packages. Perhaps the electronic goods and gifts of money are not enough to pull someone out of poverty, but the contributions from Internet contacts are enough to keep many folks at the Internet café "gold digging."

At the dawn of the personal computer age, Albanese (1988) wrote an article explaining how thievery techniques and opportunities have always shifted in response to existing technology. He predicted that computers would create new opportunities for theft and in response would require new security measures to protect online commerce. His predictions have become a reality in the twenty-first century. The Ghana credit card criminals are a case in point.

The processing of stolen credit cards is not unique to Ghana, but extends across the globe. The great distance between the offenders and the victims help the criminal rationalize their actions as harmless. They do not perceive that the individuals shipping items are at risk of loss and feel the credit card companies painlessly absorb most of the merchandise costs. Most importantly, they are motivated to take advantage of opportunities to receive items they could not otherwise obtain in their lifetime.

In conclusion, I believe the deviant and criminal uses of the Internet answered my initial research question. The illegal Internet activity appears to be informed by available computer technologies, human nature, and environmental circumstances. Ghanaians are using the Internet for communication like the rest of the world are, but since they live in a developing country, their keystrokes are more likely to focus on acquiring money than on education purposes. A case can be made that individuals engaged in online begging or using fraudulent credit cards are adapting the technology to their circumstances.

There is scant scholarly attention of these crimes originating from Ghana. In the United States, there is a general awareness and fear of identity theft and credit card fraud. However, when we think of identity thieves, we rarely think of our global neighbors.

In browsing the Internet for consumer alerts about the credit card problem in Ghana and other African countries, I have found very little information. The Ghana Consular warns an increasing "number of travelers have been victims of credit card fraud after using their credit cards in Ghana. You may wish to settle bills using traveler's checks or cash. If you elect to use credit cards in Ghana, take all possible precautions" (U.S. Department of State 2006). A further precautionary statement is given. "Another type of fraud is by persons claiming to live in Ghana who profess friendship or romantic interest over the Internet. Once a relationship has been established, the correspondent typically asks the American to send money for living expenses, travel expenses, or visa costs" (U.S. Department of State 2006). When I prepare students traveling with me to Ghana for summer school credit, I instruct them to "leave home without your credit cards," or the cards "will be everywhere you don't want to be."

KEY TERMS

Computer technology
Credit card fraud
Internet cafés

REFERENCES

Albanese, J. S. 1988. Tomorrow's thieves. *Futurist* 22: 24–28.

Central Intelligence Agency. 2006. *World Fact book*, https://www.cia.gov/cia/publications/factbook/geos/gh.html

Cloward, R. A., and L. E. Ohlin. 1960. *Delinquency and Opportunity: A Theory of Delinquent Gangs.* NY: The Free Press.

Pew Internet & American Life Project. 2006. Who's online. Retrieved December 12, 2006, from http://www.pewinternet.org/trends/User_Demo_4.26.06.htm

U.S. Department of State. 2006. http://travel.state.gov/travel/cis_pa_tw/cis/cis_1124.html

Zachary, G. P. 2004. Black star: Ghana, information technology and development in Africa. *First Monday* 9 (3). Retrieved July 8, 2004, from http://www.firstmonday.org/issues/issue9_3/zachary/index.html

Chapter 8

Regulating Cyberstalking

Subhajit Basu
Queen's University Belfast, UK

Richard Jones
Liverpool John Moores University, UK

Subhajit Basu is lecturer in information and technology law at Queen's University Belfast. He did his Ph.D. from the Liverpool John Moores University, on "Taxation of E-Commerce from a Global Perspective," in 2003. He is the Book Review Editor for *International Review of Law Computers and Technology* (IRLCT); Reviewer for the Editorial Reviewer Board of the *International Journal of E-Government Research* (IJEGR), IRLCT, *Journal of Law and Technology* (JILT), and *Scientific Journals International* (SJI); International Reviewer of *Social Science Computer Review* (SSCORE); Member of the Editorial Advisory Board (EAB) of the *Advances in Electronic Government Research* (AEGR) Book Series; and Member of the Editorial Board of *Journal of Information and Communication Technologies and Human Development*. Subhajit is extensively involved in research related to E-government-developing countries and the issue of digital divide; governance of cyberspace and role of politics, technology, and law in IT; precipitators of e-commerce crime as new form of white-collar crime; implication of information and communication technologies for the growth of criminal and deviant identities and behavior on the Internet; and role of technology in economic development of developing countries. He is a member of the Executive Committee of the British and Irish Legal Educational Technology Association (BILETA). He is a Fellow of the Higher Education Academy, and Member and Reviewer of LEFIS (EU Project on IT and Legal Education). He is also the author of *Global Perspectives on E-Commerce Taxation Law*.

Richard Jones is reader in law and information technology at Liverpool John Moores University. Richard teaches information technology law, intellectual property law, and family law in the undergraduate law degree and offers cyberspace law for other schools in the university. Richard's research interests are in the law of ethnic minorities, technology and the law, and law teaching and technology. He was invited by the Council of Europe to work on a recommendation for teaching technology to law students and was awarded a Research Fellowship with IBM to investigate legal expert systems. He was Chair of the British and Irish Legal Educational Technology Association (BILETA) and a Council member of the Society for Computers and the Law. Richard is assistant editor of the *International Review of Law, Computers and Technology*. He has published articles recently in the International Review on E-Commerce, IT Law in S.E. Asia and Creative Commons Licences. In 1998, 2003, and 2005 he edited issues of the *International Review on IT and Criminal Justice, E-Commerce and IT Law in S.E. Asia*. Richard is a member of the Editorial Board and joint editor of *Journal of Law and Technology* (JILT) and of the Liverpool Law Review (Kluwer Publications). He is also the author (with Welhengama, G.) of *Ethnic Minorities in English Law*.

Abstract

Through the use of examples of cyberstalking, the chapter will consider the nature of regulation required in relation to this behavior in cyberspace. The chapter will consider the differences between offline and cyberstalking, and review how these differences affect the regulation of such activities. The chapter will review the boundaries between public and private laws, between national and international laws, and between state law and self-regulation, and consider whether the traditional positivist methodology of law, within these boundaries, offers an adequate intellectual framework in which to consider the nature and form of regulation in cyberspace.

INTRODUCTION

> Right, you've got as far as finding yourself attracted to a guy on the net. But do you really know anything about him? He's said he's 39, divorced, has 2 kids, is tall, blond and enjoys driving fast cars and going to the theatre. How can you know for sure that he's not 46, married, 2 kids, 5'4", drives a Ford Fiesta and spends most of his time either in front of the PC or down the local watering hole with his mates? ASK! "Oh yeah," you may well think he's likely to say "yes Sally, I've been lying to you all along." Of course he isn't. It's a matter of asking the right questions.

As illustrated from the above extract from a guide to cyber-flirting, flirting in **cyberspace** is different from that in physical space. These differences (an ever growing number) give an insight into the difficulties in regulating behavior in cyberspace. Yet the perspectives offered by lawmakers, judges, and scholars are all grounded in various premises about online life, and the search for solutions has been approached from the perspective that cyberspace is merely an extension or continuation of the real world. The peculiarities of cyberspace, particularly **anonymity**, mean it is not simply a question of transferring behaviors across from the physical world; individuals and communities in cyberspace are different and so is their behavior. This chapter will illustrate how the key concepts of social interaction, social bonding, and empirical experience differ in cyberspace from those in the physical world. Such differences should inform the debate about the nature and form of **regulation** of cyberspace. Cyberspace is a distinct place for purposes of legal analysis with a legally significant border.[1] As pointed out by Lessig (1999), "Cyberspace presents something new for those of us who think about regulation and freedom. It demands a new understanding of how regulation works and of what regulates life there?"

Legislations can profoundly alter social relations. But the way we frame this development substantially affects our understanding of what is at stake and how we should respond to it. Through the examples of **cyberstalking**, the chapter will consider the nature of regulation

---

[1]At the outset, it is acknowledged that the call for a body of law regulating cyberspace is not uniformly accepted in the legal community. The usual arguments are that (1) there is no consensus concerning the many possible designs or architectures that may affect the functionality we now associate with cyberspace; (2) very few bodies of law are defined by their characteristic technologies; and (3) the best legal doctrine reexamines, expands, or applies existing doctrines to a new arena. Whatever the validity of such comments concerning activities within single nation states, the capability of the Internet to cut across many national jurisdictions at lightning speed argues that we look anew. It recommends that nations seek a comprehensive reexamination of the many relevant, sometimes conflicting legal doctrines, practices, and procedures to produce a comprehensive, universal, and uniform legal framework for handling the issues (Gelbstein and Kamal 2002).

required in relation to such behavior in such a place. We suggest that the boundaries between public and private laws, between national and international laws, and between state law and self-regulation, and indeed the traditional positivist methodology of law, no longer offer an adequate intellectual framework in which to consider the nature and form of regulation in cyberspace. For example, the process may conveniently proceed as follows: as the *Protection from Harassment Act, 1997* makes no attempt to define the term "stalking" it may, by judicial interpretation, be extended to cyberstalking (some have suggested that cyberstalking represents nothing more than an additional behavior that can be associated with "offline stalking"); therefore, with minor amendments to deal with the "technology," this Act is able to regulate cyberstalking. This approach, we would suggest, ignores the nature of the community in which this is happening and the nature and form of the behavior itself. New technology inevitably leads to effects on culture and on forms of deviant behavior that will naturally arise in order to exploit new opportunities. Cyberstalking, for example, encompasses a wide range of new behaviors that are not associated with offline stalking. Cyberstalking can be associated with the activities of pedophiles, and has been seen to include intimidation to achieve a variety of ends. Drawing on literature that analyses the nature of the activities, the space in which they occur, and the effect of technology on culture, the chapter will argue that the foundation should be an investigation and an analysis of the community space over which the regulation is to apply. Such an analysis, will it is hoped, illustrates the inadequacies of traditional "legal" deterministic approaches and offers workable approaches to the problem of regulation and enforcement.[2]

While there is no universally accepted definition of cyberstalking, the term generally refers to using the Internet or other telecommunication technology to harass or menace another person. Although the behavior widely identified as stalking has existed for centuries, the legal system has only codified its presence in the statutes in recent decades. As a result, cyberstalking could truly be identified as a crime of the '90s owing to its reliance on computer and communications technology, which has only reached maturity in the past decade. The Crown Prosecution Service defines cyberstalking as:

> Cyber stalking generally takes the form of threatening behaviour or unwanted advances directed at another using the Internet and other forms of online communications. Cyber stalkers can target their victims through chat rooms, message boards, discussion forums, and e-mail. Cyber stalking can be carried out in a variety of ways such as: threatening or obscene e-mail; spamming (in which a stalker sends a victim a multitude of junk e-mail); live chat harassment or flaming (online verbal abuse); leaving improper messages on message boards or in guest books; sending electronic viruses; sending unsolicited e-mail; and electronic identity theft amongst others.

STALKING

In the United States, California was the first state to adopt stalking laws, most often identified as a result of the murder in 1989 of actress Rebecca Schaeffer by Robert Bardo, an obsessed fan (Zona, Sharma, and Lane 1993). Legislation was subsequently enacted in 1990. Other

---

[2]We fear that much of our current thinking about the law of cyberspace is impressionistic, reductionist, and ultimately counterproductive.

states followed but most of the states' laws do not refer specifically to nor can be interpreted to include the concept of cyberstalking. Stalking directly impacts upon the individual lives of victims creating in them a fear for personal safety and security; anxiety for the future and a loss of quality of life; uncertainty and unpredictability, as the uncontrolled acts intrude upon the lives of victims in a random fashion, making the reestablishment of a normal life difficult (Miller 2001).

In the United Kingdom without specific legislation to deal with stalking and harassment, case law had begun to expand the concept of bodily harm found in the *Offences Against the Person Act*, 1861 to cover the rapidly developing social phenomena of stalking and harassment. In *R. v Ireland (Robert Matthew) R. v Burstow (Anthony Christopher)* (HL) [1998] A.C. 147 (1997) 141 S.J.L.B. 205, the defendant had made several malicious telephone calls to women. It was held that a recognizable psychiatric illness suffered by a victim of malicious telephone calls amounted to "bodily harm" within the meaning of the Act. The relevant UK domestic laws on harassment (of which stalking is a form) are a rag bag of statutes, many predating the explosion of the Internet and the development and use of mobile phones. The *Telecommunications Act*, 1984, *Malicious Communications Act*, 1988, and the *Protection from Harassment Act*, 1997 provide a number of options to deal with stalking but none attempt to define the term. Section 1 of the *Malicious Communications Act*, 1988 make it an offence to send an indecent, offensive, or threatening letter, electronic communication, or other article to another person. In addition section 43 of the *Telecommunications Act*, 1984 creates a similar offence to send a telephone message which is indecent, offensive, or threatening. The 1988 Act is the wider ranging, although still rather dated in its language, making provision for the "punishment of persons who send or deliver letters or other articles for the purpose of causing distress or anxiety." Under section 1, an offence is committed by a person "who sends a letter or other article which conveys

i.   a message which is indecent or grossly offensive;

ii. a threat; or

iii. information which is false and known or believed to be false by the sender; or any other article which is, in whole or part, of an indecent or grossly offensive nature."

Should there be more than one offensive event, then it will be possible to prosecute under the *Protection from Harassment Act*, 1997. The 1997 Act was introduced following a campaign by Diane Lamplugh whose daughter Suzy was murdered. The 1997 Act requires a "course of conduct" before an offence is committed. The Act introduces both civil and criminal wrongs and enables the court to make a Restraining Order (s.5) preventing the offender from contacting the victim again. Such an order is not available under the 1984, nor the 1988 Act. The 1997 Act introduces two main criminal offences under section 2; a person who pursues a course of conduct (harassment) in breach of section 1 is guilty of an offence. The more serious offence is in section 4 where a person whose "course of conduct causes another to fear, on at least two occasions, that violence will be used against him is guilty of an offence if he knows or ought to know that his course of conduct will cause the other so to fear on each of those occasions." More seriously, if the harassment is racially aggravated, then charges could be brought under section 32 of the *Crime and Disorder Act*, 1998. If the offender is "associated" with the victim, then a nonmolestation order may be available under the *Family Law Act*, 1996 (section 42, 62).

TECHNOLOGY

Technological change does not occur within a social vacuum (Kuhn 1996), and social upheaval in the face of technological change is not new. Some of this change is undesirable, as Postman (1992) states:

> That is not to say that the computer is blight on the symbolic landscape; only that, like medical technology, it has usurped powers and enforced mindsets that a fully attentive culture might have wished to deny it. (p. 107)

Cyberspace brings together the potentially exciting cocktail of technology, and its unique group of users, within the context of anonymity and an environment lacking in consistent norms. Whilst the potentially democratizing effect is to be welcomed, the potential for perverse activity is not (Lessig 1999). It is this dichotomy—the democratic versus the perverting role of the Internet within the context of the less discussed forms of crimes and deviance— that makes the subject of this paper. As Sherizen (1992) comments:

> Seldom is there an integrated socio-technological approach to the computer crime problem . . . [W]e need to establish where the social and psychological lines are drawn between normal and deviant, between allowed and disallowed, between expected and unexpected, between wanted and unwanted. (p. 39)

Societies throughout the history of mankind have incorporated into their fabric technologies that have had a profound cultural effect. However, what is arguably significant about Internet revolution is the nature and pace of change; the pace surpasses any of the previous technological revolutions. This technological change has now reached a speed that is increasingly difficult for both society and individuals to accommodate, a situation expressed by the novelist William Gibson (1984) in his description of a typically urban environment of the near future:

> Night City was like a deranged experiment in social Darwinism, designed by a bored researcher who kept one thumb permanently on the fast-forward button. Stop hustling and you sunk without a trace, but move a little too swiftly and you'd break the fragile surface tension of the black market; either way, you were gone, with nothing left of you but some vague memory . . . though heart or lung or kidneys might survive in the service of some stranger. (p. 14)

Crime follows opportunity. Crime in "Night City" is very different from crime in the physical world. Technology has provided an efficient and more effective means to commit the "old" crimes; however, the extent of their impact on our day-to-day life is much more profound and much more intrusive. In less than a decade, the full spectrum of immorality covered in the real world transferred to the virtual world: cyber warfare, cyber terrorism, identity theft, racial hate speech, organized crime, brutal child pornography, cyberstalking, chat room crimes, and questionable forms of hacking pervaded cyberspace. Activities have not only replicated those in the virtual world but also have taken on their own character fuelled by an environment where anonymity is the norm. Policies for policing and prevention of some cyber crimes are ineffective, we would argue, without an analysis of the society in which they occur.

CYBERSPACE SOCIALITY—SPACE AND COMMUNITY

The notion of physical space saturates our ordinary everyday lives. It is a basic concept which underlies our understanding of the world around us, the entities within it, and our own and other people's movements through it. Philosophy has traditionally understood questions about the nature of space in terms of the dichotomy between substantivalism (or absolutism) and relationalism, with Newton and Leibniz as the two key proponents. "Does something exist over and above spatial relationships between entities, something in which those entities inhere (i.e. absolute space)? Or does our concept of space amount to nothing more than those entities and the spatial relationships between them?" (Bryant 2001, 138–55). Paul Teller (1991) explains this dichotomy:

> Is it [space] a substance, a collection of particulars ("points," or "regions"), existing independently, and providing an objective framework of spatial reference ("substantivalism")? Or should we say that substantival space is an illusion, there being nothing more than the spatial relations holding between physical objects or events ("relationalism")? (pp. 363–97)

Is cyberspace a *space* existing in the penumbral ether between the networked computers? In a rough conceptual equivalence of space and cyberspace: can cyberspace exist as an independent entity over and above those entities that it accommodates?

> In early days of computer networks it seemed a slightly far-fetched metaphor to describe . . . sites as "places", since bandwidth was narrow . . . [A]s bandwidth burgeons and computing muscle continues to grow, cyberspace will present themselves in increasingly multi-sensory and engaging ways . . . [W]e will just look at them; we feel present in them. (Mitchell 1995, 114–15)

Most notable within the postmodernist view has been Jean Baudrillard's exposition of "hyper-reality" (Baudrillard 1988), as it relates to the development of cyberspace and especially the potential capabilities of virtual reality technologies. Although based primarily upon mass communications media, Baudrillard's contention that such technologies are constructing an entirely new social environment, an electronic reality, has clear resonance for those arguing that cyberspace represents an alternative, virtual reality. In this hyper-reality of cyberspace it is contented that time, place, and individual identity are separated from modernist physical locations. However, what accompanies discourses on both these latest technologies and the new articulations of space-time that they express—whether utopian, dystopian, or measured—is an impoverished understanding of the real and the virtual. This lack of understanding infiltrates both the virtual and the real, to the point where the virtual is invariably collapsed into a badly analyzed version of the real—wherein the real and virtual are no longer distinguishable according to qualities, but only according to quantities. Regardless of the nature of the space what cannot be questioned is the fact that cyberspace is everywhere, omnipresent, in other words ubiquitous.

So, is cyberspace a place? Whatever answer we give to the normative question, there is significant evidence that, purely as a descriptive observation, individuals do think of cyberspace as a place. Cognitive science investigations into how people think provide ample evidence of this. The legal fraternity has unwillingly accepted that our physical assumptions about property should also apply to this new "space." Owners of Internet resources consider their Web site or e-mail address as their own little "claim" in cyberspace which should give similar level of protection against any infringement to that which would be provided in the physical world.

The sociology of cyberspace raises some crucial questions, not only about the emergence of new forms of community and sociality, but also of how these are best understood. Viable "societies" exist in cyberspace. It is a space where people experience all that they may experience in real space, or almost all anyway. It is also an international community with social interaction, social bonding, and empirical experience . . .

> . . . rather than being constrained by the computer, the members of these groups creatively exploit the systems' features so as to play with new forms of expressive communication, to explore possible public identities, to create otherwise unlikely relationships, and to create behavioural norms. In so doing, they invent new communities. (Reid 1995, 164–83)

Defining "community" will help frame the ensuing legal discussion, and will enable us to better evaluate various forms of crimes against the virtual community. So, what do we mean by community? Many scholars have noted the elusiveness of a definition of "community" (Post 1997, 473), a term that is complicated by its central position in the debate between communitarians and liberals (Alexander 1989). Traditionally, geography has helped to indicate community. Although geography arguably remains important in defining virtual community, we are better served in the Internet context by an "experiential" conception of community, rather than a geographic one (Alexander 1989). Is the use of the phrase "virtual community" a perversion of the notion of community? Not all scholars accept that cyber subcultures are worthy of our attention or whether they are simply ephemeral, imagined communities, too fleeting, too superficial, and too "virtual" to warrant serious exploration. Calhoun (1991) argued that the modern condition is one of "indirect social relationships" in which connectivity with others is more imagined, or parasocial, than "real." The media's ability to broaden the range of our experiences creates the illusion of greater contact or membership in large-scale social organizations. Rather than creating "communities," however, we are merely developing "categorical identities" or "imagined communities" that are nothing more than the "feeling" of belonging to some group. He further argues that a true "community" requires direct relationships among its members:

> . . . that there is a great deal of difference between social groups formed out of direct relationships among their members, although often sharing an imaginatively constructed cultural identity, and social categories defined by common cultural or other external attributes of their members and not necessarily linked by any dense, multiplex, or systematic web of interpersonal relationships. (Calhoun 1991, 95–121)

In contrast, Oldenburg (1989) argues "online communities might fill a need that has been all but abandoned in modern societies, where the closeness and social bonding of the gemein-schaft has been replaced by the emotional disconnect of the gesellschaft. An individual moves about through three basic environments: where he works, where he lives, and the place where he joins with others for conviviality." According to Thomsen, Straubhaar, and Bolyard (1998), it is in the latter environment, the place of "idle talk and banter with acquaintances and friends," where the sense of membership in a "community" is often achieved and experienced. According to some theorists, this environment also maximizes individual's creativity, imagination. Cafes, barbershops, and pubs once provided this envi-ronment, but in the age of shopping malls, drive-in fast food, shrinking public space, and res-idential "cocooning," this need for conviviality is left unfulfilled (Thomsen, Straubhaar, and Bolyard 1998). Modernity, Oldenburg (1989) argues, has established a culture in which the home and the workplace remain as the only two interactive spheres of existence. It should not be surprising, then, that millions of people throughout the world turn to the Internet to re-create and reestablish the third sphere of conviviality. Cerulo (1997) has argued that in order to effectively study online communities, sociologists and communication researchers must reframe the way in which they view the computer-mediated world and past assumptions about human interactions:

> [R]ecent developments have touched issues at the very heart of sociological discourse—the definition of interaction, the nature of social ties, and the scope of experience and reality. Indeed, the developing technologies are creating an expanded social environment that requires amendments and alterations to ways in which we conceptualize social process. (pp. 48–58)

"Technology does not have to dictate the way our social relations change, but we can only influence change if we understand how people use technologies." Hence, technologically gen-erated communities have forced us to reformulate the way in which we view three key ana-lytic concepts: social interaction, social bonding, and empirical experience, the traditional stance in sociological analysis. Cerulo explained that physical co-presence is the determining factor in judging the significance and quality of a communicative exchange. So, is there something disturbing about finding community through a computer screen? "We speak of the closeness and trust born of such mediated connections using terms such as pseudo-gemeinschaft, virtual intimacy, or imagined community. Such designations reify the notion that interactions void of the face-to-face connection are somehow less than the real thing." Purcell (1997) contradicted this view, suggesting:

> Co-presence does not insure intimate interaction among all group members. Consider large-scale social gatherings in which hundreds or thousands of people gather in a location to perform a ritual or celebrate an event. In these instances, participants are able to see the visible manifestation of the group, the physical gathering, yet their ability to make direct, intimate connections with those around them is limited by the sheer magnitude of the assembly. (pp. 101–12)

If accepted then interactions within cyberspace are considered by the participants to be real, such a conclusion will impact upon consideration of the motive and the nature of harm in stalking.

REGULATION OF CYBERSPACE

As we commented earlier, it is apparent that owners of Internet resources consider their Web site or e-mail address as their own little "claim" in cyberspace, which should give a similar level of protection against any infringement to that which would be provided in the physical world. Such views have found acceptance in the courts.[3] It is questioned whether such acceptance has occurred through an understanding of virtual community or space or merely through a process where the virtual is collapsed into a badly analyzed version of the real.

Regulation is required and will occur in cyberspace (Mnookin 1996). In general, communities generate and perpetuate their own legal norms (Giordano 1998). Community norms receive deference when "community standards" are used to determine whether a crime or tort has been committed (Byassee 1995, 207–8). Legal rules, statutes, court decisions, and deference to extralegal mechanisms such as norms, markets, and programming code (Lessig 1998) are crucial in determining what sorts of communities thrive in cyberspace and what sorts of communities do not. Territorial sovereigns can recognize communities not only by leaving these groups alone but also by enforcing community rules. The law may give communities a sphere of autonomy through the principle of freedom of association, or it may grant communities such as churches, corporations, and civic associations the power of self-governance, enforceable in courts of law. As cyberspace becomes more entwined with real-space life, the rules governing virtual communities may also in time begin to influence our real-space communities.

The nature and extent of regulation is where the debate lies. For some the virtual is the same as the physical. The perspectives offered by lawmakers, judges, and scholars are all grounded in various premises about online life and have been approached with the idea that cyberspace is an extension or continuation of the real world. For others cyberspace is a distinct "place" for purposes of legal analysis with a legally significant border between the cyberspace and the "real world." Johnson and Post (1997), for example, argued that cyberspace should have "its own law and legal institutions," and that state-based government would generally have no **jurisdiction** over online activity. To Johnson and Post (1997), then, the law of cyberspace is, quite literally, the law of another place (p. 62). It is the law of cyberspace—the same way that we might think of the law of the State of New York or the law of the United Kingdom.[4] Latterly there has been recognition of distinctions between the real and the virtual but also a merging of the idea of how we think about cyberspace with the normative question of how cyberspace is or may be regulated. This is most clearly seen where Lessig (1999) comments: "cyberspace presents something new for those of us who think about regulation and freedom. It demands a new understanding of how regulation works and of what regulates life there" (contrast Post 2000).

We argue that the debate has been wrongly constrained and that we need to retrace our route and begin again; we suggest, with an analysis of space and community, a space and

---

[3]*Ebay Inc v. Bidders Edge Inc*, 100 F. Supp. 2d 1058 (N.D. Cal. 2000); *America Online Inc v. LCGM Inc*. Civ. Act. No. 98-102-A (E.D. Va., Nov. 10, 1998); *Shetland Times v. Wills* [1997] FSR 604.

[4]Those critical of such a view, including Goldsmith, argued that cyberspace was not a unique challenge and that similar challenges had been resolved by unexceptional jurisdictional rules and legal mechanisms derived from conflict of laws. Transactions in cyberspace, it is argued, are no different from those occurring in the "physical space" of international trade or international crimes (Goldsmith 1998).

community with distinct interactions, social ties, and experiences. A virtual[5] community is one in which the balance between law and sanctions and legal and self-regulation is subtly different, and where the nature of the interactions requires a review of the acceptance or nonacceptance of various behaviors.[6] Simple legislative extension to cyberspace is unlikely to lead to a reduction in criminal Internet activity; such responses have been inadequate in the peculiar environment of cyberspace. Will Internet citizens be forced to resort to forms of situational crime prevention either individually or in consort with Internet service providers to provide adequate protection from such behavior? The debate is often encapsulated in the terminology of Lessig (1999, 53–4, fn. 5) between East Coast responses, centering on the law, and West Coast responses, based upon technology. The failure of the traditional legal responses in cyberspace has led to fallback response relying unthinkingly on technology rather than an examination of the reasons why laws have failed to regulate behavior effectively. A fundamental review will free the debate to enable a breach of the traditional conceptual boundaries that have railroaded the debate so far. These boundaries include but are not limited to the divisions between public and private law, between national and international law, and between state law, self-regulation, and code, within the nature of the community itself (Paliwala 2004; Brownsword 2005).

THE "ANONYMOUS" WORLD OF CYBERSPACE

As we previously commented, technologically generated communities have forced us to reformulate the way in which we view three key analytic concepts: social interaction, social bonding, and empirical experience. Before considering the nature and form of regulation that will establish and enforce baseline rules of conduct that is unique for cyberspace and define, punish, and prevent wrongful actions that harm others through online means (Paliwala 2004), we begin as we have suggested with an analysis of the nature of the community and in particular one aspect of the virtual community—anonymity.

Anonymity in the cyberspace can be seen as the norm and not a deviation. Anonymous interaction in cyberspace has become commonplace. Cyberspace makes anonymity easy so long as no physical manipulation is involved. Some benefits of social interaction can be achieved, whilst still maintaining a sense of privacy. In short, cyberspace has created infinitely new possibilities to the deviant imagination, for contemporary life has been described as a world of spectacle, narcissism, and performance (Abercrombie and Longhurst 1998), cyberspace provides a space for all three. The virtual worlds are "laboratories for the construction of identity," where individuals frequently feel more like their "real" selves than in the physical world (Turkle 1996). In this space, one can excogitate new identities.

Identity is a complex and multifaceted concept that plays a central role in delineating the parameters of *inter alia* ethnicity, nationality, and citizenship, thus generating an immense amount of debate across various disciplines (Bendle 2002). Individual identity can be seen as

---

[5]Lessig (1999) argues a community based on code.

[6]A large number of self-help and self-regulatory bodies exist on the Internet to deal with harassment and stalking. Internet users can use blocking and filtering systems. Net Nanny, Safe Surf, and Surf Watch provide directories of offensive sites; Internet Watch and Cyber Angels provide mechanisms for reporting offenders.

the sense of self that is based upon the internationalization of all that is known about oneself. For Goffman (1959) the key characteristics of what he termed—after Freud—"id" (re felt) identity are subjectivity and reflexivity. Hence individual identity is more than simply self-perception; rather it is the subjective construction of self that is modified by reflections on the views of others and the individual interactions in the social world (Goffman 1963). As such, individual identity is not a static construction but one that is constantly evolving and readjusting in line with an individual's life experience (Finch 2002, 87).

Identity plays a key role in virtual communities. In communication, which is the primary activity, knowing the identity of those with whom you communicate is essential for understanding and evaluating an interaction. Yet in the disembodied world of the virtual community, identity is also ambiguous (Detwiler 1993). In the physical world there is an inherent unity to the self, for the body provides a compelling and convenient definition of identity. The norm is: one body, one identity. Although the self may be complex and mutable over time and circumstance, the body provides a stabilizing anchor. The virtual world is different. It is composed of information rather than matter. Information spreads and diffuses; there is no law of the conservation of information. The inhabitants of this impalpable space are also diffuse, free from the body's unifying anchor. One can have, some claim, as many electronic personas as one has time and energy to create.

A single person can create multiple electronic identities that are linked only by their common progenitor; that link, though invisible in the virtual world, is of great significance. What is the relationship among multiple personas sharing a single progenitor? Do virtual personas inherit the qualities—and responsibilities—of their creators? Such questions bring a fresh approach to ancient inquiries into the relationship between the self and the body—and a fresh urgency. Online communities are growing rapidly and their participants face these questions, not as hypothetical thought experiments, but as basic issues in their daily existence. Large amount of text-based affairs embodies part of the cyberspace, while people's illusion embodies other parts of it. In the everyday world of cyberspace strangers meet, exchange some right or wrong information, and shift more or less their personality.

A man creates a female identity, a high school student claims to be an expert on viruses; other explorers in virtual space develop relationships with the ostensible female, relationships based on deep-seated assumptions about gender and their own sexuality, believing them to be backed by real-world knowledge (Mnookin 1996). Identity is essential for assessing the reliability of information and the trustworthiness of a confidant. And care of one's own identity and one's reputation is fundamental to the formation of community. This is the misfortune of the Internet, for it allows people to experiment with their identity and instantly change their gender with a few strokes of the keyboard.

Identity cues are sparse in the virtual world, but not nonexistent. People become attuned to the nuances of e-mail addresses and signature styles. New phrases evolve that mark their users as members of a chosen subculture. Virtual reputations are established and impugned. By looking closely at these cues, at how they work and when they fail, we can learn a great deal about how to build vibrant online environments. Instead of being judged by others through birthright, and other social and economic categories, interacting in cyberspace allows to choose where and how to belong. It becomes very easy to send e-mails, messages, and information without anyone knowing who sent it and without having to account for the actions.

In Goffman's analysis, he sees us performing in different types of settings. Usually, the setting stays constant during our performance and it is only rarely that the setting follows us. Basically, we fit into the setting (Goffman 1959). When looking at the interaction in cyberspace, we see that the setting forces the user to transform them, and the setting fits the user. The Internet offers different scenarios and creates a setting that is conducive to anonymity and pseudonymity; many find it easy and sometimes necessary to change their persona or to change their front. Being anonymous in cyberspace is helpful to those who live in countries where freedom of speech and press may not be so widely upheld. It creates an open forum to communicate and inform others without danger to themselves. Also, anonymity creates a situation where there is no gender, race, or prejudice; it transcends these boundaries and everyone can be seen as equal. The cyberspace environment is constantly changing, the setting is never constant, and thus it makes it easier for people to remain "hidden." Anonymous interaction maintains privacy, but not at the expense of social isolation. What other medium will allow you to enter new worlds and meet new people without having to follow rules of specific conduct? It becomes possible to exit a setting or change a setting that you do not like, whereas in face-to-face communication, this is not easy. But what are the consequences of operating this way in cyberspace?

Just as anonymity conceals an individual's real identity in online communication, pseudonymity also serves to disguise it. Similar to anonymity, pseudonymity involves the sender changing his or her name as opposed to not sending one at all. And, just like anonymity, pseudonymity is both untraceable and traceable (Jacobson 1996). With untraceable pseudonymity, the sender will change his or her real name to something else. If the sender becomes worried that someone may try to masquerade under their pseudonym, the sender can sign his or her name with a digital signature created specifically for the pseudonym. This will help detect any forged signatures and create a digital persona or a "nym" (Froomkin 1996). Traceable pseudonymity is communication with a "nom de plume" attached which can be traced back to the author. Why would people want to communicate in such a manner?

There are many benefits to anonymous interaction on the Internet, but do these benefits outweigh the social reality? In our lives, we do present various fronts, but when we do, we are accountable for our actions. This is a disadvantage to anonymity, because there is no face-to-face communication or interaction. You no longer have to be accountable for what you say or do. Often, Internet users evade or hinder accountability which allows them to express feelings without taking into perspective how someone else may feel. In the real world of face-to-face communication, such outbursts of inappropriate behavior would bring about retaliation. Also, with anonymity, the Internet's communal nature is broken. The once open forum of open communication and debate is vastly transferred when you are bombarded with anonymous rhetoric. Since the user is able to put on as many fronts without being held accountable, a high level of uncertainty is created among users. Therefore, positive personal relationships on the Internet are rare and infrequent. It takes longer to move toward shared points of views and it becomes easier to engage in more verbal aggression. Unfortunately, there is no easy way to balance the benefits from the consequences, which means that all users out there must beware because things may not be as they seem. The key concepts of social interaction, social bonding, and empirical experience differ in cyberspace from the physical world. Such differences should inform the debate about the nature and form of regulation of cyberspace. We will now illustrate how this appreciation of community and identities can inform the debate on regulating stalking in cyberspace.

"WHERE EVIL DARE: STALKING IN CYBERSPACE"[7]

When you're growing up your parents tell you not to talk to strangers, but the whole point of the Internet is to talk to strangers.

The nature and extent of cyberstalking is difficult to quantify.[8] It is perhaps more difficult to assess than physical stalking, given the anonymity and breadth of electronic communication. In addition, cyberstalking is difficult to assess in terms of its incidence and prevalence within any given population because some victims may not consider the behavior to be dangerous, indeed they may even be unaware they are stalked. There is no comprehensive data on the extent of cyberstalking, and limited research has been carried out in the area of cyberstalking. In August 1999, the U.S. Justice Department published a report examining the problem of **online harassment** and cyberstalking. The report accepts that the nature and extent of cyberstalking is difficult to quantify; however, the report suggests that the potential magnitude of the problem may be estimated by reference to the problem of real-life stalking (Ellison 2001, 142).

In the United Kingdom, the findings of the 1998 British Crime Survey suggested that only 11.8 percent of the population had been victims of stalking in the past (Budd, Mattinson, and Myhill 2000 as cited in Bocij 2003); as yet there are no separate statistics for cyber crimes but overall harassment rose 23 percent to 137,460 incidents in 2002–03. There are no reliable estimates of the number of cyberstalking incidents that take place each year.[9] That it may be more common has been suggested by Bocij and McFarlane (2002a) who argue that

> A number of factors may encourage an otherwise peaceful and law-abiding individual to take part in deviant or criminal acts via the Internet. One such factor is that modern technology helps to . . . enable participation without fear of sanctions. Technology provides both the mechanism through which the individual can act and the protection needed against arrest or other punishment.

We would suggest that cyberstalking is not merely stalking using the Internet but that there are qualitative differences between stalking in the physical and cyberspace. As to the differences between physical world crimes and cyberworld crimes, Wall (2005) has suggested a so-called "elimination test" to define differing forms of "cyber crimes." Using this

---

[7]Parts of this section are drawn from Bocij (2002) and are used with his permission.

[8]Detailed statistics on cyberstalking are difficult to obtain. The very nature of the online crime means the victims do not know their harasser nor do they have any information about them. Add to this the potential for anonymity and this presents potentially insurmountable problems for law enforcement agencies. Of statistics on reported crime e-mail is the most popular stalking method used followed by message boards (including news groups), messaging, then chat.

[9]Published statistics do not separate out cyberstalking from general harassment. In the United States, there are over 1.5 million reported incidents of harassment every year. It is not possible to separate cyberstalking, although Working to Halt Online Abuse comment "Currently there are over one billion people online worldwide—if only one percent become victims, that's ten million people!" (Yet this organization only reports 372 incidents in 2006.) (Working to Halt Online Abuse, Online Harassment/Cyberstalking Statistics, http://www.haltabuse.org/resources/stats/index.shtml; accessed April 3, 2007). Similarly in the United Kingdom, separate statistics are not collated. However, harassment offences show approximately 10 percent increase year on year since 2003 (Home Office Statistics, http://www.crimestatistics.org.uk; accessed April 3, 2007), where in 2004–5 of the 2.4 million reported incidents 18 percent were harassment involving no physical injury to the victim (Social Trends 2006, accessed at http://www.statistics.gov.uk/socialtrends36/).

test he concludes that there are three types of cyber crimes: firstly, traditional crimes where the Internet is simply a tool to assist in the crime, an example of this would be the use of e-mail by those planning a robbery. Secondly, hybrid crimes which he describes as where "the internet has opened up entirely new opportunities" for existing criminal activities; and finally, true cyber crimes which are "solely the product of the internet and can only be perpetrated within cyberspace" (e.g., spamming). Using this analysis, cyberstalking would appear at first sight to be a hybrid crime. However, the significant differences between offline and online stalking are such that we are hesitant to describe cyberstalking as a mere variant of physical stalking. This may not be what Wall and the elimination test are implying, but the use of the term hybrid for us has a diluting effect, which may hide the true characteristics and effects of this activity and as a result lead to the misinterpretation of its consequences.

What then are these substantial differences? Firstly, the nature and form of the behavior lead to differences. For the investigator or concerned Internet user, information relating to the behavior often exhibited by a stalker will be important, as this may provide insight into possible motivations behind the offender. The fact that cyberstalking does not involve physical contact may create the misperception that it is more benign than physical stalking. This is not necessarily true. As the Internet becomes an ever more integral part of our personal and professional lives, stalkers can take advantage of the ease of communications as well as increased access to personal information. In addition, the ease of use and nonconfrontational, impersonal, and sometimes anonymous nature of Internet communications may remove disincentives to cyberstalking. Where a potential stalker may be unwilling or unable to confront a victim in person or on the telephone, he or she may have little hesitation sending harassing or threatening electronic communications to a victim. This lack of knowledge means that the harm suffered by victims of cyberstalking is often dismissed. However,

> to argue that an act of cyberstalking is less serious than stalking will grant an would-be offender the right to harass, humiliate or defame individuals simply on the basis that it is not "real". There is always attempt made by some commentators to oversimplify what is a far complex act of crime for "the sake of a presumed theoretical, methodological or philosophical bias." (Williams 2004, 153)

The second area of difference surrounds the relationship of stalker and victim. We can speculate that a significant number of cyberstalking victims do not know the identity of their harassers. Given the enormous amount of personal information available through the Internet, a cyberstalker can easily locate private information about a potential victim with a few mouse clicks or keystrokes. This contrasts with offline stalking, where research has shown that the majority of stalkers know their victims. However, the nature of Internet and the proximity it creates make it possible for cyberstalking to be committed by strangers. This would lead to a qualitative difference between offline and online stalking. The third difference surrounds the nature of the acts; cyberstalkers tend to concentrate on very different activities from physical stalkers. Particularly cyberstalking has been said to comprise three major types:

> Email Stalking: Direct communication through email. Internet Stalking: Global communication through the Internet. Computer Stalking: Unauthorized control of another person's computer. (Ogilvie 2000)

To these should be added SMS and text messaging through mobile phones.[10] These show obvious parallels between offline and online stalking; for instance, "attempting to cause damage to data by inserting a computer virus onto the victim's computer system is comparable to the vandalism experienced by some victims of offline stalking, yet there are also a number of important differences in the behaviors associated with offline and online stalking" (Standage 1998). Ogilvie (2000) and Jenson (1996), who have investigated the characteristics of cyberstalking, claim cyberstalkers have similar characteristics to the offline stalkers, with most cyberstalkers motivated to control the victim (Maxwell 2001). A cyberstalker can dupe other Internet users into harassing or threatening a victim by utilizing Internet bulletin boards or chat rooms. For example, a stalker may post a controversial or enticing message on the board under the name, phone number, or e-mail address of the victim, resulting in subsequent responses being sent to the victim. "The harm caused by 'cyber-smearing' is often far more serious than any equivalent offline acts. This is because information posted to the Internet is available to a huge audience and can remain easily accessible for a great deal of time." Because of lack of detailed evidence, it also difficult to estimate the timescale over which a typical cyberstalking case unfolds. Jenson argues "that as internet provides anonymity and simplicity for stalkers whereby, the cyberstalkers identity can be concealed which allows the cyberstalking to continue longer than offline stalking" (Jenson 1996), whilst it is possible to argue that cyberstalking cases take place over a shorter period.

REGULATING CYBERSTALKING

Whilst significant, the above differences do not tell the whole story. The nature of the community and those who populate it are fundamentally different from the physical world such that the nature and form of any regulation should be different. What does this brief analysis of the nature of cyberstalking does is to enable us to reflect upon the nature of regulation required for this activity. Fundamentally the nature of cyberspace is such that it is seen to encourage stalking. However, it can be argued that merely having the ability to do something does not necessarily motivate a person to carry out that action. As we previously suggested, a key element in the cyber community is the sense of anonymity which reduces inhibitions; users of the Internet often manifest reduced self-restraint and a significant percentage of them engage in behaviors in this medium that are not in concordance with social norms which includes both pro- and antisocial behaviors, including self-disclosure, and causes variety of interpersonal behavior (Bubaš 2001). It is well known that people engage in behaviors they would normally deem inappropriate in physical world.[11] They feel more uninhibited, express themselves more openly. Researchers call this the "disinhibition effect." Kiesler, Siegal, and

---

[10]It is somewhat ironic that the latest forms of cyberstalking have reverted to the telephone network given the Internet has grown out of this network (Standage 1998).

[11]Social regulation is effective when people feel the need to conform to social norms. In cyberspace, social norms do not operate as a regulatory force; there are many incidents of people abusing the freedoms that the digital world provides. For example, as discussed in "A Rape in Cyberspace," one individual chose to use his account to harass others, resulting in collective aggravation without a real mechanism for stopping the behavior (Dibbell 1993). (Boyd, D. 2002. *Faceted Id/Entity: Managing Representation in A Digital World* (MIT)).

McGuire (1984) have argued that Internet encourages antinormative, aggressive, uninhibited behavior.

> The most general cause of problematic behaviours when using Internet is related to the phenomenon of behavioural disinhibition. In face-to-face communication, individuals are constrained by the social rules that govern interpersonal interaction, immediate negative feedback, and visible consequences of their inappropriate behaviour, as well as by possible social sanctions. However, when using the Internet the users reside in relative anonymity and physical safety, distant from others in interaction, often unaware of their identities and personalities, as well as of the negative consequences of their risky or potentially damaging behaviour. This contributes to the expression of anger or aggression, inappropriate self-disclosure, or personal use of socially doubtful material on the Internet, like pornography.

It is possible to offer several explanations for this, including the freedom to idealize that the lack of visual cues provides the ability for communicators to choose which aspects of the self to disclose and when to disclose them; however, according to Kiesler, Siegal, and McGuire (1984) "computer-mediated communication seems to comprise some of the same conditions that are important for 'deindividuation.' " Furthermore, Rowland (2000) suggests,

> Over the last century there have been a number of social psychological studies of what has been termed "deindividuation," the state of alienation, reduced inhibition and lack of self-awareness which occurs when a personal sense of identity is overwhelmed and subjected to the group.

Disinhibition experienced by many Internet users has been identified as a result of "deindividuation." Isolation is one of a number of factors that produce a condition that Zimbardo (1969) termed "deindividuation." "Deindividuation occurs when people are in anonymity-producing situations that reduce their concerns about being evaluated by others. They lose self-consciousness and, in turn, are more likely to do things that they would otherwise not do" (Diener 1980). It can be argued that when deindividuation occurs, this actually increases the individual's sensitivity and disobedience to situational norms. These situational norms and cues would normally indicate what appropriate and desirable behavior is in a particular context. "Hence deindividuation effects on private self awareness, as result of a group membership, can impair the ability to regulate one's behaviour" (Willison 2001). However, this view of the average Internet user as deindividuated has been strongly criticized (Lea et al. 1992). Although there is some evidence that both task-focus and negative, antisocial behavior do occur, Lea et al. (1992) rejected the assumption that the lack of contextual cues and the relative anonymity lead to crass antinormative behavior, and argued that "may represent a more intrinsically 'social' medium of communication than the apparently richer context of face-to-face interaction, and one that gives fuller rein to fundamentally social psychological factors."

Joinson (1998) criticized the idea that many Internet users may be deindividuated. He recommended from a social identity explanation of deindividuation effects an alternative explanation for the hostile or aggressive behavior of some Internet users. Joinson (1998) cites Reicher (1984) to suggest "most deindividuation effects reported by Zimbardo onwards can be explained without recourse to deindividuation. Anonymity, because of the lack of focus on the self as an individual, tends to lead to the activation of social identities rather than the activation of personal identities. This would lead to the regulation of behaviour based on the norms associated with the salient social group" (Joinson 1998, 27). Many studies of online communities have described how groups develop norms for their interaction and that some users take on the norms associated with the social group(s) to which they belong (Barzilai-Nahon and Neumann 2005; Kling and Courtright 2003; Preece 2001). The term "ways of speaking" is used in the ethnography of communication to describe how group values, beliefs, and social structures are embodied in a culture's language form and use. If this stereotype is known to somebody identifying with that group, the person will strive to adhere to the group norms in order to stay in favor with the group.

McKenna and Bargh (2000) claim that "it is not surprising then that de-individuation and the negative results that often accompany it . . . readily occur on the Internet" so it is reasonable to believe that people belonging to groups in which aggression is not the exception, but the norm, and which promote hate speech or racist ideologies may eventually take on the norms of these groups and begin to behave accordingly. In this view, group members following group norms that are at odds with wider social norms are not engaging in antinormative behavior.

> When people pursue activities that are harmful to others for reasons of personal gain or social pressure, they avoid facing the harm they cause or minimize it. If minimization does not work, the evidence of harm can be discredited. As long as the harmful results of one's conduct are ignored, minimized, distorted or disbelieved, there is little reason for self-censure to be activated. It is easier to harm others when their suffering is not visible and when injurious actions are physically and temporally remote from their effects. (Bandura 1999)

It can be argued that cyberspace helps to support such behavior on pretext of anonymity and a false sense of power. Hidden in cyberspace is the mystery of the invisible hand of aggression, of control without authority. The manifestation of this misconduct is most likely to be charged under statutes in place in the respective jurisdictions. The range of activities associated with cyberstalking is such that the content of e-mails and texts may contravene laws on pornography, blasphemy, and incitement to racial hatred. The regulation relating to cyberstalking is merely using or an adaptation of existing laws to extend and cover the behaviors evident in cyberstalking. The UK's Protection from Harassment Act would clearly cover cyberstalking activities whilst the Criminal Justice and Police Act 2001 extend the Malicious Communications Act 1988 to include electronic communications. This is in addition to the relevance of specific computer crime offences created by the Computer Misuse Act 1990.[12] The Act was designed in a time of mainframes and terminals, but the offences are deemed sufficiently broad to cover several cyberstalking activities including Internet stalking and computer stalking.[13] How effective then are the laws adapted from those primarily designed to

---

[12]The 1990 Act creates three new offences: unauthorised access (s.1), unauthorised access with intent to commit or facilitate the commission of further offences (s.2), and unauthorised modification of computer material (s.3).
[13]The All Party Internet Group (2004) of Parliament was of the view that the Act had adapted to contemporary events reasonably well.

deal with physical stalking?[14] A recent case before the English Court of Appeal (Criminal Division) *R Debnath (Anita)* [2005] EWCA Crim 3472 shows the use of enforcement orders designed for physical stalking in a cyberstalking case. The court had to review the width of a restraining order under the UK's Protection from Harassment Act, section 2. In this case, Anita Debnath had undertaken a 12-month campaign against her former lover and his fiancée. This had involved sending e-mails, interfering with his e-mail account, and paying a group of hackers to sabotage his e-mail account. The restraining order made prohibited her from contacting directly or indirectly him or his fiancée and publishing any information about them whether or not it be true. In the context of the Human Rights Act, it was held that in the case of noncelebrities, an order restraining the publication of the truth could be proportionate to protect them from furthest harassment. As such, the original order was upheld.

Comparisons with other cyber crimes show that, for example, SPAM increased following the introduction of the U.S. antispam legislation (Gaudin 2004 cited by Wall 2004, 332). Using Wall's definitions of cyber crimes (Wall 2005, fn. 13), SPAM is true cyber crime and these may be less receptive to solution through strictly legal means. Cyberstalking, which in Wall's terms is not a true cyber crime, does not seem to sit comfortably within the hybrid definition, particularly when the impact of cyber society and deindividuation are considered. Brenner (2001) has taken a first step in this analysis by examining the nature of the behavior in cyber crimes; she concludes:

> Unlike the offences heretofore discussed, cyber-stalking cannot be addressed simply by tweaking the principles we use to impose liability for stalking in the physical world . . . [W]e have to create a new crime, one that encompasses the actus reus, mens rea and attendant circumstances characteristic of the activity we now call cyber-stalking. We can do this in two different ways: One is to revise the elements we use to impose liability for traditional stalking so that they remedy the deficiencies noted above and identify the result as a new crime: cyber-stalking. A better approach is to study the components of this activity as it exists and as we think it may come to exist, and parse these components into the constitutive elements (actus reus, mens rea, attendant circumstances and harm) of one or more new crimes.

We respectfully agree, but would comment that this analysis moves from the assumption of criminalizing the activity, and from considering regulation only through law. Cyberspace has, as we commented earlier, rekindled the debate between regulatory forms, often encapsulated in the terms East Coast (law) and West Coast (technology) (Brownsword 2005, 2006). Whilst writers vacillate between the two, we would suggest that a wider analysis involving the

---

[14]Beginning with California in 1990, states and the federal government drafted statutes to address the crime of stalking. By 1993 all 50 states and the District of Columbia had passed some form of antistalking legislation. In 1996, Congress enacted federal legislation to combat stalking. The first U.S. state to include online communications in its statutes against stalking was the state of Michigan in 1993. Other states which have antistalking laws that include electronic harassment include Arizona, Alaska, Connecticut, New York, Oklahoma, and Wyoming. Arizona Criminal Code (1995): 13-2921, Alaska Criminal Law Sec. 11.41.270; Connecticut Penal Code Sec. 53a-183; New York Penal Code § 240.30; Oklahoma Code (1996): §21-1173; and Wyoming Code: 6-2-506. Of the 22 states that have so far enacted cyberstalking laws, the majority have merely expanded existing stalking laws to include cyberstalking. In the United States, the constitutionality of state antistalking legislation remains undecided. Antistalking legislation has been challenged on the grounds of being too vague and too broad.

nature of cyber communities would enable a consolidation of the three elements we consider fundamental to the discussion of the nature of the regulation (role of self help, etc.) required to deal with cyberstalking: the differences between physical and cyberstalking, the character of cyberspace and its community and the effects on the social interactions, the nature of social ties, and the scope of experience and reality. With such an analysis, it is not obvious that either form of regulatory regime is not appropriate (Brownsword 2006), nor is it obvious how formal legal identities and responsibilities can be imposed upon such "virtual" actors.

For example, the scope, timescale, and anonymity of the perpetrator of cyberstalking impact upon the harm suffered by the victim. The scale of the cyberstalking may be considerable in terms of its breadth, covering e-mails, chat rooms, and even the victim's computer; this could be seen to be aggravated by the fact that the perpetrator is unknown to the victim. Yet the context is such that the threat is a nonphysical one and the victim may themselves have taken advantage of anonymity, may have created and furthered an imaginary character and life which is now the subject of the attack. To what extent is the victim who is happy to play the part of an imaginary character be able to complain if that character is stalked or indeed requisitioned by others, given that self-help may be both simple and effective? What would be the place of traditional defenses and sanctions in this scenario? To which legal identity does one impose regulation and liability? Political reactions to this situation often jump at measures aiming at restoring the transparency of potentially criminal behavior without understanding the true nature of the crime and against whom it is being perpetrated. There is a symbiotic relationship between an individual and social identity which Goffman argued is based upon the categorization of an individual to determine the acceptability of the membership of certain social group. The imaginary character and life of the victim has that social identity just because of belonging to a community that exists in the cyberspace. It is also the very anonymity of the Internet that raises the question of what constitutes "normal" and "deviant." In a society dominated by the social norms that protects "social identity," any behavior that infringes the "norm" is deviant and is open to sanctions.

Regulation of cyberstalking will not only hinge upon laws which are flexible enough to deal with electronic harassment (Ellison 2001, 146). Cyberstalking is a relatively new criminal phenomenon. Often law enforcement agencies do not have the resources or the technology to deal with the offences. In several instances, victims have been told by the law enforcement agency simply to turn off their computers (Ellison 2001). Therefore, victims of online harassment and threats, often in collaboration with victim service providers and advocates, have had to step in to fill the void by developing their own informal support networks and informational Web sites to exchange information about how to respond to these crimes effectively (United States Attorney General 1999).

Further, many of the solutions to cyberstalking will come about through personal intervention. A mixed solution is one involving not only regulation but also a mix of personal and technological strategies.[15] A move to gender and age neutral identities would clearly reduce the risk of stalking, as again would the use of ISPs that provide specific policies, schemes, and technological deterrents prohibiting harassment and abusive behavior. Situational crime prevention, self-help responses, or joint activities between users and ISPs are not without their

---

[15]Purely technological solutions could make matters worse by hardening the resolve of the stalker.

difficulties; those involving regulations or strategies are unlikely to be transparent or account-able as would legislation (Katyal 2003).

While many may object that personal protection strategies are an infringement upon people's right to travel freely in cyberspace, the fact is that personal prevention is taken on a daily basis in the physical world, and the cyberworld is no different; and as Ogilvie (2000) argues people should therefore become more responsible and should follow simple strategies such as not providing personal information to strangers that are just as, if not more, applicable in cyberspace. People who participate in the cyberworld will minimize the likelihood of their being stalked by using techniques such as gender neutral and age neutral names. Personal information should not be recorded on the Internet and people should hesitate before filling in electronic forms which request names, age, addresses, together with personal likes and dis-likes. Similarly, people can be proactive before signing on to an ISP provider by researching beforehand on whether there are specific policies prohibiting harassment, abusive behaviors, and cyberstalking.

But this then must bring us back to regulation. Are we, as Brenner (2001) suggests, merely tinkering at the edges of the problem of regulation? For Wall (2004) the nature of the regulation depends upon the categorization of the crime; for him a clear distinction can be made between pure and hybrid cyber crime—the former requiring "a mix of private legal action and technology" as he describes a "digital realist approach." This would lead us to sub-categorize cyberstalking to differentiate between mere extension of physical stalking, where the victim is known to the stalker and technology is merely being used to provide new oppor-tunities, and pure cyberstalking, where the victim and stalker may be hidden in pseudo char-acters, in a virtual world far removed from reality. Whilst there would appear to be little to prevent the former hybrid stalking from being rightly brought within existing criminal law (stalking with new tools), it would be equally perverse to simply extend legislation to cover pure cyberstalking. As Lacey (2002) comments,

> Criminal Law is therefore implicitly justified not only in terms of its role in proscribing, condemning, and (perhaps) reducing conduct which causes or risks a variety of harms, but also in treating its subjects with respect, as moral agents whose conduct must be assessed in terms of attitudes and intentions and not merely in terms of effects.

Whether cyberstalking is considered a hybrid or as a pure cyber crime, we would argue that the nature of the activity and the community requires a more radical review of the issues and not fall back on merely extending existing legislation and/or technological solutions. Whereas a digital realist perspective would suggest that Internet users should tolerate some stalking as users choose to enter cyberspace with knowledge of the nature of the community and perva-sive anonymity, we would question whether the behavior should be categorized as criminal. Is not this behavior acceptable within that community? Put more starkly looking at the differ-ences between physical and cyberstalking, the character of cyberspace and its community and the effects on the social interactions, the nature of social ties, and the scope of experience and reality—should we be criminalizing or indeed even regulating this behavior? In essence the question comes down to the perceived need to regulate this particular behavior in cyberspace and criminalize this behavior. The attraction of regulation depends very much on who one is, where one stands, and the community in which this behavior operates. Legislators and writers steeped in rule of law see the only solution to be some form of regulation fixed on legal identities (Lessig 1999; Bocij and McFarlane 2002b; Brownsword 2006). Fixed within the physical world imposed, formal and bureaucratic regulation is a given. This need not be the case. Communities and activities thrive both within and without formal regulatory mechanisms (Jones and Cameron 2005; McCann 1998). Cyberspace has stretched the applicability of such regulation beyond breaking point, and we would question whether, given the nature of the community and the often anonymous actors, it is appropriate to impose a formal identity and regulation. There is a place for nonregulatory environments, and cyberspace is such an example. Regulation may destroy the very form and nature of the behavior, and the environment will be left the poorer. Two examples may serve to illustrate the point. Firstly, spam where East Coast technologies could be used to prevent all unsolicited e-mails. However, cyberspace with all spam removed would be a very different, and some would say a poorer, place (Wall 2004). Secondly, the opportunities for creativity in cyberspace and the clash with tradition rules of intellectual property. Whilst noting the oppressive nature of intellectual property regimes, writers have struggled to hold down the emancipating role of cyberspace in the creative environment and have succumb to the need for some regulation albeit in a more limited form (Lessig 2004; Gowers Review of Intellectual Property 2006). Such watered down regulatory forms have failed to find favor with either the creative industries or the artists and are seen as used only by nerds or hobbyists. Regulation may therefore be at best futile and at worst damaging.

CONCLUSION

The main problem of the cyberspace is linked to its ubiquitous nature and its immateriality: cyberspace is not rooted in a kind of material reality; it is, instead, the result of its substitution with its iconic counterpart. The concept of border limits disappear and then the concept of nationality. The peculiarities of cyberspace, particularly anonymity, mean it is not simply a question of transferring behaviors across from the physical world, communities in cyberspace are different and so is their behavior. We would reiterate the key concepts of social interaction, social bonding, and empirical experience differ in cyberspace from the physical world. Such differences should inform the debate about the nature and form of regulation of cyberspace. The debate we have argued has taken a wrong turn, and we would suggest the debate should now rethink the basic concepts upon which regulation is based. These boundaries between public and private law, between national and international law, and between state law and self-regulation, nor indeed the traditional positivist methodology of law, no longer offer an adequate intellectual framework in which to consider the nature and form of regulation in cyberspace. As with all analysis of the process and concept of law, the foundation should be an investigation of the community over which the regulation is to apply; we cannot regulate cyberspace without an understanding of cyberspace. In the case of pure cyberstalking, the nature of the community, the activity, and the actors lead us to the conclusion that rather than considering the form of the regulation, we should consider whether there can be any regulation at all. Rather than accept inappropriate regulation, we would urge that in relation to pure cyberstalking consideration be given to a regulatory-free approach. As Bowrey (2005) comments, in relation to the imposition of intellectual property rules in cyberspace, ". . . a law free sign still has some currency in it."

KEY TERMS

Anonymity	Jurisdiction
Cyberspace	Online harassment
Cyberstalking	Regulation

REFERENCES

Abercrombie, N., and B. Longhurst. 1998. *Audiences*. London: Sage.

Alexander, G. S. 1989. Dilemmas of group autonomy: Residential associations and community. *75 Cornell Law Review* 1: 17–33.

Bandura, A. 1999. Moral disengagement in the perpetration of inhumanities. *Personality and Social Psychology Review* 3: 193–209.

Barzilai-Nahon, K., and S. Neumann. 2005. Bounded in cyberspace: An empirical model of self-regulation in virtual communities, system sciences, HICSS '05. Proceedings of the 38th Annual Hawaii International Conference on, Volume 7, January 3–6, 2005.

Baudrillard, J. 1988. *Selected Writings*, edited by M. Poster. Cambridge: Polity Press.

Bendle, M. F. 2002. The crisis of identity in high modernity. *British Journal of Sociology* 53: 1–18.

Bocij, P. July 11, 2002. Corporate cyberstalking: An invitation to build theory. *First Monday*, http://firstmonday.org/issues/issue7_11/bocij/

Bocij, P. August 10, 2003. Victims of cyber stalking: An exploratory study of harassment perpetrated via the Internet. *First Monday*, http://firstmonday.org/issues/issue8_10/bocij/index.html

Bocij, P., and L. McFarlane. 2002a. Online harassment: Towards a definition of cyber stalking. *Prison Service Journal* 139: 31–8.

Bocij, P., and L. McFarlane. 2002b. Cyber stalking: Genuine problem or public hysteria? *Prison Service Journal* 140: 32–5.

Bowrey, K. 2005. *Law and Internet Cultures*. Melbourne: Cambridge University Press.

Brenner, S. W. April 1, 2001. Is there such a thing as "virtual crime"? *California Criminal Law Review*.

Brownsword, R. 2005. Code, control, and choice: Why East is East and West is West. *Legal Studies* 25 (1): 1.

Brownsword, R. 2006. Neither East nor West, is Mid-West best? *Script-ed* 1 (3).

Bryant, R. 2001. What kind of space is cyberspace? *Minerva—An Internet Journal of Philosophy* 5: 138–55.

Bubaš, G. 2001. Computer mediated communication theories and phenomena: Factors that influence collaboration over the Internet. Paper presented at the 3rd CARNet Users Conference, Zagreb.

Budd, T., J. Mattinson, and A. Myhill. 2000. *The Extent and Nature of Stalking: Findings from the 1998 British Crime Survey*. London: Home Office Research, Development and Statistics Directorate.

Byassee, W. S. 1995. Jurisdiction of cyberspace: Applying real world precedent to the virtual community, *30 Wake Forest Law Review* 197: 207–8.

Calhoun, C. 1991. "Indirect relationships and imagined communities: Large-scale social integration and the transformation of everyday life." In *Social Theory for a Changing Society*, edited by P. Bourdieu and J. S. Coleman. San Francisco, Oxford: Boulder.

Cerulo, K. A. 1997. Reframing social concepts for a brave new (virtual) world. *Sociological Inquiry* 67 (1): 48–58.

Detwiler, L. 1993. Identity, privacy, and anonymity on the Internet. Available from the World Wide Web at: http://www.eff.org/pub/Privacy/Anonymity/privacy-anonymity.faq

Dibbell, J. 1993. A rape in cyberspace or how an evil clown, a Haitian trickster spirit, two wizards, and a cast of dozens turned a database into a society. *Village Voice*.

Diener, E. 1980. "Deindividuation: The absence of self-awareness and self-regulation in group members." In *The Psychology of Group Influence*, edited by P. B. Paulus, 209–42. Hillsdale, NJ: Lawrence Erlbaum.

Ellison, L. 2001. "Tackling harassment on the Internet." In *Crime and the Internet*, edited by D. Wall. London: Routledge.

Finch, E. 2002. "What a tangled web we weave: Identity theft and the Internet." In *Dot. Cons*, edited by Y. Jewkes. Devon: Willan Publishing.

Froomkin, A. M. 1996. Flood control on the information ocean: Living with anonymity, digital cash and distributed databases. *U. Pittsburgh Journal of Law and Commerce* 15: 395. Online via http://www.law.miami.edu/~froomkin/articles/ocean1.htm

Gaudin, S. July 1, 2004. U.S. sending more than half of all spam. Internetnews.com, http://www.internetnews.com/stats/article.php/3376331

Gelbstein, E., and A. Kamal. November 2002. *Information Insecurity: A Survival Guide to the Uncharted Territories of Cyber-Threats and Cyber-Security*. 2nd ed. United Nations ICT Task Force and United Nations Institute of Training and Research. http://www.un.int/kamal/information_insecurity

Gibson, W. 1984. *Neuromancer*. London: Grafton.

Giordano, P. 1998. Invoking law as a basis for identity in cyberspace. *Stanford Technology Law Review* 1, 8, http://stlr.stanford.edu/STLR/Articles/98_STLR_1/

Goffman, E. 1959. *The Presentation of Self in Everyday Life*. London: Penguin Books.

Goffman, E. 1963. *Stigma: Notes on the Management of Spoiled Identity*. Englewood Cliffs, NJ: Prentice-Hall.

Goldsmith, J. 1998. Against cyberanarchy. *University of Chicago Law Review* 65: 1239–40.

Gowers Review of Intellectual Property. 2006. http://www.hm-reasury.gov.uk/independent_reviews/gowers_review_intellectual_property/gowersreview_index.cfm

Jacobson, D. 1996. Contexts and cues in cyberspace: The pragmatics of naming in text-based virtual realities. *Journal of Anthropological Research* 52 (4): 461–79.

Jenson, B. 1996. Cyberstalking: Crime, enforcement and personal responsibility of the on-line world. *S.G.R. MacMillan*. Available at http://www.sgrm.com/art-8.htm

Johnson, D., and D. Post. 1997. "And how shall the net be governed? A meditation on the relative virtues of decentralized, emergent law." In *Coordinating the Internet*, edited by B. Kahin and J. Keller, 62. Cambridge, Mass: MIT Press.

Joinson, A. 1998. "Causes and implications of disinhibited behaviour on the Internet." In *Psychology and the Internet: Intrapersonal, Interpersonal, and Transpersonal Implications*, edited by J. Gackenbach. San Diego, CA: Academic Press.

Jones, R and E. Cameron. 2005. Full fat, semi-skimmed no milk today—Creative commons licences and English folk music. *International Review of Law, Computers and Technology* 19 (3): 259–75.

Katyal, N. K. 2003. Digital architecture as crime control. *Yale Law Journal* 112: 2261–89.

Kiesler, S., J. Siegal, and T. W. McGuire. 1984. Social psychological aspects of computer mediated communication. *American Psychologist* 39: 1123–34.

Kling, R., and C. Courtright. 2003. "Group behavior and learning in electronic forums: A socio-technical approach." In *Building Online Communities in the Service of Learning*, edited by S. Barab, R. Kling, and J. Gray. Cambridge, UK: Cambridge University Press.

Kuhn, T. 1996. *The Structure of Scientific Revolutions*. 3rd ed. University of Chicago, IL: Chicago Press.

Lacey, N. 2002. "Legal Constructions of Crime." In *The Oxford Handbook of Criminology*, edited by M. Maguire, et al. 3rd ed. Oxford: OUP.

Lea, M., T. O'Shea, P. Fung, and R. Spears. 1992. " 'Flaming' in computer-mediated communication." In *Contexts in Computer-Mediated Communication*, edited by M. Lea. London: Harvester Wheatsheaf.

Lessig, L. 1998. "What things regulate speech: CDA 2.0 vs. filtering." *Jurimetrics Journal* 38 (4): 629–69.

Lessig, L. 1999. *Code and Other Laws of Cyberspace*. London: Routedge.

Lessig, L. 2004. *Free Culture. How Big Media Uses Technology and Law to Lock Down Culture and Control Creativity*. Penguin: New York, and the Creative Common movement, http:// creativecommons.org/ about/legal/

Maxwell, A. 2001. Cyberstalking. Auckland University Department of Psychology. Available at http:// www.netsafe.org.nz/ie/downloads/cyberstalking.pdf

McCann, A. 1998. Traditional music and copyright—The issues. Presented at "Crossing Boundaries," the seventh annual conference of the International Association for the Study of Common Property, Vancouver, British Columbia, Canada, June 10–14, 1998, p. 9.

McKenna, K. Y. A., and J. Bargh. 2000. Plan 9 from cyberspace: The implications of the Internet for personality and social psychology. *Personality and Social Psychology Review*, 4.

Miller, N. 2001. Stalking laws and implementation practices: A national review for policymakers and practitioners. Institute for Law and Justice. Available at http://www.ilj.org/stalking/FinalRpt.pdf

Mitchell, W. J. 1995. *City of Bits—Space, Place and the Infobahn*, 114–15. Cambridge, Mass: MIT Press.

Mnookin, J. 1996. "Virtual(ly) law: Emergence of law on LambdMOO." In *Special Issue on Emerging Law on the Electronic Frontier, Journal of Computer-Mediated Communication* 2/1, edited by A. Branscomb.

O'Connell, R., J. Price, and C. Barrow. 2004. Cyberstalking, abusive cyber sex and online grooming: A programme for education of teenagers. pp. 5–6. Cyberspace Research Unit, University of Lancaster, www.uclan.ac.uk/cru

Ogilvie, E. 2000. Cyberstalking trends and issues in crime and criminal justice, no. 166. Australian Institute of Criminology. Available at http://www.aic.gov.au/publications/tandi/ti166.pdf

Oldenburg, R. 1989. *The Great Good Places*. New York: Paragon House.

Paliwala, A. 2004. Information society e-legal education: Integrating the social economic and political context. LEFIS Workshop Proceedings, University of Durham. Available at http://www.lefis.org

Post, D. 2000. What Larry doesn't get: Code, law and liberty in cyberspace. *Stanford Law Review* 52: 1439.

Post, R. C. 1997. Community and the first amendment. *29 Arizona State Law Journal* 473.

Postman, N. 1992. *Technopoly: The Surrender of Culture to Technology*. New York: Knopf.

Preece, J. 2001. Sociability and usability: Twenty years of chatting online. *Behavior and Information Technology Journal* 20 (5): 347–56.

Purcell, K. 1997. Towards a communication dialectic: Embedded technology and the enhancement of place. *Sociological Inquiry* 67 (1): 101–12.

Reicher, S. D. 1984. Social influence in the crowd: Attitudinal and behavioural effects of deindividuation in conditions of high and low group salience. *British Journal of Social Psychology* 23: 341–50.

Reid, E. 1995. "Virtual worlds: Culture and imagination." In *Cybersociety: Computer-Mediated Communication and Community*, edited by S. G. Jones, 164–83. London: Sage.

Rowland, D. 2000. Anonymity, privacy and cyberspace. Available at http://www.bileta.ac.uk/ Document%20Library/1/Anonymity,%20Privacy%20and%20Cyberspace.pdf

Sherizen, S. 1992. The end of the (ab)user friendly era. *NCCV* 39.

Standage, T. 1998. *The Victorian Internet*. Walker: New York.

Teller, P. 1991. Substance, relations, and arguments about the nature of space-time. *Philosophical Review* 100: 363–97.

The All Party Internet Group. 2004. Revision of the Computer Misuse Act. Available at http://www. apig.org.uk/CMAReportFinalVersion1.pdf

Thomsen, S. R., J. D. Straubhaar, and D. M. Bolyard. 1998. Ethnomethodology and the study of online communities: Exploring the cyber streets. *Information Research* 4 (1).

Turkle, S. 1996. Virtuality and its discontents: Searching for community in cyberspace. *American Prospect* 24: 50–7.

United States Attorney General. 1999. Report on cyberstalking—A new challenge for law enforcement and industry. Available at www. usdoj. gov/ criminal/ cybercrime/ cyberstalking. htm

Wall, D. S. 2004. Digital realism and the governance of spam as cybercrime. *European Journal on Criminal Policy and Research* 10: 309–55.

Wall, D. S. 2005. "The Internet as a conduit for criminals." In *Information Technology and the Criminal Justice System*, edited by A. Pattavina, 77–98. Thousand Oaks, CA: Sage.

Williams, M. 2004. "The language of cybercrime." In *Crime and the Internet*, edited by David Wall, 153. London: Routledge.

Willison, R. 2001. The unaddressed problem of criminal motivation in is security: Expanding the preventive scope through the concept of readying, Working Paper Series. London: London School of Economics.

Zimbardo, P. G. 1969. "The human choice: Individuation, reason, and order vs. deindividuation, impulse and chaos." In *Nebraska Symposium on Motivation*, edited by W. J. Arnold and D. Levine, 237–307. Lincoln: University of Nebraska Press.

Zona, M. A., K. K. Sharma, and M. D. Lane. 1993. A comparative study of erotomanic and obsessional subjects in a forensic sample. *Journal of Forensic Sciences* 38: 894–903. Available at http://www.crimelibrary.com/criminal_mind/psychology/cyberstalking/1.html

Chapter 9

Internet Gambling

Gilbert Geis
University of California, Irvine

Gregory C. Brown
California State University

and

Henry N. Pontell
University of California, Fullerton

Gilbert Geis is professor emeritus in the Department of Criminology, Law and Society, University of California, Irvine. He is a former president of the American Society of Criminology and recipient of its Edwin H. Sutherland Award for outstanding contributions to the field. His most recent books are *White-Collar and Corporate Crime* (2007) and *Criminal Justice and Moral Issues* (with Robert F. Meier 2006).

Gregory C. Brown is an assistant professor of criminal justice at the California State University, Fullerton. He received his MA and Ph.D. from the University of California, Irvine, with an emphasis in criminology. He has published articles in *International Journal of Cyber Criminology*, *Journal of Medical Education*, and *Western State University Consumer Law Journal*. His teaching and research interests include corrections, street gangs, prisons, and punishment theory and practices.

Henry N. Pontell is professor of criminology, law and society and of sociology at the University of California, Irvine. His writings in criminology, criminal justice, and law and society span the areas of white-collar and corporate crime, punishment and corrections, deviance and social control, crime seriousness, and most recently, cyber crime and identity fraud. His recent books include *Profit Without Honor* (4th ed., Prentice Hall, 2007) and *International Handbook of White-Collar and Corporate Crime* (Springer, 2007). A former president of the Western Society of Criminology and vice president of the American Society of Criminology, he has received the Albert J. Reiss, Jr. Distinguished Scholarship Award from the American Sociological Association, and the Donald R. Cressey Award for lifetime contributions to fraud deterrence and detection from the Association of Certified Fraud Examiners.

Abstract

Internet gambling represents, as one writer puts it, the "elusive speeding car on the information superhighway." It presents unique and challenging opportunities and problems throughout the world. For the Third World countries, the opportunity to inaugurate a low-cost Internet structure to attract overseas gambling, especially Americans and Asians, is highly appealing. This chapter traces developments in the world of Internet gambling and, in particular, the efforts of the federal government in the United States to interdict such activity. It considers litigation before the World Trade Organization (WTO) involving the United States and Antigua, and discusses the arrest of several persons involved with Caribbean betting organizations. Finally, it offers some ideas about what the future holds for gambling on the Internet.

INTRODUCTION

The realm of **Internet gambling** at this time is in a state of flux, although some matters are reliably known. We can be certain of the appeal of the enterprise to actual and prospective consumers. We also know that Internet gambling is a tempting target for governments seeking to increase their revenue in a relatively painless manner. That is the demand side of the equation. On the supply side there are moral, social, political, and legal forces seeking to prohibit the introduction and spread of Internet gambling both domestically and across national borders.

How these competing interests will play out remains a matter of speculation. Interpreters may reasonably forecast differing unfolding scenarios. In this chapter, we present information about various developments in the contest between those favoring unrestricted Internet gambling and the forces seeking to ban it. We also attend to those advocating intermediate positions. Since the battle to date primarily has been fought in the legal realm, we summarize case law and legislative developments, including the involvement in the United States of Native-American **casinos**. We also provide cross-cultural insights to convey how jurisdictions other than that of the United States have responded to this new arrival on the gambling scene.

There are a number of reasons why people find gambling attractive. It offers recreation and challenge, heightens emotions, and provides a sense of excitement. The word gambling itself derives from the Middle English term *gamen*, meaning to amuse oneself. This entertainment element of gambling is reflected in a study of 100 Ohio State University students that found that 77 of them had bet online at least once, and, of these, 31 did so at least once a week. Wagering on sports events, they said, added excitement to the games they watched on television (Meier and Geis 2006, 219).

Gambling also plays into a common contemporary human desire to acquire money, perhaps a great deal of it, without the need to work. Wagers represent economic choices made under conditions of varying certainty of the consequences. As such, they can be seen as no different than other ventures in which the odds and the outcomes are in doubt. If your house does not burn down or break up in an earthquake, you forfeit the money you had bet when you purchased a home insurance policy.

Betting casinos also can provide an attractive social atmosphere. There typically is a great deal of activity, a mélange of fellow players and onlookers, a mood of anticipation, and the highs and lows of success and failure. These circumstances are the major underpinnings of an industry that has come to play a prominent role in present-day American life. Las Vegas and Atlantic City dominate the scene. There also are burgeoning gambling sites on Indian reservations, state lotteries, riverboat gambling facilities, **poker** clubs, bingo parlors, pari-mutuel, and offtrack betting venues as well as slot machines, which are now finding their way into horse racing tracks.

In the United States today, only Utah and Hawaii do not allow some form of gambling within their borders. No longer do cash-starved jurisdictions pay heed to the warnings of Cotton Mather, the fire and brimstone preacher of the colonial period, who insisted that gambling defied divine will: "Lots, being mentioned in sacred oracles of scriptures," Mather preached, "are used only in weighty cases, and as an acknowledgement of God's sitting in judgment, cannot be made the tools and parts of our common sports, without, at least, such an appearance of evil as is forbidden by the word of God" (Chafetz 1960, 19). Mather's words form part of a lingering element of the colonial Puritan ethic that maintained that people should prosper and enjoy the good life only through their own toil (or that of their forebears from whom they have inherited wealth) and not by means of luck and chance.

DIFFUSION OF INTERNET GAMBLING

Internet gambling is but another form of wagering, but, as one writer notes, "the nascent challenges imposed by Internet gambling are vast and unique" (Massoud 2004, 989). Another commentator observes that Internet gambling "is the elusive speeding car on the information superhighway, weaving through traffic and seemingly immune to efforts to slow its charge" (Friedrich 2000, 389). A General Accounting Office survey echoes this point: "Internet gambling is an essentially borderless activity that poses regulatory and enforcement challenges" (Jenkins and Keller 2002, 3).

Internet gambling spread dramatically throughout the world after the mid-1990s. At first it involved simulated bets with imaginary money, but the appeal soon led to commercial enterprises, unlike the now deeply entrenched domestic establishments. Internet gambling has aroused strong opposition from politicians, especially on the federal level, aided and abetted by law enforcement agencies. Persons and groups whose moral disapproval of gambling had been pushed aside by governments in their quest for additional sources of tax revenue found themselves in concert with forces who fear the loss of the revenue generated by current forms of wagering if Internet gambling flourishes. Municipalities and states see Internet gambling reducing their income not only from gambling but also from corollary kinds of enterprises, such as restaurants, shops, and motels and hotels.

Internet gambling is vulnerable to such opposition because it lacks some of the key ingredients that have sustained other forms of wagering. It can be, and often is, a solitary activity, and therefore one in which no external checks, such as concerned friends or family, can moderate the behavior. It has been wryly observed that Internet gambling is like placing a slot machine in every home. As Ann Geer, the chair of the National Coalition Against Gambling Expansion, observes, Internet gamblers can "literally click their mouse and bet the house" (Hammer 2001, 108).

A vital matter is that to date no method has been found by means of which Internet gambling revenues can be taxed locally when the transactions involve a person in the United States placing bets on the Internet that are taken in and paid out from a foreign country.

Federal Legislation

Federal legislation to criminalize Internet gambling has become the most prominent vehicle for control, although it must overcome the fundamental objection that the regulation of gambling is a matter that exclusively belongs to the states. Article X of the United States Constitution reads: "The powers not delegated to the United States by the Constitution, nor prohibited by it to the States, are reserved to the States specifically, or to the people." Several court decisions have placed control of gambling exclusively within the domain of state governments. In Nevada, for instance, Frank ("Lefty") Rosenthal was denied a license to operate a gambling facility on the ground that, among other matters, he had been convicted in North

Carolina of a conspiracy to bribe an amateur athlete and had been barred from racetracks and pari-mutuel betting in Florida. A Nevada court upheld the state's Gaming Commission's decision not to license Rosenthal. It ruled that his claim that he had been denied his constitutional rights in the proceedings was irrelevant, since there was no federal issue, only a state concern (*State v. Rosenthal* 1979; Pileggi 1995). Similarly, a United States House of Representatives (2000) report on a gambling bill noted:

> Since the founding of our country, the Federal Government has left gambling regulation to the States. The last two Federal Commissions Congress created to look into gambling have concluded that States are best equipped to regulate gambling within their own borders, and recommended that Congress continue to defer to the States in this regard. (p. 54)

Nonetheless, the federal government has resorted to its right to legislate on interstate commerce to intrude itself into the regulation of gambling. That right was legitimized as far back as 1903 when the United States Supreme Court in a 5-4 decision affirmed the power of Congress to supplement the actions of states in order to further protect citizens against the illegal sale of lottery tickets. Charles Champion and others had traveled from Dallas in Texas to Fresno, California to sell tickets in the Pan-American lottery, a monthly drawing held in Ascension, Paraguay. The dissenters in the case insisted that this was a state not a federal concern, but Champion's conviction remained in place (*Champion v. Ames* 1903).

In recent years, legislative efforts to address Internet gambling stalled in either the House or the Senate or faced irresolvable disagreements between the two bodies in conference committee. Proponents were persistent, however, or, as a columnist in the *Washington Post*, who expressed his displeasure with the bill's continuous reappearance, noted: "It's hard to keep a bad idea down" (Boyer 1999, D1). The truth of that sentiment (putting aside the moral judgment) was demonstrated in 2006 when the Senate leadership inserted a clause in a bill dealing with the safety at seaport sites that mandated that banks and credit card companies could not permit Internet gambling transactions using their facilities. The measure, the Unlawful Internet Gambling Enforcement Act (31 U.S. Code §§5361–5367), was adopted by a late-night vote in the closing moments of the Congressional session and without either committee hearings or floor debate.

The new law supplemented the thrust of a 1988 court decision in which the Providian National Bank had sued Cynthia Haines, a California resident, to recover the $70,000 that she had run up on her credit card through Internet gambling. Haines countersued Providian and a dozen other credit card companies and banks, maintaining that they had engaged in unfair business practices and aided and abetted a crime by giving online betting establishments' merchant accounts to process wagers by customers who lived in places where such gambling is outlawed (Patterson 2002, 641; Gold 2000). Rather than contest the issue, the countersued companies settled, letting Haines escape her debts (*Providian National Bank v. Haines* 1998).

Among the arguable aspects of the 2006 measure was that it focused on trying to prevent Internet gambling rather than on arrangements that might permit satisfactory regulation of the pursuit so that it would satisfy both consumers and the tax collector. Opponents argued that it was much like the ill-fated Volstead Act that sought to outlaw the sale of alcoholic beverages, a measure doomed because it lacked the support of the general public.

Fantasy sports games were excluded from the reach of the new law. Baseball officials believe that these games have exerted a strong influence in the resurgence in baseball attendance figures. In fantasy sports leagues, participants become managers of self-assembled sports teams, choose and trade players, and are rated on the performance of their team. Their activity often involves wagers and the use of the Internet to transmit up-to-date information on injuries and other considerations pertinent to calculating odds (Davidson 2002; Walker 2006).

A large hole in the new statute is the existence of other routes that have been developed for the transfer of funds that thwart blocking the use of credit cards. Firms such as Neteller and FirstPay allow customers to deposit funds that are forwarded to offshore casinos. Neteller, founded in 1999 and traded on the London Stock Exchange, is located in the city of Douglas, on the Isle of Man off the coast of England, and in a recent year served 2.5 million customers, handling $7.5 billion in betting money. Cynics believe that the federal law would be no more than a slight inconvenience. As one lawyer observed: "Money, like water, will find its way. The money will find a way to get to offshore sites" (Schmidt and Garabaldi 2006, A01).

The 2006 bill was opposed by the Poker Players Alliance, which is reported to have 75,000 members and which claims that the federal law against Internet poker games merely will "drive the business of poker underground" (Nakashima 2006, C19).

Some believed that the Congressional attempt to control Internet gambling primarily was a symbolic gesture to distance members facing reelection campaigns from the illegal lobbying efforts of Jack Abramoff, who had spread bribes on behalf of Native-American casinos among legislators, including $50,000 to the wife of an aide of Representative Tom DeLay of Texas, then the Majority Leader of the House of Representatives, to encourage opposition to the proposed Internet gambling act. Abramoff, who pled guilty, received a 70-month prison sentence (Schmidt and Garabaldi 2006, A01).

Native-American Internet Gambling

There are now 310 casinos run by 200 of the 556 federally recognized Native-American tribes. In 1987, a 6-3 decision by the United States Supreme Court declared that neither state nor local laws could be used to ban gambling on tribal grounds (*California v. Cabazon Band of Mission Indians* 1987). The following year, the Congress enacted the Indian Gaming Regulatory Act (IGRA), which legalized gambling on Indian reservations while imposing some mild restrictions. The IGRA sought to promote "tribal economic development, self-sufficiency, and strong tribal government" (18 U.S. Code §2701).

A Native-American casino figured in the first court cases on Internet gambling in the United States. Interactive Casinos, Inc., which had opened on August 15, 1995, accepted bets on 15 of the usual casino forms of play as well as on sports events and on the National Indian Lottery (Girdwood 2002). The Lottery had been created by the Couer d'Alene tribe under a compact with the State of Idaho. Most players were out-of-state residents who had established accounts by check or with credit cards, then purchased chances by telephone or via the Internet. The Internet aspect of the National Indian Lottery was challenged by AT&T, which sought a judgment regarding whether it was obligated to furnish toll-free "800" numbers for the lottery's operation. The tribe won the case on appeal on the ground that the courts had no jurisdiction over reservation of gambling activities (*AT&T v. Couer d'Alene Tribe* 1998).

Matters went otherwise for the Couer d'Alene tribe when the Missouri attorney general sought to enjoin it from selling lottery chances to Missouri residents. The tribe argued that the Indian gaming law provided it with full control over how it went about its wagering program, but a federal appellate court declared that the law specified that this power applied only to gambling conducted on Indian lands and did not extend to territory outside its boundaries (*Missouri v. Couer d'Alene Tribe* 1999). The contrary judgments in the two cases involving the Idaho tribe remain to be reconciled by an opinion from a higher court or by Congressional action.

MGM Mirage

Particularly telling in the story of Internet gambling was the outcome of the effort of the MGM Mirage gambling conglomerate to establish a foothold in the realm of such gambling. MGM Mirage advertises itself as an entertainment, hotel, and gaming enterprise. It has almost two dozen subsidiaries in the United States and on three continents, with the Bellagio in Las Vegas its flagship. MGM Mirage in 2002 became one of three organizations licensed for Internet gambling by the Isle of Man. MGM launched its operation in tandem with Silicon Gaming, a business that develops interactive slot machines.

Bets at MGM Mirage were accepted exclusively from European and other non-American sites, but 20 months after its inception the project was shut down. The reason offered by Terri Lanni, the company's chair and CEO, was that the unstable legal and political situation in the United States made the status of its enterprise unclear and thereby treacherous. Lanni mourned the demise of the experiment. "We set out to prove that online gambling could be implemented with the same high standards of regulatory integrity as land-based operations," Lanni declared. "We were successful in demonstrating a working model." He could not resist a jab at the forces that led to the end of the Internet operation. "On-line gambling is a multi-million dollar industry," Lanni observed, "and it's ridiculous that we can't be part of it." He also pointed out that the United States government was losing close to a billion dollars a year in tax revenues by not legalizing this type of gambling, considering that the largest number of wagers going to offshore sites come from the United States (Mark 2003, 1).

One of Lanni's colleagues speculated that the hounding of Internet gambling efforts by federal authorities in the United States would be alleviated. "From our company's perspective," he noted, "in terms of keeping ourselves in the online gambling space, it is too long to wait [for a resolution of current uncertainties]. But if and when things change, we will come back to it because of our competency" (Mark 2003, 1).

Internet Gambling in Australia

Australia offers an example of permissible, but closely regulated and restricted, Internet gambling. As in the United States, the Australian federal government proclaims that it gives to its states and territories the prerogative to regulate gambling, but, as in the United States, the national legislature has been an active force in molding the country's Internet regimen. The federal Interactive Gambling Act 2001 outlaws the provision of Internet casino gambling to a person physically present in the country whether or not that person is an Australian. Online sports betting remains permissible. The act also prohibits broadcasting, data casting, and publishing an advertisement for Internet gambling.

Otherwise, the Australian federal government defers to the states to determine whether or not to license Internet providers and thereby put them beyond the reach of the Commonwealth statute. The states and territories addressed Internet gambling by appointing a working party in May 1997. Its report opted for state licensing of Internet gambling. Queensland made the first move by adopting most of the major recommendations of the working party. Under its rules, which were largely duplicated by Victoria and the Australian Capital Territory, applicants for a license must demonstrate integrity, suitability, solvency, and a willingness to submit to regulation. They also must agree to periodic inspections and adhere to a Code of Conduct. Minors are to be excluded from gambling on the Internet, credit cannot be extended to customers, and the payout schedule for slot machines has to be made public. Licenses to run an Internet gambling enterprise must be obtained by directors, CEOs, and any person with a 5 percent or greater financial interest in the company. In addition, the organization must permit regular audits of its books. In the Northern Territories and Tasmania, the local laws were amended to regulate Internet gambling. New South Wales, South Australia, and Western Australia have not addressed the issue by statute, but have permitted some operators to engage in Internet gambling.

The issue of compulsive gambling is dealt with in Queensland with the following admonition:

> If a person is concerned about another player's welfare and believes that the gambling habit poses a threat to the player or the player's family, an application may be made to have the player banned from participating in interactive gambling which is licensed in Queensland or in any other participating state (Kelly 2000, 217–18).

Objections to Internet Gambling

Among the more broadly condemnatory attacks on Internet gambling is the sweeping argument by two legal scholars that "policymakers worldwide generally failed to identify the large socio-economic costs associated with Internet gambling, as well as the ability of Internet gambling and other forms of cyberspace gambling to destabilize local, national, and even international economies by disrupting financial institutions" (Kundt and Joy 2002, 111). This seems overstated, but there is no question that there are significant arguments against Internet gambling. Internet gambling sites are "particularly pernicious," a Department of Justice court filing observed, "because they can be accessed so easily by anyone in the country, including particularly vulnerable populations such as children and compulsive gamblers, via a computer or telephone, and also due to the potential for fraud and money laundering" (Frese 2005, 588). For public relations reasons, the loss of revenue tends to be downplayed, probably because it seems less compelling in a roster of more emotionally tinged items, such as protecting children and people with mental problems. Rarely are the theological and other moral reservations about gambling that so characterized its earlier history in the United States raised today, although they assuredly play a part in the current campaign against Internet gambling.

Money Laundering

There is no hard evidence to date that Internet gambling has been used to facilitate the laundering of illegally acquired funds, but that possibility is an argument constantly employed to support control of such gambling (Schopper 2002). How such laundering would work is rather simple. A drug dealer has made $100,000 from the sale of cocaine that he desires to put into a bank account without the likelihood that it will be regarded as ill-gotten. He therefore places two Internet bets at offshore sites. At one, he bets $100,000 that Notre Dame will whip the University of Michigan, and at the other that Michigan will prevail. Whichever team wins, he ends up with $100,000, minus fees, that he can now satisfactorily maintain was the product of wagering and not the income from drug sales.

Some writers suggest that terrorists might also take advantage of Internet gambling sites to launder money, but it is arguable whether this is more in the nature of a scare tactic, an emotional appeal rather than a likely possibility.

Loss of Revenue

The inability to collect taxes on wagers that are made in offshore jurisdictions is probably the most compelling reason for efforts to make such endeavors illegal. One writer had observed that some people believe that "derailing Internet gambling is not about protecting Americans from the scourge of fraud or compulsive gambling: it's about government eliminating an untaxed competitor" (D. Schwartz 2005, 8). Ryan Hammer maintains that Internet betting "not only deprives the economy of valuable tax revenues, but also costs the economy valuable jobs and assorted fees associated with traditional gambling." Hammer offers representative illustrations: Iowa in 2001 collected more than $17 million in taxes and fees from casinos and racetracks. The Casino Queen Riverboat in East St. Louis, Illinois, annually generates between $10 and $12 million in tax money and creates more than 1,200 jobs. It is noteworthy that 16 of the 22 states with the greatest increase in unemployment in the 1980s created lotteries. It is much easier and safer for politicians to support a lottery or a casino riverboat than to propose a tax increase (Hammer 2001, 104, 117–18). In addition, the licensing fees levied against domestic gambling operations are lost when the enterprise is housed overseas. Besides, if wagering moves from established casinos to the Internet, the decline in tourism to gambling sites, such as the 30 million annual visitors to Las Vegas, would constitute a serious economic deprivation.

Addiction

Particularly prominent in the debate on Internet gambling is the position that it can produce a pattern of addiction that has dire consequences both for the gambler and for those dependent upon him or her. In this respect, the highly regarded commentator George Will has called Internet gambling "electronic morphine" (Will 2002, 92). There exists a very large number of case studies of individuals who have been plunged into despair or have committed suicide or have perpetrated crimes, both against property and against persons (as, for instance, to collect insurance or an inheritance), in order to seek to extricate themselves from the financial consequences of a compulsive commitment to wagering.

The major criteria to determine what is said to be pathological gambling are set out in the fourth edition of the diagnostic manual of the American Psychiatric Association (1994) (DSM-IV). The Association maintains that about 4 percent of the American population suffers from a maladaptive gambling disorder during their lifetime. If 5 of the following 10 items are present, then the DSM-IV maintains that we are dealing with a pathological gambler:

1. is preoccupied with gambling;

2. needs to gamble with increasing amounts of money in order to achieve the desired excitement;

3. has repeated unsuccessful efforts to control, cut back, or stop gambling;

4. is restless or irritable when attempting to cut down or stop gambling;

5. gambles as a way of escaping from problems or of relieving a dysphoric mood;

6. after losing money gambling often returns another day to get even;

7. lies to family members, therapist, or others to conceal the extent of involvement with gambling;

8. has committed illegal acts such as forgery, fraud, theft, or embezzlement to finance gambling;

9. has jeopardized or lost significant relationships, jobs, or educational or career opportunity because of gambling; and

10. relies on others to provide money to relieve a desperate situation.

It has been argued that this jerry-built roster of diagnostic clues has no empirical basis. Why do five items instead of six or four provide diagnostic assurance? There also is the unfounded assumption that each of these items is of equal weight. Note further that a wealthy person has an advantage in avoiding the label of pathological gambler: he or she need not resort to the criminal behaviors listed in Item 8 to finance gambling and, if living at leisure, will not jeopardize a job or other commitments found in Item 9. Presumably, such considerations should not render a person less of a pathological gambler, though they do so. Item 9 indicates that a spouse can also give you a push toward a defined mental disorder by resenting your gambling behavior.

This is not to say that compulsive gambling cannot create serious problems for an individual and for those who might suffer from his or her behavior. By its private nature, an Internet gambling compulsion is more difficult to pinpoint than more overt gambling overindulgence. Arizona Senator Jon Kyle, the leader force in the effort to get antigambling legislation through Congress, cited the case of Greg Hogan, a 19-year-old sophomore and president of the class of 2008 at Lehigh University in Bethlehem, Pennsylvania. Hogan had run up a $5,000 Internet gambling debt. On December 9, 2005, he entered a bank in Allentown, Pennsylvania, claimed to be armed, and left with $2,871. Captured that evening, he received a 22-month prison sentence.

The difficulty is that the same scenario can be played out in regard to any outlay of money that cannot be afforded. The woman who runs up considerable debt to clothe herself in a fashion she desires and the man who purchases cars or stamps or other items that seriously overextend him financially seem little different in terms of the impulses and their consequences than the person who has been singled out as mentally disturbed because of gambling activity. To most of us, such disabling behavior may seem inappropriate, but it is arguable if it provides a sufficient basis for employing the force of the criminal law to ban Internet gambling.

There also is a question whether online gambling is more or less likely to aggravate personal problems than casino wagering. As one writer has asked: "Are gamblers more likely to self-destruct from their home office than at Caesar's Palace, surrounded by high rollers, alluring hostesses and dazzling décor?" (Chapman 2006). Not likely, the writer surmises, and points out that casinos build in many lures that are not found in Internet gambling, such as windowless rooms that have no clocks and free-flowing alcoholic liquor refreshments.

In the United States, the courts have generally been inhospitable to allegations that a compulsion to gamble provides an excuse to overcome or reduce a criminal charge. A leading case is *United States v. Scholl* (1997). William Scholl, a Tucson, Arizona, superior court judge, was charged with filing false income tax returns and structuring money transactions to avoid Treasury Department regulations. His defense was that his compulsion to gamble prompted these violations, and that the compulsion overrode his law-abiding instincts. The trial judge was not impressed with the testimony on Scholl's behalf by a psychologist. "Something doesn't become 'scientific knowledge' just because it's uttered by a scientist," she observed. The judge found the diagnostic label irrelevant to the crime with which Scholl was charged, indicating that there was no evidence that he did not understand the requirements of the tax law and his need to file an honest return. Scholl's appeal was dismissed (Geis 2004).

Underage Gamblers

A particularly strong prong of the attack on Internet gambling is the argument that minors, persons as young as their early teens, are strikingly conversant with the intricacies of the computer. A cartoon makes the point well. Two youngsters are talking: "For a father's day present," says one, "I gave my dad two hours of free computer training." That underage boys and girls can manipulate computers for illegal ends is demonstrated by recurring accounts of their hacking access to supposedly secret and protected information and their perpetration of Internet scams. Hackers, it is pointed out, could infiltrate Internet gambling sites and alter the algorithm to increase payouts and could pilfer identifying information supplied by wagering customers.

Youths readily can engage in Internet gambling when they are beyond the supervision of their parents or other adults. Anecdotal evidence abounds that such involvement is not uncommon. But attempts to keep youngsters from Internet Webs pose what appear to be almost insurmountable obstacles. In addition, precedent law suggests that such an action might arouse constitutional objections similar to those raised in *Reno v. ACLU* (1997) when the U.S. Supreme Court unanimously struck down the Communications Decency Act, a law that sought to protect persons under the age of 18 from Internet materials deemed harmful or pornographic. The primary justification for the decision was that the law was a violation of First Amendment free speech rights (Is Internet gambling free speech?). The Child Online Protection Act, a sequel to the earlier statute, suffered the same fate in the courts (*Ashcroft v. ACLU* 2004).

Fraud

The arguments that offshore betting may be haphazardly monitored assuredly have a certain weight. "There is no way for the user to know if the dice are actually being rolled," one writer observes, "if the roulette table is really spinning, if the cards are dealt randomly, or if they are part of a programmed sequence to cheat customers" (Karadabil 2002, 439). By being beyond the reach of American authorities, offshore operators may be able to manipulate odds to a greater extent than they are free to do so domestically. They also are not susceptible to penalties. There may, in addition, be trouble collecting winnings.

A hint of how collection difficulties likely would be handled by American courts can be found in the decision of a Texas appellate court in *Thompson v. Handa-Lopez, Inc.* (1998). Tom Thompson, a Texas resident, had gambled on an Internet site operated by Handa-Lopez, Inc. of San Jose, California, called "Funscope's Casino Royale" with tokens ("funbucks") he had purchased. He won $193,728.40, but the proprietor declined to pay him. The Texas court proved totally sympathetic to the claim that his case could be tried in Texas, rather than being filed in California as the defendant wished. We can presume that Thompson either prevailed on his claim that the Internet company had breached a contract, committed fraud, and violated the Texas Deceptive Trade Practices Act or, more likely, that a settlement agreement was reached.

The position of those who dispute this likelihood of significant fraud is that unfair Internet gambling operations would be deserted by customers seeking more equitable arrangements. The Internet itself could serve as a check on unscrupulous operations since word of irregularities can be circulated very rapidly and very widely. At the moment, two Web sites exist as consumer advocates that monitor offshore gambling sites: www.therx.com and www.MajorWager.com.

Additionally, new technologies can avoid the anonymity that may underlie fraudulent practices. A casino would be able to determine with a high degree of accuracy the geographic location of an Internet user and thereby to block betting from areas where it is illegal. Other technologies, like retinal scans and biometric fingerprinting, though costly, are nearly foolproof tactics to identify the party online (Cabot and Faiss 2002). Also, sports betting, unlike roulette or poker wagers, is not easily susceptible to manipulation. The bettor knows the odds and the point spread he or she has and can readily determine whether the wager was successful or not.

The issue of fraud surfaced early in the story of Internet gambling, but involved not shady tactics by the wagering entities, but by customers who engaged in what was called "bonus hustling." Internet offshore gambling establishments commonly offered a bonus to those who deposited wagering funds with them. Typical is an advertisement that recently appeared in one of the present writer's e-mail:

Gamble Online!

$888

FREE BONUS

Just for trying Casino

- Slots

- Blackjack

- Roulette

- Video Poker

Click here to try

Good luck!!

$888

FREE BONUS is ON THE HOUSE!!!

The e-mail was signed "Priscilla," and later the same day a duplicate appeared, this time signed by "Vladimir." Hustlers would deposit, say, $200 and receive the $888 bonus. Before they could collect, they had to bet a minimum amount. If they spent $3,000 on blackjack and played sensibly, their total loss would come to $15, and they could ask for the $1,073 credit they had with the company. Offshore Internet companies in time caught on to the ruse and introduced controls to eliminate it (Hainey 2006).

Christine Hurt (2006) has compared Internet gambling to stock transactions carried out on computers, and though she grants that there are important distinctions, she believes that fundamentally one form is no more disreputable or dangerous than the other, although prevailing legal doctrines are hospitable to the stock market and hostile to Internet gambling. Another writer maintains that "day [stock] trading appears more closely related to traditional forms of gambling than traditional forms of investing" (Kailus 1999, 1074–75). Internet gambling, although it rarely does, can provide funds for worthy causes. Plus Lotto, the first Internet lottery, run out of Liechtenstein, invites bets on keno, lotteries, bingo, and scratchpads, with 25 percent of the earnings going to the International Federation of the Red Cross and Red Crescent Societies.

THE LEGAL SITUATION

Five American states at present outlaw Internet gambling: Illinois, Louisiana, Nevada, Oregon, and South Dakota (Jenkins and Keller 2002, 3). Nevada takes a notably self-serving position. Its law forbids an Internet operator from anywhere in the world accepting a bet from a Nevada resident and imposes criminal liability on the person placing the bet as well as on the online server. But the statute exempts any wagers that are made online to a licensed Nevada operation (Rodefer 2002). For its part, South Dakota specifically exempts Internet wagers on its own state lottery from the prohibition against Internet betting. In 1989, South Dakota had introduced the first VLTs (video lottery terminals) in the United States when its lottery was struggling with total sales of $21 million annually. A decade later that sum had risen to more than $500 million (La Fleur and La Fleur 2002).

On the federal level, as so often happens, it took a prominent scandal to motivate the Congress to try to remedy what came to be regarded as a serious social problem. Pete Rose, a colorful baseball star, was a compulsive gambler and was discovered betting on the Cincinnati Reds, the team that he managed. The federal legislature in 1992 enacted the Professional and Amateur Sports Protection Act (28 U.S. Code §3701), which bans wagers on sports anywhere in the country besides Nevada, Oregon, Delaware, and Montana, where it already was sanctioned (Weiler 2000). The Act was opposed by the U.S. Department of Justice because it was deemed an interference with the rights of states to regulate gambling. The law makes it illegal for a government entity to sponsor, advertise, operate, promote, license, or authorize a lottery, sweepstakes, or other betting scheme based on one or more competitive games in which amateur or professional athletes compete. The law exempts jai alai games and dog and horse racing from its embrace.

Legal sports betting is said to amount to about $80 billion a year in the United States (Weiler 2006, 813). One of the more unusual venues for such wagers is Betbug, located in Toronto, Canada, where individuals are matched who will take opposing teams in a sports contest and set their own odds and point spreads. The house siphons off 5 percent or less, a figure that compares favorably with the usual 10 percent commission and the 15 percent house slice customary for Kentucky Derby bets.

The Wire Act

Actions against Internet gambling have relied primarily on the Interstate Wire Wager Act, a federal statute enacted in 1961 (18 U.S. Code §1084). The law was part of Attorney General Robert Kennedy's crusade against organized crime. Kennedy made his target clear when he testified in favor of the bill during a Congressional hearing:

> The [hoodlums and racketeers who have become so rich and powerful] use interstate commerce with impunity in the conduct of their unlawful activities. If we could curtail their use of interstate communications and facilities we could inflict a telling blow to their operations. We could cut them down to size. (United States Senate 1961, 4)

Kennedy declared that the primary source of organized crime's wealth was illicit gambling. From huge gambling profits flowed the funds to bankroll other illegal activities (D. Schwartz 2005, 86). The Wire Act became outmoded when organized criminals largely abandoned gambling to concentrate on the narcotics trade, and 9 years later the much more powerful Racketeer Influenced and Criminal Organizations Act (RICO) was passed to deal with that threat. But the Wire Act has come to the forefront again as the heavy artillery weapon to be employed against Internet gambling.

The Act prohibits the use of "a wire communication facility for the transmission in interstate or foreign commerce of bets or wagers or information assisting in the placing of bets or wagers on any sporting event or contest" (Doyle 2003). To be liable under the Act, the perpetrator must earn the larger share of his or her income from the operation, and not merely engage in the casual acceptance of wagers (DeMarco 2001). Ambiguity exists over what precisely is a "wire communication facility" and whether, for instance, online poker is a "sporting event or contest." An appeal failed that argued that a single transaction was inadequate to convict since the law specified "bets" and "wagers." The plural usage, the judge reasoned, "was not of design" but rather "imprecise conversational language" and one act of wrongdoing was meant by the legislators as well as several (*Sagansky v. United States* 1966). Significantly, the Act does not criminalize persons who place bets.

Decades earlier the courts had settled the question of whether an overseas gambling act that involved persons in American territory could be prosecuted domestically. In the *Horowitz v. United States* case, four persons were charged with sponsoring a lottery on radio station XED in Reynosa, Mexico, and selling chances to residents of McAllen, Texas, which lay just across the Rio Grande River. The judge concurring in the decision to hold the defendants guilty settled the jurisdictional issue with the following reasoning:

> If pistol or poison takes intended criminal effect from Mexico in the United States, the United States may punish it if it can catch the criminals. The effect in the United States of the act done in Mexico draws to it jurisdiction to punish those who are responsible for it. It may properly be alleged as done in the United States. The mailed lottery receipts and checks are little bullets that hit their mark. Jurisdiction exists from the standpoint of international law. (*Horowitz v. United States* 1933, 709)

Travel Act

The Travel Act (18 U.S. Code §1952) is a 1961 law that at times has been employed to prosecute Internet gambling. The Travel Act, like the Wire Act, was directed against organized crime. The Act prohibits interstate and international travel or the use of an interstate facility to engage in racketeering, with a primary emphasis on gambling (Breen 1986). The legislative report on the bill specified that the outlawed business had to be a continuous activity. Use of the mail, telephone or telegraph, newspapers, or tickertapes has been determined to be sufficient to establish that a defendant employed "a facility of interstate commerce" to further an activity in violation of the Travel Act.

The Illegal Gambling Business Act (18 U.S. Code §1952), passed in 1970, also was put in place as a weapon against organized crime, making it a federal offense to operate a gambling business that violates state law, providing that other conditions are met, such as the involvement of at least five persons who "conduct, finance, manage, supervise, direct or own a or part" of the entity. The operation also has to be in place for more than 30 days and to have taken in $2,000 or more on any given day.

The Interactive Gambling Case (1997)

The first state foray into control of overseas Internet gambling came in 1997 when a grand jury in Missouri indicted the Interactive Gaming and Communications Corporation, which was registered in Delaware but operated out of the Caribbean island of Grenada. The charge was operating a gambling Web site. The court granted a permanent injunction against the company, forbidding it to receive bets from Missouri residents and fined it $67,053. The company president was assessed $20,000 to pay the state for the prosecution of the case and an additional $5,000 as a fine for the violation (*Nixon v. Interactive Gaming & Communications Corp.* 1997; Scharf and Corin 2002). Similarly, a Minnesota case resulted in a casino in Nevada being enjoined from taking wagers from residents of Minnesota, where Internet gambling is illegal (*Minnesota v. Granite Games Resorts* 1997). Although these moves were successful, there has been a dearth of further such state actions.

The Jay Cohen Case (2000)

The landmark case—and one of very few of any kind—on Internet gambling is *United States v. Cohen*. Jay Cohen had studied nuclear engineering at the University of California, Berkeley, and then worked as a trader for Group One on the floor of the Pacific Stock Exchange. He and several other American citizens in early 1997 established the World Sports Enterprise (WSE) in the Caribbean island of Antigua with $600,000 start-up capital. Antigua had taken a lead in Internet gambling by edging out competitors with the development of an undersea fiber-optic link with the United States that guaranteed American gamblers continuous telecommunications access, even in the event of a hurricane (D. Schwartz 2005, 9).

WSE, which would become the island's second largest employer, required customers to transmit at least $300 before they were able to bet. The Antigua group took 10 percent off the top of bets for what in the trade is called "vig," short for "vigorish"—a commission. In 15 months of operation, the company took in $3.5 million. Its problems began when the WSE

accepted bets from undercover American agents who telephoned from Connecticut and
Illinois, where betting by phone is illegal. Subsequently, Cohen was charged in a New York
court with violation of the Wire Act. Twenty-one others were also indicted: most pled guilty
to conspiracy, some to misdemeanor charges, while seven remained fugitives from American
justice. In his opening presentation to the jury, Cohen's lawyer contended that the Wire Act
could not apply to Internet gambling since such procedures did not exist when it was passed.
His defense of his client took the following form:

> You will learn from Mr. Cohen that he became an outstanding advocate of this new business,
> and I submit to you that's why he is here . . . . He spoke out for the right of a new business
> idea, to be run in a country where it is legal, and he went out front [on] the cover of
> *Newsday*, a several page article in *Sports Illustrated*, debating issues with former attorney
> generals on radio, publicly speaking on Internet gambling symposiums, questioning, prob-
> ing, learning, . . . and trying to make this a business that could work honestly, and even pub-
> licly inviting regulation by the United States so that the United States could learn from its
> operation. (J. Schwartz 2005, 207)

The judge's instructions after the 10-day trial offered the jury no room to exonerate Cohen,
even if it was so inclined. He told them that if Cohen had accepted bets over the telephone,
and the proof was overwhelming that he had done so, they were obligated to find him guilty.
Cohen was sentenced to a 21-month prison term for each of eight counts, the time to be served
concurrently, and incurred a $5,000 fine, a penalty much lighter than what he could have
received (*United States v. Cohen* 2001). He resigned from BetOnSports and served 18 months
in the minimum-security prison at Fort Nellis, a federal prison located in Nevada on an army
base. He was paroled after 18 months, and assigned to a halfway house in Las Vegas. Cohen
later explained why he had returned home to press his case while many of his colleagues
remained in their Antiguan haven:

> I came back to the United States because I wanted to clear my name and felt this was
> wrong . . . . Here I sit in the shadow of the [Las Vegas] Strip while billion-dollar corpora-
> tions engage in the same activity every day for which I am serving a sentence. And for what?
> For running a legal business in another country. (Massoud 2004, 996)

Cohen also defended the Internet gambling business that he had organized, maintaining that it
was no different from the stock market transactions he had conducted in San Francisco and a
good deal more aboveboard. "I came from the stock market," he asserted, "and if that isn't
gambling, I don't know what is. Internet gambling is the same as my last career, except the
folks I work with [now] are less sleazy" (Lubben 2003, 321–22).

The Cohen case, despite the success of the prosecution, illustrated the observation of a
law review writer that "the explosion of Internet gambling in this past decade has caught officials in the United States off guard and forced courts to improvise and cobble together precedent based on statute and case law, neither of which are on point" (McBurney 2006, 337). The
Wire Act clearly was not targeted at Internet gambling and its meaning has to be stretched
considerably to employ it on that kind of mission. The impact of the prosecution of Cohen,
whatever symbolic and precedent value it may possess, apparently has had little practical
significance. WSE continues in business and registers approximately 30,000 members.
At the same time, though, another company, owned by American nationals, sold out to

Sportingbet.com, an English entity, for £15 million (about $25 million). Its owner told the media that legal advice had assured him he would not be subject to an American court process. But that view is challenged by a law review writer who argues that the new owner "should not be surprised if a U.S. court choose to assume jurisdiction on the basis of a territorial nexus [between the U.S. and the English company] which only requires that some element of the crime take place within the forum's territory" (August 2002, 44).

DAVID VERSUS GOLIATH: ANTIGUA CHALLENGES THE UNITED STATES

Disconcerted by the Cohen decision, and prodded by Cohen himself (Blustein 2006), Antigua and Barbuda, two islands with a total population of about 76,000 persons that form a single nation (Dyde 2000), presented to the WTO a claim of commercial discrimination by the United States in regard to Internet gambling. The WTO, headquartered in Geneva, Switzerland, has as members 148 countries who together are responsible for 95 percent of international trade.

The case first was assigned to a specially created hearing panel. Following an appeal by both parties on different points, it was heard by an appellate body. Media reports and law review assessments on the outcomes vary widely. There is no question that the first decision went against the United States, holding it in violation of the 1995 General Agreement on Trade in Services (GATS). The appellate decision moderated the panel's judgment and has variously been described as a victory for the United States, a mixed bag, a victory for Antigua, and a standoff. The parties were told to mediate their differences. When that failed to work, another panel was appointed to arbitrate the issues, but at the moment the two countries have been unable to agree on what exactly the findings truly mean and what policy implications they possess. There also is a possibility that, thwarted by the ruling, the United States may disengage from the WTO as it has from the Kyoto treaty on global warming and the International Criminal Court.

The dispute was titled "United States—Measures Affecting the Cross-Border Supply of Betting and Gambling Services." Antigua had filed its complaint on March 13, 2003, maintaining that a treaty obligation of the United States was to open the American market to global competition in "recreational, cultural and sporting services." Here we shall seek to highlight in an understandable way the complicated and often ambiguous (and perhaps deliberately so) content of the decisions.

Gambling had become a crucial component of economic life in Antigua, helped along by tax advantages offered to those who operated it. The cost of a casino license is $100,000 a year and $75,000 for a business taking bets on sporting events. The law also requires that employees of Internet gambling enterprises must be local residents (Andrle 2004).

In its suit, Antigua maintained that the objections by the United States to Internet gambling had been adequately dealt with by measures it had implemented. It pointed out that notices were posted on its Web warning against overindulgence in wagering and supplying instructions on how to get in touch with groups such as Gamblers Anonymous. Antigua also claimed that it had installed a verification system that barred underage persons from its gambling sites (Bissett 2004; J. Schwartz 2005). Antigua granted that it is more difficult to police an activity that is taking place abroad, but pointed out that this consideration is true of all offshore activities and that it is hardly a reason to ignore the requirements of the GATS fair trade treaty (World Trade Organization 2004, 80).

The first panel's report highlighted three issues:

1. The GATS treaty covered international trade in betting and gambling services.

2. The United States was in violation of the Treaty when it relied on the Wire Act and other federal laws to interdict Internet gambling with Antigua. These statutes, so employed, violated the intent of fair trade and access to markets in Antigua by persons living in America.

3. The United States had failed to demonstrate that its interdiction of Internet gambling with Antigua was necessary in regard to exceptions permitted by the Treaty to protect "public morals," which were defined as "standards of right and wrong conduct maintained by or on behalf of a community or a nation." To the panel this American claim must have appeared as patent hypocrisy given the legal status of gambling throughout most of the United States. The panel called the United States' position "a disguised restraint on trade" that "amounts to arbitrary and unjustifiable discrimination between countries" (Weiler 2006, 815). The panel insisted that nation-states cannot unilaterally define what constitutes "public morals" (Maxell 2006).

The appeals panel reached the following pair of major conclusions:

1. It upheld the earlier finding, although for different reasons, that the United States' obligation under the Treaty required it to grant full market access to gambling and betting services and that the United States had acted inconsistent with its treaty obligations by maintaining certain limitations on Internet gambling.

2. It reversed the panel's finding, although for different reasons, that American federal laws were not necessary to protect public morals and maintain public order (World Trade Organization 2005).

But the matter did not end there. Antigua announced that it would request the formation of another WTO panel to decide what action the United States should take, when it was required to do so, and what penalties would be imposed on it if it failed to follow instructions. Mark Mendel, Antigua's lawyer, took an optimistic view of the likely outcome of Antigua's efforts: "We fully expect they [the United States] will be found woefully noncompliant, and that will give further impetus to our efforts to get the U.S. to stop being hypocritical and comply with the [WTO] ruling" (Wissman 2006). Against this expectation is the conclusion of a comprehensive examination of WTO law and practice that notes significant shortcomings in its adjudication approach. "A problem with the implementation of WTO dispute settlement recommendations and rulings is a lack of guidance over what exactly a losing party must do to comply," Mitsuo Matsushita and his colleagues write, and then add wryly: "The tendency has been for the losing party to take minimal steps and declare itself in full compliance. The losing party often disagrees" (Matsushita, Schoenbaum, and Mavroidis 2003, 30).

THE GOLDEN CHIPS CASE (1999)

The Attorney General in New York filed a case against the World Interactive Gaming Corporation (WIGC), the holding company for the Golden Chip Corporation, which accepted bets in Antigua via the Internet. New York launched the case because its constitution forbids gambling operations without prior state legislative consent. The WIGC, incorporated in Delaware, had its headquarters in Bohemia, New York, a suburban hamlet of New York City located on Long Island. It had employed Impax Studios in New York City to design graphics for its appeals to customers. It also had solicited $844,665 from 114 investors located throughout the country, including many residents of New York. The court declared that WIGC was violating the federal Wire Act, the Travel Act, and the Wagering and Paraphernalia Act (18 U.S. Code §1953). The decision resulted in a fine and an injunction ordering the company to cease its business in New York state (*People v. World Interactive Gaming Corp.* 1999). Subsequently, in 2002, the New York State Attorney General reached an agreement with PayPal and Citibank that they would stop processing payments for Internet casinos by blocking transactions through the monitoring of embedded merchants' codes.

FIRST AMENDMENT ISSUES

The hard-line posture by American federal enforcement agencies has been said by one writer to be an "obsession with sinful activities" that has led to "aggressive (and aberrational) approaches to Internet gambling" (Crawford 2005, 597). Advertisers for Internet gambling facilities have been threatened with prosecution for "aiding and abetting" an illegal enterprise, an act defined as including, besides aiding and abetting, counseling, commanding, inducing, or procuring the commission of a criminal act. So forewarned, New York City buses removed Internet gambling advertising placards from their vehicles, and both Google and Yahoo eliminated solicitations from Internet gambling operations. Yahoo noted that "a lack of clarity in the environment [of offshore betting]" made it seem "too risky" to continue to provide details about such betting sites (Frese 2005, 555). In addition, U.S. Marshals seized $3.2 million from Discovery Communications that had been paid to it by offshore gambling groups as advertising fees. Legal conflict, yet unresolved, has arisen between the federal Department of Justice and Casino City Inc., a company that is the leader in the field of disseminating information about online gambling. The Casino City group insisted that the Department of Justice was interfering with its right of free speech (Lindner 2006), and that the Wire Act applied only to sports betting, not to casino games, and not to Internet bets (*In re Master Card International, Inc.* 2001). In that case, two men had mounted a civil suit against several credit card companies and banks that issue cards, claiming that they had violated the RICO by involving themselves in illegal gambling as collectors of debts run up by offshore Internet bettors. The district court concluded that the Wire Act prohibited only wagers on sports. "A plain reading of the statutory language," the court declared, "clearly requires that the object of the gambling be a sporting event or contest" (*In re Master Card International, Inc.* 2001, 480). The court further noted that unsuccessful Congressional attempts to amend the Wire Act to include casino-style gambling supported the idea of the limited reach of the statute.

More generally, the Casino City supporters quoted the view of Congressman Barney Frank (D-Mass.) to give added credence to their position:

> I would have hoped that the American experience with alcohol [prohibition] in the '20s and '30s would have made my colleagues far more skeptical of new forms of prohibition than they have been. This Act violates the principle of leaving the Internet unregulated, and violates as well the privacy of millions of Americans. While I do not myself gamble, I think it is a choice that adults should be able to make for themselves. (Frese 2005, 597)

The decision was affirmed on appeal (*In re Master Card International, Inc.* 2002).

Gambling, and by implication advertising of Internet gambling sites, became the focus of another First Amendment controversy when GamblingPalace.com began to pay boxers to display "body billboards" tattoos placed on their backs advertising the casino. The first instance arose in September 2001, involving Bernard "The Executioner" Hopkins who was fighting Felix Trinidad for the middleweight title. "It's like freedom of speech," Hopkins declared regarding the tattoo. "It's like something that no one can tell me what I do with my own body. This was my own decision. My own kingdom." Subsequently, the casino arranged with at least 30 additional boxers to have the same advertisement tattooed on their backs. The Nevada Athletic Commission filed a court case protesting the procedure, arguing that it was "demeaning," a health hazard, and a distraction to the judges of the boxing match. The casino claimed that the tattooing was permitted under the constitutional guarantee of freedom of speech and commercial sponsorship and that the process involved a nontoxic substance that has been harmlessly in use for tattoos for more than 300 years. In March 2002, a district court agreed, ruling against the Athletic Commission (McKelvey 2003).

More generally, in 1999 the United States Supreme Court decided that it was an unconstitutional violation of the First Amendment to forbid advertising of Native-American casinos but to allow it for private casinos. The court noted as well that "the federal policy of discouraging gambling in general, and casino gambling in particular, is now decidedly equivocal" and that Congress appeared unwilling "to adopt a single national policy" (*Greater New Orleans Broadcasting Association v. United States* 1999, 187).

THE DAVID CARRUTHERS CASE (2006)

It would be 5 years following the arrest of Jay Cohen before the federal government made another aggressive move against an offshore gambling entrepreneur. The target was Scottish-born David Carruthers, the chief executive officer of BetOnSports.com, a leading Internet gambling establishment with headquarters in Britain. Internet gambling had been made legal there by the 2005 Gambling Act, which sought to regularize gambling, including Internet betting which it labels "remote gambling," and to prevent proceeds from going to criminal elements. The company had gone public in July 2004, and investors included some of the major American Wall Street firms and mutual funds, including Merrill Lynch and Goldman Sachs. Trading in the stock was halted on the London Stock Exchange the day Carruthers was arrested. The stock almost immediately had lost 40 percent of its value (Richtel 2006a: C3).

Carruthers was arrested by FBI agents in mid-July 2006 in the Dallas-Fort Worth international airport while on a layover between the United Kingdom and Costa Rica, where his company has its headquarters. It also is licensed in Antigua. Carruthers was charged with 22 counts in a St. Louis federal court, including violation of the Wire Act as well as with involvement in a racketeering conspiracy. In short order, he was fired from his job on the ground that he no longer was in a position to perform his duties and, perhaps, because the company sought to protect itself against the court order that it forfeit $4.5 billion, plus several vehicles and its computers (Nakashima 2006).

The government also issued a warrant for the arrest of Gary Kaplan, the company's founder and an American citizen, and filed charges against 10 additional BetOnSports employees as well as three marketing companies situated in Florida that were promoting the enterprise. Kaplan remained outside the United States, where he was charged with 20 felony counts including violation of the Wire Act, RICO, interstate transportation of gambling paraphernalia, and income tax evasion. It was noted that he had been arrested in 1993 in New York City for operating a sports book, and then moved to Florida before relocating in Costa Rica and Antigua. A news report observed that the arrest of the BetOnSports workers raised "complex legal and political questions" and further noted the discrepancy between the government position on Internet gambling in the United States and that in a large part of the remainder of the world:

> The charges [against Carruthers] reinforce a growing divide between the United States' policy on Internet gambling and its popularity in much of the rest of the world, not just among gamblers but also with investors. Some popular sites have sold shares to the public and are experiencing growing revenue and, in turn, interest even from major American investment houses, which hold shares of online casinos in their mutual funds. (Richtel 2006b: C6)

The arrest sent a message to Internet offshore gambling officers that they would be well advised to avoid setting foot in the United States. Nonetheless, any prosecution of Carruthers, who could face a 20-year sentence if convicted of conspiring to operate an illegal gambling business, will first have to demonstrate that his company had what the courts call "minimum contact" with Americans. The minimum contact doctrine declares that a court will not accept jurisdiction in a case unless the contacts of the party being charged in the state in which the court lies are such that the accused could reasonably expect to be hauled into court in that state. The case, on this ground, "must not offend traditional notions of fair play and substantial justice" (*Milliken v. Meyer* 1940, 463). BetOnSports had no physical presence in the United States. The most optimistic reading of the impact of Carruthers' arrest was that it demonstrated that offshore gambling could be harassed and curtailed, but that it could not be eliminated. But the harassment could have potent consequences. Less than a month after Carruthers' arrest, BetOnSports informed 800 employees in Costa Rica and Antigua that it was closing down its operations there and planned to relocate its business in other parts of the world, most notably in Asia, where it had 300 employees in Kuala Lumpur. It declared that it would pay off Americans to whom money was owed, but would have to do so through third parties, involving what could prove to be complex negotiations. Market experts thought the move of BetOnSports was unfortunate. They insisted that it had needlessly caved in to highhanded American enforcement tactics, and that, besides, the Asian Internet gambling market was but one-third the size of the American market. They did grant that Japan and China, especially the Chinese people's traditional cultural enthusiasm for gambling, could in time provide a lucrative market.

A leading stock analyst indicated his belief that the BetOnSports case would continue to "haunt" the trading in shares of Internet gambling companies for a long time. On the London Stock Exchange, the indictment of Carruthers had prompted a big sell-off of Internet gambling company shares, but they had rebounded somewhat during the following month. It almost appeared that dedicated gamblers themselves were placing bets on the quite uncertain future of the companies, seeing the panicky sell-off as an opportunity to get on board cheaply. Another analyst maintained that investors viewed the arrest of Carruthers as no more than "American bluster." They noted that PartyPoker.com had been named as one of the world's 10 fastest growing Web sites, with its traffic up 185 percent between July 2005 and the same month in 2006 (Richtel and Timmons 2006a).

The Carruthers case also reminded onlookers that there is a longstanding rule in American jurisprudence that in criminal cases courts will not inquire how a defendant was brought before them (i.e., he might have been kidnapped overseas by American agents) but will proceed to adjudicate the allegations. In this regard, any overseas Internet gambling entrepreneur is vulnerable to being seized by American agents in an overseas setting in a process known as rendition and being brought and tried before a court in the United States (DiMento and Geis 2006).

FOREIGN JURISDICTIONS

Five foreign jurisdictions have prohibited Internet gambling entirely. They are Estonia, Hong Kong, Iceland, Norway, and Uruguay. The Hong Kong situation is illustrative. Gambling there, which is heavy, is the monopoly of the Hong Kong Jockey Club, which contributes considerable tax revenue to the government. The government and the club joined together with religious groups and social service agencies to impose a ban on Internet gambling that included a possible 9 months in prison for bettors as well as a heavy fine (Wong 2005).

On the other side of the spectrum, approximately 50 countries have legalized the practice, including European nations, Caribbean islands, and the countries in the Australia/Pacific region. There also is legal Internet gambling in the self-governing Canadian aboriginal territories in the northern regions of the country. American customers are believed to contribute 50–70 percent of the overseas Internet gambling business. About 8 percent of the offshore sites engage in casino gambling, 49 percent offer sports banks, 22 percent horse and dog race bets, and 6 percent lotteries (Jenkins and Keller 2002, 6, 53).

CONCLUSION

Scrutinizing past and current developments in the campaign by lawmakers and prosecutors in the United States against Internet gambling, a national newspaper adopted a guarded position. The headline reads: "U.S. May Push Crackdown, but Internet Casinos Won't Die Easily" (Richtel and Timmons 2006b). The first quotation in the main part of the news story is from a man in North Carolina who says that during the football season he places up to 70 bets a week on an Internet site of between $2,000 and $5,000 each. "They're not going to stop the offshore sports books," he predicts. A crackdown will "just force it back to the black market," where betting still flourishes in the United States, in workplaces, among friends, and at the events themselves (Richtel and Timmons 2006b: C1). A forecast that Internet gambling will prevail has been offered by I. Nelson Rose, one of the leading authorities on legal issues concerned with wagering, who writes:

> Ultimately, those states who wish to license operations and allow casinos to operate will be allowed to do so. As more developing countries turn toward legalization, taxation, and regulation, and as more states pass enabling statutes, the United States federal government will be forced to shift away from a complete prohibition position to one of reluctant tolerance. Federal permission will, at first be limited to state-licensed operations, if for no other reason that that foreign and non-licensed operations have no lobbying presence in Washington. (Rose 2000, 40)

Internet gambling enterprises are relatively easily established, and the amount of capital required to begin such ventures is strikingly small compared to the cost of brick-and-mortar gambling parlors. Developments to date have followed Craig Lang's observation that "when Internet met gambling" it was "a love story in the making" (Lang 2002, 533). Nonetheless, it is at this time a rocky romance, and divorce, remains a possibility. But events have to be seen in terms of the report of the federal commission that three decades ago reviewed gambling in the United States. "Gambling is inevitable," the Commission concluded, adding: "No matter what is said or done by advocates or opponents of gambling in its various forms, it is an activity that is practiced, or tacitly endorsed by a majority of Americans" (United States 1976, 1).

Legal jousting regarding Internet gambling, which we have summarized above, has largely relied on anecdotal evidence, ideological preferences, and juridical precedents. The April 18, 2007 issues of *The Wager* points out that only 11 articles have appeared in print that report empirical research on the subject and that virtually all of these have but a limited sample and other flaws. "To move forward, the field of gambling studies needs to conduct rigorous research on . . . the distribution of Internet gambling problems, and the risk factors for these problems," the writer notes. "It is time to provide legislators with empirical research using representative samples and real-time observations . . . so that they can make informed decisions" (Internet Gambling Caught in the Web 2007, 2). It is a call that we heartily second.

KEY TERMS

Casino
Internet gambling
Poker

REFERENCES

American Psychiatric Association. 1994. *Diagnostic and Statistical Manual of Mental Disorders*. 4th ed. Washington, DC: Author.

Andrle, J. 2004. A winning hand: A proposal for an international regulatory scheme for the growing online gambling dilemma in the United States. *Vanderbilt Journal of Transportation Law* 37: 1389–422.

Ashcroft v. ACLU. 2004. 542 U.S. 656.

August, R. 2002. Cyber jurisdiction: A comparative analysis. *American Business Journal* 39: 531–72.

Bissett, C. 2004. All bets are off(line): Antigua's trouble in virtual paradise. *University of Miami Inter-American Law Review* 35: 367–403.

Blustein, P. August 4, 2006. Against all odds. *Washington Post*: D1.

Boyer, A. March 31, 1999. Racing industry gambles on Internet. *Washington Post*: D1.

Breen, B. 1986. *The Travel Act (18 U.S.C. sec. 1952): Prosecution of Interstate Acts in Aid of Racketeering.* Washington, DC: Criminal Division, U.S. Department of Justice.

Cabot, A. N., and R. D. Faiss. 2002. Sports gambling in the cyberspace era. *Chapman Law Review* 5: 1–45.

California v. Cabazon Band of Mission Indians. 1987. 480 U.S. 202.

Chafetz, H. 1960. *A History of Gambling in the United States from 1492 to 1955.* New York: Potter.

Champion v. Ames. 1903. 188 U.S. 321.

Chapman, S. July 26, 2006. Odds are with online gambling. *Orange County* (CA) *Register*: Local 9.

Crawford, S. P. 2005. Responsibility on the Internet: Shortness of vision: Regulatory ambition in the digital age. *Fordham Law Review* 74: 695–745.

Davidson, N. 2002. Internet gambling: Should fantasy sports leagues be prohibited? *San Diego Law Review* 39: 201–50.

DeMarco, J. V. March 2001. Gambling against enforcement—Internet sports books and the Wire Wager Act. *Computer Crimes and International Property* 49: 33–7.

Dempsey, J. A. 2001/2002. Surfing for wampum: Federal regulation of Internet gambling and Native American sovereignty. *American Indian Law Review* 25: 133–52.

DiMento, J., and G. Geis. 2006. The extraordinary condition of extraordinary rendition: The F.B.I., the C.I.A., the D.E.A., kidnapping and the law. *War Crimes, Genocide, and Crimes Against Humanity.* 32: 35–64.

Doyle, C. 2003. *Internet Gambling: Overview of Federal Criminal Law.* New York: Novinka.

Dyde, B. 2000. *A History of Antigua: The Unsuspected Isle.* London: Macmillan Education.

Frese, M. E. 2005. Rolling the dice: The online gambling advertisers "aiding and abetting" criminal activity in exercising first amendment-protected commercial speech. *Fordham Intellectual Property, Media & Entertainment Law Journal* 15: 547–622.

Friedrich, T. J. 2000. Internet casino gambling: The nightmare of lawmaking, jurisdiction, enforcement, and the dangers of prohibition. *CommLaw Conspectus* 11: 369–88.

Geis, G. 2004. Pathological gambling and insanity, diminished capacity, dischargeability, and downward sentencing departures. *Gaming Law Review* 8: 347–60.

Girdwood, R. S. 2002. Place your bets . . . on the keyboard: Are Internet casinos legal? *Campbell Law Review* 25: 135–50.

Gold, D. I. 2000. Internet gambling debt liability: Trouble ahead?: A consideration of *Providian v. Haines. Thomas Jefferson Law Review* 33: 219–37.

Greater New Orleans Broadcasting Association v. United States. 1999. 527 U.S. 173.

Hainey, J. August 14, 2006. Jeff Hainey on a dying scheme to hustle online casinos. *Las Vegas Sun*: 2, 6.

Hammer, R. D. 2001. Does Internet gambling strengthen the U.S. economy? Don't bet on it. *Federal Communications Law Journal* 54: 103–27.

Horowitz v. United States. 1933. 63 F.2d 706 (5th Circuit).

Hurt, C. 2006. Regulating public morals and private markets: Online securities trading, Internet gambling, and the speculation paradox. *Boston University Law Review* 86: 371–441.

In re Master Card International, Inc. 2001. 132 F. Supp. 2d 468 (Eastern District of Louisiana).

In re Master Card International, Inc. 2002. 313 F.3d 257 (5th Circuit).

Internet Gambling Caught in the Web. April 18, 2007. *The Wager* 12: 1–3.

Jenkins, W. O., Jr., and B. I. Keller. 2002. *Internet Gambling: Report to Congressional Requesters: Overview and Issues.* GAO 03-80. Washington, DC: General Accounting Office.

Kailus, M. P. 1999. Do not bet on unilateral prohibition of Internet gambling to eliminate cyberspace casinos. *University of Illinois Law Review* 1999: 1045–81.

Karadabil, J. F. 2002. Casinos in the next millennium: A look at the proposed ban on Internet gambling. *Arizona Journal of International and Comparative Law* 17: 413–47.

Kelly, J. M. 2000. Internet gambling. *William Mitchell Law Review* 26: 157–72.

Kundt, J. W., and S. W. Joy. 2002. Internet gambling and the destabilization of national and international economies: Time for a comprehensive ban on gambling over the World Wide Web. *Denver University Law Review* 80: 111–53.

La Fleur, T., and B. La Fleur. 2002. *La Fleur's 2001 World Lottery Almanac*. Boyd, MD: TLF Publications.

Lang, C. 2002. Internet gambling: Las Vegas logs in. *Loyola of Los Angeles Entertainment Law Review* 22: 525–58.

Lindner, A. 2006. First amendment as last resort: The Internet gambling industry's bid to advertise. *Saint Louis University Law Journal* 50: 1289–325.

Lubben, T. A. 2003. The federal government and the regulation of Internet sports gambling. *Sports Lawyers Journal* 10: 317–34.

Mark, R. June 15, 2003. MGM online casino proves to be a mirage. *Online.news.com*

Massoud, S. 2004. The offshore quandary: The impact of domestic regulation on licensed offshore gambling companies. *Whittier Law Review* 25: 989–1009.

Matsushita, M., T. J. Schoenbaum, and P. C. Mavroidis. 2003. *The World Trade Organization: Law, Practice, and Policy*. Oxford, UK: Oxford University Press.

Maxell, J. C. 2006. Trade and morality: The WTO public morals exception after gambling. *New York University Law Review* 81: 802–30.

McBurney, J. J. 2006. To regulate or to prohibit: An analysis of the Internet gambling industry and a need for a decision on the industry's future in the United States. *Connecticut Journal of International Law* 21: 337–65.

McKelvey, S. M. 2003. Commercial "branding": The first frontier or false start for athletes' use of temporary tattoos as body billboard. *Journal of Legal Aspects of Sports* 13: 1–32.

Meier, R. F., and G. Geis. 2006. *Criminal Justice and Moral Issues*. Los Angeles: Roxbury.

Milliken v. Meyer. 1940. 311 U.S. 457.

Minnesota v. Granite Games Resorts. 1997. 568 N.W.2d 715 (Minnesota Court of Appeals), affirmed 576 N.W.2d 747.

Missouri v. Couer d'Alene Tribe. 1999. 164 F.3d 1102 (8th Circuit), cert. denied 527 U.S., 1039.

Nakashima, R. August 6, 2006. Legality of online poker is on the table. *Los Angeles Times*: C12.

Nixon v. Interactive Gaming & Communications Corp. 1997. CV97-7808 (Circuit Court, Jackson County, Missouri).

Patterson, J. 2002. Internet gambling and the banking industry: An unsure bet *North Carolina Banking Institute* 6: 665–688–9.

People v. World Interactive Gaming Corp. 1999. 174 N.Y.S.2d 844.

Pileggi, N. 1995. *Casinos: Love and Honor in Las Vegas*. New York: Simon & Schuster.

Providian National Bank v. Haines. 1998. CV 980858 (California Superior Court).

Reno v. ACLU. 1997. 521 U.S. 844.

Richtel, M. August 11, 2006a. BetonSports, after indictment, folds its hand and decides to move to Asia. *New York Times*: C3.

Richtel, M. July 18, 2006b. An arrest in Internet gambling. *New York Times*: C1, C6.

Richtel, M., and H. Timmons. August 21, 2006a. Web casinos becoming a riskier bet for investors. *New York Times*: C1, C3.

Richtel, M., and H. Timmons. July 25, 2006b. The gambling is virtual, the money is unique. *New York Times*: C1, C2.

Rodefer, J. R. 2002. Internet gambling in Nevada: Overview of federal law affecting assembly bill 466. *Gaming Law Review* 6: 393–415.

Rose, I. N. 2000. Gambling and the law: The future of Internet gambling. *Villanova Sports and Entertainment Law Journal* 71: 29–53.

Sagansky v. United States. 1966. 358 F.2d 195 (1st Circuit.), cert. denied 385 U.S. 816 (1972).

Scharf, M. P., and M. K. Corin. 2002. On dangerous ground: Passive personality and the prohibition of Internet gambling. *New England International and Comparative Law Journal* 8: 9–35.

Schmidt, S., and J. V. Garabaldi. January 6, 2006. Abramoff pleads guilty to 3 counts. *Washington Post*: A01.

Schopper, M. D. 2002. Internet gambling, electronic cash, and money laundering: The unintended consequences of a monetary control scheme. *Chapman Law Review* 5: 303–30.

Schwartz, D. B. 2005. *Cutting the Wire: Gaming Prohibition and the Internet*. Reno: University of Nevada Press.

Schwartz, J. 2005. Click the mouse and bet the house: The United States' Internet gambling restriction before the World Trade Organization. *University of Illinois Journal of Law, Technology & Policy* 2005: 125–40.

State v. Rosenthal. 1979. 559 P.2d 830 (Nevada).

Thompson v. Handa-Lopez, Inc. 1998. 998 F. Supp. 738 (Western District, Texas).

United States Commission on the Review of the National Policy Toward Gambling. 1976. *Final Report*. Washington, DC: U.S. Government Printing Office.

United States House of Representatives. 2000. Internet Gambling Act of 2000. Report No. 106-655. 106 Congress, 2nd Session.

United States Senate. 1961. Committee on the Judiciary. Hearings on the Attorney General's Program to Curb Organized Crime and Racketeering. 87 Congress, 1st Session.

United States v. Cohen. 2001. 260 F.3d 68 (2nd Circuit), cert. denied 536 U.S. 926 (2002).

United States v. Scholl. 1997. 959 F. Supp. 1189 (District Arizona.), cert. denied 541 U.S. 873.

Walker, S. 2006. *Fantasyland: A Season Baseball's Lunatic Fringe*. New York: Viking.

Weiler, P. C. 2000. *Leveling the Playing Field: How the Law Can Make Spots Better for Fans*. Cambridge, MA: Harvard University Press.

Weiler, P. C. 2006. Renovating our recreational crimes. *New England Law Review* 40: 809–30.

Will, G. E. November 25, 2002. Electronic monitoring. *Newsweek*: 92.

Wissman, K. August 14, 2006. Antigua lead counsel in WTO case Mark Mendel sits down with 911. *Gambling 911*, www.gambling911.com

Wong, K. C. 2005. Computer crime and control in Hong Kong. *Pacific Rim and Policy Law Journal* 14: 337–82.

World Trade Organization. November 10, 2004. *United States—Measure Affecting Cross-Border Supply of Gambling and Betting Services*. Report of Dispute Settlement Panel. Document WT/D285/R. Geneva, Switzerland: WTO.

World Trade Organization. April 7, 2005. *United States—Measures Affecting Cross-Border Supply of Gambling and Betting Services*. Report of the Appellate Body. Document WT/D528/AB. Geneva, Switzerland: WTO.

Chapter 10

Nature and Distribution of Phishing

Anthony Stroik and Wilson Huang
Valdosta State University, Georgia

Anthony Stroik is a political science graduate from Valdosta State University. He had served in the Air Force for 6 years. He is currently a member of the VSU Honors program and the University's mock trial team. He plans to pursue a law degree.

Wilson Huang, Ph.D., is associate professor in the Department of Sociology, Anthropology, and Criminal Justice at Valdosta State University. He received his Ph.D. in criminal justice and criminology from the University of Maryland, College Park. His teaching and research interests include police–community relations, comparative criminal justice, research methodology, and cyber crime.

Abstract

Phishing is an online solicitation of sensitive personal information through the impersonation of another legitimate entity. The typical scam involves an e-mail message pretending to be from a financial institution, leading the recipient to an authentic-looking Web site asking for account numbers and other data, which the criminal then intercepts. Efforts within the criminal justice system appear to lack the speed and sophistication of phishers, but multiple existing statutes can be combined to prosecute these perpetrators. This article details the growth of this scheme, techniques employed by the criminals, and descriptions of offenders and victims, as well as real examples of phishing. The study also suggests ways average Internet users may safeguard themselves from such an attack.

INTRODUCTION

Internet fraud is a rapidly growing area of cyber crime that can potentially affect anyone with Internet access. The anonymity and relative ease of access provided by the Internet, coupled with a general trust and/or lack of knowledge on behalf of the public, create an avenue for savvy criminals to destroy computer systems or embezzle large sums of money. One area of fraud that is particularly noteworthy, since the victims volunteer their own personal information, is **phishing**. Phishing is a technique used by scammers to gather personal information from their victims online, typically by sending e-mails that purport to be from reputable companies or simulating legitimate Web sites. The criminals then use the information, such as bank account number, birth date, address, or social security number, to swindle money

191

(Symantec Corporation 2004; University of Houston 2005). To summarize this swindling process, the U.S. Department of Justice (USDOJ 2004) provides that:

> "Phishing" is a general term for criminals' creation and use of e-mails and websites—designed to look like e-mails and websites of well-known legitimate businesses, financial institutions, and government agencies—in order to deceive Internet users into disclosing their bank and financial account information or other personal data such as usernames and passwords. (p. 1)

The term "phishing" is conceptually analogous to the fraudulent use of online communications as hooks to "fish" for account usernames, passwords, and other private information from the sea of Internet users in the cyberspace. The term originated in early 1996 on the alt.2600 **hacker** newsgroup, where members discussed computer hacking and telephone "phreaking" (Anti-Phishing Working Group n.d.). Some members of the newsgroup who had knowledge in cracking the telephone network for making free long-distance calls were referred to as phreakers (Britz 2004). Phreakers are known as the precursors of computer hackers (Britz 2004, 39), while hacked accounts are referred to as "phish." In fact, phish have been traded between hackers for their needs. The Anti-Phishing Working Group (APWG n.d.) reported that some hackers routinely traded 10 active AOL phish for a copy of hacking software. Over the past decade, the simple stealing of AOL dial-ups has progressively transformed into a solely greedy act for financial gains.

Like other crimes that are rising with the growth of the Internet, phishing is an increasingly common and serious problem. In 2005, the number of U.S. adults who reported receiving phishing e-mails was 109 million, almost twice the amount received in 2004 (Howell 2006). Howell further revealed that approximately 25 percent of people who reported receiving a suspicious e-mail in 2006 admitted to following the links provided, and 2 percent lost money as a result. Symantec, a company well known in the Internet security industry, also discovered a sharp increase in phishing e-mails. In the first 6 months of 2005, the company's security teams detected 97,592 unique phishing messages. During the same period in 2006, the number increased by 61 percent to 157,477 (Symantec Corporation 2006). What is significant about the number of these messages is that people cannot faithfully rely on social networks to inform them of dangerous e-mails. While one certain e-mail may become notorious, and therefore friends and family will warn one another about it, they will remain vulnerable to the other 157,476. Even people who are aware of phishing can fall prey to it. A study conducted by the Internet security company MailFrontier (2004) found that 10 percent of people who examined an e-mail previously marked as suspicious by MailFrontier surprisingly still divulged the personal information the message requested. The follow-up to a phishing e-mail is the Web site where users enter their personal data. According to records from the Anti-Phishing Working Group (2006a, b), the average monthly unique phishing Web sites detected by the group in 2006 was around 17,824; the largest number of phishing Web sites recorded in a single month was 37,444 in October 2006. That number was nearly nine times the number for the same time the previous year.

This chapter will examine phishing issues by detailing the escalation of this Web-based fraud, damages resulting from phishing attacks, methods employed by phishers to trick their victims, descriptions of offenders and victims, and governmental responses. Avoidance and containment strategies will be assessed with a focus on improving the effectiveness of various preventive tactics. While a certain technical savoir faire and specialized antiphishing software are undoubtedly beneficial to protect end users, the factors that can best prevent phishing victimization ultimately are likely to center on education. By educating the public of the increased prevalence and sophistication of phishing rouses, thereby increasing personal cognizance of e-mail **scams**, this study functions to mitigate the unguarded susceptibility to a phishing ploy.

THE GROWTH AND SPREAD OF PHISHING

Phishing is by no means a uniquely American problem. According to a Korean phishing trends report, the monthly figures of phishing sites between 2004 and 2006 grew in that country by 10 percent on average (Korea Internet Security Center 2006). In Germany, phishing attacks increased 90 percent in 2006 (Kurtz 2006). A survey of Canadians conducted by VISA Inc. (2005) showed that 60 percent of respondents reported that they would likely provide personal information in response to legitimate-sounding phishing e-mails, and 4 percent had been phishing victims. The survey also reported that 65 percent of respondents expressed concern about the scams. In terms of monetary losses, Rudd (2004) noted that Australian banks have spent $2 million to cover losses from phishing, and banks in Great Britain have lost £1 million through phishing scams. Since international access is practically limitless with the Internet, phishing will flourish wherever computers and Internet access exists. Also, a fraudster need not be in the same part of the world as his or her intended victims. Countries that are uninformed about phishing remain the most vulnerable to attack. Nowadays, phishers are sending messages in Spanish, French, German, Dutch, and other languages (MailFrontier 2004). Though the largest percentage of phishing sites was found in the U.S. (25 percent), the other top ten countries— China (10.16 percent), South Korea (9.5 percent), France (4.43 percent), Germany (4.1 percent), Japan (3.02 percent), Russia (2.34 percent), the Netherlands (1.92 percent), the United Kingdom (1.82 percent), and Chile (1.66 percent)—accounted for almost 40 percent of phishing sites worldwide (APWG 2007). This scattering of countries in various continents clearly indicates that phishing is a global problem across national boundaries.

Along with an increase of the number of phishing e-mails and Web sites, the dollar amount lost per person has risen. In 2006, victims lost an average of $1,244, compared to $256 in 2005 (Howell 2006). Fraudulent ATM transactions resulting from phishing scams in particular have risen dramatically. A total of 1,407 debit card numbers were reported as compromised in 2003, followed by 13,507 debit card numbers in 2004, and a staggering 17,642 in just the first quarter of 2005 (Fair Isaac Corporation 2005).

Phishing victims recovered slightly over half of their financial losses, with the majority of revenue coming from banks; credit cards followed (Howell 2006). This introduces another category of phishing victims: financial institutions and the entire e-commerce industry. Financial losses in excess of $1.2 billion plagued victims in 2003 (Rusch 2004), but economic damages from electronic banking soared past $32.2 billion (MailFrontier 2004). Phishing is responsible for the loss of much greater amounts of money than what ends up missing from people's bank accounts. Money spent on security programs aimed at preventing phishing, time spent training and educating employees, efforts to beef up security measures using new technology, and the hiring of Internet security specialists are examples of quantifiable expenditures. McMillan (2006a) quotes a study by Gartner that reveals U.S. businesses paid $2.8 billion out in 2006 because of phishing scams. Another damaging effect of phishing is a growing mistrust of the Internet among online visitors. While the Internet user should very well be cautious, many are simply shying away from using it for purchases and financial transactions. A survey of 1,501 adult Internet users conducted by *Consumer Reports* in 2005 found that 9 out of 10 Internet users have altered online habits and practices due to the risk of identity theft (Anderberg 2005; Binational Working Group on Cross-Border Mass Marketing Fraud 2006). Of these, 30 percent reduced their time spent online, and one-quarter stopped purchasing goods over the Internet. This is a crippling blow to a popular means of business and can potentially damage more on online services.

PHISHING STATUTES AND TYPES

Suspects accused of phishing are likely subject to a number of current federal laws. Generally, a combination of multiple statutes is applied to a given crime involving phishing. These statutes fall under the scope of various sections of Title 18 of United States Codes. Some of the most pertinent to a fraudulent phishing are identity theft, wire fraud, bank fraud, access device fraud, and computer fraud and abuse (Rusch 2004). Codified as 18 U.S.C. §1028(a)(7), identity theft occurs when a person illegally obtains, transfers, or uses another person's means of identification and is somehow connected with criminal activity. Penalties for a violation of this code include a maximum of 15 years' imprisonment, a $2,500 fine, and forfeiture of any property used or intended to be used to commit the offense. Although identity theft is indeed a major aspect of phishing, that alone does not entail a comprehensive application of statutes for the crime. Computer Fraud and Abuse, 18 U.S.C. §1030, is another primary violation that occurs during a phishing scam. This section explains the use of computers beyond authorized access to obtain information across state or national borders. Penalties for breaking this law are 5 years' imprisonment and a fine. One can be found guilty of phishing by breaking only the two aforementioned statutes. However, if the criminals do, in fact, use the stolen information to gain money, they are committing access device fraud, wire fraud, and/or bank fraud, with penalties reaching 30 years' imprisonment and a $250,000 fine. The access device is not limited just to credit cards or other tangible identification items. As defined by 18 U.S.C. §1029(e), the term "access device" can include:

> any card, plate, code, account number, electronic serial number, mobile identification number, personal identification number, or other telecommunications service, equipment, or instrument identifier, or other means of account access that can be used, alone or in conjunction with another access device, to obtain money, goods, services, or any other thing of value, or that can be used to initiate a transfer of funds (other than a transfer originated solely by paper instrument).

The following example illustrates how a phishing case can be tried for violations of multiple federal statutes. In September 2006, a federal grand jury in New Haven, Connecticut, charged six men for a fairly elaborate phishing scheme (State News Service 2006). This scheme first involved employing a spammer to send out e-mails with electronic greeting cards to thousands of AOL subscribers. Once a subscriber clicked on the card, his or her computer was be infected with a malicious Trojan that blocked the user from accessing AOL unless personal identification items such as name, birth date, and social security number were entered. The fraudsters then utilized the vital information to produce counterfeit debit cards for use at ATMs and retail outlets. Charges filed by federal prosecutors in this indictment included wire fraud, bank fraud, access device fraud, computer fraud and abuse, and identity theft. These charges resulted in 12 counts of fraud against the defendants.

The most current federal statute related to phishing was enacted through the CAN-SPAM Act passed in 2003. Codified in 18 U.S.C. §1037, the act prohibits anyone from knowingly using a protected computer to transmit multiple commercial e-mails with the intent to deceive or mislead recipients. Also prohibited are accessing a protected computer without authorization, falsifying header information on e-mails, registering five or more false e-mail accounts or Internet Protocol addresses. Given that phishing is not too difficult to generate and deploy, phishers can use a single e-mail address possibly from their own computer, set up a false Web site to receive personal information for 5 days, and then perform fraudulent activities outside of the scope of the CAN-SPAM Act. Few other related federal statutes have a similar limitation. For example, current fraud and identity theft statutes are not effective in deterring and prosecuting phishing cases. As explained by Senator Patrick Leahy (D-VT) in his Anti-Phishing Act of 2005, traditional fraud statutes allow prosecutors to charge the accused only after victims have been defrauded—these statutes are "not sufficient to respond to phishing." Because of these loopholes, Senator Leahy proposed the Anti-Phishing Act at the first session of the 109th Congress in 2005. This bill focused on the two main elements of phishing: fraudulent e-mails and Web sites. The act proposed a maximum sentence of 5 years for those who use e-mail or Web sites "with the intent to carry on any activity," which would be a fraud or identity theft (GovTrack 2005a). The act inherently permits prosecutors to press charges against phishers without specific financial damage to any individuals (Stevenson 2005). Nevertheless, the proposed bill was not passed at the end of the session; it has been referred to the Judicial Committee. This bill currently remains at the initial stage of the legislative process; it seems concerns of the First Amendment protection need to be addressed. The bill may undergo major changes in later markup sessions (GovTrack 2005b).

Phishing encompasses a number of features inherent in many other fraudulent criminal acts. Jonathan Rusch (2004), Special Counsel for Fraud Prevention of the U.S. Department of Justice, cautioned that fraudsters have employed multiple varieties of phishing schemes to deceive targets. Rusch categorizes three main types of phishing as: Dragnet, Rod-and-Reel, and Lobsterpot. The Dragnet type is the most common of the three. Phishing attempts in this category consist of e-mails bearing authentic-looking corporate identification, designed to persuade a large group of people to visit an equally authentic-looking, but phony, Web site. Those who visit the Web site are then prompted to divulge sensitive information. Another feature of the Dragnet method is that it does not target specific potential victims; the messages are written in such a way as to prompt a sudden reaction by whoever reads them. The scammers send out mass quantities of e-mail supposedly from companies with a wide client base, figuring the odds of reaching an actual customer are high. Another instance of a Dragnet e-mail is one claiming the receiver of the e-mail has just been awarded an inheritance or won the lottery. The potential victims are then asked to provide bank information in order to receive their money quickly. The Rod-and-Reel type acts just as one might imagine, aiming for a specific, predetermined target. Phishers make harmless contact at first, and then once they feel they have gained the trust of the individual, they proceed with their scam. For instance, a phisher may send fraudulent bank letters and IRS forms to members of a target group, and instruct them to fax personal information and financial account number to a fake bank or seemingly IRS unit. These personal records are then used by the scammer to transfer money from the victim's account to an overseas account. The last type described by Rusch (2004) is the Lobsterpot method. With this strategy, the criminals create Web sites that closely resemble legitimate Web sites, in hopes that a specific class of people will mistakenly visit the counterfeit Web site and disclose financial data. This type of technique differs from the others significantly, in that it does not involve the distribution of an enticing e-mail. In contrast, the phishers plant the falsified Web site and wait for victims to come to it.

Phishing Methods

Technical artifice and social engineering are two basic methods phishers employ to steal valuable personal identification (APWG n.d.). The technical artifice method involves infecting personal computers with malicious software. This software is capable of recording keystrokes entered by the user, and sending that information to the phisher. Also, it can redirect Internet users from legitimate Web sites to false ones via a remote connection. Social engineering can be defined as "gaining intelligence through deception or also as using human relationships to attain a goal" (Yoo 2006, 8). Similar to social engineers who apply sociological doctrines to specific problems, phishers using these methods utilize deceptive devices to trick Internet users into a situation where they are willing to disclose sensitive information. Usually, the social engineering methods launch a false e-mail urging the receiver to click on a linked Web site appearing to come from a genuine business. After clicking the link, the user is actually brought to a fraudulent site asking for personal financial information such as credit card or bank account numbers. Phishers then use the obtained records to swindle money from the credit card or bank, or to apply for a new credit card with a false identity.

Social engineering phishing tactics and targets vary. Some simpler e-mails contain fill-in forms, while other more complex ones direct victims through a variety of synthetic Web sites. As phishing is performed mostly for financial reasons, the most commonly attacked sector in 2006 was financial services, which registered 84 percent of reported phishing activity for that year (Symantec Corporation 2006). The next most active area of phishing was the Internet service provider sector, at 8 percent. Although fraudsters are not as likely to produce monetary gain in this area, it is probable they are using stolen information and accounts to further their phishing activities, such as sending mass e-mailings through the stolen accounts. The third most lucrative segment for phishers is retail, accounting for 5 percent of phishing attacks. Phishers attempt to purchase goods online and request that the items to be shipped to a location which the phisher has access to. The Symantec study (2006) revealed that the great disparity between financial scams (84 percent) and all other areas (16 percent) lies in the relative ease and immediate fiscal reward for successful deceit.

A historical catalog of phishing attacks categorized by company further illustrates the tendency of phishers to imitate financial institutions. As of December 2005, more than 5,003 attacks had used the name of the online auction giant eBay, and 4,632 had used the name of its online payment service, PayPal (Secure Computing 2006). Completing the top five were Citibank, SunTrust Bank, and AOL, which were named in 655, 603, and 440 attacks, respectively. The most attacked overseas banks are Bank of the West (385) and Barclays Bank (322) (Secure Computing 2006). While banks experienced a downward trend of attack frequency in 2005, the number started to swing upward again in 2006 (Kurtz 2006). This trend continued steadily into November 2006, when financial institutions accounted for 91.7 percent of phishing attacks that month (APWG 2006a). Moreover, phishers posing as financial institutions have become increasingly sophisticated. In late 2006, phishing ploys made use of dual authentication, which is a process that is supposed to ensure higher security for online transactions (Clarke 2006). What makes this especially deceiving is that the Federal Financial Institutions Examination Council (FFIEC) had just previously issued a guidance requiring banks and credit unions to use stronger authentication methods. The hackers had this procedure in place and operable before the FFIEC's due date (Clarke 2006).

One feature common to phishing e-mail messages is the imitation of another entity. In November 2006 alone, 120 brand names were mimicked during phishing attempts (APWG 2006a). This number increased to 146 the next month (APWG 2006b). Tricks that fraudsters have used to appear legitimate have included the use of company graphics, working links to the real company's Web site, and a falsified return address (MailFrontier 2004). The next stage of the phishing process is creating a message that prompts the recipient to take some specified action, such as sending an e-mail reply, completing a form within the e-mail, or clicking on a hyperlink. Message content varies, with the most common form claiming to require information for account verification, or in response to a security upgrade. Another common ploy scammers use is to pretend to be collecting for humanitarian reasons, such as hurricane relief efforts. A growing category is one of fake e-mails maintaining that the addressee must enter financial data to claim lottery/sweepstakes prizes (Musgrove 2005). Since fraudulent Web sites and e-mail messages are caught fairly quickly, the messages must strive to instill a sense of urgency in the reader (MailFrontier 2004). In November 2006, the average length of time a site was online was 4.5 days (APWG 2006a). In November 2007 that was shortened to 4 days (APWG 2007). Crooks urge their victims to respond hurriedly by threatening account expiration or termination if there is not a prompt reply (MailFrontier 2004).

Once the messages have successfully convinced the reader to click on a hyperlink, the ensuing Web page must be equally believable. Company graphics, page layout, fonts, and color schemes are essential to satisfying a user's preliminary impression of the Web site (MailFrontier 2004). Many Internet-savvy phishers have been effective not only in replicating the graphic look of legitimate Web sites, but also in adding or circumventing some of the signs users are advised to look for in evaluating a Web site's safety and authenticity, such as a yellow padlock in the lower right corner, an "https" in the beginning of the URL, and a "TRUST-e" symbol, all of which are indicators of increased security protection (University of Houston 2005). In 2005, over 450 phishing Web sites operated using a secure socket layer, which is a certification that provides the gold padlock in a browser window, plus an "https" designation (Miller 2005). Examining a Web site's URL used to be a more reliable way to detect a counterfeit, since earlier phishers used domain names only somewhat similar in appearance to the valid company they were spoofing. For example, a phisher attempting to imitate eBay used the following Web site address: http://ebay-securitycheck. easy. dk3. com (MailFrontier 2004). Today, however, fraudsters can make the company's actual domain name visible, such as www.paypal.com, but when the user clicks on the hyperlink, it really directs the user to http://218.246.224.203, the phisher's Web site (APWG n.d.). On two separate occasions in March 2005, phishers attacked Charter One Bank using a new technique in which the hackers placed a layer over the company's real Web site. So while users were on the correct Web page, and any antiphishing software would have recognized the site as trustworthy, the section where a user enters information was superimposed by the phisher. Any information entered there would then go to that scammer instead of the bank (Miller 2005).

Other tricks phishers adopt to hide the addresses of their fake Web sites include using an @ symbol after the real company's address, and then putting the fraudulent domain name after that symbol. This technique redirects the user to the second Web site, while most phishing filters only examine the Web site before the @ symbol (MailFrontier 2004). Also, placing %00 in the address essentially makes everything after that invisible, and some fraudsters further use a string of hexadecimal character codes to hide their IP addresses. For instance, a

deceitful Web site with the address http://www.visa.com%00@%32%32%30%2E%36%
38%2E%32%31%24%2E%32%31%33 would only show the user http://www.visa.com
because the %00 after that renders the rest of the address invisible. In addition, the fraudster's
IP address http://220.68.214.213 is hidden in the hexadecimal character string %32%32%
30%2E%36%38%2E%32%31%34%2E%32%31%33 (MailFrontier 2004, 14).

While the institutions that phishers imitate and the complexity of individual scams differ, most phishing attempts share two characteristics: the impersonation of another entity and
a request for personal information. Simple messages can be just as deceiving as an elaborate
hoax, and both are potentially financially devastating to the victim. Phishing attempts can
come from practically anywhere in the world, pretending to be from any of a countless number of sources, and endeavoring to convince the receiver of any imaginable claim.

Phisher Characteristics

Although it may appear that a person needs to be highly proficient in computers to operate a
successful phishing scheme, it is not necessarily true. An instance of phishing in 2003 highlights just how easy it is to create a scam to successfully con people out of their money. In this
case, a minor sent fake e-mail messages that warned AOL subscribers their accounts would be
terminated if their personal data was not updated immediately. The messages provided a link
to a fake information update page, with authentic AOL logos, colors, and design. After the
victims entered their billing information, the youth bought things online and opened more
false accounts with the freshly stolen data. To close the case, the juvenile agreed to pay $3,500
to the Federal Trade Commission to settle the fine (Rusch 2004).

The ages and backgrounds of convicted phishers vary widely. One 23-year-old
Connecticut man simply entered a chat room, copied the screen names of other participants,
and began sending e-mails under the guise of AOL to those individuals asking for personal
information (Rusch 2004). Another scammer trying to swindle money while pretending to be
AOL-affiliated was a 55-year-old from Ohio (Rusch 2004). One self-taught phisher was candid during an interview with CNN (2006), in which he told reporters phishing is "extremely
easy," and that he could find a person's social security number, date of birth, and bank account
number in "two or three hours." The fraudster went on to say law enforcement does not "have
enough manpower or knowledge" to catch the phishers, and things "go on that they're never
going to find out about."

Potential phishers nowadays have an even easier avenue to conduct their deceit. RSA
Security, Inc., recently announced the presence of a new phishing software kit (Krebs 2007),
which is easily installable and functions straightforward via a point-and-click interface. This
kit allows the user to intercept data by means of a "man-in-the-middle" technique. The program can interface in real time with the legitimate site being imitated, granting the phisher
seamless and invisible access to a victim's personal information (Buckley 2007). Man-in-the-
middle tactics render a traditional way of checking authenticity useless. Previously, one could
enter a gibberish password, and if it were accepted, one would know the site was a fraud. If
the password was not accepted, one could assume the site was legitimate. Now, with this kit,
phishers instantly check the acceptability of the password through the real company and reject
it if the company does too. This type of kit is commonly priced between $50 and $100 (Krebs
2007). Using this kit, practically anyone with Internet access may silently rob thousands of
innocent people of valuable cash and credit.

The fact that many convicted phishers fit the description of ordinary people, however, does not negate the existence of highly skilled, computer-literate criminals. The previous examples only illustrate the diversity of individuals who have decided to commit this particular type of Internet fraud, and how easy it can be. Information about a convicted phisher who appears to be demographically representative of any regular person may be more prevalent than the information about so-called masterminds. The reason for this is that, even though common criminals may perform phishing easily, chances are they are not well versed in methods of avoiding law enforcement. This is in contrast to the entity called Rock Phish, a leading phishing force of whom virtually nothing is known (McMillan 2006b). As researched by McMillan, Rock Phish is attributed with approximately half of all current phishing attacks, and its innovative methods have earned it an estimated $100 million since 2004. Security experts are unsure whether Rock Phish is an individual or a group, or based in one country or many. Rock Phish is credited with pioneering image spam and single-use URL's, as well as any other cutting-edge schemes in use. Image spam plants the deceitful message in an e-mail as an image, rather than text, to avoid text-based filters. Single-use URLs are Web sites that self-destruct after a single use, thereby rendering phishing filters that use a blacklist useless since there is no time for the particular Web site to be recognized as fraudulent and blocked as such. McMillan (2006b) noted that Rock Phish does not particularly target eBay or PayPal, but it has been associated with attacks on 44 companies in nine different countries. It utilizes domain names from countries that are rarely, if ever, linked with phishing, such as Moldovia and São Tomé.

Phishing Victims

Despite the diversity among phishers, victims of their phishing may be even more diverse. Ages, occupations, and geographic location range greatly. A 38-year-old man from Houston, Texas, lost $1,500 online, and the phishers even locked him out of his bank account by changing his password (Krebs 2004). Several months later, someone tried to open a $25,000 line of credit in his name. A 44-year-old businessman became aware he was a phishing victim after $5,000 worth of car parts was charged to his account in a different state, and a slew of new computers were purchased in another state (Krebs 2004). A 31-year-old Los Angeles high school teacher, a 55-year-old retiree, and a Wisconsin woman operating a cleaning business from her home are all examples of phishing victims (Krebs 2004, Swartz 2006). So is a 77-year-old Washington woman, who lost hundreds of dollars over the course of multiple deceitful purchases (Krebs 2004). Military members are increasingly attacked in cyberspace as well. The Air Force issues its members credit cards for official business from Bank of America. Recently, scammers have been targeting Air Force members using a Bank of America façade, which has prompted officials to issue warnings and additional Internet security training (AF Portal 2007). Sometimes, the speed with which phishers act is astonishing. A California attorney lost $100 less than one minute after he released sensitive information, and in less than 15 minutes hackers had purchased $1,200 worth of plane tickets, electronic equipment, and other items with his credit card (Swartz 2006).

Although virtually anybody who uses the Internet is a potential victim for phishing, certain qualities and attributes seem to make some groups at greater risk than others. One of those groups is young adults aged 18 to 25 (Krebs 2004). It appears that individuals in this age range tend to spend more time online and to bank online. In addition, Krebs (2004) noted that a high level of complacency exists among 18- to 25-year-olds, and their perception of Internet fraud is that it is inevitable. To them, extra precautions are useless and there is no point in being careful. Exemplary of this attitude is a 25-year-old Brooklyn, New York, woman whose information became compromised. She did not fret, figuring since her credit card was nearly at its limit, the crooks would not be able to buy much. She continues to shop online without any safety measures since, according to her, "it really wasn't a big deal. It didn't end up costing [her] anything" (Krebs 2004).

Another group vulnerable to phishing is online job seekers. As indicated by Shin (2007), phishers have taken advantage of individuals looking for employment on job Web sites such as Monster.com and Yahoo HotJobs. The scammers act as if they are working for the employment company and send an e-mail requesting additional information, in exchange for an exciting career. People are required to proffer more information on employment Web sites than on banking sites, and in an attempt to become hired, they are more likely to fulfill requests for sensitive information.

Another social-demographic that has slightly elevated susceptibility is income. Based on a survey of 5,000 American adults, the research firm Gartner (2006) found that high-income earners, classified as individuals who earn over $100,000 annually, are more likely to receive phishing e-mails. The survey showed that these affluent adults were reported to receive 112 e-mails, in comparison to 74 for other income groups. This finding is possibly due to the fact that high-income earners are more likely to conduct electronic transactions and utilize online services. Although individuals in this income classification responded less often to phishing messages, when they did, they lost about four times the amount of money as other victims (Gartner 2006).

In addition to individual victims, financial institutions and service providers in the e-commerce industry are both negatively impacted by this growing Internet fraud (Goth 2005). Banks and credit unions are the primary sources of monetary recovery for phishing victims (Howell 2006). These institutions not only pay the first time when the criminals make purchases but also when the victims demand restitution. Credit card companies are also a source of reimbursement. Altogether, victims were able to recover a little over half of money lost (Howell 2006). All financial institutions face a problem, regardless of whether they have to disburse compensation to account holders or not. Operating costs, in the form of issuing new cards, changing passwords, and updating databases, are factors financial institutions deal with (Organisation for Economic Co-operation and Development 2005). Moreover, companies must strengthen their online authentication and Internet security programs to combat this threat, which may require hiring an expert third party (Clarke 2006). For example, BT Group, formerly British Telecom, purchased a security firm called Counterpane for almost $40 million (Raisbeck 2007). A technological effort to dissuade phishing attempts by Microsoft is redesigning the address bar at the top of the browser, which unfortunately burdens small companies, sometimes unbearably (Chafkin 2007). This coloring procedure displays a green background in the bar for approved Web sites, and a red shade for potentially hazardous Web sites. In order to purchase green shading, a company must be over 3 years old and not be a sole proprietorship or LLC. Quite possibly, customers might turn away from a legitimate young business if the business' URL is shown in a shaded red box.

Trust is another sensitive area for financial institutions and e-commerce merchants alike. With an estimated 30 percent of Internet users reducing time spent online, and 25 percent discontinuing online purchasing, businesses that rely on Internet sales and marketing are all but ruined (Anderberg 2005; Binational Working Group on Cross-Border Mass Marketing Fraud 2006). Anderberg further indicates that nearly one-third of Internet users do not trust messages that are from banks, and over half do not trust stockbroker sites. As a result of this mistrust, companies are forced to use more expensive means of communicating, either by more sophisticated e-mails, phoning directly, or traditional paper mail (Organisation for Economic Co-operation and Development 2005). Ironically, paper mail or other hard-copy documents are not only more expensive but can be less secure than online banking (Beaumier 2006, MailFrontier 2004). As indicated by Beaumier, fraud via traditional methods such as searching the trash of households and businesses, stealing wallets and checkbooks, and cheating by the insiders are more common than online fraud.

CRIMINAL JUSTICE RESPONSES

While the Anti-Phishing Act remains to be passed by Congress, the criminal justice system must rely on other applicable laws to convict phishers, some of which have been previously mentioned. Four years after its enactment, the CAN-SPAM Act saw its first jury conviction (Technology News 2007). A 45-year-old California man was not only charged under the CAN-SPAM Act, but also with "10 other counts, including wire fraud, aiding and abetting the unauthorized use of an access device, possession of more than 15 access devices, misuse of the AOL trademark, attempted witness harassment, and failure to appear in court" (Technology News 2007, 1). Many different agencies cooperated in the investigation. Officers of the Ontario Police Department initiated the case in 2005, and then contacted the Federal Bureau of Investigation (FBI), which ultimately combined forces from the United States Secret Service, the Los Angeles Police Department, California Highway Patrol, the Los Angeles County District Attorney's Office, and the United States Attorney's Office (FBI 2006).

This task force is illustrative of the need for law enforcement agencies to work hand in hand with one another, private entities, and foreign organizations due to the highly technical nature, global presence, and widespread damage of phishing. The Anti-Phishing Working Group is a focal point for government and businesses alike, with over 2,600 members from sectors as diverse as law enforcement agencies, banks, Internet service providers, and technological security firms such as RSA Security, Inc., SecureWorks, and Websense (Krebs 2007, Clarke 2006). Businesses sometimes have a separate department just for Internet fraud. For example, Microsoft employs an Internet Safety Enforcement Team consisting of 65 lawyers, professional investigators, and others worldwide (Kornblum 2006). Kornblum, an attorney of the Microsoft team, claimed that the first global phisher investigated by his group has resulted in a 21-month sentence for an Iowa resident with 3 years' supervised release, and a fine of $57,494.07.

Phishers can operate from wherever there is Internet access, and affect any other location online. Even more, the multiple facets of a complex phishing scheme, such as writing malicious code, hosting a server, and channeling funds, are suspected to be divided geographically, even between different countries. This international spread leaves already difficult-to-follow tracks even more vague. Additionally, time constraints arise when phishing take-down groups from one nation attempt to investigate and remove the fraudulent site in a previously unrelated country (McMillan 2006b). Global interaction among antiphishing organizations is visible through a number of working groups and bilateral partnerships. Canadians and Americans have been working together since 2004 in a Canada–U.S. Cross-Border Group, with participation from the U.S. Department of Justice and the Public Safety and Emergency Preparedness Canada. Another interesting international effort occurs at the Black Hat briefings and trainings (Black Hat n.d.). Government and corporation officials, Internet security experts, independent fraud researchers, and underground hackers have formed the Black Hat network to develop innovative mechanisms in protecting the newest vulnerabilities. Raisbeck (2007) notes that phishers are increasingly operating out of poorer countries and ones with lax regulations on Internet use. Global efforts will have to concentrate on these countries and fully explore all relevant legislations to stay competitive enough to combat phishing crimes.

EDUCATION AND AWARENESS

Ultimately, the best defense against phishing attacks is educating the general population. Social engineering techniques that hinge on exploiting the victim's trust are paramount to a successful phishing attack (MailFrontier 2004). Communication occurs directly between the criminal and the victim, with the facelessness of e-mail providing sufficient disguise for phishers. The fraudster's speed is quite impressive, and the short length of time a phishing Web site is operable creates much difficulty for law enforcement and danger for consumers (Swart 2006, APWG n.d.). Responsive, *post facto* policing suffers even more from diplomatic interactions between nations and the ease with which hackers have to conceal their tracks (McMillan 2006b).

These factors contributed to the birth of technological defenses against phishing attacks, to act as frontline barriers. Microsoft recently released a new version of Internet Explorer that has a phishing filter installed, and an e-mail authentication device called Sender ID (Kornblum 2006). Netcraft Toolbar is another phishing filter, praised for its "great repository of phishing sites" (Brandt 2006). However, the major flaw of phishing filters is that they scan URLs for already known phishing Web sites. Criminals have devised numerous techniques to maneuver around phishing filters. One is by diluting the text with letters matching the background color, rendering them invisible to the human eye (Gallagher 2004). Another method is called cross-site scripting. This technique automatically directs the user to a Web site through the credentials and address of another, which fools most phishing filters because they only examine the first Web site in a URL (Brandt 2006). Additionally, 28,531 never-before-seen phishing Web sites appeared in December 2006, with an average online time of 4 days, which makes updating a blacklist a monumental task (APWG n.d.). Combined with the development of single-use URLs, phishing filters are not a stand-alone solution (McMillan 2006b).

A list of items for consumers to perform in order to safeguard themselves from phishing attacks commonly contains instructions on searching for a yellow padlock in the browser window, submitting an unacceptable password and seeing if the Web site accepts it, and looking for "https" at the beginning of an address (University of Houston 2005, Musgrove 2005). Nevertheless, knowledgeable phishers are able to navigate around most of the aforementioned practices. Over 450 phishing attacks in 2005 had used Web sites with the golden padlock and "http" at the beginning of the address (Miller 2005). Krebs (2007) also noted that the man-in-the-middle kit has been utilized by some phishing sites to intercept data transmitted between the customer and the legitimate Web site. Though the number of such sites is small, Krebs (2007) warned that this type of attack may become the norm in the near future.

Preventative strategies that remain the most useful, according to Musgrove (2005), include typing an address into the browser instead of following and clicking on an embedded hyperlink, never entering account information into an e-mail, and directly telephoning the company who is supposedly attempting to contact you. Above all, a basic understanding of the tactics and prevalence of phishing, paired with constant skepticism, will prepare the average person against phishing attacks. One would find helpful information from the Anti-Phishing Working Group, the Federal Trade Commission, and the Department of Justice. People more adept at computer technology might discover beneficial details from security specialists or firms mentioned previously. The Microsoft attorney Kornblum (2006) adds that "educating consumers about the dangers of phishing, spyware, etc., is also a key strategy" (p. 1).

CONCLUSION

Phishing and its related Internet scams are sure to keep increasing monetary gains. This trend is the same to phishers who will continue to sharpen their skills to avoid detection and increase their criminal profits. As technologies continue to improve, a new generation of Internet con artists will begin to develop greater challenges to the criminal justice system. Legislators will have to act more quickly to keep up the full control of the growing problem. Meanwhile, criminal justice agencies should strengthen their collaborations in the network of cyber crime enforcement and prevention. Agencies, community members, and researchers also share a sense of responsibility to combat Internet phishing in a collaboratively effective manner. It is hoped that the combination of legislation, criminal justice and community responses, and citizen education and awareness can work together in a way that Internet phishing schemes are fully under control.

KEY TERMS

Hacker
Phishing
Scam

REFERENCES

AF Portal. February 1, 2007. Internet scam—Bank account holders beware!!! Retrieved February 28, 2007, from https://www.my.af.mil/gcss-af/afp40/USAF/ep/contentView.do?contentType=EDITORIAL&contentId=1026065&programId=1024980&pageId=9374&channelPageId=-1073755231

Anderberg, K. December 2005. We have a problem [Electronic Version]. *Communication News* 4.

Anti-Phishing Working Group. 2006a. Phishing activity trends: Report for November, 2006. Retrieved January 10, 2007, from http://www.antiphishing.org/reports/apwg_report_november_2006.pdf

Anti-Phishing Working Group. 2006b. Phishing activity trends: Report for December, 2006. Retrieved February 15, 2007, from http://www.antiphishing.org/reports/apwg_report_december_2006.pdf

Anti-Phishing Working Group. 2007. Phishing activity trends: Report for the Month of February, 2007. Retrieved April 20, 2007, from http://www.antiphishing.org/reports/apwg_report_february_2007.pdf

Anti-Phishing Working Group Website. n.d. What is phishing and pharming? Retrieved January 3, 2007, from www.antiphishing.org

Beaumier, C. February, 2006. Multifactor authentication: A blow to identity theft? *Bank Accounting & Finance*. Retrieved April 20, 2007, from http://www.protivit.net/downloads/PRO/pro-us/Multifactor_Authentication.pdf

Binational Working Group on Cross-Border Mass Marketing Fraud. 2006. Report on phishing: A report to the minister of public safety and emergency preparedness Canada and the attorney general of the United States. Retrieved February 8, 2007, from http://www.usdoj.gov/opa/report_on_phishing.pdf

Black Hat. n.d. Retrieved March 15, 2007, from http://www.blackhat.com

Brandt, A. October 2006. How bad guys exploit legitimate sites [Electronic Version]. *PC World* 39.

Britz, M. 2004. *Computer Forensics and Cyber Crime: An Introduction*. Upper Saddle River, New Jersey: Pearson Education Inc.

Buckley, M. January 2007. RSA discovers new universal man-in-the-middle phishing kit; New kit helps fraudsters easily launch increasingly-sophisticated and automated online fraud attacks. *PR Newswire*. Retrieved January 11, 2007, from LexisNexis Academic database.

Chafkin, M. January 2007. Plan to stop phishing could hurt small business [Electronic Version]. *Inc. Magazine* 24. Retrieved April 5, 2007, from http://www.inc.com/magazine/20070101/priority-theweb.html

Clarke, E. W. 2006. SecureWorks warns of phishing schemes using dual authentication signup process to scam bank and credit union customers. *PR Newswire*. Retrieved January 2, 2007, from LexisNexis Academic database.

CNN. 2006. Convict: Stealing your identity was easy fun. Retrieved March 2, 2007, from http://www.cnn.com/2006/US/05/18/cnna.identitythief/index.html

Fair Isaac Corporation. 2005. Identifying and controlling debit card phishing scams. Retrieved February 8, 2005, from http://www.fairisaac.com/NR/rdonlyres/99668780-A4D9-4936-A2BA-61EDDD2EF2F6/0/Debit_Solutions_Phishing_WP.pdf

FBI. November 1, 2006. Cybercrime fugitive arrested in azusa for operating phishing scheme, failing to appear and witness harassment. Press Release. Retrieved March 1, 2007, from http://losangeles.fbi.gov/pressrel/2006/la110106.htm

Gallagher, D. F. 2004. Users find too many phish in the Internet sea. *New York Times*, Technology 1.

Gartner, Inc. 2006. Number of phishing e-mails sent to U.S. adults nearly doubles in just two years. *Business Wire*. Retrieved April 5, 2007, from LexisNexis Academic database.

Goth, G. 2005. Phishing attacks rising, but dollar losses down [Electronic Version]. *Security & Privacy Magazine*, IEEE, 3, 8.

GovTrack. 2005a. S. 472—109th Congress, Anti-phishing Act of 2005. *GovTrack.us* (database of federal legislation). Retrieved April 21, 2007, from http://www.govtrack.us/congress/billtext.xpd?bill=s109-472

GovTrack. 2005b. S. 472—109th Congress, Anti-phishing Act of 2005, Bill Status. *GovTrack.us* (database of federal legislation). Retrieved April 21, 2007, from http://www.govtrack.us/congress/bill.xpd?bill=s109-472

Howell, D. 2006. Line on phishing scams: We're getting deeper; Study finds folks losing more money than before to these Website ruses [Electronic Version]. *Investor's Business Daily* A05.

Korea Internet Security Center. 2006. Korea Phishing Activities Trends Report, Retrieved April 18, 2007, from APWG Web site http://www.antiphishing.org/reports/200612_KoreaPhishingActivityReport_Dec2006.pdf

Kornblum, A. 2006. Enforcement takes the fight to the phishers. *IEBlog, The Microsoft Internet Explorer Webblog*. Retrieved April 5, 2007, from http://blogs.msdn.com/ie/archive/2006/06/22/643173.aspx

Krebs, B. 2004. Phishing schemes scar victims. *Washington Post*. Retrieved March 1, 2007, from http://www.washingtonpost.com/ac2/wp-dyn/A59349-2004Nov18?language=printer

Krebs, B. 2007. Great strides in phishing. *Washington Post*. Retrieved January 17, 2007, from http://blog.washingtonpost.com/securityfix/2007/01/the_threat_in_the_scams_and_fa.html

Kurtz, L. 2006. Cloudmark reports spikes in European phishing attacks, cautions U.S. brands against complacency; Banks in Germany and U.K. at center of current attacks. *Market Wire*. Retrieved January 2, 2007, from LexisNexis Academic database.

MailFrontier, Inc. 2004. Anatomy of a phishing email, 2004. Retrieved April 5, 2007, from http://www. mailfrontier.com/docs/MF_Phish_Anatomy.pdf

McMillan, R. November 2006a. Gartner: Consumers to lose $2.8 billion to phishers in 2006. *Network World*. Retrieved April 5, 2007, from http://www.networkworld.com/news/2006/110906-gartner-consumers-to-lose-28b.html

McMillan, R. December 2006b. "Rock Phish" blamed for surge in phishing. *InfoWorld*. Retrieved January 10, 2007, from http://www.infoworld.com/article/06/12/12/HNrockphish_2.html

Miller, R. 2005. More than 450 phishing attacks used SSL in 2005. *Netcraft*. Retrieved February 8, 2007, from http://news.netcraft.com/archives/2005/12/28/more_than_450_phishing_attacks_used_ssl_in_2005.html

Musgrove, M. 2005. "Phishing" keeps luring victims. *Washington Post*. Retrieved April 5, 2007, from http://www.washingtonpost.com/wp-dyn/content/article/2005/10/21/AR2005102102113.html

Organisation for Economic Co-operation and Development. 2005. Phishing as a threat to the financial industry. Retrieved March 2, 2007, from https://oecd.org/dataoecd/52/26/34594162.pdf

Raisbeck, F. February 8, 2007. Schneier: Cyber crime goes global. *SC Magazine*. Retrieved February 8, 2007, from http://scmagazine.com/uk/news/article/631650/schneier-cyber-crime-goes-global/

Rudd, B. 2004. An analysis of phishing and possible mitigation strategies. SANS Institute. Retrieved April 19, 2007, from http://www.giac.org/certified_professionals/practicals/gsec/3994.php

Rusch, J. August 2004. *Phishing and Federal Law Enforcement*. Washington, DC: U.S. Department of Justice. Retrieved January 3, 2007, from http://www.abanet.org/adminlaw/annual2004/Phishing/PhishingABAAug2004Rusch.ppt

Secure Computing. 2006. Phishing attacks by company. Retrieved January 9, 2007, from http://www. ciphertrust.com/resources/statistics/phishing.php

Shin, A. 2007. Taking the bait on a phishing scam; Job seekers are targets, victims of sophisticated phishing ploy. *Washington Post*. Retrieved February 27, 2007, from LexisNexis Academic database.

State News Service. 2006. Six men charged in Internet phishing scam, three plead guilty. *State News Service*. Retrieved January 20, 2007, from LexisNexis Academic database.

Stevenson, R. L. 2005. Plugging the "phishing" hole: Legislation versus technology. *Duke Law & Technology Review*. Retrieved April 21, 2007, from www.law.duke.edu/journals/dltr/articles/PDF/2005DLTR0006.pdf

Swartz, J. 2006. Good cybercitizens keep watch over ID-theft victims; They let people know they've been duped. *Gannett Company*. Retrieved March 11, 2007, from LexisNexis Academic database.

Symantec Corporation. 2004. Mitigating online fraud: Customer confidence, brand protection, and loss minimization. Retrieved April 16, 2007, from http://antiphishing.org/sponsors_technical_papers/symantec_online_fraud.pdf

Symantec Corporation. September 2006. Symantec Internet security threat report trends for January 06–June 06. Retrieved January 9, 2007, from http://www.symantec.com/specprog/threatreport/ent-whitepaper_symantec_internet_security_threat_report_x_09_2006.en-us.pdf

Technology News. 2007. Spam act conviction for phishing scheme. *Technology News Daily*. Retrieved March 1, 2007, from http://www.technologynewsdaily.com/node/5716

University of Houston. 2005. Phishing scams. Retrieved January 2, 2007, from University of Houston, Information Technology Website http://www.uh.edu/infotech/news/story.php?story_id=802

U.S. Department of Justice. 2004. Special report on "phishing." Retrieved March 21, 2007, from http://www.usdoj.gov/criminal/fraud/Phishing.pdf

Visa Inc. 2005. Phishing as a threat to financial industry. Retrieved January 2, 2007, from https://www. oecd.org/dataoecd/52/26/34594162.pdf

Yoo, J. 2006. Phishing: A survey. Retrieved April 20, 2007, from Yale University Website http://zoo.cs. yale.edu/classes/cs490/05-06b/yoo.dunne.pdf

Chapter 11

You Can't Cheat an Honest Man: Making ($$$s and) Sense of the Nigerian E-mail Scams

Adam King and Jim Thomas
Northern Illinois University

Adam King, Ph.D., is an assistant professor at Northern Illinois University, where he primarily studies social psychology, culture, and information technology. He welcomes comments and questions at: adking@niu.edu. Dr. King holds a Ph.D. in sociology from Indiana University.

Jim Thomas, Ph.D., emeritus professor in sociology/criminology at Northern Illinois University, specializes in research on cultures of marginalized groups, including computer hackers, prisoners, and Internet subcultures. Dr. Thomas holds a Ph.D. in sociology from Michigan State University. His teaching focus includes corrections, social theory, and ethnographic research ethics and methods. He is currently completing two monographs: *Revisiting Critical Ethnography* (Sage, 2008) and *Communicating Prison Culture* (in progress).

Abstract

The Nigerian e-mail scam, although neither the most costly nor the most frequent Internet crime, remains the most ubiquitous and well known of all cyber crimes. Although many Internet service providers utilize spam filters, randomly generated solicitations reach an estimated 10 million recipients worldwide each day. Many suggest that those who fall prey to such scams are naïve and gullible whereas we suggest otherwise. We introduce affect control theory (ACT) to describe how Nigerian con artists are able to elicit desired behaviors in their victims by blocking the normal inhibitors to such con games. Victimization statistics indicate that the scam has cost victims worldwide over $28 billion since its inception. To accomplish such a task, the scammers create a compelling and believable intellectual narrative to overcome the doubts of their victims using persuasive, yet manipulative tactics.

INTRODUCTION

It begins with an e-mail, one with a plaintive subject heading and a return address that you do not recognize. The author of the e-mail purports to be a former member of the Nigerian royal family (or banking official or terminally ill Christian). Due to ongoing civil unrest (or imminent death from cancer, or impending persecution), the author must surreptitiously move a large sum of money out of the country. After searching the Internet for a reliable partner, the author has selected you as the most trustworthy. As a reward for your help, you will receive a surprisingly large portion of the total amount, millions of dollars. If you continue the communication with the author, you eventually will be asked for personal banking information. If you are "lucky," not long after providing the requested information (and often additional money to cover "transfer fees" or "legal expenses"), your checking account is cleared out and your refugee vanishes with your money. If you are less fortunate, your checking account is left alone, but a long series of follow-up demands for advance payments begins, leading you to liquidate assets, borrow money, and you may even be asked to make a hasty flight to Africa in order to obtain the payday lying just beyond your reach. You have just been made a victim of the Nigerian 419 scam.

The Nigerian scam is neither the most costly nor the most frequent Internet crime. More common forms include auction fraud, which accounts for about 63 percent of reported incidents and 42 percent of financial losses, and nondelivery of goods, which accounts for 16 percent of reported crimes and 15 percent of the losses. However, the Nigerian e-mail scam, despite constituting less than 1 percent of reported Internet fraud complaints and only 2.7 percent of reported financial losses in 2005 (ICCC 2007), remains the most ubiquitous and well known of all cyber crimes. Although many Internet service providers have spam filters that keep most such solicitations out of users' mailboxes, the sheer volume of the randomly generated solicitations results in them reaching an extremely conservative estimate of over 10 million recipients worldwide each day.

There has been no lack of commentary on the Nigerian scam both in the academic literature and in the popular media. However, many of these accounts are built on the assumption that victims fall prey to the scam because they are ignorant, naïve, or simply greedy. We suggest that neither gullibility nor stupidity is an adequate explanation for the growing success of the Nigerian scams, nor—by extension—to the success of con games in general. Instead, we build on previous work in affect control theory (ACT) to describe how Nigerian con artists are able to elicit desired behaviors in their victims by creating an affective scenario that blocks the normal inhibitors that normally raise a caution flag in everyday social interactions. We describe common variants of the Nigerian e-mails and then examine how the common threads of these e-mails are built on the affective symbolic foundations underlying everyday social life.

BACKGROUND

Between 1990 and 2006, the number of people with Internet access exploded from 13.5 million worldwide to 1.1 billion (Global Policy Forum 2003; Minwatts Marketing Group 2007). As with any new frontier, as the population of cyberspace expanded, hustlers and con artists followed, and the Internet has become fertile ground for a new breed of international electronic con artists. The Nigerian scam and others like it typify how crimes that require interaction face-to-face are easily imported into the digital world.

The Nigerian 419 scam, named after the section of the Nigerian Criminal Code devoted to it (ICNL 2007), provides a dramatic and visible example of a successful Internet scam. Also known as an **"advance fee fraud"** (AFF) because it requires the victim to pay the scammer in advance with the promise of obtaining seemingly lucrative rewards later, it is hardly new. Variants date back nearly 900 years (re-quest.net 2007) and became more fully developed in the sixteenth century as the "Spanish Prisoner Scam." Purists might argue that the Nigerian AFF scam is not a true cyber crime, because it primarily uses e-mail to make contact and then shifts to more traditional forms of communication such as telephone and fax. However, we categorize it as a cyber crime because the initial computer-based e-mail and spam-generated outreach are required for the critical first contact, and details of credibility are often supplied through Internet-based interaction.

In 2006, most perpetrators of AFF Internet scams, about 97 percent, were based in Nigeria (UAGI 2007). In addition, many other online schemes are also Nigerian-based: Ultrascan Advanced Global Investigations (UAGI 2007) estimates that 95 percent of Internet lottery fraud and 76 percent of Internet check fraud solicitations are of Nigerian origin. Despite increased media visibility, online warnings, FBI, and Secret Service alerts, and growing awareness among computer users as to the dangers of these scams, both the frequency of victimization and the dollar amounts lost continue to increase dramatically. Between 2005 and 2006 in the United States, reported financial losses increased by 8 percent.

One reason why Nigeria became a base for Internet scammers lies in the nation's politics and economy. For decades, the Nigerian government was considered one of the most corrupt in the world. Because government officials profited both directly through bribes and indirectly through the influx of foreign currency, there was little incentive to impede the lucrative scams and every incentive to nurture them. When a new democratically elected government assumed power in 1999, one of the first goals was to reduce corruption. Although the current government in Nigeria has begun cooperating with other countries in combating the scam, decades of corruption in which government officials and other participants have created a "culture of larceny" neither quickly nor easily altered (Ribadu 2006).

Although there may be freelancing individuals who initiate contact and solicit information, the scammers generally work in small teams with a specialized division of labor. Unlike con artists who hope for a quick score by taking their gain in a single transaction, called "short cons," Nigerian scammers work on a **long con**, one designed to play out over time and gradually deplete a victim's resources. Contrary to public perceptions, the goal of most Nigerian AFF scam variants is not to simply empty a bank account by immediately obtaining financial information as some other scams do:

> It is also a misconception that the victim's bank account is requested so the culprit can plunder it—this is not the primary reason for the account request—merely a signal they have hooked another victim. (United States Secret Service n.d.)

Rather than a "quick score," the scammers intend to draw increasingly large sums from the victim, who is manipulated into seeking additional sources of funds to supply them. The life cycle of the relationship between the scammer and the victim can drag out for months, and the permutations, diagramed as a flowchart, can be complex (.NExT 2007). The U.S. Secret Service (n.d.) adds that, if carried to the conclusion, the victim often will be enticed to come to Nigeria for the final financial coup de grace.

The seductive lure of the long con has been demonstrated a number of times in popular fiction. Train's (1910) short story provides a rich illustration of how a seemingly wealthy, well intentioned, and savvy victim was drawn into the Spanish Prisoner con. Believing he could secure the release of a political prisoner held by the king, the victim would—for a small investment to cover costs—receive a handsome reward and a beautiful young woman in matrimony. Instead, the scheme snared the victim in a beautiful mess after he complied with continued requests for money to meet continuous "unexpected problems." In the end, he was forcibly robbed of the entire sum that he, and other investors he innocently drew into the plot, had collected.

The Spanish Prisoner scam has been around for several hundred years, and the Nigerian AFF scam operates in much the same way, enticing the victims to gradually increasing their investment and into accessing an ever-widening pool of funds obtained from a growing number and variety of sources. The Nigerian scam predates the Internet, dating back at least to the 1970s as a mail fraud scheme targeting especially small businesses (UAGI 2007), and one author of this paper received periodic Nigerian-based hardcopy solicitations over conventional postal mail as late as the 1990s. However, with the growth of the Internet in industrialized countries, it has become a predominantly online epidemic especially since 2000.

The scam has many variants, but they all share the same basic characteristics. First, a large sum of money becomes available because of a tragic event. Often, the event will be specific, such as a plane crash, major catastrophe (World Trade Center in 2001 or the 2004 Indonesian tsunami), an auto accident, political strife, or a fatal disease. Legitimate names of the wealthy victim may also be included. This allows the scammer to provide a URL link to a legitimate source that "confirms" both the incident and the actual death, providing initial credibility. Second, the scammer reports that the money remains unclaimed and provides a reason why haste is needed in order to claim it, and secrecy must be maintained to protect the project. Third, a reason for the need to expedite the transfer, usually because of political unrest or a looming deadline in which the money reverts to the bank or the government, adds a sense of urgency to the transaction. Fourth, the scammer invariably implies that the transaction needs help from a "foreigner" in order to skirt laws, outwit others who are also after the funds, or to avoid disclosure that the "fortune" exists. This underscores the compelling requirement of secrecy. Finally comes the direct attempt to establish direct personal contact between the scammer and the recipient. Occasionally, this may be a direct request for information, including personal details and bank account number and bank's routing number. However, in most variants, the scammer initially requests only a reply, which can lead to extended, even comic, e-mail exchanges or phone calls (Sturgeon 2003). On occasion, the e-mails will include attachments containing pictures or other information to enhance credibility. However, the attachments may also contain malware that includes spyware or worms capable of extracting the recipients e-mail address book or allows the users' PC to be used to relay future e-mails through a legitimate system.

Given the improbable scenarios, the seemingly random good fortune of being the beneficiary of such largesse, and the often stunning illiteracy of the solicitation, it might seem unlikely that any Internet users, presumably people with some sophistication and basic literacy skills, would fall prey to the scams. At least, it would seem that, with the increasing visibility and awareness of the scam, the prevalence of victimization would decrease. Yet, victimization increases.

One international firm that provides approximations of Nigerian AFF activity acknowledges that there are no reliable victimization statistics (UAGI 2007). All such figures are, at best, rough estimates for several reasons. First, the scam is international, and there is no centralized data source to provide an accurate accounting of those who have lost money. Second, as with all types of fraud, the complaints to authorities represent a small fraction of victims. An estimated 90 percent of fraud victimization goes unreported, and this may be even higher for Internet fraud. Third, the scam can take months to unfold, and much longer before the victim realizes what occurred.

How successful is the scam? One Secret Service investigator suggested that 1 percent of those who receive the solicitation in the United States respond at least once (Emery 2002).

This estimate may be inflated, but with millions of solicitations sent out daily, if only one person in 10,000 responded, that still leaves 1,000 potential victims for every one million solicitations. With an average loss in the United States of $5,000 per victim, the potential profits are astronomical. Data compiled by Ultrascan Advanced Global Investigations (UAGI), the most comprehensive source for Nigerian AFF victimization statistics, indicate that the scam has cost victims worldwide over $28 billion since its inception, and in 2006 alone cost over $3.8 billion (UAGI 2007).

Why does this scam remain so lucrative that, according to one 2007 estimate, there are over 300,000 perpetrators worldwide, a number growing at a rate of about 3 percent annually (UAGI 2007)? Longtime Internet commentator Jerry Pournelle (2001) has suggested a tongue-in-cheek explanation for the success of the scam by asking: "What percentage of the US adult population is (a) far dumber than average, (b) greedy, and (c) has an email account?" He concludes that, by creating a population "two standard deviations below the norm" as a base population and from it culling those with an e-mail account who are greedy, this leaves more than 10,000 likely victims. However tempting his hypothesis, we suggest that the explanation is more complex. While a touch of avarice and an e-mail account are prerequisites, we argue that stupidity is neither a necessary nor sufficient explanatory factor.

THEORETICAL FRAMEWORK

We cannot, of course, know the inner motives, emotional state, or intellectual prowess of victims of the Nigerian AFF scams. However, a casual search of media stories and court cases suggests that "stupidity" does not provide a useful explanation for victimization, as victims are often well educated and quite successful in other intellectual arenas despite falling for such a seemingly obvious scam. The only two things that our nonrandom reading of victims' accounts revealed is that the victims shared two primary characteristics, neither of them stupidity. First, they had an e-mail account. Second, they were enticed by a large sum of money with no credible explanation of the source. Some victims succumbed to this unusual circumstance because of greed, others out of well-intended concern to help somebody in need, but few, if any, seemed to succumb due to any overt mental defect.

There is a third characteristic victims shared, one basic to most social interaction: They engaged in a form of communicative activity that entailed a process of information exchange containing an explicit affective component. Because Nigerian AFF scam teams are well organized and attempt to tailor their narratives to appeal to specific affective states, they can cast a wide net that increases the probability of finding the right affective key to unlock the barriers that would ordinarily alert the wary and otherwise intelligent targets. By examining the affective content of e-mails, we can begin to tease out how the rhetoric of Nigerian e-mails produces affective frames that make the e-mails effective even when they are dealing with smart people.

Goffman, Cons, and "Expression Gaming"

The Nigerian scam is not intended as a one-hit mugging, but rather as a sustained interaction in which the target becomes increasingly enmeshed into the plot as a willing partner, drawn in by the scammer's ability to manipulate a narrative and establish rapport and trust without giving away the game. Goffman's (1969) rather cynical view of interaction as a dance of secrets illustrates a key ploy in establishing the necessary affective bond between victim and the mark. Goffman contends that every social situation contains elements of information control, in which participants have something to gain by manipulating the process by revealing, tailoring, concealing, or fabricating information, which, he says, makes us all a bit like "secret agents" (Goffman 1952, 81). He calls this "expression gaming." The control of information generates different types of secrets that must be team-managed in the dance of information control. The participants team up in a secrecy-managing expression game in which the players manipulate the secrets both to the outside world and to individual players. This conspiracy in secrets establishes a seemingly shared affective bond while simultaneously serving to prevent the potential mark from obtaining external information that might reveal the con.

Goffman's conception of the "mark" refers to an intended victim in a plan of illegal exploitation. A scammer obviously does not send out invitations inviting others to be a mark. In a "short con," the scammer intends a short period of interaction in which the scammer hopes to make off with the mark's money in a one-time interaction. The pigeon drop, dramatized in the opening scenes of the movie *The Sting*, illustrates this. Robert Redford and Paul Newman were two street hustlers who convinced a mark to give up a sum of money for the promise of even more money. The premise of a short con, such as the pigeon drop, is that the mark is willing to engage in illegal exploitation of another by working with one scammer to seemingly steal money from another person who is the scammer's secret accomplice. Both the scammer and accomplice disappear, leaving the mark with a bag of shredded paper instead of money.

The Nigerian scam, by contrast, is a "long con," which is intended to keep the mark on the hook for as long as possible in order to gradually drain the mark of resources. In a long con, the mark must be carefully groomed from the beginning, first with a lure and set-up, next with the actual exploitation, and finally with the breaking off of the game. Because the long con requires sustained interaction and steady depletion of the mark's resources, the initial lure and set-up are critical to establishing the context to provide a credible framework that will justify subsequent exploitation and reduce the mark's suspicion. Therefore, the narrative of the lure must include a complex set of threads that can be woven into an explanatory tapestry that calms the mark at the onset and keeps the money flowing once the tap has been turned in. One way that this occurs in the Nigerian scam is by a narrative lure that contains a strong affective component that simultaneously anticipates and defuses suspicion by portraying the scam as a set of shared secrets that can be manipulated for financial gain.

AFFECTIVE CONTROL THEORY

Affect control theory (ACT) (Heise 2007, 1979; Smith-Lovin and Heise 1988) offers a fruitful way to examine the symbolic lures used by Nigerian scammers to create a credible narrative to hook potential victims into prolonged bleeding for a long con. The underlying ACT premise is that the rhetoric of Nigerian scam e-mails taps the affective (emotional) sentiments and cultural meaning structures with sufficient credibility to sustain the scam. The affective nature of the e-mail narratives also contributes to the longevity of the continued success of the con. ACT provides a lens into how cultural affective meanings are manipulated and presented as a framework of shared secrets and conspiracy that lure people into the electronic equivalent of buying the Brooklyn Bridge and then paying for its maintenance.

Based on the measurement work of Charles Osgood et al. (1969, 1975), ACT argues that people process and act on cultural meanings in ways that confirm their affective sentiments toward familiar things, including their sentiments toward their behaviors, social location, and identities. When the components of a situation do not match their previous emotional sentiments toward them, people will attempt to take corrective action to reframe the situation to one that is more compatible with their preexisting emotional sentiments. For example, when someone who is normally associated with positive sentiments does something evil (e.g., a father is observed hitting a child), the observer will try to resolve the affective dissonance by either recasting the situation (the father is punishing the child, not beating him) or by taking another corrective action to restore the balance (the father is labeled as a criminal and sent to jail).

An ACT approach would frame Nigerian scams as an achievement of social engineering, one that allows deceptive expression gaming by manipulating a narrative lure to capitalize on preexisting affective sentiments. This manipulation and the corresponding definition of the situation build on the affective structure laid out in the e-mail narrative of the initial solicitation, and through it, the scammer can make handing over money appear as a rational and inevitable course of action. Thus, the initial solicitation is crucial to the scam, because it sets the stage and provides the affective logic for the subsequent playing out of the game.

Method

Our data draw from 4,893 different Nigerian scam e-mails collected between January 2002 and March 2007. For parsimony, we excluded from this database other AFF schemes such as lotteries, false job offers, and other lures that do not share the standard Nigerian AFF motif. Our data totaled over 180 Megabytes, but about 80 percent of that included large binary attachments. Although we opened few attachments, a scan of their contents indicated that they were often malware intended to use the recipient's PC as a proxy server, provided jpgs or other graphics files presumably in support of the narrative, or were text files with instructions, "evidence" of the truth of the narrative, or additional instructions or forms. The e-mails were received on nine different e-mail accounts on six different servers in four states. In addition, one author, a Unix system administrator on two university servers, examined daily spam logs that identified and filtered the servers generating the most egregious sources of all spam, including scam-spam. A preliminary examination of the originating addresses of the Nigerian AFF e-mails suggests that, unlike previous years, in the last few years the originating address was not forged or "spoofed." Instead, the addresses of the sender were legitimate. About 80 percent in our database originated from an eastern European or Asian country. This probably occurs because the scammers need a stable address in order to communicate with potential victims over a period of weeks or months. We also drew from additional Nigerian AFF posts on urgentmessage.org (available at: http://www.urgent.org, accessed October 24, 2007), a homepage that provides an extensive database of Nigerian scam and related e-mails.

Because the e-mails were sent automatically and randomly to a vast number of potential victims, there is little reason to believe that the examples in our data are atypical or significantly different from other Nigerian scam e-mail solicitations. As other researchers have indicated (Kich 2005), although Nigerian scam e-mails vary considerably in minor details, their basic structure is formulaic and generally homogenous. This comprehensive body of e-mail sent to diverse accounts provides an accurate and reliable picture of the consistency of the narratives.

This analysis also draws from a semantic "dictionary," a database of 300 common concepts and affective sentiment ratings assigned to them by American college students in 2003 (Heise 2007). Analysis of the affective sentiments of Internet users has demonstrated that Internet users develop strong and nuanced affective sentiments toward online-only identities, settings, and behaviors (King 2001). Like affective sentiments held toward offline phenomena, the sentiments of Internet users form a meaning system that motivates and regulates their online interactions.

To examine the affective sequences that are played out in the Nigerian AFF e-mails, concepts matching the tone and content of the e-mails in our e-mail database are compared to those in the 2003 semantic dictionary as a means of assessing the affective weight of sentiments associated with phrases, words, or motifs in online messaging. For example, in one common step in Nigerian scam e-mails, the scammer self-describes as a prestigious or important business person or functionary (VIP) and suggests a business deal. Drawing from the 2003 affective dictionary of status terms, the affective concept ratings of "VIP," "businessman," and the action of "doing business" are high status and powerful images that enhance a narrative suggesting exciting and exclusive dealings. Although we do not attribute affective responses to the recipients of AFF e-mails, we suggest that they represent a reasonable approximation of the emotional content that persuasively frames the lure. Because scammers do not know in advance who will be receiving their pitch, they must cast a wide narrative net and construct a message that they believe will be substantially persuasive in tapping the affectivity that corresponds to meanings that are culturally relevant in the recipients' culture. In this paper, we focus only in U.S. culture.

Analysis

Nigerian scam e-mails gain some of their legitimacy because they bear some resemblance to the kinds of sales promotion letters that are often sent out by legitimate businesses. However, Nigerian scam e-mails differ in several important ways from legitimate sales promotion letters: They include an unusually lengthy background story to set the stage for the interaction; they assure the receiver of transaction safety (usually taken for granted in legitimate sales promotion e-mails); and they overtly flatter the recipient (Budge 2006). It may well be that these variations are what signal most recipients that something is not "on the level" with Nigerian scam e-mails. That being the case, why would Nigerian e-mail scammers include these kinds of tip-offs in their notes, rather than making them more similar to legitimate sales promotion e-mails? Our affective examination of Nigerian e-mails suggests that these *cognitively* suspicious elements are included precisely because they satisfy an *affective* purpose in luring the mark.

In an insightful rhetorical analysis, Budge (2006) describes Nigerian AFF e-mails as a unique genre of communication reflecting a type of "discourse community" that builds meaning through shared symbols that function to establish rapport and shared goals. In a phase analysis of the structure of the e-mails, Kich (2005, 134) provides a typology of the formulaic series of steps that Nigerian AFF e-mails tend to follow. Our analysis draws both from Budge and Kich to examine the affective rhetorical content in the sequenced structure of the solicitations. Our categories are ideal types, which sometimes overlap in the narratives. Some of the following categories blur together or do not follow the precise sequence, but all contain the same essential structure.

Introduction to the Sender

The subject headers of Nigerian AFF e-mails vary dramatically, but all are designed to get attention, and nearly all tend to be short, four words or less. They are designed to get the recipient's attention. The most common greetings were "Subject: Urgent" (15 percent), followed by variations of "Subject: From [sender's name]" or some combination of "Subject: [business/investment] [opportunity]/Proposal," each comprising 12 percent of the subjectheaders in our database. Other common subject headers included variations of "Subject: Assistant!" (8 percent), "Subject: Please Help!" (7 percent), or "Subject: ATTENTION!" and "Subject: URGENT!," each constituting 5 percent of the subject headers.

Most e-mails begin with a simple greeting, such as "Dear," "Dear Friend," "Esteemed Partner to Be," or more generically, "Dear Sir/Madam." They are invariably polite and often apologetic, and often include the sender's status-identifying information. The sender of the e-mail is typically described as related to a country's nobility or a powerful government official or business person:

> Dear Friend,
>
> I am the first son of the late JOSEPH . MOBUTU, the former President of the ZAIRE now democratic republic of congo.
>
> (Fri, 6 Dec 2002, 09:39:47) ($20.5 million)

> Dearest: Friend,
>
> My Name is Mr. Andre Koffi a credit officer with the one of the leading (Finance Trust House) here in Cotonou Republic Du Benin. In my department I discovered an abandoned funds (USD 32 M) in an account that belongs to one of our foreign customer (MR. ANDREAS SCHRANNER from Munich, Germany) who died along with his entire family in July 2000 in a plane crash.
>
> (Thu, 01 Sep 2005, 12:21:12)

> Dear Friend, [no name given in first paragraph]
>
> I guess this letter may come to you as a surprise since I had no previous correspondence with you. I the chairman tender board of Independent National Electoral Commission (INEC). I got your contact in my search for a reliable person to handle a very confidential transaction involving the transfer of US$20.5 million.
>
> (15 Aug 2005, 21:20:52) ($37 million)

Sometimes, the status identification is sufficiently precise that it can be "verified" with a Google search. In the example above of the "first son" of Joseph Mobutu, a search would indicate that the identifying details do correspond to an actual person. Similarly, a "Mr. Andreas Schranner" was featured in a BBC online story, including a picture, describing the plane crash in 2000. However, the "chairman" of "INEC" is more dubious. Of 19 similar e-mails between 2002 and 2006 with the initiating poster identify as "chairman" of "INEC," all had a different signatory, none of which corresponded to the chairperson of INEC in Nigeria during that period. In a spot check of the accuracy of the "facts" in a narrative, nearly 10 percent contained easily Googled fundamental factual errors that subverted the entire premise.

As the Nigerian scam has evolved, the status identity of the sender also shifted to cast a broader net. These identities retained the same generic status-identifying introduction, but shifted from a neutral salutation to one that assumed a shared sentiment based on religious belief:

DONATION FOR THE LORD

From: Mrs. Sarah Rowland

PLEASE ENDEAVOUR TO USE IT FOR THE CHILDREN OF GOD.

I am the above named person from Malaysia. I am married to Dr. Alan George Rowland who worked with Malaysia embassy in South Africa for nine years before he died in the year 2000. We were married for eleven years without a child. He died after a brief illness that lasted for only four days. Before his death we were both born again Christians. Since his death I decided not to re-marry or get a child outside my matrimonial home which the Bible is against.

(11 Jan 2003 14:03:39) ($27.6 million)

Dearest one in the lord,

I am Mrs Maria Koffi, from Ivory Coast, Cote D'Ivoire. I was married to Mr. Stephen Koffi who was a contractor with the government of Cote D'Ivoire before he died in the year 2003 after few days in the hospital The doctor said his death was as a result of poison.

(Mon, 29 Jan 2007 03:21:39) ($10 million).

The greetings and introductions serve the rhetorical purpose of establishing a positive tone and identity claim that are consistent with the subsequent story about to unfold. From a cognitive point of view, all that is necessary is that the claimed identity appears consistent with the story and cannot be easily refuted. From an affective point of view, the greeting and identification of the sender provide a vital affective component of the situation, the identity of the sender, and all the sentiments that are attached to such identities (Heise 2007).

The identities commonly used in Nigerian scam e-mails (bankers, government officials, lawyers, millionaires, VIPs) are rated as extremely good, extremely powerful, and quite dynamic in the 2003 affective sentiment database. These ratings suggest that most Americans feel that people with these sorts of identities are good, powerful, reputable people. To establish affective affinity, the senders' names tend to be common and anglicized, invoking credible identity images. The most common English-based name used was "Smith," occurring 452 times in our database, and "Jones" appeared 131 times. Familiar African names appearing in the news were also common, such as Abacha (1009), Seko (210), or Mobuto (200).

One of the most powerful influences in a social situation is the push toward affective consistency. When the actions taken by someone carry affective meanings that are inconsistent with the identity of the person performing them, the situation will seem strange or inexplicable. When this occurs, the mark may invoke a process of reducing dissonance to reestablish balance in the "reality gaps" that might otherwise subvert credibility. Therefore, by establishing the sender of the Nigerian scam e-mail as a familiar, powerful, dynamic kind of person, the introduction of the e-mail creates a social situation where lucrative, powerful, dynamic actions taken by the sender will seem consistent and reasonable rather than inconsistent or improbable. This provides the critical foundation of the subsequent narrative.

Explanation of Recipient Selection

After the initial greeting, the AFF e-mails continue with an explanation for why the recipient was selected to receive the message. The explanation for the recipient's selection rarely provides detail, and may allude to a general search for a partner that might seem plausible.

> Let me start by first introducing myself properly to you. I am Dr. ABBA GANA, a director general in the Petroleum Ministry and I head a Six-man tender board in charge of Contracts Awards and payment Approvals. I came to know of you in my search for a reliable and reputable person to handle a very confidential business transaction which involves the transfer of a huge sum of money to a foreign account requiring maximum confidence.
>
> (Fri, 31 May 2002, 14:52:49) ($400 million)

> Dear:
>
> I got your contact through the Internet in my earnest search for a reliable and trustworthy individual who can render me assistance. And I am so much trusting on you because of the content of your profile in the internet, and I am applying more carefullness because I have falling a victim of fraudlers in my search for someone I can trust.
>
> (Wed, 25 Oct 2006, 05:03:44),($28 million)

> I have lost confidence with anybody within the country. . . . I got your contacts through my personal research, and out of desperation of wanting to invest this money I decided to reach you through this medium. I will give you more information as to this regard as soon as you reply.
>
> (Fri, 05 Aug 2005, 13:03:53) ($700 million)

Sometimes, the scammer does not directly solicit the help of the mark, but only dangles the lure by requesting assistance to search for a reputable and honest intermediary:

> Hello, We want to transfer to overseas the sum of One hundred and Forty Two Million United States Dollars (U.S.$142,000,000.00) from South Africa here. (Great Opportunity) I want to ask you to kindly look for a reliable and honest person who will be capable and fit to provide either an existing bank account or to set up a new bank account immediately to receive this money, though an empty bank account could serve this purpose as long as you will remain honest to me till the end of this important business trusting in you and believing in God that you will never let me down either now or in time to come. (URGENT TRANSACTION)
>
> (Sun, 2 Oct 2005, 03:09:32)

The generality allows the recipient to fill in details with some logical specificity for it to "make sense." This suggests that what makes the Nigerian e-mail scam successful is that even when cognitive consistency is lacking and rational evidence is scanty, creating affective consistency with the pitch can be both necessary and sufficient to slip the scam past the victim's radar. In short, sometimes less is more.

For recipients who already hold positive affective sentiments toward themselves, the characteristics implied by the author's explanation of why the mark was selected are affectively consistent with the mark's already-established beliefs. If the mark self-defines as respectable and socially well situated, then it is plausible that the sender, also so situated, would seek a person of similar status. The affective traits of the narrative reinforce the mark's self-perception of intellectual status, fueling the scenario that seems otherwise implausible. Ironically, this may explain why some victims of the Nigerian e-mail scam are otherwise sophisticated and intelligent people such as doctors, lawyers, and other professionals: Their affective sentiments about themselves are consistent with the sentiments expressed in the note, and they lower their guards to the otherwise unconvincing narrative. Cautious recipients who either did not accept the credibility of the author's self-identification, or do not already hold affective sentiments toward themselves that are consistent with the professional senti-ments played on in the note, fall out of the pool of potential victims.

Description of Situation

The initial greeting, identification of the author, and explanation for the selection of the recip-ient are crucial to the scam's success. Failure of this opening to achieve affective resonance with the reader will likely engender suspicion and distrust and the likely collapse of the scam. However, if these opening elements have achieved an affectively consistent narrative, one that fits the recipient's sentiments toward their self-identity and their mental image of the sender, the next stage presents a story to justify the offer. The requirement is to build a scenario that has as much intellectual consistency as possible while also achieving the consistency of affec-tive sentiments that will subvert the affect control system's ability to detect emotionally improbable scenarios.

There is a variety of motifs describing the scenario requiring the money transfer, often long and detailed. Here, we limit our illustration to the three most common ones.

The first, comprising about 1/3 percent of the solicitations in our database, is the "coun-try in turmoil" ploy. Here, the sender alludes to easily checked details of political or govern-mental disarray. Although these tend to allude to African countries such as Nigeria or Zaire, sometimes they include Iraq or central European countries such as Bosnia. These can contain lengthy, easily checked descriptions of a political situation with considerable detail:

> Until his death, our father was the General overseer of the Diamond Mine in Kanema Sierra Leonne. On November 6 2005 the military forces loyal to the Government of Ahmed TIJAN KABBAH invaded the diamond mine and assassinated our father, mistaking him for his brother SIMON ANTHONY who is the deputy to the leader of the revolutionary United Front (RUF) FODAY SANKOH. When the news reached us, we hurried gathered some valuables in our family villa and escaped for our dear life. Among the valuables was a file that contained details of a deposit our father made in a BANK, although our late father has secretly told us before the incedent that he has a sum of (US$20,000,000.00 Twenty Million United States dollar) that he deposited in BANK in my name CHARLES ANTHONY as the only son, the money he made at his time as General overseer of the Diamond Mine in Kanema Sierra Leonne Now that we are in Abidjan and verified the deposit with the BANK as the rightfull owner, we need your assistance to move this fund out of Cote d,Ivoire . . .

(Thu, 2 Nov 2006, 19:29:53)

A second scenario, found in about 25 percent of the e-mails, invokes serendipitously discovered funds. In this narrative, a wealthy client died, and the funds sit dormant. The scammer indicates, usually without subtlety, that the transfer of funds requires illicit bending of rules. The example below typifies both the explicit description of the deception and a justification for it:

> On June 6,1997, a FOREIGN Oil consultant/contractor with the Nigerian National Petroleum Corporation, Mr. Barry Kelly made a numbered time (Fixed) Deposit for twelve calendar months, valued at US$8,000,000.00 (Eight Million Dollars) in my branch. Upon maturity, I sent a routine notification to his forwarding address but got no reply. After a month, we sent a reminder and finally we discovered from his contract employers, the Nigerian National Petroleum Corporation that Mr. Barry Kelly died from an automobile accident. On further investigation, I found out that he died without making a WILL, and all attempts to trace his next of kin was fruitless.
> I therefore made further investigation and discovered that Mr. Barry Kelly did not declare any kin or relations in all his official documents, including his Bank Deposit paperwork in my Bank. This sum of US$8,000,000.00 is still sitting in my Bank and thinterest is being rolled over with the principal sum at the end of each year. No one will ever come forward to claim it. According to Nigerian Law, at the expiration of 5 (five) years, the money will revert to the ownership of the Nigerian Government if nobody applies to claim the fund. Consequently, my proposal is that I will like you as an Foreigner to stand in as the next of kin to Mr. Barry Kelly so that the fruits of this old man's labor will not get into the hands of some corrupt government officials.
>
> (Mon, 17 Jun 2002, 04:37:28)

A third common narrative, one that may be merged with other scenarios, invokes an appeal to religious compassion and play on the affective sentiment of Christian charity. This narrative was spun through about 15 percent of the posts in the database. The following example plays on invocation of sympathy for a terminally ill woman (the scammer is always "female") and the possibility of distribution of funds for charitable purposes:

> Beloved in Christ
>
> Calvary greetings in the name of our Lord Jesus Christ, I am former Mrs Fatima Aisha Williams, now Mrs Joy williams, a widow to Late Usman Danjuma Alamin Williams, I am 61 years old, I am now a new Christian convert, suffering from long time cancer of the breast. From all indications, my condition is really deteriorating and is quite obvious that I may not live more than six months, because the cancer stage has gotten to a very severe stage.
>
> Lastly, I want you/your ministry to be praying for me as regards my entire life and my health because I have come to find out since my spiritual birth lately that wealth acquisition without Jesus Christ in one? life is vanity upon vanity. If you have to die says the Lord, keep fit and I will give you the crown of life. May the Grace of our Lord Jesus Christ, the love of God, and the sweet fellowship of the Holy Spirit be with your. I await you. reply.
>
> (Fri, 07 Oct 2005, 01:12:23) ($10 Million)

Affectively, these scenarios each set up a situation in which the forthcoming offer and requests for help appear reasonable. This illustrates one of the fundamental characteristics of

an individual's affect control system: All social events are iterative, with the affective sentiments evoked by previous social acts acting as a guide to the interpretation of subsequent
actions in the game. At this point in the pitch, the scammer has established credentials as a
reputable potential partner (RPP) and the recipient as a canny and generous potential partner. For example, for an RPP (a powerful identity) to ask for help (a weak act) from the recipient would be affectively inconsistent with the positive impressions of the scammer's power
and integrity. Therefore, the narrative must be modified to explain the weakness. One way this
is done is by the "victimization" ploy in which the scammer has apparently unjustly lost
power and needs help to reestablish it, enticing the mark into conspiratorial collusion.

Resolution and Payoff

Having been appropriately primed by the previous step in the original solicitation, the mark is
now ready to learn the next step in the scheme, usually in a terse, cryptic summary:

> I will require your telephone and fax numbers so that we can commence communication
> immediately and I will give you a more detailed picture of things. In case you don't
> accept please do not let me out to the security as I am giving you this information in total
> trust and confidence I will greatly appreciate if you accept my proposal in good faith.
> Please expedite action.
>
> (Fri, 05 Aug 2005, 13:03:53) ($700 million)

In the following examples, after setting up the justification, the scammers request only
a "response of interest":

> The Banking law here stipulates that if such money remains unclaimed for five years,
> it will be forfeited to the Bank treasury as an unclaimed bill. It is only a foreigner that
> can stand as a next of kin and It is upon this discovery that I decided to contact you to
> collaborate with you to pull out this dormant fund . . . . .
>   What I want from you is for you to act as the deceased next of kin. I have in
> my possession, all the necessary Documents to successfully accomplish the operation.
> Bear in mind that this proposal is 100% risk free. Further Information will be given
> to you as soon as I receive your positive response. I suggest you get back to me as
> soon as possible stating your wish. Find in the attachment of my Family Picture,
> to proof who I am. If your interested Please forward the following information to:
> attn_henryokoye@yahoo.co.in
>
> (Thu, 4 Aug 2005 05:05:06) ($35 million)

There are actually two affective sentiment manipulations here that can motivate the
mark to respond to the pitch at this point. First, the scammer's normal affective aura of
power and beneficence has been reduced slightly by the preceding narrative step in the pitch,
which usually suggests illicit actions to accomplish the goals. Although the mark presumably has no vested interest in the scammer's well being, ACT suggests that people will
engage in rebalancing to preserve their impressions toward *all* parts of a situation, not just to
those parts of the situation in which they have a personal interest. Thus, the mark has been
predisposed by the preceding narrative to act in a way that will allow the scammers to

reclaim the normal power appropriate to their position. In this case, the mark does so by aiding the scammer's attempt to smuggle money out of the country, which will restore to the scammer some of the power and affective dynamism they had previously established as being accustomed to. Importantly, the illicit actions being requested are framed to sound minor and almost casual. This is consistent with the manipulation; the scammer's status has been reduced, but only slightly. A massive illicit action would seem incongruous with the relatively minor decrease in the scammer's positive affective impression, while a minor one seems reasonable and sufficient for restoring the affective impressions back to their normal order.

The second affective manipulation draws from the earlier praise and flattery expressed to the mark when identifying the reasons for selection as the recipient. The flattery slightly elevates the positive affective self-sentiments of the marks; if believed, the mark will find the idea of providing assistance to a slightly deflated RPP to be quite affectively consistent with their own elevated sentiments toward themselves. Complying with the requested action will "feel right." They will feel like they are exactly the kind of person who *would* assist a temporarily humbled RPP.

This phase of the manipulation is delicate; while elevating the mark's affective sentiment increases the predisposition to comply with the next step, this escalation phase cannot be so extreme that it sets off the contrary reaction of raising suspicion. Here lies another clue to why some people fall for the Nigerian scam and others do not: People whose opinion of themselves is already elevated will more easily find it credible when additional flattery and ego reinforcements added.

The Request for Action

At this point in the game, the affective chess pieces that have been carefully moved into place by the previous steps are put into motion with a request for action. This step is the most important, the one that will determine if the mark continues with the scheme or withdraws. All of the affective manipulations in the earlier steps of the note have been building to this point.

Following a lengthy narrative establishing the premise and the context, typical requests-for-action reemphasize the need for secrecy and provide the steps to obtain the money:

> In the light of the above, I have been mandated by my family to contact a reliable and trustworthy foreign partner who can help us invest this money abroad especially in Europe, we have decided to solicit your assistance in helping to invest this money in your country. The family has unanimously agreed to compensate you with 25% of this money for your full assistance. You can contact me immediately by via this email address for any further explanation on how we are to evacuate the said money am_hammed@mail.com.
>
> Finally, the members of the family and I are praying that the confidentiality of this transaction should be maintained, hence all our hope are hinged on this money. My heart greetings go to your family.
>
> Regards,
>
> AHMED MOHAMMED.

NOTE: DUE TO THE CONFIDENTIALITY BEHIND THIS ISSUE, WE PREFER
THIS MEANS OF CONTACT FOR NOW.

(Wed, 29 May 2002) ($25 million).

Other endgames provide seemingly plausible specificity:

I HAVE DEPOSITED THE SUM THIRTY MILLION UNITED STATE DOLLARS
(US$ 30,000,000,00.) WITH A SECURITY COMPANY, FOR SAFEKEEPING. THE
FUNDS ARE SECURITY CODED TO PREVENT THEM FROM KNOWING THE
CONTENT. WHAT I WANT YOU TO DO IS TO INDICATE YOUR INTEREST
THAT YOU WILL ASSIST US BY RECEIVING THE MONEY ON OUR BEHALF.
ACKNOWLEDGE THIS MESSAGE, SO THAT I CAN INTRODUCE YOU TO MY
SONDUKE) WHO HAS THE OUT MODALITIES FOR THE CLAIM OF THE SAID
FUNDS. I WANT YOU TO ASSIST IN INVESTING THIS MONEY, BUT I WILL
NOT WANT MY IDENTITY REVEALED. I WILL ALSO WANT TO BUY
PROPERTIES AND STOCK IN MULTI-NATIONAL COMPANIES AND TO
ENGAGE IN OTHER SAFE AND NON-SPECULATIVE INVESTMENTS. MAY I
AT THIS POINT EMPHASISE THE HIGH LEVEL OF CONFIDENTIALITY,
WHICH THIS BUSINESS DEMANDS, AND HOPE YOU WILL NOT BETRAY
THE TRUST AND CONFIDENCE, WHICH I REPOSE IN YOU. IN CONCLUSION,
IF YOU WANT TO ASSIST US, MY SON SHALL PUT YOU IN THE PICTURE OF
THE BUSINESS, TELL YOU WHERE THE FUNDS ARE CURRENTLY BEING
MAINTAINED AND ALSO DISCUSS OTHER MODALITIES INCLUDING
REMUNERATION FOR YOUR SERVICES. FOR THIS REASON KINDLY
FURNISH US YOUR CONTACT INFORMATION, THAT IS YOUR PERSONAL
TELEPHONE AND FAX NUMBER FOR CONFIDENTIAL PURPOSE.

BEST REGARDS,

MRS M. SESE SEKO

(Fri, 31 May 2002, 11:25:39) ($30 million)

At this point, a mark who has been sufficiently prepared will be predisposed to take
action on behalf of the RPP. Offering a massive reward to the recipient both reconfirms the
customary affective sentiment held toward RPPs (that they are very good, very powerful, and
quite dynamic, the kinds of people who would bestow massive rewards upon their apparent
peers), and confirms the sentiments held by the marks toward themselves (that they are astute
business people, the kind who deserve massive profits on a business deal).

Whether the mark takes the next steps depends in part on the success of the prior
affective manipulations. Did the scammer convince the mark of the elevated RPP's status? Did
the RPP successfully elevate the mark's sentiments to create the perception of being entitled to
the reward? Did the scammer successfully present the narrative in such a way that any negative
sentiments held toward the "RPP" are temporarily suppressed, and the action required to raise
them back to normality relatively minor? Ultimately, did the scammer nudge the affective presentation of the narrative such that the mark will feel comfortable, or at least willing, to participate further? This requires narrative reassurance. If the process of manipulation in the pitch
has gone well, the mark will now see further collusion as normal, and even inevitable.

CONCLUSION

Successful cons require affectively structured symbolic representations of legitimacy and a mutually shared discourse that appear to put both mark and scammer on the same team, in the same ballpark, playing the same game. Trying to lure a mark into a basketball game and then showing up to play baseball dooms the con. It also demonstrates that affective manipulation is not a useful tool for persuasion if it is not used by a skilled persuader. To continue the sports metaphor, the best bat in the world will not help you if you cannot connect with the ball.

We have argued that emotion and the affective response systems are an overlooked and underappreciated diagnostic and validation system in everyday social interaction. This is especially true in the case of con schemes, in which the mark must detect inconsistencies in the scammer's story to avoid victimization. This detection can occur in two ways. First, one means of detecting such inconsistencies is through cognitive processing, which compares the denotative characteristics of the elements of the situation to determine whether they are cognitively consistent with each other. The story, or "setup," of a con game is designed to defeat such "thinking through" of the game by creating a believable scenario in which all mental inconsistencies are accounted for, or at least discounted as irrelevant. However, it is presumably successful in protecting the mark part of the time, enough so that some observers wonder how any thinking person could fall for such an obvious scam? In the example, there is no reading-off by the scammer of the cues given off by the recipient that could lead to building on the narrative and lure the mark further into the Web.

A second means by which people detect inconsistencies in social situations is through the affect control system from which they draw to socially construct elements of a situation based upon their affective or connotative meanings. If a situation does not combine these visceral reactions or "emotional flavors" in a way that is consistent with their fundamental character, the participants in that situation will experience a feeling of strangeness or improbability (a sensation referred to as "deflection") that will alert them that there is something wrong with the situation and will motivate them to resolve the inconsistency. When a mark decides to go through with the scheme because it "feels right," or decides to forego participation in the scheme because "something just doesn't feel right about it," they are tacitly describing the feelings of normality and abnormality that are the primary diagnostic signals of the affect control system. These feelings alert the mark to the relative affective consistency of the situation, related to, but separate from, the cognitive consistency of the situation and acts as a secondary decision mechanism when evaluating the pitch and deciding what course of action to follow in relation to it.

A scammer thus cannot simply create a compelling and believable intellectual narrative to overcome the doubts of their victims. They must also create an affectively or emotionally consistent narrative that will avoid setting off an emotional response that alerts the victim to the problematic nature of the situation they are experiencing. The need to satisfy both the cognitive and the affective consistency needs of the victim is likely one reason why the skilled scammer must be both an expert in the intellectual details of the specific con game as well as a master of the arts of empathy and rapport. Kich (2005) describes this in Nigerian scam e-mails, where the consistent use of words with positive associations and avoidance of words with negative associations tends to compensate for otherwise jarring intellectual errors in the narrative.

We have also suggested that affective states and emotions are not simply "noise" that corrupts the rational thinking process and must be expunged for valid reasoning to take place. The Nigerian scam is successful not simply because it elicits base emotions to cloud the judgment. Rather, as Alberto Damasio's "Descartes' Error" (1995) argues, affect and emotions serve a vital role in our interpretation of situations and social decisions, acting as a sort of "evaluative filtering mechanism." The Nigerian scam works because it manipulates this filtering process, turning this validation and legitimating mechanism against itself.

Although we argue that emotions and affective processing are important mechanisms for establishing the believability of a con game or, conversely, for creating skepticism toward the pitch, we would not go so far as to claim that the affect control system is the only important factor in determining the believability of a con. Many factors influence the success of a con, including (a) cognitive consistency, (b) affective consistency, (c) persuasive skill (which influences a and b), and (d) importantly, the mark's preexisting biases toward themselves and the future. People who fall for cons are often people who have inflated views of their intelligence and competence, and, furthermore, have the "will to believe" the scenario presented by the con artist. It is not strictly necessary for the scammer to present a scenario that is entirely cognitively and affectively consistent; it is enough to present a scenario that is sufficiently internally consistent and believable so that a mark with a will believe in the possibility of the implausible.

One of the ironies of the Nigerian e-mail scam is that it leverages the same efficiencies and cost benefits as legitimate online businesses like Amazon or eBay. Like more legitimate online businesses, Nigerian e-mail scams have very low overhead costs, flexibility in location, and the ability to advertise widely with little effort or expense. Maurer's (1957) classic study of confidence men describes how early twentieth century scammers tired of moving around to find new marks, and so they created physical "con stores" where potential marks would come to the store to be fleeced, perhaps in response to a token supply of cheap merchandise or word of mouth. There being a tradition of con enterprises aping actual retail stores, perhaps it was just a matter of time before brick-and-mortar "con stores" followed their legitimate cousins online to taste the commercial benefits of the information age. It is a brave new world indeed, whether you are selling books or snake oil.

KEY TERMS

Advance free fraud
Long con
Reputable potential partner (RPP)

REFERENCES

.NExT Web Security Services. 2007. 419 Nigerian advanced fee fraud scam lifecycle. Available at http://www.nextwebsecurity.com/419LifeCycle.asp, accessed January 31, 2007.

Budge, S. B. 2006. To deceive the receiver: A genre analysis of the electronic variety of Nigerian scam letters. Unpublished manuscript, School of Humanities, Department of English. Vaxjo University, Vaxjo, Sweden. Available at www.diva-portal.org/diva/getDocument?urn_nbn_se_vxu_diva-627-2__fulltext.pdf, accessed January 3, 2007.

Damasio, A. 1995. *Descartes' Error: Emotion, Reason, and the Human Brain.* New York: Harper Perennial.

Emery, D. 2002. The Nigerian e-mail hoax West-African scammers take to the Net. SFgate.com, March 14. Available at http://www.sfgate.com/cgi-bin/article.cgi?file=/gate/archive/2002/03/14/nigerscam. DTL, accessed December 11, 2006.

Enos, L. 2001. Online auctions top FBI Net fraud list. Ecommercetimes, March 7. Available at http://www.ecommercetimes.com/story/7986.html, accessed January 29, 2007.

Global Policy Forum. 2003. Internet users: 1996–2002. Available at http://www.globalpolicy.org/globaliz/charts/internettable.htm, accessed February 3, 2007.

Goffman, E. 1952. On cooling the mark out: Some aspects of adaptation to failure. *Psychiatry* 15 (November): 451–63.

Goffman, E. 1969. "Expression games: An analysis of doubts at play." In *Strategic Interaction,* 1–81. Philadelphia: University of Pennsylvania Press.

Heise, D. R. 1979. *Understanding Events: Affect and the Construction of Social Action.* New York: Cambridge University Press.

Heise, D. R. 2007. *Expressive Order: Confirming Sentiments in Social Actions.* New York: Springer.

International Center for Nigerian Law (ICNL). 2007. Nigerian criminal code. Available at http://www.nigeria-law.org/About%20ICFNL.htm, accessed January 3, 2007.

Internet Crime Complaint Center (ICCC). 2007. IC3 2005 crime Internet crime report. Available at http://www.ic3.gov/media/annualreports.aspx, accessed February 1, 2007.

Kich, M. 2005. A rhetorical analysis of fund-transfer-scam solicitations. *Cercles* 14: 129–41. Available at http://www.cercles.com/n14/kich.pdf, accessed January 3, 2007.

King, A. B. 2001. Affective dimensions of Internet culture. *Social Science Computer Review* 19 (4): 414–30.

Maurer, D. W. 1957. *The Big Con.* 1999 ed. New York: Random House.

Minwatts Marketing Group. 2007. Internet world stats: Usage and population statistics. Miniwatts Marketing Group. Available at http://www.internetworldstats.com/stats.htm, accessed February 3, 2007.

Osgood, C. E. 1969. On the why's and wherefore's of E, P, and A. *Journal of Personality and Social Psychology* 12: 194–99.

Osgood, C. E., et al. 1975. *Cross-Cultural Universals of Affective Meaning.* Urbana, IL: University of Illinois Press.

Pournelle, J. 2001. The Nigerian and other scams. Available at http://www.jerrypournelle.com/reports/jerryp/scams.html, accessed January 15, 2007.

Re-quest.net. 2007. Nigeria e-mail scam aka 419 scam aka advance fee fraud. Available at http://www.re-quest.net/internet/myths/nigeria/index.htm#history, accessed January 23, 2007.

Ribadu, M. N. 2006. Nigeria's struggle with corruption. Paper presented to the US Congressional House Committee on International Development, Washington DC, May 18. Available at http://www.nigeriavillagesquare.com/content/view/3072/55/, accessed February 4, 2007.

Smith-Lovin, L., and D. R. Heise, eds. 1988. *Analyzing Social Interaction: Advances in Affect Control Theory.* New York: Gordon and Breach Science Publishers.

Sturgeon, W. 2003. "Nigerian" money scam: What happens when you reply? Silicon.com: The Spam Report, February 18. Available at http://www.silicon.com/research/specialreports/thespamreport/0,39025001,10002928,00.htm, accessed January 21, 2007.

Train, A. 1910. The Spanish prisoner. *Cosmopolitan*, March. Available at http://www.hidden-knowledge.com/funstuff/spanishprisoner/spanishprisoner1.html, accessed February 1, 2007.

Ultrascan Advanced Global Investigations (UAGI). 2007. 419 unit AFF statistics and estimates. January 23. Available at http://www.ultrascan.nl/html/419_statistics.html and http://www.ultrascan.nl/assets/applets/2006_Stats_on_419_AFF_jan_23_2007_1.pdf, accessed February 3, 2007.

United States Secret Service. n.d.. Public Awareness Advisory Regarding "4-1-9" or "Advance Fee Fraud" Schemes. Washington, D.C. Originally available at http://www.secretservice.gov/alert419.htm. Now cached at http://cc.msnscache.com/cache.aspx?q=5878476907408&lang=en-US, accessed February 4, 2007.

Chapter 12

Identity Theft Causes, Correlates, and Factors: A Content Analysis

Sara E. Berg
University at Albany

Sara E. Berg is a doctoral student in the School of Criminal Justice at the University at Albany. She also holds a BS and MS in information technology from the Rochester Institute of Technology and an MA in criminal justice from the University at Albany. Her primary research interest is computer crime, specifically examining the intersection between technology and crime as it relates to offending and victimization. For the past 4 years, she has been carrying out identity theft victimization research, with a focus on information protection and security.

Abstract

This study employs content analysis of 577 newspaper articles published between 1985 and 2003 to determine causes, correlates, and factors surrounding identity theft. Findings show that identity theft is a complex sociotechnological problem that follows predictable patterns of victimization and offending behaviors, which are modeled using network view diagrams produced with Atlas.ti content analysis software. These diagrammatic models illustrate relationships between key variables and have important implications for fraud prevention policies and practices beyond those addressed by existing legislation, regulations, and recommendations of the federal government, especially as the use and power of computing and Internet technologies continue to grow.

INTRODUCTION AND LITERATURE REVIEW

Identity theft is one of the fastest growing crimes in the United States today, and its numbers don't seem to be diminishing. Also known as identity fraud, these two labels are relatively interchangeable umbrella terms[1] that refer to the commission of several fraud crimes in the United States and in other nations, although naming conventions vary in crime statutes and in practice vary throughout the world. Identity theft is committed by obtaining unique personal information and then using that information to impersonate one or more victims, in one or

---

[1]Although both identity theft and identity fraud refer to the same incident type inside the United States, there is often more differentiation internationally. Similarly, it has been proposed to break apart the term "identity theft" and instead further distinguish each individual type (Cheney 2005).

more locations, across a time period spanning hours to years. Various methods are used in order to gain access to information for identity theft purposes, of which a key piece of data is a person's Social Security Number (SSN). It causes both financial and emotional harm to its victims, making this "crime of the Internet" as dangerous to consumers as traditional "off-line" crimes.

While most people would generally want security, privacy, and protection of their self and their assets, other people desire assets not theirs and will take whatever steps necessary to get them. Greedy people are driven by these desires, often independent of criminal laws prohibiting behaviors for acquiring assets, and may thus commit fraud. Although identity theft is one specific form of fraud, multitudes of other crimes are also fraud, regardless of what form they take—**credit card fraud**, bank fraud, loan fraud, mail fraud, wire fraud, telephone fraud, etc. These types of fraudulent acts are accomplished using deceit or trickery. The offender misrepresents himself or herself as another person, typically for financial or material gain. Over the years there have been numerous definitions offered for fraud, with assorted terms for these criminal acts used interchangeably. As Dick Johnston (1996), former director of the National White Collar Crime Center noted, "If I say fraud, you may say economic crime, while somebody else says corporate crime or business crime and others say white collar crime" (p. 1). There has been a steady stream of evolving labels attached to these sorts of acts, especially once computing technology became involved: from fraud, to white-collar crime, to financial crime, to computer abuse, to computer crime, to computer-related crime. Further spin-offs include economic crime, corporate crime, and cyber crime, as well as the more recent high tech crime (McQuade 2005).

Types of Identity Theft

Corresponding to every form of identity theft are forms of specific **victimization**, including for example, credit card fraud, phone or utility service fraud, bank fraud, etc. Recent data provided by the Federal Trade Commission (FTC) indicate relatively high rates of fraud-related victimization among 246,035 reporting identity theft victims. As listed in Table 12-1 these range from a high of 25 percent from credit card fraud to 5 percent for loan fraud.

TABLE 12-1 Identity Theft Fraud-related Victimization

Credit card fraud	25%
Phone or utilities fraud	16%
Bank fraud	16%
Employment-related fraud	14%
Government document or benefits fraud	10%
Loan fraud	5%
Other assorted incidents	24%
Attempted identity theft	6%

Source: Federal Trade Commission [FTC] (2007)

Data from Table 12-1 are explained as follows:

- *Credit card fraud*: This is the most common incident. The offender uses their victim's identity in order to apply for and obtain new credit cards or fraudulently use an existing card belonging to the victim.

- *Unauthorized phone or utility service:* The offender uses the stolen identity to obtain such services as a cell phone, landline phone, or other utility or may rack up charges on an existing account.

- *Bank fraud*: The offender opens a new account using the victim's information, makes fraudulent withdrawals or writes checks against the victim's existing account, or engages in electronic funds transfers.

- *Employment fraud*: The offender obtains employment in the victim's name.

- *Government identification or benefits fraud*: Offenders can use a victim's identity to obtain or forge a driver's license or other government-issued identification papers, or file fraudulent tax returns.

- *Loan fraud*: Many types of loans (e.g., business, real estate, and auto) can be easily obtained using victim information.

- *Other assorted incidents*: These can include obtaining medical services, signing lease agreements, evading legal sanction or criminal warrants, or engaging in Internet-based "phishing" schemes.

- *Attempted identity theft*: The victim's personal information may have been obtained, but no completed act using that information was committed.

Many victims will experience multiple types of identity theft together, such as when an offender obtains both new credit cards and loans in the victim's name. In CY-2006, 18 percent of complaints included more than one identity theft type (FTC 2007).

Methods of Committing Identity Theft

Although some victims are not aware of how an offender obtained their personal identification information, there are a number of different methods that enable the theft to occur (see, for example, Newman 2004; National Center for Victims of Crime 2001). Unlike many other high-tech crimes that necessitate the use of computing or Internet technologies to commit, identity theft can begin with any number of traditional ways to obtain tangible information. Offenders may steal the victim's purse or wallet to gain access to data such as name, address, date of birth, driver's license, phone number, credit cards, and, most importantly, SSN. In a technique known as "dumpster diving," offenders search through garbage belonging to individuals or businesses in order to find documents that might contain SSNs or other sensitive data. Mail theft is a similar method in which documents, such as preapproved credit card applications, are stolen directly from a physical mailbox. Perpetrators could also fill out a change-of-address form in order to divert a victim's mail, potentially containing personal information, to the offender; this could be done after the mail theft as a means to obtain the newly applied for credit card. In the corporate sector, information could be stolen by dishonest employees with access to sensitive data—the so-called "insider threat." Finally, it could be a relative, friend, or someone else with a personal relationship with the victim who may divulge their information to a third party and/or use it themselves.

However, the information superhighway has, without a doubt, made it faster and easier to steal personal information. Just as technology may be used to help people protect what is theirs, it can also help the people who want to steal from others. According to the theory of technology-enabled crime, as technology—tools and techniques—becomes more complex, criminals may adopt these in order to perform new types of illicit acts (McQuade 1998). Online information brokers sell both publicly available and sensitive data to those who are willing to pay; this can include name, address, date of birth, driver's license, phone number, or SSN (often obtained through the headers of credit reports). One hazard of e-commerce (Internet-based shopping) is that credit card information could be stolen from insecure Web sites. Hackers may gain unauthorized access to corporate databases to steal SSNs and credit card numbers. Through the use of "phishing" e-mails that purport to be from a financial institution or other similar company, offenders may entice users to click on a fake link given in order to submit real username and passwords; these can then be used to access the victim's financial accounts. Clicking on an e-mail attachment could install a keylogger program on the victim's computer, which will collect sensitive information and/or account passwords and send them to the offender. "Skimming" devices on automated teller machines can record someone's debit card number, account information, and password, data which is used by the offender to imprint a new card and withdraw funds. As new technologies emerge so do new ways of committing crimes, creating no limits on the Internet and computing-based methods that could be used for illicit purposes.

Laws Concerning Identity Theft

McQuade's (1998) technology-enabled crime theory also reveals that understanding and managing relatively complex crimes is initially quite difficult, and there is continual competition between the criminals and law enforcement for technological advantage. As criminals do something new and innovative, law enforcement must catch up in order to avert, control, deter, and prevent new forms of crime. Until the new forms of criminality are understood, there is a policy lag before statutes are passed to criminalize the behavior. Behaviors themselves are not "inherently criminal or deviant"; this only comes through the label that society confers upon it, though necessarily because it incurs harm (Lilly, Cullen, and Ball 2002, 106). A label of "crime" will not occur until there is an "organized social-legal reaction against some form of behavior" (Pfohl 1981, 69). The terms "identity theft" and "identity fraud" as labels to describe the act of financial identity misrepresentation were first used in 1991 (Neuffer 1991a, b). It would be another 7 years, however, before the associated behaviors were criminalized via the October 1998 passage of the Identity Theft and Assumption Deterrence Act (ITADA) (U.S. Public Law 105-318, 1998).

The ITADA made "knowingly transfer[ring] or us[ing], without lawful authority, any name or number that may be used, alone or in conjunction with any other information, to identify a specific individual with the intent to commit, or to aid or abet, any unlawful activity that constitutes a violation of Federal law, or that constitutes a felony under any applicable State or local law" the legal definition for criminal purposes. This act created identity theft as a crime against an individual victim, as opposed to being only a crime against a business, and called for

25-year sentences against offenders. The follow-up Identity Theft Penalty Enhancement Act of 2004 (U.S. Public Law 108-275, 2004) adds 2 years onto the sentence of anyone convicted of identity theft–related offenses, including using stolen credit card numbers. If identity theft was used as a means to commit terrorism, provisions in this act would add 5 extra years to the sentence (McGuire 2004). As of 2007, all 50 states, as well as the District of Columbia, Guam, and the U.S. Virgin Islands, have their own laws against identity theft.

Even though the offender is not stealing the true identity of the victim (the sum of their thoughts, feelings, knowledge, and experience), their misrepresentation of the victim's financial identity (unique pieces of computerized data that identify individuals and tie them to financial and information databases) is a unique sociotechnological phenomenon that causes harms. However, there has been little to no research undertaken to explore the experiences of victims in an identity theft incident. Most of the published statistics refer solely to descriptive victim characteristics, including age and location of victim, if law enforcement or a credit reporting agency was contacted, and the specific type of victimization experienced (FTC 2007). No studies have been done to look at the process by which identity theft generally occurs, or how such crimes affect those individuals who are victimized in various ways. Therefore, the purpose of this work is to answer the following primary research question: What in general are the causes, correlates, and factors surrounding the occurrence of identity theft?

METHODOLOGY

Ultimately, the value of any research will be determined by the amount and quality of data collected and analyzed, which simply means that a researcher's methodology is crucial. Generally speaking there are two basic approaches to research, namely, quantitative and qualitative, which derive their labels from the types of data collected and analyzed and the way in which research is done (Tesch 1990). While quantitative data gathering and analysis is appropriate when researching a known or understood phenomenon, a qualitative approach is better for the study of phenomenon which are unknown or not well understood (Creswell 1994). The primary goal of qualitative research is "to produce findings through systematic gathering and analysis of data" (McQuade 2001, 64). For this study, the qualitative method that I have chosen to focus on is content analysis.

Content analysis is a subjective technique in which data is systematically and objectively examined for meaning. The researcher seeks patterns in the data, which are then classified (coded) according to operational definitions that they have created, and relationships between the codes are modeled visually. While this data is most often textual, the method can be used with any form of data (e.g., graphical image, musical scores, etc.). Software programs, such as Atlas.ti, are designed to assist the researcher with coding by providing a computer-based interface. However, it is the researcher who creates all the codes and sets up relationships between them. The software program is a tool; it does not do the work by itself. There is also a quantitative component to the method, regarding the number of codes created and frequency counts of those codes (McQuade 2001). By analyzing nearly 20 years worth of newspaper articles, it was possible to advance models of code relationships, specifically looking at the roles of the criminal justice system, offenders, victims, negative effects of victimization, and prevention.

DATA COLLECTION AND CONTENT ANALYSIS[2]

Articles were collected from ProQuest's National Newspaper Database, which provides access to 30 papers from around the United States. There were five major search terms that were used for the purposes of this study: "identity theft," "identity fraud," "ID theft," "ID fraud," and "credit card fraud." Given that credit card fraud is the most common form of identity theft, the reasoning was that these terms should produce the best selection of newspaper articles. In all, 577 newspaper articles published between 1985 and 2003 were selected by both purposeful and random sampling. An examination of counts of articles published between 1980 and 2006 (see Figure 12-1), however, reveals a slow growth of media activity concerning identity theft in the mid-1990s and an explosion beginning around 2000.[3] This is consistent with the increase in Internet traffic, Internet users, and registered domain names (for Internet hosts, see Figure 12-2) for Web sites experienced in the mid-to-late 1990s (U.S. Department of Commerce 1998). Additionally, it is consistent with the expected rise in newspaper attention following the ITADA being passed in 1998, as more cases of identity theft were made public and victims' voices became more outspoken.

I performed content analysis on these newspaper articles in order to view how identity theft has come about over the last 20 years, therefore advancing my thesis and beginning to

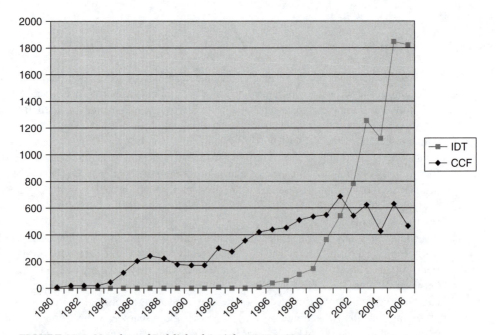

FIGURE 12-1 Number of Published Articles (1980–2006)

[2]For a detailed methodology, including sampling procedure, refer: Berg, S. 2005. What in general are the causes, correlates and factors surrounding the occurrence of identity theft? Unpublished manuscript, Rochester Institute of Technology.

[3]At the time of the original study, full text of articles was only available starting with 1985, and it was only possible to obtain all articles through the end of 2003.

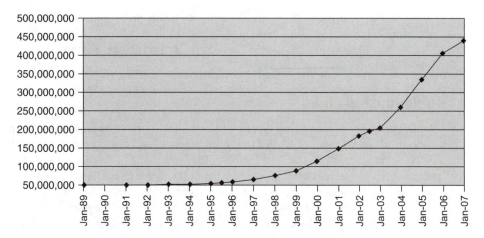

FIGURE 12-2 Number of Internet Hosts (1989–2007)

Source: Constructed by author from Internet Systems Consortium (www.isc.org) Domain Survey data

answer my primary research question. While manual open coding was time consuming, new codes continually emerged during my process of coding and recoding the data. After coding the 577 newspaper articles, I had derived a total of 117 conceptual codes on the basis of my interpretation of the data. It was my determination that any further code creation beyond this analysis would not result in anything new. In addition, during the process of open coding, I also refined my operational definitions to create a better definition for certain codes.

ANALYTICAL FINDINGS

Conceptual Codes

In the course of the data analysis, I developed 117 conceptual codes to represent how I interpreted the data. These included three major subsets: 77 substantive codes that represented factors involved in identity theft events, 18 background codes for fraud incidents that were not identity-theft-related, and 22 background codes for any other incidental data. Of the 77 substantive codes, 56 were the most important and appear in the relationship models developed.

The most frequent codes, appearing over 100 times each, were Offender Action (411 occurrences), Offender Name (264 occurrences), Charges (202 occurrences), Offender Info (190 occurrences), Monetary Harm (173 occurrences), Offender Age (169 occurrences), Prevalence (143 occurrences), Offender Location (126 occurrences), and Prevention (113 occurrences). These frequencies are not surprising given how related they are. Each instance of an Offender Action may not have been individual identity theft events but instead been a single event with multiple actions, such as where the offender used a stolen credit card and applied for a loan. Because the majority of events are discovered due to the offender's actions, a greater number of newspaper articles contain details about the offender—such as their name, age, location, and other information—than about the victim. As laws and statutes were passed to criminalize identity theft offending behaviors, more individuals were charged with those crimes, and many offenders were charged with multiple offenses. Monetary Harm, comprised of both financial losses and material goods purchased, is a large component of offending behavior and again may be coded as multiple instances within a single event. As identity theft began to occur more frequently, its Prevalence was noted more often, and Prevention efforts increased as a result.

Relationship Links

Additionally, seven major link types were developed to represent the relationships between conceptual codes (Table 12-2). A *Causal* link exists when I determined that one code concept is the direct cause of another. An *Enabling* link exists when one code concept facilitates the occurrence of a second code, as against being the direct cause. A *Contributing* link exists when one code concept contributes to the existence of another; the outcome of the second code is directly affected by the circumstances of the first. A *Codependent* link refers to two codes which are dependent on each other in an interplay situation. A *Providing* link exists when one code concept provides the means for a second code concept to occur. An *Is Part Of* link signifies that one code is a piece of a second, more encompassing code. An *Associated* link indicates that two code concepts are similar to each other.

The most frequent link type was Contributing, followed by Enabling, Causal, Is Part Of, Codependent, Providing, and Associated. The counts for each link appear in Table 12-3.

IDENTITY THEFT MODELS

I developed five major models using Atlas.ti's network view diagrams in order to represent the relationships between key variables in an event. These views show portions of an identity theft event as a whole, focusing specifically on the Criminal Justice System, the Offender, the Victim, the Negative Effects of Victimization, and Prevention. Based on my judgment as the researcher, these models emerged from the data as being the most conceptually sound, in deference to the set of codes developed.[4]

TABLE 12-2 Types of Coding Links

Link Type	Link Color	Link Symbol
Causal	Red	=>
Enabling	Blue	->
Contributing	Orange	~>
Codependent	Purple	<->
Providing	Green	-->
Is Part Of	Black	[]
Associated	Black	==

[4]Refer "Berg, S. 2005. What in general are the causes, correlates and factors surrounding the occurrence of identity theft? Unpublished manuscript, Rochester Institute of Technology" for a full explanation of how the analyzed newspaper articles fit each part of the model.

TABLE 12-3 Counts of Relationship Link Types

Link Type	Count
Contributing	96
Enabling	29
Causal	12
Is Part Of	8
Codependent	2
Providing	1
Associated	1

Criminal Justice System

An identity theft event begins with an Initial Incident, which is at the point in time when an offender is able to gain control of a victim's personal information. It could be through the theft or loss of a purse or wallet containing credit cards or ID cards, a computer error, the retrieval of discarded paperwork ("dumpster diving"), mail theft, an employee mistakenly revealing sensitive information, or unauthorized copying of information. Many victims, however, do not know how their data gets taken. Regardless of the method, it is the Initial Incident that provides the Key information used to commit identity theft—most often an SSN, but potentially a physical credit/bank card or account number, name, address, date of birth, or mother's maiden name. This Key thus enables an identity theft event to occur through one or

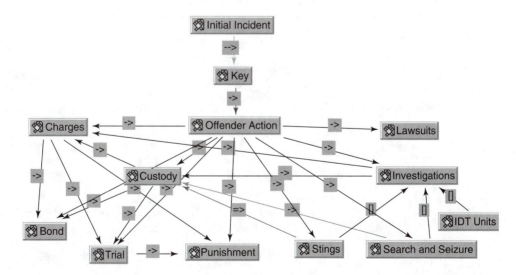

FIGURE 12-3 Model of the Criminal Justice System

a series of Offender Actions, ranging from a single use of a credit card to multiple forms of victimization. In the criminal justice system, it is these Offender Actions which enable law enforcement and corrections to investigate, prosecute, and punish the criminals. Generally an offender will be taken into Custody, when they are arrested and/or questioned. This then allows for the offender to be Charged with any number of fraud crimes, if not identity theft/fraud specifically. The offender may also be taken into Custody after being Charged, depending on the specifics of the case. They may be able to post Bond or bail at their arraignment, if they are not held without it. The offender may then go to Trial and be given Punishment if found guilty; they might also be Punished if they plead guilty as part of a plea bargain. Punishment is often time imprisoned, but some offenders are also required to pay restitution for their crimes. Law enforcement may also undertake criminal Investigations of cases, sometimes which involve (undercover) Sting operations and lead to the Search and Seizure of evidence. Occasionally it will be an IDT Unit, an investigative team specifically focusing on identity theft, which will handle the case. Certain Search and Seizure operations will contribute to the taking of an offender into Custody, while Stings may lead directly to a Custodial state. Some victims, both commercial and consumer, will later file Lawsuits as a result of their victimization. Consumers may file against credit reporting agencies, while commercial organizations have filed suit against the offenders.

Offender

Again, the Initial Incident is what provides an individual the means to obtain a Key to enable an identity theft event via Offending Actions. There are two major contributing factors to obtaining information from the Initial Incident. First, Internet Information is easily and readily accessible as a way to obtain Key data. Various online databases contain such information as names, addresses, phone numbers, dates of birth, and SSNs; these are available at low cost, while many public records are now publicly accessible for free. Second is the Insider Threat, where an offender uses his or her trusted Employment status as a means to gain access to victim data. Offender characteristics, namely Location (of residence or business), Name,

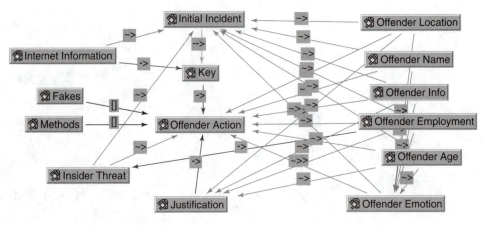

FIGURE 12-4 Model of the Offender

Employment, Age, and other Information about them, contribute to the opportunity to partake in an Initial Incident and later commit various criminal Actions. Their Emotion at the time may also play a part in their decision to offend. Various Methods are used to engage in Offender Actions, including dumpster diving, mail theft, debit or credit card tampering, and card skimming, and they might also use various Fake cards or identification during the identity theft event. Offenders may Justify why they partake in their criminal Actions, and their personal characteristics also contribute to this decision.

Victim

Once an offender has committed the Action(s) that comprise(s) an identity theft event, it is hoped that the victim will then gain Awareness of their victimization. This will then cause them to Respond to the victimization, to such entities as commercial merchants, financial institutions, credit reporting agencies, and the criminal justice system. These elements, all part of a larger "System," will, in turn, Respond to the victim. Thus a codependency of sorts occurs, as how the Victim Responds to the System will determine its response, and vice versa. A System Response to the victim might be informing them of their victimization and making them Aware of it if they do not discover it first. As with assorted offender characteristics, Victim characteristics—including Location, Name, Employment, Age, other Information, and their Emotions—can contribute what Key(s) may be obtained, what Actions the offender takes, how they Respond after victimization, how the System Responds to them, and how they Initially React upon learning of the identity theft. Similarly, these victim characteristics can contribute to the negative effects they suffer as a result of victimization, including Loss of Time, Monetary Harm, credit-related Consequences, Emotional harm including Frustrations

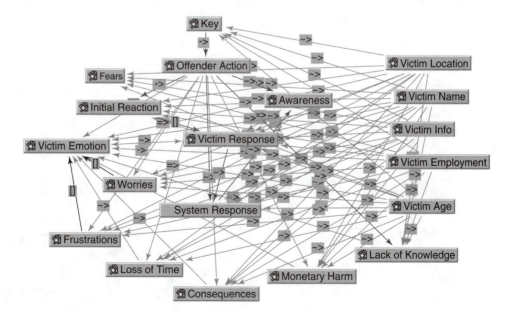

FIGURE 12-5 Model of the Victim

and Worries, and a Lack of Knowledge about how to proceed toward recovery. Individuals may also have Fears that certain activities may cause them or others to become victims, even if they had not been personally victimized by identity theft; in this respect, we can all be considered victims.

Negative Effects on Victims

The types of harms experienced by identity theft victims are not very different from those experienced as a result of other crimes. An Offender's Actions are the direct cause of a number of negative effects experienced by both consumer and commercial victims. A Loss of Time generally comes about during recovery, when a victim must contact various organizations including financial institutions, credit reporting agencies, and commercial merchants about their victimization. It may range from hours to months, to even years, with individuals who have suffered from long-term victimization requiring the most time to repair their credit and name. Monetary Harm comes in the forms of consumer financial liability, offender-purchased goods, and offender-spent money, and it could range from a few hundred dollars to a few hundred thousand dollars. Businesses, especially financial institutions, may even lose millions or billions due to credit card fraud. Consumers often have credit-related Consequences such as incorrect credit reports and an inability to take out loans or mortgages. A more serious Consequence is facing arrest arrested for acts committed by the offender in the victim's name, while other victims have actually been arrested. Victims also experience strong Emotional hurt including Frustrations about the investigative, recovery, or prevention process and Worries about other possible consequences of victimization. They may also experience Run around on the part of the "System," by being directed to multiple individuals or organizations in the course of recovery, contributing directly to Frustrations.

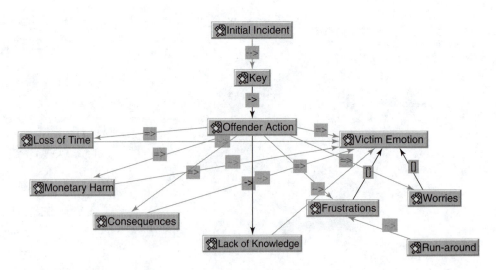

FIGURE 12-6 Model of Negative Effects on the Victim

Prevention

The increasing number of Offender Actions being committed has caused a rise in the Prevalence of identity theft, notably beginning in the late 1990s. In turn, this has led to a number of Prevention efforts taking place in an attempt to curb its growth. These have included Laws passed in order to criminalize identity theft and prevent it, Educational programs, financial Incentives for employees and consumers to help prevent identity theft and provide information leading to the arrest of offenders, and the development of Good Practices that commercial organizations and financial institutions should follow to aid in prevention. Continued Recommendations on how Prevention should occur contributes to these efforts. However, while a positive result of Prevention efforts has been Financial Savings to organizations and potentially Averted Incidents, these efforts are not without assorted Problems, including many that bring up concerns about Privacy. In addition, even with these types of protective measures in place, if any Bad Decisions are made by individuals or organizations when handling financially based situations, criminal Actions by an offender can still occur.

DISCUSSION

The Key to Identity Theft

Clearly, with regards to identity theft, the concept of the Key is everything. Bits and pieces of data unique to each individual can be—and are—easily used for illicit purposes. However, it is important to recognize the advances in society which made this possible in order to understand how identity theft could become so prevalent. Although SSNs are an easy way to keep track of an individual, and while electronic banking and credit card use have made modern life convenient, the theft of these ubiquitous SSNs and credit cards is the major method in committing identity theft today.

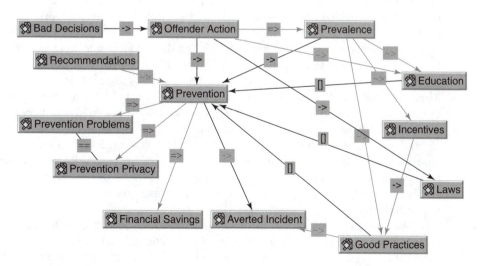

FIGURE 12-7 Model of Prevention

Social Security

In the midst of the Great Depression, there was a need in the United States to improve the economic security of its citizens. President Franklin D. Roosevelt, elected in 1932, felt that "social insurance" as opposed to welfare assistance was the key—a plan where workers would contribute through taxes while employed and later on receive benefits as retirees (Social Security Administration 2003). A year after its initial promotion, the Social Security Act was signed into law on August 14, 1935, creating general welfare programs and providing for a system by which retired workers over age 65 could be paid a continuing income after retirement (Social Security Administration 2003). To implement the Act, every worker would be assigned an SSN so they could begin acquiring credits toward retirement. While the original intent was that this unique identifier would solely be used within the Social Security Administration, this proved not to be the case.

In 1943 President F. D. Roosevelt authorized the use of the SSN as a primary key for other government databases (Berghel 2000). Fueled by this decision, a number of other federal agencies also adopted the SSN as an official identifier in subsequent years (Social Security Administration 2000). Starting in 1987, a project was initiated for parents to automatically obtain SSNs for their newborn infants when the state registered their birth (Social Security Administration 2000). This led the way for other, nongovernment organizations to use the SSN, including medical offices, utility companies, insurance companies, and schools, especially once nearly everyone in the United States had one. The widespread usage of the SSN as an everyday form of personal identification was inevitable, which set conditions for its misuse and easy availability.

Banking and Automated Teller Machines

During the 1900s the use of paper money increased, which led to the growth of consumer banking and the development of formal credit systems. The existence of various technologies surrounding the banking industry, starting with the early days of paper-based payment ledgers built on trust, provided a framework in which identity theft was able to evolve and grow. At the beginning of the twentieth century, hotels, oil companies, and department stores began issuing payment cards to customers to identify that they had a charge account with them, but these were not networked together in any fashion (Evans and Schmalensee 2003). In early 1950, the Frank McNamara distributed a few hundred cards to people in Manhattan and got local restaurants to bill a portion of the meal tab to the Diners Club—the first organizational charge card (Evans and Schmalensee 2003). Barclay's Bank, in 1967 London, began operating a cash-dispensing machine—the first automated teller machine (ATM) in the world (Bátiz-Lazo and Wood 2002). This was followed by Chemical Bank's opening of the first American cash-dispensing machine on September 2, 1969, in Rockwell Centre, Long Island, allowing customers to cash checks (Florian, Burke, and Mero 2004). By the mid-1970s, these ATMs could also perform additional banking functions, including deposits and balance inquiries (Florian, Burke, and Mero 2004).

As computing technologies became more powerful, ATMs from different banks could be networked together, and then different networks connected. Customers could use cards issued at one bank in ATMs belonging to another bank. Credit cards were issued by every financial institution and many commercial merchants. Banking had shifted from local commerce to a transnational affair, paving the way for the dependence on interconnected financial databases and the ease of accessing this information for illicit purposes.

IDENTITY THEFT AND THE OFFENDER

Offender Motivations

To date, very little has been written about the offender in an identity theft event. Prior surveys conducted have addressed only the victim, without going to the criminal source to obtain more data. One study using a Florida police department database found that identity theft offenders were most often unemployed African-American females who worked alone and were unknown to the victim, but it did not address their motives (Allison, Schuck, and Lersch 2005). From the analyzed newspaper articles, however, we see they are driven by financial desires. By looking at the types of purchases that offenders make, it is possible to see the inherent greed which precipitates an identity theft event. They buy new vehicles, computers and computer equipment, furniture, jewelry, airline tickets, and assorted electronic devices; obtain mortgages or rental apartments; open utility or landline/cellular phone service; and run up thousands, if not hundreds of thousands, of dollars on credit cards.

Clearly, the majority of offenders are not committing identity theft for altruistic purposes. This would seem to fit the category of strain theories in criminology, where offenders engage in criminal activity as a response to blocked goals. They cannot obtain what they want, often money or luxury items, through legitimate means and so they turn to crime to get them. Offenders in this mostly American sample used identity theft in order to buy "stuff," consistent with Messner and Rosenfeld's (2001) idea of the American Dream as it relates to crime. In their theory, American culture strongly emphasizes monetary success over a weaker commitment toward obtaining it through legitimate means ("playing by the rules"), and the balance of the institutional social structure is tipped toward the economy (Messner and Rosenfeld 2001). They discuss how "the American Dream" is implicated in violent crime but also apply it to financial crime, making it well suited toward better understanding why identity theft can be committed.

Criminal Charges and Punishments

When it comes to the statutes under which offenders are generally charged, most are various fraud or theft crimes, especially credit card fraud. In the context of labeling deviant behavior, it is not surprising that it took until 1999 for an offender to be charged specifically with identity theft (ProQuest 1999b). Because general fraud was understood and labeled before the 1998 passage of the ITADA, existing fraud and theft statues already criminalized the behavior now called identity theft and were more familiar to use. By 2001, it was seen that prosecutors began to combine fraud and identity theft charges, potentially in part to include the lesser offense of fraud underneath the larger-encompassing crime of identity theft and thus have a better change of punishing the offender.

Initial punishments for these crimes were similar in that they would be stated for the fraud and theft statues as opposed to identity theft. Most offenders found guilty of fraud were both incarcerated and ordered to pay restitution to victims, with sentences ranging from a sailor being "restricted to base for 30 days and fined $880" (Associated Press 1994) for credit card fraud to "fac[ing] up to 20 years in prison and up to $750,000 in fines" (Brooks 2003) for conspiracy, mail fraud, and credit card fraud. However, while the sanctions for identity theft have begun to increase in recent years, it remains difficult to investigate, arrest, and punish offenders. This stems, in part, from the jurisdictional issues created by the offender and victim often living in different states, if not different countries. As mentioned previously, the fraud acts which comprise an identity theft incident are not new crimes. However, computers and the Internet have eliminated the need for interpersonal contact to be a part of the crime act and make it easier to commit identity theft literally anytime and anywhere.

IDENTITY THEFT AND THE VICTIM

Victim Characteristics

According to the lifestyle-exposure theory, the basic premise is that "demographic differences in the likelihood of victimization can be attributed to differences in the personal lifestyles of victims" (Meier and Miethe 1997, 232). Thus, variations in lifestyle—a person's occupation, education, residence, age, gender, marital status, and family income and race—all factor into the likelihood that they will become a victim of crime. Because victimization occurs disproportionately as opposed to uniformly, certain lifestyles may increase the risk (Hindelang, Gottfredson, and Garofalo 1978). For example, with regards to identity theft, individuals with more education will generally have higher incomes, which may mean that individuals have more credit cards, more money in bank accounts, and clean credit histories. Married couples, especially if both individuals work, may have more assets than a single individual.

Previous research on fraud victims has found that they were more likely to be young (Titus, Heinzelman, and Boyle 1995; Van Wyk and Mason 2001; Van Wyk and Benson 1997), and have at least some college education or a college degree (Titus, Heinzelman, and Boyle 1995). Of the 246,035 complaints to the Identity Theft Data Clearinghouse in 2006 where respondents reported their age, 29 percent came from victims aged 18–29, with another 23 percent being 30–39 (FTC 2007, 7). Demographic data collected within the 577 newspaper articles display the range of victim types. They are both male and female, living in various locales across the United States, and working in a range of jobs. This sample ranges in age from 22 to 59, though victims can certainly be younger and older than this. Generally most victims are over 18, however, as adults are more likely to have credit cards, credit history, and bank accounts than minors. One weakness of the articles, however, is that they do not offer insights into why these victims were targeted by offenders, nor do they give enough information to develop a good victim profile.

Effects of Victimization

Because criminal victimization so violates a victim's sense of self, trust, and autonomy, it results in emotional harm to the victim (Kennedy 1983). Identity theft victims suffer a myriad of emotions upon becoming aware of their victimization, and some have a notable initial reaction to this news. Their emotions remain strong as they work toward recovery, but recovery itself can be difficult. Offenders that engage in long-term patterns of victimization will create greater harms for their victims, making it much more difficult to find relief. Additionally, victims will often experience revictimization due to the treatment received by "System" (e.g., criminal justice system, financial institutions, and commercial merchants).

Individuals against whom the offense was not originally perpetrated often experience sufferings from the criminal violation, resulting in indirect victimization (Shichor 1989). If a direct victim is suffering from negative, emotional impacts, their friends and family—will also be affected by their victimization. This could include marriages being affected due to stress (O'Connor and Possley 1996) or because a victim's spouse is the primary individual working toward the victim's recovery efforts (Hunt 1988). One couple postponed their wedding to ensure that the victim's credit record was clear before they bought a house (Lowry 1999).

There can also be tertiary victimization that extends to the societal level. Taxpayers fund the criminal justice system services "designed to prevent, prosecute, punish, and recompense crimes" (Elias 1986, 110). Financial institutions and commercial organizations pass the costs of fraud losses to everyday consumers in the form of higher fees or costs for goods and services. Finally, it is also striking to examine the general fear that identity theft produces, in part due to the media's role in coverage, even individuals who have not been personally victimized experience fears that they will become victims, or that someone else will be. In 1986, a businessman expressed a worry that his credit cards could be stolen after "hearing about the growth of credit card fraud" (Diamond 1986). Ten years later, the director of a company's shredding division noted that there was a "growing paranoia in the U.S." concerning "people [being] worr[ied] about their private becoming public" (Lalley 1996). Surveys done in the late 1990's showed that consumers were "reluctant to buy . . . over the Internet" due to "concern about security of their card numbers" (Lewis 1999). One such survey reported that 42 percent of Internet users had such a fear that it was "not safe to use their plastic in online transactions" (McIntosh 1999). Crime and victimization do not merely touch the original, direct victim; they affect all layers of the surrounding society.

Emotional Harm

In one of the few empirical studies on this subject, 37 identity theft victims completed a victim questionnaire, with 30 of them also completing a Brief Symptom Inventory (Sharp et al. 2004). It was found that the victims suffered a number of strong emotional responses two weeks after learning of their victimization, including irritability and anger, fear and anxiety, and frustration. After 26 weeks, participants felt distressed and desperate. A related study looking at 77 victims of a white-collar crime found that 29 percent "experienced a major depressive episode as defined by DSM-III criteria in the first 20 months after their [monetary] loss," five victims "developed suicidal ideation," and 45 percent showed "generalized anxiety disorder" (Ganzini, McFarland, and Bloom 1990, 59). Another study, looking at the effects of financial crime on victims of pension fraud, found that they experienced a "psychological, emotional, physical, financial, and behavioural impact" due to their victimization and suffered from anger and anxiety (Spalek 1999). Shover, Fox, and Mills (1994), in researching the long-term effects of victimization, found victims had emotional stress and protracted psychological suffering and that these "enduring and pervasive effects, for some individuals, [continued] nearly a decade after their victimization" (p. 319). Victims also displayed fear, worry, depression, intense anger, bitterness, and resentment after having suffered from a "catastrophic financial or emotional loss," and for some, the psychological harm was greater than the monetary (Shover, Fox, and Mills 1994, 312).

It is this emotional or psychological harm that is most notable among identity theft victims. In describing their experience, victims used like "fear," "frustrated," "nightmare," "overwhelming," "angry," "hard," "depressing," and "violated." Because society may view victims of financial crimes as having a hand in their victimization, there could be a stigma attached. Victims feel embarrassed by their situation, which in turn may lead to low rates of reporting. One victim who had criminal acts committed by the offender in his name said that "sometimes [he] feel[s] like [he] can't even go out because people will assume [the offender's] crimes are [his] crimes" (Lowry 1999). Even though there is usually no physical injury present in this type of crime due to lack of interpersonal contact, especially if the act is occurring solely within the confines of cyberspace, it is clear that victims are affected deeply.

PREVENTION OF IDENTITY THEFT

When it comes to preventing identity theft and protecting consumers, there are always blocks that various elements of the commercial business system place on being legislated or otherwise regulated. These commercial organizations want to make money, and they may be resistant to anything that forces them to change the way they do business. This leads to a conflicted existence between businesses and consumers. Consumers want to stay safe. They want their information protected and want organizations to do everything in their power to keep them from becoming victims of identity theft. Businesses, however, want to make money and are, literally, in the business of making money. Where is the incentive for them to change their business practices when profits are high enough, especially for large financial institutions, that fraud losses are a mere cost of doing business? In the end, the key may be reputation. If an organization is discovered to have a large number of actual victimized customers, or if breaches of sensitive personal information belonging to customers are made public, potential clients could take their business elsewhere. It will be a combination of loss of reputation or monetary fraud losses exceeding profits before businesses will change their mindset.

There have also been a number of problematic issues that come about when looking at measures to prevent identity theft. There is a large concern with the need to balance the availability of information with an individual's desire for privacy. Public records are increasingly becoming available on the Internet. In 1998, six states and the District of Columbia required the use of SSNs on driver's licenses as a deterrent against illegal immigration, but this information could then be used to commit identity theft (Alonso-Zaldivar 1998). A New Hampshire company hoping to build a national database of photographs and personal information to help retailers prevent identity theft found resistance from consumer groups who opposed the sale of the information and later abandoned their plans (O'Harrow 1999a, b; Obmascik 1999). Additionally, some technical preventative solutions are not without fault. In one such fraud detection service, there was a worry that "false positives" could occur, in which legitimate transactions were rejected (Bank 1999). Biometric systems, using an individual's biological characteristics for identification purposes, may be incompatible with one another (Schofield 1999). While large businesses may be able to absorb the costs to implement preventative solutions, it may be too expensive for small organizations (ProQuest 1999a). As more information continues to be made available online, and as technologies constantly improve, the debates over protection—whether through information technology or human-based means—will become more pressing.

IDENTITY THEFT AND THE MEDIA

While not present in any of the models, the media's role cannot be denied when it comes to helping to shape society's views about identity theft. In 1990, there was a credit card fraud case where the offender "became the identity" of the victim, according to the investigating detective (Chavez 1990). It was during the following year that the term "identity theft" appeared in a Boston Globe article (Neuffer 1991a), succeeded by "identity fraud" in a follow-up article two months later (Neuffer 1991b). These two articles were unique in two major ways, compared to the majority of articles subsequently published. First, they reported a number of victim accounts about their identity theft victimization. Second, the author interviewed the offender and offered insights into his mental state in the first article. The early victims profiled expressed frustrations about how system was not set up to help them remedy their situation, words that would echo later that decade and into the twenty-first century. Victims were told by officials to change their name. There was no single place to report their victimization so they instead had to make numerous calls. Agencies were slow to investigate their cases. In Massachusetts, state and local prosecutors recognized that SSN misuse could lead to greater crimes, but judges did not.

In February 1995, an author and victim wrote of the offenders "appropriating [his] identity" (McQuaid 1995). By mid-1996, identity fraud was "the latest in credit card fraud," and the FTC began to step in to look for solutions (Meckler 1996a). One requirement of the Identity Theft and Assumption Deterrence Act, passed on October 30, 1998, was that the FTC would help consumer victims. This led to the opening the Identity Theft Data Clearinghouse on November 1, 1999, to take consumer complaints. By the end of 2003, it was estimated that 10 million Americans were victims of identity theft, based on a phone survey of households across the United States (Schwartz 2003).

Finally, beginning in the late 1990s, the language used to describe identity theft became stronger, with journalists calling it "rampant" (Sinton 1997), "epidemic" (O'Harrow and Schwartz 1998; Dugas 1999; Pankratz 1999), and "a disturbing trend" (Liu 2000). Numerous articles written before this period refer to the prevalence of credit card fraud, such as one talking about its "seemingly intractable rise" (Fickenscher 1994), but they generally do not use the same sort of powerful adjectives as those that describe the prevalence of identity theft. As Jodie Bernstein of the FTC said in 2000, "the fear of identity theft has gripped the public as few consumer issues have" (ProQuest 2000). Around early 1997 the tone of articles began to shift toward the sensational, unsurprising since during this time the story of an identity theft victim was becoming "increasingly common" (Meckler 1996b), and victims started to become more vocal about their experiences.

A credit card fraud incident which was a clear case of identity theft was called a "nightmare for victims" (Robinson 1997), which preceded a large number of articles discussing identity theft's prevalence. A month later identity theft was referred to as "a disturbing trend" (Yavorsky 1997). By late 1997 we were in an "era of rampant IDT and financial fraud" (Sinton 1997). Comments about how fast-growing identity theft continued through the late 1990s and early 2000s, with "epidemic" and "exploding" being common descriptors. Journalists noted that: "such crimes have become almost epidemic in recent years" (O'Harrow and Schwartz 1998, 257); an "exploding number of unsuspecting citizens['] . . . identities have been stolen" and there has been an "alarming rise in identity theft" with an "explosion of cases" (Lowry 1999); "identity theft isn't new, but in the last five years it has exploded"

(Scott 1999); "identity theft has become epidemic" (Dugas 1999); "identity theft schemes have reached 'epidemic proportions' in the Denver area" (Pankratz 1999); a "surging number of Americans [are] reporting the crime to police" and identity theft has been a "dangerous trend fueled by the use of forged IDs" (Liu 2000); and it has "ensnared a number of prominent victims" and "the trend is soaring" (Greenberger and Simpson 2001). In one of the final articles published in 2003, it was noted that "the crime is growing exponentially" and "number of identity theft cases has exploded nationwide," then called a "hot-button topic in every state of the union" (Schwartz 2003). This was a very fitting end statement to an extremely large problem, especially as it was made following survey results that extrapolated that as many as 10 million Americans may have been victims. After a slow response to the crime, followed its growth, identity theft had finally been recognized as being a serious threat.

CONCLUSION

Identity theft has traditionally been easy to commit, and it results in lucrative gains. Offenders have rarely been apprehended, even more rarely convicted, and often received what victims would see as minimal punishment. Perhaps a solution is to start shifting the focus of identity-theft-related laws toward the prevention end instead of the prosecutorial end, especially for prevention in the commercial and financial sector. While many companies have taken a lead in developing technologies that are used to prevent identity theft, these solutions will only be as strong as the humans behind them. Computers and machines are not personally processing loan and mortgage applications. They are not behind a bank teller's counter dispensing money. They are not the department store cashier who fails to ask for picture identification when a credit card is presented. As the saying goes, security is only as strong as the weakest link. Although these sorts of organizations may fight against being regulated, regulation may be what is necessary to force companies into following good practices to prevent identity theft. Recent laws, such as the Health Insurance Portability and Accountability Act (HIPAA) to control the privacy and security of health care records and the Sarbanes–Oxley Act requiring financial audits, have changed the way organizations are doing business. Similarly, more acts addressing identity theft and the protection of personal information could be passed. As the news becomes filled with frequent articles about losing customer and employee data, perhaps it is time to take the choice out of business' hands concerning what measures they take and instead hold them to a federal standard of information protection.

Today, technology is omnipresent. It is in our homes, in our offices, in our cars, and even in our bathrooms. Electronic storage devices are continually developed to hold more data even as the physical media gets smaller. Information can be located in "usual" places, such as hard drives and compact discs, as well as places that might not be viewed as so common, including digital cameras, cellular phones, and Xbox gaming consoles. The Internet has grown from a handful of nodes (sites) in the United States into the large, worldwide distributed network that it is today, with data located at multiple points instead of at a single location. This ubiquity is what both helps and hurts. A user can access practically any information that they want with the click of a button or the press of a mouse—but this comes at a price. SSNs and credit card numbers are available from many sources and often are protected by lax information security measures, if protected at all. Sensitive information can be easily obtained and then stored on portable media, making it easier to steal. Businesses may have poor security training in place for employees, compounded by lack of accountability in the case of an information breach.

Now firmly in the digital age, we cannot go back to an older era. We also cannot police the expanse of the Internet with a cadre of "cybercops." Instead, we must move forward with better protection over electronic information. The identity theft incident models presented here detail how information moves from being obtained to being used in a fraudulent manner. Just as the key to committing identity theft stems from the acquisition of pieces of sensitive information, the key to stopping identity theft stems from protecting it. Businesses must use a combination of better information technology and better understanding of human factors to keep information safe from offenders. Security standards concerning company policies, network architecture, and data encryption, such as those developed by the PCI Security Standards Council (http://www.pcisecuritystandards.org) for the payment card industry, should be mandated for all sectors using and storing personal information. Scaling back SSN usage would eliminate it from a vast number of databases and thus scale back the potential places in which it could be found. Better training for employees would alert them potential identity theft situations and require them to notify authorities instead of authorizing transactions. Anyone handling credit cards should be sure that the current card user is the actual card owner and check for some kind of identity verification. These are merely a few of the improved security and training measures that could be implemented to stop identity theft before it is begun. Today's "crime of the Internet" does not need to belong to tomorrow too.

KEY TERMS

Credit card fraud
Identity theft
Victimization

REFERENCES

Allison, S. F. H., A.M. Schuck, and K. M. Lersch. 2005. Exploring the crime of identity theft: Prevalence, clearance rates, and victim/offender characteristics. *Journal of Criminal Justice* 33: 19–29.

Alonso-Zaldivar, R. November 27, 1998. Privacy to get attention of Congress. *Los Angeles Times*: 49. Retrieved March 26, 2005, from National Newspapers via ProQuest.

Associated Press. June 16, 1994. Probe: Son of former Navy secretary was treated far too leniently. *Chicago Tribune*: 18. Retrieved March 26, 2005, from National Newspapers via ProQuest.

Bank, D. May 10, 1999. HNC to offer its antifraud service for the Web. *Wall Street Journal*: 1. Retrieved March 26, 2005, from National Newspapers via ProQuest.

Bátiz-Lazo, B., and D. Wood. 2002. An historical appraisal of information technology in commercial banking. *Electronic Markets* 12 (3): 192–205.

Berghel, H. 2000. Digital village: Identity theft, Social Security numbers, and the Web. *Communications of the ACM* 43 (2): 17–21. Retrieved October 1, 2003, from the ACM Digital Library.

Brooks, N. R. February 12, 2003. How to be a CEO without trying hard. *Los Angeles Times*: C1. Retrieved March 26, 2005, from National Newspapers via ProQuest.

Chavez, S. February 22, 1990. Credit scam suspect pleads not guilty. *Los Angeles Times*: 2. Retrieved March 26, 2005, from National Newspapers via ProQuest.

Cheney, J. S. 2005. Identity theft: Do definitions still matter? Federal Reserve Bank of Philadelphia Payment Cards Center Discussion Paper. Available at SSRN: http://ssrn.com/abstract=815684

Creswell, J. W. 1994. *Research Design: Qualitative & Quantitative Approaches*. Thousand Oaks, CA: Sage Publications.

Diamond, S. J. February 2, 1986. Charge card services may not be needed. *Houston Chronicle*: 18. Retrieved March 26, 2005, from National Newspapers via ProQuest.

Dugas, C. July 2, 1999. Protect your Social Security number: Don't be a victim of identity theft. *USA Today*: 6B. Retrieved March 26, 2005, from National Newspapers via ProQuest.

Elias, R. 1986. *The Politics of Victimization: Victims, Victimology, and Human Rights*. New York: Oxford University Press.

Evans, D., and R. Schmalensee. 2003. *Paying with Plastic: The Digital Revolution in Buying and Borrowing*. Cambridge, MA: MIT Press.

Federal Trade Commission. 2007. Identity theft victim complaint data: January 1, 2006–December 31, 2006. Retrieved May 21, 2007, from the Federal Trade Commission Web site http://www.ftc.gov/ bcp/edu/microsites/idtheft/downloads/clearinghouse_2006.pdf

Fickenscher, L. 1994. Fraudulent cash advances decline as Visa and MasterCard fight back. *American Banker* 159 (7): 16. Retrieved March 26, 2005, from National Newspapers via ProQuest.

Florian, E., D. Burke, and J. Mero. 2004. The money machines. *Fortune* 150 (2): 100–4.

Ganzini, L., B. McFarland, and J. Bloom. 1990. Victims of fraud: Comparing victims of white collar and violent crime. *Bulletin of the American Academy of Psychiatry and the Law* 18 (1): 55–63.

Glaser, B. G., and A. L. Strauss. 1967. *The Discovery of Grounded Theory: Strategies for Qualitative Research*. New York: Aldine Publishing Company.

Greenberger, R. S., and G. R. Simpson. April 12, 2001. Identity theft dogs credit firms in the Supreme Court, Congress. *Wall Street Journal*: A18. Retrieved March 26, 2005, from National Newspapers via ProQuest.

Hindelang, M. J., M. R. Gottfredson, and J. Garofalo. 1978. *Victims of Personal Crime: An Empirical Foundation for a Theory of Personal Victimization*. Cambridge, MA: Ballinger Publishing Company.

Hunt, D. January 17, 1988. Questions cloud tale of Lalor's arrest in London. *Houston Chronicle*: 1. Retrieved March 26, 2005, from National Newspapers via ProQuest.

Johnston, D. 1996. "Introductory remarks." In *Definitional Dilemma: Can and Should There Be a Universal Definition of White Collar Crime?* edited by J. Helmkamp, R. Ball, and K. Townsend, 1–4. National White Collar Crime Center.

Kennedy, D. B. 1983. Implications of the victimization syndrome for clinical intervention with crime victims. *Personnel & Guidance Journal* 62 (4): 219–22.

Lalley, H. August 15, 1996. Paper shredder popularity: Prudence or paranoia? *Houston Chronicle*: 1. Retrieved March 26, 2005, from National Newspapers via ProQuest.

Lewis, P. H. February 7, 1999. The cybercompanion. *New York Times*: 5, 13. Retrieved March 26, 2005, from National Newspapers via ProQuest.

Lilly, J. R., F. T. Cullen, and R. A. Ball. 2002. *Criminological Theory: Context and Consequences*. 3rd ed. Thousand Oaks, CA: Sage Publications.

Liu, C. January 16, 2000. Identity theft is on the rise, tough to solve; Crime: Stolen IDs can be used to get credit cards in victims' names. Effect can be devastating. *Los Angeles Times*: 1. Retrieved March 26, 2005, from National Newspapers via ProQuest.

Lowry, T. April 6, 1999. Stolen identity hostages: Thieves cash in on others' names, credit and future. *USA Today*: 1B. Retrieved March 26, 2005, from National Newspapers via ProQuest.

McGuire, D. July 14, 2004. Bush signs identity theft bill. Retrieved April 4, 2005, from the Washington Post Web site http://www.washingtonpost.com/wp-dyn/articles/A51595-2004Jul15.html

McIntosh, N. September 16, 1999. Net users losing fear of buying: In the last year, the proportion of web users who shop online has doubled; Neil McIntosh reports on the state of e-commerce. *Guardian*: 4. Retrieved March 26, 2005, from National Newspapers via ProQuest.

McQuade, S. C. 1998. Towards a theory of technology-enabled crime. Unpublished manuscript, Institute of Public Policy, George Mason University.

McQuade, S. C. 2001. Cops versus crooks: Technological competition and complexity in the co-evolution of information technologies and money laundering. Unpublished doctoral dissertation, George Mason University.

McQuade, S. C. 2005. *Understanding and Managing Cybercrime*. Boston: Allyn & Bacon.

McQuaid, J. February 18, 1995. Following the money writer discovers he has a clone in a world of credit card fraud. *St. Louis Post—Dispatch*: 1D. Retrieved March 26, 2005, from National Newspapers via ProQuest.

Meckler, L. August 21, 1996a. FTC trying to combat theft of credit identity. *Times – Picayune*: A6. Retrieved March 26, 2005, from National Newspapers via ProQuest.

Meckler, L. August 25, 1996b. Credit-Card fraud soars as technology unlocks personal information. *Los Angeles Times*: 16. Retrieved March 26, 2005, from National Newspapers via ProQuest.

Meier, R. F., and T. D. Miethe. 1997. Understanding theories of criminal victimization. *Crime and Justice: A Review of Research* 17: 459–99.

Messner, S. F., and R. Rosenfeld. 2001. *Crime and the American Dream*. 3rd ed. Belmont, CA: Wadsworth.

National Center for Victims of Crime. 2001. Get help series: Identity theft. Retrieved September 17, 2003, from the National Center for Victims of Crime Web site http://www.ncvc.org/gethelp/identitytheft/

Neuffer, E. May 27, 1991a. One name's double life: David Lombardi lost his ID cards, acquired coworker's debts and crimes. *Boston Globe*. Retrieved March 26, 2005, from National Newspapers via ProQuest.

Neuffer, E. July 9, 1991b. Victims urge crackdown on identity theft: Say officials often fail to act on complaints. *Boston Globe*. Retrieved March 26, 2005, from National Newspapers via ProQuest.

Newman, G. R. 2004. Identity theft. Problem-Oriented Policing Guides for Police No. 25. U.S. Department of Justice Office of Community Oriented Policing Services and Center for Problem-Oriented Policing.

Obmascik, M. February 2, 1999. Fla. judge bans sale of photos; Colorado DMV prepares to sell 5 million this week. *Denver Post*: B1. Retrieved March 26, 2005, from National Newspapers via ProQuest.

O'Connor, M., and M. Possley. December 29, 1996. Credit card impostor thrived for 2 decades. *Chicago Tribune*: 1. Retrieved March 26, 2005, from National Newspapers via ProQuest.

O'Harrow, Jr., R. January 22, 1999a. Posing a privacy problem?; driver's-license photos used in anti-fraud database. *Washington Post*: A1. Retrieved March 26, 2005, from National Newspapers via ProQuest.

O'Harrow, Jr., R. November 12, 1999b. Firm changes plan to acquire photos; drivers' pictures ignited privacy furor. *Washington Post*: E3. Retrieved March 26, 2005, from National Newspapers via ProQuest.

O'Harrow, Jr., R., and J. Schwartz. May 26, 1998. A case of taken identity; thieves with a penchant for spending are stealing consumers' good names. *Washington Post*: A01. Retrieved March 26, 2005, from National Newspapers via ProQuest.

Pankratz, H. August 6, 1999. Police seek three indicted in identity theft. *Denver Post*: B1. Retrieved March 26, 2005, from National Newspapers via ProQuest.

Pfohl, S. J. 1981. "Labeling criminals." In *Law and Deviance*, edited by H. L. Ross, 45–64. Vol. 5. *Sage Annual Reviews in Studies of Deviance*. Beverly Hills, CA: Sage Publications.

ProQuest. July 18, 1999a. Small businesses up in arms over new private mailbox rules. *Houston Chronicle*: 5. Retrieved March 26, 2005, from National Newspapers via ProQuest.

ProQuest. September 28, 1999b. Metro briefs: News from around the region. *Times—Picayune*: B2. Retrieved March 26, 2005, from National Newspapers via ProQuest.

ProQuest. July 13, 2000. Washington briefs: From wire reports. *Times—Picayune*: A9. Retrieved March 26, 2005, from National Newspapers via ProQuest.

Robinson, M. April 4, 1997. Wrong side of the law: Cop finds crooks who assumed his identity. *Denver Post*: B3. Retrieved March 26, 2005, from National Newspapers via ProQuest.

Schofield, J. May 20, 1999. The eyes have it: The days of the PIN are numbered as computers learn to identify us by our fingerprints or irises, writes Jack Schofield. *Guardian*: 2. Retrieved March 26, 2005, from National Newspapers via ProQuest.

Schwartz, M. December 11, 2003. County looks to fight rise in identity theft: Specialized unit could be state's first. *Houston Chronicle*: 37. Retrieved March 26, 2005, from National Newspapers via ProQuest.

Scott, J. July 1, 1999. Buyer's edge: Your Thursday guide to saving time and money on the cutting edge: Identity theft crimes drive shredder sales. *Atlanta Constitution*: D1. Retrieved March 26, 2005, from National Newspapers via ProQuest.

Sharp, T., A. Shreve-Neiger, W. Fremouw, J. Kane, and S. Hutton. 2004. Exploring the psychological and somatic impact of identity theft. *Journal of Forensic Sciences* 49 (1): 131–36.

Shichor, D. 1989. Corporate deviance and corporate victimization: A review and some elaborations. *International Review of Victimology* 1: 67–88.

Shover, N., G. L. Fox, and M. Mills. March 1994. Long-term consequences of victimization by white-collar crime. In *Victims of Crime and the Victimization Process*, edited by M. McShane and F. P. Williams III, 301–24. New York: Garland Publishing. Criminal Justice: Contemporary Literature and Practice. (Reprinted from *Justice Quarterly* 11 (1): 75–98.)

Sinton, P. October 20, 1997. A confidentiality penalty. *San Francisco Chronicle*: B3. Retrieved March 26, 2005, from National Newspapers via ProQuest.

Social Security Administration. March 1, 2000. Social Security Number chronology. Retrieved January 4, 2005, from the Social Security Administration Web site http://www.ssa.gov/history/ssn/ssnchron.html

Social Security Administration. March 2003. A brief history of Social Security. Retrieved January 4, 2005, from the Social Security Administration Web site http://www.ssa.gov/history/briefhistory3.html

Spalek, B. 1999. Exploring the impact of financial crime: A study looking into the effects of the Maxwell scandal upon the Maxwell pensioners. *International Review of Victimology* 6 (3): 213–30.

Strauss, A., and J. M. Corbin. 1990. *Basics of Qualitative Research: Grounded Theory Procedures and Techniques*. Newbury Park, CA: Sage Publications.

Tesch, R. 1990. *Qualitative Research: Analysis Types and Software Tools*. New York: Falmer Press.

Titus, R. M., F. Heinzelman, and J. M. Boyle. 1995. Victimization of persons by fraud. *Crime and Delinquency* 41 (1): 54–72.

U.S. Department of Commerce. 1998. *The Emerging Digital Economy*. Washington, DC: U.S. Government Printing Office.

U.S. Public Law 105-318. October 30, 1998. 105th Congress, 112 Stat. 3007. Identity Theft Assumption and Deterrence Act of 1998.

U.S. Public Law 108-275. July 12, 2004. 108th Congress, 115 Stat. 831. Identity Theft Penalty Enhancement Act.

Van Wyk, J., and M. L. Benson. 1997. Fraud victimization: Risky business or just back luck? *American Journal of Criminal Justice* 21 (2): 163–79.

Van Wyk, J., and K. A. Mason. 2001. Investigating vulnerability and reporting behavior for consumer fraud victimization: Opportunity as a social aspect of age. *Journal of Contemporary Criminal Justice* 17 (4): 328–45.

Yavorsky, S. 1997. Forget cops and robbers: It's age of the inside job. *American Banker* 162 (99): 15. Retrieved March 26, 2005, from National Newspapers via ProQuest.

Appendix A

Coding Rules, Principles, and Procedures

1. **Assigning Codes:** To ensure accurate and consistent coding, newspaper articles were recoded as many as five times. Upon the emergence of new identified concepts, I reanalyzed previous articles again to check for the presence of those concepts.

2. **Operational Definitions:** I established conceptual codes to represent different substantive concepts. When a new code was created, it would be labeled and assigned an operational definition. These definitions were occasionally refined as my understanding of conceptual nuances increased (Glaser and Strauss 1967, Strauss and Corbin 1990)

3. **Code Application and Level of Abstraction:** I used two forms of open coding, in vivo and interpretive. *In vivo coding* was used when a newspaper article statement was logically taken at face value, with a code being assigned regardless of the context in which the statement was made. *Interpretive coding* was used when a newspaper article statement was applied to a concept.

4. **Data Cleaning:** Some of the article text was reformatted to fit in the primary document window within Atlas.ti, and sentences were brought together in the same paragraph structure present in their original source. However, none of the article's words were changed in any other way.

5. **Relational Code Links and Construction of Network Views:** During analysis of the 577 newspaper articles, I developed seven major types of links that I used to represent relationships between code concepts. These links were developed on the basis of my interpretation of the article data, but they were not assigned unless statements by one or more articles supported them.

6. **Checking Potential Researcher Bias:** As a check against potential researcher bias, I assigned codes and code links as objectively as possible, even though the research itself required subjective analysis of the data.

7. **Overlapping Code Data:** To ensure comprehensive analysis, I coded short phrases, incomplete sentences, or even single words, but other times I coded an entire paragraph with a single code. These overlapping code assignments were necessary to capture the relationships between codes. This procedure resulted in a handful of double counting (i.e., the same code applied more than once to the same text).

8. **Merging Codes:** While I originally had certain separate open code categories, they were later merged to represent more encompassing concepts. For example, I had originally created *Positive System Response* and *Negative System Response*, for quotations referring

to activities/responses that were either positive towards or negative against the victim of an identity theft incident. After determining that having separate codes was not justified, I merged them into the single code *System Response* and deleted them from the code list.

9. **Open Coding Reflective Memos:** During manual open coding of the 577 newspaper articles, I wrote 18 reflective (note taking) memos to myself to document my thoughts about the emerging data and keep track of ongoing analysis that was occurring in the course of my research.

Chapter 13

Internet Fraud and Cyber Crime

Wendy Cukier, Avner Levin
Ryerson University

Wendy Cukier, Ph.D., is the associate dean of the Faculty of Business, Ryerson University where she is a full-time professor in Information Technology Management. She has an MA and an MBA from the University of Toronto and a Ph.D. in Management Science from York University. She co-authored *The Global Gun Epidemic* published by Praeger in 2006 as well as the best-selling business book, *Innovation Nation*, published by Wiley in 2002. She has published more than 200 articles and papers and presented at conferences around the world. Currently she holds a large grant for research on technology and the media. Wendy has served on many industries, academic and government committees—she is on the expert panel for the Computer and Information Technology Council as well as the Canadian Information Productivity Award. She has also been a member of the Ad Hoc Council on Crime Prevention, The Canadian Advisory Committee on Firearms and the National Commission on Small Arms. As a consultant, she has worked for UN agencies, governments, business and nonprofit organizations. Recently she has completed a project on Quality Assurance for the Canadian Association of Chiefs of Police as well as a Business Process Reengineering project for the South African Police Service. Her volunteer work has been recognized with many awards including honorary doctorates in Law (Concordia) and Medicine (Laval), the Canadian Public Health Association's Award of Merit, the Canadian Criminal Justice's Public Education Award, and a Women of Distinction award from the YWCA. In 2000, the University of Toronto named her among the "alumni who had shaped the century." She is also a recipient of the Meritorious Service Cross, one of Canada's highest civilian honors.

Professor **Avner Levin** is the coordinator of the Law Area at the Ted Rogers School of Management at Ryerson University. His research interests include the legal regulation and protection of privacy and personal information in various sectors across jurisdictions, both within Canada and internationally. Professor Levin heads the Privacy and Cyber Crime Institute at Ryerson University. Professor Levin's recent research has focused on privacy in the workplace, and his research team has been funded by the Privacy Commissioner of Canada's Contributions Program. The team's report, titled "Under the Radar: The Employer Perspective on Workplace Privacy" was published in the summer of 2006 to widespread media attention in Canada.

Abstract

In this chapter, we review the various forms of fraud and crime committed online. Following the review, we discuss the laws in place to prevent Internet fraud and cyber crime in major jurisdictions such as the United States and the European Union and the effectiveness of the existing legislative framework. We then offer some suggestions on how to reduce online crime, building upon theories of victimization and crime-prevention insights from a criminological perspective, as well as on an international legal perspective. We conclude with some necessary immediate steps that can be taken to reduce Internet fraud and cyber crime.

INTRODUCTION

Many of the qualities that make the Internet an important vehicle for legitimate business also make the Internet a near-perfect instrument for fraud. The broad reach of the Internet means that a large number of potential victims can be reached quickly from virtually anywhere in the world. The fragmentation and limitations of legislative frameworks has led some to argue that more protection of consumers is needed domestically and internationally (Broadhurst 2005). The lack of international standards provides "safe haven" for many Internet criminals. Not only does the Internet dramatically expand the reach of potential criminals, but it dramatically reduces the chances that they will be detected, apprehended, and successfully prosecuted. Sophisticated criminals base their operations outside the jurisdiction of the United States, in countries with no extradition treaties with America. They also operate in countries, as in the case of Nigeria, with weak legal and policing systems (Cukier, Nesselroth, and Cody 2007). They have sophisticated technologies that reduce the links between them and their victims and protect their identity. Free and therefore relatively untraceable, e-mail accounts are readily available from a number of online companies, and because no financial payment information is required to establish and use such an account, the identity of the account owner easily can be falsified and rendered largely indiscernible. Criminals are also able to exploit standard security features in most online auctions where buyers and sellers register at the auction Web site and subsequently communicate by e-mail, but with their true identities masked (Loza 2001). Law enforcement resources are limited, less sophisticated and hampered by outdated legislation. As a result only a small fraction of **Internet frauds** are successfully prosecuted.

Spam accounts for the vast majority of communications now on the Internet, estimated to be almost two-thirds of all e-mail traffic (Moustakas, Ranganathan, and Duqenoy 2005). Spam is defined in the United States as unsolicited commercial electronic mail (Controlling the Assault of Non-Solicited Pornography and Marketing Act, known by its acronym, CAN-SPAM). These are unsolicited or unwanted electronic messages sent to a large number of users (in bulk), without regard to the identity of the individual user, and having commercial purposes (Zeltsan 2004). While spam is not in and of itself criminal in the United States (although spammers often violate policies concerning acceptable use and privacy), it is often a vehicle for perpetrating crime (Chhabra 2005). Legally, fraud is commonly defined as an intentionally misleading representation of fact which cause a person that relied on it to suffer a loss. Internet fraud may be associated with:

- Altering computer input in an unauthorized way. This requires little technical expertise and is not an uncommon form of theft by employees altering the data before entry or entering false data, or by entering unauthorized instructions or using unauthorized processes.

- Altering, destroying, suppressing, or stealing output, usually to conceal unauthorized transactions: this form of fraud difficult to detect.

- Altering or deleting stored data.

TABLE 13-1 Federal Trade Commission Released January 25, 2006

	Fraud Complaints	Identity Theft	Total
2003	327,479	215,177	542,656
2004	406,193	246,847	653,040
2005	431,118	255,565	686,683

- Altering or misusing existing system tools or software packages, or altering or writing code for fraudulent purposes.

- Hacking into financial databases via the Internet in order to get access to confidential client information for the purpose of obtaining credit by use of false identity (identity theft). (Bainbridge 2000)

Internet fraud schemes may use e-mail, Web sites, chat rooms, or message boards to present fraudulent solicitations to prospective victims, to conduct fraudulent transactions or to transmit the proceeds of fraud to financial institutions or to others connected with the scheme. Spam has become one of the major mechanisms for perpetrating fraud via the Internet. While some of the schemes distributed by spam are highly improbable, the sheer volume of the audience reached results in a surprisingly high number of victims (Cerf 2005).

During 2005, the Federal Trade Commission (FTC) received over 685,000 Consumer Sentinel complaints. Of these 63 percent represented fraud and 37 percent were identity theft complaints (Table 13-1). The total number of fraud complaints has increased every year since data were collected but the investigations are very difficult and prosecutions are relatively rare considering the extent of the problem (Fishman et al. 2002).

FORMS OF INTERNET FRAUD

In 2005, consumers reported fraud losses of over $680 million. Internet-related complaints accounted for 46 percent of all reported fraud complaints, with monetary losses of over $335 million and a median loss of $345. The Internet is used to perpetrate frauds in a number of ways including Internet auctions (12 percent), foreign money offers (8 percent), shop-at-home/catalog sales (8 percent), prizes/sweepstakes and lotteries (7 percent), Internet services and computer complaints (5 percent), business opportunities and work-at-home plans (2 percent), advance-fee loans and credit protection (2 percent), and telephone services (2 percent). The percentage of Internet-related fraud complaints with "wire transfer" as the reported payment method more than tripled between the calendar years of 2003 and 2005, increasing by 12 percentage points. In more than half of the reported fraud complaints (55 percent) the perpetrator's initial contact was through electronic mail (35 percent) and the Web (see Table 13-2; Federal Trade Commission 2006).

Auctions

Twelve percent of the complaints reported in 2005 were associated with Internet auctions. These schemes, and similar schemes for online retail goods, typically purport to offer high-value items likely to attract consumers—ranging from expensive watches to computers to collectibles.

TABLE 13-2 Top Internet Fraud Complaints, 2005 (Federal Trade
Commission 2006)

Fraud	Percentage of All Complaints	Average Loss ($)
Auctions	42	1,155
General merchandise	30	2,528
Nigerian money offers	8	6,937
Fake checks	6	4,361
Lotteries/lottery clubs	4	2,919
Phishing	2	612
Advance fee loans	1	1,426
Information/adult services	1	504
Work-at-home plans	1	1,785
Internet access services	1	1,262

The victims send money for their successful bids but receive nothing or substitute items which
are often counterfeit (McQuillen 2003). A Connecticut woman was sentenced to almost five
years in prison and fined $10,000 for taking $880,000 from eBay customers who bid for computers she never delivered. Officials called the case the largest Internet auction fraud prosecution
ever (McQuillen 2003).

     Recently, charges were laid in what has been called the "largest Internet fraud case in US
history" (Kouri 2006). An international fraud scheme based in Romania is alleged to have
allowed 21 defendants to obtain more than $5 million in an Internet-based scheme in which vic-
tims were led to believe that they were purchasing items that were listed for sale on the Internet,
typically via auctions on eBay, but then did not receive the goods that they paid for. The money
was collected mostly in the Chicago area over three years from more than 2,000 victims who
were led to believe that they were purchasing items that were listed for sale on the Internet, typically via auctions on eBay, but then did not receive the goods that they paid for. Each of the
21 defendants was charged with one count of wire fraud. Law enforcement agencies reviewed
records from Western Union and currency exchanges of more than 2,000 wire transfers of funds
believed to be related to the alleged fraud scheme. The victims who bid unsuccessfully on items
were led to believe that they were being given a "second chance" to purchase items and were
instructed over the Internet to send money via Western Union to be picked up by the seller or the
seller's agent (Kouri 2006). The 21 defendants participated in the fraud scheme in the United
States by obtaining multiple alias identification documents to use when receiving fraud proceeds from Western Union or recruiting other individuals to receive fraud proceeds from
Western Union. In many instances, victims provided copies of the fraudulent Internet solicitations and other online communications with the "sellers." This material shows that solicitations
often share identical features, such as bogus eBay logos and other graphics, and false assurances
that buyers would be protected by insurance and escrow of funds. Through the records of wire
transfers from Western Union and currency exchanges, investigators were able to trace many of

the individuals who received the payments (Kouri 2006). A review of these identification documents, along with other identity documents seized by numerous local police departments at various times, allowed investigators to identify dozens of aliases that allegedly were used by the defendants as part of the fraud scheme (Kouri 2006).

However, many cases are never resolved. For example, in one case, an eBay buyer decided to buy an expensive automobile listed in one of eBay's auctions. Although he did not have the highest bid, he was contacted by the "seller" and offered the car for the $61,000 he bid. He did offer to provide car title and other verification information and appeared to be a legitimate car dealer located in the United States. That payment went to Eastern Europe but the car did not arrive. An accomplice saw the car when it was offered for sale and obtained the vehicle information number, title number, and other information while acting as a prospective buyer. That information was used to create the eBay auction notice that looked convincing (Wingfield 2004).

While there are many cases of successful prosecutions being undertaken for auction fraud, some have argued that the lack of specific regulation means that many victims have little effective recourse. For example, Albert (2002) suggests that the FTC should use its substantial regulatory authority to craft binding regulations for online auction sites rather than relying on the auction sites to take appropriate steps concerning the authentication of identities, verifying credit, authenticating the goods for sale, and taking any other steps needed to ensure the highest possible level of consumer protection (Albert 2002). Albert (2002) argues, for example, that because the auctioneers do not take title to the goods they are selling, under current law, they have no liability for fraud occurring on their sites and therefore have limited incentive to take steps to prevent fraud from occurring.

General Merchandise

There is also widespread fraud perpetrated in connection with Internet sales. The FTC has prosecuted Internet fraud involving a diverse range of products, as follows (Federal Trade Commission 2006):

1. Purported learning-enhancement products

2. Computer and computer peripheral equipment sold online and by mail and auctioned online

3. Purported laundry detergent substitutes

4. Textile and apparel products

5. Purported beauty and health care products, including therapeutic methods and devices, medicinal products, dietary supplements, diagnostic test kits, weight-loss products, exercise equipment, sexual enhancement products, and illicit drug and tobacco substitutes

This category of fraud (related to general merchandise) appears to utilize the Internet as a traditional communication channel, similar to regular mail, for example, rather than capitalize on the unique characteristics of the Internet as described above. We will therefore not analyze this category in greater detail. However, the following category is one that has reached almost unparalleled notoriety thanks to the Internet.

Advance Fee Fraud: Nigerian Letters

One of the most identifiable forms of Internet fraud perpetrated via spam is the "Nigerian letter," an adaptation of a direct mail fraud scam dating back to the 1990s. The proliferation of these letters was so great that The United States Secret Service (n.d.) actually issued an "Advance Fee Fraud Advisory" regarding Nigerian letters. The Federal Trade Commission also identified the "Nigerian letter" in its study of false claims in spam. This is a U.S.$5 billion worldwide scam that emerged in 1989 under successive Governments of Nigeria. It is also referred to as "Advance Fee Fraud" and "419 Fraud" after the relevant section of the Criminal Code of Nigeria (Edelson 2003).

The target receives an e-mail from an insider or alleged "official" representing a present or former foreign government or agency. Initially targeting businessmen, the scam has now expanded to include the average citizen due to the low cost of e-mail transmission in relation to potential gains. Either initially or eventually you must provide further fees and payments, usually by wire transfer, for various taxes and expenses to complete the transaction (Edelson 2003).

All of these scams use the same tactic—the victim must pay a series of fees to process the transaction, and the sender claims that "just one more" fee, stamp, duty, form, etc. must be processed before the millions can be deposited. In addition, the victim either sets up an account in Nigeria, or uses his own account to transfer fees from stolen checks. Often on their home turf, this makes the victim the criminal who will be charged with fraud for passing stolen checks. The process is predicated on escalating commitment—the more the victim invests the less likely they are to walk away.

Victims are convinced of the authenticity of the proposal by the numerous documents bearing official looking Nigerian government letterhead, stamps, and seals. There have been cases where victims have had meetings with genuine Nigerian Government officials in their offices to discuss a 419 "deal" during office hours. There have also been cases of victims verifying the phone number of the relevant Parastatal from the Lagos directory assistance, calling that number (CBN, for example), asking for their scammer by name, and getting put through during office hours (Cukier, Nesselroth, and Cody 2007).

The scams can become extremely dangerous as the process proceeds and the stakes escalate. In the final phase, the victim will be asked to meet someone in Nigeria (or New York or Amsterdam). At that point they may be killed, extorted, kidnapped for ransom, or be given a trunk of black money—for which he will be charged a "laundering fee" to wash the blackened bills. When given the "cleaned" money, it will, of course, be counterfeit or just blank slips of paper (Cukier, Nesselroth, and Cody 2007). To add insult to injury, victims who call the police and lay charges in the hopes of getting their money back, often receive calls back from) someone claiming to be a Nigerian official. The official will state that their stolen funds have been recovered, but in order to get the money back, they must pay a fee—and the whole scam begins again (see Table 13-3; Cukier, Nesselroth, and Cody 2007).

Phishing

One of the principal ways in which spam perpetrates fraud is through **phishing**: the mass e-mailing of messages from apparently legitimate organizations such as Citibank, Bank of America, or VISA. Phishing is aimed at acquiring confidential financial information such as account numbers and passwords (Anti-Phishing Working Group 2007). For example, many

TABLE 13-3 Advance Fee Fraud in 37 Countries (Cukier, Nesselroth, and Cody 2007)

Jurisdiction	Active Scam Rings	Active Scammers	Profits per Scam Ring (million U.S.$)	Losses to private Sector (million U.S.$)
United States	8	3,800	370	720
United Kingdom	20	2,030	284	520
Spain	18	2,530	262	320
Japan	1	3	21	320
Germany	10	1,270	137	210
Canada	5	3,200	410	172
South Africa	3	780	80	136
France	7	810	119	130
Italy	8	200	70	120
Switzerland	3	120	65	102
Nigeria	36			
Other				434
Totals	**119**	**14,743**	**1,818**	**3,184**

phishing ploys claim to be from a major bank or firm and to be confirming customer information. The message is often written to sound alarming—"your account is suspended"—and the recipient is told to visit a Web site to confirm their identity. Phishers often employ the ruse that the security arm of a bank or credit card company needs to verify an account-holder's name, address, account number, and password to "protect" them from unscrupulous criminals who would drain the accounts. The messages include a response link to the firm that appears to be authentic (Anti-Phishing Working Group 2007). Subsequently, the response Web sites look as professional and authentic as the originals. The statistics show that the response rate to this type of fraud is around 5 percent. Often, it takes a long time before victims realize that their personal information has been stolen and it can cost thousands of dollars to recover from identity theft. The number of unique phishing Web sites detected by Anti-Phishing Working Group rose to 55,643 in April 2007. While financial institutions are the preferred targets in over 90 percent of phishing expeditions, there is evidence of growth in attacks on nonfinancial brands such as social networking, voice over Internet protocol (VOIP), and numerous large Web-based e-mail providers (Anti-Phishing Working Group 2007).

Business Opportunity/"Work-at-Home" Schemes Online

Business opportunities advertised through spam are becoming a leading form of Internet fraud. These ads offer individuals the chance to earn thousands of dollars a month in "work-at-home" ventures. The schemes usually require the individuals to pay a fee or purchase products, but then do not deliver the goods or services which were purchased. For example, in 1999 in Los Angeles, four individuals were criminally charged for their roles in conducting a fraudulent scheme. The scammers sent out approximately 50 million e-mails that falsely advertised work-at-home opportunities. In reality, there were very few opportunities for those people who paid the $35 advance fee (United States Department of Justice 2007).

Penny Stock Spam and Securities Fraud

This form of spam began appearing in 2006 in response to the increasing successful technological measures such as spam filters have had. Penny Stock spam has two characteristics. First, it is graphic in nature—an e-mail incorporating an image of a page. In this fashion spammers circumvent text-reading filters, although the recipient is still exposed to the content of the message (Byrne 1998). The second characteristic is the content of the spam, promoting some obscure and close to worthless (i.e., "penny") stock. As with all forms of spam, this form of fraud increases in success with an increase in the number of recipients, since statistically, inevitably some percentage of recipients will respond to the offer to purchase stock. Spammers profit in the traditional market way—buying low and selling high—and in a unique way by sending out a promotional spam message to facilitate the increase in price in between.

Prosecutions for securities fraud enabled by the Internet are not new. For example, in August 1999 four spammers were charged in New York for their alleged roles in the fraudulent promotion of eight stocks through misleading Internet Web sites and spam. Also in 1999, two individuals pleaded guilty in North Carolina to fraud for their roles in offering securities in a nonexistent bank that offered, a "guaranteed" 20 percent return on savings (United States Department of Justice 2007).

Other Investment Schemes

Some other schemes combine the Internet with other channels of communication such as telemarketing. In one case the Internet and telemarketing were used to promote "general partnerships" that would invest in online shopping malls and Internet service providers. The scheme allegedly defrauded more than 3,000 victims nationwide of nearly $50 million (United States Department of Justice 2007).

Credit Card Schemes

These schemes involve the use of unlawfully obtained credit card numbers to order goods and services over the Internet. For example, "sellers" will offer victims expensive items, such as video cameras, at a very attractive price. When the victim contacts the "seller," they will even be promised that the item would be shipped prior to payment. Naturally, victims tend to agree. The "seller" then uses the victim's real name, without the victim's knowledge, together with a credit card number belonging to another person, to buy the item online (United States Department of Justice 2007). Once the real seller ships the item to the victim, the victim, believing all along that the transaction is legitimate, authorizes the credit card to be billed by "seller" or sends payment directly to the "seller." There are actually two victims here: the real seller, and the consumer who paid after receiving the goods (United States Department of Justice 2007).

Pyramid Schemes

The defendants in *FTC v. Fortuna Alliance* promoted Internet investments in a pyramid scheme in effect, a "high tech chain letter." We discuss this case in greater detail below. *FTC v. Cano* saw the use of purported pre-approved unsecured VISA or MasterCard credit cards to perpetrate a combined pyramid-investment scheme. In the case of the *FTC v. Five Star Auto Club, Inc.*, defendants operated an illegal pyramid scheme through supposedly free "dream car" leases. Finally, the illegal conduct in *FTC v. Martinelli* linked a pyramid scheme with a work-at-home ploy (Loza 2001). Similarly, in 2000, four people were indicted in Ohio, on charges including conspiracy to commit and committing mail and wire fraud for a pyramid scheme. A company with which the defendants were affiliated allegedly collected more than $26 million from "investors" without selling any product or service, and paid older investors with the proceeds of the money collected from the newer investors (Loza 2001).

Family Status Schemes

There are Web sites that offer U.S. citizens an opportunity to divorce quickly in the Dominican Republic or other foreign countries for $1,000 or more, without even having to leave the United States (United States Department of Justice 2007). These sites often contain inaccurate if not false information about divorce procedures in such jurisdiction (e.g., no need for physically visiting the jurisdiction in order to get divorced). The Web sites will even send out legal "certificates" of divorce upon receipt of payment from the victims, while in fact, victims have not changed their legal status at all (United States Department of Justice 2007).

Telecommunication Theft

Theft of telecommunications services is another common form of fraud. In several cases, online adult entertainment operators purport to offer "free" viewing of pornographic images. In fact, the operators used downloaded executable files that surreptitiously rerouted the viewer's Internet access through international telephone calls, which then were billed deceptively to the consumer's regular telephone account. In other cases, adult entertainment operators sent false e-mail messages that induced consumers to call a fraudulent customer service telephone number, which resulted in charges to consumers for undisclosed international calls and routed these consumers to sexual audio content, instead of a customer service representative (Loza 2001).

"Spoofing" or "Page-jacking": Fake or Fraudulent Web Sites

Web spoofing or creating hoax Web sites that mirror real sites is used to extract personal information and is a major way in which Internet fraud is perpetrated (Dinev 2006). "Page-jacking" is the term used to describe the appropriation of Web site descriptions, key words, or meta-tags from other sites. The page-jacker inserts these items into his or her own site, seeking to draw consumers to a particular site. This is because the descriptions, key words, and meta-tags are used by search engines when sorting and displaying sites on a particular topic requested by an individual (Dinev 2006). Pharming crimeware misdirects users to fraudulent sites or proxy servers, typically through domain name system (DNS) hijacking or poisoning.

When the sites for a particular topic appear, an individual might see two or three descriptions for what appear to be the same site (Dinev 2006). If a person happens to click on one of the duplicated descriptions, he or she will be directed to the fake site which offers false promises, fake products and services, or unwanted products (such as pornography).

Web sites are often used to perpetrate fraud often in combination with spam or telemarketing. The registration of Web sites is relatively unregulated with few checks and balances and consequently consumers are falsified Web site name registrations greatly complicate investigations and prosecution of Internet fraud (United States President's Working Group on Unlawful Conduct on the Internet 2000). For example, the defendants in *FTC v. Crescent Publishing Group, Inc.*, commonly owned 65 affiliated corporations, each held one or more registered domain name (often a pornographic site). Complicating matters even further is that page-jackers often "mouse-trap" a user's browser so that attempts to close the browser's windows or to use the back or forward button will simply direct the user to another pornographic site (United States President's Working Group on Unlawful Conduct on the Internet 2000).

Homographs

Internationalized domain names (IDNs) were introduced to the Internet in 2003. An IDN allows the use of language characters other than ASCII in a domain name, and therefore provides users of other languages with the ability to create and access domain names in their character set of preference. A homograph is a character from another language that visually resembles an ASCII character. For example, this "a" is actually the Cyrillic letter "a." Can you visually spot the difference? IDNs therefore introduce the possibility of phishing through the creation of domain names that are visually similar to familiar, well-established domain names, but are in fact fraudulent since they incorporate homographs into the domain name. In such a manner, a criminal could construct any Web site, for example, the Web site paypal.com, where the first "a," would, in fact, be a Cyrillic character (as it is in the line above). The criminal would then redirect traffic from the legitimate PayPal Web site to the fraudulent Web site by spamming victims with the fraudulent link.

Homograph phishing can be greatly reduced providing all IDN registrars adhere to policies and guidelines established in 2003 by the Internet Corporation for Assigned Names and Numbers (ICANN), the American nonprofit corporation in control of the Internet. This (adherence) would prevent misleading homograph-based domain names, and by the implementation of international character screening by Internet browsers. With the addition in late 2006 of such capabilities to Microsoft's Internet Explorer it is anticipated that the threat of homograph phishing will be greatly reduced (Krammer 2006).

Homograph phishing and page-jacking exploit the vulnerability of the Internet's regulatory framework, which is in fact set by ICANN. ICANN is an American corporation and the only prohibitions against fraudulent domain name registration are set in ICANN's Uniform Domain Name Dispute Resolution Policy (UDRP). Section 2 of the UDRP stipulates that owners of domain names must make complete and accurate statements and must not register the domain name for an unlawful purpose, or use the domain name in violation of any applicable laws or regulations. However, since it is not federal law but a corporate policy the FTC is unable to enforce it directly. That fact has not stopped the FTC from pursuing page-jackers by other means. In September 1999, the FTC announced that it had obtained temporary restraining orders in federal district court against several Web site owners for page-jacking. The FTC alleged that the Web site owners engaged in deceptive and unfair trade practices in violation of the FTC Act, 15 U.S.C. § 45(a). Page-jacking can also potentially violate federal intellectual property laws, if a page-jacker copies substantial portions of the imitated sites, they may be criminally liable for copyright infringement (United States President's Working Group on Unlawful Conduct on the Internet 2000). In addition, if a page-jacker hacks into a domain name server and changes the data to redirect visitors to the hacker's site, that person could also be in violation of federal computer crime statutes, such as 18 U.S.C. § 1030, which protects the integrity of computer systems against hackers (United States President's Working Group on Unlawful Conduct on the Internet 2000).

In *FTC v. Pereira* (Atariz.com) the defendants counterfeited more than 25 million Web pages belonging to third parties, ranging from pages for the Harvard Law Review to the Japanese Friendship Garden. These counterfeit pages included the so-called "hooks" (common Internet search engine search terms, e.g., "toys") found in the authentic pages (Loza 2001). The defendants organized these counterfeit pages under a single Web site domain name, i.e., Atariz.com. The page-jacking conduct came about when hyperlinks to the counterfeit pages, along with links to the authentic pages, were returned in the results of an Internet search engine search by way of these copied hooks. Upon clicking on one of these hyperlinks, the consumer, however, was not directed to the authentic Web page about children's toys, rather a "redirect" command was inserted in the illicitly copied pages to send the viewer's browser software to a pornographic Web site (Loza 2001).

In another case the Australian respondents' Web site, internic.com, mimicked the Web site internic.net, the then only official U.S. Internet domain name registration service, InterNIC. The scheme grossed at least U.S. $3.5 million before the FTC and Australian authorities closed it down. In *FTC v. Oliver*, another defendant made his Web site to look like a legitimate government-affiliated consumer protection agency, using, among other tricks, a logo mimicking the FTC seal (Loza 2001).

Defrauders also use downloaded executable software files like stealth weapons to deceive and steal from online consumers. In both *FTC v. Audiotex Connection, Inc.* and *FTC v. Beylen Telecom*, for example, the defendants maintained a number of pornographic Web sites and promised "free" images by means of "david.exe," a so-called "viewer" software program that was downloaded and executed by consumers. In fact, the "david.exe" program disconnected their computers from their contracted Interact service providers, turned off the computers' speakers and dialed an international telephone number purportedly in Moldavia. The program then reconnected the computers to the Internet through these international calls. Moreover, the computers remained connected to these calls until consumers completely shut down their computers. Victims were charged $2.00 per minute for these calls (Loza 2001).

Identity Theft

Spam is one way of perpetrating identity theft and associated frauds. Identify theft refers to the wrongful acquisition and use of someone else's personal data in some way that involves fraud or deception, typically for economic gain. Often spam advertisements are not intended to sell goods but rather to collect personal information. This personal information is then used to obtain credit or to purchase goods and services. In 2005 credit card fraud (26 percent) was the most common form of reported identity theft followed by phone or utilities fraud (18 percent), bank fraud (17 percent), and employment fraud (12 percent). Other significant categories of identity theft reported by victims were government documents/benefits fraud (9 percent) and loan fraud (5 percent) (United States Federal Trade Commission 2006).

"Electronic Fund Transfer" related identity theft was the most frequently reported type of bank fraud during calendar year 2005. In one federal prosecution, the defendants allegedly obtained the names and Social Security numbers of U.S. military officers from a Web site, and then used more than 100 of those names and numbers to apply via the Internet for credit cards with a Delaware bank. In another federal prosecution, the defendant allegedly obtained personal data from a federal agency's Web site, and then used the personal data to submit 14 car loan applications online to a Florida bank (U.S. FTC). One large undercover operation, dubbed "Operation Firewall," resulted in indictments against 21 individuals was the "Shadowcrew" gang, who ran a Web site with approximately 4,000 members dedicated to facilitating malicious computer hacking and the dissemination of stolen credit card, debit card, and bank account numbers and counterfeit identification documents, such as drivers' licenses, passports and Social Security cards (United States Department of Justice 2007). They used account numbers and counterfeit identity documents to complete identity theft and defraud banks and retailers, for example, through gift card vending (i.e., purchasing gift cards from retail merchants at their physical stores using counterfeit credit cards and reselling such cards for a percentage of their actual value). In addition to possessing and using stolen credit card numbers to obtain things of value, gang members were also charged with possessing equipment used to encode counterfeit credit cards with stolen numbers (United States Department of Justice 2007).

RELEVANT LEGISLATION

Under American law, the term "fraud" is a generic term covering a variety of ways in which a party can lie or suppress the truth for financial gain. Generally, a successful plaintiff must show the defendant's misrepresentation of a past or present material fact; the defendant must be shown to have had the intent to induce reliance by the plaintiff. The plaintiff must also show their justifiable reliance on the misrepresentation (Albert 2002). Fraud includes the claims of fraudulent inducement when a party is enticed into a contract through misrepresentation or fraud, as well as fraud in the factum when the fraud occurs during the process of obtaining execution or delivery (Albert 2002).

Currently, criminal and civil laws make no distinction between fraudulent representations over a telephone or fax machine and fraudulent representations posted on an online bulletin board or Web site. The FTC has, on the basis of existing laws, brought hundreds of Internet-related cases to court, obtained permanent injunctions against dozens of Internet-related schemes, collected millions of dollars in redress for victims of online fraud, and frozen millions of dollars of assets in cases currently in litigation.

The regulation of electronic commerce, including the fraudulent activities discussed in this chapter falls in the United States largely to the FTC and to a lesser extent to the Department of Justice (DOJ), which can conduct criminal prosecutions of these fraud schemes and seek civil injunctive relief under 18 U.S.C. § 1345. The U.S. Constitution grants Congress the authority to supervise interstate commerce, of which electronic commerce, including spam, phishing, and other fraudulent activity conducted over the Internet, is considered a part (U.S. Constitution § 1.8.3). Individual states still retain jurisdiction over commerce conducted electronically, but within the jurisdiction of the state. For example, the State of California would have jurisdiction over an e-commerce transaction between a buyer in Los Angeles and a seller in San Francisco.

The FTC was created by Congress, through the FTC Act, on the basis of this constitutional power. The Act, and subsequent legislation, provide the FTC with its authority and supervisory role, and allow it to regulate various aspects of e-commerce, issue orders, levy fines, and commence litigation against individuals and corporations which it finds in violation of the legislation and regulations created by the FTC to oversee electronic interstate commerce (15 U.S.C. § 45(a), § 53(b)). The FTC has also been known, through its general prohibition against unfair and deceptive conduct, to enforce corporate policies against corporations that fail to follow their stated policy, even in the absence of legislation regulating the area of commerce governed by the corporate policy. For example, the FTC has repeatedly enforced privacy policies against corporations such as Microsoft, and drug maker Eli Lilly, although there is no comprehensive data protection legislation in the United States. Some of the legislations relevant to spam, fraud, and crime on the Internet are listed in Table 13-4.

TABLE 13-4 U.S. Legislation Relevant to Internet Fraud (Wikipedia)

Title	Code	Description
ACCESS DEVICE FRAUD	18 U.S.C. § 1029	Fraud and related activity in connection with access devices.
COMPUTER FRAUD AND ABUSE ACT	18 U.S.C. § 1030	Fraud and related activity in connection with computers.
CAN-SPAM ACT	18 U.S.C. § 1037	Fraud and related activity in connection with electronic mail.
CREDIT CARD FRAUD	15 U.S.C. § 1644	
EXTORTION AND THREATS	18 U.S.C. § 875	
FINANCIAL INSTITUTION FRAUD	18 U.S.C. § 1344	
IDENTITY THEFT AND ASSUMPTION DETERRENCE ACT	18 U.S.C. § 1028	Fraud and related activity in connection with identification documents, authentication features, and information.
MONEY LAUNDERING	18 U.S.C. § 1956	
WIRE FRAUD	18 U.S.C. § 1343	Fraud by wire, radio, or television.
NO ELECTRONIC THEFT ("NET") ACT	17 U.S.C. § 506	Criminal copyright infringement.
DIGITAL MILLENNIUM COPYRIGHT ACT (DMCA)	17 U.S.C. § 1201	Circumvention of copyright protection systems.
ELECTRONIC COMMUNICATIONS PRIVACY ACT	18 U.S.C. § 2701	Stored wire and electronic communications and transactional records access.
TRADE SECRETS ACT.	18 U.S.C. § 1832	Theft of trade secrets.
ECONOMIC ESPIONAGE ACT	18 U.S.C. § 1831	Economic Espionage.

Other Federal agencies besides the FTC and the DOJ with authority over crime and fraud over the Internet include the FBI, that has jurisdiction to investigate violations of each of these statutes, the Postal Inspection Service, with jurisdiction to investigate most of these violations as they relate to mail fraud schemes, the Secret Service, with jurisdiction to investigate credit card fraud and identity theft, and the Internal Revenue Service, with jurisdiction to investigate money laundering. The Customs Service and Secret Service also have jurisdiction over some of the predicate offences related to money laundering, and the Securities and Exchange Commission has jurisdiction to investigate violations of the federal securities laws. The multiple agencies and jurisdictions make prosecution of cases particularly complex.

Legislation and Spam

Spam is used for a wide range of purposes: at best it is a form of legitimate marketing; at worst it is a vehicle for perpetrating fraud, stealing identities or spreading viruses. Many countries, including the United States, Australia, and the European Union (but not Canada) have implemented legislation in an attempt to combat spam (Table 13-5). Legislation varies from jurisdiction to jurisdiction, however, with slightly different definitions of spam, different standards, and different approaches to spam control. These add to the inherent difficulty of enforcing any illicit cross-jurisdictional activity. The implementation and enforcement of the law in a global environment is still to be resolved. Enforcing antispam legislation is a challenge (Delaney et al. 2003).

To date, no country has criminalized spam. Commercial e-mail, in itself, is considered a legitimate, if annoying at times, marketing tool. The concerns about spam that legislation has attempted to address have been about spam as a vehicle for more nefarious activity, such as fraud, and about the increasing burden imposed by the phenomenon of spam on individuals, corporations, and the information systems that they use. The second concern is akin to concerns raised against unsolicited telemarketing, junk mail, and the like. Two main alternatives have been formulated in legislation to deal with it, the opt-out, and the opt-in mechanisms (Byrne 1998).

Opt-in legislation typically allows the sender of spam to send one unsolicited e-mail. The spammer must then receive permission from the e-mail recipient to send more commercial messages, which are therefore solicited from this point forward. The recipient has, in effect, opted in to the commercial message service. A person that would continue to send

TABLE 13-5 Antispam Legal Environment

Australia	European Union	United Kingdom	Japan	United States
Spam Act (2003)	Article 13(1) of the Privacy and Electronic Communications Directive (2002)	EU—Privacy and Electronic Communication Regulations 2003 (UK)	The Law on Regulation of Transmission of Specified Electronic Mail July 2002	CAN-SPAM Act (2003)
Opt-in	Opt-in	Opt-in	Opt-out	Opt-out

TABLE 13-6 A Spoof Protection Strategy for Individual Users (Dinev 2006)

Do	Don't
Pay attention to the salutation in the e-mail. It should mention your full name.	Believe an e-mail if it greets you by your e-mail address or "Dear Customer."
Open your browser and type the link into the site on the address bar yourself.	Click on a link to a site from an e-mail or from a chat room.
If spoofing is suspected, login by typing any characters. Some new spoof versions display "login failed" in any case, so it doesn't raise suspicions. Thus, your login failure is not an indication that the Web site is authentic. Watch for further clues.	Try to login immediately. Look for suspicious giveaways. Even if a "Login Failed" message asks you to try again, do not enter your real login name and password, but watch for more clues.
Know that financial institutions are very aware of spoofing and will avoid contacting you by e-mail if there are account problems.	Panic, if you receive an e-mail account problem.
Know that no bank will ask you to enter your credit/debit card PIN numbers, or drivers' license number online for authentication purposes. Most will not ask for SSN, though some insurance companies do that. This is bad practice even if the connection is secure.	Enter your PIN number. No bank will request such information, online or by phone.
Examine the URL, on the address bar. If it contains numbers followed by the Web site's name, it is a spoof. A hijacked URL bar is shifted and blurry. Examine cookies and status bar.	Continue if the address bar doesn't clearly show the real Web address. If in doubt close the browser, then reopen and retype.

---

unsolicited commercial e-mail to a recipient who has not opted-in would then commit an offence for which the typical remedy would be a fine. As indicated in Table 13-6, the European Union and Australia have adopted opt-in regimes, which are generally considered to be stricter than the alternative, the opt-out mechanism (Canada, Task Force on Spam 2005).

The United States and Japan allow spammers to offer recipients the option to opt-out of further communication, but do not insist that senders of commercial e-mail receive the approval of recipients ahead of time. The opt-out option is therefore less strict in its control of spam than its opt-in alternative, since the opt-out option allows spam to continue unfettered unless recipients actively request it to stop.

U.S. Legislation—CAN-SPAM Act 2003

The introduction of U.S. Federal legislation regulating spam in 2003 received a surprisingly lukewarm response. The lack of warmth emanated from the analysis that the CAN-SPAM Act had in fact watered down what little spam legislation already existed in the United States at the state level. The watering-down effect was the result of the stipulation within the CAN-SPAM Act that it replace similar state legislation, other than, for example, serving as a minimal standard upon which states can build stricter restrictions if they so choose (15 U.S.C. § 7707). In particular, the state of California, with a market size larger than Canada, introduced strict antispam legislation with an opt-in mechanism and private legal action. That legislation was superseded by the CAN-SPAM Act which offers neither.

The CAN-SPAM Act does not prohibit unsolicited commercial e-mail as such. However, it does include prohibitions against fraudulent and deceptive commercial e-mail, and allows recipients to opt-out of further communications. The Act is therefore a "compromise" between the various spam stakeholders and allows e-mail marketers to send unsolicited commercial e-mail until the recipient opts out from receiving future messages. The Act suggests certain standards, for example, e-mail marketers must identify their messages as advertisements (by using the tag ADV in the subject line) and include warning labels on messages that contain sexual material (15 U.S.C. § 7710).

Fraudulent messages, not only in terms of their content (such as a misleading subject), but in terms of their format (such as a false message headers) are prohibited by the Act (15 U.S.C. § 7704). It also prohibits spammers from disguising or hiding their identities, which, as noted above is a serious problem (15 U.S.C. § 7703). The Act prohibits harvesting addresses from Web sites and prohibits "dictionary attacks" in which spammers attempt different permutations of e-mail addresses until they are successful (15 U.S.C. § 7704). Many spammers use automated software to collect e-mail addresses through the Internet by searching Web sites, newsgroups, mail lists, or other online resources that could possibly contain e-mail addresses. Those violating these provisions could face penalties of up to five years in prison (15 U.S.C. § 7704).

The Act required that the FTC study the feasibility of a do-not-spam list of e-mail addresses, and the FTC has concluded that for now such a list would be counterproductive, and would in fact serve as a potential target list for spammers.

Canada

Canada currently has no antispam legislation in place in spite of the recommendations of a task force in 2005. The task force recommended the adoption of legislation with an opt-in mechanism, and the adoption of prohibitions found worldwide against dictionary attacks, address harvesting and the like. It also recommended that the government explore creating an antispam commissioner, with a mandate to create a registry of spammers (also known as a spam freezer) which the commissioner would then be able to enforce Internet service providers not to carry (Canada, Task Force on Spam 2005). None of these, or other, recommendations regarding spam have been adopted by the federal government. As a result there are no Canadian restrictions, with the exception of the prohibition of fraud in general, on unsolicited commercial e-mail (Canada, Task Force on Spam 2005).

European Union (EU) Directive

The European Parliament and the Council voted to ban spam. The resulting EU Directive requires that safeguards be provided for subscribers against the intrusion of their privacy by unsolicited communications for direct marketing purposes. The directive specifies in particular automated calling machines, telefaxes, e-mails, and SMS messaging. Since these forms of unsolicited communications are on the one hand relatively easy and cheap to send, and on the other hand, impose a burden and/or cost on the recipient who wishes to avoid such forms of unsolicited communications for direct marketing. The EU concluded that it is justified to require that senders of such communications obtain the explicit consent of the intended recipients before such communications are addressed to them. Therefore, the EU adopted an "opt-in" approach, unlike the approach taken in the United States. An exception is allowed where there is an existing customer relationship. The implementation of the directive varies among states as does the enforcement (Moustakas, Ranganathan, and Duqenoy 2005).

Other International Approaches

Internet crime is a global problem which requires a global solution. Without an international minimum standard spammers simply migrate to the least regulated environments or where enforcement is least effective (Gerard 2005). Progress has been made with a number of multi-lateral agreements to establish common standards and cooperation. For example, the Council of Europe's Treaty of Cybercrime requires parties to:

1. Establish substantive laws against cyber crime

2. Ensure that their law enforcement officials have the necessary procedural authorities to investigate and prosecute cyber crime effectively

3. Provide international cooperation to other parties in the fight against computer-related crime

There are 43 signatories and 15 parties to the Convention—about a third of the world's nations (Huang, Radkowski, and Roman 2007). However, harmonization is not an easy matter as many countries have legislative regimes based on different assumptions. For example, as mentioned above, the United States and EU have opposing opt-out/opt-in approaches.

CHALLENGES TO INVESTIGATION AND PROSECUTION

Classical criminology suggests that the deterrent effect of any legislative regime is dependent less on the severity of the penalties and more on the certainty of apprehension and prosecution. Nowhere is this true than in "white collar crimes" such as fraud (Smith 2004; Wells 2004). Unfortunately there is limited evidence that the existing legislation regime concerning Internet fraud is effectively enforced and while there have been successful prosecutions they are only a small tip of a very large iceberg.

The technical sophistication of the frauds, the ability to conceal identity, and the fact that many Internet frauds involve multiple jurisdictions and the significant costs associated with pursuing them are significant impediments. Law enforcement is often unfamiliar with the technology and many private and commercial enterprises are reluctant to report fraud because of the negative publicity (Huang, Radkowski, and Roman, 2007).

The scale of some of these operations is immense. For example, let us return to the Fortuna Alliance case mentioned above. In 1996, Fortuna Alliance, a business headquartered in the United States, advertised on the Internet an investment opportunity, in which investors could earn as much as $5,000 per month, in perpetuity, after recruiting 300 new investors. The case was essentially a pyramid scheme facilitated by the use of the Internet. After the FTC brought enforcement action against Fortuna Alliance and its principals, the head of the company left the country and transferred nearly $3 million of Fortuna's receipts to offshore bank accounts. Ultimately, the FTC reclaimed $5.5 million from other Fortuna assets to 15,625 victims in 71 countries (United States President's Working Group on Unlawful Conduct on the Internet 2000).

Often cases are not worth the cost of the pursuit. For example, the FTC reported a case of an individual in a Western European country who accessed an online Web site based in Chicago, Illinois, to purchase stereo speakers costing over $2,000. The Web site merchant ran the individual's credit card and received authorization for the transaction and shipped the speakers. Subsequently, the true owner of the credit card disputed the charge, and the merchant had the full amount of the charge deducted from his merchant account. Even if the buyer were identified and apprehended, prosecution of the perpetrator abroad would most likely have been not be worth the expense of trial, particularly if witnesses had to be flown from the U.S., given the relatively low (though significant to the merchant) monetary loss (United States President's Working Group on Unlawful Conduct on the Internet 2000).

Pursuing transnational Internet fraud schemes requires extensive cooperation among agencies and significant resources. Investigators must determine the validity of foreign addresses, the true identities of participants in the scheme, the location and content of banking information, and the location of suspects' assets. In many cases, the authorities can rely on existing mechanisms, such as mutual legal assistance treaties or letters rogatory (a letter of request for assistance from one country's judicial authority to that of another country; see, e.g., 28 U.S.C. § 1782) that can be effectively employed to gather investigative information. However, often perpetrators deliberately locate in jurisdictions where they know it will be more difficult to pursue them. Cooperation among government agencies and law enforcement agencies is critical and being promoted actively through mechanisms such as the "London Action Plan," the product of an antispam enforcement summit jointly hosted by the United Kingdom and the United States. However, some countries which are major producers of spam, such as Russia and China do not participate in such plans (Swartz 2004a).

Other challenges include competing values: there is no consensus on the appropriate balance between the interests of law enforcement versus personal privacy and in many countries the debates about lawful access to electronic information and records continue. Technological and administrative impediments—more than legal ones—are the cause of most difficulties experienced in **cyber crime** investigations and prosecutions, specifically: insufficient basic record keeping by telecommunications and Internet service providers; inability to effect data preservation extraterritorially; inability to circumvent encryption; and, a lack of common data-sharing protocols (Young 2004).

Another challenge to enforcement is the difficulty of proving according to a legal standard that a communication was unsolicited. Due to the insecure nature of the SMTP protocol even records of a double opt-in confirmed subscription can be easy to fake and as a result unreliable as proof. For example, it is possible that an individual might sign in to a list and then claim to be spammed. As a result U.S. legislation does not allow for private legal action in such circumstances. Other concerns about the U.S. spam legislation concern the penalties that, it is argued, are insufficient to act as a real deterrent (Moustakas, Ranganathan, and Duqenoy 2005).

There are limited resources available to pursue investigations and prosecutions and companies, such as PayPal and eBay, have indicated that although they report cases of online fraud to the police, they are often not investigated. In addition, many companies, sensitive to bad publicity, are reluctant to report Internet crime (Espiner 2006). Increasingly, private sector companies are enhancing their capacity to support fraud protection. This is one of the fastest growing areas of private security (Parisi and Grady 2006).

While an enabling legal framework is a fundamental element for the development of e-commerce, there are technical issues as well. In an effort to promote trust in ecommerce among consumers, many companies have developed systems to reduce the chances of Internet fraud. For example eBay has developed a "seller protection plan" that uses its PayPal payment service. PayPal reports that it aims at protecting its sellers against chargebacks due to fraud. Therefore, sellers will not be held liable for chargebacks due to the fraudulent use of credit cards or false claims of nonshipment if the seller follows the rules of the seller protection policy. The rules are complicated but can be followed (Cukier, Nesselroth, and Cody 2007).

As quickly as corporations develop tools to prevent fraud, criminals seem to find ways to get around them. While surveys suggest that financial institutions remain most concerned with types of fraud such as phishing where consumers are duped into giving out sensitive information online (71 percent of institutions surveyed), almost as many (65 percent of institutions surveyed) are concerned or very concerned about technology used to commit fraud, such as malware and Trojan horses (Aite Group LLC Survey, cited in Anonymous 2007). Many of the tools used to perpetrate Internet fraud are also relatively easy to acquire or develop. While the use of technologies to further a fraud scheme would constitute crime (15 U.S.C. § 1644 and 18 U.S.C. § 1029) it is difficult to control access to them. These concerns are driving technology decisions at banks and credit unions which are focusing on ID verification solutions for new accounts as well as stronger user authentication (Aite Group LLC Survey, cited in Anonymous 2007). For example, ensuring that all e-mail systems use authentication technologies so that spammers will not be able to hide the origins of their e-mail would have a significant impact. Although major Internet Service Providers (ISPs) including Yahoo, America Online, Microsoft, and Earthlink support authentication in principle, there is no common approach (Swartz, 2004b).

Work continues worldwide to explore additional measures to reduce Internet fraud. For example, one way to reduce spam would be to increase the cost of spam. Currently most of the costs of spam are born by the recipients rather than the senders. Requiring spammers to pay "e-postage" fees would translate into significant cost. Given the relatively small rate of consumers who respond to spam scams, the economics of many Internet fraud schemes rest on the low costs of mass mailings (Bambauer 2005).

UNDERSTANDING AND PREVENTING VICTIMIZATION

Scholars interested in electronic commerce have begun to examine Internet fraud as a threat to the electronic market place, arguing that "even a small number of deceptive sellers might 'poison' a market driving out good products and eventually consumers" (Grazioli and Jarvenpaa 2003). Empirical consumer research has been applied to the exploration of how consumers detect (or fail to detect) fraud over the Internet and the elements of communication which can trigger the detection of deception (Grazioli and Jarvenpaa 2003). To date criminologists have tended to focus less attention on "white-collar crime," such as consumer fraud, compared to other forms of crime. As a result, criminological understanding of the problem and effective responses is limited (Holtfreter, Van Slyke, and Blomberg 2006). Some frauds, such as spoofing, are extremely sophisticated and complex; others, such as the Nigerian letters, seem obviously ridiculous. Yet the wide reach afforded by the Internet means that even if only a small percentage of recipients respond the gains can be significant. Efforts have been made to better understand how the frauds are perpetrated in order to develop effective **crime prevention** strategies (Rusch 1999).

According to the Theory of Deception, which is based on a model of human cognition, deception exploits systematic weaknesses in our cognitive systems. Internet fraud relies on a range of deceptive tactics including masking, dazzling, decoying, mimicking, inventing, relabeling, and double play, which are intended to undermine our normal defenses (Grazioli and Jarvenpaa 2003). Rusch (1999) notes that Internet fraud employs techniques of persuasion which can overcome normal resistance to deception. For example, often frauds will trigger strong emotional responses in an effort to interfere with the victim's logical thinking. Nigerian letters often attempt to develop empathy and seek to create the impression the sender is sincere, using unsophisticated malapropisms in order to make it less likely that the victim will scrutinize the content of the message.

Rusch (1999) suggests that Internet fraud uses six basic appeals:

- **Authority.**   People are highly likely, in the right situation, to be highly responsive to assertions of authority, even when the person who purports to be in a position of authority is not physically present.

- **Scarcity.**   People are also highly responsive to indications that a particular item they may want is in short supply or available for only a limited period.

- **Liking and similarity.**   Our identification of a person as having characteristics identical or similar to our own—places of birth, or tastes in sports, music, art, or other personal interests, to name a few.

- **Reciprocation.**   A well-recognized rule of social interaction requires that if someone gives us (or promises to give us) something, we feel a strong inclination to reciprocate by providing something in return.

- **Commitment and consistency.**   Society also places great store by consistency in a person's behavior.

- **Social proof.**   In many social situations, one of the mental shortcuts on which we rely, in determining what course of action is most appropriate, is to look to see what other people in the vicinity are doing or saying. Many Internet scams rely on complicated and sophisticated layers of falsehoods (including links to testimonials etc.) in an effort to reassure their victims.

"Target hardening" is a well-established approach to preventing crime. Education can, in some cases, reduce **victimization** or at least displace it. Education can raise awareness of consumers and businesses regarding the tactics used in Internet fraud and reduce their vulnerability. Given the significant costs and difficulties associated with prosecuting Internet fraud, deterrence measures have had limited impact, even though the FTC and other law enforcement agencies have focused on preventing crime by educating consumers through a wide range of campaigns, and major corporations and government agencies such as Microsoft, the FBI, and the Internal Revenue Service (IRS) all offer guidelines on how to spot Internet deception and fraud. One emerging focus of research is designing multi-layered protection strategies (Dinev 2006). See, for example, Table 13-6.

Another dimension to prevention is improving detection. Many consumers are not aware that they have been defrauded, and increased vigilance, for example, double checking credit card statements against receipts, can help identify anomalies. The Federal Bureau of Investigation and National White Collar Crime Center have created an Internet Fraud Complaint Centre to increase reporting (Grazioli and Jarvenpaa 2003).

CONCLUSION

Internet fraud is a significant threat to the growth of legitimate e-commerce and imposes an economic burden on consumers, legitimate business and law enforcement. It takes a variety of forms. While some argue that well-established principles of law, such as those related to fraud and theft can be adapted to cover Internet fraud, others argue that more regulation is needed to protect consumers. As with many other forms of crime, the regulatory systems and tools available to law enforcement have not kept pace with the problem. Although the FTC has demonstrated successes in successfully prosecuting many Internet frauds, the frauds prosecuted are only the tip of the iceberg and many victims of Internet fraud find themselves without effective recourse undermining confidence in e-business.

Effectively combating Internet fraud requires a higher degree of international cooperation than the one that exists presently, on an integrated crime prevention strategy that will address primary prevention, target hardening, and deterrence. Such a strategy would incorporate:

- An effective "antispam" law in all countries
- Cross-border cooperation on enforcement in specific cases
- Self-regulatory solutions by market players, for example on contractual and marketing practices
- Technical solutions to manage or reduce spam, like filtering and other security features
- Greater consumer awareness about, for example, how to minimize spam and how to react to spam and complain (Organization for Economic Cooperation and Development 2004)

Until major e-markets such as the United States, the EU and other jurisdictions increase their cooperation along the lines discussed above we fear that Internet fraud and cyber crime will continue to exact a heavy toll on the confidence and pocketbooks of individuals worldwide.

KEY TERMS

Crime prevention	Phishing
Cyber crime	Spam
Internet fraud	Victimization

Appendix A

Computer Crime Cases

Below is a summary chart of recently prosecuted computer cases in the United States. Many cases have been prosecuted under the computer crime statute, 18 U.S.C. §1030.

Computer Crimes Case Chart: Colloquial Case Name (District) Press Release Date	Interest Harmed: Confid. (C), Integrity (I), Avail. (A)	Estimated Dollar Loss	Target: Private, Public, or Threat to Public Health or Safety	Perpetrator Charged: Juvenile	Group	Geography: International	Sentence in Months	Fine, Forfeiture, Restitution	Notes
U.S. v. Arabo (D.N.J.) August 25, 2006	CIA	504K	Private				30	504K	
U.S. v. Kwak (D.D.C.) May 12, 2006	C		Public				5	40K	
U.S. v. Ancheta (C.D. Cal.) May 8, 2006	IA		Public				57	75K	First U.S. "botnet" prosecution
U.S. v. Maxwell (W.D. Wash) May 4, 2006	CIA	252K	Threat to public health or safety				TBD	TBD	"Botnet" case
U.S. v. McCarty (C.D. Cal.) April 20, 2006	CIA		Private				TBD	TBD	
U.S. v. Levine (E.D. Ark) February 22, 2006	C		Private				96		Massive data theft

(continued)

Computer Crimes Case Chart: Colloquial Case Name (District) Press Release Date	Interest Harmed: Confid. (C), Integrity (I), Avail. (A)	Estimated Dollar Loss	Target: Private, Public, or Threat to Public Health or Safety	Perpetrator Charged		Geography: International	Punishment		Notes
				Juvenile	Group		Sentence in Months	Fine, Forfeiture, Restitution	
U.S. v. Flury (N.D. Ohio) February 18, 2006	C	384K	Private		✓		32	300K	Online trafficking: id theft, credit **and** debit cards, and bank fraud
U.S. v. Li (D. Utah) February 17, 2006	CI		Private				TBD	TBD	Student
U.S. v. Fisher (D. Utah) February 15, 2006	CIA		Private				TBD	TBD	Former employee
U.S. v. Benimeli (N.D. Ohio) July 13, 2006	CIA		Private				TBD	TBD	Former employee; indictment
U.S. v. Ancheta (C.D. Cal.) January 23, 2006	IA		Public				TBD	TBD	First U.S. "botnet" case prosecution

Case	Code	Amount	Sector					Notes
U.S. v. Miller (S.D. Ohio) January 19, 2006	C		Private			TBD	TBD	
U.S. v. Clark (N.D. Cal.) December 28, 2005	CIA		Private	✓		TBD	TBD	"Botnet" case
U.S. v. Zhang (N.D. Cal.) December 22, 2005	C		Private			TBD	TBD	Economic Espionage Act Case
U.S. v. Kwong (E.D. TX) November 21, 2005	CIA	600K	Private		Yes	TBD	TBD	
U.S. v. Mantovani (D. N.J.) November 17, 2005	C	4M	Private	✓	Yes	TBD	TBD	Online trafficking: id theft, credit and debit cards
U.S. v. Hatten (S.D. TX) November 1, 2005	C		Private			TBD	TBD	
U.S. v. An Unnamed Junveile II (D. Mass.) September 8, 2005	CIA	1M	Public, private			11 (juvenile detention)	TBD	
U.S. v. Shea (N.D. Cal.) September 8, 2005	IA	100K	Private	✓		12 mos.	TBD	
U.S. v. Perez et al. (S.D. Cal.) August 26, 2005	CIA		Private	✓		TBD	TBD	

(continued)

Computer Crimes Case Chart: Colloquial Case Name (District) Press Release Date	Interest Harmed: Confid. (C), Integrity (I), Avail. (A)	Estimated Dollar Loss	Target: Private, Public, or Threat to Public Health or Safety	Perpetrator Charged		Geography: International	Punishment		Notes
				Juvenile	Group		Sentence in Months	Fine, Forfeiture, Restitution	
U.S. v. Levine (E.D. Ark.) August 12, 2005	C		Private				TBD	TBD	
U.S. v. Carlson (E.D. Pa.) July 14, 2005	CA		Private				48		
U.S. v. Meydbray (N.D. Cal.) June 8, 2005	CIA	5K	Private				TBD	TBD	Former employee
U.S. v. Chavet (N.D. Cal.) May 9, 2005	CI		Private				TBD	TBD	
U.S. v. Heckenkamp (N.D. Cal.) April 25, 2005	C	5K	Private				8	268K	
U.S. v. Lyttle (N.D. Cal.) March 11, 2005	CI	70K	Public				TBD	TBD	Member of hacking group "The Deceptive Duo"

Case								
U.S. v. Jiang (S.D. N.Y.) February 28, 2005	CI		Private			27	201K	Also plead to software piracy
U.S. v. Jacobsen (C.D. Cal.) February 15, 2005	CI	5K	Private			TBD	TBD	
U.S. v. An Unnamed Juvenile (W.D. Wash.) February 11, 2005	IA		Private	✓		18		Created RPCSD-BOT variant of "Blaster" worm
U.S. v. Parson (W.D. Wash.) January 28, 2005	CIA		Private		Yes	18	TBD	
U.S. v. Salcedo et al. (W.D. N.C.) December 15, 2004	CI		Private	✓	Yes	108	0	
U.S. v. Mantovani et al. (D. N.J.) October 28, 2004	C	4M	Private	✓	Yes	TBD	TBD	Online trafficking: id theft, credit and debit cards

United States Department of Justice, Computer Crime and Intellectual Property Section, Computer Crime Cases, http://www.usdoj.gov/criminal/cybercrime/cccases.html, accessed January 20, 2007.

REFERENCES

Albert, M. R. 2002. E-buyer beware: Why online auction fraud should be regulated. *American Business Law Journal* 39 (4): 575.

Anonymous. 2007. Fraudsters are starting to score successes against online banking. *Digital Transactions*. http://www.digitaltransactions.net/newsstory.cfm?newsid=1309, accessed July 15, 2007.

Anti-Phishing Working Group. 2007. http://www.antiphishing.org, accessed January 14, 2007.

Bainbridge, D. 2000. *Introduction to Computer Law*. 4th ed. Harlow: Pearson.

Bambauer, D. 2005. Solving the inbox paradox: An information-based policy approach to unsolicited e-mail advertising. *Virginia Journal of Law & Technology* 10 (5).

Broadhurst, R. 2005. Developments in the global law enforcement of cyber-crime. *Policing: An International Journal of Police Strategies and Management* 29 (3): 408.

Byrne, J. 1998. Squeezing spam off the Net: Federal regulation of unsolicited commercial e-mail. *Journal of Law and Technology*. http://www.wvu.edu/~law/wvjolt/Arch/Byrne/Byrne.htm, accessed September 20, 2006.

Canada, Task Force on Spam. 2005. Stopping spam: Creating a stronger, safer internet report of the task force on spam. http://strategis.ic.gc.ca/epic/internet/inecic-ceac.nsf/en/h_gv00317e.html, accessed January 14, 2007.

Cerf, V. G. 2005. Spam, spim and spit. *Communications of the ACM* 48 (4): 39.

Chhabra, S. 2005. Fighting spam, phishing and email fraud. Unpublished Masters Thesis, University of California, Riverside.

Cukier, W., E. Nesselroth, and S. Cody. 2006. Genres of spam: Expectations and deceptions, Lihue, HICCS.

Cukier, W., E. Nesselroth, and S. Cody. 2007. The Nigerian Letter, Hilo, HICCS.

Delaney, E. M., C. Goldstein, J. Gutterman, and S. Wagner. 2003. Proposed legislation targets unsolicited commercial email. *Intellectual Property & Technology Law Journal* 15 (8).

Dinev, T. October 2006. Why spoofing is serious Internet fraud. *Communications of the ACM* 49 (10): 77.

Edelson, E. 2003. The 419 scam: Information warfare on the spam front and a proposal for local filtering. *Computers and Security* 22 (5): 392.

Espiner, T. 2006. UK failing to fight Internet fraudsters. http://news.zdnet.co.uk/security/0,1000000189,39279915,00.htm?r=1, accessed July 15, 2007.

Fishman, R., K. Josephberg, J. Linn, and J. Pollack. 2002. FTC announces international Internet fraud efforts. *Intellectual Property & Technology Law Journal* 14 (7): 32.

Gerard, P. 2005. Co-operating internationally against spam. Proceedings from ASEM, London 4th Conference on eCommerce Tackling Spam, London, England.

Grazioli, S., and S. L. Jarvenpaa. 2003. Deceived; Under target online. *Communications of the ACM* 46 (12): 196.

Holtfreter, K., S. Van Slyke, and T. G. Blomberg. 2006. Sociolegal change in consumer fraud: From victim-offender interactions to global networks. *Crime, Law and Social Change* 44 (3): 251.

Huang, X., P. Radkowski, and P. Roman. 2007. Computer crimes. *The American Criminal Law Review* 44 (2): 285.

Kouri, J. 2006. Largest Internet fraud case in US history exposed. Axcess News. http://www.axcessnews.com/modules/wfsection/article.php?articleid=12377, accessed December 16, 2006.

Krammer, V. 2006. Phishing defense against IDN address spoofing attacks. *Privacy, Security, Trust Annual Proceedings*: 275–84.

Loza, E. 2001. Internet fraud: Federal trade commission prosecutions of online conduct. *Communications and the Law* 23 (2): 55.

McQuillen, W. 2003. States, feds target online-auction fraud. *Seattle Times, Business & Technology*. http://archives.seattletimes.nwsource.com/cgi-bin/texis.cgi/web/vortex/display?slug=netfraud010&date=20030501&query=software, accessed January 14, 2007.

Moustakas, E., C. Ranganathan, and P. Duqenoy. 2005. Combating spam through legislation: A comparative analysis of US and European approaches. Proceedings from CEAS, Second International Conference on Email and Anti-Spam. Stanford University, Stanford, California.

Organization for Economic Cooperation and Development. November, 2005. Anti-spam regulation. http://www.oecd.org/dataoecd/29/12/35670414.pdf

Parisi, F., and M. F. Grady. 2006. *The Law and Economics of Cybersecurity*. Cambridge University Press.

Rusch, J. J. 1999. The 'social engineering' of Internet fraud. Proceedings from INET99, The Internet Global Summit. San Jose, CA.

Smith, R. G. 2004. Understanding tertiary crime prevention in controlling fraud: The effectiveness of criminal justice system responses. Australian Fraud Summit 2004, Sydney, March 30, 2004.

Swartz, N. 2003. The international war on spam. *Information Management Journal* 37 (5): 18.

Swartz, N. 2004a. The worldwide war on spam continues. *Information Management Journal* 38 (2): 16.

Swartz, N. 2004b. What spam law? Next up . . . spim. *Information Management Journal* 38 (3): 12.

Tillman, B. 2002. Spamming gets a closer look. *Information Management Journal* 36 (2): 10.

Treese, W. 2004. The state of security on the Internet. *ACM Guide to Computing Literature* 8 (3): 15.

United States Department of Justice. 2007. Computer Crime and Intellectual Property Section, Computer Crime Cases. http://www.usdoj.gov/criminal/cybercrime/cccases.html, accessed January 20, 2007.

United States Federal Trade Commission. 2003. False claims in spam. A Report by the FTC's Division of Marketing Practices. http://www.ftc.gov/reports/spam/030429spamreport.pdf, accessed January 14, 2007.

United States Federal Trade Commission. 2006. *Consumer Fraud and Identify Theft Complaint Data: January-December 2005*. Washington, DC: Federal Trade Commission, http://www.usdoj.gov, accessed January 14, 2007.

United States President's Working Group on Unlawful Conduct on the Internet. 2000. The electronic frontier: The challenge of unlawful conduct involving the use of the Internet. http://www.usdoj.gov/criminal/cybercrime/unlawful.htm, accessed January 14, 2007.

United States Secret Service. n.d. Public awareness advisory regarding '4-1-9' or 'advance fee fraud.' http://www.dced.state.ak.us/bsc/pub/publicawareness.pdf, accessed January 14, 2007.

Wells, J. February 2004. The fraud beat: It's time to take a new look at the auditing process. *Journal of Accountancy*.

Wingfield, N. 2004. Cat and mouse problem for cops on ebay beat: Crooks keep getting smarter. *Wall Street Journal*. http://wsjclassroomedition.com/archive/05feb/related_05feb_online_ebay.htm, accessed July 5, 2007.

Young, J. 2004. Surfing while Muslim: Privacy, freedom of expression and the unintended consequences of cybercrime legislation. *Yale Journal of Law & Technology* 7.

Zeltsan, Z. 2004. General overview of spam and technical measures to mitigate the problem. ITU-T SG 17 Interim Rapporteur Meeting. http://strategis.ic.gc.ca/app/sitt/spamforum/servlet/JiveServlet/download/2-282-983-70/ITU-%20SG17-Interim%20Rapporteur-Spam.ppt, accessed January 14, 2007.

PART III

Criminological Perspectives on Cyber Crime

Chapter 14

Space Transition Theory of Cyber Crimes

K. Jaishankar
Manonmaniam Sundaranar University, India

Dr. K. Jaishankar is a lecturer in the Department of Criminology and Criminal Justice, Manonmaniam Sundaranar University, Tirunelveli, India. He is the founding editor-in-chief of the *International Journal of Cyber Criminology* and the founding editor of *Crime and Justice Perspective*—the official organ of the Criminal Justice Forum (CJF), India, and the founding managing editor of the *International Journal of Criminal Justice Sciences*. He serves in the international editorial boards of *Journal of Social Change* (U.S.), *Electronic Journal of Sociology* (Canada), *Crime, Punishment and Law: An International Journal* (U.S.), *Journal of Physical Security* (U.S.), and *Graduate Journal of Social Science* (UK). He is the National Focal point for India for the International Police Executive Symposium's working paper series and expert of world police database at www.coginta.com. He is a co-investigator of the international project on cyber bullying funded by SSHRC, Canada, involving eight countries, along with the principal investigator Dr. Shaheen Shariff, McGill University. He is a pioneer in developing the new field "cyber criminology," and is the proponent of *Space Transition Theory*, which gives an explanation for the criminal behavior in cyberspace. He is a recognized expert in the field of cyber criminology and invited by various universities in United States to deliver lectures on his space transition theory of cyber crimes. He is a member of the UNODC (United Nations Office on Drugs and Crime) Core group of experts on identity-related crime. His areas of academic competence are cyber criminology, crime mapping, GIS, communal violence, victimology, policing, and crime prevention.

Abstract

Some researchers have tried to explain cyber crimes with traditional theories such as social learning theory (Skinner and Fream 1997; Rogers 1999, 2001), Kohlberg's moral development theory and differential reinforcement theory (Rogers 2001), Cohen's strain theory (O'Connor 2003), deindividuation theory (Demetriou and Silke 2003), Gottfredson and Hirschi's general theory of crime (Foster 2004), routine activities theory (Adamski 1998; McKenzie 2000; Grabosky 2001; Pease 2001; Yar 2005a) and multiple theories (McQuade 2005; Taylor et al. 2005; Walker, Brock, and Stuart 2006). However, those theoretical justifications have proved to be inadequate as an overall explanation for the phenomenon of cyber

The author wish to express his profound gratitude to Professors Susan Brenner, Eric Suler, Keith Harries, and Eric Lambert for reviewing this chapter on request and for their wise comments and constructive criticisms which enabled to improve the quality of this chapter. The author also sincerely thanks Prof. Dipika Halder for editing and proofreading the theoretical propositions.

crimes. To fill the gap in explaining cyber crimes, the space transition theory has been developed. This theory is presented and discussed in this chapter.

INTRODUCTION

The **Internet** has become a powerful force in today's world (Burney 2001). The access of the Internet into the everyday lives of millions of population across the world has begun to transform many different aspects of life. Some of the transformations have occurred because of the manner in which Internet users are directed to negotiate their relationship with the real and virtual spaces they now inhabit (Mitra and Schwartz 2001). In the past five years, the number of Internet users has skyrocketed from 0.5 million to 6.5 million—a 13-fold increase. In the process, an entirely new universe has been created—the world of **cyberspace**. Cyberspace is a virtual space that has become as prominent as real space for business, politics, and communities.

The term cyberspace is sometimes treated as a synonym for the Internet, but is actually a broader concept. The term cyberspace emphasizes that it can be treated as a place (Byassee 1995). The word cyberspace (a portmanteau of cybernetics and space) was coined by William Gibson, a Canadian science fiction writer, when he sought a term to explain his vision of a global computer network, linking all people, machines, and sources of information in the world, and through which one could move or navigate as through a virtual space (Heylighen 1994), in 1982 in his novelette *Burning Chrome* in *Omni* magazine and was subsequently popularized in his novel *Neuromancer*.

In the early 1980s, Gibson observed young players in video game parlors and extrapolated a future of communication and control through game-like globally linked graphical computer systems. His space is "consensually hallucinated," not real (a "nonspace of the mind"), but effective and dominant (Aarseth 1998). In his novel *Neuromancer* (1984), Gibson invented the notion of cyberspace as a computer-available location where all the existing information in the world was collected. Later, John Perry Barlow described the real world of connected computers using exactly the same term as Gibson used. In 1990, Barlow first applied the science-fiction term cyberspace to the Internet (or precisely, as Barlow states on his Web site, to the "already-existing global electronic social space now in most instances referred to by that name"). Until his citing it, it had not been considered any sort of place (Barlow 1991). Some claim, therefore, that cyberspace, as it exists today, should be called "Barlovian cyberspace" in order to distinguish it from the fictional "Gibsonian cyberspace" of cyberpunk literature (Jordan 1999). In this chapter, the concept of cyberspace means the global aggregate of digital, interactive, electronic communication networks; cyberspace thus includes the constituent networks comprising the global inter-network (the "Internet") as well as the Internet itself as a separate, emergent phenomenon.

Suler (2005) has accentuated that the term cyberspace has been hackneyed and overly commercialized. He explains that the experience created by computers and computer networks can in many ways be understood as a psychological "space." Many users who have connected to a remote computer or explored World Wide Web will describe the experience as "travelling" or "going someplace." On an even deeper psychological level, users often describe how their computer is an extension of their mind and personality—a "space" that reflects their tastes, attitudes, and interests. In psychoanalytic terms, computers and cyberspace may become a type of transitional space that is an extension of the individual's intrapsychic world. It may be experienced as an intermediate zone between self and other that is part self and part other (Suler 2005).

Mitra (2003) has clearly examined the two significant differences between the physical space and cyberspace, as well as brought out a new space that he calls as "cybernetic space," which is an intersecting space of physical and cyber (Mitra and Schwartz 2001). The first difference between the physical space and cyberspace is that cyberspace defies boundaries. The second component of the cyberspace is its discursive nature which suggests that experience of space moves away from the realm of the sensory to an interpretation of texts, images, and sounds. Simply put, it is not possible to "touch" the virtual but it is only possible to "read" the virtual. Cyberspace, within a modernistic epistemology, does not exist, but can only be interpreted (Tyner 1998; Mitra 2003). Brenner (2004a) has provided another two important differences between the cyberspace and the real space, that is, absences of physical constraints and lack of hierarchical constraints. Lessig (1998) brings the very important difference between physical space and cyberspace, anonymity. Menthe (1998) argued that, for jurisdictional analysis, cyberspace should be treated as a fourth international space along with other three international spaces, Antarctica, outer space, and the high seas. However, these three physical spaces are nothing at all like cyberspace, which is a nonphysical space (Menthe 1998; Mann and Sutton 1998) and is perfectly different from physical space (Lessig 1998).

The cyberspace presents an environment in which both healthy and pathological behaviors may be pursued (Suler 1999, 2004; Suler and Phillips 1998). Joinson (1998, 2003), in a thoughtful review, examined how modern electronic tools have valuable, positive aspects for people's advancement and success, as well as destructive, negative aspects that humiliate, terrorize, and block social progress. Cyberspace at the new millennium resembles the frontier at the beginning of the eighteenth century: bullies and criminals swagger electronically through the commons, stealing what they want, breaking what they don't, and interfering with people's activities (Kabay 2005).

In the present chapter, an effort is made to construct a theory that explains the criminal behavior in the cyberspace. This chapter is structured in the following way. Firstly, a brief description of the criminal behavior of cyberspace is provided that includes **cyber crime** definition, typology of cyber crime, definition and typology of cyber criminal, and the differences between the crimes of physical space and cyberspace. Secondly, the need for a new theory for the criminal behavior in cyberspace is emphasized. Thirdly, the *space transition theory* of *cyber crime* is established and, discussed.

CRIMINAL BEHAVIOR IN CYBERSPACE

The vast majority of people in our society are productive, law-abiding citizens, including when they are on the Internet (Danda 2001). Many users of cyberspace are well behaved. They are sensitive to nuance, capable of expressive and articulate prose, careful not to hurt feelings, and responsible in spreading verified information and not rumor. But you can always find a fraction of people in society who act inappropriately, break the law, or otherwise use illicit means to take advantage of others. Many of the dangers, threats, and annoyances that plague society in general can also be found on the Internet. The users of cyberspace display a varied set of behaviors. Some are business competitors or bargain-seeking consumers who are not above stealing intellectual property or services. Others set loose viruses and other malicious code or they deface Web sites or destroy data files. Still others are criminals who use the Internet to perpetrate fraud, theft, and extortion. Terrorists, noting the increasing dependence of many societies on the Internet, may use it as a target or channel for the expression of their views, or to harass, coerce, or destroy social institutions (Lukasik 2001). We also find the cyberspace equivalents of slum lords, drug pushers, boors, and bully boys. There are people running private Web sites and blogs that cater to thieves, drug users, terrorists (e.g., Al-Qaeda) (Coll and Glasser 2005), and pedophiles (Kabay 2005).

Cyber Crime: Definition and Conceptualization

A primary problem for the analysis of cyber crime is the absence of a consistent and statutory definition for it (PJCACC 2004; Yar 2005a) and also defining cyber crime raises conceptual complexities (Smith, Grabosky, and Urbas 2004). Varied definitions of cyber crime are available in the literature. Like varied definitions, cyber crimes is also called by variety of terms such as computer crime, computer-related crime, digital crime, information technology crime (Matt 2004), Internet crime (Wall 2001), virtual crime (Lastowka and Hunter 2004), e-crime (AIC 2006) and netcrime (Mann and Sutton 1998). Cyber crime could reasonably include a wide variety of criminal offenses and activities.

The Oxford Reference Online defines cyber crime as "crime committed over the Internet." The scope of this definition becomes wider with a frequent companion or substitute term "computer-related crime." Some writers are also of the opinion that "computer crime" refers to computer-related activities that are either criminal in the legal sense of the word or just antisocial behavior where there is no breach of the law (Lee 1995). Examples of activities that are considered computer-related crime can be found in the United Nations Manual on the Prevention and Control of Computer-Related Crime (1997). The manual includes fraud, forgery, computer sabotage, unauthorized access, and copying of computer programs as examples of computer crime.

At the Tenth United Nations Congress on the Prevention of Crime and Treatment of Offenders, in a workshop devoted to the issues of crimes related to computer networks, cyber crime was broken into two categories and defined thus: (a) *Cyber crime in a narrow sense*: any illegal behavior directed by means of electronic operations that targets the security of computers systems and the data processed by them; (b) *Cyber crime in a broader sense*: any illegal behavior committed by means of, or in relation to, a computer system or network, including such crimes as illegal possession and offering or disturbing information by means of a computer system or network.

Also in the Council of Europe's Convention on Cybercrime (2001), cyber crime is used as an umbrella term to refer to an array of criminal activity including offenses against computer data and systems, computer-related offenses, content offenses, and copyright offenses (AIC 2006). The convention covers cyber crimes in four main categories: (1) offenses against the confidentiality, integrity, and availability of computer data and systems; (2) computer-related offenses; (3) content-related offenses (e.g., child pornography); and (4) offenses related to infringements of copyright and related rights. A working definition along these lines is offered by Thomas and Loader (2000), who conceptualized cyber crime as those "computer-mediated activities which are either illegal or considered illicit by certain parties and which can be conducted through global electronic networks." The working definition for cyber crime offered by the Canadian Police College has increasingly been accepted by Canadian law enforcement agencies: "a criminal offence involving a computer as the object of the crime, or the tool used to commit a material component of the offence" (Statistics

Canada 2002). Matt (2004) proposed a definition for cyber crime: "Cybercrime encompasses all illegal activities where the computer, computer system, information network or data is the target of the crime and those known illegal activities or crimes that are actively committed through or with the aid of computers, computer systems, information networks or data." It is significant to note that there is no consistent and statutory definition for cyber crime.

Apart from the issues of definition of cyber crime, the usage of the term cyber crime in varying contexts is also debated. Smith, Grabosky, and Urbas (2004) have argued that a distinction should be made between the two contexts when the term cyber crime is used: (i) a singular concept of crime that could encompass new criminal offenses perpetrated in new ways and (ii) a descriptive term for a type of crime involving conventional crimes perpetrated using new technologies. Smith, Grabosky, and Urbas (2004) have preferred to use the term cyber crime to encompass any proscribed conduct perpetrated through the use of, or against, digital technologies. The same context will be employed in this chapter as well.

Classification and Typology of Cyber Crimes

According to many research sources (Carter 1995; Davis and Hutchison 1997; Goodman and Brenner 2002; Deflem and Shutt 2006), there are two broad categories of cyber crime. The first category is defined where the computer is the tool of the crime. This category includes crimes that law enforcement has been fighting in the physical world but is now seen with increasing frequency on the Internet. Some of these crimes include child pornography, criminal harassment, fraud, intellectual property violations, and the sale of illegal substances and goods. The second category is defined where the computer is the target of the crime by means of attacks on network confidentiality, integrity, and availability (Statistics Canada 2002).

Adamski (1998) classified computer crimes or cyber crimes as one of two categories: (i) crimes geared specifically to the network and the related data-processing systems (i.e., offenses against computer and information security) and (ii) crimes for which computer networks provide a new opportunity for the commission of traditional offenses (such as fraud, industrial espionage, and child pornography). The Council of Europe's Convention on Cybercrime (2001), covered cyber crimes in four main categories: (1) offenses against the confidentiality, integrity, and availability of computer data and systems; (2) computer-related offenses; (3) content-related offenses (e.g., child pornography); and (4) offenses related to infringements of copyright and related rights (Aldesco 2002).

The above classification of cyber crimes is more oriented toward technology and less toward criminology. The classification evolved by Wall (2001) and Smith, Grabosky, and Urbas (2004) is more pertinent in the criminological parlance. Wall (2001) has divided cyber crime into four categories:

1. **Cyber trespass**—crossing boundaries into other people's property and/or causing damage, e.g., hacking, defacement, and viruses.

2. **Cyber deceptions and thefts**—stealing (money, property), such as credit card fraud or intellectual property violations (a.k.a. piracy).

3. **Cyber pornography**—activities that breach laws on obscenity and indecency.

4. **Cyber violence**—bringing psychological harm to or inciting physical harm against others, thereby breaching laws pertaining to the protection of the person, such as hate speech or stalking.

Yar (2005a) agreed that Wall's (2001) classification is helpful in relating cyber crime to existing conceptions of proscribed and harmful acts and has criminological utility. Smith, Grabosky, and Urbas (2004) classified cyber crime as that:

- involving the use of digital technologies in the *commission of the offence,*
- *directed* at computing and communications technologies themselves, or
- *incidental* to the commission of other crimes.

Within the first category are cases involving dissemination of offensive material electronically, online fraud and financial crime, electronic manipulation of share markets, and the dissemination of misleading advertizing information. Also included are traditional crimes such as fraud or deception in which the involvement of computers constitutes a statutory aggravating element, such as unauthorized access to computers and computer networks, crimes involving vandalism and invasion of personal space, and denial-of-service attacks, and theft of telecommunications and Internet services. The third category involves conduct that has been described as computer-supported crime (Kowalski 2002, 6), such as the use of encryption (i.e., the translation of data into secret code) or steganography (i.e., in which information is embedded within other, seemingly harmless data such as pictures) to conceal communications or information from law enforcement. It also includes the use of electronic databases to store and organize information concerning proposed or completed criminal activities (Smith, Grabosky, and Urbas 2004).

In a study of 30 countries with statutory laws against cyber crimes, Drozdova et al. (1999) identified seven types of cyber crimes : (1) unauthorized access; (2) illicit tampering with files or data (e.g., unauthorized copying, modification, or destruction); (3) computer or network sabotage (e.g., viruses, worms, Trojan horses, denial of service attacks); (4) use of information systems to commit or advance "traditional" crimes (e.g., fraud, forgery, money laundering, acts of terrorism); (5) computer-mediated espionage; (6) violations against privacy in the acquisition or use of personal data; (7) theft or damage of computer hardware or software. These seven acts were referred as "consensus crimes" (Drozdova et al. 1999; Putnam and Elliot 1999), because of the availability of laws related to cyber crimes in the 30 countries studied. Graycar (2000) first brought out nine types of cyber crimes, and later Grabosky (2000) developed it to 11 types. Grabosky's (2000) 11 types of cyber crimes are: theft of services; communications in furtherance of criminal conspiracies; information piracy and forgery; the dissemination of offensive materials; cyberstalking; extortion; electronic money laundering; electronic vandalism and terrorism; sales and investment fraud; illegal interception; and electronic funds transfer fraud.

Definition and Types of Cyber Criminals

Cyber criminals come in all forms, from the street drug dealer to the identity theft mastermind. Cyber criminals can range from teenagers who vandalize Web sites to terrorists who target a nation. History has shown that cyber crime is committed by a broad range of persons: students, amateurs, terrorists, and members of organized crime groups. Unlike traditional crimes, the perpetrators of cyber crimes are more likely to have more affluent socioeconomic backgrounds (Williams 2005). Kelly (2001) defined cyber criminal as "someone whose knowledge and use of computers and/or the Internet has enabled him or her to commit the crime of choice." This definition covers everyone from the first-time offender to chronic whose cyber crime activities span more than a decade (Kelly 2001).

Cyber criminal behavior cuts across a wide spectrum of society, with the age of offenders ranging from 10 to 60 years and their skill level ranging from novice to professional. Cyber criminals, therefore, are often otherwise average persons rather than super criminals possessing unique abilities and talents. Any person of any age with a modicum of skill, motivated by the technical challenge, by the potential for gain, notoriety or revenge, or by the promotion of ideological beliefs, is a potential cyber criminal (UN Manual 1997). Almost any technically/analytically oriented person has the potential to become a computer criminal. Indeed, even technically unsophisticated individuals are capable of such acts given sufficient motivation and opportunity (Morrison 1990). The typical skill level of the computer criminal is a topic of controversy. Some claim that skill level is not an indicator of a cyber criminal (see, for example, Mann and Sutton 1998), while others claim that potential cyber criminals are bright, eager, highly motivated subjects willing to accept a technological challenge (Kishore et al. 2005). They argue that it may be easier than ever to use the Net, send e-mail, etc., but to get unauthorized access into another network or someone else's computer requires much more knowledge (Kishore et al. 2005).

The types of cyber criminals have changed since the late 1980s and 1990s, when computer crimes primarily related to the infiltration of large computer systems by hackers (Berwick 1999). Commercial crime offenders joined the hacker problem in the early 1990s. With the public adoption of the Internet, beginning in 1995, the extent and nature of computer-based offenses have changed fundamentally and irreversibly (Berwick 1999). Considerable work has been done to define cyber criminals (ACPR 2000). For example, the FBI has defined three types of cyber criminals linked to the outcome of their criminal activities (Icove 1998):

- **crackers** (generally young offenders who seek intellectual stimulation from committing computer crimes)

- **criminals** (often adults subgrouped into those who commit fraud or damage systems and those who undertake espionage)

- **vandals** (usually not pursuing intellectual stimulation; motivation often rooted in revenge for some real or imagined wrong)

A typology for cyber criminals was developed by Kishore et al. (2005), who designed a Web site on cyber crimes to create awareness of cyber crimes among the public. They classified five types of cyber criminals as:

- *White-collar criminals* (which were further classified as vengeful criminals, patient criminals, and desperate criminals). Dumped lovers or spouses, retrenched employees, businessmen who feel cheated or ripped off, etc. belong to the category of vengeful criminals.

- *Hackers.* Teenagers characteristically belong in this group.

- *Crackers.* This term generally refers to people who infringe copyrights for the benefit of those refuse to pay for copyrighted materials, such a software and music.

- *Psycho-criminals.* Pedophiles, cyberstalkers, and fanatic cyber terrorists belong to this category.

- *Con artists.* They are perhaps the most cunning and deceitful type of cyber criminals. They are like chameleons, being able to mould their personality and behavior as and when they like, to cheat their unsuspecting victims of their money. However, not all con artists are in this game for monitory gains alone.

Crimes in Physical Space versus Crimes in Cyberspace

Burney (2001) tried to analogize crimes of physical space and cyberspace. The analogy was of burglary of physical space and hacking of cyberspace. He concludes that it is appropriate to analogize crimes in physical space and cyberspace. He warned that we must proceed with extreme caution to make sure that the analogy is complete and successful. However, his analogy is limited for two reasons. One, hacking is only one form of crime of cyberspace and two, the analogy of crimes of physical space and cyberspace can never be complete and successful, as properties of both the spaces are entirely different. Apart from Burney (2001), few authors have tried to analogize crimes of physical space with crimes in cyberspace (Brenner 2001, 2002a, 2004b; Wall 2004; Williams 2005; Deflem and Shutt 2006). Of these analyses, Brenner's analysis stands distinctively apart. She has meticulously analyzed the differences between the cyber crimes and crimes in real space. She has brought out significant characteristics of cyber crimes to differentiate it with crimes in physical space.

The characteristics developed by Brenner (2001, 2002a, 2004a, b) are:

- *Transnational nature and jurisdictional issues.* "Cybercriminals can defy the conventional jurisdictional realms of sovereign nations, originating an attack from almost any computer in the world, passing it across multiple national boundaries, or designing attacks that appear to be originating from foreign sources" (Brenner 2004a; McConnell International 2000).

- *Physical constraints.* "The constraints that govern action in the real, physical world do not restrict the perpetrators of cybercrime. Cybercrimes can be committed instantaneously and therefore require a rapid response; law enforcement, however, is accustomed to dealing with real-world "crimes," the investigation of which proceeds at a more deliberate pace" (Brenner 2004b).

- *Proximity.* "Unlike real-world "crime," cyber crime does not require any degree of physical proximity between the victim and the victimizer at the moment the "crime" is committed" (Brenner 2004a). It can be committed against a victim who is in another city, another state, or another country (European Commission 2001).

- *Scale and multiple victimization.* Cyber crime is different because it is automated crime. Whereas a nineteenth-century fraudster would have to defraud victim A, then victim B, then victim C, and so on, an early twenty-first-century cyber fraudster can automate the process, defrauding many victims simultaneously and with essentially the same effort. "Automated crime" is using technology to multiply the number of "crimes" someone can commit in a given period of time (Parker 1999, 2002; Arena 2001); automation gives perpetrators the ability to commit many cyber crimes very quickly (IPWatchdog.com 2003).

- *Conduct at issue may not be illegal.* "Another characteristic of cybercrime is that the conduct at issue may not be illegal" (Brenner 2001). In May 2000, the "Love Bug" virus raced around the world in two hours and caused billions of dollars of damage in over 20 countries. It was quickly traced to the Philippines, where FBI agents and local authorities identified a suspect. But since Philippines law did not criminalize virus dissemination, it took days to get a warrant to search his apartment, giving him time to destroy evidence. Then there was the problem of prosecution. The perpetrator could not be charged locally because virus dissemination was not a crime in the Philippines; since virus dissemination was not a local crime, he could not be extradited for prosecution in the United States, where it was a crime.

Extradition treaties require "double criminality" (i.e., require that conduct be a crime in the jurisdiction where it was committed as well as in the jurisdiction seeking to extradite an offender). So, the "Love Bug" virus affected millions of computer users in more than 20 countries, causing billions of dollars in damage, but no one was ever prosecuted for disseminating it (Brenner 2004a).

- *Perfect anonymity.* Cyberspace also lets perpetrators conceal or disguise their identities in a way that is not possible in the real world (Brenner 2002a; Post 1996). In the real world, an offender can wear a mask and perhaps take other efforts to conceal his identity, but certain characteristics—such as height, weight, accent, and age—will still be apparent. In cyberspace, one can achieve perfect anonymity or perfect pseudonymity; a man can be a woman, a woman can be a man, a child can be an adult, a foreigner can pass for a native, all of which makes the apprehension of cyber criminals difficult (Lessig 1998; Brenner 2004a).

- *Velocity.* "Velocity is an important characteristic of cybercrime" (Brenner 2002a). The Love Bug virus spread around the world in two hours, hitting tens of thousands of users. On the first night of the Love Bug, ABC TV news described it as a hyper-speed crime wave. Velocity raises a big challenge in security.

Even though some researchers feel cyber crimes as a case of "old wine in new bottles" (Grabosky 2001), "old wine in bottles of varying and fluid shape" (Yar 2005a), or "new wine in no bottles" (Wall 1999), cyber crimes are still different from the crimes of physical space. There exists a fine line of demarcation between the crimes of physical space and crimes of cyberspace. The demarcation lies in the involvement of the virtual cyber medium (Pati 2003), lack of geographical boundaries (Hafner and Markoff 1995; Mitra 1999), and their occurrence in a diffuse, fluid, evolving (Brenner 2004b) and spatiotemporally disorganized environment (primarily the collapse of spatial–temporal barriers, many-to-many connectivity, and the anonymity and plasticity of online identity) (Yar 2005a; Williams 2005). Yar (2005a) ascertains after analyzing cyber crime with routine activities theory that cyber crime is a new and distinctive form of crime. Cyber crime is an entirely new form of crime.

THE NEED FOR A THEORY EXPLAINING CRIMINAL BEHAVIOR IN CYBERSPACE

Cyberspace presents an exciting new frontier for criminologists. Virtual reality and computer-mediated communications challenge the traditional discourse of criminology, introducing new forms of deviance, crime, and social control (McKenzie 1996). Since the 1990s, academics have observed how the cyberspace has emerged as a new locus of criminal activity (Thomas and Loader 2000; Littlewood 2003; Yar 2005a, b), but in general, criminology has been remiss in its research into the phenomena of cyber crime and has been slow to recognize the importance of cyberspace in changing the nature and scope of offending and victimization (Mann and Sutton 1998; Jewkes 2006, 2007). As such, very few theoretical explanations of cyber crime exist.

Some researchers have tried to explain cyber crimes with traditional theories, such as social learning theory (Skinner and Fream 1997; Rogers 1999, 2001), Kohlberg's moral development theory and differential reinforcement theory (Rogers 2001), Cohen's strain theory (O'Connor 2003), deindividuation theory (Demetriou and Silke 2003), Gottfredson and Hirschi's general theory of crime (Foster 2004), routine activities theory (Adamski 1998;

McKenzie 2000; Grabosky 2001; Pease 2001; Yar 2005a), and multiple theories (McQuade 2005; Taylor et al. 2005; Darin, Brock, and Stuart 2006). However, these theoretical explanations were found to be inadequate as an overall explanation for the phenomenon of cyber crimes, because cyber crimes are different from crimes of physical space.

Rogers (2000) analyzed hacking with some criminological theories and concluded traditional psychological theories are deficient with regard to explaining cyber criminal behavior. He also argued that Kohlberg's moral development theory, differential reinforcement theory, and social learning theory were only partially effective in explaining the initial involvement and continuation of cyber criminal behaviors. Rogers (2000) also argued that psychoanalytic theories of crime were primarily suited for those types of crimes that resulted from unconscious conflicts (Blackburn 1993; Hollin 1989) and they are not well suited for explaining crimes that incorporate planning and rational goals, such as white collar and computer crimes (Blackburn 1993; Feldman 1993; West 1988; Rogers 2000). Forster's (2004) research offered only a moderate support for Gottfredson and Hirschi's general theory of crime for cyber crimes. Forster's research found direct and positive effects for self-control and opportunity on computer offending, but not for the interaction between self-control and opportunity. Yar's (2005a) analysis on cyber crimes in relation with routine activities theory concluded that, although some of the theory's core concepts can be applied to cyber crime, there remained important differences between "virtual" and "terrestrial" worlds that limited the theory's usefulness.

There does not appear to be any one theory that accounts for all types of conventional criminal behaviors (Blackburn 1993; Ellison and Buckhout 1981; Hollin 1989; Rogers 2000). This problem is compounded when dealing with cyber crimes. At best some of the traditional theories reviewed can only be applied to a limited portion of cyber crimes (Rogers 2000). Darin, Brock, and Stuart (2006) analyzed cyber crimes with several conventional theories of crime (e.g., classical criminology or choice theory, rational choice theory, and routine activities theory) from a policing perspective, and they developed a concept called Faceless Oriented Policing (FOP). Though the authors call it a policing theory, it is a rudimentary explanation for cyber crimes. Nevertheless, it lacks a criminological approach. There is a need for a theory for cyber crimes. Therefore, this chapter is directed at theory building for the explanation of criminal behavior in the cyberspace, and presents the *space transition theory*.

SPACE TRANSITION THEORY OF CYBERSPACE

Space transition theory is an explanation about the nature of the behavior of the persons who bring out their conforming and nonconforming behavior in the physical space and cyberspace. This theory is aimed at explaining only cyber crimes and not physical space crimes. Space transition involves the movement of persons from one space to another (e.g., from physical space to cyberspace and vice versa). Space transition theory argues that, people behave differently when they move from one space to another.

Propositions: Explanation of the Criminal Behavior in the Cyberspace

1. Persons with repressed criminal behavior (in the physical space) have a propensity to commit crime in cyberspace, which otherwise they would not commit in physical space, due to their status and position.

2. Identity flexibility, dissociative anonymity, and lack of deterrence factor in the cyberspace provides the offenders the choice to commit cyber crime.

3. Criminal behavior of offenders in cyberspace is likely to be imported to physical space, which may be exported to cyberspace as well.

4. Intermittent venture of offenders in to the cyberspace and the dynamic spatiotemporal nature of cyberspace provide the chance to escape.

5. (a) Strangers are likely to unite together in cyberspace to commit crime in the physical space; (b) Associates of physical space are likely to unite to commit crime in cyberspace.

6. Persons from closed society are more likely to commit crimes in cyberspace than persons from open society.

7. The conflict of norms and values of physical space with the norms and values of cyberspace may lead to cyber crimes.

DISCUSSION

1. Persons with repressed criminal behavior (in the physical space) have a propensity to commit crime in cyberspace, which, otherwise they would not commit in physical space, due to their status and position.

Arbak (2005) in his model of social status and crime argued that individuals feel varying degrees of self-reproach if they commit criminal acts. In addition, they are concerned with their social status in society, based on others' perceptions of their values. In making their decisions, individuals weigh both the material and social risks of being a criminal as compared to being a law-abiding person. Therefore, an individual with a low propensity of guilt may nevertheless choose not to be engaged in illegal activities in order to maintain their social status, or to avoid embarrassment. In other words, if individuals are sufficiently concerned about their social status, they may be inclined to act "as if" they are moral. However, Arbak's (2005) arguments find relevance only to the behavior of individuals in physical space. The same persons who are concerned about their social status in the physical space are not bothered about their social status in the cyberspace because there is no one to watch and stigmatize them. Those persons, who are worried about their status in the physical space hack, stalk, harass, steal, and threaten in the cyberspace.

In this proposition, repressed criminal behavior does not mean any criminal behavior that is repressed from childhood (repression concept of Sigmund Freud). Here, repressed criminal behavior means the behavior that is repressed in the physical space due to status and position and shown during the transition of persons from physical space to cyberspace.

2. Identity flexibility, dissociative anonymity, and lack of deterrence factor in the cyberspace provides the offenders the choice to commit cyber crime.

Suler (2005) highlighted the concepts of identity flexibility and dissociative anonymity while describing the psychology of cyberspace. "Anonymity has a disinhibiting effect that cuts two ways. Sometimes people use it to act out some unpleasant need or emotion, often by abusing other people, or it allows them to be honest and open about some personal issue that they could not discuss in a face-to-face encounter. That anonymity works wonders for the disinhibition effect. When people have the opportunity to separate their actions from their real world and identity, they feel less vulnerable about opening up. Whatever they say or do cannot be directly linked to them. They do not have to own their behavior by acknowledging it within the full context of who they really are. When acting out hostile feelings, the person does not have to take responsibility for those actions. In fact, people might even convince themselves that those behaviors 'aren't me at all.' In psychology this is called dissociation" (Suler 2005).

A critical problem in cyberspace is not knowing with whom you are interacting. A famous cartoon (Steiner 1993) popularized the idea that "on the Internet, nobody knows that you are a dog," let alone a Ph.D. holder or a Nobel Prize winner. Instead, a person is only as good as his or her last e-mail (Steiner 1993). Currently, a person cannot determine accurately the identity of people in cyberspace or the information presented by them (Abelson and Lessig 1998). A study by Demetriou and Silke (2003) found out that persons believing that they were anonymous entered a Web site trap and were caught downloading illegal material. Demetriou and Silke (2003) argued that deindividuation was the reason for the cyberspace deviant behavior they observed. Deindividuation is a psychological state where inner restraints are lost when individuals are not seen or paid attention to as individuals (Estinger, Pepitone, and Newcomb 1952, 382). The loss of restraints can lead people to behave less altruistically, more selfishly, and more aggressively. While deindividuation can be caused by a number of factors, anonymity has been identified as one of the key causes (Demetriou and Silke 2003). However, it should be noted that the research of Demetriou and Silke (2003) was unable to determine the exact identity of the persons who were caught in their Web site trap. Still, identity flexibility is the norm of the cyberspace. Furthermore, Demetriou and Silke (2003) pointed out that the acts observed in their study occurred in a situation of perceived anonymity for the perpetrators, and there were immediate personal rewards for the visitors to do what they did. This research has only brought out a small tip of the iceberg and there are several million of criminal activities undergoing anonymously on a day-to-day basis in cyberspace.

One of the key elements that keeps most members of any society honest is fear of being caught—the deterrence factor. Cyberspace changes two of those rules. First, it offers the criminal an opportunity of attacking his victims from the remoteness of a different continent and secondly, the results of the crime are not immediately apparent (The Financial Express 2004). Cyber crimes may cause real psychological, social, and financial harms to their victims, and they may grossly transgress reasonable and sensible civic expectations of behavior, but they are not activities that tend to fall within the scope of existing criminal prohibitions due, in part, to the unique nature of cyberspace (Lastowka and Hunter 2004).

3. Criminal behavior of offenders in cyberspace is likely to be imported to physical space which, in physical space, may be exported to cyberspace as well.

Before 2000, cyber criminals acting alone committed the bulk of computer-related crimes. For these individual cyber offenders, publicity and notoriety—not profit—were the main motivation. In the last few years, however, cyber crime has moved from amateurs and occasional criminals to professional criminals. Criminals have realized that huge financial gains can be made from illegal cyberspace activities with relatively little risk. They bring the skills, knowledge, and connections needed for large-scale, high-value criminal enterprise that, when combined with computer skills, expand the scope and risk of cyber crime (McAfee 2005a, b).

In the last two years, cyber crime has become less open to ordinary criminals (e.g., hackers) as criminal organizations have started to realize the potentially huge financial gains to be made from the Internet. Traditional crime gangs are starting to use the Internet not only for communication but also as a tool to commit crimes such as extortion, fraud, money laundering, intimidation or theft, more efficiently and with less risk, and to move into new fields of crime. Due to the Internet's global reach, the temptation is highly attractive and the scale of the problem is massive. The growth of e-business and Internet usage as part of everyday business has made it easier for organized crime gangs to facilitate and cover up their criminal activities. Money can be moved rapidly, and it is difficult for law enforcement to monitor and follow the financial transactions of international criminal gangs. Furthermore, the creation of virtual identities gives a greater anonymity to the activities of organized criminals (McAfee 2005a, b).

4. Intermittent venture of offenders in to the cyberspace and the dynamic spatiotemporal nature of cyberspace provide the chance to escape.

Cyberspace is a transit space for many people, including offenders. While people do not live in cyberspace, they visit and exit like they do in any other place. This nature provides the offenders a chance to escape after the commission of cyber crime. Cyberspace is of dynamic nature. Web sites can be created and removed quickly. This can encourage terrorist-related activities in cyberspace. The characteristics of cyber crimes can vary from those of traditional crimes, because, cyber crimes has little adherence to the spatial-temporal restrictions (Woolgar 2002). Networked societies allow for time and space to be distanced, meaning that an action in one spatial-temporal boundary may have an effect outside of that restriction (Giddens 1990). In relation to criminal activity this means that individuals are able to attack their victims at-a-distance. The temporal dimension of crime is also affected; cyberspace allows criminals to commit crimes in compressed periods of time and potentially across long distances (Williams 2005; Yar 2005a,b). Because of the spatiotemporal problem of cyber crimes, mapping of cyber crimes has become a question. Cyberspace erases the importance of geography, because of the difficulty that lies in determining the location of crimes (Brenner 2004a). The irrelevance of geography has important implications for people with antisocial motivations, and this is a negative feature of cyberspace (Suler 2005).

5. (a) Strangers are likely to unite together in cyberspace to commit crime in the physical space; (b) Associates of physical space are likely to unite to commit crime in cyberspace.

The Internet is an effective medium for criminal recruitment and the dissemination of criminal techniques (Mann and Sutton 1998). Most of the newsgroups in the cyberspace are almost all unmoderated and their ease of access and openness make them ideal places to collect and disseminate information with like-minded people (Sterling 1992; Durkin and Bryant 1995; Mann and Sutton 1998). Another major threat of cyberspace is the insider threat. Frustrated individuals from organizations can play the role of mole and potentially destroy the future of companies by spying, engaging in sabotage, or leaking sensitive information.

6. Persons from closed society are more likely to commit crimes in cyberspace than persons from open society.

Persons from an open society have an option of venting out their feelings, such as anger, in the form of protests and demonstrations. However, persons from closed society do not have an option to vent their feelings. Those individuals from the closed society may find solace in the cyberspace, and they may engage in all types of criminal activities, ranging from ordinary hate messages in blogs to cyber terrorist attacks (Denning and William 1999; Shelley 2003; Weimann 2004; Devilette, 2005).

7. The conflict of norms and values of physical space with the norms and values of cyberspace may lead to cyber crimes.

Cyberspace is an international space where people from various nations conglomerate. This space has its own norms and values which may be in conflict with the norms and values of different groups of people. In cyberspace, the behavior of one person may be different from the behavior of another person. This could lead to conflict among people in cyberspace, which may ultimately lead to cyber crimes.

CONCLUSION

Criminological theories are as diverse as their proponents and practically every criminologist's thought has been elevated to independent theory status, partly because of criminology's lack of a common and unifying theoretical thread (Cullen and Agnew 1999). However, all criminology theories have one distinctive common factor—they have all been conceived to examine criminality in the physical space and not in cyberspace. Since criminology has started viewing the emergence of cyberspace as a new locus of criminal activity, a new theory is needed to explain why cyber crime occurs. The Space Transition Theory presented in this chapter provides an explanation for the criminal behavior in the cyberspace, and this theory is different past criminological theories. There is a need to test the space transition theory to see if it explains cyber criminal activity. In the end, it is hoped this theory will open new vistas for research in cyber criminology.

KEY TERMS

Cyberspace   Space transition theory
Cyber crime   Internet

REFERENCES

Aarseth, E. 1998. Allegories of space: The question of spatiality in computer games. Retrieved December 15, 2006, from http://www.hf.uib.no/hi/espen/papers/space/

Abelson, H., and L. Lessig. 1998. Digital identity in cyberspace. White Paper Submitted for 6.805/Law of Cyberspace: Social Protocols, December 10, 1998.

Adamski A. 1998. Crimes related to the computer network. Threats and opportunities: A criminological perspective. Helsinki, Finland: European Institute for Crime Prevention and Control, affiliated with the United Nations (HEUNI). Retrieved December 15, 2006, from http://www.ulapland.fi/home/oiffi/enlist/resources/HeuniWeb.htm

Aldesco, A. I. 2002. The demise of anonymity: A constitutional challenge to the convention on cybercrime. *Loyola of Los Angeles Entertainment Law Review* 23 (81): 81–123.

Arbak, E. 2005. Social status and crime. Documents De Travail—Working Papers W.P. 05–10, Novembre 2005, GATE Groupe d'Analyse et de Théorie Économique Écully—France. Retrieved December 15, 2006, from ftp://ftp.gate.cnrs.fr/RePEc/2005/0510.pdf

Arena, K. August 8, 2001. U.S. targets porn site's customers. CNN.com Web Site. Retrieved December 15, 2006, from http://www.cnn.com/2001/LAW/08/08/ashcroft.childporn/

Australian Centre for Policing Research (ACPR). 2000. The virtual horizon: Meeting the law enforcement challenges—Developing an Australasian law enforcement strategy for dealing with electronic crime. Scoping paper. Report Series No. 134.1 Police Commissioners' Conference Electronic Crime Working Party, Australasian Centre for Policing Research, 298 Payneham Road, Payneham SA 5070.

Australian Institute of Criminology (AIC). 2006. Cybercrime: Definitions and general information. Retrieved January 12, 2007, from http://www.aic.gov.au/topics/cybercrime/definitions.html

Barlow, J. P. 1991. Coming into the new country: Cyberspace, the new datasphere. *Communications of the ACM* 34 (3): 19–22.

Berwick, D. 1999. Keynote address: Trends in information technology crime, Australasian Crime Conference and Seminar, November 15, Australasian Crime Conference, Adelaide.

Blackburn, R. 1993. *The Psychology of Criminal Conduct: Theory, Research and Practice.* Toronto: John Wiley and Sons.

Brenner, S. W. 2001. Is there such a thing as virtual crime? *Boalt Journal of Criminal Law,* 4. Retrieved December 15, 2006, from http://www.boalt.org/bjcl/v4/v4brenner.htm

Brenner, S. W. 2002a. Organized cybercrime? How cyberspace may affect the structure of criminal relationships. *North Carolina Journal of Law & Technology* 4 (1). Retrieved December 15, 2006, from http://www.jolt.unc.edu/Vol4_I1/Web/Brenner-V4I1.htm

Brenner, S. W. 2002b. The privacy privilege: Law enforcement, technology and the constitution. *Journal of Technology Law & Policy* 7 (2): 123–94. University of Florida. Retrieved December 15, 2006, from http://grove.ufl.edu/~techlaw/vol7/issue2/brenner.pdf

Brenner, S. W. 2004a. The challenge of cybercrime. *CEB Case 'n Point Newsletter*, 6. Retrieved December 15, 2006, from http://ceb.ucop.edu/newsletterv6/criminal_Law.htm

Brenner, S. W. 2004b. Toward a criminal law for cyberspace: Distributed security. *Boston University Journal of Science & Technology Law* 10 (2).

Brenner, S. W., and M. D. Goodman. 2002. In defense of cyberterrorism: An argument for anticipating cyber attacks. *University of Illinois Journal of Law, Technology & Policy*: 1–57.

Brenner, S. W., and J. Schwerha IV. 2002. Transnational evidence-gathering and local prosecution of international cybercrime, 20. *J. Marshall J. Computer & Info. Law* 347: 375–77.

Burney B. 2001. The concept of cybercrimes—Is it right to analogize a physical crime to a cybercrime? University of Dayton School of Law. Retrieved December 15, 2006, from http://cybercrimes.net/Virtual/Burney/page1.html

Byassee W. S. 1995. Jurisdiction of cyberspace: Applying real world precedent to the virtual community, 30. *Wake Forest L. Rev.* 197: 198 n.

Carter, D. 1995. Computer crime categories: How techno-criminals operate. *FBI Law Enforcement Bulletin* 64 (7): 21.

Coll, S., and S. B. Glasser. August 7, 2005. Terrorists turn to the Web as base of operations. *Washington Post*: A01. Retrieved December 15, 2006, from http://www.washingtonpost.com/wp-dyn/content/article/2005/08/05/AR2005080501138_1.html

Council of Europe's Convention on Cybercrime. 2001. Final Draft, released June 29, 2001. Retrieved December 15, 2006, from http://www.cybercrime.gov/newCOEFAQs.html

Cullen, F. T., and R. Agnew. 1999. *Criminological Theory: Past to Present: Essential Readings* Los Angeles: Roxbury Pub. Co.

Danda, M. 2001. Protect yourself online. Microsoft Corporation. Retrieved December 15, 2006, from http://www.microsoft.com/mspress/books/sampchap/4801b.asp

Darin, W., D. Brock, and T. R. Stuart. 2006. Faceless-oriented policing: Traditional policing theories are not adequate in a cyber world. *Police Journal* 79 (2): 169–76.

Davis, R., and S. Hutchison. 1997. *Computer Crime in Canada*. Toronto: Thomson Canada Limited.

Deflem, M., and J. Eagle Shutt. 2006. "Law enforcement and computer security threats and measures." In *The Handbook of Information Security*. Vol. 2, *Information Warfare; Social, Legal, and International Issues; and Security Foundations*, edited by H. Bidgoli, 200–9. Hoboken, NJ: John Wiley and Sons.

Demetriou, C., and A. Silke. 2003. A criminological Internet 'sting': Experimental evidence of illegal and deviant visits to a website trap. *British Journal of Criminology* 43: 213–22.

Denning, D. E., and W. E. Baugh, Jr. 1999. Hiding crimes in cyberspace. *Information, Communication and Society* 2 (3).

Devilette, S., ed. 2005. Reporters without borders: Handbook for bloggers and cyber dissidents. Reporters without Borders International Secretariat Paris, France. Retrieved December 15, 2006, from http://www.rsf.org/IMG/pdf/handbook_bloggers_cyberdissidents-GB.pdf

Drozdova, E., M. Goodman, J. Hopwood, and X. Wang. 1999. Emerging international consensus on cybercrimes: Results of global cyber law survey of fifty countries in Africa, the Americas, Asia, Europe, the Middle East, and Oceania. (Source: Ekaterina Drozdova, prepared for the Conference on International Cooperation to Combat Cybercrime and Terrorism, December 6–7, 1999, Hoover Institution, Stanford University.)

Durkin, K. F., and C. D. Bryant. 1995. Logon to sex: some notes on the carnal computer and erotic cyberspace as an emerging research frontier. *Deviant Behavior: An Interdisciplinary Journal* 16: 179–200.

Ellison, K., and R. Buckhout. 1981. *Psychology and Criminal Justice*. New York: Harper and Row.

Estinger, L., A. Pepitone, and T. Newcomb. 1952. Some consequences of deindividuation in a group. *Journal of Abnormal and Social Psychology* 47: 382–9.

Etter, B. 2002. Critical issues in high-tech crime, presentation to the Commonwealth Investigations Conference at the Australasian Centre for Policing Research. Retrieved December 15, 2006, from http://www.acpr.gov.au/pdf/presentations/ciinhi-tech.pdf

European Commission. 2001. Communication from the European Commission to the Council and the European Parliament 1.1, COM, 890 final, at 9 (Brussels, January 26, 2001). Retrieved December 15, 2006, from http://europa.eu.int/ISPO/eif/InternetPoliciesSite/Crime/CrimeCommEN.html

Feldman, P. 1993. *The Psychology of Crime a Social Science Textbook*. Cambridge: Cambridge University Press.

Fernandes, A. 2002. Ethics in online communities. Assignment submitted to Visual Culture and Communication programme of the University of Toronto, Canada. Retrieved December 15, 2006, from http://home.utm.utoronto.ca/~alison_f/Assignment%20Two.doc

Financial Express. 2004. Remoteness of cybercrimes makes it different. January 17, 2004. Retrieved December 15 2006, from http://www.nasscom.org/artdisplay.asp?Art_id=3933

Foster, D. R. 2004. Can the general theory of crime account for computer offenders: Testing low self-control as a predictor of Computer crime offending. Unpublished Master's Thesis, University of Maryland, College Park.

Gibson, W. 1984. *Neuromancer*. New York: Ace Books.

Giddens, A. 1990. *The Consequences of Modernity*. Polity Press: Oxford.

Grabosky, P. 2000. Computer crime: A criminological overview. Paper presented at the Workshop on Crimes Related to the Computer Network, Tenth United Nations Congress on the Prevention of Crime and the Treatment of Offenders, Vienna, April 15, 2000.

Grabosky, P. 2001. Virtual criminality: Old wine in new bottles? *Social & Legal Studies* 10: 243–49.

Graycar, A. 2000. Nine types of cybercrime. Speech delivered in the conference "Cybercrime: Old Wine in New Bottles?" Centre for Criminology, The University of Hong Kong, February 24, 2000.

Hafner, K., and J. Markoff. 1995. *Cyberpunks: Outlaws and Hackers on the Computer Frontier*. Toronto: Simon and Schuster.

Heylighen. 1994. Cyberspace Principia Cybernetica web. Retrieved December 15, 2006, from http://pespmc1.vub.ac.be/CYBSPACE.html

Hollin, C. 1989. *Psychology and Crime: An Introduction to Criminological Psychology.* New York: Routledge.

Icove, D. 1998. Catching cybercrooks. Computer Security. December 1997/January 1998. Retrieved December 15, 2006, from http://www.engaust.com.au/ew/12crime.html

IPWatchdog.com. 2003. About cybercrime. IPWatchdog.com Web Site. Retrieved December 15, 2006, from http://www.ipwatchdog.com/cybercrimes.html

Jewkes, Y. 2006. Comment on the book *Cybercrime and Society* by M. Yar, Sage Publications. Retrieved December 15, 2006, from http://www.sagepub.co.uk/booksProdDesc.nav?prodId=Book227351

Jewkes, Y. 2007. *Crime Online.* Devon: Willan Publishing.

Joinson, A. N. 1998. "Causes and implication of disinhibited behavior on the Internet." In *Psychology and the Internet: Intrapersonal, Interpersonal, and Transpersonal Implications,* edited by J. Gackenbach, 43–60. San Diego, CA: Academic Press.

Joinson, A. N. 2003. *Understanding the Psychology of Internet Behavior.* Basingstoke, UK: Palgrave Macmillan.

Jordan, T. 1999. *Cyberpower: The Culture and Politics of Cyberspace in the Internet.* London and New York: Routledge.

Kabay, M. E. April 2005. *Totem and Taboo in Cyberspace: Integrating Cyberspace into Our Moral Universe.* 5th ed. Division of Business and Management, Norwich University,

Kamal, A. 2005. *The Law of Cyberspace: An Invitation to the Table of Negotiations.* Geneva: United Nations Institute for Training and Research, Palais des Nations.

Kelly, B. J. 2001. Supervising the cybercriminal. *Federal Probation.* Special issue on Technology and Corrections, 65 (2): 8–10.

Kishore, Ushnish, Shafeeq, and Amos. 2005. Cybercrime: Piercing the darkness. Retrieved December 15, 2006, from http://library.thinkquest.org/04oct/00460/

Lastowka, F. G., and D. Hunter. 2004. Virtual crimes. *New York Law School Law Review* 49: 293–316.

Lee, M. K. O. 1995. Legal control of computer crime in Hong Kong. *Information Management & Computer Security* 3 (2): 13–19. Retrieved December 15, 2006, from http://mustafa.emeraldlibrary. com/vl=4775179/cl=50/nw=1/rpsv/~1177/v3n2/s3/p13

Lessig, L. 1998. The laws of cyberspace. Paper presented at the Taiwan Net '98 conference, Taipei, March 1998. http://cyber.harvard.edu/works/lessig/laws_cyberspace.pdf

Littlewood, A. 2003. Cyberporn and moral panic: An evaluation of press reactions to pornography on the Internet. *Library and Information Research* 27 (86): 8–18.

Lukasik, S. J. 2001. "Current and future: Technical capabilities." In *The Transnational Dimension of Cybercrime and Terrorism,* edited by A. D. Sofaer and S. E. Goodman, 125–82. Hoover Institution Press Publication, Stanford University. Retrieved December 15, 2006, from http://www.oas.org/ juridico/english/stanford.htm

Mann, D., and S. Mike. 1998. NetCrime. More change in the organisation of thieving. *British Journal of Criminology* 38 (2): 201–29.

Matt, S. M. 2004. Cybercrime: A comparative law analysis. Unpublished Dissertation submitted for the Degree of Magister Legum (LLM) at the University of South Africa.

McAfee. 2005a. McAfee Virtual Criminology Report: North American study into organized crime and the Internet, July 2005.

McAfee. 2005b. McAfee Virtual Criminology Report: The first Pan-European study into organized crime and the Internet, February 2005.

McConnell International. 2000. Cybercrime . . . and punishment? Archaic laws threaten global information. A Report. Retrieved December 15, 2006, from http://www.mcconnellinternational. com/services/cybercrime.htm

McKenzie, S. 1996. Examining the political realities of crime prevention implementation. Unpublished manuscript.

McKenzie, S. 2000. Child safety on the Internet: An analysis of Victorian schools and households using the routine activity approach. A thesis submitted to the University of Melbourne, February 2000. Retrieved December 15, 2006, from http://www.criminology.unimelb.edu.au/research/internet/childsafety/index.html

McQuade, S. C. 2005. *Understanding and Managing Cybercrime*. New Jersey: Allyn & Bacon.

Menthe, D. C. 1998. Jurisdiction in cyberspace: A theory of international spaces, 4. *Mich. Telecomm. Tech. L. Rev.*, 69. Retrieved December 17, 2006, from http://www.mttlr.org/volfour/menthe.pdf

Mitra, A. 1999. Characteristics of the WWW text: Tracing discursive strategies. *Journal of Computer Mediated Communication* 5 (1). Retrieved December 17, 2006, from http://jcmc.indiana.edu/vol5/issue1/mitra.html

Mitra, A. 2003. Cybernetic space: Our new dwelling place. Proceedings of the Hawaii International Conference on Social Sciences, June 12–15, 2003. Retrieved December 20, 2006, from www.hicsocial.org/Social2003Proceedings/AnandaMitra.pdf

Mitra, A., and R. L. Schwartz. 2001. From cyberspace to cybernetic space: Rethinking the relationship between real and virtual spaces. *Journal of Computer-Mediated Communication* 7 (1). Retrieved December 15, 2006, from http://jcmc.indiana.edu/vol7/issue1/mitra.html

Morrison, P. 1990. Computer crime: The improvement of investigative skills. Final Report Part One. Report Series No. 96.1. Australasian Centre for Policing Research, Payneham.

O'Connor, T. 2003. Glee, elation, and glory as motives for cybercrime. Paper presented at the annual meeting of the Southern Criminal Justice Association, Nashville, March, 2003.

Parker, D. 1999. Automated crime, information security. Retrieved December 15, 2006, from http://www.infosecuritymag.com/articles/1999/autocrime.shtml

Parker, D. October 16, 2002. Automated crime, WindowSecurity.com Web Site. Retrieved December 15, 2006, from http://secinf.net/misc/Automated_Crime_.html/

Parliamentary Joint Committee on the Australian Crime Commission (PJCACC). 2004. *Cybercrime*. Canberra: Parliament of the Commonwealth of Australia.

Pati, P. 2003. Cybercrime. Retrieved December 15, 2006, from http://www.naavi.org/pati/pati_cybercrimes_dec03.htm

Pease, K. 2001. "Crime futures and foresight: Challenging criminal behavior in the information age." In *Crime and the Internet,* edited by D. Wall. London: Routledge.

Post, D. G. 1996. Pooling intellectual capital: Thoughts on anonymity, pseudonymity, and limited liability in cyberspace, 11. *University of Chicago Legal Forum* 139: 149–52. Retrieved December 15, 2006, from http://www.temple.edu/lawschool/dpost/pseudonym.html

Putnam, T. L., and D. D. Elliott. 1999. "International responses to cybercrime." In *The Transnational Dimension of Cybercrime and Terrorism,* edited by A. D. Sofaer and S. E. Goodman, 35–67. Hoover Institution Press Publication, Stanford University. Retrieved December 15, 2006, from http://www.oas.org/juridico/english/stanford.htm

Rogers, M. 1999. Modern-day Robin Hood or moral disengagement: Graduate studies paper. University of Manitoba, Winnipeg, Manitoba. Retrieved December 15, 2006, from http://homes.cerias.purdue.edu/~mkr/moral.doc

Rogers, M. 2000. Psychological theories of crime and hacking. *Telematic Journal of Clinical Criminology*. International Crime Analysis Association. Retrieved December 15, 2006, from http://homes.cerias.purdue.edu/~mkr/crime.doc

Rogers, M. 2001. A social learning theory and moral disengagement analysis of criminal computer behavior: An exploratory study. Unpublished Ph.D. thesis submitted to the University of Manitoba, Winnipeg, Manitoba. Retrieved December 15, 2006, from http://homes.cerias.purdue.edu/~mkr/cybercrime-thesis.pdf

Shelley, L. I. 2003. "Organized crime, terrorism and cybercrime." In *Security Sector Reform: Institutions, Society and Good Governance*, edited by A. Bryden and P. Fluri, 303–12. Baden-Baden: Nomos Verlagsgesellschaft.

Skinner, W., and A. Fream. 1997. A social learning theory analysis of computer crime among college students. *Journal of Research in Crime and Delinquency* 34: 495–518.

Smith R., P. Grabosky, and G. Urbas. 2004. *Cybercriminals on Trial*, 5–10. Cambridge: Cambridge University Press.

Statistics Canada. 2002. *Cyber-Crime: Issues, Data Sources and Feasibility of Collecting Police-Reported Statistics*. Ottawa: Canadian Centre for Justice Statistics.

Steiner, P. 1993. Cartoon: On the internet nobody knows you are a dog. *New Yorker* 69 (20): 61.

Sterling, B. 1992. *The Hacker Crackdown: Law and Disorder on the Electronic Frontier*. London: Penguin Books.

Suler, J. 1999. To get what you need: Healthy and pathological Internet use. *CyberPsychology and Behavior* 2: 385–93.

Suler, J. 2004. The online disinhibition effect. *CyberPsychology and Behavior* 7: 321–26.

Suler, J. 2005. The psychology of cyberspace. Retrieved December 15, 2006, from www.rider.edu/suler/psycyber/psycyber.html

Suler, J., and W. Phillips. 1998. The bad boys of cyberspace: Deviant behavior in multimedia chat communities. *CyberPsychology and Behavior* 1: 275–94.

Taylor, R., T. Caeti, K. Loper, E. Fritsch, and J. Liederbach. 2005. *Digital Crime and Digital Terrorism*. UK: Pearson.

Tedeschi, B. January 28, 2003. Crime wave washes over cyberspace. *International Herald Tribune*.

Thetard, T. N. 2002. Gender swapping on the Internet. Spark-Online, Media, Version 28.0, January. Retrieved December 15, 2006, from http://www.spark-online.com/issue28/thetard.html

Thomas, D., and B. Loader. 2000. "Introduction—cybercrime: Law enforcement, security and surveillance in the information age." In *Cybercrime: Law Enforcement, Security and Surveillance in the Information Age*, edited by D. Thomas and B. Loader. London: Routledge.

Tyner, K. 1998. *Literacy in a Digital World*. New Jersey: Lawrence Earlbaum Associates.

United Nations. 1997. United Nations Manual on the Prevention and Control of Computer-Related Crime, International Review of Criminal Policy Nos. 43 and 44. United Nations: New York. Retrieved December 15, 2006, from http://www.uncjin.org/Documents/EighthCongress.html

Van Gelder, L. 1991. "The strange case of the electronic lover." In *Computerization and Controversy: Value Conflicts and Social Choices*, edited by C. Dunlop and R. Kling, 364–75. London: Academic Press.

Wall, D. S. 1999. Cybercrimes: New wine, no bottles? In *Invisible Crimes: Their Victims and Their Regulation*, edited by P. Davies, P. Francis, and V. Jupp, 105–39. London: Macmillan.

Wall, D. S. 2001. "Cybercrimes and the internet." In *Crime and the Internet*, edited by D. Wall. London: Routledge.

Wall, D. S. 2004. "The Internet as a conduit for criminal activity." In *Information Technology and the Criminal Justice System,* edited by P. April. Thousand Oaks, CA: Sage Publications.

Weimann, G. 2004. WWW.terror.net: *How Modern Terrorism Uses the Internet*. Washington DC: United States Institute of Peace. http://www.usip.org/pubs/specialreports/sr116.pdf

West, D. 1988. Psychological contributions to criminology. *British Journal of Criminology* 28: 77–92.

Williams, M. 2005. "Cybercrime." In *Encyclopaedia of Criminology,* edited by J. Mitchell Miller. London: Routledge.

Woolgar, S. 2002. *Virtual Society?—Technology, Cyberbole, Reality*. Oxford: Oxford University Press.

Yar, M. 2005a. The novelty of "cybercrime": An assessment in light of routine activity theory. *European Journal of Criminology* 2 (4): 407–27.

Yar, M. 2005b. Computer hacking: Just another case of juvenile delinquency? *Howard Journal* 44 (4): 387–99.

Chapter 15

Routine Activity Theory and Internet Crime

Raymond W. Cox III
University of Akron

Terrance A. Johnson
Lincoln University of Pennsylvania

George E. Richards
Edinboro University of Pennsylvania

Raymond W. Cox III is a professor in the Department of Public Administration and Urban Studies at the University of Akron. He holds a Ph.D. in Public Administration and Public Affairs from Virginia Polytechnic Institute and State University. He is the author of nearly 50 academic and professional publications, including two books. His recent work has been focused on issues of discretion in decision-making and police ethics.

The late **Dr. Terrance A. Johnson**, CBM, CFE, was an associate professor at Lincoln University (PA) where he taught public administration and criminal justice courses. He researched and wrote on contemporary law enforcement issues, with an emphasis on misconduct. He was a member of peer-review editorial boards for four criminal justice journals. He began his teaching career following a 20-year profession in policing, law enforcement, government investigations, and corporate security. He retired as a special investigator 2 for the Office of Chief Counsel, Department of Transportation, and the Commonwealth of Pennsylvania. He was the principal in an asset protection-consulting group.

George E. Richards, CPP, a native of Kentucky, he is an assistant professor of criminal justice at Edinboro University of Pennsylvania. Dr. Richards is currently the second Vice-President of the Ohio Council of Criminal Justice Education and is also the immediate past president of this association. In addition to his work in the classroom, he has an active research agenda that focuses primarily on crime prevention and security-related issues. He has published in several peer-reviewed and popular publications, among these being *The Journal of Contemporary Criminal Justice, Journal of Security Administration*, and *The American School Board Journal*.

Abstract

The advent and growth of the Internet has not only altered how people communicate, but has also added a new dimension to criminal behavior. This chapter addresses Internet-based crime in conjunction with theoretical frameworks: opportunity theory, situational crime prevention, and routine activity theory. The displacement of Internet-based crime and victim characteristics are also addressed.

INTRODUCTION

Crime continues to be a global concern. Recent technological advances have changed the one element essential for violent confrontations to occur: "places" where victims and perpetrators meet. The opportunity for incidences of physical harm during the commission of crime has been reduced as a result. Victims and violators, for the most part, never come face-to-face because their location is often unknown to each other. The Internet that has revolutionized our communicative abilities worldwide has increasingly been used as a locale to commit crimes or a location for people to engage in activity that might result in their criminal victimization. The information super highway allows criminals and would-be criminals to operate with a high probability of privacy. The **Internet Crime Complaint Center** (ICCC) operated by the Federal Bureau of Investigation (FBI) and the **National White Collar Crime Center** (NWCCC) have collected data since 2001 that shows Internet crime continues to be a growing problem. Crimes committed via the Internet routinely employ trickery, deceit, and deception as the weapons of choice (Internet Crime Complaint Center).

The privacy of the Internet (mostly at one's computer) has also encouraged victims and potential victims to travel to unknown and unprotected places for lewd and lascivious activities because they too believe their identities are protected (Regoli and Hewitt 2006; Doerner and Lab 1998, 2002, 2005). Siegel (2007) notes that research has shown victims may play a part, which can range from passive to aggressive behavior, in their own victimization. The Internet represents both the best and worst place for such unobtrusive observation. This chapter will explore those theories (**routine activity theory**, adjunct **displacement theory**, and **opportunity theory**) that help to better enlighten the community as to how these crimes are carried out and the interconnection between these theories and the Internet.

While the responsibilities of police largely focus on detecting and deterring crimes (Johnson 2006a, b, Doerner and Lab 1998, 2002, 2005), the academic community has begun to examine Internet crime from a theoretical approach involving the concealment of the criminals' and victims' identity. Past research reveals many in the general public do not violate the law because of the informal social control of being ostracized by people in their life they revere like family and friends. Others are influenced to obey the law because of formal social controls. The social contract people agree to obey when joining a community gives them status and a sense of belonging. This obliges them to follow the tenets of the legal system. Thus, they obey the law. The similar component of these controls is the perceived fear and embarrassment of getting caught that acts as a strong deterrent for most people. However, global advances in technology have allowed criminals to commit crimes without a direct connection to a person or group and/or a location.

For three decades, routine activity theory (RAT) (Cohen and Felson 1979, Felson and Clarke 1998) has been applied to help understand the relationship between the actions of the criminal and the crime victim. Felson and Clarke's displacement theory argues that moving the place of a crime does not deter it, but rather changes the opportunity. Some displacement occurs, but the underlying element in crime is the aforementioned "opportunity."

Routine activity theory, displacement theory, and opportunity theory emphasize the idea that "place" is the key to the commission of crimes. The physical location allows the criminal to identify potential victims by studying their day-to-day activities and determining their suitability as targets. Simply put, these two conditions must be present for the theory to unfold— a pattern of behavior by the victim that can be identified by the criminal and an unobtrusive place for observation so the criminal might discover and confirm that behavior. It is important to note such "observation" does not generally rise to the level of criminality. Rather it is the opportunity to plan a crime that is afforded by the confirmation of a routine behavior by the eventual victim. It is in this distinction between mere "observation" and recognition of a routine behavior and the decision to use that behavior to criminal advantage upon which the utility of RAT for understanding Internet crime hinges.

ROUTINE ACTIVITY THEORY

RAT proposes that for a crime to occur three things must happen at the same time and in the same space (Cohen and Felson 1979):

- a suitable target is available
- there is a lack of a suitable guardian to prevent the crime from occurring
- and a motivated offender is present

RAT looks at crime from the offender's or potential criminal's point of view. A crime will only be committed if a potential criminal thinks a target is suitable and a capable guardian is absent. It is the assessment of a situation that determines when or if a crime will take place.

A Suitable Target

The first condition for crime is that a suitable target must be available. A target can be categorized in the following three ways (Cohen and Felson 1979):

- a person
- an object
- a place

Under RAT a suitable target is one that has come to the attention of a person searching for a criminal opportunity. The criminal observes the victim. The observation affirms that the intended victim is a worthy target of means. The potential victim's behavior and their location helps make the criminal act ripe for success. The suitability of a target is tempered by the presence or absence of a capable guardian. The presence of a guardian is a significant deterrent to the commission of a crime. The guardian may be either a mechanism (locks, alarms, etc.) or an "animate" being (guard dog or security officer). Thus, a target may be "suitable," but may not become a victim. It is the absence of a guardian that makes the suitable target a victim of crime. Simply stated, the most important crime deterrent mechanism is the sentinel.

Absence of a Capable Guardian

The second condition in the analysis of the potential for success in the commitment of a crime is that a capable guardian whose presence would discourage a crime from taking place must be absent. Many times a guardian is seen as a human element. A person's mere presence would deter potential offenders from perpetrating an act on a victim. Some of the guardians are formal and deliberate, such as security guards; some are informal and inadvertent, such as neighbors. However a "capable guardian" could also be a machine or mechanism. These mechanisms can be as simple as a lock or as complex as a closed-circuit television (CCTV), providing that someone is monitoring it at the other end of the camera. Some examples of capable guardians are:

- police patrols
- security guards
- neighborhood watch
- door staff
- vigilant staff and coworkers
- friends
- neighbors
- CCTV systems

The critical variable is that the guardian is "capable," that is, the guardian can serve the purpose of providing deterrence to crime. It is possible, for example, for a guardian to be present, but ineffective. Also, a CCTV camera is not a capable guardian if it is set up or sited wrongly. Staff might be present in a store or building, but may not have sufficient training or awareness to be an effective deterrent.

Motivated Perpetrator

There can be no victim without the *intentional* actions of another individual. Criminal behavior is exactly that—acting in an illegal manner. The perpetrator generally does not commit a crime by happenstance. As suggested by routine activity theory it is the combination of the behavior of the potential victim as those behaviors take the victim into contact with the perpetrator that contributes to the commission of the crime.

According to Meier and Miethe (1993), RAT has many similarities with lifestyle exposure theory in that both emphasize how patterns of routine activities or lifestyles in conventional society provide an "opportunity structure" for crimes to occur (p. 470). They note both theories deemphasize the role of offender motivation and the social ecology of crime.

> . . . . [S]tructural changes in routine activity patterns influence crime rates by affecting the convergence in time and space of three elements of direct-contact predatory crime . . . Drawing from work in human ecology (e.g. Hawley, 1950), Cohen and Felson (1979) argue that humans are located in ecological riches with a particular tempo, pace, and rhythm in which predatory crime is a way of securing those basic needs or desires at the expense of others. (pp. 470–71)

OPPORTUNITY THEORY

While it has been suggested that the confluences of circumstances and events play a significant role in the criminal act, it should also be noted that merely removing the opportunity for crime or seeking to prevent a crime by changing the situation in which it occurs does not actually prevent crime, but merely moves it around.

There are five main ways in which crime is moved:

- crime can be moved from one location to another (geographical displacement)
- crime can be moved from one time to another (temporal displacement)
- crime can be directed away from one target to another (target displacement)
- one method of committing crime can be substituted for another (tactical displacement)
- one kind of crime can be substituted for another (crime type displacement) (Felson and Clarke 1998)

Opportunity Knocks

Felson and Clarke (1998), building upon the work of Cohen and Felson (1979), argue opportunity is a cause of crime and, indeed, a *root* cause of crime (see Table 15-1). Critics often downplay opportunities or temptations as true causes of crime. This is a mistake. No crime can occur without the physical opportunities to carry it out. Whatever one's criminal inclinations, crime opportunities are necessary conditions for crime to occur. This makes them causal factors (Doerner and Lab 2005; Regoli and Hewitt 2006).

This does not mean that other factors explaining why some individuals have a propensity to commit crime are unimportant, merely that they are complex, controversial and not necessarily helpful to today's practitioner. Felson and Clarke (1998) aggressively assert the point that crime opportunities are at least as important as individual factors and are far more tangible and relevant to everyday life.

> . . . . Accepting that opportunity is a cause of crime equal in importance to those personal and social variables that are usually thought of as causes, results in a criminology that is not only more complete in its theorizing, but also more relevant to policy and practice. (Felson and Clarke 1998, 31)

TABLE 15-1 Ten Principles of Crime Opportunity Theory

1. Opportunities play a role in causing all crime.
2. Crime opportunities are highly specific.
3. Crime opportunities are concentrated in time and space.
4. Crime opportunities depend on everyday movements of activity.
5. One crime produces opportunities for another.
6. Some products offer more tempting crime opportunities.
7. Social and technological changes produce new crime opportunities.
8. Crime can be prevented by reducing opportunities.
9. Reducing opportunities does not usually displace crime.
10. Focused opportunity reduction can produce wider declines in crime.

Source: Felson and Clarke (1998, v–vi)

The argument that reducing the opportunity for crime results in reductions in crime is straightforward. Those with the responsibility for situational prevention have long predicated their work upon intuition and common sense. Opportunity reduction can take many forms:

- the design and layout of dwellings and commercial premises to reduce burglary and other crimes
- design and management of stores to reduce shoplifting
- targeted policing
- identification requirements and cash handling procedures to reduce fraud
- personal safety advice to reduce robbery
- target "hardening" to make property more difficult to steal, property marking to deter theft and reduce profit
- improving street lighting to facilitate natural surveillance

Felson and Clarke (1998) take the argument further by their assertion that opportunity plays a role in causing *all* crime, not merely property crime. They argue, for example, that homicide rates in the United States are many times higher than in Britain and other European countries (although overall crime is lower) because of the widespread availability of handguns. They assert the availability of handguns means a much greater opportunity to carry out a quick and deadly attack, often on the spur of the moment and perhaps for reasons that later seem trivial. The question is, if the assailants did not possess a handgun at the moment of the crime, would they plausibly kill with fists or knives? Zimring (1972) found the likelihood of death in a violent encounter was directly related to the lethality of the instrument used. Even otherwise mature and reasonable people lose their tempers and control. Put a gun in their hand during this brief period of rage and the result may be tragic. Again, the people and the circumstance do not change. The key variable is the opportunity to squeeze a trigger. The logic is similar to that found in relation to suicide.

Felson and Clarke (1998) observe the importance of opportunity in relation to sexual offences against children, domestic violence, drug dealing, prostitution, and welfare fraud. Thus, there is no class or category of crime in which opportunity does not play a role. Therefore, altering the volume of crime opportunities at any level will produce a change in criminal outcomes.

> Accepting opportunity as a cause of crime also opens up a new vista of crime prevention policies focused upon opportunity-reduction. These policies do not merely complement existing efforts to diminish individual propensities to commit crime through social and community programs or the threat of criminal sanctions. Rather, the new policies operate on circumstances much closer to the criminal event and thus have a greater chance to reduce crime immediately. (Felson and Clarke 1998, 31)

Displacement

If a primary focus of crime reduction is opportunity reduction, the logical question is whether or not such efforts simply displace or move the crime to another locale. This will be discussed in more detail later in this chapter. For the moment we wish to focus on two questions: first is the significance of displacement in general and whether the displacement of crime is always negative. By focusing on the affects of the displacement of crime it is possible to see some positive, or at least nonnegative or neutral results, from crime displacement. Studies in the United Kingdom conclude the displacement of crime yields a range of outcomes:

- Positive—a crime is displaced to a less serious type of crime or a crime with greater risk, with lower rewards, or causing less serious damage. It represents a success since it produces a net gain.
- Neutral—a crime is displaced to one of the same seriousness, of the same risk, rewards, and damage.
- Even-handed—prevention is concentrated on those who are repeatedly victimized in order to achieve a more equitable distribution of crime.
- Negative—a crime is displaced to a more serious crime, a crime with greater reward, or greater social cost.
- Attractive—activities and/or places attract crime from other areas or activities (e.g., red light districts attract customers from other areas, as well as other criminal activities).

Yet there are studies which report displacement did not occur at all, or only to a limited extent. Furthermore, displacement is always a problem for crime prevention efforts. Displacement begs the question of crime reduction. There are strong theoretical reasons for believing it is far from inevitable. Even when it can be shown to occur, it may be far from complete displacement, giving important net reductions in crime (Doerner and Lab 2005; Regoli and Hewitt 2006).

Displacement theory is discussed in connection to prevention initiatives. More recently a look at displacement from the standpoint of the offender has emerged. This perspective is known as "perpetrator displacement" (Barr and Pease 1990). Town (2001), citing the work of Hill and Pease (2001), comments

> The closest one can imagine to complete displacement would be in respect to what has come to be known as 'perpetrator displacement', whereby a crime opportunity is so compelling that the removal of any number of offenders will not prevent the crime. The obvious example concerns drug importation from a third world country, in which poverty generates an unlimited pool of volunteers to be 'mules'. . . . The displacement theory is widely accepted because it is instinctively seen as 'common-sense,' which is reinforced by our understanding of the way the world works—or is thought to work. Criminals are, after all, criminals. Stop them in one location and surely they just find another. Common sense is a valuable commodity, but it has its limitations and changes with time. (p. 4)

Poverty is not the only generator of new perpetrators. An unguarded, vulnerable, and tempting target produces the same effect. From this perspective, victimization seems to breed victimization. Whether the result of living or working in a risky environment, or because of targeting, it is well known by the police that time and again perpetrators return to the same premises, often despite a number of arrests. The cause may be the inherent vulnerability of the premises, or the high desirability of the products found there.

The Internet has proven to be a fruitful locale for victimization. **"Phishing"** is one method by which identity thieves can obtain personal information to obtain access to steal money from your bank account and use your credit card to pay for online purchases. In the typical phishing scam, the victim receives an e-mail from a company they routinely do business with or a government agency. The message encourages the reader to submit personal information such as their Social Security Number or other confidential information so their identity might be verified. The victim may even be told this information is necessary to prevent identity theft. Success breeds success. The lack of knowledge of the dangers posed by phishing creates an environment rich with criminal opportunity.

The anonymity the Internet provides to cyber offenders is also appealing. Business is routinely conducted over Web sites that offer a means of both buying and selling between two parties that may never meet and may be separated geographically by thousands of miles. While some auction sites such as eBay make all possible efforts to ensure the security of transactions and take measures to educate those who bid on items for sale on their Web sites, there can be no controls implemented on the intentions of those who may offer bogus items for sale.

Research on Crime Displacement

According to Town (2001), research on crime displacement became more systematic in the 1990s when research in Canada (Gabor 1990) and the United States (Eck 1993) specifically studied displacement and found it to be much less of problem than had generally been supposed. Eck (1993) suggested where displacement did occur it was most likely to be to similar targets or similar and adjacent areas. The seminal work on this issue occurred in 1994 when the Ministry of Justice of Holland released a systematic analysis of all the available literature on crime prevention measures in which researchers had specifically looked for evidence of displacement (Hesseling 1994). The study took 14 months and involved reviewing dozens of published articles, including those of Gabor (1990) and Eck (1993). The works reviewed came from throughout the developed world, but most (about 85 percent) came from the United Kingdom, the United States, or the Netherlands. Forty percent of the studies found no displacement and another 12 percent found evidence that crime prevention measures had produced a beneficial effect in adjacent areas. While 60 percent of the studies found some form of displacement, most displacement was limited and no study found complete displacement of crime. The summary of the final report asserts that while displacement is possible and even likely, it is not an inevitable consequence of crime prevention. Furthermore, if displacement does occur, it will be limited in scope and affect (Hesseling 1994).

One critical point of the Hesseling study is that the extent of displacement varies across the types of crime. A number of studies found the sale and distribution of illegal goods is susceptible to displacement (Rengert 1990; Sherman 1990; Eck 1993). However, the commonly asserted belief that the behavior of drug addicts is fixed and impervious to logic or a change in opportunity was not confirmed. Town (2001) summarizes this research by noting that "prevention does not always lead to displacement" (p. 3). For example, he noted heroin addicts appear to be more capable of controlling their habit than previously suspected.

> [R]esearch revealed numerous instances where an addicted offender planned a burglary and
> was deterred temporarily. Occasionally the deterred burglar located another burglary target
> and committed a burglary, as intended. Just as often the planned crime was not committed.
> (Town 2001, 6)

Why Isn't Crime Displaced?

For crime to be displaced it first has to be prevented. The first task, then, is to examine the circumstances under which crime is successfully reduced and then answer the question of why it is then not displaced. Clarke (1997) wrote criminologists have generally shown little interest in **situational crime prevention**. This neglect stems from what he regards as two mistakes of modern criminology:

- Explaining crime has been confused with the problem of explaining the criminal
- Confusing the problem of controlling crime with that of dealing with the criminal

Moss and Pease (1999) make the same point. They note that the problem of crime tends to be reduced to the problem of what to do about the criminal. Clarke (1997) argues these assumptions are based directly on the mistaken belief that offenders faced with situational impediments will merely be displaced elsewhere. In contrast *situational* crime prevention can quickly and clearly deliver dramatic results. Clarke (1997) commented on the manner in which this phenomenon occurs. Well-designed measures can produce results far exceeding expectations. The key is reducing opportunity.

Displacement may occur in cyberspace through routine, and well-advertised, security measures. A prominent statement on a Web site that informs visitors that Internet addresses will be logged may prohibit some criminals from targeting those who do business with or patronize that particular Web site. As wealthier companies and organizations incorporate more stringent security measures, perpetrators will be encouraged to target Web sites with more lax security measures (Tomorrow Project Home 2007).

Opportunity Theory Redux

Opportunity theory seems to be a form of common sense when explained to people. However, while it explains one means to reduce crime, it does not explain *why* prevented crime is simply displaced. It would seem that criminals, when faced by barriers to crime, would simply move on to an area where opportunity remains unaltered. A surprising answer that comes from a study in the United Kingdom by Paul Wiles and Andrew Costello (2000) suggests most criminals are relatively place-bound. The area within which they commit crimes is small and close to home. "The most general and consistent [finding] is the fact that offenders do not appear to travel very far" (Town 2001, 10). Crime, it seems, is generally "local." Wiles and Costello (2000) found that the average distance travelled to commit domestic burglary was 1.8 miles.

Concern about displacement is natural. However, when plausible, but unsubstantiated beliefs, affect policy and decision making, the results can be harmful. The findings of the Hesseling review (1994) are routinely affirmed in research in the United Kingdom and in the United States, but opinions are overwhelmingly still based on beliefs or simplistic assumptions. This is not to say that partial displacement does not exist or that some crimes are not more prone than others. However, the conclusion is clear: crime prevention initiatives can produce very substantial net gains with little or no displacement. Reducing the level of opportunity reduces crime.

ROUTINE AND CRIMINAL ACTIVITY AND THE INTERNET

Since the early 1960s, the Internet has helped speed globalization through the rapid transmission of data. It provides international signaling capability, acts as an instantaneous highway for transporting information, and sets the stage for which individuals and groups can easily interact from every geographic location worldwide. The boundaries of the Internet continue to expand. The continued technological advancement of the Internet has helped not only to improve the quality of personal life but also our professional life. Having a computer at home or at work being able to communicate with others provides a sense of unlimited connection. The use of the Internet is duly noted and continues to improve the quality of life. Being able to communicate with people for a variety of reasons at a moment's notice and the complete or partial secrecy has allowed people to engage in activity that may have just been a thought and not acted out. The privacy of the Internet reduces the possibility of public shame (Internet Society).

The question to be asked is how the crime triangle is affected by the mediation of the Internet. It seems obvious that the *opportunity* for crime is multiplied by the simple fact the criminal is no longer "place-bound." The potential victim is far more likely and more frequently to be exposed to an offender, through the Internet. Furthermore, the issue of **guardianship** is both more straightforward and more difficult in the era of Web surfing. Thus, for example, "parental control" devices on computers may substitute for direct contact by a guardian and thus serve as a significant deterrent. The Internet and the World Wide Web is not designed to make value judgments on data, but to rapidly transmit data.

The ability of the computer criminal to shift easily to new targets is greatly enhanced by mobility created by the ability to "surf" the Web. Traditional crimes are explained by routine activity theory as the result of the confluence of physical circumstance (both potential victim and offender are intentionally in the same place) and events (the victim is "unguarded" and the offender is motivated). The crime act is the by-product of the opportunity resulting from events and circumstances. The deterrence of such crimes comes from shifting either the events (the presence of a guardian) or the circumstances (changing the place). Internet crimes are more difficult to deter for the simple reason that neither the circumstances nor the events are readily altered. Using the Web per se is what makes potential victims vulnerable. The place is always an integral element of the criminal act. However, the Internet is one place to which the potential victim of necessity willingly returns. Avoiding Internet usage (changing the circumstance by changing the place) can only prevent Internet crime. In contemporary society, this is simply not possible. Therefore, unlike traditional crimes, which require a physical place for them to occur, the opportunity for Internet crime has more to do with the effectiveness of indirect guardianship.

The FBI has dedicated significant resources to fighting Internet crime. The Bureau and the National White Collar Crime Center (NWCCC) have partnered to develop an Internet Crimes Complaint Center (ICCC) in which the victims of alleged Internet crimes can register complaints. Specifically, the FBI produces an annual report on Internet Crimes from the complaints that have been lodged on the ICCC site. Since 2000 and in 2001 with the first ICCC report there has been a steady increase in the reporting of alleged Internet crimes. From 2004 to 2005, there was an 11.6 percent increase in reported victimizations. Auction crime tops the list of the most reported allegations from 2001 to 2005, along with other fraudulent claims that appear to involve minimal contact between the victim and criminal.

During 2005, the ICCC determined geographically where many of the alleged criminal activities have been initiated. Seventy-five percent of the alleged perpetrators resided in California, New York, Florida, Texas, Illinois, Pennsylvania, and Ohio. Although child pornography complaints are often highly publicized, they were the least reported to the ICCC in 2005. This specific type of Internet crime was not a part of the categories listed in the ICCC reports of 2001–2004 (Internet Crime Complaint Center).

Committing a crime against a person or property does not necessarily mean a physical encounter taking place. Although society tends to link criminal activity with a victim and violator meeting face-to-face, a crime can occur with the two ever seeing each other. The Internet has provided the cover to criminals and would-be criminals they need to feel comfortable that their identity will not be easily revealed if they engage in criminal behavior. Furthermore, the Internet has also provided cover to victims and unsuspecting victims who often are deterred from engaging in abnormal behavior because of being exposed by their respective community brethren.

As Grabosky (1998) notes:

> . . . . the global village has its dark alleys . . . . The rapid mobility of people, money, information, ideas, and commodities generally, has provided new opportunities for crime, and new challenges for law enforcement agencies . . . . Of equal concern is the lack of international consensus on what constitutes criminal behavior . . . Given the limited capacity of governments to control crime in cyberspace...the first line of defense lies in the exercise of prudent behavior by prospective victims. Just as the first step in the control of burglary is to lock one's doors and windows, so too the basic principles of information security should be honored. (p. 2)

THE VICTIM AND CRIME

For decades criminological theory has focused on the criminal violator when trying to explain crime causation. According to Doerner and Lab (1998, 2002, 2005), the focus shifted away from the victim when he or she lost the right to pursue criminals who had wronged him or her and state assumed responsibility. The unintended consequence of pitting the accused against the state regulates the victim to second- or third-class status.

About five decades ago, sociologists who studied criminology began to investigate to determine if victims played a part in their own victimization. Their significance can be subtle to extreme and be based on factors that are out of their control such as race, gender, age, and mental capacity. When a suitable target is unprotected by a capable guardian, the chances that a crime will take place increases. All that is needed is the final element; the presence of a likely offender. Crime is a matter of circumstance and opportunity. Victims knowingly and unknowingly put themselves in harm's way. It is the repetition of behavior of the potential victim that brings them to the attention of the potential criminal, who can then gage the likelihood of success at a particular moment in time and in a particular place (Regoli and Hewitt 2006; Doerner and Lab 1998, 2002, 2005).

Victim precipitation theory explains some victims start the confrontation which can often lead to death. The precipitation can be both active and passive in nature. Fighting words or even attacking first are examples of active precipitation, and the exhibition of personal characteristics such as a woman's costume or unaware dispute with someone are examples of the passive version. The correlation between the victim and his or her own victimization has resulted in the American criminal justice system advancing this notion and has lead to unprofessional treatment of victims at the hands of criminal justice professionals. Detectives and police officers have been accused of less than sympathetic treatment of rape victims, treating them as though they were being investigated for committing a crime. The insensitive behavior of these law informant professionals led the victims in these cases to believe the focus was on what they did to provoke the perpetrators to forcibly rape them. These misguided ideas about victims are slowly changing as the American criminal justice system looks at ways to improve the manner in which it handles victims.

The potential victim of an Internet crime is different than other crime victims. As noted it is the simple fact of using the Internet that makes Internet crime possible. We cannot turn back the clock to the time when the Internet was not an integral part of daily life. The necessity of being connected to cyberspace sets the stage for possible victimization. There is a second element of self-victimization. To protect against crimes in the physical world we can consciously and actively solicit a guardian (walking home from school or to the parking garage with others, locking the car doors while inside, etc.). While not perfect, such guardians reduce criminal opportunity and will persuade even relatively highly motivated offenders to find other victims. While firewalls, virus protection, and other barriers exist, the effectiveness of these security precautions is dependent upon the user to routinely and correctly employ them. We use computer systems without much consciousness of the quality of the guardianship. It is not so much that we "trust" our technological guardians, as we are ignorant of their capacity and thus unaware of their effectiveness. We make the choice to step into the world of the offender. The computer and the Internet is an integral part of our everyday life. This technological familiarity leads individuals into a false sense of security. Meier and Meithe (1993) conclude:

> Current theories of victimization highlight the symbiotic relationship between conventional and illegal activities. Regardless of their particular terminology, routine activities and lifestyle-exposure theories emphasize how criminal opportunities develop out of the routine activities of everyday life. Routine activity patterns that increase proximity to motivated offenders, increase exposure to risky and dangerous situations, enhance the expected utility or attractiveness of potential crime targets, and reduce the level of guardianship are assumed to increase aggregate rates and individuals' risks of predatory crime. (pp. 494–95)

In the physical world of crime, the guardians are both machines and humans. The machines can be both simple (a lock) and complex (burglar alarm systems). They provide very specific forms of deterrence. The very purpose of the machine or mechanism is to provide that specific form of deterrence. It is the singleness of purpose that makes these mechanical devices and machines, once activated, effective. Mechanical devices are reactive. On the other hand, human guardianship can serve multiple roles in deterring the offender. Moreover, compared to most mechanical deterrence, humans have the advantage of the capacity to think, anticipate, and change. Humans are effective as deterrence device because they can play change roles and behaviors during an event. The capacity to change in response to circumstances and events is what makes the human effective as guardians. The central problem in guarding against Internet crime is that there are no other humans we can bring with us. No matter how sophisticated and complex the "guardians" for the users of the Internet are, these are all mechanical devices. They are reactive. They are designed to prevent actions that have already been identified. They cannot respond to new intrusions and criminal activity.

As Shytov (2005) reminds us the Internet is a technological phenomenon. In his discussion of how to control pornography on the Internet, he offers suggestions that are directly related to the issue of "guardianship":

> It is important to exercise surveillance of the Internet with the purpose of identifying the web sites containing pornographic materials and eliminating or a least blocking them. It can be practical to hold the ISP (Internet Service Providers) responsible for surveillance and blocking access to the porn sites. . . . One way to efficiently reduce pornography on the Internet is to oblige all users of the Internet to use protective software. Even though this software may not be perfect to block all indecent materials, the technological advances through investment, creativity and effort can improve it. (p. 279)

All crimes require a willing and motivated perpetrator. While motivations may vary, the motivations are indeed there. No crime can occur in the absence of someone who wants to commit an illegal act. Yar (2005) describes four types of cyber crimes:

1. Cyber-trespass—crossing boundaries into other people's property and/or causing damage, e.g. hacking, defacement, viruses.

2. Cyber-deceptions and thefts—stealing (money, property), e.g. credit card fraud, intellectual property violations (a.k.a. 'piracy').

3. Cyber-pornography—activities that breach laws on obscenity and decency.

4. Cyber-violence—doing psychological harm to, or inciting physical harm against others, thereby breaching laws pertaining to the protection of the person, e.g. hate speech, stalking. (p. 410)

The question for us is whether or not these crimes require a different kind of criminal. Yar (2005) asserts that the criminals do not follow the behavioral patterns of "traditional" criminals. Yet Kovacich (1999) and Grabosky (2001) argue that attitudes and behaviors of offenders are still driven by routines and opportunities.

CONCLUSION

There are some environments that are more prone to certain types of crime. Certain communities suffer from higher domestic violence rates than other communities, while addiction to certain types of narcotics may vary from locale to locale. The problem confronting law enforcement in regards to cyber crime is that cyberspace is not a static environment. An individual can "travel" from place to place with the click of a mouse. The lack of personal interaction with the authors of Web pages, or merchants who utilize auction sites for their products, reduces the ability of a person's intuitive ability to determine the level of risk for victimization.

An Internet criminal has a wealth of possible targets depending on their motivations. eBay, one of the largest Internet auction sites, claims to have over 100 million members with an excess of $40 million being transferred on the site daily With the advent of the Internet and the growth of personal computer usage in every corner of the world, cyber terrorism is a growing concern of law enforcement and public officials. Weimann (2004) maintains that the cyber terrorist has a wealth of possible weapons and avenues in which to use these weapons at their disposal. From the theft of sensitive data to the manipulation of utilities systems to releasing viruses designed to destroy or corrupt data, the multiplicity of targets available on the Internet are boundless.

The grounds for sexual predation and murder can be derived from a cyber environment. John Robinson, a Kansas farmer, has been awarded the sobriquet of the "Internet's First Serial Killer." A con artist and thief who had served time for felony theft, Robinson lured his victims via Internet chat rooms where, using the nickname "Slave Master," he would ingratiate himself to women he met there. One of the young women Robinson made contact with over the Internet brought her four-month-old daughter to meet him. After murdering her, Robinson offered to let his brother adopt her baby. Robinson was convicted in 2002 of three murders and received a death sentence (Gribben and Robinson 2007).

The best way to describe the current state of interdiction efforts regarding computer criminals is "catch up." The exponential growth of computer technology and communication devices demands that law enforcement exhibits some degree of "guardianship" over cyberspace. The problem is that too few officers are trained in computer crime investigative techniques. This includes computer forensics. This knowledge is not wasted on the criminals who, for a variety of reasons, operate in a cyber environment.

KEY TERMS

Displacement theory
Guardianship
Internet Crime Complaint Center
National White Collar Crime Center

Opportunity theory
Phishing
Routine activity theory
Situational crime prevention

REFERENCES

Barr, R., and K. Pease. 1990. "Crime placement, displacement, and deflection." In *Crime and Justice: A Review of Research*, edited by M. Tonry and N. Morris. Vol. 12. Chicago: University of Chicago Press.

Clarke, R. V. 1997. *Situational Crime Prevention: Successful Case Studies*. 2nd ed. Albany, NY: Harrow and Heston.

Cohen, L. E., and M. Felson. 1979. Social change and crime rate trends: A routine activity approach. *American Sociological Review* 44: 588–608.

Doerner, W. G., and S. P. Lab. 1998. *Victimology*. 2nd ed. Cincinnati: Anderson.

Doerner, W. G., and S. P. Lab. 2002. *Victimology*. 3rd ed. Cincinnati: Anderson.

Doerner, W. G., and S. P. Lab. 2005. *Victimology*. 4th ed. Cincinnati: Anderson.

Eck, J. E. 1993. The threat of crime displacement. *Criminal Justice Abstracts* 25: 527–46.

Felson, M., and R. V. Clarke. 1998. *Opportunity Makes the Thief. Policing and Reducing Crime Unit, Research, Development and Statistics Directorate, Paper 98*. London: Home Office.

Gabor, T. 1990. Crime displacement and situational prevention: Towards the development of some principles. *Canadian Journal of Criminology* 32: 41–74.

Grabosky, P. N. 1998. Crime and technology in the global village. Paper presented February 1998 at the conference Internet Crime in Melbourne, Australia.

Grabosky, P. N. 2001. Virtual criminality: Old wine in new bottles. *Social and Legal Studies* 10 (2): 243–49.

Gribben, M., and J. E. Robinson Sr. 2007. The slavemaster. Retrieved February 14, 2007, from http://www.crimelibrary.com/serial_killers/predators/john_robinson/index.html

Hesseling, R. B. P. 1994. "Displacement: A review of the empirical literature." In *Crime Prevention Studies 3*. Monsey, NY: Criminal Justice Press.

Hill, I., and K. Pease. 2001. "The wicked issues: Displacement and sustainability." In *Secure Foundations*, edited by S. Ballantyne, et al. London: IPPR.

Johnson, T. A. 2006a. Who are the police and why do we train them? *Police Forum* 15 (1): 1–10.

Johnson, T. A. 2006b. The future of law enforcement: Can community policing survive a post 9/11 era? *Law Enforcement Executive Forum* 6 (5): 23–38.

Kovacich, G. L. 1999. I-way robbery: Crime in the internet. *Computers and Security* 18: 211–20.

Meier, R. F., and T. D. Miethe. 1993. Understanding theories of criminal victimization. *Crime and Justice* 17: 459–99.

Moss, K., and K. Pease. 1999. Crime and Disorder Act 1998: Section 17, A Wolf in sheep's clothing? *Crime Prevention and Community Safety: An International Journal* 1 (4): 15–19.

Regoli, R. M., and J. D. Hewitt. 2006. *Delinquency in Society*. New York: McGraw-Hill.

Rengert, G. F. 1990. Drug purchasing as a routine activity of drug dependent property criminals and the spatial concentration of crime. Paper presented at the American Society of Criminology annual conference.

Sherman, L. W. 1990. "Police crackdowns: Initial and residual deterrence." In *Crime and Justice: A Review of Research*, edited by M. Tonry and N. Morris. Vol. 12. Chicago: University of Chicago Press.

Shytov, A. 2005. Indecency on the internet and international law. *International Journal of Law and Information Technology* 13 (2): 260–80.

Siegel, L. J. 2007. *Criminology: Theories, Patterns and Typologies*. Belmont, CA: Thompson/Wadsworth.

Tomorrow Project Home. April 20, 2007. Tomorrow Project Home. Retrieved June 8, 2007, from Tomorrow Project Home Web site http://www.tomorrowproject.net/pub/1__GLIMPSES/Globalisation/-1243.html

Town, S. 2001. Crime displacement: The perception, problems, evidence, and supporting theory. Retrieved on January 4, 2007, from http://www.crimereduction.gov.uk

Weimann, G. 2004. Cyberterrorism: How real is the threat? Retrieved February 15, 2007, from http://www.usip.org/pubs/specialreports/sr119.html

Wiles, P., and A. Costello. 2000. *The "Road to Nowhere": The Evidence for Travelling Criminals*. Home Office Research Study 207. London: Home Office Research, Development and Statistics Directorate.

Yar, M. 2005. The novelty of cybercrime: An assessment in light of routine activity theory. *European Journal of Criminology* 2 (4): 407–27.

Zimring, F. E. 1972. The medium is the message: Firearm calibre as a determinant of death from assault. *Journal of Legal Studies* 1: 97–123.

Chapter 16

The Rhetoric of Hackers' Neutralizations

Orly Turgeman-Goldschmidt
Bar-Ilan University

Orly Turgeman-Goldschmidt (Ph.D., Hebrew University, 2002) is a lecturer at the Interdisciplinary Department of Social Sciences, Bar-Ilan University, Israel. Her research interests include computer crime, hacking, digital culture, and gender differences in language. She can be contacted at turgemo@mail.biu.ac.il

Abstract

Stories about computer pirates, hackers, and phone phreaks have become all too common. Few studies, however, have examined hacking activities from the perspective of the operators themselves. This chapter shows how hackers use neutralization techniques. The research is based on 54 unstructured, in-depth, face-to-face interviews with Israeli hackers. The findings showed that hackers do not employ two of the commonly used neutralization techniques, "denial of responsibility" and a "sad tale," indicating that they do not rely on the external justifications frequently used by deviants. Instead, similarly to political criminals, hackers assume responsibility for their acts by means of neutralization techniques based on internal justification.

INTRODUCTION

According to Sykes and Matza (1957), delinquents usually sense a moral obligation to be bound by the law, as their values, beliefs, and attitudes are similar to those of law-abiding citizens. When they violate social norms, they justify their behavior by means of a specific set of justifications, called **neutralization techniques**, which enable them to temporarily neutralize those values, beliefs, and attitudes and drift back and forth between conventional and illegitimate behaviors. Techniques of neutralization "free the individual from a large measure of social control" (Matza and Sykes 1961, 713). According to Scott and Lyman (1968), neutralization techniques are "socially approved vocabularies that neutralize an act or its consequences when one or both are called into question . . .To *justify* an act is to assert its positive value in the face of a claim to the contrary." (p. 51).

The author wishes to thank Leonard Weller for his helpful comments on an earlier version of this chapter. Most importantly, she also thanks the interviewees, who shared their life stories with her.

Hacking, or unauthorized computer intrusion (Jordan and Taylor 1998), is usually categorized as a particular type of computer crime (Bequai 1990; Parker 1989; Rosoff, Pontell, and Tillman 2004; Stewart 1990). The purpose of this study is to determine the extent to which hackers use the common neutralization techniques. The following are some examples of the neutralization techniques.

> Neutralizing attitudes include such beliefs as, "Everybody has a racket," "I can't help myself, I was born this way," "I am not at fault," "I am not responsible," "I was drunk and didn't know what I was doing," "I just blew my top," "They can afford it," "He deserved it," and other excuses and justification for committing deviant acts and victimizing others. (Akers 2000, 77)

Neutralization has become an important theory of deviant behavior, extending beyond juvenile delinquency to adult deviancy and to different forms of deviance. Although reported nearly five decades ago, neutralization theory still arouses scholars' interest (e.g., Cromwell and Thurman 2003; Piquero, Tibbetts, and Blankenship 2005; Topalli 2005). In the present chapter, I have analyzed the use of neutralization techniques (Sykes and Matza 1957; Scott and Lyman 1968) by hackers and compared it with the use of such techniques by other types of deviants.

According to Sykes and Matza (1957), there are five neutralization techniques used by deviants in order to protect themselves from feelings of guilt and from blame by others: denial of responsibility, denial of injury, denial of victim, condemnation of condemners, and appeal to higher loyalties. These techniques are critical for reducing the effectiveness of social control and are used by a wide range of deviants. In the case of *denial of responsibility*, the subjects are passive rather than active. The delinquents claim that their acts are due to forces beyond their control. For example, "It wasn't my fault." Sykes and Matza include in this technique the claim by delinquents that unloving parents, bad companions, or slum neighborhoods caused their behavior (1957, 667). In the case of *denial of injury*, the subjects perceive their behavior as harmless. For example, "everybody does it" or the victim can "afford it." In the case of *denial of the victim*, subjects view their behavior as retaliation; the victims deserved it. For examples, when attacking homosexuals or minority groups, the delinquents feel that their victims got what they deserved (Sykes and Matza 1957, 668). In the case of *condemnation of the condemners*, subjects blame lawmakers and law-enforcement, so that those who condemn them are themselves involved in questionable behavior: "The system is corrupt." In the case of *appeal to higher loyalties*, subjects claim that their acts were necessitated by loyalty to others: "I did it for my friends."

Scott and Lyman (1968) have added two other justifications: *sad tale* (first described by Goffman 1961), and *self-fulfillment*. The sad tale is a "selected (often distorted) arrangement of facts that highlight an extremely dismal past, and thus 'explain' the individual's present state" (Scott and Lyman 1968, 52). Scott and Lyman exemplify this technique by citing a mental patient who related: "I was going to night school to get an M.A. degree, and holding down a job in addition, and the load got too much for me" (Goffman 1961, 152). Self-fulfillment is "a peculiarly modern type of justification" (Scott and Lyman 1968, 52) in which deviant behavior is justified by pointing to the individual's need for self-fulfillment. Scott and Lyman (1968) exemplify this technique with an "acid head" who related: "The whole purpose in taking the stuff is self-development. Acid expands consciousness. Mine eyes have seen the glory—can you say that? I never knew what capacities I had until I went on acid."

Different types of deviants, violent and nonviolent alike, utilize neutralization techniques. For example, Scully and Marolla (1996) examined the justifications and excuses of rapists and found that those who denied their actions also justified them, or claimed that what they did was for the good, or that it was allowed under certain circumstances. Deniers referred to their victims' sexual reputation and argued that the women got what they deserved. Those who admitted their acts claimed that they were done under the influence of an external factor or agent, such as alcohol, drugs, or emotional problems. Neutralization techniques were also found among hard-core, active, noninstitutionalized (uncaught) drug dealers, street robbers, and carjackers (Topalli 2005), and among professional contract killers (Levi 1981). According to Levi (1981), a professional killer (hit man) starts his career by adapting to his new role and by learning to view killing as "just a job" or as "just business." This enables him to deny responsibility for his act; he views himself as a "hired gun," and his victims as "targets" rather than people.

Nonviolent deviants were also found to use neutralization techniques. Cromwell and Thurman (2003) found that many shoplifters neutralized their activities by claiming loss of self-control due to alcohol or drug use, which is a common form of denial of responsibility. For example, one female respondent claimed: "I don't know what comes over me. It's like, you know, somebody else is doing it, not me" (Cromwell and Thurman 2003, 541). Others attributed their behavior to "poor parenting, bad companions or internal forces (the devil made me do it)" (p. 542).

In his book about professional criminals and organized crime, *The Criminal Elite*, Abadinsky (1983) claimed that professional criminals are very skilled, "smart guys" (p. 166), and do not rely on violence. Professional jewelry thieves use neutralizing techniques such as denial of injury (e.g., "yesterday in the paper I read where Sears had the biggest year in history, made more money than ever before," p. 60), and denial of the victim (e.g., "they get it back from insurance," p. 60). Abadinsky's principal informant argues that he was a victim of circumstances. "Poor and devoid of remunerative skills, yet ambitious and possessing an outstanding physique and physical stamina, he was simply a 'natural' for jewel theft" (p. 55). Thus, he denies his responsibility and regards himself as a victim of circumstances.

Another example of a neutralization technique is found in a study conducted by Jesilow, Pontell, and Geis (1996), who studied physicians involved in medical fraud cases. Among other neutralizations, the physicians used denial of responsibility; they called their activities "mistakes," and some blamed themselves for not being careful enough. For example, "a psychiatrist who illegally submitted bills under his name (and took a cut) for work done by psychologists not qualified for payment under Medicaid blamed the therapists . . . 'There were times I wanted to quit, but the therapist would say that these people are in need of therapy, and it is going well . . . I couldn't do it myself; I wasn't there all the time'" (Jesilow, Pontell, and Geis 1996, 76).

Neutralization techniques were found also among white-collar deviants. Benson (1985) examined the justifications used by white-collar offenders who had committed securities and exchange fraud, antitrust violations, false claims, and tax evasion to explain their involvement in criminal activities. He found that the most consistent pattern was denial of criminal intent. Tax violators, for instance, "were more likely to have acted as individuals rather than as part of a group and, as a result, were more prone to account for their offenses by referring to them as mistakes or the product of special circumstances" (Benson 1996, 69). For example, "I didn't cheat. I just didn't know how to report it" (p. 69). Cromwell (1996) claimed that the main theme in occupational crime is that offenders create elaborate justifications, excuses, and rationalizations to be able to deny to themselves responsibility for their criminal behavior. Piquero et al. (2005), who evaluated the decisions of MBA students to commit corporate offenses in the promotion of a hypothetical pharmaceutical drug, found that the "denial of responsibility" techniques had positive effects on the intention to commit corporate crime. The statement "The government exaggerates the danger to consumers from most products" exemplifies both denial of injury and denial of responsibility. "This statement allows the individual to deny the injury of the act by claiming that the government is overly cautious in assessing the danger to the public. This belief also relates to denial of responsibility in the sense that it implies that there is minimal danger in the use of marketed products, so the companies that produce such items should not be held responsible if injuries do happen to occur from usage" (p. 170). Interviewee statements often contain more then one neutralization technique. Jesilow, Pontell, and Geis (1996, 76) noted that "Commonly, denials of responsibility were blended with other self-justifications."

In sum, various types of deviants utilize a range of neutralization techniques and explicitly tend to deny responsibility for their actions. In the present chapter, I investigate techniques of neutralization (Scott and Lyman 1968; Sykes and Matza 1957) as possible explanations for the way in which hackers reduce their perceived guilt about their illegal conduct involving computers.

THE PHENOMENON OF HACKING

Given the authorities' rush to discourage and cope with forms of crime borne from rapidly advancing technologies, hacking has important ramifications for policy, enforcement, and prevention. Understanding of the fundamental mindsets of hackers (also known as members of the computer underground) underlies any effective response to the problem.

Rosoff, Pontell, and Tillman (2004, 477) conceptualized computer crimes as electronic embezzlement and financial theft, computer hacking, malicious sabotage such as the dissemination of viruses, use of computers and computer networks for the purposes of espionage, and use of electronic devices and computer codes for making unauthorized long-distance telephone calls (phone phreaking). Tavani (2000) named the following types of computer crimes: piracy, break-ins, and sabotage in cyberspace. His categories seem more appropriate because he separates genuine computer crimes from criminal activities in which computer technology is merely at hand or used as just another tool (Tavani 2000, 6).

According to the 2006 Internet Crime Report of the National White Collar Crime Center of the FBI (Internet Crime Complaint Center; IC3), the vast majority of cases of Internet crime was fraudulent in nature and involved a financial loss on the part of the complainant. Internet auction fraud was by far the most reported offense, followed by nondelivery of merchandise and/or payment, check fraud, credit and debit card fraud, computer fraud, confidence fraud, other financial institutions fraud, identity theft, investment fraud, and child pornography confidence fraud. Of individuals who reported financial losses, the highest median losses were found among Nigerian letter fraud, check fraud, and other investment fraud complainants.

The 2006 CSI/FBI Computer Crime and Security Survey lists the following reported misuses (in order of decreasing frequency): virus, laptop/mobile theft, insider abuse of Net access, unauthorized access to information, denial of service, system penetration, abuse of wireless network, theft of proprietary information, financial fraud, telecom fraud, misuse of public Web application, Web site defacement, and sabotage. The survey indicates that unauthorized use is "a broad category, covering undesired uses of computer and network resources in addition to abuses that are traditionally classified as "attacks." Trading offensive jokes among colleagues using a corporate e-mail server or storing downloaded music on an enterprise workstation in defiance of corporate policy would both constitute unauthorized use, but wouldn't be reflected in traditional cybercrime categories" (p. 11). The survey found that the top four categories of losses were viruses, unauthorized access, laptop or mobile hardware theft, and theft of proprietary information, which together accounted for 74.3% of total losses.

Hacking is an exclusive and relatively new form of deviance. The techniques of neutralization used by hackers have not yet been examined. Examining these techniques is important because hackers, more than other types of deviants, arouse ambivalent reactions, including positive ones.

The first generations of hackers were pioneers in the use of computers; they were the enthusiasts, the "heroes of the computer revolution" (Levy 1984). Currently, however, the label "hackers" is used negatively and refers to electronic criminals or vandals (Chandler 1996). Hackers of the old school use the term "cracker" to distinguish the malicious type, but the contested nature of the term is worth bearing in mind (Yar 2005, 390). Although the hacker label may suggest people who are a threat to national security or the intellectual property of others (Halbert 1997, 369), the term still retains its original connotation of "bitheads" who have mastered computer technology at very high levels (e.g., Upitis 1998). Skibell (2002, 353) called the computer hacker a myth, claiming that few **computer hackers** possess sufficient skills or the desire to commit more than nuisance crimes.

Hackers are involved not only in deviant activities, but have also developed the computer, the Internet, computer programs, and peripheral devices (Chandler 1996; Himanen 2001; Kitchin 1998; Wall 2001). Hackers "are not TV celebrities . . . but everyone knows their achievements, which form a large part of our new, emerging society's technological basis: the Internet and the Web (which together can be called the Net), the personal computer, and an important portion of the software used for running them" (Himanen 2001, vii). Their ethical stand is that information should be free (Levy 1984) and shared (Himanen 2001), as demonstrated by the open-source movement, the best-known example of which is the development of the Linux operating system (Ljungberg 2000). The Linux project enables all computer users to use, test, and develop their programs as scientific researchers (Himanen 2001, 180). Gunkel (2001) applied the term "hacking" as an analytical tool in his book *Hacking Cyberspace*, using the analogy of penetrating the theories of cyberspace in the way that hackers penetrate computer systems. These positive qualities are being attributed to the hacker community even now, despite the process of criminalization (Hollinger and Lanza-Kaduce 1988) that has gradually changed the meaning of the hacker label from computer pioneer to computer burglar (Voiskounsky and Smyslova 2003, 172).

According to Denning (2000), journalists and the public are fascinated by any kind of computer attack. Voiskounsky and Smyslova (2003) noted that Russian hackers are informally treated as heroes, and not as criminals. In a survey of public attitudes toward computer crimes, Dowland et al. (1999) reported that a high proportion of respondents were indifferent to illegal activities such as the unauthorized viewing of someone else's data or the copying of data or software. White and Pooch (1994, 172) urge that we "stop glorifying the exploits of the abusers of this electronic frontier. We need to use appropriate terms, such as software theft, instead of adding an air of legitimacy to actions by using terms such as 'piracy.'" Although it is difficult to estimate the losses due to software piracy, it is an extremely costly problem (Rosoff, Pontell, and Tillman 2004).

Part of the ambiguity surrounding the perceptions of hackers has to do with the changing attitudes toward hackers over the years, but it is also due to the many types of hackers and hacking activities. A hacker may be a specialist programmer who explores, tests, and pushes computers to their limits (Stewart 1990), and is not engaged in criminal acts. Alternatively, the hacker may be a specialist in obtaining unauthorized access to computer systems (Jordan and Taylor 1998; Meyer and Thomas 1990), which is usually a criminal activity.

There are significant differences between hackers. The term "hackers" includes a variety of types. Leeson and Coyne (2006) divide the community of hackers into three types, based on their motivation: The "good" hackers illegally penetrate computer systems but share security weaknesses with the people in charge of the systems. The "bad" hackers are fame-driven and commit unethical hacking by penetrating into computer systems. The third type is that of "greedy" hackers who are driven by profits; they may be "good" (when they work for or operate computer security firms) or "bad" (when they engage in activities such as credit card fraud, selling sensitive information stolen from one firm to the other, or work in the service of other criminals). In a study based on interviews of hackers attending hackers' conventions, Schell and Dodge (2002) found that 36% said they hacked to "advance network, software, and computer capabilities," 34% claimed to do so "to solve puzzles or challenges," and 5% said they hacked to "make society a better place to live." They found that only a small proportion of bad hackers were malevolent. The data in this paper is derived mainly from hackers who are not driven by profit.

A hacker may also be a political activist. "Hacktivists" often define themselves as hackers with political consciences (Denning 2000; Jordan and Taylor 2004). Recently, more and more cases of hackers' political activities have been reported. Since the "Al-Kuds Intifada," the Palestinian uprising that began in October 2000, we frequently hear and read about "virtual battles" between Israeli and Arab hackers taking place over the Web. Politically driven "cyber wars" also took place during the tension between the United States and China following the collision of a U.S. spy plane and a Chinese jet fighter. On May 10, 2001, the online edition of *The New York Times* featured news that Chinese hackers had attacked 1,000 U.S. Web sites, and that American hackers penetrated into hundreds of Chinese sites, leaving messages such as "We will hate China forever and we will hack its sites."

In sum, it seems that the attitude toward hackers conforms to Lemert's concept (2000) of unstable equilibrium in societal reaction to deviance, as it arouses positive evaluations and reactions as well. Our question, therefore, is whether in light of this ambivalent societal reaction the neutralization techniques used by hackers are different from those used by other types of deviants.

METHOD

Stories about computer pirates, hackers, and phone **phreaks** have become common. In view of the growing concern about computer crime and the expectation that a significant part of future transgressions will involve cyber crime (e.g., Denning 2000; Stephens 1998), it is important to investigate hacker activities and understand their neutralization processes. Few studies have examined hacking activities from the perspective of the operators themselves, that is, their perceptions, attitudes, behaviors, etc. According to Skinner and Fream (1997, 496), "Most studies on computer crime have been carried out on the victims of computer crime rather than the perpetrator." For example, both the 2006 CSI/FBI survey and the 2006 Internet Crime Report of the National White Collar Crime Center of the FBI are based on responses or complaints by victims rather than reports by perpetrators, and they do not analyze perpetrator accounts. The academic literature on crime and delinquency has neglected this area (Yar 2005). Specifically, little is known about the hackers' drive.

Researchers have only vague ideas on what really pushes hackers to hack, that is, what their motivation is. Although this is a key issue, too little efforts have been made to understand motivation of the modern generation of hackers. Since only anecdotal and self-reported evidences are available, we might conclude that research in this problem area is not advanced enough (Voiskounsky and Smyslova 2003, 172).

Despite the difficulties researchers face in gaining access to the hacker community, (see Jordan and Taylor 1998; Voiskounsky and Smyslova 2003), I was able to conduct 54 unstructured, in-depth, face-to-face interviews with Israeli hackers. I used the narrative interview technique (Rosenthal and Bar-On 1992) to obtain the life stories of the participants. In the biographic narrative interpretive method (Wengraf 2001), the first part contains the main narrative, usually the life story, told without interruptions. I used nonverbal means and paralinguistic expressions of interest and attention to encourage interviewees to open up: body language (an attentive listening posture and a degree of eye contact) and nonverbal sounds such as "hmm" to indicate that I was listening. The second part was the "asking questions" stage. I collected information based on the narrative, elaborating on the biographical events mentioned earlier by the interviewees, and about additional aspects of the main story.

Locating interviewees required intensive efforts to establish connections and make the acquaintance of various informants and of suitable potential candidates. I located seven interviewees through media reports (one was interviewed on TV and six appeared in magazine reports); five at Israeli hacker conferences (one called Movement, a demo scene party, and the other called Y2Hack); one interviewee at an Israeli conference about information security; two through the Internet (arranging a face-to-face interview on ICQ); and six with the aid of other informants (journalists, a radio broadcaster, and the owner of a computer company). Two interviewees approached me when I was lecturing on computer crime (each at a different lecture). Acquaintances and family members were the source of six other interviews. The remaining 25 interviewees came as a result of snowball or chain referrals. I asked participants to recommend others. I had many small chains of referral (16) because the initial interviewees did not always recommend additional ones. For example, of two interviewees who approached me after the lectures, one referred me to another interviewee, the other did not.

The interviews were conducted in 1998 and 1999 in the hackers' homes or in such public places as coffee shops, according to interviewee preferences. I took notes during the interviews, recording the words of the interviewees almost verbatim. I assigned each interviewee an identification number, without any identifying details. The interviews lasted an average of three hours (the shortest was two hours, the longest eight). In a few cases, more than one meeting was necessary to complete the interview. At the end of the interview, I asked whether there was anything they wanted to add or felt that they had missed, then thanked them and ended the session. Later, I sent them a thank you note by e-mail. In most cases, interviewees responded positively, saying that they should be thanking me.

I analyzed the data using qualitative techniques that included two main stages: the generation of categories and the forming of hypotheses (Glaser and Strauss 1967, 35). Generating categories is referred to as "encoding"; Strauss (1987, 25) called it "the concept-indicator model." After a close reading of the interviews, I assigned names to classes of actions or events based on a series of indicators. Comparing indicators and comparing and contrasting similarities, differences, and inconsistencies helped generate the coded categories. After I defined a set of categories that covered the hackers' neutralization techniques, based on their accounts of hacking activities, I generated a series of hypotheses or theoretical propositions (Strauss and Corbin 2000). These propositions were based on conceptual relationships between categories and sub-categories. I continued this process until the categories and propositions were verified by constantly referring back to the data for impressions, and saturated; that is, despite new data and additional detail, they remained stable.

Hackers were mostly males (51 out of 54 interviewees). They were white, nonviolent, from upper-middle-class families, mostly with no prior criminal records (only six reported a criminal record, of which five were in computer crime). Average age was 24, with a range between 14 and 49, and the most common age group between 20 and 30, indicating that the phenomenon does not reflect only adolescent delinquent behavior. This profile matches other findings in the literature that most hackers are young adult males, have no previous criminal record, are white, nonviolent, and come from upper-middle-class backgrounds (Ball 1985; Forester and Morrison 1994; Gilbora 1996; Hollinger 1991; Hollinger and Lanza-Kaduce 1988).

NEUTRALIZATION TECHNIQUES OF HACKERS

Hackers used accounts to justify three types of computer offenses they had committed: (1) software piracy (unauthorized duplication of pirated software, unauthorized distribution of pirated software, cracking software or games, and selling cracked pirated software); (2) hacking (unauthorized accessing of computer systems, using illegal Internet accounts, development and/or distribution of viruses, browsing or reading other users' files, stealing computer-stored information, causing computer systems to crash, using stolen credit cards from the Internet); and (3) phreaking (using either technology or telephone credit card numbers to avoid charges for long-distance phone calls). Most of these offenses are of the same type as attacks or instances of misuse detected by the 2006 CSI/FBI survey (such as viruses, unauthorized access to information, denial of service, system penetration, theft of proprietary information, system penetration, Web site defacement, and sabotage).

Indeed, although the nature of cyber crime is constantly changing, hackers who are not motivated primarily by greed are still a group apart with unique characteristics. Hackers' activities not driven by profit and similar to those described in this paper continue to make headlines. For example, Netherby reported on HD DVD encryption code broken and posted online by a hacker for the benefit of tech-savvy users to break the content protection on HD DVDs; the popular Web site Digg.com allows posts containing this crack (www.videobusiness.com, March 5, 2007). Spero news reported the editors of a Catholic Web site claiming that their site was brought down by Muslim hackers from Turkey (www.speroforum.com, May 22, 2007). The following is an analysis of hackers' accounts of their use of neutralization techniques.

Denial of Injury

Deviants make a distinction in assessing the extent of damage caused by their behavior, and justify their behavior by determining the amount of harm it may have caused, if any. Hackers try to prove that although their behavior deviates from the norm it does not hurt anyone or that the harm is insignificant. Sykes and Matza (1957) noted that a deviant could define vandalism as mischief because the people whose possessions were destroyed or stolen can easily afford it. Interviewees used this technique to report copying, cracking, and distributing protected software, using other people's Internet accounts, browsing through other people's files, programming and sending viruses, and using other people's credit cards. Even when it was clear that damage had been done, hackers found it comfortable to claim that they had no malicious intentions.

For example, Ran (all names are fictitious), who developed viruses "for the challenge in it, and to see how it works," said that sometimes when he wanted to get back at someone he would send him a virus. He felt surprisingly at ease with it, claiming that he had no malicious intentions:

> I wrote viruses. I was also interviewed about how they work. I became quite good at it, though today I'm not up to date. I wrote some for myself, I didn't distribute them that much. I didn't mean to do any harm, it was all for the challenge. I wanted to see how it works . . . That's the thing about being a hacker. You don't know when it'll kick in [the virus]. That's the "human" thing—it'll do unexpected things at unexpected times. It's smart, the way it multiplies.
>
> Q: How did you feel the first time you wrote a virus?
>
> A: It was fun; I was satisfied, creating something so perfect, working, multiplying. I was the least interested in the damage it does. What interested me was that I tell it what to do. It's inside [the system], and you program it what to do, what not to do. I was never into destruction, it never interested me. (All quotations have been translated from Hebrew.)

Computer-related offenses are a new type of offense that is not physically tangible. The domain of computer hacking is generally considered to be virtual space, or a "space without bodies" (Thomas 1998). According to Michalowski and Pfuhl (1991), hacking is an offense in which the offender might not feel, in the physical sense, that damage has been done, because electronic information in computer systems can be "stolen" without physically taking or touching it. The following example refers to the intangibility of the offense:

> First of all, where did it all start? The first stage is developing the software. Software is a strange bird. It's not a product, it's definitely an outcome of something, but it's not something tangible. You cannot see it with your eyes but you can download it through the net, so it is difficult (Ronen).

According to hackers, downloading information is copying, not stealing (Denning 1990). Gad says, "It's not that I'm stealing somebody else's cucumber. The cucumber stays there. I don't have the money, Microsoft does. If I have to pay, I wouldn't be able to afford my breakfast; Microsoft could, even if I don't pay it." When the interviewees claim that damaging an institution or an organization is different from damaging an individual person, they mean that companies are not really damaged and can easily overcome such invasions; they neutralize their sense of guilt by denying the injury.

Hackers who offered accounts based on weak deterrents tried to show that, although their behavior was deviant, its consequences were insignificant (Sykes and Matza 1957). Uri presented his and his friends' behavior—breaking into computer systems—as "mischievous acts" that should not be punishable. Only when he saw friends arrested and sentenced did he decide to stop ("Once it became dangerous, and I became aware of the danger, I saw the ground burning, so I decided to stop."). Aviram said:

> [I would copy software] but I'm afraid to sell and make a business out of it. It depends on the chances of someone actually knocking on my door and punishing me for copying software. I know that what I'm doing is a crime, but I'm OK with it. It's the norm; it doesn't feel like a crime. It never bothered me.

Hackers who explained their unauthorized browsing the contents of other people's computers as "voyeuristic" curiosity often neutralized their guilt by claiming that as long people are not aware that somebody is browsing through their files they are not harmed and no damage is being done:

> That's the motive for browsing through other people's content (Tiran).

> I want to have access to all the things people do all the time, preferably without their knowledge. Information must be free (Gad).

> After I have satisfied my curiosity, they're useless to me (Oren).

Denial of the Victim

Using this technique, deviants can neutralize their guilt by persisting in the idea that any damage done was justifiable under the circumstances. The victim is in fact not a victim but a person deserving of punishment (Sykes and Matza 1957). According to Scott and Lyman (1968), deviants who use this technique describe four categories of punishable people as legitimate targets: (a) close enemies who have harmed the offender directly; (b) people who do not conform to normative social roles, such as homosexuals and prostitutes; (c) groups with tribal stigmas, such as ethnic minorities; and (d) remote enemies, who hold positions perceived as questionable or corrupt, such as politicians. By extension, objects and possessions that represent such people are also targeted. Here, the offender assumes the role of "avenger" and "crusader for justice," and the victim is a sinner needing to be punished. In a similar way, a thief would justify stealing from a store owned by a person he believes to be a criminal.

Hackers who committed offenses such as spreading viruses, crashing computer systems, removing other users from the network, or deleting content from other people's computers justified their actions by revenge. For hackers, the easiest way to "pay someone back" is to employ malicious practices (viruses and such), as these capabilities are readily available within their toolbox.

Hackers can cause intentional damage to whoever is marked as "the enemy." Sending a virus to someone who "deserves it" makes the offense guilt-free. Ben, for instance, uploaded a Trojan type of computer virus to a bulletin board because the operator was not nice to him. Ben said, "He was a stinker to me. Not a problem. Don't forgive—get back, get even. Scene of solely revenge . . . he deserved it, you feel a cool kind of satisfaction." Shaul spoke about a large factory that decided to discontinue his employment and refused to pay him the money they owed him, so he ran "one of mine Trojans that take over on the computer system remotely." He smiled: "three weeks of crashing systems, then the check arrived." In most cases, the victims belonged to the "close enemy" category of punishable people—people who hurt them, insulted them, spread rumors, etc.

Hackers often perceived Microsoft as a remote enemy against whom any offense was justified. Oren, for instance, stated that "we're the only ones who can confront the giant corporations, we have the knowledge, and knowledge is power. Because of Microsoft's dominance, we see it as our enemy." Boaz, who described himself as someone who has neither the opportunity nor the need to hurt people he knows ("I don't fight with people that much"), directs his vandalism against Nazi sites. He is a hacktivist:

> Vandalism in Israel is also about [attacking] Nazi sites; it's just one of the methods. You make a homemade virus, it's very easy. All you need is a little know-how. The problem is getting it into the server, according to the specific virus, what it does; but from then on, it's quite easy . . . The thing about Nazi sites is erasing and destroying the content, or changing—replacing everything that's there with an anti-Nazi site I prepared. It is about revenge, vandalism, anger at other people.

Condemnation of the Condemners

Offenders use this technique to divert attention from their offense to the motives and behaviors of those who criticize and accuse them. Use of this technique is based on the fact that most people violate some norms from time to time; the deviants point out the deviations of their accusers, thereby dismissing their right to accuse or prosecute them. The offenders might call the accusers hypocrites, deviants in disguise, or driven by malice (Sykes and Matza 1957).

In today's world, in which giant corporations control the economy (Duff and Gardiner 1996), hackers (Levy 1984) mistrust the authorities and promote decentralization. They view the freedom of information as an ethical point of utmost importance, and confront the giant corporations that attempt to limit, in their opinion, free information. According to Hollinger (1991), from a hackers' point of view, infringing on software copyrights, distributing passwords, and illegal logging and browsing are not deviant behaviors but symbolic expressions of their resentment against the large bureaucracies that control the media and the sources of information. They see the "real" criminals of the computer world as the private corporations, institutions, and government agencies that try to prevent access to the abundance of information they control. When Bar asks "if there is a software that can make someone in the world do something good, why should he be deprived of it?" he criticizes the software companies and presents himself as fighting for a common cause, the freedom of information. When Ronen says "The software giants are unrealistic. Instead of saying 'you're criminals,' do something about it," he diverts attention from his illegal practices to the software manufacturers' conduct.

Hackers often divert attention from their acts to what they define as tyrannical and overpowering bureaucracies that, in their eyes, are the real criminals of the computer world. Gil's words ("I'm willing to donate ten shekels [approximately $4.00] a month toward the pie that

Bill gets in the face every month.") and Ami's words ("I feel a moral commitment to screw Microsoft.") illustrate the hackers' feelings against Microsoft, and were echoed by many other interviewees. Hackers have indeed affected the development of the open-source movement, and they usually practice what they preach. For example, Linux users are encouraged to use, test, and further develop their programs.

Hackers showed a fundamental reluctance to pay the prices charged by the software companies, which they say are too high and unfair. In addition to claims about high prices ("insane"), hackers often perceive themselves as "crusaders," struggling for free and open information. As Amir said, "everything is free—that's the way it should be." The hackers' claims about the requirement to pay large amounts of money can be seen as an attempt to dictate a new social order, in which the reality (more and more people copying software) would dictate terms to software developers.

Hackers also justify their actions by the ease with which they operate, placing the onus on the victims who failed to protect their computer systems. Using the 'condemnation of condemners' technique, hackers blame the company owners and information security experts for their violations; had they properly protected their information, leaving no "back-doors" open, nobody would have broken into their systems. For example, some claim that massive virus and worm attacks are often caused by Microsoft issuing alerts to its many users about a potential breach in Windows security, which was previously known only to a few academics. Microsoft then supplies a patch, but only a portion of users apply it. In the meantime, hackers are alerted by Microsoft and write worms to take advantage of the advertised breach. Sykes and Matza (1957, 669) maintained that the "orientation toward the conforming world may be of particular importance when it hardens into a bitter cynicism directed against those assigned the task of enforcing or expressing the norms of the dominant society." This attitude is exemplified by Ran's words: "If I succeeded in doing it, it must be legitimate. If I got in there, it was open. I don't enter closed places." He blames inadequate security rather than himself.

Appeal to Higher Loyalties

Deviants using this strategy admit committing the offense and do not deny possible damages but justify the offense by claiming that it was committed to protect higher values, such as loyalty to the group, responsibility toward the family, or love for one's spouse, which are more important than obeying the law. Deviants must break one norm to observe another, more important one (Sykes and Matza 1957).

Sykes and Matza (1957) may not have referred only to normative, acceptable loyalties. For example, Piquero et al. (2005), who investigated techniques of neutralization in corporate crime, found the company's profit as the criminals' primary (if not only) loyalty. Hackers assign utmost importance to the freedom of information ethics. For hackers, curiosity generates a desire to learn and know as much as possible and a need to explore the boundaries of whatever is within discoverable range. Hackers who contend that their conduct was a result of craving for information and knowledge actually regard knowledge as a socially revered value. Ben wants "to be the most up-to-date, to know a lot about everything. For me, it's about communication. To find out things, also about people . . . it's like a library." He actually represents this desired value and ignores the practices he uses to obtain the information. This is how he repudiates any feelings of guilt.

Self-Fulfillment

The "self-fulfillment" technique (Scott and Lyman 1968) is used to justify conduct regarded by others as undesirable. For example, people who abuse drugs claim that the drugs expand their consciousness. Accounts of fun, enjoyment, and thrill, and of computer virtuosity, which are most prevalent among hackers (Turgeman-Goldschmidt 2005), exemplify the self-fulfillment neutralization techniques. These accounts are given in general for a variety of computer offenses. Mor's account is typical:

> I did it for the fun of it, breaking into places, doing illegal things . . . I liked the feeling that they might catch me, the feeling that you're communicating with somebody and you know you're smarter than he is, and he doesn't know it. It gives you a feeling of superiority and control. That's the feeling. Basically, it all comes from the same place—you're doing something that nobody else thought of. You have the power to do things that are more sophisticated; it's competing with the world—to do things that others think I can't. Stealing students' computer access codes is one thing, but I'm talking about much more difficult things . . . I helped friends get good jobs in the army, it gave me a sense of an ego trip, like a girl walking down the street and everybody looking at her even if she doesn't want anything. Computers sent me on an ego trip, everyone knew I was the best, I proved it to everybody and to myself. A real ego trip . . . The thrill of hiding. Voyeurs like prying. It's about curiosity. It's one of the strongest human urges. When I discovered my sexuality, I would go to the university dorms to see if anybody was doing anything. We would watch through binoculars for hours. My friend had a neighbor, a great looking girl. It's about watching her and knowing she can't see you, the same with hpc [hacking, phreaking, cracking].

Hackers view their activity as a type of "self-fulfillment" (Scott and Lyman 1968) that enables them to achieve enjoyment and to demonstrate their ability and superiority in the use of computers and software. In Gil's words, it is "to do the impossible," or, as Ami said, "to break the boundaries, to be smarter than someone else." Shay said: "It's all my work, totally . . . what I like is to compete totally with the computer. I call it 'computer masturbation' . . . taking a software I don't know and establishing control over it." His emphasis is on knowledge of the computer and its programs and on control over them.

> I'm a hacker, enter my world . . . mine is a world that begins with school . . . I'm smarter than most of the other kids, this crap they teach us bores me . . . Yes, I'm a criminal. My crime is that of curiosity . . . My crime is that of outsmarting you, something that you will never forgive me for (Hacker called "The Mentor" in *Phrack*, 1986).

In sum, hackers used neutralization techniques employed by other deviants: *denial of injury*, *denial of the victim*, *condemnation of the condemners*, and *appeal to higher loyalties* (Sykes and Matza 1957), as well as a sense of *self-fulfillment* (Scott and Lyman 1968), but not two common neutralization techniques: *denial of responsibility* (Sykes and Matza 1957) and the *sad tale* (Scott and Lyman 1968).

DISCUSSION

Hackers used most of the neutralization techniques. *Denial of injury* appears in their claims of lack of malicious intentions, intangibility of the offense, weak deterring factor, and "voyeuristic" curiosity. *Denial of the victim* is present in their claims for revenge. *Condemnation of the condemners* is manifest in their claims of the need to confront the giant corporations that limit the freedom of information and charge high prices, and in the ease of execution that the victims make possible by not protecting their systems. *Appeal to higher loyalties* appears in their claims of curiosity for desire for knowledge. *Self-fulfillment* is demonstrated by describing hacking as an activity that enables them to achieve enjoyment, thrill, and computer virtuosity.

But hackers are unique in the two neutralization techniques that they did not use: *denial of responsibility* and the *sad tale*. The common denominator of these techniques is that they are external, with the operators presenting themselves as not being responsible for their actions, as passive actors controlled by external forces. Rotter (1966) studied how individuals attribute the outcomes of their actions. People who view themselves as being able to "control" events are referred to as "internals," whereas those who believe that events are beyond their control are characterized as "externals" (external locus of control). Externals believe that reinforcements in their life are the consequence of outside forces such as luck, fate, or chance rather than their own efforts (Rotter 1966). Hackers use only neutralization techniques based on internal neutralization—denial of injury, denial of the victim, condemnation of the condemners, and appeal to higher loyalties, as well as a sense of self-fulfillment, in which they act in the name and for the purpose of something. They do not use external techniques in which the actors are being acted upon rather than acting themselves.

In denial of responsibility, the deviants define themselves as not responsible for their deviant actions: "In so far as the delinquent can define himself as lacking responsibility for his actions, the disapproval of self or others is sharply reduced in effectiveness as a restraining influence" (Sykes and Matza 1957, 666). This technique is based on such claims as mistakes or accidents. More important, deviants can claim that their behavior is the consequence of uncontrollable external powers such as unloving parents, an unsupportive spouse, or poverty (Sykes and Matza 1957). The individual who uses this technique has a "billiard ball conception of himself in which he see himself as helplessly propelled into new situations" (Sykes and Matza 1957, 666).

Other types of deviants (violent, nonviolent, and white-collar) used the denial of responsibility technique widely. They view themselves as being acted upon rather than acting. For examples, the rapist who claims that his alcohol and drug use "brought out what was already there but in such intensity it was uncontrollable" (Scully and Marolla 1996, 111); the shoplifter who says, "I never boost when I'm straight. It's the pills, you know?" (Cromwell and Thurman 2003, 543); or the transgressing physicians who "typically laid the blame on a wide variety of persons other than themselves" (Jesilow, Pontell, and Geis 1996, 75). It is reasonable to believe (and worth examining) that profit-driven hackers, such as those who steal electronically stored information or money, show greater similarity to other types of deviants and use denial of responsibility techniques, unlike hackers who are not motivated by profit.

External factors are also used to explain deviation by means of the "sad tale" technique (Scott and Lyman 1968), where deviants structure their biography in a way that accounts for their deviance, and spin a tale of selective and distorted facts that emphasizes their dark and difficult past. For instance, the violator of financial trust, who tells the following story (Benson 1996, 70): "As a kid, I never even—you know kids will sometimes shoplift from the dime store—I never did that. I had never stolen a thing in my life . . . but there are some psychological and personal questions that I wasn't dealing with very well. I wasn't terribly happily married. I was married to a very strong-willed woman and it just wasn't working out." In this example, the offender goes further "to explain how, in an effort to impress his wife, he lived beyond his means and fell into debt" (Benson 1996, 70).

The nonuse of external justification to neutralize hacking activities is meaningful. The fact that hackers do not feel the need to deny their responsibility or to tell a sad tale implies that they take pride in who they are and in what they are doing, and feel no shame or guilt. Although they are perfectly aware of the fact that they are breaking the law, hackers oppose labeling their actions as offenses.

Hackers do not develop a deviant identity in its negative meaning. They are usually not after economic gain and view their actions positively, which leads them to view themselves as information warriors rather than criminals. Hackers perceive themselves as "positive deviants." Dodge (1985, 18) defines positive deviance as "those acts, roles/careers, attributes and appearances . . . singled out for special treatment and recognition, those persons and acts that are evaluated as superior because they surpass conventional expectations." According to Heckert (1989), acts or attributes that deviate from the norm constitute deviance. Geniuses, artists, and exceptional athletes are examples of positive deviance, located at the other extreme of the same continuum on which negative deviants and criminals reside. Hackers view themselves as "positive deviants" because they demonstrate qualities and behaviors that are extraordinary and desirable (Ben-Yehuda 1990; Heckert 1989), such as computer knowledge and virtuosity, and because they regard themselves as agents of positive social change (Ben-Yehuda 1990) in the struggle for free information. "There is a strong romance to outlaw cultures and some of the hacker attacks seem to be youthful modern versions of keyboard bandits wishing to be Billy the Kid or Bonnie and Clyde" (Kling 1996, 5).

Other offenders who do not attribute their activities to external forces are the **political criminals**. Studies of political crime or political deviance are often occupied with the contrasting perceptions of such behaviors as heroism and crime (Ben-Yehuda 1990, 1992; Hagan 1997; Schafer 1974). Schafer (1974, 2–3) explained:

> In the Classical sense, a hero (from the Greek heroes) signifies a man of great courage, strength, and skill who sometimes possesses supernatural powers, who stands up against destructive monsters, demons, and other ruinous forces, or who excels in wars and exploits against other worlds, sometimes superhuman worlds, or against oppressors who are of his own nation, tribe, or family . . . In more sophisticated societies, new elements have altered the traditional ancient image of the hero . . . Not only have those who battled external powers been regarded as heroes but also, more and more, those who fought internal evils as well.

The political deviant is particularly interested in publicity, unlike regular deviants, who are usually interested in concealing their activity (Ben-Yehuda 1990). Publicity enables political deviants to attain recognition and prestige, as is often the case with hackers. This is not to say that there are no significant differences between the nature of the activities and the rhetoric used by hackers and political activists; but there is a definite similarity between these two groups of offenders.

Ben-Yehuda (1992) offered a typology based on three types of political deviance: challenges to rulers, challenges from rulers, and contests between symbolic moral universes from different cultures. It seems that there is a common denominator between hackers and political criminals in the first type (challenges to rulers), which includes symbolic acts from the periphery toward the center that challenge the right of the rulers to rule. This is the most dangerous type, because it challenges the legitimacy of the center.

Examples for this type are civil disobedience, rebellion, and guerrilla and terrorist attacks. A contemporary example is the Palestinian uprising in the Israeli-occupied territories

(*Intifada*) that began in October 2000. Thus, the definition and evaluation of the consequences of deviancy are relative and depend on the point of view of the observer (Ben-Yehuda 1993, 12); the assassin can be stigmatized as negative, criminal, and dangerous, or revered as a revolutionary hero. In the latter case, deviants also have such attributes as respectability, legitimacy, and heroism (Ben-Yehuda 1992). This means that any deviant act can be perceived as either negative or positive deviance (Ben-Yehuda 1990, 1993; Heckert 1989).

While many in Israeli society perceive those who make or deliver bombs or explosive materials and the terrorists and suicide bombers who deliberately murder innocent people as criminals, for many Palestinians they are "martyrs," heroes, sanctified avengers, who earn a reward in heaven. Sacrifice is redefined as heroic death and hailed as the harbinger of national renewal (Cromer 2001, 6). The perpetrators of what appears to Israelis as terrorist acts do not view themselves as criminals and do not deny their responsibility for their activity. Cromer (2001) argued that terrorist acts always include claims of responsibility. Like hackers, the perpetrators of terrorist acts claim responsibility for their acts and use internal justifications.

CONCLUSION

The common factor that enables both hackers and political offenders to present themselves as heroes or as positive deviants is that both groups receive support and sympathy from a significant group within the societies in which they operate, which enables them to view their own actions as positive. They can, therefore, structure their identities as positive deviants, instrumental in achieving positive social change in the long run. Deviance always involves a challenge to power or the dominant morality (Ben-Yehuda 1992, 80). The ambivalent attitudes displayed by parts of the population and even by the legal system can be explained partly, as Lemert says, by "a generalized culture conflict which affects such a large majority of the population that little consistent action is possible" (Lemert 2000, 34). Thus, hackers become a political challenge aimed at the existing social order of the "information age" (Forester 1985), in which people trust computer information technologies implicitly.

This chapter has shown that the use and nonuse of specific techniques of neutralization can shed light on the differences and similarities between various forms of deviance. Although there are significant differences between hackers and political deviants in their rhetoric and the nature of their activities, there is also a significant amount of intriguing similarity between the two groups of deviants. Their choice not to use the common neutralization techniques based on external factors (denial of responsibility and sad tale) reveals more about how society looks upon these two groups than about the deviants themselves.

KEY TERMS

Computer hackers   Phreaks
Hacking   Political criminals
Neutralization techniques

REFERENCES

Abadinsky, H. 1983. *The Criminal Elite: Professional and Organized Crime*. Westport, CT: Greenwood Press.

Akers, R. L. 2000. *Criminological Theories: Introduction, Evaluation, and Application*. Los Angeles, CA: Roxbury.

Ball, L. D. 1985. "Computer crime." In *The Information Technology Revolution*, edited by F. Tom, 532–45. Oxford, UK, and Cambridge, MA: Basil Blackwell and MIT Press.

Ben-Yehuda, N. 1990. *The Politics and Morality of Deviance*. Albany, NY: State University of New York Press.

Ben-Yehuda, N. 1992. Criminalization and deviantization as properties of the social order. *Sociological Review* 40: 73–108.

Ben-Yehuda, N. 1993. *Political Assassination by Jews: A Rhetorical Device for Justice*. Albany, NY: State University of New York.

Benson, M. L. 1985. Denying the guilty mind: Accounting for involvement in white collar crime. *Criminology* 23: 583–607.

Bequai. August. 1990. *Computer-Related Crime*. Federal Republic of Germany: Strasburg, Council of Europe.

Chandler, A. 1996. The changing definition and image of hackers in popular discourse. *International Journal of the Sociology of Law* 24: 229–51.

Computer Security Institute and Federal Bureau of investigations. 2006. CSI/FBI Computer Crime and Security Survey. Available at http://i.cmpnet.com/gocsi/db_area/pdfs/fbi/FBI2006.pdf

Cromer, G. 2001. *Narratives of Violence*. Burlington: Ashgate Dartmouth.

Cromwell, P. ed. 1996. *In Their Own Words, Criminals on Crime*. Los Angeles, CA: Roxbury.

Cromwell, P., and Q. Thurman. 2003. The devil made me do it: Use of neutralizations by shoplifters. *Deviant Behavior* 24: 535–50.

Denning, D. E. 1990. Concerning hackers who break into computer security systems. Paper presented at the 13th National Computer Security Conference, Washington, D.C., October 1–4.

Denning, D. E. 2000. Activism, hacktivism, and cyberterrorism: The Internet as a tool for influencing foreign policy. *Computer Security Journal* 16: 15–35.

Dowland, P. S., S. M. Furnell, H. M. Illingworth, and P. L. Reynolds. 1999. Computer crime and abuse: A survey of public attitudes and awareness. *Computers & Security* 18: 715–26.

Duff, L., and S. Gardiner. 1996. Computer crime in the global village: Strategies for control and regulation-in defence of the hacker. *International Journal of the Sociology of Law* 24: 211–28.

Forester, T. ed. 1985. *The Information Technology Revolution*. Cambridge, MA: The MIT Press.

Forester, T., and M. Perry. 1994. *Computer Ethics: Cautionary Tales and Ethical Dilemmas in Computing*. London: Massachusetts Institute of Technology.

Gilbora, N. 1996. "Elites, lamers, narcs and whores: Exploring the computer underground." In *Wired Women: Gender and New Realities in Cyberspace*, edited by L. Cherny and E. R. Weise. Seattle, WA: Seal Press.

Glaser, B. G., and A. L. Strauss. 1967. *The Discovery of Grounded Theory: Strategies for Qualitative Research*. Chicago, IL: Aldine Publishing Company.

Goffman, E. 1961. *Asylums: Essays on the Social Situation of Mental Patients and other Inmates*. New York: Anchor Books.

Gunkel, D. 2001. *Hacking Cyberspace*. Boulder, CO: Westview Press.

Hagan, F. E. 1997. *Political Crime: Ideology and Criminality*. Boston: Allyn & Bacon.

Halbert, D. 1997. Discourses of danger and the computer hacker. *Information Society* 13: 361–74.

Heckert, D. M. 1989. The relativity of positive deviance: The case of the French impressionists. *Deviant Behavior* 10: 131–44.

Himanen, P. 2001. *The Hacker Ethic and the Spirit of the Information Age.* London: Vintage.

Hollinger, R. C. 1991. Hackers: Computer heroes or electronic highwaymen? *Computers and Society* 2: 6–17.

Hollinger, R. C., and L. Lanza-Kaduce. 1988. The process of criminalization: The case of computer crime laws. *Criminology* 26: 101–26.

Jesilow, P., H. M. Pontell, and G. Geis. 1996. "How doctors defraud Medicaid: Doctors tell their stories." In *In Their Own Words, Criminals on Crime*, edited by P. Cromwell, 74–84. Los Angeles, CA: Roxbury.

Jordan, T., and T. Paul. 1998. A sociology of hackers. *Sociological Review* 46: 757–80.

Jordan, T., and T. Paul. 2004. *Hacktivism and Cyberwars: Rebels with a Cause?* New York, NY: Routledge.

Kitchin, R. 1998. *Cyberspace: The World in the Wires.* Chichester: John Wiley & Sons.

Kling, R. 1996. Beyond outlaws, hackers and pirates: Ethical issues in the work of information and computer science professionals. *Computers and Society* 26: 5–15.

Leeson, P. T., and C. J. Coyne. 2006. The economics of computer hackers. *Journal of Law, Economics and Policy* 1: 511–32.

Lemert, E. M. 2000. "Rules, deviance, and social control theory." In *Crime and Deviance: Essays and Innovations of Edwin M. Lemert*, edited by C. C. Lemert and M. F. Winter. Lanham, MD: Rowman & Littlefield.

Levi, K. 1981. Becoming a hit man: Neutralization in a very deviant career. *Urban Life* 10: 47–63.

Levy, S. 1984. *Hackers: Heroes of the Computer Revolution.* Harmondsworth: Penguin.

Ljungberg, J. 2000. Open source movements as a model for organising. *European Journal of Information Systems* 9: 208–16.

Matza, D., and G. M. Sykes. 1961. Delinquency and subterranean values. *American Sociological Review* 26: 712–19.

Mentor, The. 1986. The conscience of a hacker. *Phrack* 1 (3).

Meyer, G., and J. Thomas. 1990. "The baudy world of the byte bandit: A postmodernist interpretation of the computer underground." In *Computers in Criminal Justice*, edited by F. Schmalleger, 31–67. Bristol, IN: Wyndham Hall.

Michalowski, R. J., and E. H. Pfuhl. 1991. Technology, property, and law—The case of computer crime. *Crime Law and Social Change* 15: 255–75.

National White Collar Crime Center and the Federal Bureau of Investigation. 2006. IC3 2006 Internet Crime Report. Available at www.ic3.gov/media/annualreport/2006_IC3Report.pdf

New York Times. May 10, 2001. Online Web, Hackers report a truce.

Parker, D. B. 1989. *Computer Crime: Criminal Justice Resource Manual.* Washington, DC: Stanford Research Institute (SRI) International.

Piquero, N. L., S. G. Tibbetts, and M. B. Blankenship. 2005. Examining the role of differential association and techniques of neutralization in explaining corporate crime. *Deviant Behavior* 26: 159–88.

Rosenthal, G., and D. Bar-On. 1992. A biographical case study of a victimizer's daughter's strategy: Pseudo-identification with the victims of the holocaust. *Journal of Narrative and Life History* 2: 105–27.

Rosoff, S. M., H. N. Pontell, and R. H. Tillman. 2004. *Profit Without Honor.* Upper Saddle River, NJ: Prentice Hall.

Rotter, J. B. 1966. Generalized expectancy for internal versus external control reinforcement. *Psychological Monographs* 80: 609–16.

Schafer, S. 1974. *The Political Criminal.* New York: The Free Press.

Schell, B., and J. Dodge. 2002. *The Hacking of America: Who's Doing It, Why, And How.* Westport, CT: Quorum Books.

Scott, M. B., and S. M. Lyman. 1968. Accounts. *American Sociological Review* 33: 46–62.

Scully, D., and J. Marolla. 1996. "Convicted rapists' vocabulary of motive: Excuses and justifications." In *In Their Own Words, Criminals on Crime*, edited by P. Cromwell, 107–16. Los Angeles, CA: Roxbury.

Skibell, R. 2002. The myth of the computer hacker. *Information, Security & Society* 5: 336–56.

Skinner, W. F., and A. M. Fream. 1997. A social learning theory analysis of computer crime among college students. *Journal of Research in Crime and Delinquency* 34: 495–518.

Stephens, R. E. 1998. "Cyber-biotech terrorism: Going high tech in the 21st century." In *The Future of Terrorism: Violence in the New Millennium*, edited by H. W. Kushner, 195–207. Thousand Oaks, CA: Sage.

Stewart, J. K. 1990. *Organizing for Computer Crime: Investigation and Prosecution.* Medford: Davis Association.

Strauss, A. L. 1987. *Qualitative Analysis for Social Scientists.* New York: Cambridge University Press.

Strauss, A., and J. Corbin. 2000. "Grounded theory methodology: An overview." In *Handbook of Qualitative Research*, edited by N. K. Denzin and Y. S. Lincoln, 273–85. Thousand Oaks: Sage.

Sykes, G. M., and D. Matza. 1957. Techniques of neutralization: A theory of delinquency. *American Sociological Review* 22: 664–70.

Tavani, H. 2000. Defining the boundaries of computer crime: Piracy, break-ins, and sabotage in cyberspace. *Computers and Society* 30: 3–9.

Taylor, P. A. 1999. *Hackers: Crime and the Digital Sublime.* New-York: Routledge.

Thomas, D. 1998. Criminality on the electronic frontier: Corporality and the judicial construction of the hacker. *Information, Communication and Society* 1: 382–400.

Topalli, V. 2005. When being good is bad: An expansion of neutralization theory. *Criminology* 43: 797–835.

Turgeman-Goldschmidt, O. 2005. Hackers' accounts: Hacking as a social entertainment. *Social Science Computer Review* 23: 8–23.

Upitis, R. B. 1998. From hackers to luddites, game players to game creators: Profiles of adolescent students using technology. *Journal of Curriculum Studies* 30: 293–318.

Voiskounsky, A. E., and O. V. Smyslova. 2003. Flow-based model of computer hackers' motivation. *CyberPsychology & Behavior* 6: 171–80.

Wall, D. S. ed. 2001. *Crime and the Internet.* London: Routledge.

White, G. B., and U. W. Pooch. 1994. "Computer ethics education: Impact from societal norms." In *Proceedings of the Conference on Ethics in the Computer Age. Gatlinburg, Tennessee*, 170–73. New York: ACM Publishing.

Yar, M. 2005. Computer hacking: Just another case of juvenile delinquency? *Howard Journal of Criminal Justice* 44: 387–99.

Chapter 17

Lone Hacks or Group Cracks: Examining the Social Organization of Computer Hackers

Thomas J. Holt
The University of North Carolina at Charlotte

Dr. Thomas J. Holt, Ph.D., is assistant professor in the Department of Criminal Justice at the University of North Carolina at Charlotte, specializing in computer crime, cyber crime, and technology. His research focuses on computer hacking, malware, and the role that technology and the Internet play in facilitating all manners of crime and deviance. He works with computer and information systems scientists, law enforcement, businesses, and technologists to understand and link the technological and social elements of computer crime. Dr. Holt has published many articles in academic journals, and has presented his work at various computer security and criminology conferences. He is also a memberof the editorial board of the *International Journal of Cyber Criminology*.

Abstract

Computer hackers represent an increasingly significant yet misunderstood problem for computer users across the globe (Furnell 2002). Academic research from a variety of disciplines has contributed to our understanding of the hacker. However, there has been very little research on the way these individuals operate individually and in group contexts. This study examines hackers' current level of organization through complexity of divisions of labor, coordination of roles, and purposiveness of associations between hackers (Best and Luckenbill 1994; Decker, Bynum, and Weisel 1998). Three qualitative data sets were created, analyzed, and triangulated to address this question. These analyses indicate that hackers operate along a continuum of organizational sophistication. The implications of this research on the academic study of computer hackers are explored.

INTRODUCTION

Internet use has dramatically affected the way people communicate and do business across the world (see Jewkes and Sharp 2003). Businesses depend on the Internet to draw in commerce and make information available on demand. The banking and financial industries have

The author wishes to thank Jody Miller, Scott Decker, G. David Curry, and Vicki Sauter for helpful comments and assistance on previous drafts. This paper was originally presented on November 18 at the 2005 American Society of Criminology meetings in Toronto, Canada.

implemented new technology, enabling customers to gain access to their funds and accounts with relative ease. As the world comes to rely on computers and rapidly changing technologies, the threat posed by computer criminals has become increasingly significant (see Furnell 2002; Holt 2003; Wall 2001).

The threat posed by one particular kind of computer criminal, the hacker, is of most concern (see Furnell 2002, 28). **Computer hackers** are individuals with a profound interest in computers and technology who have used their knowledge to access computer systems (Schell, Dodge, and Moutsatsos 2002). Many in the general public identify hackers as a primary threat to computer security, and there is significant media attention given to dramatic computer crimes attributed to hackers (Furnell 2002, 29). Individual nations and international bodies have recently created legislation to combat hacker-related crimes (Norman 2001). In fact, the U.S. federal sentencing guidelines for hacking have been expanded to provide life sentences if a hack leads to injury and death (Krebs 2003). The business community has also taken action to proactively fight against hackers. For example, Microsoft recently announced they would offer monetary rewards for information leading to the capture of computer hackers and virus writers (Lemos 2003a).

Researchers from a variety of fields, including criminology (Holt 2007), computer science (Furnell 2002), and psychology (Woo 2003), have developed a diverse literature on computer hackers. This scholarship has improved our knowledge of the attack methods and subculture of computer hackers, though few have examined the way hackers operate individually and in group contexts (except Meyer 1989). Most deviants have relationships with one another and form associations, especially in the context of subcultures (see Best and Luckenbill 1994). A study by Meyer (1989) found hackers had connections with others online, though they overwhelmingly offended alone.[1]

The insights generated by Meyer's research have been used by law enforcement agencies to combat the threats from hackers and hacker groups (Best and Luckenbill 1994); however few have subsequently explored this issue with on- or offline data. Considering the vast shifts in computer technology over the past two decades, it is entirely possible that the structure and nature of hacker relationships have changed on- and offline. For example, hackers have become involved in online terrorism (Williams 2001) and organized crime (Kleen 2001), but it is unknown how prevalent these groups are in hacker subculture. Thus, it is critical to explore hacker **social organization** to improve our knowledge of modern hackers and better combat their activities.

This qualitative study attempts to address this gap using three data sets, including 365 strings from six hacker **Web forums**, interviews with active hackers, and observations at a hacker convention. Grounded theory techniques (Corbin and Strauss 1990) were used to analyze these data, and the results are compared against previous research to consider any similarities or changes that have occurred. The significance of these findings for the larger academic study of hackers is also discussed.

[1]Meyer's (1989) research was based on the first edition of Best and Luckenbill's work from 1982. The current study works from the second edition of Best and Luckenbill's (1994) work, though there have been relatively minor substantive changes across the versions (p. vi).

THEORIES OF SOCIAL ORGANIZATION

Social organization frameworks provide a way to account for relationships between deviants, and how they form, persist, and operate (Best and Luckenbill 1994). Sociologists have developed organizational frameworks to examine deviant behavior (Cressy 1972; Miller 1978), however, Best and Luckenbill (1994) provide the most comprehensive theoretical framework for understanding the organizational features of deviant subcultures. Their classification scheme for examining the organizational sophistication of groups was measured based on four characteristics: associations between deviants; participation in deviance individually or collectively; the division of labor within the group; and how long their deviant activities "extend over time and space" (Best and Luckenbill 1994, 12). These characteristics create a continuum of organizational sophistication along which Best and Luckenbill (1994) classify five forms of deviant organization: loners, colleagues, peers, teams, and formal organizations (see Table 17-1; Best and Luckenbill 1994, 12).

Loners are the least sophisticated group, as they associate with one another infrequently and do not participate in deviant acts together (Best and Luckenbill 1994, 12). Colleagues are the next most sophisticated group, because individuals create a deviant subculture based on their shared knowledge. Despite this connection, colleagues are not very sophisticated by measures of social organization: they do not offend together, have no division of labor, and do not exist over time. Peers have all the characteristics of colleagues and offend together. However, they are relatively short lived, with no division of labor (Best and Luckenbill 1994, 12). Teams are more sophisticated than peers. They last for longer periods of time and have an elaborate division of labor for engaging in deviance (Best and Luckenbill 1994, 23). The formal organization is the most sophisticated deviant organization that Best and Luckenbill include in their framework. Formal organizations have all the elements of teams, as well as extended duration across time and space (Best and Luckenbill 1994, 12).

TABLE 17-1 Best and Luckenbill's (1994) Social Organization Framework

Organization Characteristics

	Mutual Association	Mutual Participation	Division of Labor	Elaborate Extended Organization
Loners	No	No	No	No
Colleagues	Yes	No	No	No
Peers	Yes	Yes	No	No
Teams	Yes	Yes	Yes	No
Formal Organizations	Yes	Yes	Yes	Yes

Source: Best and Luckenbill (1994, p. 12)

Previous Research on Hacker Social Organization

Using this framework, Meyer (1989) examined hackers with ethnographic data generated from 17 months of participant observation online, including Bulletin Board Systems (BBSs), e-mail, and phone communications with hackers. He found that computer hackers functioned as colleagues because they developed a subculture centered on communications technology (Meyer 1989, 63). This subculture created a network where hackers could socialize and exchange information with others, as well as indoctrinate new members into their subcultural norms and values (Meyer 1989, 63).

Still, the majority of hacking was performed alone because of the sheer physical distance separating individuals online. Additionally, a great deal of competition existed between hackers because only a finite number of security flaws existed. This drove individuals to identify and exploit or fix these holes before anyone else does (Meyer 1989, 66). Thus, hackers were colleagues based on the Best and Luckenbill framework (1994), since they formed a subculture and shared information, but did not hack with others (Meyer 1989, 63).

There were also instances in which hackers resembled peer organizations, particularly when individuals organized into cooperative working groups (Meyer 1989, 63). Hacker groups formed through private and public BBS, where hackers could connect and share information with others if they showed some knowledge of the computer underground (Meyer 1989, 51). If one gained access to such BBS, they had the potential to join the group that ran it. This had a significant benefit: access to valuable information otherwise kept from the general hacker population (Meyer 1989, 67). Since sensitive information could be abused or could draw unwanted attention from law enforcement agencies, such knowledge was shared only between members of groups (Meyer 1989; Landreth 1985).

Meyer (1989) found that associations with a group could lead to mutual participation in actual hacks against systems (p. 68). Such relationships moved these hacker groups beyond collegial associations to create peer organizations. However, most hacker groups were short lived, had small memberships, no set division of labor, were leaderless, and allowed individuals to do whatever they desired (Meyer 1989, 73). These characteristics limited hacker groups to peer associations rather than more sophisticated organizations. This assertion has been supported by some recent research indicating that hackers operate in gangs (Slatalla and Quittner 1995; Mann and Sutton 1998).[2]

Yet, Best and Luckenbill (1994) caution that "a particular type of deviant can organize in various ways in different societies or at different times" (Best and Luckenbill 1994, 13). The social organization of any given group is mutable over time and may fall outside of their classification schema. In that regard, recent research suggests that hackers have grown more sophisticated and may now, in some instances, constitute teams. Several hacker groups appear to meet the team criteria, including the Chaos Computer Club, the Cult of the Dead Cow, and the l0pht (see Furnell 2002). There is also growing evidence that hackers are involved in organized crime (Williams 2001) and terrorist groups (Kleen 2001), indicating that some hackers

---

[2]This structural similarity between hacker groups and gangs is relatively unsubstantiated in the text by Mann and Sutton (1998). Additionally, it is unclear why Slatalla and Quittner use the term "gang" throughout their research other than to create a sort of moral panic around hacking (see Thomas 2002). Thus, the similarities between hacker groups and gangs are not fully understood or supported at this time.

may now operate in formal organizations. However, it is unclear how common these organizational forms are in hacker subculture.

THE PRESENT STUDY

Given these questions, it is critical to reexamine the current state of the social organization of computer hackers. This study expands from the previous research (Meyer 1989) through the use of grounded theory techniques to examine hacker social organization with three qualitative data sets. These techniques allow the identification of important issues and concepts to emerge from research subjects. Qualitative data were used to assess hacker social organization as they provide an insider's perspective on the topic of inquiry (see Silverman 2001). Multiple data sets were developed to more fully address this research question and gain access to a large sample of hackers who are otherwise difficult to access (see Gilboa 1996; Wysocki 2003).

The three data sets examined for this research include 365 strings from six hacker Web forums, interviews with active hackers, and observations made at the 2004 Defcon Hacker Convention. Each of these unique sources allows hackers to be viewed in different social settings and from individual and group perspectives. The inductive nature of this study also provides a way to move beyond the parameters of Best and Luckenbill's (1994) ideal types and generate new evidence of hackers' social organization.

Web Forum Data

The first data set used was a series of 365 posts to six different hacker Web forums. Forums have been used with some success by researchers examining hackers (Loper 2000; Mann and Sutton 1998), and function as online discussion groups where individuals can discuss a variety of problems or issues. An individual creates a post within a forum, asking a question or giving an opinion. Other people respond to the remarks with posts of their own that are connected together to create strings. Thus, strings are composed of posts that center on a specific topic under a forum's general heading. Since posters respond to the ideas of others, the exchanges present in the strings of a forum may "resemble a kind of marathon focused discussion group" (Mann and Sutton 1998, 210). As a result, forums demonstrate relationships between individuals, provide information on the quality and strength of ties between hackers, and specify what information hackers exchange in public forums.

The forums identified for this data set were selected based on several criteria, including size, traffic, and public accessibility. Forums with both large and small user populations were identified to represent the range of forums currently operating online. Additionally, high traffic forums with a large number of existing posts were selected, as frequent posts suggest high activity. Finally, public forums were selected because they do not require individuals to register with the site to examine previous posts.[3]

---

[3]The Web addresses and names of groups and users of all sites and forums used will not be provided in this analysis in an effort to maintain some confidentiality for the hacker groups and forum users. Pseudonyms are used to refer to all interviewees, unless otherwise stated. In addition, because of the relatively high number of males involved in hacking (see Jordan and Taylor 2004; Taylor 1999), masculine pronouns are used, unless it is known that the referent is female.

TABLE 17-2 Descriptive Data on Forums Used

Forum	Total Number of Strings	User Population	Timeframe Covered (Months)
1	48	109	11
2	50	20	2
3	50	101	9
4	117	179	2
5	50	110	6
6	50	400	30

A snowball sampling procedure was used to identify the six forums used in this analysis. An initial publicly accessible forum was identified through searching on Yahoo.com using the term "hacker Web forum." The "Links" section of the site was examined for connections to other public forums. Five other forums were identified that met the sampling criteria to create the total sample. The six forums that compose this data set include a total of 365 strings, providing copious amounts of data to analyze (see Table 17-2 for forum information breakdowns). These strings span two and a half years, from August 2001 to January 2004. Moreover, they represent a range of user populations, from only 20 to 400 users.

Interviews with Active Hackers

The second data set collected was a series of in-depth interviews (N=13) with active hackers. These interviews considered individual experiences as a hacker and any associations or affiliations with hacker groups. This provided information on both the computer hacker subculture and its social organization. Interviewees were identified through the use of a fieldworker, word-of-mouth solicitations at a Midwestern University, Defcon 12 hacker convention, and IT listservs. Two methods were used: face-to-face and e-mail interviews. A fieldworker/key informant was employed, and solicitations were made at a hacker group meeting to generate interviews locally. Hackers who could be met in person were asked to participate in an open-ended interview, lasting between two and three hours. These interviews (N=5) were taped and transcribed verbatim (see Table 17-3).

To expand the sample size and likelihood of respondents, interviews were also conducted via e-mail (N=8). This method helped expand the pool of respondents beyond geographic limitations. Solicitations were posted to two e-mail listservs, and made verbally at the Defcon 12 hacker convention. These requests often precluded interpersonal contact or did not allow the respondent enough time to complete a face-to-face interview. Consequently, respondents were asked to engage in e-mail interviews using the same questions as the in-depth interview instrument. This allowed respondents to answer the instrument at their leisure. Once the respondent completed the form, they were returned to the researcher for analysis. Regardless of the type of interview conducted, the instrument consisted of questions about individual experiences as a hacker in cyberspace and the real world.

TABLE 17-3 Interviewees for This Study

Interviewee	Interview Method	
	Face to Face	E-mail
Bob Jones	Face to Face	
Dark Oz		E-mail
Indiana Tones	Face to Face	
jRose		E-mail
Kamron	Face to Face	
Mack Diesel	Face to Face	
MG		E-mail
Mr. J		E-mail
Mutha Canucker		E-mail
R. Shack	Face to Face	
Spuds		E-mail
Supa Jew		E-mail
Vile Syn		E-mail

Observational Data

The third data source developed were first-hand observations of hackers at Defcon 12, the largest hacker convention held in the United States. This three-day convention, held annually during the last weekend of July, draws participants from around the world, as well as researchers who use the convention as a way to gain access to the hacker population (e.g. Schell, Dodge, and Moutsatsos 2002). The convention is open to the public, and draws in law enforcement agents, technophiles, attorneys, and hackers of all skill levels. Attendees must pay $80 at the door to enter the convention. This fee provides individuals with a convention program, conference identification badge, and data disk containing files and information for panels, events, and other conference-related materials. There are multiple events, including panels of speakers and games where individuals and teams compete to hack different systems. A marketplace is also set up in the hotel, giving individuals the opportunity to purchase equipment, videos, books, clothing, and various goods.

Written and tape-recorded field notes were made during panels, games, and social situations throughout the convention. These observations provided insight on social organization based on hackers interacting in this distinctive real-world social setting. Furthermore, the convention program, data disk, and other onsite materials were included in this analysis. These materials contain notes from the organizers and founders of the convention on their perspectives of hackers and hacking culture. Thus, Defcon provides a unique, diverse setting to examine hacker social organization in action within social situations that are relatively uncommon.

Measurement and Analysis Techniques

To assess hacker social organization, grounded theory methodology was used to derive concepts and information from the data, along with guiding questions from Best and Luckenbill (1994). Their framework was developed from inductive analyses of empirical research, considering how "deviant actors organize themselves to pursue their deviant activities" and how "these basic forms differ in organizational features, such as division of labor, coordination among the deviant actors, and objectives" (Best and Luckenbill 1994, 9). Best and Luckenbill (1994) also assessed how these forms develop and persist through the following questions: "what conditions shape the development and transformation of organizational forms," and "how do organizational forms change over time, and what conditions account for these changes?" (p. 9).

These concepts were applied along with specific questions from a study on the social organization of gangs performed by Decker, Bynum, and Weisel (1998) to direct this analysis of organizational sophistication.[4] Decker and his associates (1998) identified and examined elements of social organization that mirror the larger conceptual questions of Best and Luckenbill (1994). They used questions assessing the elements of groups, including any formal or informal regulations on behavior and relationships within and across groups.

Specifically, the first series of questions used centers around the *complexity of division of labor*, asking whether deviants offend together and about the nature of their division of labor (Best and Luckenbill 1994, 11). This includes questions about the presence of groups, their number of members, their relationship to one another, stratification, and the degree of role specialization. Second, the *coordination of roles* examines relationships between individuals (Best and Luckenbill 1994, 12). Here, any codes or rules on the regulation of relationships, and how these rules are defined and enforced are assessed. Finally, *purposiveness* assesses relationships between groups and how they specify, strive toward, and achieve goals (Best and Luckenbill 1994, 12). This includes any meetings between groups, their relationships, crimes committed by multiple groups, and any leisure time spent with other groups (Decker, Bynum, and Weisel 1998, 77).

Thus, these questions were used after the initial phases of data analysis were complete to refine the analyses. The three data sets were analyzed by hand using grounded theory methodology to examine the social organization of hackers. Grounded theory techniques permit the researcher to "develop a well integrated set of concepts that provide a thorough theoretical explanation of social phenomena under study" (Corbin and Strauss 1990, 5). Inductive analyses of the data were performed to produce findings based on the respondent's repeated comments or observations relating to social organization. The value of a concept was based on the positive or negative stances of respondents to an issue. In turn, the results were compared against the Best and Luckenbill (1994) framework to assess the organizational sophistication of hacker subculture. The data were also triangulated, or compared for similarities and differences, to identify the distinct features of each data set to be connected while situating each in its specific social setting and context (Silverman 2001, 235).

---

[4]Their research does not explicitly use concepts derived from Best and Luckenbill (1994), but they are concise and link well with this framework.

FINDINGS

These methods are used to critically explore the social organization of hackers on- and offline. The analysis is presented based on the four characteristics of social organization identified by Best and Luckenbill (1994). The contours and connections of relationships between hackers are described utilizing quotes from the data sets when appropriate.

Mutual Association

In assessing hacker social organization, it was apparent that there were clear interpersonal relationships between hackers across all data sets. In all, 10 of the 13 (76 percent) interviewees said they had friends who hacked, though such friends represented a relatively small percentage of their overall friendship network. Vile Syn emphasized this point stating, "I have a few friends that people would classify as 'hackers', but most of my friends really don't know much about computers at all." Often, these friendships are developed during school, such as j.Rose who wrote that "through school, I always had friends who worked with computers."

Social relationships were also evident at Defcon. The conference provides a way to facilitate mutual associations between hackers by providing a place to interact with others in the real world. For instance, several Defcon attendees frequent the convention to catch up with old friends and make new acquaintances. Individuals could be seen sitting together talking, or in large room-based parties with alcohol and music. This suggests that Defcon provides a significant, yet unique, opportunity to foster social relationships in the real world that may not be possible online.

Forum users also had relational ties, structured through their comments and attitudes toward each other while online. Because the forums were utilized to exchange information, hackers' relationships were based largely on the quality of information they shared. If an individual gave good information, they would receive thanks or praise from others. For example, a forum user made the following post after receiving useful information from another poster: "lol [laughing out loud] thanks for the link Mr. Holmes. I researched this last night . . . but that was still helpful." Hackers could also gain a reputation if they were uncooperative or unwilling to help others. This was exemplified in a post lambasting a user named 0b10ng for his treatment of others:

> 0b10ng is one of those guys that come to this board dying to fit in somewhere or atleast [sic] have some sort of status somewhere because in life he is at the bottom of the totem pole . . . this is the same thing we learned in kindergarten, people make fun of others to feel better about themselves, or compensate for inadequate penis size.

Hackers also appeared to have relationships and contact outside of the forums through e-mail and instant messaging. Posters often put their e-mail addresses at the end of their posts, or in the text of a message. In some instances, posters discussed making outside contact in the forums, as in the following exchange:

> DOOCEBIGELEOW: My last question about this subject (hope that's allright.) You people
>   gave me a lot of great programs to burn dvd's, but do you also know some

programs with which I can burn burn-protected cd's (like games) (It's legal to backup your own games as ☺).

Thanx Doocebigeleow

B0B0F377: I sent you a link [via] im [Instant Message] PM [tonight], let me know when you have read it.

However, hackers did not have demonstrably strong or deep relationships with other hackers on- or offline. The interviewed hackers suggested that relationships with other hackers represented a relatively small percentage of their overall offline friendship network. Vile Syn emphasized this point stating, "I have a few friends that people would classify as 'hackers', but most of my friends really don't know much about computers at all." In fact, the majority of interviewees described having "a few" or "two" friends that hack, like Bob Jones who suggested "there were like three or four of us who did this [hacking]."

The social connections between hackers online were also relatively shallow. Interviewees noted this fact, such as Mack Diesel, who said, "there were some bulletin boards that I would visit and maybe throw a shout to some people if I recognized their screen names, but it's not like I had a bunch of people that I was really tight with." The forum data also reflected weak connections between users, since the majority of all posters in the six forums posted less than three times (see Table 17-4). Between 40 and 87 percent of all posters made less than three posts, indicating that the majority of forum traffic was composed of individuals making a relatively small number of posts (see also Herring 2004). At the same time, a small percentage of posters accounted for a high number of posts. For example, 10 posters accounted for 48.6 percent of all posts in the forum with 101 users. In the forum with 21 total users, 5 posters made 73.8 percent of all posts. As such, the user populations from all six forums fit the "J-curve form" found in studies of differential participation in group activity (Robinson 1984, 25).

The depth of relationships between hackers in cyberspace was also affected by the use of multiple forums. It was clear that individuals used more than one forum based on comments from users like Hackwieser who wrote that he belonged to a forum on "a shitty site and everyone knows it, I'm SilentWolf from over there, hope you enjoy this place." Hackers also appeared to have multiple online identities, which could limit their ability to fully connect

TABLE 17-4 Forum Users Who Made Less Than Three Posts

Forum	Posters Who Made Less Than Three Posts	Total Forum Users	Percentage of All Posters
1	71	101	70.3
2	131	179	73.2
3	85	110	77.2
4	8	20	40.0
5	341	392	87.0
6	78	109	71.5

with others. Forums do not allow two individuals to have the same username, forcing some users to create alternative nicknames if their usual handle was already registered. This was exemplified in the following post by UltramegaChicken:

> I notice there is (or was) a HackHell here (which is why I used UltramegaChicken), but just to clear it up, that wasn't me. I'm HH from [a different forum]

As a result, the use of handles and multiple forums appeared to reduce the knowledge hackers had of one another (Thomas 2002).

Despite the weak nature of hackers' social ties, they utilized their social networks to share information, whether in person or online (see Meyer 1989; Schell, Dodge, and Moutsatsos 2002). For example, Defcon attendees sat at communal tables between and during panels discussing issues. Individuals lined the halls and common areas of the hotel with laptops connected together to share files and information. In much the same way, the forums provided access to a wealth of information about hacking. Myriad questions were posed in the forums, and answers given in different forms, including tutorials, Web links, posts, and downloadable content. Nine of the 13 interviewees also reported using Web forums or BBS to obtain information about targets or download different tools and software. Thus, hackers functioned as colleagues because of their mutual associations rather than as loners. This supports Meyer's (1989) claim that "it is impossible to be a part of the social network of the computer underground and be a loner" (p. 63).

Mutual Participation

While hackers had clear associations with others, there was some variation across the data regarding their mutual participation in offending. Hacker groups were prevalent offline at Defcon where 46 distinct groups were observed or mentioned in the program. These groups formed prior to the convention, and were, in some cases, well established. For instance, the Salt Lake City and San Francisco 2600 chapters that helped implement certain games at the convention had 13 or more members as well. Groups of various sizes readily participated in the full gamut of events at Defcon. Three-to-four-person groups commonly competed in different games like the Scavenger Hunt, while larger groups were present in a "capture the flag"-style hacking challenge called "Root Fu."[5]

Less formal peer groups were also present, but they had little outward evidence of stratification or leadership. The 2600 chapters were the only notable exception, based on evidence in the Defcon program. For instance, a biographical program note on a speaker named Grifter referenced his leadership role for two groups, stating he "currently runs 2600SLC, the Salt

---

[5]This was an elaborately staged game where eight teams defended their own fictional savings banks. Teams were connected to a main router and scoring system, which would make deposits into each specific "bank." The system would try to retrieve its deposits every few minutes. Teams would earn a defensive point if the deposit was retrieved. At the same time, teams could attempt to steal other teams' deposits. If a team could register a stolen deposit with the scoring system and claim ownership until the retrieval time, that team could earn an offensive point. Penalties were issued based on the network traffic created by each team. The team who scored the most points through offense, defense, and penalty deductions won. Therefore, teams had to win by defending themselves while hacking the other teams' systems.

Lake City 2600 meeting, and the DC801 [Def Con Group], the Utah Defcon meeting; where he often lectures on a range of security related topics." These 2600 groups demonstrate that formal hacker groups may have had a leadership structure, though it was not immediately evident to the public (see Meyer 1989, 73). Rather, stratification was made known when those affiliated with a group specified its structure.

The generally large number of groups at Defcon may be due to its unique social nature. Since Defcon is an annual gathering with some importance among hackers, groups may be more likely to attend as a way to learn, meet others, or participate in challenges. Furthermore, there were over 5,000 people at Defcon 12, which may have increased the likelihood of group attendance. Hence, Defcon may over-represent the importance of groups in everyday contexts.

This was exemplified by the hackers interviewed for this research who did not commonly report membership in hacker groups. Four (30 percent) belonged to a group at any point in time, with eight distinct groups described. Three of the four interviewees claimed to be involved in multiple groups over their hacking career. Three of these hackers belonged to local 2600 chapters, or to formal BBS groups. Finally, they described belonging to private groups that were offshoots of larger associations. For example, Vile Syn participated in a programming club, which soon led to involvement in a smaller group:

> Shortly after [going to the programming club meetings], we were attending private gatherings with certain members with an array of abilities. One was one of the first true hackers I had ever met, who could crack almost any software within a five-hour period of time. Another had a forte in electronics.

Indiana Tones described belonging to "a little group that was kind of on the side of 2600, but a lot of them also came from 2600." This smaller group was decidedly less organized, and more of a teen peer group as he explained:

> Sometimes we'd go down to the [club] and try to pick up girls and stuff. Uh, spent a lot of time there and a lot of time in the [downtown area]. Goin' to punk shows and things like that. When we were driving around getting from place to place, man, we were always talking about the newest technology, you know, and how the rules could be bent and everything.

Hackers who were members of hacker groups provided little detail on their membership or size, except for Indiana Tones who suggested the two groups he was affiliated with ranged in size from 10 to 15 members. There was also no real membership stratification and weak evidence of any rules on relationships within or between groups.

However, the interviewees clearly indicated that their involvement in hacker groups did not lead to group-based attacks. Instead, membership in these groups provided contacts that facilitated information sharing. For example, Indiana Tones explained that belonging to a 2600 club increased his level of knowledge because of the members' willingness to share information:

> I would help someone learn to program in visual basic if they taught me how to do web page design, you know. Or this guy here will teach this guy web page design if that guy will teach him networking. And it was basically about sharing knowledge.

Yet, the relatively small incidence of group affiliation reported by interviewees suggests that this was not a necessary part of the hacker experience. Instead, the hackers interviewed used forums and BBSs to connect with others and exchange information (see also Meyer 1989, 63). In fact, some hackers felt they did not want to be affiliated with any group. For example, Mack Diesel said, "a lot of these clubs were . . . guys out for trouble, because you know . . . once you got into being in a club then you were more apt to be either a gray hat or a black hat [malicious hacker]."

This may explain why eight of the hackers interviewed for this project said they almost always hacked alone (see also Meyer 1989; Schell, Dodge, and Moutsatsos 2002). For instance, Dark Oz wrote, "I most often work alone, but I'll discuss things with others whenever I get the chance." Only 10 of the 33 (30 percent) incidents reported by interviewees involved more than one hacker. For example, Kamron wrote that he had to "co-create a program" that could be used to attack and "ruin a corrupt game server." Spuds worked with others to hack a university e-mail account system, stating "we would print the list [of e-mail addresses] and then . . . try the accounts and find the ones that had not been used an[d] then change the password to the password we wanted. Then we would use that account until [sic] it was removed or claimed by the student."

Beyond these instances, 70 percent of the hacks described by interviewees were completed on their own. This supports the notion that "the actual performance of the phreak/hacking act is a solitary activity" (Meyer 1989, 66). However, hackers did go to each other for advice and opinions such as Spuds who wrote, "I do my work alone more times than other times. It depends on the lives of those around me. I prefer to have friends around when I do my work, since there's always more than one solution."

There was also little evidence that forum users hacked together. Posts in two of the six forums provided information on group-based hacks, but these were mainly hacks performed by individuals with real-world relationships. For example, RatzofftoYA posted a message stating, "Me and my mates (we got a hackers team) we were expelled we install a trojan [malicious program] on my school's se[r]ver (we got a network) and we were having illegal access to my teachers pc, what we did was to use his connection fo[r] 2 months and his acount [sic] to get logged on to the net." These sorts of posts were relatively infrequent and did not appear in the other four forums in the data set.

In fact, most of the posts on hacks involving individuals with offline relationships came from the forum with the largest population. Otherwise, there was little evidence to support the notion that forum users hacked together, though posters did however share information and guidance with others (see also Meyer 1989). Thus, the findings are consistent with Best and Luckenbill's (1994) peer categorization, and supports the notion that "in some cases the computer underground is socially organized as peers" (Meyer 1989, 74).

Division of Labor

The data also provided limited support for the existence of teams with a sophisticated division of labor. For instance, the groups that participated in the Root Fu competition appeared to have some specialized roles within groups. The teams competed and worked in the open, where each person or, in some cases, pairs worked on specific components of the game. Individuals were running different programs and involved in different tasks, such as programming attack tools. The rigidity of role specialization within each team was not completely clear, but members were involved in completing specific tasks.

There was further evidence of specialization and sophistication at the awards ceremony when the winning team was announced. The Sk3wl of R3wt won because they were able to protect their network while attacking other teams heavily. Competing teams had different strategies, and most spent time building tools to attack others. Yet, the Sk3wl of R3wt prevailed because they actively identified exploits and flaws in the system to maximize the effectiveness of their attacks.

It must be noted that the specialization observed is likely an artifact of the structure of Root Fu. The game was designed to defend a "fictional" savings bank network while attacking other systems, engaging participants in multiple roles and tasks. These teams clearly had some skill and understood how members needed to operate to be successful. Capture-the-flag games like Root Fu reflect real-world attacks and system vulnerabilities, and the game's organizers suggest that it demonstrates the ability of skilled hackers (Lemos 2003b). Therefore, while it is a unique event, the role specialization and teams involved gave some insight into more sophisticated hacker groups.

There was some evidence of stratification and division of labor in the forums as well. Each forum was a unique association composed of two distinct subgroups. One was a core group of forum users with specific titles, such as "Administrator," "Sysop," and "Moderator" that were responsible for rule enforcement on the forum. They monitored and deleted posts when necessary and sanctioned users based on their actions. For example, a user made a 10-page post that was clearly plagiarized from a book. In response, the sysops, administrators, or moderators, of the board made the following posts:

> SYSOP: It seems to me like you do not want to hear me out on the credits issue.
>
> **Your posts have been reported to the admins and mods of each forum.** [poster's emphasis]
>
> SR. SYSOP: Plagiarism is illegal and not condoned by [the forum], If your going to copy and paste PLEASE give the proper credits to the writer by posting the URL also.
>
> Thread Closed

The moderator group represented a relatively small proportion of the overall user population in each forum (see Table 17-5 for detail). For example, eight moderators posted in the forum with 392 members; they composed 2 percent of the entire user population. Across all

TABLE 17-5 Proportion of Moderators to General Forum Population

Forum	Number of Moderators	General Population	Percentage
1	10	179	5.49
2	1	110	0.50
3	1	20	5.00
4	5	101	4.95
5	2	109	1.83
6	8	392	2.04

six forums, moderators represented 5 percent or less of all users. There may have been more operating on each board, but they were not present in the data.

The second forum subgroup comprised the larger population of users that discussed issues and exchanged information with one another. These posters provided and consumed information and, in some cases, took a role in rule enforcement. The members of this group were much more loosely affiliated with the forum than the moderators. Yet, there was some stratification within the user groups, via a distinct ranking system and user hierarchy. Individuals were given a rank signifying how long they had been on the forum. The labels varied across forums, and included terms like "newcomer," "newbie," or "peewee" for new users. More established users had titles like "member," "master," or "forum junkie," though the ranking structures were not well explicated in most forums.[6]

Forums also had specific written rules for their members to follow that were not evident in the interviewees' or Defcon's observations. Four of the forums had their own Frequently Asked Questions (FAQ) post or section outlining the rules for posters and moderators. One common rule across the forums was to search the board for answers to questions before posting. This was because, as one forum's FAQ stated, "the chances are good that the question you're asking today has already been answered before—numerous times." Three of the four forums required users to respect the moderators because "showing respect is the only way to get respect." This was an important unwritten rule, since those who disrespected the moderators or their rules in any forum were subject to sanctions.

In addition, forums required users to respect each other, and avoid making flaming posts. Flames are comments and exchanges between individuals, including "many subtle varieties of insult and verbal jab" (Loper 2000, 52). Such negative comments were viewed as unproductive and disrespectful:

> Do not start a flame against people who you do not agree with, it is best to post nothing at all then [sic] to flame someone. If you don't agree with a post and want to see it closed, then send a PM [private message] to the moderator of that forum. Flaming will get you nowhere, you will not get any respect for flaming.

The notion that moderators should handle problematic posts and users was outlined in two of the forums' FAQs. This was an unwritten rule in forums as well, yet the general user populations ignored this rule. Thus, the larger population of users took a role in rule enforcement, despite this being the purview of the core group. This led to unnecessary posts and traffic that detracted from the overall mission of the forum. Moderators attempted to control the self-help of forum users at times, as in the following post from a forum moderator:

> I realize that many of you are dedicated to upholding the rules of [the forum], and that some of you may become annoyed when people appear to break them. I appreciate your dedication. However, arguments about whether or not a post is rule breaking, or even several posts telling the author that his post is against the rules does nothing to help the situation. The "report this post to a moderator" button is there for a reason, so please use it . . .

---

[6]Only one forum provided a table of their ranking structure, which limited the number of posts a user could make during the course of a day. For instance, lower-ranked users could make fewer posts per day, while higher-ranked users had more freedom to post at any time.

Generally, there was limited evidence of hacker teams, or at least within the Best and Luckenbill (1994) framework. A small number of groups at Defcon had clear divisions of labor, specialized roles, and operated to achieve a specific goal: win a competition. The moderator groups of forums also fit within the ideal team category since they were small, and had specialized roles and rules on behavior. At the same time, there was no evidence that they hacked in groups. The larger group of users seemed to constitute colleagues, or peers, because of the relationships between individuals that were used to exchange information, and occasional mutual participation in hacking. Thus, the complex nature of forums suggests they may or may not constitute teams in the Best and Luckenbill (1994) frame.

Extended Duration

The final element of organizational sophistication to be considered is extended duration. Across all of the data, there was no clear evidence of any group with an extensive history. Most relationships and groups appeared transitory, particularly with regard to the forums. In fact, three of the six used for this research no longer exist. Two of the groups no longer support forums on their Web sites, and the entire site for the third forum was taken down. This is especially remarkable as this third forum billed itself as the largest online hacker community. Similarly, Meyer (1989, 41) found the life spans of the BBS he studied to be relatively short, ranging from one month to one and a half years. As such, the forums appeared to be relatively transitory groups.

In turn, relationships within forums were somewhat weak and short-lived. Most users posted less than three times in each forum. There was no guarantee that an individual used a specific forum every day. Drains on users' time may keep them from actively participating in a forum, as exemplified in this exchange:

> SAZZAZZA: i have twice msg [messaged] cr@ckh3@d according to his commitment. ☹ but he dosnt [sic] respond [to] any one of them so here i m again. 🙂 Thanks! 😎

> CRACKHEAD: well just came online and saw your msgs [messages] . . . for your information Sazzazza . . . some people have to work during the day and cant be online every single day. . . . . so dont expect to get a reply as soon if someone msgs me . . .

There was no real evidence of purposive relationships between forum users either. Examples of group hacks were in the data, though there was nothing to suggest they involved users from different forums. There was also no indication of meetings between forum operators or members on- or offline. Users had some knowledge of other forums, and used them because of specialized content or knowledgeable members. However, there was no evidence of interactions between core members of different forums.

There was also no evidence on the lifespan of the groups involved with Defcon, but the convention is in its 12th year. Defcon has become the oldest hacker convention in the United States, and an important part of the hacker subculture. Long-standing groups like the Cult of the Dead Cow have used Defcon as a launch party for different security/hacking tools (see Furnell 2002). Hence, the convention, its organizational hierarchy, and communal atmosphere have persisted.

Furthermore, Defcon provided some evidence of multiple purposive relationships between groups. Several different organizations worked together to promote or sponsor events. For example, members of Defcon Group 801 and Rootcompromise.org organized a movie network on the hotel's closed circuit television system. Multiple groups also organized and sponsored two of the games held during the convention.

However, the Defcon organization was not openly or outwardly involved in deviance. Information was given to facilitate deviant behavior, but the Defcon convention organizers did not support deviant behavior or condone any sort of illegal hacking or otherwise criminal behavior. Defcon's private security "goons" and local law enforcement were on hand to ensure that individuals did not engage in such activities. Since Best and Luckenbill (1994) define deviant organizations as organizations that are involved in deviance (p. 72), Defcon constitutes a legitimate, rather than deviant, formal organization. Furthermore, there were no real deviant formal organizations evident across the data.

Discussion

As a whole, this research found that hackers operate in various stages along the continuum of deviant and nondeviant organizational sophistication. Specifically, hackers act as colleagues in social networks with other hackers in the real world and cyberspace (see also Meyer 1989). The on- and offline social ties between hackers were used to share information, tools, and introduce subcultural norms to new hackers. At the same time, the act of hacking was an overwhelmingly solitary behavior, regardless of an individual's social ties.

There was also evidence that hackers belonged to groups of various sizes with little stratification or role specialization offline, particularly at Defcon. Membership in hacker groups was not heavily reported by interviewees or forum users, and there was weak supporting evidence that they performed group-based hacks. Instead, hacker groups created and fostered relationships between individuals who could provide access to information and resources. This suggests that peer groups are prevalent in hacker subculture, though they do not offend together (see also Meyer 1989).

This study also goes beyond Meyer (1989) by identifying limited numbers of teams with specialized roles and divisions of labor when hacking offline. For instance, teams were present at Defcon in the Root Fu competition where they competed against each other. There was also conflicting evidence of teams online in the forum data. The small groups of forum moderators could constitute teams based on their clear division of labor, stratification, and rules on the behavior of members. However, members of the broader user group were loosely tied to each other and did not offend collectively. Thus, forum groups did not clearly fit within the continuum of organizational sophistication.

There were similar complications regarding the Defcon convention as a whole. The convention could not operate without the cooperation of multiple groups to sponsor and organize the various events. Roles were coordinated in advance, ranging from security "goons" to speakers. Defcon has become the longest operating hacker convention in the United States and an important part of the hacker subculture (see Furnell 2002). As such, it constitutes a formal organization because it has all the characteristics of organizational sophistication including extended duration across time and space and purposive relationships between groups. Furthermore, Defcon may be a legitimate formal organization, based on the convention organizers' insistence that they do not support deviant or criminal behavior.

Considering the range of relationships and levels of sophistication present, this study does not support Meyer's (1989) finding that "there is no evidence to support assertions that the CU [Computer Underground] is expanding" and "is not likely to do so on a large scale" (p. 80). In fact, hackers may now constitute a community that Best and Luckenbill (1994) define as "groups which share a common territory and a higher degree of institutional completeness," meaning there are various institutions and resources that serve the interests of community members (Best and Luckenbill 1994, 68). The deviant community is the most sophisticated organizational form, though it is excluded from Best and Luckenbill's (1994) framework, as they are unable to develop in modern society due to the increased penetration of law enforcement (Best and Luckenbill 1994, 72).

However, there is evidence that hackers have the defining characteristics of a community, including their use of common territories. Hackers did not necessarily share common territory offline, as they had relatively small peer groups and limited involvement in hacker groups. At the same time, shared spaces were evident online, since hackers communicated and connected with others via Web forums, e-mail, and other forms of computer-mediated communication allowed hackers to develop shared online spaces. Many of the hackers interviewed for this project used online resources and forums to make contact with others and share information. Conventions like Defcon may also constitute a sort of shared space, providing a location for individuals across the country or globe to come together in one place to discuss issues and socialize. Hence, while hackers do not have a specific territory in a traditional sense, they have spaces that allow them to connect with other hackers.

Communities are also "institutionally complete," in that they have institutions that serve the interests of their members (Best and Luckenbill 1994, 68). Numerous businesses and conventions cater to hackers, which was evident at Defcon where clothing companies, magazines such as the 2600 and Blacklisted, and products were marketed specifically to hackers (see also Furnell 2002). An inordinate number of Web forums exist, providing social links to other hackers, as well as resources to facilitate hacking activities. Hackers have also banded together to generate social support and legal funds, as in the case of the hacker Kevin Mitnick (see Loper 2000). Thus, hackers appear to be institutionally complete due to the myriad institutions providing goods and services for hackers. This is a significant advancement beyond Meyer's (1989) findings, and illustrates that hacker relationships have become increasingly sophisticated over time.

CONCLUSION

Taken as a whole, this study demonstrates that hacker social organization has changed in the past two decades to function in more sophisticated and complex ways. At the same time, this research illustrates several areas for future research, including the need to refine and further develop the Best and Luckenbill (1994) framework. Their continuum of organizational sophistication allowed for differentiation between forms of organization based on the peer relationships of hackers, and the impact of organizational involvement on hackers' ability to offend. However, not all facets of hacker organization fit within Best and Luckenbill's (1994) ideal types. For example, the categorization of Web forums is complicated by their two-population composition: forum users and forum operators or moderators. Thus, research is needed to explore and refine and operationalize the concepts that structure Best and Luckenbill's (1994) classification scheme, with particular emphasis on virtual relationships. Such clarification is critical to better understand the social relationships between deviants and criminals, especially in light of deviants' increased reliance on the Internet to share information and identify others that share their interests (see Holt 2007; Jewkes and Sharpe 2003).

Researchers should also continue to examine the structure of hacker organizations with larger and more diverse samples of hackers. While there was some evidence of sophisticated hacker organizations, there was limited detail on their leadership, rules, and operations. This was due in part to the small number of interviewees who belonged to hacker groups, and was compounded by the researcher's limited access to many of the groups at Defcon. Developing a sample of hackers who have belonged to groups of various sizes could refine our understanding of the nature of these groups, and the benefits provided by membership. Sampling at hacker conventions around the country may enable greater access to hackers of all skill levels, and provide a more representative sample of this subculture. Moreover, such a broad strategy may clarify the importance of groups and formal organizations within this relatively collegial hacker subculture.

Finally, this study emphasizes the need for greater explorations into computer hacker subculture, and computer crime generally. The literature on hackers and computer attackers is growing and encompasses a number of different issues of importance to the social and computer sciences. Yet, there is a strong likelihood that the form and shape of hacking and all crime may change due to shifts in technology over time. As a consequence, research on computer hackers and computer crime must be carefully considered, reexamined, and subject to critical analyses in order to improve and cultivate sound understandings of computer criminals and their offending behaviors.

KEY TERMS

Computer hackers
Social organization
Web forum

REFERENCES

Best, J., and D. F. Luckenbill. 1994. *Organizing Deviance*. 2nd ed. New Jersey: Prentice Hall.

Corbin, J., and A. Strauss. 1990. Grounded theory research: Procedures, canons, and evaluative criteria. *Qualitative Sociology* 13 (1): 3–21.

Cressy, D. R. 1972. *Criminal Organization*. New York: Harper & Row.

Decker, S. H., T. Bynum, and D. Weisel. 1998. "A tale of two cities: Gangs as organized crime groups." In *The Modern Gang Reader*, edited by J. Miller, C. L. Maxson, and M. W. Klein, 73–93. Los Angeles, CA: Roxbury Publishing Co.

Furnell, S. 2002. *Cybercrime: Vandalizing the Information Society*. Boston, MA: Addison-Wesley.

Gilboa, N. 1996. "Elites, lamers, narcs and whores: Exploring the computer underground." In *Wired Women: Gender and New Realities in Cyberspace*, edited by L. Cherny and E. R. Weise, 98–113. Seattle, WA: Seal Press.

Herring, S. C. 2004. "Computer-mediated discourse analysis: An approach to researching online behavior." In *Designing for Virtual Communities in the Service of Learning*, edited by S. A. Barab, R. Kling, and J. H. Gray, 338–76. New York: Cambridge University Press.

Holt, T. J. 2003. Examining a transnational problem: An analysis of computer crime victimization in eight countries from 1999 to 2001. *International Journal of Comparative and Applied Criminal Justice* 27 (2): 199–220.

Holt, T. J. 2007. Subcultural evolution? Examining the influence of on and off-line subcultural experiences on deviant subcultures. *Deviant Behavior* 28: 171–98.

Jewkes, Y., and K. Sharp. 2003. "Crime, deviance and the disembodied self: Transcending the dangers of corporeality." In *Dot.cons: Crime, Deviance and Identity on the Internet*, edited by Y. Jewkes, 1–14. Portland, OR: Willan Publishing.

Jordan, T., and P. Taylor. 2004. *Hacktivism and Cyberwars: Rebels with a Cause.* New York: Routledge.

Kleen, L. J. 2001. Malicious hackers: A framework for analysis and case study. Master's thesis, Air Force Institute of Technology. Retrieved January 3, 2004, from http://www.iwar.org.uk/iwar/resources/usaf/maxwell/students/2001/afit-gor-ens-01m-09.pdf

Krebs, B. 2003. Hackers to face tougher sentences. *Washington Post.* Retrieved February 4, 2004, from http://www.washingtonpost.com/ac2/wp-dyn/A35261-2003Oct2?language=printer

Landreth, B. 1985. *Out of the Inner Circle.* Washington: Microsoft Press.

Lemos, R. 2003a. Microsoft to offer bounty on hackers. Retrieved November 15, 2003, from http://news.com.com/21007355_3-5102110.html?tag=nefd_top

Lemos, R. 2003b. Hacking contest promotes security. Retrieved August 11, 2004, from http://msn.com.com/2100-1009_22-5059827.html?

Loper, D. K. 2000. The criminology of computer hackers: A qualitative and quantitative analysis. Doctoral diss., Michigan State University. *Dissertation Abstracts International,* vol. 61-08, sec. A, p. 3362.

Mann, D., and M. Sutton. 1998. Netcrime: More change in the organization of thieving. *British Journal of Criminology* 38 (2): 201–29.

Meyer, G. R. 1989. The social organization of the computer underground. Master's thesis, Northern Illinois University. Retrieved December 29, 2003, from http://csrc.nist.gov/secpubs/hacker.txt

Miller, G. 1978. *Odd Jobs.* Englewood Cliffs, NJ: Prentice Hall.

Norman, P. 2001. "Policing 'high tech' crime within the global context: The role of transnational policy networks." In *Crime and the Internet*, edited by D. S. Wall, 184–94. New York: Routledge.

Robinson, M. 1984. *Groups.* New York: John Wiley and Sons.

Schell, B. H., J. L. Dodge, with S. S. Moutsatsos. 2002. *The Hacking of America: Who's Doing It, Why, and How.* Westport, CT: Quorum Books.

Silverman, D. 2001. *Interpreting Qualitative Data: Methods for Analysing Talk, Text, and Interaction.* 2nd ed. Thousand Oaks, CA: SAGE Publications.

Slatalla, M., and J. Quittner. 1995. *Masters of Deception: The Gang That Ruled Cyberspace.* New York: Harper Collins Publishers.

Taylor, P. A. 1999. *Hackers: Crime in the Digital Sublime.* New York: Routledge.

Thomas, D. 2002. *Hacker Culture.* Minneapolis, MN: University of Minnesota Press.

Wall, D. S. 2001. "Cybercrimes and the Internet." In *Crime and the Internet*, edited by D. S. Wall, 1–17. New York: Routledge.

Williams, P. 2001. Russian organized crime, Russian hacking, and U.S. security [Online]. Retrieved November 20, 2003, from http://www.cert. org/research/isw/isw2001/papers/Williams06-09.pdf

Woo, H. J. 2003. The hacker mentality: Exploring the relationship between psychological variables and hacking activities. Doctoral diss., The University of Georgia. *Dissertation Abstracts International,* vol. 64-02, sec. A.

Wysocki, M. D. 2003. Cracking the hacker code: An analysis of the computer hacker subculture from multiple perspectives. Doctoral diss., Northwestern. *Dissertation Abstracts International,* vol. 64-04, sec. A, p. 1125.

Chapter 18

"It's like Printing Money": Piracy on the Internet

Johnny Nhan
University of California–Irvine

Johnny Nhan is a doctoral student in the Department of Criminology, Law, and Society at the University of California–Irvine. Nhan holds bachelor degrees in criminology and economics. He has published and presented research pertaining to the subject of policing cyber crimes, which is the focus of his doctoral dissertation.

Abstract

The explosion of digital media coupled with the rapid development of high-speed computer networks has resulted in a spike in piracy, indicating that control mechanisms are lagging behind. Companies have long used technology to fight this problem. However, these efforts have been overwhelmed by increasing sophistication and organization of piracy groups. As a result, a hierarchical distribution chain of piracy, known as "Darknet," has developed, allowing digital files to be distributed efficiently to millions of file sharers. Industry has turned to the government and law enforcement for assistance, but technical and structural issues, as well as little public support, hinder these efforts. This chapter uses interviews and relevant data with these key stakeholders in fighting piracy to examine points of cooperation and structural conflict in the California security network. Findings suggest a growing collaboration between industry and law enforcement, but factors such as organizational culture, politics, and general apathy has resulted in underfunding and limited efforts to niche enforcement.

INTRODUCTION

The ubiquitous digitization and storage of information coupled with the widespread use of distributed network technology, such as the Internet, has exponentially increased media piracy. **Piracy** is defined as the unauthorized replication and distribution of intellectual property (IP) in violation of U.S. copyright law (Title 17, U.S. Code).[1] The development of the affordable and user-friendly high-speed computers connected to broadband networks and the Internet has

Special thanks to the guidance of professors John Dombrink, Laura Huey, Paul Jesilow, Henry Pontell, Michael T. Goodrich, Simon Cole, David H. Bayley, Benoît DuPont, and Jennifer Wood.

[1]http://www.copyright.gov/circs/circ1.html

given the general public access to technology once reserved for researchers, government, and highly technical individuals.[2] However, the drive to satisfy growing public demands for digital content and services has outpaced traditional forms of social controls, such as law enforcement, laws, and companies' abilities to self-police. The lack of enforcement deterrence, ease of duplication and distribution, and general public apathy in recognizing piracy as a real crime, has resulted in widespread distribution of copyrighted material. The Institute for Policy Innovation (IPI) estimates that movie piracy costs U.S. workers $5.5 billion in lost earnings annually, with an estimated total lost output of $20.5 billion impacting the associated industries (Siwek 2006). The recording industry estimates $1.1 billion in losses, which excludes a ripple effect in consequent jobs lost and the overall impact to the U.S. economy from potential tax revenues.[3] A 2004 report by the Department of Justice describes online media distribution as "one of the greatest emerging threats to intellectual property ownership."[4]

A holistic overview of Internet piracy in film, music, and software will be presented in this chapter. This includes structural variables affecting policing, policy, and security in each industry and government entity. Interview data from a larger research study on policing the Internet with movie industry professionals, specialized high-tech crime units in California, California state emergency services representatives, and tech-industry security experts will be used. In addition, legal procedures will be analyzed using data from civil court cases and documents. Surveys, such as the Pew Internet and American Life Project[5] survey, will give insight into public attitudes toward piracy. Furthermore, antiforensics technologies and organizational structures of piracy groups will be analyzed. Throughout the chapter, sociological frameworks, economic and social ramifications of Internet piracy, and policing policies will be explored. The goal of this chapter is to give insight and overview of a significant and growing crime occurring in a new medium that challenges the effectiveness of existing paradigms of social and crime control.

METHODS

Interviews were conducted with several industry and law enforcement groups considered significant to music, movie, and software piracy in the Western United States (see Table 18-1). These groups include industry security practitioners from the film industry, security experts from the technology sector, California state emergency services representatives, and members of California regional high-tech crimes **taskforces**. Due to the limited scope of this research, representatives from the recording industry and general public were not interviewed. Data from the general public were derived from the Pew Internet and American Life Project and various Internet and printed sources.

Respondents were selected using a snowball sample from known contacts in the Southern California law enforcement community. The film industry and information technology industry were chosen for its significance in the piracy scene. Both industries have a large

[2]For a history of the Internet, visit URL http://www.isoc.org/internet/history/cerf.shtml
[3]The losses over Internet piracy is largely debated, with some research showing that loss figures are exaggerated and published estimates are "self-serving" and "unverified" (McClellan 2006).
[4]http://www.cybercrime.gov/IPTaskForceReport.pdf
[5]http://www.pewinternet.org

TABLE 18-1 The Development of Software and Media Piracy on the Internet

Participant Category	Number of Respondents
Law enforcement personnel	12
Private industry	
Film industry security	8
Information technology	18
State representatives	2
Total	**40**

presence in California and the Western United States. California is the largest piracy hub in the United States., serving as a piracy gateway to East Asia. Samples from these industries include participants of the California High Tech Crime Advisory Committee, and security experts from Arizona and Washington. Subjects were asked open-ended questions related to piracy in their field, their role in the piracy security network, and the strengths, limitations, and structural complications within their profession. In addition, subjects were asked about the effectiveness of the criminal justice and legal system in terms of piracy. Interviews were semi-structured and lasted approximately one hour or more.

Electronic piracy can be interpreted as an old crime adapted to a new medium. Piracy and counterfeiting can be traced back to the unauthorized replication and distribution of items such as hard currency, artwork, apparel, and other goods associated with the open market-place. Widespread electronic piracy began in the form of unauthorized duplication of data and software digitally stored in physical magnetic and optical mediums that were distributed by physically carrying them from one source to another, informally known as the "sneakernet" (Boutin 2002). Audio-visual media were duplicated and distributed in a similar fashion. The speed and efficiency of duplication and distribution were bound by the operating capacity of replication machines and human distribution channels. The risk of detection and apprehension of larger-scale operations were significant since physical items, or "hard goods," required large storage and physical delivery. Physical evidence can be collected from commonly used legitimate distribution channels. Moreover, hard goods were often more easily identified from lower-quality packaging and media quality degradation with music and films.

The transition from sneakernets to the Internet allows for the exponential increase in the volume and speed of piracy. The Internet is a decentralized network of interconnected smaller networks (Tanenbaum 2003). Digital information electronically delivered from one computer system to another, known as "soft goods," has eliminated the temporal and geographic limitations of sneakernets. Compared to hard goods, the borderless distribution channels allows for rapid simultaneous information broadcasting and sharing without any information degradation and at a fraction of the cost. The Motion Picture Association (MPA) projects that a single movie file can be virally copied and distributed to over 3.7 million computer systems from a single source within a 70-hour period.[6] One Internet security expert in the film industry

---

[6]http://mpaa.org/avalancheofpiracy.htm

describes the impact of Internet technology as a traditional crime that occurs at a "phenomenally larger scale."

Industry enforcement and legal actions perpetuate a cycle of more robust soft goods technology and sophistication. Each technological generation of soft goods piracy has evolved from the increased threat of legal actions by companies and studios. As companies and studios utilize more sophisticated detection and forensic tools, they are countered by technologies designed to prevent detection and **forensics**. One film industry security expert who has witnessed these changes explains:

> Initially, websites such as Geocities[7] etc. allowed hosting [unauthorized copyrighted] content that users can download. Detection was very simple, and these sites were taken down easily. Then it shifted to [File Transfer Protocol] sites, [Internet Relay Chat Direct Client-to-Client protocol known as Fserves] etc. This advancement in technology makes it harder in the cat and mouse game to detect and shut down sites.

Counter technologies used to circumvent detection and enforcement are also intended to make legal prosecution difficult. The shift from client-server to peer-to-peer (P2P) network infrastructures reduces data stored on servers, where forensic evidence can be gathered in one location and easily linked to the registered individual or group. Instead, a decentralized client-to-client infrastructure, where data is stored locally on individual computers, makes identifying a main source of copyrighted files more difficult to detect and hold legally liable. Popular P2P protocols and services such as Napster,[8] Kazaa,[9] and BitTorrent,[10] have argued that legal responsibility should fall on individual users, since no files are stored on their servers.

Each generation of P2P technology has been designed to further insulate networks from industry and legal interference. One film industry Internet security expert explains:

> It's a battle between [the film industry] and P2P networks. [Pirates] keep coming up with more robust technologies. For example, [P2P] networks are running on servers currently, but [server administrators] have anticipated that the servers will be the next target of litigation and policing, so torrents have built in abilities to 'flip a switch' and go completely decentralized.[11] This makes it virtually impossible to police. This is a nightmare scenario.

The first widespread P2P network, Napster, used a centralized server to manage searches and file indexing. To insure against future liability, next-generation technology can be completely decentralized using distributed hash tables,[12] which shifts all indexing and

---

[7]http://www.geocities.com

[8]http://www.napster.com

[9]http://www.kazaa.com/us/index.htm

[10]http://www.bittorrent.com

[11]An example of a completely decentralized P2P network is Kademlia.

[12]Distributed hash tables (DHTs) are a class of decentralized, distributed systems and algorithms being developed to provide a scalable, self-configuring infrastructure with a clean programming interface. This infrastructure can then be used to support more complex services. DHTs can be used to store data, as well as route and disseminate information. http://en.wikipedia.org/wiki/Distributed_hash_table

routing functions from servers to individual computers on the network (Borland 2004). The same security expert expresses frustration from the difficulties of even current technology, stating, "We haven't even taken down the servers yet."

The difficulty of using enforcement and legal remedies against file sharing organizations is exemplified by the replacement effect of organizations targeted from the film industry. In May 2006, Swedish-based P2P file-sharing portal The Pirate Bay's[13] headquarters were raided by Swedish police in a joint effort by the Swedish government and the Motion Picture Association of America (MPAA).[14] Despite mass equipment confiscations and arrests, the site was fully operational within a month, with new servers located in The Netherlands (Harrison 2006). The Pirate Bay is an example of the evolution of P2P networks.

File sharing has evolved into a sophisticated network of technologies operated by a highly organized hierarchy of individuals and organizations, known as "Darknet," or simply "The Scene" (Biddle et al. 2002; Howe 2005; Lasica 2005). According to Lasica's (2005) in-depth interview, Bruce Forest, who has a unique position of being in an exclusive circle of top-level pirates while working legitimately for a Hollywood studio, Darknet is described as the cyberspace equivalent to a "lawless, ethics-free frontier" where "epic battles over copy protection and file sharing" take place. Darknet consists of groups that often operate by pseudonyms and anonymity but have developed a set of norms, economic models, and efficiently organized distribution.

The organization of the piracy network is described by the MPAA as a "pyramid."[15] Piracy begins with a supplier, or the source of pirated material, such as individuals who have illegally obtained a prerelease copy of a movie, music, or software. According to a film industry security expert, suppliers are often compensated thousands of dollars for a copy of an unreleased movie by release groups, depending on the quality of the digital copy. A screener DVD, or advanced copy sent to critics and award judges, can be sold for $5,000 or more. Release groups, consisting of top members often only known by pseudonyms, place these digital copies on "topsites," or high-speed hosts for download by other release group members. According to Forest, membership to this ultra-exclusive group requires earning a high level of trust from existing members and the value added by the prospective member, such as access to unreleased digital media or software, equipment, or high-level hacking skills.[16]

Digital files are placed on *facilitators*, or P2P Internet portals such as BitTorrent that manage searching and organizing public downloads by lower-level *file sharers* and *downloaders*. Once a file is downloaded, that computer can become a "seeder," or client computers with a copy of the file available to share with other downloaders. More seeders can exponentially increase the amount of download sources, making downloading much quicker.

Piracy networks can be very lucrative, with relatively lower risk as compared to street crimes, making it a natural fit with organized crime groups. Many consider piracy as a form of organized crime. According to Peter Reuter (1983), "Organized crime consists of organizations

---

[13]http://www.thepiratebay.org. A video documentary on the Pirate Bay entitled, "Steal this Film" can be found at http://video.google.com/videoplay?docid=-4116387786400792905&q=steal+this+film
[14]A video documentary on the Pirate Bay raid, entitled, "Steal this Film" can be found at http://video.google.com/videoplay?docid=-4116387786400792905&q=steal+this+film
[15]http://mpaa.org/pyramid_of_piracy.pdf
[16]http://mpaa.org/pyramid_of_piracy.pdf

that have durability, hierarchy, and involvement in a multiplicity of illegal activities." One film industry security expert explains how piracy is an avenue of organized crime:

> [Piracy] crimes are real and there is a lot of money. Organized crime has taken a hold of the piracy industry, with high organization, 'taxation,' enforcement etc. It is a high stakes business and they have the resources to invest in piracy. They have been performing illegal activities for a long time and have savings and resources to invest to keep one step ahead of any anti-piracy policies and/or activities. They have integrated this into part of their activities. This is in addition to other illegal activities. This persists because this crime is seen as less risky than drugs.

Suppliers not only provide source material, but serve to insulate organized crime groups from any risk of apprehension. A studio security expert explains, "[pirates are] supplying organized crime with the masters, [who are in turn] leveraging talent," adding, "Organized crime pulls the strings and the minions follow." In addition, a film industry Internet security expert explains, "[top pirates] are similar to the Don in a crime family, who sells to trusted distributors and in turn, those sell to smaller groups."

The adoption of the Internet by organized crime groups has heightened the stakes due to incentives created by the low risk of detection and apprehension. A network security expert at a large software corporation explains during an interview:

> [Organized crime groups] are considered the *real* criminals, not the script kiddies.[17] Crime has fundamentally shifted from the kids using code to try to hack for fame. Now, organized crime will employ this guy and use them to commit further crime. The structure of organized crime has changed the dynamics of computer crime. The structure of the crime organization is no different from traditional organized crime. But instead of using drug dealers, script kiddies and hackers are employed, which insulates the top of the organization. These organizations are extremely well funded and are very dangerous when the top involves terrorists and nation-states.

In some smaller markets where legitimate distribution is nonexistent, pirates fill the demand. A film industry professional explains, organized criminals are like "businessmen; you have demand, and there's no legitimate alternative." He questions, "Who fills the gap?," adding, "[In small markets], piracy is the only way to watch certain movies, so piracy is at 100%."

The low risk, high returns, and light penalties of piracy make it a viable alternative to risky street crimes. One studio security expert compared piracy with the drug trade, stressing that heroin on the street has anywhere from a 200–300 percent markup with high risk, while "movies and music have a 1,000 percent markup and upwards." He adds, relative to drugs, "possession of pirated goods is not a big deal and barriers to entry are low with rewards very high." For the casual downloader or file sharer only interested in consumption, a variety of free software client applications can be easily found on the Internet. In popular P2P networks, users can easily search and download files without any knowledge of computer networks.

---

[17]A "script kiddie" is a low-end computer hacker that uses preexisting software code or "scripts" to gain unauthorized entry into computer systems. These individuals are considered unsophisticated and viewed in disdain by the hacker community because they do not create new code or make any contributions.

The popularity of services depends on the available files on the network. Users are drawn to networks with a large amount of content, such as unreleased movies or software, and fast download speeds. To prevent users from exclusively downloading without sharing files and computing resources, or "leeching," most client software automatically scan local computers to share files. To spread content quickly and maintain fast download speeds, it is important to have a minimum ratio of seeders to downloaders. Software algorithms allow for several seeders to simultaneously stream data to a single downloader who, in turn, becomes another seeder. Each seeder, in addition to contributing content, provides bandwidth, or channel capacity. Some P2P protocols begin seeding before the complete file is finished downloading. This cycle of seeding and downloading occurs simultaneously across all P2P networks, growing exponentially with viral momentum and resulting in what the MPAA calls an "avalanche" of piracy.

To prevent this avalanche of piracy, the strategy by the film industry is to target the top source of piracy. According to the MPAA, release groups are considered the "first source of piracy on the Internet."[18] Gaining access and gathering member information on topsites is not an easy task. A film industry security expert explains, "[Release groups] are similar to the Don in a crime family, who sells to trusted distributors and in turn, those sell to smaller groups," adding, "It may take years to establish trust and to take down a major site or top guy." This exclusive group operates in secrecy, being cloaked by cryptic monikers, anonymous online communication mediums such as Internet Relay Chat (IRC), and distributes files via password-protected File Transfer Protocol (FTP) servers. Information, such as "most wanted" film lists and their prices, are often exchanged through these channels.

Memberships to release groups are only extended to trusted individuals. There are three forms of membership, explains one film industry security coordinator: those who pay for subscription, those who supply equipment, and those who supply content. For example, rogue network administrators using company equipment to supply mass storage space and bandwidth are oftentimes offered membership. For example, in July 2004, employees of an IT service company in Australia contracted by the Commonwealth Bank were alleged to have used company servers to host pirated adult pornography (Krone 2005). In addition, individuals who can consistently supply highly sought after content such as "clean" digital copies[19] of movies still playing in theaters or newly released software with copy protections removed[20] are release group candidates. However, one film industry security coordinator warns, "If you offer too much content, it's very suspicious, so it's very difficult to infiltrate these groups."

Release group membership can be very lucrative and prestigious. Being associated with one group can create membership opportunities in other groups in *the scene* to create enough income equivalent to full employment. Release groups are not in competition, but share content and memberships. "You're looking at the top dog," explains a film industry security

---

[18]http://mpaa.org/pyramid_of_piracy.pdf

[19]A clean digital copy of a movie is digitally recorded directly from the source, such as replicating a digital versatile disc (DVD), as opposed to recording indirectly using a camcorder.

[20]Modern computer software is often copy protected using authentication of serial numbers to activate the full product. Copy protection is "cracked," when users can bypass authentication or activate the product using fictitious or illegally obtained serial numbers. Sophisticated hackers create fictitious serial generators that use algorithms similar to authentic serial numbers that are accepted by the system.

expert, "He can go from site to site and make a lot of money. It's a full time job communicating and being on IRC channels organizing."

While the lucrative nature of Darknet can explain partially why piracy is prevalent and a growing problem, many argue that it is not necessarily bad. Choi and Perez (2006) argue that online piracy has actually created a market that parallels and improves legitimate markets through (1) pioneering new technologies, (2) identifying market demand, (3) creating new market demand for digital downloadable content, and (4) the creation of new and legitimate business models. Stier and Richards (1987) explains the development of a symbiotic relationship between organized crime and the public is the most difficult to police, due to public perceptions of legitimacy and market integration (Lupsha 1988). Despite the unintended positive consequences of the illegitimate market brought about by competition, legitimate distribution channels may find it much more difficult to compete and appeal to potential customers with the constraints of a traditional business model.

THE PUBLIC MENTALITY

To understand the mentality of file sharers, it is necessary to understand what the Internet represents to the public at large. The Internet is largely perceived as being disconnected from the physical world. In researching the difficulties of policing the cyber environment, Huey (2002) explains, "Instead of viewing computers as physical phenomena, for many, they come to represent magic boxes that mysteriously obey commands upon direction." This disjuncture between the physical and the abstract borderless space allows for many to perceive the Internet as a "free" and "neutral" frontier for information and communication. One film industry security expert explains that, in terms of public perception, "The Internet is the last bastion of freedom, an uncontrollable free space to express ideas and share information." The mentality stems from the notion that no one person or group *owns* the Internet. "Net Neutrality," or "Internet Neutrality," is a controversial principle regarding the Internet as an open free space. This principle asserts that no one group or technology should be privileged and that any type of technological or economic regulation should only be used to ensure neutrality.[21] Companies trying to implement security technologies and pricing are perceived as violating this space.

The mentality of most high-level file sharers is rooted in the hacker subculture that emerged the 1980s. The once prestigious term, "hacker," referred to individuals with an elegant mastery of computer coding. These individuals began to fraternize in pre-Internet chat rooms such as direct dial-in bulletin board services (BBSs). Common traits and norms emerged from this culture that has carried on to the file sharing mentality. Steven Levy (2001) in the early 1980s introduced "the Hacker Ethic," a set of norms adhered by early hackers. The beliefs included unrestricted and complete access to computers, all information should be free, a cynicism toward authority, and promotion of decentralization. Under these principles, attacks on large company computer systems are perceived as being harmless and even justified under certain circumstances. A 2006 Australian survey asking network security professionals what motivates hacking computer systems found that 27 percent of respondents cited

---

[21]An updated list of articles on Net Neutrality can be found on CNET news http://news.com.com/2009-1028_3-6055133.html

a demonstration of technical skill.[22] Applied to file sharers, this is significant in understanding the public apathy towards piracy as a serious crime.

Growing demand for digital content may explain public apathy toward release groups. A Pew Internet and American Life Project survey of 2,515 adults in 2003 shows that 67 percent of unauthorized music downloaders say they do not care if the music downloaded is copyrighted, increasing from 61 percent in 2001 (Madden and Lenhart 2003). The same survey estimates that 35 million U.S. adults download unauthorized music files, with 26 million sharing music files.[23] This number is expected to be higher today with increased broadband penetration and more Internet users. However, the increase may be slightly offset by the increased threat of litigation and legitimate music downloading services such as iTunes.[24]

Public loathing against copyright can be further explained by the perception that large companies and corporate conglomerates have stymied artistic progress and collective creativity through copyright. According to interviewed file sharers, downloading is considered a punitive action against large corporations who refuse to share their work as a foundation for creativity. Lasica (2005) argues that true societal progression can only occur when the public transitions from passive consumers to active agents of creativity in the arts and media. The Creative Commons[25] is a grassroots nonprofit organization dedicated to create a range of creative works in media, art, and software, with "flexible" and "reasonable" copyright that allows for open community enjoyment and creative modification of works, while avoiding exploitation of artists.

The current copyright system, it is argued, is exploitive by nature. For instance, record labels in the recording industry have been known to underpay artists, who surrender ownership of the copyright and master copies. For example, Nirvana producer Steven Albini outlined a typical scenario where a band owed a record company $14,000 in costs despite selling 250,000 copies and earning $710,000 for the label.[26] This is consistent with findings by The Future of Music Coalition, which examined music contracts and found that the controlled composition clause in a typical contract contained language that amounts to a net loss to the artist, stating, "Each record sold puts her deeper in the hole, and farther away from ever recouping."[27]

Computer software companies face similar demands by the public to loosen or remove copyright. "Open Source" is a philosophy in the software industry that emphasizes open community development and ownership of source code for better and more creative products. According to opensource.org, "When programmers can read, redistribute, and modify the source code for a piece of software, the software evolves. People improve it, people adapt it, people fix bugs."[28] The result is software that is less bound by restrictive licenses and more beneficial to the end-user instead of companies. Perens (1999) explains the three tenets of open source: (1) the right to copy and distribute the software, (2) the right to source code for

---

[22] 2004 Australian Computer Crimes and Security Survey. http://www.auscert.org.au/images/ACCSS2006.pdf
[23] 2004 Australian Computer Crimes and Security Survey. http://www.auscert.org.au/images/ACCSS2006.pdf
[24] http://www.apple.com/itunes/
[25] http://creativecommons.org/
[26] http://creativecommons.org/
[27] Future of Music Coalition: Contract Critique. http://www.futureofmusic.org/images/FMCcontractcrit.pdf
[28] http://www.opensource.org

changes, and (3) the right to make improvements in the program. The benefit of such a model is essentially free[29] software for end-users that can be tailored to individual or organizational needs that is more secure and bug-free. Moreover, the exploitive adversarial relationship between proprietary software vendors and clients is removed in favor of more mutually beneficial relationships. Open-source software widely in use today include Netscape/Mozilla Firefox[30] web browsers, Linux[31]–kernel-based operating systems, Apache[32] web server, MySQL[33] database, and OpenOffice[34] office productivity suite.

In addition to the significantly lower or no cost of open source software, some argue that software development results in better and more secure products. Open source advocates reason that flaws in the software code can be detected and addressed early in development. For example, the computer security industry relies heavily on cryptography and encryption to secure data transmissions and authentication. Encryption works by encoding plain text in to ciphertext using different algorithms and decrypted using a secret key, such as a password. In the early 1970s, the National Bureau of Statistics and National Security Administration (NSA) sponsored Digital Encryption Standard (DES), a universal encryption standard developed by IBM to ensure safe data transmission. The encryption algorithm used in DES was kept secret and used a 56-bit key (Denning and Baugh 1996).[35] Once released, it soon became clear that the standard was not secure and could be broken by a variety of attacks. DES was criticized for the lack of public input during development that would have prevented flaws. Instead, the classified methods of encryption were criticized as being "security through obscurity," or security through secrecy. The public opted for stronger open source developed standards based on transparent but computing-intensive mathematical equations such as Rivest, Shamir, Adleman (RSA)[36] encryption algorithm based on factoring extremely large variable-length prime numbers (Kaufman, Perlman, and Speciner 2002).

The disdain toward large corporations and proprietary copyrights reflect the critique of hegemonic forces of capitalism on laborers. Influenced by Marxist theory of worker alienation, Harry Braverman (1974, 52–53) explains the exploitive nature of the modern corporation that transforms "working humanity" into a "labor force." He writes, "Employers hire workers in order to expand their capital base, while employees seek employment because they have no viable alternative by which to sustain their lives and those of their families." Gartman (1999) writes of the effects of the corporate machinery on creativity and individual craftsmanship using Ford's assembly-line automobile production during the 1930s as an example. He explains, "The aesthetic consequence of such product standardization was the increasingly homogenized appearance of cars—the individuality and distinction of craft-built cars gave way to the cookie-cutter sameness of mass-produced ones." Similarly, copyright and copy

---

[29]Some open source software is sold at a cost to cover technical support, such as Red Hat Linux.

[30]http://www.netscape.com, http://www.mozilla.com/en-US/firefox/

[31]http://www.linux.org/

[32]http://www.apache.org/

[33]http://www.mysql.com/

[34]http://ww.openoffice.org

[35]The 64-bit key was controversially lowered to 56 bits by the NSA, which significantly lessened the possible combinations. The remaining 8 bits was supposedly used for parity (error checking) but many argue that it was weakened to allow backdoor entry by the government.

[36]RSA was developed in 1977 by Ron Rivest, Adi Shamir, and Len Adleman. http://www.rsasecurity.com

protection technologies are seen as an affront to free will, free choice, and creativity. Community-based open source and public domain development of technology and the arts eliminates the exploitive relationship between producers and consumers, essentially shifting power to every consumer by giving them the ability to become a potential producer and contributor.

Public apathy can be further explained by a variety of neutralizations to justify file sharing activities. File sharing is often considered a form of victimless crime. A victimless crime is a behavior that is illegal but perceived as not serious or injurious, and some believe should be legal. According to Rossi et al. (1974), measures of perceived seriousness of crimes are not derived from the actions of the criminal justice system but as a combination of societal consensus and individual lifetime learning processes. Individually learned motives and justifications for deviant behavior are applied through neutralization mechanisms that include: (1) denial of responsibility, where offenders are not personally accountable for the crime due to existential circumstances, (2) denial of injury, where offenders claim their actions cause no harm to victims, (3) denial of victim, where the actions of the offender are blamed on victims as being deserving of the harm, (4) condemnation of the condemners, where offenders claim to be the true victims, and (5) appealing to higher authorities, where the actions of offenders are justified by something of more significance (Sykes and Matza 1957). Similarly, white-collar criminals apply neutralizations for unethical business practices where economic pressures, lack of social and legal controls including gatekeepers, and normative organization culture of deviance led to the collapse of the energy firm Enron and the consulting firm Arthur Anderson (Coffee 2002).

High-level hackers and release groups members are often guided by the ideology of protecting the free Internet from privatization and ownership. Marc Canter, cofounder of the software company Macromedia, expresses, "Today, no more than 5 percent of the populace can create" (Lasica 2005, 13). This is consistent with a studio Internet security expert who explains the benefits of piracy, stating, "It's like printing money and at the same time you're draining the money from your enemies." Another studio security expert and former high-level pirate described his past mentality as, "I can beat the Man, and it's fun to beat the Man!"

INDUSTRY

Industry professionals perceive file sharing and unauthorized downloading as criminal regardless of intent. "It's theft, plain and simple," claims a film industry security supervisor. Others in the industry echo his opinion, questioning the relevance of the Internet as a medium. "What's the difference between walking in to a store and stealing a CD or DVD?" questions another film industry Internet security supervisor. When asked about industry overpricing, the security expert pointed out the disadvantage the studios have against file sharers. "[Studios] can't compete against free," he explains. Furthermore, he questions the motives and rhetoric behind file sharers, stating, "It's not free speech, it's free movies." He goes on:

> I think Mercedes' costs too much but I don't get to steal them. Yes, the studios are slow but that's irrelevant; these are basically excuses by criminals who are after profit, not freedom. Profit does not necessarily mean money. What's your motivation? There is always a motive of gain behind

the actions of pirates. Bandwidth and equipment costs aren't free. For file-sharers, their gain is the music they obtained. For some, it may be the notoriety or fame associated with the activity. For others, maybe the service is free but the ad space sold is not. So in some way, there is always personal or group benefit at the cost of someone else.

This industry perspective points out the totality of benefits by file sharers. This is consistent with observations by researchers on hacker motivation, which includes monetary gain, intellectual challenge, power, peer recognition, and youthful mischief (Grabosky and Smith 1998; Krone 2005). These individuals and groups find online social status and reputation meaningful, despite real-life anonymity.

In the movie industry, individuals and groups motivated by monetary incentives record motion pictures in theater using inexpensive camcorders that end up on Darknet. According to one film industry security manager, release groups can offer up to $10,000 or more for a good-quality camcorder copy. He explains, "[Release groups] will even pay off projection technicians. When these teens get caught, they're still juveniles so the risk is extremely low." Camcorder copies, either analog or digital, are digitized to video files that can be copied on to an optical disc and/or released on to Darknet. To ensure sound quality, one studio security expert explains the sophistication of pirates: "[Pirates] use the hearing impaired signal to get a clean [audio] signal. They used to plug it in to the handicap seat jack but now they're using [wireless Infrared] instead."

Industries also cite the countermeasure technologies used by Internet malefactors as proof of monetary and malicious motivation. According to the 2004 Australian Computer Crimes and Security Survey,[37] various industry security professionals' polls suggested that 20 percent of hackers were motivated by financial gain, while 31 percent used company system resources such as bandwidth and storage without authorization. One type of technology utilized by top-level attackers are Botnets, or networks of remotely controlled computers (bots) used for attacks, extortion, and other types of technology-enabled crimes. One film industry security expert explains:

> In one instance, people are hacking already hacked systems and stealing their bots. What they do is hack an insecure server, plant a bot, and secure the server from other bot thieves. The result is the creation of a massive botnet. When you have 100,000 computers at your disposal, that's power. You pay me $50,000 or I take down your online gambling site for 3 days. That's real money.

A network security engineer at a large software company underscores the harm caused by sophisticated malefactors, explaining these botnets "serve as a middleman, making it *very* difficult to find out who's in charge." He adds, "Teens are not a big concern for [our company], sharing software or minor piracy, but the real threat is the professional hacker who is contracted out. It's just like business outsourcing."

Similar to a legitimate business, professional pirates also operate with hard goods, using authentic equipment and facilities. According an MPA report on organized movie piracy in Asia, optical discs are distributed in a supply chain with manufacturers, wholesale distributors,

---

[37]2004 Australian Computer Crimes and Security Survey. http://www.auscert.org.au/images/ACCSS2006.pdf

exporters, and territorial overlords who supply street peddlers.[38] The quality of pirated goods can be very good. One computer network security expert explains:

> The biggest threat [to our company] are [the] professional middlemen. These are the people with professional equipment that can handle producing large volumes of authentic-looking software packages that sell near or at retail prices. Some have duplicated some, not all, of overt (visible physical security on disc and packaging) and covert (invisible) security measures.

This is further facilitated in countries that may share similar motives in undermining economies of other nations. While there is growing pressure to curb piracy, piracy can generate a tremendous amount of revenue for some countries that turn a blind eye. One security expert hypothesizes, "China will not significantly shift to protect our [intellectual property] until they have IP to protect."

The decentralized and borderless nature of the Internet creates many layers of enforcement and political difficulties in protecting IP by U.S. industries. One studio security expert explains, "Pirates will move their operations to Europe, and if that's clogged up, they'll move it to Asia, then Africa, until there's a rogue nation with the bandwidth willing to host everything for a fee." Nations with lax copyright laws and enforcement requires companies to develop strategies and partnerships that pool technological, enforcement, legal, and political resources to create a security framework.

The film and recording industry has employed a variety of technologies to fight piracy. The studios are aware that overaggressive technological solutions can trigger a public backlash and stronger antiforensics countermeasures. To protect against soft goods piracy, movie studios rely on the MPA, which handles international piracy, and the MPAA, which handles piracy in North America. This chapter will use both organizations' names interchangeably.[39] The MPA employs both technical and legal staffs, many with law enforcement and investigation backgrounds. Some studios go further by employing their own security staff who monitor and searches communication mediums used by piracy networks.

Some technical services are outsourced to vendors specializing in piracy. Companies such as Safenet[40] (MediaSentry), MediaDefender,[41] Ranger Online, and MediaForce are considered P2P "bounty hunters," who perform security activities using tools such as search engines more sophisticated than Google[42] (Ahrens 2002; Hanley 2003). In addition, these companies employ covert disruptive technologies such as adding distortion to digital music files and uploading partial and tracking files. However, one studio security expert warns, "if you employ too many countermeasures, the account will be banned which includes an IP block, making it difficult to infiltrate top [release group] members."

---

[38]Motion Picture Association Organized Crime and Motion Picture Piracy Asia/Pacific Report. November, 2005.

[39]The Motion Picture Association of America (MPAA) handles U.S. piracy, while the Motion Picture Association (MPA), deals mainly with international piracy. They are both part of the same organization.

[40]Formerly MediaSentry. http://www.safenet-inc.com/

[41]http://www.mediadefender.com/

[42]http://www.google.com

To maintain flexibility and allow managed copying and licensing of media, software, and hardware, companies have employed Digital Rights Management (DRM), a controversial set of technologies used to set limitations on the uses and duplication of copyrighted material. For example, the software company Microsoft[43] verifies the authenticity of their software using Microsoft Genuine Advantage (MGA)[44] to check the Validation Key or Certificate of Authenticity (COA). However, loopholes have been exploited by pirates. According to one network security professional:

> Where fraud occurs very frequently is with Volume License Keys (VLK). VLKs are used in large companies with hundreds of clients where single installation on all machines is not practical. This installation method is installed on one machine and cloned on all other machines using the same key. An IT staff cannot sit there and type in every COA. Licenses are often abused when they pay for example, 8,000 machines and there are 200,000 installs. This occurs quite frequently.

This highlights the opportunistic nature of pirates. Most software developers use similar schemes that require product registration and serial number checks. The digital music download service iTunes[45] Music Store limits the number of computers and iPod portable music devices from playing its copy-protected music using its FairPlay DRM. However, FairPlay's DRM security has been circumvented, or "cracked," by hackers, making downloaded music playable on any portable device (Fisher 2004).

Progressively cheaper technology has made pirating easier. Optical disc recorders, or "burners," have dropped in price to a point where it is affordable to the average consumer. These CD and DVD burners can quickly and cheaply make perfect replicas of original discs. While DVDs contain a Content Scrambling System (CSS) DRM encryption scheme, it has long been easily circumvented by freely downloaded utilities that have decoded the encryption algorithm (Patrizio 1999). Once decrypted, the digital bits can be copied or "ripped" on to a computer and transferred over the Internet. It is important to note that DRM and copy protection technology is not new. Before the Internet, Macrovision[46] technology distorted video copying from multiple video cassette recorder (VCR) devices. However, soft goods piracy has allowed for unprecedented distribution speed without any quality degradation. The music recording industry has been profoundly affected by the lowered cost of technology and increased Internet bandwidth. Small music files are especially vulnerable to soft goods piracy due to the lack of copy protection technology built in from its inception.

Sony BMG highlighted the difficulties of using technology to fight piracy by unsuccessfully implementing CD copy protection schemes. In 2002, Sony's Extended Copy Protection (XCP) embedded Key2Audio technology in CDs designed to prevent disc ripping, and duplication was easily circumvented by "scribbling around the rim of a disk with a felt-tip marker."[47] Similarly, in 2005, Sony BMG drew harsh criticism and later retracted its copy

---

[43]http://www.microsoft.com/windows/windowsmedia/forpros/drm/default.mspx
[44]http://www.microsoft.com/genuine/default.mspx?displaylang=en
[45]http://www.apple.com/itunes/
[46]http://www.macrovision.com/
[47]Wired News via Reuters May 20, 2002. http://www.wired.com/news/technology/0,1282,52665,00.html

protection for its music CDs that installed a Trojan-horse-like[48] rootkit, or hidden files that compromised Microsoft Windows-based PCs to hacker attacks (Schneier 2005). One studio security expert stressed the ineffectiveness of using only technology to stop piracy, likening copy protection to "snake oil." Moreover, technologies that are designed to secure systems against piracy such as Trusted Computing, a closed system architecture of dedicated hardware designed to only run approved software, "can be employed to better protect pirates and their P2P distribution networks from the entertainment industry" (Schechter, Greenstadt, and Smith 2003). Consequently, part of the strategy used by companies is using law enforcement for assistance.

ENFORCEMENT AND INVESTIGATIONS

The main reason why piracy occurs is the low risk of detection and apprehension. As part of an overall strategy, industries have partnered with law enforcement to incapacitate offenders. Unlike other industries such as banking, which tend to underreport crime in fear of the negative ramifications associated with insecurity,[49] piracy is very compatible with policing objectives and capabilities. Police specialize in forensics for the purpose of gathering evidence to build cases for prosecution. Evidence collection can involve seizing computer equipment or temporarily stopping operations. For companies that rely on continuous business functionality, the priority is restoring or maintaining operations, which can destroy ephemeral digital evidence required for case building. One network security expert at a computer hardware company explains, "[During a criminal event, it might be too late if the system is already up and running." Moreover, sensitivity of information, such as trade secrets, can be exposed during public hearings. Several interviewed network security professionals warned that any attempts at deterrence from aggressive technical and legal actions can be seen as an affront and challenge to the hacker community, which can lead to a spike in attacks from more sophisticated hackers.

The piracy enforcement philosophy, however, embraces high-profile investigations and arrests. The film industry, for instance, targets high-profile top sites, suppliers, and high-level distribution channels to disrupt P2P networks and supply chains. According to a film industry security expert, "Disruption of a top site does two things: sends a message to other distributors that a major site can be taken down, and sends a ripple effect to other servers that get overloaded." In addition, high-profile raids are often reported by media outlets, and details are made available through MPAA publications that advertise literally tons of counterfeit optical discs seized, with an estimated street value of billions. In a 2006 MPA piracy report, New York City police seized 91,685 optical discs during a raid on May 11, weighing nearly as much as two adult elephants and four baby elephants.[50]

---

[48]A Trojan horse is a program that hides malicious code inside innocuous files that can be activated to cause harm such as allowing unauthorized access to computer systems. Unlike a computer virus, Trojan horses do not self-replicate and spread.

[49]According to the 2006 CSI/FBI Computer Crime and Security Survey, only 25% of respondents reported security incidents to law enforcement (Gordon et al. 2006).

[50]The Film Piracy Report, Issue 01, July 2006.

Investigations leading to big busts are a result of active partnerships between industry and law enforcement. Neither law enforcement nor the film industry has the capacity to deal with piracy. Modern society is described by Ericson and Haggerty (1997) as "risk society," where the complexities of technology that require expertise have overwhelmed traditional forms of social control. As a result, social institutions such as the police have adopted a business model in dealing with risk by allocating limited resources and becoming "experts" in specialized fields. According to one network security engineer, the "pain," or potential losses to companies, has increased to a point where public assistance is deemed a necessary part of a comprehensive security plan. A studio security expert echoes this opinion, explaining, "State law allows for the MPA to do complete investigations all the way up to the arrest. They can even obtain search warrants. However, they don't do this. They share the responsibility with police." Several film industry investigators and security experts have law enforcement backgrounds. The "instant trust and rapport," according to one security supervisor with a law enforcement background, helps ensure a reliable evidentiary chain during an investigation.

A typical online movie piracy investigation starts when the MPAA or studio identifies a file sharer, usually with a substantial amount of copyrighted files on his or her local drive or file server. Once evidence is collected, such as screen captures of the suspect's file directory showing movie titles and other identifiers, a file sharer's unique Internet Protocol (IP) address is recorded. Similar to telephone numbers, IP addresses are a series of numbers that give location information on the Internet of a particular piece of hardware, which can be used to find a physical location. The Internet works by transferring information that is broken up into smaller "packets" that are routed to an end destination and reassembled using the IP delivery protocol. Similar to telephone number area codes, the first series of digits belong to different Internet Service Providers (ISPs), such as cable and telecommunication companies.

Once an IP address is identified, the MPAA or studio can identify and contact the registered ISP, who has the actual end-user information. Each ISP subscriber is assigned a specific IP address within the ISP network. To obtain private customer information, a legal order or subpoena is acquired. After customer information is obtained, the MPA can pursue two avenues: contact the party directly or contact law enforcement for apprehension.

One complication is the conflict between media companies interested in protecting their intellectual property and ISPs who have an interest in protecting customer privacy to prevent losing subscribers. In 2002, the ISP Verizon[51] refused to serve an RIAA partial subpoena that requested end-user subscriber information. RIAA President Cary Sherman (2002) filed a brief stating, "Verizon disingenuously implies that they are protecting the 'privacy' of their subscribers. But they are not." The refusal by Verizon to release customer information began a chasm that has also caused a discord with the motion picture industry. One film industry security expert explains, "Collaboration between the film industry and ISPs were on a very good basis *until* the RIAA wanted user info. When that lawsuit [between the RIAA and Verizon] happened, we were shut out." He adds, "This situation is still contentious. Cable companies have been more cooperative over [telecommunication ISPs]," reasoning, "Smaller companies want to protect their bandwidth." Through a series of ongoing controversial court battles, ISPs have turned over information to media companies.

---

[51]http://www22.verizon.com/

Once end-user information is obtained, the studio or MPA usually issues a cease and desist letter, a legal letter that demands immediate termination of activities deemed in violation of law. With end-users, usually a teenager, the threat of legal action is usually enough to end file sharing activities. One studio security supervisor explains, "What usually happens is a notice is sent with some legalese and parents usually call in." However, this same studio security supervisor who signs the letter with his contact information has had countless repercussions, such as threatening phone calls and even postulates that his credit has been ruined by retributive hackers.[52]

If criminal actions are pursued, law enforcement is contacted. In California, there is no specified piracy branch of law enforcement. Piracy usually is handled by a combination of federal, state, and local agencies. When crimes that are high-tech in nature occur, they are typically assigned to one of the state's five regional high-tech crime taskforces. These taskforces operate under the Office of Emergency Services (OES) and are consulted by a steering committee consisting of public law enforcement, district attorneys, and a variety of private industry representatives. Regional taskforces consist of a variation of federal agents from different agencies, including the California Highway Patrol, county sheriff departments, local police departments, and state and local district attorneys.

These taskforces serve to enforce crimes sanctioned under California Penal Code 13848,[53] specifying activities such as unlawful access to computer systems, copyright infringement, white-collar crime, and theft of trade secrets. Crimes are often reported at local police stations and referred to the taskforce. Taskforce officers are given ongoing extensive training and have been successful in numerous cases, including a $200 million bust in Southern California in 2004, the largest in U.S. history.[54] The taskforce only accepts cases filed by regional police departments or victim company representative directly, not the general public.

Depending on the nature of the case, the primary role of law enforcement is to identify the suspect(s) and to obtain the probable cause. Probable cause is the threshold of evidentiary standard necessary for searches and arrests. According to a regional taskforce member, 90 percent of all cases involve time- and labor-intensive computer forensics to build evidentiary proof of a crime.

Computer forensics is a systematic analysis of computer hardware and software to collect evidence for the purpose of building a case. A taskforce supervisor explains, once a computer is brought in, the first step is to take a "snapshot" of the system configuration and time logs using special forensics software to prevent accusations of evidence tampering. Next, the storage drive is imaged, or an exact duplicate is made, to prevent altering data or time-sensitive files and logs. Preserving digital evidence is an important step because any automated system process or investigator input can alter the drive content. To further preserve evidence integrity during the file transfer process, computer transfers take place in a locked room inside the substation when unsupervised. The duplicate drive is then scanned for viruses before being installed in an isolated computer. Finally, a search is performed to look for evidence. According to several investigators and district attorneys interviewed, law enforcement experience can minimize the time required for locating files for prosecution. Outsourcing

---

[52]Sample legal letters sent to The Pirate Bay can be found at http://thepiratebay.org/legal.php
[53]http://law.onecle.com/california/penal/13848.html
[54]http://www.dvd-recordable.org/Article1694-mode=thread-order0-threshold0.phtml

forensics work to private vendors and hiring purely technical civilian personnel are not considered by law enforcement for this reason.

Public apathy also adversely affects law enforcement priorities and budgets. One task-force investigator explains, "Banks don't make good victims. Technology doesn't make good victims. [Companies are] already rich!" He adds, "The problem is public perception. [Piracy] will never be prioritized." Since budgets are set by elected officials who reflect the concerns the majority, street crimes are given supremacy over protecting company profits. One state government emergency services representative explains how public indifference towards piracy can impact budgets:

> We just need someone to bang on Washington's door and say we need funding. It's getting worse, it's not getting better. You have funds for victims against women and they get funding, but based on identity theft, that's devastating [also]. But since it's not violent, it doesn't qualify. You talk to any law enforcement agency [and they will confirm that] we just don't have enough funds. We're on a shoestring budget.

The lack of funds has significantly limited the capacity of piracy enforcement in California. Each regional taskforce is given approximately $2 million annually from the OES in grants and is required to match 25 percent of state contributions. Most taskforces' contribution far exceeds the minimum 25 percent match requirement, citing personnel, training, and equipment costs. One taskforce supervisor estimates departmental contributions closer to $6 million. This amounts to roughly .01 percent of the overall department budget for the 2005–06 fiscal year. Moreover, the five regional taskforces do not cover the entire state, leaving gaping holes in the security infrastructure.

The lack of funding and limited capacity has resulted in more discriminating case selection. One taskforce investigator explains a typical scenario, stating "A case is usually picked up when there are multiple victims by the perpetrator and reaches a $2,500 loss or damage threshold." He adds, "The taskforce is extremely busy, with each detective typically working five forensics cases and three intrusion cases." According to another investigator, each case takes approximately three times longer and generates significantly more paperwork than typical street crime, describing her work as "never ending." Each industry must vie for limited investigatory time. With hard goods piracy, the same investigator estimates the minimum threshold for taking a case is approximately 500 CDs and 100 DVDs to make it "worthwhile."

In addition to small budgets and limited manpower, cultural factors also limit availability of police to industry. Law enforcement has developed a strong subculture from real and perceived dangers inherent to the profession that has resulted in a strong loyalty to other officers (Christopher Commission Report 1991; Skolnick and Fyfe 1993). While the taskforce is designated to enforce corporate crimes under PC13848, a large proportion of their workload involves handling cases received from local agencies requiring technical assistance in crime scenes. Cases range from extracting and analyzing surveillance video stored on a digital medium to child pornography. Cases brought in from officers or law enforcement agencies are not turned away but are placed in queue and often take priority over company cases. According to one federal agent assigned to the taskforce, "Cases are given priority by court dates and if imminent danger is present." This added workload diverts time dedicated to companies, who often find it difficult to compete with cases involving children. During one committee meeting, an industry representative voiced his frustration, stating "We can't compete with children."

Another structural issue of law enforcement is whether police, who are generally reactive by nature, should take on a more active prevention role. Some industry critics question the usefulness of forensics, which allocate resources after a crime has been committed, versus prevention-based corporate network security and critical infrastructure protection models. One state emergency services representative questions if taskforces are necessary, given that many large companies employ their own team of investigators. She uses one large software company as an example, commenting, "They have their own team now, their own investigations." She questions, "Maybe the trend is we need to re-look at [our strategy]. Are we duplicating [their functions]?"

A network security expert at a large software company reaffirms the need for law enforcement's role in forensics. He stresses, "Local law enforcement is the biggest area of need," adding, "It's a pipeline problem and forensics is the single biggest critical element. Law enforcement should focus on what they're good at, forensics." He further emphasizes the need to significantly increase collective investigatory capacity by increasing the base knowledge of all law enforcement officers at the street level. He states, "The local level is lagging the most and there needs to be a pipeline of information starting at the community colleges to offer mandatory training to law enforcement recruits and cadets to get them thinking and integrated into the forensics realm." One taskforce supervisor agrees, stating that the need for forensics is growing, with more digital evidence not just from computers, but from cellular phones to personal data assistants (PDAs). He states, "One, the [taskforce] is important and needs to be expanded and two, there needs to be some sort of training curriculum and base knowledge [at the street officer level]." Implementing expensive high-tech training may be difficult for the vast majority of local officers who have little to no background in computers. According to one taskforce supervisor, it takes approximately four years to fully train an investigator.

Even if funding for the taskforce is increased, it remains difficult to expand personnel. The rigid bureaucratic structure of law enforcement often promotes officers away from taskforce divisions to higher-ranking positions supervising street officers. One former taskforce detective used the taskforce as a steppingstone to become sergeant. Another member took mandatory leave of the taskforce for a couple of years after being promoted to sergeant before returning. In addition, members of the taskforce are frequently "pulled" from the taskforce and reassigned to home agencies in need of personnel for street duties. Despite "free" training and equipment offered to departments who assign officers to the taskforce, who are essentially "gaining a full function computer crime lab," understaffed departments remain reluctant. Moreover, there is the constant possibility of losing officers to private industry positions offering higher salaries. Furthermore, outsourcing or hiring nonsworn investigators is not considered.

Prosecutorial willingness to accept cases is another limiting factor to law enforcement effectiveness in handling Internet crimes. The factors that can influence decisions can range from threshold of losses to jurisdictional issues. As mentioned, computer crime cases are significantly more time consuming to prosecute than street crimes. Despite special district attorneys assigned to the taskforce, prosecutors face similar issues of prioritizing cases ranging from identity theft to piracy to child pornography. One taskforce investigator explains, "A lot of crimes are considered misdemeanors with penalties being [very] light, such as probation. In addition, with things such as IP tracking, it's hard to prove who was on the computer," concluding, "It's just not worth the time." For example, fraud cases relayed by the FBI and

National White Collar Crime Center's (NW3C) Internet Crime Complaint Center (IC3)[55] are not pursued by the taskforce. She explains that the taskforce is too busy, and oftentimes companies will write off losses as a routine cost of doing business.

The borderless nature of the Internet is also a factor adding to prosecutorial difficulties. International cases require extensive concerted efforts based on the cooperation and assistance of foreign governments. According to one investigator, "Cases are dropped immediately once they cross international lines." One studio security expert confirms the criminal justice bottleneck, stating "[In order for the studio] to pursue more criminal cases, we need support from the government, the U.S. Attorneys Office," explaining, "Those are hit and miss." More research needs to be conducted to explore the factors and variables contributing to case acceptance.

The bottlenecks that limit the capacity of law enforcement to operate effectively and efficiently in a cyber environment can be explained by Pontell's (1984) systems capacity theoretical framework. According to systems capacity theory, "the effectiveness of criminal justice is dependent upon the willingness and ability of the criminal justice system to enforce laws and mete out punishment."[56] Variables affecting law enforcement and industry such as prosecutorial decision-making, budgets, bureaucratic structures, public apathy, and the strong countermeasures of Darknet can limit the overall capacity of criminal justice. This is substantially compounded by a borderless cyberspace environment.

Two major variables that allow for the flexibility to deal effectively with the Internet environment are an inverse relationship between organizational hierarchy and individual autonomy. The major difference between the taskforce and street patrol units is the significant flattening of the hierarchical command structure with high-level investigator autonomy. According to one taskforce supervisor, rank is seldom exercised. Investigators generally operate independently and autonomously on cases. One potential problem with such a large degree of freedom may be the lack of direct supervision of investigators with a significant amount of fieldwork. However, the supervisor explains that autonomy is necessary and worth the tradeoff, stating "A lot of it is based on trust." Furthermore, symbols of rank and authority such as uniforms and service weapons are disregarded and replaced by business casual attire. The autonomy also allows investigators to build personal rapport with individuals within companies who contact investigators directly for enforcement needs.

Despite the negative ramifications of aggressive enforcement by companies, legal actions are undoubtedly the most controversial strategy used against file sharers and distributors. The main legal apparatus used against online file sharers are copyright laws.

COPYRIGHT LAW AND LEGAL ACTIONS

The United States copyright law was established to protect "authors of 'original works of authorship,' including literary, dramatic, musical, artistic, and certain other intellectual works" (Title 17, U.S. Code).[57] This was derived from an international agreement at Bern,

[55]http://www.ic3.gov/
[56]http://www.ic3.gov/
[57]http://www.copyright.gov/title17/

Switzerland, on September 9, 1886, at The Bern Convention for the Protection of Literary and Artistic Works.[58] Copyright laws affecting Internet piracy includes published and unpublished literary work, musical work, pictorial and graphic work, motion pictures, and sound recordings. Today, Title 17 is part of an international agreement called the World Intellectual Property Organization (WIPO) Copyright Treaty. There are many caveats to the copyright law that are too lengthy for discussion, but for the purposes of this chapter, the focus will be on the Digital Millennium Copyright Act of 1998[59] (DMCA, H.R.2281 Public Law 105–304) amendment to Title 17, U.S. Code, which focuses specifically on newer computer technologies.

The DMCA makes important modifications to traditional copyright law. Specifically, it addresses technologies used in online file sharing. There are two main sections of the act. Title I (§1201) of the DMCA makes it illegal to use circumvention technologies used to block user access without permission. For example, using technologies that unlock cable television channels to access premium content is in violation of the DMCA. Title II (§1201) of the DMCA criminalizes trafficking of circumvention technologies, such as distribution of code that decrypts DVD DRM software. The DMCA also makes illegal the tampering or removal of Copyright Management Information (CMI) that identifies copyrighted work, such as authorship, embedded company information, and limitations of use, such as End User License Agreements. Criminal penalties for violation of the DMCA, specified under §1204, are fines up to $500,000 and/or imprisonment of up to five years for violation of one section. If a violation occurs in both §1201 and §1202, offenders may face up to a $1 million fine and/or imprisonment for up to 10 years. Exception to the DMCA include nonprofit libraries, archives, educational institutions, and public broadcasting entities with a statute of limitation of up to five years.

Companies can also file civil suits in federal district courts against groups or individuals. Civil penalties are based on judiciary discretion. A judge can order monetary restitution, including legal fees and profits earned from piracy. Furthermore, injunctions can be issued stopping the distribution or destruction of circumvention tools and products. Judges can also order probationary conditions that restrict computer access. A repeat violation within a three-year period can result in tripling the damages awarded.[60]

The most publicized legal actions began with the RIAA, who sued P2P organizations. In December 1999, the first mainstream P2P operation Napster was sued for violation of the DMCA from music files shared. RIAA counsel Cary Sherman justified the civil suit, stating "Napster is about facilitating piracy, and trying to build a business on the backs of artists and copyright owners" (Menta 1999). The RIAA sued for violation of Title I and Title II of the DMCA, resulting in $100,000 for each copy-protected song file being shared, totaling approximately $20 billion from a library of over 200,000 downloadable songs at the time. In defense, Napster cited the "fair use" doctrine of the Copyright Act of 1976 §107,[61] which allows for limited duplication of copyrighted material without permission. The doctrine takes into account the purpose of use, nature of the copyrighted work, the amount and substantiation of the copied work, and market effects of the copying. Napster's argument that it was merely facilitating users to share files for noncommercial fair use and not all files were copyrighted

---

[58]http://www.law-ref.org/BERN/index.html

[59]http://www.copyright.gov/legislation/dmca.pdf

[60]http://www.chillingeffects.org/anticircumvention/faq.cgi#QID123

[61]http://www.law.cornell.edu/uscode/html/uscode17/usc_sec_17_00000107——000-.html

music files was criticized by the RIAA as being "baseless" (Borland 2000). The Ninth Circuit District Court agreed, reasoning that since Napster routed all songs through its own internal servers, Napster has a responsibility to prevent copyright infringement (McGuire 2005). The result was Napster shutting down operations in 2001 after an injunction to stop operations and a $36 million settlement. Napster eventually reemerged after a bankruptcy buyout to become a legal DRM-compliant pay service. Many subsequent P2P services have been sued since.

The RIAA drew the most controversy in 2003 when it began filing mass lawsuits against individual file sharers. After winning legal battles with ISPs to obtain end-user information, such as Verizon, 261 lawsuits were filed in the United States in what was described as "driftnet fishing" tactics.[62] Almost all users were unable to pay for legal fees in a lengthy court battle and settled out of court for an average of $3,000 each case. In 2004, after a legal setback with ISPs, the RIAA began suing "John Does," or anonymous individuals known only by their IP addresses linked to high-volume "gregarious" file sharing activities (Roberts 2004). Since end-user information was limited, individuals who were sued ranged in age from children to senior citizens, with an infamously dubious lawsuit filed against a deceased 83-year-old grandmother that was later withdrawn (Bangeman 2005).

In 2005, file sharing entered the U.S. Supreme Court in *Metro-Goldwyn-Mayer Studios Inc. (MGM) v. Grokster Ltd.* (545 U.S. 913),[63] cementing the legal liability of P2P download services. In a landmark unanimous ruling, the Court found Grokster's[64] online P2P service: (1) similar to Napster, aimed to satisfy a known source of demand for copyright infringement, (2) it did not attempt to develop software to curtail piracy activity, and (3) Grokster was making money by selling advertising space in their free software. This ruling has settled any uncertainties regarding the legal position of P2P operations. One studio Internet security expert explains that when civil cases are brought forth by the MPA, "There is no defense," adding, "It's not a case where there's any gray areas. With Grokster, now everyone has a much better understanding and everything is rock solid [when cases are filed]."

In *Arista Records LLC et al. v. LimeWire LLC* (Civil Action No. 06 CV. 5936 2006), defendants accused the recording companies of using strong-arm tactics to win cases and undermine P2P technology. According to P2P service LimeWire,[65] the studios' refusal to license content for digital distribution while not developing their own equivalent technology in a timely manner constitutes a "conspiracy to destroy innovation" and threatens to "destroy P2P technology." LimeWire cited denied requests for legitimate distribution. Studios declined requests for DRM licensing and hashes (encryption codes used for authenticity identification) used in content filtering. Moreover, the defendants accused the studios of anticompetitive pricing. LimeWire has currently filed a countersuit demanding a jury trial. The suit is unlikely to win from mounting legal precedent in cases such as Napster and Grokster.

For individual file sharers who have tried to defend cases, it has been very difficult to find compelling evidence. In *Arista Records LLC et al. v. David Greubel* (Civil Action No. 4:05-CV-531-Y, 2005), the defendant argued that the lawsuit was too vague without specifying the actual time and acts of infringement, reasoning that merely the *availability* of the files does

---

[62]*RIAA v. The People: Two Years Later.* Electronic Frontier Foundation. http://www.eff.org
[63]http://fairuse.stanford.edu/MGM_v_Grokster.pdf
[64]http://www.grokster.com/
[65]http://www.limewire.com/english/content/home.shtml

not constitute distribution. In addition, the defendant argued that the studios failed to properly register the sound recordings. Using the semantics of the law, the defendant also argued that §106(3) of the Copyright Act does not cover electronic transfers, only specifying "copies or phonerecords." The judge, however, denied a request by the defense for case dismissal.

The film industry has also exercised legal action against threats to their IP. According to one studio security expert, "there is a limited palette of legal options to choose from," citing "the DMCA is used on a daily basis." Among the legal options available are "cybersquatting" laws, which are laws preventing extortion-like registration of online domain names associated with a company and charging inflated prices to return them. In addition, the film industry frequently utilizes federal laws targeting camcordering in movie theaters. The "No Electronic Theft Act," or Net Act (17 U.S.C. § 101),[66] criminalizes profiting from copyrighted material, and the Family Entertainment Act[67] under the Copyright Act further specifies penalties and actions associated with infringements of motion picture copyrighted material.

Unlike the RIAA, civil cases against end-users are less frequently pursued by the MPAA, which uses a top-down approach. According to one studio security expert, targeting file sharers is "a lot of expenditure for someone without a whole lot of money." He adds, "Studios don't have an interest in bankrupting people and holding the judgment over their heads," explaining, "We do it when we feel there are some [public relations] benefit." He warns of the negative ramifications of overaggressive legal actions, stating "The more [the industry applies] ever-thicker layers of lawyers to this problem, the more lawyer-proof new technologies [will be] that emerge." This is consistent with a deterrence model study that found short-term legal victories are negated by long-term losses from stronger resistance (Oksanen and Valimaki 2006). Instead, the industry sees a bigger impact by targeting release groups and dismantling top sites.

Aggressive legal actions have failed to significantly deter file sharers. According to a 2004 Pew report, unauthorized music downloads had increased from an estimated 18 million in 2003 to 23 million in 2004 (Rainie et al. 2004). A recent study found that while file sharing has decreased due to legal threats, a substantial amount of files shared on P2P networks remain (Bhattacharjee et al. 2006). According to an EFF report, empirical evidence shows P2P network usage increasing despite earlier self-report surveys "suggesting a modest reduction in file sharing since the recording industry lawsuits against individuals began."[68]

CHANGING THE PUBLIC DISCOURSE: WINNING "HEARTS AND MINDS"

The most important and effective long-term strategy to permanently curtail piracy, as emphasized by all three industries, is to change the public discourse through education. While most file sharers know their activities are prohibited, it is difficult for industry to convince them to stop. According to all three industries, community self-policing can be formed through internalization of morals. One film industry security expert comments, "One of the most challenging things for us is in [the public relations] and education side of the house. We can say [our message] but it

[66]http://www.usdoj.gov/criminal/cybercrime/17-18red.htm
[67]http://www.copyright.gov/legislation/pl109-9.html
[68]*RIAA v. The People: Two Years Later.* Electronic Frontier Foundation. http://www.eff.org

really doesn't translate." He questions, "How do we educate the public? How did we become the bad guys?" These are the major challenges developing a permanent solution to online piracy.

It remains extremely difficult for industry to convey the overall societal impact of online piracy to change public perceptions that are fixated on the hacker mentality. "It's an issue of legitimacy," explains one movie industry security expert. "To win the hearts and minds and [change the perception that] it's easier to buy than to steal." While some losses are absorbed as business losses to multimillion-dollar companies, the negative ramifications of piracy can permeate throughout society. The same security expert explains:

> What's the big deal about piracy? The big deal is one, the tremendous money involved and two, the money doesn't go back to the community, ultimately hurting the community. It may seem like free stuff and fun initially. The effects are huge on our economy overall. Our economy is based on innovation, not production.

When asked about the positive competitive effects of piracy such as driving down prices, progressing innovation, and better, more robust products, the movie security expert did not see any positive effects. He explains, "You're actually driving *down* competition," adding, "Small companies are affected the most. For example, why buy $30 software when the bootleg high-end stuff is for free?" He emphasizes, "It's hard to explain to the average person who feels they're spending too much; hard to make them understand production coming to their town." One network security engineer at a large software company explains, "All forms of computer crime creates an 'IP tax,' costing everyone money." The added cost of vigilance in security and piracy are absorbed by higher retail prices for goods and services, perpetuating a disadvantageous cycle for companies competing against Darknet. Changing public mentality through education requires the right combination of education and deterrence strategies targeted towards different groups.

The major challenge facing companies battling piracy is balancing rigorous enforcement and education. As seen in the music industry, overaggressive enforcement and legal actions against the general public can undermine educational strategies, creating adversarial relationships. One network security engineer explains, "There is a big chasm between public consciousness and the reality of computer crime." One strategy used by the film industry is convincing casual file-sharers sympathetic to topsites and release groups that there are real "bad guys" running these operations. It is important for all industries to tailor specific strategies toward specific groups. Using strong enforcement and technological efforts can be effective against release groups, but not a majority of the file sharing population.

The largest concentration of piracy is tech-savvy teenagers, highlighting the importance of early intervention and prevention strategies. According to a 2004 Harris Interactive poll conducted for the Business Software Alliance (BSA), in comparison to children aged 8 to 12, more teenagers believe it is okay to download copyrighted material. Teenagers are also less likely to worry about getting in trouble with their parents and more likely to know peers who illegally download copyrighted material. The Harris poll concluded, "Teaching respect for digital copyrighted works is critical as young people grow up."[69]

---

[69]*New Survey Shows that Teens are more Likely to Illegally Download Than Tweens.* http://www.bsa.org/usa/press/newsreleases/New-Survey-Shows-that-Teens-Are-More-Likely-to-Illegally-Download.cfm

According to Farrington (2003), crime is best prevented by targeting onset deviant behavior before a spike during the teenage years. The same data show that targeting criminals later in life is a less optimal allocation of resources from the general desistence in deviant behavior, or "aging-out," during adulthood stemming from higher incomes and greater responsibilities. This is consistent with one security expert interviewed who gave up hacking to pursue a legitimate career at a studio when his wife became pregnant with his first child. This security expert, aware of the aging-out effect warns, "Going after [teenagers] is just a bully tactic. The reality is that there are true bad guys who run these [piracy] operations at a large scale."

CONCLUSION

In summary, piracy of intellectual property is a growing problem magnified by increasingly affordable and faster computer technology and the Internet. To curtail this problem, security alliances have been formed between industry, public law enforcement, and domestic and international political bodies. However, a critical partnership must be formed with the general public, currently fixated on the discourse of companies getting just deserts in losses from the new generation of Robin Hood–like freedom fighters only worsens the problem. Without changing public perceptions that online piracy is often used to fund other dangerous illegal activities and requires more resources than traditional street crimes, public policing will remain limited to small taskforces.

It has been determined that using technology alone is ineffective and often leads to more robust countermeasures by sophisticated individuals and groups in Darknet. Using California as the focus of this research, it has been shown that collaborations between policing and industries are forming to deal with the problem. However, with structural and cultural barriers in place, full and successful partnerships have not come to fruition. To achieve this, significant changes in the hierarchical command structure must take place that gives officers more autonomy and, moreover, keep trained investigators from being promoted to other duties. Furthermore, law enforcement is at a pivotal moment to invest in increasing the technical knowledgebase of all agents and officers or face falling further behind increasingly organized and sophisticated criminal bodies. Partnerships must be expanded beyond certain industries to create a unified security network that transcends geographic borders.

Major structural changes must take place in the legal system to allow for the necessary flexibility to deal with the borderless nature of the Internet. Without such changes, specialized taskforces will be constrained to local jurisdictions. The rigidity of the legal system forces all law enforcement to follow evidentiary protocol for both physical and digital evidence for a public trial. These requirements discourage many industries from seeking law enforcement assistance and, moreover, prevent law enforcement from forming active partnerships based on areas of greatest impact: piracy prevention and network security.

A true paradigm shift is required to acknowledge that Internet piracy is more than a niche "computer crime" that affects large corporations. New theoretical models in the social sciences must be developed to understand the social mechanisms that drive file sharers and multifaceted online social networks. In addition, cross-disciplinary research should include economic models and technological perspectives in computer sciences, engineering, and informatics. More research and funding for research are vital. Unfortunately, without public and political acknowledgement that computers and the Internet are no different than ordinary crimes, funding for enforcement and research of Internet-enabled crimes will remain marginal and limited.

KEY TERMS

Forensics
Piracy
Taskforce

REFERENCES

Ahrens, F. June 19, 2002. "Ranger" vs. the movie pirates: Software is studios' latest weapon in a growing battle. *The Washington Post*: H0. Retrieved November 11, 2006, from http://www.washingtonpost.com/ac2/wp-dyn/A5144-2002Jun18?language=printer

Bangeman, E. 2005. I sue dead people. *Ars Technica*. Retrieved December 14, 2006, from http://arstechnica.com/news.ars/post/20050204-4587.html

Bhattacharjee, S., R. D. Gopal, K. Lertwachara, and J. R. Marsden. 2006. Impact of legal threats on online music sharing activity: An analysis of music industry legal actions. *Journal of Law and Economics* 49 (2006): 91–114.

Biddle, P., P. England, M. Peinado, and B. Willman. 2002. The darknet and the future of content distribution. Microsoft Corporation: 2002 ACM Workshop on Digital Rights Management. Retrieved December 2, 2006, from http://www.crypto.stanford.edu/DRM2002/prog.html

Borland, J. July 13, 2000. Recording industry calls Napster defense "baseless." CNET News. Retrieved December 15, 2006, from http://news.com.com/2100-1023-243162.html

Borland, J. October 6, 2004. Super-powered peer to peer. CNET News. Retrieved December 20, 2006, from http://news.com.com/Super-powered+peer+to+peer/2100-1032_3-5397784.html

Boutin, P. August 26, 2002. Sneakernet Redux: Walk your data. Wired News. Retrieved October 19, 2006, from http://www.wired.com/news/culture/0,1284,54739,00.html

Braverman, H. 1974. *Labor and Monopoly Capital: The Degradation of Work in the Twentieth Century*. New York: Monthly Review Press.

Choi, D. Y., and A. Perez. 2006. Online piracy and the emergence of new business models. USASBE/SBI 2006 Joint Conference Proceedings, Tucson, AZ. Retrieved September 2, 2006, from http://www.sbaer.uca.edu/research/usasbe/2006/pdffiles/papers/cases/016.pdf

Christopher Commission Report. 1991. Independent Commission on the Los Angeles Police Department (the Christopher Commission). *Report of the Independent Commission on the Los Angeles Police Department*. Los Angeles: International Creative Management. Retrieved December 1, 2004, from http://www. parc.info/client_files/Special%20Reports/1%20-%20Chistopher%20Commision.pdf

Coffee, J. C. 2002. Understanding Enron: It's about the gatekeepers, stupid. Columbia Law School Center for Law and Economic Studies. Retrieved June 20, 2005, from http://ssrn.com/abstract_id=325240

Denning, D., and W. Baugh. 1996. Decoding encryption policy. *Security Management* no. 2: 59–62. Retrieved September 13, 2006, from http://www.securitymanagement.com/library/000065.html

Ericson, R., and V. Haggerty. 1997. *Policing the Risk Society*. Toronto: University of Toronto Press.

Farrington, D. P. 2003. "Advancing knowledge about the early prevention of adult antisocial behaviour." In *Early Prevention of Adult Antisocial Behaviour,* edited by D. P. Farrington and J. W. Coid. Cambridge: Cambridge University Press.

Fisher, K. June 5, 2004. Apple's FairPlay DRM cracked. *Ars Technica*. Retrieved March 1, 2006, from http://arstechnica.com/news/posts/1081206124.html

Gartman, D. 1999. "Dialetics of the labor process, consumer culture, and class struggle." In *Rethinking the Labor Process,* edited by M. Wardell, T. L. Steiger, and P. Meiskins. Albany: State University of New York Press.

Godon, L. A., M. P. Loeb, W. Lucyshyn, and R. Richardson. 2006. *2006 CSI/FBI Computer Crime and Security Survey*. Computer Security Institute Publications. http://www.gocsi.com/forms/fbi/csi_fbi_survey.jhtml

Grabosky P., and R. Smith. 1998. *Crime in the Digital Age*. Sydney: Federation Press.

Hanley, R. March 5, 2003. Web bounty hunters help in anti-piracy war. *Stanford Daily*. Retrieved December 2, 2006, from http://daily.stanford.edu/article/2003/3/5/webBountyHuntersHelpIn AntipiracyWar

Harrison, A. March 13, 2006. The pirate bay: Here to stay? Wired News. Retrieved December 2, 2006, from http://www.wired.com/news/technology/0,70358-0.html

Howe, J. January 2005. The shadow Internet. Wired Magazine no. 13: 1. Retrieved October 3, 2006, from http://www.wired.com/wired/archive/13.01/topsite.html

Huey, L. J. July 2002. Policing the abstract: Some observations on policing cyberspace. *Canadian Journal of Criminology*: 243–54.

Kaufman, C., R. Perlman, and M. Speciner. 2002. *Network Security: Private Communication in a Public World*. 2nd ed. New Jersey: Prentice Hall.

Krone, T. 2005. High tech crime brief: Hacking motives. Australian Institute of Criminology. Retrieved October 9, 2006, from http://www.aic.gov.au/publications/htcb/htcb006.html

Lasica, J. D. 2005. *Darknet: Hollywood's War against the Digital Generation*. New Jersey: Wiley and Sons.

Levy, S. 2001. *Hackers: Heroes of the Computer Revolution*. Penguin: New York.

Lupsha, P. A. 1988. Organized crime: Rational choice not ethnic group behavior: A macro perspective. *Law Enforcement Intelligence Analysis Digest*. Winter.

Madden, M., and A. Lenhart. 2003. Music downloading, file-sharing, and copyright. PEW Internet Project Data Memo. Retrieved October 14, 2006, from http://www.pewinternet.org/PPF/r/96/report_display.asp

McGuire, D. March 28, 2005. At a glance: MGM vs. Grokster. *Washington Post Online*. November 3, 2006, from http://www.washingtonpost.com/wp-srv/technology/articles/groksterprimer_033805.htm

Menta, R. 1999. RIAA sues music startup Napster for $20 Billion. MP3 Newswire. Retrieved September 29, 2006, from http://www.mp3newswire.net/stories/napster.html

Oksanen, V., and M. Valimaki. 2006. Theory of deterrence and individual behaviour: Can lawsuits control file sharing on the Internet? *Review of Law and Economics*. Retrieved December 21, 2006, from http://www.valimaki.com/org/oksanen_valimaki_rle.pdf

Patrizio, A. November 2, 1999. Why the DVD hack was such a cinch. Wired News. Retrieved December 14, 2006, from http://www.wired.com/news/technology/0,1282,32263,00.html

Perens, B. 1999. "The open source definition." In *Open Sources: Voices from the Open Source Revolution: O'Reilly,* edited by C. DiBona, S. Ockman, and M. Stone. Retrieved November 4, 2006, from http://www.oreilly.com/catalog/opensources/book/toc.html

Pontell, H. N. 1984. *A Capacity to Punish*. Bloomington: Indiana University Press.

Rainie, L., M. Madden, D. Hess, and G. Mudd. 2004. The state of music downloading and file-sharing online. Pew Internet Project and Comscore Media Metrix Data Memo. http://www.pewinternet.org/PPF/r/124/report_display.asp

Reuter, P. 1983. *Disorganized Crime: The Economics of the Visible Hand*. Cambridge: MIT Press.

Roberts, P. January 21, 2004. RIAA sues 532 "John Does": Alleged file swappers identified only by the IP address of their computer. PC World. Retrieved December 1, 2006, from http://www.pcworld.com/article/id,114387-page,1/article.html

Rossi, P. H., E. Waite, C. E. Bose, and R. Berk. 1974. The seriousness of crimes: Normative structure and individual differences. *American Sociological Review* 39 (2): 224–37.

Schechter, S. E., R. A. Greenstadt, and M. D. Smith. 2003. Trusted computing, peer-to-peer distribution, and the economics of pirated entertainment. The Second Workshop on Economics and Information Security. Retrieved December 1, 2006, from http://www.eecs.harvard.edu/~stuart/papers/eis03.pdf

Schneier, B. November 17, 2005. Real story of the rootkit. Wired News. Retrieved December 27, 2006, from http://www.wired.com/news/privacy/0,1848,69601,00.html

Sherman, C. September 11, 2002. Sherman on dispute with Verizon. Recording Industry Association of America Press Room. Retrieved December 20, 2006, from http://www.riaa.com/news/newsletter/091102_2.asp

Skolnick, J. H., and J. J. Fyfe. 1993. *Above the Law: Police and the Excessive Use of Force.* New York: The Free Press.

Siwek, S. E. September 2006. The true cost of motion picture piracy to the U.S. economy. Institute for Policy Innovation Policy Report 186. Retrieved June 13, 2006, from http://www.ipi.org/ipi%5CIPIPublications.nsf/PublicationLookupExecutiveSummary/A6EB1EAC4310AF6F862571F7007CB6AF

Stier, E., and P. Richards. 1987. Strategic decision making in organized crime control: The need for a broadened perspective. In *Major Issue in Organized Crime Control,* edited by H. Edelhertz. Washington, DC: National Institute of Justice.

Sykes, G., and D. Matza. 1957. Techniques of neutralization: A theory of delinquency. *American Sociological Review* 22 (6): 664–70.

Tanenbaum, A. S. 2003. *Computer Networks.* 4th ed. New Jersey: Prentice Hall.

Chapter 19

The Warez Scene: Digital Piracy in the Online World

Lucille M. Ponte
Florida Coastal School of Law (ABA-approved), Jacksonville, FL

Lucille M. Ponte, J.D., B.A., Certificate in Mediation, is an associate professor of law at the Florida Coastal School of Law, Jacksonville, Florida, where she teaches cyber law and contracts. She has written two books, several manuals, and numerous national and regional law review articles on cyber law, workplace privacy, and alternative/online dispute resolution (ADR/ODR). She has also taught undergraduate and graduate cyber law courses and writes extensively on cyber law topics. She serves on the advisory boards of both the Centre for Electronic Dispute Resolution, at the Computer Law Institute of Vrije University in Amsterdam, The Netherlands, and the Bentley College Global Cyberlaw Center in Waltham, Massachusetts. A licensed attorney since 1983, Dr. Ponte was previously inhouse counsel for technology firms as well as government agencies in Massachusetts and Washington, DC.

Abstract

Highly organized domestic and international "Warez release groups" compete to illegally amass huge stores of digital media, including movies, music, games, and software programs. The secretive world of the "Warez scene" presents complicated legal, ethical, cultural, and sociological issues. This chapter examines the development of the Warez community and the evolution of criminal copyright infringement laws targeting Warez traders. In addition, this chapter considers persistent challenges facing law enforcement and policymakers seeking to prevent and prosecute online intellectual property theft. This chapter concludes with several practical proposals aimed at decreasing illegal Warez trading and promoting a global environment that better respects creativity and innovation.

INTRODUCTION

Drink Or Die, Pirates with Attitude, Rogue Warriorz, and Razor 1911. These names may be unfamiliar to the general public, but they are well known to law enforcement in the United States and overseas as well as to digital media producers. These designations identify some of the top online piracy groups recently prosecuted for criminal copyright infringement of tens

The author wishes to acknowledge and thank Joseph Ferrandino, Master's in Criminal Justice and Ph.D. candidate in Public Affairs, for his research assistance on this article.

of thousands of software programs, songs, video games, and movies. These loosely affiliated, but highly organized, domestic and international groups compete to illegally amass huge stores of digital media in the secretive online world known as the *Warez scene* (Department of Justice n.d.). **Warez** release groups actively operating online are considered to be responsible for the vast majority of illegal digital media available on the Internet (Department of Justice n.d.), resulting in billions of dollars in lost revenues to the entertainment industry every year (Motion Picture Association of America 2005, 2006). Digital media producers fear that the rapid pace of technological advances and the greater technical skills of Warez community members will lead to continuing increases in intellectual property theft worldwide (Hinduja 2001; Yang and Hoffstadt 2006). This chapter examines the development of the Warez community and the evolution of criminal copyright infringement laws to target Warez traders. In addition, this chapter considers the persistent challenges facing law enforcement and **policymakers** to prevent and prosecute online intellectual property theft in the Warez scene. This chapter concludes with several practical proposals aimed at better deterring online piracy in the Warez community.

THE DEVELOPMENT OF THE "WAREZ SCENE"

The early 1990s witnessed explosive growth in the information technology industry. Millions obtained faster Internet access on the job, at school, and at home, while increased capacity for data storage made it quick and easy to upload and download a wide range of information and materials from the Web. Newly developed CD burners became inexpensive commodities allowing individuals to rapidly and easily burn CDs of downloaded materials for further use or even resale. These technological innovations improved overall communications and productivity, and also led to the proliferation of illegal activities on the Internet, including illegal infringement or theft of copyrighted materials (Granade n.d.; Hinduja 2001). Popular games, music, movies and software programs were soon being illegally traded on the Internet. The term Warez (pronounced "wares") is a play on the word software, with the addition of the "z" indicating that the software program has been illegally copied (Granade n.d.). Therefore, *gamez* refers to video games illegally copied, or *moviez* meant films illegally copied, and so forth (Granade n.d.).

Clandestine groups of individuals, later referred to as *Warez release groups*, began to race to illegally collect and/or exchange these valuable business assets, sometimes days or weeks before the digital media producers ever publicly released or distributed these products (Hinduja 2001; Department of Justice n.d.; States News Service 2006a). Some Warez groups may specialize in particular types of Warez, while others may aim merely to collect as much illegal digital media as possible. Members of Warez traders may actively use and barter their Warez with other groups while some Warez groups only collect Warez to impress others with the level of their technical abilities and the breadth of their collections (Goldman 2003; Granade n.d.). Certain Warez groups consider themselves to be archivists of older or out-of-date video games, called *abandonware* or *abandonwarez* (Costikyan 2000; Goldman 2003; Granade n.d.). These abandonwarez groups collect earlier versions of gamez that are no longer supported by their original vendors but are still protected under copyright laws (Costikyan 2000; Goldman 2003; Granade n.d.).

Over time, Warez release groups began to develop a typical kind of hierarchy and methodology that best facilitated their Warez access and trading activities. Normally, at the top of the Warez group are site operators, or *SiteOps*, who run and maintain the Warez site and directing the activities of the group (Nasheri 2004; Department of Justice n.d.; States News Service 2006a). The SiteOps also control access to the site by group members or other Warez traders through various security measures, such as encrypted e-mails, virtual hosts to disguise their IP addresses, invitation-only instant messaging channels, unusual screen names to mask individual identities, and password-protected sites (Nasheri 2004; Department of Justice n.d.; States News Service 2006a). In the initial stages, *scripters* aid in the programming necessary to build the Warez Web site, while *equipment suppliers* obtain the hardware necessary to support the site, such as hard drives or servers (Department of Justice n.d.; States News Service 2006a). *Brokers* try to recruit other individuals to participate in the Warez group's actions or contact other Warez traders for exchanging or bartering pirated goods (Department of Justice n.d.; States News Service 2006a).

Usually, a Warez group receives an illegal copy of a desired game or other media products from *suppliers*, individuals with prerelease and/or unauthorized access to the copyrighted goods (Department of Justice n.d.; *Computer & Internet Lawyer, The* 2002). At times, the suppliers may be employees within a media company, such as in *United States v. Sarna*, 2004, when six former Fox Cable Network employees were accused of using the company's computer network for their own Warez operation (*Entertainment Litigation Reporter, The* 2004b). Suppliers may also be company outsiders, such as film critics or game reviewers, who gain access to products before public release (States News Service 2006b; *Entertainment Litigation Reporter, The* 2004a; States News Service 2006a). In another criminal case, *United States v. Breen*, 2004, the suppliers posed as game reviewers for nonexistent game magazines to get their hands on prerelease versions of video games (*Entertainment Litigation Reporter, The* 2004a). In other instances, suppliers may be individuals who obtain early access to publicly distributed products materials, such as movie projectionists or *cammers*, individuals who illegally use digital camcorders to record films at the theater (Motion Picture Association of America 2005; States News Service 2006).

In turn, *couriers* gather the stolen materials from their suppliers and then upload them to one of the Warez group's drop sites (Department of Justice n.d.; States News Service 2006a). The most technologically advanced members of the Warez group are the *crackers* who retrieve the copyrighted materials and defeat any antitheft or copyright protection controls built into the pirated goods. Once these devices have been removed, the cracker will test the product to make certain it still functions properly. The cracker then breaks the successfully cracked item up into manageable file packets for further distribution and downloads it to the drop site (Department of Justice n.d.; States News Service 2006a; *Computer & Internet Lawyer, The* 2002).

Then prerelease couriers or *preers* make certain that the illegal goods are disseminated worldwide within minutes to secure file transfer protocol (FTP) sites that store the group's Warez. Secure FTP archive or storage sites may contain 10,000 and 25,000 copies of illegal Warez. These FTP sites permit certain group members and other associated Warez groups to upload and download the illegal Warez. An information file (.nfo file) is attached to the cracked Warez announcing which Warez group deserves credit for the new release (Department of Justice n.d.). Most drop sites and FTP archive sites are illicitly hosted, abusing the limited computer resources of large universities and major commercial businesses (*Computer & Internet Lawyer, The* 2002).

The Warez community thrives on the competition for collecting new goods that others do not possess or have not yet cracked, battling for *0-Day* Warez releases that occur before or within 24 hours of the release of a new game, movie, software program or music CD (Goldman 2003; Department of Justice n.d.). In one instance, DrinkorDie, an elite Warez group that originated in Russia, released copies of Microsoft 95 two weeks before its official company launch (Nasheri 2004).

Individuals in Warez groups often crave the attention and ego boost they get from beating out other Warez groups by cracking and releasing hot items first and then proclaiming their technical superiority to others in the Warez community. In addition, each Warez group attempts to build their goods collection and their overall reputation in the Warez scene, thereby increasing their group's free access to pirated goods from other leading release groups (Goldman 2003; Department of Justice n.d.). Some people join Warez groups for the excitement of being involved in an underground community locked in a cat-and-mouse game with law enforcement and industry giants (Goldman 2003). One Warez site operator admitted that "deep down everyone is a little scared [of criminal prosecution] but that is also what keeps us going" (Goldman 2003, 407). The Warez scene also fosters a sense of community and camaraderie amongst individuals who may feel estranged from society in the off-line world (Goldman 2003).

Unlike other criminal gangs, most Warez groups neither pursue commercial gain nor undertake entrepreneurial distribution of their Warez (National Institute of Justice [NIJ] 2004). Many in the Warez community disdain any sale of their cracked items, preferring to view their group's activities as akin to an online "Robin Hood," offering goods to a deserving public oppressed by the media and entertainment industries' unfair pricing and licensing practices (Goldman 2003). Similarly, some Warez groups see themselves as cyber anarchists, believing that all forms of creative media should be given away to the public for free (Goldman 2003). Since most Warez groups did not pursue economic gain, but personal aggrandizement, Warez release groups were originally outside of the purview of prosecution under earlier criminal copyright infringement laws.

Recognizing that Warez groups can account for up to 90 percent of all pirated materials on the Internet (*Computer & Internet Lawyer, The* 2002), the information technology and entertainment industries have long demanded greater legal protection from **digital piracy**. In 2005, the Institute for Policy Innovation, a nonprofit research organization, indicated that the movie industry alone lost about $2.3 billion due to Internet piracy, with about $447 million from domestic online piracy and more than $1.8 billion from international online piracy (Motion Picture Association of America 2005). In addition, online movie piracy resulted in approximately 141,030 lost jobs and $837 million in lost tax revenues (Motion Picture Association of America 2006).

The software industry estimates its losses to all forms of piracy, including Internet piracy, at about $12 billion annually, with about half of all piracy losses coming from Asia, particularly China, Indonesia, and Vietnam (NIJ 2004; Software & Information Industry Association [SIIA] n.d.). The greatest dollar losses due to software piracy are about $2.4 billion in China and about $2.2 billion from the United States (NIJ 2004). Although the United States has a relatively low piracy rate of about 25 percent, the software industry's high revenue losses are due to its high percentage of computers and computer users in the United States (SIIA n.d.). The Recording Industry Association of America [RIAA] also indicates that its industry loses about $4.2 billion every year to piracy worldwide, including online piracy (RIAA 2003a).

It is important to recognize that pirated items posted by even the most well-meaning Warez groups often trickle outside of the confines of the scene on to the broader Internet. In some cases, the cracked items end up on peer-to-peer (P2P) file-sharing sites with millions of copies being downloaded illegally. In addition, some Internet sites lure visitors with offers of free access to goods, then victimizing them through identity theft, fraudulent schemes, or computer viruses (Sag 2006). In other instances, cracked items find their way to offline organized crime gangs or terrorist groups. These criminal groups often have established and operate bricks-and-mortar optical disc factories that allow them to generate hundreds of thousands of counterfeit discs for sale in the real world (Nasheri 2004; Department of Justice n.d.). The sale and distribution of counterfeit hard goods help to fund their criminal activities and their cheaper prices seriously damage the market for legitimate products (Nasheri 2004; Department of Justice n.d.).

Subsequently, industry pressure compounded by concerns about online consumer protection and the need to prevent pirated goods from being used to support organized crime and terrorism, led Congress to reevaluate existing copyright laws. Since the 1990s, Congress has consistently acted to revise criminal copyright infringement laws and to increase the associated penalties in an effort to specifically target Warez release groups (Yang and Hoffstadt 2006).

THE EVOLUTION OF CRIMINAL COPYRIGHT INFRINGEMENT LAWS

The Constitution directs Congress "[t]o promote the Progress of Science and useful Arts, by securing for limited Times to Authors and Inventors the exclusive Right to their respective Writings and Discoveries" (U.S. Const., art. I, §8). Copyright law protects original, creative works in a fixed form, such as software programs, movies, songs, and video games (17 U.S.C. §102 (2005)). Congress determined that in order to promote creativity the copyright laws must reward creative people and entities with ownership and control over their creative works for certain time periods (cf. Ferrera et al. 2004). In general, creators possess the exclusive right to reproduce or copy the copyrighted work, to prepare derivative works, to distribute copyrighted works, to sell, license, or transfer ownership to others, and to perform and/or publicly display their creative works (17 USCS § 106 (1-5) (2004); cf. Ferrera et al. 2004; Latham 2003; Szymanski 1996). Since 1998, the protected term for copyright for individuals is the life of the author or creator plus 70 years or copyright owners for works created after January 1, 1978 (17 U.S.C. §302 (1998); cf. Ferrera et al. 2004). For copyrights owned by corporations or e-businesses, the copyright term is 95 years from the date of first publication or 120 years from the date of creation, whichever is shorter (17 U.S.C. §302 (1998); cf. Ferrera et al. 2004). During the life of the copyright, the creators would be allowed to maximize potential revenues through such avenues as licensing fees or royalty payments (Blessing 2004; Kartha 1996–1997; Kravis 1993).

Opportunities for creative control and economic gain are considered the prime incentives for creative activities that promote the public good under copyright law (NIJ 2004; Piquero and Piquero 2006). The revenues generated by creative works are considered central to funding future creative endeavors that provide more products and services for consumers (NIJ 2004; RIAA 2003a). Economists and other experts opine that creativity and innovation will decline if creative people and entities are not rewarded economically for their efforts (NIJ 2004; Morea 2006). Third parties who violate the copyright holder's exclusive rights without their consent are "free riders" on the creative efforts of others and are therefore subject to the civil and/or criminal penalties for copyright infringement (Nasheri 2004).

Types of Copyright Infringement

Digital piracy is one type of copyright infringement which allows illegal file sharers to "free ride" off the creative efforts of others. This infringing behavior harms innovation and creativity (Hinduja 2001; Nasheri 2004; Morea 2004), often robbing artists and businesses of the funds needed to encourage the creation of new works, to develop and market the creative talent of the future, and to provide future consumers with a continuing range of musical options (Nasheri 2004; RIAA 2003a). For example, the RIAA contends that 85 percent of all released recordings do not bring in sufficient sales to cover their costs (RIAA 2003a). The industry asserts that it must rely on the 15 percent of profitable recordings to subsidize these losses and to be able to continue to develop new artists and more musical choices for consumers (RIAA 2003a). Similarly, the movie industry claims that illegal downloading harms its ability to produce new films, since only 1 in 10 films ever repays its initial investment (Taylor 2005).

Under the law, there are three basic forms of liability for copyright infringement; direct, contributory, and vicarious infringement (Ferrera et al. 2004). Generally speaking, the direct infringer is the primary party who has violated one or more of the copyright holder's exclusive rights (Ferrera et al. 2004), such as an individual who illegally downloads a song or a supplier in a Warez group who uploads an illegal copy of a video game to a drop site. Contributory infringement only exists if there is an underlying direct infringement, and the party knew or should have known of the infringing conduct and caused or contributed to the acts of the direct infringer (Ferrera et al. 2004). Members of Warez groups who do not undertake the direct infringement but recruit others to infringe copyrighted works for the group's collection or illegal P2P file-sharing services that provide access to unauthorized copies of copyrighted material are good examples of contributory infringers. Lastly, vicarious infringement occurs when an individual or business receives a direct financial benefit from another's infringing acts and has the right and ability to supervise the party's infringing conduct (Ferrera et al. 2004). Bulletin board services or online auction sites that post pirated goods and receive a direct economic gain through ad revenues, subscriptions, or commissions may be held responsible for vicarious infringement. Warez groups might be considered vicarious infringers because they direct the infringing activities of their members and may receive the economic benefit of enjoying free games, movies, music and software programs or bartering their goods with other Warez groups.

Main Exemptions to Copyright

The law balances the creative control of copyright holders with promoting the public good in having access to creative materials (Blessing 2004; Ferrera et al. 2004; Kartha 1996–1997; Kravis 1993). To achieve this goal, the copyright laws contain certain limitations on the rights of the copyright owner, including the fair use and first sale doctrines as well as public domain. Under the fair use doctrine, parties can use copyrighted materials without the consent of the copyright holder depending upon the purpose and character of the use, the character of the copyrighted material, the amount or substantiality of the material used in relation to the work as a whole, and the impact of the use on the potential market for the copyrighted materials (17 U.S.C. 107; cf. *Campbell v. Acuff-Rose Music, Inc.*, 510 U.S. 569 (1994); Erekosima and Koosed 2004; Ferrera et al. 2004). The court will balance these elements to determine if the use is a fair or legitimate one under copyright law. Generally speaking, an instructor providing a couple of pages from a 300-page informational text as part of a classroom handout may be protected under fair use (Ferrera et al. 2004) since the purpose is educational, the work at issue is primarily informational, the amount copied is small in comparison to the work as a whole, and the conduct is unlikely to have a serious impact on the marketability of the item. Warez groups would not be expected to succeed in claiming fair use since they are not copying for nonprofit or educational purposes, they copy all or most of a creative, rather than an informational work, and their efforts are viewed as having a substantially negative impact on the market for these goods.

However, abandonwarez sites may have a potential claim under fair use. Although these groups copy the entire work, they do so primarily for educational purposes, desiring to maintain the cultural and technological history of gaming by preserving vintage video games no longer supported by their original producers (Gentile 2006). Furthermore, abandonwarez sites do not impact the market for these video games since these items are no longer sold, distributed, or supported and may actually help to stimulate interest in forgotten games or promote a market for revised versions of these older games for a new audience. For example, abandonwarez sites helped to revitalize interest in the 1981 video game, Frogger, which subsequently led to the legal development and marketing of a highly successful 1999 version, one of the top ten of the best-selling video games that year (Gentile 2006). To date, it is uncertain how courts will apply fair use to civil and/or criminal infringement actions brought against abandonwarez groups.

The first sale doctrine concerns one's right to sell or dispose of a copy of a legally obtained item, such as a book, wherein the seller does not retain any rights to the sold or disposed item (17 U.S.C. §109 (2000); cf. Erekosima and Koosed 2004; Ferrera et al. 2004). Typically, under the first sale doctrine, university students may legally buy a text for a class and then resell it at the end of the semester, giving up all rights to the book (Ferrera et al. 2004). Since Warez groups do not legally purchase the items they trade in, they would not be protected under the first sale doctrine. Even if a group member had legally obtained a creative work, uploading the item for Internet access and copying would not come within the doctrine because the original purchaser does not give up rights to the item, but enjoys it along with many other users.

Lastly, the notion of public domain largely applies to works for which the copyright protection period has expired or works created by the U.S. government, such as court decisions or legislative materials (Ferrera et al. 2004). Warez groups try to crack and distribute copyrighted commercial works, often before or shortly after their public release, so this defense would also not likely apply to their activities.

Updating Criminal Copyright Infringement Laws

Initially, digital media producers tried to deter Warez activities through traditional civil lawsuits (cf. Groennings 2005; NIJ 2004). Under civil copyright actions, copyright holders may call for monetary damages for their actual losses, statutory damages ranging from $200 to $100,000 per work infringed, attorney's fees, and injunctive relief (Ferrera et al. 2004). Industry members, especially the Recording Industry Association of America (RIAA), brought hundreds of civil lawsuits against individuals who illegally downloaded or allowed others to download from their computers unauthorized copies of copyrighted materials (NIJ 2004). These lawsuits, coupled with the development of legal downloading sites, led to a steep decline in illegal file-sharing from 29 percent (approximately 35 million users) to 14 percent (about 18 million users) in 2003 (Rainie et al. 2004; cf. Groennings 2005).

The movie industry also claims that illegal downloading impacts its ability to develop new movies, since only one in ten films ever recovers its initial investment (Taylor 2005).

At the outset, this copyright litigation mainly succeeded in moving individuals, already prone to legal behavior, to use properly licensed media services (Clark 2006; Sag 2006; Sohn 2006), such as iTunes or the new Napster, with little effect on hard-core infringers, such as Warez groups. In the wake of these lawsuits, there was actually an increase in illegal downloaders, including Warez groups who sought out and began to utilize more unorthodox Internet channels to exchange Warez, pushing Warez activities even further underground (cf. Groennings 2005). Successful civil actions against sophisticated Warez groups had some limited success, but became problematic due to the difficulty in identifying the actual individuals involved in Warez groups (Goldman 2003; Yang and Hoffstadt 2006). Also the fact that many Warez defendants are judgment-proof meant that they were not deterred by the threat of damage awards (Goldman 2003; Yang and Hoffstadt 2006). Therefore, the information technology and entertainment industries began to lobby Congress for more severe criminal penalties for Warez activities (Morea 2006).

Prior to 1997, in order to prove criminal copyright infringement, the prosecution had to meet its burden of proof as to four basic elements (Copyright Act of 1976, 17 U.S.C. §506 (2000); cf. Erekosima and Koosed 2004). First, the prosecution must provide evidence to show that a third party had a valid copyright, such as a musician or video game creator (Copyright Act of 1976, 17 U.S.C. §506 (2000); cf. Erekosima and Koosed 2004). Individuals or companies can register a copyright and use that certificate of registration to provide prima facie evidence of ownership (Erekosima and Koosed 2004). Second, the prosecution must prove that the defendant infringed the valid copyright by violating one of the exclusive rights of the copyright owner (Copyright Act of 1976, 17 U.S.C. §506 (2000); Erekosima and Koosed 2004). Third, the prosecution must show that the defendant's conduct was willful in infringing another's copyright (Copyright Act of 1976, 17 U.S.C. §506 (2000); Erekosima and Koosed 2004). Although courts have taken different approaches to willfulness in the past, most courts interpret willfulness as the intention to violate copyright law with the jury typically making a factual determination as to intent (*United States v. Cheek*, 498 U.S. 192 (1991); cf. Clark 2006; Goldman 2003; Yang and Hoffstadt 2006). Lastly, the government has to prove that the defendant's infringement was for either commercial advantage or private financial gain (Copyright Act of 1976, 17 U.S.C. §506 (2000); cf. Erekosima and Koosed 2004).

Congress took its first step in enacting the Anticounterfeiting Consumer Protection Act of 1996, which permitted Racketeer Influenced and Corrupt Organizations Act (RICO) violations to extend to all intellectual property theft, including criminal copyright violations. Copyright counterfeiting became a predicate offense that may trigger a RICO prosecution and more severe criminal penalties for organized criminal activity (Erekosima and Koosed 2004). In light of the growing concerted actions of the Warez scene, digital media producers tried to prod law enforcement to track down and prosecute members of Warez release groups. Yet earlier copyright laws tied the hands of state and federal prosecutors since prosecutors could only bring criminal actions against those who sought commercial advantage or financial gain from their infringing activities. Therefore, the lack of a profit motive originally kept most Warez release groups outside of the scope of prior criminal copyright infringement laws.

Ultimately, the criminal case of *United States v. LaMacchia* 1994, pushed Congress to revise the provisions of and penalties for criminal copyright infringement. David LaMacchia, an MIT student, used pseudonyms and an encrypted address on his university's computer network to create password-protected bulletin boards that Web surfers to upload and download a broad array of then-popular software programs and video games, including Excel 5.0, WordPerfect 6.0, and Sim City 2000. In 1994, a grand jury returned a single indictment against the student under the federal wire fraud statute (*United States v. LaMacchia*, 871 F. Supp. 535 (D. Mass. 1994); cf. Clark 2006). The indictment indicated that LaMacchia violated the statute by illegal copying and distributing copyrighted software, thereby defrauding the effected manufacturers and vendors of more than $1 million in licensing fees and royalty payments. Although not part of a Warez release group, LaMacchia could be considered the first Warez SiteOp to be prosecuted for criminal copyright infringement (*United States v. LaMacchia*, 871 F. Supp. 535 (D. Mass. 1994)).

But like most Warez release groups today, LaMacchia did not charge for access to these pirated programs and games posted on his two Web sites, but made them available for free. Unable to show either commercial advantage or financial gain, the court dismissed the criminal indictment as an inappropriate use of the wire fraud statute. The court indicated that prosecutors could not try to turn conduct legal under the existing criminal copyright laws into illegal crimes through the wire fraud statute (*United States v. LaMacchia*, 871 F. Supp. 535 (D. Mass. 1994); cf. Clark 2006; Goldman 2003). The *LaMacchia* court concluded that the student's actions might be unethical or immoral, but that Congress would need to update existing copyright laws in order to make his actions criminal (*United States v. LaMacchia*, 871 F. Supp. 535 (D. Mass. 1994); cf. Goldman 2003).

In the aftermath of the *LaMacchia* decision, Congress responded by enacting several major laws to deal directly with digital piracy. The No Electronic Theft Act of 1997 (NET Act) sought to close the "LaMacchia Loophole" under then-existing copyright laws, specifically targeting Warez release groups (Clark 2006; Goldman 2003; Goldman and Gladstone 2003; Morea 2006). The NET Act expanded the definition of financial gain to include expectations of gain through the sharing or bartering of pirated goods (18 U.S.C. §2319 (1997); cf. Andrews 2005; Goldman 2003), a common practice among Warez groups. More importantly, the Act revised the criminal copyright laws allowing prosecution in instances where there was no profit or economic motive (18 U.S.C. §2319 (1997); cf. Clark 2006; Goldman 2003; Goldman and Gladstone 2003; Morea 2006).

Under the new law, Congress took a shoplifting approach to online piracy, finding that illegal file-sharing was akin to stealing items from a bricks-and-mortar store (Copyright piracy, and H.R. 2265; Goldman 2003). The shoplifter in a retail store is looking for a "five-finger discount," enjoying the item for themselves or sharing it with others with no intention to resell the goods for a profit (cf. Copyright piracy, and H.R. 2265). Similarly, illegal file-sharers take something for free that they would otherwise have to pay for in a store, enjoying it alone or sharing it with others for free, and should also be prosecuted for the theft, like a shoplifter (Copyright piracy, and H.R. 2265; cf. Goldman 2003). Typically, public service announcements on TV and at the start of many DVDs picked up this shoplifting theme in which online piracy is portrayed as no different than stealing an item from a bricks-and-mortar store.

Under the Net Act, any person who illegally shared online one or more copies of copyrighted material, with a retail value up to $1,000 in a 180-day period, could be charged with a federal misdemeanor (18 U.S.C. §2319 (b)(1)(1997); cf. Clark 2006; Goldman 2003; Goldman and Gladstone 2003; Morea 2006). The misdemeanor penalties included fines and possible prison time of up to one year (18 U.S.C. §2319 (b)(1)(1997); cf. Goldman 2003). Felony charges could be lodged for a first offense involving illegal file-sharing of 10 or more copies valued at $2,500 or more retail with fines and possible imprisonment up to three years. Subsequent offenses could ratchet up the fines and the prison time up to six years (18 U.S.C. §2319 (b)(1)(1997); cf. Goldman 2003).

In 1999, the Department of Justice brought its first action under the NET Act against Jeffrey Levy, a University of Oregon student, who established a bulletin board, similar to the one in the *LaMacchia* case (Goldman 2003; Goldman and Gladstone 2003; Morea 2006). His site allowed others to download thousands of copies of software programs, video games, music and movies (Goldman 2003; Goldman and Gladstone 2003; Morea 2006) with the actual retail value considered to be approximately $70,000. Levy pleaded guilty to illegally distributing software (reduced down to $5,000) and was sentenced to two years probation (Goldman 2003; Goldman and Gladstone 2003; Morea 2006). Prosecutions of other individuals followed, but over time law enforcement began more aggressive efforts to investigate and prosecute the growing Warez community with the enactment of two other major copyright laws.

Congress then passed the Digital Millennium Copyright Act (DMCA) in 1998, which among other things, made it a felony to try to circumvent or to manufacture, offer, or seek to provide devices that would circumvent copyright protection measures on copyrighted works (17 U.S.C. §1201; cf. Ferrera et al. 2004; Fitzdam 2005; Morea 2006; Erekosima and Koosed 2004). The DMCA indicated that violators could be fined up to $500,000 and/or imprisoned for up to 5 years for a first offense. Any subsequent offenses could result in fines up to $1 million and/or imprisonment for up to 10 years (17 U.S.C. §1204; cf. Morea 2006). Therefore, Warez groups which cracked antitheft devices on copyrighted items, such as using DeCSS software to break the copy protection code on DVDs (Nasheri 2004), would now be violating copyright under the terms of the DMCA. Warez groups that provide others with or traffic in online tools for circumventing copyright protection could also be criminally liable under the DMCA.

David Rocci, who established a Web site for Warez groups, www.ISONEWS.com, became the first person convicted under the DMCA. The site provided the latest news on piracy developments and the illegal Warez scene. It also sold mod chips that allowed Warez group members to by-pass copyright protections on game consoles, such as the Microsoft X-Box and Sony Playstation, and to engage in unlimited play of pirated video games. The site received more than 140,000 hits per day and had more than 10,000 registered members. The site operator was prosecuted for violating the DMCA, was sentenced to five months, and fined $28,500.00 (*Computer & Internet Lawyer, The* 2003; Nasheri 2004).

In addition, the DMCA recognized the difficulties that Internet service providers (ISPs) would face if they had to monitor and deal with potential copyright violations committed by their subscribers (Erekosima and Koosed 2004; Fitzdam 2005). The DMCA granted immunity to ISPs from direct infringement liability if an ISP adopted and implemented reasonable policies for terminating online services to repeated infringers and does not interfere with online technical measures taken by copyright owners to identify and protect copyrighted materials (17 U.S.C. §512 (i); cf. Ferrera et al. 2004; Fitzdam 2005). Most ISPs require subscribers to agree to terms of use that allow the ISP to terminate those who abuse their Internet access through repeated acts of copyright infringement (17 U.S.C. §512 (i); cf. Ferrera et al. 2004; Fitzdam 2005). Also ISPs normally do not hamper or impede automated Web crawler devices that help copyright owners to detect and pursue online piracy (RIAA 2003c).

One of the more controversial provisions of the DMCA allows digital media producers to use expedited information subpoenas that require ISPs hosting a site that allows access to pirated materials to disclose the identity and contact information of the site operator

(17 U.S.C. §512(h); cf. Morea 2006). These subpoenas do not require that the subscriber be informed in advance or given an opportunity to block the disclosure of this personal information (17 U.S.C. §512(h); cf. Electronic Frontier Foundation 2006). The RIAA has vigorously used information subpoenas to determine the identity of an infringing party and to take measures to halt the infringing activity (RIAA 2003c). In some cases, the RIAA will send an e-mail warning the individual to remove their site and stop their illegal conduct (RIAA 2003c). In other instances, the RIAA has brought civil lawsuits and so far has sued hundreds of individuals for civil copyright infringement, serving both a deterrent and educative impact on potential online infringers (RIAA 2003c; Sohn 2006).

In its efforts to root out digital piracy, the RIAA sought to extend the DMCA's provisions to include access to subscriber information in instances in which the individual was alleged to be using P2P software programs to share music files from their own computers, and not from sites hosted on the ISP's server. Some ISPs voluntarily turned over subscriber information for those involved with P2P file-sharing to the RIAA. However, Verizon challenged the legality of these subpoenas under the provisions of the DMCA as well as First Amendment free speech issues and existing privacy laws (*RIAA v. Verizon* 2003; cf. Morea 2006; Electronic Frontier Foundation n.d.). While the District Court sided with the RIAA, the appellate court overruled the lower court's decision (*RIAA v. Verizon* 2003; cf. Morea 2006; Electronic Frontier Foundation n.d.).

The D.C. Circuit court determined that the language and legislative history of the DMCA did not yet envision the practice of P2P file-sharing and, therefore, such expedited subpoenas did not apply to pirated materials residing on an individual's own computer. The RIAA appealed to the Supreme Court, which rejected its request for further review, leaving the appeals court decision in favor of Verizon in tact. However, the decision does not prevent copyright holders from using expedited subpoenas to learn the identities of individuals posting pirated materials on sites hosted on an ISP's server, such as illegal Warez trading sites (*RIAA v. Verizon* 2003; cf. Electronic Frontier Foundation n.d.; Morea 2006).

Subsequently in 2005, Congress sought to further deter Warez operations under certain provisions of the Family Entertainment and Copyright Act (FECA) (18 U.S.C. Appx. §2B5.3). Under FECA, the penalties under the Federal Sentencing Guidelines are increased two levels for those who post prerelease copies of copyrighted works online (18 U.S.C. Appx. §2B5.3(b)(2)) as well for individuals who store copyrighted work as an openly shared file (18 U.S.C. Appx. §2B5.3(b)(3)).

Major Law Enforcement Operations against Warez Groups

Starting in 2000, the FBI, in coordination with other government agencies, undertook a number of undercover investigations of domestic Warez groups (cf. Goldman 2003). In 2002, Operation Bandwidth, a two-year covert investigation, pursued Rogue Warriorz (RWZ), a well-known Warez group established in 1997 (Nasheri 2004; Department of Justice 2003c). A highly organized group, its potential members were required to submit applications and complete a successful probationary period before becoming full-fledged members of the group. The Warez group communicated with each other through a password-protected instant messaging channel and Web page, which also stored "achievement" statistics for those members who brought in the greatest number of pirated items (Department of Justice 2003c).

The FBI set up an undercover Warez site, Shatnet, loaded with thousands of copies of copyrighted goods. The site was used to lure in RWZ members who wished to barter or trade items with another Warez group. The FBI estimated that during a six-month period, the RWZ group uploaded more than $1 million in pirated software programs, video games, and movies to the Shatnet site. The investigation led to the indictments of 21 people associated with RWZ, ranging in age from 23 to 52 years old from 11 different states. One RWZ member from Saskatchewan faced prosecution in Canada. Each U.S. defendant faced a maximum of five years in prison and $250,000 in fines, while also agreeing in a plea bargain to pay restitution to the copyright holders, to hand over the copyrighted works, and to forfeit the computer equipment used by the group (Department of Justice 2003c).

Other early domestic operations, such as Operation Cybersweep (2003) (Department of Justice 2003b), Operation Safehaven (2003) (Department of Justice 2003a), which involved a Warez site using the computer resources of SUNY-Albany, Operation Jolly Roger (2005) (Department of Justice 2006), and Operation CopyCat (2005) (States News Service 2006a, b) took further aim at the domestic Warez community. Investigations into the domestic activities of Warez groups are ongoing.

Yet as the Warez scene became more global, both U.S. domestic and international law enforcement agencies recognized the need to coordinate their efforts in order to be successful against Warez traders (Department of Justice 2004). Simultaneous executions of search warrants or *takedowns* were essential to avoid the destruction of evidence or shifting of files to other drop sites. The first global investigation was Operation Buccanneer, conducted by U.S. Customs and the Department of Justice's Computer Crime and Intellectual Property Section, which targeted Warez members from such high-profile release groups as DrinkOrDie, Razor 1911, and Pirates with Attitude (PWA) (Nasheri 2004). After a 14-month investigation in concert with international authorities, 37 search warrants in 27 U.S. cities, and 19 search warrants in 5 foreign nations (Australia, England, Finland, Sweden, and Norway) were executed simultaneously. It was estimated that these Warez groups established 10 major drop sites in the United States and overseas abusing the computer resources of several major universities and corporations. Each Warez site stored between 5,000 and 10,000 pirated items, accounting for a total of approximately 10 terabytes of data (equivalent to approximately 7,000,000 floppy disks). The operation netted 40 convictions worldwide, including the leaders of DrinkOrDie, Razor 1911, and PWA, with sentences ranging from 24 to 30 months to 4 years in prison, fines in excess of $600,000, and the property seizure of 230 computers (Department of Justice 2002; Department of Justice n.d.; SIIA n.d.).

Law enforcement has continued to follow Operation Buccaneer's approach of simultaneous search warrants or takedowns in attacking global Warez operations. Subsequent international Warez investigations, such as Operation FastLink (2004) and Operation Site Down (2005), involved the coordinated effort of various U.S. federal and international law enforcement agencies from more than 12 nations with more than 55 convictions resulting from these two investigations as of 2006 (*U.S. Fed News* 2006; cf. *Computer & Internet Lawyer, The* 2005; Department of Justice 2004).

THE CHALLENGES OF THE WAREZ SCENE

Despite these impressive efforts, digital piracy persists and the Warez community continues to expand internationally (Goldman 2003). The increasing numbers of technically savvy individuals with high-level computer and programming skills coupled with their willingness to create user-friendly tools that aid the illegal behavior by less technologically astute people will result in a further increase in cyber crimes, including online intellectual property theft (Yang and Hoffstadt 2006). It is important to explore in greater depth the main challenges facing law enforcement and government policymakers in order to determine what proposals might best aid in the prevention or deterrence of online piracy in the Warez scene.

Low Priority of Criminal Copyright Infringement Cases

Since the start of major operations against Warez groups, there has been a chorus of voices questioning whether or not limited law enforcement resources should be utilized for such "victimless" crimes (Nasheri 2004). Despite the changes in the copyright laws, investigations of criminal copyright are clearly a lower priority for most law enforcement authorities than dealing with more serious public safety threats, such as terrorism or drug trafficking (Nasheri 2004; Yang and Hoffstadt 2006). Significant interagency coordination is required to undertake these actions as well as outreach to global law enforcement agencies which may result in squabbles over appropriate priorities for criminal investigations, proper procedures, jurisdictional concerns, direction and control of the Warez investigation, and ultimate credit for prosecuting global Warez trading operations (Nasheri 2004; Zacharia 2006). Agencies also struggle with finding and retaining adequately trained personnel (Nasheri 2004). Operations against Warez groups may receive plaudits from the effected industries, but generally little acknowledgement or support from the general public or elected officials for their efforts (Nasheri 2004).

Aside from the low priority given these matters in the law enforcement community, other policymakers have criticized the use of limited public safety resources to vindicate the economic rights of the lucrative information technology and entertainment industries (Nasheri 2004). Some experts indicate that civil lawsuits should be brought by these private businesses and underwritten by their own monies, rather than taxpayer funds (Clark 2006; Nasheri 2004). A return to the days before the NET Act would mean that the civil courts would once again become the venue for these kinds of intellectual property disputes, which had previously been largely effective against average downloaders, yet ineffectual against most members of secretive Warez release groups.

Furthermore, prosecutions of Warez groups have been spotty and the severity of penalties imposed has fluctuated, with courts rarely exacting the highest statutory penalties (Andrews 2005; Goldman 2003; Goldman and Gladstone 2003). In the anonymous world of the Internet, this lack of predictability may make many feel that the risks of detection are low, that prosecution is unlikely, and that any penalties will not be very stiff (Andrews 2005; Goldman 2003; Hinduja 2001). In this context, many Warez traders may perceive the benefits of free and easy access to games, movies, music, and applications as outweighing the chances of detection and serious prosecution (cf. Andrews 2005).

Questioning the Value of Tougher Criminal Penalties

While suing Warez groups proved an unsuccessful route for copyright holders, many believed that toughening penalties for criminal copyright infringement may not be a better alternative. Two years after the passage of the NET Act, a 1999 Business Software Alliance (BSA) study reported that Warez sites actually grew from about 100,000 to about 900,000 Web pages with software piracy revenue losses climbing from $11.3 billion to $12.2 billion worldwide (Goldman 2003; Goldman and Gladstone 2003). A 2001 Websense, Inc., report similarly found that Warez sites had increased after the NET Act, estimating the existence of about 5,400 Warez sites with in excess of 800,000 individual Web pages for Warez trading (Fisher 2001). Strengthening the penalties seems to have fueled greater interest in Warez, in part, because of unique sociological factors attributable to participants in the Warez scene (Goldman 2003; Goldman and Gladstone 2003).

As discussed earlier, many Warez participants consider themselves to be "cyber-Robin Hoods" (Goldman and Gladstone 2003, B9), fighting against powerful industries who have lobbied for unfair laws (Goldman 2003; Goldman and Gladstone 2003). Making penalties stiffer only reinforces this group's view of its own martyrdom and the need for members to continue to battle the unjust authority forces within government and industry that persecute Warez traders (Goldman 2003; Goldman and Gladstone 2003). In addition, some Warez members thrive on the thrill that goes with being in an underground community involved in illicit activities (Goldman 2003; Goldman and Gladstone 2003). Tougher sanctions against Warez groups only heighten the excitement for these individuals and may promote Warez activities (Goldman 2003; Goldman and Gladstone 2003). Their egos become inflated with the thought that federal and international law enforcement are chasing them which makes their ability to avoid detection and prosecution even more impressive (Goldman 2003). Furthermore, those who join the Warez scene for camaraderie they cannot find in the offline world may become even more closely bonded to others in that community (Goldman 2003). Although tougher criminal penalties may deter some individuals, the criminal sanctions fuel an "us versus them" perspective that may solidify these personal bonds and exacerbate the shared outlaw mentality (Goldman 2003).

In addition, others outside of the Warez scene have criticized the potential impact of these criminal laws on developing technologies (cf. Morea 2006). Individuals and companies involved in researching and developing new technologies are concerned that revisions to existing copyright laws have diluted the protections for fair use and dampened the willingness of entrepreneurial individuals and firms to finance and create new technological tools (Clark 2006; Fitzdam 2005). This concern is exemplified in the Supreme Court case of *MGM Studios, Inc. v. Grokster* 2005. In that case, the entertainment industry called upon the courts to expand civil contributory and vicarious liability to defendant companies who developed P2P software programs that could be used for both legal file-sharing and illegal downloading activities (*MGM v. Grokster* 2005). Although the Supreme Court found in favor of the entertainment industry, many legal experts decried the outcome as placing a "chilling effect" on valuable future technologies that would benefit society as a whole.

In his concurring opinion in *Grokster*, Justice Breyer gave voice to this concern. He contended that the majority's strict interpretation and application of copyright standards from earlier precedent might

[s]ignificantly weaken the law's ability to protect new technology. . . . To require defendants to provide, for example, detailed evidence, say business plans, profitability estimates, projected technological modifications, and so forth, would doubtless make life easier for copyrightholder plaintiffs. But it would simultaneously increase the legal uncertainty that surrounds the creation or development of a new technology capable of being put to infringing uses. Inventors and entrepreneurs (in the garage, the dorm room, the corporate lab, or the boardroom) would have to fear

(and in many cases endure) costly and extensive trials when they create, produce, or distribute the sort of information technology that can be used for copyright infringement. . . . The additional risk and uncertainty would mean a consequent additional chill of technological development. (*MGM v. Grokster* 2005, 2792–2793)

Clearly, if the threat of civil liability might harm technological exploration and development, then the threat of criminal penalties, such as fines and prison time, would potentially create a more serious obstacle to future technological growth. It is important to note that the creation and distribution of P2P software eventually resulted in the development of legitimate legal file-sharing services, such as iTunes and the new Napster. Had it not been for the originally illegal files-sharing sites that had initially developed P2P software programs, one may legitimately ask whether or not there would have been the evolution of legal sites that have benefited both industry and the consuming public.

Incompatibility between Revised Laws and Societal Values

In enacting changes to the copyright laws, Congress attempted to draw an analogy between shoplifting in the bricks-and-mortar world and illegal file-sharing in the online world. Unfortunately, many in the public do not agree with this analogy. Surveys consistently show that most Americans, especially teenagers, think illegal file-sharing is acceptable, and not stealing, so long as there is no profit motive involved (Clark 2006). Some 78 percent of people who download music do not think it is theft, while Internet users in general agree by a margin of 53 percent. Of teenagers, one of the largest groups involved in illegal downloading, two-thirds oppose any criminal fines for file-sharing and 8 out of 10 teens think file-sharing should be legal (Fitzdam 2005).

Furthermore, Americans have also become accustomed to information and entertainment on demand and tailored to their needs (Goldman and Gladstone 2003; Morea 2006; Sohn 2006). File-sharing allows individuals to select what they want, when they want it, leading many to become desensitized to these activities as intellectual property theft (Goldman and Gladstone 2003; Morea 2006; Sohn 2006). A 2002 Business Software Alliance survey found that 80 percent of Internet users admitted to having downloaded commercial software illegally and for free, while about 25 percent of all Web surfers claim to never pay for software (Goldman 2003; Goldman and Gladstone 2003).

A subsequent 2003 survey by the Pew Internet Project backs up the notion of increased disrespect for copyright laws and the rights of copyright holders (Madden and Lenhart 2003). In that survey, about two-thirds of those who share files online indicated that "they don't care whether the files are copyrighted or not" (Madden and Lenhart 2003, 1). This lack of concern was particularly strong amongst young Americans, aged 18 to 29, with 72 percent claiming not to care if the files they downloaded were copyrighted (Madden and Lenhart 2003). Four out of five full-time students expressed no concern about the copyright status of the files they downloaded (Madden and Lenhart 2003). Furthermore, adults aged 30 to 49 were in general agreement with these two groups, since 61 percent of these adults also had a lack of concern about downloading copyrighted work (Madden and Lenhart 2003). Coupled with the anonymity of the Internet and the low risks of prosecution, many individuals regularly download copyrighted materials with little knowledge or concern about legal mandates. Many people now scoff at copyright laws, in part, due to the prevalence of P2P networks and illegal file-sharing, by the public, in general, and Warez traders, in particular.

Some people may rationalize their illegal file-sharing by claiming that these downloads help them to sample music before buying it or arguing that prices for digital media are too high and do not adequately reward artists (Madden and Lenhart 2003). Other individuals may believe that lucrative digital media industries will not miss the few dollars they might spend on copyrighted materials (Madden and Lenhart 2003; RIAA 2003a). Others assert that they must download abandonware since these items are not readily available in offline markets (Madden and Lenhart 2003). None of these reasons takes into account the big picture; the cumulative effect of millions of illegal downloads on jobs, tax revenues, artist royalties or industry profits.

Clearly, there is a disconnect between legal policies on file-sharing and public perception's of right and wrong as regards this activity in the United States. Professor Steven Penney stated that most Americans believe that "criminal law should not be used for things most people reckon are not really wrong, or if wrong, merely trivial" (Morea 2006, 228) and view copyright infringement as too minor for criminal penalties (Morea 2006). Further, Professor Joel Feinberg opined that criminal sanctions are not justified for copyright infringement due to the lack of potential and substantial harm to others (Morea 2006). He asserts that copyright violations should only be criminalized if there are no other alternatives to preventing such activities (Morea 2006). Legal experts suggest that this discrepancy between public policy and public morality may make it difficult to successfully prosecute Warez traders before juries who may hand down verdicts nullifying the revised criminal copyright laws as inconsistent with public values (Yang and Hoffstadt 2006).

Similarly, in a global context, not all cultures take the same approach to the legality and/or morality of intellectual property laws and associated online downloading practices (NIJ 2004; Piquero and Piquero 2006). In Canada, individuals are allowed to download copyrighted materials from file-sharing sites provided that these items are limited to personal or private use (NIJ 2004). Taxes are imposed upon recording products, such as rewritable CDs, and these taxes fund artist royalties (NIJ 2004). Through this approach, Canadian officials attempt to compensate artists while freeing up limited law enforcement resources for more serious intellectual property violations (NIJ 2004).

Differences can also arise from long-held cultural and social mores that may be very difficult to change with the legalistic stroke of a government pen (NIJ 2004; Piquero and Piquero 2006). For example, a survey in Singapore found that students were more knowledgeable about copyright laws than North Americans, but were more likely to view the morality of downloading through the lens of the overall benefits to family, friends, and themselves, rather than strict legal mandates regarding such copying (Piquero and Piquero 2006). Furthermore, the enforcement of intellectual property laws may be seen by some as just another opportunity for rich, powerful countries to coerce poorer, less industrialized nations into protecting the assets of wealthy elites (Piquero and Piquero 2006).

PROPOSALS FOR DETERRING ONLINE PIRACY IN THE WAREZ COMMUNITY

Taking these various issues into consideration, legal commentators have hotly debated what should be done to deal with the Warez scene. There has been a consistent tug-of-war between those experts calling for steady increases in criminal penalties while others propose the abandonment of criminal penalties in favor of civil lawsuits, seeking court injunctive relief and monetary damages (cf. Goldman 2003; Groennings 2005; Morea 2006). As each side pulls for its perspective, neither approach has proved sufficient on its own to address illegal download-ing, particularly amongst active participants in the Warez scene. Other additional creative pro-posals could be considered in order to help more effectively address copyright infringement concerns relative to Warez release groups.

Promote Industry Proactive Measures to Reduce Warez Trading

One of the best ways to reduce Warez trading is for effected industries to shoulder greater responsibility in helping to prevent Warez activities. Industry can take proactive steps to reduce Warez activities including, the development of technological measures that reduce Warez cracking efforts, employee education efforts and confidentiality agreements aimed at potential Warez suppliers, improvements to network security to block the creation of Warez storage sites, and the purchase of "hacker insurance" to help spread potential industry losses. By undertaking a multi-pronged approach, industry can help itself avoid the expenses of civil lawsuits and the revenue and productivity losses associated with Warez groups' activities while preserving limited law enforcement resources.

First of all, digital media producers need to continue to develop new technologies to stop illegal copying and to facilitate the authentication of legitimate products (Morea 2006; Nasheri 2004). Many firms recognize existing defects in their products and the limitations of their antitheft measures, but ship the products nonetheless in order to generate revenues. Rather than expecting public resources to be used to protect their business assets after-the-fact, impacted industries could strive for fewer defects in their products as well as employ new technologies, such as advanced encryption, security holograms or biometric codes (Nasheri 2004), or digital watermarking (*MGM v. Grokster* 2005); all options aimed at deterring the ability to crack items, and hack systems for FTP while making it easier to detect infringers The burden of avoiding product defects that create opportunities for infringement and keeping pace with future product protection tools should fall primarily on the industries that would benefit the most from halting illegal file-sharing (*MGM v. Grokster* 2005; Nasheri; 2004; Yang and Hoffstadt 2006).

Alternatively, the industry needs to find better ways to allow consumers to make use of items they have legally downloaded (Clark 2006; Fitzdam 2005). Many consumers are upset that once they have legally downloaded an item, they are prevented from making back-up copies of a DVD or CD or transferring legally obtained songs or games to multiple platforms, within the consumer's own household (Clark 2006; Fitzdam 2005). The DMCA needs to be revised to insure that those who legally download materials are not penalized for using legiti-mate sites and are not required to buy multiple copies of the same item in order to make full use of these materials (Clark 2006; Fitzdam 2005).

In addition, insiders in the information technology and entertainment companies play key roles in leaking valuable company assets to Warez groups. Digital media producers should take a proactive role in training employees about the value of copyright ownership to company revenues and employee job security as well as their employees' legal duty to keep confidential company information private. Companies also need to better supervise employee compliance with their legal and fiduciary obligations relative to their employer's copyrighted products. Companies should also properly screen requests for review copies of forthcoming products to insure that the requestors are actually bona fide product reviewers.

Furthermore, employees and other insiders, such as game reviewers, should be required to sign confidentiality agreements prohibiting them from disclosing or distributing copyrighted materials. Any breach of these confidentiality agreements would result in civil damages and injunctive relief. Any current employee who passes along copyrighted materials, would also be subject to appropriate discipline or discharge for violating their fiduciary duty of confidentiality and their legal obligations under the confidentiality agreement.

It is also important to note that many Warez groups have exploited the resources of legitimate business and major universities to house their FTP sites. These institutions need to better protect and monitor their own networks to avoid this abuse. Those companies that fail to adopt reasonable network security measures could be held civilly liable for failing to keep Warez groups from misusing their resources. Legal theorists already have acknowledged that tort theories may be applied to these situations, including the breach of the duty of reasonable care for a company's failure to develop and maintain a secure computer network. The potential for such liability might increase vigilance by firms most likely to be targeted by Warez groups to house their illegal copies. Educational and business entities could try to spread their losses among insurance companies by obtaining "hacker insurance." About 25 percent of U.S. businesses have hacker insurance while other companies are self-insured, choosing to take steps on their own to prevent illegal and damaging network intrusions (Yang and Hoffstadt 2006).

Educating the Public about Value of Copyright Protections

The government and business have developed and implemented a number of educational campaigns aimed at children, teens and adults (cf. RIAA 2003b). Despite these educational programs, many in the public do not seem to know about the changes to previous copyright laws and lack an understanding of and appreciation for the importance of copyright protection to national and international commerce (cf. Morea 2006; Nasheri 2004). The commercial sector, with its vast marketing resources, may wish to study ways in which it can best get its message across to a broad spectrum of the public, especially young people (cf. Andrews 2005). These education efforts can also be tailored to reach people in other nations for whom preexisting cultural values may impact their views on file-sharing. Serious and concerted efforts need to continue and be broadened to better educate the public about how copyright laws help to promote individual and corporate creativity, to provide valuable information and products for the public, and to protect company revenues and the associated jobs of individual employees. This educational process could also stress the ease and convenience of legitimate file-sharing sites.

In this campaign, universities and colleges have a special obligation to educate their students about their legal and ethical obligations as to legal file-sharing (Groennings 2005; Hinduja 2001; Morea 2006). College students are more likely than nonstudents to participate in illegal downloading and are often key members of Warez groups (Hinduja 2001; Morea 2006). In part, university computing resources, especially high-speed Internet access, provide cheap and easy downloading opportunities for students (Hinduja 2001; Morea 2006). As indicated earlier, university networks also have become prime targets for Warez storage sites.

To help students to form legal and ethical online conduct, these institutions could better educate students about the value of copyright laws, the social and economic harms of illegal downloading, and the potential penalties under copyright laws as well as under school policies (Groennings 2005; Morea 2006). Educational institutions should establish clear computer resource and Internet usage policies (Hinduja 2001; Morea 2006), including blocking known illegal file-sharing sites and potential suspending the Internet privileges of repeat student infringers (Hinduja 2001). Schools might utilize orientation sessions, e-mail updates, announcements from key college officials, guest speaker events, and articles in the school newspaper to reinforce the importance of legal downloading conduct (Hinduja 2001; Morea 2006).

Broaden Copyright Dialogue between Appropriate Stakeholders

In the battle over illegal downloading, effective lobbying by industry groups has often overshadowed or blocked out any dissenting voices in the debate over intellectual property laws. A wider range of domestic and international stakeholders need to be engaged in a dialogue that will help to communicate the diverse concerns and values that permeate this field, including the general public and Warez release groups. In the past, federal law enforcement created an online bulletin board that allowed open discussion and debate about online copyright issues (NIJ 2004). The forum opened a channel for online visitors to make comments, raise objections, and learn about copyright law and other forms of intellectual property protection (NIJ 2004). Aside from educating the online public, law enforcement agencies had a unique chance to hear blunt criticism from and learn more about the values underlying the Warez community (NIJ 2004). Through a better understanding of the Warez community, government policymakers and law enforcement may recognize the sociological factors that impact their decision making, and consider these factors in trying to constructively address copyright concerns in the ware scene.

Similarly, an international forum could also provide a global conduit for dialogue aimed at building a broader international consensus about online file-sharing activities. These improved communication channels could aid international law enforcement agencies in sharing information, discussing investigatory procedures, and breaking down cultural barriers to the enforcement of intellectual property rights (NIJ 2004). Opening the dialogue to more diverse global stakeholders may aid in formulating future public policy in the intellectual property arena and promoting more precise targeting of those Warez groups who advance organized crime and terrorist activities that truly endanger public safety (NIJ 2004).

Continued Promotion of Quick and Legal Access to Copyrighted Products

Initially, much of the success of illegal file-sharing sites was derived from the demand for more individual choice and faster, cheaper access to copyrighted materials. Cash-strapped students sought to pick and choose individual songs, rather than pay the price for an entire CD for which they desired only one or two songs. Lawsuits and criminal prosecutions may have helped to decrease some illegal downloading. But the development of legal file-sharing sites ultimately has better served consumer demands, while providing lucrative opportunities for showcasing new artists and promoting new digital media from industry (cf. Groennings 2005; Morea 2006).

In February 2006, iTunes announced that its media services Web site had surpassed one billion legally downloaded songs (Apple Computer, Inc. 2006). Apple's CEO, Steven Jobs, stated that, "[o]ver one billion songs have now been legally purchased and downloaded around the globe, representing a major force against music piracy and the future of music distribution as we move from CDs to the Internet" (Apple Computer, Inc 2006). The iTunes site not only offers legal downloads of music, but also access to more than 60 hit TV programs, more than 3,500 music videos, 35,000 audio podcasts, 16,000 audio books, and 2 million songs (Apple Computer, Inc. 2006). Most experts agree that the continuing availability of cheap and fast access to digital products will help deter illegal file-sharing (Groennings 2005; Morea 2006; Rainie et al. 2004).

However, since Warez traders thrive on 0-Day releases, the sooner products are made legally available the less exciting or awe-inspiring it may become to have a certain movie or video game before others can obtain it. In 2006, award-winning director Steven Soderbergh of *Traffic* and *Ocean's Eleven* fame, teamed up with Magnolia Pictures, Landmark Theaters, and HDNet Movies, a cable TV channel, to propose making six films that would be released on DVD and cable television on the same day as the theatrical release of a film. Referred to as the *day and date* release strategy, this approach may further help to thwart the driving competition amongst Warez groups for obtaining items since the general public will similarly be able to view or download copyrighted items immediately. Already, the FX channel allows viewers to watch programs prior to their initial broadcast date and other stations make some TV shows available online the day after they are broadcast (Gentile 2006). As consumer demand for copyrighted materials continues to evolve with increasing expectations of day and date releases and on demand viewing, Warez traders may find that these legitimate options will help reduce the illicit thrill of collecting or trading Warez since everyone else will already have legal access to these desired materials.

Preservation Efforts for Vintage Games or "Abandonwarez"

Within the Warez community, about 100 online sites allow others to download older video games no longer technically supported nor distributed by their original producers. Abandonwarez collectors view themselves as archivists trying to preserve vintage games, such as Atari 2600's Missile Command and Space Invaders. Since these games are no longer available in retail stores or through online sites, abandonwarez sites fill a variety of needs inside and outside of the gaming world (Costikyan 2000).

Older gamers may enjoy the nostalgia and fun of playing the video games of their youth while younger players enjoy experiencing these old-time games for the first time. Media scholars also consider older video games as aiding our understanding of important aspects of cultural history and theory. In addition, many game designers view the preservation of older video games as essential for a better understanding of the art and key design techniques needed for the creation of future games (Costikyan 2000). Richard Carlson, a Rogue Entertainment game developer, indicated that vintage games are "about the history of art, storytelling, music, animation, programming, level design and all of the other disciplines involved in making classic game entertainment" (Costikyan 2000, 11).

While copyright holders are striving to shut down abandonwarez sites, other alternatives may be available to help curb the growth of abandonwarez sites. First, many more video game producers could consider re-releasing and supporting classic games to meet the playing interests of both older and younger gamers and the scholarly and development needs of cultural theorists and game designers. Second, game publishers could consider the creation of a virtual or online museum to preserve the art, history and design of these games. Brick-and-mortar museums have exhibited displays of vintage arcade games and an online nonprofit counterpart for video games could preserve older versions and provide access to these classic games for gamers, scholars, and designers. By creating these legitimate sites, there would be little need for separate abandonwarez sites. In turn, video game publishers may be able to assess public interest in classic favorites that may be suitable for re-release or updated for distribution to today's audiences (Costikyan 2000).

CONCLUSION

The Warez scene presents complicated legal, ethical, cultural, and sociological issues. More research on and dialogue with members of the Warez community is necessary to help formulate appropriate policies. At present, it is clear that civil liability and criminal prosecution alone will not fully deter Warez scene activities. A multipronged approach may help lessen the threat of illegal Warez trading through greater industry responsibility for product quality, technological protections, and network security, broader and more effective education campaigns to raise employee and public awareness and understanding about the value of copyright laws, improved channels of domestic and international communication to gain a consensus on file-sharing issues, and greater efforts to preserve vintage games. Collaboration between industry, educational institutions, government agencies, law enforcement, and the general public provides the best opportunity to decrease illegal Warez trading and to promote a global environment that better respects the creativity and innovations of both individuals and businesses.

KEY TERMS

Digital piracy
Policymakers
Warez

REFERENCES

Andrews, R. 2005. Copyright infringement and the Internet: An economic analysis of crime. *Boston University Journal of Science & Technology Law* 11: 259, 266–7, 281–2.

Apple Computer, Inc. February 23, 2006. iTunes music store downloads top one billion songs. Press Release. Retrieved December 28, 2006, from http://www.apple.com/pr/library/2006/feb/23itms.html

Blessing, D. S. 2004. Who speaks Latin anymore? Translating de minimis use for application to music copyright infringement and sampling. *William and Mary Law Review* 45: 2406.

Campbell v. Acuff-Rose Music, Inc., 510 U.S. 569 (1994).

Clark, J. B. 2006. Copyright law and the Digital Millennium Copyright Act: Do the penalties fit the crime? *New England Journal on Criminal and Civil Confinement* 32: 379–81, 383–5, 390–02, 395, 402–03.

Computer & Internet Lawyer, The. February 2002. U.S. Customs dismantles sophisticated internet piracy network. *The Computer & Internet Lawyer* 19: 18. Retrieved December 18, 2006, from LexisNexis.

Computer & Internet Lawyer, The. May 2003. Justice Dept. seizes top internet site involved in copyright conspiracy. *The Computer & Internet Lawyer* 20: 30. Retrieved December 18, 2006, from LexisNexis.

Computer & Internet Lawyer, The. September 2005. Justice Department conducts international Internet piracy sweep. *The Computer & Internet Lawyer* 22: 34. Retrieved December 18, 2006, from LexisNexis.

Copyright Act of 1976, 17 U.S.C. §506 (2000).

Copyright piracy, and H.R. 2265. The No Electronic Theft (NET) Act: Hearing before the Subcommittee on Courts and Intellectual Property of the House Committee on Judiciary. 105th Cong., 1st Sess., 10-12 (1997) (testimony of Rep. Bob Goodlatte). Retrieved January 1, 2007, from http://commdocs.house.gov/committees/judiciary/hju48724.000/hju48724_0f.htm

Costikyan, G. May 18, 2000. New front in the computer wars: Out-of-print computer games. *New York Times*. Retrieved December 22, 2006, from http://www.nytimes.com/library/tech/00/05/circuits/articles/18aban.html

Department of Justice. July 2, 2002. Member of "DrinkOrDie" Warez group sentenced to 41 months. Press Release. Retrieved August 29, 2006, from http://www.usdoj.gov/criminal/cybercrime/Pattanay.htm

Department of Justice. October 2, 2003a. Federal investigation leads to prosecution of Internet software pirates. Press Release. Retrieved August 30, 2006, from http://www.usdoj.gov/criminal/cybercrime/myersPlea.htm

Department of Justice. November 20, 2003b. Attorney General Aschcroft announces "Operation Cyber Sweep"—Five men charged in New Hampshire with software piracy. Press Release. Retrieved August 30, 2006, from http://www.usdoj.gov/criminal/cybercrime/zielenCharge.htm

Department of Justice. December 18, 2003c. Twelve "Operation Bandwidth" software pirates enter into group guilty plea. Press Release. Retrieved August 31, 2006, from http://www.usdoj.gov/criminal/cybercrime/bandwidthPlea.htm

Department of Justice. April 22, 2004. Justice department announces international Internet piracy sweep. Press Release. Retrieved August 28, 2006, from http://www.cybercrime.gov/fastlink.htm

Department of Justice. February 1, 2006. Nineteen indicted in $6.5 million "RISCISO" software piracy conspiracy. Press Release. Retrieved August 14, 2006, from http://www.usdoj.gov/criminal/press_room/press_releases/2006_4428_otoole.pdf

Department of Justice. n.d. "Operation Buccaneer." Illegal "Warez" organizations and Internet piracy. Retrieved Aug. 29, 2006, from http://www.usdoj.gov/criminal/cybercrime/ob/OBorg&pr.htm

Digital Millennium Copyright Act (DMCA) of 1998, 17 U.S.C. §§512(h-i), 1201 & 1204 (2005).

Electronic Frontier Foundation. March 9, 2006. DMCA subpoena provision still endangers privacy. Retrieved December 22, 2006 from http://www.eff.org/deeplinks/archives/004468.php

Electronic Frontier Foundation. n.d.. *RIAA v. Verizon case archive*. Retrieved December 22, 2006 from http://www.eff.org/legal/cases/RIAA_v_Verizon/

Entertainment Litigation Reporter, The. April 30, 2004a. E-Piracy leader gets four years in prison, must pay $690,000. *The Entertainment Litigation Reporter*. Retrieved December 18, 2006 from LexisNexis.

Entertainment Litigation Reporter, The. June 30, 2004b. Six former Fox Cable employees face criminal copyright charges. *The Entertainment Litigation Reporter*. Retrieved December 18, 2006 from LexisNexis.

Erekosima, O., and B. Koosed. 2004. Intellectual property crimes. *American Criminal Law Review* 41: 830–8, 846.

Family Entertainment and Copyright Act (FECA), 18 USC Appx §2B5.3 (2006).

Ferrera, G. R., S. D. Lichtenstein, M. E. K. Reder, R. C. Bird, and W. T. Schiano. 2004. *Cyber Law: Text and Cases*. 2nd ed. Ohio: West Legal Studies in Business.

Fisher, D. November 2001. Sites offering pirated software on the rise. *ExtremeTech*. Retrieved December 22, 2006, from http://findarticles.com/p/articles/mi_zdext/is_20011/al_ziff17652

Fitzdam, J. D. 2005. Private enforcement of the Digital Millennium Copyright Act: Effective without government intervention. *Cornell Law Review* 90: 1105, 1089–91, 1093–95, 1115–6.

Gentile, G. January 18, 2006. 'Bubble' hits theaters, TV, DVD on same day. *USA Today*. Retrieved December 22, 2006, from http://www.usatoday.com/tech/news/2006-01-18-bubble-theater-threat_x.htm

Goldman, E. 2003. A road to no Warez: The No Electronic Theft Act and criminal copyright infringement. *Oregon Law Review* 82: 369–76, 398–400, 402–12, 420.

Goldman, E. and J. A. Gladstone. March 17, 2003. 'No Electronic Theft Act' proves a partial success. *National Law Journal*: B9. Retrieved December 18, 2006, from http://ericgoldman.org/Articles/nljnet.htm

Granade, S. n.d.. Warez, abandonware and the software industry. Retrieved December 22, 2006 from http://brasslantern.org/community/companies/Warez-b.html

Groennings, K. 2005. Costs and benefits of the recording industry's litigation against individuals. *Berkeley Technology Law Journal* 20: 572–84, 586–88, 595–99, 600–01.

Hinduja, S. 2001. Correlates of Internet software piracy. *Journal of Contemporary Criminal Justice*. Retrieved August 26, 2006, from http://ccj.sagepub.com/cgi/content/abstract/17/4/369

Kartha, N. 1996–1997. Comment: Digital sampling and copyright law in a social context: No more color-blindness!! *University of Miami Entertainment & Sports Law Review* 14: 225.

Kravis, R. S. 1993. Does a song by any other name still sound as sweet? Digital sampling and its copyright implications. *American University Law Review* 43: 258–9.

Latham, S. J. 2003. Newton v. Diamond: Measuring the legitimacy of unauthorized compositional sampling—a clue illuminated and obscured. *Hastings Communication & Entertainment Law Journal* 26: 125–6.

Madden, M. and A. Lenhart 2003. *Pew Internet Project data memo.* pp. 1–2, 5–6. Retrieved December 22, 2006, from Pew Internet & American Life Project: http://www.pewinternet.org/pdfs/PIP_Copyright_Memo.pdf

MGM Studios, Inc. v. Grokster, Ltd. 2005. 545 U.S. 913, 125 S. Ct. 2764, 2792-2793

Morea, L. A. 2006. The future of music in a digital age: The ongoing conflict between copyright law and peer-to-peer technology. *Campbell Law Review* 28: 201–02, 209, 215–18, 222–25, 228–29, 231–35.

Motion Picture Association of America (MPAA). 2005. 2005 U.S. piracy fact sheet. Retrieved October 5, 2006, from http://www.mpa.org/USpiracyfactsheet.pdf

Motion Picture Association of America (MPAA). September 29, 2006. Motion picture piracy costs U.S. economy thousands of jobs, billions in lost wages. Press Release. Retrieved from October 5, 2006, from http://www.mpaa.org/press_releases/ipi%20release%209%2029%2006.pdf

Nasheri, H. 2004. *Addressing global scope of intellectual property law* (Document No. 208384). National Institute of Justice, The International Center Department of Justice. pp. 7–8, 12, 15–17, 28, 41, 53–58, 65–66, 69, 71. Retrieved August 29, 2006, from National Criminal Justice Reference Service: htpp://www.ncjrs.gov/pdfiles1/nij/grants/208384.pdf

National Institute of Justice. 2004. *Intellectual property and while-collar crime: Report of issues, trends, and problems for future research* (Document No. 208135). pp. 4, 11, 17–18, 21–22, 26, 33–34, 36. Retrieved August 31, 2006, from National Criminal Justice Reference Service: htpp://www.ncjrs.gov/pdfiles1/nij/grants/208135.pdf

No Electronic Theft (NET) Act of 1997, 18 U.S.C. §2319 (2005).

Piquero, N. L., and A. R. Piquero. 2006. Democracy and intellectual property: Examining trajectories of software piracy. *Annals* 605: 106, 108–109, 121.

Rainie, L., M. Madden, D. Hess, D., and G. Mudd. 2004. *Pew Internet Project and Comscore Media Metrix data memo.* pp. 1, 3. Retrieved December 22, 2006, from Pew Internet & American Life Project: http://www.pewinternet.org/pdfs/PIP_File_Swapping_Memo_0104.pdf

Recording Industry Association of America, Inc (RIAA)., v. Verizon Internet Services, Inc., 351 F.3d 1229 (D.C. Cir. 2003), *rehearing denied en banc*, 2004 U.S. App. LEXIS 3564 (D.C. Cir. 2004), *cert. denied,* 543 U.S. 924 (2004).

Recording Industry Association of America (RIAA). 2003a. Anti-piracy. Retrieved January 1, 2007, from RIAA web site: http://www.riaa.com/issues/piracy/riaa.asp

Recording Industry Association of America (RIAA). 2003b. Copyright educational efforts. Retrieved January 1, 2007, from RIAA web site: http://www.riaa.com/issues/piracy/riaa.asp

Recording Industry Association of America (RIAA). 2003c. What the RIAA is doing about piracy. Retrieved December 22, 2006 from RIAA web site: http://www.riaa.com/issues/piracy/riaa.asp

Sag, M. 2006. Piracy twelve year-olds, grandmothers, and other good targets for the recording industry's file sharing litigation. *Northwestern Journal of Technology & Intellectual Property* 4: 142–143, 149, 155.

Software & Information Industry Association. n.d. The dimensions of the piracy problem. Retrieved December 20, 2006, from http://www.siia.net/piracy/whatis.asp#Internet

Sohn, G. B. 2006. Digital rights management: Don't mess with success: Government technology mandates and the marketplace for online content. *Journal on Telecommunications & High Technology Law* 5: 74–75, 84–85.

States News Service. June 20, 2006a. Thirtieth copyright conviction as part of Operation Copycat. *States News Service.* Retrieved August 28, 2006, from LexisNexis.

States News Service. August 1, 2006b. Four men sentenced and another film critic pleads guilty in Operation Copycat. *States News Service.* Retrieved August 28, 2006, from LexisNexis.

Szymanski, R. M. 1996. Audio Pastiche: Digital sampling, intermediate copying, fair use. *UCLA Entertainment Law Review 3*: 299.

Taylor, R. September 22, 2005. Piracy on campus: An overview of the problem and a look at emerging practices to reduce online theft of copyrighted works. Presentation to the Subcommittee on Courts, the Internet, and Intellectual Property. Retrieved February 20, 2007, from http://www.mpaa.org/MPAAtestimonyfor9.22.05hearing.pdf

U.S. Fed News. April 27, 2006. Five additional defendants charged in crackdown against worldwide Internet piracy groups. *U.S. Fed News.* Retrieved August 28, 2006, from LexisNexis.

U.S. Const. art. I, §8. Retrieved May 15, 2005, from House of Representatives web site: http://www.house.gov/Constitution/Constitution.html

United States v. Cheek, 498 U.S. 192 (1991).

United States v. LaMacchia, 871 F. Supp. 535 (D. Mass. 1994).

Yang, D. W. and B. M. Hoffstadt. 2006. Countering the cyber-crime threat. *American Criminal Law Review* 43: 205, 208–09, 211–12, 214.

Zacharia, J. H. August 2006. Criminal enforcement of intellectual property rights. Presented at the annual meeting and conference of the Academy of Legal Studies in Business (ALSB), Technology Section, St. Petersburg, FL.

Chapter 20

Internet and Crime Trends

Marc Ouimet
Université de Montréal

Marc Ouimet received his Ph.D. in criminal justice from Rutgers University in 1990. He is now full-time professor at the School of Criminology, Université de Montréal. He teaches courses in crime analysis, delinquency theories, and statistics. His areas of research include the analysis of crime rates across time and space, as well as the study of criminal careers. He has published many books, book chapters, and articles in refereed journals.

Abstract

This chapter discusses the potential impact of Internet on traditional crime. After examining available research on the impact of media on crime, such as comic books, television, or video games, we discuss the potential effects of Internet on recent crime trends. In agreement with the routine activity approach (Cohen and Felson 1979), according to which changes in life habits are related to changes in the volume of crime, we wonder if Internet has changed our lives enough to have any effect on crime trends. Our reflection brings us to think that Internet does lower crime for three principal reasons. First, Internet usage generally confines the user to his house or workplace, environments of relative security. Second, since Internet usage leaves almost permanent traces, motivated offenders might refrain from crime once realizing that they can be somehow identified. Finally, Internet swarms with information that has crime protection potential.

INTRODUCTION

The number of Internet users recently surpassed the billion and the growth is not over. Commercial activities over the Internet will also notice a boom since, at the present time, online purchases only constitute a fraction of the sales of goods and services. Considering the importance of the phenomenon, it is obvious that the problem of cyber crime will grow during the upcoming years. Grabosky and Smith (1988) made the junction between the famous quote "As Willie Sutton the bank robber said when asked why he robbed banks, 'because that's where the money is'" and cyber crime. So, as human and economic activities migrate more and more toward cyberspace, we will see more predations committed or attempted over the Internet.

The present chapter discusses the impact of the Internet on traditional forms of crimes that do not entail the use of new technologies. To our knowledge, this subject matter has never been addressed in the scientific literature. Nevertheless, there are pieces of research and dispersed data that may help us provide a tentative prediction and explanation for the eventual impact of computer technologies on crime.

Before approaching this subject directly, it will be useful to recall how science has reacted to past innovations in the media such as comic strips, television, or **video games**. Then, we are going to look at the major trends in crime over the last decades. Finally, the possible impact of the Internet on recent trends in crime will be discussed. More specifically, we will see if and how the Internet can be considered as a factor in the recent decline in crime rates.

FROM COMIC BOOKS TO THE INTERNET

In the '50s, several specialists in child development and moral entrepreneurs warned the public on the dangers of "comic books." According to Wertham (1954):

> Badly drawn, badly written, and badly printed—a strain on the young eyes and young nervous systems—the effects of these pulp-paper nightmares is that of a violent stimulant. Their crude blacks and reds spoil a child's natural sense of colour; their hypodermic injection of sex and murder make the child impatient with better, though quieter, stories. Unless we want a coming generation even more ferocious than the present one, parents and teachers throughout America must band together to break the 'comic' magazine.

The crusade against the "comic books" industry raged on for a decade. There had even been a U.S. Senate commission formed to study the possible effects of this type of material. The title of the report, *Comic Books and Juvenile Delinquency* (1954) leaves no doubt in the seriousness of the matter at this time. For several people, the *Wonder Woman* promoted bondage fetishism and the duet *Batman and Robin* characterized a homosexual relationship. As a result, large publishing corporations provided themselves with guidelines to insure that **violence** is not promoted and to make sure the villains at the end of the story always get punished.

In the '70s, television had come under scrutiny. Violence on television and its effect on child behaviors had been the subject of countless studies to date. Many famous psychiatrists, psychologists, and moral crusaders believe that exposing children to images of violence will increase the likelihood that they themselves will engage in violent behavior. However, the research on the relation between television violence and violent behavior is far from convincing (Ouimet 2002). One finds counterexamples, incoherent and contradictory results and a lot of low quality research designs. The experimental or corelational studies on the subject obtain results which appear weak in the context of other factors (i.e., parental supervision, socioeconomic status of the household, etc.). Centerwall (1992) published a paper evaluating the effects of television on violence between 1945 and 1973. He indicated that the arrival of television in a country is followed, 10 years later, by an increase in crime. This study is often used by promoters of a less violent television, one which would not show the *Ninja Turtles*, the *Power Rangers*, or movies such as *Die Hard*, or *Rambo*. As argued by Jensen (2001), the Centerwall macro-research design does not withstand a more complete statistical modeling. Would anyone want to assert that the Internet is causing a decrease in violence simply because crime has declined in the last decade?

In the recent history of the crusade against violence in the media, the next target became video games. There are a few studies on the possible connection between video game playing and aggressive behaviors (Anderson and Dill 2000; Gentile et al. 2004). It is often believed that since violent behavior is omnipresent and even rewarded in video games, it should lead to greater violent dispute resolutions amongst gamers. Not all studies have found a significant relationship between video game playing and other negative behaviors, social integration, or even school performance. One study has even found a significant positive link between video gaming and intelligence (Van Schie and Wiegman 1997; Ivory 2001). In fact, most young hardcore video gamers, often called geeks or nerds, are far from resembling traditional delinquents.

Surprisingly, the idea that the Internet can in some way be related to an increase in delinquency among teenagers has not (yet) surfaced in the scientific community. Although the Internet is thought to facilitate criminal behaviors and to promote ideas and values leading to violence, no known research has questioned the possible influence of the Internet on the etiology of criminal behavior amongst youths. The attention of the media in regard to the Internet–crime connection has mostly been placed on the dangers associated with online chatting, personal information theft, phishing, and the like. Although the content on the Internet can be several times more offending than what is shown on television or in video games, the link between Internet usage and criminality remains difficult to establish.

It is not the object of this chapter to examine the possible impact of the Internet on the explanation of the initiation or continuation of the criminal career. However, our guess would be that its influence would be very limited since much more fundamentals factors, such as family violence, erratic disciplinary systems used at home, weak socialization, or poverty, have been shown to strongly predict delinquency (Shoemaker 2004). The typical delinquent, at an early age, usually spend much time outside the home, frequently with peers in parks and in the street and devotes himself quickly to pleasures that are not virtual (Cusson 2005).

GENERAL TRENDS IN CRIMES

It has been established many times in criminology that trends in homicide rates are a fairly good indicator of a nation's violent crime levels. When there are more thefts, burglaries, robberies, rapes, and family violence, there will be more homicides. The homicide rate has a unique quality as an indicator of violence since most murders and nonnegligent manslaughters are known to police and therefore counted in the annual statistical reports (crimes such as rapes or aggravated assaults suffer from changes in definitions and reporting levels over time and space). Figure 20-1 displays the homicide rates in Canada and the United States from 1950 to 2005. The trends in both countries appear as very similar, although the prevalence of homicide is three to four times higher in the United States.

The curves in Figure 20-1 show that the homicide rate tripled in Canada and doubled in the United States from the early 1950s to the late 1970s. Then, a 20-year plateau in homicide rates occurred over the next two decades, before the homicide rate started to plunge from 45 percent in the United States and 25 percent in Canada during the 1990s. Finally, the last five years show a new stable plateau.

Many explanations have been put forward in order to explain the surge in crime during the 1960s and 1960s. Demography has certainly played a major role in shaping the trends in crime since crime is a phenomenon strongly associated with age (most crimes are committed by the youths). Also, it is probable that increases in divorce and family instability during the 1970s impacted on crime, as well as other economic variables (poverty, inequality, etc.). Although many other concepts have been used to explain the trends in crime, Cohen and

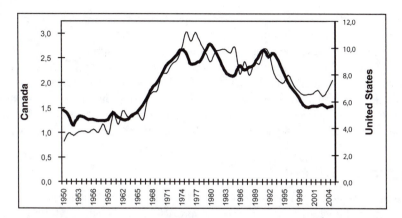

FIGURE 20-1 Trends in Homicide Rates in Canada (light) and the United States (bold) from 1950 to 2005

Source: Statistics Canada (Juristat) and the FBI (Crime in the United States)

Felson (1979) proposed a unique explanation to account for the upward trends in crime during the 1960s and 1970s—a theory now known as the **routine activity approach**. In this model, it is believed that what accounts for changes in the level of crime are changes in the routine activities of the people. In particular, a greater dispersion of human activities away from homes has lead to more crimes. The arrival of automobiles and public transport, and the integration of women in the job market (leaving homes unattended and teens unsupervised) are two examples of changes that have affected the number of crimes recorded.

There is now a growing body of research on what may have caused the recent drop in crime in Canada and the United States. In fact, almost all types of crimes have declined substantially in almost all regions of the two countries. There are currently a few well-established explanations for the drop in crime. First, demographic changes (fewer teenagers and young adults) appear to be important. Second, many people think that the massive incarceration policy created in the 1990s has finally paid off. Third, it is possible that the hiring of more police officers and security personnel has had an effect. Finally, the improvements in the job markets in the 1990s have certainly helped. There are also more marginal explanations, such as the waning of the crack market, improvements in the hospital emergency procedures, changes in values, and so on that may very well have had some impact.

We have just seen a number of factors that may have played a role in the downward trends in crime in the 1990s. However, we will discuss another explanation that mirrors the Cohen and Felson (1979) routine activity approach. We will argue that the arrival and greater use of the Internet has had a profound impact on our routine activities and made us either less likely to engage in crime or less likely to being victimized.

INTERNET AND TRENDS IN TRADITIONAL CRIMES

Research focusing on cyber crime has mainly concentrated on new forms of attacks and predations. As a general phenomenon, it is clear that the arrival and popularization of the Internet has brought new breeds of crime and modify the way certain forms of crime are perpetrated. Cyber crimes are generally divided into two general categories according to the fact the computers or databases are the object of the attack or computers and the Internet are means used to perpetrate a traditional form of crime.

There is, however, very little, if anything at all, on the impact of Internet on traditional forms of crime. We have seen that crime in Canada and the United States has increased tremendously in the 1960s and 1970s, has leveled off in the 1980s and has decreased significantly in the 1990s. Several factors are known to explain the drop in crime during the 1990s, but we think that the arrival of the Internet and its greater use is responsible for a share of the downward trend in crime. We divided the pretended impact of the Internet in three general dimensions.

Routine Activities

Personal computers became popular in the 1980s. However, for the first decade, applications were mostly limited to word processing, spreadsheet applications, databases, and gaming. The interconnection between computers only arrived later. One can assert that the birth of the contemporary Internet happened in 1994 and 1995 when Netscape and Internet Explorer became standard in operating systems. It is therefore between 1995 and 2000, that the Internet became part of a large portion of the population. The popularization of Napster in 1999, the first large-scale file-sharing system, contributed to the growth of the Internet, especially among youths. Also, it was around 1999 that popular games like Half-Life/Counterstrike, Quake, Starcraft, and Unreal became popular (McCreary 2002).

Nowadays, approximately 70 percent of the population in North America is using the Internet.[1] Estimates of the weekly time spent over the Internet vary from one source to the other, but if the average user spent 10 hours a day surfing, reading e-mails, or searching for information, it means that the total number of hours spent on the Internet in America totals 520 billion hours. Among certain groups, the time spent over the Internet now equals or surpasses the time devoted to television viewing.

According to the Stanford Institute for the Quantitative Study of Society, there is a strong correlation between time spent over the Internet and other social activities.[2] Heavy Internet users report spending less time talking to friends or family over the phone, spending less time with family and friends and spending less time attending social events outside the home. They also report spending less time shopping or commuting in traffic. For youngsters and teenagers, the popularization of gaming consoles and computers may have had a bigger impact on their daily routines. Since they now spend so much time playing electronic games, they spend much less time on the streets, in public parks, and school playground. Parents may not like it, and it may have some implications with regard to health issues or even socialization with peers (Markoff 2004), but kids spending more time inside homes protects them from many types of victimizations and other forms of accidents.

A poll conducted by the Health Canada in 1990 and 1998 show changes in the employment of time among youths (Boyce 2004). For the 15 years, the percentage of boys playing electronic games at least seven hours a week was of 10 percent in 1990, 19 percent in 1998 and doubtless much more now. Using the cycle 14 of the Canadian General Social Survey (Statistics Canada 2000) concerning the use of the new technologies by Canadians also show interesting

[1]http://www.internetworldstats.com
[2]http://www.stanford.edu/group/siqss

results. In the group of men aged between 15 and 29 years of age declaring having a computer at home and an Internet connection, the average number of hours spend surfing averages 10. Questioned on whether or not respondents felt that their Internet habits had any impacts on their other activities, 41 percent felt they watched television less often, 13 percent said they spent less time shopping, 7 percent said they read less, 2.1 percent said they worked less, 21 percent said they slept less, and 8.3 percent said they spent less time visiting friends. In light of these results, it then appears that the use of the Internet drives down the time spent on various other activities, some of which are criminogenic or related to victimization (Sacco and Johnson 1990).

The time spent in front of the computer affect the risks of victimization in several manners. For example, if windows-shop online (finding the good product and the beat place to buy it), it will then require much less subsequent movement in going to buy the good. Of course, buying the goods online and having them delivered to the door even decreases movement outside one's home. Hence, potential robberies, car thefts, or potential burglaries are avoided and teens are more supervised. Another example of the anticrime virtues of the Internet is online dating. Online dating appears much less risky for women than meeting at a bar or tavern. If ICQ chat rooms of the past may have been somewhat dangerous for lone women, one can assume that dating sites are more secure since clients are electronically known to the company (via credit card for example). The communications over Internet leaves a lot more traces than what was possible over telephone conversations.

On the whole, the greater use of the Internet has brought a transformation in the daily routines of people. An increase of the time spent at home would, under Cohen and Felson's model, lead to a decline in criminal opportunities and, therefore crime. Of course, such changes in the life habits have not only beneficiary, since it might lead to a decrease in physical activity and a growing social isolation growing.

Traceability

When Foucault published "Discipline and Punish" in 1975, he could not have foreseen the information and communication revolution that would take place two decades later. Foucault proposed a new reading of history based on the notion of surveillance and supervision. If modern society has brought much greater surveillance and identification of the citizens, recent technological advances have made giants leaps in that direction. However, the Orwellian society, one in which "Big Brother is watching you" has not materialized. What has been taking place instead are growing capabilities of retro-surveillance by authorities, as well as rising inspection capabilities by ordinary citizens over their fellow citizens or other entities such as corporations and government.

The history of the telephone is instructive. One of the virtues of the telephone is, or was, the anonymity it provided. Kids could pester school friends or order pizza for the neighbor just for the simple pleasure of annoyance. The arrival of the digital era changed it all. Every call is logged somewhere. It is then probable that the number of obscene and harassing phone calls have plummeted. The simple idea is that activities leaving traces, or spoors, do rarely lead to crime.

At first, the Internet was believed to provide anonymity for the user, a notion that contributed to its growth. This idea is, of course, part true and part false (Newman and Clarke 2003). It is true because users can surf the Internet, post comments, send messages, etc., without having others knowing about it. However, since most actions made over the Internet are logged, surfing is in fact done behind a screen of anonymity. As a general rule, traces of the communication such as time, origin and destination, bytes transferred are being kept for longer time periods than the content of the communication. Yet, the content of the communications may be retrieved later. Besides communication traces left on various servers, people also leave their imprint on various discussion groups, personal Web pages, and so on.

The traceability of online activity became much greater in the early 2000s when various companies, universities, and other semi-public obligated users to log on with their personal account in order to communicate. Yet, the recent arrival of Wi-Fi connections may complicate the matter. But in an era obsessed by the fear of terrorism, there are new and will be new tools for tracing communications, and always larger communications storage data sets. But who will monitor the custodians of all this information (Thomas and Loader 2000)? Thus, when one decides to use Internet, one accepts also to be traced.

Tracking is a new control and supervision form that works in a retrospective way. No one reads or looks at our communications in real time. However, if a person gets involved in a criminal act, duly authorized investigators will be able to dig out quantities of information that may relate to the case. The computer traces are then used as support to the investigation. Thus, since normal Internet activities leave traces, someone who has bad intentions may refrain from committing a crime once he realizes he trapped himself using a computer.

The tracking notion developed here for the Internet also applies for a variety of other technologies. In fact, our daily routines leave more and more traces every day: buying goods or services with a credit card leaves traces whereas unlocking a door with an access card also leaves traces. Moreover, communicating with a portable phone or using a car equipped with a GPS device also leaves traces. Computer systems nowadays archive considerable quantities of data that can be consulted in a more or less distant future. To these advances, one could add the growing number of CCTV positioned in public or private places.

Information

The Internet is essentially a vast information world. Although some crimes can be committed using it or some crimes might be helped by the information it contains, it is also clear that Internet has important anticrime virtues. For example, for the person preparing a trip to another country, a good itinerary planning can reduce victimization risks. As another example, if a teenager puts GHB into Google just to look, he might decide later to refrain from using it because of what he learned.

There are many specific applications nowadays available over the Internet that may reduce crime. For Example, in Quebec, the government has given access to citizens to the registry of personal rights on movable property, allowing a person interested in buying a given car, boat, or aircraft to check for real ownership. Close to 500,000 information requests were made by the public in 2003–2004 (Ministry of Justice 2004). This public service is an information tool that can reduce in a significant way fraud occasions and opportunities.

CONCLUSION

The object of this chapter was to discuss the impact of the Internet on traditional crime. Our reflection leads us to think that the arrival and the growth of Internet usage are in many ways related to a crime decline. Three principal reasons would support a causal relationship between both variables: change in routine activities, tracking, and information.

Alongside the Internet, many other new technologies have significantly changed our life habits, and therefore might have affected crime. This is certainly the case for portable phones; which certainly help drug dealers to operate their businesses. Nevertheless, cell phones have increased the teenager's level of parental supervision and allow teens to get in touch with parents more readily in case of a problem. Also, teens do not have to congregate as much in specific places, such as parks or street corners, since they can now communicate more easily. Also, there are little doubts that the proliferation of the portable phones may have complicated the life of certain types of criminals who use to have seconds or minutes before the police could be alerted.

If Internet is explaining part of the traditional crime decline, Internet crime is on the rise. Since a large portion of human activities will in the future be done in cyberspace, crime will also migrate. It is therefore pressing to invest in Internet crime prevention research. At some point, it will be necessary to better specify the role of each person involved: legislator, ISP, private sector, and police. According to Grabosky and Smith (2001), if prevention and self-help are the foundation of a secure Internet experience, the police still have to adapt itself to this new reality.

KEY TERMS

Routine activity approach
Video games
Violence

REFERENCES

Anderson, C. A., and K. E. Dill. 2000. Video games and aggressive thoughts, feelings, and behavior in the laboratory and in life. *Journal of Personality and Social Psychology* 78 (4): 772–90.

Boyce, W. 2004. *Young People in Canada: Their Health and Well-Being.* Public Health Agency of Canada. http://www.phac-aspc.gc.ca/dca-dea/publications/hbsc-2004/index_e.html

Centerwall, B. 1992. Television and violence: The scale of the problem and where to go from now. *Journal of the American Medical Association* 267 (22): 3059–63.

Cohen, L. E., and M. Felson. 1979. Social change and crime rate trends: Routine activity approach. *American Sociological Review* 44 (4): 588–608.

Cusson, M. 2005. *La Délinquance: Une Vie Choisie.* Montréal: HMH.

Foucault, M. 1975. *Surveiller et Punir: Naissance de la Prison.* Paris: Gallimard.

Gentile, D. A., P. Lynch, J. Linder, and D. Walsh. 2004. The effects of violent video game habits on adolescent hostility, aggressive behaviors, and school performance. *Journal of Adolescence* 27: 5–22.

Grabosky, P., and R. Smith. 1998. *Crime in the Digital Age: Controlling Telecommunications and Cyberspace Illegalities.* New Brunswick, NJ: Transaction Publishers, and Sydney: Federation Press.

Grabosky, P., and R. Smith. 2001. Telecommunication fraud in the digital age. In *Crime and the Internet*, edited by D. S. Wall, 29–43. Londres: Routledge.

Ivory, J. D. 2001. Video games and the elusive search for their effects on children: An assessment of twenty years of research. Presented at the Association for Education in Journalism and Mass Communication's Annual, Washington, DC, Disponible: http://www.unc.edu/~jivory/video.html

Jensen, G. 2001. The invention of television as a cause of homicide: The reification of a spurious relationship. *Homicide Studies* 5 (2): 114–30.

Markoff, J. December 30, 2004. Internet use said to cut into TV viewing and socializing. *New York Times*. http://medialit.med.sc.edu/internet_news_story.htm

McCreary, S. 2002. Trends in wide area IP traffic patterns. San Diego: Rapport de recherche, Cooperative Association for Internet Data Analysis (CAIDA): http://www.caida.org/outreach/papers/2000/AIX0005/AIX0005.html.

Ministère de la justice. 2004. Rapport annuel de gestion: Direction des registres et de la certification. Disponible sur le site du gouvernement du Québec: http://si1.rdprm.gouv.qc.ca/rdprmweb/html/publication.asp

Newman, R. G., and R. V. Clarke. 2003. *Superhighway Robbery: Preventing E-Commerce Crime.* Portland, OR: Willan Publishing.

Ouimet, M. 2002. La violence à la télévision et les tendances de la criminalité au Canada. *Revue Internationale de Criminologie et de Police Technique* 55 (3): 358–73.

Sacco, V., and H. Johnson. 1990. *Profil de la Victimisation au Canada.* Ottawa: Statistique Canada, Enquête sociale générale.

Shoemaker, D. 2004. *Theories of Delinquency.* 5th ed. New York: Oxford University Press.

Statistique Canada 2000. *Access to and Use of Information Communication Technology.* Ottawa: Statistics Canada, Cycle 14 de l'enquête sociale générale.

Thomas, D., and B. D. Loader. 2000. "Cybercrime: Law enforcement, security and surveillance in the information age." In *Cybercrime: Law Enforcement, Security and Surveillance in the Information Age*, edited by D. Thomas and B. D. Loader, 1–14. Londres: Routledge.

U.S. Congressional Senate. 1954. *Comic Books and Delinquency.* Committee on the Judiciary. Library of Congress.

Van Schie, E. G. M., and O. Wiegman. 1997. Children and videogames: Leisure activities, aggression, social integration, and school performance. *Journal of Applied Social Psychology* 27: 1175–94.

Wertham, F. 1954. *Seduction of the Innocent.* New York: Reinhart. *See also* Coville, J., *The Comic Book Villain.* http://www.psu.edu/dept/inart10_110/inart10/cmbk4cca.html

Chapter 21

Internet Gambling: The Birth of a Victimless Crime?

David Giacopassi, Wayne J. Pitts
The University of Memphis

David Giacopassi has a Ph.D. in sociology from the University of Notre Dame. He is currently a professor in the Department of Criminology and Criminal Justice at The University of Memphis. He has published widely in a variety of social science journals, with more than a dozen of his articles examining the impact of gambling on individuals and communities.

Wayne J. Pitts is currently an assistant professor in the Department of Criminology and Criminal Justice at the University of Memphis in Tennessee. His current research interests include: internet gambling, corrections, Latin American prisons, occupational stress, and a variety of topics in comparative research methods. Dr. Pitts completed his Ph.D. in sociology at the University of New Mexico in 2003.

Abstract

Several states and the federal government have passed laws against various types of Internet gambling. This chapter discusses the category of offense labeled "victimless crimes" to determine how well Internet gambling fits this theoretical conceptualization. A discussion of the harm that may accrue to the individual and to society from Internet gambling is presented, along with an analysis of the scope of the activity and a typology of Internet gamblers. Regulatory issues of national and international scope and some practical difficulties in enforcing a ban on Internet gambling are also discussed.

INTRODUCTION

> Has online gambling caused you any grief? "Grief? Naw. I broke even last week which is great, because I needed the money."— *A San Francisco Chronicle reader's comment following an article on gambling addiction by Berton (2006)*

Despite the humorous anonymous quote at the beginning of this chapter, it is clear that some people do lose large sums of money gambling on the Internet and, as a result, these individuals and their families may suffer greatly as a result of **Internet gambling**. It appears, however, that most who gamble on the Internet have no serious gambling problems. Yet, in most instances, the simple act of placing a bet, or hosting an Internet site that receives wagers, is against American law.

In the classic book *Crimes Without Victims*, Edwin Schur states that numerous acts, such as homosexuality, abortion, and drug addiction, lie at "the borderline of crime" where there is no consensus as to whether these acts should be considered crimes, sins, vices, diseases, or simply as patterns of social deviance (Schur 1965, V). Schur notes that in a variety of **victimless crimes**, there is a willing and private exchange of strongly demanded yet officially proscribed goods and services. Schur believes that the element of consent, especially when it applies to adults, "precludes the existence of a victim—in the usual sense of the word" (Schur 1965, V). He acknowledges, however, that his definition of victimless crime is somewhat arbitrary. For example, Schur's definition of victim is limited to "harm to the participating individuals themselves" (p. 170). Clearly, in a variety of victimless crimes, such as prostitution and gambling, the harm may extend beyond the immediate, willing participants to wider social groupings such as the family, community, and society.

Schur concludes that two elements, a willing exchange transaction and lack of apparent harm to others, are at the core of the concept of victimless crime. He acknowledges that even dispassionate and objective analyses of the same social act may differ in their conclusions relative to the attendant social harm. Finally, Schur notes that there does appear to be one feature that characterizes all crimes without victims: the unenforceability of laws intended to prohibit or regulate crimes due to their low visibility and absence of a willing complainant (Schur 1965, 171).

Other criminologists have elaborated and parsed Schur's formulation of "victimless crime." Stitt (1988), for example, deals with the concept of victim and the concept of harm and whether an individual who knows (or should know) the risks accompanying an act is a "victim" if the chosen behavior results in the individual harming oneself. Stitt argues that an individual cannot truly be wrongfully harmed and thus victimized if the individual is informed of what the consequences of an act may be and consents to be a party to said act. According to Stitt, the fact of informed consent is most important in conceptualizing victimless crime. The consent does not obviate the harm but does negate the responsibility in a legal sense. Following this line of reasoning, Stitt (1988, 95) states that criminal harm can "only come to an individual who does not consent or who is incapable of making a reasonable judgment, or who is forced or deceived into participation in the act."

Goode (1984) focuses on the cost of victimless crimes to society, noting that "one may harm others by harming oneself." Thus, even when one willingly and knowingly engages in behavior that will (or may) harm oneself, there may be an unacceptable cost to another. Drug addiction's harm frequently extends beyond the individual to the addict's family or to society due to crime, lost productivity, or medical expenses borne by society. Goode concludes that the distinction between victimless behavior and victimization is often difficult to formulate, especially where the harm is indirect, and that "both intervention and tolerance entail dilemmas" (pp. 291–2).

Skolnick and Dombrink's (1978) article "The Legalization of Deviance" helps put societal reaction to Internet gambling in an historical and theoretical perspective. They agree with Bedau (1974) that it is difficult to see consistency or logic in contemporary social reaction to the behaviors traditionally categorized as vices and victimless crimes. They note that many traditional vices have been decriminalized and that a variety of formal and informal social responses are elicited by the legalization or decriminalization of the previously prohibited conduct. The societal responses are not based on a consistent legal theory but rather are the product of both historical and ideological circumstance and frequently driven by powerful economic forces. The result is often a period of social turbulence before administrative regulations replace the criminal enforcement of moral prohibitions embodied in the victimless crime statutes.

Internet gambling is a behavior that is perceived by many as a new form of vice. It is clearly a behavioral choice freely entered into by the individual, but one that just as clearly can have direct and disastrous consequences for the individual and, indirectly, the wider society of which the Internet gambler is a part. In this chapter, we will review the nature and extent of Internet gambling before reviewing the potential harms and efforts at regulation.

INTERNET GAMBLING

The Internet is the new gambling frontier. While large numbers of people are tentatively exploring its boundaries, Internet gambling is often beyond the ken of laws and regulatory bodies that seek to establish some order in cyberspace. Many see the virtual casino as liberating and its lure of readily accessible 24 hours a day entertainment as not only highly desirable but inevitable. Others see the virtual casino as embodying a multitude of dangers that will magnify the problems associated with conventional casino gambling while introducing new and perhaps as yet unimagined dangers to vulnerable populations.

The National Gambling Impact Study Commission (NGISC) stated that Internet gambling posses "serious legal, economic, and social concerns" (1999, 25). It noted the legal uncertainties, the potential for various types of criminal activities, and the potential for a myriad of negative social consequences surrounding Internet gambling. While the Commission admitted the difficulty of regulating an industry "whose parameters have yet to be defined," the members of the NGISC nevertheless unanimously endorsed "total prohibition of gambling on the Internet" (p. 27). The Chairman of the Federal Trade Commission, one of the regulatory bodies charged with Internet gambling oversight, stated that "there is a growing problem with kids engaged in online gambling" (FTC Consumer Alert 2002). Griffiths (1999) noted that addiction is essentially tied to rewards and speed of rewards and he believes that the evolving technology of Internet gambling will almost inevitably lead to more problem gamblers. Shaffer, the director of Harvard Medical School's Division on Addiction Studies, stated, "As smoking crack cocaine changed the cocaine experience, I think electronics is going to change the way gambling is experienced" (NGISC 1999, 5–5). Yet, despite the dire warnings, little hard information exists to support the various claims made against Internet gambling.

Few studies have investigated the prevalence of Internet gambling or of problem gambling on the Internet. Prevalence studies conducted in England by Griffiths (2001) of 2,098 people found only 24 percent were Internet users. Of this group, only 1 percent had gambled on the Internet and no one was a weekly Internet gambler. In a Canadian study by Ialomiteanu and Adlaf (2001) of 1,294 adults living in Ontario, 5.3 percent had gambled on the Internet in the last month. Petry and Mallya's (2001) study of Internet gambling among a sample of 907 university health center employees in the northeast found that just 1.2 percent had gambled on the Internet. In a survey of dental patients at this same health center, 8.1 percent of the 389 individuals who returned usable questionnaires were found to have gambled on the Internet. Of these, 3.7 percent participated at least weekly in Internet gambling. Internet gambling was associated with being younger and with being a member of a minority group. Of those who gambled, 22 percent without Internet gambling experience were found to have a gambling problem (level 2 or 3 on the South Oaks Gambling Screen) (Lesieur and Blume 1987). Of those who have participated in Internet gambling, 74 percent were found to have a gambling problem (Ladd and Petry 2002). From these studies, it is apparent there are great variations, possibly due to international differences in Internet gambling policies, regarding the prevalence of Internet gambling and problems associated with the behavior.

Given the newness of Internet gambling, we first discuss the nature of Internet gambling, outlining its growth and the various forms that this evolving technology has taken. We then discuss some of the regulatory issues, economic issues, and the social concerns that surround the phenomenon of Internet gambling. The chapter concludes by assessing whether Internet gambling should be considered a victimless crime and the consequences for the criminal justice system and society of criminalizing online gambling.

THE GROWTH OF INTERNET GAMBLING

The explosive growth of lotteries and casino gambling in the United States in the last decade may be only the first leg of gambling's growth spurt. Internet gambling began on the World Wide Web in 1995 (Yures 2002). The National Gambling Impact Study Commission estimated revenue earned from Internet gambling more than doubled from 1997 to 1998, rising from $300 million to $651 million (NGISC 1999). By 2002, there were more than 1,800 virtual casinos taking in $3.5 billion in lost wagers from the 2 million weekly players worldwide (Horn 2002). One English Web site, which holds a lottery drawing once every minute, has attracted 200,000 customers daily and one million bets in the first month (New Media Age 2001). According to one estimate, nearly 23 million people gambled nearly $12 billion on the Internet in 2005, with almost 8 million residing in the United States (CCA 2007). This same research group expects the amount gambled online to double by 2010. These numbers suggest that Internet gambling is one of the most popular and profitable applications of the Internet, taking in more than three times the revenue of porn sites (Horn 2002).

The Government Accounting Office in 2002 conducted a randomized study of 162 Internet gambling sites. The purpose of the study was to analyze the content, dispersion, and global reach of Internet gambling. The results of the Internet gambling Web site survey show the majority of Internet gambling sites offer casino type gaming opportunities (79.6 percent) while nearly half of those surveyed had sports book betting (49.4 percent). Less prevalent were horse and dog racing (22.8 percent) and sites with lottery options (6.8 percent). Visa (85.8 percent) and MasterCard (85.1 percent) were accepted at most sites but American Express (4.9 percent) and Discover (1.2 percent) cards were also valid methods of payment. Third-party payment transfer services are a common method for making payments and receiving winnings. The three leading online third-party fund transfer services were PayPal (66.7 percent) NETeller (32.7 percent), and FirePay (21.0 percent), but sites also accepted direct wire transfers via Western Union (46.9 percent) or direct bank wires (59.3 percent). Other forms of checks are also accepted by some online gambling Web sites. Bank drafts, cashier's checks, and certified checks (40.1 percent) appear to be the most commonly accepted checks, although some sites allow money orders (27.8 percent), traveler's checks (8.0 percent), and, surprisingly, even personal checks (29.6 percent). In short, Internet gambling sites offer a wide range of convenient methods for online bettors to move winnings and losses (Government Accounting Office 2002). Table 21-1 further demonstrates the global reach of Internet gambling through the 2002 GAO study.

To understand the popularity of Internet gambling, one should envision having 24 hours a day, 365 days a year access to casino-style gambling from the comfort and privacy of one's own home. To entice the uninitiated, many of the virtual casinos offer a try-out run where the

---

TABLE 21-1 Live Web Sites Listing Licensing Countries and Contacts

Licensing Country	Number of Sites	Contact Location	Number of Sites
Antigua	27	Antigua	13
Australia	2	Australia	1
Barbuda	8	Barbuda	1
Canada, Kahnawake	4	Belize	3
Costa Rica	8	Canada	2
Curacao	21	Costa Rica	6
Dominica	3	Curacao	19
Grenada	1	Dominican Republic	1
Isle of Man	1	Ireland	1
Netherlands Antilles	1	Isle of Man	1
South Africa	1	Korea	1
Trinidad	1	Panama	1
Tobago	1	Netherlands	1
United Kingdom	7	Netherlands Antilles	2
United States	1	New Zealand	1
Venezuela	1	St. Kitts	1
		South Africa	1
		United Kingdom	13
		United States	3
		West Indies	3

Note: Table sums were derived from the electronic survey conducted by GAO analysts.

Source: GAO electronic survey (Government Accounting Office, 2002, 52)

---

play is for fun, without any money being wagered. Once the player feels comfortable, a credit card number allows credits to be deposited in an account. Whether the online gamblers budget money monthly for this type of entertainment, or whether it is an occasional outlet for the bored, or a one-time fling, or an irresistible attraction for compulsive gamblers, it is clear that Internet gambling is a "killer app" of the Internet (Horn 2002). According to the Pew Internet and American Life Project (2006), 97 million Americans representing 66 percent of American adults log onto the World Wide Web daily (up from 52 million in 2000 and 66 million in 2003). It is clear from these numbers that there is a vast potential for increase in Internet gambling, but who are the online gamblers?

Research from a survey of 2,900 Internet users by the River City Group, an online gaming industry research company, shows that 74 percent of online gamblers are male. The study goes on to establish that online gamblers are among the highest income, highest educated, and youngest group of people who use the Internet (Cabot and Balestra 2003). These findings are supported by other studies as well (Jay 2003). The River City Group study concludes that the majority of all gamblers gamble online (83 percent). However, only about one-third of these online gamblers wager real money. The other two-thirds play free online games. Of those who play for real money, almost three-fourths reported online losses in the month prior to the survey while a slightly higher percentage of gamblers who did not play online reported losses during the same period. The study does show that online gamblers tend to lose greater amounts of money than other gamblers. Online gamblers lost more than twice the amount of money as exclusively offline players which are not surprising since the data also expose the fact that online players are more than four times more likely to make especially large wagers (Cabot and Balestra 2003).

In addition to the convenience of Internet gambling, the array of games that can be easily accessed via the Internet is greater than any casino offers. The technology allows for downloads of games traditionally played in casinos, such as video slots, video poker, roulette, and blackjack. In addition, the Internet offers innumerable variations of the traditional casino games, where the player can change games without leaving one's seat. While the sophistication of the Internet gambling sites varies, many sites offer spectacular sound and graphic displays to enhance the sense of excitement upon a big win. Other sites allow interactive, real-time gaming where the player views the actual turn of a card or spin of a roulette wheel in a casino that may be operating thousands of miles from the Internet player's home.

Beyond the traditional casino games, one of the attractions of the Internet is that it allows gambling on games not found in most casinos. Sports betting is one of the most popular types of gambling and obviously opens a vast market to the American (or any nationality) sports fan. Lotteries, bingo, and keno, games that run at varying intervals if they are offered in casinos, can be speeded up and played whenever the player wishes. In addition, Internet gambling sites can offer types of betting not found in casinos. Person-to-person sites allow an individual to post a wager (on the academy awards, an election, who will win a reality TV show, etc.) to determine if anyone wants to accept the bet. On any given day, there are approximately 10,000 bets available and the host site will take a percentage of the money wagered (Bentley 2001). Other innovative sites offer betting (as opposed to investing) on which stocks will go up or down in a given day or week. What Internet gambling offers is convenience gambling that is limited only by one's imagination and one's ability to find a site (or individual) willing to accept the wager.

TYPOLOGY OF INTERNET GAMBLERS

Wykes (1964) reports that the word gambling comes from the Anglo-Saxon word *gamenian,* which means to joke, to play, or to sport. Devereux (1968), a pioneer in gambling studies, defines gambling as the betting or wagering of valuables on events of uncertain outcome. Scimecca (1971) developed one of earlier attempts to systematically classify gamblers based on a range of behavioral and attitudinal characteristics, including the motivation for gambling, the degree of ego involvement, the amount of skill involved, the degree of superstition, and societal reaction. Several others have subsequently attempted to create a typology of gamblers (Clotfelter and Cook 1989; Fisher 1993; Hayano 1984; NORC 1999). In a report to Congress on Internet gambling, the U.S. Government Accounting Office defined Internet gambling as "an activity that takes place through a non-redirected, live Web site that allows monetary transactions in one or more of the following categories of gaming: casinos, lotteries, sports betting, or horse or dog racing" (Government Accounting Office 2002). Perhaps due to the relatively recent emergence or the confusing forms and constant evolution of Internet gambling, there have been few systematic attempts to create a typology of Internet gamblers.

Clotfelter and Cook (1989) suggest that all gambling behavior can be distinguished through a consideration of three dimensions: personal motivations, willingness to take risks, and the overall intensity of the behavior as evidenced by the amount of time and money gambling. One of the most important and frequently cited factors considered in assessing gambling behavior is an individual's propensity to engage in games of chance. Rooted in certain personality and other psychological factors, there are individual differences among potential gamblers that affect the decision to gamble. The second dimension considers the willingness of an individual to risk a wager given the perceived likelihood of being unsuccessful. Finally, how intense is the gambler? How much time and money do they invest in gambling activities? The magnitude of the financial risk and the amount of time spent gambling online serves as the third dimension to characterize gamblers.

While these dimensions help to explain gambling behavior generally, the newness and uniqueness of the Internet culture and the total access to Internet gambling it provides deserve careful analysis. It is possible to use these dimensions to further profile Internet gamblers. Consider the following theoretical subtypes of Internet gamblers.

- ***The Accidental Tourists:***   These gamblers are casual Internet users. They are willing to take a look at free online games but rarely provide credit card information to access a site. As indicated by the name, this type of would-be gambler does not access the Internet for the expressed goal of gambling. They are skeptical of online gambling methods and could be characterized as a spontaneous gambler seeking to win on the basis of luck and not skill.

- ***Beachcombers:***   Unlike the Accidental Tourist whose use of the Internet is fairly limited, Beachcombers are Internet vagrants who waste time almost ritually spending hours per day combing the net. Their gambling is sporadic although some gambling binges may occur. Although the Beachcombers are familiar with online gambling sites, their risk taking behavior is usually minimal. Their main motivation seems to be to avoid boredom.

- ***Recreational Surfers:***   Also a casual online user, this type of gambler usually has experience in other types of gambling and generally prefers the atmosphere and personal side of traditional gambling outlets. Because these users are somewhat aware of gambling methods, they are not reticent about playing, but their investments of both time and money are typically small. This type of Internet gambler is situational in that they will make bets on high profile events like the Superbowl or American Idol.

- ***Card Sharks:***   The primary focus of these Internet gamblers is card playing. While many are motivated to play online for recreation, this type of Internet gambler may also believe their skills will lead them to turn a profit. Their risk taking can vary from minimal to substantial. Usually, Card Sharks are experienced card players in non-Internet settings. It is suspected that Card Sharks invest large amounts of time on the Internet.

- ***Steamers:***   Initially motivated by recreation, this type of user is attracted to fast-paced, flashy games of limited or no skill. Almost all Steamers have been to a casino before. We suspect that Steamers have a higher likelihood of developing addictions because they have a tendency to "chase" lost bets. Steamers often fall into "bait and switch" schemes as initially free games evolve into expenses. Risk generally starts small and increases.

- *Wi-Fi Trekkers:*   Mobile gambling refers to gambling done on a remote wirelessly connected device. These devices can include wireless tablet PCs, mobile phones, and other nontraditional middle-level networked computing devices. While these users also access the Internet through stationary machines, Wi-Fi Trekkers are accustomed to accessing gambling sites while on the go. Some online casinos and online poker card rooms offer mobile options. In fact, many Trekkers are also Card Sharks. Trekkers often believe that their gambling skills can contribute to their income.

- *Handicappers:*   The primary focus of these gamblers is sport event gambling. Most online Handicappers are veteran sports gamblers. In fact many Handicappers will cast wagers both online and through conventional channels. According to one account, Handicappers wager as much as $6 billion annually through the Internet with about half of all bets originating in the United States (Richtel and Timmons 2006). Almost all handicappers are motivated to gamble because they believe their skills will lead to financial benefits.

- *Fad Gamers:*   Also known as imagination gamblers, these online players place wagers on almost anything. Common bets include wagers on events such as reality shows, various Winner-of-the-Year Awards, etc. The Fad Gamers may also place bets on the stock market, whether a certain stock increases or declines and by how much. Many gamblers of this type are motivated to gamble as a form of entertainment only. Most are situational gamblers stimulated by current events.

It is important to note that these subtypes are not necessarily mutually exclusive and that this list may not be exhaustive. Indeed there is very likely a high degree of blurring between the categories of the abbreviated typology presented here. Moreover, with ever-emerging technologies and gambling innovations available, these characterizations will no doubt evolve. Change may also occur in reaction to social as well as legal responses to Internet gambling.

CONCERNS OVER INTERNET GAMBLING

Internet gambling concerns generally fall in three areas. First, there is concern over whether the individuals or organizations that operate Internet gambling sites are honest and law abiding. Second, there is concern that, even if casino games and operations are run honestly, Internet gambling may appeal to and exploit vulnerable populations (youth, problem gamblers, etc.). A third area of concern involves the regulatory issues that surround the Internet generally. How can a jurisdiction regulate, or perhaps prohibit, Internet gambling in an effective manner? Each of these issues will be dealt with in the following section of the paper.

Organizational Concerns

One of the concerns of both government and individuals is whether the organizations running Internet gambling sites are legitimate. The concern is whether criminal enterprises may be funding and profiting from Internet gambling. This concern recognizes both the huge profits believed available to those running Internet gambling sites and also the historical fact that organized crime for decades profited from illegal gaming operations, such as illegal casinos or numbers operations, and was attracted to Las Vegas in its early years. Clearly, to the extent that Internet gambling is a hugely profitable operation where government oversight is minimal, Internet gambling may be fertile ground for traditional or new Internet-based organized crime organizations.

The honesty of Internet gambling organizations also affects the Internet gambler. Are the games run honestly? Will wins be paid in full and in a timely fashion? Can customers trust that their credit card numbers and other personal information (social security number, bank accounts, gambling activity) will be kept confidential? Griffiths and Parke (2002) note that some of the more unscrupulous companies might embed programs or plant "cookies" on a gambler's home computer. These serve to not only invade one's privacy by gathering information about how one uses the computer but can also steer users to their virtual casino through "free bet" offers or having their Web sites appear regardless of what the user is accessing. The more doubt that potential Internet gamblers have regarding the integrity of the organizations running Internet gambling sites, the less willing they will be to participate in Internet gambling.

The trend clearly appears to be for more established and trusted companies to become involved in Internet gambling. Initially, many casino and other types of betting operations in the United States and elsewhere (England and Australia) opposed Internet gambling as a threat to their established, legitimate betting operations (witness the NGISC recommendation). Many established companies now seem willing to operate Internet gambling sites. For example, many of the legal bookmaking companies in England are operating Internet gambling sites. Similarly, some of the major American casino companies (as Caesar Casinos, Playboy, and MGM Mirage) have planned to launch Internet casino sites (Carter 2002). Even Disney is operating an Internet gaming site (called Skillgames), although Disney differentiates itself from casino gambling by stating that its site, while accepting wagers, will be based on games of skill, such as solving puzzles or winning trivia games, and there will be a $300 limit on monthly wagers (Kurlantzick 2001). Clearly, there is growing interest in Internet betting from both casino and other entertainment companies.

There appears to be at least two reasons for the established gaming and entertainment companies to enter the Internet market. First, it appears that profit potential from Internet gaming is huge. A corporation could choose to build a new casino in Las Vegas for perhaps a billion dollars, or invest considerably less in technology and develop a virtual casino whose payback on a percentage basis is many times that of a brick and mortar casino (Horn 2002). Secondly, many of the companies believe that if they do not offer their customers Internet gambling, they will be at a competitive disadvantage and will lose customers to companies that provide a full range of gambling options (Carter 2002).

Perhaps somewhat paradoxically, to the degree that government is successful in eliminating criminal enterprises from the realm of Internet gambling, the confidence in the legitimacy of the operations is enhanced. The result may be removal of a barrier to many attracted to this form of entertainment and, consequently, further growth of online gambling. Also, as more well-known and trusted companies get in the Internet gambling business, various tie-ins can be established which will further spur business. For example, companies such as Playboy, Hard Rock Cafe, or Caesars can have Internet "players cards," where playing on the Internet can lead to credits and more tangible experiences, such as trips to Playboy Mansions or to Las Vegas or other similar benefits for those who patronize their online casinos (Carter 2002).

Social Concerns

A second major concern about Internet gambling is the social problems that may result from millions of individuals taking advantage of round-the-clock Internet gambling. Although the research is somewhat ambivalent, problem gambling, crime, bankruptcy, suicide, and divorce are some of the problems popularly associated with traditional casino gambling. Countering these perceived negative effects, economic benefits are frequently associated with casinos in the form of added employment, municipal and state tax revenue, and growth in tourism. Internet casinos potentially bring all the problems of traditional casinos with none of the potential benefits.

In addition, Internet casinos are seen as presenting a new set of problems. In casinos, drinking and gambling are often paired activities, as most casinos serve complimentary drinks to those gambling. The practice enhances the enjoyment of the gambling experience for many while benefiting the casino as the alcohol acts to impair the gambler's judgment. State Gaming Control rules, however, prohibit the serving of alcohol to the point of intoxication to protect the gamblers from their own excesses. Gambling within the privacy of one's own home eliminates this check, as gamblers are free to imbibe and gamble to the point of intoxication which would lead to impaired judgment and potentially disastrous gambling losses.

Another social concern that may be exacerbated by Internet gambling is problem gambling. According to the National Gambling Impact Study Commission published in 1999, the societal costs of pathological gambling includes the expenditure of unemployment benefits, physical and mental health problems, bankruptcy, suicide, domestic violence, and child abuse and neglect (NGISC 1999). Research indicates that perhaps 1.6 percent of adults are pathological gamblers while another 3.9 percent are problem gamblers (individuals exhibiting problems with gambling but who are not yet at the most extreme stage) (Shaffer, Hall, and VanderBilt 1999). Although somewhat debatable as to their effectiveness, many casinos have programs, ranging to exclusion, for individuals identified as problem gamblers. Additionally, gambling in a social setting with friends may act as a moderating force for some individuals tempted to engage in problematic gambling. These controls are obviously lacking when one gambles in the privacy of one's own home over the Internet. The anonymity the Internet provides may serve to insulate the gambler from conventional social pressures and free the individual to engage in behaviors unthinkable in a social setting.

In addition, some have argued that the nature of Internet gambling may actually serve to induce more problem gambling than does casino gambling, because "where accessibility of gambling is increased there is an increase not only in the number of regular gamblers but also an increase in the number of problem gamblers" (Griffiths 1999, 266–7). Also, because of the choice of games, many of which can be tailored to one's particular preferences, and because of the speed of the action (not having to wait for other players or an interval in games such as keno or a lottery), the excitement and reinforcement potential of the games are higher than in an actual casino. Furthermore, in a traditional casino setting, players must wait for the dealer to shuffler or reset the game and additional time is spent socializing with other players. Online gambling requires less social interaction and less downtime allowing players to experience instant gratification or especially fast losses (Smith 2004).

Finally, the wagers bet (and lost) on the Internet are even more distant than the betting and losing of casino tokens (Griffiths and Wood 2000). In the casino, it is generally accepted that playing with tokens gives the house an advantage as they are a step removed from players having to physically bet real money, whether coins or currency, which many treat as a precious commodity not to be spent frivolously. Over the Internet, bets are even less tangible than tokens and even more removed from the reality of money as individuals provide a credit card number and may bet over an extended period of time without ever having to confront the fact that significant sums are being lost that will eventually have to be accounted for.

Perhaps the major concern voiced by opponents of Internet gambling is the inability to impose minimum age limits on those gambling. The NGISC (1999), the Federal Trade Commission (FTC Consumer Alert 2002), and Elliot Spitzer (Horn 2002), former Attorney General of the State of New York, have all decried the lack of effective controls. Anyone who has access to a credit card (or credit card number) can log on and register to gamble. A study by the Federal Trade Commission of 100 Internet gambling sites found that few had more than minimal notice of minimum age requirements and none had adequate controls to prevent the underage from gambling online.

Research confirms that the overwhelming majority of youths have engaged in some form of gambling (Ladouceur and Mireault 1988; Lesieur and Klein 1987; Winters, Stinchfield, and Fulderson, 1993; Fisher 1993). Although prohibited, many underaged individuals have also engaged in casino gambling. For example, Arcuri, Lester, and Smith (1985) found that 64 percent of 1,120 high school students in Atlantic City had gambled in a casino. Stitt, Giacopassi, and Vandiver (2000) found that 52 percent of underage students at the University of Nevada, Reno, had casino gambled, and Oster and Knapp (1994) found that 92 percent of the students at the University of Nevada, Las Vegas, under the age of 21 had gambled in a casino, 22 percent doing so weekly. Although research is just beginning to examine Internet gambling and youth, a national survey of 14- to 22-year-olds found that 11 percent of males had gambled over the Internet, a figure that is a dramatic increase from even a few years ago (Tresniowski 2003).

Griffiths and Wood (2000) note that Internet gambling potentially poses a greater threat to young people than to other segments of the population. They note that youth appear more susceptible to becoming problem gamblers and may experiment with online gambling in the same way they experiment with alcohol, drugs, or other delinquent activities during adolescence. In addition, their familiarity with computers and Internet technology almost certainly surpasses many of their elders and may serve to make them more comfortable in engaging in Internet gambling. Griffiths and Wood note similarities between video game playing and video gambling and also note that the Internet may provide an alternate reality for many adolescents who are experienced with video games and chat rooms. These factors combined with others, such as poor grades and the seeking of escape or an alternate reality, serve as risk factors for adolescent males in particular (Griffiths and Wood 2000).

Finally, it is important to consider the effect of Internet gambling on lost state tax revenues. Hammer (2001) provides an analysis of the tax losses due to Internet gambling. Based on Illinois riverboat gambling taxes and estimates of the total Internet bets from the United States that might reasonably be from Illinois, he concludes that the state loses millions of dollars annually as a result of Internet gambling. This estimate does not take into account lost employment and losses in revenue from ancillary services that casinos and casino gamblers normally purchase. Overall, Hammer concludes that the lost revenue is staggering. This loss of revenue undoubted has an impact on basic government services and an additional undetermined negative social impact.

Regulatory Issues

Since the origin of Internet gambling in 1995, legal scholars have been debating the legality of various aspects of Internet gambling (Masoud 2004). The National Gambling Impact Study Commission noted in 1999 that "the legalities of gambling in cyberspace are unclear" (1999, 27). Federal prosecutors, however, have been moving decisively to limit Internet gambling. In 2004, over $3 million was seized from Discovery Communications, a media company that had accepted the money from a Costa Rica–based Internet gambling company. The money was to be used to advertise an Internet gambling site legally operating in Costa Rica. Prosecutors contended that media companies, by advertising Internet gambling, were aiding and abetting an activity illegal in the United States (Richtel 2004). Although prosecution of a company for advertising Internet gambling was an untested legal theory, it served to send a message to media outlets that by accepting ads from Internet companies involved in gaming, the media companies were placing themselves in legal jeopardy.

In an escalation of enforcement efforts, in July 2006, federal authorities arrested David Carruthers, a British citizen and the chief executive of BetOnSports, an Internet gambling company listed on the London stock exchange, while he was changing planes at the Dallas airport. Although Internet gambling is legal in England, by landing on American soil, he was subject to arrest for violating U.S. law prohibiting the taking of Internet bets from Americans. Prosecutors indicated that, as a result of a 22 count indictment, they would seek a $4.5 billion penalty against the company and its executives (Richtel 2006).

In September 2006, a second British-based Internet gambling executive was arrested. This time, Peter Dicks, chief executive of Sportingbet, was arrested at Kennedy Airport in New York by agents of the Port Authority of New York, executing an arrest warrant issued by the state police in Louisiana (Richtel and Crampton 2006). Louisiana is one of nine states that prohibit some form of Internet gambling (New Media Age 2006).

The effect of these arrests and threatened future arrests was to send a message to executives of Internet gambling companies that Internet gambling is illegal in the United States and for the executives to stay out of the United States. However, because their businesses are legal in the countries where they are based, the arrests did not prevent the continued operation of the companies from their home soil or their operation in most of the world.

Until 2006, the legality of Americans gambling on the World Wide Web was obscured by the federal government attempting to limit or prohibit Internet gambling through the use of outmoded laws. The Wire Act passed by Congress in 1961 was the primary legal instrument used to attempt to limit Internet gambling. The Wire Act, however, was written to hinder the organized crime activity of bookies who typically took horse race or sports bets over the telephone. Consequently, federal regulation of "wire communication" was specified in the law. Legal scholars doubted whether such terminology could be applied to the technology inherent in Internet gambling and also skeptical that the forms of gambling covered by the Wire Act could be applied to the myriad forms of gambling now available on the Internet.

To remedy this confusion in the law, Representative James Leach of Iowa had for several years sponsored a bill to specifically curtail Internet gambling. A variety of business interests opposed the law and had successfully blocked its passage. A prior version of the bill passed the House in 1999 but failed in the Senate due largely to the influence of discredited lobbyist Jack Abramoff. In September of 2006, however, the Unlawful Internet Gambling Enforcement Act was attached to the Security and Accountability for Every Port Act of 2006 (known as the

SAFE Port Act). The SAFE Port Act was enacted to provide security at the nation's ports to prevent terrorists from shipping into the United States materials, such as nuclear or radioactive substances, that could harm the health or welfare of the nation. The bill passed with minimum attention paid to the Internet gambling provisions attached to the harbor protection plan. Those who opposed prohibition of Internet gambling did not believe they could vote against a politically popular port security bill and the law passed with overwhelming support.

The Unlawful Internet Gambling Enforcement Act makes it a felony for banks and other financial institutions (such as credit card companies) to transfer funds to unlawful Internet gambling sites that engage in poker, sports betting, or casino-type gaming (blackjack, slots). Since the act prohibits funding illegal Internet gambling, it remains legal to engage in those forms of Internet gambling permitted under state or other federal law. It remains legal in some instances to buy lottery tickets, play keno, place bets through off-track betting on horse races, and to participate in fantasy sports leagues. The Internet betting activities that remain legal have been permitted by various states and remain legal under the federal law.

The focus of the federal Internet prohibition law is not on individual gamblers but on the businesses that process the financial transactions necessary to run the various Internet gambling Web sites. These legitimate financial institutions are required to identify and block payments or money transfers relating to unlawful Internet gambling.

The possible penalties against legitimate banking and credit card companies found in violation of the Unlawful Internet Gambling Enforcement Act could be formidable. Prosecutors would have a range of options, including threats of prosecution under the Racketeer Influenced Corrupt Organizations (RICO) Act. The RICO Act was originally formulated to aid in prosecution of organized crime by allowing long prison sentences, seizure of personal assets derived from illegal activities, and forfeiture of company assets used to violate the law (Schmalleger 2006).

Immediately after passage of the federal law against Internet gambling, the impact on the industry was evident. Several of the Internet gambling companies announced that they would take measures to prohibit Americans from gambling on their Web sites. Since Americans accounted for a large proportion of the worldwide revenue, with 8 million Americans betting $6 billion annually on the Internet (Richtel and Timmons 2006), the stocks in these companies plummeted as the industry's future prospects darkened. Banks, such as Citibank, Bank of America, and Wells Fargo, and credit card companies such as Visa had already announced they would no longer process transactions involving Internet gambling (Rose 2003).

Without the gamblers being able to use credit cards or use sites such as PayPal to deposit funds or pay debts owed to betting sites, Internet gambling cannot exist as a major industry. Easy access to a transferable currency is essential for the industry to thrive. Although the Unlawful Internet Gambling Enforcement Act appears to provide prosecutors with a powerful new tool to curtail Internet gambling, questions remain as to both its legality and possible effectiveness.

PROBLEMS/FEASIBILITY OF ATTEMPTING TO LIMIT INTERNET GAMBLING

The United States is attempting to limit its citizens' Internet gambling by choking off the financial transactions that are the lifeblood of the gambling industry. The focus is on the companies running the gambling sites and the peripheral industries (financial and media) that support or promote Internet gambling.

This strategy of focusing on the providers of a disapproved product or service and those who profit from its purchase, rather than the consumers or users of the service, is a classic description of traditional vice enforcement. Law enforcement traditionally focused on prostitutes and pimps rather than those who procured their services, on the illegal gambling houses and numbers operators rather than the gamblers themselves, on the purveyors of obscene materials rather than the consumers of the pornography.

While there are legal questions as to the adequacy of the laws attempting to accomplish these tasks, their legality, and how effective they will be in dissuading Internet gamblers from continuing to gamble, there are a host of other questions surrounding the anti-Internet gambling crusade.

Since Internet gambling is legal in a multitude of countries around the world, the attempts to limit Americans' access to the gambling sites and to prosecute foreign nationals from engaging in a business legal in their own countries becomes subject to international law. In a number of small Caribbean countries, the employment and taxes from the Internet gambling companies are significant to their economies. Consequently, Antigua and Barbuda have accused the United States of restraint of trade in the World Trade Organization. They argue that laws that make it difficult for Americans to transfer funds to partake in a legal activity in the source nation violate various trade agreements. The World Trade Organization has not issued a conclusive ruling, but some believe that the United States is on a "collision course" with other nations over Internet gambling (Batt 2006).

Even if the U.S. position is ruled legal in the international arena, there are numerous questions as to the ability of a single government to limit the Internet's uses. In testimony before the National Gambling Impact Study Commission, Tom Bell listed several reasons why an American prohibition against Internet gambling would be ineffective. First, he argued that the "open architecture" of the Internet and that continual technological advances insure that any prohibition would be futile. Second, he stated that the Internet's world-wide scope and ability to transfer data from place to place make it easy to detour around any country's prohibition. Bell notes that it takes only one country to provide a "safe harbor" to enable Internet applications prohibited elsewhere to flourish. He compares Internet communications to letters sent through the postal service. If the service is available, it becomes nearly impossible to control the content of the messages. Lastly, it should be noted that Internet gambling is a $5 billion industry, accounting for 4.3 percent of all e-commerce (Parke and Griffiths 2004). Bell concludes that the financial incentives combined with consumer demand will almost certainly ensure that prohibition will not succeed (Bell 1998).

Bell believes that aggressive law enforcement against Internet gambling companies will not succeed and will have the effect of insuring that the business activity, employment, and tax benefits accrue overseas. Further, the more that established and legitimate companies are threatened for engaging in any activity connected with Internet gambling, the more opportunity it provides for marginal and perhaps unethical companies to enter the field and reap tremendous profits (Bell 1998; Parke and Griffiths 2004). The combination of consumer demand and legal prohibition for goods or services has traditionally been an invitation for organized crime organizations to flourish. Some Internet gambling companies are already seeking to disguise credit card transactions through use of "ghost" intermediary firms so that payments are not flagged and identified as associated with Internet gambling (Parke and Griffiths 2004).

Given the demand for the product and the amount of money at stake, some companies are skirting the legal boundaries by arguing that games of skill are in a different legal category than are games of chance. Companies such as Disney have introduced a "Skillgames" Web site where players pay to play and possibly win prizes based on their skill. These sites are attempting to take a middle ground between Internet sites that allow games to be played for free and gambling sites where individuals risk money on games of chance.

Among the most popular forms of Internet gambling are the poker sites. These sites are viewed as a form of traditional gambling and therefore prohibited under law. The PartyPoker Web site was among the most popular of all betting Web sites, having had 7.5 million users in September 2006. After the law prohibiting companies from handling financial transactions went into effect, the number of users dropped to 2.5 million the following month (Ahrens 2006). An organization called "Poker Players Alliance," which claims 100,000 members, has formed to lobby for changes in the law to allow poker online (Berton 2006).

Another complication in the prohibition of Internet gambling in the United States is that some Native American tribes, already successful in operation of traditional casinos on tribal land, see an opportunity to initiate Internet gambling from their reservations. Once again, there are conflicting ideas on whether these activities by Native Americans would be subject to the Unlawful Internet Gambling Enforcement Act. One tribe is considering making the legal question even more complicated by applying for a license in a Caribbean nation, where Internet operations are legal, thereby adding additional layers to the legal puzzle (Rose 2000). Finally, state laws are, at this point, inconsistent. Rose (2001) notes that some state laws passed in the 1800's are being utilized to regulate Internet gambling in the twenty-first century.

Britain's culture secretary has compared America's approach to Internet gambling as reminiscent of America's approach to alcohol during Prohibition. By attempting to prohibit a popular activity rather than regulating it, a lawless environment that encourages disrespect for law seems likely. The offshore Internet companies become the equivalent of the "speakeasies" of prohibition, operating outside the law in a totally unregulated environment (Wardell 2006).

One of the dangers of prohibiting Internet gambling is that it provides a fertile ground for those willing to violate the law. Abadinsky (1985) observed, "Organized crime evolved out of moralistic laws that created opportunity for certain innovative actors. As circumstances changed, so did available opportunity, and organized crime proved quite dynamic" (p. 322). In the modern world, Internet access and expertise are worldwide. Given the chance, few doubt that criminal syndicates will form and attempt to take advantage of the opportunity presented by the Unlawful Internet Gambling Act of 2006. From a law enforcement perspective it is clear that cyber crime is difficult to detect and investigate, making the enforcement of such laws problematic (Grant and Terry 2005).

Bell (1998) argues that a more practical strategy than prohibition and criminalization is regulation. By permitting legitimate and established corporations open to public scrutiny to participate in Internet gambling, the government would have more control over the activity. It could insure fairness in the gambling activity and payments to and from bettors. It would also allow better compliance with regulations concerning who is allowed to gamble, providing at least some measure of control of under-age gambling. Regulation would also provide opportunities for American companies to benefit from the huge profit potential of Internet gambling. Several U.S. companies, including MGM and Harrah's Entertainment, have lobbied for regulating and taxing Internet gambling (Benston 2006).

Andrle (2004) contends that an effective mechanism can be developed to both control underage and problem gambling while enabling American companies and the American government to raise revenue. He believes a regulatory schema, such as Australia's Queensland Interactive Gambling Player Protection Act, is viable and much more beneficial than prohibition in controlling the multitude of potential problems associated with Internet gambling.

CONCLUSION

The question of whether online gambling builds on an existing urge to gamble, or creates one, will require additional investigation. Similarly, an objective assessment of the pros and cons of Internet gambling cannot yet be made.

However, judging by the popularity of traditional forms of gambling in the United States, it is apparent that gambling is widely accepted by Americans as a legitimate form of recreation. Given this, is the attempt to prohibit Internet gambling a laudable attempt to save Americans from exposure to the "crack cocaine" of gambling, or is it a misguided and doomed-to-fail crusade to impose on society a moral standard not accepted by a large proportion of the population?

Internet gambling can now be added to the list of other offenses in the "victimless crime" debate that includes a variety of traditional vices subject to law enforcement, including other forms of gambling, drug use, prostitution, and pornography. The appropriateness and effectiveness of laws against Internet gambling will continue to be debated, along with the other offenses in the victimless crime category.

The nature of the debate on vice control is familiar: should government have the right to regulate personal conduct, even if the conduct is freely chosen, when the conduct has the potential to harm the individual and possibly the wider society? A corollary to this question is can the government, assuming it has the right to prohibit the disapproved behavior, be effective in its enforcement efforts? Alternately, if it is shown that prohibition is not effective and that government cannot exert reasonable control over the presumed deleterious behavior, is it more socially beneficial to license, tax, and regulate?

Internet gambling is even newer than the Internet. As such, it is in a formative stage with dimensions yet undiscovered. The answers to the questions posed above may well affect millions of people for better or worse. One thing we do know is that traditional ways of thinking about gambling are no longer sufficient. When lotteries run every minute, when person-to-person Internet gambling is increasingly prevalent, and when a form of betting on hybrid games of skill is promoted by Disney, it is clear that we are entering a brave new world that presents new challenges for governments and governmental agencies whose task is to enforce the law, whether it entails prohibition or regulation.

KEY TERMS

Internet gambling
Victimless crimes

REFERENCES

Abadinsky, H. 1985. *Organized Crime.* Chicago: Nelson Hall.

Andrle, J. 2004. A winning hand: A proposal for an international regulatory schema with respect to the growing online gambling dilemma in the United States. *Vanderbilt Journal of Transnational Law* 37 (5): 1389–422.

Arcuri, A. F., D. Lester, and F. O. Smith. 1985. Shaping adolescent gambling behavior. *Adolescence* 20 (80): 935–8.

Batt, T. 2006. Lawyer: Net ban violates WTO ruling. *Gaming News.* Retrieved October 9, 2006, from casinocitytimes.com

Bedau, H. A. 1974. "A world without punishment." In *Punishment and Human Rights,* edited by M. Goldinger. Rochester, VT: Schenkman Books, Inc.

Bell, T. May 21, 1998. Congressional testimony, Internet gambling: prohibition v. legalization. Retrieved December 16, 2006, from http://www.cato.org

Benston, L. October 3, 2006. New gambling law could land hard on big gaming companies. *Las Vegas Sun.* Retrieved December 17, 2006, from LexisNexis.

Bentley, R. March 29, 2001. Are web wagers addictive? You bet! *Computer Weekly*: 115.

Berton, J. August 27, 2006. On-line poker players face new prohibition. *San Francisco Chronicle.* Retrieved August 27, 2006, from http://sfgate.com

Cabot, A., and M. Balestra. 2003. *Internet Gambling Report.* 6th ed. St. Louis: The River City Group.

Carter, B. July 18, 2002. Wheel of fortune. *New Media Age*: 29.

CCA. 2007. Internet gambling estimates. Retrieved January 5, 2007, from Christiansen Capital Advisors at http://www.cca-i.com

Clotfelter, C. T., and P. J. Cook. 1989. *Selling Hope: State Lotteries in America.* Cambridge: Harvard University Press.

Devereux, E. C. 1968. Gambling. *International Encyclopedia of the Social Sciences* 6: 53–62.

Fisher, S. 1993. Gambling and pathological gambling in adolescents. *Journal of Gambling Studies* 9 (3): 277–88.

FTC Consumer Alert. June 26, 2002. Online gambling and kids: A bad bet. Federal Trade Commission. www.ftc.gov/gamble

Goode, E. 1984. *Deviant Behavior.* Englewood Cliffs, NJ: Prentice Hall.

Government Accounting Office. 2002. Internet gambling: An overview of the issues. GAO-03-89. Washington DC: U.S. Government Accounting Office.

Grant, H., and K. Terry. 2005. *Law Enforcement in the 21st Century.* Boston: Pearson.

Griffiths, M. 1999. Gambling technologies: Prospects for problem gambling. *Journal of Gambling Studies* 15 (3): 265–83.

Griffiths, M. 2001. Internet gambling: Preliminary results of the first UK prevalence study. *Electron Journal of Gambling Issues.* Retrieved from www.camh.net/egambling/issue5

Griffiths, M., and J. Parke. 2002. The social impact of internet gambling. *Social Science Computer Review* 30 (3): 312–20.

Griffiths, M., and R. Wood. 2000. Risk factors in adolescence: The case of gambling, videogame playing, and the internet. *Journal of Gambling Studies* 16 (2/3): 199–225.

Hammer, R. 2001. Does internet gambling strengthen the economy? Don't bet on it. *Federal Communications Law Journal* 54 (1): 103–29.

Hayano, D. M. 1984. The professional gambler: Fame, fortune and failure. *Annals of the American Academy of Political and Social Science* 474: 157–67.

Horn, J. October 28, 2002. Point and bet: Internet gambling's explosive growth has made it the Web's killer app. Now critics are trying to pull the plug. *Newsweek*: 50.

Ialomiteanu, A., and E. Adlaf. 2001. Internet gambling among Ontario adults. *Electronic Journal of Gambling Issues.* Retrieved from www.camh.net/egambling/issue5

Jay, R. 2003. A profile of the online gambler. Center for Gambling Research, University of Nevada Las Vegas. Retrieved from http://gaming.unlv.edu/reading/online_profile.pdf

Kurlantzick, J. May 28, 2001. Disney's risky bet. *U.S. News & World Report* 130 (21): 38.

Ladd, G., and N. Petry. 2002. Disordered gambling among university-based medical and dental patients: A focus on internet gambling. *Psychology of Addictive Behaviors* 16 (1): 76–9.

Ladouceur, R., and C. Mereault. 1988. Gambling behaviors among high school students in the Quebec Area. *Journal of Gambling Studies* 4 (1): 3–12.

Lesieur, H., and S. Blume. 1987. The South Oaks Gambling Screen (SOGS): A new instrument for the identification of pathological gamblers. *American Journal of Psychiatry* 144: 1184–8.

Lesieur, H., and R. Klein. 1987. Pathological gambling among high school students. *Addictive Behaviors* 12: 129–35.

Masoud, S. 2004. The offshore quandary: The impact of domestic regulations on licensed offshore gambling companies. *Whittier Law Review* 25 (4): 989–1004.

National Gambling Impact Study Commission. 1999. Final Report. Retrieved January 12, 2007, from http://govinfo.library.unt.edu/ngisc/reports/finrpt.html

New Media Age. 2001. Ladbrokes lottery draw pulls in over 200,000 clients a day. Retrieved December 17, 2006 from LexisNexis.

New Media Age. October 30, 2006. What the unlawful internet gambling enforcement act of 2006 means. Retrieved December 17, 2006, from LexisNexis.

NORC. 1999. Gambling impact and behavior study. Report to the National Impact Gambling Study Commission. National Opinion Research Center at the University of Chicago.

Oster, S., and T. Knapp. June 1994. Casino gambling by underage patrons: Two studies of a university student population. Paper presented at the Ninth International Conference on Gambling and Risk-Taking, Las Vegas, NV.

Parke, A., and M. Griffiths. 2004. Why internet prohibition will ultimately fail. *Gaming Law Review* 8 (5): 295–99.

Petry, N., and S. Mallya. 2001. Gambling participation and problems among health center employees. Unpublished paper cited in Ladd & Petry, 2002.

Pew Internet and American Life Project. 2006. Retrieved December 22, 2006, from http://www.pewinternet.org

Richtel, M. May 31, 2004. U.S. steps up push against online casinos by seizing cash. *New York Times.* Retrieved May 31, 2004, from http://www.nytimes.com

Richtel, M. August 11, 2006. BetOnSports, after indictment, folds its hand and shifts focus to Asia. *New York Times.* Retrieved August 11, 2006, from http://www.nytimes.com

Richtel, M., and T. Carampton. September 8, 2006. Arrest of second major online gambling figure is a first for state officials. *New York Times.* Retrieved January 12, 2007, from http://www.nytimes.com

Richtel, M., and H. Timmons. July 25, 2006. The gambling is virtual; the money is real. *New York Times.* Retrieved July 25, 2006, from http://www.nytimes.com

Rose, I. N. 2000. Indian nations and internet gambling. Center for Gaming Research, University of Nevada, Las Vegas. Retrieved December 15, 2006, from http://gaming.unlv.edu

Rose, I. N. 2001. Why Disney won't take bets from Vermont. Center for Gaming Research, University of Nevada, Las Vegas. Retrieved December 15, 2006, from http://gaming.unlv.edu

Rose, I. N. 2003. Why Visa is dropping online gambling. Center for Gaming Research, University of Nevada, Las Vegas. Retrieved December 15, 2006, from http://gaming.unlv.edu

Schmalleger, F. 2006. *Criminology Today.* Upper Saddle River, NJ: Pearson/Prentice Hall.

Schur, E. 1965. *Crimes Without Victims.* Englewood Cliffs, NJ: Prentice Hall.

Scimecca, J. A. 1971. A typology of the gambler. *International Journal of Contemporary Sociology* 8 (1): 56–71.

Shaffer, H., M. Hall, and J. VanderBilt. 1997. *Estimating the Prevalence of Disordered Gambling Behavior in the United States and Canada: A Meta-Analysis*. Kansas City, Missouri: National Center for Responsible Gaming.

Skolnick, J., and J. Dombrink. 1978. The legalization of deviance. *Criminology* 16 (2): 193–208.

Smith, A. D. 2004. Controversial and emerging issues associated with cybergambling (e-casinos). *Online Information Review* 28 (6): 435–43.

Stitt, B. G. 1988. Victimless crimes: A definitional issue. *Journal of Crime and Justice* 11 (2): 87–102.

Stitt, B. G., D. Giacopassi, and M. Vandiver. 2000. A minor concern? Underage casino gambling and the law. *Social Science Journal* 37 (3): 361–73.

Tresniowski, A. 2003. Gambling online: How to go deep into debt without ever leaving your living room. *People Weekly* 60 (October 13): 119–21.

Wardell, J. October 27, 2006. Britain attacks U.S. online gambling ban. *AP Business Wire*. Accessed December 15, 2006.

Winters, K., R. Stinchfield, and J. Fulderson. 1993. Patterns and characteristics of adolescent gambling. *Journal of Gambling Studies* 9 (4): 371–86.

Wykes, A. 1964. *The Complete Illustrated Guide to Gambling*. Garden City, NY: Doubleday.

Yures, E. 2002. Gambling on the internet: The states risk playing economic roulette as the Internet gambling industry spins onward. *Rutgers Computer & Technology Law Journal* 28 (1): 34+.

PART IV

Investigating and Prosecuting Cyber Crimes

Chapter 22

Investigating Computer Crime

Sameer Hinduja
Florida Atlantic University

Sameer Hinduja, **Ph.D.**, is an assistant professor in the Department of Criminology and Criminal Justice at Florida Atlantic University. He received his Ph.D. and MS in criminal justice from Michigan State University and his BS in criminal justice (with a minor in legal studies) from the University of Central Florida Honors College. He studies various forms of computer-related deviance and crime from both social and technological perspectives, and works nationally and internationally with school districts, law enforcement, and the private sector toward its understanding and response. He has written one book and his interdisciplinary research is widely published in a number of academic journals. He can be reached via email at hinduja@fau.edu.

Abstract

Many traditional crimes are now being aided or abetted through the use of computers and networks, and wrongdoing previously never imagined has surfaced because of the incredible capabilities of information systems. Computer crimes are requiring law enforcement departments in general and criminal investigators in particular to tailor an increasing amount of their efforts toward successfully identifying, apprehending, and assisting in the successful prosecution of perpetrators. In the following text, key research findings in the area of traditional American criminal investigations are summarized. Similarities and differences between traditional and computer crime investigations are then presented, and consequent implications are discussed. Pragmatic suggestions as to how American computer crime investigative task forces can most competently fulfill their intended objectives are given in conclusion via a hypothetical example of a specialized unit. It is hoped that past knowledge can be assimilated with current observations of computer-related criminality to inform and guide the science of police investigations in the future.

INTRODUCTION

Criminal **investigation** has been a topic of study for academics and practitioners alike, and is defined as "the process of legally gathering evidence of a crime that has been or is being committed" (Brown 2001, 3). It seeks to identify the truths associated with how and why a

This article was originally published in volume 1, issue 1, of the *International Journal of Cyber Criminology*. A special thanks goes out to Dr. K. Jaishankar, Editor in Chief of the journal. The article was originally published under the title *Computer Crime Investigations in the United States: Leveraging Knowledge from the Past to Address the Future*. http://www.cybercrimejournal.co.nr/

crime occurred, and works toward building a case that may lead to the successful prosecution of the offender(s). Many research studies have sought to determine the best way in which the investigative process can be conducted and managed. The overarching goal of these studies has been to enable police departments to reflect upon their own practices against the backdrop of the findings, and then to implement salient positive changes which would improve the day-to-day operations of their organization. Practices of investigation have been modified and refined over the years, taking into account changes in social, political, economic, and scientific domains. These practices have infused "science" into an activity that was once primarily considered an "art" (Beveridge 1957), and have consequently enhanced the investigative process.

In his law of insertion, Gabriel Tarde ([1890] 1903) asserted that novel forms of criminal behavior are fostered through the superimposing of new practices onto traditional ones, often through technological advances or innovation. Due to the exponential growth of information technology in modern society, many traditional crimes are now being aided or abetted through the use of computers and networks, and criminality heretofore never conceived has surfaced because of the incredible capabilities of information systems. These **computer crimes**[1] will require **law enforcement** departments in general and criminal investigators in particular to tailor an increasing amount of their effort toward successfully identifying, apprehending, and assisting in the successful prosecution of perpetrators.

In order to develop a sound strategy in this regard, it is crucial to learn from past research in the area of investigations, and to incorporate into law enforcement organizations those policies deemed most fruitful. In the following text, a summary of the two most important studies on traditional investigations in America is presented for the purposes of providing a historical and comparative position. Next, the similarities and differences between traditional and computer crime investigations are given, and consequent implications are discussed in terms of: the role of the first-responding officer and investigator(s); information, instrumentation, and interviewing; evidence collection and processing; jurisdictional issues; reactive and proactive strategies; and utility of symbolic investigations. The current work concludes with some pragmatic suggestions as to how computer crime investigative task forces should be created and managed to competently fulfill their intended objectives. This is presented via a hypothetical example of a specialized unit.

SEMINAL RESEARCH ON INVESTIGATIONS

RAND Study of Criminal Investigation

In the 1970s, the RAND Corporation in the United States conducted a nationwide study of criminal investigations by law enforcement departments with over 150 sworn officers or serving a population over 100,000. Through analyses of various agencies with differing investigative philosophies, comparison with official crime statistics to determine investigative efficacy,

---

[1]The focus of this chapter is on investigations of: (1) traditional crimes in which a computer is used in an ancillary manner, and (2) nontraditional or high-tech crimes in which a computer is the primary object of, instrument in, or repository of evidence related to, a crime.

and a review of detailed case studies, a comprehension of how agencies managed and organized investigations was sought. Four main conclusions were set forth:

1. *Case solution:* The most important determinant of case solution was the information provided to the responding officer by the victim (Greenwood, Chaiken, and Petersilia 1977). It was also discovered that follow-up investigations were largely ineffective. Specifically, if the victim was not able to provide identifying information of the perpetrator, it was unlikely that apprehension would result. The importance of the responding officer highlighted the need for well-trained patrol personnel with a larger investigative role, who are then singularly capable of closing many cases rather than turning them over to another person (see also Block and Weidman 1975; Greenberg et al. 1977). As a consequence, this would allow specialized investigative forces to address only those incidents that absolutely require expert abilities, and would keep their caseload to a manageable size.

2. *Investigative effectiveness:* Differences in investigative organization, training, staffing, workloads, and procedures did not proportionately affect crime rates, arrest rates, or clearance rates.

3. *The processing of physical evidence:* While law enforcement departments collected a great deal of physical evidence, much of it was not processed in an effective manner. As such, the suggested policy involved the allocation of more resources to the processing of collected evidence, which would thereby have a positive impact on crime solving.

4. *Investigative thoroughness:* Investigators were generally failing to thoroughly document all of the important evidentiary facts that would strengthen the ability of prosecutors to obtain the most appropriate convictions. Incompleteness in documentation, it was argued, may have contributed to an increase in the number of case dismissals and a weakening in the plea bargaining position of prosecutors (Greenwood et al. 1977). This deficiency in comprehensive recordkeeping necessitated immediate attention.

PERF Study on the Investigation of Burglary and Robbery

In another important study led by John Eck under the auspices of the Police Executive Research Forum (PERF), more than 3,360 burglary and 320 robbery investigations over a 2-year period were analyzed in three jurisdictions: DeKalb County, Georgia; St. Petersburg, Florida; and Wichita, Kansas. The PERF study differed from the earlier research by RAND in that it focused on the entire investigative process, rather than only on the cases cleared by arrest. As such, Eck was able to determine the impact of a host of variables which affected the outcome to disproportionate degrees.

A primary finding was that both detectives and patrol officers contributed equally to the solving of cases, and that it was a disservice to emphasize one over the other (Eck 1983). The research also found that individuals in both positions should be less reliant on information provided by the victim and more proactive in exploring leads provided by others related to the incident (Eck 1983). The practice of neighborhood canvassing and the use of informants were asserted as important techniques to increase the effectiveness of investigations. It appeared that while most information came from the victims of the crime during the initial police response, much of those leads were unfruitful. When other sources were consulted, however, much more useful information was discovered.

The necessity of being sensitive to victims was also underscored by Eck, who asserted the relative uselessness of reinterviewing the victim during follow-up investigations. Physical evidence was found to be most useful to corroborate preexisting identifications rather than as a means to identify suspects who were previously unknown (Sanders 1977; Wilson 1976). Cooperation, information sharing, and information management among police departments were also extolled as key factors in successful investigations (Eck 1983).

One of the most practical recommendations to stem from Eck's study concerned the categorization of cases into three groups—those that could be solved, those that have been solved, and those that may be solved through some effort (Brown 2001). This "triage system" was devised to assist law enforcement personnel in making objective decisions as to which cases were worthy of resource expenditure. Through this form of case screening, investigations could proceed in a targeted and informed manner after determining the presence of certain solvability factors that would most likely lead to a case clearance. In addition, this procedure also allowed law enforcement to tailor their efforts toward the small group of habitual offenders or "career criminals" who commit the majority of serious crimes (Wolfgang, Figlio, and Sellin 1972). Eck felt that these recommended changes would go a long way in refining the process and improving its utility and success rate.

From these two intensive research endeavors in the United States, some important lessons can be learned. First, the role of the responding officer is crucial in investigations, and oftentimes the information provided to him or her is the deciding factor in solving a case. Additionally, it appears that expanding the breadth of investigations by exploring other avenues of information acquisition may prove valuable, as informative qualitative data can be gained in this manner. Allocating resources only to those cases most likely to be solved is another wise strategy that law enforcement departments can employ. Finally, thoroughness in evidentiary documentation is seemingly critical to building a strong case and increasing the likelihood of a successful conviction by the prosecuting team.

DEFINITIONAL DIFFERENCES

As mentioned, investigative practices and procedures for both traditional crimes and highly developed forms of computer crime are similar in many respects simply because of a recursive process inherent in the modification of traditional crimes through innovation or technological development (Tarde [1890] 1903). Nonetheless, vital differences exist in the investigative process, and these must be accommodated to best address computer crime. These differences are largely revealed by the definitional distinctions therein.

Traditional crimes generally concern personal or property offenses that law enforcement has continued to combat for centuries—such as the Type I offenses of the FBI's Uniform Crime Report in the United States. *Nontraditional crimes*, for the purposes of the current work, encompass those involving a computer. These historically have not received a proportionate amount of attention as compared to traditional crimes, despite their gravity and the substantive harm they often cause (Braithwaite 1985; Hinduja 2004; Newman and

Clarke 2003; Parker 1976; Rosoff, Pontell, and Tillman 2002; Webster 1980). Furthermore, they do not elicit the same visceral and emotionally charged reaction from the American public and political system as do the conventional personal and property crimes that **police** largely work to address (Benson, Cullen, and Maakestad 1990; Cullen, Link, and Polanzi 1982). Since these entities significantly influence the policies and actions of the U.S. criminal justice system, the result is a comparatively small amount of effort and resources allocated for computer crime.

Computer crime has been defined as "any illegal act fostered or facilitated by a computer, whether the computer is an object of a crime, an instrument used to commit a crime, or a repository of evidence related to a crime" (Royal Canadian Mounted Police 2000; Wallace, Lusthaus, and Kim 2005). Some of the most prominent types include e-commerce fraud (Philippsohn 2001; Tan 2005), child pornography trafficking (O'Grady 2001; Taylor and Quayel 2003), software piracy (Hinduja 2001, 2003), and network security breaches (Power 2000; Reames 2000). Investigative difficulties are introduced when attempting to tackle computer crime because of its generally technologically advanced nature, the fact that it can occur almost instantaneously, and because it is extremely difficult to observe, detect, or track (Leibowitz 1999; United Nations 1994; Wittes 1994). These problems are compounded by the relative anonymity afforded by the **Internet** as well as the transcendence of geographical and physical limitations in cyberspace, both of which render difficult the detection of criminals who are able to take advantage of a virtually limitless pool of victims.

APPLICATION AND EXTENSION TO COMPUTER CRIME

A multitude of aspects related to investigations are necessarily implicated when considering how traditional practices must be modified, augmented, or even restructured to compensate for differences inherent in computer crime. While there is no panacea, it appears that acknowledging and accommodating the following points will result in greater investigative efficacy when addressing **high-technology** wrongdoing. Before proceeding, though, it must be stated that while this work specifically concentrates on investigations of computer crime, some examples of white-collar crime that can occur through the use of computer systems are presented to support the assertions.

Role of the First-Responding Officer

As previously stated, one of the most important findings of the RAND study concerned the role of patrol officers who first respond to a crime scene. It was suggested that these first responders be granted additional investigatory responsibilities to ease the caseload burdens of specialized investigators, and because their initial presence on the scene often gave them information to use as leads to explore (see e.g., Block and Weidman 1975; Greenberg et al. 1977). By extension, the role of the first-responding law enforcement officer in computer crime cases is of critical import because the evidence associated with a computer crime is often intangible in nature. Certain precautions must be taken to ensure that data stored on a system or on removable media is not modified or deleted—either intentionally or accidentally (Lyman 2002; Parker 1976). Even the simple shutting-down of a computer can change the last-modified or last-accessed timestamp of certain system files, which introduces questions associated with the integrity of the data. In sum, to preclude vulnerabilities in the prosecutor's case and to adequately defend against any related challenges, grave care must be exercised by first responders during the search and seizure of computer equipment (Wallace, Lusthaus, and Kim 2005).

Depicting some parallels to the subject matter at hand is the collection of hair, bodily fluids, and clothing samples from which DNA is extracted. They have no obvious use or meaning until a criminalistics expert analyzes them and consequently determines their forensic significance. Once cogent knowledge and proof is obtained from these samples by properly trained personnel, however, the investigation and its attendant efforts toward achieving **justice** are often simplified. In a similar vein, specialized skills must be taught to first-responding officers who might encounter technological evidence, which on the surface may appear meaningless, but upon further analyses by computer forensic examiners might prove crucial in clearing a case.

Role of the Investigator

The research of Greenwood et al. (1977) stated that over 50 percent of traditional street crimes are solved based on information provided to the responding officer by the victim(s), and that in cases where incomplete or unusable information is provided by a victim, most are not subsequently solved through investigative efforts. Other research has likewise shown that little is gained through police effort to aid in offender apprehension following the commission of a crime (Block and Bell 1976; Skogan and Antunes 1979). Indeed, Skogan and Antunes (1979, 223) have specifically stated that "investigatory follow-up work, the gathering of physical evidence, and the ferreting out of criminals through detective work, play a relatively unimportant role in identifying and apprehending offenders."

Nonetheless, the role of the investigator in computer crime cases will be much more important in clearance and arrest rates than information presented to him or her by the responding officer, victims, or witnesses. Due to the veiled nature of the techniques associated with computer crime and even the actual victimization itself, much effort will seemingly be expended in order to identify evidentiary facts, interpret clues, follow leads, and gather data to make a compelling case against the suspect(s). In addition, the PERF study recommended that officers work to locate witnesses through a neighborhood canvass; a similar procedure can be fruitful in an organizational context where computer crime has occurred. The scope of the investigation can be expanded to include interviews with other persons who might provide qualitative information related to pressures, demands, constraints, motives, and rationalizations that affect behavior. Accordingly, a sense of how the organization shapes and impels behavior may be captured, and can thereby assist the investigator in better comprehending possible stimuli for crime commission.

Information, Instrumentation, and Interviewing

O'Hara and O'Hara (1980) have written that there are three components of the criminal investigation: information, instrumentation, and interviewing. While technology and technique might change, these fundamentals persist across time and are therefore worthy of delineation. *Information* simply refers to the fact that criminal investigation is centered around the gathering, organizing, and interpreting of data directly or tangentially related to the case. Second, *instrumentation* is related to forensic science and the specific techniques afforded to crime-solving investigators. For example, technological advances such as biometrics, DNA analyses,[2] and audio/video data processing will continue to enhance the accuracy of law enforcement in clearing cases. Third, *interviewing* involves the process of soliciting and lawfully extracting information from individuals who are knowledgeable about the circumstances of a crime in some capacity.

These three fundamentals have been—and will continue to be—utilized in the investigation of traditional offenses in the United States in a relatively straightforward manner. However, their application to computer crime is less clear and seemingly more nuanced. Information accumulation will continue to be the "bread and butter" of the investigation of these nontraditional crimes. In fact, the skill of the investigator is largely rendered irrelevant if he or she is not provided with enough useful information to move toward case clearance during the course of the investigation. Similarly, even the most adept investigator will encounter difficulties if information culled during its course is incomplete or generally inapplicable. With this in mind, though, instrumentation and interviewing—which are simply other methods to gather information—should be executed in a distinctively different manner.

Instrumentation in investigating *financially related* crimes involving computer systems primarily revolves around the tracking and analysis of records and logs to determine discrepancies or irregularities in the normal order. For example, money laundering with the use of computers concerns the process of concealing the source of illegally obtained money and often involves the creation, fabrication, or alteration of documents to create a legitimate paper trail and history (Lyman 2002; Van Duyne, Groenhuijsen, and Schudelaro 2005). Financial institutions are presumed to keep detailed records of all transactions, currency exchanges, and the international transportation of funds exceeding a certain amount. Additionally, the Bank Secrecy Act of 1970 requires these institutions to maintain records that "have a high degree of usefulness in criminal, tax and regulatory investigations and proceedings" and authorizes the Treasury Department to require the reporting of suspicious financial activity that might be related to a law violation (Office of Technology Assessment 1995; Van Duyne et al. 2005).

Another example testifies to the importance of instrumentation when dealing with computer-related wrongdoing. Before the exponential growth of the Internet, the investigation of credit card fraud often involved accurate identification by witnesses and the collection and identification of condemning physical evidence. When an offender made a purchase at a retail establishment through the use of a fraudulent credit card for payment, sales clerks and store—employees trained in accurately observing and remembering physical and behavioral details of perpetrators were able to assist in the investigation. Catching an offender in possession of the fraudulently acquired merchandise was also easier since purchases were made in a physical location. Finally, the handwriting sample obtained when the goods were signed for, and fingerprints left at the scene of the crime, also served as corroborating evidence. With the advent and growth of electronic commerce, however, the assistive role of witnesses and

---

[2]Though outside the scope of this work, it is interesting to consider how the expertise of DNA evidence collection and analyses migrated into the police organization, and whether the development of that specialized component can serve as an instructive template for the introduction and maturation of computer forensics expertise.

physical evidence—sources of information previously (and even heavily) relied upon—has now been largely eliminated. Combined with interjurisdictional complications, a deficiency of available investigatory resources, and the fact that these crimes occur in such an unconstrained and unregulated manner in cyberspace, the problem is further confounded. Investigators of computer crime must consequently pursue other avenues of inquiry and learn to master information retrieval from these sources, or else continue to struggle in their case clearance attempts.

The third component—interviewing—appears to be less salient as a *direct* method to investigate computer crime, largely because the victim is often unaware (either immediately or even for a great length of time) that a crime has occurred and that harm has resulted (Parker 1976; Webster 1980). Information useful in the solving of these cases is sometimes only identified after ferreting through reams of data on a computer system, and often the victim's only role in these investigations is to report the crime and provide access to the data storage machines. Furthermore, witnesses in computer crime are relatively rare since these offenses tend to occur behind closed doors (Rosoff, Pontell, and Tillman 2002). The only witnesses in most cases are those who commit the crimes either individually or collectively, and therefore, other techniques to gather information must be utilized (Lyman 2002).

Interviewing, then, may provide *indirect* utility for the investigator—such as insight into the motives and possibly the specific techniques employed, particularly if the offender was an "insider." Motive for a crime such as embezzlement [the siphoning off of funds from an employer by an employee—often through the use of computer systems (Lyman 2002; Rosoff, Pontell, and Tillman 2002)], for example, might stem from organizational variables—such as pressure from supervisors or managers to demonstrate productivity or effectiveness, or from a "culture of competition" that permeates the enterprise (Coleman and Ramos 1998). It might also stem from individual-level variables such as a personality characterized by laziness, vengeful inclinations, a tendency to mock authority, or an inability to deal with stress in a prosocial manner (Krause 2002). Coworkers of a possible suspect may provide useful secondary information in this regard, while also outlining the capabilities of (and methods potentially used by) the individual to bypass access controls to commit the crime. The task of the investigator would then be to evaluate the viability of the anecdotal feedback received, and to follow leads that may uncover stronger evidence that would hold substantive weight in a court of law.

Evidence Collection and Processing

In terms of evidentiary issues, the preliminary investigation strategies associated with computer crime should be executed as any other type of crime. Law enforcement departments have procedural requirements for evidence collection that should be followed, but certain subtleties endemic to computer crime must be noted. For example, Lyman (2002) points to the complexity associated with the lack of tangible evidence and an actual scene to be examined. As such, it is suggested that the investigator learn as much as possible about the victim and the possible suspects in a case. Though not exclusive in their impact, this highlights the salience of understanding individual-level variables as predictors of this form of criminality. Furthermore, the detailed analyses of logs, records, and documents associated with the unlawful transaction or action must occur (Lyman 2002). The collection and use of physical evidence has been documented as vital (Eck 1983), and while this procedure in investigating computer crime is very time-intensive, it often yields key clues that can lead to an apprehension.

The manner in which evidence is procured in computer crime cases remains a sizable challenge for law enforcement. Specific information related to the computer system requiring search and possible seizure must be detailed in the warrant in order to be approved, and also so that the prosecutor can counter any evidentiary challenges brought by the defense staff (Wallace, Lusthaus, and Kim 2005). Consistent investigative standards and protocols for computer crimes have not yet become firmly ensconced in most police departments, and this can lead to evidence being deemed inadmissible—evidence that otherwise might have led to a conviction (Lyman 2002; Webster 1980).

Relatedly, search warrant proceedings for traditional crimes are familiar and routine to the courtroom workgroup. Due to the relative newness of search warrant applications for computer crimes, however, some states are specifically designating individual judges to deal with these specialized requests (New Jersey Attorney General Commission of Investigation 2000). Nonetheless, requests must still be presented in a manner that allows ease of comprehension. The judge must not be confused by the technical details associated with the investigation, but should understand the nuances of what is involved so that the court can make an informed decision (Brungs and Jamieson 2005). The goal is to clearly articulate probable cause that a crime has been committed, and that the items described in the warrant are related to that crime. Likewise, technological jargon is often used by victims to communicate the specifics of the victimization and possible sources of investigative clues, and many law enforcement officers themselves may not be able to fully understand the information, nor assimilate it to direct or refine the investigation (Lyman 2002). More police agencies are employing technicians who can assist responding officers or detectives in the proper preservation, collection, and processing of evidence, as well as with interpretation and presentation of the technological details of crime commission.

Once evidence associated with a computer crime is lawfully discovered, multiple safeguards should be instituted to preserve its continuity and integrity. Extreme attention must be given to the specifications on the search warrant so that all relevant items are properly and legally seized. Moreover, it is paramount to protect physical and removable media because of their sensitive nature. Magnetic fields and even static electricity have the potential to render unusable and unreadable certain electronic equipment such as data storage devices or disks. Another critical point is that suspects in a case should be restricted from the computing environment because of the possibility that digital evidence might be altered or deleted (Lyman 2002).

At this point, the forensic analysis of computer hard drives has proven to be beneficial in building a case against a suspected criminal. This method of evidence acquisition, however, is technically complex and laborious. While the number is increasing, many law enforcement departments do not have the expertise to perform these techniques and must outsource their forensic analysis requirements to other agencies that do have skilled personnel. Unfortunately, with the continued increase of computer crime and the limited resources available for law enforcement to deal with traditional crimes—let alone novel instantiations of them—backlogs are invariably created and rows of computers often become lined up in evidence rooms awaiting analyses by a technician (Bhaskar 2006; Bogen and Dampier 2004; Newville 2001). In accordance with intuition, priority is given to computer crime cases involving potential or actual physical harm to individuals. Nonetheless, backlogs invariably compromise the celerity with which justice is served to perpetrators of other offenses, and consequently undermine the viability of the system itself.

Finally, the RAND study (Greenwood et al. 1977) underscored the necessity to refine and optimize evidence processing efforts, and the PERF Study (Eck 1983) highlighted the utility of collecting evidence to corroborate and strengthen the case against a suspected offender, rather than used to identify a suspect. These policy suggestions have been assisted and supported by recent technological advances, such as software that can analyze hundreds of gigabytes of electronic financial data for the purposes of detecting inconsistencies, and programs that can parse log files quickly to hone in on the specific activities of offenders. Unquestionably, more equipment, personnel, and training are essential to further improving the efficiency of the process.

Jurisdiction

Since national boundaries effectively disappear when considering many computer crimes, jurisdiction is another complicated matter. While a complete examination of jurisdictional issues is beyond the scope of this work, it merits comment that countries differ in civil and criminal offense standards, substantive and procedural law, data collection and preservation practices, and other evidentiary and juridical factors (Brungs and Jamieson 2005; Lyman 2002; Speer 2000). Moreover, it is often ambiguous as to whose responsibility it is to address a particular crime or spearhead an investigation, or how best to collaborate through extradition and mutual assistance policies. This plays out not only on an international level, but also within nations where multiple law enforcement departments are implicated (Wallace, Lusthaus, and Kim 2005).

Reactive and Proactive Investigations

Another distinction illumined in the literature is between reactive and proactive investigations (Lyman 2002). Intuitively, reactive investigations attempt to solve crimes that have already occurred; this is the most frequent type. Proactive investigations attempt to deal with crime prior to the victimization, rather than after it has exacted harm on an individual, a corporation, or society. This often takes place through novel and innovative programming designed by criminal justice organizations and assisting entities, such as situational crime prevention strategies (Newman and Clarke 2003). When law enforcement is able to anticipate the commission of certain crimes, personnel are often deployed to surveil and target resources toward a known group of criminals or to counter a specific type of crime. This type of investigation is primarily intelligence-led, which underscores the importance of collecting and appropriately responding to useful data from viable sources while concurrently accounting for issues related to civil liberties and evidentiary rules.

For example, the monitoring of bulletin boards and chat rooms by investigators has led to the detection and apprehension of those who participate in sex crimes against children (Meehan et al. 2001; Mitchell, Wolak, and Finkelhor 2005; Penna, Clark, and Mohay 2005). In addition, participants in online communities have contributed to preventing crimes by informing authorities about questionable behavior, who then are able to provide that information to investigators. For example, self-policing on Internet auction sites has led to the identification of attempted and completed sales of counterfeit and fraudulent items, and to the perpetrators of such crimes (Enos 2000; Fusco 1999). Partnerships in the United States between the private and public sector involving the sharing of computer crime victimization data have also assisted law enforcement in its investigative endeavors.

"Symbolic" Investigations

Lastly, Brandl and Horvath (1991) discovered that the effort expended by law enforcement through investigative practices is positively related to victim satisfaction rates. That is, victims are more pleased with the police response when the department is able to demonstrate that due attention was given to the incident. This can occur through the acts of fingerprint dusting, mug shot showing, and the questioning of witnesses—which in truth are often performed to maintain a media-generated "image" rather than to productively contribute to the investigation of a crime (Greenwood et al. 1977). This cumulatively underscores the importance of "symbolic" investigations that serve purposes oriented more toward "public relations" than "crime solving" (Greenwood et al. 1977).

Extending this finding to computer crime, it appears that in order for the police to demonstrate that they are motivated and able to address these nontraditional offenses, they must respond in a similar fashion. Otherwise, individual and corporate victims will lose faith in the capacity of law enforcement to control crime, and a shaken confidence in the most prominent arm of the criminal justice system forebodes greater problems for society (Webster 1980). Victims may also choose against reporting suspected or actual wrongdoing, and may turn to their own means of investigating and punishing transgressors—perhaps in an unlawful manner (Johnston 1996; Silke 2001). Trust must be developed to create and perpetuate a candid and constant line of communication between victims and law enforcement, so that each party can help the other in their collective goals of preempting and addressing computer crime.

COMPUTER CRIME INVESTIGATIVE TASK FORCES

As computer crime originating in the United States often implicates interstate and international laws, many cases fall under federal jurisdiction. Federal collaboration with local law enforcement and prosecutors to share intelligence and efforts through teamwork has demonstrated effectiveness in addressing traditional crimes involving drugs, weapons, gangs, and violence[3] (McGarrell and Schlegel 1993; Russell-Einhorn 2004). By extension, many scholars and practitioners have asserted the importance of forming comparable teams to combat computer crime with the hope of similar positive outcomes (see, e.g., Conly and McEwen 1990).

Research has recently been conducted to determine how such task forces might best meet the needs of law enforcement, the private sector, and societal members at large (Hinduja 2004). The findings have provided some insight into the formation and organization of these dedicated teams. Most importantly, it appears that their investigative functions should be structured in a way that concentrates effort and attention on equipping personnel to accomplish their goals. Characteristics of three areas should distinguish a specialized computer

---

[3]The United States Department of Justice's Weed and Seed Program and Project Safe Neighborhoods are two examples.

crime task force from a traditional police unit: recruiting, mentorship, and promotion practices; training requirements; and outsourcing to the private sector. In the following text, each of these characteristics is elaborated in the context of a hypothetical computer crime unit.

Recruiting, Mentorship, and Promotion

To begin, individuals who seek to become a part of the unit must have at least 3 years of experience as sworn law enforcement officers to ensure familiarity with their role as an agent of the state, as well as insight into the dynamics of the U.S. criminal justice system. They should also be recommended by their supervising officer as highly technically inclined and possessing character qualities essential to succeeding as an investigator—such as attention to detail, patience, excellent communication skills, and first-rate integrity. New recruits would then be charged with obtaining experience in some of the more mundane duties of the department. For example, new members of the unit would be responsible for assisting veterans with the acquisition, safeguarding, and analysis of evidence, the processing of paperwork to meet the requirements of the prosecuting team, the completion and archiving of reports for the department's data collection purposes, and the numerous telephone and face-to-face conversations related to specific incidents with victims, witnesses, and informants.

The key point is that new initiates would be specifically assigned to the tutelage and supervision of a veteran investigator who would have the responsibility to assimilate him or her into the culture of the unit and the investigation of computer crime cases in general. This "probationary" period would last one year, after which time new members would be assigned their own cases. The investigation of crimes with comparatively little at stake—such as online credit card fraud, hate group propaganda on the Internet, the digital counterfeiting of checks or currency less than $1,000, software piracy, and minor unauthorized use of computing resources—would be relegated to these neophytes. Ensconced veterans would be in charge of crimes with more significant potential or actual repercussions, such as cyber terrorism, child pornography and identify theft rings, network intrusions causing large-scale denial of service or data damage, hefty financial losses to a victim, and those offenses with possible organized crime ties.

Concerning promotion, one would incorporate a typical hierarchical ladder of positions through which officers would ascend incrementally after demonstrating proficiency at their current level. If an investigator shows much promise and has commendable case clearance and arrest rates with the type of crimes currently assigned, he or she will be evaluated for promotion to the next level where crimes with graver implications are addressed. With the increased responsibility will come greater autonomy and, of course, greater rewards contingent upon success at the new position. Greater autonomy will ultimately result in authorization to conduct proactive investigations to preempt the commission of computer crime before it occurs. Due to the controversial nature and human rights implications of proactive strategies, only long-term, highly skilled veterans will be afforded this opportunity.[4]

---

[4]Proactive investigations introduce a host of techniques that alarm human rights activists and privacy advocates, such as wire-tapping, database mining and knowledge discovery, and grants of immunity and protection to informants. The ethical nature of these techniques will continue to warrant debate, and violations to civil rights must be precluded at all costs through policy and procedural guidelines developed by agencies for their investigators (Brown 2001).

Training Requirements

During the aforementioned probationary period, new recruits will be required to attend numerous training workshops to deepen their knowledgebase with regard to crimes facilitated by a computer.[5] Technical sessions—on topics such as network protocols, operating systems, encryption schemes, and forensic analysis—will be complimented with legal sessions on topics such as the application for, and execution of, search warrants in these cases, and the importance of properly preserving and documenting evidentiary items and facts.[6] In the United States, many of these training workshops are organized by federally funded entities and are administrated to law enforcement personnel at no charge.[7] Certification exams will also be administered to recruits to ensure that they have truly learned the material taught, and can apply it to practical situations. Such intensive training is essential to equip unit investigators to excel in their positions.

Outsourcing to the Private Sector

The previous discussion appears to give no regard to the limited resources—time, personnel, equipment, and knowledge—with which most law enforcement departments continually struggle. Accordingly, the hypothesized computer crime unit would develop partnerships with the private sector to mitigate the relevance of initially inadequate resources. For example, it is presumed that American corporations would want to act in ways that demonstrate an investment in their local community for the purposes of maintaining and increasing consumer allegiance, and to receive tax breaks. As such, many of these companies could donate equipment to the unit in the form of hardware, software, and peripherals to meet law enforcement's needs for investigative tools. Even the time of a private sector employee might be provided *non grata* to the law enforcement agency if and when a technical or legal question arises that investigators are unable to answer, or when advice as to how to proceed in a case is required. A simple telephone call between these entities may be immeasurably beneficial to crime solution and successful prosecution.

With regard to computer crime, some might argue that the *entire* investigative process be outsourced to the business community. Historically, the privatization of investigations has assisted public law enforcement by allowing them to concentrate on other responsibilities, and has prevented their resources from being allocated in too sparse a manner to be useful. For example, Pinkerton's National Detective Agency was created in 1852 (Kuykendall 1986; Lyman 2002), largely stemming from vigilante forms of justice that prevailed in eighteenth- and

---

[5]Hinduja (2004) found through a survey of law enforcement agencies that when presented with the options for more training, personnel, or equipment, law enforcement agencies overwhelmingly declared a need for training over and above the other resource provisions.

[6]Hinduja (2004) discovered that the greatest training demands were in the areas of search and seizure training, and evidence collection and processing. This speaks to the importance of accumulating knowledge and experience related to the legal aspects of computer crime investigations over the need to acquire more technical expertise.

[7]For example, the National White Collar Crime Center holds workshops on basic and advanced data recovery analysis at locations across the country throughout the year.

nineteenth-century rural America. Vigilante justice has also reared its head in cyberspace, most prominently with the defacement of Web sites related to the Taliban and the governments of Afghanistan, Pakistan, and Iran following the September 11, 2001, terrorist attacks on America. Indeed, the federal government and private corporations have also engaged in "self-help" and have launched counterattacks on computers that are used to penetrate or afflict their systems (Schwartau 1999). A primary sentiment shared by organizations who strike back on their own terms is that law enforcement is impotent to competently respond due to limited resources and intelligence, the slow pace at which computer crime investigations tend to proceed, and the possibility that the vulnerability will become public knowledge (Kshetri 2006; Schwartau 1999).

Regardless of the effectiveness of these retributive acts, these corporations are technically engaging in criminal behavior subject to prosecution if caught. A mandate of any partnerships between law enforcement and the private sector should outline appropriate investigative and punitive responses by the latter, so that law violation does not occur in an attempt to obtain justice. With this caveat in mind, it appears a wiser solution would be to call upon American private sector organizations to partially fulfill essential duties related to criminal investigations. Their actions, in fact, may be more fruitful in facilitating an arrest or case clearance than those of the public sector agency.

A host of companies have arisen—some with solely "virtual" storefronts on the Internet—that are available for the outsourcing needs of individuals and businesses seeking services of network security development and management, hard-drive forensic analyses and data recovery, and various other security-related tasks. It might be argued that these firms possess the skills sets and resources to competently assist law enforcement in their investigative duties, much like the Pinkerton Detective Agency. Due in part to the comparatively lucrative nature of the business world, many of those who are technologically skilled seek employment in the private, rather than the public, sector. Additionally, businesses are much more financially able to select and retain the most proficient workers. They are also in a better position to compile the resources and develop the infrastructure necessary to provide computer crime investigative services to other organizations—and, of course, to profit from it.[8]

By building a solid infrastructure around the components of: recruiting, mentorship, and promotion practices; training requirements; and outsourcing to the private sector, the likelihood of successful computer crime investigations is increased. In time, it is very possible that some other unexpected consequence will arise and affect either the investigative or prosecutorial effort, and policies will have to be adapted toward closing any loopholes or vulnerabilities in the process. Structuring a department in this manner, however, appears to hold the most promise with which to assess and address computer-related criminality.

---

[8]Underscoring the utility of employing a private business to aid in a criminal investigation; a victim of auction fraud on eBay.com contracted a private business to perform a reverse cellular-telephone lookup, which resulted in the discovery of the home address of the perpetrator of the crime. After this information was retrieved, the victim then got in contact with the law enforcement department that had jurisdiction over the area in which the offender lived, and a sting was orchestrated which led to an arrest and case clearance of not only the current incident, but an impressive array of similar auction frauds by the same individual (Smith 2002).

DISCUSSION

Law enforcement will have to expand their investigative practices to competently respond to the problem at hand; thankfully, they are not starting from "square one." A solid foundation has been laid through the years of modification and refinement of traditional investigations, and through empirical research assessing the relevance and efficacy of their techniques and procedures. While not all are equally applicable to computer crime, much insight can be gained from the past when developing sound policy to guide investigators in the future. The preceding text has summarized key points from previous research on traditional investigations in the United States, and has extrapolated and applied certain "best practices" to computer crime investigative efforts. Suggestions as to how to suitably create and manage a specialized unit were also presented to inform American police departments called to address these crimes in their jurisdiction.

The preceding recommendations are not sizable deviations from traditional methods, but stem intuitively from principles with which law enforcement officials are currently familiar. All that is generally required is awareness of particular nuances associated with high-technology crimes to prevent investigative mistakes from invalidating the criminal justice effort. The knowledgebase associated with computer crime investigations will grow and be refined over time. Indeed, the techniques and strategies should eventually become as second nature to investigators as are those they utilize to solve traditional forms of crime. The hope is that with additional research by academics and experience accumulated by practitioners, that time will come soon rather than later, as the significance of crimes involving computers demands it.

KEY TERMS

Computer crime   Justice
High-technology   Law enforcement
Internet   Police
Investigations

REFERENCES

Benson, M. L., F. Cullen, and Maakestad, W. 1990. Local prosecutors and corporate crime. *Crime and Delinquency* 36: 356–72.

Beveridge, W. I. B. 1957. *The Art of Scientific Investigation*. New York: Norton.

Bhaskar, R. 2006. State and local law enforcement is not ready for a cyber Katrina. *Communications of the ACM* 49 (2): 81–3.

Block, P., and J. Bell. 1976. *Managing Investigations: The Rochester System*. Washington, DC: Police Foundation.

Block, P., and D. Weidman. 1975. *Managing Criminal Investigations: Perspective Package*. Washington, DC: U.S. Government Printing Office.

Bogen, A. C., and D. A. Dampier. 2004. Knowledge discovery and experience modeling in computer forensics media analysis. *ACM International Conference Proceeding Series* 90: 140–5.

Braithwaite, J. 1985. White-collar crime. *Annual Review of Sociology* 11: 1–25.

Brandl, S. G., and F. Horvath. 1991. Crime-victim evaluation of police investigative performance. *Journal of Criminal Justice* 19 (3): 293–305.

Brown, M. F. 2001. *Criminal Investigation: Law and Practice*. 2nd ed. Boston: Butterworth-Heinemann.

Brungs, A., and R. Jamieson. 2005. Identification of legal issues for computer forensics. *Information Systems Management* 22 (2): 57–66.

Coleman, J. W., and L. L. Ramos. 1998. Subcultures and deviant behavior in the organizational context. *Research in the Sociology of Organizations* 15: 3–34.

Conly, C. H., and J. T. McEwen. 1990. *Computer Crime*. National Institute of Justice, U.S. Department of Justice.

Cullen, F., B. Link, and C. Polanzi. 1982. The seriousness of crime revisited: Have attitudes towards white-collar crime changed? *Criminology* 20: 83–102.

Eck, J. 1983. *Solving Crimes: The Investigation of Burglary and Robbery*. Washington, DC: Police Executive Research Forum.

Enos, L. 2000. Group takes aim at net auction pirates. Retrieved December 28, 2002, from http://www.newsfactor.com/perl/story/6077.html

Fusco, P. 1999. eBay confirms federal investigation. Retrieved December 29, 2002, from http://www.internetnews.com/ec-news/article.php/4_73961

Greenberg, B., C. V. Elliot, L. P. Kraft, and H. S. Proctor. 1977. *Felony Decision Model: An Analysis of Investigative Elements of Information*. Washington, DC: U.S. Government Printing Office.

Greenwood, P. W., J. Chaiken, and J. Petersilia. 1977. *The Criminal Investigation Process*. Lexington, MA: D. C. Heath and Company.

Hinduja, S. 2001. Correlates of Internet software piracy. *Journal of Contemporary Criminal Justice* 17 (4): 369–82.

Hinduja, S. 2003. Trends and patterns among software pirates. *Ethics and Information Technology* 5 (1): 49–61.

Hinduja, S. 2004. Perceptions of local and state law enforcement concerning the role of computer crime investigative teams. *Policing: An International Journal of Police Strategies & Management* 27 (3): 341–57.

Johnston, L. 1996. What is vigilantism? *British Journal of Criminology* 36 (2): 220–36.

Krause, M. S. 2002. *Contemporary White Collar Crime Research: A Survey of Findings Relevant to Personnel Security Research and Practice*. The Personnel Security Managers' Research Program. Accessed December 29, 2002, from http://www.navysecurity.navy.mil/White%20Collar%20Crime.pdf

Kshetri, N. 2006. The simple economics of cybercrimes. *IEEE Security & Privacy Magazine* 4 (1): 33–9.

Kuykendall, J. 1986. The municipal police detective: An historical analysis. *Criminology* 24 (1): 175–201.

Leibowitz, W. R. 1999. How law enforcement cracks cybercrimes. *New York Law Journal* 5.

Lyman, M. D. 2002. *Criminal Investigation: The Art and the Science*. 3rd ed. Upper Saddle River, NJ: Prentice Hall.

McGarrell, E. F., and K. Schlegel. 1993. The implementation of federally funded multijurisdictional task forces: Organizational structure and interagency relationships. *Journal of Criminal Justice* 21 (3): 231–44.

Meehan, A., G. Manes, L. Davis, J. Hale, and S. Shenoi. 2001. Packet sniffing for automated chat room monitoring and evidence preservation. Proceedings of the 2001 IEEE Workshop on Information Assurance and Security, pp. 285–88.

Mitchell, K. J., J. Wolak, and D. Finkelhor. 2005. Police posing as juveniles online to catch sex offenders: Is it working? *Sexual Abuse: A Journal of Research and Treatment* 17 (3): 241–67.

New Jersey Attorney General Commission of Investigation. 2000. Computer crime. A joint report.

Newman, G., and R. V. Clarke. 2003. *Superhighway Robbery: Preventing E-Commerce Crime*. Portland, OR: Willan Publishing.

Newville, L. 2001. Cybercrime and the courts: Investigating and supervising the information age offender. *Federal Probation* 65 (2): 11–20.

Office of Technology Assessment. 1995. *Information Technologies for Control of Money Laundering.* Washington, DC: U.S. Government Printing Office.

O'Grady, R. 2001. Eradicating pedophilia: Toward the humanization of society. *Journal of International Affairs* 55 (1): 123–40.

O'Hara, C. E., and G. L. O'Hara. 1980. *Fundamentals of Criminal Investigation.* 5th ed. Springfield, IL: Charles C. Thomas.

Parker, D. B. 1976. *Crime by Computer.* New York: Charles Scribner's Sons.

Penna, L., A. Clark, and G. Mohay. 2005. Challenges of automating the detection of paedophile activity on the Internet. First International Workshop on Systematic Approaches to Digital Forensic Engineering, pp. 206–22.

Philippsohn, S. 2001. Trends in cybercrime—An overview of current financial crimes on the internet. *Computers & Security* 20 (1): 53–69.

Power, R. 2000. *Tangled Web: Tales of Digital Crime from the Shadows of Cyberspace.* Indianapolis, IN: Que.

Reames, J. E. 2000. Computer crimes, hacking, and cybernetic warfare. *Journal of California Law Enforcement* 34 (1): 17–26.

Rosoff, S. M., H. M. Pontell, and R. Tillman. 2002. *Profit Without Honor: White-Collar Crime and the Looting of America.* Upper Saddle River, NJ: Prentice Hall.

Royal Canadian Mounted Police. 2000. Computer crime, can it affect you? Retrieved November 10, 1999, from http://www3.sk.sympatico.ca/rcmpccs/cpu-crim.html

Russell-Einhorn, M. L. 2004. Federal–local law enforcement collaboration in investigating and prosecuting urban crime, 1982–1999: Drugs, weapons, and gangs (No. NCJ 201782). National Institute of Justice.

Sanders, W. 1977. *Detective Work.* New York: Free Press.

Schwartau, W. 1999. Cyber-vigilantes hunt down hackers. Retrieved December 20, 2003, from http://www.cnn.com/TECH/computing/9901/12/cybervigilantes.idg

Silke, A. 2001. Dealing with vigilantism: Issues and lessons for the police. *Police Journal* 74 (2): 120–33.

Skogan, W. G., and G. E. Antunes. 1979. Information, apprehension, and deterrence: Exploring the limits of police productivity. *Journal of Criminal Justice* 7: 217–41.

Speer, D. L. 2000. Redefining borders: The challenges of cybercrime. *Crime Law and Social Change* 34 (3): 259–73.

Tan, H. S. K. 2005. E-fraud: Current trends and international developments. *Journal of Financial Crime* 9 (4): 347–54.

Tarde, G. Ed. [1890] 1903. *Gabriel Tarde's Laws of Imitation.* New York: Henry Holt.

Taylor, M., and E. Quayel. 2003. *Child Pornography: An Internet Crime.* New York: Brunner-Routledge.

United Nations. 1994. International review of criminal policy—United Nations manual on the prevention and control of computer-related crime. Retrieved June 20, 1999, from http://www.ifs.univie.ac.at/~pr2gq1/rev4344.html

Van Duyne, P. C., M. S. Groenhuijsen, and A. A. P. Schudelaro. 2005. Balancing financial threats and legal interests in money-laundering policy. *Crime, Law and Social Change* 43 (2–3): 117–47.

Wallace, R. P., A. M. Lusthaus, and J. H. Kim. 2005. Computer crimes. *American Criminal Law Review* 42 (2): 223–76.

Webster, W. H. 1980. An examination of FBI theory and methodology regarding white-collar crime investigation and prevention. *American Criminal Law Review* 17 (3): 275–86.

Wilson, J. Q. 1976. *The Investigators: Managing FBI and Narcotics Agents.* New York: Basic Books.

Wittes, B. 1994. Perils of policing the internet: Law enforcement lacks the tools needed to go after a new breed of online criminal. *Recorder.*

Wolfgang, M. E., R. M. Figlio, and T. Sellin. 1972. *Delinquency in a Birth Cohort.* Chicago: University of Chicago Press.

Chapter 23

Criminal Profiling and Cyber Criminal Investigations

Daniel Shoemaker, and Daniel B. Kennedy
University of Detroit Mercy

Dan Shoemaker, Ph.D., is the director of the Centre for Assurance Studies, a National Security Agency (NSA) Center of Academic Excellence in Information Assurance Education at the University of Detroit Mercy. He is also a professor at UDM, and he has been the chair of the Computer and Information Systems Program within the College of Business Administration since 1985. He obtained his Ph.D. from the University of Michigan, Ann Arbor, and he subsequently spent a career in various professional IS roles at that institution, as well as at Michigan State University.

Dr. Shoemaker is coauthor of McGraw-Hill's global best seller, "*Information Assurance for the Enterprise—A Roadmap to Security.*" He serves as an expert panelist on three national working groups within the Department of Homeland Security's National Cybersecurity Division (NCSD). The most prominent of these is the Software Assurance Common Body of Knowledge (SWA-CBK). Dr. Shoemaker is an author and domain editor for that document. He also serves on the Assurance Business Case Working Group and the Workforce Education and Training—FISMA Certification Working Group.

Dr. Shoemaker has written and lectured on cyber security and information assurance topics throughout the Eastern United States and Canada. He founded the International Cybersecurity Education Coalition (ICSEC), which is an NSA sponsored consortium of higher education institutions located in Michigan, Ohio, and Indiana. ICSEC's mission is to extend and support the teaching of standard information assurance curricula within the Midwest. He is also a member of the Advisory Panel for Automation Alley, which is the State of Michigan's Economic Development initiative in information security.

Dr. Daniel B. Kennedy, Ph.D., is a professor of criminal justice and security administration at the University of Detroit Mercy. He brings both practical experience and an extensive academic background to the study of criminal behavior and security issues. Dr. Kennedy has served as an urban renewal worker, a probation officer, and an inmate counselor for the Federal Bureau of Prisons in Detroit. He also directed a police academy in Macomb County, Michigan.

Dr. Kennedy earned his BA, MA, and Ph.D. at Wayne State University in Detroit, concentrating his studies in sociology and criminology. He has had extensive training in security administration at the National Crime Prevention Institute at the University of Louisville and at specialized security training seminars around the United States. Dr. Kennedy has published several books and over 90 technical articles dealing with crime, policing, and security administration. He has lectured at the FBI Academy and at various national legal seminars dealing with inadequate security issues as well as police and corrections practices.

Dr. Kennedy is licensed by the State of Michigan as a Certified Social Worker. He is also designated a Certified Sociological Practitioner by the Sociological Practice Association and a Certified

456

Protection Professional by the American Society for Industrial Security. Dr. Kennedy has been accepted as a security expert in numerous state and federal courts across the country.

Abstract

This chapter relates the methods and assumptions of classic criminal profiling to the identification of perpetrators of crime in cyberspace. The use of behavioral signatures to identify "unknown perpetrators of known crimes" seems to be the only option for addressing most types of cyber crime. That is because of the unique situation that cyberspace creates. Offenders are often not present at the scene of the crime and their crimes are often electronic and virtual rather than physical. This suggests some concrete ways to approach the investigation based on common profiling techniques, as well as a series of 12 typical inductive profiles of cyber criminals developed using those methods. These typologies are based on traditional motive, intent, and post-offense behavioral assumptions.

INTRODUCTION: THE CHANGING NATURE OF CYBER CRIME

In the 1980s and 1990s, a typical cyber crime was a criminal trespass or Web site defacement and the victims tended to be government institutions and corporations who were frequently in the public eye. **Cyber criminals** themselves were inclined to be counterculture types who worked alone and on the fringes. That situation has changed as the Internet has become the medium of choice. Now, instead of being inspired by a need to prove their art, cyber criminals are often motivated by financial gain. As a consequence, the old stereotypical image of the kid living on Skittles, while doing 72-hour hacks, has been replaced by a much darker and more complex persona, one who is well organized and much more focused on making trouble (Bednarz 2004).

Crime in cyberspace today is about making money (Hochmuth 2004). And just like the bank robbers of old, organized groups of cyber criminals perpetrate large-scale raids on financial institutions. Worse, much of that activity originates in places like China, India, Russia, Romania, and Latin America, which puts those perpetrators out of reach of U.S. law enforcement agencies (Gudaitis 2005).

With financial institutions, the repertoire for cyber criminal activity ranges from extortion and fraud to outright electronic theft (Gudaitis 2005). In fact, the opportunities for financial gain from cyber crime are so great that established criminal syndicates have gotten into the business of electronic crime (Garretson and Duffy 2004). As a result, security experts generally agree that law enforcement has to learn a lot more about the skill level, personality traits, and various methods of operation of computer criminals (Rogers 2003)

Cyber criminals count on the remoteness and anonymity that the Internet provides. As a result, it is essential to be able to understand what cyber criminals actually know and, more importantly, what motivates them (Bednarz 2004). That is the point of this discussion.

ADAPTING INVESTIGATIONS TO A STRANGE NEW WORLD

It would be incorrect to assume that all cyber crimes are alike. In fact, cyber crimes and cyber criminals differ as much in motive, intent, and outcome as any type of physical criminal. Moreover, the general set of assumptions that underlie the investigation of cyber crime are the same as they would be for crimes in physical space. What is different is the form of the evidence. Evidence arising out of the electronic discovery process is not part of the physical world, so cyber evidence is not the same as the evidence that investigators typically work with (Heiser and Kruse 2002). Consequently, criminal investigators who in the past have relied on such concepts as physical artifacts, eyewitnesses, and confessions to solve crimes will now have to accommodate the fact that in most cyber crimes the bulk of the actual evidence will be in electronic or digital format (Rogers 2003).

Yet, cyber criminals, just like physical criminals, still adhere to Locard's "Exchange Principle," in that the perpetrator leaves some form of evidence at the scene and takes away some form of evidence that links them to the crime (Saferstein 2001). In its raw, electronic form, none of that evidence is easy to read or understand, so the task of evidence gathering and analysis in cyberspace is not an easy one.

The role of the discipline of digital forensics is to make that virtual or electronic evidence meaningful to the conventional investigator. Digital evidence typically consists of binary data inscribed on a mass storage device, like a hard drive or a flash memory stick. The evidence itself can comprise everything from executable code artifacts, to the contents of a system table, all the way up to plaintext, or encrypted electronic content, or pictures. Sometimes, for example, there are even very tiny pictures placed within pictures, which is known to cyber forensic investigators as steganography.

Although forensics is a useful tool in the evidence discovery process, there are a variety of other investigative techniques that are also important to the solution of any type of crime. Any or all of those approaches might be relevant to some aspect of the investigative process (Rogers 2003). The problem is that cyberspace creates unique situations that no conventional investigative practice can accommodate. For instance, the actual perpetrators might be on the other side of the planet when they commit the crime. Because of conditions such as this, new investigative approaches have to be employed. For example, IP tracing techniques are common tools. These allow authorities to determine the origin of an Internet action even if it is located in a faraway place. The disconnectedness that the Internet provides raises another important issue, which is the location of the actual crime scene. The investigator has to answer the practical question: Is the real crime scene located where the perpetrator performed the act, or is it the victim's location?

Because of all of these complications, cyberspace gives new meaning to the concept of the unknown perpetrator of a known crime. That is, one of the wonders of electronic criminality is that it is possible to commit a criminal act that could best be described by a layman as a "bank robbery" from the safety of a location 6,000 miles away from the actual scene of the crime. The virtuality of cyberspace permits that sort of "uninvolved criminality." It creates a physical separation between the actual crime scene and the perpetrator, which then imposes unique complications of access and timing on the investigation of the crime.

It is almost impossible to be able to use physical evidence to identify criminals who are operating under cyberspace's anonymous conditions. This can only be done by utilizing the single piece of evidence that will be available to investigators: the behavioral signatures of the individual perpetrator. In order to obtain that highly technical information, evidence from unfamiliar sources like system logs and system level reconstructions of attack behavior has to be factored into the investigative process (Gudaitis 2005).

The behavioral characterization of unknown subjects forms the basis of the discipline of **criminal profiling**. The ability to use unique individual behavioral factors as a means of sorting out and identifying a specific criminal is not new. As a formal practice, some form of behavioral approach has been a part of the investigation of physical crimes for well over a century. The earliest example of a behavioral profile was done by Dr. Thomas Bond in the "Jack the Ripper," case in the late 1880s (Hicks and Sales 2006). It would seem logical then, to consider the usefulness of profiling when it comes to the investigation of cyber crimes as well. The only constraint is that those conventional profiling methods and techniques have to be modified to meet the unique conditions and requirements of virtual space.

UTILIZING CRIMINAL PROFILING AS AN AID TO CYBER CRIMINAL INVESTIGATIONS

In the investigation of traditional crimes, it is essential to understand three fundamental things: What motivated the offenders (motive); how did they choose their particular victim (opportunity); and what are the details of the crime (means). In the case of cyber crimes, common investigative techniques have to be modified to allow the investigator to approach the computer and its network as if it were a physical crime scene where those three factors can be studied. The investigator then gathers all of the electronic evidence present at the scene, for the purpose of painting a meaningful picture of the specific motive and methods of a given offender (Bednarz 2004).

Behavioral analysis is a key factor in this effort because, according to Steven Branigan (2004), "Companies aren't going to solve computer security issues just by throwing technology at the problem." "It is about understanding how people behave" (Bednarz 2004, 1). In the case of a cyber crime, which is typically anonymous and can originate from an almost infinite number of places on the Internet, the ability to differentiate the unique behavioral characteristics of the perpetrator is an invaluable aid to the investigation.

As is the case with conventional investigations, profiling does not solve the crime itself. Instead, it focuses the investigator down to a workable set of suspects. This is done by building a profile of the criminal's distinguishing characteristics, which in turn is based on the unique set of behaviors that the offender exhibits during the commission of the crime. The investigator can use those distinctive behaviors to differentiate a particular offender from a group of potential suspects with similar modus operandi (MO). Because profiling is based on evidence gathered at the crime scene, the description of the perpetrator does not depend on the presence of witnesses. Thus, the ability to characterize a person who is otherwise not known, based strictly on signature behaviors, is one of the reasons why criminal profiling is such a productive contributor to the investigation of such offenses as serial crimes, where there are no witnesses to describe the suspect.

Profiling assumes that the psychological landscape of every individual criminal is different and so each perpetrator will behave slightly differently. As a consequence, profiling helps the investigator "see" the person behind the crime. This more intimate understanding is independent of other factors, such as the criminal's method of operation (MO), which can typically be inferred from the physical evidence. Because it is important to understand the difference between the MO and the offender's personal behavioral "signature," we are going to elaborate on this idea a little further.

Most classes of crime, even cyber crimes, have a common MO. For example, many **hacking** exploits rely on "canned" scripts that people pull down off the Internet. Knowing that a Web site was violated by a "script kiddy," as this type of offender is called, will not narrow the field of potential suspects down to a workable set. However, even script kiddies exhibit distinctive individual behaviors that are a result of their unique psychological composition. Some of the more immature types like to leave unique markings on a violated site to tell the world that (in effect) "Kilroy was here." Other more politically motivated offenders like to leave political manifestos, some like to make intricate changes or additions to the Web site that they can subsequently display to their friends as a personal "trophy" of their great intellectual prowess and some will make surreptitious alterations, such as installing "back doors," that essentially mean that the hacker now controls that Web site.

All of these actions are distinctive behaviors that can potentially be used as identifiers and each can be used to eliminate the other class of individual. For instance, a script kiddy who leaves simple markings is usually just a novice hacker, more often than not a high school kid. On the other hand, a script kiddy who leaves political messages can be inferred to be motivated by activist ideologies and thus more mature. Script kiddies who need to collect trophies are typically more broadly disturbed and, therefore, exhibit deviant behavior in other aspects of their life. Some, for example, have become involved in Internet stalking and sexual predation in the past (McGrath and Casey 2002). Other hackers may display characteristics reminiscent of Asperger's syndrome, an autism spectrum disorder that has surfaced in the background of a variety of other types of serial offenders (Murrie et al. 2002; Silva, Leong, and Ferrari 2004).

An investigator can use the "clues" that these simple behavioral differences provide to narrow the search down to a workable group. For instance, since the script kiddy who leaves simple markings is often just immature, one of the likeliest places to find the culprit is in high school near the Internet origin of the offense. As a practical matter, however, it is probably a waste of time to look for trophy hunters in the local high school, unless one of the kids there has a history of deviant behavior in other aspects of school life.

The ability to differentiate anonymous individuals based on their psychological characteristics is a particularly important aid to the investigation of cyber crime. That is because; the gathering of the behavioral evidence and even its analysis can be automated. The one advantage that cyberspace provides to criminal investigators is the ability to look at an infinite number of individual actions in an infinite number of places, all at computer speed. That degree of data gathering and analysis would be impossible in physical space. However, because of the processing and retention capabilities of modern computer technology, it is not only possible but relatively easy to monitor and analyze in great detail the actions of each individual user on any network. Therefore, whether their identity were actually known or not, it would conceivably be possible to differentiate every person in cyberspace if a detailed enough profile of the unique individual behaviors associated with each person could be constructed. The assumption behind this is straightforward. Since computers are operated by people, and every person has a different set of personal capabilities and psychological terrain, it can theoretically be assumed that, if sufficient computing power was available, it would be possible to differentiate every user from every other user based on their unique capabilities and behaviors.

BASIC PROFILING CONCEPTS

Profiling seeks to differentiate behavior patterns in order to narrow the range of suspects in a given crime. Essentially, investigators hope to reduce the suspect pool to the few likeliest candidates. For instance, in the physical universe, a robber might adopt a range of approaches based on personal capabilities and psychological makeup in the commission of a robbery. In one case, an individual might be unskilled in the use of a weapon or adverse to violence in the actual commission of the crime and, therefore, would not carry a gun or knife. Another individual might be highly skilled in gun use and would carry one. The decision to carry a weapon is part of their MO.

More important the actual behavior in committing the crime will be different; one robber might actually have a sadistic desire to harm the victim. Therefore, this perpetrator might not only carry a knife but would use it in every crime. This is known as a signature because the violence itself was not necessary for the successful execution of the crime. Instead, that action serves a specific emotional need of that particular criminal. This behavior can be used to narrow the field of investigation down to those suspects who have shown a need to injure a victim in the past. If the injury takes place in a unique or sadistic fashion it is an even more powerful individual trademark and therefore an even greater differentiator.

Logically, additional actions which are irrelevant to the purpose of the crime but which are consistently carried out by the person can sometimes be used to build a particularized description of that individual (Rogers 2003; Turvey 2002). Moreover, since these actions are all part of the fundamental psychological makeup of the individual and are, therefore, unlikely to change, those behaviors when viewed as a whole can serve in the investigative process as a uniquely identifying fingerprint, or signature.

In terms of the practical investigation, however, it has to be remembered that the signature behaviors that go into building a profile are elements separate from the common aspects of a criminal investigation, such as determination of primary motive, method of operation and postoffense behavior (Rogers 2003). In actual application, signature behaviors are unique to each perpetrator. Therefore, the gathering of that type of evidence should be carried out irrespective of considerations of the general motive and MO.

For instance, in the robbery examples, both of the robbers who used weapons employed the same MO. In one example, nobody was hurt; but in the other example, the victim was purposefully and needlessly harmed. The difference between the two criminals lies in the psychological structure of each criminal. This knowledge could constitute an investigative lead that may be developed into a solution of the crime, perhaps by rounding up prior offenders who have histories of similar gratuitous violence.

Nevertheless, the clues in the examples that we have used so far are all part of the physical universe and relatively easy to gather and analyze. That is not the case with cyber crime. In that world most evidence is virtual rather than physical in form. As such, a different set of evidence-gathering techniques has to be used. As we said earlier, because evidence is processed and stored by some form of computing device, the investigator has to employ evidence and analysis techniques that are primarily technological. Therefore the investigation must pay scrupulous attention to the details of system processing. This includes such meticulous exercises as time-stamp/time-pattern analysis, which uses data in the system logs, or analysis of programming behavior, which involves differentiating the stylistic and linguistic characteristics of the offender's coding technique (Gudaitis 2005). In fact, if the right data-gathering utilities are in place, there might even be the capability to obtain a range of physio-logical observations, such as keystroke timing and even keyboarding technique (Rogers 2003).

Finally, these micro-focused and somewhat arcane technical practices are all very use-ful in building an individual profile of a particular cyber offender. However, it should also be noted that it is equally important to be able to view the actions of each individual from the standpoint of the big picture, including factors like changes in the internal and external cor-porate environment (Gudaitis 2005). There is nothing like a layoff, mass firing, or plant clo-sure to motivate individuals to mischief. Thus, knowledge of broader political, economic, and social conditions is also useful to the professional cyber profiler (Gudaitis 2005).

The remainder of this chapter will review the history and possible applications of crim-inal profiling to future cyber crime investigations. This discussion will be built around an examination of the various current methodologies and how each of these methods adds to the investigation of common types of cyber crime. In addition, we will present and discuss some basic generic profiles the authors have developed using these techniques.

HOW IS CRIMINAL PROFILING DONE?

By definition, criminal profiling is a method for identifying the personal and behavioral characteristics of an unknown perpetrator of a crime. Profiling is based on an analysis of the nature of the offence and the manner in which it was committed (Canter 2000; Douglas and Olshaker 1995; Kocsis 2006; Petherick 2006; Turvey 2002). Profiling can either be reactive or proactive. With reactive or retrospective profiling, the investigator builds a profile in order to solve a crime that has already been committed. In the case of proactive or prospective pro-filing, the investigator is specifically attempting to prevent a crime from occurring (Reddy et al. 2001).

One ordinary example of the use of a proactive offender profile is the current Transportation Safety Administration (TSA) profiling of potential airplane hijackers. Pro-active profiles such as these are not developed from the evidence of a specific crime scene, rather they are meant to inform TSA workers about behaviors that might be indicative of a potential hijacker, such as buying a one-way ticket with cash. Other examples of proactive offender profiling include drug dealer and pedophile profiles (Homant and Kennedy 1998). It should be noted, however, that, in the past when proactive profiles have been used, they have tended to be controversial because they are liable to generate false-positives that can be used to support a claim of bias or prejudice. As a result the more common use of profiling by police agencies is retrospectively, to support investigators after the occurrence of the crime.

As we stated earlier, various aspects of the criminal's personality and psychological makeup can be determined by studying the actions that he or she takes before, during, and after the crime. This information can then be combined with any other relevant details and the physical evidence to build a working description of the unknown criminal. That description can then be compared with the characteristics of personality types and abnormalities of known offenders and other people of interest to create a list of suspects. As it might apply to the investigation of cyber crime, this general definition should also include the investigation, analysis, assessment, and reconstruction of data from a behavioral/psychological perspective extracted from computer systems, networks, and the actions of the humans committing the crimes (Radcliff 2003).

The general aim of all profilers is to isolate identifiable behaviors or actions that describe how the offender is fulfilling a basic psychological or physical need above and beyond the commission of the crime itself (Petherick 2005). Profilers do this by comparing the behavior at a specific crime scene with the behavior of criminals who were "profiled" in the past (Turvey 1998). That comparison then allows them to make specific inferences about the lifestyle and offending history of an unknown person (Canter 2000).

It is a common myth that the FBI's Behavioral Sciences Unit developed the techniques of profiling during the 1970s (Petherick 2005). In fact, however, the earliest handbook for profilers might be the *Malleus Maleficarum*, which was published circa 1486. That little manual provided helpful practitioner advice to professional witch hunters about ways that people of interest could be identified for the Inquisition (Turvey 2002). There have been many examples of the use of profiles in the history of criminology starting as early as the 19th century with the work of Jacob Fries and Cesare Lombroso. It should be kept in mind, however, that no approach to profiling has been conclusively determined by rigorous scientific research to be theoretically and empirically correct (Palmero and Kocsis 2005).

INDUCTIVE PROFILES

Whether the approach is retrospective or proactive, profiling methods fall into two basic categories: inductive and deductive (Petherick 2005). With the inductive approach, the profiler assumes that people who have committed similar crimes in the past share characteristics with people who commit the same type of crime now. Thus, the characteristics of an unknown offender can be inferred from the characteristics and behavior of known similar offenders with the same general method of operation or even similar signature. Criminal investigators and profilers have found it useful to construct typologies of rapists (Hazelwood and Burgess 2001), sexual murderers (Keppel and Walter 1999), arsonists (Canter and Fritzon 1998; Kocsis, Irwin, and Hayes 1998), and child molesters (Lanning 1992) based on their experiences with prior crimes and criminals who have manifested similar crime scene behaviors.

Detailed explanations of the deductive approach to profiling, which characterizes much of the FBI method, can be found in treatises by Douglas et al. (1986) and by Ressler et al. (1986). Finally it should be noted that the organized–disorganized dichotomy that is the centerpiece of the FBI model also has its critics (Canter et al. 2004; Hicks and Sales 2006; Turvey 2002), as has the entire discipline of profiling (Allison et al. 2002).

DEDUCTIVE PROFILING

As the name implies, deductive profiles are the outcome of the application of logic (Petherick 2005). They are more highly focused, in the sense that they are based on the specific evidence gathered at the scene of each crime (Petherick 2005). Thus, unlike inductive profiles, which are built on generalized conclusions from the known characteristics of prior cyber crimes and cyber criminals, deductive profiles are built from the explicit conclusions that are drawn from actual evidence in the current case under investigation (Turvey 2002).

Deductive profiles are constructed bottom-up, in that the profile is developed from evidence gathered at the crime scene of the particular case in question. Although there is some disagreement about whether it is inductive, or deductive, the most popular example of profiling is the FBI's Behavioral Evidence Analysis (BEA) approach, which is based on a characterization of the perpetrator as either organized or disorganized. Organized types commit crimes that are planned, involve control over the victim and leave little forensic evidence (Douglas 1998). The disorganized type commits crimes that are impulsive, opportunistic, and haphazard (Woodworth 2001).

The classic BEA model involves four component activities: equivocal forensic analysis, case victimology, crime scene characteristics, and offender characteristics (Turvey 2002). Equivocal forensic analysis, presumes there are no preset interpretations of cyber crime behaviors. Preexisting typologies may be considered by the investigator, but will not determine the a priori importance of any given fact of the case. Case victimology includes an analysis of the victim of cyber crime, including vulnerabilities and defenses. The key goal is to determine why this particular victim was chosen and which of its vulnerabilities might be known by insiders or outsiders. Crime scene characteristics require a complete understanding of how the cyber attack was carried out (what? how? why? when? and where?) The "who" part of this classic set of investigative questions is what comprises the offender characteristics component of the BEA. The answer to that question is determined by the answers to the other three parts of the process.

This approach can also apply to the investigation of cyber crime. Because cyber crimes can only be committed within certain technological boundaries, there are really only two ways that a cyber criminal can execute a cyber crime: (i) through the introduction of some type of malicious agent (in the form of computer code) and (ii) through targeted attacks. Each of these approaches calls for different assumptions about the motivations associated with the crime, and conclusions can be drawn about the degree of proximity and competence of the individual who has committed the crime based on the specific behaviors associated with each exploit. This will be discussed in much greater detail when we talk about cyber crime types but these constraints on behavior should be kept in mind as we discuss our particular method for cyber criminal profiling.

A SUGGESTED PROFILING METHOD FOR CYBER CRIMINALS

Although there are no practical examples of the application of profiling to victimless crimes, it should be understood that when we use the term cyber crime we are talking about intentional crimes that harm a specific victim, or victims. In that respect, cyber crimes follow the same common set of rules as crimes in the physical universe do. They can be targeted (organized), or untargeted (disorganized), they involve an MO, and they will leave behind specific behavioral signatures depending on the individual attacker. There is also a victimology associated with cyber crimes that can accurately suggest the type of criminal involved. Moreover, there is always some form of geographic component. For instance, it is almost impossible to pass a logic bomb through a firewall. Therefore, proximity is required that fits within the parameters of geographical profiling. Our point is that the classic methods of profiling can all contribute to the prevention and solution of cyber crime.

In application, the organized-disorganized dichotomy is useful when it comes to understanding perpetrators of cyber crimes. For instance, untargeted worm-based denial of service (DOS) exploits, which are the most common source of harm on the Internet, rarely fit the organized typology. Although the code exploit itself is planned, its impacts are unknown. Thus, the motive and intent are more typically characteristic of unfocused social patterns and psyche.

Just as physical crimes are often characterized by mixed motives, so too are many cyber crimes. As cyber profiling efforts become more sophisticated, the organized-disorganized dichotomy may be replaced by a more appropriate heuristic model. Until such time, however, the beginning profiler may wish to consider the methodology that we have evolved. This approach is based both on the FBI's method of profiling, known as Criminal Investigative Analysis, and a second approach known as Turvey's Behavioral Evidence Analysis. Using these two models, we believe that there are five sequential stages to the cyber criminal profiling process. These stages are sequential and they all apply directly to the investigation of cyber crime:

Evidence gathering. Whether it is called an assimilation phase, or equivocal forensic analysis, the first step in any investigation is the collection of forensic evidence. This is no different for cyber crimes; and the entire discipline of cyber forensics, which is a separate and much larger topic, has been created to address it.

Behavioral analysis. No matter if it is equivocal or based on pattern determinations, behavioral analysis is an attempt to derive a meaningful set of characteristic behaviors from the facts of the crime. This stage of the process is a logical follow up to evidence gathering and is a critical part of any criminal investigation, cyber crime, or otherwise. An unknown perpetrator can only be characterized and distinguished by the describable behaviors he exhibits.

Victimology. is the next part of the puzzle. This is as true for cyber crime investigation as it is for the investigation of crimes in physical space. In fact, the victim profile can tell the investigator a lot about the type of perpetrator since there are well-known signatures associated with different types of crimes in cyberspace. For instance, an attack on a Microsoft product without an obvious motive beyond the actual attack is usually a statement, and statements are associated with counterculture behavior. That narrows the list of suspects down to cyber punks who are frequently well known to authorities.

Crime pattern analysis. This is the "what and how." This stage combines all of the things that are already known with any other considerations, such as geography and timing, into a logical theory of the actors and events of the crime. This is obviously a critical element of a typical physical investigation. Notwithstanding that fact, however, it would be impossible to approach a cyber crime intelligently without a fact-based, working hypothesis about the execution of the crime.

Profile development. Once the crime itself is reconstructed, it is possible to formulate a profile of the offender. While these methods support deductive reasoning about the nature of the offender, it may be helpful to have generalized inductive typologies on hand to aid in the interpretation of fact patterns.

TWELVE CYBER CRIMINAL PROFILES

Using this approach we developed 12 profiles of cyber criminals which might be routinely encountered by law enforcement and information assurance professionals. We differentiated each of these types based on their motive, intent, and postoffense behavior. These are inductive profiles. They are derived from cyber criminal acts, which have been well documented in the literature as well as the media.

It should be noted, however, that although most of these profiles are unique, several of them, specifically the "kiddie" (cf. Fitzgerald 2004), the "cyberpunk" (cf. Hafner 1991), the "cyberthief" (cf. Goodell 1996), and the "cyberstalker" (cf. Bocij 2004) have had varying degrees of coverage in both academic publications and the popular literature.

Kiddies are technologically inept. They use preprogrammed scripts, their intent is almost always to trespass, and their motivation is ego. More advanced kiddies will engage in invasion of privacy exploits. Kiddies can be of any age, but they are always outsiders and not technologically hip. They are usually new to crime and can be tracked by matching a crime to the individual who has downloaded a suitable toolset from hacker Web sites.

Cyberpunk hackers are members of the counterculture. Because they are ego-driven, their intent is almost always trespass or invasion. If their purpose is invasion, the motive is exposure. Cyberpunks will engage in theft and sabotage but only of what they perceive as legitimate targets. Cyberpunks are responsible for many virus, application layer, and DOS attacks targeted on establishment organizations, companies, and products. A cyberpunk is invariably young, technologically proficient, and an outsider.

Old-timer hackers are perhaps the most technologically proficient members of the hacker community. They are ego driven and the last of the Old Guard whose only intent was to prove their art by trespassing. They are relatively harmless because they know what they are doing and their motives are relatively benign. Where their actions cause harm they generally specialize in Web site defacement. An old-timer is middle aged or older with a long personal and/or professional history in technology and possibly hacking.

Code warriors are the first of the more destructive profiles. In the past they were driven by ego or revenge. Now, they are almost strictly driven by monetary gain. As such they engage in either theft or sabotage. Their crimes are built around code exploits, specifically application layer attacks and Trojan horses. Like old-timers they are technologically superb with long and visible histories in technology. They are likely to have been identified as having committed hacking exploits in the past. They can be of any age but, because their art is a profession in and of itself, most of these individuals fall into the 30-to-50 age range. They are likely to have a degree in technology but are not employed in that sector or may even be unemployed. Code warriors are almost always socially inept and show signs of social deviance.

Cyberthieves are motivated by monetary gain, either through coming into possession of valuable information illicitly or by outright theft. Their crimes are built around any means to that end. They are specifically adept at surreptitious network attacks such as sniffing or spoofing. As such, the individuals in this profile use network tools and simple programming exploits such as Trojans and malware rather than targeted code. They are also very adept at social engineering, which amounts to running a classic con game. They can be any age, but this profile does not require a long history in technology; therefore, these perpetrators can be younger than the code warrior. Most are organizational insiders but some are found outside the organization.

Cyberhucksters are the spammers and general purveyors of malware. Their motives are monetary gain, and their intent is commercialization. They are adept at social engineering. They also use spoofing. This profile employs methods like tracking cookies, spyware, and even legitimate data mines to find victims. They tend to be older business types who are already well known to local law enforcement. Cyberhucksters are not prosecuted as conscientiously as they should be because their actions are more irritating than criminal (although they have been committing crimes since early 2005).

Unhappy insider is perhaps the most dangerous profile in the entire set. These people are inside most organization's defenses. This individual is motivated by revenge or monetary gain and uses extortion or exposure of company secrets for the purpose of theft, or sabotage. His intent is to steal, or harm items of value to the company. He can steal information, set destructive logic bombs, or perform other malicious acts on the system. A distinctive characteristic of this perpetrator is his unhappiness with the organization. These individuals are insiders who can be of any age and employed at any level. The only protection against this type of perpetrator is to identify signs of unhappiness and closely monitor further actions.

Ex-insider is the terminated former employee motivated by extortion, revenge, sabotage, or disinformation. These individuals are focused on harming the organization that dismissed them. If they can see the dismissal coming, they might set logic bombs or perform other destructive acts. Otherwise, they will make use of insider information to harm or discredit the company from the outside. They can be of any age and work at any level. The only protection from this type of malcontent is to plan a dismissal to ensure a clean break. A sure sign of the work of an ex-insider are attacks on company vulnerabilities that were not public knowledge.

Cyberstalker is an individual motivated by ego and deviance. The primary intent of this perpetrator is invasion of privacy for the purpose of learning something to satisfy some specific personal need (like jealousy). The chief tool of the perpetrators in this category is the key-logger; however, more sophisticated cyberstalkers will use targeted Trojan horses or sniffers. This profile is differentiated from the other ego-driven profiles by the fact that these invasions of privacy are driven by a psychological need. Identification of that need, which is their fingerprint, will often point to the cyberstalker.

Con man is an individual motivated by simple monetary gain, and his intent is primarily theft, or some form of illicit commercialization. This type is adept at social engineering and spoofing. Members of this group run traditional con games like the Nigerian scam, as well as newer exploits like phishing. These attacks are typically untargeted and anonymous. Because of that anonymity, con men are very difficult to catch once they have hit. Since the con man depends on the ignorance of his victim, the best defense is awareness.

The *mafia soldier* is organized crime's entry into the field of cyber crime and is differentiated from all other categories by its purposefulness and high level of organization, which is second only to that of the warfighter. Mafia soldiers are motivated by the same goals that motivate their nontechnical brethren in crime—monetary gain. This end is achieved by the same means: theft, extortion and, occasionally, invasion of privacy for the purposes of blackmail. Mafia soldiers have the distinguishing characteristics of the code warrior or con man. However, they always work in highly organized groups; often with the best technology money can buy. The most common incarnation of this type currently works out of the Far East and Eastern Europe. However, given the ease and profitability of Internet crime, it is expected that every organized crime group in the world will eventually be into this business.

Warfighter is not a criminal type when he is fighting on your side. However, when the warfighter is on the other side of the law, his actions would be viewed as destructive. The warfighter is motivated strictly by Infowar. His aim is strategic advantage for friends and harm to the enemy. These individuals are technologically superb so they are extremely dangerous. They can wreak havoc on the physical infrastructure of a country by attacking the electronic underpinnings. This is most frequently accomplished through application layer attacks and logic bombs delivered by surreptitious means over a long period of time. DOS is another form of attack. Warfighters can spread disinformation. This might occur by targeted attacks on the media or through social engineering. Warfighters can be of any age, highly organized, and frequently are the best and brightest that the country has to offer. Since this profile really just characterizes the members of any elite government agency, the best defense against a warfighter is another friendly set of warfighters.

TYPES OF CYBER CRIMINAL EXPLOITS: MALICIOUS CODE

As we said earlier, all forms of cyber crime are constrained by technology. Therefore, there are a limited number of ways that the perpetrator can go about committing a cyber crime, no matter what the typology is. Fundamentally, all computer-based crimes are limited to two general categories, the injection of some form of **malicious code**, or a technological exploit aimed at a selected target. The latter type of attack can be either electronic, or physical. Any of the profiles we have just discussed could execute either of these two types of exploits. But since the approach is usually shaped by the intent there are good logical reasons to assume that certain types of criminal exploits can be more closely associated with particular criminal types.

For instance, much of the malicious code currently encountered by cyber investigators is a hangover from the earlier days of cyber crime when the motivation was ego, not profit or revenge (Honeynet Project, The 2001). When ego is the motivator, most of this code is a product of two of the profile types we discussed earlier: cyberpunks and code warriors. Script kiddies have also been involved in spreading some viruses, but, since they depend on the other two categories for the tools, they will be discussed separately.

Most malicious code exploits may be defined as "disorganized," in that there is no particular target involved, ego is a primary motivator, and there is no financial profit motive that would accrue directly to the perpetrator. Where profit from a malicious code exploit is involved, the typology is clearly organized. That is because the crime is conceived, targeted, and executed with a plan for criminal gain or revenge and utilizes a certain degree of care.

Most of the targeted malicious code is being written to put in bot-nets, key loggers, or steal databases, or to harvest computers and then sell the bandwidth off to spammers (Hochmuth 2004, 1). Based on some degree of past study, the people who carry out the organized type of malicious code exploits fit the characteristics of the "organized" typology (Saita 2001; Honeynet Project, The 2001; Casey 2000).

There are four accepted categories of malicious code: viruses, logic bombs, Trojan horses, and malware. Each of these has a slightly different criminal application; therefore, each involves a different typology.

Viruses are probably the most common types of malicious code. These are tiny code segments that attach themselves to host programs and then propagate when the host is executed. They are almost by definition a disorganized exploit since it is impossible to say who the victim of a particular virus will be.

In general, a virus is a harmless example of an ego-driven exploit. Viruses are generally created as a demonstration of programming technique; rather than from any focused attempt to take over the world. On the other hand worms, which are a specialized type of virus, might have features that would be associated with an organized type of perpetrator since they are responsible for DOS. When activated, they carry out preprogrammed attacks on a network or networks.

Because they cause denials of service, worms are increasingly being used for purposes of extortion and sabotage. The motivation behind a worm is almost always aggressive and destructive. Therefore, people who construct worms are more likely to have specific criminal motives. Criminals who have carried out acts in this category and who have been apprehended and studied tend to fit very solidly into the organized typology.

The first example of a worm-based exploit is the Great Worm of 1988, which specifically targeted the UNIX operating system. The perpetrator was almost immediately tracked down and arrested, because the authorities were able to associate the intent of that worm with critical comments made about that specific vulnerability. Thus, in effect, this case also becomes the first instance of the use of a profile to solve an Internet cyber crime.

Logic bombs, on the other hand are examples of planned exploits. They are programs set in a host machine and only activated based on parameters. They are almost impossible to detect once they are set and invariably destructive because they are there for a reason. They are a key tool for crimes like extortion, sabotage, and even infowar. Their weakness is that close or hands-on access is usually required to set a logic bomb, unless it is delivered by a Trojan horse. As such, they are also almost perfect examples of an organized type of crime. They can be extremely dangerous because, if set by hand, it is possible to build a great deal of malicious functionality into a logic bomb's programming.

Profiles are extremely useful in the case of a logic bomb because it invariably requires physical access to set them. Therefore, the perpetrator can be profiled just as he or she would for a physical crime. Crime scene evidence can be gathered and analyzed, and even geographic profiling can be used. The only problem with profiling in this respect is that it is mostly after the fact, since logic bombs are usually discovered after the harm is already done.

Trojan horses are like their namesake. They are typically wrappers for malicious payloads attached to innocuous looking programs. Because they are hard to detect, Trojan horses are the primary means of delivering a range of malicious objects. Therefore, the criminals who use Trojan horses are very similar to the type of serial killers that inhabit the physical world. They are hard to catch or even identify because they exhibit the same characteristics of high intelligence and detachment that a serial killer might have. But unlike serial killers, the criminals who employ Trojan horses are never near the scene of their crime nor do they leave a physical footprint. Thus, they are the classic unknown subject. Almost the only way to track down a person who writes Trojan horse code is by building a profile sufficient to identify a limited set of suspects in a narrow physical location.

Finally, if commercialization and cyberstalking are issues, there is the special case of malware. Malware is a code that is transferred to a visitor's computer when his browser visits a site preselected by the cyber criminal. Malware can include such innocuous things as data miners and adware. But malware can also deliver things like home page hijackers and keyloggers. Adware is an example of Internet commercialization.

The more malicious forms of malware are always set for specific criminal purposes such as theft. The problem with profiling this category is that malware offenders exhibit both organized and disorganized characteristics. Although the primary purpose of their endeavor is known and planned in advance with a certain degree of remorselessness, the actual victim can be any person who visits the site. The dispersal of the adware exhibits some of the characteristics of "sin" type victimologies in the sense that the Web sites associated with "mainstream" activity do not set malicious objects. Consequently, the most likely place to pick up a botnet hijacker is from a site associated with "fringe" type commerce, a pornography site for instance. In that respect, some of the attitudes and criminal motivations for people who set highly malicious objects match those of their sin-trade counterparts.

The problem with investigating malware is that those malicious agents are usually unfocused in their intent. Since the victim is almost by definition randomly self-selecting, the perpetrators of those crimes are hard to profile deductively. Plus, because the malware itself is usually picked up from a fringe site, the crime is not as likely to be reported. The only way to profile the writer of malware is through inductive profiling techniques, which are generally always less accurate. Because of the constraints of geographic space, this almost never produces a workable list of suspects.

TARGETED ATTACKS

Profiling is particularly useful in the case of targeted attacks. A good profiler can differentiate the general characteristics of the attacker based on attack type (Petherick 2005). This makes it possible to prepare a defense in advance where the attack can be anticipated from an inductive typology, or it can facilitate tracking down and prosecuting otherwise anonymous attackers by analyzing their signature or MO.

Targeted attacks are just like any other kind of organized criminal activity. They are motivated, they have a method, and they usually have a specific victimology associated with them. Targeted attacks fall into eight generic types: insider, password, sniffing, spoofing, man-in-the-middle, application layer, denial of service, and social engineering.

Insider Attacks

The insider attack has always been the number-one threat, and probably always will be. No one knows the security system better than someone who's on the inside. If that person becomes disgruntled, they can easily steal privileged information by loading it on a memory stick, for example, and walking out the door with it. They can also send that information to any external place since the firewall is outward facing. That is, most firewalls are designed to detect potential inbound violations not outbound ones. Finally, besides violations of confidentiality, insider attacks can also be extremely destructive since, "until just a few years ago, most security appliances didn't even look internal within the network" (Hochmuth 2004, 2). As a result, insider attacks account for up to three-quarters of the reported annual loss to cyber crime in the United States (Garretson and Duffy 2004; CSI 2004). Since these crimes center on human behavior, insider attacks can be profiled; and the ability to predict who might execute them can help get monitoring in place to prevent the acts before they occur.

Although some insider attacks might be directed on targets of opportunity and thus fit the disorganized typology, most are planned; and the characteristics of the perpetrator almost always fit the organized type. The victim is overwhelmingly the insider's place of work. However, there are a significant number of instances where an insider uses his or her status with a business partner to carry out a crime. No matter the victimology, insider attacks fit the general motivation and method of an organized type of crime aimed at criminal profit.

Password Attacks

Password attacks are simple exploits. The aim of a password attack is to either guess a password or obtain it through confidence scams, called social engineering. In the past the aim of most password attacks was trespass merely for the sake of ego. However, access can also lead to theft and sabotage. In both cases, the attack has to be carefully planned and executed. Therefore, it is invariably classifiable as an organized type of exploit and the general characteristics associated with that typology apply.

Password attacks are often social engineering exploits but they can also originate from Trojan horses, network sniffing, or specific application assaults, such as dictionary attacks. If the attack is electronic in origin, for instance, from the Internet and very little harm is done, then the basic hacker profile for kiddies, cyberpunks, or old-timers apply. If the aim is sabotage, extortion, or theft, code warriors, cyberthieves and even the mafia warrior fit the profile.

Nevertheless, given the reliance on social engineering, which is the manipulation of people in order to trick them out of sensitive information such as passwords, the most likely method of attack is through personal contact. Social engineering-type password attacks constitute up to 90 percent of the total attacks of that type (Garretson and Duffy 2004; CSI 2004). As such, the likeliest person to perpetrate a password attack is an individual who is in close physical proximity to where the attack originated, such as an insider or client.

Sniffer-Based Attacks

Sniffing, spoofing, man-in-the middle, and application layer attacks are all varieties of technological exploit that closely fit the organized typology. Sniffing involves stealing information from a transmission through the use of a standard network utility called a Sniffer. Because network topology and operation of netware utilities are involved, this is a carefully planned and executed exploit that requires technological know-how and technical proficiency. Thus, the likeliest people to try this exploit are cyberpunks, cyberthieves, and cyberstalkers.

The simplest word to describe sniffing is "snooping." Sniffing is primarily designed to steal something like a password in order to gain access. Another purpose is to acquire account or social security information, which can support theft and sabotage. If the aim of sniffing is theft or sabotage, then the criminal is more likely to fit the code warrior, mafia soldier, or warfighter typology. The sniffing exploit itself is passive, so it only serves to provide information, such as passwords and account data. It will not support active exploits that are performed using that information.

Finally, in addition to the types of criminal behavior that we have discussed so far, deviants also use sniffing exploits for the purpose of invasion of privacy. These are almost always motivated in the same way as other types of personal crimes, such as sex crime.

The aim of this behavior is to gain some form of advantage or control over the victim by securing knowledge that is either private or personal. In cases such as this, the perpetrator almost always has some form of direct relationship to the victim, or the victim fulfills some type of common fantasy. In both cases, this type of offender fits the typical methods and doctrines as physical profiling does.

Spoofing-Based Attacks

Spoofing is another example of an organized type of crime because it requires careful planning and execution to convince others that the sender of an Internet packet or message is legitimate. As such, the attributes of the organized typology are just as accurate for spoofers as it is for other criminals of this type.

There is one difference, however. Because spoofing has become something of a business enterprise in various third-world countries (Bednarz 2004; Garretson and Duffy 2004; Gudaitis 2005), the spoofer is almost never a classic loner. Instead, he is part of a large and well-organized group of criminal participants. Just like sniffing, spoofing is done in order to perpetrate more destructive crimes such as theft or sabotage. At the technological level, this exploit typically involves spoofing an IP address by changing the packet-header information. At the behavioral or social engineering level, this can entail simple or elaborate phishing scams or spamming using recognizable addresses.

Spoofing is almost always done for the purpose of gaining access for profit. It is a common technique used by every category of criminal; however, it is the chief technique of the electronic con man. In order for the spoof to work properly, the victim has to be tricked into believing something that is not true. One of the interesting asides of this method is that, because of IP spoofing, the computer itself is as likely to be the target victim as any human dupe.

The likeliest type of individual to employ IP spoofing is the cyberthief or code warrior. The more powerfully malicious categories, such as the mafia soldier and the warfighter, also employ this technique but, compared to the other categories there are relatively few of those latter types in the game. The common thread for all of these types however is their technical proficiency. As such, the list of suspects in an IP spoofing incident is fairly easy to compile compared to the practitioners of the behavioral spoof.

The individuals who engage in behavioral spoofing are exactly like the old-fashioned con men of literary fame. In fact, many of these spoofing exploits bear the same time-worn names, like the Nigerian Scam, the Lottery Scam, and the ever popular Pigeon Drop. In a behavioral exploit of this type, the victim is unknown to the criminal until they respond to the spoof. The spoof itself is usually a "mass-mailing" exploit involving a very large number of unknown but potential victims. Because the behavioral spoof does not involve specifically targeting a victim, the victimology can also fit into the disorganized typology (e.g., the specific behavior of the victim creates the target).

Man-in-the-Middle and Application Layer Attacks

Man-in-the-middle (MITM) and application layer attacks are explicit code exploits. MITM involves inserting a malicious code entity into a two-party conversation as a third party (MITM). This usually takes place on a network, typically by the placement of a Trojan horse.

However, it can also be a direct physical attack if the agent is a keylogger placed on the victim's system by the criminal party.

On the other hand, application layer attacks come at a specific application through a defect or vulnerability in the code (buffer overflow, for example). Application layer attacks are the most common direct exploits in the cyberuniverse. These attacks require careful planning and execution. They also invariably require a reasonable level of technical knowhow and skill. As such, the perpetrators in this case have attributes that are very close to the typology associated with the organized criminal.

These exploits occur most frequently for the purposes of theft, extortion, sabotage, and Infowar (CSI 2004; Garretson and Duffy 2004; Bednarz 2004). As such, where profit is involved, they tend to best describe the mafia soldier, cyberthief, and the code warrior profiles, or the cyberpunk if the target is an institution like Microsoft. The more sinister types like the warfighter could also use these exploits to commit the sort of mayhem that is typically international in significance.

The majority of the crimes that are rated as significantly destructive by agencies such as the FBI's Computer Security Institute (CSI 2004) and the U.S.-CERT are application layer attacks. The problem for law enforcement is that the perpetrator is almost always unknown and to some extent unknowable. Because of the level of technical proficiency required to carry out such an attack, the attacker is ensured in advance there will be no evidence. As such, almost the only option available is a good solid profile.

Denial-of-Service Attacks

Last but not the least, DOS is an explicit attack aimed at preventing a host from gaining access to the Internet. Targeted attacks can be technological, or they can be simple physical assaults, such as vandalizing the server. There can also be untargeted, broad-spectrum attacks, such as worm-based DOS attacks. Monetarily this category of exploit is the most harmful type in the entire group of potential attacks. It is estimated that one DOS exploit alone, MyDoom, cost companies up to $250 million in lost productivity and prompted Microsoft to offer a $250,000 reward for the capture of the criminals involved (Stein 2004).

Since targeted DOS attacks are done for profit or revenge, these perpetrators fit squarely into the organized typology. If the purpose of the attack is profit, the perpetrator is likely to be a code warrior or a mafia soldier. If the attack is strategic, the perpetrator is a warfighter. All of these individuals display skill and careful planning and execution. They can be counted on not to leave any useful evidence. However, because of the nature of the exploit, which typically involves overwhelming the transmission medium with a large number of messages or requests, it is almost impossible to target a DOS attack to a single victim. Therefore, a targeted DOS attack is nowhere near as common or harmful as a broad spectrum or untargeted DOS.

Broad-spectrum or untargeted DOS attacks are typically motivated by personality issues or even occur by accident. Therefore, they fit into the disorganized typology. In fact, if the assumption is made that the perpetrator did not have mass destruction in mind, it can be said that every worm-based crime, from Code Red to Santy, displays the same lack of organization.

Accidental DOS, which is an attribute of the disorganized type, is a particularly common occurrence and is a consequence of a lack of knowledge. For instance, the person who perpetrated the first DOS attack, the Great Worm, claimed that he was only trying to discover the limits of the Internet. Untargeted attacks are characteristic of the cyberpunk who typically has an axe to grind, such as SQL Slammer (aka the Sapphire Worm) or MyDoom. A cyberpunk motivated DOS could be considered to be targeted in the sense that companies such as Microsoft are frequently the intended victim. However, since the actual victims are the millions of users of their products, it is hard to classify that type of attack as specifically targeted.

Every cyber criminal could conceivably engage in DOS attacks; however, recently kiddies have been among the most notorious. The attributes of a script kiddy are also a perfect example of the attributes of a disorganized cyber criminal: technologically inept, a younger, or immature personality and a fringe worker in a nontechnical field.

The Special Case of Social Engineering

Social engineering is a strictly behavioral exploit. It is also a very common form of attack. Social engineering scams can vary in sophistication from dumpster diving to actually running short- and long-term con games and stings. These are always organized type crimes, and they almost perfectly fit the attributes of that category of cyber criminal.

If they are *not* ego driven, social engineering attacks are typically done to steal something like a password or account information. However, they are also used for everything up to Infowar and strategic, political, or disinformation purposes. Since social engineering gambits are behavioral, they can generally be classified based on what the attacker seeks to gain (Hochmuth 2004). The only true practitioner of a strictly social engineering exploit is the con man type. However, social engineering is part of the art of the cyberpunk, the cyberthief, and the cyberstalker.

CONCLUSION

In conclusion, we have introduced and discussed herein the practice of cyber profiling. Just as physical world crimes are sometimes quite amenable to criminal profiling, so too are cyber crimes. Many physical crimes leave behind insufficient evidence to support criminal profiling, and this may be true of certain cyber crimes as well. Because the art of cyber profiling is evolving so rapidly, we fully expect portions of our discussions on this chapter to be somewhat outdated in the near future.

Motivations such as money, entertainment, ego, allow entrance to social groups and status (Kilger, Arkin, and Stutzman 2004) have been with us for a long time and are unlikely to disappear soon. Perhaps a better model for understanding and identifying cyber criminals may evolve through the creation of a typology which more intricately blends the concept of organized and disorganized cyber attacks with the motives mentioned above. We hopefully await this development.

KEY TERMS

Criminal profiling   Hacking
Cyber criminals   Malicious code

REFERENCES

Alison, L., C. Bennell, A. Mokros, and D. Ormerod. 2002. The personality paradox in offender profiling: A theoretical review of the processes involved in deriving background characteristics from crime scene actions. *Psychology, Public Policy and the Law* 8: 115–35.

Bednarz, A. November 29, 2004. Profiling cybercriminals. *Network World* 1–2. www.networkworld.com. Accessed December 2006.

Bocij, P. 2004. *Cyberstalking: Harassment in the Internet Age and How to Protect Your Family.* Westport, CT: Praeger Publishers.

Branigan, S. 2004. *High-Tech Crimes Revealed: Cyberwar Stories from the Digital Front.* Boston: Addison-Wesley.

Canter, D. 2000. Offender profiling and criminal differentiation. *Legal and Criminological Psychology* 5: 23–46.

Canter, D., L. Alison, E. Alison, and N. Wentink. 2004. The organized/disorganized typology of serial murder: Myth or model? *Psychology, Public Policy, and Law* 10: 293–320.

Canter, D., and K. Fritzon. 1998. Differentiating arsonists: A model of firesetting actions and characteristics. *Legal and Criminal Psychology* 3: 73–96.

Casey, E. 2000. Criminal profiling, computers and the Internet. *Journal of Behavioral Profiling* 1. Retrieved February 3, 2007, from http://www.profiling.org/journal/vol1_no2/jbp_toc_may2000_1-2_pub.html

Computer Security Institute. 2004. *Annual Survey of Computer Crime in America.* Washington, DC: Federal Bureau of Investigation.

Douglas, J., and M. Olshaker. 1995. *Mindhunter: Inside the FBI Elite Serial Crime Unit.* London: Mandarin Paperbacks.

Douglas, J. E., R. K. Ressler, A. W. Burgess, and C. R. Hartman. 1986. Criminal profiling from crime scene analysis. *Behavioral Science and the Law* 4: 401–21.

Fitzgerald, M. January 13, 2004. "Hackers, crackers and script kiddies, oh my!" *Yahoo! Tech Tuesday.* Accessed January 2007.

Garretson, C., and J. Duffy. November 29, 2004. Cybercrime: The story behind the stats. *Network World* 1–2. www.networkworld.com. Accessed December 2006.

Goodell, J. 1996. *The Cyberthief and the Samurai: The True Story of Kevin Mitnick—And the Man Who Hunted Him Down.* Dell.

Gudaitis, T. April 6, 2005. Profiling cybercrime. *ITBusinessedge.* Retrieved September 2006 from www.ITBusinessedge.com

Hafner, K. 1991. *Cyberpunk: Outlaws and Hackers on the Computer Frontier.* Touchstone.

Hazelwood, R., and A. Burgess, eds. 2001. *Practical Aspects of Rape Investigation: A Multidisciplinary Approach.* 3rd ed. Boca Raton, FL: CRC Press.

Heiser, J. G, and W. G. Kruse. 2002. *Computer Forensics: Incident Response Essentials.* Boston: Addison Wesley Professional Series.

Hicks, S., and B. Sales. 2006. *Criminal Profiling: Developing an Effective Science and Practice.* Washington, DC: American Psychological Association.

Hochmuth, P. November 29, 2004. Profiling cybercrime—"Network threats and defence strategies." *Network World* 1–2. www.networkworld.com. Accessed December 2006.

Homant, R., and D. Kennedy. 1998. Psychological aspects of crime scene profiling: Validity research. *Criminal Justice and Behavior* 25: 319–43.

Honeynet Project, The, ed. 2001. *Know Your Enemy: Revealing the Security Tools, Tactics and Motives of the Blackhat Community.* Boston: Addison-Wesley.

Keppel, R., and R. Walter. 1999. Profiling killers: A revised classification model for understanding sexual murder. *International Journal of Offender Therapy and Comparative Criminology* 43: 417–34.

Kilger, M., O. Arkin, and J. Stutzman. 2004. "Profiling." In *Know Your Enemy: Learning about Security Threats,* edited by The Honeynut Project, 505–56. 2nd ed. Boston: Addison Wesley.

Kocsis, R. 2006. *Criminal Profiling.* Totowa, NJ: Humana Press.

Kocsis, R., H. Irwin, and A. Hayes. 1998. Organized and disorganized criminal behavior syndromes in arsonists: A validation study of a psychological profiling concept. *Psychiatry, Psychology and Law* 5: 117–31.

Lanning, K. 1992. *Child Molesters: A Behavioral Analysis.* Alexandria, VA: National Center for Missing and Exploited Children.

McGrath, M., and E. Casey. 2002. Forensic psychiatry and the Internet: Practical perspectives on sexual predators and obsessional harassers in cyberspace. *Journal of the American Academy of Psychiatry and Law* 30: 81–94.

Murrie, D., J. Warren, M. Kristiansson, and P. Dietz. 2002. Asperger's syndrome in forensic settings. *International Journal of Forensic Mental Health* 1: 59–70.

Palermo, G. B., and R. N. Kocsis. 2005. *Offender Profiling: An Introduction to the Socio-Psychological Analysis of Violent Crime.* Springfield, IL: Charles C Thomas Publisher.

Petherick, W. 2005. *The Science of Criminal Profiling.* New York: Barnes and Noble.

Petherick, W., ed. 2006. *Serial Crime: Theoretical and Practical Issues in Behavioral Profiling.* London: Academic Press.

Radcliff, D. 2003. Profiling defined. *Network World Fusion.* Retrieved January 2005 from www.nwfusion.com

Reddy, M., R. Borum, J. Berglund, B. Vossekuil, R. Fein, and W. Modzeleski. 2001. Evaluating risk for targeted violence in schools: Comparing risk assessment, threat assessment and other approaches. *Psychology in the Schools* 38: 157–72.

Ressler, R. K., A. W. Burgess, J. E. Douglas, C. Hartman, and R. D'Agostino. 1986. Sexual killers and their victims: Identifying patterns through crime scene analysis. *Journal of Interpersonal Violence* 1: 288–308.

Rogers, M. 2003. The role of criminal profiling in the computer forensics process. *Computers and Security* 22: 292–98.

Saferstein, R. 2001. *Criminalistics: An Introduction to Forensic Science.* 7th ed. Upper Saddle River, NJ: Prentice Hall.

Saita, A. 2001. Hacker psychology, understanding peopleware. *Information Security Magazine.* http://infosecuritymag.techtarget.com/articles/june01/features_hacker_psychology.shtml

Silva, J., G. Leong, and M. Ferrari. 2004. A neuropsychiatric developmental model of serial homicidal behavior. *Behavioral Sciences and the Law* 22: 787–99.

Stein, A. January 30, 2004. Microsoft offers MyDoom reward. *CNN/Money.* Retrieved December 2006 from http://money.com

Turvey, B. 1998. Deductive criminal profiling: Comparing applied methodologies between inductive and deductive criminal profiling techniques. Knowledge Solutions Library, http://www.corpus-delicti.com/Profiling_law.html

Turvey, B. 2002. *Criminal Profiling: An Introduction to Behavioural Evidence Analysis.* 2nd ed. New York: Academic Press.

Woodworth, M., and S. Porter. 2001. Historical foundations and current applications of criminal profiling in violent crime investigations. *Expert Evidence* 7: 241–61.

Chapter 24

Digital Evidence

Kathryn E. Scarborough
Eastern Kentucky University

Marc Rogers
Purdue University

Kelli Frakes
Eastern Kentucky University

Cristina San Martin
Purdue University

Kathryn E. Scarborough, **Ph.D.**, professor at the Department of Safety, Security, and Emergency Management at Eastern Kentucky University, earned her Ph.D. in criminal justice from Sam Houston State University. She also has an MA in applied sociology with a certificate in women's studies from Old Dominion and Norfolk State Universities, and a BS in criminal justice from the University of Southern Mississippi. Prior to her teaching at Eastern Kentucky University, she was a police officer in Portsmouth, Virginia, a United States Navy Hospital Corpsman/Emergency Medical Technician, and a chemical dependency technician. In addition to her faculty role, Dr. Scarborough is Director for Research, Evaluation and Testing for the Justice and Safety Center. Her current teaching and research interests include criminal investigation, law enforcement technology, cyber crime and security, and police administration.

In her role as director for research, testing and evaluation, she has oversight of more than 70 projects funded by the Department of Homeland Security, the National Institute of Justice/Office of Science and Technology, the State of Kentucky, and the Department of Defense. She also serves as project director or codirector of the following projects: National Study on Criminal Investigation, the Digital Evidence Assessment of Local and State Law Enforcement Organizations, the Rural Cyber Crime Response and Prevention Team project, Cyber PAAL, and the ASIS International Security Trends project.

Marc Rogers, **Ph.D.**, CISSP, CCCI, is the Chair of the Cyber Forensics Program in the Department of Computer and Information Technology at Purdue University. He is an associate professor and also a research faculty member at the Center for Education and Research in Information Assurance and Security (CERIAS). Dr. Rogers was a senior instructor for (ISC)2, the international body that certifies information system security professionals (CISSP), is a member of the quality assurance board for (ISC)2's SCCP designation, and is Chair of the Law, Compliance and Investigation Domain of international Common Body of Knowledge (CBK) committee. He is a former police detective who worked in the area of fraud and computer crime investigations. Dr. Rogers sits on the editorial board for several professional journals and is a member of various national and international committees focusing on digital forensic science and digital evidence. He is the author of numerous book chapters, and journal publications in the field of digital forensics and applied psychological analysis. His research interests include applied cyber forensics, psychological digital crime scene analysis, and cyber terrorism.

Kelli Frakes is currently pursuing a doctoral degree in Public Policy Administration from Walden University. She is currently employed by the Justice & Safety Center at Eastern Kentucky University. Kelli also works part time to maintain her certification as a police officer in Paris, Kentucky.

Cristina San Martin is a graduate student in the Cyber Forensics Lab at the Department of Computer and Information Technology, Purdue University. She received her bachelor's degree in electronic and communications engineering from the University of Panama, Panama. Her research interests are network forensics and wireless networks.

Abstract

This chapter focuses on the understanding of, and issues that surround the prevention, detection, and investigation of electronic crime. Law enforcement officers and prosecutor's perceptions are measured using survey research. Each group is asked questions about their perceptions about their own work and the work of others in the criminal justice system. This is part of a larger study that examines all relevant criminal justice system actors' perceptions about digital evidence and their role in dealing with it.

INTRODUCTION

Technology has produced new means for committing crime. Whether it is called electronic crime, computer crime, or cyber crime the end result is the same: a loss, damage, or invasion. According to Myers and Myers (2003, 247), an estimated "$555 million to $13 billion is lost each year because of the high technology crime problem," many of which go unreported.

Identity theft and embezzlement are a few of the more well-known crimes committed using computers, but there are other crimes often less considered. For example, drug dealers use computers and other electronic devices in the commission of crimes. They use computers to maintain their "customer" list and record accounting and transaction information. With the means to communicate and do business "beyond or without borders," it is crucial for **law enforcement** to understand exactly how to prevent, detect, and investigate electronic crimes (Oates 2001). If computer crime is continued to be given such little attention, especially at the state and local levels, it will become an even greater significant challenge for law enforcement than DNA was when it was initially used as evidence in legal cases. We have yet to recover from the backlog of DNA evidence that was generated in U.S. crime laboratories. While officers had to learn how to identify and collect DNA evidence at crime scenes using practices that they were unfamiliar with, expectations for **digital evidence** (DE) are more extensive. As with DNA evidence officers must learn how to identify and collect DE, it is most often necessary for them to also learn how to investigate a computer crime, and conduct a forensic analysis of the evidence. These procedures are not taught at most basic or in-service training classes and require much more time and resources to teach. So, it is necessary to immediately deal with some of the previously identified issues in hopes of preventing another situation similar to what occurred with DNA.

BACKGROUND

According to Palfrey (2000, 174), "Cyberspace spans jurisdictions and state power may have no control over instantaneous information flow across borders." Even more confounding is that not everyone agrees on the definition of cyber crime. Commonly thought of cyber crimes in the United States include: hacking, viruses, and denial-of-service attacks that creates chaos for those affected (Groves 2003). According to Wall (1998) and Palfrey (2000) there are four categories of cyber crime: "cyber-trespass (hackers, spies, terrorists), cyber-theft (credit, cash and intellectual piracy), cyber-obscenity (pornography and the dissemination of obscene material) and cyber-violence (stalking, hate speech, 'bomb talk')." Other researchers have placed computer crimes into the categories of computer as a target, computer as an instrument of the crime, computer as incidental to crime, and crimes associated with the prevalence of computers (Casey 2001; Taylor 1999). However, it is possible that crimes may overlap among categories as these are not mutually exclusive. While the categorization of computer crime might not be as important to the forensic analysis of the DE, understanding this categorization makes it easier for officers to think of evidence associated with these various types of crimes as well as shedding light on an investigation.

Due to the changing nature of technology, "collecting, managing, processing, and sharing information" has never been easier (Hinduja 2004, 38). With one click of a button, an individual can submit personal information such as name, address, phone number, social security number, and bank account numbers. According to Correia and Bowling (1999, 228), the widespread increase in technology has left many vulnerable because it has "provided a new arena for criminal activity." "Broken windows" exist in cyberspace because of easy targets online (Correia and Bowling 1999). There are many obstacles for law enforcement in maintaining some sort of order in cyberspace. According to published studies, law enforcement is struggling to keep pace with the changes in technology and the sheer volume of potential evidence and data that is generated by computer and online technology (Rogers and Zeigfried 2004; Stambaugh 2000), as previously discussed.

What were once traditional crimes of theft, larceny, and vandalism have bred a technologically advanced criminal who understands the workings of a computer system. Not only are criminals able to commit crimes via the computer, but many are hiding evidence on them (e.g., steganography). Law enforcement must widen their scope and learn new ways to investigate these crimes with appropriate identification of DE in order to apprehend and, more importantly, convict criminals.

Debate over whose job it is to "police the Internet" has existed for years continues to be a problem (Wall 1998). The debate focuses on the notion that there should be personal responsibility, industry responsibility, and responsibility on the part of Internet Service Providers (ISPs). Regardless of whose responsibility the public feels it should be, there is a needed response by law enforcement and the private sector to deal with the changing nature of technological crimes by preventing and investigating computer and cyber crime. Certainly, though, if citizens accept personal responsibility as well, this can only benefit law enforcement and the private sector in carrying out their duties.

Policing the Internet has taken on a self-regulation approach with many doing what they can on a personal level to protect themselves (Wall 1998). Users are reminded to update antivirus definitions, update software patches, install personal firewalls, and use encryption with private data. Only after a violation occurs are law enforcement called in to investigate, if, in fact, they are ever called at all. Report rates of computer crime are likely not accurate and many are never reported, because of embarrassment of the victim, unawareness that they are a victim, and the low prosecution rate of this sort of offense (Wall 1998). Additionally, victims often do not know who to report a computer crime too. This makes sense based on the question of who is really responsible for investigating crimes of this kind.

Most local agencies have less or no persons responsible for investigating computer crime. Additionally, in a study conducted by Cheurprakobkit and Pena (2003), they found that only a small percentage of agencies (14 percent) had a dedicated cyber crime unit. Reasons cited for limited numbers of cyber crime units are attributed to the lack of training, funding, and support from superiors, which affects the likelihood of even having one officer allocated to computer crimes. Likewise, Huey (2002) found that many officers were fearful of investigating online crimes due to lack of human resources, funds, and training. With such resource deficits, law enforcement agencies cannot be prepared to handle computer-related crimes and much less develop computer crime units (Correia and Bowling 1999).

It is through proper training that Huey (2002) contends that law enforcement will gain confidence to address the cyber front; however, officer training is difficult for many to obtain and costly if it is available. According to Cheurprakobkit and Pena (2003), half of their respondents received less than two days training. Another complicating factor affecting training is that in order to stay current with the changing nature of computer crime, officers must continually receive up to date training (Correia and Bowling 1999). This proves challenging for many agencies, especially small ones, because of limited personnel and funding.

In order for a computer crime unit to succeed there must be a positive "officer's attitude, institutional support, personnel, and networking" (Cheurprakobkit and Pena 2003, 24). Ideally, agencies will be willing to work with other agencies because small departments generally do not have as much resources to handle computer crime investigations as larger ones do. Most officers are not familiar with advanced technologies and do not know how to investigate computer crimes. Computer crime training is needed; a basic knowledge of computers assists an officer in grasping the material faster. However, Myers and Myers (2003) indicate that there is not enough law enforcement or security personnel with even the foundational knowledge or interest to keep up with the growing demand.

Organizational support is extremely important for an officer engaged in cyber investigation. Proper training and equipment is needed and in addition, a deeper understanding about the nature and extent of computer crime by upper administration is necessary (ISTS 2002; Stambaugh 2000).

Despite the increase in computer crime, results from a study conducted by Correia and Bowling (1999) found that approximately 70 percent of agencies surveyed indicated that computer crime was a low priority. A correlation between size of agency and anticipation of increasing computer crime was found, indicating that larger agencies believe it was more likely to impact their department (Correia and Bowling 1999).

Part of the problem in responding to cyber and computer crimes is the lack of attention it has received. Investigating crimes with no jurisdictional boundaries presents a significant challenge for law enforcement and security personnel. Many acts taking place against Americans are occurring in other countries too, with minimal legislation to effectively deal with international computer crime incidents (Litt 1999).

Law enforcement is not at a complete loss. There is software available that assists digital examiners in collecting crucial evidence from seized computers (O'Brien 2005). Several *ad hoc* and formal associations have been set up to assist investigators in dealing with the complexities of computer investigations (e.g., International Association of Computer Investigative Specialists—IACIS, High Technology Crime Investigators Association—HTCIA). The FBI has also created the Scientific Working Group on Digital Evidence (SWGDE) in order to standardize investigative protocols and methods of dealing with DE. Academia and the private sector are also helping with basic and applied research, and publications related to computer investigations and DE.

Court is an additional concern of law enforcement and security personnel. Typically, the question is asked about whether the examiner had the needed "level of expertise" to conduct the forensic examination or better yet, testify in court (O'Brien 2005, 159). The field of digital forensics is currently pushing for scientific and legal recognition in order to be treated like DNA analysis. In fact, the American Academy of Forensic Sciences (AAFS), the professional organization for primarily those who work in crime laboratories, is currently developing a section within the organization for Digital and Multimedia Analysis, which would include those individuals who have knowledge of computer forensics.

The purpose of this chapter is to present preliminary findings of state and local law enforcement officers and their knowledge and perception of DE. This work is a part of a larger study examining roles of those working in the **criminal justice system**, their perceptions of DE training, and how DE moves through the criminal justice system.

METHOD

The respondents chosen to participate in the survey were state and local law enforcement agencies (State & Local Entities—SLE) selected from the National Public Safety Information Bureau database and district and county attorneys that prosecuted criminal cases from around the country. The SLE sample consisted of the top 199 largest agencies, and a stratified random sample of municipal and county agencies (n = 400), and State Police and Bureaus of Investigation (n = 72).

The SLEs and prosecutors were contacted via mail outs and were asked to answer a series of questions about DE. A total of 661 SLE surveys were mailed and 280 were returned, resulting in a 42 percent response rate. A total of 310 prosecutor surveys were distributed with a preliminary return of 85 surveys. The prosecutor response rate is 27.4 percent.

Attached to each survey questionnaire was a cover letter outlining objectives of the study, the principal investigator's contact information, a guarantee of anonymity and adherence to the University's Human Subjects Guidelines. A self-addressed stamped envelope was included for returning the completed questionnaire.

Agency Demographics

SLE agency demographics are presented in Table 24-1. Almost half (49.3 percent) of the respondents were from Municipal agencies. City Sheriffs, State Sheriffs, and Merged County and Municipal agencies each represented 0.4 percent of the respondents. Prosecutor agency demographics show county attorneys represented 38.8 percent of respondents with district attorneys representing 28.2 percent (see Table 24-2).

Survey responses for each discipline came from varying states. The state with the most SLE responses was California (7.1 percent), followed by Georgia (6.0 percent), Texas

TABLE 24-1 SLE Agency Demographics

Type	Frequency	Percent
Municipal	138	49.3
County Sheriff	70	25.0
State Police	44	15.7
County Police	19	6.8
Marshal	3	1.1
Bureaus of Investigation	3	1.1
Merged County and Municipal	1	0.4
State Sheriff	1	0.4
City Sheriff	1	0.4
Total	280	100

TABLE 24-2 Prosecutor Agency Demographics

Type	Frequency	Percent
County	33	38.8
District	24	28.2
Circuit	14	16.5
Combination	10	11.8
Juvenile	2	2.4
City	1	1.2
Missing	1	1.2
Total	85	100

(5.0 percent), and Ohio and Florida (both 4.3 percent). The highest response for the prosecutor survey came from Kentucky and West Virginia (both 7.1 percent). Minnesota and Montana each represented 6.0 percent of respondents.

FINDINGS

Status of Digital Evidence

Findings reveal that more than half (56.6 percent) of respondents did not have a dedicated computer crime and/or digital forensics unit that includes one or more fulltime employees. Approximately 43 percent indicated having a computer crime unit that investigates and examines DE as opposed to only having the examination capability. Units ranged from 1 to 54 people with one to four officers being the most common.

Questions regarding agency policies concerning who can seize, duplicate, examine, or analyze DE were asked. Approximately 31 percent reported they had such a policy. Almost 64 percent indicated that the handling of DE is restricted to certain personnel. With regard to training, 48 percent indicated that their agency requires specific training to seize DE. Numbers were slightly higher (54 percent) for respondents answering whether or not their agency requires specific training to duplicate DE. Fifty-six percent reported that their agency requires specific training to examine DE. Lastly, 59 percent reported that their agency requires specific training to analyze DE.

Training and Certifications

Several questions were asked about training and certifications. Two-thirds (76 percent) of the respondents indicated that their agency does not certify individuals to perform any duties related to DE. Additionally, 59 percent indicated that their agency does not require an outside certification to perform such duties. Responses to types of training offered revealed that almost 50 percent of respondents stated that they received specialized training in DE, while roll call training was the least utilized method for training about DE (Figure 24-1). Private organizations were found to be the most common trainers for DE (43.6 percent), followed closely by federal agencies (41.4 percent) (Figure 24-2).

It is important to examine the specific types of training associated with DE to better determine agency capabilities. The two most common types of training were basic data recovery and acquisition (60.7 percent) and basic online technical skills (59.3 percent). Least commonly identified were basic local area network (LAN) investigations (Table 24-3).

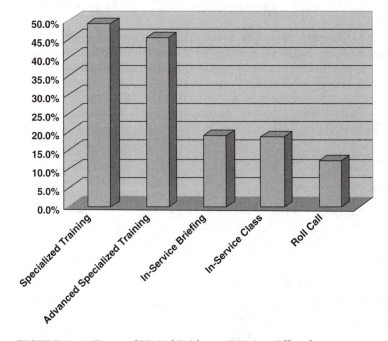

FIGURE 24-1 Types of Digital Evidence Training Offered

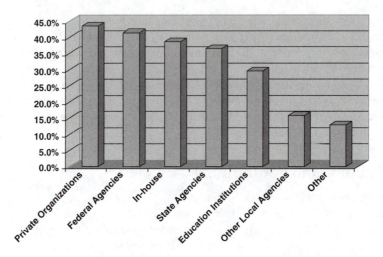

FIGURE 24-2 Providers of Digital Evidence Training

Law Enforcement and Prosecutor Perceptions

Both law enforcement and prosecutors were asked if DE is routinely (over 50 percent of the time) considered in all of the criminal cases they investigate and prosecute. Approximately 51 percent of law enforcement respondents indicated that DE is considered during investigations by their agency, as opposed to 37 percent of prosecutors. On average, however, 18 percent of cases investigated by law enforcement and 21 percent of cases prosecuted by prosecutors include DE.

Surprisingly, prosecutor's perceptions of law enforcement and law enforcement's perception of prosecutors are quite similar (Figure 24-3). Approximately one-third of each group thought that the other discipline was moderately knowledgeable about DE.

TABLE 24-3

Types of Training	Percent
Basic data recovery and acquisition	60.7
Basic online technical skills	59.3
Intermediate data recovery and analysis	50.7
Investigation of online child exploitation	47.9
Advanced data recovery and analysis	46.4
Undercover chat investigations	41.1
Windows Internet trace evidence	40.7
Windows NT operating system	39.6
Basic Local Area Network (LAN) investigations	32.9

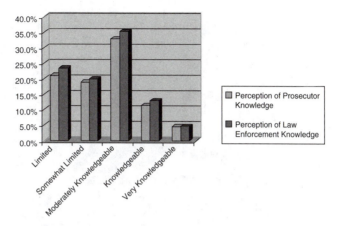

FIGURE 24-3 What Law Enforcement and Prosecutors Say about Each Other

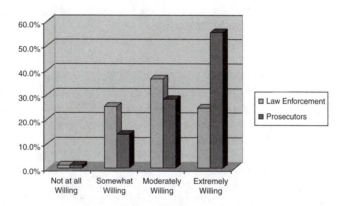

FIGURE 24-4 How Willing Prosecutors to Prosecute Cases with DE Are

Only 5 percent of each discipline felt that the other was very knowledgeable about DE. These perceptions are important because this could affect the response or willingness to work with DE. If law enforcement feels prosecutors are not very knowledgeable, they might be less likely to collect such evidence for fear of wasting their own time. Similarly, if prosecutors feel that law enforcement is not well versed in handling DE they could possibly feel that evidence was not collected adequately and decide not to prosecute.

Despite prosecutors and law enforcement having similar perceptions about each other's knowledge, significant differences were found for perceptions of willingness to prosecute cases with DE. The mean for prosecutors was 3.39 (s.d. = .78) and the mean for law enforcement was 2.96 (s.d. = .80). The difference between the means indicates a significant difference between groups (t = –4.29, df = 327, p <.001) (Figure 24-4).

Significant differences were not found for law enforcement's and prosecutors' perceptions about judges' knowledge. Responses primarily indicate that judges are somewhat limited

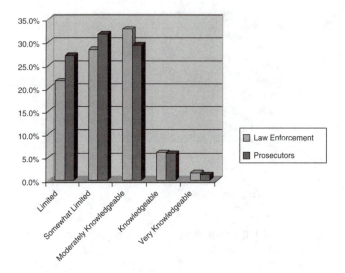

FIGURE 24-5 What Law Enforcement and Prosecutors Say about Judges Knowledge

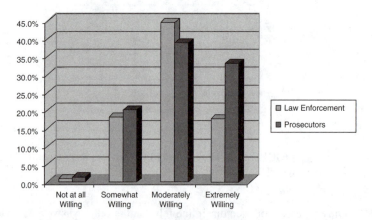

FIGURE 24-6 Perceptions of Judges Willingness to Admit DE at Trial

to moderately knowledgeable about DE. The mean for prosecutors was 2.19 (s.d. = .96) and the mean for law enforcement was 2.31 (s.d. = .97). The difference between the means does not indicate a significant difference between groups (t = .996, df = 305, p>.05) (Figure 24-5). Similarly, means were closely related for both prosecutors (mean = 3.11, s.d. = .78) and law enforcement (mean = 2.98, s.d. = .69) on perceptions of judges' willingness to admit DE at trial. No significant difference exists between groups (t = −1.454, df = 302, p > .05) (Figure 24-6). Caution should be used in interpretation of these results due to the fact that ordinal scales are being treated as if they have been measured at the interval/ratio level.

DISCUSSION

A response is needed and much of the responsibility falls on local and state law enforcement. With this is mind, police organizations have had a difficult time keeping up with the changing nature of information systems, oftentimes because of limited resources. Law enforcement must begin to consistently identify, collect, and analyze DE more than they have in the past, but they should also be engaged in *preventing* cyber crimes, which will be a challenging transition to make. Historically law enforcement has operated in a reactive mode, primarily responding to calls. Cyber crime prevention will likely require even more training than was previously discussed and means that decision makers must reevaluate their resource allocation and perhaps even goals and objectives of the organization. The changing nature of information technology will also be a factor for continuous consideration.

Despite critics, as more and more crimes are committed via computers, smaller departments must find a way to address this problem. No community will be, or is, immune from cyber- or computer crimes. Cheurprakobkit and Pena (2003) found that discrepancies exist between the number of computer crimes reported to agencies with and without computer crime units. Law enforcement has a responsibility to do what they can to prevent, investigate, and prosecute these crimes. Unlike in the past, dealing with cyber crime and, consequentially, DE will take more than just the resources of one law enforcement organization. Law enforcement must engage other law enforcement agencies at various levels, including federal law enforcement, which in many cases already have capabilities as well as resources for cyber crime investigations. The private sector has been dealing with cyber crime much longer than public law enforcement, so it would be wise for them to collaborate and take advantage of the experience and expertise available in the private sector.

CONCLUSION

It is apparent from the current study and previous works that resources and training are among the primary concerns of law enforcement in dealing with DE due to the increased commission of cyber crime. Law enforcement may have to reprioritize their budget requests to include additional personnel and training for developing cyber crime investigative capabilities.

Law enforcement is not the only agent within the criminal justice system that needs training. Prosecutors and judges must also have a level of familiarity with which they can effectively do their jobs when dealing with DE resulting from cyber crime. Laboratory personnel, in cases where DE is analyzed outside of the law enforcement agency, must have computer forensic capabilities to deal with the DE.

Ideally we would not get in the same situation with DE as we have with DNA evidence. If a more proactive stance is taken to deal with DE, then hopefully a backlog of DE that can easily overwhelm crime labs will not be created. However, the situation is more complicated with DE because law enforcement, in many cases will be expected to develop their own forensic analysis capabilities within their agencies, whereas with DNA, the greatest challenge was to train the officers to identify and collect DNA evidence. The laboratory analysis is left to the laboratory personnel, because law enforcement officers would not have the same capabilities as forensic scientists who analyze DNA evidence do.

It is imperative to understand the various roles of individuals in the criminal justice system that might have to deal with DE. With greater understanding, agencies are better positioned to collaborate with other agencies in not only reacting to cyber crime but hopefully, in time, being able to take preventive measures that will facilitate a decrease in cyber crime and less strain on the agency.

If agencies are capable of dealing with DE, policies and procedures must be developed to guide all of the associated processes. The International Association of Chiefs of Police (IACP) develops Model Policies for law enforcement organizations that can be used in these efforts. Additionally, agencies should collaborate with each other in not only developing adequate policies and procedures, but also in identifying promising practices that agencies can use as benchmarks for guidance.

KEY TERMS

Criminal justice system
Digital evidence
Law enforcement

REFERENCES

Casey, E. 2001. *Handbook of Computer Crime Investigation: Forensic Tools and Technology*. San Diego, Calif.: Academic Press.

Cheurprakobkit, S., and G. Pena. 2003. Computer crime enforcement in Texas: Funding, training, and investigating problems. *Journal of Police and Criminal Psychology* 18 (1): 24–37.

Correia, M., and C. Bowling. 1999. Veering toward digital disorder: Computer-related crime and law enforcement preparedness. *Police Quarterly* 2 (2): 225–44.

Groves, S. 2003. The unlikely heroes of cyber security. *Information Management Journal* 37 (3): 34–40.

Hinduja, S. 2004. Theory and policy in online privacy. *Knowledge, Technology, & Policy* 17 (1): 38–58.

Huey, L. 2002. Policing the abstract: Some observations on policing cyberspace. *Canadian Journal of Criminology* 44 (3): 243–54.

Myers, L., and L. Myers. 2003. Identifying the required knowledge elements for the effective detection, investigation, and prosecution of high technology crime: The perspective of academe. *Journal of Criminal Justice Education* 14 (2): 245–67.

Oates, B. 2001. Cyber crime: How technology makes it easy and what to do about it. *Information Systems Security* 9 (6): 45–50.

O'Brien, M. 2005. Clear and present danger? Law and the regulation of the Internet. *Information & Communications Technology Law* 14 (2): 151–64.

Palfrey, T. 2000. Surveillance as a response to crime in cyberspace. *Information & Communications Technology Law* 9 (3): 173–93.

Rogers, M. and K. Ziegfried. 2004. The future of computer forensics: A needs analysis survey. *Computers and Security* 23 (1): 12–16.

Stambaugh, H. and National Institute of Justice (U.S.). 2000. *State and local law enforcement needs to combat electronic crime*. Washington, DC: U.S. Dept. of Justice, Office of Justice Programs, National Institute of Justice.

Taylor, P. 1999. Hackers: *Crime in the digital sublime*. New York, Routledge.

Wall, D. 1998. Catching cybercriminals: Policing the internet. *International Review of Law, Computers & Technology* 12 (2): 201–17.

Chapter 25

The Dateline Effect: Internet Stings

Lorie Rubenser
Sull Ross State University

Gregory Orvis
University of Texas in Tyler (online teaching)

Jeffrey P. Rush
The University of Louisiana

Dr. Lorie Rubenser is currently an associate professor of criminal justice at Sull Ross State University. Her research interests include policing issues and minority issues in criminal justice. She also serves as the Secretary/Treasurer of the Texas Association of Criminal Justice Educators. She is a coeditor of the *Police Forum* publication of the Academy of Criminal Justice Sciences Police Section featuring peer reviewed research articles and other items of interest relating to policing.

Gregory Orvis earned his JD from the Tulane School of Law (1978) and his Ph.D. in political science from the University of Houston (1988). He actively practiced law in New Orleans for many years, and is still a member in good standing with the Louisiana State Bar. Dr. Orvis has been teaching criminal law and public administration for the last 20 years, most recently as a tenured associate professor for the University of Texas in Tyler, with many publications on topics ranging from constitutional issues to victims rights. He currently resides in semi-retirement with his family in Pacifica, California, researching and writing on current practices in criminal justice and teaching online courses for UTT.

Dr. Jeffrey P. Rush is an assistant professor of criminal justice at The University of Louisiana at Monroe, and is the author/coauthor of several books and book chapters as well as numerous professional journal articles. His research interests include gangs, terrorism, and policing. A past president of the Southern Criminal Justice Association, he is the current chairman of the juvenile justice section of the Academy of Criminal Justice Sciences. He is also the coeditor of the *Police Forum* publication of the Academy of Criminal Justice Sciences Police Section featuring peer reviewed research articles and other items of interest relating to policing.

Abstract

Change occurs in everyone's life, and nowhere is that change perhaps more important or significant than with the Internet. Vitagliano notes that "[T]he Internet has changed nearly everyone's life—and for millions of people, it's for the better. But like any realm, the Web has its predators waiting to snatch up the unsuspecting, and children and teens are especially vulnerable" (2007, para 1). Unfortunately, law enforcement is behind the curve on this issue.

As such, the teaming of criminal justice with the private sector in developing Internet stings is increasing. This is perhaps most prevalent with the teaming of *Dateline NBC*, Perverted-Justice.com, and law enforcement. As many police agencies struggle with their relationship to the community, the cyber crime area is a golden opportunity to reach out in numerous ways developing strong positive relationships and partnerships with many aspects of the community. Such relationships could (and should) help to assist the police in improving relationships in all aspects of service delivery. It is an opportunity that should not be squandered, even if it only "works" in the area of cyber crimes and cyber stings.

Vitagliano notes that "[T]he Internet has changed nearly everyone's life—and for millions of people, it's for the better. But like any realm, the Web has its predators waiting to snatch up the unsuspecting, and children and teens are especially vulnerable" (2007, para 1). Donald Daufenbach, a U.S. Customs and Border Protection Senior Special Agent notes that "the Internet is like anything else: It can be bent or perverted for nefarious purposes . . . The Internet has absolutely changed the way people communicate with each other . . ." (Schmalleger 2007, 67). There's certainly no question that the **Internet** has changed how we do business, literally and figuratively. Unfortunately, as Daufenbach notes, "law enforcement is lagging behind miserably in this whole endeavor" (Schmalleger 2007, 67).

If law enforcement is "lagging miserably behind" and it no doubt is, the media certainly is not. Like *Crime Stoppers* and *America's Most Wanted* before it, *Dateline NBC* has taken up the mantle of trying to catch or at least stop some of these predators. Their success has been indeed phenomenal as evidenced from their most recent visit to Long Beach, California (broadcast on Tuesday 30 January 2007), that was "leaked" on CraigsList online, and still quite a number of men responded to the online decoys (a "young" girl and a "young" boy). Admittedly, a few men (and they were all men) apparently changed their minds, some making a u-turn before arriving at the house, others leaving upon seeing the decoy, yet the vast majority were coming to have sex (or so they thought) with someone younger than 14, and that's what they were prepared to do.

Almost everyone who arrives at the decoy house has condoms. In addition to condoms, one "perp" also has a vibrator and baby oil. Others bring additional sex accoutrements, and of course, for all of them this is their first time as observed from one of the Dateline NBC's series:

> GALEANO: 'cause I never chatted with anybody like that.
>
> HANSEN: So this is the first time?
>
> GALEANO: First time.
>
> HANSEN: Did you bring condoms?
>
> GALEANO: I don't carry 'em—well—they're in my car.
>
> HANSEN: You have condoms in your car?
>
> GALEANO: Yeah.
>
> HANSEN: What does that say about your intent here?
>
> GALEANO: No, well, if I was gonna bring condoms here, I would have just brought them.
>
> HANSEN: Right. Or you could see how things go, and go out to the car and get them.
>
> GALEANO: Yeah. But—
>
> HANSEN: In case somebody caught you here. And you had them in your pocket.

GALEANO: Right.

HANSEN: Well, what do you think should happen to you?

GALEANO: I know I really regret this.

HANSEN: You regret it?

GALEANO: Right. (*Dateline NBC* 2007).

After all this comes the *Candid Camera* moment, when it gets deadly serious:

HANSEN: I'm Chris Hansen with Dateline NBC. And we're doing a story on adults who try to meet . . .

GALEANO: Oh!

HANSEN: . . . kids on the Internet for sex (*Dateline NBC* 2007).

And then follows the apologies, the "I've never done anything like this before," and finally the exit—right into the waiting arms of the local constabulary.

In addition to the sex accoutrements, some of the perps bring food, drink, smokes, pretty much anything one could think of. And many of them are well aware of *Dateline NBC*, the show and its purpose, yet they come and go . . . to jail—38 over a 3-day period (*Dateline NBC* 2007). Of course, as is always the case with bad guys, some do not want to go quietly, preferring a more difficult or painful trip to the hoosegow. In this particular episode, one of the bad guys, failing to adhere to the reasonable and lawful demands of the Long Beach police, was tased:

HANSEN: Why was it necessary to use the taser on this guy?

SGT. LEE DEBRABANDER: He's already demonstrated that he's not going to listen to the orders of the police officers. A lot of these guys, they are confronted with the reality that they are about to be exposed for what they did. And a lot of them may try violence to get away. The taser was used to prevent any injury to him and also to any police officers.

Amazingly, one of the perps arrested in this episode had been arrested in an earlier episode shot just up the road in Riverside, California. This particular individual has a criminal record (of violence) and apparently engaged in a number of chats with individuals he believes to be 14 or younger, clearly a sexual predator. **Perverted-Justice.com**, the Web site with whom *Dateline NBC* works, noted "a TCAP (To Catch A Predator) first, a man exposed and arrested at the third TCAP sting that shows up nine months later for the Long Beach sting. We've had many head-scratching moments, but witnessing obsession in the form of a man meeting Chris Hansen for a second time in less than a year definitely ranks up there" (Perverted-Justice.com 2007).

The Web site Falsely Accused suggests that "Cyber Sex is a Masquerade Ball—But the Police Just Don't (Won't) Get It!" (Internet Stings 2007). While perhaps true for consenting adults, it is clearly not the case for those who wish to prey on children and teens as *Dateline NBC* continues to demonstrate. The reality is that there are those who for whatever reason wish to prey on our children and teenagers, many of whom simply know no better, and of course many who are simply ignorant of what's happening. If Falsely Accused, North American Man Boy Love Association (NAMBLA), and the American Civil Liberties Union (ACLU) think there is nothing wrong with cyber sex or even sex with children, the Web site that probably started all this, Perverted-Justice.com, clearly disagrees.

Perverted-Justice.com bills itself as "trained adult citizen-contributors who enter regional chat rooms as underage kids and, if solicited for sex by adults, work with police to prosecute and convict those adults" (Perverted-Justice.com 2007). Since 2004, those convictions number 138. The Web site offers itself up for working with and training law enforcement: "The benefits for law enforcement and government working with us are immense. First, we cost no money to local government for the hours we put in. No overtime, no health care, no need to purchase equipment . . . we're a self-contained unit that funds itself. Secondly, we can work any hour of the day, any time of the year . . . if a predator wants to chat at midnight on January 1st, we can do that. Thirdly, unlike traditional detectives, our people are taught, trained and drilled in one specific crime, that of internet predators and their effects. We're a specialized unit, experts in our field. Each day we're keeping up on this specific crime. That level of specialization isn't typically found in a traditional detective. Fourth, we have numbers. When we do a large-scale police sting, we bring dozens of trained contributors in on the task. We spend thousands upon thousands of man-hours on each sting. The level of engagement we bring to the table would cost local governments hundreds of thousands to possibly over a million dollars if they attempted it themselves. Fifth, post-stings, we bring to the table a [sic] immense level of evidence coordination, handling a good load of 'the paperwork'" (Perverted-Justice.com 2007).

They suggest that "Our results in both individual sting and large-scale stings have been impeccable. Nary has an acquittal nor dropped case resulted to date. We bring high-impact results for law enforcement at no cost to law enforcement. That's why you see law enforcement contacting us about participating in large-scale police stings. Our methods work, which is why we've received kudos after kudos from the law enforcement we've worked with" (Perverted-Justice.com 2007).

Additionally, the Web site offers itself up as an avenue of training for law enforcement, "targeting companies" who "allow the online organized pedophilia movement to flourish online," offer forums for survivors of sexual abuse, work on Internet-related abductions, provide internships for criminal justice, and "seek to raise awareness regarding internet predator to the public via our media efforts" (Perverted-Justice.com 2007).

In other words, Perverted-Justice.com serves as the decoys awaiting those who wish to prey on children and teens. And they feel good about their efforts in this area, noting, "[W]e're very good at catching predators, evident from the fact that we've shattered national records when it comes to large-scale sting operations" (Perverted-Justice.com 2007).

With the exceptions noted above, few people, institutions or organizations believe that child predators are a good thing. The problem or question, if one exists, is with the way in which these predators are apprehended, with "the sting." With accusations of corruption, entrapment and the like when stings and undercover operations are used in the non–cyberworld, the questions of their use in the cyberworld to combat **cyber crime** could be even more important. And with the November 2006 suicide of a suspect in a Perverted-Justice.com/*Dateline NBC* sting, their use will be scrutinized all the more, especially since the man who committed suicide was a felony prosecutor (Eaton 2006).

WHAT IS CYBER CRIME?

The prefix cyber refers to things that are being done online through a modem or networking device. Cyberspace refers to the "place" where this behavior occurs. Over 72 million persons in 135 countries access the Internet everyday. Each year this number increases and the Internet itself triples in size. The content of this enormous entity is intellectual rather than physical and is not "owned" by a central authority. Access to cyberspace has revolutionized our world, including how we communicate, learn and do business. Along with the changes to our ordinary world, cyberspace has changed the way people go about committing crimes (O'Connor 2007).

A loose definition of cyber crime is "committing a crime through the use of a computer or the Internet" (Wagner 2002). Although there are many more specific definitions of cyber crime, a widely cited definition is "any crime that involves computers and networks, including crimes that do not rely heavily on computers" (Britz 2004). How much damage is done by cyber crimes is not as simple to define.

Just focusing on the Federal Bureau of Investigation's nationwide initiative against cyber crime, code named Operation Web Snare, which was begun in 2004 and is ongoing, the result is more than 150 investigations in 100 arrests, 116 indictments, and the execution of 130 search warrants. These investigations also revealed 870,000 victims who collectively lost more than $210 million. The FBI admits, "These investigations represent only a fraction of the cyber crime problem" (Federal Bureau of Investigation 2007).

Who Polices Cyberspace?

The problem of crimes in cyberspace is not limited to a single city or state, but exists around the world. A single crime can cross multiple jurisdictions in multiple countries. This creates some difficulty in determining who is responsible for a particular case and which laws are applicable.

In the United States, cyber crimes may be reported to any local law enforcement agency which may then make a determination of what agencies should become involved. Citizens may also call on several offices of the federal government when they believe a crime has occurred. For domestic cases of child pornography or exploitation, the FBI is generally the lead agency. Where these cases cross international boundaries, the U.S. Customs Service becomes the lead agency (Keytlaw 2001).

What is a Cyber Sting?

Drs. Archambeault and Archambeault (1984, 32) wrote in one of the first books linking computer science and criminal justice, albeit more in the tune of criminal justice management than criminal investigation, that "The information society and its economic reality will define the parameters of the operational environment within which today's criminal justice organizations must function." The statement is true in the new millennium from investigative methods of criminal justice agencies to how those agencies manage the myriads of information collected by them during the investigation through the punishment of crimes.

A sting operation by law enforcement is a particular type of crime investigation technique. Dr. Hay (2003, 2) notes that "The defining feature of a sting operation is that through covert means the authorities create, or facilitate, the very offense of which the defendant is convicted. Normally this is done by having an undercover agent hold out some sort of bait or opportunity, to commit a crime, and then punishing the person who takes the bait." Dr. Hay further notes that sting operations further both an "informational" function, which is identifying and investigating those committing or likely to commit a crime, and a "behavioral" function, which is deterring those who might contemplate committing said crime (Hay 2003, 3).

Early American court decisions upheld the use of such sting operations by law enforcement wholeheartedly, holding little sympathy for the defendant. In an 1864 decision, one state judge opined, "The allegation of the defendant would be the repetition of the plea as ancient as the world, and first interposed in Paradise: 'The serpent beguiled me and I did eat.' That defense was overruled by the Great Lawgiver, and whatever estimate we may form, or whatever judgment pass upon the character or conduct of the tempter, this plea has never since availed to shield crime or give indemnity to the culprit" (*Board of Commissioners v. Backus* 1864, 33). Another state court judge held more simply, "The courts do not look to see who held out the bait, but to see who took it" (*People v. Mills* 1904, 289). Although still recognizing the sting operation by law enforcement as legitimate although distasteful, the courts began backing away from absolute support in 1932 when the U.S. Supreme Court recognized the legal defense of entrapment, stating that the court must "protect itself and the government from such prostitution of the criminal law" (*Sorrells v. United States* 1932, 457).

A definition of the **cyber sting**, similar to that of the cyber crime, would be a sting operation conducted by law enforcement where the criminal inducement or bait is offered through the use of the computer or the Internet. More specifically, law enforcement would, through an undercover agent, create an opportunity to commit a crime, using a computer or the Internet as the medium for creating that opportunity.

Many cyber stings have been initiated by law enforcement agencies at all levels of government—federal, state, and local—and often organized in task forces with representatives from many police agencies. The landmark year for the beginning of the proliferation of cyber stings appears to be 2000, with the advent of the federal report on cyber crime by the President's working group on unlawful conduct on the Internet, which made three recommendations:

- First, any regulation of unlawful conduct involving the use of the Internet should be analyzed through a policy framework that ensures that online conduct is treated in a manner consistent with the way offline conduct is treated, in a technology-neutral manner, and in a manner that accounts for other important societal interests such as privacy and protection of civil liberties.

- Second, law enforcement needs and challenges posed by the Internet should be recognized as significant, particularly in the areas of resources, training, and the need for new investigative tools and capabilities, coordination with and among federal, state, and local law enforcement agencies and coordination with and among our international counterparts.

- Third, there should be continued support for private sector leadership and the development of methods—such as "cyber ethics" curricula, appropriate technological tools, and media and other outreach efforts—that educate and empower Internet users to prevent and minimize the risks of unlawful activity (United States Department of Justice 2000, 54).

It is the second recommendation, along with the requisite government funding, that induced the proliferation of cyber stings and the promotion of interagency cooperation, along with concerned citizens in the private sector and even law enforcement from other nations, in creating a wide variety of elaborate schemes to catch cyber criminals who were using the computer and Internet as the medium for committing a wide variety of traditional crimes. The cyber stings of child predators has received much of the public's and the media's attention, thanks to the *Dateline* television show's focus on cyber stings by the public interest group Perverted-Justice.com, whose citizen volunteers pretend to be underage in online chat rooms, and when solicited for sex, turn the transcripts of the chats over to law enforcement, who then arrange an offline sexual liaison with the would-be child molester, who is subsequently arrested on *Dateline*'s cameras. In one such cyber sting initiated by the Harris County Sheriff's Office in Georgia and who asked for Perverted-Justice.com's help, 100 child predators were identified and 73 were arrested. It was further reported by the Harris County Sheriff's Office that the Atlanta Metro Narcotic Task Force, the Georgia Bureau of Investigation, the United States Marshal Service, and the United States Secret Service helped investigate and execute the offline portion of the cyber sting (Leathers 2006).

There have been many other cyber sting operations for other crimes as well. Just a few examples, stating the traditional crime in bold print:

- Operation Firewall, that began in 2003 as a joint effort by the United States Justice Department and Secret Service, ended in indictments of 28 individuals from eight states and six countries for *identity theft* and *credit card fraud* involving 1.7 million credit card numbers (Ely 2004). The group, who collectively operated as "Shadow crew," operated as "a kind of underworld bazaar," where stolen credit card numbers and fake credit cards were used to buy and sell through pawn shops, e-commerce sites, and even online auction sites like eBay, making an illicit profit of $4.3 million in just over a year. Although criminal applicants to "shadow crew" were carefully screened by its members, one of the arrested leaders of the Shadow crew is a 17-year-old living with his parents in the suburbs of Canada (Staples and Skelton 2005).

- According to Inspector Ed Del Carlo of the vice crimes division of the San Francisco Police Department in an interview with *CyberCrime*, prostitution is rampant on the Internet, with prostitutes setting up Web sites to offer their sexual services and set up appointments under the guise of such code terms as "escort." Inspector Del Carlo explained, "Release is a big word, full service is a big word. In-calls means you come to her place, out-calls means she comes to your place. I mean, it's pretty obvious." Del Carlo insisted that the San Francisco Police Department takes complaints about online *prostitution* seriously, stating, "Whether it's on the internet or on the street, prostitution is still illegal. It's just like a woman is walking on Capp Street and charges a man $40 for a specific sex act." When pressed by the *CyberCrime* reporter as to what the police would do, he replied, "We will set up an undercover sting operation, where we use a police officer posing as a john" (*CyberCrime* staff 2003).

- Extortionists led by a 21-year-old Russian college student used thousands of hacked personal computers to temporarily shut down online businesses that would not pay their *extortion* demands, costing those businesses hundreds of thousands of dollars. The owner of an online gambling Web site based in Costa Rico became disgusted when the protection money demanded by the online cyber gang was raised from $500 to $40,000, so he hired a private investigator. The private investigator successfully infiltrated the gang through a cyber sting operation, learned the identities of several gang members, and then turned the case over to law enforcement in the United States, the United Kingdom, and Russia, who then made the arrests (Brandt 2004).

- Local Belmont police occasionally "patrol" popular Web sites like CraigsList and eBay in order to catch criminals and *recover stolen goods* via cyber stings. However, there is no one officer designated to the task and the officers are more often likely to follow up on a tip from the public then to find the crime online themselves. Belmont police Lt. Dan DeSmidt remarked, "In the last year or so we've been making more of an effort when it comes to our attention to Web sites like that. We need to learn how to make ourselves comfortable in that arena" (Yates 2006).

Substantive Laws Concerning Cyber Crimes and Cyber Stings

For the most part, cyber criminals are prosecuted under the same laws forbidding conduct that is deemed criminal by society just as if they had committed the acts without use of computers or the Internet, and this fact is unlikely to change soon. The President's Working Group on Unlawful Conduct on the Internet concluded that ". . . existing substantive federal laws generally do not distinguish between unlawful conduct committed through the use of the Internet and the same conduct committed through the use of other, more traditional means of communication. To the extent these existing laws adequately address unlawful conduct in the offline world, they should, for the most part, adequately cover unlawful conduct on the Internet" (United States Department of Justice 2000, 54).

Although the United States along with 29 other nations signed the European Council of Europe's Convention on Cybercrime (2001) that mandated that all signature nations create specific laws punishing specific cyber crimes, American federal and state governments have followed the belief in the existing substantive criminal laws forbidding traditional crimes. One major exception where new substantive law has been legislated is in the area of "computer crimes," or "crimes against computers or their services, and it includes obtaining illegal access to a system, preventing access by others, theft of services, and causing damage to a computer system or its data" (Wagner 2002, 458). There are specific provisions of the federal code that address computer crime (Federal Code, 18 USC @ 1029-1030, 1362, 2511, & 2701); although other cyber crime is prosecuted under the generic provisions covering traditional crimes. Some states, such as Alabama (Alabama Criminal Code 2007, Article 5) and Texas (Texas Penal Code Chapter 33), have also created specific laws in their criminal codes to punish computer crime, while leaving the punishment of other cyber crimes to existing laws covering traditional crimes.

Legal Defenses Concerning Cyber Stings

The greatest obstacle in American procedural criminal law to cyber stings is the one that has existed for decades for traditional sting operations: Entrapment. Entrapment is an affirmative defense in which the defendant, simply put, claims "that government trickery induced him or her to commit a crime that he or she was otherwise not predisposed to commit" (Abadinsky 1991, 215).

The U.S. Supreme Court recognized the legitimacy of a police sting operation in *Sorrells v. U.S.* (1932, 441) by stating that "The fact that officers or employees of the government merely afford opportunity or facilities for the commission of the offense does not defeat the prosecution." But the court also first recognized the entrapment defense in the same case when it opined, "Artifice and stratagem may be employed to catch those engaged in criminal enterprises . . . [But] the processes of detection and enforcement [are] abused by the instigation by government officials of an act on the part of persons otherwise innocent in order to lure them to its commission and to punish them."

Lower courts have tried to develop a judicial test for entrapment ever since, with two very different tests for entrapment emerging. The "objective test," which is used by only a few jurisdictions, focuses on the probable affect of the government's conduct on a hypothetical law-abiding citizen. If the governments conduct could induce such a hypothetical person to commit a crime then illegal entrapment has occurred. Since the actual defendant's character or predisposition to criminal activities is not allowed under the objective test, it is hard for the state to get a conviction; although it is equally unlikely that a defendant will be convicted because of his or her bad character (Carlson 2002).

The "subjective test" for entrapment is recognized by the federal jurisdiction and the majority of states. The U.S. Supreme Courts stated the test in *Jacobsen v. U.S.* (1992, 548), "In their zeal to enforce the law . . . government agents may not originate a criminal design, implant in an innocent person's mind the disposition to commit a criminal act, and then induce commission of the crime so the government may prosecute." Also called the predisposition test, the subjective test requires that the defendant overcome the initial burden of proving that the government provided inducement or encouragement for the crime, and then the question becomes whether the government seduced an otherwise innocent citizen into committing said crime. "Inducement can be any government conduct creating a substantial risk that an otherwise law abiding citizen would commit an offense including persuasion, fraudulent representations, threats, coercive tactics, harassment, or pleas based on need, sympathy, or friendship" (*U.S. V. Davis* 1994, 1430). Once government inducement is established, and unlike in the objective test, the bad character of the defendant in question may be used to show a criminal predisposition, including his or her past criminal record, thus ensuring successful prosecution and much less likely a finding of entrapment (Carlson 2002).

Although there has not yet been a U.S. Supreme Court case concerning entrapment and cyber stings, there is precedent from the Federal Court of Appeals for the Ninth Circuit. The three-judge appeals court found that a cross-dressing defendant with a foot fetish from Florida was entrapped by California law enforcement officials when they posed online as an adult mother who wanted the defendant to be a sex "mentor" to her three underage daughters. The defendant frequented online chat rooms looking for an adult companion who would be accepting of his sexual eccentricities, when he met "Sharon," the online "disguise" of a police undercover officer. The defendant initially only wanted an adult relationship with "Sharon," including marriage and father role to the daughters, but after 3 months of e-mails agreed to what "Sharon" demanded. The defendant came to California and was promptly arrested at the airport for the federal crime of crossing state lines to have sex with a minor. Although convicted by a federal jury at the trial court, the Court of Appeals for the 9th Circuit found that the defendant had been induced by the government's promises of "friendship, sympathy, and psychological pressures" and had no predisposition to cross state lines to have sex with minors (*U.S. v. Poehlman* 2000).

Entrapment was thus set as a precedent as a legitimate legal defense in cyber sting cases and has been used successfully since, although not enough to deter law enforcement across the nation from increasingly engaging in cyber sting operations. For example, a federal district court judge in Kansas City recently acquitted a defendant because the minor he was accused of enticing online was in fact a police officer. Whether this case poses any long term ramifications remains to be seen (*Columbia Daily Tribune* 2005).

Overzealous police officers can have their cyber sting cases thrown out if they falsify the affidavits supporting search warrant applications, as occurred at least twice in the FBI's "Operation Candyman." The FBI affidavit supporting search warrant requests in "Operation Candyman" stated that anyone who had joined the online Candy man group automatically received child pornography from other members via an e-mail list. In truth, members of the Candyman group could participate in the chat room and surveys, but could opt out of joining the e-mail list; and if fact, most members of the group did opt out of the e-mail list subscription. A Bronx man did just that, but a search warrant for his home and computer was issued anyway based on the misleading affidavit, and incriminating evidence was found. His case went to the New York Federal District Court, where Judge Denny Chin found the FBI "acted with reckless disregard for the truth" in obtaining the search warrant, thus excluding the evidence that was found. Another defendant in St Louis also caught in the Candyman cyber sting had his case thrown out of a Federal District Court for the same reason. More than 1,800 people have been investigated by the FBI in "Operation Candyman," with over 100 arrests, and 60 convictions, many by plea bargains. It is feared that these federal court rulings may put many of these prosecutions in jeopardy (Weiser 2003).

Other Problems as Well

Cyber sting investigators still complain about a lack of resources and personnel, as well as uneven cooperation when investigations cross international borders. One particular problem is extraditing cyber criminals, especially when legal jurisdiction is unclear (Staples and Skeleton 2005).

The lack of cyber crime prevention is also mentioned as a problem for cyber law enforcement. There is a need to educate the public in "cyber ethics," which includes "(a) recognizing that copying software and other digital media without permission is illegal, (b) teaching children to be aware of dangers lurking on the Internet, (c) creating aids for parents to protect their children from potential harm from cyber criminals, and (d) informing the public that not all information and offers that are found on the Internet are credible" (Wagner 2002, 462). If educated in cyber ethics, the public can engage in an internet "neighborhood watch," such as the one which occurred recently when a California man trolling for teens on CraigsList (the seventh largest Internet site in terms of activity, with 4 billion page views a month) was caught by a local police cyber sting because the police were first alerted by a parent whose daughter brought the criminal's posting to her mother's attention (Yates 2006).

Possibilities for the Future

First, the whole idea of cyber crime and cyber stings is still relatively new to law enforcement and creates an excellent way to involve the community in partnering with law enforcement. As parents get more information on how to better monitor their children's Internet use many will notice attempts to solicit their children in many and various ways. They need to feel comfortable in taking this information to the police and in partnering with them to go after the perpetrator(s).

This, of course, will require law enforcement to reach out to their community in various ways to insure that the community knows not only what to look for but how and when to contact and involve law enforcement. This can be done by law enforcement speaking to educational groups (e.g., PTO), community groups (e.g., garden clubs, Rotary, etc.), and potentially even during employee training at various companies. Such "training" must included what to look for, how to respond, how to access law enforcement, and the like. Further, law enforcement must make sure they act on these reports and share with the parents their results.

Second, there must be in-service training to patrol officers so that they know how to respond when receiving the call for service. Are they to take a report, what needs to be in the report, how will it be "flagged" are just some of the topics that need to be included.

Third, this topic should be included in recruit training. Police academies need to modify their curriculum to include at least the basics of cyber crime and cyber stings. We recognize that this might require changing the Peace Officer Standards and Training (POST) legislation. If so, then police agencies should work diligently to bring their POST training into the 21st and 22nd centuries.

Fourth, does the whole idea of cyber crime and cyber stings necessitate a change in the kind of officer being hired? Police agencies around the country are having difficulty finding recruits, and we are in no way suggesting a lessening of standards. What we are suggesting is that dealing with cyber crime might require rethinking the kind of person who is recruited and the kind of skill sets that might be needed. It might also produce a re-thinking of how assignments are being made. As we have done for years with vice and narcotics, perhaps a recruit with the necessary computer skills (or willingness to learn) should be moved on into investigations after completing probation (and the Field Training Officer (FTO) process). Why should someone with these skills serve 3, 5 or even 10 years "on the street" before being moved into this highly specialized and increasingly important area?

In addition to changing the type of officer recruited, departments will be forced to make changes in salary to attract persons with these skills. Changes to budgets will also have to be made in order to purchase the necessary electronic equipment to conduct appropriate investigations. Cyber crime is not cheap.

Fifth, this area of criminality is an opportunity for law enforcement to partner with a variety of different "groups" or individuals with a particular interest or expertise in this area. Already noted is the relationship between *Dateline NBC*, Perverted-Justice.com, and law enforcement and the success of this partnership. Miss America Lauren Nelson, Suffolk County New York police, and America's Most Wanted teamed up recently to catch online predators. Using a profile created by Suffolk County and photos of Miss Nelson as a teenager, the sting was on! "I got to chat online with the predators and made phone calls, too," Nelson said, "The Suffolk County Police Department was there the whole time" (Associated Press 2007). Miss Nelson posed as a 14-year-old and actually met many of the predators at a home in Long Island. Says Miss Nelson, "It would only take a matter of time before it got pretty explicit" (Associated Press 2007). Like the *Dateline* sting, once inside the house, Miss Nelson would excuse herself and John Walsh would appear confronting the perp. Though there were some reports that Miss America would not be testifying, apparently those reports are false and Miss America "plans to—and has always planned to—fully cooperate with the Suffolk County Police Department and will continue to champion her cause" (Fox News Channel 2007).

The social networking site MySpace.com is even getting into the act. After first refusing to cooperate, it now says that it will "release information to authorities about convicted sex offenders who had registered profiles on its web pages" (Monstersandcritics.com 2007). According to the Attorney General of Connecticut, "there are 'at least' 5,000 registered sex offenders with MySpace profiles who pose 'an immediate, urgent risk to children'" (Monstersandcritics.com 2007). Another example of law enforcement (in this case Attorneys General) partnering up with a specialized "group" to investigate and ultimately prosecute those who would prey on the least and most vulnerable—the children—our children.

This is only the tip of the iceberg. A brief search of the Internet will demonstrate the proliferation of Web sites and organized groups dedicating to protecting children from Internet predators. Services available range from searches for children sold into the international sex trade all the way to providing instructions for parents about how to keep their children safe, and programs that can be downloaded to create filters for home computers.

As many police agencies struggle with their relationship to the community, the cyber crime area is a golden opportunity to reach out in numerous ways developing strong positive relationships and partnerships with many aspects of the community. Such relationships could (and should) help to assist the police in improving relationships in all aspects of service delivery. It is an opportunity that should not be squandered, even if it only "works" in the area of cyber crimes and cyber stings.

The fact that so many services exist outside the policing world suggests a strong need for police to interface with these groups in the community. Normally police have the specialized expertise in investigations. In this area it would be wise for police to work smarter by working with these groups rather than working harder by developing their own expertise from scratch.

These interfaces with community groups may also be beneficial to police in more than just improved community relations. Budget constraints that would normally limit the technical expertise police can pay to hire or place limits on the equipment police can purchase can be overcome by using the resources of these community groups.

CONCLUSION

The solution for cyber crime appears not to be a change in the substantive or procedural laws, as they appear to be adequate. Cyber criminals can be successfully prosecuted for crimes already listed in state and federal criminal codes, and the procedural defense of entrapment, long established by case law, still adequately protects those accused of cyber crimes from police overzealousness.

Cyber stings, if done properly and legally, are valuable tools for catching cyber criminals. However, the public needs to be more educated about the criminal dangers of the Internet, so they in turn can inform law enforcement of cyber crimes in progress. While law enforcement is getting better at policing the Internet, or at least engaging those who use the Internet for criminality, those law enforcement officers engaged in cyber stings need both adequate resources and training to guarantee success. Furthermore, such training should not only be in computer science but in procedural law as well. Both technical success in the cyber sting and legal success in the subsequent criminal prosecution will thus be more likely to occur.

KEY TERMS

Cyber crime   Internet
Cyber sting   Perverted-Justice.com

REFERENCES

Abadinsky, H. 1991. *Law and Justice*. Chicago: Nelson Hall.

Alabama Criminal Code. 2007. Article 5: Alabama Computer Crime Act @ 13A-8-100–13A-8-103.

Archambeault, W. G., and B. J. Archambeault. 1984. *Computers in Criminal Justice/Administration and Management*. Cincinnati OH: Pilgrimage.

Associated Press. April 24, 2007. Miss America Tries to Catch Sex Predators. Associated Press. Retrieved May 23, 2007, from *http://www.msnbc.msn.com/id/18299072/*

Board of Commissioners v. Backus, 29 How. Pr. 33 (1864).

Brandt, A. October 26, 2004. Internet extortion ring arrested in Russia. *PC World*. http://www.crime-research.org/news/26.10.2004/741/

Britz, M. T. 2004. *Computer Forensics and Cyber Crime*. Old Tappan, NJ: Pearson Education, Inc.

Carlson, J. C. 2002. "Entrapment." In *Encyclopedia of Crime and Punishment,* edited by D. Levinson. Thousand Oaks, CA: Sage Publications.

Columbia Daily Tribune. August 3, 2005. Judge tosses Internet sting. http://www.columbiatribune.com/2005/Aug/20050803News019.asp

Council of Europe. November 23, 2001. Convention on cybercrime. http://conventions.coe.int/treaty/EN/Treaties/html/185.htm

Dateline NBC. 2007. Scary Chats and a Repeat Predator. *Dateline NBC*. Retrieved January 31, 2007, from http://www.msnbc.msn.com/id/16895737/page/2/

Eaton, T. 2006. Prosecutor kills himself in Texas raid over child sex. Retrieved February 16, 2007, from http://www.nytimes.com/2006/11/07/us/07pedophile.html?ex=1320555600&en=9a849fc4db0d28ce&ei=5088&partner=rssnyt&emc=rss

Ely, C. December 20, 2004. Organized (cyber)crime. http://www.suite101.com/print_article.cfm/crime_stories/105089

Federal Bureau of Investigation. January 8, 2007. Investigative programs—Cyber investigations: Operation Web snare. http:www.fbigov/cyberinvest/inetschemes.htm

Federal Code. 18 USC @ 1029. Fraud and related activity in connection with access devices.

Federal Code. 18 USC @ 1030. Fraud and related activity in connection with computers.

Federal Code. 18 USC @ 1362. Communication lines, stations or systems.

Federal Code. 18 USC @ 2511. Interception and disclosure of wire, oral, or electronic communications prohibited.

Federal Code. 18 USC @ 2701. Unlawful access to stored communication.

Fox News Channel. May 1, 2007. Organization: Miss America Will Help Sex Sting "Any Way She Can." Fox News Channel. Retrieved May 23, 2007, from http://www.foxnews.com/story/0,2933,269357,00.html

Hay, B. October 2003. Sting operations, undercover agents, and entrapment. Discussion Paper No. 441. The Harvard John M. Olin Discussion Paper Series. http://www.law.harvard.edu/programs/olin_center/

Internet Stings. 2007. The Crime de Jour of the 90's. Retrieved January 31, 2007, from http://www.accused.com/clients/cases/internet.stings.html

Jacobson v. United States, 303 U.S. 540 (1992).

Keytlaw. November 16, 2001. How to report Internet-related crime. http://www.keytlaw.com/netlaw/reportcrime.htm

Leathers, B. August 1, 2006. Local man arrested in Internet predator sting. *The Post-Searchlight* (Bainbridge, GA). http://www.zwire.com/site/printerFriendly.cfm?brd=2068&dept_-d=387472&newsid=1699

Monstersandcritics.com. May 21, 2007. My Space to cooperate with attorneys on sex offenders. Retrieved from http://tech.monstersandcritics.com/news/article_1307476.php/MySpace_to_cooperate_with_attorneys_on_sex_offenders

O'Connor, T. Cybercrime: The Internet as a crime scene. Retrieved from http://faculty.ncwc.edu/toconnor/315/315lect12.htm

People v. Mills, 178 N.Y. 274 (1904).

Perverted-Justice. 2007. Retrieved from *http://www.perverted-justice.com/*

Rebovich, D. J. 2002. "Entrapment." In *Encyclopedia of Crime and Punishment*, edited by D. Levinson. Thousand Oaks, CA: Sage Publications.

Schmalleger, F. 2007. *Criminal Justice Today*. 9th ed. Upper Saddle River, NJ: Pearson Prentice-Hall.

Sorrells v. United States, 287 U.S. 274 (1932).

Staples, S., and C. Skelton. October 12, 2005. Internet fraud: con men nabbed. *Canda.com*. http://www.crime-research.org/news/12.10.2005/1546/

Texas Penal Code. Chapter 33 Computer Crimes @ 33.01–33.05 (2007).

United States Department of Justice. March 2000. The electronic frontier: The challenge of unlawful conduct involving the use of the Internet—A report of the president's working group on unlawful conduct on the Internet. http://www.usdoj.gov/criminal/cybercrime/unlawful.htm

United States v. Davis, 36 F3d 1424 (9th Cir., 1994).

United States v. Poehlman, Case# 98-50631. 9th Circuit Court of Appeals (June 10, 2000).

Vitagliano, E. January 27, 2007. Online porn, predators threaten children, teens. *OneNewsNow.com*. Retrieved from http://www.onenewsnow.com/2007/01/online_porn_predators_threaten.php

Wagner, S. C. 2002. "Cybercrime." In *Encyclopedia of Crime and Punishment,* edited by D. Levinson. Thousand Oaks, CA: Sage Publications.

Weiser, B. March 6, 2003. Judge discards FBI evidence in Internet case of child smut. *New York Times*. http://www.injusticebusters.com/2003/Candyman_entrapment.htm

Yates, D. March 3, 2006. Web crime targeted by police. *San Mateo Daily Journal*. http://www.smdailyjournal.com/article_preview_print.php?id=56826

Chapter 26

Evidence Issues Involved
in Prosecuting Internet Crime

Cliff Roberson
Professor Emeritus, Washburn University; Adjunct Professor, Kaplan University

Cliff Roberson, LLM, Ph.D., is a professor emeritus at Washburn University. His previous academic experiences include Associate Vice-President for Academic Affairs, Arkansas Tech University; Dean of Arts and Sciences, University of Houston, Victoria; Director of Programs, National College of District Attorneys; Professor of Criminology and Director of Justice Center, California State University, Fresno; and Assistant Professor of Criminal Justice, St. Edwards University. He has authored or coauthored 47 books and texts.

Dr. Roberson's nonacademic experience includes U.S. Marine Corps service as an infantry officer, trial and defense counsel and military judge as a marine judge advocate; and Director of the Military Law Branch, U.S. Marine Corps. Other legal employment experiences include Trial Supervisor, Office of State Counsel for Offenders, Texas Board of Criminal Justice and judge pro-tem in the California courts. Cliff is admitted to practice before the U.S. Supreme Court, U.S. Court of Military Appeals, U.S. Tax Court, Federal Courts in California and Texas, Supreme Court of Texas and Supreme Court of California.

Educational background includes: Ph.D. in Human Behavior, U.S. International University; LLM in Criminal Law, Criminology, and Psychiatry, George Washington University; JD, American University; BA in Political Science, University of Missouri; and one year of postgraduate study at the University of Virginia School of Law.

Abstract

This chapter discusses several evidentiary issues in the prosecution of crimes involving computers and the Internet. Issues discussed include preserving evidence that is in electronic form and search and seizure issues involving computers and electronic files. The chapter also points out that the Internet is a great vehicle for individuals involved in financial fraud and child pornography.

INTRODUCTION

In this chapter, several of the more important evidentiary issues concerning the prosecution of crimes committed by use of the Internet will be discussed. This chapter is designed, not for trial lawyers, but for criminal justice professionals and to provide them with some of the evidence issues involved in the prosecution of crimes involving the Internet and the

computer. Two major classes of crimes committed by using the Internet include financial fraud and child pornography. The Internet has been a great vehicle for individuals involved in both financial fraud and child pornography. In prosecuting both types of cases, one of the most frequent evidence issues is the right to search and seize a suspect's computer. Accordingly, a fair amount of discussion will be devoted to that issue. Two other issues discussed in this chapter are the problems of proving venue and criminal intent.

In criminal cases, the primary purpose of the rules of evidence is to secure a defendant's constitutional right to a fair trial. One scholar defined the **study of evidence** as the study of the legal regulations of proof of facts and the inferences and arguments that arise from such proof, in the trial of a civil or criminal lawsuit (Rothstein, Raeder, and Crump 2003).

The first murder trial in the American Colonies occurred in September 1630. It is also one of the first reported cases that discussed the rules of evidence. John Billington, who came over on the Mayflower, was convicted of murdering John Newcomen. After a heated argument between the two, Billington fatally shot fellow colonist John Newcomen in the back with a blunderbuss. The Massachusetts Bay Colony Governor William Bradford advised that Billington ought to die and his land be purged of blood (forfeited to the state). Billington was tried for the English common law crime of murder using the common law rules of evidence; he was found guilty and hanged (Collected Essays of Albert Borowitz 2005).

The rules of evidence have evolved almost entirely from decisional law handed down by the courts. At the time that Billington was tried in 1630, evidentiary rules were based entirely upon decisional law. Later those decisions were codified in statutes and rules of court. The most influential codification of the rules of evidence is the Federal Rules of Evidence (FRE)[1] The federal rules were drafted by a distinguished panel of lawyers, judges, and evidence scholars. The U.S. Supreme Court approved the rules and transmitted to Congress where they were adopted and became effective July 1, 1975. Most states have used the FRE as the basis for their rules of evidence.

FIRST INTERNET BANK ROBBERY

Vladimir Levin, a biochemistry graduate of St. Petersburg's Tekhnologichesky University in mathematics, led a Russian hacker group in one of the first publicly revealed international bank robberies. Levin used a laptop computer in London to access the Citibank network, and then obtained a list of customer codes and passwords. Then he logged on 18 times over a period of weeks and transferred $3.7 million through wire transfers to accounts his group controlled in the United States, Finland, the Netherlands, Germany, and Israel. Citibank later retrieved all but about $400,000 of the money.

When Citibank noticed the transfers, they contacted the authorities, who tracked Levin down and arrested him at a London airport in March, 1995. He fought extradition for 30 months, but lost, and was transferred to the US for trial. He was convicted and sentenced to three years in jail, and ordered to pay Citibank $240,015. Four members of Levin's group pleaded guilty to conspiracy to commit bank fraud, and served various sentences (Carley and O'Brien 1995).

---

[1]28 U.S. Code (Rules Appendix).

EVIDENCE IN BANK COMPUTER HACKING CASES

According to Professor Orin S. Kerr, the process of collecting electronic evidence in computer hacking cases is generally divided into three steps with each step presenting unique facts and requiring special considerations. Kerr's three steps are (1) collecting digital evidence that is in transit, (2) collecting digital evidence stored with friendly third parties, and (3) collecting digital evidence stored with hostile parties such as the target (Kerr 2005).

The most basic step, according to Kerr, is obtaining stored records from the system administrators of the various computer servers used in the attack. In this step, the investigator must contact the system administrator to determine if they have any records of the connection to the bank at the particular time that the attack occurred. Investigations are rarely simple. The trail of evidence is usually interrupted somewhere along the way. In step 2, the biggest problem is that few system administrators keep comprehensive records, and those records that are kept often are deleted after a brief period of time. In addition, hackers routinely target intermediary computers known to keep few or no records so as to frustrate investigators.

Kerr contends that the key in most cases is step 3, recovering the computer used to launch the attack. If the police can find and analyze the computer, it will likely yield damning evidence. The records kept by most operating systems can allow forensics experts to reconstruct with surprising detail who did what and when. Even deleted files often can be recovered, as a delete function normally just marks storage space as available for new material and does not actually erase anything. An analysis of the computer may reveal a file containing the bank password used to set up the unauthorized account. It may reveal records from that account, or records taken from some of the intermediary computers. Even if no such documents are found, it may be possible to tell whether the attack was launched from the computer.

SEARCH WARRANT PROBLEMS

> A search warrant should be issued only upon a showing of probable cause to believe that the legitimate object of a search is located in a particular place, and therefore safeguards an individual's interest in the privacy of his home and possessions against the unjustified intrusion of the police. (*Steagald v. United States,* 451 U.S. 204, 213 (1981))

One U.S. Court of Appeals noted that the Fourth Amendment incorporates a great many specific protections against unreasonable searches and seizures (*United States v. Beusch,* 596 F.2d 871 (9th Cir. 1979)). The contours of these protections in the context of computer searches pose difficult questions. Computers are simultaneously filing cabinets (with millions of files) and locked desk drawers; they can be repositories of innocent and deeply personal information, but also of evidence of crimes. The former must be protected, the latter discovered. As society grows ever more reliant on computers as a means of storing data and communicating, courts will be required to analyze novel legal issues and develop new rules within the established Fourth Amendment jurisprudence (Probst and Wright 2006). The Court noted that the fact of an increasingly technological world is not on us as we consider the proper balance to strike between protecting an individual's right to privacy and ensuring that the government is able to prosecute suspected criminals effectively.

As former Supreme Court Justice Lewis Brandeis's noted in *Olmstead v. United States,* "Ways may some day be developed by which the Government, without removing papers from secret drawers, can reproduce them in court, and by which it will be enabled to expose to a jury the most intimate occurrences of the home. Can it be that the Constitution affords no protection against such invasions of individual security?" (*Olmstead v. United States,* 277 U.S. 438, 474 (1928)).

In *United States v. Rogers* (No. 05-1455-cr (2d Cir. 12/19/2005)), the defendant-appellant, Jan Elijah Rogers, was convicted of two counts of advertising to receive, exchange, and distribute child pornography,[2] and one count of transporting child pornography by computer.[3] He was sentenced to 20 years' imprisonment.

Rogers challenged the search warrant pursuant to which most of the evidence against him was discovered. He argued that the warrant was without probable cause because no images of child pornography had been found prior to the issuance of the warrant. In response to that argument, the court cited *United States v. Singh* (390 F.3d 168, 181 (2d Cir. 2004)) and stated:

> In reviewing a magistrate's probable cause determination, we accord substantial deference to the magistrate's finding and limit our review to whether the issuing judicial officer had a substantial basis for the finding of probable cause."The warrant was based, among other things, on a chat room advertisement in which Rogers advertised" a server for fans of panty/diaper, swimsuit, and action pix (0–8 yrs), a post by Rogers stating "remember, the higher the quality, the younger the girl (or boy), and the better the action, the more bonus credits you receive," and a file directory indicating files with names like "BBRAPE." The court held that given all the circumstances set forth in the affidavit, there was a fair probability that evidence of a crime would be found in Rogers' residence and the magistrate judge had a substantial basis for finding probable cause.

Rogers also attached the search warrant because of the Fourth Amendment requirement that a search warrant must particularly describe the things to be seized. He claimed that because of the many files and e-mails on his computer, that the warrant should have listed which files and e-mails that could be seized under the warrant. He also contended a warrant to seize all files on a computer was overly broad and violated the Fourth Amendment. The court held that the warrant was sufficiently specific to enable the executing officer to ascertain and identify with reasonable certainty those items that the magistrate has authorized him to seize.

In *United States v. Adjani* (No. 05-50092 (9th Cir. 07/11/2006)), while executing a search warrant at the home of defendant Christopher Adjani to obtain evidence of his alleged extortion, agents from the Federal Bureau of Investigation (FBI) seized Adjani's computer and external storage devices, which were later searched at an FBI computer lab. They also seized and subsequently searched a computer belonging to defendant Jana Reinhold, who lived with Adjani, even though she had not at that point been identified as a suspect and was not named as a target in the warrant. Some of the e-mails found on Reinhold's computer chronicled conversations between her and Adjani that implicated her in the extortion plot. Relying in part on the incriminating e-mails, the government charged both Adjani and Reinhold with conspiring to commit extortion in violation of 18 U.S.C. § 371 and transmitting a threatening communication with intent to extort in violation of 18 U.S.C. § 875(d).

---

[2]18 U.S.C. § 2251(c) (now 18 U.S.C. § 2251(d)).
[3]18 U.S.C. § 2252A(a)(1).

With respect to the computer search, the search warrant in question prescribed the process to be followed: "In searching the data, the computer personnel will examine all of the data contained in the computer equipment and storage devices to view their precise contents and determine whether the data falls within the items to be seized as set forth herein." Additionally, it noted that "in order to search for data that is capable of being read or intercepted by a computer, law enforcement personnel will need to seize and search any computer equipment and storage device capable of being used to commit, further, or store evidence of the offense listed above."

The defendants brought motions to suppress the e-mails, arguing that the warrant did not authorize the seizure and search of Reinhold's computer and its contents; but if it did, the warrant was unconstitutionally overbroad or, alternatively, the e-mails fell outside the scope of the warrant. The district court granted the defendants' motion to suppress the e-mail communications between Reinhold and Adjani, finding that the agents did not have sufficient probable cause to search Reinhold's computer, and that once they discovered information incriminating her; the agents should have obtained an additional search warrant. The government appeals this evidentiary ruling, but only with respect to three e-mails. The district court had indicated that the warrant was overly broad regarding the computer search.

The Court of Appeals reversed the district court decision as to the three e-mails and held that the government had probable cause to search Reinhold's computer, and that the warrant satisfied the test for specificity and the seized e-mail communications fell within the scope of the properly issued warrant.

The Court of Appeals held that the warrant was supported by probable cause, because the affidavit submitted to the magistrate judge established that there was a fair probability that contraband or evidence of a crime would be found in computers at Adjani's residence. The Court stated that the extensive 24-page supporting affidavit described the extortion scheme in detail, including that Adjani possessed a computer-generated database and communicated with Paycom over e-mail, requiring the use of a computer. The court also noted that the agent's affidavit explained the need to search computers, in particular, for evidence of the extortion scheme: "I know that considerable planning is typically performed to construct and consummate extortion. The plan can be documented in the form of a simple written note or more elaborate information stored on computer equipment."

The court in addressing the issue of ownership of the computer noted that the agents, acting pursuant to a valid warrant to look for evidence of a computer-based crime, searched computers found in Adjani's residence and to which he had apparent access. That one of the computers actually belonged to Reinhold did not exempt it from being searched, especially given her association with Adjani and participation in some of his activities as documented in the agent's supporting affidavit. The officers therefore did not act unreasonably in searching Reinhold's computer as a source of the evidence targeted by the warrant.

Reinhold argued that the e-mails were outside the scope of the warrant because they implicated her in the crime and supported a charge of conspiracy to commit extortion (a crime not specifically mentioned in the warrant), the Court rejected the argument and stated that there is no rule or case law suggesting that evidence turned up while officers are rightfully searching a location under a properly issued warrant must be excluded simply because the evidence found may support charges for a related crime or against a suspect not expressly contemplated in the warrant.

The Court of Appeals stated that there was no need for the agents expressly to claim in the affidavit that they wanted to arrest Reinhold, or even that Reinhold was suspected of any criminal activity. The government needed only to satisfy the magistrate judge that there was probable cause to believe that evidence of the crime in question—here extortion—could be found on computers accessible to Adjani in his home, including—as it developed—Reinhold's computer. By setting forth the details of the extortion scheme and the instrumentalities of the crime, augmented by descriptions of Reinhold's involvement with Adjani, the government satisfied its burden. The Court held that the magistrate judge properly approved the warrant, which in turn encompassed all the computers found at Adjani's residence.

The Court of Appeals stated that the Fourth Amendment's specificity requirement prevents officers from engaging in general, exploratory searches by limiting their discretion and providing specific guidance as to what can and cannot be searched and seized. And that general warrants are prohibited. The Court stated that nothing is left to the discretion of the officer executing the warrant. However, the level of detail necessary in a warrant is related to the particular circumstances and the nature of the evidence sought. Warrants, according to the court, which describe generic categories of items, are not necessarily invalid if a more precise description of the items subject to seizure is not possible.

The Court noted that the warrant in question objectively described the items to be searched and seized with adequate specificity and sufficiently restricted the discretion of agents executing the search. The warrant affidavit began by limiting the search for evidence of a specific crime—transmitting threatening communications with intent to commit extortion. And that reference to a specific illegal activity can, in appropriate cases, provide substantive guidance for the officer's exercise of discretion in executing the warrant. The specificity of the items listed in the warrant combined with the language directing officers to obtain data as it relates to the case from the computers was sufficiently specific to focus the officer's search.

In *United States v. Hay* (231 F.3d 630 (9th Cir. 2000)), the defendant made an argument similar to Reinhold's, challenging the district court's ruling allowing evidence of child pornography found on his computer to be used against him at trial. Hay claimed that the affidavit submitted by officers to obtain a warrant did not establish probable cause to engage in a search of Hay's computer because there was no evidence that he fell within a class of persons likely to collect and traffic in child pornography because the affidavit did not indicate that he was a child molester, pedophile, or collector of child pornography and sets forth no evidence that he solicited, sold, or transmitted child pornography. The Court of Appeals rejected Hay's challenge, holding that it is well established that a location can be searched for evidence of a crime even if there is no probable cause to arrest the person at the location. The correct inquiry was whether there was reasonable cause to believe that evidence of misconduct was located on the property that was searched. Property owned by a person absolutely innocent of any wrongdoing may nevertheless be searched under a valid warrant (*United States v. Melvin,* 596 F.2d 492, 496 (1st Cir. 1979)).

In one federal court case involving the search of a business, the Court of Appeals for the Ninth Circuit held that the search warrant was impermissibly general where the only limitation on the search and seizure of appellants' business papers was the requirement that they be the instrumentality or evidence of violation of the general tax evasion statute. The Court noted that the officers' discretion was unfettered, there was no limitation as to time and there is no description as to what specific records were to be seized (*United States v. Cardwell,* 680 F.2d 75 (9th Cir. 1982)).

In drafting a search warrant for electronic files on a computer, care should be taken to narrow the scope of the warrant to prevent the issue of an overly broad search warrant. For example the computer used to draft this paper had 94,178 files on it, with less than 20 percent of its hard drive being used. A warrant to search the contents of a computer, that is, all files on the computer may too broad to withstand a challenge.

SEARCHES THAT EXCEED THE SCOPE OF THE WARRANT

The problem that was addressed in *United States v. Carey* is a common problem in computer searches (172 F.3d 1268 (10th Cir. 1999)). Patrick J. Carey was charged with one count of possessing a computer hard drive that contained three or more images of child pornography produced with materials shipped in interstate commerce.[4] Following a conditional plea of guilty, he appealed an order of the district court denying his motion to suppress the material seized from his computer on grounds it was taken as the result of a general, warrantless search.

Carey had been under investigation for some time for possible sale and possession of cocaine. Controlled purchases had been made from him at his residence, and six weeks after the last purchase, police obtained a warrant to arrest him. During the course of the arrest, officers observed in plain view a "bong," a device for smoking marijuana, and what appeared to be marijuana in defendant's apartment. Alerted by these items, a police officer asked Carey to consent to a search of his apartment. The officer said he would get a search warrant if Carey refused permission. After considerable discussion with the officer, Carey verbally consented to the search and later signed a formal written consent at the police station. Because he was concerned that officers would "trash" his apartment during the search, Carey gave them instructions on how to find drug-related items.

Armed with this consent, the officers returned to the apartment that night and discovered quantities of cocaine, marijuana, and hallucinogenic mushrooms. They also discovered and took two computers, which they believed would either be subject to forfeiture or evidence of drug dealing.

The computers were taken to the police station and a warrant was obtained by the officers allowing them to search the files on the computers for names, telephone numbers, ledger receipts, addresses, and other documentary evidence pertaining to the sale and distribution of controlled substances. Detective Lewis and a computer technician searched the contents of the computers, first viewing the directories of both computers' hard drives. They then downloaded onto floppy disks and printed the directories. Included in the directories were numerous files with sexually suggestive titles and the label "JPG." Lewis then inserted the disks into another computer and began searching the files copied from Mr. Carey's computers. His method was to enter key words such as, money, accounts, people, etc., into the computer's explorer to find text-based files containing those words. This search produced no files related to drugs.

Lewis continued to explore the directories and encountered some files he was not familiar with. Unable to view these files on the computer he was using, he downloaded them to a disk which he placed into another computer. He then was "immediately" able to view what he later described as a "JPG file." Upon opening this file, he discovered it contained child pornography.

Lewis downloaded approximately 244 JPG or image files. These files were transferred to 19 disks, only portions of which were viewed to determine that they contained child

---

[4]A violation of 18 U.S.C. § 2252A(a)(5)(B) (1996).

pornography. Although none of the disks was viewed in its entirety, Lewis looked at about five to seven files on each disk.

Defendant Carey moved to suppress the computer files containing child pornography. During the hearing on the motion, Lewis stated although the discovery of the JPG files was completely inadvertent, when he saw the first picture containing child pornography, he developed probable cause to believe the same kind of material was present on the other image files. When asked why, therefore, he did not obtain a warrant to search the remaining image files for child pornography, he stated, that question did arise, and my captain took care of that through the county attorney's office. No warrant was obtained, but the officer nonetheless continued his search because he believed he had to search these files as well as any other files contained in the computer.

Upon further questioning by the government, Lewis retrenched and stated until he opened each file, he really did not know its contents. Thus, he said, he did not believe he was restricted by the search warrant from opening each JPG file. Yet, after viewing a copy of the hard disk directory, the detective admitted there was a "phalanx" of JPG files listed on the directory of the hard drive. He downloaded and viewed these files knowing each of them contained pictures. He claimed, however, "I wasn't conducting a search for child pornography that happened to be what these turned out to be."

At the close of the hearing, the district court ruled from the bench. Without any findings, the court denied the motion, saying: "at this point, the Court feels that the . . . Defendant's Motion to Suppress should be denied. And that will be the order of the Court, realizing that they are close questions."

The Court of Appeals noted that Carey argued the search of the computers transformed the warrant into a "general warrant" and resulted in a general and illegal search of the computers and their files. And that the Fourth Amendment requires that a search warrant describes the things to be seized with sufficient particularity to prevent a general exploratory rummaging in a person's belongings. Defendant also argued that the requirement that warrants shall particularly describe things to be seized makes general searches under them impossible and prevents the seizure of one thing under a warrant describing another. And as to what is to be taken, nothing is to be left to the discretion of the officer executing the warrant.

The Court of Appeals stated that:

> The essential inquiry when faced with challenges under the Fourth Amendment is whether the search or seizure was reasonable—reasonableness is analyzed in light of what was reasonable at the time of the Fourth Amendment's adoption. It is axiomatic that the 4th Amendment was adopted as a directed response to the evils of the general warrants in England and the writs of assistance in the Colonies.

The Court noted that despite the specificity of the search warrant, files not pertaining to the sale or distribution of controlled substances were opened and searched, and according to Mr. Carey, these files should have been suppressed.

The government had argued that the plain view doctrine authorized the police search (*Coolidge v. New Hampshire*, 403 U.S. 443, 465 (1971)). Under the plain view doctrine, a police officer may properly seize evidence of a crime without a warrant if: (1) the officer was lawfully in a position from which to view the object seized in plain view; (2) the object's incriminating character was immediately apparent, that is, the officer had probable cause to believe the object was contraband or evidence of a crime; and (3) the officer had a lawful right of access to the object itself (*United States v. Soussi,* 29 F.3d 565, 570 (10th Cir. 1994), citing *Horton v. California,* 110 S. Ct. 2301, 2307 (1990))).

The government had contended that "a computer search such as the one undertaken in this case is tantamount to looking for documents in a file cabinet, pursuant to a valid search warrant, and instead finding child pornography." Just as if officers had seized pornographic photographs from a file cabinet, seizure of the pornographic computer images was permissible because officers had a valid warrant, the pornographic images were in plain view, and the incriminating nature was readily apparent as the photographs depicted children under the age of 12 engaged in sexual acts. The warrant authorized the officer to search any file because any file might well have contained information relating to drug crimes and the fact that some files might have appeared to have been graphic files would not necessarily preclude them from containing such information.

The Court of Appeals held that the warrant obtained for the specific purpose of searching defendant's computers permitted only the search of the computer files for names, telephone numbers, ledgers, receipts, addresses, and other documentary evidence pertaining to the sale and distribution of controlled substances. The scope of the search was thus circumscribed to evidence pertaining to drug trafficking. The Court opined that the government's argument the files were in plain view is unavailing because it is the contents of the files and not the files themselves which were seized. Detective Lewis could not at first distinguish between the text files and the JPG files upon which he did an unsuccessful word search. Indeed, he had to open the first JPG file and examine its contents to determine what the file contained. Thus, until he opened the first JPG file, he stated he did not suspect he would find child pornography. At best, he says he suspected the files might contain pictures of some activity relating to drug dealing.

The Court noted that his suspicions changed immediately upon opening the first JPG file. After viewing the contents of the first file, he then had "probable cause" to believe the remaining JPG files contained similar erotic material. Thus, because of the officer's own admission, it is plainly evident each time he opened a subsequent JPG file, he expected to find child pornography and not material related to drugs. Armed with this knowledge, he still continued to open every JPG file to confirm his expectations. Under these circumstances, the Court stated that it could not find that the contents of each of those files were inadvertently discovered. Moreover, the Court noted, Lewis made clear as he opened each of the JPG files he was not looking for evidence of drug trafficking. He had temporarily abandoned that search to look for more child pornography, and only "went back" to searching for drug-related documents after conducting a five hour search of the child pornography files.

The Court stated that it was clear from his testimony that Lewis knew he was expanding the scope of his search when he sought to open the JPG files. Moreover, at that point, he was in the same position as the officers had been when they first wanted to search the contents of the computers for drug-related evidence. They were aware they had to obtain a search warrant and did so. These circumstances suggest Lewis knew clearly he was acting without judicial authority when he abandoned his search for evidence of drug dealing.

The Court stated:

Although the question of what constitutes "plain view" in the context of computer files is intriguing and appears to be an issue of first impression for this court, and many others, we do not need to reach it here. Judging this case only by its own facts, we conclude the items seized were not authorized by the warrant. Further, they were in closed files and thus not in plain view.

The Court of Appeals noted that since the case involved images stored in a computer, the file cabinet analogy may be inadequate since electronic storage is likely to contain a greater quantity and variety of information than any previous storage method, computers make tempting targets in searches for incriminating information. According to the Court, relying on analogies to closed containers or file cabinets may lead courts to oversimplify a complex area of Fourth Amendment doctrines and ignore the realities of massive modern computer storage.

In *United States v. Turner* (1999 WL 90209 (1st Cir. February 26, 1999)), the defendant's neighbor was the victim of a nighttime assault in her apartment, and police officers obtained the defendant's consent to search his apartment for signs of the intruder and for evidence of the assault itself. While searching the apartment, an officer noticed the defendant's computer screen suddenly illuminate with a photograph of a nude woman resembling the assault victim. He then sat at the computer and itemized the files most recently accessed. Several of the files had the suffix ".jpg," denoting a file containing a photograph. The officer opened these files and found photographs of nude blonde women in bondage. After calling the district attorney's office for guidance, the officer copied these adult pornography files onto a floppy disk and then searched the computer hard drive for other incriminating files. He opened a folder labeled "G-Images" and noted several files with names such as "young" and "young with breasts." After opening one of these files and observing child pornography, the officer shut down and seized the computer, and the defendant was charged in a single count of possessing child pornography. The government contended the "consent was so broad—authorizing search of all the defendant's 'personal property' that it necessarily encompassed a comprehensive search of his computer files." But the First Circuit Court of Appeals affirmed the suppression of the computer files on grounds "the consent did not authorize the search of the computer" because an objectively reasonable person assessing in context the exchange between the defendant and these detectives would have understood that the police intended to search only in places where an intruder hastily might have disposed of any physical evidence of the assault.

CONSENT TO SEARCH A THIRD PERSON'S COMPUTER

Valid consent is a well-recognized exception to the Fourth Amendment prohibition against warrantless searches (*Schneckloth v. Bustamonte,* 412 U.S. 218 (1973)). Consent to search in the absence of a warrant may, in some circumstances, be given by a person other than the target of the search (*United States v. Block,* 590 F.2d 535, 539 (4th Cir. 1978)). Two criteria must be met in order for third party consent to be effective. First, the third party must have authority to consent to the search (*Stoner v. California,* 376 U.S. 483 (1964)). Second, the third party's consent must be voluntary (*Bumper v. North Carolina,* 391 U.S. 543 (1968)).

The *Trulock v. Freeh* (275 F.3d 391 (4th Cir. 12/28/2001)) case presented an interesting issue regarding a third party's consent to search a computer. Notra Trulock served as the Director of the Office of Intelligence of the U.S. Department of Energy (DOE) from 1994 to 1998. From 1995 to 1998, Trulock also served as the DOE's Director of the Office of Counterintelligence. Trulock alleged that he uncovered evidence that Chinese spies had systematically penetrated U.S. weapons laboratories, most significantly the Los Alamos Nuclear Laboratory. Trulock contended that the White House, the FBI, and the Central Intelligence

Agency (CIA) ignored his repeated warnings about the espionage. Congress eventually learned of the security breach and in 1998 invited Trulock to testify, which he did on several occasions. That same year, Trulock was demoted within the DOE; he was ultimately forced out in 1999.

In early 2000, Trulock wrote an account of his findings, which criticized the White House, the DOE, the FBI, and the CIA for turning a blind eye to the security breach. Trulock claimed that the manuscript did not include any classified information. Nonetheless, in March of 2000, Trulock submitted the manuscript to the DOE for a security review, but the DOE declined to examine it. Afterward, Trulock sent the manuscript to the National Review, which published an excerpt in an edition that was circulated in early July of 2000. Although neither side placed the article in the record, the parties agree that it charged the administration with incompetence.

Linda Conrad had been the Executive Assistant to the Director of the Office of Intelligence at the DOE for more than six years. Trulock and Conrad lived in a Falls Church, Virginia townhouse, which Conrad owned. Conrad alleged that on the morning of July 14, 2000, when she arrived at work, her supervisor took her aside to say that the FBI wanted to question her about Trulock. The supervisor warned her that the agents had a warrant to search the townhouse and would break down the front door, in the presence of the media, if she refused to cooperate.

The agents queried Conrad about Trulock's personal records and computer files. Conrad responded that she shared a computer with Trulock, but that each of them maintained separate, password-protected files on the hard drive. Conrad and Trulock did not know each other's passwords and could not, therefore, access each other's private files. The agents questioned Conrad for about three hours. Towards the end of the interview, the agents gave Conrad a form, which they asked her to sign. The complaint alleges that the agents did not explain the form to Conrad and that Conrad did not read it, learning only afterwards that she had consented to a search of her house. The complaint does not allege that the agents claimed to have a search warrant, threatened to break down Conrad's door if she refused to sign, or mentioned the media. Conrad does maintain, however, that she was fearful, crying and shaking.

At the end of the questioning, the agents followed Conrad to her townhouse, where Trulock was waiting. When Trulock asked to see the search warrant, the agents responded that they had no warrant but that Conrad had consented to the search. The complaint does not contend that Conrad tried to withdraw her consent or that Trulock tried to bar the search on the ground that his consent, as a resident of the house, was also necessary.

The agents located the computer in the bedroom. An unidentified FBI computer specialist and Agent Carr searched the computer's files for about 90 minutes. The complaint alleged that Agent Carr looked at Trulock's password-protected files. When the search was over, the specialist, after giving Conrad a receipt, took the hard drive away.

Trulock argued that the search of his password-protected files violated his Fourth Amendment rights. He asserted even if Conrad's consent were valid, she did not have the authority to consent to a search of his password-protected files. The Court held that Conrad's consent to search was involuntary and even if her consent was voluntary, it would not authorize a search of Trulock's private, password-protected files. The Court stated that the authority to consent originates not from a mere property interest, but instead from "mutual use of the property by persons generally having joint access or control for most purposes, so that it is reasonable to recognize that any of the co-inhabitants has the right to permit the inspection in his own right and that others have assumed the risk that one of their numbers might permit the common area to be searched. Conrad lacked authority to consent to the search of Trulock's files.

The Court noted that Conrad and Trulock both used the computer located in Conrad's bedroom and each had joint access to the hard drive. Conrad and Trulock, however, protected their personal files with passwords; Conrad did not have access to Trulock's passwords. Although Conrad had authority to consent to a general search of the computer, her authority did not extend to Trulock's password-protected files. Trulock's password-protected files are analogous to the locked footlocker inside the bedroom. By using a password, Trulock affirmatively intended to exclude Conrad and others from his personal files. Moreover, because he concealed his password from Conrad, it cannot be said that Trulock assumed the risk that Conrad would permit others to search his files. Thus, Trulock had a reasonable expectation of privacy in the password-protected computer files and Conrad's authority to consent to the search did not extend to them. The Court held that Trulock had alleged a violation of his Fourth Amendment rights.

EVIDENCE ESTABLISHING VENUE

To convict a person of a crime, the prosecutor must establish that the crime was committed within the venue of the court, i.e., judicial district, unless the defendant has waived his or her right under the Sixth Amendment, U.S. Constitution to be tried in the judicial district in which the crime occurred. As noted by the court in *United States v. Rowe* (414 F.3d 271 (2d Cir. 2005)):

> We must therefore discern the location of the commission of the criminal acts. Where a crime consists of distinct parts which have different localities the whole may be tried where any part can be proved to have been done. Where the acts constituting the crime and the nature of the crime charged implicate more than one location, the Constitution does not command a single exclusive venue. . . . The government maintains that what it calls a "continuing offense" is defined in 18 U.S.C. § 3237(a), which states in part that "any offense against the United States begun in one district and completed in another, or committed in more than one district, may be inquired of and prosecuted in any district in which such offense was begun, continued, or completed."[5]

As discussed earlier, in *United States v. Rogers* (No. 05-1455-cr (2d Cir. 12/19/2005)), the defendant-appellant, Jan Elijah Rogers, was convicted of two counts of advertising to receive, exchange, and distribute child pornography,[6] and one count of transporting child pornography by computer.[7] He was sentenced to 20 years' imprisonment.

Rogers challenges his conviction and sentence on several grounds. Rogers argued that venue in the Southern District of New York was improper because he was a resident of Colorado whose only connection with New York was that his Internet crime was discovered here. The court held that venue in the Southern District of New York was proper because Rogers's Internet advertisement could be, and was, viewed in the Southern District of New York, and because its placement on the Internet supports a strong inference that Rogers contemplated that it would be accessible everywhere that access to the Internet can be had. The court concluded that venue was proper in any jurisdiction where the Web site could be accessed.

---

[5]All states have a similar venue provision by state constitution, statute, or court rule.
[6]18 U.S.C. § 2251(c) (now 18 U.S.C. § 2251(d)).
[7]18 U.S.C. § 2252A(a)(1).

In *United States v. Thomas* (74 F.3d 701 (6th Cir. 1996)), the Sixth Circuit affirmed a couple's conviction for operating an electronic bulletin board from which paying subscribers could download obscene images. The couple ran the bulletin board from California, but was prosecuted in the Western District of Tennessee after a federal postal inspector there, acting on the complaint of a private individual, subscribed to the bulletin board and obtained the images found to be obscene. To gain access to the bulletin board, the inspector—and every other subscriber—had to submit a signed application form, along with a $55 fee, indicating the applicant's age, address, and telephone number. After the inspector pseudonymously submitted the form and fee, one of the defendants called him at his undercover telephone number in Memphis, Tennessee, acknowledged receipt of his application, and authorized him to log on with the defendant's personal password.

The Sixth Circuit Court of Appeals reasoned that there was no constitutional impediment to the government's power to prosecute pornography dealers in any district into which the material was sent. The court held that venue in Tennessee was proper pursuant to 18 U.S.C. § 3237(a) because defendant Robert Thomas knew of, approved, and had conversed with a bulletin board member in the Western District of Tennessee who had his permission to access and copy the images that ultimately ended up there.

PROVING CRIMINAL INTENT IN OBSCENITY CASES

It is often difficult to prove that the defendant had the necessary criminal intent required for successful prosecution in certain crimes. For example, the Communications Decency Act of 1996 (CDA)[8] prohibited the *knowing* transmission over the Internet of obscene or indecent messages to any recipient under 18 years of age.[9] The phrase "knowing transmission to any recipient under 18 years of age" requires that the prosecution establish that the defendant knowingly transmitted the obscene material to a person under the age of 18 years. This issue was discussed in by the U.S. Supreme Court in *Ashcroft v. American Civil Liberties Union* (122 S. Ct. 1700, 152 L.Ed.2d 771 (2002)).

In Ashcroft, the Court noted that the Internet offers a forum for a true diversity of political discourse, unique opportunities for cultural development, and myriad avenues for intellectual activity. While "surfing" the World Wide Web, the primary method of remote information retrieval on the Internet today, individuals can access material about topics ranging from aardvarks to Zoroastrianism. One can use the Web to read thousands of newspapers published around the globe, purchase tickets for a matinee at the neighborhood movie theater, or follow the progress of any Major League Baseball team on a pitch-by-pitch basis.

The Court also noted that the Web contains a wide array of sexually explicit material, including hardcore pornography (the court cited *American Civil Liberties Union v. Reno*, 31 F. Supp. 2d 473, 484 (ED Pa. 1999)). In 1998, for instance, there were approximately 28,000 adult sites promoting pornography on the Web.[10] The Court stated that because navigating the Web is relatively straightforward and access to the Internet is widely available in homes, schools, and libraries across the country children may discover this pornographic material

---

[8] 110 Stat. 133.
[9] See 47 U.S.C. § 223(a).
[10] See H. R. Rep. No. 105-775, p. 7 (1998).

either by deliberately accessing pornographic Web sites or by stumbling upon them. The Court opined that a child with minimal knowledge of a computer, the ability to operate a browser, and the skill to type a few simple words may be able to access sexual images and content over the World Wide Web.

In Ashcroft, the Court noted that Congress first attempted to protect children from exposure to pornographic material on the Internet by enacting the CDA, which also forbade any individual from knowingly sending over or displaying on the Internet certain "patently offensive" material in a manner available to persons under 18 years of age. The prohibition specifically extended to "any comment, request, suggestion, proposal, image, or other communication that, in context, depicted or described, in terms patently offensive as measured by contemporary community standards, sexual or excretory activities or organs.[11]

The CDA provided two affirmative defenses to those prosecuted under the statute. The first protected individuals who took good faith, reasonable, effective, and appropriate actions to restrict minors from accessing obscene, indecent, and patently offensive material over the Internet.[12] The second shielded those who restricted minors from accessing such material by requiring use of a verified credit card, debit account, adult access code, or adult personal identification number.[13]

In *Reno v. American Civil Liberties Union*, the U.S. Supreme Court held that the CDA's regulation of indecent transmissions and the display of patently offensive material violated the First Amendment's freedom of speech clause. The Court concluded that "the CDA lacked the precision that the First Amendment requires when a statute regulates the content of speech" because, in order to deny minors access to potentially harmful speech, the CDA effectively suppressed a large amount of speech that adults had a constitutional right to receive and to address to one another.[14]

The Court noted that its holding was based on three crucial considerations. First, the existing technology did not include any effective method for a sender to prevent minors from obtaining access to its communications on the Internet without also denying access to adults. Second, the breadth of the CDA's coverage was wholly unprecedented. Its open-ended prohibitions embraced not only commercial speech or commercial entities, but also all nonprofit entities and individuals posting indecent messages or displaying them on their own computers in the presence of minors. In addition, because the CDA did not define the terms "indecent" and "patently offensive," the statute covered large amounts of nonpornographic material with serious educational or other value. The Court noted that the CDA regulated subject matter extended to discussions about prison rape or safe sexual practices, artistic images that include nude subjects, and arguably the card catalog of the Carnegie Library. Third, the Court found that neither affirmative defense set forth in the CDA constituted the sort of narrow tailoring that would save an otherwise patently invalid unconstitutional provision. Consequently, only the CDA's ban on the knowing transmission of obscene messages survived the Supreme Court's scrutiny because the Court noted "obscene speech enjoys no First Amendment protection."

[11]47 U.S.C. § 223(d)(1).
[12]47 U.S.C. § 223(e)(5)(A).
[13]47 U.S.C. § 223(e)(5)(B).
[14]521 U.S. 874.

After the Supreme Court's decision in *Reno v. American Civil Liberties Union*, Congress explored other avenues for restricting minors' access to pornographic material on the Internet. In particular, Congress passed and the President signed into law the Child Online Protection Act, (COPA).[15] COPA prohibits any person from "knowingly and with knowledge of the character of the material, in interstate or foreign commerce by means of the World Wide Web, making any communication for commercial purposes that is available to any minor and that includes any material that is harmful to minors.[16]

Apparently responding to the Supreme Court's objections to the breadth of the CDA's coverage, Congress limited the scope of COPA's coverage in at least three ways. First, while the CDA applied to communications over the Internet as a whole, including, for example, e-mail messages, COPA applies only to material displayed on the World Wide Web. Second, unlike the CDA, COPA covers only communications made for commercial purposes. And third, while the CDA prohibited "indecent" and "patently offensive"communications, COPA restricts only the narrower category of "material that is harmful to minors."

Drawing on the three-part test for obscenity set forth in *Miller v. California* (413 U.S. 15 (1973)), COPA defines material that is harmful to minors as any communication, picture, image, graphic image file, article, recording, writing, or other matter of any kind that is obscene or that (1) the average person, applying contemporary community standards, would find, taking the material as a whole and with respect to minors, is designed to appeal to, or is designed to pander to, the prurient interest; (2) depicts, describes, or represents, in a manner patently offensive with respect to minors, an actual or simulated sexual act or sexual contact, an actual or simulated normal or perverted sexual act, or a lewd exhibition of the genitals or postpubescent female breast; and (3) taken as a whole, lacks serious literary, artistic, political, or scientific value for minors.[17]

Like the CDA, COPA also provides affirmative defenses to those subject to prosecution under the statute. An individual may qualify for a defense if he, in good faith, has restricted access by minors to material that is harmful to minors (A) by requiring the use of a credit card, debit account, adult access code, or adult personal identification number; (B) by accepting a digital certificate that verifies age; or (C) by any other reasonable measures that are feasible under available technology.[18] Persons violating COPA are subject to both civil and criminal sanctions. A civil penalty of up to $50,000 may be imposed for each violation of the statute. Criminal penalties consist of up to six months in prison and/or a maximum fine of $50,000. An additional fine of $50,000 may be imposed for any intentional violation of the statute.[19]

One month before COPA was scheduled to go into effect, a lawsuit was filed challenging the constitutionality of the statute in the United States District Court for the Eastern District of Pennsylvania. The respondents were a diverse group of organizations, most of which maintain their own Web sites. While the vast majority of content on their Web sites is available for free, respondents all derive income from their sites. Some, for example, sell advertising that is displayed on their Web sites, while others either sell goods directly over their sites or charge artists for the privilege of posting material.[20] All respondents either post

[15]112 Stat. 2681-736 (codified in 47 U.S.C. § 231 (1994 ed., Supp. V)).
[16]47 U.S.C. § 231(a)(1).
[17]47 U.S.C. § 231(e)(6).
[18]47 U.S.C. § 231(c)(1).
[19]47 U.S.C. § 231(a).
[20]31 F. Supp. 2d, at 487.

or have members that post sexually oriented material on the Web. Respondents' Web sites contained resources on obstetrics, gynecology, and sexual health; visual art and poetry; resources designed for gays and lesbians; information about books and stock photographic images offered for sale; and online magazines.

In their complaint, respondents alleged that, although they believed that the material on their Web sites was valuable for adults, they feared that they would be prosecuted under COPA because some of that material could be construed as "harmful to minors" in some communities. Respondents' facial challenge claimed, inter alia, that COPA violated adults' rights under the First and Fifth Amendments because it (1) created an effective ban on constitutionally protected speech by and to adults; (2) was not the least restrictive means of accomplishing any compelling governmental purpose; and (3) was substantially overbroad.

The district court granted respondents' motion for a preliminary injunction, barring the government from enforcing the Act until the merits of respondents' claims could be adjudicated.[21] Focusing on respondents' claim that COPA abridged the free speech rights of adults; the district court concluded that respondents had established a likelihood of success on the merits. The district court reasoned that because COPA constitutes content-based regulation of sexual expression protected by the First Amendment, the statute, under this Court's precedents, was "presumptively invalid" and "subject to strict scrutiny." The district court then held that respondents were likely to establish at trial that COPA could not withstand such scrutiny because, among other reasons, it was not apparent that COPA was the least restrictive means of preventing minors from accessing "harmful to minors" material.

The Attorney General of the United States appealed the District Court's ruling (*American Civil Liberties Union v. Reno*, 217 F.3d 162 (CA3 2000)). The United States Court of Appeals for the Third Circuit affirmed. Rather than reviewing the District Court's "holding that COPA was not likely to succeed in surviving strict scrutiny analysis," the Court of Appeals based its decision entirely on a ground that was not relied upon below and that was "virtually ignored by the parties and the amicus in their respective briefs." The Court of Appeals concluded that COPA's use of "contemporary community standards" to identify material that is harmful to minors rendered the statute substantially overbroad. Because "Web publishers are without any means to limit access to their sites based on the geographic location of particular Internet users," the Court of Appeals reasoned that COPA would require "any material that might be deemed harmful by the most puritan of communities in any state" to be placed behind an age or credit card verification system. Hypothesizing that this step would require Web publishers to shield "vast amounts of material," the Court of Appeals was persuaded that this aspect of COPA, without reference to its other provisions, must lead inexorably to a holding of a likelihood of unconstitutionality of the entire COPA statute.

The Supreme Court granted the Attorney General's petition to review the Court of Appeals' determination that COPA likely violates the First Amendment because it relies, in part, on community standards to identify material that is harmful to minors.[22] The Supreme Court reversed the Court of Appeals' judgment.

The Supreme Court noted that the First Amendment states that Congress shall make no law abridging the freedom of speech. And that this provision embodies our profound national commitment to the free exchange of ideas. The Court opined that as a general matter, the First

---

[21]31 F. Supp. 2d, at 499.
[22]532 U.S. 1037 (2001).

Amendment means that government has no power to restrict expression because of its message, its ideas, its subject matter, or its content (the court cited *Bolger v. Youngs Drug Products Corp.,* 463 U.S. 60, 65 (1983) and *Police Dept. of Chicago v. Mosley,* 408 U.S. 92, 95 (1972)). However, the Court stated that this principle, like other First Amendment principles, is not absolute.

The Court stated that obscene speech, for example, has long been held to fall outside the purview of the First Amendment (*Roth v. United States,* 354 U.S. 476, 484–485 (1957)). But this Court struggled in the past to define obscenity in a manner that did not impose an impermissible burden on protected speech. The difficulty, the Court noted, resulted from the belief that in the area of freedom of speech and press the courts must always remain sensitive to any infringement on genuinely serious literary, artistic, political, or scientific expression.

The Court noted that the Court of Appeals had concluded that community standards jurisprudence has no applicability to the Internet and the Web because Web publishers are currently without the ability to control the geographic scope of the recipients of their communications.[23] The Court stated that for the purposes of this case it was sufficient to note that community standards need not be defined by reference to a precise geographic area. Absent geographic specification, a juror applying community standards will inevitably draw upon personal knowledge of the community or vicinage from which he comes.

The Court noted that because juries would apply different standards across the country, and Web publishers currently lack the ability to limit access to their sites on a geographic basis, the Court of Appeals feared that COPA's "community standards" component would effectively force all speakers on the Web to abide by the most puritan community's standards. And such a requirement, the Court of Appeals concluded, imposes an overreaching burden and restriction on constitutionally protected speech.

The Court noted that the COPA applies to significantly less material than did the CDA and defines the harmful-to-minors material restricted by the statute in a manner parallel to the Miller definition of obscenity. To fall within the scope of COPA, works must not only depict, describe, or represent, in a manner patently offensive with respect to minors, particular sexual acts or parts of the anatomy, they must also be designed to appeal to the prurient interest of minors and taken as a whole, lack serious literary, artistic, political, or scientific value for minors.[24]

According to the Supreme Court the additional restrictions substantially limit the amount of material covered by the statute. Material appeals to the prurient interest, for instance, only if it is in some sense erotic. Of even more significance to the Court was COPA's exclusion of material with serious value for minors. In Reno, the Court emphasized that the serious value requirement is particularly important because, unlike the "patently offensive" and "prurient interest" criteria, it is not judged by contemporary community standards. This is because "the value of a work does not vary from community to community based on the degree of local acceptance it has won." Rather, the relevant question is whether a reasonable person would find value in the material, taken as a whole. Thus, the serious value requirement allows appellate courts to impose some limitations and regularity on the definition by setting, as a matter of law, a national floor for socially redeeming value—a safeguard not present in the CDA.

---

[23]217 F.3d, at 180.
[24]47 U.S.C. § 231(e)(6).

KEY TERMS

Computer
Study of Evidence

REFERENCES

American Civil Liberties Union v. Reno, 31 F. Supp. 2d 473, 484 (ED Pa. 1999).

American Civil Liberties Union v. Reno, 217 F.3d 162 (CA3 2000).

Ashcroft v. American Civil Liberties Union, 122 S. Ct. 1700, 152 L.Ed.2d 771 (2002).

Bolger v. Youngs Drug Products Corp., 463 U.S. 60, 65 (1983).

Bumper v. North Carolina, 391 U.S. 543 (1968).

Carley, W. M., and T. L. O'Brien. September 12, 1995. How Citicorp system was raided and funds moved around world. *Wall Street Journal*: A1.

Collected Essays of Albert Borowitz. 2005. The Mayflower Murderer. *Legal Studies Forum* 29 (2): 596–99.

Coolidge v. New Hampshire, 403 U.S. 443, 465 (1971).

Kerr, O. S. 2005. Essay, digital evidence and the new criminal procedure. *105 Columbia Law Review* 279: 290–92.

Miller v. California, 413 U.S. 15 (1973).

Olmstead v. United States, 277 U.S. 438, 474 (1928) (Brandeis, J., dissenting).

Police Dept. of Chicago v. Mosley, 408 U.S. 92, 95 (1972).

Probst, E. L., and K. A. Wright. January 30, 2006. Using their e-words against them. *New Jersey Law Journal*: S1 (noting that tens of billions of e-mails are sent daily).

Roth v. United States, 354 U.S. 476, 484–485 (1957).

Rothstein, P., M. S. Raeder, and D. Crump. 2003. *Evidence in a Nutshell*: 1. St. Paul: Thompson West.

Schneckloth v. Bustamonte, 412 U.S. 218 (1973).

Steagald v. United States, 451 U.S. 204, 213 (1981).

Stoner v. California, 376 U.S. 483 (1964).

Trulock v. Freeh, 275 F.3d 391 (4th Cir. 12/28/2001).

United States v. Adjani, No. 05-50092 (9th Cir. 07/11/2006).

United States v. Beusch, 596 F.2d 871 (9th Cir. 1979).

United States v. Block, 590 F.2d 535, 539 (4th Cir. 1978).

United States v. Cardwell, 680 F.2d 75 (9th Cir. 1982).

United States v. Carey, 172 F.3d 1268 (10th Cir. 1999).

United States v. Hay, 231 F.3d 630 (9th Cir. 2000).

United States v. Melvin, 596 F.2d 492, 496 (1st Cir. 1979).

United States v. Rogers, No. 05-1455-cr (2d Cir. 12/19/2005).

United States v. Rowe, 414 F.3d 271 (2d Cir. 2005).

United States v. Singh, 390 F.3d 168, 181 (2d Cir. 2004).

United States v. Soussi, 29 F.3d 565, 570 (10th Cir. 1994), citing *Horton v. California* 110 S. Ct. 2301, 2307 (1990).

United States v. Thomas, 74 F.3d 701 (6th Cir. 1996).

United States v. Turner, 1999 WL 90209 (1st Cir. February 26, 1999).

Chapter 27

The Politics of Internet Crimes

Nancy Marion
University of Akron

Nancy Marion, Ph.D., is professor of political science at the University of Akron, Akron, Ohio. She holds a Ph.D. in political science/public policy from the State University of New York at Binghamton. She is the author of several books and numerous scholarly articles on the public policy of crime and criminal justice. Her research interests revolve around the interplay of politics and criminal justice.

Abstract

In recent years, Internet crimes have proliferated as computer technology has evolved. Politicians have been forced to react to the public's concerns with statements and new laws that are intended to decrease the incidence of crimes committed with the use of the Internet. Various political actors, including nonelected organizations such as interest groups, courts, and bureaucracies, as well as elected officials such as presidents and Congress, have all been active in the legal battles against Internet crimes. This chapter is a description and analysis of the actions taken by elected and nonelected officials to prevent criminal victimization through the Internet. It covers topics such as file sharing, online pornography, online gambling, identity theft, counterfeit goods, cyber security, privacy, and money laundering.

INTRODUCTION

In recent years, the proliferation of crimes committed on the Internet or with the help of the Internet has forced politicians and policymakers to react with statements, laws, and policies that are attempts to reduce the incidences of such crimes. As these crimes become more common, citizens want to see lawmakers, **bureaucracies**, **courts**, and other actors "do something" to protect them and their families from a variety of crimes, such as **identity theft**, child pornography, or even terrorism.

There have been many political actors, both elected and nonelected, who have decided to, or have been forced to, get involved in protecting the public from Internet crimes. Elected officials such as the President and **Congress** have addressed the issues during their campaigns, and once elected, have attempted to address voters' concerns with proposed legislation to combat Internet-related crimes. Nonelected officials, such as **interest groups**, the courts, and bureaucracies, have done the same.

The current research is a description and analysis of the actions taken by both elected and nonelected political actors to prevent Internet offenses. It will show how political actors have reacted to the problem, and how the issues have become a permanent part of the political process.

CAMPAIGNS AND ELECTIONS

Crime in general has been a campaign issue for presidential candidates since the 1960s (Rosch 1985, 20), and is considered to be a "safe" issue that will tend to increase support from voters (Rosch 1985, 20; Jacob et al. 1982, 3). It is assumed that most voters will support those candidates who back tougher anticrime measures. Crime is considered to be a "valence" issue, which are those that most people support and over which there is not much disagreement (Salmore and Salmore 1985, 117). When it comes to Internet crime, most people will be in favor of actions to prevent it, making the issue a valence issue. At the same time, however, there might be disagreements on individual pieces of legislation, or disagreements about the best method for preventing Internet crime. Because of this, the issue becomes a positional issue, which is one where a candidate must choose between one position over another (Marion 1995, 94).

During the most recent presidential campaign, many of the candidates talked about Internet crime, but none extensively. For example, Governor Bush, the Republican nominee for president, supported parental filtering devices for television and the Internet. He was concerned that with the advent of the Internet, personal **privacy** is at risk. He claimed to be committed to protecting personal privacy for every American. He promised, if elected, to criminalize identity theft and guarantee the privacy of medical and sensitive financial records. He promised to make it a criminal offense to sell a person's social security number without his or her consent (Connolly 2000; Sobeira 2000). Another candidate, John Edwards, the Democratic nominee for vice president, was a member of the Congressional Internet Caucus, a group of Congressional members who worked to educate their colleagues about the promise and potential of the Internet. As such, he supported tools to keep inappropriate material away from children. Another candidate for the presidency, John McCain, supported filtering software for all public school and library computers as a way to keep children from potentially harmful Internet sites (Marion 2007). He wanted to legalize the development and sale of encryption devices (Senate Statements S 798, April 14, 1999). Overall, each of these candidates supported tougher stances on some aspects of Internet crime, but chose different positions within the broader topic area.

BUREAUCRACIES

It is the role of bureaucracies and agencies to carry out, or implement, the policies and laws passed by Congress. Because they are aware of the issues facing constituents, the bureaucracies are often the ones that are most knowledgeable about issues facing Congress. Thus, bureaucrats become involved in the legislative process by helping Congress write bills, or they may lobby for bills, or even testify for or against proposed bills. Some of the agencies involved are the Department of Justice, the Federal Bureau of Investigation (FBI), the Federal Communications Commission (FCC), and the Department of Homeland Security.

The Department of Justice has many ways to fight Internet crimes. One of those is the Computer Crime and Intellectual Property Section (CCIPS). This part of the Justice Department is responsible for implementing our national strategies developed to combat computer and intellectual property crimes around the world. It attempts to halt electronic penetrations, data thefts, and cyber attacks on critical information systems. Their personnel have worked to crack down on computer piracy, fraud, **money laundering**, identity theft, spyware, pornography, sports betting, cyberstalking and harassment, and even cases concerning e-bay auction scams. It also investigates and prosecutes computer crimes by working with other government agencies, the private sector, and academic institutions. The attorneys not only investigate offenses, but litigate cases or provide litigation support to other prosecutors as well. They also train federal, state, and local law enforcement personnel. In the legislative process, members of CCIPS often comment on, or propose legislation dealing with Internet crimes. Finally, they initiate and participate in international efforts to combat computer and intellectual property crime (see the Web site of U.S. Department of Justice 2006).

In 1995, another division of the Department of Justice, the Office of Juvenile Justice and Delinquency Prevention (OJJDP), decided to create the Internet Crimes Against Children (ICAC) Task Force Program as part of their Missing Children's Program. This was in response to the increasing number of children and teenagers using the Internet, the proliferation of child pornography, and the heightened online activity by predators searching for unsupervised contact with underage victims. The purpose of the new program was to combat the threat of offenders who use the Internet to sexually exploit children. ICAC members speak to families, children and parents about the dangers of the Internet. They help to train law enforcement personnel in ways to combat Internet crimes against children, and assist them in developing specialized multijurisdictional, multiagency teams that work to prevent, investigate, and prosecute those people who commit Internet-related sexual crimes against children. Each task force is composed of federal, state, and local law enforcement personnel, as well as federal and local prosecution officials, local educators, and service providers such as mental health professionals. In 2005, the Department of Justice awarded more than $13 million in grants to fund ICAC task forces nationwide (U.S. Department of Justice 2005).

As part of the Department of Justice, the FBI has many options for fighting Internet crimes. Agents regularly pose as teenagers in online chat rooms in order to identify and thwart online sexual predators, and those who use the Internet to meet young people for sexual purposes or to produce, share, or possess child pornography. The FBI investigates computer hacking to stop computer intrusions and the spread of malicious codes. They also have programs to counteract operations that endanger our national security, and to dismantle national and transnational organized criminal enterprises that may engage in crimes such as Internet fraud.

To do this, the FBI has created Cyber Action Teams (CATs), which are small, highly trained teams of agents, analysts, and computer forensic and malicious code experts. They have also created the Innocent Images program to focus specifically on computer-facilitated child sexual exploitation.

A more recent program developed by the FBI is the Internet Crime Complaint Center (IC3). In this program, the FBI works with the National White Collar Crime Center (NW3C). The mission of IC3 is to serve as an agency that will receive, develop, and refer criminal complaints regarding cyber crime. The IC3 gives victims of cyber crime an easy, online method for reporting criminal behavior, both criminal and civil. It also provides a central referral mechanism for complaints involving Internet related crimes to law enforcement.

Another agency involved in preventing Internet crimes is the Federal Communications Commission (FCC). The FCC is responsible for, among other things, regulating the decency of broadcasting and wired communications. In the early 2000s, the FCC began increasing enforcement of their indecency regulations, mainly because of Janet Jackson's "wardrobe malfunction" during the halftime show of Super Bowl XXXVIII. However, the FCC is frequently criticized for violating the First Amendment right of Free Speech when it comes to regulating indecency. The FCC has often had disagreements with conservatives and family-oriented groups for not censoring or restricting sexually explicit and violent material that they believe might be harmful to children.

Because of these concerns, the House of Representatives in 1996 considered a bill (HR 3957) that would, among other things, bar the FCC from regulating the Internet. If passed, it would declare that the FCC had no jurisdiction or authority over the Internet or other interactive computer services (Healey 1996b, 2594). The bill did not have enough support to pass.

Another agency involved with Internet crimes is The Department of Homeland Security. It has a National Cyber Security Division that works to secure cyberspace and any assets on it. The goals of the agency are to maintain an effective cyber response system, and to implement a cyber risk management program to protect our critical infrastructure from attack. To do this, they have created the National Cyberspace Response System that analyzes threats made to the system, and prepares for such an attack if one should occur. They do this by staging attacks to test our preparedness, and by reducing software vulnerabilities (see the Web site of Department of Homeland Security 2006).

COURTS

The federal courts are involved in helping to define the laws against Internet crimes. It is the courts' responsibility to review the actions of the Congress and through their power of judicial review, determine if a law is Constitutional. The federal courts have made many decisions regarding Internet crimes. Some of these are described below.

File Sharing

In 2001, a federal appeals court slammed Napster (an Internet company that distributed song files for free) by affirming a lower court ruling that Napster encouraged copyright infringement by allowing people to swap music without cost. In April 2003, a lower federal court in Los Angeles ruled that two Internet **file sharing** companies could not be held liable for piracy committed by their users. The entertainment industry appealed the ruling to the Supreme Court. In 2005, The Supreme Court decided in *MGM Studios Inc v. Grokster Ltd* (545 U.S. 125; S. Ct. 2764) that Internet file sharing companies could be held legally liable for copyright infringement if they encouraged the use of their software to trade pirated music and movies (Tessler 2005b, 1792). This decision restricted the behavior of online file sharing companies.

Pornography

A law passed by Congress in 1996 (PL 104-208), the Child Pornography Prevention Act (CPPA), prohibited individuals from creating, possessing or distributing computer-simulated sexual images of children or young-looking adults who were portrayed as underage children engaging in sex acts. This was referred to as "virtual child pornography" or "morphed" child pornography. The Supreme Court, in *Ashcroft v. Free Speech Coalition* (535 U.S. 234), struck down the law as too broadly written and unconstitutional because it could apply to virtual pornography that did not depict actual children, and to material that was not obscene. The Court said that the law might prohibit otherwise legal material from being permitted (Palmer 2002a, 1028; Dlouhy 2002a, 1675).

That same year, Congress passed a Telecommunications Act (PL 104-104), part of which made it a crime to send a message that is "obscene, lewd, lascivious, filthy, or indecent with intent to annoy, abuse, threaten or harass another person" (Carney 1999, 968). The Supreme Court reviewed the Act in 1997 in the case of *Reno v. ACLU* (117 S. Ct. 2329). In a 7-2 decision, the Court struck down the decency provisions of the telecommunications law and ruled that a ban on "obscene" e-mail and faxes violated the Constitution. They ruled that indecency provision violated the First Amendment and was a violation of free speech rights. The Court described the law as so broad that it would have imposed limits on adult conversation. The Court also said that the law was so vague that it would halt the speech of people who might be uncertain of whether they might be prosecuted. The Court's decision established that the same free speech protections would be applied to online communications as they are to as print media such as newspapers and magazines (Carney 1997, 1519).

In 1998, the Congress passed another attempt to block children from accessing pornographic material online. The Child Online Protection Act (COPA) (PL 105-277) was designed to protect children from material with adult content. The statute was immediately challenged in court, and the court placed a ban on the enforcement of the new law. The ban was later extended for another two months because the judge expressed concern that it violated free speech (Ota 1999b, 334). In June of 2004, the Supreme Court ruled in a 9-0 decision *Ashcroft vs. ACLU* (542 U.S. 656) that COPA was unconstitutional and upheld the injunction against the law. The court sent the case back to the U.S. District Court for the Eastern District of Pennsylvania for further review.

Congress then passed the Children's Internet Protection Act (CIPA) (PL 106-5554), which required schools and public libraries that receive federal funding to use Internet filters (Williams 2002, 1464). CIPA was challenged by groups such as the American Library Association, the ACLU, and other pro-pornography groups. A lower federal court struck down the law. The decision was appealed to the Supreme Court When it reached the Court in 2003 in the case of *ALA v. United States* (American Library Association) it ruled that CIPA was Constitutional. This meant that libraries that received federal funds for computers with Internet access must put filters on those computers. The court said that CIPA was legal because libraries can turn off filters for any adult patrons who ask. In addition, every library can reject federal funds if it wishes to continue giving children unrestricted access to pornographic materials.

Copyrights

In 1999, a complaint was filed in the U.S. District Court in the District of Columbia concerning an earlier law passed by Congress (the Copyright Term Extension Act) that extended copyright terms. The plaintiff argued that the extension was unconstitutional. The District Court decided that the Congress had the power to extend terms. The case was appealed to the Court of Appeals in May 2000, which upheld the decision of the District Court. In 2001, the case went to the U.S. Supreme Court. In *Eldred v. Ashcroft* (537 U.S. 186; 2003) the Supreme Court decided, in a 7-2 decision, that Congress did not overstep its power when it passed legislation that added twenty years to the life of copyrights (Dlouhy 2003, 154). Their ruling focused on Congress' power to legislate on copyright issues.

PRESIDENTS

Presidents can influence policies in many ways, but they often influence the actions of Congress by suggesting potential legislation (Oliver 2003). Presidents often give speeches about issues in hopes of getting those issues on the Congressional agenda (Marion 1994). Since the issue of Internet crimes is a more recent concern, only two presidents have expressed concerns about them: **William Clinton** and **George W. Bush.**

President Clinton often mentioned the general dangers of the Internet in quotes such as this:

> All this wonderful technology and this easily accessible information has its dark underside. You can get on the Internet now and tap into one of these fanatic extremists, and they will explain to you how you too can make a bomb just like the one that blew up the Federal building in Oklahoma City. The explosion of technology means that a radical religious group in Japan can figure out how to get a little bitty vial of gas and walk into a subway and break it open and kill a bunch of totally innocent people and put hundreds of others in the hospital. (Public Papers of the President 1995a, 932)

Because of these dangers, Clinton in 1999 issued an Executive Order that created a Working Group that was to analyze unlawful conduct on the Internet and to make recommendations about the need for legislation.

Clinton went on to discuss specific Internet crimes, such as **online pornography**. With regards to this issue, Clinton said, "The truth of the matter is that the Internet is being used to promote child sexual abuse" (Public Papers of the President 1996b, 2212). He also said that "It means that our children can get on the Internet, and how, without even paying any money, can be exposed to hardcore porn" (Public Papers of the President 1995b, 982).

Another specific crime with which Clinton was concerned was that of tax evasion:

> We will work with you to make sure that the Internet never becomes a vehicle for tax evasion or money laundering (Public Papers of the President 1998a, 297). Of course, the Internet could be used for other things, too: cyber-criminals can use computers to raid our banks, run up charges on our credit cards, extort money by threats to unleash computer viruses. (Public Papers of the President 1998b, 741)

Clinton also discussed Internet fraud. In 1999, he said, "Listen to this: Complaints of Internet fraud have tripled in the past 6 months—just in the last 6 months. Therefore, I will work with Congress and Chairman Levitt to provide the additional resources for the SEC necessary for enforcement, beyond what I have already requested in our balanced budget" (Public Papers of the President 1999b, 685). A few years later, Clinton said, ". . . we have announced new initiatives on Internet fraud and identity theft that call on law enforcement to step up their efforts on behalf of consumers" (Public Papers of the President 1999c, 2003).

Clinton discussed how the Internet could be used to further illegal gun sales in a speech in 2000:

> . . . the Internet is fast becoming a new outlet for illegal gun sales. This past May, two teenagers, using a forged Federal firearms license, were able to order guns over the Internet for delivery to their home in Montclair, New Jersey. Because they used a forged license, there was no scrutiny, no background check, no questions asked . . . Unfortunately, the Internet, despite all its benefits, is making it easier for guns to fall into the wrong hands. There are now 4,000 firearm sales-related sites on the Internet, and there are 80 sites where you can actually buy a gun at auction. Clearly, we must do more to ensure that every sale over the Internet is legal and that no one uses the anonymity of cyberspace to evade our nation's gun laws. (Public Papers of the President 2000, 1910)

In some of his later speeches, Clinton focused on the dangers of the Internet when it came to terrorism. He said, "But in an open world of easy information, quick technology, and rapid movements, we are all more vulnerable than we used to be to terrorism and its interconnected allies, organized crime, drug running, and the spread of weapons of destruction" (Public Papers of the President 1996a, 551). Clinton was concerned that terrorists could attack America's computer infrastructure. He told Americans that

> We must be ready—ready if our adversaries try to use computers to disable power grids, banking, communications and transportation networks, police, fire and health services, or military assets. More and more, these critical systems are driven by and linked together with computers, making them more vulnerable to disruption . . . And we already are seeing the first wave of deliberate cyber attacks, hackers break into Government an business computers, stealing and destroying information, raiding bank accounts, running up credit card charges, extortion money by threats to unleash computer viruses. The potential for harm is clear. (Public Papers of the President 1999a, 87)

Throughout his administration, Clinton was concerned with the privacy of consumers' information, particularly of medical information. He said, "Congress should follow the new medical privacy guidelines we issued last week and pass legislation to make sure records now stored in computers stay just as confidential as records locked in a file cabinet" (Public Papers of the President 1997, 1166).

President Bush

Like President Clinton, privacy of Internet users was a concern for President Bush, who supported legislation (HR 4380) that would increase requirements on financial services companies to get consent from consumers before sharing information about their records or personal spending habits with affiliated companies (Ota 2000c, 1273).

During the Bush Administration, The White House proposed a comprehensive program to combat cyber crime and address issues surrounding electronic surveillance, despite a low probability of passing through Congress. The program included a provision allowing law enforcement to trace Internet communications across state lines. It also would require law enforcement to show probable cause before seeking access to a suspect's e-mail, similar to the procedures for obtaining permission for a wiretap (Bettelheim 2000d, 1776).

When he signed the Patriot Act, Bush reiterated his opinion that the law would "allow surveillance of all communications used by terrorists, including e-mails, the Internet, and cell phones" (Public Papers of the President 2001a, 1307). His concern for the safety of cyber-space branched out to his discussions with other nation's representatives. After talks with offi-cials from India, the White House released a Joint statement between the United States and India, about which President Bush announced the establishment of a Joint Cyberterrorism Initiative (Public Papers of the President 2001b, 1370).

Overall, both of these presidents discussed the issue of Internet crimes, but had different ideas about the best ways to stop the harm done by such offenses. These offenses were both on the general agendas of these presidents, but their specific proposals differed.

INTEREST GROUPS

Interest groups attempt to influence legislation by lobbying, providing testimony about a bill, or even educating the public about an issue (Marion 1995, 90). There have been multiple interest groups that have become active in issues surrounding Internet crimes. For example, social conservative advocacy groups, including the Eagle Forum and the Traditional Values Coalition, have objected to bills that would allow for **online gambling** (HR 3125) (Ota 2000e, 1617). Instead, the Traditional Values Coalition supported the Unlawful Internet Gambling Funding Prohibition Act (HR 556) because "Internet gambling is the crack cocaine of gam-bling and will contribute to an increase in gambling addictions, family break down, and crime. Gambling is a highly addictive sport that destroys communities and degrades all who become involved in it" (see the Web site of Traditional Values Coalition 2006). More recently, in 2006, the Traditional Values Coalition was concerned about HR 4777, the Internet Gambling Prohibition Act, because it would expand gambling in a number of ways, including allowing intrastate lottery Internet use, interstate horse racing, Internet gambling, and online wagers on fantasy sports teams.

Victims' rights groups, in particular the National Center for Victims of Crime, lobbied lawmakers for legislation that would protect victims of identity theft. The proposed legisla-tion would require courts to issue specific findings that these victims are innocent of any crimes committed using their personal information (Bettelheim 2000c, 543).

Other groups are concerned with theft of intellectual property on the Internet. The Recording Industry Association of America (RIAA 2003), a lobbying organization for music companies and the recording industry, is concerned with online piracy, which is the unautho-rized uploading of a copyrighted sound recording and making it available to the public, or downloading a sound recording from an Internet site, even if the recording is not resold. It helped to lead the fight against Napster by hiring former Senate Majority Leader Bob Dole and former Montana Governor Marc Racicot to lobby for stronger copyright protections (Bettelheim 2001b, 715). The group's representatives lobbied in support of a measure (HR 4077) that would make it easier for federal prosecutors to pursue criminal copyright infringement cases. RIAA has a team of Internet specialists that work to stop Internet sites that make illegal recordings available (RIAA 2003).

A similar organization, the Motion Picture Association of American (MPAA), was founded in 1922 as an advocate of the American motion picture, home video and television industries. It attempts to influence policies surrounding file sharing programs such as Kazaa, eDonkey, and Grakster by announcing its intention to file lawsuits against these groups who distribute films using the file sharing programs (Sharma 2004b, 2585).

TABLE 27-1 Contributions to Federal Candidates, Political Action Committees, and Parties by Gambling Industry Political Action Committees

Political Action Committees	1998 Election Cycle	2000 Election Cycle
Boyd Gaming	$102,500	$31,397
Circus Circus	$45,500	$15,700
Harrah's	$428,650	$77,000
International Game Technology	$53,600	$7,000
MGM Grand	$73,024	$17,000
Mirage	$164,596	$29,000
Station Casinos	$70,700	$36,500
Tropicana Resort	$29,000	$1,000

Source: FEC Info (accessed September 9, 2006).

The Information Technology Association of America (ITAA) is a trade association that represents Internet and software companies. It has been wary of legislation that would crack down on nefarious activities, such as online piracy and identity theft, that may put restraints on legitimate software products.

A final example is The Center for Democracy and Technology, a nonprofit public policy organization that promotes the democratic potential of the Internet. Their mission is to develop and implement policies that preserve and enhance free expression, privacy, and other democratic values. The agency does research in public policy development, and promote their policy positions in Congress (Center for Democracy and Technology 2006).

Each of these groups, and many others, not only lobby for their interests in front of Congress, but also contribute money to political campaigns. In exchange for large contributions, the agency hopes that the legislator will return their "favor," so to speak, and support legislation in the best interest of the groups. Table 27-1 provides information on the contributions made by gaming corporations to different candidates in campaigns. This shows that the major gaming corporations have donated large sums of money to candidates and political parties in recent years. Table 27-2 provides more details about their political contributions over a longer time span. Obviously, these groups hope that the candidates, if elected, will support progaming legislation.

CONGRESS

Members of Congress have struggled to keep up with the ever-changing technology of the Internet and crimes that are a byproduct. The Internet has increased the ease and speed with which companies and individuals can collect vast amounts of information about consumers, including children. It has become easy for thieves and sex offenders to get personal information of Internet users, leading to identity theft and sexual offenses against children. There are

TABLE 27-2 Contributions to Casinos/Gambling Organizations Long-Term Contribution Trends

Election Cycle	Total Contributions	Donations to Democrats	Donations to Republicans	Percentage to Democrats	Percentage to Republicans
2006	$7,660,868	$3,938,695	$3,696,052	51%	48%
2004	$11,255,936	$6,503,963	$4,745,613	58%	42%
2002	$15,019,998	$7,536,653	$7,482,881	50%	50%
2000	$12,588,017	$6,922,353	$5,638,115	55%	45%
1998	$6,571,268	$2,576,547	$3,993,432	39%	61%
1996	$7,118,257	$3,776,622	$3,338,885	53%	47%
1994	$3,049,449	$1,646,569	$1,401,980	54%	46%
1992	$1,562,919	$1,036,893	$520,241	66%	33%
1990	$466,869	$332,669	$134,200	71%	29%

Source: Center for Responsive Politics. http://www.opensecrets.org/industries/indus.asp?Ind=NO7&Format=print (accessed September 9, 2006).

now hundreds of online sites that offer pornography and gambling. In recent years, Congress has had to react to these new threats the Internet poses to citizens. One indication of the growing importance of the Internet was a name change approved for the Subcommittee on Courts and Intellectual Property. Chairman Sensenbrenner and the Judiciary Committee members approved changing the name to the Subcommittee on Courts, the Internet and Intellectual Property.

For the most part, Congress' attitude toward regulating the Internet can be described as "hands off." In general, lawmakers seem to be content to let the digital marketplace set its own rules (Bettelheim and Ota 2000, 110). Lawmakers have been reluctant to pass new policies concerning the Internet that could become burdensome and hinder its development (Bettelheim 2001a, 412). But in recent years, Congress has been forced to deal with issues relating to Internet crimes. In the early years, they focused on issues such as Internet fraud, pornography, or gambling. One of the first laws concerning the Internet was passed in 1986, when Congress passed the Computer Fraud and Abuse Act (CFAA). The CFAA prohibits computer fraud, including unauthorized use, access and transmission. The legislation made it a felony to enter computer systems operated by the federal government or federally insured financial institutions, with punishments of up to five years in prison. The law also made it a crime to exchange computer passwords with the intent of committing interstate fraud (Hansen and Bettelheim 2002, 1769).

But the focus of Congressional action concerning the Internet shifted after the terrorist attacks of September 11, 2001. Members of Congress now had to deal with more intense topics such as cyber terrorism. Congress also became concerned with the possibility of an attack on America's infrastructure, including computers, especially because telecommunications networks, power grids, pipelines, nuclear plants and refineries had become largely automated, making them vulnerable to computer hackers, viruses, worms and other devastating forms of electronic intrusion (Bettelheim and Adams 2001, 2260). Millions of computers were now interconnected, and officials were worried about malicious acts that potentially could shut down critical government applications and business transactions (Bettelheim and Adams 2001, 2260). The problem was confounded since federal, state and local governments did not communicate easily with each other. But lawmakers in Congress were unsure what they could or should do to prevent such an attack in the future (Bettelheim and Adams 2001, 2259).

At that time, Congress was also forced to struggle with defining the balance between citizens' liberty and the security of the nation. Some members of Congress were in favor of changes that would make it easier for law enforcement to snoop on electronic communications such as e-mails (Bettelheim and Palmer 2001, 2210), primarily because it was believed that Osama bin Laden and his associates used e-mail, messages embedded in computer files and encryption software that was used to scramble electronic messages to communicate with each other (Bettelheim and Palmer 2001, 2210). The new Director of Homeland Security, John Ashcroft, asked Congress for additional powers that would make it easier for law enforcement agencies to track e-mails and allow them to obtain "roving wiretaps" to follow suspects to any telephone lines (Palmer 2001, 2263). Of course, other Congressional members as well as groups such as the ACLU saw these proposals as unnecessary limits on the Freedom of Speech.

Over the years, Congress has passed many laws concerning Internet crime. Table 27-3 indicates the issues that were discussed by Congressional Session, and Table 27-4 is a summary of the issues discussed by year. A description of some of the Congressional action to keep cyberspace safe is below.

TABLE 27-3 Internet Offenses Introduced in Congress

Issue	Sessions
Copyright	102, 104, 105, 106, 107
Decency	103
Pornography	104, 105, 106, 107, 108
Gambling	104, 105, 106, 107, 109
Encryption	104, 105, 106
Counterfeit Goods	104, 106, 108
Alcohol Sales	106
Privacy	105, 106, 107
Schools	106, 107
Security	105, 106, 107, 108
Hacking	106
Identity Theft	106, 107, 108, 109
Stocks	106
Pharmacy Drug Sales	109

TABLE 27-4 Internet Crimes Discussed in Congressional Sessions

Session	Topics
102 (1991–1992)	Copyright
103 (1993–1994)	Decency Standards
104 (1995–1996)	Pornography, Gambling, Encryption, Counterfeit goods, copyrights
105 (1997–1998)	Encryption, Pornography, Cyber security, Copyright, Gambling
106 (1999–2000)	Gambling, Alcohol sales, Drugs, Pornography, Encryption, Privacy, Schools, Copyrights, Security, Identity Theft, Stock trading
107 (2001–2002)	Internet Filters, Copyrights, Cyber security, Pornography, Privacy, Identity Theft, Gambling
108 (2003–2004)	Pornography, Copyrights, Identity Theft, CyberSecurity
109 (2005–2006)	Copyrights, Privacy, Cyber attacks, Identity Theft, Cyber security, Online Pharmacy Sales, Gambling

Decency Standards/Pornography

Congress first tackled the issue of the decency of the information available on the Internet during the 103rd Congress (1993–1994). It began when the Senate added an amendment to a telecommunications bill (S 1822) that would assure that the information superhighway did not turn into a "red-light district," and that the telecommunications networks met the same standards of decency that the federal government applied to other forms of communication (Healey 1994, 2565). The bill proposed that commercial services could provide indecent material only to adults upon their request.

Even though the bill later died in session, Congress continued to discuss it in the following session. The Senate members of the 104th Congress (1995–1996) added an amendment to a larger telecommunications bill (S 314) that would ban anyone from knowingly transmitting indecent material to minors, or even making it available to them. The bill, known as the Communications Decency Act, would also make it illegal to use telecommunications devices, such as computer e-mail systems and fax machines, to abuse, harass, annoy, or threaten others (Healey 1995a, 803). The Senate also proposed S 652 that included a provision that outlawed obscene communications over computer networks, and required those networks to keep indecent material away from minors (Healey 1995b, 1995).

President Clinton signed S 652 into law, and it became PL 104-104. Once the bill was signed, lawsuits were brought in court to determine the Constitutionality of the law. One of the lawsuits was filed in the U.S. District Court in Philadelphia by the American Civil

Liberties Union (ACLU). The ACLU wanted to see the section of the new law that banned the dissemination of "indecent" materials to minors struck down by the Court as unconstitutional (Carney 1996a, 359). The Supreme Court later ruled that the indecency provisions were unconstitutional in *Reno v. ACLU* (117 S. Ct. 2329).

The House members also got into the issue of decency standards. They proposed HR 1240 to strengthen the penalties for criminals who sexually exploit children. The House wanted the U.S. Sentencing Commission to increase the penalties for making or trafficking in child pornography, with additional time for offenders who use a computer for distribution or recruiting (Congressional Quarterly Weekly Report 1995, 1030). House members also wanted longer sentences for those individuals who transport a child across state lines for the purpose of engaging in criminal sexual activity (Congressional Quarterly Weekly Report 1995, 1030). This proposal was also signed into law, becoming PL 104-71.

But that did not stop Congress from being concerned about the problem of Internet pornography. In the 105th Congress (1997–1998), the Senate discussed S 1482 that would ban the sale of material that is "harmful to minors" who are less than seventeen years old. Further, any pornography distributors would be forced to remove free images from their Web pages and would have to get a credit card number or personal identification number from any buyer. Violators would face penalties of up to six months in jail and a $50,000 fine (Ota 1997, 3028). This proposal did not pass. In the House, the members debated HR 774 that would require Internet providers to offer to sell or give customers software allowing them to screen Web sites (Ota 1997, 3028). This was called the Internet Freedom and Child Protection Act, but it did not have enough support to pass and become a law.

The 105th Congress (1997–1998) also debated HR 3494, the Child Protection and Sexual Predator Punishment Act of 1998. This addressed the growing use of the Internet by pedophiles to contact and distribute pornography to minors. Under the proposal, if a pedophile contacted a minor through the Internet for the purpose of engaging in sexual activity or transferring obscene materials, they could be sent to prison for up to five years and face fines. The bill would also increase penalties for other crimes against children, including a sentence of up to 15 years or a fine for transporting a child across state lines with the intent of forcing him or her to engage in prostitution or another illegal sexual activity (Gruenwald 1998c, 1227). The proposal was signed by the president (PL 105-314).

There were many other bills concerning Internet pornography addressed in the 105th Congress. These included those listed in Table 27-5. None of these proposals passed.

Congressional members again returned to the issue of online pornography during the 106th Congress (1999–2000). After a federal judge placed a temporary ban on the enforcement of the Child Online Protection Act (PL 105-277) expressing concern that it violated free speech (Ota 1999b, 334), Congress responded with more antipornography proposals. For example, S 97 would require schools to install filtering software on classroom computers to prevent access to Web sited that feature pornographic material. If schools did not install the software, they would not qualify for grants to pay for telecommunications services (Ota 1999b, 334; Ota 1999e, 1555). Similar legislation in the House was HR 543. Neither passed.

In the 107th Congress, lawmakers proposed new legislation (HR 4623) that would ban "virtual" child pornography (Palmer 2002b, 1161). The Senate also proposed antipornography legislation (S 2520). The House and Senate bills were only slightly different. The House bill would ban any computer-generated image that is nearly indistinguishable from that of a minor engaging in sexually explicit conduct, but the Senate measure would make it a crime to pander,

TABLE 27-5 Anti-Internet Pornography Bills Proposed in 105th Congress

1. S 1482: to prohibit the distribution of material harmful to minors on the Internet

2. S 1619: to direct the FCC to study systems to filter or block matter on the Internet; would require installation of such on schools and libraries computers

3. S 3783: would require distributors of online pornography to limit access to adult material; set penalties of up to six months in prison and a fine of $50,000 for businesses that make any online communication for commercial purposes that is harmful to minors under the age of 17

4. HR 1180: would require internet Service Providers to offer screening software to subscribers: called the Family-Friendly Internet Access Act

5. HR 3783: would require companies to verify a person's age before they could view pornography on Internet websites. Under the bill, Web sites would be required to ask potential viewers for proof, such as a credit card or other means of identification, to ensure that only adults could access their sites. Violators could face a $50,000 fine and six months in jail (did not pass)

6. HR 1964: would require internet access providers to offer screening software to customers with children

7. S 1356 and HR 2791: would prohibit Internet Service Providers from providing services to sexually violent predators

8. S 1619: would require schools to use blocking technology as a condition of receiving subsidies

9. S 1482: would make it illegal to distribute sexual material to those under seventeen via the Internet

10. HR 3442: would require schools and libraries receiving universal service support for discounted telecommunications services to establish policies governing access to material that is inappropriate for children

11. HR 3177 and S 1619: Safe Schools Internet Act: would require schools to install systems to filter or block inappropriate Internet material on school computers

12. HR 2815: Protecting Children from Internet Predators Act: would penalize using the Internet to target children under 16 years of age for sexually explicit messages or contacts

Source: Ota (1998, 2499), Gruenwald (1998a, 388).

or solicit, child pornography. It also would require the pandering to be linked to material that had been determined to be obscene (Dlouhy 2002c, 2816). Neither proposal was turned into law.

Online Gambling

The availability of Internet gambling was discussed by Congress at many points. During the 104th Congress (1995–1996), the House approved the creation of a nine-member commission that would spend two years studying the proliferation of legalized gambling in the United

States (Salant 1995, 3463). In HR 497 (PL 104-440), the House voted to establish the National Gambling Impact and Policy Commission, which would be comprised of three members named by the president, three by the house speaker, and three by the Senate majority leader. The Commission's recommendations were made in 1999, and included a moratorium on any further growth of the industry (Ota 1999d, 1035). They also proposed outlawing Internet gambling, "Web" betting on collegiate sports and gambling by those under 21.

During the 105th Congress (1997–1998), the issue of online gambling was again addressed by Congress. The law at the time banned interstate gambling over a telephone or other wire communication, but it did not specifically outlaw wagering on the Internet (Gruenwald 1997b, 2597). So the Senate Judiciary Committee approved S 474 that would prohibit gambling on the Internet by criminalizing, placing, or receiving bets or wagers on the Internet (Gruenwald 1997b, 2597). It was simply a ban on Internet gambling. The bill was passed by the Senate by a vote of 90 to 10, but it did not become law. The companion bill in the House was HR 2380. This would also prohibit Internet gambling and allow law enforcement officials to order Internet service providers to cut off service to gambling sites (Gruenwald 1998e, 2409). This was approved by the House Judiciary Committee's Crime Subcommittee, but went no further.

The issue of Internet gambling came up again in the 106th Congress (1999–2000). There was a proposal that would establish a $500 fine and three months in jail for Internet bettors and a $20,000 fine and four years in jail for Internet gambling operators (Ota 1999a, 192). S 692, the Internet Gambling Ban, had many exceptions and circumstances under which computer services or businesses would be immune from penalty. Groups such as fantasy sports leagues or state lotteries would be immune. If the law passed, gamblers would not be allowed to place bets with just a computer and a credit card. The bill would prohibit the operation of gambling sites on the Internet, closing a loophole in federal gambling laws that ban betting over phone lines (Pierce 1999, 1470). The law did not pass.

At the same time, the House members considered HR 3125, the Internet Gambling Prohibition Act that would prohibit online gambling. The House version would permit online advertising for legal gambling operations, which was not in the Senate version. Both measures would ban gaming businesses and gamblers from using the Internet to place or receive bets, but the senate bill would permit Indian tribes to take online bets from customers on Indian reservations (Bettelheim and Ota 2000, 111). The House did not pass the bill.

The House also proposed HR 4419, the Internet Gambling Funding Prohibition Act that would ban the use of certain bank instruments for Internet gambling. This did not pass.

The 106th Congress chose to focus on the problem of sports betting. The House Judiciary Committee approved HR 3575 that would ban gambling on high school and collegiate sports nationwide, which would essentially eliminate it in Nevada, the only state that allowed such wagering (Palmer 2000, 2149). But the bill did not become law.

The House during the 107th Congress (2001–2002) passed a bill, HR 556, that would crack down on online gambling by cutting off the flow of money to such operations (Dlouhy 2002b, 2600). The new law would give law enforcement agencies the power to stop banks from processing financial transactions involving such operations. Gambling Web sites, for example, often take bets by credit card. Investigators also could force Internet service providers to stop providing Web links to gambling sites and offering services to those businesses (Dlouhy 2002b, 2600). The bill did not change state authority to regulate gambling. The bill did not have enough support to pass.

The problem of Internet gambling continued in the 108th Congress (2003-04). The Senate proposed S 627 that would prohibit banks and credit card companies from receiving funds for Internet gambling sites. In brief, the bill would make it illegal for credit card companies and other financial institutions to handle Internet bets (Anselmo 2003, 1976). The bill did not pass.

In the 109th Congress, the House members are debating HR 4411, the Unlawful Internet Gambling Enforcement Act of 2006. The bill would prohibit acceptance of any payment for unlawful Internet gambling.

Encryption

Over the years, Congress tackled issues surrounding encryption devices, which are data-scrambling technologies that allow computer users to encode communications such as e-mail and credit card orders (McCutcheon 2000, 92) and can prevent unauthorized access to electronic communications (Congressional Quarterly Weekly Report 1998a, 561). Early on, the government prohibited the export of certain types of encryption hardware or software (Carney 1996b, 986). However, since that law was passed, encryption devices had become a crucial technology not only to governments but to private companies and individuals as well, as they could be used to protect major financial transactions, corporate documents and other types of sensitive private conversations (Carney 1996b, 985). The Clinton administration supported the ban on exporting encryption devices because of national security issues and law enforcement interests. They argued that unrestricted use of encryption might prevent them from keeping tabs on nations like Iraq and Libya and working to combat terrorism (Carney 1996b, 985). The administration argued that use of strong encryption technology could hamper law enforcement and intelligence gathering (Gruenwald 1997a, 802), and they were reluctant to relax export controls on encryption.

The Congress discussed the encryption issue during the 105th Congress (1997–1998). The computer industry wanted Congress to loosen the export restrictions on encryption products (Gruenwald 1997a, 802). Legislation (S 376) called the Encrypted Communications Privacy Act was proposed that would prohibit mandatory key escrow and release of decryption keys to government officials without a court order. HR 695, the Security and Freedom through Encryption (SAFE) Act, would reduce export controls. These proposals did not pass.

But some Congressional members supported another proposal, HR 2281, that would outlaw the manufacture, importation or trafficking of devices "primarily designed or produced" to circumvent technology, such as encryption, aimed at preventing access to copyrighted materials (Gruenwald 1998b, 484). This proposal became law (PL 105-304).

During the 106th Congress (1999–2000), encryption remained an issue for Congress. A House bill (HR 850) was proposed that would give businesses and individuals easier access to technology to protect sensitive information (Ota 1999c, 615), and would give people the right to buy and use the best encryption technology. The proposal would also limit the government's ability to restrict the export, manufacture or use of encryption technology. It would also prevent the government from requiring manufacturers to give federal officials the ability to unlock encrypted data (Ota 1999c, 615). This did not pass.

Members of the House asked President Clinton to develop a compromise bill on the export of encryption products (Ota 1999f, 1723). In the end, the Clinton Administration agreed to end most controls on the export of technology used to encode wireless telephone calls, e-mail, and online credit-card purchases (Ota 1999j, 2171). The administration announced that it was lifting almost all restrictions on the export of data encryption software. Under their proposal, companies would still have to ask permission to sell encryption products to a foreign government or military, and exports will be banned to countries accused of supporting terrorism: Iran, Iraq, Libya, Syria, Sudan, North Korea, and Cuba (McCutcheon 2000, 92). The administration explained their change in policy was to allow U.S. companies to compete with foreign rivals (Ota 1999j, 2171).

COUNTERFEIT GOODS

The problems surrounding the ease of counterfeiting goods were first discussed by the 104th Congress (1995–1996). This term, the House proposed HR 2511 that was aimed at curbing **counterfeit goods**, including software. The bill was not passed. The topic of counterfeit goods was not discussed again until the 108th Congress (2003–2004). This time, the House Judiciary Committee approved legislation that would make it more difficult for counterfeiters to sell fake products (Stern 2004, 1565). Under HR 3632, it would be more difficult to buy and sell authentication devices, such as holograms and special inks that mark copyrighted works as genuine. The measure also would apply to the gear used to attach the devices to books, records, software, videotapes, artwork, packaging or packaging inserts (Stern 2004, 1565). This was passed by both the House and the Senate, becoming law (PL 108-482).

COPYRIGHT LAW

During the 102nd Congress (1991–1992), the Senate proposed and passed S 893 to impose criminal penalties for illegally copying computer software. The bill made copyright infringements of motion pictures and audio recordings a felony no matter of the value (Healey 1996a, 2719). The House proposed a different version of the bill. Their version made the penalty for the offense dependent upon the value of the copies made. For instance, if a defendant made copies worth $5,000 or more, it would be a felony (Healey 1996a, 2719). The Senate version became PL 102-561.

Copyright infringements were also discussed in the 104th Congress (1995–1996). HR 2441 was an attempt to impose copyright law on the Internet, but no one could agree on the bill (Carney 1996c, 1752) and it did not pass.

In the 105th Congress (1997–1998), many proposals concerning copyrights were proposed, but none passed. These included those listed in Table 27-6.

In 1998, Congress passed the 1998 Digital Millennium Copyright Act (PL 105-304) that was intended to provide protection against the proliferation of online music and film (Kady 2004, 493). That same year, HR 2265 was signed into law (PL 105-147). The No Electronic Theft Act (NET) modified copyright law to impose criminal liability on one who willfully infringes copyright for personal as well as commercial financial gain. The new law prohibited unlawful electronic transmission of copyrighted works for commercial advantage or private financial gain.

During the 106th Congress, HR 1671 was proposed in the House to increase the statutory penalties in copyright infringement cases. It raised the limit on individual statutory damage awards, with even stiffer penalties for repeat offenders. After passing the bill, the House passed the Senate's version, S 1257 and inserted HR 1761 into it (Gravely 1999, 1953). Neither proposal passed.

TABLE 27-6 Copyright Proposals in the 105th Congress

1. HR 2180: the On-Line Copyright Liability Limitation Act: would exempt Internet Service Providers such as bulletin board operators from liability for copyright infringement

2. HR 2589: to extend the term granted to copyright owners by 20 years

3. HR 3209: the On-Line Copyright Infringement Liability Limitation Act: to provide online service providers with some protection from legal liability for copyrighted works stolen over their networks; would limit liability of Internet Service Provider based solely on the intermediate storage of material and protect the provider from claims based on the removal of material believed to be infringing. This was the same as HR 2180; neither passed

4. S 2037: to provide limitations on copyright liability relating to material online

5. HR 2652: would amend copyright law to create liability for extracting or using in commerce information gathered or maintained by another through investment of resources so as to cause harm

6. S 1146: Digital Copyright Clarification and Technology Education Act: would limit the liability of Internet Service Providers for copyright infringement, expand the fair use by teachers and librarians of copyrighted works, and amend federal copyright law to implement the 1996 WIPO Copyright Treaty

The 106th Congress also had to deal with "cybersquatting," or the unauthorized use by some Internet users of register World Wide Web addresses that suggest a connection to a brand name, major company, or political candidate (Ota 1999h, 1870; Koszczuk 1999, 1951). There were many proposals to prevent unauthorized use of brand names such as "Coca-Cola" and "Porsche" (Ota 1999h, 1870). These included S 1259 (PL 106-43) and HR 3028 (did not pass). The Senate Judiciary Committee approved S 1255, which created statutory damages in civil suits of at least $1,000, but not more than $100,000 for "cybersquatting." This went no further.

The issue continued to be an issue for Congress, who struggled with the issues surrounding copyrighted material. That session, they focused on the illegal downloading and copying of material on the Internet. Much of the demand for this legislative action came from musicians, authors, publishers and entertainment companies such as the Walt Disney Company because their work was being reproduced nearly perfectly, but without authorization (Bettelheim 2002, 894). One of the main offenders was Napster, which had a system for distributing song files for free (Bettelheim 2001b, 715). The major question for Congress became what collections of data should be protected, and for how long.

The 108th Congress (2003–2004) introduced legislation in the Senate (S 2560) that would hold companies that "intentionally induce" copyright infringement liable for theft of digital property. The House also proposed similar legislation. The House Judiciary Committee approved HR 4077 that would give prosecutors tools to go after such companies. The bill would set new standards for criminal online copyright infringement and authorize $15 million to the Justice Department for enforcement (Sharma 2004a, 2120). Neither bill passed.

The 109th Congress (2005–2006) proposed legislation that would deter movie piracy and legalize technology that lets parents filter objectionable content from films. The proposal was passed by the House Judiciary Committee (Tessler 2005a, 663). The Senate proposed

S 167 that would make it a federal crime to use a camcorder in a movie theater or distribute a copyrighted work before its release or commercial distribution. It also would protect companies that produce movie-filtering technology that can screen sexually graphic, violent and profane content (Tessler 2005a, 663). This became PL 109-9.

Another bill, HR 6052, was proposed in the current Congressional session. It would provide for licensing of digital delivery of musical works and to provide for limitation of remedies in cases in which the copyright owner cannot be located. So far, the bill has not passed.

Cyber Security

During the 105th Congress (1997–1998), both Congress and the Clinton administration took an interest in the possible vulnerability of U.S. computer networks to hackers, thieves and terrorists. They had been warned of possible serious weaknesses in computer networks at the State Department and other agencies. In addition, there had been recent disclosures that hackers had broken into public Internet sites at the Pentagon and other government departments. Government officials were concerned that more serious attacks could disrupt banks, telephone networks, air-traffic control centers, and other public or commercial networks (McCutcheon 1998a, 1404).

In fact, in June 1997, the Pentagon conducted tests to simulate electric power failures and 911 emergency telephone service overloads. Then they staged an actual unannounced invasion of the Defense Department's unclassified computer networks, using two people to gain access to data that could have seriously disrupting troop movements (McCutcheon 1998b, 1622). The exercise was not a success. The President's Commission on Critical Infrastructure Protection held a series of hearings and heard about the problem, and recommended that the government develop a real-time warning system for computer break-ins similar to the military's air-defense system (Congressional Quarterly Weekly Report 1998b, 676).

During the 106th Congress (1999–2000), the House Science Technology Subcommittee approved legislation that was aimed at protecting the federal government's computer systems from break-ins. The bill updated a 1987 law and give the Commerce Department's National Institute of Standards and Technology authority over computer security at nondefense agencies (McCutcheon 1999, 2534).

S 1993 was proposed in the Senate, and was aimed at protecting federal government information systems. The bill would require federal agencies to develop information security plans and submit to annual audits. This did not pass. Another proposal, S 1314/HR 2816 would set up a $25 million grant program for states to draw from annually for education, training, enforcement and prosecution of computer crimes. The House version was passed, and became PL 106-572.

As a result of increasing cyber attacks on popular Internet sites such as Amazon.com and eBay, Senators chose to increase protection for databases and infrastructure (Bettelheim 2000a, 420). The Senate Judiciary Technology, Terrorism and Government Information Subcommittee considered S 2092 that would give federal law enforcement agencies nationwide authority to use "trap and trace" devices to detect hacking. These devices capture electronic signals that identify the originating number of a computer. The bill also would lower barriers to prosecuting computer criminals (Bettelheim 2000a, 420; 2000b, 474). This did not pass.

The Senate Judiciary Committee of the 106th Congress approved an electronic crime bill proposal (S 2448) that was designed to help federal law enforcement agencies prevent and prosecute computer crimes. The new bill would establish a deputy assistant attorney general to oversee the Justice Department's computer crime and intellectual property division (Fagan 2000b, 2354). This did not pass.

The 107th Congress (2001–2002), after hearing that computer crimes range from simple pranks to sophisticated fraud schemes, proposed new ways to punish hackers. The House Judiciary Committee approved HR 3482, a cyber crime bill that built on portions of the antiterrorism law (PL 107-56). The new law would amend federal sentencing guidelines to address computer hacking. It would also give Internet service providers the authority to disclose the content of suspicious communications to law enforcement (Hansen and Bettelheim 2002, 1763). This did not pass.

After the 9/11 terrorist attacks, House members of the 107th Congress (2001–2002) overwhelmingly passed cyber security legislation (HR 3394) that authorized $880 million over five years aimed at preventing terrorist attacks on private or government computers. The Senate also proposed S 2182, similar legislation, and replaced their version with the House version. This was passed and became PL 107-305.

Even today, members of the 109th Congress (2005–2006) are trying to increase protections against poorly protected government computers, knowing that the possibility of a massive cyber attack—which could bring e-commerce to a halt, with devastating consequences for financial networks and the economy—to the theft of classified intelligence documents that could help terrorists stage another 9/11-style attack (Kady 2005, 347). In the House, members proposed HR 5318, the Cyber-Security Enhancement and Consumer Data Protection Act of 2006. The bill is an attempt to better assure **cyber security** by protecting personal records, and by increasing punishments for such offenses. House members also proposed HR 4982, the SAFER NET Act. This would improve public awareness in the United States regarding safe use of the Internet through the establishment of an Office of Internet Safety and Public Awareness within the Federal Trade Commission.

Privacy

For many years, member of Congress were concerned about maintaining the privacy of medical records and other personal information appearing on the Internet with more frequency. There were many Internet Privacy Bills introduced in the 105th Congress concerning privacy matters, none of which passed. They are described in Table 27-7.

During the 106th Congress (1999–2000) there were concerns over protecting the privacy of consumers who surf and shop on the Internet (Ota 2000a, 637). These concerns resulted in two bills, HR 354 that would punish unauthorized uses of such information with civil and criminal penalties, and HR 1858, which proposed only civil penalties for the same offense. Neither of these bills became law.

President Clinton promised to try to do more to protect the information related to consumers who used the Internet. He promised to ask Congress to support his proposal for new safeguards for medical and financial records (Ota 2000a, 637), and to restrict corporate use of personal financial information. Clinton's plan became HR 4380. It would strengthen privacy protection requirements for financial service companies (Ota 2000b, 1051). This did not pass.

TABLE 27-7 Internet Privacy Bills in the 105th Congress

---

1. **HR 98**: would require Internet Service Providers to get a subscriber's permission before releasing personal information about the person
2. **HR 1287**: would ban computer services from disclosing a Social Security number without the persons permission
3. **HR 1330**: Would ban federal agencies from releasing personal information about citizens on the Internet without consent
4. **HR 2368**: Would prohibit the commercial marketing of government information about an individual obtained via the Internet and displaying an individual's Social Security number on the internet. Also would ban the commercial marketing of personal medical information obtained from the Internet without consent
5. **S 600**: would prohibit credit card bureaus from releasing personal information such as Social Security numbers
6. **HR 1330**: American Family Privacy Act: would prohibit federal officers and employees from providing online access to information from Social Security accounts, earnings and benefit statements, and tax returns
7. **HR 1964**: Communications Privacy and Consumer Empowerment Act: would direct the FTC to protect the privacy of consumers on the internet
8. **HR 1287**: Social Security On-Line Privacy Protection Act: would prohibit interactive computer services from disclosing Social Security numbers and information protected by such numbers
9. **HR 1813**: to protect the privacy of the individual with respect to the social security number and other personal information

---

Source: Gruenwald (1998d, 1987), Congressional Quarterly Weekly Reports.

The House Government Reform Subcommittee on Government Management, Information and Technology approved HR 4049 to create a commission to study the issue of Internet privacy and how to better protect consumer privacy (Ota 2000d, 1466). They were given eighteen months to complete their investigation.

Internet privacy was again an issue of the 107th Congress (2001–2002). In an attempt to protect the privacy of Internet users, a House Energy and Commerce subcommittee released a draft bill (HR 4678) that would allow consumers to remove their names addresses, phone numbers and other personal information from customer lists that were compiled and sold by retailers. House members also proposed HR 237 that would require Web site operators to post their privacy guidelines and give consumers a chance to opt out of sharing information. These did not pass.

In the 108th Congress, HR 3261 would make it illegal to take information from a copyrighted database and then use that data for commercial or competitive gain. It would allow the victims of such actions to sue the violators for monetary damages (Kady 2003, 2572). This did not pass.

The current Congress is debating S 3568, a bill to protect information relating to consumers, and to require notice of security breaches. This bill was introduced on June 26, 2006, and has not yet been passed.

Internet Alcohol Sales

In the 106th Congress (1999–2000), members of the House proposed a bill to help states crack down on the interstate sale of liquor to minors through the Internet. Liquor distributors, who supported the bill, were afraid that direct sales via the Internet would steal their customers (HR 2031). Other supporters argued that the bill would prevent sales of liquor to minors by allowing states to get federal court injunctions against Internet sales of alcohol to those under a minimum age set by states (Ota 1999g, 1795; Ota 1999i, 1949). But owners of small wineries opposed the bill, arguing that their products get little shelf space in retail stores, and Internet sales were helping expand their businesses (Ota 1999g, 1795; Fagan 2000a, 480). The proposal did not become law.

Identity Theft

The Identity Piracy Act of 1998 (HR 3551) was introduced in the 105th Congress. It would establish a federal offense of identity theft, which involves stealing credit card and Social Security numbers and other personal information (Hansen and Bettelheim 2002, 1764). This did not pass. The Senate also acted to stop identity theft. The Senate Judiciary Technology, Terrorism and Governmental Information Subcommittee argued that cases of identity theft were growing and required more vigilance on the part of government and private services that track consumers' credit histories (Bettelheim 2000c, 543). They passed, and Clinton signed, the Identity Theft and Assumption Deterrence Act (HR 4151; PL 105-318) enacted in October 1998. Under the law, identity theft would be punishable by a prison sentence of up to fifteen years, in addition to fines and forfeiture of personal property used to commit the crime.

The concern about identity theft continued into the 107th Congress (2001–2002). In an attempt to halt such offenses, the Senate Judiciary Committee approved legislation to protect the credit records of identity theft victims. S 1742 would prohibit credit reporting companies from issuing reports on consumers who prove someone has stolen their social security numbers and other identifiers to impersonate them. The bill also would extend the time that victims of identity theft would have to file lawsuits alleging that a credit reporting company improperly released a bad credit report on them (Clarke 2002, 1320). This did not pass. In the House, members considered HR 91 that would make it harder for Internet scammers to commit identity theft by stealing social security numbers. Similarly, the Senate considered S 30 that would restrict how banks trade customers' personal information with affiliated companies. Neither of these passed.

The 108th Congress (2003–2004) also debated the issue of what to do to stop identity theft. They proposed HR 1731, which became PL 108-275, that established tougher criminal penalties for identity theft and made it easier for prosecutors to go after the perpetrators. They also proposed HR 1745, the Social Security Number Privacy and Identity Theft Prevention Act. In the Senate, the members introduced S 768, the Comprehensive Identity Theft Prevention Act. This bill would create an Office of Identity Theft, help consumers recapture their stolen identities, and require reasonable steps to protect sensitive personal information such as social security numbers. The Senate also proposed S 1408, the Identity Theft Protection Act, which was also an attempt to protect sensitive personal information such as social security numbers. In addition, they proposed S 3514, the Social Security Number

Online Protection Act of 2006. This bill would restrict the public display on the Internet of the last four digits of social security account numbers by state and local governments.

More recently, the Senate proposed S 472, the Anti-phishing Act of 2005. The bill would criminalize Internet scams involving fraudulently obtaining personal information, commonly known as phishing. This bill was also proposed in the House, as HR 1099.

Money Laundering

The Senate Banking Committee of the 107th Congress (2001–2002) proposed anti-money-laundering legislation to begin a financial war on terrorism (Perine 2001, 2328). The House also proposed similar legislation. HR 3004, the Financial Anti-Terrorism Act, would tighten government regulation of U.S. and foreign banking. It would forbid U.S. banks from offering correspondent accounts that offer services such as wire transfers and currency exchanges, to shadowy foreign shell banks with no physical presence. Such correspondent accounts have been used by drug traffickers and organized crime. The White House signaled its support for this money-laundering legislation (Perine 2001, 2328). Parts of the legislation were incorporated into the Patriot Act (HR 3162).

CONCLUSION

Internet crimes are evolving as technology changes, develops, and improves. The political response to Internet crimes has sometimes been slow, but shows an interest in stopping victimization by use of the Internet. All of the major political actors have become involved in this new battle, including elected officials such as the president and Congress, and nonelected officials such as interest groups and the courts. Despite their actions, many issues remain unresolved. There continues to be debate over how to prevent or punish Internet crimes in an age of rapid and accessible information. There is no doubt that the issue of Internet crimes will continue to be an important part of the political realm, especially with regard to Internet fraud, identity theft, and terrorism. There will continue to be major debates concerning the balance of citizen freedom and the power of government to peek into people's lives in an effort to protect the country from future cyber attacks. As the Internet grows, making information more readily available, the debate will continue.

KEY TERMS

Bureaucracies
Congress
Counterfeit goods
Courts
Cyber security
File sharing
George W. Bush
Identity theft

Interest groups
Money laundering
Online gambling
Online pornography
Presidents
Privacy
William Clinton

REFERENCES

Anselmo, J. C. August 2, 2003. Internet betting bill a serious game. *Congressional Quarterly Weekly Report*: 1976.

Bettelheim, A. February 26, 2000a. Senators introduce anti-hacking bill. *Congressional Quarterly Weekly Report*: 420.

Bettelheim, A. March 4, 2000b. Lawmakers, industry debate how to tackle "cybercrime" without jeopardizing privacy. *Congressional Quarterly Weekly Report*: 473–4.

Bettelheim, A. March 11, 2000c. Congress urged to do more to combat identity theft and ensure victims' rights. *Congressional Quarterly Weekly Report*: 543.

Bettelheim, A. July 22, 2000d. Clinton's cyber-proposal won't have legs. *Congressional Quarterly Weekly Report*: 1776.

Bettelheim, A. February 24, 2001a. Policing consumer privacy: Congress prepares to opt in. *Congressional Quarterly Weekly Report*: 412–17.

Bettelheim, A. March 31, 2001b. Congress steps into clash of copyright, consumer rights. *Congressional Quarterly Weekly Report*: 715–19.

Bettelheim, A. April 6, 2002. Hill contemplates copyrights: Does innovation trump piracy? *Congressional Quarterly Weekly Report*: 894–900.

Bettelheim, A., and R. A. Adams. September 29, 2001. America's infrastructure at risk: What is the federal role? *Congressional Quarterly Weekly Report*: 2259–61.

Bettelheim, A., and A. K. Ota. January 22, 2000. Governing the Internet. *Congressional Quarterly Weekly Report*: 110–11.

Bettelheim, A., and E. A. Palmer. September 22, 2001. Balancing liberty and security. *Congressional Quarterly Weekly Report*: 2210–14.

Carney, D. February 10, 1996a. Indecency provision attacked as Clinton signs bill. *Congressional Quarterly Weekly Report*: 359.

Carney, D. April 13, 1996b. Software firms seek to end ban on exporting encryption codes. *Congressional Quarterly Weekly Report*: 985–7.

Carney, D. June 22, 1996c. Cyberspace bill appears dead. *Congressional Quarterly Weekly Report*: 1752.

Carney, D. June 28, 1997. Court strikes down ban on Internet "indecency." *Congressional Quarterly Weekly Report*: 1519.

Carney, D. April 24, 1999. Obscene e-mail ban upheld. *Congressional Quarterly Weekly Report*: 968.

Center for Democracy and Technology. 2006. Accomplishments and objectives. http://www.cdt.org/mission/, Accessed September 21, 2006.

Clarke, D. May 18, 2002. Bill to protect credit records approved by senate panel. *Congressional Quarterly Weekly Report*: 1320.

Congressional Quarterly Weekly Report. April 8, 1995. Child Pornography Bill heads back to House. *Congressional Quarterly Weekly Report*: 1030.

Congressional Quarterly Weekly Report. March 7, 1998a. Coalition wants to liberalize laws on encryption exports. *Congressional Quarterly Weekly Report*: 561.

Congressional Quarterly Weekly Report. March 14, 1998b. Cyberspace invaders. *Congressional Quarterly Weekly Report*: 676.

Connolly, C. October 6, 2000. A light day for ticket toppers. *Washington Post*: A16.

Department of Homeland Security, National Cyber Security Division. 2006. http://www.dhs.gov/dhspublic/interapp/editorial/editorial_0839.xml, Accessed September 24, 2006.

Dlouhy, J. June 22, 2002a. Ban takes another shot at ban on virtual child porn. *Congressional Quarterly Weekly Report*: 1675.

Dlouhy, J. October 12, 2002b. Bill to curb online betting passes in house. *Congressional Quarterly Weekly Report*: 2600.

Dlouhy, J. October 26, 2002c. Hatch substitute amendment to "virtual" pornography bill pushes constitutional envelope. *Congressional Quarterly Weekly Report*: 2816.

Dlouhy, J. January 18, 2003. Supreme Court's copyright ruling could mean broad powers for congress. *Congressional Quarterly Weekly Report*: 154.

Fagan, A. March 4, 2000a. Bill would curb online alcohol sales. *Congressional Quarterly Weekly Report*: 480.

Fagan, A. October 7, 2000b. Substitute electronic crime bill adopted by senate judiciary. *Congressional Quarterly Weekly Report*: 2354.

Gravely, B. August 7, 1999. House passes tougher penalties for theft of intellectual property. *Congressional Quarterly Weekly Report*: 1953.

Gruenwald, J. April 5, 1997a. A scramble to safeguard encryption exports. *Congressional Quarterly Weekly Report*: 802–4.

Gruenwald, J. October 25, 1997b. Ban on cyberspace gambling gets first push in senate. *Congressional Quarterly Weekly Report*: 2597.

Gruenwald, J. February 14, 1998a. Panel again looks to limit internet porn to children. *Congressional Quarterly Weekly Report*: 388–9.

Gruenwald, J. February 28, 1998b. Panel moves copyright bills as debate escalates. *Congressional Quarterly Weekly Report*: 484.

Gruenwald, J. May 9, 1998c. Bill may curb Internet use by pedophiles. *Congressional Quarterly Weekly Report*: 1227.

Gruenwald, J. July 25, 1998d. Who's minding whose business on the Internet? *Congressional Quarterly Weekly Report*: 1986–90.

Gruenwald, J. September 12, 1998e. House panel approves bill to sharply restrict gambling on the Internet. *Congressional Quarterly Weekly Report*: 2409.

Hansen, B., and A. Bettelheim. June 29, 2002. Cybercrime: Congress addresses the breach in online security. *Congressional Quarterly Weekly Report*: 1761–71.

Healey, J. September 17, 1994. Exon plan to sweep indecency from superhighway criticized. *Congressional Quarterly Weekly Report*: 2565–6.

Healey, J. March 18, 1995a. Exon wants shield for children. *Congressional Quarterly Weekly Report*: 803.

Healey, J. July 8, 1995b. Clashing over obscenity in cyberspace. *Congressional Quarterly Weekly Report*: 1995.

Healey, J. September 12, 1996a. House panel OKs software bill. *Congressional Quarterly Weekly Report*: 2719.

Healey, J. September 14, 1996b. Panel approves bill on FCC revisions. *Congressional Quarterly Weekly Report*: 2594.

Jacob, H., R. Lineberry, A. M. Heinz, J. A. Beecher, J. Moran, and D. H. Swank. 1982. *Governmental Responses to Crime: Crime on Urban Agendas*. Washington, D.C.: U.S. Department of Justice, National Institute of Justice.

Kady, M., II. October 18, 2003. Database piracy bill approved by judiciary subcommittee. *Congressional Quarterly Weekly Report*: 2572.

Kady, M., II. February 21, 2004. Standing still may be best action for congress on technology issues. *Congressional Quarterly Weekly Report*: 493.

Kady, M., II. February 14, 2005. Cybersecurity a weak link in homeland's armor. *Congressional Quarterly Weekly Report*: 347.

Koszczuk, J. August 7, 1999. Senate passes penalties for misuse of trademarks in Internet addresses. *Congressional Quarterly Weekly Report*: 1951.

Marion, N. E. 1994. *A History of Federal Crime Control Initiatives, 1960–1993.* Westport, CT: Praeger.

Marion, N. E. 1995. *A Primer in the Politics of Criminal Justice.* New York: Harrow and Heston.

Marion, N. E. 2007. *A Primer in the Politics of Criminal Justice.* New York: Criminal Justice Press, p. 46.

McCutcheon, C. May 23, 1998a. Alarm but no answers at senate hearing on threats to nation's computer networks. *Congressional Quarterly Weekly Report*: 1404–5.

McCutcheon, C. June 13, 1998b. Pentagon's simulated attacks on computers succeed too well. *Congressional Quarterly Weekly Report*: 1622–33.

McCutcheon, C. October 30, 1999. House bill would give agencies more computer security options. *Congressional Quarterly Weekly Report*: 2534.

McCutcheon, C. January 15, 2000. Administration ends ban on export of encryption devices. *Congressional Quarterly Weekly Report*: 92.

Oliver, W. M. 2003. *The Law and Order Presidency.* Upper Saddle River, NJ: Prentice Hall.

Ota, A. K. December 6, 1997. Internet industry hopes self-policing will click. *Congressional Quarterly Weekly Report*: 3028–9.

Ota, A. K. September 19, 1998. On-line smut curb criticized as too tough. *Congressional Quarterly Weekly Report*: 2499.

Ota, A. K. January 23, 1999a. The virtual casino. *Congressional Quarterly Weekly Report*: 192.

Ota, A. K. February 6, 1999b. Judge blocks Internet smut law, reopening child-access debate. *Congressional Quarterly Weekly Report*: 334.

Ota, A. K. March 13, 1999c. Pro-encryption bill gains traction, but administration reiterates law enforcement objections. *Congressional Quarterly Weekly Report*: 615.

Ota, A. K. March 20, 1999d. Gambling restrictions to be proposed. *Congressional Quarterly Weekly Report*: 1035.

Ota, A. K. June 26, 1999e. Senate panel approves Internet bills. *Congressional Quarterly Weekly Report*: 1555.

Ota, A. K. July 17, 1999f. Deeply divided over encryption bill, house looks to Clinton for a deal. *Congressional Quarterly Weekly Report*: 1723–4.

Ota, A. K. July 24, 1999g. Intended to protect minors, bill on Internet alcohol sales is stage for industry showdown. *Congressional Quarterly Weekly Report*: 1795.

Ota, A. K. July 31, 1999h. Senate poised to prohibit misuse of brand names in Web addresses; separate trademark bill clears. *Congressional Quarterly Weekly Report*: 1870.

Ota, A. K. August 7, 1999i. Curb on sale of alcohol on-line passes. *Congressional Quarterly Weekly Report*: 1949.

Ota, A. K. September 18, 1999j. White house drops controls on encryption. *Congressional Quarterly Weekly Report*: 2171.

Ota, A. K. March 25, 2000a. Internet privacy issue beginning to click. *Congressional Quarterly Weekly Report*: 637–40.

Ota, A. K. May 6, 2000b. Clinton unveils financial privacy plan. *Congressional Quarterly Weekly Report*: 1051.

Ota, A. K. May 27, 2000c. FTC asks lawmakers for expanded authority to protect Internet privacy. *Congressional Quarterly Weekly Report*: 1273.

Ota, A. K. June 17, 2000d. House panel seeks Internet privacy study. *Congressional Quarterly Weekly Report*: 1466.

Ota, A. K. July 1, 2000e. Online gambling curbs approved. *Congressional Quarterly Weekly Report*: 1617.

Palmer, E. A. September 16, 2000. Panel OKs bill to ban college sports betting. *Congressional Quarterly Weekly Report*: 2149.

Palmer, E. A. September 29, 2001. Committees taking a critical look at Ashcroft's request for broad new powers. *Congressional Quarterly Weekly Report*: 2263–5.

Palmer, E. A. April 20, 2002a. Foes of "virtual" child pornography seeking a very real remedy after court strikes down ban. *Congressional Quarterly Weekly Report*: 1028.

Palmer, E. A. May 4, 2002b. Bill narrows "virtual" porn definition. *Congressional Quarterly Weekly Report*: 1161.

Perine, K. October 6, 2001. Money-laundering bill gets new life as financial tool against terrorists. *Congressional Quarterly Weekly Report*: 2328–9.

Pierce, E. June 19, 1999. Web gambling is the target of senate bill. *Congressional Quarterly Weekly Report*: 1470.

Public Papers of the President. June 23, 1995a. Remarks at the America's hope, Arkansas' pride luncheon in little rock, Arkansas, 929–37.

Public Papers of the President. June 29, 1995b. Remarks at a fundraiser in Chicago, Illinois, 979–86.

Public Papers of the President. April 5, 1996a. Remarks at the University of Central Oklahoma in Edmond, Oklahoma, 549–53.

Public Papers of the President. December 16, 1996b. The President's news conference with European Union leaders, 2211–18.

Public Papers of the President. September 15, 1997. Remarks to the Service Employees International Union, 1162–7.

Public Papers of the President. February 26, 1998a. Remarks to the Technology 98 Conference in San Francisco, 295–8.

Public Papers of the President. May 12, 1998b. Remarks on the international crime control strategy, 740–2.

Public Papers of the President. January 22, 1999a. Remarks at the National Academy of Sciences, 85–8.

Public Papers of the President. May 4, 1999b. Remarks announcing the financial privacy and consumer protection initiative, 682–5.

Public Papers of the President. November 6, 1999c. Memorandum on protecting consumers from fraud, 2003–4.

Public Papers of the President. September 23, 2000. The President's radio address, 1909–10.

Public Papers of the President. October 26, 2001a. Remarks on signing the USA PATRIOT ACT of 2001, 1306–7.

Public Papers of the President. November 9, 2001b. Joint statement between the United States of America and the Republic of India, 1369–70.

Recording Industry Association of America. 2003. About us. http://www.ria.com/issues/piracy/riaa.asp, Accessed September 9, 2006.

Rosch, J. 1985. "Crime as an issue in American politics." In *The Politics of Crime and Criminal Justice*, edited by E. Fairchild and V. A. Webb. Beverly Hills: Sage Publications.

Salant, J. D. November 11, 1995. Panel would study impact of legalized gambling. *Congressional Quarterly Weekly Report*: 3463.

Salmore, S. A., and B. G. Salmore. 1985. *Candidates, Parties and Campaigns*. Washington, D.C.: CQ Press.

Sharma, A. September 11, 2004a. Panel OKs bill to prevent copyright theft. *Congressional Quarterly Weekly Report*: 2120.

Sharma, A. November 6, 2004b. Film industry joins the battle against Internet pirates. *Congressional Quarterly Weekly Report*: 2585.

Sobeira, S. October 6, 2000. Bush, Gore spout similar rhetoric to Michigan voters. *Cleveland Plain Dealer*: 19A.

Stern, S. June 26, 2004. Anti-counterfeiting measure approved by house judiciary. *Congressional Quarterly Weekly Report*: 1565.

Tessler, J. March 14, 2005a. Film piracy measure OKd. *Congressional Quarterly Weekly Report*: 663.

Tessler, J. July 4, 2005b. What SCOTUS didn't grok: File-sharing won't fade. *Congressional Quarterly Weekly Report*: 1792.

Traditional Values Coalition. 2006. Support the unlawful Internet Gambling Funding Prohibition Act. http://www.traditionalvalues.org/pring.php?sid=478, Accessed September 9, 2006.

U.S. Department of Justice. 2005. Department of Justice awards more than $13 million in grants to combat Internet crimes against children. http://www.ojp.gov/newsroom/2005/ICAC06242005.htm, Accessed September 21, 2006.

U.S. Department of Justice. 2006. Internet Crimes Against Children Task Force Program. http://www.usdoj.gov/criminal/cybercrime/ccips.html, Accessed September 21, 2006.

Williams, B. June 1, 2002. Court overrules Internet filters. *Congressional Quarterly Weekly Report*: 1464.

Chapter 28

The Fourth Amendment Impact on Electronic Evidence

Evaristus Obinyan
Benedict College, Columbia

Patricia Ikegwuonu, Seyi Vanderpuye
Albany State University, Georgia

Dr. Evaristus Obinyan is associate professor of criminology in the Department of Social Science and Criminal Justice at Benedict College, Columbia. Dr. Obinyan earned his BA in liberal arts and science from the University of Illinois at Chicago; MSc from Chicago State University, and Ph.D. in Criminology and Criminal Justice from the University of South Florida, Tampa. Dr. Obinyan has worked in both the field and in academia as a criminologist. Dr. Obinyan has publications in peer-reviewed journals. His book *Adolescent Delinquency Tolerance* was published in 2005. Dr. Obinyan was Director of the Fort Valley State University's Georgia Center for Juvenile Justice for five years. He will be director of the Albany State University Homeland Security Program starting Spring 2008.

Patricia Ikegwuonu is assistant professor of criminal justice at Albany State University.

Seyi Vanderpuye is associate professor of forensic science at Albany State University, Georgia. Dr. Vanderpuye has several publications in peer-reviewed journals.

Abstract

The twenty-first century has begun to witness incredible and amazing evolutionary advancements in science and technology. We are also witnessing the use of technology by disgruntled elements and other cyber criminals to threaten our democracy. This chapter examines the impact that the Fourth Amendment of the United States constitution has on the legal phenomena known as electronic evidence. The legal implications of investigating evidence stored electronically and the forensic nature of the computer evidence is carefully presented. The chapter provides analysis of conceptual definitions and the importance of exclusionary rule and the Fourth Amendment in electronic investigations. The court's, particularly the federal court's, assessment of the E-Discovery and the guidelines for E-Discovery are presented. The chapter also provides some explanation of the process of investigation of electronic evidence, types of electronic evidence, the analysis of electronic evidence, and the misconceptions of digital evidence.

INTRODUCTION

The **Fourth Amendment** is derived from a factual but historical document, and the policies associated with this law are and have been a significant contributor to our ever-evolving democracy. The Fourth Amendment states very clearly, but forcefully, that "The right of the people to be secure in their persons, houses, papers, and effects, against unreasonable searches and seizures, shall not be violated, and no warrants shall issue, but upon probable cause, supported by Oath or affirmation, and particularly describing the place to be searched, and the persons or things to be seized." This law is absolutely clear and is a valued American individual right and guarantees against unlawful intrusion to our privacy or personal space. Since the implementation of the "Bill of Rights," court decisions have strengthened this American valued fundamental right. The former Attorney General of the United States in 1997 said it best when he commented, "The state's interest in crime fighting should 'NEVER' vitiate THE CITIZEN's Bill of Rights."

Unfortunately, the Fourth Amendment since its implementation in 1791 has gradually eroded and slowly, but steadily, roasted in the blazing heat of political funk just as cancer does to the human body. This chapter is concerned with the trend in the legal environment where courts in both civil and criminal cases allow Internet data files, otherwise known as electronic evidence found in computers, to be admissible as evidence in court proceedings. The chapter focuses precisely on the impact that the Fourth Amendment has and may continue to have on this relatively new evidentiary phenomenon. It will explore the forensic nature of electronic evidence, how it is collected, managed, and prepared for courtroom presentation. We will discuss generally the restrictions and/or limitations the Fourth Amendment has on the use of electronic evidence. Certain cases and issues the cases present will be addressed.

The Fourth Amendment impedes government official access to evidence without a search warrant. The position of the United States' Department of Justice is that a warrant-less search does not necessarily violate the Fourth Amendment if one of two conditions is satisfied in accordance with the Supreme Court ruling. In the first instance, the government's conduct must not have violated a persons' "reasonable expectation of privacy" ; therefore, it does not constitute a Fourth Amendment search in which a warrant is unnecessary (*Illinois v. Andreas*, 463 U.S. 765, 771 (1983).

WHAT IS ELECTRONIC EVIDENCE?

Electronic evidence may be defined as information that has evidentiary, investigative, and cyber-forensic value, which are stored in an electronic device such as the computer or transmitted on an electronic device. The relationship between the Fourth Amendment and electronic evidence has become very interesting due to the evolving digital crimes and incredible technological creativity of modern-day society. As the technological evolution of society becomes more complex, so are those who intend on using the same technological advancements to assault the quality of life of members of the society. Therefore, the demand for policy change to meet the needs of a growing criminal global underground has increased tremendously. The Fourth Amendment will play a crucial role in the manner by which the American society should be able to win the war on cyber crimes in general and cyber terrorism in particular. The next section will briefly examine the fundamentals of the Fourth Amendment and the manner in which the law enforcement community is contributing to the evolution of the relationship between the Fourth Amendment and electronic evidence.

BACKGROUND

The Fourth Amendment of the United States' Constitution is one of the most revered of the guaranteed rights that citizens of the United States have when compared with the other amendments. In fact, it is so highly regarded that any intrusions or violations of it, have been accorded the most stringent of penalties. The Fourth Amendment reads as follows:

> The right of the people to be secure in their persons, houses, papers, and effects, against unreasonable searches and seizures, shall not be violated, and no Warrants shall issue, but upon probable cause, supported by Oath or affirmation, and particularly describing the place to be searched, and the persons or things to be seized.

This amendment establishes the fundamental right to privacy against governmental intrusion, except for just cause. Just cause has been interpreted as probable cause and is an indication that a violation of the law has occurred and therefore a higher need, to preserve an orderly society, must be met. It is only when a determination of probable cause is found that the government is said to have a right to intrude into our property and our very beings. So precious is this right to privacy that even the laws surrounding the determination of probable cause are strict. The government, usually through law enforcement, had concluded that probable cause is formed through observation and information, and has stated a plethora of examples to be had in each category. Some of the more noteworthy examples of observation would include any of the inferences derived from any of the governmental agent's sensory perceptions: sight, hearing, touch, taste, and/or smell. Examples of information-producing probable cause would include a wanted poster, and statements from an informant.

In both the areas of observation and information gathering are even more regulations, each to heighten the scrutiny involved when a risk that one's privacy rights might be violated. For instance, once the governmental agent believes that he or she has found probable cause to search a person or a place and to arrest a person, our constitution further provides that the agent must acquire a warrant. This legal document granting permission to search and/or seize things and suspects also must pass legal muster.

A warrant must state with specificity, the person or place to be searched, and/or the person to be arrested, and/or thing or things to be seized; the warrant must be signed by the officer or officers seeking the warrant, who by their signatures swears to the fact that they are operating in good faith, and that the evidence thus far amounts to probable cause. It must clearly indicate the probable cause that underlies the warrant, and renders it necessary. It must be signed by a neutral and detached magistrate, which is intended to be an indication that he or she has read the warrant and agrees that probable cause exists. If a search warrant is granted, it must specify the exact places and locations to be searched, yet must not be unduly broad or unnecessarily vague.

The stringent requirements inherent in the process entitling the government to intrude into our privacy clearly show the importance of the Fourth Amendment, and the fact that this most basic right is so zealously guarded. The warrant requirement, whether for a search or an arrest, is intended to prevent law enforcement from random, unprovoked, unjustified intrusions and seizures. It is intended that all citizens of the United States be free from such invasions.

UNITED STATES SUPREME COURT

There are instances when, in the interest of security and to preserve an orderly and just society, our law has deemed a warrant to be unnecessary. In the instance of a search warrant, the following circumstances are deemed to justify a warrant-less search: (1) consent to the search has been granted; (2) the item being searched for is in plain view; (3) emergency or exigency necessitates that it is unwise to take the time to secure a warrant; (4) the item being searched for is an automobile or is suspected of being contained in an automobile, and because of the automobile's ability to move, the agent's leave to get a warrant would likely cause him or her to lose the evidence, and therefore would be unreasonable; (5) the item being searched for is in an open field and/or is a curtilage, which means that it is annexed to or adjoins a site within the purview of a warrant, although the open field or curtilage is not specified; (6)when the evidence to be gained would be greatly compromised if those who control it are alerted to the fact that it is being searched for via a warrant, and therefore the government utilizes electronic surveillance (i.e., wiretapping); (7) when the search is incident to a lawful arrest, for the arresting officer's protection; and (8) when the search occurs at the border of the country, the rationale being that the evidence could disappear altogether, or the person being searched would be outside the jurisdiction of U.S. law enforcement, should he be allowed to cross the border. The expended time to secure a search warrant might make this very likely.

From a slightly broader perspective, the Supreme Court has upheld warrant-less searches by administrative authorities in public schools, government offices, and penal institutions. Further, the Court has upheld drug testing of public and transportation employees. In each of these instances, warrant-less searches with no probable cause showing were affirmed on the basis of reasonableness. The reasonableness standard balanced the government's regulatory interest against the individual's privacy interest, and found that the government's interest outweighed the individual's. One of the justifications for a warrant-less search, incident to a lawful arrest, while at one time limited to the immediate reach (wingspan) of the arrested suspect, was expanded to a search of the entire home ("protective sweep") if there is a reasonable belief that the home harbors an individual who may pose a danger (FindLaw.com: U.S. Constitution, Fourth Amendment).

Exclusionary Rule

To underscore the constitution's emphasis of the importance of a citizen's privacy rights, and to demonstrate to law enforcement that unreasonable, invalid searches (i.e., without probable cause searches) would be disregarded, the exclusionary rule was born. This judge-made rule of law dictates that evidence obtained by law enforcement that violates the Fourth Amendment is not admissible in a criminal trial. Intended to dissuade police officers from obtaining evidence unlawfully, there yet exists some exceptions to the exclusionary rule. In other words, there are instances where, even when the evidence seized by law enforcement is seized unlawfully, it may still be admissible in a criminal trial, if law enforcement is able to prove that the evidence was obtained (1) in good faith, or that it is a (2) harmless error, or that the same evidence was later obtained via a (3) valid independent source, and, lastly, that the evidence would (4) inevitably has been discovered anyway.

ELECTRONIC EVIDENCE AND THE COURTS

The emergence and proliferation of electronic evidence, has raised numerous other and legitimate legal issues. Questions surrounded jurisdiction, ownership, culpability, privacy rights, and overall Fourth Amendment protections abound. For instance, "Internet access raises difficult legal issues to which standard Fourth Amendment analysis cannot easily be applied" (Swaminatha 2004–2005, 52). Thus far, it is settled that courts consider two questions to determine if a warrant-less search of a computer, conducted by the government violates the Fourth Amendment. The courts want to know (1) if the search violates one's reasonable expectation of privacy, and if so, (2) whether the search is reasonable, precisely because it would constitute an exception to the warrant requirement (Swaminatha 2004–2005, 59).

The tremendous upsurge in the use of computers to carry out criminal activity as well as actual or direct computer crimes is documented. There is no doubt that experienced and savvy computer criminals pose a substantial challenge to law enforcement. On the issue of warrant-less searches and "no-knock" warrants in particular, the Federal Guidelines for Searching and Seizing Computers point out, with respect to computers, the ease of destroying data. In fact, the Federal Guidelines for Searching and Seizing Computers recognize a whole "host" of challenges presented by electronic evidence, adding to the ease involved in destroying data, is the ease of creating, altering, storing, copying and moving, with unprecedented ease. The guidelines go on to discuss scenarios where digital photos are easily altered without a trace, and the potential use of digital signatures to create electronic seals.

To counteract this activity, electronic surveillance has emerged as one of the most valuable tools in law enforcement's crime-fighting arsenal. In many instances, the criminal activity has been either thwarted, or if crimes have been committed, the criminals have been apprehended due to legally authorized electronic surveillance (CALEA).

ELECTRONIC EVIDENCE DISCOVERY

The guidelines recommend the use of experts in all computer searches and seizures. These include local, state, and federal personnel, as well as local universities and the victims of crimes themselves. In the 1980 well-relied-upon case of *Payton v. New York,* the Court held that a person has a reasonable expectation of privacy in property that is located within that person's home. The *Kyllo, Katz, and U.S. v. Ross* cases extended that reasonable expectation of privacy to different rooms in the home revealed through thermal imaging, phone conversations in enclosed phone booths, and contents found within opaque containers. Under present law, law enforcement agencies cannot open a closed container to obtain evidence.

The courts have looked at the issue surrounding electronic storage devices, and have ruled that these are akin to opening a closed container; therefore, one can expect a reasonable level of privacy (Salveggio 2004, 4). In *Oliver v. U.S., California v. Greenwood,* and *Rakas v. Illinois,* the Court held that one had no reasonable expectation of privacy in items found and activities taking place in open fields, trash, or garbage left on the periphery of one's property, or in a stranger's home that the person entered with the intent to steal.

For purposes of analyzing the issue of the Fourth Amendment and electronic evidence, it is also critical to emphasize that the restrictions imposed by the Fourth Amendment apply not only to private citizens but also to government officials/agents. When we are mindful of the fact that the purpose of the Fourth Amendment is to preserve one of our most treasured rights, the right to privacy, against governmental intrusion, we understand that this amendment was not created to be applied to private citizens alone. Of course, what comes up most with respect to the government and private citizens in situations like this is the impact of "private" citizens who act on behalf of the government, thereby being "elevated" to the status of a government agent.

FEDERAL COURTS AND E-DISCOVERY

The 1994 case of *U.S. v. McAllister* found that whether a confidential informant (i.e., private citizen) is acting as a government agent would be determined on a case-by-case basis. The Fourth Amendment is "wholly inapplicable to a search and seizure, even an unreasonable one, effected by a private individual" (*U.S v. Jacobsen*, 466 U.S 109 (1984)). On the other hand, it is settled that should the court find that one was acting as an "arm" of the government when conducting the search, that search would then be subject to Fourth Amendment restrictions (*Mcallister v. Detroit Free Press CO.*, 76 Mich. 338, 43 NW (1976)).

The federal courts, in *U.S. v. Crowley* (2002), have introduced a three-part, or multipart, test to determine if a private citizen is acting or has acted as an agent of the government. This test asks the following questions: (1) Is the government aware of the search and have they acquiesced to it? (2) Was the private citizen's purpose to assist law enforcement or was it independently motivated? (3) Did the government request the search or had it offered a reward for it?

According to *U.S. v. Ellyson* and *U.S. v. Koenig,* determining whether a private citizen is indeed acting on behalf of the government requires a "fact-intensive inquiry," and according to *U.S. v. Feffer,* not all factors are weighted equally. In Feffer, where a private citizen found that one had submitted false tax returns, and thereafter searched the person's financial documents again, the court weighed the following factors, namely, that the private citizen had a purpose for searching in addition to assisting the government. Secondly, the government neither requested anything from the private citizen, nor expected anything from either search, and finally, the government did not directly participate in amassing the evidence. In *U.S. v. Shahid* (1977) and *U.S. v. Koenig* (1998) the courts concluded that a private citizen's search could be converted to a government search when the government exercises power over the private citizen. Yet, in the comparatively recent case of *U.S. v. Jarrett* (2003), the test to determine if a private citizen is a government agent for Fourth Amendment purposes was significantly relaxed.

So, while the Fourth Amendment protects private conversations (*Berger v. NY.* '67; Katz. '67), it does not cloak information, even personal information, where there is no individual justifiable expectation of privacy, Situations concerning telephone records, and bank records would apply (Kerwin 2005, 1). By extension, the relevant question would be, "Is there an individual justifiable expectation of privacy stemming from one's personal computer and with respect to one's electronic communications and transactions?" John Perry Barlow, songwriter for the world-renowned rock band, the Grateful Dead, and cofounder of the Electronic Frontier Foundation, an Internet civil liberties group, in his "Declaration of the Independence of Cyberspace" to governments, wrote, "I declare the global social space we are building to be naturally independent of the tyrannies you seek to impose on us. You have no moral right to rule us nor do you possess any methods of enforcement we have true reason to fear . . . Cyberspace does not lie within your borders."

After the courts decided Berger and Katz, the U.S. Congress enacted Title III of the Omnibus Crime Control and Safe Streets Act of 1968, which generally prohibited electronic eavesdropping on phone conversations, face-to-face conversations, or computer and other forms of electronic communications. The Act "reached" to allow for electronic surveillance as a last resort in serious criminal cases (Kerwin 2005, 1). The court orders provided for in Title III describe the duration and the scope of the surveillance permitted, along with the conversations which may be seized.

The next level of privacy protection, subject to Title III, relates to some matters that the Supreme Court has designated as "beyond the reach of the Fourth Amendment protection." These include telephone records and e-mail held in third-party storage (18 USC 2701-2709, Ch. 121). In cases such as these, the law permits access, if there is a search warrant, or court order, if in connection with a criminal investigation (18 USC 2703).

The then Chairman of the Senate Commerce Committee on Consumer Affairs, Foreign Commerce and Tourism, John Ashcroft, stated, "The state's interest in crime-fighting should never vitiate the citizen's Bill of Rights." For some time now, many cyber criminals use the Internet to achieve their selfish goals and violate the Internet ethics and law. These offenders are violating others' rights to privacy and this behavior is increasing tremendously and is documented in governmental archives. Over the recent years, millions of people have spent time and money via the computer, whether using e-mail, making purchases, surfing the Net, or managing databases. Included in the "mix" are criminals, who are using this technology to carry out, for the most part anonymously, their criminal activities. The noncriminal citizen's rights, particularly ones privacy rights, are being eroded in the pursuit of the criminal segments of our society (Salveggio 2004, 2).

From the Katz case emerged four criteria for determining whether one could expect one's privacy to be invaded. Salveggio describes them as follows: (1) General Legal Principles means that anything you do or say in a public place is subject to being accessed. You would have no expectation of privacy. (2) Vantage Point refers to the fact that any space or area from which you can be seen can serve as a "vantage point" for law enforcement to conduct surveillance of you, so long as they do not trespass, illegally inhabit or occupy a space. (3) Degree of Privacy Awarded by Building and Places refers to the fact that any public place, if uncovered, is considered "fair game" for placing one under surveillance. (4) Technology refers to the fact that even for information given via technology, it is still subject to a Fourth Amendment reasonable search.

Digital data is now routinely requested during the course of litigation. Just as e-mail has become critical to the operation of many businesses, so it has to the discovery process in both civil and criminal litigation. Retrieving such data, placing it within a useful context, and maintaining its integrity can be critical to its authentication and use at trial (Kerwin 2005, 3).

MISCONCEPTIONS OF DIGITAL DATA

There existed a common misconception at one time that once a file was "deleted," it was gone permanently; now we know that is rarely the case. The public has learned that computer operating systems use various methods to store data, and even though a file has been deleted, with the name of the file removed from the operating system's file-tracking table, the data itself remain intact until it is overwritten or specifically erased. So, to facilitate discovery for trial, parties are usually ordered to disclose passwords or encryption systems, in place to "protect the data." If this is not the case, then a "hacker" will be employed to access the data (Kerwin 2005, 3).

SEIZING DIGITAL EVIDENCE

According to the Federal Guidelines for Searching and Seizing Computers issued by the Department of Justice, it is recommended that the "independent component doctrine" be utilized to determine if a there is a "sound" and legitimate reason to seize each separate piece of hardware. Prosecutors should seize only those pieces of equipment for basic input/output that would justify execution of the warrant. Additionally, the guidelines note that often computers and accessories are incompatible, and therefore it might be advisable to seize all of the related equipment, with irrelevant material returned quickly.

In general, warrants are required for searches of computers unless one of the recognized exceptions (articulated above) to the warrant requirement exists. For computers utilized by more than one person, the Federal Guidelines indicate that consent by one user is sufficient to authorize a search of the entire system. If, by chance, users have taken "special steps" to protect their privacy (i.e., password or encryption), a search warrant is necessary. There is a suggestion in the guidelines that users do not have an expectation of privacy on large mainframe systems because users should know that system operators have the technical ability to read all files on those systems.

In addition, where there is no warrant, prosecutors might argue successfully that "reasonable users" might expect system administrators to be able to access any data on the system. The guidelines indicate that employees may also have an expectation of privacy that is reasonable, such would prohibit employers from granting consent to search to law enforcement, and that the Fourth Amendment protects public employees and searches of their computers are prohibited except for "noninvestigatory, work-related intrusions" and "investigatory searches for evidence of suspected work-related employee misfeasance."

In keeping with the "spirit" and actual purpose of the Fourth Amendment, the Electronic Communications Privacy Act (ECPA) of 1986 advised that, concerning computers that contained private e-mail, prosecutors inform the judge that private e-mail may be present and avoid reading portions not covered in the warrant. Pursuant to the ECPA, a warrant is required for e-mail on a public system that is stored for less than 180 days, and if stored for more than 180 days, then it can be obtained via a subpoena or a warrant without notice.

For computers that contain confidential information, the guidelines suggest that forensic experts restrict their inspection of irrelevant files. Alternatively, court-appointed special masters may be enlisted to search systems containing confidential information. A grant of limited immunity may be necessary prior to compelled disclosure of encryption keys from suspects.

United States v. Simons (2000) held that public sector workplace employees have limited, if any, privacy rights in their workplace computers, e-mail, and other electronic communications. Findings as a result of Simons include the following: (1) Employers should draft an Internet policy when they allow Internet access to their employees, and this policy should be disclosed to all employees with the employer prepared to prove that employees were aware of it; (2) The Internet policy should clearly indicate that the computer, in addition to all communications sent or received, are the property of the employer; (3) The policy should articulate that the computer should be used only for business purposes, and that other purposes, such as personal or illegal use, is prohibited; (4) The policy should provide specific illustrations of inappropriate communications and utilization; (5) The policy should clearly inform employees that employers audit and/or monitor their employees' Internet activity; (6) The policy should clearly indicate that warrant-less searches may be conducted; and finally (7)

The policy should be coordinated with the employer's e-mail policy. A general derivation citing the best approach is for the employer to adopt a comprehensive policy governing the use of computers in the workplace, including e-mail and the Internet (Hogge 2007, 4–5).

RELEVANT FOURTH AMENDMENT ELECTRONIC EVIDENCE CASES

A summary review of earlier case and statutory law concerning the Fourth Amendment and electronic evidence begins with the 1928 Olmstead Case. An issue here was the validity of evidence gained through telephone wiretapping, which was in itself, in violation of state law. The court concluded that "wiretapping was not within the confines of the Fourth Amendment," which meant that persons had no privacy rights that deserved Fourth Amendment protections. The jurists found that since there was no actual, physical trespass across property controlled by the defendant, and because the evidence obtained was a conversation, this did not amount to a seizure within the purview of Fourth Amendment.

In 1934, the Federal Communications Act was enacted, which included a provision interpreted by the Court to limit wiretapping by law enforcement. In *Nardone v. United States,* the court referenced this act to hold that wiretapping by federal agents would violate the act if the agents both intercepted and disclosed what they had overheard; as such the intercepted conversation would not be permissible at trial.

In *Goldman v. United States,* the court overruled a portion of the Olmstead decision when it concluded that conversations could indeed be seized. In Goldman, a "bug" was "planted" against a wall and conversations could be overheard on the opposite side. However, in what the Court must have interpreted as "going too far," the agents placed a microphone into a wall and when it touched a heating duct, it disseminated the defendant's conversation, resulting in a court determination that the Fourth Amendment was applicable.

As referenced earlier, the *Berger v. New York* case was pivotal, in that it invalidated a state statute that gave judges the authority to grant law enforcement the right to trespass on private property for the express purpose of installing wiretaps. Of particular significance was the "less than probable cause" showing required by the officers to access the warrants; warrants could be issued based on "*reasonable grounds* to believe that evidence of a crime occurred, and particularly describing the person or persons whose communications, conversations or discussions are to be overheard or recorded."

The court cited several serious flaws inherent in this showing requirement, one of which was that one's conversations could be intercepted without any showing that a crime occurred or was in progress. Another fatal flaw was that the property that the officers were seeking was not required to be described. Both of these areas, no doubt, seriously impacted the purpose and intent of the Fourth Amendment.

The rationale of the requirement of probable cause is to preserve the privacy rights of citizens, such that in the absence of a probable cause, which is more than a "mere suspicion," the government could not invade ones privacy. With reference to the lack of a requirement for a showing that a crime occurred or was occurring, the constitutional framers recognized the inherent wrong in invading the privacy of a law-abiding citizen.

Probable cause requires that the government has a reasonable belief, based primarily on evidence derived through observation and information, that the object searched for is where law enforcement seeks to search for it. This is intended to provide "parameters" to the government's search such that they are not given *carte blanche* into areas, outside the purview, of their stated legal concerns.

Another major distinction made in *Berger* was the ramifications of electronic surveillance over a two-month period as compared to an episodic event. The court was appropriately concerned about the breadth of the longer duration surveillance, primarily because the length of time would inevitably draw in the private conversations of persons who were not under the shadow of suspicion to begin with, thereby violating their constitutional rights for no just cause. The court, referring to the statute as a "blanket grant of permission to eavesdrop" found that it was lacking proper court monitoring and protections.

In probably the most referenced "wiretapping" case, *Katz v. United States,* the government placed a "bug" in a telephone booth that they "activated" each time the suspect used the booth. Because there was not a physical trespass of the booth, lower courts concluded that the suspect had no Fourth Amendment protection, thereby approving the government's actions. The Supreme Court, on the other hand, argued that the Fourth Amendment's application was not contingent upon an actual, physical trespass, rather an invasion of privacy, even if intangible, such as a conversation. Although the wiretapping was held invalid because it had not been approved by a magistrate, the court indicated that the surveillance in Katz was perhaps the kind of search that would have been constitutionally permitted.

Of particular interest now, in the aftermath of the terrorist attacks on America, September 11, 2001, we find that the Katz case addressed the possibility that wiretapping could be authorized by the president or even the attorney general without court approval, if national security were at risk. The presidential power would exist "against domestic subversion" and "against foreign intelligence operations." Actions of this nature would rely on the preeminence of the office of the president and on the court's interpretation of wiretapping as a *reasonable* search and seizure pursuant to the Fourth Amendment.

The court upheld the warrant requirement in cases where one was being investigated for domestic subversive activities, stating that "the Government's duty to preserve the national security did not override the guarantee that before government could invade the privacy of its citizens it must present to a neutral magistrate evidence sufficient to support issuance of a warrant authorizing that invasion of privacy."

What was also pivotal was the acknowledgment by the court that differing standards of probable cause might be used in domestic security cases; that domestic security cases raise potentially much wider ranges of injurious impact and national complications than do other crimes, and as such evidence collection, via wiretapping or other means is bound to be more complex. The court noted that evidence collection in national security cases would be lengthy and involve numerous kinds of information and sources.

The court further noted the potential difficulty in specifying the person or persons to be investigated. Therefore, while the court acknowledged a potential need for differing probable cause standards, it also emphasized the need for the standards to be reasonable, striking a balance between the need of the government for this information and the targeted person's right to privacy.

Katz left to be determined the exact breadth of the presidential powers in national security cases. Federal law granted the president the right to authorize wiretapping without a warrant to gain information crucial to national security, but provided that the surveillance is limited to conversations "between or among foreign powers and there is no substantial likelihood any United States person" will be overheard.

Nardone v. United States also held that "derivative evidence," the evidence resulting from information gained through a wiretap, is inadmissible. *Goldstein v. United States* held that testimony retrieved through "exploited" wiretap information could be admissible, and *Rathbun v. United States* held as valid the eavesdropping, upon permission of one of the parties, on a conversation via a telephone extension.

In *United States v. Knotts* (460 U.S. 276) (1983) the court concluded that there was not a violation of the Fourth Amendment, when a beeper was used as surveillance to note the whereabouts of an automobile and where the beeper was installed in the absence of judicial authorization. The court's rationale was simply that one had no valid expectation of privacy on public roads.

The *United States v. Karo* (468 U.S. 705) (1984) is an extension of *Knotts,* which held that a beeper utilized without judicial authorization could not be used to access information concerning the "continuing presence of an item within a private residence." All these cases reflect the evolution of electronic evidence and the manner the society at large has managed the technology and criminal events.

FORENSIC ASPECTS OF ELECTRONIC EVIDENCE AND THE FOURTH AMENDMENT

Introduction

The development of new technologies for electronic communication and data storage has provided new challenges for the interpretation and application of the Fourth Amendment and related legislation. In addition, information technologies have made it possible to commit crimes in ways not possible previously and have enabled new sorts of crime. In many other sorts of crime, tools of science and technology are important in the identification and analysis of evidence and can provide information used in arriving at justice. This section covers special emphasis on the effects of the Fourth Amendment on the analysis of electronic evidence by the methods of forensic science.

The Variety and Scope of Electronic Evidence

Definitions

Forensic science has been defined by many professionals. One definition (Saferstein 2004) states: "Forensic Science is the application of science to those criminal and civil laws that are enforced by police agencies in a criminal justice system." In the service of different laws, forensic science encompasses the identification and analysis of different types of evidence by using scientific techniques. Electronic evidence is one among many types of evidence that can be examined scientifically and it is useful to also provide a definition of what type of evidence is considered "electronic."

Volonino (2003) defines electronic evidence as "electronically-stored information on any type of computer device that can be used as evidence in a legal action."

Electronic evidence can also be defined as "any electronically stored information (ESI) which may be used as evidence in a lawsuit or trial." "Electronic evidence includes any documents, emails, or other files that are electronically stored. Additionally, electronic evidence includes records stored by network or Internet service providers."

The term "digital evidence" seems to be more widely used in forensic science and may be sometimes be used interchangeably with "electronic evidence." Digital evidence is defined in a National Institute of Justice (NIJ) report (NIJ 2004) as "information stored or transmitted in binary form that may be relied upon in court."

Similarly, the SWGDE (Scientific Working Group on Digital Evidence) and SWGIT (Scientific Working Group on Imaging Technology) Glossary of Terms defines digital evidence as: "Information of probative value that is stored or transmitted in binary form" (SWGDE and SWGIT 2005).

It is possible that the terms "digital evidence" and "electronic evidence" may not always overlap because electronic information may occur in a form other than digital such as analog TV or video.

SCOPE OF ELECTRONIC EVIDENCE

There are various types of Internet-related electronic evidence that may be pertinent in civil cases or in criminal investigation and these include

1. data files
2. digital images: graphics and photographs
3. digital video
4. digital sound files
5. records of Internet addresses and e-mail routing

These types of electronic evidence may now be found not only on both laptop and desk top computers and servers but on electronic devices such as PDAs, cell phones, and media players such as iPods and on portable storage such as DVDs, USB devices, and flash memory cards. All these devices are thus relevant to the investigation of electronic evidence and affected by legislation such as the Fourth Amendment.

Computer crime investigation may involve various terms such as computer-related crime, computer forensics, cyber forensics, and digital forensic science. According to Zatyko (2007) computer forensics has also been called cyber forensics and is defined by WhatIsIt.com as "the application of computer investigation and analysis techniques to gather evidence suitable for presentation in a court of law. The goal of computer forensics is to perform a structured investigation while maintaining a documented chain of evidence to find out exactly what happened on a computer and who was responsible for it." A definition of computer forensics from the SWGDE/SWGIT Glossary of Terms (2005) is "A sub-discipline of digital and multi-media evidence, which involves the scientific examination, analysis and/or examination, analysis and/or evaluation of digital evidence in legal matters."

In addition, digital forensic science is defined as: "The application of computer science and investigative procedures for a legal purpose involving the analysis of digital evidence (information of probative value that is stored or transmitted in binary form) after proper search authority, chain of custody, validation with mathematics (hash function) use of repeatability, reporting, and possible expert presentation" (Zatyko 2007).

Cyber forensics is referred by Stephenson (2005) as: "The extraction of evidence that particular digital data passed over some medium between two points in a network." Although these definitions may seem long and complicated, it may be necessary they are expressed in such form to reflect the realities and cover many essentials in a field that has a very wide scope.

Types of computer crime include fraud, malpractice, theft of trade secrets and intellectual property, privacy invasion, identity theft, violent crime, money laundering, terrorist activity, hacker activity, malware (computer viruses, etc.) illegalities involving drugs (e.g. steroids), workplace discrimination and harassment (Volonino 2003).

In the digital age, there are different types of criminals who prey on both the innocent and the ignorant. The law enforcement environment has begun to make connections between digital crimes and criminals and other types of crimes. We also are able to establish timelines, statistics regarding the most common forms of digital crimes and criminals, and major cases as example of this phenomenon are readily available in court records across the nations' jurisdictions. These records will indicate among other things the major case examples involving different electronic evidence such as e-mail, computer financial records, terrorist and their havens, copyright violations, etc., and how the Fourth Amendment relates to these and digital evidence-privacy and property rights.

ELECTRONIC EVIDENCE: FOCUS OF THE FOURTH AMENDMENT

Summary of USDOJ Analysis

The Fourth Amendment relates to search and seizure aspects of digital forensics, electronic evidence investigation and computer forensics. The Computer Crime and Intellectual Property Section of the U.S. Department of Justice produced in 2002 a report on electronic evidence and the Fourth Amendment that is available on the Internet (United States Department of Justice 2002). This 96-page (approximately) report discusses the Fourth Amendment and legislation that affect criminal investigation that involves electronic evidence. The report is divided into five sections. The first deals with searching and seizing computers without a warrant. The second covers searching and seizing computers with a warrant.

The third section addresses the electronic Communications Privacy Act. The fourth focuses on electronic surveillance in communications networks. The fifth section deals with various aspects of electronic evidence itself and ensuring the quality of analysis and admissibility.

The overall content of these sections will now be summarized. The section on searching and seizing computers in the absence of a warrant identifies the restrictions imposed by the Fourth Amendment, discusses the definitions of privacy applicable to electronic information and materials and provides different examples. Warrant-less searches are permitted under the Fourth Amendment under certain exceptions or conditions although the circumstances may require careful attention to detail and case-by-case assessment. Some examples include when someone else such as a spouse, roommate, coworker, or supervisor with shared access or authority consents to a search. Another exception allowing warrant-less searches concerns "exigent circumstances" under which there is reason to believe evidence would get destroyed. International borders are special cases in which warrant-less searches are allowed. Workplaces, either private, but especially government, are places where warrant-less searches are especially possible based on the consent of persons with authority or where the condition-of-employment allows access to information on computers used by employees.

The second section on the search and seizure of computers with a warrant covers several approaches, points, and considerations in search and seizure of computer/electronic evidence. The section provides several examples and discussions. Probable cause and oath/affirmation are stated to be required for these warrants as well as descriptions of places to be searched and items to be seized taking account of the peculiar circumstances and properties relating to electronic evidence.

Computer searches generally differ from those involving other types of evidence because the properties of electronic evidence can render the details of search and seizure unpredictable. Electronic evidence is more easily changed and destroyed than traditional physical evidence, may be hidden in more ways and its true nature or form be unknown at the time of constructing the search warrant.

Search warrants for electronic or computer evidence generally require close cooperation of experts in the different fields of criminal investigation, computer technology, and law enforcement to properly draft a warrant and create a search plan. No one type of expert usually has all the knowledge needed to craft and plan what may be needed for seizing and searching the electronic evidence.

Under some circumstances, special types of warrants may be needed to prevent loss of evidence or other difficulties with investigation. These include "no knock warrants" and "surreptitious entry" or "sneak and peak warrants." These excuse law enforcement from announcing entry and/or notifying persons whose premises are being searched. In all kinds of warrants involving electronic evidence especial care must be taken with the language of the draft.

INVESTIGATION AND ANALYSIS OF ELECTRONIC EVIDENCE

A number of publications have discussed or recommended the strategies and steps in forensic analysis of electronic (digital) evidence. Best practices for computer forensics have been published online by the Scientific Working Group on Digital Evidence (2006). The organization outlined different steps in the process of computer forensics and these were: (1) seizing evidence, (2) preparation of equipment used to investigate seized computers, (3) forensic imaging (computer hard drive imaging), (4) forensic analysis/examination, (5) documentation, and (6) reports.

In seizing evidence it was stated that attention be paid to understanding and following the proper legal authorization for investigation, ensuring no tampering with the evidence and obtaining information on the computer system involved. Investigators were also recommended to follow proper procedures regarding the power supply to computers and the different approaches best used for stand alone computers versus networked computers versus servers. Preparation of equipment used to investigate electronic evidence involves ensuring that such hardware and software are properly operating and maintained and using documented procedures in a manual.

THREAT TO E-DISCOVERY

Disk imaging is another term for forensic computer imaging and has been defined in an article by Mohd. Saudi (2007) as "creating physical sector copy of a disk and compressing this image in the form of a file. This image file can then be stored on dissimilar media for archiving or later restoration." (The term "forensic imaging" appears to be also used by Internet search engines to refer to forensic analysis of video and photographic images.)

According to the SDWGDE (2006) publication, forensic imaging (computer hard drive imaging or disk imaging) needs to include documentation and prevention of contamination or modification of the evidence. It is also essential that the evidence be imaged as a "bit stream image." Forensic analysis or examination recommendations include using examiners trained according to SWGDE guidelines. In addition, examination should use only forensic copies of the evidence and include close review of documents and legal scope from those requesting the examination. Where digital devices such as cell phones, PDAs, and iPods are forensically examined, best practices should be used and nontraditional methods should be documented and validated before use on the original media.

Documentation according to SWGDE guidelines needs to include a copy of legal authority (*for analysis*), chain of custody, count of evidence, the state of the evidence and its packaging when received by the examiner, description of the evidence and the communications concerning the case. For the reporting of forensic analysis of computers, SWGDE recommends attention to (a) the needs of the requestors of analysis, (b) investigative agency requirements, and (c) clarity of exposition.

NIJ and E-Discovery

In a publication titled "Forensic Examination of Digital Evidence: A Guide for Law Enforcement," the National Institute of Justice (NIJ) outlined the steps in investigation of digital evidence. It was recommended that at the outset, there be defined and documented policies and procedures for the steps in digital evidence investigation. The major investigative steps were listed as (1) assessment, (2) acquisition, (3) examination, and (4) documenting and reporting.

At the outset, the NIJ publication states that an investigative agency needs to have written policies and procedures for the steps in digital evidence investigation. There should be a description of qualifications required for personnel as well as job descriptions, the requirements for continuing education, evidence, and case management.

Evidence assessment involves review of the type of digital analysis requested as well as its legal authority and information about sophistication of the users or producers of the evidence. The NIJ also recommends attention as to what other types of forensic analysis may be required such as fingerprints or DNA. It is also important to consider whether the computer hosting the digital evidence is processed at the site of the crime or in the forensic laboratory. Additional considerations are the documentation of the nature of the evidence and secure storage to prevent loss of the digital information.

For evidence acquisition, the NIJ report emphasizes attention to best practices for good operating condition and documentation, verification and validation of the hardware and software to be used by the forensic examiners for the digital evidence. General technical steps for evidence acquisition from the computer in question were reviewed.

Major steps in evidence examination as outlined by the NIJ are (1) preparation, (2) extraction, (3) analysis of extracted data, and (4) drawing conclusions on the evidence. The preparation step relates to making directories on digital storage media in which to organize the captured evidentiary digital evidence. The extraction step comprises two processes: physical extraction, which relates to all the data on the system that contains the evidence, and logical extraction, which relates to files and data based on the operating system on the computer being investigated.

In the analysis step, the extracted data are studied to assess their meaning to the criminal case; for example, the time the files were created and by whom, the content of files, and whether deliberate attempts were made to hide the data. One objective is to see what overall patterns are suggested by the study of the data.

The last stage of the forensic investigation concerns documenting and reporting the findings. During the analysis it is important to make detailed notes of what was done. The report needs essential identifying information with regard to the case. The NIJ article stated that the findings on the digital evidence analysis should be summarized as well as presented in some detail in terms of the files and data found and attempts made at hiding data. The NIJ report also contained some case study examples as well as examples of forms and formats for requesting service and reporting findings and a glossary of terms.

The International Organization on Digital Evidence

A report by the SWGDE and IOCE (International Organization on Digital Evidence) (SWGDE and IOCE 2000) outlined standards and principles for working with digital (electronic) evidence. The report explained that the pervasiveness of the Internet and its economic uses mean that a crime in one country can involve digital evidence in one or more foreign countries and create the need for guidelines to facilitate exchange of digital evidence among countries.

The SWGDE emphasized the need for standard operating procedures in all judiciaries, properly trained analysts, and documentation of processes used in every investigation. SWGDE membership is international in composition although most of its members are from the United States or Western Europe. In the same article, the IOCE states that its mission is to help "international law enforcement agencies exchange information on computer crime investigation." IOCE is also involved in defining standards in digital evidence analysis and stated some general principles relating to the accuracy and proper processes in digital evidence analysis.

The Corporate Environment and E-Discovery

The growing significance of electronic evidence and computer forensics was reviewed by Volonino (2003) with emphasis on the risks to businesses that do not properly store their electronic information. The Federal Rules of Civil Procedure and Discovery and the Sabranes–Oxley Act require that businesses preserve certain sorts of electronic information and this includes e-mail because these may be regarded as business records. Volonino did discuss the interplay between these laws which strongly relate to electronic (digital) evidence and the Fourth Amendment. Several case examples were provided and these included (1) the Arthur Anderson LLP (2002) case, (2) American Home Products and their Fen-Phen diet product, (3) Credit Suisse First Boston executive Frank Quattrone, and (4) Boeing's response to a discovery request.

An article by Ciardhuáin (2004) discussed the main models for cyber crime investigations to indicate the need for standard terminology and to provide a framework for the investigative practice. The model proposed by Ciardhuáin included 13 steps, which in order are:

1. Awareness
2. Authorization
3. Planning
4. Notification
5. Search for and identify evidence
6. Collection of evidence
7. Transport of evidence
8. Storage of evidence
9. Examination of evidence
10. Hypothesis
11. Presentation of evidence
12. Proof/defense of evidence
13. Dissemination of information

This model contains more steps than previously proposed by other authors and describes them in some detail and generally tries to cover all the important steps. In the future, it will be important to examine the impact of the Fourth amendment at different criminal justice stages including but not restricted to admissibility and testimony. It is advisable that students are exposed to methods of cyber crime investigation: the materials used, technology, products, suppliers of the equipments or technology, training resources, responsibilities of each actor in cyber investigations, roles, and ethics.

DIGITAL EVIDENCE IN INVESTIGATIVE AGENCIES, SCIENTIFIC AND PROFESSIONAL BODIES

Some of the main federal agencies active in cyber crime investigation are the FBI, IRS, US DOJ, and Secret Service. There are also state and local law enforcement agencies across the United States, which are involved in investigating electronic evidence. The role of these agencies is continuing as crimes involve new technological advances and increases the scope and numbers of crimes involving digital evidence and the Fourth Amendment. It is therefore critical that the personnel associated with these law enforcement agencies must be trained thoroughly to attain the goals and successes for the departments. Therefore we must reevaluate the roles of present law enforcement personnel and begin to retrain the mass of manpower that may be technologically illiterate and provide standards for new roles, qualifications, certifications, education, ethics, and responsibilities.

FBI and Digital Files

The Federal Bureau of Investigation has several globally recognized forensic science areas of expertise that include the area of computer forensics and electronic evidence (FBI Cyber Investigation 2007). Crimes of particular interest involving electronic evidence include (a) computer intrusions (hacking), (b) online sexual predators of children, (c) theft of U.S. intellectual property, (d) Internet fraud by national and international organized crime, (e) fraud, and (f) Internet crime.

The FBI counters Internet crime by various tactics and strategies. Firstly, the FBI provides a Web site where the public can file complaints of Internet crime to which they have fallen victim (www.ic3.gov; Internet Crime Complaint 2007). This site also serves as a central national resource for law enforcement agencies who are investigating Internet-related crimes. The resource is hosted in West Virginia and in 2006 received 231,493 complaints.

The FBI also has Cyber Action Teams (CATs)

These teams combine FBI agents, computer forensics experts, and software experts who work as a rapid response team on a global level. As an example of one of their cases: Turkish and Moroccan hackers launched the Zotob code to steal credit card numbers globally. However, the software cause computers to crash and the severity and extent of the attacks brought in the FBI. A CAT team became involved with the Turkish and Moroccan authorities in forensic investigations that led to the arrest of two suspects and the case is still ongoing. The FBI has 92 computer crime task forces nationally and these collaborate with other agencies such as the US Secret Service, US Postal Inspection Service, and the Department of Defense, IRS, as well as state agencies.

FBI computer investigations started as far back as 1984. In 1999, the FBI started a program called RCFL (Regional Computer Forensics Laboratory 2007), which has been undergoing continuous growth since then (www.fbi.gov/page2/april06'rcfl042406.htm). In 2002, the RCFL National Program Office was established to oversee RCFL operations and promote technology transfer and training for law enforcement. RCFL involve interactions among federal, state, and local law enforcement agencies.

Typically an RCFL team is composed of 15 people, including 12 examiners and 3 supporting staff. The team's duties include (a) seizure and collection of digital evidence from crime scene, (b) analysis of digital evidence, and (c) expert testimony. The RCFL examiners undergo training in the use of software used for imaging of computer hard drives and other aspects of computer forensics including American Society of Crime Laboratory Directors (ASCLD) certification (www.rcfl.gov/index.cfm).

In 2007, there were 14 RCFLs in Chicago, Greater Houston, Heart of America (Kansas and Western Missouri), Intermountain West (Utah, Idaho, Montana), Kentucky, Miami Valley (Ohio), New Jersey, North Texas, Northwest (Oregon and Eastern Washington State), Rocky Mountain, (Colorado and Wyoming), San Diego, Silicon Valley, and western New York. These laboratories analyze electronic evidence from a variety of digital devices and performed analyses for 3,500 law enforcement agencies in the United States.

Accreditation by a respected organization enhances the standing of forensic laboratories when evidence is presented by their analysts in court. The north Texas, Silicon Valley, and New Jersey RCFLs are accredited by the ASCLD.

The BTK (Bind Torture Kill) serial killer case is an example of a high-profile case in which the RCFL in Kansas City played a role. Dennis Rader, the serial killer, sent a floppy disk to a radio station following an established pattern of publicly taunting the law enforcement authorities. Forensic examination of the floppy uncovered a first name, place of employment, and location which helped identify a suspect and solve the case.

Another case involving the RCFL is that of the corruption investigation of the mayor of Niles, Illinois, a city close to Chicago in the area of O'Hare airport. The mayor has been charged with fraud and bribe taking in exchange for pressuring businesses to buy insurance policies and electronic evidence is important in the case. The Kansas City area RCFL is active in another case involving murder and kidnapping charges against Richard Davis and Dena Riley. The electronic evidence in the case includes video tapes, computers and flash memory cards.

In Philadelphia, where the RCFL was opened in July 2006, an October 2006 case is that of Michael Carter Reynolds, who was arrested for terrorist organization involvement, specifically the Al-Qaida. He also tried to escape using a fraudulent passport. Incriminating evidence was found in his computer and e-mail records. The Rocky Mountain laboratory in Colorado is involved in the investigation of the leader of a polygamist sect called the Fundamentalist Latter Day Saints. He was captured in August 2006 with the help of digital forensics work.

The RCFL has a statement about privacy and civil rights in regards to the investigations that they undertake. The chief of the RCFL program, Gerry Cocuzi, was quoted "examiners do not conduct unwarranted searches" and only investigate under two conditions: (1) when granted legal authority by a judge and (2) when the party involved signs a consent of the search. It was also stated that the RCFL restricts itself in accessing evidence by searching only for items specifically requested by investigators. In addition, access to the evidence files is restricted and the evidence is kept in secure locations (www.rcfl.gov).

Electronic Crime Statistics Technology

The FBI maintains statistics on crime that also covers electronic crime (FBI Electronic Crime Statistics 2007). According to the FBI, in 2006, 207,492 complaints were made about Internet fraud and the total amount of money was $198.4 million. Of the cases, 45 percent were online auction fraud such as undelivered merchandise or payments. Other common crimes were e-mail murder threats, identity theft, investment fraud, cyberstalking, and spamming. The criminals were 75 percent male, and 61 percent were from the United States. Other nationalities prominent in Internet crime were Britons, Romanians, Nigerians, Canadians, and Italians.

The victims were of all agencies but commonly 30- to 40-year-old males in California, Florida, Texas, and New York, the most populous states. The crimes causing the most economic impact were the Nigerian e-mail fraud (419 scams) in which the median loss was $5,100.00. In this type of crime, 74 percent of Internet crime victims were contacted by e-mail and 36 percent of the crimes occurred by means of Web sites. Cases involving sex crimes against children via the Internet grew from 113 in 1996 to 2,500 in 2005 (www.fbi.gov/page2/april06/Internettrends040706.htm).

The US Department of Justice

The US DOJ has a Computer Crime and Intellectual Property Section (CCIPS). This section carries out national strategies of the US DOJ that relate to computer crime. The CCIP collaborates with both public and private organizations to fight computer crime and plays especially strong roles in intellectual property protection as well as training of computer crime professionals.

The National White Collar Crime Center (NW3C) is a private sector organization which supports law enforcement agencies in the investigation and prevention of economic and high tech crime. The NW3C does this especially by means of courses and information products relating to Internet and computer crime. However, the Secret Service, military, and other federal, state, local, and private agencies do have roles in the evolution of the Fourth Amendment and electronic evidence.

Federal, state, local, and private agencies and the judiciary must begin to develop and implement universally acceptable guidelines that establish qualifications, certifications, education, responsibilities, ethics and the Fourth Amendment applications, interpretations, timeline of activities, composition, and major roles.

CONCLUSION

In spite of current dilemmas, challenges, and predictions of what will come, according to numerous case laws, citizens are protected, and can expect to be protected (i.e., maintain a reasonable amount of privacy), when it comes to computer-related issues, unless and except we forfeit our rights to privacy by doing any number of acts already referenced. We also lose our privacy rights when we relinquish our control of information to a third party: repair shops, handing out floppy disks or CD-ROM, or even sending data across the Internet, including e-mail, instant messaging, and any type of Voice-over-Internet Protocol (VOIP), which is on the rise. As with most other aspects of our legal system, "ignorance of the law" will not ensure that our privacy rights are not violated. And we are wise to keep in mind that there is no expectation of privacy for electronic media, and if law enforcement decides to place us under surveillance, they may do so, so long as they remain within legally appropriate boundaries (Salveggio 2004).

Computers versus Servers

Preparation of equipment used to investigate electronic evidence involves ensuring that such hardware and software are properly operating and maintained and using documented procedures in a manual. Disk imaging is another term for forensic computer imaging and has been defined in an article by Mohd. Saudi (2007) as "creating physical sector copy of a disk and compressing this image in the form of a file. This image file can then be stored on dissimilar media for archiving or later restoration." (The term forensic imaging appears to be also used by Internet search engines to refer to forensic analysis of video and photographic images.)

According to the SDWGDE (2006) publication, forensic imaging (computer hard drive imaging or disk imaging) needs to include documentation and prevention of contamination or modification of the evidence. It is also essential that the evidence be imaged as a "bit stream image." Forensic analysis or examination recommendations include using examiners trained according to SWGDE guidelines. In addition examination should use only forensic copies of the evidence and include close review of documents and legal scope from those requesting the examination. Where digital devices such as cell phones, PDAs, and iPods are forensically examined, best practices should be used and nontraditional methods should be documented and validated before use on the original material.

KEY TERMS

Fourth Amendment
Electronic evidence

REFERENCES

Ciardhuáin, S. O. 2004. An extended model of cybercrime investigations. *International Journal of Digital Evidence* 3 (1).

FBI Cyber Investigation. 2007. www.fbi.gov/cyberinvest/cberhouse.htm, Accessed April 7, 2007.

FBI Electronic Crime Statistics. 2007. www.fbi.gov/page2/march07/ic3031607.htm, Accessed April 7, 2007.

Hogge, B. 2007. The knowledge revolution. http://www.opendemocracy.net

Internet Crime Complaint. 2007. www.ic3.gov, Accessed April 7, 2007.

Kerwin, D. 2005. Discovery of digital evidence. *ABA*.

Mohd. Saudi, M. 2007. An overview of disk imaging tool in computer forensics. http://niser.org.mu/resources/disk_imaging.pdf, Accessed March 12, 2007.

NIJ. 2004. Forensic examination of digital evidence: A guide for law enforcement. www.ncjrs.org/pdffiles1/nij/199408.pdf, Accessed March 8, 2007.

Regional Computer Forensics Laboratory. 2007. www.rcfl.gov, Accessed April 7, 2007.

Salveggio, E. April 28–May 4, 2004. Your (un) reasonable expectation for privacy. *Ubiquity* 5 (9).

Saferstein, R. 2004. *Criminalistics*. 8th ed., chap. 1, 2. San Diego: Pearson Prentice-Hall.

Scientific Working Group on Digital Evidence. July 2006. Best practices for computer forensics. http://ncfs.org/swgde/2006/Best_practices_for_Computer_Forensics%20July06.pdf, version 2.1, Accessed February 28, 2007.

Stephenson, P. 2005. Forensic science: An introduction to scientific and investigative techniques. In *Investigating Computer-Related Crime,* edited by S. H. James and J. J. Nordby, chap. 27, 553–70. CRC Press LIC.

Swaminatha, T. M. 2004–2005. Fourth amendment unplugged: electronic evidence issues and wireless defenses. *Yale Journal of Law and Technology.*

SWGDE and IOCE. 2000. Digital evidence: Standards and principles. *Forensic Science Communications* 2:2. www.fbi.gov/hq/lab/fsc/baackissu/april2000/swgde.htm

SWGDE and SWGIT Glossary of Terms, version 1.0. July 25, 2005. http://ncfs.org/swgde/documents/swgde2006/SWGDE_SWGIT%20Glossary%20V2.0.pdf

United States Department of Justice. July 2002. Searching and seizing computers and obtaining electronic evidence in criminal investigations. Computer Crime and Intellectual Property Section, Criminal Division, United States Department of Justice. www.usdoj.gov/criminal/cybercrime/s&smanual2002.htm, Accessed January 15, 2007.

Volonino, L. 2003. Electronic evidence and computer forensics. *Communications of the Association for Information Systems* 12: 457–68.

Zatyko, K. 2007. Defining digital forensics. *Forensic Magazine* 4 (1): 18–20.

PART V

Cyber Terrorism: The "New" Face of Terrorism

Chapter 29

The Dark Side of the Web: Terrorists' Use of the Internet

Kelly Damphousse
University of Oklahoma

Kelly Damphousse, Ph.D., is Associate Dean in the College of Arts and Sciences and Presidential Professor of Sociology at the University of Oklahoma. He earned his Ph.D. in Sociology from Texas A&M University in 1994. His research career has included studies of terrorism, homicide, drugs/crime nexus, Satanism, and several justice-related evaluation projects. He served as the Site Director of the Oklahoma City and Tulsa ADAM sites from 1998 to 2004 and has been Associate Director of "The American Terrorism Study" since 1994.

Abstract

This chapter examines how terrorists have used the Internet to communicate with a "world wide" audience. We begin by defining terrorism and placing the need for communication to a wide audience in context. Terrorists have traditionally communicated with people outside their organization to express their views, seek support, and raise money. Just as the Internet has become an increasingly important tool to society, terrorists have begun to use the Internet to achieve their goals. Indeed, terrorists were early adopters of the Internet, using bulletin boards and newsgroups before the advent of the browser-based Internet. The Internet is an extraordinary medium for the advancement of terrorist ideology because it is relatively inexpensive and attracts a large audience. The Internet also provides an outstanding tool for communicating with current and potential group members. Finally, the Internet provides access to vital information that can be used to injure terrorist targets (like governments) or to collect reconnaissance information to plan attacks. The chapter describes the proliferation of terrorists on the Internet and the ways that terrorists may use the Internet to perform acts of terrorism. Finally, we show how the Internet is being used to "counter" terrorism.

INTRODUCTION

This chapter addresses the use of the Internet by **terrorists** and those who mean to counter their activities. Before we go too far, though, we need to understand what is meant when we use the word "terrorist." For many of the people we examine in this chapter, the term is meaningless. On one extreme, these people see themselves as "freedom fighters" that are organized against an oppressive and more powerful regime (Ross 2006). It might surprise you, for example, to think that George Washington and his fellow "patriots" were considered to be rebels (or "terror-ists") by the English government. On another extreme, terrorists might think that they are only exercising their right to express themselves about a controversial issue (Hoffman 1998). Thus, someone who is opposed to **abortion** and publishes a list of abortion clinic addresses may only feel like they are "pointing toward evil," and not creating "hit lists" for which they might be criminally liable (Macavinta 1999).

Terrorism scholars have spent years trying to define terrorism and there about as many definitions of terrorism as there are scholars (Hoffman 1998). One simple definition provided by the United States government—the definition used by the FBI—states that terrorism is "the unlawful use of force and violence against persons or property to intimidate or coerce a government, the civilian population, or any segment thereof, in furtherance of political or social objectives" (28 Code of Federal Regulations Section 0.85). The two key issues in most such definitions are (1) the use of force and (2) a political motivation.

As we will see, however, this definition is problematic regarding terrorists' use of the Internet. While creating a Web page may be politically motivated, it is certainly not a *use* of force. Indeed, it is often not even a *threatened* use of force. So, by definition, most uses of the Internet by terrorists are not terrorist acts, *per se*, but may be best described as acts that are *ancillary* to terrorism—acts that support terrorist activities (Smith, Damphousse, and Roberts 2006). Many times, for example, terrorists only use the Internet to air their grievances, some-thing that such groups have done throughout the history of terrorism. Indeed, one might say that is the whole *point* of terrorism: to draw attention to a problem. Terrorists "want to impress. They play to and for an audience, and solicit audience participation" (Hacker 1976, xi). Thus, the Internet can be seen as just one more way of communicating with an audience, join-ing the **communiqué**, the poster, the placard, and the soapbox. The impact of the Internet on the ability of terrorists to communicate is enormous, of course, given its ability to reach such a wide audience so quickly. Interestingly, the Internet has given potential terrorists a tool that may preclude terrorism acts. In the pre-Internet era, a violent act was probably the only way to "get the word out." The Internet now gives politically frustrated groups a voice that does not *require* violence.

But if we stop there, we fail to recognize that the Internet also gives terrorists another weapon in its arsenal. Herein we observe a tremendous irony: as society becomes increasingly dependent on the Internet, it also becomes increasingly vulnerable to attack via the Internet. Thus, terrorists not only use the Internet to *communicate* with society, they may also use the Internet to *attack* society.

Terrorists also face a paradox when they decide to use the Internet because their new tool, like bomb parts and fingerprints, can be used by investigators to identify the attackers. In addition, the Internet can be used by **counter-terrorism** actors to warn citizens about poten-tial terrorism threats and to seek information that can aid in the capture of the terrorists. This is the same problem that terrorists face when they use the media. "Just as the media is a tool of the terrorist, it is pernicious to the terrorist groups too. It helps an outraged public to mobi-lize its vast resources and produces information that the public needs to pierce the veil of secrecy all terrorist groups require" (Rapoport 1996, viii). Making their cause public brings greater attention to the terrorist, which may result in eventual capture and arrest. Thus, the way that terrorists use the Internet can make them more vulnerable to capture.

Terrorist groups described in this chapter are composed of three types: (1) groups that hate certain types of *people* (e.g., blacks, Jews, and women) (2) groups that oppose certain types of *aspects of social life* (e.g., affirmative action, abortion, technology, and immigration), and (3) groups that oppose governments (e.g., Irish Republican Army and the **Republic of Texas**). While the ultimate focus of each of these protest groups may differ, there is certainly some overlap between the two types of groups in terms of behavior, strategy, membership, and etiology (Lofland 1996). A cautionary note is in order. We use the term "terrorist group" guardedly because we recognize that some groups that are described in this chapter might only be *potential* terrorist groups—that is, they have not committed any criminal act. At the same time, these groups are still interesting because of their marked potential for (1) engaging in terrorist acts or (2) providing for others the incentive to engage in violence (Damphousse and Smith 1997). Thus, this paper assesses the different ways that terrorist groups use the Internet (both as a manner of communicating with a wider audience and as a form of attack) and how the use of the Internet makes the terrorists vulnerable to capture. We start by discussing the need for communication by terrorist groups and then describe how terrorists and counter-terrorists use the Internet.

TERROR AND COMMUNICATION

If you consider the life course of terrorist groups, you realize that most groups started because their founding members were frustrated by some "problem" (Ross 2006). In some cases, they may have tried to "fix" the problem via legitimate means (e.g., through the political or legal system) while in other cases, they may not have felt empowered to make a change at all. At some point, the members decided that the only way that they can change the current situation is to react violently. As von Clausewitz wrote nearly 200 years ago, "War is the continuation of politics by other means" (von Clausewitz 1832/1976). By extension, terrorism is also a continuation of politics. The difference is that wars are fought between "states" while terrorism is conducted (mostly) by nonstate actors.

Terrorist groups in particular, engage in behaviors designed to send messages to outsiders. Violence, therefore, can be seen as an attempt by terrorist groups to call attention to some "problem" that needs to be "fixed" (Herman 1982; Rubenstein 1987). Indeed, some have suggested that terrorism could not even exist without the ability to communicate with people outside of the skirmish, calling to mind the proverbial "tree falling in the forest with no one to hear it" (Schmid and Graaf 1982). Acts of violence by terrorists can be considered indirect efforts at communication whereby the terrorists use the news media to inform the public about the motives of the group, in an effort to give "violent voice to the voiceless, and to awaken their sleeping brethren to the necessity of mass action" (Rubenstein 1989, 323). Hoffman (1998) details, for example, the impact of the media coverage of hijacking of an Israeli *El Al* airliner in 1968 and the killing of Israeli athletes at the Munich Olympic games in 1972 as watershed events that resulted in increased international attention to the "Palestinian question" (Said 1979).

Less extreme, though more direct, measures have also been taken by protest groups to get their message out. In general, this tactic is referred to as **propaganda** (Wright 1990). Propaganda is used by protest groups to inform the general public (or other more specific groups) about some problem in an effort to make them "feel the urgency, the necessity of some action, its unique characteristics, . . . [and] what to do" (Ellul 1969, 208). Traditionally, protest groups have used the printed word (via leaflets, fliers, posters, and newsletters) to inform others about their cause (Wright 1990). More recently, terrorist groups used faxes to communicate with each other and with selected outsiders (e.g., media and academics). The problem with the use of these media is the relatively high cost and limited scope of coverage. There is little "bang for the buck" when much of the material is discarded by uninterested members of the public.

Protest groups experimented with the use of short wave radio for a time (and still continue to do so, to a lesser extent), but access to a larger audience was still restricted. The next advance that allowed greater access to the general public was made possible by the increased popularity of nationally syndicated talk radio programs. It was talk radio that first allowed members of protest groups to be able to discuss their concerns with a host and (presumably) a national audience. Conservative talk radio shows that allowed/fostered the discussion of topics that angered groups of individuals blossomed in the late 1980s. Still, access to a wide audience by the protest groups was somewhat limited as was the information that could be provided. Even worse, the information was also limited in that it was in verbal format; easily discarded and easily forgotten. While members of protest groups were able to communicate easily with each other and with a limited sympathetic audience, they were still unable to get their message to the "uncommitted audience" (Wright 1990).

THE EVOLUTION OF REVOLUTION

The advent of the World Wide Web (as we know it) in the mid-1990s provided protest groups with access to a mode of communication that was relatively inexpensive, patently "permanent," was in text and image format, and was accessible to almost anyone in the world. To the extent that antigovernment groups were among the first to make use of the Internet for propaganda use, the information revolution coincided with the conservative revolution in an ironic twist. The Internet had been developed in the late 1960s by the federal government (United States Department of Defense) to allow for the sharing of computer files between research scientists located around the country. The irony is that the project initially developed by the federal government was now being used by protest groups to encourage its downfall.

Terrorists were not latecomers to the computer age. In fact, discussion lists (listservs), bulletin board systems, and **newsgroups** had been actively used by such groups in the decade before the browser-based Internet came into existence. The least private of these early technologies was the newsgroups and **bulletin boards**, where messages ("articles") are posted to servers that are available to most anyone who has access to the site. These were the precursors to the currently in vogue Web log (blog) and networking sites. Electronic bulletin boards began in the late 1970s but they are essentially extinct now. A bulletin board normally was composed of a local group of computer users who were interested in a certain topic. Since people were accessing the bulletin board through the phone line, the expense of a long distance phone call resulted in most bulletin boards being used locally. Indeed, it was common back then for members of a bulletin board group to meet in person. Throughout the 1980s, right wing terrorist groups and activists were heavy users of such bulletin boards. Registered users could post comments, files, and software to the bulletin board system (BBS) so that others could access them. The advent of Internet browser software led to the ultimate near-demise of the BBS.

Newsgroups were similar to bulletin boards but they provided greater access to a wide range of people beyond the local area. Newsgroups were eventually divided into different topical hierarchies in 1986 to provide order to the rapidly expanding system ("comp.*" for computers discussions, "sci.*" for discussions about sciences, etc.). The "alt.*" hierarchy was created as a catchall category for topics that did not fit the other seven hierarchies. Over time, the "alt.*" designation became synonymous with "alternative" groups including Satanists, wiccans, and illicit drug enthusiasts. Included in this category were several politically defiant groups such as alt.activism.militia, alt.society.anarchy. Eventually, many antigovernment groups were using the newsgroup technology to communicate with each other. In time, a myth suggested that alt.* stood for "Anarchists, Lunatics and Terrorists" (Salus 1995). These public forums consist of individuals posting comments or questions and allowing others to post responses in a series of "threads." Newsgroups are monitored by an administrator who can drop "inappropriate" posts to the group or delete posts when interest in the topic as waned. The problem with using newsgroups, however, was that they were relatively easy for the government and others to monitor.

Listservs, first developed in 1984, are relatively more private than bulletin boards and newsgroups, but controlling who is part of the list can be difficult. Listservs use the e-mail system as a means of communication among people with a shared interest. In most cases, a moderator operates the listserv by creating a list of e-mail addresses of people who wish to be part of the "list." Interested members subscribe to the list and receive e-mail messages from every subscriber who submit an e-mail to the listserv. Upon receipt of the e-mail, the recipient can either reply to the rest of the listserv or to the individual.

These "asynchronous" communication processes are now being replaced by real-time applications called "**chat rooms**" (e.g., Internet Relay Chat and MUDs—Multi-User Dungeons). These programs allow groups of individuals to instantly communicate with each other via their computers. In recent years, simple text-based messages have been supplemented with video and voice protocols that allow users to see and hear each other, eliminating the need to type messages.

These early computer links were important for planning and the transmission information between terrorist group members who were physically separated. But this medium was accessible to only a limited audience (mostly people who were active computer users and interested in the topic). The advent of the browser and "worldwide" access to these new Web pages changed the importance of the Internet for terrorist groups. For the first time, activists had access to people from all walks of life who were potential members, supporters, and contributors to their cause. Unfortunately for the protest groups, potential enemies also had access to the information that they made public. How protest groups and their opponents use the Internet is discussed in the following sections. But before detailing the activities of protesters on the Internet, it is necessary to provide some background regarding how the Internet works to make communication via the computer more accessible to a larger group of people.

Before the advent of Web browsers like Netscape and Internet Explorer, access to the Internet was available only to people who were technologically advanced. Knowledge of several programs was required to perform simple tasks like sharing files and sending an e-mail message. The creation of Web browsers solved most of these problems because of introduction of hypertext markup language (html). Even so, Web developers were required to learn a relatively complex software program and language to be able to create a Web page. Advances in technology over time eliminated that hurdle and now, anyone with access to the Internet can create a Web page or site. Indeed, the availability of networking sites like Facebook, Xanga, and MySpace has made even the requirement for a Web page almost obsolete. If you want to let people know about your cause, you simply register at one of these networking sites and create a "group." Like-minded people from around the world can join your "group" and everyone can post information that is accessible to the world (or just to your "friends"). A recent search from my Facebook page, for example, revealed seven "groups" that express support for the **Earth Liberation Front** (ELF). These networking programs are incredibly easy to learn such that 12-year-old children are more than proficient in their use (www.comScore. com, retrieved June 12, 2007).

This system was made even more accessible in 1993 when browsers were developed that allowed computer users to interact with other computers through a graphical interface. With the Mosaic browser (and subsequently others like Netscape, FoxFire, Safari, and Explorer), novice users were able to access the Web pages created by terrorists. Over time, the graphical interface of the home pages became increasingly sophisticated, supplementing the images and text with sound and video. People using video-sharing sites like YouTube or on private Web sites, for example, can now easily access excerpts of speeches and videos. In addition to merely visiting Web sites, advances in software development has allowed people with no formal computer training to be able to create Web pages, giving them access to literally millions of people around the world. The decreasing cost of personal computers was associated with an increased access to the Internet and modem speed resulting in an incredible increase in Internet activity. From 1993 to 1997, the number of Web sites grew from almost zero to just under 5 million. By the middle of 2007, the Netcraft Web Survey reported that there were more than 123 million Web sites. Unfortunately, this incredible tool that has changed our world in so many ways is also being used to harm us. The goal of this chapter is to describe how terrorist groups can use the Internet to further their cause.

Method of Study

The data presented in this paper were compiled over the course of a 12-year research project starting in 1995 that was originally designed to examine how terrorist groups used the Internet to communicate with each other (Damphousse and Smith 1997). As the Internet evolved, we discovered that terrorists' use of the Internet evolved along with it. Each advance in Internet technology was adopted by terrorist groups to their advantage. The data collection began by the researchers conducting Internet searches via the Yahoo search engine for the virtual presence of specific known terrorist groups (e.g., KKK, FALN, and Aryan Nations). We discovered that it was not sufficient to search for "terrorism" since these groups don't always think of themselves as "terrorists"—so the searches had to be more creative. For example, an early search on the word "terrorism" yielded 68 "hits," most of which had to do with new stories about terrorists. Back in 1995, a search on Yahoo for the word "**Aryan**," however, yielded only nine Web sites, each of which was directly related to Aryan Nations groups. Other search engines yielded different Web pages. Using AltaVista, for example, resulted in over 3,700 pages with the word "Aryan."

Times and the Internet have changed. A search on the word "Aryan" in 2007 using Google yielded over 3.5 million hits (the first being the ubiquitous Wikipedia definition). Obviously, just using a search engine is not efficient. So we found other locations were found by conducting searches for militia groups and by following links from one site to another. We discovered that a site maintained by one white supremacist group often provides links to several other similar Web sites. Thus, we followed the links located at each of the Web sites that we catalogued (and all the links on the subsequent Web sites). Each of the locations we visited was bookmarked for ease of later access and then visited regularly over the course of the 12-year period. We conducted crude content analyses of these pages, looking for patterns and trends in the way that these groups used the Internet. In addition, we scanned electronic news Web sites to see how the media was covering the topic of "terrorists and the Internet." In retrospect, we wish that we had done a better job making copies of Web sites given the frequency with which these Web sites disappeared. Unfortunately, much of the raw data has disappeared over time. Still, we believe that we understand how terrorist groups have used the Internet over the past 12 years. We discuss these tactics in the following section.

The Internet as Tool for Protest Groups

Previous examinations of how terrorists use the Internet have suggested as many as eight categories of usage (Weiman 2005). In the following sections, we provide examples of nine ways that terrorist groups can use the Internet. Some of these categories are based on exclusive properties of the Internet such as the potential ease of reaching millions of people. Some categories simply aid terrorists groups accomplish their goals. The final set of categories suggests ways that terrorists can use the Internet to attack their targets, the "**Cyber terrorism**" that has caused such concern (Collin 1996).

Leaderless Resistance and Propaganda

Until the 1980s, most terrorist groups exhibited a militaristic, hierarchical structure that allowed leaders to communicate directly with their followers. Over time, however, counterterrorist efforts evolved such that law enforcement used this structure against the group as an entity. Instead of just prosecuting those who were involved in the terrorist incident, the FBI targeted the entire group, especially its leaders. Thus, the goal of the U.S. government became the "beheading" of the terrorist group. Lower-level operatives who were arrested for a terrorist act were offered attractive plea arrangements in exchange for testifying against their leaders. This resulted in leaders being held criminally culpable for the acts of their followers and in the eventual demise of many terrorist groups (Smith and Damphousse 1998).

To counter this strategy, terrorists groups began to change their tactics. One possible option would have been the creation of a cellular structure, where a leader coordinates independent cells. This strategy reduces damage to the entire terrorist structure but continues to put the leader at risk. A more suitable option emerged in the early 1990s that has come to symbolize the contemporary terrorism structural strategy, what Michael Barkun (1994, 1997) has referred to as "uncoordinated violence" strategies.

Ironically, the most prominent of these strategies, "**leaderless resistance**," evolved from unsuccessful federal prosecutions in the late 1980s. Following the acquittal of extreme right-wing group leaders in the 1988 Fort Smith, Arkansas trial, Louis Beam spent months devising a plan to minimize civil and criminal liability for group leaders. Following the siege at Ruby Ridge, Idaho in 1992, Beam publicly called for the implementation of "leaderless resistance" at a meeting of extreme right-wing adherents in Estes Park, Colorado (Beam 1992).

Copies of Beam's document abound on the Internet, including Beam's own Web site (http://www.louisbeam.com/leaderless.htm).

Beam's call to change was indeed prescient. He was aware that, even if people are motivated to engage in violent acts by the awareness of a problem, they still need training, information, and some direction. He saw the importance of the computer as vital cog in this new leadership strategy. "Organs of information distribution such as newspapers, leaflets, *computers, etc., which are widely available to all*, keep each person informed of events, allowing for a planned response that will take many variations. No one need issue an order to anyone. Those idealists truly committed to the cause of freedom will act when they feel the need" (Beam 1992, 2, emphasis added). Thus, terrorists who have adopted this new "indirect action" strategy can "lead" without putting themselves at risk of criminal prosecution. The Internet provides the best option for such "leaders" to guide "followers" in future actions, providing a rationale for "direct action" and information about successful tactics and potential targets. Using the Internet allows followers to receive their marching orders without the leader ever knowing who the follower is.

The majority of the sites that we observed, for example, had sections that described the purported "problem" (e.g., immigration, gay and minority rights, and excessive taxation and government control) in great detail to show how society was deteriorating. The use of vivid imagery was designed to appeal to each reader's sensitivity. Frequently, the Web pages provided anecdotal "atrocity" stories like the moral entrepreneurs of other such moral panics (Victor 1993). For example, the "**Waco Holocaust Electronic Museum**" Web page suggested that the siege at the Branch Davidian compound was only part of a continuing pattern of attacks by federal law enforcement agencies against the Christian right (http://www.public-action.com/SkyWriter/WacoMuseum/, accessed February 27, 2006). To further incite passion about the threat of the government to the church, the "curator" provided links to the autopsy reports of the Waco victims, including grisly photographs of the victims of the fiery end of the siege. Bear in mind that it was frustration about the Waco siege and its outcome that motivated (in part) **Timothy McVeigh** to bomb the Oklahoma City federal building in 1995.

Other Web sites offer similarly graphic text. The Watchman newsletter was hosted by a white supremacist Web site called stormfront.org.[1] The following text relates a race-related atrocity story to seemingly unrelated events at Ruby Ridge, Waco, and Oklahoma City in a thinly veiled call for action.

"As I was preparing to mail this double issue of 'The Watchman' an event took place in the Chicago area which demands comment. Three black animals butchered a White woman and her young White children, one by torture and then cut her open to remove the half-breed baby she was pregnant with . . . It seems that they were using her as an incubator to breed a light-skinned child, and decided to eliminate her, having no further need for her reproductive ability. The one who removed the little bastard was a negress nurse who used her medical training to carry out her part in the crime . . . it is becoming more apparent with every day that passes that *unless the White Race rises up against their tormentors in a consuming fury, we will instead be consumed by them.* I do not hate these people as individuals but only a fool would believe that we will ever live together in peace. Events like this, as well as Waco, the Randy Weaver massacre and Oklahoma City portend a darkening future for America and it is

---

[1]The newsletter is not longer available because—according to the Stormfront Web site—the editor (Mark Thomas) was thought to have become an informant for the government.

becoming increasingly clear that *unless heroic measures are taken without delay*, there will be no future for us or our children" (http://www2.stormfront.org/watchman/index.html, retrieved on February 6, 1996, emphasis added).

Recruiting

The primary job of all terrorist leaders is to recruit members into their group. The traditional way of doing this is by inflaming the passion of potential followers so that they become willing to engage in activities that they would normally find repugnant—to move them from the "propaganda of word" to the "propaganda of deed" (Stafford 1971). In the past, this task was accomplished through the publication of books and pamphlets (e.g., Marx and Engels 1848/1964). In the information age of terrorism, the Internet provides the best way of showing potential new members that they have been lulled into a complacency (a false consciousness) that threatens to destroy them. As opposed to books on the subject, the Internet is free to potential members have nothing to invest to learn about the problem. The Internet also offers greater coverage than pamphlets and yelling from the street. It is also private, so that both the "speaker" and the "listener" are safe from observation during their "conversation." The following quote which appeared on the now defunct Web site called "The Patriot's Soapbox" demonstrates this line of reasoning:

> If there is one thing I want to accomplish by publishing these thoughts on the Internet, it is to stimulate you American slaves out there to WAKE UP and become sovereign Americans again. While you were slumbering, watching television, drinking beer, being amused, your 'servants' captured and enslaved you, and became your 'masters'. You could be free, but you are entangled in a Web of deceit: lies, fictions and frauds committed by your friendly public servants. (http://www.geocities.com/CapitolHill/1781/, retrieved February 14, 1996)

More contemporary examples include Web sites that are devoted to the question of abortion. Pro-life advocates worry that the very *act* of abortion has been so watered down that citizens are not offended by the act. A recent controversial tactic has been the use of large shocking photographs of aborted fetuses on billboards and 18-wheeler trailers "as a way to educate people about the realities of abortion" to that potential recruits can fully appreciate the issue at hand (Baez 2006, 1). These tactical uses of images find a natural home on the Internet and several Web sites have been created based on the same principle. The antiabortion Web page abort73.com, for example, includes a sophisticated video that begins "If ignorance is bliss, turn back now. But if you are ready to lift the curtain on one of the greatest injustices history has even known, you've come to the right place . . . while contemporary media outlets cover-up the carnage, an entire industry grows rich off of a strategically uninformed clientele . . . we dare you to know" (http://www.abort73.com/, retrieved June 1, 2007). The Web site provides statistics on the number of abortions completed each year along with graphic pictures and videos of fetuses and procedures.

It would be a stretch to call this a "terrorist" Web site but there are other sites that can capitalize on such sites to encourage direct action. A Web site called "The Nuremburg Trials" (http://www.christiangallery.com/atrocity/, retrieved June 1, 2007), for example, provides a list of abortion clinic, their respective addresses, and pictures that have been taken by "abortioncams." The impact of such Web sites has been observed in U.S. courts. In a 2003 federal criminal complaint, for example, Stephen Jordi was recorded telling an informant that "he had ordered over the Internet a book known for its 'prolific terrorist ties' and had visited the **'Army of God'** Web site . . . (www.christiangallery.com). This Web site has been called a 'hit list' for abortion clinics and providers" (*USA v. Stephen Jordi* 2003, 6–7).

Communication with the Audience

Historically, terrorists have followed attacks by issuing a communiqué—often through the media—that lets the "audience" know why the attack occurred. Indeed, the very rationale for committing a violent act is to gain public attention (Hoffman 1998). The media was used because it was the best way to reach a large audience. Having access to the Internet allowed terrorists to bypass the media to speak directly to the audience. The takeover of the Japanese embassy in Peru in 1996 by the **Túpac Amaru Revolutionary Movement** (MRTA) pro-vides the first know example of a terrorist group using the Internet to communicate with the people of the world. Over the course of the four-month long crisis, MRTA hostage-takers provided statements and electronic videos on their now defunct Web site: http://burn.ucsd.edu/~ats/mrta.htm (the Web site was retrieved at http://www.nadir.org/nadir/initiativ/mrta/ on May 24, 2007). Tellingly, the text of the communiqués was presented English (as well as in Spanish and Japanese), showing the importance they placed on reaching out to the western world. The Web site also included Italian, Turkish, and Serbian language versions. Clearly, the terrorist group seeks to communicate with a wider audience than those with whom it bat-tles.

Federal authorities have come to realize that one threat of the Internet is its ability to allow a large number of people who would never have otherwise met to be able to communi-cate with each other. Thus, an individual in Idaho who hates African-Americans can create a home page to exhibit this hatred. People living in Florida can visit this home page and read the material placed there. If the Florida readers are impressed with the page, they can add the Idaho Web address to a list of "hot" links making Idaho page now available to people who visit the Florida page. The advent of networking sites has made this kind of interaction much more possible. The importance of the Web for this capacity is exhibited in the following quote found on a right-wing Web site:

> The net is the most powerful free speech forum that has ever existed. Support all efforts to keep it uncensored. Wild claims of your children being carted away by Internet pedophiles, etc. are meant to frighten the unaware. The Internet terrifies the powers that be because they are no longer in control of the information that you can receive. Through the Internet one can set up a Web page and state his opinion to the world, literally. Everyone in the world who is interested in that subject can then access that page and read that opinion for themselves. How unbelievable! We no longer have to wait to be told what someone or some group is saying. We can now get it straight from the horse's mouth. Well, expect the world control freaks to move to crush this situation. (http://207.15.176.3:80/cause/, retrieved on February 16, 1997)

Some terrorist groups use the Internet as a method of communicating with the group as a whole. The Republic of Texas was a secessionist group that planned to re-claim Texas from the federal government and overturn the de facto (State) government. During the late 1990s, they held their meetings in small cities all over Texas. Because many members were not able to attend every meeting, the meeting minutes were published on the group's Web page. The group also published all of its press releases (communiqués) on the Web site and an interpretation of previous events that involved the group. Even more amazing, the Web site published a list of the officers of the Republic, making it very easy for the government to know who to watch. The Web site was also used for emergency purposes at times. When federal agents arrested an "ambassador," for example, an urgent alert was placed on the Web asking citizens to call the local, state, and federal law enforcement agencies demanding his release. Their original extensive Web site is no longer available electronically but one faction of the group has created a similar Web site that continues to list members of the "provisional government" and meeting minutes—although it takes a while to find it if you don't know where to look (http://www.texaspublicrecord.net/gov/index.shtml, retrieved on June 15, 2007). The new site includes the 2003 Declaration of Independence signed by more than 40 signatories.

Further efforts at the coalescing of like-minded individuals and groups have evolved into a page with a more social than political agenda. A "pro-white" record label called Resistance Records (http://www.resistance.com/, retrieved on May 24, 2007) produces and sells music suitable for those with pro-Aryan attitudes. At one time, a white power group named Alpha hosted a Web page (http://www.alpha.org, retrieved on November 21, 1996) that included "Aryan Dating Page." The "lifestyles" Web site is no longer available but it allowed men and women (white and nongay) to meet over the Internet via the posting of pictures contact information for available and interested men and women. A similar Web site with a focus on "white dating" (http://www.allwhitedating.com/, retrieved April 14, 2003) was created in 2002. Aryans who are looking to find compatible love interests can to the **Stormfront** Web site (http://www.stormfront.org/forum/, retrieved June 1, 2007), which evolved from an ordinary Web site to a forum host site. Along with a "white singles" forum, people can log in to running discussions on subjects like poetry, religion, health and fitness, and white nationalism. In addition, the Web site provides access to "Stormfront Radio," a white supremacist Internet radio station that plays right-wing oriented music and provides social commentary.

e-ffiti

The nature of Internet use is that happening upon one or another Web page is usually not a planned event but more a matter of happenstance. Indeed, one of the problems with performing research about terrorists on the Internet is that it is easy to get distracted by following interesting links. But anyone who has wasted a few hours surfing the Web is familiar with the results—it is not difficult to end up far removed from where you ever intended to go. This feature of the Internet works to the advantage of terrorist groups who want to inflict harm on others through the written word or "art" work. This is especially relevant for hate groups that are focused on race or ethnicity. As a result, an African-American who happened upon the Alpha (http://www.alpha.org, retrieved on December 12, 1996) home page would understandably be shocked and offended by reading the following messages scrolling at the bottom of the screen: "African American, what a joke, why not just call them what they are? N*****S! America for Whites, Africa for blacks, ship those apes back to those trees, send them n*****s back! Ring that bell, jump for joy, White mans day is here, no more n****r civil rights, led by n****r queers! Who needs N*****s?"

Likewise, a more recent Web site called Tightrope (http://www.tightrope.cc/forum/, retrieved June 12, 2006), which is highlighted by an image of a raised fist holding a noose, has a page dedicated to jokes aimed at African Americans and Jews and provides a set of racist songs available for download in mp3 format. In a similar vein, the several Aryan Web pages, such as White Revolution—Nebraska (http://www.whiterevolution-ne.org/, retrieved June 1, 2007) proclaim allegiance to a sacred 14-word code of honor ("We Must Secure The Existence Of Our People And A Future For White Children!") that is portrayed prominently on most of the pages. T-shirts, posters, and bumper stickers showing the **14 words** in different formats are readily available over the Web.

But race is not the only feature attacked on the Web by Aryans. The White Aryan Resistance Web page (http://www.resist.com/, retrieved June 1, 2007) exhibits cartoons and a joke book attacking both gays and Jews. The use of stereotypic humor is a common phenomenon appearing on many of these sites. The Web site also provides contact information for "prisoners of war," white power supporters who are currently serving time in federal prison.

Support Activities

Terrorist groups are normally self-sufficient (with the exception of state-sponsored terrorists) with the result being that they have to raise money in order to sustain their activities. One way many groups do this is by engaging in "preincident activities" such as bank robbery and fraud (Smith and Damphousse 1996). The Internet provides a legal way to seek external funding. The Internet's reach into millions of homes and the ease of collecting money using credit card services like PayPal makes such fund raising relatively easy (and much safer). Thus, many terrorist Web sites include the option of buying merchandise such as books and T-shirts while other sites simply plea for donations to support the efforts. The pleas used on these pages are usually addressed to "fellow travelers" who might be motivated to aid the group's need to replace failing equipment or to sustain the membership. The request for funds is often associated with a desire to provide a better service to the user. In 1996, for example, an author left the following message for his followers: "Many people have told us how they cannot access our Web site much of the time, this is due to lack of funding. Our Web site is run on an old and slow machine that allows only two people at any time to be on the site. The site is now receiving between 50 and 100 users per day with not a second of idle time. That 50–100 per day can be improved to hundreds of white people per day worldwide accessing great writings of white leaders and learning more about the movement for White Power. We must upgrade and improve our equipment a.s.a.p. Every white man or woman who can not access our site may not return to try again becoming a lost soul" (http://www.alpha.org, retrieved December 12, 1996).

Other times, the efforts at fund raising display the personal hardships endured by the host that are the result of efforts to be a "good citizen." Thus, the editor of *The Watchman* newsletter wrote in desperation "Your prayers and financial support are urgently needed at this time. I am currently under tremendous attack and the threat of criminal prosecution. In the last six months I have lost my disability allowance, had many of my belongings stolen by the feds and am being driven from my home of 18 years. I have six children and staggering legal bills. Without a miracle, I am going under, and if the feds have their way, to prison. I have given my life to this struggle on faith, without regard to the consequences to my self or even my family. Our future is in God's hands and they are attached to your forearms. We are unable to cash checks without using a bank account that could be seized at any time by the feds. Postal Money Orders made out to XXXX are best and they protect your privacy as well.

Please help us to survive and continue the struggle for His Kingdom at The watchman (http://www2.stormfront.org/watchman/, retrieved August 15, 1996)."

This plea for funds on the Internet is not limited to American terrorists. **The Shining Path**—a Peruvian terror group—regularly posts messages to its Web site urging supporters to export the revolutionary message by hawking "revolutionary" products like T-shirts, posters, and videos (http://www.csrp.org/index.html, retrieved May 12, 2007).

The Web as Weapon

The possibility that the Web will be used to conduct acts of terrorism has increased dramatically since its inception. Indeed, since corporations who are the victims of computer crime are wont to dealt with virtual invasions discretely, it is likely that there is much more cyber terrorism occurring than currently known. There are three possible threats from protest groups using the Internet to perform acts of terrorism. First, protest groups can gain access to other home pages and either deface them, or change them to provide alternative information. There are already several examples of this kind of "**hactivism**" occurring. Perhaps one of the most infamous early incidents was the defacing of the home page of the Central Intelligence Agency (CIA). On September 18, 1996, a Swedish protest group called "Power Through Resistance" vandalized the home page of the CIA. The group changed the title of the page to the "Central Stupidity Agency," and added several links to nongovernment home pages such as Playboy. Earlier, hackers had renamed the Department of Justice home page the "Department of Injustice." Although no sensitive material was available to the attackers, the fact that individuals on another continent were able to sabotage these sensitive and heavily protected Web sites is evidence of the potential for remote activity.

A second way that protest groups can use the Web as a weapon is through the impairment (or at least threatened impairment) of vital government or corporate communication processes. It is not difficult, for example, to imagine a protest group "hacking" its way into the computer system that controls the power supply to an area and then threatening to cut off power unless some demand is carried out. In fact, such a problem has occurred in Japan where groups attacked the commuter train computer system (Devost, Houghton, and Pollard 1996). The threat is even greater if one considers the impact such a threat would have on the operation of a nuclear facility. Related, protest groups could directly access financial institutions and perform account transfers, resulting in the theft of huge amount of funds. The relative ease of impairment of other computers is evidenced by the large growth in computer viruses (which "infect" computer with programs designed to destroy software or data) in the past several years. As society infrastructure becomes increasingly dependent on computers and the importance of remote access (which provides the necessary portal for terrorists), the chances of such an attack increase dramatically.

Finally, there is increasing concern among governments that information housed on their computers may be accessed by unauthorized individuals. In 1994, a British youth was arrested for suspicion in a case where a military base in New York was impaired for over a month (Wilson 1996). There are two potential problems here. First, opposition groups may more easily gain intelligence information. Second, and perhaps more deadly, false or illegitimate commands could be delivered to military forces, ordering them to unwittingly perform some terrorist act.

The fears associated with these types of virtual attacks have created a new industry of software and hardware solutions including virus protections and firewalls that are designed to protect vulnerable and important computer systems from attack. These programs are designed to only allow legitimate users access to the information housed on corporate or agency computers (Alpert 1996). In general, firewalls are designed to inspect each attempt to access a computer network. Those users who attempt to get into the network without authorization are rejected.

Virtual Reconnaissance

It is not just the publication of Web pages and the ease of communication that makes the Internet so useful to terrorists. The Internet has spawned increasingly complex sets of tools that can be used to aid terrorist efforts. These tools can aid terrorist efforts at reconnaissance—where they seek detailed information about selected targets. For example, there is increasing concern about the use of Google Earth by terrorist groups. The free and easy-to-use program provides a "bird's eye view" of potential terrorism targets by simply typing in an address or the name of a location. It has been well documented that the group that was planning the May 2007 attack on JFK Airport had used Google Earth to obtain detailed information on the airport and the location of the jet fuel tanks. Ordinary street maps would have provided some limited information but the aerial photos available from Google Earth provided the group with unparalleled information—the kind of data once only available to technologically advanced governments. To counter this tool, governments have asked Google Earth to "blur" the photos of sensitive areas, but a recent search by the author provided startlingly clear and detailed photos of airports, U.S. military bases in Europe, and symbolically important national monuments.

In a similar vein, the advent of the Internet created a huge information vacuum that governments seemed overly willing to fill. In the early days of the Internet, it was common for local, state, and federal governments to feel compelled to "put it on the Web." Thus, many documents and much information that should never have been made public were put on the Internet. This information included electrical grids, maps of water supplies, emergency response plans. As a witness testified before the Little Hoover Commission on California State Government Organization and Economy one month after the 9/11 attacks, "One cautionary note, however, is that we used available sources of information to identify and characterize the critical physical infrastructure of the state. The same information we accessed is available to individuals and terrorist groups, who may use it as a road map for designing cyber disruptions, decide which critical systems to target, and when to target them" (Riley 2001, 5). It was only after vulnerability studies were conducted after the 9/11 attacks that governments became aware of how susceptible they were to having their own information used against them. As a result of a careful reexamination of the public's right to know and the need for security, governments are working on removing much of this vulnerable information from the Internet.

Terrorism Strategy Depository (e-libris)

Terrorists often learn from other terrorists and it is not uncommon for raids on terrorist compounds to uncover copies of terrorist "manuals" and other material that can either encourage the terrorist action or show how to perform certain acts. These books range from "how to" books that describe how to build a bomb to books on successful terrorism strategies. Examples include *Military Studies in the Jihad Against the Tyrants* (allegedly used by members of Al-Qaeda), the *Mini-manual of the Urban Guerrilla* by (Marighella 1970), *The Anarchist's Cookbook* (Powell 1970) and **The Turner Diaries** (MacDonald 1978) by William Luther Pierce. Pierce's book provided the framework for McVeigh's bombing of the Murrah Building in Oklahoma City. Each of these books and others like them are widely available on the Internet. The latter three are likewise available for purchase at the Amazon bookstore Web site. Interestingly, Powell has posted a statement on several Web sites (including Amazon.com) disavowing the book he wrote when he was a teenager. Since he does not own the copyright, he has no power to stop its continued publication. Even if he did, it is very likely that his work (and the copycats it spawned) would continue to be available on the Internet indefinitely.

Coordination of Direct Action

Like all tactical units, communication among participants and between leaders and participants is vital. The ability to communicate by e-mail and, more recently, by instant messaging, greatly enhances terrorist operations. The problem for terrorists, of course, is the difficulty in keeping "private" anything that is sent by e-mail. Thus, terrorists are increasingly using **encryption** technologies that can keep the message safe from prying eyes. During the 2004 trial of Abdelghani Mzoudi, who was on trial in Germany for his alleged role in the 9/11 attacks, included testimony from a former Iranian intelligence operative who stated that Mzoudi had been trained to encrypt e-mail messages in Iran (Boston 2004).

Encryption software uses a mathematical algorithm that can scramble and then unscramble a message that is sent from one person to another through the use of a "key." If an e-mail were intercepted, it would be meaningless without the ability to decode it. The ability to communicate secretly via e-mail is a major advance for terrorist groups and a cause for great concern. In the days following 9/11, for example, policymakers called for restrictions on encrypting software once law enforcement agencies reported the use of the software by the attackers. Suggested changes included the outright ban of encryption software availability for the public to the requirement that software companies create a "back door" into the encryption code so that the government can better monitor communication between suspected terrorists (Knight 2001).

Industry experts have suggested, however, that there is no way of stopping the use of encryption software, especially since it would be available from Web sites outside of the US. In addition, experts point to the greater likelihood that terrorists would use **steganography** (i.e., "covered writing") where messages are hidden in plain sight. Ancient examples of steganography include tattooing information on a bald head that is eventually covered by the growth of hair. The microdot technology invented during the cold war also allowed information to be "hidden" on the period at the end of a typed sentence. In the electronic world, steganography takes advantage of how digital pictures are created. Briefly, a digital picture is composed of a series of pixels that represent one of the three primary colors. The more pixels in a picture, the sharper the image and the bigger the file size. Steganographic encoding software embeds the message within these pixels and a user who receives the picture (and a decoding key), can extract the image or the message from the digital photo. Steganography programs like S-tools for Windows can also use sound files (*.wav) to hide information (Johnson and Jajodia 1998).

DISCUSSION: TERRORISM IN A FLAT WORLD

Last month, I was riding in a van in central Oklahoma going 70 miles per hour when I checked my e-mail on my cell phone. I noticed that I had received an e-mail from my boss who was waiting out a rainstorm at an archeological dig in northern Italy. I replied to his request and then sent an instant message to my assistant asking her to handle the problem. Later that same day, when we got lost on the way to an event, I accessed Google Maps from my cell phone to find our way. Later, I e-mailed a picture of the event to my daughter. This "flattening of the world" has changed our lives forever (Friedman 2005). Instant access to the Internet and all that it provides also makes the task of a terrorist even easier. All of the things that the Internet provides for terrorists are now available almost anywhere in the world at almost any time—something that was unthinkable to most people just 15 years ago.

The World Wide Web is being used by protest groups in America (and around the world) to deliver their message in ways never dreamed possible before 1980. Access to the Web has allowed protest groups to proselytize more individuals than ever before. They have also become better able to communicate with each other (for political and social ends). They are also in a better position to attract funding from people with whom they would not otherwise have contact. The most serious threat, however, appears be the potential of actual terrorist acts committed via the Web. The presence of protest groups on the Web has spawned a new aspect of terrorism/counter-terrorism previously never imagined—the explosion of "citizen counter-terrorists."

Just as the Internet benefits terrorist groups, it can also increase their vulnerability. Using the Internet gives the government an opportunity to monitor their activities. One recent example occurred in China, where search engine giant Yahoo provided the e-mail addresses of political dissidents to the Chinese government (Sinn 2007). Indeed, the Chinese government has required Internet companies doing business in the country to participate in self-censorship or have censored the Web site unilaterally (Zittrain and Edilman 2003). This has resulted recently in the Internet photo company Flickr being blocked in China, apparently because photos offensive to the Chinese government were linked to the site (Perez 2007).

Other nonstate actors also use the Internet to interrupt terrorist behavior. We usually consider "counter-terrorists" as being the purview of government agencies, the military, and special terrorism task forces. The mission of these organizations is to gather intelligence about potential terrorist groups and to inform the public, when necessary, about their threat. Some social/civic groups and private individuals, however, have created Web sites whose primary function is to publicize the operations of protest type groups. The "Klanwatch" project operated by the **Southern Poverty Law Center** and the **Anti-Defamation League**, for example, focuses upon making available information about the **Ku Klux Klan** and other anti-Semitic activities. These two organizations have continued these activities in cyberspace, operating home pages that describe activities of terrorist groups. Also available at these home pages are opportunities to purchase literature describing the history of the militia groups and other terrorist groups.

What is unique with the advent of the Internet, however, is the proliferation of Web sites that have been created by private citizens who have made it their mission to document both pro- and anti-terrorism pages. A common example of civilian counter-terrorism on the Internet is the "Police Officer's Internet Directory" home page, hosted by a Boston police officer. This page provided little independent commentary, but included a large number of links to pro- and antiprotest groups throughout the early 1990s (e.g., "Hate Groups, Terrorists, & Radicals"). The commentary supplied by the host was limited to suggesting that the sites provided on the page were offensive and may be unpleasant to view. By the mid-2000s, the Web site had expanded beyond just focusing on terrorist and became a key source about all things police-related—including counter-terrorism (see http://www.officer.com, retrieved November 12, 2006).

One of the most progressive of these early citizen counter-terrorism pages was called "The **Militia Watchdog**," which grew out of a Usenet FAQ (frequently asked questions). In this location, the host (an historian who is an expert on the history of the militia in America) tracked news about terrorist groups and provides links to, and commentary about, the home pages of various protest groups. The page provided "patriot profiles" (thick descriptions of contemporary militia groups), essays (e.g., description of gun show activities), collection of news articles about terrorists (e.g., the militia follies), and special reports about events such as federal elections. By 2000, the author became an employee for the anti-defamation league and the Militia Watchdog page "died," although the archives are still available (http://www.adl. org/mwd/default.asp, retrieved on August 15, 2001).

Perhaps the most interesting development along these lines is the formation of counter-counter-terrorism on the Web. At least two home pages have been created that challenge the information provided on the Militia Watchdog and other similar pages: "[The author of the Militia Watchdog] is feeding the paranoia of the mass population, fueled by the news media, that the patriots and militias are somehow planning to commit terrorist acts. [He] and his traitorous counterparts in the government and in the media have yet to prove there to be a link between the militias and the **Oklahoma City Bombing**. Having recently re-viewed footage of the initial 2 hours following the bombing in Oklahoma City, simple things I noticed REFUTE the claims to a 4,800 pound truck bomb full of cow manure! Rather, the basic evidence supports an INTERNAL blast blowing out from INSIDE the building" (http://www.execpc.com/ ~warning/dogpound.html, retrieved on February 20, 1996).

Increasingly sophisticated tools to monitor and investigate terrorists on the Internet are currently being developed. Researchers at the University of Arizona, for example, have developed an algorithm that will allow investigators to monitor Internet chat rooms and be able to determine who is participating in the conversation (Zhou et al. 2005). The software creates a visual pattern that distinguishes among users. The algorithm is based on word pattern usage. Since people are habitual, when we write, we tend to use certain combinations of words in ways that are different from other people. The software is designed to conduct **authorship analysis**, allowing the users to determine the word-use patterns and then recognize when they are used. Thus, the text-based messages that terrorists use to communicate with each other create virtual "fingerprints" that allow investigators to know who is participating. Even more, the researchers are developing virtual "spiders" that can crawl throughout the World Wide Web looking for the identified terrorists as they move from chat room to chat room.

Clearly, the use of the Internet by terrorist groups and those who oppose them is a phenomenon that bears continued observation. The impact of the citizen counter-terrorists on the propaganda and fundraising efforts of the protest groups is uncertain at this time. The fact that counter-counter-terrorism home pages have begun to spring up is evidence that the effect is beginning to be noticed.

The creation of the Internet has been referred to as the beginning of the information revolution. How fitting, then, that the political revolutionaries of our time were among the first to make the most creative use of it. What is interesting is that the term "leaderless resistance" may take on a new meaning in this age of generating information and then making it available to the world. Serious implications await discussion concerning the liability of those whose home pages (filled with anger, hate, and protest) become the catalyst for some violent action by an unknown actor. The Oklahoma City bombing, for example, has been compared to activities described in *The Turner Diaries* (MacDonald 1978), which is now also available on the Web. It remains to be seen if the federal government will begin prosecuting individuals who foment rage while attempting to shield themselves via the leaderless resistance strategy.

In essence, individuals who operate home pages perform essentially one-way communication with other people. The information provided on the Internet is of a special case. Much like leaflets of old, the information is distributed to individuals only indirectly. That is, propaganda about the excesses of government—or some other threat—is distributed rather anonymously, where the reader and the writer may never meet. The authors of the information in the home page can claim that they did not intend for readers to take any specific action. It is certain that the Internet will continue to play an important role in how terrorist groups operate—just as the Internet has become so essential to the rest of the world.

KEY TERMS

14 words	Encryption	Stormfront
Abortion	Hactivism	Terrorist
Anti-Defamation League	Ku Klux Klan	The Shining Path
Army of God	Leaderless resistance	*The Turner Diaries*
Aryan	Militia Watchdog	Timothy McVeigh
Authorship analysis	Newsgroups	Túpac Amaru
Bulletin boards	Oklahoma City bombing	Revolutionary
Chat rooms	Propaganda	Movement
Communiqué	Republic of Texas	Waco Holocaust
Counter-terrorism	Southern Poverty Law	Electronic Museum
Cyber terrorism	Center	
Earth Liberation Front	Steganography	

REFERENCES

Alpert, B. November 1996. On fire: Fear of hackers should keep the computer firewall market smokin'. *Barrons*: 25.

Baez, A. 2006. Anti-abortion photos spark rally, debate: National organization sets up graphic panels depicting aborted fetuses in Arbor. Retrieved May 25, 2006, from http://www.dailynexus.com/article.php?a=11829

Barkun, M. 1994. *Religion and the Racist Right: The Origins of the Christian Identify Movement.* Chapel Hill, NC: University of North Carolina Press.

Barkun, M. 1997. Changing U.S. domestic threats. Presentation to the International Conference on Aviation Safety and Security, Washington, DC.

Beam, L. 1992. Leaderless resistance. Presentation made to leaders of the extreme right, October 23, 1992, Estes Park, Colorado. First published in *Seditionist* 12: 1–3.

Boston, W. 2004. Witness-box weirdness. Retrieved February 8, 2004, from http://www.time.com/time/magazine/article/0,9171,901040209-586265,00.html

Collin, B. 1996. The future of cyberterrorism: Where the physical and virtual worlds converge. Retrieved May 2, 1997, from 11th Annual International Symposium on Criminal Justice Issues Web site: http://www.acsp.uic.edu/OICJ/CONFS

Damphousse, K. R., and B. L. Smith. 1997. "The Internet: A terrorist medium for the 21st century." In *The Future of Terrorism: Violence in the New Millennium,* edited by H. Kushner, 208–24. Thousand Oaks, CA: Sage.

Devost, M., B. Houghton, and N. Pollard. 1996. Information terrorism: Can you trust your toaster? Retrieved May 2, 1997, from The Terrorism Research Center Web site: http://www.Terrorism.com

Ellul, J. 1969. *Propaganda: The Formation of Men's Attitudes.* New York: Alfred A. Knopf.

Friedman, T. L. 2005. *The World Is Flat: A Brief History of the Twenty-First Century.* New York: Farrar, Straus and Giroux.

Hacker, F. J. 1976. *Crusaders, Criminals, Crazies: Terror and Terrorism in Our Time.* New York: W. W. Norton.

Herman, E. 1982. *The Real Terror Network: Terrorism in Fact and Propaganda.* Boston: South End Press.

Hoffman, B. 1998. *Inside Terrorism.* New York: Columbia University Press.

Johnson, N. F., and S. Jajodia. February 1998. Steganography: Seeing the unseen. *IEEE Computer:* 26–34.

Knight, W. 2001. Controlling encryption will not stop terrorists. Retrieved September 30, 2001, from http://www.newscientist.com/article.ns?id=dn1309

Lofland, J. 1996. *Social Movement Organizations: Guide to Research on Insurgent Realities.* New York: Aldine de Gruyter.

Macavinta, C. 1999. Abortion "hit list" slammed in court. Retrieved February 2, 1999, from CNET News Web site: http://news.com.com/2100-1023-221054.html

MacDonald, A. 1978. *The Turner Diaries.* Arlington, VA: National Alliance.

Marighella, C. 1970. *Mini-Manual of the Urban Guerrilla.* NP: New World Liberation Front.

Marx, K., and F. Engels. 1848/1964. *The Communist Manifesto,* translated by P. M. Sweezy. New York: Monthly Review Press.

Perez, J. C. 2007. Flickr photos being blocked in China: Is Yahoo's photo tool being censored? Retrieved June 12, 2007, from http://www.pcadvisor.co.uk/news/index.cfm?newsid=9683

Powell, W. 1970. *The Anarchist's Cookbook.* New York: Lyle Stuart, Inc.

Rapoport, D. 1996. Editorial: The media and terrorism—Implications of the Unabomber case. *Terrorism and Political Violence* 8 (1): i–ix.

Riley, K. J. 2001. Statement of Jack Riley before the Little Hoover Commission. Retrieved December 1, 2002, from Little Hoover Commission on California State Government Organization and Economy Web Site: http://www.lhc.ca.gov/lhcdir/disaster/RileyOct01.pdf

Ross, J. I. 2006. *Political Terrorism: An Interdisciplinary Approach.* New York: Peter Lang.

Rubenstein, R. 1987. *Alchemists of Revolution: Terrorism in the Modern World.* New York: Basic Books.

Rubenstein, R. 1989. "Rebellion in America: The fire next time." In *Violence in America: Protest, Rebellion and Reform,* edited by T. R. Gurr, 167–82. Newbury Park, CA: Sage.

Said, E. 1979. *The Question of Palestine.* New York: First Vintage Books.

Salus, P. 1995. *Casting the Net: From ARPAnet to Internet and Beyond.* Reading, MA: Addison-Wesley Professional.

Schmid, A., and J. Graaf. 1982. *Violence as Communication: Insurgent Terrorism and the Western News Media.* Beverly Hills: Sage.

Sinn, D. 2007. Yahoo weighs in on free speech in China. Retrieved on June 12, 2007, from Associated Press Web site: http://www.ap.org

Smith, B., and K. Damphousse. 1996. Punishing political offenders: The effect of political motive on federal sentencing decisions. *Criminology* 34 (3): 289–321.

Smith, B., and K. Damphousse. 1998. Terrorism, politics, and punishment: A test of structural contextual theory and the liberation hypothesis. *Criminology* 36 (1): 67–92.

Smith, B., K. Damphousse, and P. Roberts. 2006. Final technical report: Pre-incident indicators of terrorist incident: The identification of behavioral, geographic, and temporal patterns of preparatory conduct. Washington, DC: Office of Justice Programs.

Stafford, D. 1978. *From Anarchism to Reformism*. Toronto: University of Toronto Press.

USA v. Stephen Jordi. 2003. Criminal complaint in case number 03-CR-60259.

Victor, J. 1993. *Satanic Panic: The Creation of a Contemporary Legend*. Chicago: Open Court.

von Clausewitz, C. 1832/1976. *On War*. Princeton, NJ: Princeton University Press.

Weiman, G. 2005. How modern terrorism uses the Internet. *Journal of International Security Affairs* 8: 1–10.

Wilson, D. 1996. 40 million potential spies. Retrieved on May 23, 1996, from http://www.cnn.com/US/9605/23/internet.spying/index.html

Wright, J. 1990. *Terrorist Propaganda: The Red Army Faction and the Provisional IRA, 1968–86*. New York: St. Martin's Press.

Zhou, Y., E. Reid, J. Qin, H. Chen, and G. Lai. 2005. US domestic extremist groups on the Web: Link and Content Analysis. *IEEE Intelligent Systems* 20 (5): 44–51.

Zittrain, J., and B. Edilman. 2003. Internet filtering in China. *Internet Computing* 7 (2): 70–77.

Chapter 30

Cyber Terrorism: Problems, Perspectives, and Prescription

P. Madhava Soma Sundaram, K. Jaishankar
Manonmaniam Sundaranar University, India

Dr. P. Madhava Soma Sundaram (Madhavan) is the reader and head of the Department of Criminology and Criminal Justice, Manonmaniam Sundaranar University, Tirunelveli, India. Madhavan holds masters' degree in criminology and Ph.D. in criminology from the University of Madras. His doctorate work is in the field of victimology, focusing on fear of crime. Madhavan has authored one book and several articles/papers, chapters in books, editorials, book reviews, project reports, monographs in journals and magazines. He is the founding editor-in-chief of "Crime and Justice Perspective"—the official organ of the Criminal Justice Forum (CJF), India, and the founding editor of the *International Journal of Criminal Justice Sciences*. He serves in the International Editorial Advisory Board of the *International Journal of Cyber Criminology*. In recognition of his contribution in the growth of criminology in India, Madhavan was conferred the title of Fellow of Indian Society of Criminology (FISC) by the Indian Society of Criminology (ISC) for 2001. His areas of specialization are juvenile justice, victimology, child protection, and social defense.

Dr. K. Jaishankar is a lecturer in the Department of Criminology and Criminal Justice, Manonmaniam Sundaranar University, Tirunelveli, India. He is the founding editor-in-chief of the *International Journal of Cyber Criminology* and the founding editor of "Crime and Justice Perspective"—the official organ of the Criminal Justice Forum (CJF), India, and the founding managing editor of the *International Journal of Criminal Justice Sciences*. He serves in the International Editorial boards of *Journal of Social Change* (USA), *Electronic Journal of Sociology* (Canada), *Crime, Punishment and Law: An International Journal* (USA), *Journal of Physical Security* (USA), and *Graduate Journal of Social Science* (UK). He is the national focal point for India for the International Police Executive Symposium's working paper series and expert of world police database at www.coginta.com. He is a co-investigator of the International Project on Cyber bullying funded by SSHRC, Canada involving eight countries, along with the principal investigator Dr. Shaheen Shariff, McGill University. He is a pioneer in developing the new field, cyber criminology, and is the proponent of "space transition theory," which gives an explanation for the criminal behavior in cyberspace. He is a recognized expert in the field of cyber criminology and invited by various universities in U.S. to deliver lectures on his space transition theory of cyber crimes. His areas of academic competence are cyber criminology, crime mapping, GIS, communal violence, victimology, policing, and crime prevention.

Abstract

The Internet has brought revolutionary changes to the world. One of the greatest changes has been the growing connectivity between all "corners" of the world via the Internet. In many ways, this has been a boon to humanity. However, there is also a dark side to this achievement.

A prime example of this negative side has been the rapid spread of computer viruses. The world becomes more dependent on the myriad activities carried out via the Internet, and a potential exists for much more serious consequences of this dark side of the Internet, including events related to cyber terrorism. This chapter examines cyber terrorism, one of the major negative consequences of the Internet. It also examines the potential impact of cyber terrorism, its possible methods, its prevention, and control.

INTRODUCTION

Indeed, the world is undergoing a second industrial revolution. Information technology today touches every aspect of life, irrespective of one's location on the globe. Daily activities are affected in form, content, and time by the computer. Businesses, governments, and individuals all receive the many benefits of this information revolution. While providing tangible benefits in time and money, the computer has also had an impact on everyday life, as computerized routines replace mundane human tasks. More and more businesses, industries, economies, hospitals, and governments are becoming dependent on computers. Computers are not only used extensively to aid in the performance of industrial and economic functions in society, but are also to perform many functions upon which human life itself depends. Computers are also used to store confidential data of a political, social, economic, or personal nature. They assist in the improvement of economies and of living conditions in all countries. Communications, organizational functioning, and scientific and industrial progress have developed so rapidly with computer technology that our way of living has irreversibly changed.

Defining Cyber Crimes

Defined broadly, the term "computer crime" could reasonably include a wide variety of criminal offenses, activities, or issues. The potential scope is even larger when using the frequent companion or substitute term "computer-related crime." Given the pervasiveness of computers in everyday life, even in the lives of those who have never operated a computer, there is almost always some nontrivial nexus between crime and computers. This is especially the case when factoring in the extensive use of computers in evidence, investigations, and court administration (Lewis 2002; Gregory 2000; Post 2000; Sprols and Byars 1998).

Nevertheless, something far less than such a panoramic view of "computer crime" comes to mind, when the term is used. Moreover, as the phrase is evolving into a term of art, the narrower set of meanings has become more prevalent in the literature. One noteworthy example is the FBI National Computer Crime Squad's (NCCS) (ISTS 2001) list of crime categories it investigates: Intrusions of the Public Switched Network (the telephone company)

- major computer network intrusions
- network integrity violations
- privacy violations
- industrial espionage
- pirated computer software
- other crimes where the computer is a major factor in committing the criminal offense

What is Cyber Terrorism?

A spectrum of criminal acts may be conducted via the Internet, ranging from cyber espionage and **information warfare** carried out by foreign governments to **cyber crimes** carried out by smaller groups or individuals. Although **cyber terrorism** may be carried in conjunction with cyber espionage or cyber crime, it is considered distinct from the two entities. Cyber terrorism combines both cyberspace and terrorism and it is the use of intentional violence against computer systems that support or protect the health of human communities or the information stored in these systems. Unlike cyber espionage, virtually all instances of cyber terrorism to date have been carried out by organized factions unconnected to world governments. Often, cyber terrorism is aimed at coercing a population or its government to accede to certain political or social objectives. In addition, cyber terrorism usually is more extensive and destructive than is simple cyber crime. As a result, cyber terrorism either harms the health of human communities or generates a fear of this harm.

Cyber terrorism still is in its infancy. Although there have been numerous cyber-terrorist events, there have been no large-scale incidents affecting large geographic areas. Despite the challenge of producing damage of this magnitude, the potential for large-scale, cyber-terrorist events increases as the Internet continues to expand. Furthermore, cyber terrorism may be used to:

1. help plan other terrorist activities
2. soften a target prior to a physical attack
3. generate more fear and confusion concurrent with other terrorist acts

Defining Cyber Terrorism

If one views cyber terrorism in a narrow sense, it essentially becomes an extension of traditional terrorism into the realm of information technology. Although there is no internationally agreed-upon definition of traditional terrorism *per se*, central characteristics include politically or otherwise motivated use of violence directed at civilians, by a group or individual, in order to influence public perceptions (Conway 2002). Terrorism in this sense can and does apply to the cyberworld. There is clearly the potential for individuals with political and/or religious motivations to make use of information technology **tools** to abuse, tamper, or corrupt information technology–based data or control processes, which could result in severe injury or death.

It is first important to note that no single definition of the term "terrorism" has yet gained universal acceptance. Additionally, no single definition for the term "cyber terrorism" has been universally accepted as well. In addition, labeling a computer attack as "cyber terrorism" is problematic, because it is often difficult to determine the intent, identity, or the political motivations of a computer attacker with any certainty until long after the event has occurred (Wilson 2003).

There are some emerging concepts, however, that may be combined to help build a working definition for cyber terrorism. Internationally, terrorism is defined as premeditated, politically motivated violence perpetrated against noncombatant targets by subnational groups or clandestine agents, usually intended to influence an audience. The term "international terrorism" means terrorism involving citizens or the territory of more than one country. The term "terrorist group" means any group practicing, or that has significant subgroups that practice, international terrorism[1] (U.S. Department of State 2003).

Caruso (2002) has provided an official definition for cyber terrorism in the United States. "Cyberterrorism—meaning the use of cybertools to shut down critical national infrastructures (such as energy, transportation, or government operations) for the purpose of coercing or intimidating a government or civilian population—is clearly an emerging threat." Denning's (1999) definition of cyber terrorism is slightly more elaborate:

> Cyberterrorism refers to unlawful attacks and threats of attacks against computers, networks and the information stored therein when done to intimidate or coerce a government or its people in furtherance of political or social objectives. Further, to qualify as cyberterrorism, an attack should result in violence against persons or property, or at least cause enough harm to generate fear. Attacks that lead to death or bodily injury, explosions, or severe economic loss would be examples. Serious attacks against critical infrastructures could be acts of cyberterrorism, depending on their impact. Attacks that disrupt nonessential services or that are mainly a costly nuisance would not.

Though these attacks occur in cyberspace, they still exhibit the four elements common to all acts of terrorism:

1. *Premeditated and not simply acts born of rage*: Cyber-terrorist attacks are premeditated and must be planned since they involve the development or acquisition of software to carry out an attack.

2. *Political and designed to impact political structure*: Computer terrorism is an act that is intended to corrupt or destroy a computer system (Galley 1996). Cyber terrorists are hackers with a political motivation; their attacks can impact political structure through this corruption and destruction.

3. *Targeted at civilians and civilian installations*: Cyber-terrorist attacks often target civilian interests. Denning (2000) defines cyber terrorism as an attack that results in violence against persons or property, or at least that causes enough harm to generate fear.

4. *Conducted by ad hoc groups as opposed to national armies*: Cyber terrorism is sometimes distinguished from cyber warfare or information warfare, which are computer-based attacks orchestrated by agents of a nation or state.

Cyber warfare is another term that is often used to describe various aspects of defending and attacking information and computer networks in cyberspace, as well as denying an adversary's ability to do the same (Hildreth 2001). Cyber warfare and information warfare employ information technology as an instrument of war to attack an adversary's critical computer systems (Hirsch, Kett, and Trefil 2002). Schwartau (1996) has proposed three categories for classifying information warfare: (1) personal information warfare, (2) corporate information warfare, and (3) global information warfare.

---

[1]The U.S. government has employed this definition of terrorism for statistical and analytical purposes since 1983.

Personal information warfare involves computer-based attacks on data about individuals. It may involve such things as disclosing or corrupting confidential personal information, such as those in medical or credit files. Corporate information warfare may involve industrial espionage or disseminating misinformation about competitors over the Internet. Global information warfare is aimed at a country's critical computer system infrastructure. The goal is to disrupt the country by disabling systems, such as energy, communication, or transportation.

Magnitude of the Problem

Some experts (Caruso 2001; Copeland 2000; Conway 2002; Hoopes 2005) have observed that terrorist organizations may begin to change their use of computer technology:

- Seized computers belonging to terrorist organizations indicate its members are now becoming familiar with hacker tools that are freely available over the Internet.

- As computer-literate youth increasingly join the ranks of terrorist groups, what may be considered radical today will become increasingly more mainstream in the future.

- A computer-literate leader may bring increased awareness of the advantages of an attack on information systems that are critical to an adversary, and will be more receptive to suggestions from other, newer computer-literate members.

- Once a new tactic has won widespread media attention, it likely will motivate other rival groups to follow along the new pathway.

- Potentially serious computer attacks may be first developed and tested by terrorist groups using small, isolated laboratory networks, thus avoiding detection of any preparation before launching a widespread attack.

Potential Cyber Terrorists

Cyber terrorism potentially can be carried out by anyone with access to the Internet. This includes anyone with a computer (and a modem), and as the technology becomes more sophisticated, may include anyone with cellular phones, wireless personal digital assistant (PDAs), and other wireless, handheld devices. The next cyber terrorist may be a world away or right next door as long as they have Internet access and the requisite knowledge. Accordingly, cyber terrorists may be domestic or foreign, with few limits on their actual location.

Cyber terrorists may act alone, as members of terrorist groups, or as proxies for terrorist groups. For example, in Hanover, Germany, in the 1980s, criminal hackers hired out their services to a terrorist group. Potential cyber terrorists also may include disgruntled current or former employees of a variety of private or public institutions. Cyber terrorists are likely to be very comfortable using computers and the Internet. In everyday life, people use the tools that they know and are comfortable with, including tools for criminal or destructive activities. As the Internet becomes an increasingly more central part of daily life, future terrorists increasingly will be more likely to use the Internet to plan and carry out terrorist activities. Why endanger one's life with explosives or weapons of mass destruction when you can sit in front of a computer and attack your enemy with almost total anonymity?

Today, most criminal hacking, or "cracking," is accomplished by one of three methods: (1) DoS (denial of service), in which the attacker overloads the server and shuts the system down; (2) actual destruction of information (although erasure of information usually is difficult to do effectively if their backup systems are in place); and (3) alteration of information, or "spoofing" (which is more difficult to safeguard against, but also can be mitigated with the use of backup systems).

Hackers are able to access computers via a number of routes, including poorly protected passwords, liberal access privileges, or dormant accounts of former employees. Hacking is facilitated by laxly enforced security policies (Copeland 2000). Currently, "parasites" are of great concern as a type of cyber attack. Parasites are small computer programs that remain in computer systems and slowly corrupt the system and its backups, thus, damaging the information in the system. These parasitic programs can cause systems to perform the wrong tasks. They also can spoof data, thus causing record alterations with troublesome effects.

Much of the basic knowledge needed to carry out acts of cyber terrorism is readily available through the Internet. Many hacking tools can be downloaded freely from the Internet through quick and easy searches. The beginner requires only knowledge of English and the capability to follow directions. However, in order to crack the better-protected computer systems ("hardened systems"), more extensive knowledge is required. This includes several years of experience with computer languages (e.g., C, C++, Perl, and Java); an understanding of general UNIX and NT systems administration, local-area network/wide-area network theory, remote access and common security protocols, and sufficient time would be required. Much of this advanced education and training is available over the Internet or may be obtained through readily available classes at public educational facilities (Galley 1996).

Cyber Terrorism: The Dynamics

Galley (1996) discusses three types of attacks against computer systems: (1) physical, (2) syntactic, and (3) semantic. A physical attack uses conventional weapons, such as bombs or fire. A syntactic attack uses virus-type software to disrupt or damage a computer system or network. A semantic attack is a more subtle approach. Its goal is to attack users' confidence by causing a computer system to produce errors and unpredictable results.

Syntactic attacks are sometimes grouped under the term "malicious software" or "malware." These attacks may include viruses, worms, and Trojan horses. One common vehicle of delivery for malware is e-mail.

Semantic attacks involve the modification of information or dissemination of incorrect information (Schneier 2000). Modification of information has been perpetrated even without the aid of computers, but computers and networks have provided new opportunities to achieve this process. In addition, the dissemination of incorrect information to large numbers of people quickly is facilitated by such mechanisms as e-mail, message boards, and Web sites.

There are five basic steps traditionally used by computer hackers to gain unauthorized access, and subsequently take over computer systems. These five steps may be used to plan a computer attack for purposes of cyber crime or cyber espionage, and may be employed for purposes of cyberterror (Wilson 2003). The steps are frequently automated through use of special hacker tools that are freely available to anyone via the Internet.

Step 1: Reconnaissance

In the first step, hackers employ extensive preoperative surveillance to find out detailed information about an organization that will help them gain later unauthorized access to computer systems. The most common method is social engineering, or tricking an employee into revealing sensitive information (such as a telephone number or a password). Other methods include dumpster diving, or rifling through an organization's trash to find sensitive information (such as floppy disks or important documents that have not been shredded). This step can be automated if the attacker installs in an office computer, a virus, worm, or "Spy ware" program that performs surveillance and then transmits useful information, such as passwords, back to the attacker. "Spy ware" is a form of malicious code that is quietly installed in a computer without user knowledge when a user visits a malicious Web site. It may remain undetected by firewalls or current antivirus security products, while monitoring keystrokes to record Web activity or collect snapshots of screen displays and other restricted information for transmission back to an unknown third party.

Step 2: Scanning

Once in possession of special restricted information, or a few critical phone numbers, an attacker performs additional surveillance by scanning an organization's computer software and network configuration to find possible entry points. This process can be quite slow, sometimes lasting months, as the attacker looks for several vulnerable openings into a system.

Step 3: Gaining Access

Once the attacker has developed an inventory of software and configuration vulnerabilities on a target network, he or she may quietly take over a system and network by using a stolen password, to create a phony account, or by exploiting a vulnerability that allows them to install a malicious Trojan Horse, or automatic "bot" that will await further commands sent through the Internet.

Step 4: Maintaining Access

Once an attacker has gained unauthorized access, he or she may secretly install extra malicious programs that allow them to return as often as they wish. These programs, known as "Root Kits" or "Back Doors," run unnoticed and can allow an attacker to secretly access a network at will. If the attacker can gain all the special privileges of a system administrator, then the computer or network has been completely taken over, and is "owned" by the attacker. Sometimes the attacker will reconfigure a computer system, or install software patches to close the previous security vulnerabilities just to keep other hackers out.

Step 5: Covering Tracks

Sophisticated attackers desire quiet, unimpeded access to the computer systems and data they take over. They must stay hidden to maintain control and gather more intelligence, or to refine preparations to maximize damage. The "Root Kit" or "Trojan Horse" programs often allow the attacker to modify the log files of the computer system, or to create hidden files to help avoid detection by the legitimate system administrator. Security systems may not detect the unauthorized activities of a careful intruder for a long period of time.

CYBER TERRORISM: THE TOOLS

Cyber terrorists use various tools and methods to unleash terrorism. Some of the major tools and methodologies are:

a. Hacking

"Hacking" is a generic term for all forms of unauthorized access to a computer or a computer network. Many technologies, the major ones being packet sniffing, tempest attack, password cracking, and buffer overflow facilitate hacking (Nagpal 2002).

- ### Packet Sniffing

  When information is sent over computer networks, it gets converted into hex and broken into lots of packets. Each packet is identified by a header, which contains the source, destination, size of packet, total number of packets, serial number of that packet, etc. If a hacker wants to see this information, he uses packet sniffing technology that reconverts the data from hex to the original. This technology is like putting the equivalent of a phone tap on a computer. Sniffing can be committed when a packet leaves the source or just before it reaches the destination. For this, the hacker would need to know only the IP address (the unique number that identifies each computer on a network). A packet sniffer can log all the files coming from a computer. It can also be programmed to give only a certain type of information (e.g. only passwords).

- ### TEMPEST (Transient Electromagnetic Pulse Emanation Standard)

  This technology allows someone not in the vicinity to capture the electromagnetic emissions from a computer and thus view whatever is on the monitor. A properly equipped car can park near the target area and pick up everything shown on the screen. There are some fonts that remove the high-frequency emissions, and thus severely reduce the ability to view the text on the screen from a remote location. Shielding computer equipment and cabling can avoid this attack.

- ### Password Cracking

  A password is a type of secret authentication word or phrase used to gain access. Passwords have been used since Roman times. Internal to the computer, passwords have to be checked constantly. Therefore, all computers try to "cache" passwords in memory so that each time a password is needed the user does not need to be asked. If someone hacks into the memory of a computer, he can sift the memory or page files for passwords. Password crackers are utilities that try to "guess" passwords. One way, the dictionary attack, involves trying out all the words contained in a predefined dictionary of words. Readymade dictionaries of millions of commonly used passwords can be freely downloaded from the Internet. Another form of password cracking attack is "brute force" attack. In this attack, all possible combinations of letters, numbers, and symbols are tried out one by one till the password is found out.

- *Buffer Overrun*

  Also known as buffer overrun, input overflow, and unchecked buffer overflow, this is probably the simplest way of hacking a computer. It involves input of excessive data into a computer. The excess data "overflows" into other areas of the computer's memory. This allows the hacker to insert executable code along with the input, thus enabling the hacker to break into the computer.

b. Trojans

Similar to the wooden horse, of the Troy War, in ancient Greece, a Trojan horse program pretends to do one thing while actually doing something completely different, but damages the software in a computer. Trojans are of various types, the important ones are:

- *Remote Administration Trojans*

  They let a hacker access the victim's hard disk, and perform many functions on his computer (copy files, shut down his computer, open and close his CD-ROM tray, etc.).

- *Password Trojans*

  Trojans search the victim's computer for passwords and then send them to the attacker or the author of the Trojan. There are Trojans for every kind of password. These Trojans usually send the information back to the attacker via e-mail.

- *Privileges-Elevating Trojans*

  These Trojans are usually used to fool system administrators (the system administrator is considered the king of the network as he has the maximum privilege on the network). They can either be bound into a common system utility or pretend to be something harmless and even quite useful and appealing. Once the administrator runs it, the Trojan will give the attacker more privileges on the system.

- *Key Loggers*

  These Trojans log all of the victim's keystrokes on the keyboard (including passwords), and then either save them on a file or occasionally e-mail them to the attacker. Key loggers usually do not take much disk space and can masquerade as important utilities, thus making them very hard to detect.

- *Destructive Trojans*

  These Trojans can destroy the victim's entire hard drive, encrypt, or just scramble important files. Some might seem like joke programs, while they are actually destroying every file they encounter.

c. Computer Viruses

A computer virus is a computer program that can infect other computer programs by modifying them in such a way as to include a copy of it. Viruses are very dangerous, in that they spread faster than being stopped, and even the least harmful of viruses could be fatal. For example, a virus that stops a hospital life support computer could be catastrophic.

d. Computer Worms

A computer worm is a self-contained program (or set of programs) that is able to spread functional copies of itself or its segments to other computer systems (usually via network connections). Unlike viruses, worms do not need to attach themselves to a host program. There are two types of worms: *host computer worms* and *network worms*.

e. E-mail-Related Crimes

E-mail has emerged as the world's most preferred form of communication. Like any other form of communication, criminals also misuse e-mail. The ease, speed, and relative anonymity of e-mail have made it a powerful tool for criminals. Some of the major e-mail-related crimes are e-mail spoofing, spreading Trojans, viruses, and worms; e-mail bombing, threatening e-mails, defamatory e-mails, and so forth.

f. Denial of Service Attacks (DoS)

Denial of Service (DoS) attacks are aimed at denying authorized persons access to a computer or computer network. These attacks may be launched using a single computer or millions of computers across the world. In the latter scenario, the attack is known as a distributed denial of service (DDoS) attack. The main reason for the vulnerability of computer systems to DoS attacks is the limited nature of computer and network resources, be it bandwidth, processing power, storage capacities, or other resources. DoS attacks pose another challenge, namely timely detection and source identification. These attacks are usually launched from "innocent" systems that have been compromised by the attackers. All the attacker need to do, to launch a DDoS attack is install a Trojan in many computers, gain control over them, and then employ them in sending a lot of requests to the target computer.

g. Cryptography

A disturbing trend that is emerging nowadays is the increasing use of encryption, high frequency encrypted voice/data links, steganography (steganography, literally meaning covered writing, involves the hiding of data in another object; it can be used to hide text messages within image and audio files) etc., by terrorists and members of organized crime cartels. Notable examples are those of Osama bin Laden,[2] Ramsey Yousef,[3] Leary,[4] the Calicartel,[5] the Dutch underworld[6] and the Italian mafia.

---

[2]The alleged mastermind behind the September 11 attacks on the World Trade Center in the United States is believed to use steganography and 512-bit encryption to keep his communication channels secure.

[3]He was behind the bombing the World Trade Center in the USA in 1993 and an aircraft belonging to Manila Air in 1995.

[4]He was sentenced to 94 years in prison for setting off firebombs in the New York (USA) subway system in 1995. Leary had developed his own algorithm for encrypting the files on his computer.

[5]This cartel is reputed to be using sophisticated encryption to conceal their telephone communications, radios that distort voices, video phones which provide visual authentication of the caller's identity, and instruments for scrambling transmissions from computer modems.

[6]Dutch organized crime syndicates use PGP and PGPfone to encrypt their communications. They also use palmtop computers installed with Secure Device, a Dutch software product for encrypting data with IDEA. The palmtops serve as an unmarked police/intelligence vehicles database.

Weapons of Mass Annoyance[7]

A detailed examination of some of the scenarios for attacks on critical infrastructures helps place cyberattacks more accurately in a strategic or national security context.

- Dams used for water storage and for power generation are often cited as a likely target for cyber attack. Analysts in the United States believe that "by disabling or taking command of the floodgates in a dam, for example, or of substations handling 300,000 volts of electric power, an intruder could use virtual tools to destroy real-world lives and property" (Gellman 2002).

- Assuming that a terrorist could find vulnerability in a water supply system that would allow him to shut down one city's water for a brief period, this vulnerability could be exploited to increase the damage of a physical attack (by denying fire fighters access to water; DeNileon 2001).

- Many analyses have cyber terrorists shutting down the electrical power system. One of the better cyber-security surveys found that power companies are a primary target for cyber attacks and that 70 percent of these companies had "suffered a severe attack" in the first 6 months of 2002 (Riptech 2002).

- Interference with national air traffic systems to disrupt flights, shut down air transport, and endanger passenger and crews is another frequently cited cyber threat. The high level of human involvement in the control and decision-making process for air traffic reduces the risk of any cyber attack.

- Manufacturing and economic activity are increasingly dependent on computer networks, and cyber crime and industrial espionage are new dangers for economic activity. However, the evidence is mixed as to the vulnerability of manufacturing to cyber attack. A virus in 2000 infected 1,000 computers at Ford Motor Company. Ford received 140,000 contaminated e-mail messages in 3 hours before it shut down its network. E-mail service was disrupted for almost a week within the company (Keith 2000).

- Cyber attacks are often presented as a threat to military forces and the Internet has major implications for espionage and warfare. Information warfare covers a range of activities of which cyber attacks may be the least important (Buchan 1999).

- Terrorist groups like Al Qaeda do make significant use of the Internet, but as a tool for intra-group communications, fund-raising, and public relations. Cyber terrorist could also take advantage of the Internet to steal credit card numbers or valuable data to provide financial support for their operations.

- Terrorist groups are likely to use the Internet to collect information on potential targets, and intelligence services can not only benefit from information openly available on the Web but, more importantly, can benefit from the ability to clandestinely penetrate computer networks and collect information that is not publicly available.

- The financial costs to economies from cyber attack include the loss of intellectual property, financial fraud, damage to reputation, lower productivity, and third-party liability (*The Financial Times* 2002; Swartz 2001; *Sunday Herald Sun* 2001).

---

[7]Weapons of mass annoyance: a phrase originated by Stewart Baker.

- India and Pakistan have engaged in a long-term dispute over Kashmir. The dispute moved into cyberspace when pro-Pakistan hackers began repeatedly attacking computers in India. The number of attacks has grown yearly: 45 in 1999, 133 in 2000, and 275 by the end of August 2001 (Vatis 2002). At least one of these groups, the Pakistan Hackers Club, has also attacked American assets, namely, Web sites maintained by the U.S. Department of Energy and the U.S. Air Force.

- The Israel–Palestine conflict saw its first cyber attacks in October 2000 when some Israeli teenagers launched DoS attacks against computers maintained by the Palestinian terrorist organizations Hezbollah and Hamas (Kraft 2000). Anti-Israel hackers responded almost immediately and crashed several Israeli Web sites by flooding them with bogus traffic. Among the Israeli sites attacked by the Palestinians were sites belonging to the Knesset (parliament), Israeli Defense Forces, the Foreign Ministry, and the Bank of Israel.

- Some of the other possible situations are given below:

HYPOTHETICAL SITUATIONS

Several commentators discussing the capabilities of cyberterrorists have posited numerous hypothetical situations where cyberterrorists attack critical infrastructures within the United States.

Situation 1: A possible cyber terrorist attack could target children through a cereal manufacturer. A cyber terrorist could hack into the manufacturer's production computer and change the iron content to be added to the cereal. The cyber terrorist tells the computer to add 80 percent iron to the cereal instead of two percent. Many children eat the cereal and become very ill or possibly even die. Although several experts agree that this is a possible situation, many argue that the plan's success is unlikely.

Situation 2: A possible cyber terrorist attack could target airline passengers through the air traffic control tower of an airport. The cyber terrorist hacks into the computer system of the air traffic control tower and adds false information about the airplane's location, speed, etc., causing the air traffic controller to give the airplane pilot wrong information. The airplane then crashes into another plane, or into the ground, depending on the misinformation.

Situation 3: A cyber terrorist will place computerized bombs all throughout a city. These bombs will transmit a code to one another, and can be detonated by a timer or a computer. The bombs are also programmed to explode if one of the other bombs is disarmed.

Situation 4: A cyber terrorist disrupts bank software, interrupts financial transactions, and hacks into the stock market, deleting and changing stock prices. The cyber terrorist also introduces false information to the media concerning corporate mergers, stock prices, and corporate earnings. The disinformation causes a rapid decrease in stock prices, a loss of market capitalization, and a destabilization of the market. The citizenry lose faith in the economic systems and economic destabilization is achieved.

Situation 5: A cyber terrorist hacks into a pharmacy chain's computer network and changes information regarding drug interaction information. A large number of the elderly receive different medications, which have negative combined effects. Many become ill and some die.

—Adapted from Pollitt 2000.

Potential Effects

Cyber terrorism has the potential to greatly affect the healthcare infrastructure of a modern society. In many countries, as healthcare systems have become rapidly more dependent on the Internet, a number of instances of cyber crimes against healthcare systems already have been reported. While to date, most cyber crimes have been minor, they likely are harbingers of acts to come. Areas of particular concern to healthcare facilities include the potential for cyber terrorism–related events to erase or alter computerized medical, pharmacy, or health insurance records.

Cyber terrorism also may target other institutions that directly or indirectly affect the health of communities. Industries or public service agencies at particular risk of cyber terrorism include: (1) water supplies; (2) electrical power supplies; (3) emergency services; (4) telecommunications systems; (5) transportation systems; (6) banking and financial systems; and (7) government.

There have been numerous attacks against these infrastructures. Hackers have invaded the public phone networks, compromising nearly every category of activity, including switching and operations, administration, maintenance, and provisioning (OAM&P). They have crashed or disrupted signal transfer points, traffic switches, OAM&P systems, and other network elements. They have planted "time bomb" programs designed to shut down major switching hubs, disrupted emergency services throughout the eastern seaboard, and boasted that they have the capability to bring down all switches in Manhattan. They have installed wiretaps, rerouted phone calls, changed the greetings on voice mail systems, taken over voice mailboxes, and made free long-distance calls at their victims' expense—sticking some victims with phone bills in the hundreds of thousands of dollars. When they cannot crack the technology, they use "social engineering" to con employees into giving them access.

Cyber terrorism against the telecommunications system may have critical implications for the public health of communities. From the healthcare system perspective, attacks against the telecommunications system not only have the potential to disrupt the flow of health information, but also the multiple logistical systems upon which the operations of healthcare facilities depend (e.g., the acquisition of supplies). From the public safety perspective, cyber attacks against the telecommunications system may disrupt crucial information-sharing networks. For example, in March 1997, a teenage hacker penetrated and disabled a telephone company computer that provided service to the Worcester Airport in Massachusetts, cutting off service to the airport control tower, fire department, security, and weather service for 6 hours.

Public safety may be affected adversely by cyber terrorism in other ways. For example, in 1992, a disgruntled former employee of Chevron Corporation's emergency alert network, hacked into computers in New York and San Jose, California and reconfigured the firm's emergency alert system so that it would fail during an event. The disabled system was not discovered until an emergency arose at the Chevron refinery in Richmond, California, and the adjacent community could not be notified during an accidental chemical release. During the 10-hour period in which the system was down, thousands of people in 22 states and six areas in Canada with Chevron facilities went without the Chevron emergency alert system. As suggested above, hackers also have attacked traffic regulation systems, disrupting traffic lights, with the potential for an increase in motor vehicle collisions.

Cyber attacks against the essential services, such as the water and electrical supply systems, comprise another major area of concern. Hospitals and communities alike are highly dependent on water and only can subsist for limited periods without water. Fortunately, the majority of water system authorities in the United States are protected against cyber attacks by supervisory control and data acquisition (SCADA) systems, though these systems may be still circumvented by other means. While hospitals in the United States almost always have back-up generators should the electrical supply system fail, communities almost always are immediately vulnerable. The longer a community remains without power, the more likely it is to suffer food and selected medication spoilage due to loss of refrigeration and deaths due to medical equipment failure (i.e., ventilators outside of hospitals).

Finally, cyber terrorism also can cause environmental contamination, with the potential for adverse health effects in the community. For example, in 2000, a perpetrator in Australia allegedly penetrated the Maroochy Shire Council's computer system and used radio transmissions to create overflows of raw sewage into the Sunshine Coast, causing widespread contamination. By extrapolation, a dedicated terrorist group could use cyber terrorism to cause more widespread, more enduring, or more toxic environmental contamination, with an almost incalculable impact on public health.

Cyber Terrorism and Civil Aviation

One of the methods where cyber terrorism has distinct but dangerous consequence is in the field of the civil aviation. This image of civil aviation as a potential target for cyber terrorists is a chilling one, but it paints a worst-case scenario that, in many respects, misses the point about cyber terrorism.

The range of potential perpetrators and intentions in the civil aviation environment is probably the most troubling aspect of this new reality. The availability on the Internet of easy-to-use tools to disable, disrupt, or corrupt systems is astonishing. In addition, the anonymity provided by the Internet may facilitate or encourage individuals to engage in activity or behavior that they otherwise avoid, and there is little likelihood of being caught. Several high-profile cases involving concerted attacks directed against American government systems were what appears to be the work of thrill-seeking teenagers. The civil aviation environment, therefore, is one of multiple, often unknown attackers, and a wide array of targets, whereas cyber terrorism per se represents a small but potential growth area.

Prevention and Control

Up-to-date **computer security** systems and firewalls, personal vigilance, and adherence to best-practice guidelines are essential in maintaining the security of computer systems. While the knowledge of how to hack into a computer system is readily available on the Internet, this same knowledge also allows system managers to understand how better to protect their systems. In addition, the Internet offers many resources, which can assist in protecting computer systems from cyber attacks. Nevertheless, even with the best security systems, safety measures can be rendered ineffective by lapses in security-conscious behavior.

The Need for International Technical Coordination

Networked information systems are being rapidly adopted by governments and businesses worldwide to improve communications, operational control, and ultimately, competitiveness. Reliance on these systems, especially where the Internet exists as the primary infrastructure, is likely to increase. It is a complex technical and political task for nations and their commercial enterprises to protect information assets and ensure that critical operations continue even if attacked. The growth of world markets and an increase in transnational mergers only serve to compound this complexity.

Governments are recognizing the need to protect their information and critical infrastructures in response to these threats and are responding accordingly. Some governments recognize that it is not sufficient to address only the local or national aspects of safeguarding information and critical infrastructures. Because attacks against the Internet typically do not require the attacker to be physically present at the site of the attack, the risk of being identified is significantly reduced. Besides the technological challenges this presents, the legal issues involved in pursuing and prosecuting intruders adds a layer of difficulty as they cross multiple geographical and legal boundaries. An effective solution can only come in the form of international collaboration.

In the area of law enforcement, the Internet constitutes a new patrol area in many respects. Unlike jurisdictions based on national and political borders, the digital information infrastructure does not have a central location in the physical world. So not only is responding to attacks difficult technically but also many of the accepted methods for practicing law enforcement are ineffective. Recent G8 (Group of Eight Advanced Industrial States) and OPEC (Organization of Petroleum Exporting Countries) activities are examples of increasing recognition of this international need. The problems that we must address to improve our critical information infrastructures require the involvement of diverse parties including governments, policy and lawmakers, law enforcement, software vendors, the research community, and practitioners such as FIRST (Forum of Incident Response and Security Teams) members who have experience responding to computer security incidents. Attempting to address the problems in one group without input and feedback from the others is likely to result in flawed or incomplete solutions. The U.S. government legislation (the Digital Millennium Act, 1998) resulting from the World Intellectual Property Organization (WIPO) treaty resulted in a flurry of panic throughout the Internet security community. Practitioners, researchers, software vendors, and incident response teams realized that aspects of their work that address security flaws to reduce risk to our critical infrastructures might become illegal under the proposed legislation. This was clearly not the original intent of the treaty or the resulting legislation. This is just one example of the urgent need for ongoing communication among policymakers, technologists, and others to ensure that future policies and agreements on a national and international scale are practical and effective.

Current Difficulties

Many network protocols that now form part of the information infrastructure were designed without computer security in mind. Without a secure infrastructure, it is difficult to avoid security problems and resolve computer security incidents. The combination of rapidly changing technology, expanding use, and new, often unimagined uses of the information infrastructure creates a volatile situation in which the nature of threats and vulnerabilities is difficult to assess and predict.

It is inexpensive (the cost of a personal computer and Internet access), quick (less than a minute), and easy (using freely available intruder tools) for anyone to launch attacks against our critical information infrastructures. Conversely, it is expensive (international effort and funding), long-term (research, development, and deployment), and complex (technically and politically) to take the steps needed to *harden* the information infrastructure to make it less susceptible to attack, and to enable us to respond more effectively and efficiently when attacks do happen.

In general, incident response and computer security teams consist of practitioners and technologists who have a wealth of operational experience but lack authority to make policy and security decisions in their organizations. They also may have limited funding and lack professional recognition. This has negative consequences; a given team's organization may not allow enough staff to respond effectively to security incidents. Similarly, a team may not have sufficient authority to influence and ensure improved computer security and comprehensive response. Moreover, at this time, there is no infrastructure to support a coordinated global incident response effort, although there are a few components in place that can form the basis of this infrastructure.

A variety of issues must be addressed when considering how to promote an effective global incident response infrastructure. These include discussions about which organizations will coordinate and participate in the development effort, how current groups and forums can fit their mission and objectives into an agenda to create a global infrastructure, and what possible structures and mechanisms might be required and effective in the future.

Countering Cyber Terrorism

In order to counter this form of terrorism, it is required that the following actions need to be taken immediately. In order to prevent damage, risk analysis needs to be performed for the information systems of the target critical infrastructures, and measures will have to be implemented as needed according to the importance of the information system. It is also necessary to continually raise security level in each of the fields with critical infrastructure (Erbschloe 2001).

- Raising security level in private sector critical infrastructure fields.
- Communication and coordination systems for private sector, etc. Critical infrastructure groups build a communication and coordination system between operators associated with cyber terrorism countermeasures, while making use of existing communication mechanisms, to fulfill the following roles:
  - Collect, distribute, and share the common security information in the various fields, as well as the warning information
  - A communication system for when a cyber attack occurs, or when there is a danger of such an attack
  - Implement unified, centralized communications for the government and related agencies
- Communication and coordination systems with other critical infrastructure operators.
  - In cases of interconnection to other information systems and operators of important infrastructure in other fields through networks, develop, as needed, the communication and cooperation systems for cyber terrorism countermeasures.

- Establishing a communication and cooperation system for government The government, will have to fill the following roles in developing the communication and cooperation systems:
  - Collecting, distributing, and sharing security information and warning information
  - Collecting information when a cyber attack occurs, or when there is a danger of such an attack
  - Within government departments, communication with related agencies and the private sector critical infrastructure groups
- Establishing an emergency response plan:
  - To establish countermeasures and an emergency response plan in the event of a cyber attack, or when there is a danger of such an attack on the private sector critical infrastructure operators, investigate while making use of the communications systems established. Expected issues for the emergency response plan include communication, containment of damage, verification of safety, recovery (temporary measures), prevention of recurrence, etc.
  - The actions during an emergency will sometimes require a high-level judgment, so procedures like the emergency response plan will be determined so that the appropriate persons, having the proper authority and responsibility, can make decisions quickly.
- Promote research and development:
  - The government and private sector critical infrastructure operators will promote cooperation and communication between the government and the private sector on research of the technology, countermeasures, threat analysis, and development of the required technology to build a strong foundation against the threat of cyber terrorism.
- Add and revise legislation:
  - The government needs to consider changes to the law, such as the basic criminal law, from the perspective of maintaining safety for the telecommunications networks and international harmony.
- International cooperation:
  - Cyber attacks can be made without regard for national boundaries, so international cooperation and coordination is required in order to handle such attacks.
  - The government and private sector key infrastructure operators will work to accumulate information from information security organizations outside our country.
  - The government needs to promote cooperation with the international organizations related to cyber terrorism.
  - The government will have to work to strengthen international cooperation, information exchanges and shared training with the counterparts in other nations.

CONCLUSION

The threat posed by cyber terrorism has grabbed the attention of the mass media, the security community, and the information technology (IT) industry. Journalists, politicians, and experts in a variety of fields have popularized a scenario in which sophisticated cyber terrorists electronically break into computers that control dams or air traffic control systems, wreaking havoc and endangering millions of lives (Wiemann 2004). Though, cyber terrorism has become the fancy word of today's terror lexicon, many argue that it does not pose the threat as it is perceived (Green 2002; Forno 2002; Wiemann 2004). In addition, some argue that it is a ploy created by the media (Green 2002; Forno 2002). Government officials in the United States, including Caruso (2001) argue that media has exaggerated the issue of cyber terrorism, but agree that cyber terrorism has a threat to the information infrastructure (Caruso 2002). Hence it is found that there are two alternative perspectives with regard to threat of cyber terrorism. Even though we do not see any threat of cyber terrorism, as the cyberspace is explored day by day, the threat of cyber terrorism might increase in the near future.

KEY TERMS

Cyber crimes	Cyber terrorism
Computer security	Information warfare
Tools	

REFERENCES

Buchan, G. C. 1999. "Implications of information vulnerabilities for military operations." In *Strategic Appraisal: The Changing Role of Information in Warfare,* edited by K. Zalmay, J. P. White, A. W. Marshall, 283–323. Santa Monica: Rand.

Caruso, J. T. October 11, 2001. Inaccurate media reports of potential terrorist attack. Before the House Intelligence Subcommittee on Terrorism and Homeland Defense.

Caruso J. T. March 21, 2002. Combating terrorism: Protecting the United States. Before the House Subcommittee on National Security, Veterans Affairs, and International Relations.

Conway, M. 2002. What is cyberterrorism? *Current History* 101 (659): 436–42.

Copeland, T. E. 2000. *The Information Revolution and National Security.* Carlisle, PA: Strategic Studies Institute, United States Army War College.

DeNileon, G. P. 2001. The who, what, why, and how of counterterrorism issues. *Journal AWWA* 93 (5): 78–85.

Denning, D. 1999. "Activism, hacktivism, and cyberterrorism: The Internet as a tool for influencing foreign policy." In *Networks and Netwars: The Future of Terror, Crime, and Militancy,* edited by A. John and D. Ronfeldt, 239–38. Santa Monica: Rand.

Denning, D. 2000. *Cyberterrorism.* Testimony before the Special Oversight Panel on Terrorism Committee on Armed Services U.S. House of Representatives. Retrieved December 15, 2006, from http://www.cs.georgetown.edu/~denning/infosec/cyberterror.html

Erbschloe, M. 2001. *Information Warfare: How to Survive Cyberattacks.* New York: Osborne/McGraw-Hill.

Financial Times, The [London]. November 22, 2002. A long, hard look at the hackers: 14.

Forno, R. 2002. Shredding the paper tiger of cyberterrorism. Retrieved December 15, 2006, from http:// www.securityfocus.com/columnists/111

Galley, P. 1996. Computer terrorism: What are the risks? [English translation July 1, 1998, by Arif M. Janmohamed] Retrieved December 15, 2006, from http://home.worldcom.ch/pgalley/infosec/sts_en/

Gellman, B. June 27, 2002. Cyberattacks by Al Qaeda feared: Experts: Terrorists at threshold of using Web as deadly tool. *Washington Post.*

Green, J. 2002. The myth of cyberterrorism. *Washington Monthly.* Retrieved December 15, 2006, from www.washingtonmonthly.com/features/2001/0211.green.html

Hildreth, S. 2001. Cyberwarfare [CRS Report for Congress]. Retrieved December 15, 2006, from http:// www.fas.org/irp/crs/RL30735.pdf

Hirsch, E., Jr., J. Kett, and J. Trefil. 2002. *The New Dictionary of Cultural Literacy.* 3rd ed. Boston: Houghton Mifflin.

Hoopes, N. August 16, 2005. New focus on cyberterrorism. At risk: Computers that run power grids, refineries. *Christian Science Monitor.* Retrieved April 26, 2006, from http://www.csmonitor.com/2005/0816/p01s02-stct.html

Institute for Security Technology Studies (ISTS) at Dartmouth College. September 22, 2001. *Cyberattacks During the War on Terrorism.* Hanover, NH.

Keith, B. May 8, 2000. With its e-mail infected, ford scrambled and caught up. *New York Times.*

Kraft, D. October 26, 2000. Islamic groups "attack" Israeli Web sites. Retrieved December 15, 2006, from http://www.landfield.com/isn/mail-archive/2000/Oct/0137.html

Lewis, J. A. 2002. Assessing the risks of cyberterrorism, cyber war and other cyber threats. *NATO Review* 49 (Winter): 16–18.

Nagpal, R. 2002. Cyberterrorism in the context of globalization. Paper presented at the II World Congress on Informatics and Law Madrid, Spain, September 2002. Retrieved December 15, 2006, from http://www.ieid.org/congreso/ponencias/Nagpal,%20Rohas.pdf

Pollitt, M. M. 2000. Cyberterrorism—Fact or fancy? Retrieved December 15, 2006, from www.cs.georgetown.edu/~denning/infosec/pollitt.htm

Post, J. M. 2000. From car bombs to logic bombs: The growing threat from information terrorism. *Terrorism and Political Violence* 12 (2): 97–122.

Riptech Internet Security Threat Report. 2002. Retrieved December 15, 2006, from http://www.securitystats.com/reports/Riptech-Internet_Security_Threat_Report_vII.20020708.pdf

Schneier, B. 2000. Semantic network attacks. *Communications of the ACM* 43 (12): 168.

Schwartau, W. 1996. *Information Warfare.* New York: Thunder's Mouth Press.

Sprols, J., and W. Byars. 1998. *Cyberterrorism.* Retrieved December 15, 2006, from http://www-cs.etsu-tn.edu/gotterbarn/stdntppr/

Sunday Herald Sun [Melbourne]. November 18, 2001. How terror stalks the Web: 43.

Swartz, J. October 9, 2001. Experts fear cyberspace could be terrorists' next target. *USA Today.*

U.S. Department of State. 2003. Patterns of global terrorism, 2003. Retrieved December 15, 2006, from http://www.state.gov/s/ct/rls/pgtrpt/2001/html/10220.htm

Vatis, M. 2002. Cyberattacks: Protecting America's security against digital threats. Discussion paper ESDP-2002-04, John F. Kennedy School of Government, Harvard University.

Wiemann, G. December 2004. Cyberterrorism: How real is the threat? Special Report No. 119. United States Institute of Peace. Retrieved December 15, 2006, from http://www.usip.org/pubs/specialreports/sr119.html

Wilson, C. 2003. Computer attack and cyberterrorism: Vulnerabilities and policy issues for congress. CRS Report for Congress Congressional Research Service, The Library of Congress, U.S. Department of State.

Chapter 31

Cyber Terrorism and the Law

Clive Walker
University of Leeds, UK

Clive Walker, Ph.D., is professor of criminal justice studies at the School of Law, University of Leeds. He was Dean of the School between 2000 and 2005. He has written extensively on criminal justice issues, with many published papers not only in the UK but also in several other countries, especially the USA, where he has been a visiting professor at George Washington and Stanford Universities. His books have focused upon terrorism and the law, including, *The Anti-Terrorism Legislation*, published by Oxford University Press in 2002. In 2003, he was a special adviser to the UK Parliamentary select committee, which was considering what became the Civil Contingencies Act 2004. A further book commentating upon that Act, *The Civil Contingencies Act 2004: Risk, Resilience and the Law in the United Kingdom*, was published by Oxford University Press in 2006. He has also been called upon to provide advice to other UK Parliament committees on terrorism and to the UK Government's independent adviser on terrorism. He teaches in criminal justice and constitutional issues, with innovative postgraduate courses in terrorism laws. He also supervises postgraduate research students, including some from the Middle East region.

Abstract

The nature of the threat of terrorism and cyber terrorism will be considered. An important distinction emerges between the use of the Internet in an ancillary role in furtherance of terrorism ("ancillary cyber activities") and those uses which do themselves terrorize by using the Internet as the mode or the object of attack ("cyber attack"). The ambit of cyber terrorism is found to encompass information warfare, communications usages, personnel and logistical support, intelligence gathering, and propaganda. The chapter next considers legal responses within the United Kingdom, chosen as a jurisdiction with a much longer and richer history than most of laws against terrorism. The limitations of a legalistic approach are also considered.

THE ETHICS OF RESPONDING TO TERRORISM

The continuing capacity of terrorists to terrorize even the battle-hardened must be taken seriously. Governments and citizens of countries such as Spain, Sri Lanka, and the United Kingdom might be expected to have become inured to the phenomenon of **terrorism** after campaigns of political violence that have persisted for decades or longer. Nevertheless, the impact of September 11 upon policy formation and response has been striking, not only within the United States but in many other countries, including those already mentioned with long experience of terrorism.[1] The disbelief and incomprehension as to what lies behind the attacks, the wayward calculations of danger, and the reactive destruction of revered norms and processes are all evidence of a traumatized polity (See generally Lawyers Committee for Human Rights 2003, documenting the expansion of executive authority and the abandonment of democratic procedural safeguards; Posner and Vermeule 2006, on the miscalculation of terrorist danger and the allocation of costs). Because of this evident capacity of terrorism to destabilize and damage otherwise just and democratic societies, those societies have a right to engage in forward planning and counter measures.[2] In the words of one American judge, a democracy is not a "suicide pact," and measures can be taken against clear and present dangers (*Terminiello v. Chicago* 337 U.S. 1, 37 (1949) (Jackson, J., dissenting)). This point is also reflected in Article 17 of the European Convention on Human Rights and Fundamental Freedoms of 1950, which states:

> Nothing in this Convention may be interpreted as implying for any State, group or person any right to engage in any activity or perform any act aimed at the destruction of any of the rights and freedoms set forth herein or at their limitation to a greater extent than is provided for in the Convention. (European Convention on Human Rights and Fundamental Freedoms 1950; Council of Europe 2005)

While terrorism in general is certainly to be counteracted, we must consider whether there exists a subphenomenon called "cyber terrorism," whether there is any need to react against it, and, if so, to what extent? Some would express astonishment at the need to ask the first two questions and argue that there is no more need to discuss these issues than there is to deliberate upon whether we need to respond to arson or murder. However, such a response betrays a shallow understanding of the strategy of terrorism and of how laws come to be passed against it. The point of terrorism is to destabilize and delegitimize the governments they oppose, a result which can be secured, for example, by legislative overreaction. So, it is always worth considering whether new laws against terrorism (often including severe penalties or procedures which infringe normal constitutional safeguards) are truly needed or whether existing laws may be adequate in practice. It is also worth underlining the normative constraints, which should be observed in those aspects where extra laws might become unavoidable. The overall goal of counter-terror strategy should be "to reduce the risk from international terrorism, so that people can go about their daily lives freely and with confidence" (Home Office 2006). Excessive and repressive laws are counterproductive in that quest.

The first step in the inquiry should therefore be to impose firm principle on any legal initiative. As has been explained elsewhere, full constitutional governance requires continual application of a number of elements (Walker 1997; Walker and Broderick 2006, chapters 6–7).

---

[1]There has been an almost global response by virtue of the requirements of UN Security Council Resolution 1373 (S/RES/1373, 28 September 2001), backed by reviews by the Counter-Terrorism Committee.

[2]However, there is the danger that societies, especially the unjust and undemocratic, will seize the pretext of the "war on terrorism" to repress their opponents, whether "terrorists" or not. This problem is the remit of the UN Special Rapporteur on the promotion and protection of human rights while countering terrorism (see http://www.ohchr.org/english/issues/terrorism/rapporteur/srchr.htm).

The first is a "rights audit" which means that the rights of individuals are respected according to traditions of the domestic **jurisdictions** and the demands of international law. The latter will include the periodic review of the very existence of any emergency or special measures. The second element is "democratic accountability" which includes attributes such as information, open and independent debate, and an ability to participate in decision making. The third element is "constitutionalism"—the subjection of government to norms, whether legal or extra legal (such as codes). More specific requirements in the field of special powers include the public articulation of reasons in support of particular actions taken for the public welfare, assurances through effective mechanisms that the crisis cannot be ended by normal means and that powers will not be used arbitrarily and are proportionate to the threat, and adherence to the overall purpose of the restoration of fundamental features of constitutional life. Constitutionalism also requires that, at a more individual level, excesses can be challenged, including through the courts.

Bearing these standards in mind, especially the latter, the nature of the threat of terrorism and cyber terrorism should next be considered. As for "terrorism," it must be borne in mind that resort to violence is almost certainly a breach of law—relating to murder, destruction of property, or the possession of explosives or firearms—without any need for reliance upon special measures to bring about that depiction. Consequently, in light of the need for proportionality under the heading of constitutionalism, let us consider why special laws might be needed. The answer lies not in the motivation *per se*. Whilst motivation may be a necessary defining factor in the ascription of the label "terrorism" (Silke 2002, 3), it is not a sufficient defining factor in the invocation of a special legal response. A special response may typically be justifiable when terrorism is emanating from a group with capacities to organize collectively on a sustained basis, to engage in sophisticated plans and operations, and to operate independently from normal life or to have the capacity to intimidate normal society into tolerating its presence. If those factors are present, one might concede the need to depart from normal laws of criminal detection and process which often assume (and rely upon) the opposites: lone individuals, inadequate, bungling operations, and individuals who in most cases cannot help but leave traces of their wrongdoing. Groups such as the Irish Republican Army (IRA) certainly fall into the former rather than the latter criteria. By contrast, the Unabomber (Whittell 1998; *Sacramento Bee, The* 2006)[3] or an assailant like David Copeland (whose case is discussed below) could be said to engage in terrorism, but lack the capacity to create a threat of a kind which requires special laws. Even organizations which seek political change and use violence to achieve it, but do not have the sophistication, size or threat of the likes of Irish paramilitary groups, should be tackled through normal laws rather than special laws. In practice, this demarcation is recognized by the United Kingdom authorities who have as a matter of policy declined to treat amateurish animal rights extremists as "terrorists" even though they apparently fit the definitional profile (Home Office 2001) and have been described as replicating "a quasi-terrorist cellular structure" (United Kingdom Department of Trade and Industry 2004).[4] It follows that any definitional precision surrounding the term

---

[3]Theodore Kaczynski was sentenced to life imprisonment in 1998 for bombings over a number of years which killed three people and maimed two others.

[4]As a result, the UK police response to these groups is through the National Extremism Tactical Coordination Unit (NETCU) rather than the Metropolitan Police Counter Terrorism Command or corresponding regional units.

"terrorism" may be more apparent than real and, even if achieved, there would still be a role for further modes of governance over police action in response to terrorism.

The reality is that the legal definition of "terrorism" is often far from precise (Walker 2007; Lord Carlile 2007). The legal definition adopted in the United Kingdom, in section 1 of the Terrorism Act 2000, states as follows:

(1) In this Act 'terrorism' means the use or threat of action where
    (a) the action falls within subsection (2),
    (b) the use or threat is designed to influence the government or an international governmental organisation or to intimidate the public or a section of the public, and
    (c) the use or threat is made for the purpose of advancing a political, religious or ideological cause.

(2) Action falls within this subsection if it
    (a) involves serious violence against a person,
    (b) involves serious damage to property,
    (c) endangers a person's life, other than that of the person committing the action,
    (d) creates a serious risk to the health or safety of the public or a section of the public, or
    (e) is designed seriously to interfere with or seriously to disrupt an electronic system.

(3) The use or threat of action falling within subsection (2) which involves the use of firearms or explosives is terrorism whether or not subsection (1)(b) is satisfied . . . . (Walker 2002, 20–21)[5]

The essence of the definition is in section 1(1), which contains three conjunctive legs, all of which must normally be satisfied (subject to section 1(3)). Perhaps the most relevant aspect of this formulation is the reference to an "electronic system." There was a concern to include within the definition acts which might not be violent in themselves but which can have a devastating impact. These could include disrupting key computer systems or interfering with the supply of water or power where life, health, or safety may be put at risk on a broad scale (Secretary of State for the Home Department and Secretary of State for Northern Ireland 1998, para 10). The IRA's bombs in the City of London in 1992 and 1993 and in London Docklands in 1996 may be actual illustrations. In a late modern society, the state is "hollowed out," and power is diffused across both public and private sectors (for the concept of "hollowing out," see Rhodes 1994, 1997; Stewart 2001). Power relates more to finance, knowledge and security. Consequently, the likely targets of terrorists shift in line with the new centers of power and the new power holders—such as financial institutions in the City of London. Thus, terrorism becomes less focused upon states and territories, while the terrorist groups themselves become more fluid and hybrid in objectives, forms and tactics (Raufer 1999). In this light, section 1(2) seeks to protect against (b) risks to property, (d) risks to safety and (e) interference with computer systems. At the same time, the emphasis on "serious" is important—"a costly nuisance" should not be dealt with as cyber terrorism (Iqbal 2004). In his recent review for the government of the UK legal definition of terrorism, Lord Carlile concluded that, as currently formulated, section 1(2)(e) was justifiable because of the huge potential for economic damage and injury to persons from cyber terrorism (Lord Carlile 2007, para. 71).

---

[5]As amended by the Terrorism Act 2006 s.34. Terrorism Act, 2000, c. 11, § 1 (U.K.).

Returning to the precepts of constitutional governance, how does this definition fit with the needs of society? It could be argued it is too broad because it is indeterminate as between what were referred to earlier as direct attacks and indirect attacks on the individual. The indirect form is not sufficiently linked to the Millian notion of "harm to others" to warrant intervention. It is true that the forms of intervention, such as arrest under section 41 of the Terrorism Act 2000 and the various forms of investigative powers in Parts IV and V of that Act, do not directly criminalize the activity designated as terrorism. But they do chill such behavior and demonize it in the eyes of the public. As mentioned at the outset, a state may also be worthy of protection—at least if it has sufficient attributes of legitimacy—but just as laws of subversion and sedition have become increasingly discredited (Walker 1992), so they should not be reintroduced by a backdoor extension of the term "terrorism."

As for definitions of cyber terrorism (Denning 1999; Stephens 1998; Sofaer and Goodman 2001), the threat potentially emerges through the development of a late modern, information society. As one commentator observed, "Why assassinate a politician or indiscriminately kill people when attack on the electronic switching will produce far more dramatic and lasting results?" (Laqueur 1996). But what is meant by the cyber-terrorist threat? We must at the outset distinguish various possible meanings before mapping them onto legal normative standards and actual legal responses. This task can and must be undertaken in the abstract for the purposes of legislative contingency planning, but whether action is taken at any point should also reflect the proportionate seriousness of the challenge.

An important distinction emerges from the literature between the use of the Internet in an ancillary role in furtherance of terrorism ("ancillary cyber activities") and those uses which do themselves terrorize by using the Internet as the mode or the object of attack ("cyber attack"). There is a strong line of literature which contends that only the latter fall within the definition of cyber terrorism and that a failure to make this distinction leads to an exaggeration of the threat. For example, perhaps the leading analyst of cyber terrorism, Professor Dorothy Denning, has argued that:

> Cyberterrorism is the convergence of terrorism and cyberspace. It is generally understood to mean unlawful attacks and threats of attacks against computers, networks, and the information stored therein when done to intimidate or coerce a government or its people in furtherance of political or social objectives. Further, to qualify as cyberterrorism, an attack should result in violence against persons or property, or at least cause enough harm to generate fear. Attacks that lead to death or bodily injury, explosions, plane crashes, water contamination, or severe economic loss would be examples. Serious attacks against critical infrastructures could be acts of cyberterrorism, depending on their impact. Attacks that disrupt nonessential services or that are mainly a costly nuisance would not. (Denning 2000, 2006)

This limited range is also reflected, amongst others (Stohl 2006), by Professor Gabriel Weimann, who posits that cyber terrorism means only "the use of computer network tools to harm or shut down critical national infrastructures (such as energy, transportation, government operations)" (Weimann 2005, 129, 130; 2006a, b) Likewise, it is said that "[c]ybercrime and cyberterrorism are not coterminous . . . . Terrorist use of computers as a facilitator of their activities, whether for propaganda, recruitment, data mining, communication, or other purposes, is simply not cyberterrorism" (Weimann 2005, 132–133).

Based upon these formulations, only a fraction of what is discussed below will fall within the term cyber terrorism. One can readily concur that special laws against terrorism should be confined to attacks which result in serious harm to persons or property (Iqbal 2004). Yet, it is increasingly common for the law not only to deal with a core mischief but also with the organization and finance which produces and sustains that core mischief (Crimm 2004; Parkel 2004; U.S. Customs Service Office of Investigations 2006).[6] Consequently, it is necessary for the purposes of this paper to ignore the observations that the wider, more ancillary uses should be viewed as beyond the strict definition. It is not that the strict view is wrong, but rather that, to provide a short hand for the full range of legal concerns and legal responses, a wider notion of cyber terrorism will be adopted in this paper. In effect, it will include not only cyber terrorism as a form of offence or attack, as above, but also the various ways in which the Internet is being used to sustain and further terrorism. This wider ambit is consistent with the uses of terrorism elsewhere—those who assist terrorism through finance or the supply of materials become depicted as terrorists and are dealt with accordingly under special legislation.

A TYPOLOGY OF CYBER TERRORISM

Moving from definitions to typologies, the variants of cyber terrorism include both the ancillary and offensive (Thomas 2003).

Information Warfare (Cilluffo et al. 1999–2000, 131; Brenner and Goodman 2002)

In this aspect of activity, information technology is the means and object of attack. This mode of use is how cyber terrorism is often conceived and is at the heart of Dorothy Denning's definition of cyber terrorism mentioned earlier. An example of this scenario arose in July 1997, when Spanish protestors, who it must be emphasized might fall within the definition of "activist" or "hacktivist" but not "terrorist" (Denning 2006), attacked the Institute for Global Communications (IGC; 2006) with thousands of bogus e-mail messages which swamped the Internet Service Provider's system and blocked other traffic. The objective was that IGC stop hosting the website for the *Euskal Herria Journal*, a New York-based publication supporting Basque independence, which included reports on the activities of Euskadi Ta Azkatasuna (ETA), the militant Basque group (Sullivan 1988). IGC staff members were reluctant to succumb to the pressure, but they said they had to remove the site because the attack had been crippling the entire service for the company's estimated 13,000 other subscribers. Similar tactics were used in 1998 by Tamil activists who attacked Sri Lankan embassies with an overload of e-mail messages. More insidious was the attempt by Serb sympathizers during the war in

---

[6]For post 9/11 laws in the United States which relate to terrorist finances, see especially Exec. Order No. 13224, 66 Fed. Reg. 49079 (September 23, 2001); USA PATRIOT Act of 2001, Pub. L. No. 107-56, 115 Stat. 272. Operation Green Quest was created in October 2001 as a multiagency financial crimes task force to enforce these and other laws.

Kosovo to target NATO with viruses in 1999 (Cilluffo et al. 1999–2000, 149; Wingfield 2000).[7] Nevertheless, fears of terrorists' aircraft falling from the sky through sabotaged air traffic control systems or of pharmaceutical products becoming corrupted (Collin 2006) have not materialized. Systems are generally suitably robust and resilient (Weimann 2006b, 166). Furthermore, the death of people has more allure for terrorists than the death of machines. Consequently, whilst information technology networks represent an important aspect of the critical national infrastructure[8] which may be a target for the enemies of the state (including other states) (Halpin 2007),[9] there is no clear evidence that more serious attacks on critical infrastructure via the Internet have been successfully perpetrated by terrorists, so that computers are more often the means to achieving terrorist purposes rather than the objects of attack (Gordon and Ford 2002; Weimann 2005, 129, 130).

Communications

The Internet is a widely available, fast and cheap mode of communication. It is especially accommodating for those groups which have transnational networks. Its facility for encryption is additionally a boon to those who wish to plot in the shadows. An interesting example arises from the case of Zacarias Moussaoui, who was charged as a conspirator in the September 11 attacks (for the indictment against him, see U.S. Department of Justice 2006; Lewis 2006 (he was sentenced to life imprisonment)). The FBI only discovered that Moussaoui had utilized three Hotmail accounts through his written pleadings in July and August 2002. Amongst the challenges faced by investigators in that case is the initial problem that the identities of account holders are not verified by Microsoft, the owners of Hotmail. Provided the account holder gives a false identity (*U.S. v. Moussaoui* 2006),[10] does not use a traceable IP address (which can be achieved by using an Internet terminal in a public library, an Internet café such as the Kinko's branch frequented by Moussaoui or a shopping mall), and does not download information to a traceable storage mechanism like a hard disk or floppy disk, the usage can remain anonymous. Microsoft can in theory trace messages by a combination of IP address and date/time of the message, provided the information has not been erased from its records because an account has been inactive for 30 days; however, the company refuses to do this as a matter of policy. Even this potential path to detection can be defeated by the use of more sophisticated anonymous Web browsing systems such as Anonymizer.com (Walker and Akdeniz 2003, explaining Anti-Terrorism, Crime and Security Act, 2001, c.24, §§ 102-07 (U.K.); Privy Counsellor Review Committee 2003–04, para 410; Home Office

---

[7]Likewise, hackers caused an Irish ISP, Connect-Ireland, to suspend the East Timorese domain (.tp) which it hosted. The Indonesian embassy in London denied that the Indonesian government sponsored the attack.

[8]The term has no legal definition in the UK but has administrative importance. See http://www.cpni.gov.uk/About/whatIs.aspx, 2007.

[9]Denial of service attacks on Estonian governmental Web sites followed the controversial relocation of a statue commemorating the Russian liberation of the country from Nazi occupation, an attack which was alleged to be perpetrated by Russian state agencies.

[10]Moussaoui's accounts were called xdesertman@hotmail.com, pilotz123@hotmail.com and Olimahammed2@hotmail.com, with his registered name in one case as Zuluman Tangotango.

2004).[11] Even Al Qa'ida has fleetingly made an appearance through Web sites[12] which have either been hosted by unwitting legitimate ISPs or furtively embedded within other Web sites without the owners' knowledge, with potential readers being informed of their locations through bulletin boards (Delio 2006).[13] It is said that these sites are:

> . . . central to al-Qaida's strategy to ensure that its war with the US will continue even if many of its cells across the world are broken up and its current leaders are killed or captured. The site's function is to deepen and broaden worldwide Muslim support, allowing al-Qaida or successor organizations to fish for recruits, money and political backing. (Eedle 2002)

Personnel and Logistical Support

Recruitment may be a byproduct. The Web presence increases public consciousness of the group, but security demands will not normally allow any direct approaches (Tsfati and Weimann 2002; Weimann 2004, 317, 327). Nevertheless, some enthusiasts do risk prosecution, such as Sheikh Omar Bakri Mohammed (Hall 2005; O'Neill 2005b),[14] who is said to have used Internet chat rooms to encourage support for his organization, Al-Muhajiroun, and for Jihadist groups in general (O'Neill 2005a). Likewise, security considerations limit the role of open Web sites in fund-raising operations, but Web sites for fund-raising have still been more commonly found than Web sites for recruitment (Tsfati and Weimann 2002, 317, 327).

Intelligence Gathering

Since all manner of life is present on the Web, it is possible to obtain information about possible targets, such as defense facilities (Silke 2002, 15),[15] as well as the addresses of individual targets.[16] It is also not just a myth that it is possible to find instructions on how to make a

---

[11]The Regulation of Investigatory Powers Act 2000 (c.23) Part III contains powers to allow the issuance of notices which require the disclosure of encryption keys, refusal of which is an offence. Part III is not yet in force, though the Home Office has recently made proposals with a view to commencement: Home Office, Investigation of Protected Electronic Information (http://www.homeoffice.gov.uk/documents/cons-2006-ripa-part3/ripa-part3.pdf?view=Binary, last visited December 21, 2006).

[12]According to Thomas (2003), the sites include the following: aljehad.online; almuhrajiroun.com; alneda.com; aloswa.org; alsaha.com; assam.com; drasat.com; islammemo.com; jehad.net; jihadunspun.net; mwhoob.net; 7hj.7hj.com.

[13]The domain name, Al Neda was later taken over by a private US citizen, Jon Messner.

[14]Under pressure from the Home Office because of his activities, Sheikh Omar Bakri Mohammed left the United Kingdom and has taken up residence in Lebanon. As a Syrian national, he was later banned from returning to the United Kingdom on grounds that his return would not be conducive to the public good or to national security.

[15]British Army facilities in Northern Ireland used to be listed on Sinn Féin's Web site. The Alfred P. Murrah building in Oklahoma, attacked in 1995, had been listed on the U.S. militia sites as a facility especially vulnerable to car bombs.

[16]The Criminal Justice and Police Act of 2001 (c.16, U.K.) s.45 amends company law to allow the suppression of personal details of directors so as to protect them from animal rights activists.

nuclear weapon[17] or, perhaps more realistically, a pipe or nail bomb.[18] In the case of Mohammed Naeem Noor Khan, who was arrested in Pakistan in July 2004, his computer materials revealed plans to attack targets, especially financial institutions, in London, New York, and New Jersey. A degree of panic ensued, though it was later confirmed that the plans were three or four years old (Hussain 2004; McGrory 2004a; Evans and O'Neill 2004).[19] Khan is reported to have admitted that "most of al-Qaeda's communication was done through the Internet" (Hussain 2004; McGrory 2004a; Evans and O'Neill 2004). Khan, who is also known as Abu Talha, "is said to have helped in evaluating potential American and British targets for terror attacks" (Hussain 2004; McGrory 2004a; Evans and O'Neill 2004). It should be noted that the nature of the intended attacks was probably "conventional" rather than a cyber attack, as was the case with other incriminating data from laptops found in Afghanistan in 2002 (Weimann 2005, 143). Nevertheless, former Defense Secretary Donald Rumsfeld observed that an Al Qa'ida training manual recovered in Afghanistan said, "Using public sources openly and without resorting to illegal means, it is possible to gather at least 80 percent of all information required about the enemy" (Thomas 2003, 117).

Propaganda

In this section, we are moving from Web activities which relate to the preparation or conduct of terror through to the "theater of terror," which is aimed at onlookers rather than at victims (Weimann and Winn 1993). In this way, terrorists can amplify their actions and importance and evade the usual restraints of state or legal controls imposed upon the other mass media, as well as benefiting from low production costs and anonymity (Weimann 2006b, 30). Some groups operate their own sites (Tsfati and Weimann 2002, 317; Weimann 2006b, chap. 3). Examples include Harakat ul Mujahideen (HM),[20] a militant group based in Pakistan and operating primarily in Kashmir, which was formed in 1993 as Harakat ul-Ansar. Its prime goal is to oppose Indian security forces, but it has also attacked civilians and Western tourists. It is claimed that HM has supporters in several areas of the United Kingdom, as a result of which its actions are proscribed by Part II of the Terrorism Act 2000. Another example is the Kurdistan Workers' Party (Partiya Karkerên Kurdistan or PKK).[21] The PKK was founded in 1974 and seeks an independent Kurdish state in south-eastern Turkey. It engaged in armed attacks from 1984 until after the capture of its leader, Abdullah Öçalan (*Öçalan v. Turkey*, App. No. 46221/99, Judgment 12 May 2005), following which a ceasefire was called for on

---

[17]The Nuclear Weapon Archive: A Guide to Nuclear Weapons,http://nuclearweaponarchive.org (last visited December 18, 2006).

[18]Many sites offer a version of the *Anarchist Cookbook*. The original version by William Powell, is not in print, as the author has renounced his former views. See Amazon.com Books Page, http://www.amazon.com/Anarchist-Cookbook-C-066-William-Powell/dp/0962303208 (last visited December 18, 2006).

[19]The files on Khan's computers included a plan of the layout of Heathrow and information from reconnaissance of the Canary Wharf complex. There were also suggestions for "picture postcard" targets, such as the Houses of Parliament and Windsor Castle.

[20]See Harkat-ul-Mujahideen: Latest News & Articles on Jihad & Kashmir, http://www.harkatulmujahideen.org (last visited December 18, 2006).

[21]See Partiya Karkerên Kurdistan Worker's Party, http://www.pkk.org (last visited December 18, 2006).

September 1, 1999. It broke down (save for a short period) after 2004, though a further cease-fire was unilaterally declared in 1st October 2006. The Liberation Tigers of Tamil Eelam, which was founded in 1972 and is the most powerful group in Sri Lanka fighting for a distinct Tamil state, has maintained a Web site since 1997.[22] Likewise, Hizbollah (The Party of God) is the Lebanese-based Islamic movement founded after the Israeli military seizure of Lebanon in 1982. It seeks the creation of an Iranian-style Islamic republic in Lebanon and the removal of all Israeli and Western influences in the area, including by kidnappings and suicide bombs. It has in the past maintained a Web site,[23] though the site has now ceased to operate. The Web master made the following comments concerning the site's value to the organization:

> 'In this technological revolution,' explained Hussein Naboulsi, who runs the website, 'one is obliged to get involved in it one way or another—we can't live outside our era or time. The use of websites has become like water to human beings, thus it is more than necessary to keep pace with the means of expression in our time.' Asked if the site has made a difference to the way that Hezbollah is perceived in the world, Naboulsi was philosophical. 'We don't expect to gain support and sympathy overnight . . . though the feedback is great. The good thing is that thousands of westerners are able to get a picture about the party directly from our mouth. We receive thousands of e-mails, and we answer the questions of the people. I remember a westerner, an old man, wrote to me saying: I need you to answer my questions. His questions were aggressive, but after a week of exchanging Q&A e-mails, he wrote to me saying: Thanks to God that I know the truth before I die.' (Mueller 2003)

The objective of these sites is primarily informational. They contain details of history, ideology, leadership and news; violent activities tend to be downplayed, although their vindication is explained (Tsfati and Weimann 2002, 317, 321). The audience includes both supporters and "the international 'bystander' public and surfers," with some sites even seeking to enter the homes and minds of the "enemy" (Tsfati and Weimann 2002, 326).

Because of harassment and threats from the authorities, which often translate into closure proceedings taken by Internet Service Providers (ISPs), the sites are operated by sympathizers who speak in more guarded language. In addition to sites related to organizations, the "propaganda of the deed" (Garrison 2004)[24] has been very much adopted by some insurgent groups in Iraq who have used Web sites to show attacks on military convoys and the killings of western hostages. These postings often vanish quickly, as they are stripped out by the unwitting hosts, but not before they have been publicized and replicated by legitimate sources as well as the more outlandish inhabitants of the Internet.[25]

As regards the videos of armed attacks, numerous examples have been posted on open sites such as YouTube and Google Video (Glaser 2006; Goldenberg 2006). As regards the killings of hostages, the series began with Nick Berg in May 2004 (Camera/Iraq 2006). The Web addresses that posted the Nick Berg decapitation video were based on a Web server in

---

[22]See Tamil Eelam Home Page, http://eelam.com (last visited December 18, 2006).

[23]The now defunct Web site was originally located at http://www.hizbollah.org.

[24]"Propaganda of the Deed" derives from the doctrine that spectacular action by an individual or an activist group may inspire further action by others. It was associated with anarchists such as Kropotkin, who is associated with the epigram that "[a] single deed is better propaganda than a thousand pamphlets."

[25]See, World of Death, http://www.everwonder.com/david/worldofdeath/ (last visited December 18, 2006); LiveLeak (incorporating Ogrish.com) at http://www.liveleak.com/ (last visited December 18, 2006).

Malaysia with Web masters in London, England, and Nurnberg, Denmark.[26] The technique was borrowed from the case of U.S. reporter Daniel Pearl, who was beheaded by Islamists in Pakistan in February 2002; a video was released of his killing (See Hussain 2002, describing Sheikh's pending appeal; Irish News 2002).[27] Another widely publicized event was the killing of Ken Bigley, the first British hostage to be killed, by the group Tawhid wa al-Jihad, which proclaimed allegiance to Abu Musab al-Zarqawi in October 2004 (Farrell and Evans 2004; McGrory 2004b; McGrory and Hider 2004). Bigley was seized along with Americans Eugene Armstrong and Jack Hensley, who were also beheaded. The drama was enhanced by the dressing of several hostages in orange overalls and placing him in a cage, intended to be reminiscent of equivalent uniforms worn by prisoners of the U.S. Government in Guantánamo Bay's Camp Delta. It should be noted that such distributed film making is not confined to irregular forces, and soldiers of governmental forces have also published pictures and videos of their exploits (Harkin 2006), most notably of the abuse of prisoners in Abu Ghraib (Taguba 2004; Schlesinger 2004; Fay 2004; ACLU v Department of Defense 389 F Supp 2d 547, SDNY, 2005). The U.S. Army tightened restrictions on Web publishing by soldiers in May 2007 on the grounds of protecting sensitive military information and saving bandwidth. The effects are mainly to ban combat zone access and also regulate postings by members of the armed service who have returned from war zones by requiring them to consult with their supervisors and operational security officers (Sipress and Diaz 2007). At the same time, the Multi-National Force Iraq (principally the U.S. Army) has launched its own channel on YouTube, with footage of firefights and attacks.[28]

LEGAL RESPONSES

In terms of legal reactions, we can again corral them into just two headings: hostile cyber attacks and ancillary cyber activities. There is a legal reaction to each, and the danger in each case is that the legal reaction may be excessive because of a failure to adhere to the legal principles adduced earlier. This section will examine responses, built up over a decade or so, within the United Kingdom law (For U.S. law, see Weimann 2006b, chap. 6).

Hostile Cyber Attack

The first category of cyber terrorism contemplates various forms of hostile activity. In short, this category encompasses "information warfare." Information warfare is terrorist activity designed seriously to interfere with or to harm or disrupt communication. Information warfare might involve direct incursions on computer systems which could trigger threats to life, such as interference with air traffic control systems or hospital records. However, information warfare is more likely to involve the defacing of Web site text or images, the use of viruses, or the denial of service attacks through multiple key striking software, called "ping" engines, or through e-mail bombs, none of which causes physical damage but may fundamentally

---

[26]The sites were originally located at www.al-asnar.net and www.al-asnar.biz
[27]Omar Sheikh was convicted of the murder.
[28] http://www.youtube.com/profile?user=MNFIRAQ

compromise the provision of information and services (Denning 1999; Mitliaga 2002; Post et al. 2002; Valeri and Knights 2002; Schwartan 2006).

Does all of this activity have the capacity to terrorize as opposed to damage or offend or inconvenience? In legal principle, only the truly terrorizing, based on the organizational capacity outlined previously, might require a special legal response. One should distinguish the direct from the indirect threat and should identify a threat to the well-being of an individual rather than to a machine. A direct threat might include interference which could cause aircraft to collide or cause hospitals to administer the wrong treatment. These could be paralyzing challenges to the capacity of the state to run civil life and, if carried out, could harm individuals. To the contrary, activities such as defacing, corrupting or denying are unlikely to have the same impact on the lives of individuals, even if the potential disruption to the capacities of state agencies remains large and of increasing significance. These activities also shade into forms of political activism which we should hesitate to demonize with the title "terrorism" even if they infringe such elements of the criminal law as the Computer Misuse Act 1990 (c.18 (U.K.)) or the Criminal Damage Act 1971 (c.48 (U.K.)). Is it "terrorism" for teachers to go on strike and thus deny to the public important public services any more than it is terrorism for animal rights protestors to try to bring down a Web site? While the direct and indirect may sometimes be conflated in political discourse (Silke 2002, 17), it would ignore principles of various rights (such as the right to protest and to express opinions) and of proportionality to use draconian antiterrorism powers against the latter.

Bearing these criticisms in mind, there is greater justification for offences relating to **intelligence gathering**, including intelligence gathering via the Internet, where the outcome could be some kind of murderous attack on individuals. There are two overlapping offences in the Terrorism Act 2000 (c.11 (U.K.)) which deal with this activity. One is section 58 of the Act—offences of the collecting or recording or possessing information of a kind likely to be useful to a person committing or preparing an act of terrorism. A "record" includes photographic or electronic formats as well as writings and drawings, but mental notes and knowledge, which is not recorded in any form, are not covered.

The main controversy surrounding section 58 concerns the equivocal nature of the actions involved and the fact that it is left to the defendant to prove as a defense, under subsection (3), that he had a reasonable excuse for his action or possession. The indeterminate range of the offence has also given rise to alarm on the part of journalists: "What journalist worth his or her salt does not have a contacts book? A cuttings file? A file on the activities and personal details of prominent public figures?" (Hickman 2001). Indeed, one could add that a wide range of people, including academic scholars, can become effective investigators and collators of information by using Internet sources such as the Web site directory 192.com[29] or by using documents freely available on the Web, such as *The Terrorist's Handbook* and *The Big Book of Mischief*. It follows that it is not necessary under section 58 to show that the information was obtained or held in breach of the law; the possession of Army manuals was the basis for conviction in R v. Lorenc [1988] N.I. 94.

Section 58 is augmented for Northern Ireland by section 103 which relates to the protection of specified security force personnel and other public officials.[30] For example, the pos-

[29]192.com Home Page, http://192.com (last visited December 18, 2006).
[30]Terrorism Act, 2000, c. 11, § 103 (U.K.).

session of Army manuals was the basis for conviction in *R v. Lorenc* [1988] N.I. 94 and the possession of planning and training materials was the basis in *Re Kerr's Application* [1997] N.I. 225. Though the penalties are the same, section 103 is broader than section 58 in several respects. For example, the *actus reus* includes publishing, communicating or attempting to elicit, as well as collecting or recording.[31] As with section 58, the main controversy concerns the equivocal nature of the actions involved and the fact that it is left to the defendant to prove as a defense, under subsection (5), that he had a reasonable excuse for his action or possession. In *R v. McLaughlin* [1993] N.I. 28, a radio enthusiast was able to show reasonable excuse for possessing a list of RUC radio frequencies. There is the further presumption in subsection (4) that if it is proved a document or record: "(a) was on any premises at the same time as the accused, or (b) was on premises of which the accused was the occupier or which he habitually used otherwise than as a member of the public," the court may assume that the accused possessed the document or record, unless he proves that he did not know of its presence on the premises or that he had no control over it. According to section 118, which applies to both subsections (4) and (5), if evidence is adduced which is sufficient to raise an issue, the court shall treat it as proved unless the prosecution disproves it beyond reasonable doubt.

The case of David Copeland might be considered as a test for whether there should be offences against intelligence-gathering activities (Silke 2002, 17). David Copeland carried out a series of three bombings in London in 1999 out of racist and homophobic motives (Tendler and Reid 2000). Part of the evidence at his trial was that he had obtained the information on how to make bombs from Internet sources, such as *The Terrorists' Handbook* and *How to Make Bombs Book Two*. These and other relevant materials, like *The Anarchist's Cookbook* and *The Big Book of Mischief*, are readily available through any search engine. There are, however, two caveats. The first is that such information is also available in books, including books written for lay people (see e.g., Grivas-Dignhenis 1964). Second, it turned out that David Copeland could not assemble the necessary ingredients indicated in the Web-based guides and instead resorted to an even less sophisticated bomb made out of fireworks material (Wolkind and Sweeney 2001; McGrory and O'Neill 2005; Home Office 2005–06).[32] Further reflection shows the dangers of overreaching. If possession of the addresses of government buildings amounts to terrorist intelligence, then are we to ban telephone directories and the use of the Internet to provide government services? Inevitably, an open society may be more vulnerable to attack than a closed society, but the better strategies against terrorism lie in activities such as state intelligence gathering rather than in shutting down the open society.

Support Cyber Activities

Other forms of computer use by terrorist groups exist to support their political or military objectives. The use includes internal and external communications, fund raising, recruitment, and propaganda (Damphousse and Smith 1998). These activities do not terrorize *per se*, so only if they are linked to a terrorist group should legal action be taken under special laws. In other words, legal action should be taken not because of a direct capacity to terrorize but

---

[31]Terrorism Act, 2000, c. 11, § 103 (U.K.).

[32]Likewise, the perpetrators of the London suicide bombings of July 7 and July 21, 2005, allegedly manufactured their bombs from peroxide materials which can be derived from common household goods.

because of the need to reduce the viability of organizations with the capacity to terrorize by other means. However, if these activities are not linked to a terrorist, and preferably proscribed (Walker 2002, chap. 2),[33] group, then there is again the danger of crossing over into political activism which, palatable or not, or even legal or not, should not be equated with terrorism.

The Terrorism Act 2000 does deal with support cyber activities relating to proscribed organizations in section 12 of the Act.[34] Part III of the Act is wider still and deals with "Terrorist Property" even if the organization is not proscribed.[35] There are again some elements of overreaching. One example is the offence of possession of items useful to terrorism under section 57 of the Terrorism Act 2000 (Privy Counsellor Review Committee 2003–4, para. 276, expressing no objections to the offences in Part VI of ATCSA. The penalties under section 57 are increased by the Terrorism Act 2006 (c.11) § 13).[36]

The offence of possession of items for terrorist purposes in section 57 had been an offence in Northern Ireland since the time of section 30 of the Northern Ireland (Emergency Provisions) Act 1991[37] and was later set out in section 32 of the Emergency Provisions Act 1996.[38] The offence originated pursuant to the recommendation of the Review of the Northern Ireland (Emergency Provisions) Acts 1978 and 1987,[39] though the idea was then confined to possession in public places. Then, section 63 of the Criminal Justice and Public Order Act 1994 extended a possession offence to Britain by way of section 16A of the Prevention of Terrorism Act.[40] Continuance was supported by Lord Lloyd as allowing early police intervention,[41] and so the offence now appears as section 57 of the Terrorism Act 2000 for the whole of the United Kingdom.

According to section 57(1), a person commits an offence if he "possesses an article in circumstances which give rise to a reasonable suspicion that his possession is for a purpose connected with the commission, preparation or instigation of an act of terrorism." The penalties are the same as for section 54. There is no need for any proof of a terrorist purpose in the mind of the possessor. It is notable that there is again no link to proscribed organizations, so the perpetrators may include, in accordance with the definition in section 1, animal liberation

---

[33]Proscription is allowed under Part I of the Terrorism Act, 2000, c. 11, § 103 (U.K.). Some groups (both Irish-based and foreign) are listed in the Act itself (section 3(1)). Others (all foreign based) have been added by statutory instruments on the authority of the relevant government Minister (section 3(3)). This form of proscription triggers offences in sections 11 to 13 against membership or speaking or organizing on behalf of the proscribed group. The Act therefore includes, but goes well beyond, the prohibition on the funding of listed nondomestic groups in Title IIIA of the Anti-terrorism and Effective Death Penalty Act, 18 U.S.C. § 2339B (2005). The grounds for proscription under the Terrorism Act 2000 were to be further widened by the Terrorism Act 2006, c.11 (U.K.), § 21 to cover organizations which directly or indirectly incited terrorism.

[34]Terrorism Act, 2000, c. 11, § 12 (U.K.).

[35]Terrorism Act, 2000, c. 11, §§ 14–31 (U.K.).

[36]Terrorism Act, 2000, c. 11, § 57 (U.K.).

[37]Northern Ireland (Emergency Provisions) Act, 1991, c. 24, § 30 (U.K.).

[38]Northern Ireland (Emergency Provisions) Act, 1996, c. 22, § 32 (U.K.).

[39]Review of the Northern Ireland (Emergency Provisions) Acts 1978 and 1987 (Cm. 1115, London, 199) at para. 2.9.

[40]Criminal Justice and Public Order Act, 1994, c. 33, § 63 (U.K.); Prevention of Terrorism (Temporary Provisions) Act, 1989, c. 4, § 16A (U.K.).

[41]Inquiry into Legislation against Terrorism (Cm. 3420, Stationery Office, 1996), para. 14.6.

activists seeking to attack a laboratory. The articles concerned will be lawful in themselves and even commonplace; in this regard, section 57 differs markedly from offences such as possession of an offensive weapon or going equipped for theft. There is no need for section 57 to deal with those caught red handed in possession of explosives and firearms. Rather, items such as wires, batteries, rubber gloves, scales, electronic timers, overalls, balaclavas, agricultural fertilizer, and gas cylinders, especially in conjunction, are the concern of section 57. The wide range of articles which may attract suspicion highlights the problematic nature of section 57. The actions of the suspects at this stage are highly equivocal—persons with overalls and balaclavas may be preparing for an attack on a police patrol or on a rabbit warren. In this way, there is an extension of the criminal law to put people in the dock for activities which do not require actions directly related to terrorism or the intention of being involved in terrorism.

Proof of "possession" is aided by subsection (3). If it is proved that an article: "(a) was on any premises at the same time as the accused, or (b) was on premises of which the accused was the occupier or which he habitually used otherwise than as a member of the public," the court may assume that the accused possessed the article, unless he proves that he did not know of its presence on the premises or that he had no control over it.

Recognizing the possible overreach of section 57, subsection (2) offers a defense for a person charged with an offence to prove that "his possession of the article was not for a purpose connected with the commission, preparation or instigation of an act of terrorism." In addition, under section 57(3), it is open to the defendant to show that he either did not know of the presence of the item on the premises or had no control over it. It has been argued that this defense does not alleviate the unfairness of the offence and in fact perpetrates another by switching the burden of proof to the defense, contrary to Article 6(2) of the European Convention on Human Rights and Fundamental Freedoms.[42]

The meaning of the offence and its possible breach of article 6(2) by undermining the presumption of innocence have been considered by the House of Lords in *R v. Director of Public Prosecutions,* ex parte *Kebilene* [2000] 2 AC 326. Their Lordships ultimately decided the case on the technical ground of the nonreviewability of prosecution decisions, but opinions were divided between the House of Lords and the Court of Appeal on the complaint of a breach of Article 6(2). Following the illuminating analysis provided in the speech of Lord Hope (*R v. Director of Public Prosecutions,* ex parte *Kebilene* [2000] 2 AC 378-80), it is desirable to ensure that the interpretation of section 57(3) imposes an initial evidential burden—a requirement to raise evidence in support of an issue in a case—on the defense but thereafter the burden is taken up by the prosecution to disprove there is any defense. It is also important to emphasize that the final burden of proof of guilt beyond a reasonable doubt, including proof of all essential facts, such as possession and reasonable suspicion of a terrorist purpose, remains on the prosecution. Such restraint is more likely to satisfy article 6(2) as interpreted in the jurisprudence of the European Court of Human Rights, which does allow for some flexibility in the issue of proof, especially where it can be shown that important social concerns are at stake and that the defendant has ready access to the information required for the defense (*Salabiaku v. France*, App. No. 10519/83, Ser. A 141-A (1988); *Brown v. Stott (Procurator*

---

[42]European Convention on Human Rights and Fundamental Freedoms, art. 6(2), November 4, 1950, ETS 5, 213 U.N.T.S. 17.

Fiscal, Dunfermline) and another [2003] 1 A.C. 681; *R v. Benjafield* [2002] UKHL 2; *R v. Lambert* [2001] UKHL 37.).

In light of these concerns and conflicting factors, section 118 was added to the Terrorism Act 2000 and affects both sections 57(2) and 57(3). According to section 118(4), if evidence is adduced which is sufficient to raise an issue, the court "shall treat it as proved unless the prosecution disproves it beyond reasonable doubt." This formula was intended to be merely declaratory.[43] In so far as it does impact on the problem, however, it would seem to prevent section 57 from placing any "legal" or "persuasive" burden upon the defendant by ensuring that, once raised, the issue remains for the prosecution to prove (Emmerson and Ashworth 2001; Rowe 2000). It may also slightly ease the evidential burden placed on the defendant by requiring simply that the issue be raised to negate the presumption in the statute, unless the prosecution can prove otherwise (Emmerson and Ashworth 2001; Rowe 2000).

Some commentators suggest that the dispute in *Kebilene* was misconceived on the grounds that the prosecution must prove beyond a reasonable doubt not only the possession of the items relevant to section 57 but also reasonable suspicion of the terrorist's purpose. In other words, the burden of proof is not shifted at all (Roberts 2002, 41). A comparison is made with other offences relating to preparatory stages, such as going equipped for theft or possession of an offensive weapon. It is suggested that these analogies are misplaced. The presence of items covered by section 57 is far less suggestive of crime than is the presence of items covered by the other offence. In other words, being in charge of false identity documents, counterfeit credit cards and a three-band radio (for a graphic illustration in the case of Baghdad Meziane and Brahmin Benmerzouga, see Bird 2003) is much less suggestive of terrorism than possession of a knife is suggestive of an offence against the person or against property. These are not necessarily acts, which are "not wrongful at all" (Roberts 2002, 56), though they are less wrongful than using the items in a further crime.

The fact that the offence of possession is based around, in its second leg, reasonable suspicion only serves to emphasize rather than constrain its breadth. This does not at all mean that the prosecution has "its work cut out to prove the required suspicion beyond reasonable doubt" (Roberts 2002, 51). Proof beyond a reasonable doubt of a reasonable suspicion harbored in the minds of the forces of law and order (and not even a guilty mindset on the part of the accused) is a long way away from proof, in classical Millian terms, of a harm being actually perpetrated by a wrongdoer. Rather, the presence of items can be linked, for example, to associations or expressed beliefs to weave a charge. Thus, the same commentator concedes that section 57 might be said to trivialize the prosecution's burden, especially because it also requires no direct proof of a terrorist's purpose (Roberts 2002, 67). Quite so. The fact that the defendant has to respond to such a relatively light burden is surely not much different at the end of the day than a criticism that the burden of proof is shifted. It is true an offence has to be proven at the outset by the prosecution, but if that takes no great effort, then the real task in court is for the defense, which of course was always the intention of the legislation. It should be part of the prosecution's burden to show direct proof of a terrorist's purpose in the mind of the accused as opposed to a reasonable suspicion in the mind of the police or prosecutor.

A further argument to be considered is that, if the real issue is about the formulation of criminal offences rather than burdens of proof, the European Convention has little relevance

---

[43]House of Lords Debates (5th ser.) vol. 613 col. 754 (May 16, 2000).

since it has nothing to say about substantive criminal law (Roberts 2002, 50; Buxton 2000). Yet this narrow stance is by no means assured. It is true that elements of criminal liability are substantive rather than procedural and so fall outside English conceptions of the presumption of innocence, but the European Convention's sense of fairness does seem to be much wider in that it is linked to the overall fairness of process. As was stated in another context in *(John) Murray v. United Kingdom*:

> Although not specifically mentioned in Article 6 of the Convention, there can be no doubt that the right to remain silent under police questioning and the privilege against self-incrimination are generally recognized international standards which lie at the heart of the notion of a fair procedure under Article 6.
>
> . . . [I]t is self-evident that it is incompatible with the immunities under consideration to base a conviction solely or mainly on the accused person's silence or on a refusal to answer questions or to give evidence himself.[44]

This *dictum* suggests that an offence, which made it unlawful, say, to be suspected of murder and then fail to answer police questions in response to those suspicions would not be acceptable. Is that not a statement about substantive criminal law?

It should be realized that there are inchoate offences aplenty in this field. Most obvious is conspiracy to cause explosions under section 3 of the Explosive Substances Act 1883.[45] Surely, it is fairer and more convincing to prove "conspiracy" rather than "possession" and a specific wrongful intent—for example, causing explosions rather than terrorism, which is not *per se* an offence.

Adding to the debate is the case of *Attorney General's Reference (No 1 of 2004)*,[46] which arose from the impact of section 35 of the Criminal Procedure and Investigations Act 1996 (procedural points concerning the holding of preparatory hearings).[47] The Court of Appeal gave the firm guidance that the common law and article 6(2) of the European Convention had the same effect—both permitted legal reverse burdens of proof or presumptions in the appropriate circumstances.[48] The overall burden of proof must remain on the prosecution, but there could be exceptions provided they created proportionate evidentiary burdens and were justifiable. Justifiability would be judged by the realistic effects of the reverse burden, including how easy it was for the accused to discharge or how difficult it would be for the prosecution to establish the facts, bearing in mind the seriousness of the offences and the level of penalties.

Just as important as the interpretation of section 57 has been the considerable increase in its usage over the past three years. The offence had been charged 30 times in Britain before the Terrorism Act came into force in 1996. In 2000 and 2001, there were no recorded charges.[49] Since then, there have been 22 charges in 2002, 29 in 2003, 3 in 2004, and 13 in

---

[44]App. No. 18731/91, Reports 1996-I at paras. 45, 47.
[45]Explosive Substances Act, 1883, c. 3, § 3 (U.K.).
[46][2004] EWCA Crim. 1025.
[47]Criminal Procedure and Investigations Act, 1996, c. 25, § 35 (U.K.).
[48][2004] EWCA Crim. 1025, at para. 52.
[49]House of Commons Debates (6th ser.) vol. 522 col. 966w (October 30, 2003).

2005 (Lord Carlile 2004–06). In effect, we are now close to an offence of terrorism—an offence of involvement rather than commission.

The controversial nature of section 57 is illustrated by the case of Baghdad Meziane and Brahmin Benmerzouga, as described earlier (Bird 2003). In addition, it is not clear why section 57 (or 58) was not invoked against Babar Ahmad, a computer analyst who worked at Imperial College London (McGrory et al. 2004).[50] He has been accused of material support of terrorism, support of the Taliban and Chechen rebels, conspiracy to kill (including the possession of plans for attacking U.S. warships in the Straits of Hormuz), money laundering, solicitation of funds, and conspiracy (*Humanitarian Law Project v. Ashcroft*, 309 F. Supp. 2d 1185, 1200 (C.D. Cal. 2004); Cole 2003; Chesney 2005; Stacy 2005; Schmitt 2004).[51] He was also under suspicion for raising money for terrorists through the Web sites www.azzam.com, www.qoqaz.com, and www.waaqiah.com, which Ahmad ran until their closure in November 2001 through Internet service providers in Nevada and then Connecticut. He was arrested by British authorities in December 2003 but then released, following which the U.S. authorities commenced extradition proceedings. His extradition was ordered by the Bow Street Magistrates' Court, after a diplomatic note sent to Foreign Secretary Jack Straw by the U.S. Government was produced in court, stating that Mr. Ahmad would not face the death penalty or be sent to Guantánamo Bay (McGrory 2005).[52] The decision to extradite was confirmed by the Home Secretary in November 2005 and the High Court has confirmed that the diplomatic note is a persuasive response to human rights complaints that human rights would be infringed by the extradition (*Babar Ahmad and Haroon Rashid Aswat v US* [2006] EWHC 2927 (Admin)). Contrast the current prosecution of Younis Tsouli and others, who are charged with conspiracy to murder, incitement to commit an act of terrorism and two counts of possessing a document or record likely to be useful to a person committing or preparing an act of terrorism arising from, *inter alia*, the distribution of materials over the internet in support of al Qa'ida, using the online name Irhabi007 (meaning Terrorist 007) (O'Neill 2007).

Despite all the controversies surrounding section 57, it has been augmented by a further offence in section 5 of the Terrorism Act 2006 c.11 (Joint Committee on Human Rights 2005–06), by which "A person commits an offence if, with the intention of (a) committing acts of terrorism, or (b) assisting another to commit such acts, he engages in any conduct in preparation for giving effect to his intention." The new offence covers forms of intangible preparations—giving information or advice—whereas section 57 demands that the preparation offence involve some tangible item.

Moving towards legislative action against propaganda, there is an incitement offence in section 59 of the Terrorism Act, which followed a government review (Secretary of State for

[50]For further details of his case, see FREE Babar Ahmad, http://www.freebabarahmad.com (last visited December 18, 2006).

[51]The details of the warrant for arrest are set out at http://news.findlaw.com/cnn/docs/ahmad/usahmad72804cmp.pdf (last accessed December 18, 2006). The warrant document reveals that Ahmad used PGP encryption but that the keys were readily recovered from data in his residence and in his office at Imperial College, London. The offence of material support has in part been declared unconstitutional. Sami Omar Al-Hussayen, a student at the University of Idaho, was acquitted of providing material support to terrorist groups through Web sites that prosecutors alleged, in circumstances similar to the case of Babar Ahmad, were used to recruit and raise money for Hamas and other groups.

[52]In the meantime, he had come in fourth in the general election of May 2005 in the Brent North constituency.

the Home Department and Secretary of State for Northern Ireland 1998, para. 16) and which potentially requires the United Kingdom to protect every crazy government in the world. According to section 59, a person commits an offence if: "(a) he incites another person to commit an act of terrorism wholly or partly outside the United Kingdom, and (b) the act would, if committed in England and Wales, constitute one of the offences listed in subsection (2)."[53] The listed offences are: (a) murder, (b) an offence under section 18 of the Offences against the Person Act 1861 (wounding with intent), (c) an offence under section 23 or 24 of that Act (poison), (d) an offence under section 28 or 29 of that Act (explosions), and (e) an offence under section 1(2) of the Criminal Damage Act 1971 (endangering life by damaging property). According to subsection (4), it is expressly "immaterial whether or not the person incited is in the United Kingdom at the time of the incitement." This differs from the extension of conspiracy offences under sections 5 to 7 of the Criminal Justice (Terrorism and Conspiracy) Act 1998 which give the United Kingdom courts jurisdiction over acts of conspiracy in the United Kingdom relating to any offences committed or intended to be committed abroad.[54] If, however, the conspiracy as well as the substantive offence takes place outside the jurisdiction, the conspirators cannot be prosecuted. Incitement via the Internet is likely to be the commonest form of address under this offence.

Sections 59 to 61 turn certain offences into universal crimes when they are not recognized as such elsewhere and in relation to foreign states which are not within the scope of the Suppression of Terrorism Act 1978.[55] Within the context of an incitement from the United Kingdom to intended perpetrators within a foreign country, how can it be said that the "incitement" possibly creates an immediate risk of unlawful serious violence to persons? The immediacy and causal link are diminished from what one normally thinks of as incitement. It is suggested that the offences should at least be confined in two ways. First, in terms of persons, the scope should relate to either the activities of British citizens or incitements to persons who are in the United Kingdom. This would leave a wide offence, given the indiscriminate nature of the Internet and other modern means of communications. Second, in terms of actions, the list of offences should be more clearly politically related and should not go much beyond such internationally recognized offences as hijacking, attacks on internationally protected persons (which already provide for universal jurisdiction for incitement offences) and perhaps even the wider range of terrorist bombing offences under section 62.[56] If confined in these ways, the list of offences would then more clearly reflect the core of terrorism than the current list.

In response, the Home Secretary has argued that sections 59 to 61 resolve anomalies. The aim of the incitement offences is to deter those who seek to use the United Kingdom as a base from which to promote terrorist acts abroad. It is claimed that under the Suppression of Terrorism Act 1978, there is already extra-territorial jurisdiction over a number of serious offences including murder, manslaughter, kidnapping, wounding with intent, and causing explosions, and incitement to any of those offences. It is then argued that, given the limitations of the treaty, "[t]here is no obvious justification for incitement to commit murder in

---

[53]Terrorism Act, 2000, c. 11, § 59(1) (U.K.). Corresponding offences for Northern Ireland and Scotland are set out in §§ 60 and 61.
[54]Criminal Justice (Terrorism and Conspiracy) Act, 1998, c. 40, §§ 5–7 (U.K.).
[55]Suppression of Terrorism Act, 1978, c. 26 (U.K.).
[56]Terrorism Act, 2000, c. 11, § 62 (U.K.).

Turkey or India to be an offence in the United Kingdom, whereas incitement to commit murder in Japan or Australia is not an offence."[57] But, as already mentioned, the incitement of many designated terrorist offences (hijacking and so on) already carry universal jurisdiction. Further, one wonders how many cases of incitements have resulted in prosecution instead of extradition under the 1978 Act?[58] From reported cases at least, the answer would appear to be zero, and this is also the figure given in debates by the Minister.[59] Evidential difficulties may also arise, whereby dissident groups will find it difficult to adduce evidence from overseas as to their true nature and intentions.[60] On the other hand, repressive regimes will be able to present evidence obtained by unconscionable means.

The government remained of the view that there was a need to balance free speech interests against the unacceptability of "encouraging and glorifying acts of terrorism" (Secretary of State for the Home Department and Secretary of State for Northern Ireland 1998, para. 16) However, this is one of the areas where a mature democracy should have maintained its patience with the politically immature and intemperate. Any prosecutions under sections 59 to 61 will be open to challenge under article 10 of the European Convention,[61] especially if made by a person who could be designated as a politician and especially if made against a government and especially if the words cannot be construed as a direct incitement of violence (*Incal v. Turkey*, App. No. 22678/93, Reports 1998-IV (2000); *Castells v. Spain*, App. No. 11798/85, Ser. A 236 (1992); Davis 2005).

Despite these forebodings, the encouragement and glorification of terrorism has been further criminalized by the Terrorism Act 2006. The ostensible origins of the Act can be located in the London bombings of July 2005, which sparked the Prime Minister into presenting a 12 point plan (*Times, The* 2005), though as usual, the crisis was as much a pretext as a reason. At the same time, the Act is being used to implement the Council of Europe Convention on the Prevention of Terrorism of 2005,[62] though there are major discrepancies between the Act and the Convention. The principal offence in section 1 relates to the publication of statements that are likely to be understood by their audience as a direct or indirect encouragement or other inducement to it to the commission, preparation or instigation of acts of terrorism or specified offences (Jones, Bowers, and Lodge 2006; Barnum 2006). The publisher must either intend members of the public to be directly or indirectly encouraged or otherwise induced, by the statement to commit, prepare, or instigate acts of terrorism or specified offences, or be reckless as to whether members of the public will be so directly or indirectly encouraged by the statement. By subsection (3), the indirect encouragement of terrorism includes a statement that "glorifies" the commission or preparation of acts of terrorism or specified offences (either in their actual commission or in principle) but only if members of the public could reasonably be expected to infer that what is being glorified in the statement is being glorified as conduct that should be emulated by them. Section 2 goes on to penalizes

[57]House of Commons Debates (6th ser.) vol. 341 col. 163 (December 14, 1999).

[58]See generally Suppression of Terrorism Act, 1978, c. 26 (U.K.).

[59]House of Commons Standing Committee D, Terrorism Bill (6th ser.) col. 262 (February 1, 2000) 262 (statement of Minister of State Charles Clarke).

[60]See JUSTICE, Response to *Legislation against Terrorism* (London, 1999) paras. 3.6, 3.7.

[61]European Convention on Human Rights and Fundamental Freedoms, art. 10, November 4, 1950, ETS 5, 213 U.N.T.S. 17.

[62]Council of Europe Treaty Series No. 196.

those who disseminate publications within section 1. Statements and disseminations via the internet are a particular target of this elastic crime, for section 3 expressly envisages that sections 1 and 2 can be committed where "a statement is published or caused to be published in the course of, or in connection with, the provision or use of a service provided electronically." There is also provision under section 3(3) for summary removal from the Internet—without prior judicial oversight, a constable may issue a notice which requires the recipient to take steps to remove the publication from the Internet within two days.

There were furious debates in Parliament about the breadth of this offence—whether, for example, it might criminalize anyone who glorified the armed opposition to the Apartheid regime in South Africa (such as the revered Nelson Mandela),[63] and there were calls for the future prosecution of Cherie Booth, the wife of British Prime Minister Tony Blair, for stating in a speech that, "in view of the illegal occupation of Palestinian land I can well understand how decent Palestinians become terrorists."[64] There are also concerns about how the scope of the offence extends to the glorification of terrorism throughout the world, without discrimination as to the nature of the regime attacked (by reference to section 17) (Joint Committee on Human Rights 2005–06, para. 12). For example, what if Saddam Hussein were still in power and called upon the British government to take action against self-serving statements by any surviving "terrorists" of Dujail who, in 1982, had attempted to assassinate him (reprisals against whom have now resulted in a death sentence against him)? If, for example, PKK efforts are diverted into humanitarian protests about the execution of Öcalan by the Turkish government, is that still terrorism? Given the breadth of the definition of terrorism in section 1 of the 2000 Act, its conversion into a universal offence is highly problematic—it certainly goes well beyond the internationally recognized offences such as those under the UN Terrorist Bombing Convention[65] and will therefore result in *ad hoc* and politicized prosecutorial decisions (Jones, Bowers, and Lodge 2006, para. 1.29). Plots against the Libyan regime of Ghaddafi were possibly encouraged years ago,[66] but now there is rapprochement. Conversely, plots against Syria are openly tolerated (*Times, The* 2006).

The policy of closing down channels of political discourse may be counterproductive in the long term. Surely, the experience with Sinn Fein has taught us the dubious utility of "broadcasting bans" and seeking to prohibit and demonize representative figures from political channels of communication (Michael 1988; Thompson 1989; Jowell 1990; Halliwell 1991; Morgan 1990–92; Parpworth 1994, 150; Banwell 1995; *R. v. Secretary of State for the Home Department, ex p. Brind* [1991] 2 W.L.R. 588, *In re McLaughlin's Application* (1991) 1 B.N.I.L. n. 36 (1990) 6 NIJB 4; *Purcell v. Ireland*, App. no. 15404/89; *Brind v. UK*, App no.18714/91, *McLaughlin v. UK*, App no. 18759/91; *R v. BBC ex p McAliskey* (LEXIS,1994)).[67] Whilst much of what the representatives of extreme Republicanism or Jihadism have to say is unpalatable or even reprehensible to many people, their views must be engaged with so that the onlooking public (including those who might be influenced by them, such as the bombers

---

[63]Diplomatic Conference on Reaffirmation and Development of International Humanitarian Law Applicable in Armed Conflict: Protocols I and II to the Geneva Conventions art. 49, June 8, 1977, 16 I.L.M. 1391.

[64]House of Commons Debates (6th ser.), vol. 438 col. 844, 2 November 2005, Bob Marshall-Andrews.

[65]UN International Convention for the Suppression of Terrorist Bombings (37 I.L.M. 249, 1997).

[66]Allegations were made by David Shayler: http://cryptome.org/shayler-gaddafi.htm

[67]The ban was attacked both in domestic courts and under the European Convention.

from Leeds) can be educated and can hear opposing views. These processes cannot occur if views cannot be aired in public. Driving such views underground leads to one-sided presentations on both sides.

It is commonly claimed that the use of cyberspace for incitement or propaganda purposes is its most significant terrorist use (Silke 2002, 7, 18). In reality, few terrorist groups have been able to run Web sites without attacks in turn from government agencies putting pressure on ISPs or triggering other forms of counteraction. For example, the Sinn Féin site, originally at the University of Texas, moved after protests in May 1996 (Tendler 1996).[68] Sites favoring ETA have been closed down in this way, as described earlier. No proscribed Irish group has any Web site anywhere in the world, though a few of the foreign proscribed groups do, as also noted earlier, have a direct Web presence. Of course, it is not necessarily the case that the law enforcement world would want these Web sites to be shut down—electronic intelligence-gathering works both ways. Indeed, communications, whether internal or external, can of course provide evidence of conspiracy and have indeed been used as evidence in court proceedings involving Al Qa'ida suspects (see *Al Fawwaz v. Governor of Brixton Prison* [2001] UKHL 69 (involving evidence from a facsimile)). One should not assume that encryption is always flawlessly used by terrorists.

Other offences likely to involve the Internet are more justifiable as closer to the concept of violence than politics. These include section 54, which deals with weapons training. Under this section, a person commits an offence if he "provides instruction or training in the making or use of—(a) firearms, (aa) radioactive material or weapons designed or adapted for the discharge of any radioactive material, (b) explosives, or (c) chemical, biological or nuclear weapons." This offence has its origins in successive Northern Ireland (Emergency Provisions) Acts (latterly section 34 of the 1996 version),[69] but it has now been extended throughout the United Kingdom, despite the recommendation otherwise by Lord Lloyd.[70] It is correspondingly an offence under section 54(2) to receive instruction or training, or, under section 54(3), to invite another to receive instruction or training contrary to subsections (1) or (2) even if the activity is to take place outside the United Kingdom. In this way, the offence currently also pertains to recruitment for training as well as to the training itself. By way of interpretation, under section 54(4), "instructions" and "invitations" can be general, such as by a pamphlet or via the Internet, or "addressed to one or more specific persons." In this way, no identifiable recipient is needed for the offence to be committed.

The changes in 2000 arose mainly from concerns about groups seeking to recruit British Muslims, often through the Internet, for military training in madrassas (Islamic religious schools) in Afghanistan, Pakistan, and elsewhere. Following the London bombings in 2005, it was felt that section 54 was unduly confined to weapons training and that other forms of training in the furtherance of terrorism should be criminalized, such as training in antisurveillance

[68]The site (http://uts.cc.utexas.edu/~sponge/aprn/SFhome.html) moved to a commercial Internet service provider located in Philadelphia. See Sinn Féin Online, http://www.serve.com/rm/sinnfein/index.html (last visited December 18, 2006). The site is now on an Irish internet service provider. See http://sinnfein.ie/ (last visited December 18, 2006).

[69]Northern Ireland (Emergency Provisions) Act, 1991, c. 24 (U.K.); Northern Ireland (Emergency Provisions) Act, 1996, c. 22, § 36 (U.K.).

[70]Inquiry into Legislation against Terrorism (Cm. 3420, Stationery Office, 1996) para. 14.28.

techniques or in communications skills. Therefore, by section 6 of the Terrorism Act 2006, a person commits an offence if "he provides instruction or training in any of the skills mentioned in subsection (3)" (Joint Committee on Human Rights 2005–06). Those skills are: "(a) the making, handling or use of a noxious substance, or of substances of a description of such substances; (b) the use of any method or technique for doing anything else that is capable of being done for the purposes of terrorism, in connection with the commission or preparation of an act of terrorism or Convention offence or in connection with assisting the commission or preparation by another of such an act or offence; and (c) the design or adaptation for the purposes of terrorism, or in connection with the commission or preparation of an act of terrorism or Convention offence, of any method or technique for doing anything." Mere attendance at a place of training is an offence under section 8, which means that the precise activities engaged in by the individual need not be proven, though the ambit of the crime might equally encompass an investigative journalist who harbours no intention to commit terrorism.

Sulayman Balal Zainulabidin, a chef from Greenwich, south-east London, was charged under section 54 in October 2001 arising from his activities in running an enterprise called Sakina Security Services, which had advertised on the Web training for Muslim recruits to prepare for "The Ultimate Jihad Challenge" (some of which was to occur at a facility called Ground Zero in Marion, Alabama).[71] He was acquitted of all charges in August 2002; there was no evidence to link him to al Qa'ida and, over a period of two years, only one person had even applied for the course via the Web site (Branigan 2002).

Just as the offence of weapons training has been extended to cover chemical, biological and nuclear weapons and materials, so sections 113 to 115 of the Anti-terrorism, Crime and Security Act 2001 extend offences relating to uses of weapons and threats and hoaxes concerning them from traditional areas, such as firearms and explosives, to chemical, biological, and nuclear weapons and materials. By section 113(1), it is an offence for a person to use or threaten to use a noxious substance or thing to cause serious harm in a manner designed to influence the government or to intimidate the public. The serious harm is defined further by subsection (2) as an action that:

(a) causes serious violence against a person anywhere in the world;

(b) causes serious damage to real or personal property anywhere in the world;

(c) endangers human life or creates a serious risk to the health or safety of the public or a section of the public; or

(d) induces in members of the public the fear that the action is likely to endanger their lives or create a serious risk to their health or safety; but any effect on the person taking the action is to be disregarded.

The list overall is reflective of section 1(2) of the Terrorism Act, save that there is understandably no reference to electronic systems. By section 113(3), it is an offence to make a threat to carry out an action which constitutes an offence under subsection (1) with the intention "to induce in a person anywhere in the world the fear that the threat is likely to be carried out."

---

[71]A mirror of the Web site is produced at http://www.warbirdforum.com/webarchi.htm (last visited December 18, 2006).

Section 114 deals with hoaxes with reference to "a noxious substance or other noxious thing." The law as it stood before the 2001 Act, in section 51 of the Criminal Law Act 1977 (as amended by the Criminal Justice Act 1991), made it an offence for someone to place or send any article intending to make another person believe that it is likely to explode or ignite and thereby cause personal injury or damage to property (Walker 1992, chap 2). It was also an offence under section 51 for someone to communicate any information which he knows or believes to be false intending to make another person believe that a bomb is likely to explode or ignite.[72] There were corresponding offences in Scotland[73] and in Northern Ireland.[74] A related offence is food contamination contrary to section 38 of the Public Order Act 1986 (Watson 1987a, b). It is an offence under subsection (1) to intend to cause alarm, injury, or loss by contamination or interference with goods or by making it appear that goods have been contaminated or interfered with "in a place where goods of that description are consumed, used, sold or otherwise supplied." It is also an offence to make threats or claims along these lines (section 38(2)) or to possess materials with a view to the commission of an offence (section 38(3)). Section 38 responded to a small number of well-publicized incidents of consumer terrorism, a minority of which involved animal liberationists. It follows that there was a substantial range of offences in existence before 2001, but it was felt that there remained gaps. The offences in section 51 related only to hoax devices which are "likely to explode or ignite."[75] The section 38 offences protected only the integrity of goods. Post September 11, 2001, a scare arose from the mailing of anthrax powder in the U.S. and the fear that groups like Al Qa'ida had possession of other biological or nuclear materials which could be extremely dangerous and harmful not just in the consumer chain but through any form of contact or distribution (Walker 2004). Accordingly, section 114(1) widens the offence by extending the *actus reus* to placing or sending any substance or article intending to make others believe that it is likely to be or contain a noxious substance or thing which could endanger human life or health. By subsection (2), it is an offence for a person to falsely communicate any information to another person anywhere in the world that a noxious substance or thing is or will be in a place and so is likely to cause harm or to endanger human life or health.

For the purposes of both sections 113 and 114, section 115 makes clear that for a person to be guilty of an offence, it is not necessary for him to have any particular person in mind as the person in whom he intends to induce the belief in question. Thus, threats and hoaxes issued to the whole world, such as via the Internet, can be penalized.

CONCLUSION

Cyber terrorism is a potential threat, and the United Kingdom state is justified in seeking to guard against it. As part of its commitment to that objective, it has set up the National Technical Assistance Centre, a surveillance advice and interception facility first located in the Security Services London headquarters but now in the Government Communications

---

[72]Criminal Law Act, 1977, c. 45, § 51 (U.K.), *amended by* Criminal Justice Act, 1991, c. 53 (U.K.).
[73]Criminal Law Act, 1977, c. 45, § 63 (U.K.), *amended by* Criminal Justice Act, 1991, c. 53 (U.K.).
[74]Criminal Law (Amendment) (Northern Ireland) Order, 1977, SI 1977/1249, art. 3.
[75]Criminal Law Act, 1977, c. 45, § 51 (U.K.), *amended by* Criminal Justice Act, 1991, c. 53 (U.K.).

Headquarters (GCHQ) (for further discussion on the strengthening of technological resilience, see Walker and Broderick 2006, chap. 4).[76]

In the realm of asymmetric warfare, the processor can be mightier than the sword in the hands of terrorist groups. It follows that a flexible "digital realist" response (Greenleaf 2003) is appropriate. This approach may be rather more subtle than the mantra of Lawrence Lessig that "code is law" (Lessig 1999), in that it recognizes that code (Internet technical architecture) is subject to law and that code is as malleable as is law. A digital realist approach to cyber terrorism would consider all applicable modalities of control—law and architecture as well as social factors.

First, in terms of law, the foregoing survey suggests that there are few gaps and that the difficulties of prosecution are often evidential rather than substantive. The wish to maintain the secrecy of sources and surveillance techniques are prominent amongst these, as well as the problems inevitably caused by having to deal with terrorist networks which spill into many jurisdictions, some either unsophisticated or uncooperative, and whose languages are foreign. Subject to that reservation, one possible strengthening of criminal law has recently comprised a new specific offence of denial of service, as suggested by the All Parliamentary Internet Group (2006). The Police and Justice Act 2006, section 36 (c. 48), has therefore amended section 3 of the Computer Misuse Act 1990 (c. 18 (U.K.)) offences by extending it to actions designed to impair the operation of any computer or to prevent or hinder access to, or to impair the operation of, any program or data held in any computer. Aspects of civil law may also be relevant as a discipline against those who seek to profit from, or simply enjoy, the theatre of terrorism. One might for example, provide for special funds for the victims of terrorism and their families so they can bring actions in tort (*Wainwright v. Home Office* [2003] UKHL 53; *Wilkinson v. Downton* [1897] 2 Q.B. 57.) against those who reproduce executions and other distressing episodes of terrorism.

Second, Internet architecture points towards the ability to warn and to filter, techniques, which have proven so successful against other unwanted cyber intrusions such as spam (Wall 2005). Finally, social action would involve the education of the public as to this aspect of terrorism. The vigilance of the British public has been a key factor in dealing with IRA bombings. The same could apply to attacks via the Internet. Possible outcomes might be the more effective use of filters, warnings, and reporting systems akin to those relating to child pornography (focused on the Internet Watch Foundation),[77] and even the formation of counter sites. The Internet Watch Foundation model also reminds us that the world of cyberspace, most of which rests in private hands, requires the encouragement of networks of security. This point is explicit in the U.S. government's National Strategy to Secure Cyberspace, which states that "[t]he cornerstone of America's cyberspace security strategy is and will remain a public–private partnership" (The White House 2003).

Nevertheless, any or all of these levels of response ought to be circumspect for two reasons. First, the most effective measures against any form of terrorism are, on the one hand, intelligence gathering and surveillance and, on the other hand, security counter measures.

---

[76]See House of Commons Debates (6th Series) vol. 378 col. 829w 22 January 2002, David Blunkett and vol. 451 col. 11ws 31 October 2006, Margaret Beckett.

[77]Internet Watch Foundation, http://www.iwf.org.uk (last visited December 18, 2006).

Sweeping legislation has the distinct disadvantages not only of being unproductive but also of giving a signal of undue alarm and potentially criminalizing the political rather than the violent. We must avoid the panicked conclusion that society's reliance on technology creates an unalloyed fragility. Instead, we must see it as a strength which often contains the facility for its own protection.

Next, the urge to restrict, prohibit, and to curtail must be resisted. Aside from the need to encourage dialogue with those so disaffected that they resort to political violence, Web sites can be a vital open intelligence source for the authorities, especially because propaganda is one of the main aspects of cyber terrorism. Furthermore, closed sources derived from information and communication sources are also vital. The ESCHELON[78] system is alleged to be able to "sniff" key switch points on the Internet and, in that way, intercept a huge amount of traffic. Given the absence of informants in most cases involving Al Qa'ida and other tight-knit Jihadist groups, it may be deduced that a fair proportion of the successes of the authorities in thwarting attacks and undertaking prosecutions may have been assisted by background signals intelligence. The pursuit of intelligence may be assisted by the fact that the terrorists are not as sophisticated as sometimes presented. For example, even Moussaoui did not use the encryption facilities, which are offered by the popular e-mail services. Another revealing case is that of Mohammed Naeem Noor Khan, whose seized computer materials are reported to have led to a number of further arrests (Hussein et al. 2004). His laptop was described as a "treasure trove" for Western intelligence agencies (Evans 2004; Bhatti et al. 2004; *R v Barot* [2007] EWCA Crim 1119).[79] Moreover, cell phones have been used to track terrorists and to provide evidence against them (Philips 2002; Lister 2005).[80]

Closing off modes of communication which in some eyes might amount to "propaganda" must always give liberal democracies pause for thought. One might especially recall the furious reaction to the broadcasting of "Death on the Rock" about the Gibraltar shootings in 1988. Even before this time, Prime Minister Margaret Thatcher coined a key phrase in the summer of 1985 after the TWA airline hijack in Beirut. She told the American Bar Association in London, "We try to find ways to starve the terrorist and the hijacker of the oxygen of publicity on which they depend" (Evans 1985). Outright censorship was explicitly imposed only in November 1988 under broadcast licensing powers (Henderson et al. 1990; Miller 1994; Lord Windlesham and Rampton 1989; Banwell 1995; Halliwell 1991; Morgan 1990–92; Parpworth 1994, 50; Thompson 1989; Weaver and Bennett 1989).[81] The Home

---

[78]American Civil Liberties Union, *Echelon Watch*, available at http://www.echelonwatch.org/; Committee on Foreign Affairs, Human Rights, Common Security and Defence Policy, Temporary Committee on the ECHELON Interception System 2001/2098(INI)) FINAL, A5-0264/2001 Par1.

[79]Charges were brought against eight individuals: Dhiren Barot, for possessing reconnaissance plans of the U.S. financial buildings and having notebooks with information on explosives, poisons, chemicals and related matters; Qaisar Shaffi, for owning an extract from a terrorist's handbook, which explains the use of chemicals and explosive devices; Mohammed Naveed Bhatti; Abdul Aziz Jalil; Omar Abdul Rehman; Junade Feroze; Zia ul Haq; and Nadeem Tarmohammed. Pleas of guilty to conspiring to cause explosions likely to endanger life have been accepted from Barot and six of his co-accused.

[80]However, the conviction of Colm Murphy for aiding those who bombed Omagh in August 1998 by providing mobile phones has been overturned on evidence that police interview notes had been falsified.

[81]The ban was lifted on September 16, 1994 shortly after the IRA had called a ceasefire.

Secretary, Douglas Hurd, based his actions on concern for victims, as well as on more general political concerns about the creation of fear and intimidation.[82] The ban included proscribed organizations as well as Sinn Féin, Republican Sinn Féin, and the Ulster Defence Association. The ban was upheld as lawful in *R v. Secretary of State for the Home Department, ex parte Brind* [1991] 1 A.C. 696 (See *In re McLaughlin's Application*, 1 B.N.I.L. n. 36 [1991], 6 N.I.J.B 4 (1990); *R v. BBC ex p. McAliskey* (Crown Office List), CO/3032/92 (May 27, 1994)). Likewise, the European Commission of Human Rights upheld limited broadcasting bans (*Purcell v. Ireland*, App. No. 15404/89, D.R., 70, 262 (1991); *Brind v. UK*, App. No. 18714/91, D.R., 77-A, 42 (1994); *McLaughlin v. UK,* App. No. 18759/91, 18 Eur. H.R. Rep. CD84 (1994)). One wonders whether the ban was helpful in preparing the public, especially the Unionist/Loyalist population of Northern Ireland, for the idea of accommodation and consocialism, which became the hallmark of the Belfast "Good Friday" Agreement of 1998.

Of course, some would argue that Millian concepts of harm are inadequate. There is sympathy for this view in the Canadian *Keegstra* judgment:

> [W]ords and writings that willfully promote hatred can constitute a serious attack on persons belonging to a racial or religious group. . . .
>
> [A] response of humiliation and degradation from an individual targeted by hate propaganda is to be expected. A person's sense of human dignity and belonging to the community at large is closely linked to the concern and respect accorded the groups to which he or she belongs. . . . The derision, hostility and abuse encouraged by hate propaganda therefore have a severely negative impact on the individual's sense of self-worth and acceptance. (*R. v. Keegstra*, [1990] S.C.R 697, 746 (opinion by Dickson, C.J.))

Ideally, another reaction altogether is to be encouraged. In the words of Supreme Court Justice Brandeis, "[the] remedy to be applied is more speech, not enforced silence" (*Whitney v. California*, 274 U.S. 357, 377 (1927)). Especially since the Internet facilitates easy, free, and instantaneous public discourse, self-assertion is available to all. The need for cultural education and promotion regarding the Islamic communities is suggested by the European Monitoring Centre on Racism and Xenophobia's[83] study of Islamophobia in the European Union after 9/11 and also by the House of Commons Home Affairs Committee.[84] In particular, rather than the sole pursuit of a policy of repression, "the Government must engage British Muslims in its antiterrorist strategy."[85] The UK Government has since responded positively to that representation in its counter-terrorist strategy, an element of which comprises the tactic of "Engaging in the battle of ideas—challenging the ideologies that extremists believe can justify the use of violence, primarily by helping Muslims who wish to dispute these ideas to do so."[86] That engagement should take place in cyberspace, since it has become one of the front lines in the fight against terrorism.

---

[82]House of Commons Debates (6th ser.) vol. 139 col. 1082 (1988).

[83]The EUMC was set up in 1997 by Council Regulation (EC) No. 1035/97. There are proposals to reconstitute it as the Fundamental Rights Agency of the European Union (COM(2004)693 Final).

[84]Terrorism and Community Relations (2004–05, H.C. 165).

[85]Terrorism and Community Relations (2004–05, H.C. 165), para. 225.

[86]Home Office, Countering International Terrorism (Cm.6888, London, 2006) para. 6.

KEY TERMS

Intelligence gathering
Jurisdiction
Terrorism

REFERENCES

Al Fawwaz v. Governor of Brixton Prison [2001] UKHL 69.

ACLU v. Department of Defense 389 F Supp 2d 547 (SDNY, 2005).

All Party Parliamentary Internet Group. 2006. Revision of the Computer Misuse Act: Report of an inquiry by the All Party Internet Group. Available at http://www.apig.org.uk/archive/activities-2004/computer-misuse-inquiry.html. Accessed December 18, 2006, paras. 66, 74.

Babar Ahmad and Haroon Rashid Aswat v. US [2006] EWHC 2927 (Admin).

Banwell, C. 1995. The courts' treatment of the broadcasting bans in Britain and the Republic of Ireland. *Journal of Media Law & Practice* 16: 21.

Barnum, D. 2006. Indirect incitement and freedom of speech in Anglo-American law. *European Human Rights Law Review* 258.

Bhatti, M. N., A. A. Jalil, O. A. Rehman, J. Feroze, Z. Haq, and N. Tarmohammed, S. Tendler, et al. August 18, 2004. Gang charged with plot to hit U.K. with "dirty bomb." *The Times*(London): 1.

Bird, S. April 2, 2003. Quiet existence in Leicester suburb masked complex terrorist network. *The Times* (London): 11.

Branigan, T. August 10, 2002. Cleared chef says he was terror case scapegoat: Jury dismisses first UK charges since attacks on September 11. *The Guardian*: 6.

Brenner, S., and M. Goodman. 2002. In defense of cyberterrorism: An argument for anticipating cyber-attacks. *University of Illinois Journal of Law, Technology & Policy*: 1.

Brind v. UK, App. No. 18714/91, D.R., 77-A, 42 (1994).

Brown v. Stott (Procurator Fiscal, Dunfermline) and another [2003] 1 A.C. 681.

Buxton, R. 2000. The Human Rights and the Substantive Criminal Law. *Criminal Law Review*: 331, 332.

Camera/Iraq. 2006. The war of images in the Middle East, Nicholas Berg Beheading (May 8, 2004). http://www.camerairaq.com/2004/05/nick_berg_video.html. Accessed December 18, 2006.

Castells v. Spain, App. No. 11798/85, Ser. A 236 (1992).

Chesney, R. M. 2005. The sleeper scenario: Terrorism-support laws and the demands of prevention. *Harvard Journal on Legislation* 42: 1.

Cilluffo, F., et al. 1999–2000. Bad guys and good stuff: When and where will the cyber threats converge? *DePaul Business Law Journal* 12.

Cole, D. 2003. The new McCarthyism: Repeating history in the war on terrorism. *Harvard Civil Rights-Civil Liberties Law Review* 38: 1.

Collin, B. 2006. The future of cyberterrorism: Where the physical and virtual worlds converge. *Institute for Security and Intelligence*. Available at http://afgen.com/terrorism1.html. Accessed December 18, 2006.

Council of Europe. 2005. *Guidelines on Human Rights and the Fight Against Terrorism*. 3rd ed. Strasbourg: Council of Europe.

Crimm, N. J. 2004. High alert: The government's war on the financing of terrorism and its implications for donors, domestic charitable organizations, and global philanthropy. *William & Mary Law Review* 45: 1341.

Damphousse, K. R., and B. L. Smith. 1998. "The Internet." In *The Future of Terrorism*, edited by H. W. Kushner. Thousand Oaks: Sage Publications.

Davis, H. 2005. Lessons from Turkey. *European Human Rights Law Review*: 75.

Delio, M. 2003. Al Qaeda website refuses to die. Available at http://www.wired.com/news/infostructure/ 0,1377,58356,00.html. Accessed December 18, 2006.

Denning, D. 1999. *Information Warfare and Security*. New York: ACM Press Books.

Denning, D. 2000. Cyberterrorism. http://www.fas.org/irp/congress/2000_hr/00-05-23denning.htm. Accessed December 18, 2006.

Denning, D. 2006. Activism, hacktivism, and cyberterrorism: The Internet as a tool for influencing foreign policy. http://www.cs.georgetown.edu/~denning/infosec/nautilus.html. Accessed December 18, 2006.

Eedle, P. July 17, 2002. Terrorism.com: How does Al_Qaida stay organized when its members are in hiding and scattered across the world? *The Guardian*: 4.

Emmerson, B., and A. Ashworth. 2001. *Human Rights and Criminal Justice*. paras. 9-59. London: Sweet & Maxwell.

European Convention on Human Rights and Fundamental Freedoms. November 4, 1950. ETS 5, 213 U.N.T.S. 17.

Evans, P. July 16, 1985. Thatcher unfolds strategy to beat hijack terror/British Premier addresses American Bar Association Meeting in London. *The Times* (London).

Evans, M. August 7, 2004. Al-Qaeda agent's laptop yields vital intelligence clues. *The Times* (London): 4.

Evans, M., and S. O'Neill. November 24, 2004. How Al-Qaeda's London plot was foiled. *The Times* (London): 4.

Farrell, S., and M. Evans. September 23, 2004. Help me now, Mr. Blair. You are the only person on God's earth who can. *The Times* (London): 6.

Fay, G. R. 2004. *Investigation of Intelligence Activities at Abu Ghraib*. Washington: Department of Defense.

Garrison, A. H. 2004. Defining terrorism: Philosophy of the bomb, propaganda by deed and change through fear and violence. *Criminal Justice Studies: A Critical Journal of Crime, Law and Society* 17: 259.

Glaser, M. 2006. YouTube offers soldier's eye view of Iraq war. http://www.pbs.org/mediashift/2006/01/ digging_deeperyoutube_offers_s_1.html. Accessed December 21, 2006.

Goldenberg, S. October 7 2006. Jihad videos posted on YouTube website. *The Guardian*: 24.

Gordon, S., and R. Ford. 2002. Cyberterrorism? *Computers & Security* 21: 636.

Greenleaf, G. 2003. An endnote on regulating cyberspace. *University of New South Wales law Journal* 21: 593.

Grivas-Dignhenis, G. 1964. *Guerilla Warfare and EOKA's Struggle*. London: Longmans.

Hall, B. August 13, 2005. Radical cleric Bakri barred from entry. *Financial Times* (London): 4.

Halliwell, M. 1991. Judicial review and broadcasting freedom. *Northern Ireland Legal Quarterly* 42: 246.

Halpin, T. May 18, 2007. Putin accused of launching cyber war. *The Times*: 46.

Harkin, J. August 12, 2006. War porn. *The Guardian*: 27.

Henderson, L., et al. 1990. *Speak No Evil: The British Broadcasting Ban, The Media And The Conflict In Ireland*. London: Glasgow University Media Group.

Hickman, L. 2001. Press freedom and new legislation. *New Law Journal* 151: 716.

Home Office. 2001. *Animal Rights Extremism*. para. 3.75. London: Home Office.

Home Office. 2004. *Counter Terrorism Powers*. Cm. 6147. para. 145. London: Home Office.

Home Office. 2005–06. *Report of the Official Account of the Bombings in London on 7th July 2005*. HC 1087. p. 23.

Home Office. 2006. *Countering International Terrorism*. Cm.6888. para. 41. London: Home Office.

Humanitarian Law Project v. Ashcroft, 309 F. Supp. 2d 1185, 1200 (C.D. Cal. 2004).

Hussain, Z. July 16, 2002. A lonely wait for the hangman. *The Times* (London): 3.

Hussain, Z. August 3, 2004. Confessions of a computer expert gave US vital clues. *The Times* (London): 1.

Hussein, Z., et al. August 5, 2004. Al-Qaeda's "British chief" is seized in police raids. *The Times* (London): 1.

Incal v. Turkey, App. No. 22678/93, Reports 1998-IV (2000).

In re McLaughlin's Application, 1 B.N.I.L. n. 36 [1991], 6 N.I.J.B 4 (1990).

Institute for Global Communications, The. 2006. http://www.igc.apc.org. Accessed December 18, 2006.

Iqbal, M. 2004. Defining cyberterrorism. *The John Marshall Journal of Computer & Information Law* 22: 397, 408.

Irish News. February 23, 2002. Video shows reporter killed then beheaded. p. 13. (See also *Irish Times*. February 25, 2005. p. 21.)

Joint Committee on Human Rights. 2005–06. *Counter Terrorism Policy and Human Rights: Terrorism Bill and Related Matters* (H.L. 75-I/H.C. 561).

Jones, A., R. Bowers, and H. D. Lodge. 2006. *The Terrorism Act 2006*. Oxford: Oxford University Press.

Jowell, J. 1990. Broadcasting and terrorism, human rights and proportionality. *Public Law*: 149.

Laqueur, W. 1996. Postmodern terrorism. *Foreign Affairs* 75: 24, 35.

Lawyers Committee for Human Rights. 2003. *Assessing the New Normal*. New York: Lawyers Committee for Human Rights.

Lessig, L. 1999. *Code and Other Laws of Cyberspace*. New York: Basic Books.

Lewis, N. A. May 5, 2006. One last appearance, and outburst, from Moussaoui. *The New York Times*: 21.

Lister, D. January 22, 2005. Omagh bomb retrial after police "faked evidence." *The Times* (London): 20.

Lord Carlile. 2004–2006. *Reports on the Operation in 2002–2005 of the Terrorism Act 2000*. London: Home Office.

Lord Carlile. 2007. The definition of terrorism. Cmnd. 7052. London.

Lord Windlesham and R. Rampton. 1989. *The Windlesham/Rampton Report on Death on the Rock*. London: Faber & Faber.

McGrory, D. August 4, 2004a. Al-Qaeda computer whizkid with a flawless English accent. *The Times* (London): 4.

McGrory, D. September 21, 2004b. Briton's family waits in fear as US hostage is beheaded. *The Times* (London): 1.

McGrory, D. May 18, 2005. Terror suspect loses US extradition battle. *The Times* (London): 6.

McGrory, D., and J. Hider. October 9, 2004. Ken Bigley is Beheaded. *The Times* (London): 1.

McGrory, D., and S. O'Neill. August 6, 2005. Inside the hunt for London bombers. *The Times* (London): 11.

McGrory, D., et al. August 7, 2004. Briton 'had plans to attack US warship.' *The Times* (London): 1, 4.

McLaughlin v. UK, App. No. 18759/91, 18 Eur. H.R. Rep. CD84 (1994).

Michael, J. 1988. Attacking the easy platform. *New Law Journal* 138: 786.

Miller, D. 1994. *Don't Mention The War*. London: Pluto.

Mitliaga, V. 2002. Cyberterrorism. *Legal Executive*: 4.

Morgan, D. G. 1990–92. Section 31: The broadcasting ban. *Irish Jurist* 25–27: 117.

Mueller, A. March 23, 2003. Propaganda skirmishes in cyberspace. *The Sunday Times* (London): 52.

Öcalan v. Turkey, App. No. 46221/99, Judgment (12 May 2005).

O'Neill, S. January 17, 2005a. Radical cleric who has never been prosecuted. *The Times* (London): 4.

O'Neill, S. August 9, 2005b. Radical cleric kept up inflammatory rhetoric despite becoming an outcast. *The Times* (London): 1.

O'Neill, S. April 24, 2007. Al-Qaeda's 'British propagandists.' *The Times*: 3.

Parkel, W. 2004. Note, money laundering and terrorism: Informal value transfer systems. *American Criminal Law Review* 41: 183.

Parpworth, N. J. 1994. Terrorism and broadcasting. *Journal of Media Law & Practice* 15: 50.

Philips, E. 2002. Mobile phone—Friend or foe? *Science & Justice* 42: 225.

Posner, E. A., and A. Vermeule. 2006. Emergencies and democratic failure. *Virginia Law Review* 92: 1091.

Post, J. M., et al. 2002. From car bombs to logic bombs. *Terrorism & Political Violence* 12 (2): 97.

Privy Counsellor Review Committee. 2003–04. *Anti-Terrorism, Crime and Security Act 2001 Review.* H.C. 100. Part D.

Purcell v. Ireland, App. No. 15404/89, D.R., 70, 262 (1991).

Re Kerr's Application [1997] N.I. 225.

R v. BBC ex p. McAliskey (Crown Office List), CO/3032/92 (May 27, 1994).

R v. Benjafield [2002] UKHL 2.

R v. Director of Public Prosecutions, ex parte Kebilene [2000] 2 AC 326.

R v. Director of Public Prosecutions, ex parte *Kebilene* [2000] 2 AC 378–80.

R. v. Keegstra [1990] S.C.R 697, 746 (opinion by Dickson, C.J.).

R v. Lambert [2001] UKHL 37.

R v. Lorenc [1988] N.I. 94.

R v. McLaughlin [1993] N.I. 28.

R v. Secretary of State for the Home Department, ex parte Brind [1991] 1 A.C. 696.

Raufer, X. 1999. New world disorder, new terrorisms: New threats for Europe and the western world. *Terrorism & Political Violence* 11 (4): 35.

Rhodes, R. A. W. 1994. The hollowing out of the state: The changing nature of the public services in Britain. *Political Quarterly* 65: 138.

Rhodes, R. A. W. 1997. *Understanding Governance: Policy Networks, Governance, Reflexivity and Accountability.* Buckingham: Open University Press.

Roberts, P. 2002. The presumption of innocence brought home. *Law Quarterly Review* 118.

Rowe, J. J. 2000. The Terrorism Act 2000. *Criminal Law Review*: 527, 540.

Sacramento Bee, The. 2006. Unabomber. http://www.unabombertrial.com. Accessed December 18, 2006.

Salabiaku v. France, App. No. 10519/83, Ser. A 141-A (1988).

Schlesinger, J. R. 2004. *Independent Panel to Review Department of Defense Detention Operations.* Final Report. Washington: Department of Defense.

Schmitt, R. B. June 11, 2004. Acquittal in Internet terrorism case is a defeat for patriot act. *Los Angeles Times*: A20.

Schwartan, W. 2006. Infowar.com. http://www.infowar.com. Accessed December 18, 2006.

Secretary of State for the Home Department and Secretary of State for Northern Ireland. 1998. *Legislation Against Terrorism.* Cm. 4178. Stationery Office.

Silke, A. 2002. Here be dragons. Cybercrime: Immaterial crime and policing immateriality colloquium. Economic and Social Research Council Seminar, Leeds.

Sipress, A., and S. Diaz. May 15, 2007. A casualty of war: MySpace; U.S. Military blocks popular web sites, cutting ties to home. *The Washington Post*: A01.

Sofaer, A., and S. Goodman, eds. 2001. *The Transnational Dimension of Cyber Crime and Terrorism.* Stanford: Hoover Institution Press.

Stacy, T. 2005. The 'material support' offense: The use of strict liability in the war against terror. *Kansas Journal of Law & Public Policy* 14: 461.

Stephens, R. 1998. "Cyber-biotech terrorism: Going high tech in the 21st century." In *The Future of Terrorism: Violence in the New Millennium*, edited by H. Kushner. Thousand Oaks: Sage.

Stewart, A. 2001. *Theories of Power and Domination: The Politics of Empowerment in Late Modernity.* London: Sage Publications.

Stohl, M. 2006. Cyber terrorism: A clear and present danger, the sum of all fears, breaking point or patriot games? *Crime, Law & Social Change* 46: 223.

Sullivan, J. 1988. *ETA and Basque Nationalism: The Fight for Euskadi, 1890–1986.* London: Routledge.

Taguba, A. M. 2004. *Report on the Treatment of Abu Ghraib Prisoners in Iraq: Article 15-6 Investigation of the 800th Military Police Brigade.* Washington: Department of Defense.

Tendler, S. March 25, 1996. Ulster security details posted on the Internet. *The Times* (London).

Tendler, S., and T. Reid. July 1, 2000. Soho bomber was wicked not insane. *The Times* (London): 1.

Terminiello v. Chicago 337 U.S. 1, 37 (1949) (Jackson, J., dissenting).

Thomas, T. Spring 2003. Al Qaeda and the Internet: The danger of 'cyberplanning.' *Parameters, U.S. Army War College Quarterly*.

Thompson, B. 1989. Broadcasting and terrorism. *Public Law*: 527.

Times, The. August 6, 2005. p. 1.

Times, The. June 5, 2006. The 'National Salvation Front' met at the Dorchester Hotel to 'plot the overthrow' of the Baathist regime. *The Times*: 30.

Tsfati, Y., and G. Weimann. 2002. www.terrorism.com: Terror on the Internet. *Studies in Conflict & Terrorism* 25.

U.S. Customs Service Office of Investigations. 2006. Green Quest. Available at http://www.pa-aware. org/resources/pdfs/Green_Quest_Brochure.pdf. Accessed December 18, 2006.

U.S. Department of Justice. 2006. Moussaoui indictment. Available at http://www.justice.gov/ag/ moussaouiindictment.htm. Accessed December 18, 2006.

U.S. v. Moussaoui. 2006. Government's response to court's order on computer and email evidence. Available at http://fl1.findlaw.com/news.findlaw.com/hdocs/docs/moussaoui/usmouss90402grsp. pdf, Accessed December 18, 2006.

United Kingdom Department of Trade and Industry. 2004. *Animal Welfare—Human Rights: Protecting People from Animal Rights Activists*. para. 43. London.

Valeri, L., and M. Knights. 2002. Affecting trust: Terrorism, Internet and offensive information warfare. *Terrorism & Political Violence* 12 (1): 15.

Wainwright v. Home Office, [2003] UKHL 53.

Wilkinson v. Downton, [1897] 2 Q.B. 57.

Walker, C. 1992. *The Prevention of Terrorism in British Law*. 2nd ed. Manchester: Manchester University Press.

Walker, C. 1997. Constitutional governance and special powers against terrorism. *Columbia Journal of Transnational Law* 35: 7–10.

Walker, C. 2002. *Blackstone's Guide to the Anti-Terrorism Legislation*. Oxford: Oxford University Press.

Walker, C. 2004. Biological attack, terrorism and the law. *Journal of Terrorism and Political Violence* 17: 175.

Walker, C. 2007. The legal definition of "terrorism" in the United Kingdom and beyond. *Public Law*: 331.

Walker, C., and Y. Akdeniz. 2003. Anti-terrorism laws and data retention: War is over? *Northern Ireland Legal Quarterly* 54: 159.

Walker, C., and J. Broderick. 2006. *The Civil Contingencies Act 2004: Risk, Resilience and the Law in the United Kingdom*. Oxford: Oxford University Press.

Wall, D. S. 2005. Digital realism and the governance of spam as cybercrime. *European Journal on Criminal Policy & Research* 10: 309.

Watson, S. 1987a. Consumer terrorism. *New Law Journal* 137: 84.

Watson, S. 1987b. Product contamination. *Law Society's Gazette* 84: 13.

Weaver, R. L., and G. Bennett. 1989. The Northern Ireland Broadcasting Ban: Some reflections on judicial review. *Vanderbilt Journal of Transnational Law* 22: 1119.

Weimann, G. 2004. www.terror.net: How modern terrorism uses the Internet. *U.S. Institute of Peace*. http://www.usip.org/pubs/specialreports/sr116.html. Accessed December 18 2006.

Weimann, G. 2005. Cyberterrorism: The sum of all fears? *Studies in Conflict & Terrorism* 28.

Weimann, G. 2006a. Cyberterrorism: How real is the threat? *U.S. Institute of Peace*. http://www.usip. org/pubs/specialreports/sr119.html. Accessed December 18, 2006.

Weimann, G. 2006b. *Terror on the Internet*. Washington: U.S. Institute of Peace Press.

Weimann, G., and C. Winn. 1993. *The Theater of Terror: Mass Media and International Terrorism*. UK: Longman.

White House, The. 2003. *The National Strategy to Secure Cyberspace*. Available at http://www. whitehouse.gov/pcipb/. Accessed December 18, 2006.

Whitney v. California, 274 U.S. 357, 377 (1927).

Whittell, G. May 5, 1998. Unabomber to end his days in prison. *The Times* (London).

Wingfield, T. M. 2000. *The Law of Information Conflict*. p. 24. Falls Church: Aegis Research Corporation.

Wolkind, M., and N. Sweeney. 2001. *R v. David Copeland. Medicine Science and Law* 41: 185, 190.

Index

T

U